Platinum Edition

Using

Using

Using

MICROSOFT®

Office 97

que®

Platinum Edition

Using

Using
MICROSOFT®
Office 97

que®

Kathy Ivens et al.

Platinum Edition Using Microsoft Office 97

Library of Congress Catalog No.: 97-68684

ISBN: 0-7897-1301-2

99 98 97   6 5 4 3 2

Interpretation of the printing code: the rightmost double-digit number is the year of the book's printing; the rightmost single-digit number, the number of the book's printing. For example, a printing code of 97-1 shows that the first printing of the book occurred in 1997.

Screen reproductions in this book were created using Collage Plus from Inner Media, Inc., Hollis, NH.

Contents at a Glance

I Office 97: An Integrated Environment

1 Office 97 Overview   9
2 Office 97 Interaction   27
3 The Office 97 Binder   45

II Microsoft Word

4 Document Power   61
5 Power Tools   87
6 Advanced Mail Merge   107

III Microsoft Excel

7 Advanced Templates   131
8 Advanced Work with Charts   149
9 Using Ranges   167
10 Advanced Work with Formulas   185
11 Using Worksheet Functions   209
12 Using Lists   233
13 Pivot Tables   251
14 Connecting to Access Databases   273
15 Analyzing Data   303
16 Using the Solver   323

IV Microsoft Access

17 Creating Access Tables   345
18 Working with Data   367
19 Querying Data   388
20 Database Reports   413
21 Using Multiple Tables   433
22 Macros   445

V Microsoft Outlook

23 Customizing Views   465
24 Integrating the Outlook Elements   493
25 More Power with Exchange Server   513

VI | **Microsoft PowerPoint**

26   Working with Objects   545
27   Creating a Slide Show   563
28   Creating Multimedia Presentations   585

VII | **Visual Basic for Applications**

29   Using VBA Macros   601
30   Working with Application Objects   617
31   Building Forms and Dialog Boxes   633
32   VBA Programming   657
33   Using VB Script   683

VIII | **Microsoft Publisher**

34   Manipulating Objects   711
35   Adding Publisher's Special Elements   729
36   Publishing to the Web   747
37   An Overview of Other Small Business Edition Applications   761

IX | **Office 97 on the Internet**

38   Creating Web Documents   773
39   Publishing to the Net   789
40   Understanding ActiveX   801
41   Publishing Web Sites with FrontPage 97   813
42   Making Your Web Site Interactive   833

X | **Office 97 Power User Reference for Windows 95**

43   Windows Navigation Basics   845
44   Managing Files   881
45   Adding New Hardware to Windows 95   935
46   Controlling Printers   961
47   Installing, Running, and Uninstalling Windows Applications   993
48   Backing Up and Protecting Your Data   1015

XI | **Appendixes**

A   Tips and Tricks for System Administrators   1039
B   The CD-ROM   1051
C   Business Sites on the Web   1055

Index   1087

Table of Contents

Introduction   1

Who Will Get the Most Out of This Book?   2

How to Use This Book   2

How This Book Is Organized   2

Special Features in This Book   5

I | Office 97: An Integrated Environment

1   Office 97 Overview   9

What's New in Office 97?   10

Installation Procedures   10

Network Installation Point   10

New Office-Wide Features   11

Office Binder   11

Office Art   12

New Application Features   12

New Word Features   12

New Excel Features   13

New in Access   15

New in PowerPoint   16

Outlook   17

Small Business Edition   17

Office 97 Help   18

Office Assistant   18

Help from Microsoft on the Internet   20

The Main Help System   20

Handling Document Conversions   22

Word Conversion Considerations   22

Excel Conversion Considerations   23

Access Conversion Considerations   24

PowerPoint Conversion Considerations   25

2   Office 97 Application Interaction   27

Focusing on Documents   28

Creating and Opening Documents   28

The Office 97 Common Interface   30

Customizing Office Shortcut Bars   31
  Changing the Position and Shape of an Office Shortcut Bar   31
  Making More Shortcut Bars Available   32
  Automatically Hiding Shortcut Bars   32
  Customizing Existing Shortcut Bars   33
  Creating Custom Shortcut Bars   36
  Saving Your Shortcut Bar Configuration   37

Sharing Data Among Applications   37
  Application-Specific Methods   37
  Cutting and Pasting   38
  Linking and Embedding   39

3 The Office 97 Binder   45

Getting Acquainted with Binder   46
  Creating a Binder   46
  Opening an Existing Binder   47
  Displaying a Section's Contents   47
  Using the Binder Menu Bar   48
  Editing a Binder's Sections   48
  Changing the Order of Files in a Binder   49
  Selecting Binder Sections   49
  Deleting One or More Sections   50
  Unbinding Sections   50

Printing a Binder   50
  Previewing How Sections Will Be Printed   51
  Printing the Entire Contents of a Binder   51
  Printing Individual Sections   52
  Printing a Binder with Consistent Headers and Footers   52
  Dealing with Landscape Documents   54

Sharing a Binder with Others   55
  Sharing a Binder on a Network   55
  Sending a Binder by E-Mail   55
  Sharing a Binder on the Internet   56

Using Binder Templates   57

Choosing Binder Options   57
  Options That Apply to All Binders   57
  Options That Apply to the Currently Open Binder   58

II | Microsoft Word

4 Document Power 61

The Structured Word 62

Using Templates, Wizards, and Add-Ins 63
  Basing a Document on a Template 63
  Attaching a Different Template to a Document 64
  Previewing a Template 65
  Making a Template Global 66
  How Word Resolves Template Conflicts 66
  Where Templates Are Stored 67
  Creating a Template 67
  Where Word Stores Settings and Definitions 68

Styles 69
  Catching Up on Styles 69
  Applying Styles 70
  Creating and Modifying Styles 71

Creating Forms and Responding to Forms 74
  Creating a Simple Form 75
  Forms Provided with Office 77
  Calculated Fields in a Form 78
  More Form Elements 84
  Providing Help on Forms 85
  Using a Form 86

5 Power Tools 87

Powerful Toolbars 88
  Displaying Toolbars 88
  Creating a Custom Toolbar 89

Creating Tables of Contents and Similar Tables 91
  Identifying Headings 92
  Creating a Table of Contents 93
  Creating a Table of Contents for a Multi-File Document 95
  Updating a Table of Contents 95
  Creating Tables of Figures and Other Tables 96

Mapping a Document 96

Cross-Referencing and Hyperlinks 98

Creating an Index   99
 What Is Indexing?   99
 Marking the Document   99
 Creating the Index   101
 Modifying *XE* and *Index* Fields   102
 Creating Multiple Indexes   103

Creating and Using Macros   103
 Recording and Running a Macro   103
 Examining and Editing a Macro   104

6 Advanced Mail Merge   107

What Is Mail Merge?   108
 The Main Document   109
 The Data Source   109
 Merging a Main Document with a Data Source   109
 Making Mail Merge Happen   110

Using an Existing Document as a Mail Merge Main Document   113
 Preparing an Existing Document   113
 Placing Field Codes in the Main Document   113

Creating a Data Source   113
 Using a Word Table as a Data Source   114
 Using an Access Table as a Data Source   115
 Using an Excel Worksheet as a Data Source   115
 Using Other Types of Data Sources   115
 Using an Outlook Address Book as a Data Source   116

Selecting and Ordering Records in a Data Source   116
 Selecting Records in a Data Source   117
 Sorting Records in a Data Source   118

Using Word Fields in a Main Document   118
 Including Alternative Text in Merge Documents   120
 Selecting Alternative Phrases Interactively   122
 Filling in Text   125

Printing and Distributing Form Letters   125
 Printing Directly   126
 Merging to a New Document   126
 Distributing by Conventional Mail   126
 Distributing by E-Mail or Fax   126

III | Microsoft Excel

7 Advanced Templates   131

Using Templates   132
   Opening Workbooks Based on Templates   132
   What You Can Store in Templates   133
   Finding Templates   135

Creating Templates   136
   Designing a Worksheet Template   137
   Designing a Chart Template   139

Using the Template Wizard with Data Tracking   141
   Installing the Template Wizard   141
   Choosing a Database Driver   142
   Setting Up the Template   143

8 Advanced Work with Charts   149

Understanding Chart Axes and Scales of Measurement   150
   Using a Category and a Value Axis   150
   Using Two Value Axes   152
   Putting Two Data Series on the Same Axis   155

Dealing with Data Labels   157
   Showing Values and Showing Labels   158
   Designing the User Interface   158
   Using VBA to Attach Data Labels   160
   Extending the VBA Code   161

Creating Special Effects in Charts   162
   Defining the Vertical Axis   162
   Defining the Data Marker Patterns and Error Bars   164
   Using Error Bars Instead of Data Labels   165

9 Using Ranges   167

Referring to Ranges with Reference Operators   168

Understanding Multiple Selections   169

Naming Ranges   172

Selecting, Moving, and Copying Ranges Quickly   174
   Selecting Ranges   174
   Copying and Moving Ranges   176

Working with 3-D Ranges   180
  Modifying the Characteristics of 3-D Ranges   180
  Using 3-D Ranges in Formulas   181

10   Advanced Work with Formulas   185

Referencing Cells   186
  Absolute References   186
  Relative References   186
  Mixed References   187

Using Array Formulas   188
  Using Functions that Return Arrays   188
  Using Arrays as Arguments to Array Formulas   190
  Using Array Constants   191

Naming Formulas   194
  Reviewing Names   194
  Understanding Sheet-Level and Workbook-Level Names   195
  Naming Formulas   196
  Defining Names with Relative References   198

Linking Formulas   200
  Linking Separate Workbooks   200
  The Long and Winding Link   201
  Troubleshooting Links   202

Auditing Formulas   203
  Using Excel Tracers   204
  Tracing Dependents   206
  Tracing Invalid Data   207

11   Using Worksheet Functions   209

Lookup and Reference Functions   210
  Using *OFFSET* in Charts   210
  Using *INDEX* in Array Formulas   211
  Using *COLUMN* or *ROW* to Create a Sequence of Numbers   212
  Using *INDIRECT* to Assemble Cell References   214
  Using *MATCH* and *VLOOKUP* on Multiple Columns   215

Statistical Functions   217
  Charting Normal Curves Using *NORMDIST* and
  FREQUENCY   218

Using *LINEST* and *FDIST* to Evaluate Polynomial
Trendlines   220

Financial Functions   225
Using Net Present Value to Evaluate an Investment   225
Using Internal Rate of Return to Evaluate NPV   227
Profitability Indexes   229

Excel 4.0 Functions   230

12   Using Lists   233

What's a List?   234

Filtering Lists   236
Filtering Lists with AutoFilter   236
Filtering Lists with Advanced Filter   239

Using Lists in Formulas   242
Creating Natural Language Formulas from Lists   243
Using the Database Functions with Lists   246

Using a Data Form with Lists   248

The Rationale for Lists Reviewed   250

13   Pivot Tables   251

Defining Essential Terms   252

Creating Pivot Tables from External Sources   255
Defining the Data Source   256
Using the Query Wizard   258
Using the Query Window   260
Page Fields and External Data Sources   263

Using Calculated Fields and Items   265
Calculated Items   266
Creating Calculated Fields   268
Limitations to Calculated Fields and Items   270

14   Connecting to Access Databases   273

Why Use a Relational Database?   274
Connecting Excel and Access   274
Installing DAO   275

Creating a Pivot Table Using VBA and DAO   276
Setting Up the Access Structures   276

The *Driver* Subroutine   280
The *GetQueryNames* Subroutine   282
The *DialogHandler* Subroutine   284
The *ImportData* Subroutine   286

Modifying Access Databases from Excel   290
The *SELECT* Statement   291
The *FROM* Clause   292
The *GROUP BY* Clause   293
The *ORDER BY* Clause   293
Sending SQL to Access   293
Creating Temporary Queries   295

A Sample Application   296

15   Analyzing Data   303

Creating and Managing Scenarios   304
Establishing a Scenario   305
Summarizing Scenarios   307

Using Goal Seek   310

How to Predict the Future   314
Setting Up the Baseline   315
Creating the Forecast   315
Understanding the Forecast   316
Choosing the Damping Factor   319
Dealing with Autocorrelation   321

16   Using the Solver   323

Setting the Solver Parameters   324
Structuring the Problem for the Solver   324
Specifying the Target Cell   325
Specifying the Changing Cells   326
Specifying the Constraints   328
Using the Solution   331
Understanding the Solver's Reports   333

Setting the Solver's Options   337
Controlling the Precision   337
Defining the Search   339
Influencing the Calculations   340

IV | Microsoft Access

17 Creating Access Tables 345

Creating a New Table 346

Creating a Table with Datasheet View 347

Creating a Table with Design View 348

Creating a Table with the Table Wizard 358

Creating a Table by Importing a Table 360

Creating a Table by Linking a Table 361

Modifying a Table 362

Working with Relationships 364

18 Working with Data 367

Importing and Linking Data 368

Importing versus Linking 368

Working with Other Data Sources 368

How to Import or Link Data 369

Using Linked or Imported Data 371

Adding and Editing Original Data 372

Datasheet View and Form View 372

Creating Forms 372

Switching Between Views 374

Changing Datasheet View—A Hybrid 374

Moving Around the Data 375

Adding Data 376

Editing Data in a Table 378

Deleting Data 378

Sorting Data 379

Simple Sorts 379

Multiple Sorts 380

Data Filtering 381

19 Querying Data 389

Creating a Query 390

Creating a Query with the Design View 390

Creating a Query with the Simple Query Wizard 405

Using Action Queries 407

Deleting Records with Action Queries 408

Updating Records with Action Queries   409
Appending Records with Action Queries   410
Making Tables with Action Queries   411

20 Database Reports   413

Creating Reports   414

Creating Reports with AutoReport   414
Creating an AutoReport Columnar Report   415
Creating an AutoReport Tabular Report   416

Using the Access Reports Wizard   417

Creating Mailing Labels   424

Customizing Reports   427

Publishing Reports   429
Publishing Reports in HTML   429
Publishing Reports on E-Mail   430

21 Using Multiple Tables   433

Exploring Multiple Table Relational Types   434
One-to-Many Model   434
Many-to-Many Model   435
One-to-One Model   435

Table Relationships   436

Multiple Table Queries   440

Multiple Table Forms   441

Multiple Table Reports   442

22 Macros   445

Creating and Modifying Access Macros   446
Understanding Macro Sheets   446
Creating a Macro   449
Adding Conditions   451
Assigning Macro Names   453
Manipulating Rows in the Macro Sheet   455

Referring to Controls from Within Macros   455
Breaking Down the Control Identifier Syntax   456
Using the Expression Builder   457

Using Macros in Forms and Reports   458

V | Microsoft Outlook

23 Customizing Views   465

Understanding the Elements of a View   466

Sorting the View   466

Sorting by Displayed Columns   466

Sorting by Any Available Field   467

Creating a New View from the Sort Scheme   468

Grouping the View   471

Applying Group by Box   472

Filtering the View   474

Finding Items Anywhere in Outlook   477

Working with Folders   478

Adding Folders   479

Moving Items to Folders   479

Archiving Folders   480

Designing Folder Views   483

Creating a View from an Existing View   483

Creating a New View from Scratch   485

Creating New Fields   485

Creating a Simple Field   486

Using a Simple Field in a Form   486

Creating a Formula Field   488

Creating a Combination Field   490

24 Integrating the Outlook Elements   493

Dragging Objects Between Outlook Elements   494

Some Tips About Dragging Objects   494

Create a Task from an E-mail Message   494

Create an Appointment from a Message   496

Create a Contact from a Message   496

Create a Journal Entry from a Message   497

Dragging Other Outlook Items   498

Dragging Text   500

Dragging Items Outside of Outlook   501

Keeping Journal Entries   502

Setting Journal Options   503

Using Automatic Journal Entries   504
Drag to Create a Journal Entry   507
Manually Create a Journal Entry   508

Use Categories to Connect Items   508
Add Categories   508
Assigning Categories   509
Assigning a Category to an E-Mail Message   510
View Items by Category   510
Find All Items Connected to a Category   511

25   More Power with Exchange Server   513

E-Mail Features   514
Managing Your Mailbox with Rules   514
Using the Out of Office Assistant   514
Using the Inbox Assistant   519
Voting   520
Tracking Mail   523
Specifying Delivery Options   525
Redirecting Replies   525

Additional Power for Tasks   526
How Task Assignments Work   526
Assigning Tasks   528
Accepting Task Assignments   529

Using Public Folders with Outlook   531
Using Public Folders for Outlook Features   531

Designing Outlook Forms   533
Installing the Sample Forms   533
Using the Forms   533
Modifying and Customizing the Forms   535
Saving and Publishing Customized Forms   538

More Power with Exchange Server Forms   541

VI | Microsoft PowerPoint

26   Working with Objects   545

Manipulating Objects   546
Stacking Objects   546
Grouping Objects   548

Changing an Element in a Group   549

Rotating Objects   550

Animating the Entry of Objects   552

Working with Text Objects   554

Working with WordArt   557

Linking and Embedding Objects   560

Inserting the Object   560

Converting Objects   560

Manipulating Linked and Embedded Objects   561

27   Creating a Slide Show   563

Understanding Slide Shows   564

Timing Your Slide Show   564

Setting Timings Manually   565

Setting Timings Automatically   566

Setting Slide Transitions   567

Running the Slide Show   569

Testing the Timing   569

Adjusting Slide Advances   569

Adjusting Slide Animation   570

Metering a Manual Presentation   570

Running the Show for an Audience   571

Creating Self-Running Shows   574

Configuring a Self-Running Presentation   575

Adding Action Buttons   575

Adding Actions to Slide Elements   577

Starting a Self-Running Presentation   578

Creating Presentations for the Internet   579

Using the PowerPoint Internet Assistant   580

28   Creating Multimedia Presentations   585

Understanding Multimedia   586

Technical Considerations   586

Presentation Considerations   587

Getting the Best Out of Video and Audio   588

Using Video Clips   589

Video from the Clip Art Gallery   589

Video from Other Sources   590

Editing Video   591

Configuring the Playback Action   593

Configuring the Playback Animation   594

Using Audio Clips   595

Using Sound from the Clip Art Gallery   595

Using Sound from Other Sources   596

Configuring the Sound Playback   596

VII | Visual Basic for Applications

29 Using VBA Macros   601

Creating a Macro   602

Adding the Macro to the Toolbar   604

Changing the Appearance of the Toolbar   605

Editing a Macro in VBA   607

Macro Subroutines   609

Anatomy of a Subroutine   609

Class Objects   610

Modifying VBA Code   611

Executing Macros   612

Keyboard Macro Execution   613

Auto-Execution of Macros   614

30 Working with Application Objects   617

Application Object Overview   618

Manipulating Objects   619

Using Word Objects   620

Using the *Documents* Object Collection   620

Using the *Document* Object Properties   620

Using the *Document* Object Methods   622

Using the *Document* Object Events   623

Using *Selection* Methods   624

Using Excel Objects   624

Using the *Workbooks* Object Collection   624

Using the *Workbook* Object Properties and Methods   625

Using the *Worksheets* Object Collection   626

Using *Worksheet* Object Properties   626

Using the *Range* Object   627

Using Access Objects   629

Using PowerPoint Objects   629
    Presentation   629
    Slides   629

Using Office Assistant Objects   630

31   Building Forms and Dialog Boxes   633

Beginning with an Excel Macro   634
    Adding a Form to the Project   636
    Adding Code to the Command Button   638
    Adding Text Box Controls to Our Form   639
    Using Other Controls   641
    Using the Message Box Function   642

Activating the Form from the Sheet   644
    Input Box Function   646

Exploring the Parts of VBA Environment   646
    Project Explorer Window   646
    Properties Window   647
    Control Toolbox Palette   647
    Immediate Window   648
    Object Browser   649

Common Dialog Boxes   649

Form Layout Considerations   652
    Form Properties   652
    Setting the Tab Order of Controls   653
    Aligning and Sizing Controls   654

PowerPoint Creations   654

Related Sources   655

32   VBA Programming   657

Starting VBA Programming   658
    Using Multiple Commands   659
    Creating a Subroutine   660

Using Procedures and Functions   663
    Understanding Objects   664
    Using *If...Then...Else* Statements   665
    Using *Do While...Loop* and *Do...Until*   666

Using the Debugger   666

    Using the Step Feature   668

    Setting Breakpoints   669

Creating Variables   669

Using Other Mathematical Operators   671

Including Disk Functions   671

Selecting Events   673

Accessing Databases   673

Programming with Objects   674

    Creating Objects   674

    Accessing the Excel Object   674

    Creating a Simple Application in Word   677

    Programming the Office Assistant   678

Getting Help from Visual Basic   681

Differences Between Visual Basic and VBA   681

Related Sources   682

33   Using VB Script   683

VB Script Overview   684

    VB Script versus VBA   684

    Understanding the Language   686

    Scoping Variables   690

    Using the Unicode Standard   690

    Activating Events   690

    Trapping Errors   691

    Using Objects   691

Outlook and VB Script   692

    Creating a Simple VB Script Form   693

    Creating an Effective VB Script Function   697

    Outlook Object Model   699

Using VB Script in a Web Browser   699

Using VB Script with Active Server Pages   703

Windows Scripting Host   706

Related Sources   707

VIII | Microsoft Publisher

34 Manipulating Objects   711

Manipulating Text   712
  Adding Pages   712
    Flowing Text into a New Frame   713
    Perfecting Text Appearance   714
    Adding a Continued Notice   714

Layering and Grouping Objects   716
  Arranging the Layers of Objects   716
  Layering Text Boxes   717
  Grouping Objects   719
  Creating a Group   719

Aligning and Nudging Objects   721
  Configuring Layout Guides   721
  Configuring Ruler Guides   722
  Snapping Objects   723
  Lining Up Objects   723
  Nudging Objects   724

Wrapping Text   725
  Wrapping Around Frames   725
  Wrapping Around the Picture   726
  Wrapping with Customized Settings   727

35 Adding Publisher's Special Elements   729

Using the Design Gallery   730
  Inserting Gallery Objects   730
  Altering Gallery Objects   731
  Visiting Other Galleries   732
  Creating Your Own Gallery   732

Using the Special Elements PageWizard   735
  Creating a Calendar   735
  Creating an Ad   736
  Creating a Coupon   739
  Creating a Logo   739

Inserting Special Objects   740
  Inserting a Sound Clip   740

Inserting Other Sound Files   741
Editing Sound Files   742
Inserting a Video Clip   745

36 Publishing to the Web   747

Creating a Web Publication   748
Using the Web Site PageWizard   748
Using Blank Web Pages   751

Publishing Web Pages   755
Running the Design Checker   755
Previewing the Publication   757
Putting Your Publication on the Web Site   757

Converting Publisher Documents for the Web   759

37 An Overview of Other Small Business Edition Applications   761

Understanding SBFM   762
Excel and SBFM   762
Supported Accounting Software   763
Configuring Your Accounting Software   763
Specific Software Considerations   764
Understanding What Data Is Imported   765
SBFM Built-In Reports   766
Scenarios   767

Understanding AutoMap Streets Plus   767

IX | Office 97 on the Internet

38 Creating Web Documents   773

Understanding How HTML Works   774
HTML Is a Markup Language   774
Every Web Page Follows a Basic Structure   775
Most HTML Tags Specify Formatting   776
Other Tags Perform Specialized Functions   778

Converting Existing Documents to HTML Documents   778
Word Documents   779
Excel Spreadsheets   779
PowerPoint Presentations   781
Publisher Documents   782

Creating HTML Documents with Microsoft Word   784
    Creating a New Web Page   784
    Adding Text to Your Web Page   784
    Inserting Pictures into Your Web Page   786
    Linking to Other Web Pages or Internet Resources   786
    Formatting Content with Tables   787

39   Publishing to the Net   789

Managing Your HTML Files   790
    Mirroring (or Staging) Your Web Site Locally   791
    Creating Relative References   791
    Launching Related Files   791

Finding a Home for Your Web Pages   792

Checking Your Web on Your Own Computer   792
    Check the Layout in Netscape Navigator   793
    Browse to Find Broken Links   793
    Verify that Each Image File Exists   793
    Double-Check All Custom HTML Tags   793

Publishing with the Web Publishing Wizard   794

Validating Your Web Pages Online   796
    Verifying Links Within a Web Page   797
    Checking the Performance of Your Images   798

40   Understanding ActiveX   801

Manually Working with ActiveX Controls   802
    Inserting Controls with the <OBJECT> Tag   802
    Setting a Control's Properties with the PARAM Tag   803
    Connecting Controls to Scripts   804

Introducing the ActiveX Control Pad   806
    Placing Objects into Your HTML File   807
    Editing Scripts Using the Control Pad's Script Wizard   808

Controlling Page Layout with the HTML Layout Control   809
    Inserting the HTML Layout Control into an HTML File   810
    Editing the Layout   810

41   Publishing Web Sites with FrontPage 97   813

From Web Pages to Web Sites   814
    Letting FrontPage Explorer Coordinate Your Web Site   816

A Quick Look at the FrontPage 97 Editor 817

Web Pages, Servers, and Web Sites 817

From Office Documents to FrontPage 97 Web Sites 818

Managing Web Sites with FrontPage 97 Explorer 818

Importing Web Site Components 819

Many Ways to Explore Your Web Site 820

Importing Files 821

Publishing Your Web Site to a Web Server 822

Editing Web Pages in the FrontPage 97 Editor 822

Editing and Formatting Text in FrontPage 97 Editor 823

Working with Images in FrontPage 97 Editor 825

Assigning Other Image Attributes 826

Adding Backgrounds, Clip Art, and Icons 827

Creating Text and Graphic Hyperlinks 828

Defining Image Maps 829

Saving and Testing Your Web Site 830

42 Making Your Web Site Interactive 833

Creating Interactive Web Sites 834

Timestamping Your Page 835

Generating a Current Table of Contents 836

Adding a Search Engine to a Web Page 837

Designing Input Forms 838

Creating Input Forms 838

Use FrontPage 97 Templates 841

More FrontPage 97 842

X | Office 97 Power User Reference for Windows 95

43 Windows Navigation Basics 845

Starting and Quitting Windows 846

Running Applications at Startup 847

Starting Windows After Technical Problems Occur 850

Troubleshooting in Safe Mode 854

Using a BOOTLOG.TXT to Troubleshoot Failures 855

Using Step-by-Step Mode to Interactively Test Startup 855

Frequently Used Troubleshooting Techniques   856

Restarting and Reinstalling from Your Startup Disk   857

Using the Start Menu   858

Starting a Program from the Start Menu   859

Starting a Document from the Start Menu   860

Using the Taskbar to Switch Between Programs   861

Using the Power of Shortcuts and Desktop Icons   862

Creating Shortcuts to Programs or Documents   863

Using Shortcut Icons on the Desktop   864

Creating Shortcuts to Frequently Used Folders   864

Editing a Shortcut Name and Deleting Shortcuts   864

Setting the Properties for a Shortcut Icon   865

Opening Programs and Documents from Explorer or My
Computer   867

Using Explorer to Start Programs and Open Documents   868

Using My Computer to Start Programs and Open
Documents   869

Working from Your Desktop   869

Making a Desktop Folder to Hold Other Shortcuts   870

Accessing the Desktop   870

Using Shortcuts and Icons on the Desktop   871

Arranging Icons on Your Desktop   872

Working on Your Desktop with the Keyboard   873

Changing Settings and Properties with the Right Mouse Button   875

Using the Send To Command for Frequent Operations   875

Arranging Windows from the Taskbar   877

Managing Windows After an Application Failure   877

44   Managing Files   881

Understanding Files and Folders   882

Using Windows Explorer to View Files and Folders   882

Viewing Your Computer's Resources   883

Browsing the Contents of a Folder   884

Understanding the File Icons in Windows   885

Using My Computer to Manage Files   887

Managing Your Files and Folders   888
Selecting Files and Folders   889
Renaming Files   890
Renaming Multiple Files   890
Creating New Folders   891
Moving and Copying Files and Folders   891
Copying Disks   892
Deleting Files and Folders   893
Restoring Deleted Files   895
Previewing a Document with Quick View   897
Viewing and Changing the Properties of a File or Folder   899
Opening a Document from the Explorer   901
Printing Files   902

Finding Files   902
Searching Through Compressed ZIP Files   905
Saving the Search Criteria   906

Customizing Explorer's Appearance   906
Changing the Width of Panes   906
Changing the Status Bar   907
Hiding the Toolbar   907
Changing How Folders and Files Display   907
Arranging File and Folder Icons   908
Sorting Files and Folders   909
Displaying or Hiding Different File Types   910

Starting Explorer at Specific Directories or Files   911
Opening Explorer at Specific Folders or Files   911

Customizing Explorer for Side-by-Side Views or Program
Groups   913
Opening Side-by-Side Folder Windows from a Desktop
Shortcut   914
Creating Windows 3.1-Like Program Groups   915

Working with Long File Names   916
Renaming Files and Folders   916
Using Long File Names with Older Windows and DOS
Systems   917
Administering Long File Names in a Mixed-Name
Environment   919

Modifying the Registry to Remove Numeric Tails from File Names   920

Working with Long File Names in MS-DOS   920

Synchronizing Files with the Briefcase   921

Installing the Briefcase   922

Creating a New Briefcase on the Desktop   922

Synchronizing Files with a Laptop or Another Computer on the Network   922

Checking the Status of Briefcase Files   925

Preventing a File from Synchronizing   926

Registering Documents So They Open Applications   927

Using Explorer with Shared Resources on a Network   928

Browsing Shared Folders   928

Sharing Resources on Your Computer   928

Stop Sharing a Folder   931

Mapping a Network Drive   931

Finding a Computer on Your Network   932

Using Network Neighborhood to View Network Resources   933

45   Adding New Hardware to Windows 95   935

Installing Plug and Play Hardware   936

How Windows 95 Plug and Play Works   936

Understanding Plug and Play Hardware   938

Installing Plug and Play Hardware   941

Installing Legacy (Non-PnP) Hardware   942

How Windows 95 Operates with Legacy Hardware   942

Legacy Device Detection During Windows 95 Setup   943

Setting Resource Values for Legacy Adapter Cards   943

Installing Adapter Cards with Automatic Detection   945

Installing Legacy Cards After Setting Up Drivers   948

Removing Unneeded Drivers for Legacy Devices   951

Troubleshooting Hardware Installation   952

Understanding the Device Manager   952

Changing Resource Settings   952

Checking for Resource Conflicts with the Device Manager   956

Hardware Problems with the Registry Editor   957

46 Controlling Printers   961

Installing and Deleting Printers   962
    Installing a New Printer   962
    Renaming an Existing Printer   966
    Deleting an Existing Printer   967

Configuring Your Printer   968
    Options for Your Printer   968
    Printing with Color   970
    Using the 32-Bit Subsystem   971
    Using Enhanced Meta File Spooling (EMF)   972
    Configuring the Printer Port   974

Printing from Applications   978
    Basic Windows 95 Printing Procedures   978
    Applications with Special Print Options   979
    Windows 3.1 Applications with Special Print Options   980

Managing Print Jobs   981
    The Print Manager   981
    Controlling Printing   982

Drag-and-Drop Printing from the Desktop   985
    Creating a Desktop Printer Icon   985
    Print from the Desktop   986
    Desktop Printing of Multiple Documents   987

Printing from MS-DOS Applications   987

Printing from a Docking Station   988
    Configuring a Hardware Profile   988

Common Printer Problems   990
    Before the Problem: Initial Preparation   990
    Diagnosing the Problem: A Checklist   990
    Troubleshooting Tools   991

47 Installing, Running, and Uninstalling Windows Applications   993

Understanding How Windows Runs Applications   994
    Support for Win32 Applications   994
    Support for Windows 3.1 Applications   996
    Windows 3.1 and Long File Names   996

Installing Applications in Windows 95   997
    What Does Setup Do?   997
    What If There's No Setup Program?   998

Using Windows 3.1 Applications in Windows 95   998

Installing Windows 3.1 Applications   999

Setting Up Existing Applications in a Dual-Boot Configuration   1000

Running Windows 3.1 Applications   1001

Installing Windows 95 Applications in Windows 95   1002

Adding Windows' Component Applications   1005

Adding and Removing Windows Components   1005

Installing Unlisted Components   1007

Running Applications   1008

Removing Windows Applications   1010

Removing Applications Automatically   1010

Removing Applications Manually   1011

48   Backing Up and Protecting Your Data   1015

Backing Up Your Files   1016

Understanding Backup   1018

An Overview of How to Back Up Your Hard Disk   1018

Preparing a Backup Schedule   1019

Backing Up Files   1020

Scheduling Backups Using System Agent   1022

Changing Backup Settings and Options   1023

Saving File Sets   1024

Filtering Folders and File Types Included in Backup Operations   1026

Changing the General Settings in Backup   1027

Backing Up with a Simple Drag-and-Drop   1027

Formatting and Erasing Tapes   1029

Restoring Files   1030

Restoring Files to Other Locations   1031

Changing Restore Settings and Options   1032

Verifying Backup Files   1034

Changing Compare Settings and Options   1034

Protecting Your Files from Viruses   1035

Understanding How Viruses Damage Your Computer   1035

XI | Appendixes

A Tips and Tricks for System Administrators   1039

Installation   1040

Workgroup Administration of Applications   1046

    Access Workgroup Administration   1046

    Excel Workgroup Administration   1048

    PowerPoint Workgroup Administration   1048

    Word Workgroup Administration   1049

B The CD-ROM   1051

Books   1052

Templates and Wizards   1052

Software   1052

Internet Utilities   1053

C Business Sites on the Web   1055

Business Startup and Planning   1056

Business Financing   1059

International Business and Trade   1061

Job Opportunities and Labor Resources   1063

Legal and Regulatory   1065

Magazines Online   1066

Marketing and Market Research   1068

Nonprofit Information   1071

Patents, Trademarks, and Copyrights   1072

Procurement and Contracting   1074

Small Office/Home Office (SOHO)   1077

Travel and Transportation   1082

Trade Shows and Conferences   1083

Index   1087

Credits

PRESIDENT
Roland Elgey

SENIOR VICE PRESIDENT/PUBLISHING
Don Fowley

PUBLISHER
Joseph B. Wikert

PUBLISHING DIRECTOR
Karen Reinisch

GENERAL MANAGER
Joe Muldoon

EDITORIAL SERVICES DIRECTOR
Carla Hall

MANAGING EDITOR
Thomas F. Hayes

ACQUISITIONS EDITOR
Don Essig

PRODUCT DIRECTORS
John Gosney
Joyce Nielsen
Jan Snyder

PRODUCTION EDITOR
Lisa M. Gebken

PRODUCT MARKETING MANAGER
Kourtnaye Sturgeon

ASSISTANT PRODUCT MARKETING MANAGER
Gretchen Schlesinger

TECHNICAL EDITORS
Kyle Bryant
Steve Gaines
Bradley Lindaas
Verley Nelson
Marty Wyatt

MEDIA DEVELOPMENT SPECIALIST
David Garratt

TECHNICAL SUPPORT SPECIALIST
Nadeem Muhammed

ACQUISITIONS COORDINATORS
Virginia Stoller
Tracy M. Williams

SOFTWARE RELATIONS COORDINATOR
Susan D. Gallagher

EDITORIAL ASSISTANTS
Jeff Chandler
Jennifer L. Chisolm

BOOK DESIGNER
Ruth Harvey

COVER DESIGNER
Jay Corpus

PRODUCTION TEAM
Marcia Deboy
Jenny Earhart
Christy M. Lemasters
Darlena Murray
Angela Perry

INDEXER
Charlotte Clapp

Composed in *Century Old Style* and *ITC Franklin Gothic* by Que Corporation.

Half this book is dedicated to David Madison, whose support, help, patience, and humor (especially the humor) have made such a difference throughout the writing of this book and many books before this. The other half is dedicated to E.T., who acted as guide, coach, and hand-holder for a good part of the journey to this place. They can each pick whichever half they want.

About the Authors

Kathy Ivens spent 10 years as a computer consultant and has taught diverse computer courses at a variety of institutions. She has authored and contributed to more than two dozen books on computer subjects. She is a frequent contributor to national magazines, writing articles and reviewing software.

Before becoming an expert in computing, Kathy spent many years as a television producer, where she had fun producing sports and was mildly amused producing news and entertainment programs. Preceding that career was some professional time spent as a community organizer for social agencies; she also spent a few years as a political consultant. She still doesn't know what she wants to be when she grows up.

She has three brilliant daughters, three terrific sons-in-law, and one perfect granddaughter. She keeps sending them copies of her books, but she knows they never read them.

Conrad Carlberg is president of Network Control Systems, Inc, a software development and consulting firm that specializes in the statistical forecasting of data network usage. He holds a Ph.D. in statistics from the University of Colorado, and is a three-time recipient of Microsoft Excel's Most Valuable Professional award.

Gordon Padwick is a senior programmer analyst who develops applications based on Microsoft's Office suite. He has worked with computers for more years than he cares to remember, and has experience as an engineer and manager in many hardware and software design projects. He has worked with Windows and Windows applications since Microsoft introduced the first version of Windows in 1987.

Previously, Gordon was an independent consultant who specialized in Windows applications. He has authored and contributed to many books about such subjects as word processing, spreadsheets, databases, graphics, desktop publishing, and presentation software; his most recent publications are Que's *Building Integrated Office Applications, Special Edition Using Microsoft Office 97 Professional*, and *Special Edition Using Microsoft Outlook 97*.

Padwick is a graduate of London University, has completed postgraduate studies in computer science and communications, and is a senior member of the IEEE. He currently lives in southern California.

Jerry Honeycutt provides business-oriented technical leadership to the Internet community and software development industry. He has served companies such as The Travelers, IBM, Nielsen North America, IRM, Howard Systems International, and NCR. Jerry has participated in the industry since before the days of Microsoft Windows 1.0, and is completely hooked on Windows 95 and the Internet.

Jerry is the author of several Que books, including *Special Edition Using the Internet* Third Edition, *Using the Internet* Second Edition, and *Windows NT and Windows 95 Registry and Customization Handbook*. He has been printed in *Computer Language* magazine and is a regular speaker at the Windows World and COMDEX trade shows on topics related to software development, Windows 95, and the Internet.

Jerry graduated from the University of Texas at Dallas in 1992 with a B.S. degree in computer science. He currently lives in the Dallas suburb of Frisco with Becky, two Westies, Corky and Turbo, and a cat called Scratches. Jerry is an avid golfer with a passion for fine photography. Feel free to contact Jerry on the Internet at **jerry@honeycutt.com** or visit his Web site at **http://rampages.onramp.net/~jerry**.

Dan Rahmel, a product manager for Coherent Visual, has extensive experience implementing enterprise client/server solutions using Visual Basic, VBA, and C/C++. He currently develops enterprise systems for police departments (such as the San Diego Police Department and Portland Police Department) and small- to medium-sized companies.

Kevin D. Pagan is an attorney specializing in civil trial law and most recently, representation of local governments, such as the City of McAllen, Texas, where, along with his other areas of practice, he currently serves as an assistant city attorney. Kevin has a bachelor's degree in accounting from Arkansas State University and a law degree from Southern Methodist University. He is currently a member of the Texas Bar Association and the American Bar Association.

Throughout his more than 11 years as an attorney, Kevin has served as the network system administrator for two law firms and has helped those firms, and some of his other clients, develop network solutions for common business and legal challenges.

Scott Fuller is president of IDEAS and a former employee of (EDS) Electronic Data Systems. IDEAS is a nationwide computer solutions firm that consults on a variety of MIS-related issues. Scott has extensive experience in computer systems operation, networking, software engineering, and end-user education. You can reach Scott via e-mail at **ScottFuller@msn.com**.

Scott and Nancy Warner are private consultants in the computer and publishing arenas. They have written and contributed to numerous computer books, including *Special Edition Using Microsoft Office 97 Best Seller Edition, How to Use Access 97, How to Use Outlook 97, How to Use Netscape Communicator, Easy Windows NT Workstation 4.0, Ten-Minute Guide to Microsoft Exchange 5.0, Delphi By Example, Special Edition Using SQL Server,* and *Special Edition Using PowerBuilder 5.* They both graduated from Purdue University in computer information systems, worked in computer and publishing positions, and are currently living in Arizona. Visit their Web site at **www.infinet-is.com/~warner**.

David Karlins is a Web designer, author, consultant, teacher, and amateur unpublished movie critic. He is the host of Dave's Unauthorized Image Composer site, where Image Composer designers go for help to network and to show off their creations. Drop in any time day or night at **http://www.ppinet.com**. Dave is the author or contributing author of several books on Web site design including *Special Edition Using FrontPage 97,* and *Create FrontPage Web Pages in a Weekend.* Dave enjoys hearing from readers via e-mail at **dkarlins@aol.com**.

Robert Voss, Ph.D., has made a significant contribution to many of Que's best-selling books, including *Special Edition Using Word Version 6 for Windows*. Bob is a senior trainer in Microsoft Excel and Word for Windows for Ron Person & Co.

Ron Person has written more than 18 books for Que Corporation, including *Special Edition Using Excel for Windows 97*, *Web Publishing with Word for Windows*, and *Special Edition Using Windows 3.11*. He is the lead author of *Special Edition Using Windows 97*. He has a Master's degree in physics from Ohio State University and an MBA from Hardin-Simmons University. Ron was one of Microsoft's original 12 Consulting Partners and is a Microsoft Solutions Partner.

Acknowledgments

The team that works together to get a book like this one into your hands is awesome. It's a large team, of course, but more important, it's a group of talented, bright, competent, publishing professionals. Without them, authors couldn't survive, because so much of the work begins after the authors finish.

In this case, the folks at Que Publishing worked so well together to make sure this volume met the vision we had for it that it's impossible to thank all of them properly for the work they did; it would just take up more pages than they'd let me use. So, knowing I have room for just a few, I'll acknowledge the people I worked with most directly (you can translate that as the people who had to put up with me on a constant basis). The others will have to take my word for it that my gratitude to them is deep and sincere.

Don Essig is a fun acquistions editor, and that's not a common statement (most of them are dreadful nags whose favorite phrase is "deadline is firm, no exceptions"). Don takes the same attitude, but manages to be so human and funny that somehow it's okay. Lisa Gebken is a production editor extraordinaire, and I always leap at a chance to work with her. Her professionalism, her sense of humor, and her incredible skills make the process of writing a book so much easier. There are a few terrific folks who gave their extraordinary talents to developing this book, making sure it covered what it was supposed to in an understandable way. So, grateful kudos and thanks to John Gosney, Jan Snyder, and Joyce Nielsen for a wonderful job. Technical editors Kyle Bryant, Steve Gaines, Brad Lindaas, Verley Nelson, and Marty Wyatt made sure of the accuracy of all the information in the book, and all of them spent many difficult hours going over every single word, a very intricate chore.

We'd Like to Hear from You!

QUE Corporation has a long-standing reputation for high-quality books and products. To ensure your continued satisfaction, we also understand the importance of customer service and support.

Tech Support

If you need assistance with the information in this book or with a CD/disk accompanying the book, please access Macmillan Computer Publishing's online Knowledge Base at:

> **http://www.superlibrary.com/general/support**

Our most Frequently Asked Questions are answered there. If you do not find the answer to your questions on our Web site, you may contact Macmillan Technical Support by phone at **317/581-3833** or via e-mail at **support@mcp.com**.

Also be sure to visit QUE's Desktop Applications and Operating Systems team Web resource center for all the latest information, enhancements, errata, downloads, and more:

> **http://www.quecorp.com/desktop_os/**

Orders, Catalogs, and Customer Service

To order other QUE or Macmillan Computer Publishing books, catalogs, or products, please contact our Customer Service Department:

> **Phone: 800/858-7674**
> **Fax: 800/882-8583**
> **International Fax: 317/228-4400**

Or visit our online bookstore:

> **http://www.mcp.com/**

Comments and Suggestions

We want you to let us know what you like or dislike most about this book or other QUE products. Your comments will help us to continue publishing the best books available on computer topics in today's market.

> **John Gosney**
> **Product Director**
> **QUE Corporation**
> **201 West 103rd Street, 4B**
> **Indianapolis, IN 46290 USA**
> **Fax: 317/581-4505**
> **E-mail: jgosney@que.com**

Please be sure to include the book's title and author as well as your name and phone or fax number.

We will carefully review your comments and share them with the author. Please note that due to the high volume of mail we receive, we may not be able to reply to every message.

Thank you for choosing QUE!

Introduction

Office 97 is the newest incarnation of Microsoft's popular suite, and it is a robust, feature-filled group of applications.

More important, the individual applications are more closely intertwined, and the document-centered approach of this suite is an important and obvious philosophy.

This book is a one-stop source for the advanced features and functions of Office 97.

In addition, we've provided information on Microsoft's new edition of Office 97, the Small Business Edition. The applications that are specific to that edition are covered in the chapters and on the CD accompanying this volume. ■

Who Will Get the Most Out of This Book?

Platinum Edition Using Microsoft Office 97 was conceived and written for users who have mastered the basics of Office 97 and want to take advantage of the power inherent in advanced features. It's also written with a view toward helping system administrators and help desk personnel understand what's going on behind the scenes so they can administer Office 97 more effectively.

How to Use This Book

The best way to use this book is to head right for those sections you need to advance your skills in a particular application. When you get there, you'll find plenty of technical information above and beyond the traditional numbered steps for performing tasks.

How This Book Is Organized

Platinum Edition Using Microsoft Office 97 has 48 chapters filled with information, tips, notes, and other elements. In addition, there are several chapters on the CD-ROM. The book is divided into 11 parts, with 48 chapters and 2 appendixes. Following is the information about the way we divided the subject matter.

Part I: Office 97: An Integrated Environment

In Chapter 1, "Office 97 Overview," you'll find a quick look at the new features in each application.

Chapter 2, "Office 97 Application Interaction," shows you how to use the document-centered philosophy of Office 97, covering everything from Shortcut Bars to linking and embedding.

Chapter 3, "The Office 97 Binder," is an in-depth discussion of the power of the Binder when you want to combine data from different Office applications.

Part II: Microsoft Word

Chapter 4, "Document Power," is a comprehensive explanation of Word documents, covering advanced document features such as forms.

Chapter 5, "Power Tools," explains document mapping, cross referencing, macros, and other powerful functions you can bring to your Word documents.

Chapter 6, "Advanced Mail Merge," is the place to learn all the tricks and strengths of mail merge.

Part III: Microsoft Excel

Chapter 7, "Advanced Templates," is an advanced tutorial on this powerful Excel feature.

Chapter 8, "Advanced Work with Charts," describes chart axes, scales, and data labels, and shows you how to create special effects in charts.

Chapter 9, "Using Ranges," explains the power of using ranges in functions and other documents.

Chapter 10, "Advanced Work with Formulas," is an Excel junkie's dream with lots of tricks and tips about getting the most out of Excel formulas.

Chapter 11, "Using Worksheet Functions," is a look at the Function Wizard and then a look beyond it, making the chapter a power user's playground.

Chapter 12, "Using Lists," shows you how to move outside Excel for data, set it up, and manipulate it so you can use it with Excel.

Chapter 13, "Pivot Tables," is a treatise on using this powerful feature to its maximum.

Chapter 14, "Connecting to Access Databases," gives you a chance to learn more about queries and ODBC, as you also learn to customize your query approach.

Chapter 15, "Analyzing Data," explains how to get the real power out of Scenarios and Goal Seeker.

Chapter 16, "Using the Solver," shows you the unbelievable power in this Excel feature.

Part IV: Microsoft Access

Chapter 17, "Creating Tables," teaches you how to create a new table, and work with data types and field properties. Also, we show you how to modify a table and work with relationships within a table.

Chapter 18, "Working with Data," describes all the manipulations you can perform on your Access data.

Chapter 19, "Querying Data," shows you how to create queries, work with criteria that can customize your queries, use calculations to extract summary data and perform operations on that data, and work with action queries that allow you to use a query's result set to perform an action on a table.

Chapter 20, "Database Reports," shows you all the ways you can report your Access data.

Chapter 21, "Using Multiple Tables," helps you explore multiple table relational types, queries, forms, and reports.

Chapter 22, "Macros," offers ways to create and modify macros. Learn how to refer to controls from within macros and use macros in forms and reports.

Part V: Microsoft Outlook

Chapter 23, "Customizing Views," gives you some insights (and some tricks) for storing all the information in Outlook.

Chapter 24, "Integrating the Outlook Elements," shows you how to automate the interaction between all the Outlook features.

Chapter 25, "More Power with Exchange Server," describes the extra features and power tools that you have at your disposal if your network is running Exchange Server.

Part VI: Microsoft PowerPoint

Chapter 26, "Working with Objects," is an advanced tutorial on manipulating objects in PowerPoint.

Chapter 27, "Creating a Slide Show," describes all the steps to take to have that perfect presentation.

Chapter 28, "Creating Multimedia Presentations," explains how to animate your presentation.

Part VII: Visual Basic for Applications

Chapter 29, "Using VBA Macros," is a tutorial on getting the most of out VBA when you use it for advanced macro techniques.

Chapter 30, "Working with Application Objects," describes the way you can use VBA to work with objects in all the Office applications.

Chapter 31, "Building Forms and Dialog Boxes," shows you how to use advanced VBA functions to enhance your Office configuration.

Chapter 32, "VBA Programming," presents the tricks and tips for building procedures and functions.

Chapter 33, "Using VB Script," is a close look at this application language that you can use to build forms, manipulate application objects, and increase the power of the Office applications.

Part VIII: Microsoft Publisher

Chapter 34, "Manipulating Objects," shows you how to build professional-looking pages for your publication.

Chapter 35, "Adding Publisher's Special Elements," describes the special objects that enhance publications.

Chapter 36, "Publishing to the Web," explains how to use Publisher for great, slick Web pages.

Chapter 37, "An Overview of Other Small Business Edition Applications," is an introduction, along with tips and inside information, to the Small Business Financial Manager and AutoMap Streets Plus. The detailed explanations of how to use these application are found on the chapters that reside on the accompanying CD.

Part IX: Office 97 on the Internet

Chapter 38, "Creating Web Documents," explains how to take documents from Office applications to your Web site.

Chapter 39, "Publishing to the Net," shows you how to manage your documents as you use them on the Internet or your company intranet.

Chapter 40, "Understanding ActiveX," gives you all the inside info on using ActiveX Controls effectively.

Chapter 41, "Publishing Web Sites with FrontPage 98," is where you learn how to create Web sites with FrontPage 97 Explorer and your Web server, and import files into your Web site in

FrontPage 97 Explorer. Using the FrontPage 97 Editor, learn how to polish Web page layout and edit graphic image properties.

Chapter 42, "Making Your Web Site Interactive," shows you how to timestamp your Web pages and generate a table of contents. This chapter tells you how to use search engines to enable your visitors find information quickly and provide input.

Part X: Office 97 Power User Reference for Windows 95

Chapter 43, "Navigating and Controlling Windows 95," explains what you need to know in order to best operate Windows and any Windows application, including many tips for increased productivity.

Chapter 44, "Managing Files," offers solid instruction on working with Explorer and My Computer, as well as offering advice on synchronizing files between laptop and desktop computers and viewing and changing file attributes.

Chapter 45, "Adding New Hardware to Windows 95," is a one-stop source for information on Plug and Play, as well as essential troubleshooting information regarding hardware installation.

Chapter 46, "Controlling Printers," is full of useful "must-have" information on how to best manage and use printer resources, including how to connect to and share printers across a network of multiple users.

Chapter 47, "Installing, Running, and Uninstalling Windows Applications," along with the basics, also gives instruction on how to install 16-bit applications in Windows 95 and how to add and remove Windows component applications.

Chapter 48, "Backing up and Protecting Your Data," with its information on how to back up your files, how to verify files are backed-up correctly, and how to protect your system against viruses, is essential reading for anyone who wants to work with Windows 95 in the most efficient—and safest—manner possible.

The Appendixes

Appendix A is for administrators, containing tips and information that are helpful when you need to install, configure, or troubleshoot Office 97.

Appendix B is all about the CD-ROM.

Appendix C contains a listing of related businesses and their Web sites.

Special Features in This Book

As you're used to with books from Que, we've incorporated a number of special features to make this book more informative and easier to learn from.

At the beginning of each chapter, there's a roadmap of topics covered in that chapter. This is a quick-glance way to make sure you've turned to the right place when you need information.

 N O T E Extra information (above and beyond the topic being discussed) we think you'll find helpful and interesting is placed in Notes throughout each chapter. ■

 T I P Tips are quick pieces of advice, sometimes about shortcuts or tricks, sometimes drawing on the expertise and experience of the author.

CAUTION

We'll put a caution on a page to warn you when a procedure might create a problem, and tell you the circumstances under which that problem is likely to occur.

TROUBLESHOOTING

Common problems, errors, or traps are explained in our Troubleshooting sidebars.

 ON THE WEB

Look here for sites that might be of particular interest regarding the subject at hand. For example, Que's Web site is

http://www.quecorp.com

For help in finding related information throughout the book, be on the lookout for cross references such as the following:

▶ **See** "Manipulating Objects," **p. 619**

Office 97: An Integrated Environment

1   Office 97 Overview   9

2   Office 97 Application Interaction   27

3   The Office 97 Binder   45

Office 97 Overview

The new version of Microsoft Office has a host of exciting and productive features. This book covers the applications included in Microsoft Office 97, Professional Edition. In addition, Microsoft has released a new suite called the Microsoft Office Small Business Edition, and the applications unique to that edition are part of this book, too. If you're comfortable with the applications included in either or both of these products, you'll find plenty of information about the advanced features for all of them. This chapter presents an overview of the new features in those applications. ■

New features in Office 97 applications

There are new tools and new features in all of the familiar applications.

Outlook, a new application for e-mail, scheduling, and contact management

Microsoft Outlook is a unified Personal Information Manager with robust e-mail capabilities.

Small Business Edition

The Small Business Edition offers a group of applications designed especially for small businesses that need basic business applications.

New ways to get Help

Help is everywhere, with lots of new ways to obtain assistance as you work.

Convert previous versions of documents

You can convert all your documents to Office 97 format, or adopt a system that enables files to be shared among users of various versions of application software.

What's New in Office 97?

The Office Suite has a number of new features and tools that you'll notice from the moment you first begin the installation. The Office 97 Setup program offers a larger variety of options, with special attractions for networked environments.

Installation Procedures

The installation can be performed in the typical manner, using the CD and installing directly to a computer. For networks, you can install the software to workstations from the network instead of from the CD.

If you have the Office Resource Kit from Microsoft, you can use the Network Installation Wizard to control options for the workstation user, or use a push installation that installs the files with no user intervention at the workstation.

Network Installation Point

To install Office from a network server, you create a set of folders on the server to act as the installation point. Workstation users access this group of folders to install the software. The workstation Setup program can transfer the entire suite to the local computer, or can be configured to leave some or all of the program files on the server. You can even split the program files if you have multiple servers, dividing the files in a way that uses disk space efficiently (you might want to put the Clip Art Gallery on a different server, for example).

 The term *server* refers to a computer that can be accessed by other users; it does not necessarily have to be a computer running Windows NT Server. Any computer running Windows 95 or Windows NT 3.51 or higher (either Server or Workstation) can be used as an installation server.

The server Setup process creates the folders that act as the installation point for the workstations. This process is called *Administrative Setup*, and the resulting files on the server are called the *Administrative Installation Point*.

To use Setup for an administrative installation, use Run and enter **d:\Setup/ a** (where *d*: is the drive letter of the server's CD-ROM) to launch Setup. The installation creates the following items on the server:

■ A Main Office folder that contains subfolders for all the program files, as well as Setup.Exe. By default, Setup names this folder MSOFFICE.

■ A folder for the shared application files that are included in Office, such as the spell checker, WordArt, Organization Chart, filters, converters, and so on. Setup names this folder MSAPPS.

After the installation point has been created, workstation users can connect to it and install Office.

If you have installed the Network Installation Wizard, you can control the options the workstation users see (and can respond to), or you can create a push install and have Office installed onto the workstation with no user intervention at all. Detailed information on these options is found in the Microsoft Office 97 Resource Kit.

New Office-Wide Features

There are a number of new tools and features available in all the Office applications:

- The toolbar icons and menu titles have a 3-D look when the mouse pointer is over them. Toolbars and menu bar items are unified in appearance because they are launched from a single set of toolbars. This also means there are fewer files cluttering your hard drive.

- You can customize the built-in toolbars.

- A new Web toolbar lets you access the Internet by launching your default browser while you work in an application.

- Hyperlinks can be inserted in any document to link to another document or to an Internet site. The document can be local or on any connected computer.

- Web documents can be created (saved as HTML files) and distributed over the Internet (or an intranet). (The add-on for this feature must be installed from the Office 97 CD.)

- User comments can be inserted in documents to add notes for other users, and each comment is identified with the user's name.

- Support for the Microsoft IntelliMouse is built into all the Office applications.

- Document virus checking is automatic, and you're warned if a document contains macros (there are document viruses that are spread through macros). There is an option for opening those documents without the macros. If a known macro virus is detected, the Office Virus Search add-in can usually remove it.

- Shared programming code for some functions speeds up everything because once these functions are loaded with the first Office application you open, they are not reloaded with each additional application. The shared code affects File Open and File Save dialog boxes, AutoCorrect, FastFind, and Print.

Office Binder

When you print a binder document that contains documents from different applications, you can now use headers and footers, including page numbering, in a consistent manner. And you can now use Print Preview to see every page in the binder document. This level of integration was not available when Office Binder was introduced in Office 95.

The Binder is now Briefcase-aware, and when the Briefcase is used with a binder document, the replication of the document is accomplished by section instead of as a whole. During updates between the Briefcase and the Binder, only affected sections are replaced. In a networked environment, this means that different users can work on different sections and update the shared document efficiently.

Office Art

All the Office 97 applications now have Office Art available as a tool. This is a set of drawing tools for shapes, fills, and textures that is consistent across all the applications. Office Art includes WordArt, AutoShapes, and gradation fills. (WordArt is now a tool instead of a discrete application.)

New Application Features

All the Office 97 applications have new or improved features and tools. This section presents an overview of some of those; it is not a comprehensive list.

Many of these features (and some not mentioned here) are covered in detail throughout this book.

New Word Features

Word has several new enhancements that range from major changes to minor improvements over previous versions.

The *Letter Wizard* (on the Tools menu) provides a way to format letters for consistency, and you can enter data so that important information is always a part of the document.

AutoComplete is a way to let Word offer suggestions for the rest of a partially typed word or phrase. It uses the information in your AutoText entries, and displays a ScreenTip when a matching pattern occurs. Just press Enter to accept the automatic completion of the word or phrase. In addition, AutoComplete works for dates, days of the week, days of the month, and your name and company name (the information entered during installation).

AutoSummarize creates a custom summary of your document that can be customized for length or for the way key data in the document is used. You can use it to create an abstract or summary document that is separate from the document on which it is based.

Automatic grammar checking works like automatic spell checking by offering suggestions for corrections when you right-click the marked text. In addition, the by grammar checker feature has been improved and now offers more (and better) suggestions for rewriting.

You can check spelling and grammar with one pass via the new combined *document checker*.

Tables are easier to create because you can drag the new *Draw Table tool* to set boundaries. Table cells can be formatted to any width or height you need.

A *Document Map* can be displayed on the left portion of the window to show an overview of the headings in a document (see Figure 1.1). You can scroll through the map to find the section you need and move to it quickly. The Document Map tool on the Standard toolbar toggles the feature on and off.

FIG. 1.1
Use the Document Map to navigate through a large document with great speed.

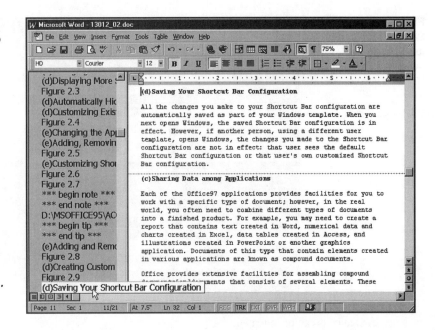

You can save multiple versions of the same document without having to resort to the SaveAs feature—instead, the versions all become part of the same file. This means you can look at earlier versions of a document (and even see who made changes to it). You can set this up automatically or use it on an as-needed basis.

New Excel Features

Excel has a number of new tools and enhancements that are the result of user requests. Some of the things about which we've all said, "I wish I could do this…" have appeared in this version.

Multiple Undo (up to 16 actions) is finally part of Excel.

Cells can contain up to 32,000 characters (quite an increase from the previous maximum of 255 characters). However, I cannot imagine making use of this feature too often.

The number of rows you can have in a worksheet is 65,536 (up from 16,384).

When you are working with multiple files, a Yes to All feature allows you to save all your open files when you exit the software, without having to answer Yes to an individual prompt for each file.

When you select a cell, the column letter and row number are bold and seem to be raised from the page, making it easier to keep track of where you are.

You can control page breaks with the Page Break Preview command on the View menu (see Figure 1.2). If you want to drag page breaks to a more logical location, Excel scales the data to fit the printed page. While you are using Page Break Preview mode, you can continue to work in the document.

FIG. 1.2

Move the page break or paper margin, and Excel works to make your data fit on your new page size.

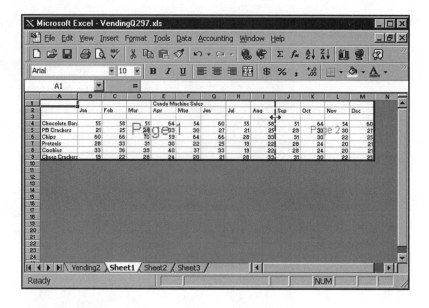

Text in cells can be indented.

Text in a cell can be rotated to any angle.

Natural language formulas permit you to create formulas that read the headings you've entered at the top of a column or in the first column of a row. This means you no longer have to enter range references for these items. For example, you could enter a formula such as =SUM(Roger) to add the column of figures under the column heading Roger.

Network users can share an open workbook, and edit the document at the same time. You cannot have multiple users editing the same cell, but if the various worksheets in the workbook contain information from different users (or departments), you do not have to work one at a time anymore. Those last-minute emergency reports will move a lot faster with this feature.

Conditional formatting means you can format a cell to display characters with certain formatting options if the conditions are right. This means that if the result of a formula matches criteria you've set, the cell characters display in a certain way. If the criteria is not met, the display changes.

The new and improved *Chart Wizard* has more options, and there are a number of new chart types. There's a new time-scale axis for charts that are built from worksheets containing dates. And, the worksheet data for a chart can be displayed beneath the chart.

You can use the new *Query Wizard* to access external databases, then select and sort the data you want to work with. You can also save a worksheet that has a query as a template—the retrieved data is not saved with the file. Then you can use the query template to retrieve the latest data. Incidentally, queries now run in the background so you can continue to work on a worksheet.

You can protect shared workbooks so that other users cannot turn off the revision tracking (nor can they turn off sharing or protection).

New in Access

Access (available in the Professional Version of Office 97) has had several improvements, and it's not surprising that some of them enhance connectivity features for networks, the Internet, and intranets.

You can place hyperlinks that connect with Internet addresses and Office 97 application documents into tables and forms.

You can now output your database tables, forms, reports, and queries to HTML format and then publish them on the Web.

Forms and reports that don't have event procedures do not contain form or report modules. This enables you to open and manipulate those simpler forms and reports much faster.

If you want to make changes to a compiled database, only the modified code is decompiled (any other dependent code is also decompiled).

Software components such as Visual Basic for Applications are not loaded with a database automatically, which speeds up retrieval and navigation of your database. Any software component that is needed is called at the time you need those functions.

Class modules now are distinguished from standard modules with a different icon.

The data in a lookup field (list box or combo box) is no longer refreshed automatically when you update the table. This makes everything move faster. You can still refresh the data as necessary by using F9.

The abbreviated year format supports the next century. For instance, if you enter **7/23/25**, the interpretation is July 23, 2025.

You can create partial replicas in order to transfer specific data to other locations. A filter (which you design) restricts the replicated data. This makes it more efficient to send relevant portions of your database to other offices and branches.

The Compact and Repair utilities can now be used on an opened database.

The Query property sheet supports `RecordSetType` so you can control the returned result set (this used to be available only for forms).

The maximum number of records to be returned can be controlled when you query an ODBC database.

You can use the new `FailOnError` property to terminate queries to an ODBC data source. This is extremely handy for bulk update queries.

You can design forms that display tabs for separate types of information.

You can use a macro to launch an Access menu command with the `RunCommand` action (replaces the old `DoMenuItem` action).

A new Visual Basic macro converter makes it easier to work with procedures.

The Macro command submenu on the Tools menu has several new items aimed at using macros you created in previous versions of Access. Those macros create the items named in these new commands:

- Create Menu from Macro
- Create Toolbar from Macro
- Create Shortcut Menu from Macro

The Edit menu has several useful new commands:

- Select All, which selects all text in the current procedure (or all text in the module if you are working in Full Module view).
- Find Next, which lets you find the next occurrence of any string you specified with Find.

The new Object Browser is an extremely useful tool that you can use to search for information about objects, properties, and constants. The Object Browser searches the current project and also any referenced object libraries. Its icon is on the Module toolbar. You can use the Object Browser dialog box to perform a number of useful manipulations:

- You can put code into your Module window with the Clipboard. Just select a property or method with the Object Browser, then use the new Copy to Clipboard button. Move to the Module window and click the Paste button.
- The Classes box displays all members that are global.
- Back and Forward buttons let you navigate through the Object Browser more easily.
- You can view the definition of a function or subprocedure you've defined.

You can now use Briefcase Replication to distribute your database or take it home over the weekend to catch up on your work.

New in PowerPoint

There are a number of exciting new features in PowerPoint, many of which involve enhanced capabilities for graphics. There are a number of new presentation templates available that you'll find useful because they're based on real business needs.

A new Summary Slide feature means you can create a recap of your total presentation. The feature uses the titles of the slides you choose to include in the summary and then automatically creates the summary. You can even use hyperlinks to create an agenda or introductory slide, then jump to the appropriate parts of the presentation by clicking the hyperlink.

The Expand Slide command separates a crowded, busy slide into several cleaner, slicker slides. Using the top-level bullets, this tool creates new slides with the sublevel bullets under the new heading.

A miniature slide appears when you work in Outline view so you can see just how crowded you're making that slide.

You can animate the way text and graphics appear on a slide with the new Animation Effects toolbar. This feature also lets you control the order in which the elements appear. Charts are included in this animation feature, so you can watch the bars grow.

You can convert your presentation to HTML format for Web publication. And you can use the PowerPoint Animation Player to create an animated Web slide show.

Outlook

Office 97 has added another application to the suite, a *Personal Information Manager*, and e-mail program called *Outlook*.

The Outlook features, all of which interact with each other, include:

- The Inbox has strong e-mail capabilities, including plenty of methods for managing, sorting, filtering, and archiving messages.
- The Outlook Calendar is a robust appointment program that displays your schedule in a wide variety of ways.
- The Outlook Contacts database provides a system for managing and tracking all your business and personal contacts. You can sort and filter the data in an endless variety of permutations and combinations.
- A task-tracking feature keeps tabs on everything from a to-do list for simple chores to complicated projects that are shared with other users.
- The journal tracks your activity in Outlook, and you can configure your own method for creating journal entries automatically.
- Outlook Notes are electronic sticky notes you use so you don't forget to visit the dentist or write a letter to your mother.

If you are connected to a network that has Microsoft Exchange Server installed, the features available in Outlook multiply several-fold.

Small Business Edition

Microsoft has issued another Office edition for organizations that don't need all the applications and networking features of the Standard and Professional editions. It's the *Small Business Edition (SBE)*, and it contains the following applications:

- Word
- Excel
- Outlook
- Publisher, Microsoft's easy-to-use publishing software, is included for businesses that need to produce newsletters, brochures, flyers, and other publications.

- Small Business Financial Manager, an add-in for Excel, has preconfigured scenarios and reports that use your accounting software data as the basis for what-if spreadsheet solvers and other advanced Excel functions.

- AutoMap Streets Plus enables you to locate customers, add notes to map locations, place pushpins on the streets where your customers live, and then ask for directions to go there.

These applications reflect the combination of software purchases made by many small businesses. The resulting Suite makes it easier and less expensive to get them.

The SBE comes on a CD-ROM and its installation differs from the other Office editions. There is no Setup program that installs all the applications; instead, the specific applications that are needed are installed discretely.

Office 97 Help

There are some new features in the Help system for Office 97 applications, including the lively Office Assistant and Microsoft Help from the Microsoft Internet sites.

Office Assistant

New in Office 97, the *Office Assistant* is an animated helpmate that replaces the Answer Wizard from previous versions of Office (see Figure 1.3).

FIG. 1.3

The Office Assistant searches for specific help and offers tips and tricks.

There are a couple of interesting advanced features in the Office Assistant:

- *Natural English queries*, which means you can ask simple questions and the Assistant finds the information (for example, you can enter **How do I print an envelope** and all the help topics on printing envelopes are listed in the Assistant's cue card).

- *Anticipated help*, which provides help before you ask. When you use certain features, the Assistant pops up with help.

- *Context-sensitive tips*, designated by a light bulb in the Assistant's box when you use certain features. The light bulb indicates that the Assistant has a tip on the currently active tool or feature. Click the light bulb to see the tip (the light bulb disappears after you read the tip and close the cue card).

N O T E Incidentally, if the Assistant is active, it takes over the job of presenting confirmation and inquiry notes (the ones usually presented by dialog boxes). For instance, if you make changes to a document and then close the document or exit the application, the cue card presents the familiar "Do you want to save changes?" query and offers the choices for responding. If the Assistant is not active, the standard dialog box displays with the query. ▨

To configure the Office Assistant, click the Options button on the cue card to open the Office Assistant dialog box (see Figure 1.4).

FIG. 1.4
Change the way the Office Assistant offers help with the Office Assistant dialog box.

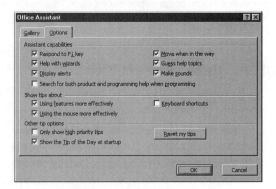

If you know your way around the Office applications, it's probably not a bad idea to deselect Show the Tip of the Day at Startup.

You can also change the persona of the Assistant with the Gallery tab of the dialog box. Be sure your Office 97 CD-ROM is in the drive because the other Assistants are kept there instead of being transferred to your hard drive during a normal installation. Continue to click Next to move through all the possibilities (see Figure 1.5).

FIG. 1.5

There are plenty of choices to replace the paper clip if you get tired of looking at it.

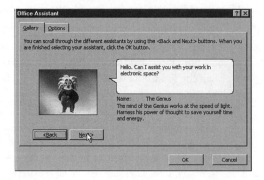

If you change the Office Assistant persona, it is changed for all of Office 97, not just the application you were working in when you made the change.

By default, the Office Assistant shows up when you first launch an Office application and sticks around while you're working. If you're an experienced user, this can be incredibly annoying. Click the X to close the Assistant; if you need it again, the Question Mark tool on the Standard toolbar brings it back.

Help from Microsoft on the Internet

The main Help menu for each application contains a Microsoft on the Web item, with a submenu covering a variety of Microsoft support topics (see Figure 1.6).

When you choose a topic from Microsoft on the Web, your default browser launches and you are sent to the appropriate Microsoft Internet site. Once there, you can go ahead and navigate through all the Microsoft information by reading, downloading, and taking advantage of all that's there. When you close your browser, you are returned to the application window.

ON THE WEB

Microsoft Internet Explorer 3.01 is available in the ValuPack folder of the Office 97 CD-ROM:

http://www.microsoft.com/ie/default.asp

The Main Help System

The way the Help files work for Office applications hasn't changed very much since the previous version of Office (Office 95), but it's amazing how few users take advantage of the customization possibilities for help. The additional power available as a result of changing the way the Find tab works is considerable.

FIG. 1.6
Go right to the source
for help by visiting
Microsoft on the Web.

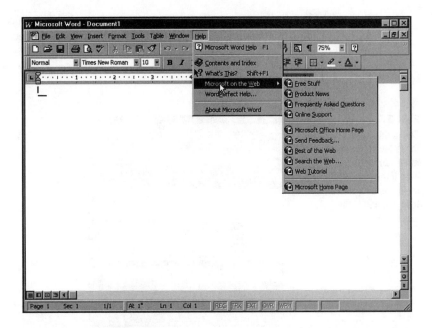

If you already configured your Find tab for the default database choice (Minimize), consider rebuilding the database to make it more robust and more useful. Begin by choosing Rebuild, then select Customize. The wizard walks you through a series of choices, and you must click Next as you make each decision.

The individual Help files available for this application are displayed, and you can eliminate any you think aren't needed. For example, you may decide that the Help files that are concerned with upgrading from the last version of Office aren't necessary.

Some Help topics don't have titles (titles are used for the basic indexing scheme), and you can eliminate these topics from your Help files. Most of the untitled topics are definitions that pop up when you click words in the Help screens that are highlighted with green text. If you include the untitled topics, the database is larger (and takes a bit longer to load), and the search for information takes longer because in the absence of a title, the text is searched. However, if you think you or the other users who are accessing the Help files need those topics, you should keep them in the database.

By default, the Find function searches for words, but you can change the configuration so it searches for phrases. As handy as this is for homing in on exactly what you need, the downside is that the Find Word list is expanded (making your Help files larger), and a search takes a bit longer.

If you do choose to search for phrases, you can configure Find to display matching phrases as you type, in the same way it moves to matching words as you enter the search word. This creates a slow-down during the process of entering the phrase to search for, so you might want to deselect this option.

There is an option to turn on similarity searches, which is a handy feature. It means that after you enter your search criteria, the list that Find displays includes a check box next to each topic (see Figure 1.7). You can select a check box and then, after you've read the Help text connected to the displayed topic, you can ask Find to search for similar information by choosing Find Similar.

FIG. 1.7

Select the check box for those topics you want more information about, even if the new information is on a similar topic instead of the exact topic.

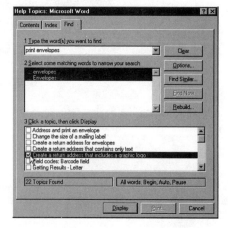

The more robust you make your Help system, the more help you'll get, of course, but there's a fairly big sacrifice in terms of speed, especially the speed with which the Find tab loads its word list.

Handling Document Conversions

Most of the time, each application in Office 97 will handle any document from a previous version without difficulty. However, in an environment that mixes versions of Office, the back-and-forth exchange of documents requires special steps.

Word Conversion Considerations

You can share most Word documents among users in a mixed environment.

Converting from WinWord 2.0, 6.0, or 95   To convert documents originally saved in Word for Windows 2.0, 6.0, or 95, just open the document in Word 97. All data and formatting is retained, and saving the document in Word 97 completes the conversion.

Converting Macros from WinWord 2.0, 6.0, or 95   If you had created WordBasic macros in Word for Windows 2.0, 6.0, or 95, they are converted for Word 97 in a format that is equivalent to Visual Basic code. For instance, here's what happened to one of my WordBasic macros.

The original macro in WordBasic (Word 95) read as follows:

```
Sub Main
Insert "Kathy Ivens, Ivens Consulting, Inc."
End Sub
```

Word 97 converted this to the following:

```
Public Sub Main()
WordBasic.Insert "Kathy Ivens, Ivens Consulting, Inc."
End Sub
```

The equivalent Visual Basic code for this macro is the following:

```
Public Sub Main()
Selection.TypeText Text:="Kathy Ivens, Ivens Consulting, Inc."
End Sub
```

This works because the Visual Basic object model in Word 97 has a WordBasic object to which all WordBasic statements (and functions) are exposed.

There are a couple of instances in which you must make changes to your WordBasic macros in order to have them convert properly:

- Any calls to custom 16-bit DLLs require you to provide a 32-bit compatibility layer (thunking layer) for the 16-bit DLL. Or you can recompile the DLL source code to a 32-bit version.

- Any call to a 16-bit Windows 3.x API must have that call replaced with a call to the equivalent Win32 API.

Converting from Word for DOS   Documents created in Microsoft Word for DOS have an entirely different file structure than those created in Microsoft Word for Windows. You must have the MS-DOS Converter that comes with the Office 97 Resource Kit to convert these documents.

Sharing Word 97 Documents with Other Users   You can save your Word 97 documents in a format that can be read by users of Word for Windows 2.0, 6.0, and 95. The Save As dialog box offers all these options. Be aware that some formatting or other special features that are unique to Word 97 may be lost during the conversion.

Excel Conversion Considerations

Microsoft Excel 97 can open files from all previous versions of Excel, and doing so converts the old documents. Saving a document in Excel 97 format completes the conversion.

For the most part, macros are also successfully converted, but there are a few known problems with VBA macros that were written for Excel 95. These involve macros that rotated text in an autoshape, or used CreateObject With DAO.DBEngine. There may be other known problems, and you should contact Microsoft support if you need a more complete list (at the time of this writing, it was still being developed).

If you have a mixed environment, the Excel Save As dialog box offers a number of solutions for sharing your Excel 97 files with other users by using the Save as Type choices:

- Use Type Excel 3.0 Worksheet
- Use Type Excel 4.0 Worksheet
- Use Type 5.0/95 Workbook
- Use Type 97 and 5.0/95 Workbook

The last option is a dual-format option that may be useful in your mixed environment (it was designed especially for organizations that are rolling out Excel 97 on a gradual basis). For one thing, it means that multiple users can work on the same workbook simultaneously regardless of their Excel platform. The downside is that files saved in this dual format are quite large and take longer to save.

Access Conversion Considerations

The conversion process for Access databases is more complicated than the processes for Word or Excel. There is a discrete conversion command (unlike Word or Excel which merely require you to open the file). And, also unlike Word or Excel, there is no opportunity to share that database in a mixed environment because there are no Save As options for saving back to an earlier Access format.

Depending upon the specific structure of a database in an earlier version, the conversion to Access 97 may or may not be totally successful. As a result, before attempting a conversion, be sure to back up the database.

Compiling Existing Databases   If the database has Access Basic or VBA code, it must be compiled before conversion, and the method varies among versions. Start by opening a module in Access, then use the Run menu command as described here:

- For Access 1.x, use Compile All.
- For Access 2.0, use Compile Loaded Modules.
- For Access 95, use Compile All Modules.

Access 97 Conversion Utility   To convert a database from a previous version to Access 97, follow these steps:

1. Launch Access and choose Cancel in the Startup dialog box.
2. Choose Tools, Database Utilities, then choose Convert Database from the submenu.
3. Select the database you want to convert from the Database to Convert From dialog box, which is like a File Open dialog box.
4. In the Convert Database Into dialog box, enter a new name for this database (don't type the .mdb extension), then choose Save.

 TIP   If you want to keep the same name for this database, choose a different location for the file.

Converting Unbound Objects   Either during or after the database conversion, you can opt to convert unbound object frame controls to image controls. This makes using forms and reports faster, but eliminates the ability to edit the controls with a double-click.

To convert during database conversion, select the Convert OLE check box in the Database to Convert From dialog box.

To convert after the database conversion, perform one of the following procedures:

- Open the form (or report) in Design view and right-click the control. Then choose Change To, Image.
- Choose Tools, Analyze, Performance. The Performance Analyzer takes care of the rest.

Database Security Issues   If the database you're converting is secured by a password, you just need to supply that password during the conversion process.

If, however, the database is secured with user-level security, you have to be more cautious about the conversion.

The workgroup information file and the secured database attached to it is downward-compatible only. If all users have converted to Access 97, you won't have a problem. If not, users of previous versions of Access will not be able to use the workgroup information files or the databases.

See Appendix A, "Tips and Tricks for System Administrators," for more information about workgroup information files.

TROUBLESHOOTING

If the conversion process seems to die before completion (you did remember to back up the original database, I hope), there is a common circumstance for the failure that you should look for.

An Access 97 table can have up to 32 indexes, and if your database has extremely complex tables that are a part of many relationships, you may exceed this limit (Access 97 creates indexes between tables on both sides of the relationships). Go back to the original database, open it in the original version of Access, and delete some of the relationships.

PowerPoint Conversion Considerations

Any PowerPoint file that is opened in PowerPoint 97 is automatically converted, and saving the file as a PowerPoint 97 file completes the conversion.

If users of various versions of PowerPoint need to share files, there are several options for saving a PowerPoint 97 file (using the file type options in the Save As dialog box):

- Save PowerPoint 97 presentations in PowerPoint 3.0 format.
- Save PowerPoint 97 presentations in PowerPoint 4.0 format.

- Save PowerPoint 97 presentations in PowerPoint 95 format.
- Save PowerPoint 97 presentations in dual PowerPoint 95 and 97 format.

The dual option (for organizations that are mixing those two versions of PowerPoint) limits users of previous versions to opening and running presentations: They cannot edit them. This is because the saving process actually creates two data streams in the file: a PowerPoint 97 data stream and a PowerPoint 95 data stream. The data stream for PowerPoint 95 limits the file to the features of the earlier version. When a PowerPoint 95 user opens the file, it must be opened as a read-only file, and only the Windows 95 data stream is read. When the PowerPoint 95 application reaches the end of the Windows 95 data stream, it ignores the rest of the file (which is the Windows 97 data stream). That means if the file is saved, the Windows 97 data stream is not saved, and the file has lost all the benefits of conversion. ●

CHAPTER 2

Office 97 Application Interaction

The Office 97 applications have three types of interactions: They interact with you, they interact with the Office 97 environment, and they interact with each other.

Therefore, you have much more than a bargain package of individual applications: You have an integrated environment that can produce documents containing text, tabular data, charts, photographs, and more. Of course, you can use Office 97's individual applications to create text documents, data documents, and presentations, but you are missing much of what Office 97 has to offer unless you consider creating integrated applications. This chapter contains plenty of suggestions that will help you create documents that take advantage of all that Office 97 has to offer. ■

Focus on documents instead of applications

Office 97 lets you focus on documents, rather than on the applications you use to work with those documents.

Use similar menus, toolbars, windows, dialog boxes, and programming

The principal Office 97 applications have similar windows, menus, toolbars, and dialog boxes. After you've learned one application, you can easily begin to work with others. You can customize applications with the shared Visual Basic for Applications programming language.

Use Office 97 Shortcut Bars to access applications and documents

The six Shortcut Bars provided with Office 97 provide a convenient way to work with documents. You can easily customize these Shortcut Bars and create your own.

Share data among applications

Office 97 provides several ways to create documents that contain elements created in various applications.

Focusing on Documents

One of the first things you notice about Office 97 is its strong focus on documents, rather than on the tools you use to work with those documents. With Office 97, you choose a document to work on, such as a spreadsheet, and then let your computer figure out that Excel is the tool you need to use to work with, or associate with, that document. In contrast, when you worked with DOS or earlier Windows applications, it was more natural to choose an application (such as Excel) and use that application to open a document.

If you stop to think about it, choosing the item you want to work on and then selecting the appropriate tool for the task is the way we normally do things. When you want slices of bread, don't you pick up a loaf and then find a knife? I don't think you start with a knife and then decide what you want to cut with it! So, a document-oriented approach is more natural and, once you become familiar with it, easier to use.

When you choose a document, Windows looks at that document's file-name extension to determine which application to use. If the document was created in Excel, its file-name extension is .XLS. Windows sees that extension, opens Excel, and then Excel opens the document so that you can work with it.

When you install Office 97 on your computer, each of the Office 97 applications is automatically associated with a file-name extension—Word is associated with .doc, Excel with .xls, and so on. The same happens when you install other Office 97-compatible applications such as CorelDRAW!, PageMaker, Visio, and many more. These associations between file-name extensions and the applications in which files were created and may be edited are maintained in the Windows 95 or Windows NT Registry.

N O T E   In Windows 95 and Windows NT, the Registry is a set of files that contains information about the computer, the computer's users, and software installed on (or accessible by) the computer. Although the Windows 95 and Windows NT Registries are similar, there are significant differences between them. For more information about the Windows 95 Registry, refer to *Platinum Edition Using Windows 95*; for more information about the Windows NT Registry, refer to *Special Edition Using Windows NT Client 4.0.* ▪

Creating and Opening Documents

In Office 97, you can use several methods to create and open documents: You can start with a document type, or you can start with an application.

Creating a New Document   The easiest way to create a new document is to start with a document type. Using this approach, choose New Office Document in the Office Shortcut Bar to display the General tab of the New Office Document dialog box shown in Figure 2.1. You can also display this dialog box by opening the Start menu and choosing New Office Document. In this tab, you can select:

- Blank Database to create a new Access database
- Blank Document to create a new Word document
- Blank Workbook to create a new Excel workbook
- Blank Binder to create a new Office binder
- Blank Presentation to create a new PowerPoint presentation
- Fax Coversheet to create a new fax as a Word document

Part
I
Ch
2

FIG. 2.1
Use the General tab of the New Office Document dialog box to create a new document of a specific type.

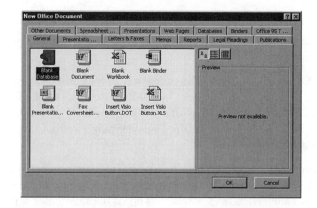

N O T E The tabs in your New Office Document dialog box might not be the same as those shown in the preceding figure, depending on how Office 97 was installed. ▪

While you're looking at the New Office Document dialog box, take a quick look at the 13 other tabs, each of which provides access to templates and wizards for specific purposes. For example, if you want to create a new database, select the Databases tab; then look at the icons for wizards that automatically create 26 different types of databases ranging from Address Book to Workout. Instead of creating a database from scratch, you can select a database type and let Office 97 automatically create the tables, forms, and reports you're likely to need. After you've let Office 97 create a database automatically, you can use Access to modify that database to suit your specific needs.

An alternative method of creating a new document is to start with the application. To do so, use Windows Explorer to locate the folder that contains your Office 97 applications. In that folder, double-click the name of the application you want to open. To open:

- Access, double-click Msaccess.exe
- Binder, double-click Binder.exe
- Excel, double-click Excel.exe
- Outlook, double-click Outlook.exe
- PowerPoint, double-click Powerpnt.exe
- Word, double-click Winword.exe

After the application opens, you can choose to create a new document or open an existing one.

N O T E   By default, the Windows Explorer doesn't display the file-name extensions of applications that are listed in the Registry. For example, after you've installed Word, Explorer shows the Word file as Winword, not as Winword.exe. If you want to see file-names with extensions, open Explorer and choose View, Options. In the Options dialog box, remove the check mark from Hide MS-DOS File Extensions For File Types That Are Registered. After you've done so, you'll see Office 97 files with their file-name extensions. ■

You can also create shortcut buttons corresponding to Windows applications on your Windows desktop and in your Office Shortcut Bar. After doing so, you can open an application by clicking its shortcut button.

Opening an Existing Document   The easiest way to open an existing document is to look for the document by name. To do so, click Open Office Document on the Office Shortcut Bar to display the dialog box that contains a list of all the documents in your My Documents folder. The My Documents folder is where Office automatically saves documents if you don't choose to save them in a specific folder.

If the document you want to open isn't in your My Documents folder, you can choose a different disk and folder in the Look In list. After you've located the file you want to open, double-click its name. Windows automatically opens the appropriate application (based on the file-name extension) and uses that application to open the file you selected.

The alternative method of opening an existing file is to open an application as described previously, and then choose File, Open (or click the Open button) in that application to select a file.

The Office 97 Common Interface

One of the benefits of using a suite of applications such as Office 97 is that the applications all have a similar interface. As a result, after you've learned one application, you can easily begin to start using another application that employs a similar interface. This benefit extends beyond the Office 97 applications themselves. You'll find the same similarities in other Microsoft applications such as Project and Publisher.

What's more, Microsoft actively encourages other software suppliers to adopt the same interfaces as the Office 97 applications. This is obviously a benefit to users; it's also a benefit to software suppliers who see a marketing advantage in being able to label their products "Microsoft Office-Compatible."

- Windows have a general appearance that includes a menu bar and toolbars at the top and a status bar at the bottom.
- Order and grouping of menu names in menu bars and buttons in toolbars.
- Names of menus and menu items.
- Design and functionality of dialog boxes.

- Methods of sharing information between documents created in the same or different applications.
- Customization by using the Visual Basic for Applications (VBA) programming language.
- Access to object structure.

N O T E Not all Office 97 applications, and certainly not all Office 97-compatible applications, share these similarities to the same extent. For example, while Access, Excel, and Word may be customized with VBA; Outlook uses Visual Basic Script (a simplified version of VBA). An application can be labeled Microsoft Office-compatible even though it does not fully support some of the characteristics of Office 97 applications. ■

Customizing Office Shortcut Bars

The default Office Shortcut Bar contains the eight buttons shown in Figure 2.2. From left to right, the buttons are New Office Document, Open Office Document, New Message, New

FIG. 2.2

The default Office Shortcut Bar is displayed at the top of your Windows desktop.

Appointment, New Task, New Contact, New Journal Entry, and New Note. You can customize the Shortcut Bar in many ways, some of which are described in the following paragraphs.

Shortcut Bar buttons, like icons on the Windows desktop, represent folders or executable files. When you click a Shortcut Bar button that represents a folder, that folder opens so you can see the files and other folders it contains. For example, when you click the Open Office Document button in the Office Shortcut Bar, you see the Open Office Document dialog box in which the files in the My Documents folder are displayed.

When you click a Shortcut Bar button that represents an executable file, that file runs, usually to start an application. For example, the New Message button points to the file Outlook.exe that starts Outlook. As you'll see in more detail later in this chapter, a Shortcut Bar button can point to an executable file with command-line options. In the case of the New Message button, command-line options open Outlook with the Message dialog box displayed.

Changing the Position and Shape of an Office Shortcut Bar

To change the position and shape of a Shortcut Bar, move the mouse pointer onto an unoccupied part of that Shortcut Bar and then drag. If you drag the Shortcut Bar to the left or right edges of the window, the Shortcut Bar becomes a column of buttons; if you drag the Shortcut Bar to the bottom edge, the Shortcut Bar remains as a row of buttons. If you drag it to any position other than the edge of the window, the Shortcut Bar becomes a rectangular array of buttons; you can change the shape of the rectangle by dragging any of its edges.

To restore a rectangular Shortcut Bar to a column or row of buttons, drag the Shortcut Bar's title bar to an edge of the window.

Making More Shortcut Bars Available

You can use the Office Shortcut Bar to make additional Shortcut Bars available. To do so, right-click an unoccupied part of the Shortcut Bar to display the shortcut menu shown in Figure 2.3.

The first few items in the shortcut menu are the names of available Shortcut Bars. In the illustration, these are:

- *Desktop*. Provides access to the applications and shortcuts represented by icons on your Windows desktop.
- *QuickShelf*. Provides access to Microsoft Bookshelf.
- *Office*. Provides access to Office applications.
- *Favorites*. Provides access to your list of favorite Web sites.
- *Programs*. Provides access to the programs listed by Programs in your Start menu.
- *Applications*. An example of a custom Shortcut Bar.
- *Accessories*. Provides access to the Accessory applications available in Windows.

As you'll see later in this chapter in the "Creating Custom Shortcut Bars" section, you can create custom Shortcut Bars, such as the Applications Shortcut Bar. After you do so, their names are listed in the shortcut menu.

To make specific Shortcut Bars available on the Windows desktop, click their names in the shortcut menu. Check marks at the left of the Shortcut Bar names indicate those that are available. Only one Shortcut Bar can be displayed at a time. Any other available Shortcut Bars are shown as buttons on the displayed Shortcut Bar.

Automatically Hiding Shortcut Bars

Shortcut Bars displayed at the top, bottom, left, or right edge of the Windows desktop can be automatically hidden, but those displayed within the desktop cannot be automatically hidden. When you automatically hide the Shortcut Bar, it will only appear when you need it so that you can use the entire area of your Windows desktop for your applications.

To activate automatic hiding, open the Office Shortcut Bar shortcut menu and click Auto Hide to place a check mark adjacent to it; if necessary, drag the Shortcut Bar to one of the edges of the Windows desktop. After you've done so, click an unoccupied place in the Windows desktop to make the Shortcut Bar disappear. To make the Shortcut Bar reappear, just move the mouse pointer to the edge of the window.

Customizing Existing Shortcut Bars

There are many ways in which you can customize Office 97 Shortcut Bars. To begin, right-click an empty space in any Shortcut Bar to display the shortcut menu, and choose Customize to display the Customize dialog box shown in Figure 2.4.

FIG. 2.4

Use the Customize dialog box to change the appearance of Shortcut Bars, add or remove buttons from Shortcut Bars, create custom Shortcut Bars, and select folders that contain templates.

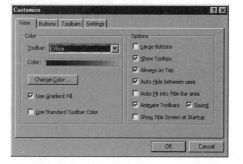

Changing the Appearance of a Shortcut Bar   To change the appearance of a Shortcut Bar, choose the View tab of the Customize dialog box, as shown in Figure 2.4. Open the Toolbar list to see the names of the Shortcut Bars available on your desktop, and choose the one you want to work with. Now you can change the color of that Shortcut Bar and choose among the options listed at the right side of the dialog box.

N O T E   You must make a Shortcut Bar available before you can change its appearance. See the previous section "Making More Shortcut Bars Available," for information about this. ■

Adding, Removing, and Renaming Shortcut Bar Buttons   To add and remove Shortcut Bar buttons, choose the Buttons tab of the Customize dialog box shown in Figure 2.5, and choose the Shortcut Bar you want to work with.

FIG. 2.5

Use the Buttons tab of the Customize dialog box to add or remove buttons from Shortcut Bars.

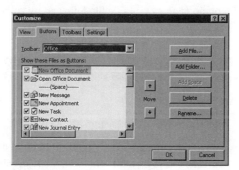

The list box at the left side of the dialog box shows folders and files that are available for display in the Shortcut Bar. Check marks in the check boxes indicate the buttons currently displayed in the Shortcut Bar. To add or remove a button from the selected Shortcut Bar, simply click the corresponding check box.

The order of buttons in the Shortcut Bar corresponds to the order they are shown in the list box. To change the order, select the name of a button, and then click one of the Move buttons to the right of the list.

The name of a button appears in a ScreenTip when you move the mouse pointer onto a button and pause momentarily. To change the name of a button, select the name of that button, click Rename, and replace the existing name with the new name.

To create a Shortcut Bar button that corresponds to a folder or file that's not listed in the dialog box, click the Add File or Add Folder button. In either case, navigate to the file or folder you want, and click OK to add it to the list in the dialog box with the corresponding check box checked.

To remove one of the Shortcut Bar buttons from the list in the dialog box, select the button's name and click Delete.

Customizing Shortcut Bar Buttons   Each Shortcut Bar button has a target property that defines the folder or file it refers to. To access this property, right-click the button in the Shortcut Bar (not in the Customize dialog box) to display the button shortcut menu shown in Figure 2.6.

FIG. 2.6
This shortcut menu lets you access a Shortcut Bar button's properties.

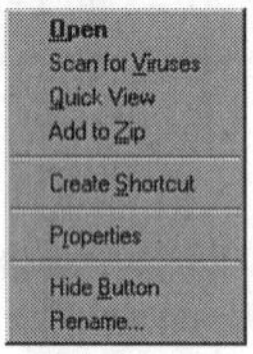

Choose Properties to display the Properties dialog box and choose the Shortcut tab. For example, if you right-click the New Message button in the Office Shortcut Bar and choose the Shortcut tab of the Properties dialog box, you'll see the dialog box shown in Figure 2.7.

The target in this case is the name of an executable file followed by some command-line options.

N O T E   For an explanation of the Outlook command-line options shown here, refer to the Starting, Outlook topic in Outlook's online Help, and look at the subtopic Control What Happens When You Start Outlook. ■

In the case of a button that refers to a folder, the `Target` property is the name of the folder.

You can edit the `Target` property in this dialog box. You might need to do this if you change the location of the file or folder referred to by a button. Also, if you create custom buttons that refer to files and need to add command-line options to the filename, you can edit the `Target` property. For example, if you create a button that starts Access and opens a specific database named `BOOKLIST`, the button's target would be something like:

`C:\MSOFFICE97\OFFICE\MSACCESS.EXE C:\WORK\BOOKLIST.MDB`

where `C:\MSOFFICE97\OFFICE\MSACCESS.EXE` is the name of the file to run, and `C:\WORK\BOOKLIST.MDB` is the name of the database to open.

FIG. 2.7

The properties of the New Message button include the button's target, the name of the file that runs when the button is clicked.

 Command-line options are particularly useful when you are creating custom applications with VBA code. By appending a command-line option such as `/cmd "value"`, you create a constant (`"value"` in this case) accessible by the `Command` function within your code. This allows you to create several buttons that open your application and run them in different ways.

While you have the Shortcut tab displayed, notice three additional text boxes in which you can supply or edit information:

- *Start In.* This text identifies a folder that contains additional files required by the application that starts when you click the Shortcut Bar button.

- *Shortcut Key.* If you want to provide a shortcut key that duplicates the action of the Shortcut Bar button, you can do so by placing the insertion point in the box and pressing the shortcut key combination you want to use.

- *Run.* Select the type of window in which the item opened by the button is to be displayed (Normal, Maximized, or Minimized).

You can also change the icon displayed in the Command Bar button by choosing Change Icon and selecting from a list of available icons.

Adding and Removing Shortcut Bars   Office 97 makes several Shortcut Bars available for display on the Windows desktop, but only one of these, the Office Shortcut Bar, is actually displayed by default. To display additional Shortcut Bars, select the Toolbars tab of the Customize dialog box shown in Figure 2.8.

FIG. 2.8
The Toolbars tab of the Customize dialog box lets you choose which of the available Shortcut Bars are displayed on the Windows desktop.

Initially, only the Office Shortcut Bar is checked in the list of Shortcut Bars. Click the appropriate option buttons to display or hide any combination of the Shortcut Bars.

You may choose any number of Shortcut Bars for display on the Windows desktop. After you choose two or more Shortcut Bars, the desktop displays one Shortcut Bar with all its buttons, together with an additional button for each of the other Shortcut Bars. Click the button corresponding to a Shortcut Bar to display its buttons.

Creating Custom Shortcut Bars

You can create custom Shortcut Bars in addition to those supplied with Office 97. Instead of cluttering your Windows desktop with many icons, you might prefer to group buttons that provide access to folders and files in custom Shortcut Bars. To do so, choose Customize in the Shortcut Bar shortcut menu, and choose the Toolbars tab in the Customize dialog box. Click the Add Toolbar button to display the Add Toolbar dialog box shown in Figure 2.9. Enter the name of a new Shortcut Bar, such as **Applications**, as shown in the figure.

FIG. 2.9
Use the Add Toolbar dialog box to name a new Shortcut Bar and, optionally, to add buttons corresponding to files in a specific folder to the new Shortcut Bar.

After you've entered a name for the new Shortcut Bar, click OK if you don't want to place buttons on it automatically. Alternatively, you can enable the Make Toolbar for this Folder option button and enter (or select) the name of a folder; if you do so, the new Shortcut Bar will contain buttons representing each file in that folder.

After you've created a new Shortcut Bar, you can add buttons to it and customize those buttons as described in the "Adding, Removing, and Renaming Shortcut Bar Buttons" section earlier in this chapter.

Saving Your Shortcut Bar Configuration

All the changes you make to your Shortcut Bar configuration are automatically saved as part of your Windows template. When you next open Windows, the saved Shortcut Bar configuration is in effect. However, if another person using a different user template opens Windows, the changes you made to the Shortcut Bar configuration are not in effect; that user sees the default Shortcut Bar configuration or that user's own customized Shortcut Bar configuration.

Sharing Data Among Applications

Part
I
Ch
2

Each of the Office 97 applications provides facilities for you to work with a specific type of document; however, in the real world, you often need to combine different types of documents into a finished product. For example, you may need to create a report that contains text created in Word, numerical data and charts created in Excel, data tables created in Access, and illustrations created in PowerPoint or another graphics application. Documents of this type that contain elements created in various applications are known as *compound documents*.

Office provides extensive facilities for assembling compound documents—documents that consist of several elements. These include:

- Application-specific methods
- Cutting (or copying) to the Clipboard, and then pasting
- Linking and embedding

Application-Specific Methods

Office 97 applications contain some built-in methods for easily and quickly copying data from one application to another. You can use data from an Access table in a Word document or in an Excel worksheet. To do so, open an Access database and display the Database window. Select a table and then open a list from the OfficeLinks button in the toolbar. You can choose:

- Merge It with MS Word to use the database table as a source of data for a Mail Merge document
- Publish It with MS Word to insert the data as a table within a Word document
- Analyze It with MS Excel to display the data in an Excel workbook

Also in Access, you can use the Report Wizard to incorporate data from an Excel workbook into a report.

In Excel, if you have the Microsoft AccessLinks Add-In installed, you can copy data from an Excel worksheet into an Access table. To check whether the add-in is installed, open the Excel Data menu and check to see whether it contains Convert to MS Access.

NOTE To install the AccessLinks Add-In into Excel, choose Tools, Add-Ins and click Microsoft AccessLinks Add-In. While you have the Add-Ins dialog box open, take the opportunity to

continues

continued

note any other add-ins you might find useful. The Microsoft AccessLinks add-in is available only if it was included in the list of options to be installed when you installed Office 97. You can install it later by running Office 97 Setup again. ■

To copy data from the Excel workbook to an Access table, open the workbook and choose Data, Convert to MS Access. You can choose to copy the data into a new database or into an existing database.

You also can copy a PowerPoint presentation into a Word document. To do so, open the Power-Point presentation and choose File, Send To, and then choose Microsoft Word. At this point, you can choose how you want text and graphics to be arranged on the pages of your Word document, or you can choose text only. You can also decide whether you want to paste the presentation into the Word document or link the presentation to the Word document (more about that in the "Linking and Embedding" section of this chapter).

Cutting and Pasting

If you need to include something created in one Office 97 application in another document, you can use the Clipboard. Open the document that contains the source object, copy that object to the Clipboard, and then paste it into your document.

ON THE WEB

As a Windows 95 user, I used to be irritated by the Clipboard's inability to deal with more than one item at a time. No more, though, because now I'm using *ClipMate*, a shareware product from Thornsoft Development. ClipMate lets me copy any number of items to the Clipboard and then choose which ones I want to paste. You can download a 30-day trial copy of ClipMate from Thornsoft's Web page at:

http://www.thornsoft.com

The straightforward way of using the Clipboard is well-known by most people. However, there are some ramifications that are not generally known.

After you select an item and then cut or copy it to the Clipboard, the Clipboard usually contains several versions of the item in different formats. You can use the Clipboard Viewer to see these formats. If the Clipboard Viewer is installed on your computer, you can usually open it by open-ing the Windows Start menu, choosing Run, and typing **C:\Windows\Clipbrd.exe**. For Windows NT, Clipboard Viewer is on the Accessories submenu.

The Clipboard Viewer isn't installed by default when you install Windows 95, but is installed with Windows NT. If you're using Windows 95 and the Clipboard Viewer isn't installed on your computer, you can install it from the Windows Control Panel by choosing Add/Remove Programs and then Windows Setup. The Clipboard Viewer is, in fact, the single executable file Clipbrd.exe in your Windows or Winnt folder.

To see the formats in which an item is saved to the Clipboard, copy an item to the Clipboard, open the Clipboard Viewer, and then open the Display menu in Windows 95 or the View menu in Windows NT 4. You'll see a list of all the formats in which the Clipboard can store that sort of item with some of them dimmed. Those formats that are not dimmed are those the application actually sent to the Clipboard, are stored there, and which you can paste into other applications. One of the formats, (named Auto in Windows 95 and Default Format in Windows NT), is the source application's native format.

When you use Paste to paste the contents of the Clipboard into an application, you don't have any choice about which format will be used: The Clipboard chooses the format it considers appropriate for the target application. In many applications, you can choose Paste Special (or a similar command); in this case, you are presented with a choice of all the formats currently available in the Clipboard.

Another capability of the Clipboard Viewer is to save the contents of the Clipboard as a file (with the extension .CLP). You can also load existing Clipboard files to the Clipboard.

Linking and Embedding

You can embed one document or object in another, or you can link one document or object to another. You'll discover the essential differences between embedding and linking in the "Understanding Linking and Embedding" section later in this chapter.

N O T E The ability to create a compound document is provided by *OLE*, an essential component of Windows 95 and Windows NT. The acronym OLE comes from the phrase *Object Linking and Embedding*. OLE has evolved into much more than just object linking and embedding, and now includes visual editing, nesting objects, dragging and dropping, and OLE automation. See Que's *Building Integrated Office Applications* for detailed information about these subjects. ■

You can use OLE to link and embed objects when you are working with applications that support linking and embedding. In addition to the Office applications themselves, certain applications from Microsoft and from suppliers other than Microsoft provide support for linking and embedding (among those I've used are Visio Professional, Visio Technical, and CorelDRAW!).

T I P Microsoft maintains a list of Office 97-compatible applications on the Microsoft Office Compatible home page at:

http://www.microsoft.com/office/compatible/

To be accepted by Microsoft as Office 97-compatible, an application must satisfy certain standards defined by Microsoft, but these standards don't include complete support of OLE. Don't assume that the applications listed support linking and embedding. If you want to know whether a specific application does support linking and embedding, you'll have to ask the supplier.

Some applications that do not satisfy Microsoft's criteria for Office 97-compatibility do support linking and embedding.

Understanding Linking and Embedding   In order to make effective use of linking and embedding to construct compound documents, you need some background information. It is incorrect to believe, as many people do, that when you provide a link in one document to an object in another document, all you are doing is inserting into the first document information about where to find the linked object. It is also somewhat misleading to believe that when you embed an object into a document, you are including the "entire" object. The following paragraphs provide the basis for a more complete understanding of linking and embedding.

Office 97 applications create documents that consist of one or more objects; for example, Excel can create a chart as an object. OLE associates two types of data about each object: The object's presentation data and its native data. The object's *presentation data* is the information required to display that object on a monitor or print it. The object's native data is the data required to edit that object. In the case of an Excel chart, you can think of the presentation as a picture of that chart and the native data as the region of the worksheet that contains the values from which the chart is created.

A *compound document* consists of a container document that contains linked objects, embedded objects, or both. Those linked and embedded objects can themselves be containers that contain other linked and embedded objects.

Suppose you have a Word document that serves as a container for an Excel chart. Table 2.1 shows what is actually included in the Word document when you link or embed the chart.

Table 2.1   Linking and Embedding Objects

Method	Data in Container Document
Link	Presentation data and reference to native data.
Embed	Presentation data and native data, but no link to the original native data.

Creating a Compound Document   Before delving deeper into the differences between linking and embedding, here's a quick review of the process, using the example of a Word document as a container and an Excel chart as a linked or embedded object. Try this exercise: Start by creating a short Word document and saving three identical copies of it; name the files Container, Embed, and Link. Also create a simple Excel chart, such as a pie chart, and save the Excel workbook, naming it Chart.

To link the chart into the Word document named Link:

1. Open the Chart workbook, select the chart, and copy it to the Clipboard.
2. Open the Link (Word) document, and place the insertion point where you want the chart to appear.
3. Choose Edit, Paste Special. In the Paste Special dialog box, choose Paste Link.
4. After a few seconds' delay, the chart appears in the Word document. Save the document.

N O T E In the Paste Special dialog box, select check boxes to determine whether or not the linked object should float over text, and whether the linked object should be displayed or represented by an icon. ■

Follow similar steps to embed a copy of the chart in the Word document named Embed. The essential difference is that you should accept the default choice of Paste (instead of Paste Link) in the Paste Special dialog box.

Part
I
Ch
2

After you've created the Word documents with linked and embedded charts, it's interesting to compare the sizes of the files. Table 2.2 contains examples of file sizes. Depending on the contents of your files, the file sizes on your computer may be different, but the effect is the same.

Table 2.2   Comparison of File Sizes for Container with Linked and Embedded Chart

File	Size (Kilobytes)
Container (without linked or embedded object)	19
Workbook (with chart to be linked or embedded)	15
Container with embedded chart	43
Container with linked chart	20

As you probably expect, the container with the linked object is considerably smaller than the one with the embedded object. But this is true only because the Excel pie chart is a very simple graphics object for which the presentation data occupies very little space.

If you perform a similar exercise using a more complex graphics object, such as a picture saved as a .TIF file, you'll see quite different results, as shown in Table 2.3.

Table 2.3   Comparison of File Sizes for Container with Linked and Embedded Picture

File	Size (Kilobytes)
Container (without linked or embedded object)	19
Illustration (.TIF file)	758
Container with embedded picture	1,284
Container with linked picture	1,283

In this case, there's very little difference between the size of the containers with linked and embedded pictures. This is because the object's presentation data is quite large.

You can learn two valuable lessons from the figures shown in these tables. First, don't assume that using linking instead of embedding necessarily saves a lot of disk space. Second, compound documents can be surprisingly large, often larger than the sum of the size of the container and the objects it contains.

Choosing Between Linking and Embedding   Common (incorrect) wisdom is that you choose linking when you want to save disk space. As you've just seen, this isn't necessarily true, despite the fact that Microsoft's help topics contain such phrases as "Use linked objects if file size is a consideration."

The principal question to consider when you're choosing between linking and embedding is whether or not you want the compound document to be independent of the files from which the inserted objects were created. When you embed an object in a compound document, any changes made to the files from which the embedded objects were created do not cause changes in the compound document. However, when you link an object into a compound document, any changes made to the files that contain the linked objects are reflected in the compound document. If you have several container documents that all contain the same linked object, any change made to the linked object is reflected in all the container documents.

Another question to consider is access to files, particularly when you share documents with other people by way of a network. A compound document that contains embedded objects is completely self-sufficient. Anyone using any computer can open a compound document that contains embedded objects and see the entire document, including the embedded objects. That person can also edit the embedded objects, as long as he has the application that will work with the embedded objects' native data. For example, if a compound document contains an embedded Excel chart, anyone who opens the document can see and print the chart; also, if Excel is installed on the computer, that person can make changes to the Excel native data from which the chart is derived and see corresponding changes in the chart.

A compound document that contains linked objects is not self-sufficient. Anyone can open a compound document that contains linked objects on any computer and see the entire document, including the linked objects. It may surprise you to know that the linked objects are visible whether or not the computer has access to the files that contain the linked objects. This is because, as explained previously, a compound document contains the presentation data for all linked objects. In order to make changes to the linked objects, however, the user's computer must have access to the linked objects' original files. One more point: If the compound document does not have access to the linked objects' original files, that document displays the linked objects as they were when the link was created (the original presentation data) and does not reflect any subsequent changes that may have been made to those files.

Tracking and Changing Links   A compound document keeps track of all the links it contains. In Word, for example, you can see a list of links by choosing Edit, Links to display the Links dialog box shown in Figure 2.10. The links listed in this dialog box show the files that are the source of each linked object.

FIG. 2.10

Select any of the links listed in the Links dialog box to see detailed information about the linked object. This information is shown below the list of links.

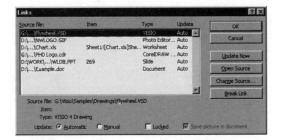

If you make changes to the locations of files containing objects that are linked, you must make sure the Links dialog box reflects those changes. If you enable the Automatic option button at the bottom of the Links dialog box, you can use Explorer to drag a file from one location to another, even from one hard disk to another, on a single computer, and Windows automatically updates the links.

It's a good idea to check the Links dialog box to verify that links have been correctly updated. Sometimes, file name conflicts interfere with automatic link updating.

If you move a file containing objects that are linked to another computer, such as your LAN server, you have to update the information in the Links dialog box manually. To do this, select one of the listed links and then choose Change Source to display the Change Source dialog box. Navigate to the folder that now contains the file, and click Open. ●

CHAPTER 3

The Office 97 Binder

When you have a major project, it probably has components scattered throughout many documents; sometimes the files are all of the same type, but very often there is a variety of document types that play a role. The Office 97 Binder (a component of Office 97 for Windows, but not in Office 97 for Macintosh) provides a convenient way to keep all these files together.

You probably already have a scheme for keeping related sets of files together; perhaps they're all in one folder, or maybe you've created a master document and embedded other files in it or linked other files to it (see Chapter 2 for information about linking and embedding). Whatever strategy you've devised has advantages and disadvantages.

The main advantages of using Binder are that you can easily work with the files separately when you need to, and you can work with them as a single entity. This is handy if you want all the pages of a set of documents to have consistent headers and footers, with all the pages of the set numbered in sequence. And, if you want to give the set of documents to another person, there's only one item to fetch and deliver. There are lots of ways to take advantage of the robust features in Binder. ■

Get acquainted with Binder

You find a fast-paced introduction to the methods available for using Binder to keep a set of related documents together.

Print a set of documents with consistent headers and footers

After combining documents in a binder, you can create a header and footer that's printed on all the pages of the documents. The header or footer can contain page numbers that are consecutive from one document to the next.

Share a set of documents with others

Binder provides a convenient way to share documents with others by way of a network, e-mail, or the Internet.

Use a template to create a binder

You can use Binder templates to create binders with preplanned formats.

Getting Acquainted with Binder

Before you dig into Binder, you should become acquainted with its basics. Binder combines several documents into a single file. Unfortunately, Binder currently works only with Excel, PowerPoint, and Word documents. However, Microsoft offers support to software suppliers who want to make their applications compatible with Binder. By the time you read this chapter, Binder may be compatible with other types of documents.

 TIP Binder isn't necessarily installed with the other Office 97 components. If Binder isn't available on your computer, you'll have to run Setup again to add Binder to your installation.

Creating a Binder

Suppose you have several related files that you want to keep together in a binder. Start by creating a new binder:

1. Open the Windows Start menu, choose Programs, and then choose Microsoft Binder to display the empty Binder window shown in Figure 3.1.

FIG. 3.1

The empty Binder window is where you create a binder's sections.

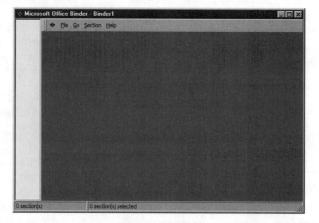

 TIP The empty Binder window should be divided into two panes as shown in the figure. If you see only one pane, click the Show/Hide Left Pane button at the left end of the Binder menu bar.

2. Open Windows Explorer and adjust the window size so that you can see the Binder and Explorer windows.

3. Find the first file you want to place in the binder, then drag that file from the Explorer window to the left pane of the Binder window. Each time you drag a document into the binder, you create a new section in the binder.

4. Repeat the previous step to create more sections by placing additional files in the binder.

5. Save the binder (binder files have .OBD extensions).

N O T E When you place a document in a binder, you are in fact embedding that document in the binder. As a result, any changes to the document you make within Binder have no effect on the original document. Likewise, any changes you subsequently make to the original document have no effect on the document embedded in the binder. Refer to Chapter 2 for more information about embedding. ■

Opening an Existing Binder

To open an existing binder:

1. Open the Windows Start menu, choose Programs, and then choose Microsoft Binder to display the empty Binder window shown previously in Figure 3.1.

2. Choose File, Open Binder to display the Open Binder dialog box, navigate to the folder that contains the binder file, select that file, and click Open.

Displaying a Section's Contents

After you've placed several documents in a binder, each document becomes a section of the binder. Each section has a name that corresponds to the file name of the document (without the file name extension). The section names are listed in the left pane of the Binder window, together with icons that indicate the type of document.

 T I P You can change a section's name by clicking the section name (or icon) and choosing Section, Rename.

One section of the binder is always active so that its contents are displayed in the right pane of the Binder window (see Figure 3.2). Initially the first section is active, as indicated by the small arrow adjacent to the section icon; you can activate a different section by clicking its section name or icon in the left pane.

N O T E Binder uses the application in which a section was created to display that section in the right pane. When you activate a section, you'll see it immediately if the required application is already open, otherwise you'll notice a delay while the application opens. ■

If you add more sections than can be seen in the left pane, scroll buttons appear at the bottom of that pane. You can click these buttons to move through the pane's entire contents. The status bar at the bottom of the window shows the total number of documents in the binder. Figure 3.2 shows the Binder window after several documents have been added.

The right pane of the Binder window shows the active section as it appears in the application in which the document was created. In Figure 3.2, for example, the active section contains an Excel workbook, and that document is displayed in an Excel window in the right pane.

FIG. 3.2

After you've added sections to a binder, those sections are listed in the left pane. The content of the active section is shown in the right pane.

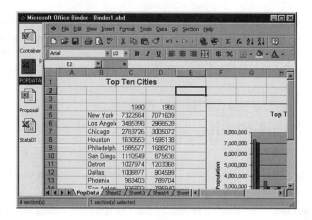

Using the Binder Menu Bar

When you create a new binder, it contains no sections and its menu bar contains only File, Go, Section, and Help menus. After you create sections in the binder, the menu bar contains additional menu items appropriate for the currently active section. For example, if you activate a section that contains an Excel document, the menu bar contains File, Edit, View, Insert, Format, Tools, Data, Go, Section, and Help; if you activate a section that contains a Word document, the menu bar is similar but Data is replaced by Table; after you activate a section that contains a PowerPoint document, Data is replaced by Slide Show. The Help menu contains help items for the active type of document and, at the bottom, Binder Help. To get help for Binder, choose Help, Binder Help, and then select the type of help you want from the Binder Help menu.

 Binder requires a lot of memory, which may be physical RAM or swap file space on a hard disk. If Binder refuses to display a file or otherwise misbehaves, the likely reason is insufficient memory. Unfortunately, Binder isn't kind enough to tell you what the problem is. If you have trouble with Binder, try increasing the size of your swap file. I've found that usually solves the problem.

Editing a Binder's Sections

While you can use a binder as a means of opening files to edit them, Microsoft states that "A binder is most effectively used as a place to assemble related, finished files. If you have a problem editing a document, use Help to troubleshoot the problem." There are three reasons for this warning:

■ A binder contains embedded documents, so any changes you make to a document in a binder do not affect the original document. You probably want each section in the binder to correspond exactly to each original document, so don't edit in the binder.

■ Although Binder displays a document in the right pane using the application in which that document was created, you have access to only the general functionality of that application, not its entire functionality.

■ Binder doesn't appear to be as well-behaved as it should be, as far as using and releasing memory is concerned. As a result, if you do a significant amount of editing within Binder, you may lose access to memory and, after a while, experience Binder error conditions.

My advice, therefore, is to finalize files before you assemble them in a binder. If you must edit a section of a binder:

■ If the document from which the section was created exists as a file on your computer, delete the section from the binder by selecting that file and then choosing Section, Delete, then edit the original file and add it back into the binder.

■ If the document from which the section was created doesn't exist on your computer, unbind the binder's sections (as described in the "Unbinding Sections" section later in this chapter) to create separate files corresponding to the sections, edit the individual files, and re-create the binder.

Open sections of a binder only to read them!

Binder isn't alone in its tendency to reduce the amount of available memory, nor is Microsoft the only source of software that does so. If, after you've been working for a while, you find your computer is becoming slow or refuses to do what it normally does, the likely reason is that you've lost access to memory. To solve this problem, close all files and then restart Windows. Also, check to make sure that some large temporary files haven't taken over most of the disk that Windows uses for swap file space.

Part
I

Ch
3

Changing the Order of Files in a Binder

One of the principle reasons for using Binder is to assemble files in a specific order ready for printing. To change the order of files in a binder, simply drag the section icons in the left pane of the Binder window to the correct position.

Selecting Binder Sections

The information Microsoft supplies about selecting sections in a binder is somewhat confusing. This is because you can select a section in two ways: You can activate a section to display its content in the right pane of the binder window, or you can manipulate a section to perform an operation. I've tried to clarify this by referring to "activating" the section you want to display and "selecting" a section (or sections) on which you want to perform an operation.

The left pane of the Binder window contains a list of sections in your binder. Only one of these sections can be activated at a time so that you can see its contents in the right pane. The small arrow at the right of the section icon indicates the active section. Activate the section you want to display by clicking its icon or name in the left pane. With one section activated, you can activate the next or previous section by choosing Section, Next Section or Section, Previous Section.

In addition to activating one section of the binder to be displayed, you can select one or more sections to perform an operation. For example, you can select one or more multiple sections and delete them, print them, or send them to somebody by e-mail.

When you click an icon in the left pane to activate a section, three things happen:

- The content of the section is displayed in the right pane.
- An arrow appears next to the section icon in the left pane to indicate which section is displayed in the right pane.
- The icon in the left pane turns blue to show that pane is selected for other operations.

Whereas only one section can be activated for display in the right pane, any number of sections can be selected so that you can perform operations on them as a group. The active section is always selected. Use the standard Windows Ctrl or Shift key actions to select multiple sections, or choose Select All from the Section menu. To deselect all sections (except the active section), choose Section, Unselect All.

Deleting One or More Sections

To delete sections from a binder, select the sections to be deleted (as described in the previous paragraph), and then choose Section, Delete.

Unbinding Sections

You can unbind a binder to create separate files corresponding to each section. In Windows Explorer, locate the binder (.OBD) file, right-click the file name and choose Unbind from the shortcut menu shown in Figure 3.3. Binder attempts to re-create the files from which the sections in your binder were created. It uses the section names as file names and adds the appropriate extensions to those names. The files are written into the same folder as your binder file, even if they were originally copied into the binder from other folders.

FIG. 3.3
A binder's shortcut menu contains the menu items shown here. Use Unbind to extract the original documents from the binder.

N O T E If the folder that contains your binder file already contains files with the names Binder proposes to use for the new files, Binder gives you the opportunity to write over the original files or to abort the unbind process. ■

Printing a Binder

One of the principal reasons for creating a binder is to print a set of documents as though it was a single document. After you have placed several documents in a binder, you can:

- Preview how the sections of a binder will be printed.
- Print the entire contents of the binder.
- Print one or more sections from the binder.
- Print the contents of a binder with consecutive page numbers across sections.

Previewing How Sections Will Be Printed

Binder lets you preview one section at a time. To preview a section, activate that section, then choose Section, Print Preview. You can only preview those sections that were created in an application that supports print preview. For example, PowerPoint doesn't have a Print Preview command, so when a PowerPoint section is active, the Print Preview command in the Section menu is disabled.

Printing the Entire Contents of a Binder

Printing the entire contents of the binder is straightforward. Simply choose File, Print Binder. Then, in the Print Binder dialog box (shown in Figure 3.4), choose the All Visible Sections option, make whatever other choices are appropriate, and click OK.

Part

I

Ch

3

FIG. 3.4

Use the Print Binder dialog box to select which binder sections to print and also to control page numbering.

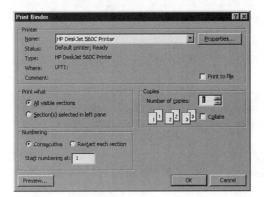

Notice that the bottom-left section of the dialog box refers to page numbering. This controls how pages are numbered, but only if you have made provisions for page numbering in the documents contained within the binder. If the original documents are formatted so that consecutive page numbers are printed in headers or footers, then the sections printed from Binder will also have page numbers. The headers and footers of the sections printed by Binder are formatted exactly as they are in the original documents, unless you have created Binder headers and footers (as explained subsequently).

By default, with the Consecutive option selected, Binder numbers pages consecutively across all the sections. If you choose the Restart Each Section option, the pages of each section are numbered separately.

The Start Numbering At box, set to 1 by default, enables you to select the number of the first page.

Printing Individual Sections

Instead of printing all the sections in a binder, you can select one or more individual sections. Select the sections you need; then, in the Print Binder dialog box, choose the Section(s) Selected in Left Pane option.

Printing a Binder with Consistent Headers and Footers

One outstanding feature in Binder is the ability to print a set of documents as one publication. To achieve this, of course, all the pages should have similar headers and footers. That means those headers and footers have to be created in Binder; otherwise, each document is printed with its own headers and footers.

To create headers and footers for a binder, choose File, Binder Page Setup to display the Header/Footer tab of the Binder Page Setup dialog box, shown in Figure 3.5.

FIG. 3.5

Use the Binder Page Setup dialog box to create headers and footers for all the documents in a binder.

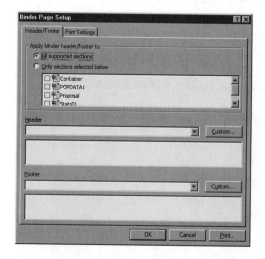

In the Binder Page Setup dialog box, choose whether you want to create headers and footers for all the sections in the binder, or only for specific sections.

You create a header and footer in the same way. For a header, open the Header list, such as that shown in Figure 3.6, and choose one of the available types of headers. The actual contents of the list are based on the information you provided when you installed Office 97, such as your name and company name, as well as the current date and document name.

After you've chosen from the list, the box below the Header text box contains a representation of how your choice will be printed, as shown by the example in Figure 3.7.

In some cases, the representation of the header shows some text in bold and other text in roman (not bold). The bold text is exactly what is printed in the header. The roman text is a placeholder for what will be printed. In the example, Container is replaced in the header by the name of the binder section.

FIG. 3.6

Binder provides a list of header options from which you can choose.

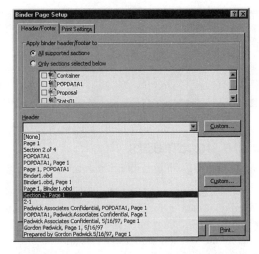

FIG. 3.7

After you've chosen a header, Binder displays a representation of how the header will appear when printed.

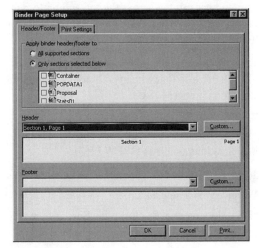

You are not limited to the headers offered by Binder. After you've chosen from the list of suggested headers, you can click Custom to display the Custom Header dialog box shown in Figure 3.8.

The Custom Header dialog box shows the three sections of the header. You can edit these three sections in the same way that you do when creating headers and footers for Word, Excel, and PowerPoint.

Instead of choosing from the list of suggested headers, you can click the Custom button and then create your header from scratch.

Binder footers are created in the same way as Binder headers.

The Binder headers and footers you create in this way replace the headers and footers in the individual binder sections.

FIG. 3.8

You can create or modify a binder header in the Custom Header dialog box.

Dealing with Landscape Documents

Here's a problem and a solution regarding print orientation for binder files.

The problem: You have two documents—one is a Word document and the other is a Power-Point document. The Word document is formatted to be printed in Portrait orientation, and the PowerPoint document is formatted to be printed in Landscape orientation. You create a binder that contains the two documents and add binder headers and footers. You print the binder on 8 1/2×11-inch paper and take the pages out of your printer. You find that the headers and footers of the Word document are printed across the top and bottom of the portrait pages the 8 1/2-inch edge), and that the headers and footers of the PowerPoint pages are printed across the top and bottom of the landscape pages (the 11-inch edge).

I don't think that's what you want. You need the headers and footers of all the pages to be printed across the 8 1/2-inch edge so that when you bind the document, the headers and footers are in the same position on every page.

Binder can't cope with this problem by itself. But, with a little ingenuity, you can solve the problem. Here's my solution. This solution uses CorelDRAW to rotate slide images, but you can use other graphics applications (such as LVIEW PRO):

1. Create a Word document to serve as a container for PowerPoint slides.
2. Open CorelDRAW and open a new document.
3. Open the PowerPoint document and select Slide Sorter view.
4. Select a slide and copy that slide to the Clipboard.
5. In the CorelDRAW window, choose Paste Special. Choose Picture (Metafile).
6. In CorelDRAW, rotate the slide image by 90 degrees and then copy it to the Clipboard.
7. Paste the image from the Clipboard into Word.

Now you have a Word page that contains the slide image rotated to fill the height of the page. Repeat this process for each slide in the presentation. It may be somewhat laborious, but it gets the job done.

 TIP If you use Windows 95, you can save a lot of time by using ClipMate (described in Chapter 2) to supplement the Clipboard. With ClipMate, you can save any number of slides in the Clipboard.

Now you can print your binder with the headers and footers across the 8 1/2-inch edge for all pages.

You can use the same method with Excel charts that you want to print vertically in your binder pages. Copy the Excel chart into a graphics application such as CorelDRAW, rotate it, then copy it into Word. However, you will probably find that the axis text in Excel charts doesn't survive the rotation process too well. Although it's time-consuming, you can use your graphics application to replace the axis text.

Sharing a Binder with Others

You can share a binder with other users in three ways:

- Place the binder file on a network drive where other people can access it.
- Send the binder file by e-mail.
- Share the binder by way of the Internet.

Part
I
Ch
3

Sharing a Binder on a Network

By copying your binder to an accessible network location, you make the documents in the binder available for other people to use. The network location should be protected so that users can read, and possibly copy, the binder file but cannot make changes to it.

If you are working on a set of documents in cooperation with other people, you can use Binder as a convenient way of sharing those documents. In that case, the people cooperating on the document should copy the shared binder into their local Briefcase. One person should be responsible for updating the master binder file so that it always contains everyone's latest contributions. Periodically, contributors can use Briefcase's Update All command to copy any changes in the master binder file to their local copy.

NOTE When you update a copy of a binder file in Briefcase, any changes to the headers and footers made by using Binder Page Setup are not copied to the Briefcase. ■

Sending a Binder by E-Mail

You can send a binder file to others by way of your local e-mail system, providing that system is compatible with the Messaging Application Programming Interface (MAPI), such as Microsoft Outlook or Microsoft Exchange, or is compatible with Vendor Independent Messaging (VIM), such as Lotus cc:Mail. You may not be able to send a binder file to someone on a remote e-mail system because mail gateways are generally not able to handle this type of file. From this, it follows that you are unlikely to be successful if you attempt to send a binder as an attachment to an Internet e-mail message.

If you want to send a binder to several people, one after the other, you can route the binder.

If you are using Microsoft Exchange as a mail server, you can post the binder in a shared folder for access by others.

TIP E-mail systems are constantly evolving, particularly in the area of capabilities for sending messages from one mail system to another. At the time of this writing, Lotus Notes doesn't let you share binder files.

To send a binder by e-mail, open the binder and choose File, Send To to see the menu shown in Figure 3.9.

FIG. 3.9
Use this menu to mail, route, or post a binder.

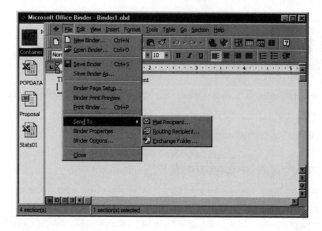

NOTE If you choose File, Send To in a routed binder you've received, the menu contains a fourth item, Next Routing Recipient. ■

You can choose from the menu as follows:

- When you choose Mail Recipient, an Outlook Message dialog box opens with the binder file ready to send.
- When you choose Routing Recipient, the Add Routing Slip dialog box opens, ready for you to list recipient names on the routing slip.
- When you choose Exchange Folder, the Send to Exchange Folder dialog box opens so that you can choose an Exchange folder.
- You choose Next Routing Recipient (available only if you've received a routed binder) to send the binder to the next person on the routing list.

Sharing a Binder on the Internet

To access binders by way of the Internet (or an intranet), start by choosing Go, Show Web Toolbar to display the toolbar shown in Figure 3.10.

FIG. 3.10
The Web toolbar con-
tains buttons you can
use to access Web sites.

The buttons in this toolbar have the same functions as corresponding buttons in Internet Explorer. You can access binder files on the Web in the same manner that you access other Web documents. Refer to Chapters 38 through 42 for additional information about using the Internet and intranets.

Using Binder Templates

As is the case with documents you create in other Office 97 applications, you don't have to create every binder from scratch. You can use one binder as a template for others. After you install Office 97, you'll usually find a Templates subfolder within your Office folder. Within the Templates subfolder, you'll find subfolders for each of the Office applications. The ...\TEMPLATES\BINDER subfolder contains a sample Binder folder: REPORT.OBT. You can double-click this file to create a new binder based on that template.

After you create a binder, you can save it as a template. Choose File, Save Binder As. Then, in the Save as Type list, choose Binder Templates. Binder automatically proposes to save the binder template in your Templates folder, but it's usually a better idea to choose the Binders subfolder so that all your binder templates are kept together.

To create a binder template, start by creating a set of documents, each of which contains the format and basic elements of each binder you eventually want to create. Then combine these documents into a binder, and save that binder as a template. Subsequently, you can open the binder template each time you want to create a standard set of documents.

Choosing Binder Options

You can choose among a few Binder options, some of which apply to all binders, and some of which apply only to the currently open binder. To access options, choose File, Binder Options to display the dialog box shown in Figure 3.11.

FIG. 3.11
The Binder Options
dialog box lets you set
a few Binder options.

Options That Apply to All Binders

By default, the Print Binder as a Single Job check box is selected. With this option selected, Binder sends the contents of all the sections of the binder to your print spooler as a single file. This is what you will normally want to happen because it quickly completes the printing operation so that you can get on with other work. The possible problem, though, is that you may not

Part
I

Ch
3

have enough space on your local or print server disk to hold all the sections. If your binder sections contain large documents, you may have to uncheck this option, in which case Binder sends the sections to the print spooler one at a time.

Also, by default, Binder assumes you want to use the My Documents folder on the disk in which you have installed Office 97 as the location for your binder files. If you create several binders, you may prefer to create a separate folder for your binder files. Also, if you have access to more than one hard disk, you may want to use a specific one for your binders. Remember that binder files can be very large; you don't want to run into problems because you don't have enough space for them. To change the default location for all binder files, click Modify and use the Modify Location dialog box to identify a location for your binder files.

Options That Apply to the Currently Open Binder

The lower portion of the Binder Options dialog box contains two options that apply to the currently open binder:

- *Show Status Bar.* This option is enabled by default. I can't imagine any reason why you wouldn't want to show the status bar (it shows the total number of sections in the current binder and the number of those that are selected), but you can disable this option if that's your preference.
- *Show Left Pane and Left Pane Button.* With this option enabled, as it is by default, the Binder window contains the left and right panes. Also, the Binder menu bar contains a button you can click to hide or display the left pane. If you disable this option, the Binder window doesn't display the left pane, and the menu bar doesn't contain a button that allows you to display the left pane. I can't imagine any reason why you might want to disable this option.

Microsoft Word

4 Document Power   61

5 Power Tools   87

6 Advanced Mail Merge   107

CHAPTER 4

Document Power

The three chapters about Word in this book are for people who already have considerable experience in working with the application. Rather than summarize what you already know, I've chosen to provide information that's intended to expand your knowledge of Word. The more you dig, the more you understand what really makes Word tick.

This chapter starts by exploring the templates on which every Word document is based. Then, the chapter delves into styles, one of the principal components of every template. The latter part of the chapter provides information about using Word to create forms: paper forms, forms shared on a network, and forms distributed by way of the Web. ■

Understand why templates are so important

Every Word document is based on one or more templates. By understanding what templates are, what they contain, and how to use them, you can take advantage of the power that's built into Word.

Learn how styles control everything

Styles control the overall layout of paragraphs as well as every character within paragraphs. Rather than routinely accept Word's default styles, you should choose styles that suit your purpose.

Use Word to create forms

Word is a versatile tool for creating and printing forms, such as forms to be accessed on your network, or forms to be published on Web pages.

The Structured Word

Most people think of Word as an application that provides tools for working on text documents. While that's largely true, it's by no means the whole truth. In fact, Word's architecture consists of three layers:

- The Word application that provides the standard menus, commands, and toolbars
- Templates that are models from which you create new documents and which provide storage for such items as styles, macros, AutoText entries, as well as custom menus, commands, toolbars, and keyboard assignments (shortcut keys)
- Documents that contain text, graphics, formatting, and settings for those documents

Word has two types of templates: global and local. The Normal template, an integral part of Word, is *global*, which means that its contents are available to every document. All other templates are local by default, although they can be made temporarily global: The contents of a *local* template are available only to those documents to which that template is applied.

Each document is based on one template which, by default, is the Normal template; in this case, that document can use only the styles and other components of the Normal template. If you create a document based on any other template, the document has access to the styles and other components of that template and also, because the Normal template is global, to the contents of the Normal template.

N O T E   Let's head off some confusion about the word *Normal*. There's a template named "Normal" and there's a style name "Normal." Within the Normal template, and within all other templates, there's a style named Normal that defines the fundamental font used in a document. Unfortunately, we're stuck with these two uses of "Normal." Just make sure when you come across the word, you understand whether a template or a style is being referred to. You'll come across this possible confusion in the next paragraph! ■

Local templates have precedence over global templates. This means that a document looks first for what it needs in its local template; if it doesn't find what it needs there, it looks in the global template. For example, suppose you've created a document based on the Elegant Report template that's supplied with Word. This template contains a Normal style that specifies the Garamond, 11-point font, whereas the Normal template (as supplied with Word) contains a Normal style that specifies the Times New Roman 10-point font. Because the local template (Elegant Report) takes precedence over the Normal template, the document uses Garamond as its Normal font.

At the risk of stating the obvious, I'll draw your attention to one very important point relating to the concept of global and local templates. Any change you make to the Normal (global) template has the potential of affecting all your documents. For this reason, you should base every document on a specific local template and, with few exceptions, modify only local templates. When you're tempted to modify your Normal template, do so only if you want that change to affect every document.

Although a document is normally based on a local template and has access to the Normal template, it can have access to other templates. To make any template temporarily global so that all documents have access to it, you can load that template, as described in "Making a Template Global" later in this chapter. This technique is often useful when you need to run a macro that's in a template different from the one on which your current document is based.

Using Templates, Wizards, and Add-Ins

Now that we have a basic understanding of how templates fit into Word's architecture and how they affect your work, it's time to look into some of the techniques for working with them. First, though, a word about the similarities and differences between templates, wizards, and add-ins.

Templates and wizards both simplify the process of creating documents and particularly of formatting documents consistently. Because templates and wizards serve similar purposes, they're usually stored in the same folders, and their icons are displayed together in dialog boxes.

A *template* provides a mold for a document and can be a container for custom features available to use while creating a document. Each template has a file name with a .dot extension. You can easily modify the templates supplied with Word, and you can create your own custom templates.

A *wizard*, on the other hand, is a specialized template that provides a simplified means of handling a complex operation. Wizards usually consist of a sequence of dialog boxes in which you make choices, answer questions, and supply information—all of which Word uses to step you through a process. Each wizard has a file name with a .wiz extension. You cannot modify the wizards supplied with Word. You can create your own wizards, though this requires programming in Visual Basic. Add-ins provide extended functionality for Word. Add-ins are available from Microsoft and from independent suppliers. You can also create your own add-ins usually, but not necessarily, by programming in Visual Basic.

Basing a Document on a Template

Microsoft provides a variety of special-purpose templates in addition to the Normal template. One way to create a document based on a specific template is to click New Office Document in the Office Shortcut Bar and choose a tab other than General in the New Office Document dialog box. For example, after you choose the Letters & Faxes tab, the dialog box contains icons representing various templates, as shown in Figure 4.1.

When you click any of the template or wizard icons, the Preview section of the dialog box shows you what a document based on that template or wizard will look like. Double-click an icon that represents a template to begin creating a document based on that template. Depending on which template you choose, you'll probably see much more than just an empty Word page.

FIG. 4.1

The Letters & Faxes tab of the New Office Document dialog box contains icons that access templates and wizards. The icon names with .dot extensions access templates; those with .wiz extensions access wizards.

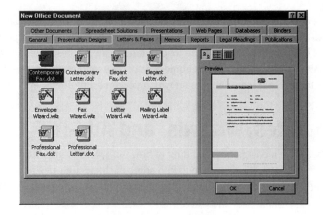

Attaching a Different Template to a Document

Suppose you start working on a document based on one template and then decide to use a different template. Choose Tools, Templates and Add-Ins to display the Templates and Add-Ins dialog box, such as that shown in Figure 4.2.

FIG. 4.2

The Templates and Add-Ins dialog box shows the template on which the document is currently based in the Document Template text box.

 TIP   You can preview the effect of attaching a template to a document before you actually make the attachment. See "Previewing a Template" later in this chapter.

To replace the current template with another, you attach a different template to the document. When you do so, you can use styles, AutoText entries, macros, custom toolbars and menus, and shortcut keys in the new template; any boilerplate text and graphics, and any page settings (such as margins) in the new template are not applied to the document.

Click Attach to open the Attach Template dialog box that lists several subfolders (each of which contains specialized templates and wizards) together with the Normal template and any other templates in your Templates folder. Navigate to the template you want, and double-click that template. The Attach Template dialog box closes and the Templates and Add-Ins dialog box reappears with the new template name in the Document Template text box.

At this stage you have a choice. Templates, as you know, contain styles that control paragraph and character formatting. Do you want the styles in the new template you're attaching to replace the styles in the original template, or do you want to retain the styles from the original template? If you leave the Automatically Update Document Styles check box unchecked, styles in the new template don't affect the document. If you check this box, styles in the new template determine the format of existing text and any new text you subsequently add to the document.

N O T E The Organizer button at the bottom of the Templates and Add-Ins dialog box provides access to a dialog box in which you can copy styles, macros, AutoText entries, and toolbars from one document or template to another. ■

Finally, click OK to attach the new template to the document.

 T I P If you forget to check the Automatically Update Document Styles check box before attaching the new template, reopen the Templates and Add-Ins dialog box and check that option.

Previewing a Template

To see what a specific document will look like if you attach a different template to it, choose Format, Style Gallery. You might reasonably expect the choice to be named "Template Gallery" rather than "Style Gallery"—you actually use it to view the effect of templates.

The Style Gallery dialog box shows a reduced version of the current document in the pane at the right and a list of templates at the left. The document is initially shown with its current template attached, as shown in Figure 4.3.

Part

II

Ch

4

FIG. 4.3

You can use the Style Gallery dialog box to preview a document with styles from any available template attached to it.

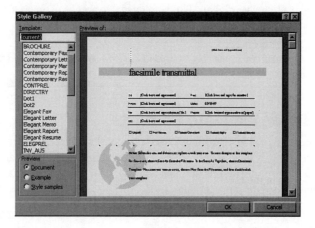

If you like what you see when you view in the Style Gallery the document with styles from another template attached to it, click OK to permanently use those styles. Otherwise, click Cancel to close the dialog box without making any changes to the document.

Making a Template Global

Although each document is based on one template and also has access to the Normal template, you may sometimes need to use macros, toolbars, or AutoText entries from other templates. You can do so by making those other templates temporarily global. Choose Tools, Templates and Add-Ins to display the Templates and Add-Ins dialog box shown previously in Figure 4.2. As before, the Document Template box shows the name of the template on which the document is based.

The Global Templates and Add-Ins list box shows the names of those templates and add-ins that are currently available to be made global. Those that are checked actually are loaded as globals. To make any listed template or add-in global, place a check mark in its check box.

N O T E   All templates and add-ins in the Word Startup folder are loaded automatically whenever you start Word. These templates and add-ins appear at the top of the Global Templates and Add-Ins list. The Word Startup folder is normally C:\Program Files\Microsoft Office\Office\Startup. You can locate your startup folder by choosing Tools, Options, and selecting the File Locations tab of the Options dialog box.

But what if the template you want to make global is not listed? In this case, click Add to display the Add Template dialog box, navigate to find the required template, then double-click to select it and return to the Templates and Add-Ins dialog box, which now contains the new template with its name checked. You can add as many templates as you like to the list, and you can check and uncheck their names to select those you actually want to be loaded as global templates. You can remove a template or add-in from the list by selecting its name, and then clicking Remove.

After you make a template global, all documents have access to macros, toolbars, and AutoText entries in that template during your current Word session.

T I P   Loaded global templates occupy memory. To avoid running low on memory, only load those templates you need to use globally. Unload global templates when you don't need them.

How Word Resolves Template Conflicts

As you've seen, a document is usually based on a local template, has access to the global Normal template, and may have access to several other temporary global templates. There may be conflicting settings or definitions in these templates; for example, the same AutoText entry may be defined in two or more templates.

Word resolves conflicts like this by looking in templates in the following order, and using the first entry it finds for the setting or definition:

1. The template on which the current document is based.

2. The Normal template.

3. Temporary global templates. If there are two or more global templates, Word looks at them in the order they're listed in the Templates and Add-Ins dialog box.

4. Add-ins.

5. The Word application layer (standard menus, commands, and toolbars).

Where Templates Are Stored

The Office installation creates a folder structure for the templates supplied with Office. This consists of a folder named C:\Program Files\Microsoft Office\Templates (or a similar name) that contains the Normal template and several subfolders, each containing specialized templates.

You can save any custom templates you create in the Templates folder or one of its subfolders. If you do so, these templates are displayed in the New Office Document dialog box so that you can easily choose them. You can also create a subfolder for your custom templates. However, even if you make this a subfolder within the Templates folder, you won't see your custom templates in the New Office Document dialog box. For this reason, I suggest placing your custom templates in one of the existing template subfolders.

 TIP If you are part of a Windows 95 and Windows NT workgroup, you can use the Systems Policy Editor to define default file locations—including those for templates—for all workgroup members. Refer to Que's *Platinum Edition Using Microsoft Windows 95* or *Platinum Edition Using Microsoft Windows NT 4.0 Workstation* for information on this topic.

Part
II

Ch
4

Word provides for storing two sets of templates: user templates and workgroup templates. *User templates* are usually stored in the default folders and subfolders on each user's computer. *Workgroup templates*, on the other hand, are stored on a disk that is available to all workgroup members. Workgroup templates offer several advantages, such as:

- Documents created by all workgroup members have a consistent format.

- All workgroup members have access to sophisticated templates created by experienced colleagues.

There is no default location for workgroup templates. To set that location, choose Tools, Options, File Locations. Select Workgroup Templates, click Modify, and use the Modify Location dialog box to navigate to the location of the workgroup templates.

Creating a Template

You can create a template from scratch, create one based on an existing template, or create one based on an existing document. The process is quite similar in each case.

To create a new template from scratch, choose File, New to display the New dialog box. In the Create New area, click Template and then click OK. Word displays a blank screen; the left end of the title bar contains `Microsoft Word - Template1`. That's your clue to the fact that you're working with a template rather than with a document. With this screen displayed, you can add any of the template components listed previously in this chapter, such as boilerplate text.

To base a new template on an existing one, open an existing template, modify it as necessary, and save it with a new name.

To create a template based on an existing document, open the document and choose File, Save As. Open the Save as Type drop-down list and choose Document Template (.dot). Word automatically opens your Templates folder. Save the new template there or in a folder of your choice.

T I P　I recommend that you save new templates in the default Templates folder, or in one of that folder's subfolders that have corresponding tabs in the New Office Document dialog box. By doing this, the new templates are visible when you start a new document by clicking the New Office Document button in the Office toolbar.

Where Word Stores Settings and Definitions

In the preceding pages of this chapter, we've concentrated on what templates can contain and how Word uses the contents of templates. To complete the picture, though, you should understand that just because a template may contain certain items, those items are not necessarily stored in a template; they may be somewhere else. For example, although macros are usually stored in templates, they may also be saved in documents. Here's where a document accesses various items:

- *AutoText Entries*. In the attached local template, in the global Normal template, and in any loaded temporary global templates.

- *Boilerplate Text and Graphics*. In the template used to create the document. Boilerplate text and graphics in a template that is subsequently attached to a document, and in any temporary global templates, are ignored.

- *Custom Menus, Shortcut Keys, and Toolbars*. In the attached local template, in the global Normal template, and in any loaded temporary global templates.

- *Default Page Settings*. In the template used to create the document. Page settings in a template that is subsequently attached to a document, and in any temporary global templates, are ignored.

- *Document Text and Graphics*. In the document file.

- *Macros*. In the document itself, in the attached local template, in the global Normal template, and in any loaded temporary global templates.

- *Styles*. In the document itself, copied from the template from which the document was created, and also from the global Normal template. If a different template is subsequently attached, you can choose between retaining the original styles or replacing them with the styles in the new template. Any styles in loaded temporary global templates are ignored.

Styles

The preceding information about templates has made frequent reference to styles because styles are the most used items in templates. Being so important and useful, styles deserve special attention in this chapter.

Catching Up on Styles

Let's start with a quick summary of some important points regarding Word styles:

- Word provides two types of styles: *paragraph* styles and *character* styles.
- You apply paragraph styles to paragraphs to control the appearance of all the text between one paragraph mark and the next.
- You apply character styles to individual characters to control the appearance of those characters; character styles override text formatting specified in paragraph styles.
- Every template, including custom templates you create, contains the full set of styles provided with Word.
- You can add custom styles to any template.
- When you create a new document, Word copies all the styles in the template on which the document is based into the document.
- Any changes you make to a document's styles don't affect the styles in that document's template.
- Any changes you make to styles in a template don't automatically affect documents based on that template (although you can update a document so that its styles match those in the template).

Each paragraph style contains a default font for the text in a paragraph. You can select any characters within a paragraph and apply a different character style to those characters, or you can manually change the font, font size, and font style.

N O T E Here we go again—one word, two different meanings! In the context of templates, a character *style* is the combination of all the factors that contribute to the appearance of characters. In the context of manually altering the appearance of characters by making choices in the Font dialog box, *style* is used for the choice made among Regular, Italic, Bold, and Bold Italic. ■

You can display a list of all the styles in a template by opening a document based on that template and pressing Shift while you click the arrow in the Style box at the left end of the Formatting toolbar. (If you don't press Shift, you only see a few basic styles and those styles used in the currently open document.) Figure 4.4 shows a section of the list of Word's built-in styles.

Part

II

Ch

4

FIG. 4.4

This is a partial list of Word's built-in styles.

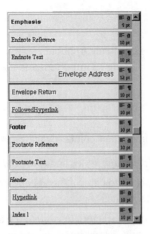

The list of styles in Word 97 provides considerably more information than the list provided by previous versions of Word. Some points to notice are:

- The horizontal position of the style name shows any indentation from the left margin that's part of the style.
- The font used to display the style's name is the font specified in that style.
- The size of the style's name is the same as the font size specified in the style, unless the specified size is smaller than 8 points (in which case the name is displayed in 8-point) or larger than 16 points (in which case the name is displayed in 16-point).
- The block at the right of each style name contains an underlined "a" to indicate a character style, or a paragraph mark to indicate a paragraph style.
- The four horizontal lines (also in the block) indicate left-aligned, right-aligned, centered, or justified.
- The block also contains the size of the font, in points.

You can delete custom styles, but Word won't let you delete any of its built-in styles, although with the exception of the Default Paragraph Font style, you can modify them.

Two styles to notice particularly are Normal and Default Paragraph Font. *Normal* is the paragraph style Word applies to all paragraphs unless you choose a different paragraph style. *Default Paragraph Font* is a character style that formats characters according to the character formatting specified in the current paragraph style. You'll see the reason for the Default Paragraph Font style in the next section, "Applying Styles."

Applying Styles

If you ignore styles, Word automatically applies the built-in Normal paragraph style to all your paragraphs. To apply a different paragraph style to a paragraph, place the insertion point anywhere within that paragraph, open the list of styles, and select the paragraph style you want—make sure you don't select a character style.

To apply a specific character style to certain characters within a paragraph, select those characters, open the list of styles, and select the character style you want.

It's important to understand that character styles override paragraph styles. For example, apply a paragraph style to a paragraph, then select some characters within that paragraph and apply a character style to them. Make sure the character style you choose makes the selected characters look quite different from the other characters in the paragraph. Now apply a completely different paragraph style to the same paragraph. You'll see that those characters to which you applied the character style retain that style, while all the other characters change to the default character style defined in the new paragraph style. Now you see what I mean by character styles overriding paragraph styles.

Also, you should know that any manual formatting you apply to text overrides paragraph styles. For example, create a short paragraph using the Normal style. Select one or two characters and make them bold by clicking the Bold button in the Formatting toolbar or by pressing Ctrl+B. With the selection point in that paragraph, select another paragraph style (one in which the default font is not bold). You'll see that the characters change to the default paragraph font in the new paragraph style, with the exception that those characters you manually bolded remain bold.

If you want all the characters in the paragraph to match the new paragraph style's default character formatting, select the entire paragraph and choose the Default Paragraph Font style. This removes the effect of any character styles or manual character formatting in the paragraph.

 TIP You can, if you like, select only some characters in the paragraph and then choose the Default Paragraph Font style. In this case, only the selected characters are affected.

Creating and Modifying Styles

You can modify existing styles, and you can create your own styles.

Modifying an Existing Style   To modify an existing style, choose Format, Style to display the Style dialog box shown in Figure 4.5.

FIG. 4.5
Use the Style dialog box to modify an existing style.

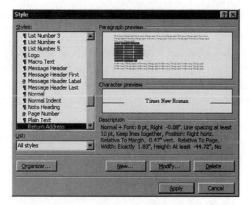

Open the List box (near the bottom of the dialog box) to choose among Styles in Use, All Styles, or User-Defined Styles; then select the style you want to modify. Notice that the Description panel contains a summary of what's defined in the selected style. Click Modify to open the Modify Style dialog box shown in Figure 4.6.

FIG. 4.6

The Modify Style dialog box is where you make changes to a style and where you tell Word how to manage those changes.

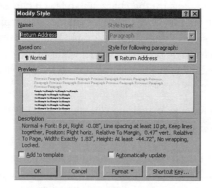

> **N O T E**   You can't modify or delete the Default Paragraph Font style. You can modify the Normal style, but Word won't let you delete it. ■

Click Format to proceed with your modifications. If you've chosen a paragraph style, you can display dialog boxes in which you can modify Font, Paragraph, Tabs, Border, Language, Frame, and Numbering; if you've chosen a character style, only Font, Border, and Language dialog boxes are available.

Each of these dialog boxes is similar to those you work with when you directly modify text in a document; you'll find detailed information about them in other books, such as *Special Edition Using Microsoft Office 97*. After you've modified a style, the Description in the Modify Style dialog box is automatically updated.

In the Modify Style dialog box, you can click Shortcut Key to display the Customize Keyboard dialog box in which you can define a shortcut key for the style you're modifying. You should define shortcut keys for the styles you frequently use so that you can apply these styles without having to open the list of styles and scroll to find the style you want.

Shortcut keys are key combinations created by holding down Alt, Ctrl, or Shift (or any combination of these) while you type an alphanumeric or punctuation character. The shortcut keys built into Word all have one part—by that I mean that each shortcut is a single key combination such as Ctrl+F. Word lets you create two-part shortcut keys, something that's very useful when creating shortcuts for styles.

To create a two-part shortcut key, select a style (such as Heading 1) in the Style dialog box, choose Modify, and then choose Shortcut Key. In the Customize Keyboard dialog box, place the insertion point in the Press New Shortcut Key box and press Alt+H; then press 1. The dialog box displays Alt+H,1 as the shortcut key. In a similar manner, create Alt+H,2 for the Heading 2 style, Alt+H,3 for the Heading 3 style, and so on. When you're working with a document, assign one of these styles to a paragraph by pressing Alt+H followed by a number (don't type the comma).

Pay particular attention to the two check boxes near the bottom of the Modify Style dialog box; it's important that you use these check boxes correctly. By default, both check boxes are unchecked.

The Add to Template check box has to do with how the modified style is saved. If you leave the box unchecked, the modified style applies only to the currently open document. On the other hand, if you check the box, the modified style is saved in the template that's attached to the current document. It's your choice! Do you want the modifications you've made to the style to apply only to the document you're currently working on, or do you want the modified style available in other documents based on the template attached to the current document?

The Automatically Update check box can be a powerful friend or a cunning enemy. Think carefully before you check it. If you do check it, it becomes very easy (perhaps too easy) to modify the style. Here's what happens after you've checked this box and saved the style.

Suppose you've modified (or created) a style (let's call the style XYZ) and checked Automatically Update. Subsequently, you're working in a paragraph that's based on the XYZ style. You decide to make a change to the format of the paragraph. The change you make affects not only that paragraph, but also every other paragraph based on the XYZ style. If that's what you want, OK. In many cases, though, you might not want a change you make in one paragraph to affect other paragraphs. I recommend you don't make a habit of checking the Automatically Update check box.

After you've finished modifying the style, click OK to return to the Style dialog box. Then click Apply to apply the changed style to your document, save the changed style, and close the dialog box.

Creating a New Style　The easiest way to create a new paragraph style is to format a paragraph in the way you want, and then save that paragraph's format as a style.

Start by creating a paragraph, then select the entire paragraph. Use the Format menu to apply font, paragraph, and whatever other formatting attributes you want. Then place the insertion point in the Style box at the left end of the Formatting toolbar. Type a name for the new format and, with the new name selected, press Enter. Now you have a new paragraph style.

But what happens if the name you propose for the new style is the name of an existing style? In that case, Word displays the Modify Style dialog box shown in Figure 4.7.

FIG. 4.7
Word displays this
dialog box if you
attempt to save a new
style with the same
name as an existing
style.

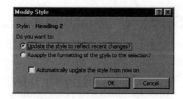

In this dialog box, choose Update the Style to Reflect Recent Changes to replace the original style with the new one. Choose Reapply the Formatting of the Style to the Selection to reapply the original style to the selected paragraph. The option Automatically Update the Style from Now On affects what happens in the future. If you check this box, the next time you use this method of creating a new style, this dialog box doesn't appear; instead, the old style is replaced with the new without giving you the choice of not doing so.

N O T E If you click Cancel in the Modify Style dialog box, the paragraph keeps the formatting changes you made manually without affecting the style. ■

 To restore access to the choice in the Modify Styles dialog box, choose Format, Style; select the style name and choose Modify. Then remove the check mark from the Automatically Update check box.

Word doesn't provide a similar way to create a new character style based on a character style in a document.

An alternative way to create a new paragraph style, and the only way to create a new character style, is by using the Format menu. Choose Format, Style to open the Style dialog box, and then choose New to display the New Style dialog shown in Figure 4.8.

FIG. 4.8

Use the New Style dialog box to begin creating a new paragraph or character style.

Enter a name for the new style, choose Paragraph or Character, choose any existing style to base the new style on (you can choose No Style for paragraph styles), and (for paragraph styles) choose a style for the following paragraph. After you've supplied this basic information, proceed to specify whatever formats are appropriate for the new style.

Creating Forms and Responding to Forms

We are all familiar with printed forms and with forms that appear on our computer screens. Examples of printed forms range from simple ones (such as those we use to tell the post office about a change of address) to complex ones (such as the infamous 1040 on which those who live in the United States have to report their income each year). Examples of forms that appear on our computer screen include those on which we supply our user name and password each time we log onto a network to those we use to apply for a subscription. Even the ubiquitous dialog boxes we work with in Windows applications are a type of form.

Forms have one thing in common: They ask questions and provide a format for us to respond to those questions. In many cases, the questions require words as a response, such as when the questions ask for first name, middle initial, and last name. In other cases, forms contain lists of items in which we can check those that are applicable.

Word is an ideal tool for creating several types of forms, and also for responding to those forms. You can use Word to create:

- A form to be printed on paper and responded to in writing.
- A form to be displayed on a computer screen and responded to interactively.

The information on the following pages deals primarily with forms to be displayed on a computer screen, although you can use some of it to create paper forms.

In addition to Word, you can use other Office 97 applications to create forms. Table 4.1 provides some recommendations about which Office application you should consider using for various types of forms.

Table 4.1   Recommended Applications for Creating Tables

Application	Form Characteristics
Access	Forms that require access to databases and are used to supply information for those databases
Excel	Forms that require sophisticated calculations
Outlook	Forms that are intended to be distributed and responded to by e-mail
Word	General forms that require no calculations or only simple calculations

There are no rigid divisions between the capabilities of these four applications. In general, choose the application with which you have relevant experience. If you run into difficulties with that application, think about choosing another one according to the recommendations in Table 4.1.

Creating a Simple Form

We deal here with creating a simple form that can be used to request a person's name, address, phone and fax numbers, and e-mail address. This form entails no calculations.

Start by making a rough sketch of the form on paper. The sketch should include the form title at the top and the various items to which you want people to provide responses. At this stage, make sure you know whether the form is going to be printed on paper or displayed on a computer monitor.

If you're creating a form to be displayed on a computer monitor, make sure the form fits on the average user's monitor. While it's acceptable to scroll down a form, people don't want to scroll across it. Unless you know for a fact that everyone who receives the form has a monitor set to a higher resolution, design the form for a standard VGA monitor (640×480 pixels).

Creating the Form   Create a form of this type much as you create any other Word document. Note, though, that the questions and space for responses are best created in a table. Proceed as follows:

1. Start with a blank Word document.
2. Enter the form title at the top of the page.
3. Under the title, create a table. The table should be two columns wide and have as many rows as there are questions to ask.

 Use the Draw Table button on the Tables and Borders toolbar if you need to create a table that has differing numbers of columns per row or cells of differing heights.

4. Enter questions (or descriptions of the information required) in the first column of the table.
5. Adjust the width of the columns and the height of the rows.
6. Use Word's facilities to improve the appearance of the form by modifying borders (those around the table and those between cells) and to add shading to cells.

 Display the Tables and Borders toolbar to make it easy to optimize tables in your forms.

If the form is to be distributed on paper, all you have to do now is to save and print your work. However, if you're going to distribute the form electronically, you need to protect it so that other people can't change the design of the form.

Protecting the Form   As your form stands at this point, anyone who opens the file can make changes to it. In order to protect the form so that people can only work in the spaces you've provided for responses, you must identify these spaces as form fields and then protect the entire form:

1. Choose View, Toolbars, Forms to display the Forms toolbar.
2. Place the insertion point in the first response space and click the Text Form Field button in the Forms toolbar. A gray bar appears in the response space to indicate the presence of a form field.
3. Repeat step 2 for all the remaining response spaces.
4. Click the Form Field Shading button in the Forms toolbar to remove the shading from the response spaces.
5. Choose Tools, Protect Document and in the Protect Document dialog box, choose Forms.

Now you'll find that you can only place the insertion point in the response spaces—those you designated as form fields. All other parts of the document are protected.

N O T E You can turn protection off by choosing Tools, Unprotect Document. To prevent other people from turning off protection, set a password in the Protect Document dialog box. ■

Saving the Form   Before you make the form available electronically for other people to use, you should save it as a template rather than as a document. Then, other people can create a document based on the template, and save that document without altering the template. To save the form as a template, choose File, Save As. In the Save as Type list at the bottom of the Save As dialog box, choose Document Template. When you do so, Word automatically proposes to save the template in your local Templates folder. Instead, you should save the form template in a folder that's accessible to other people. For example, you may want to save the template on your LAN server or, if you are part of a workgroup, in the Workgroup Templates folder.

That completes the procedure for creating the simplest of forms. Now we can turn to some more sophisticated (and very useful) aspects of using Word to create forms.

Forms Provided with Office

Microsoft provides three examples of fairly sophisticated Word forms with Office, but these are not automatically copied to your hard drive when you install Office. You can find the three forms on the Office 97 CD-ROM in the ValuPack\Template\Word folder:

- *Invoice.dot*. An invoice form.
- *Purchord.dot*. A purchase order form.
- *Weektime.dot*. A time sheet.

I suggest you copy these three templates into your local Templates folder so that you can take a detailed look at them.

N O T E If you previously had Office 95 installed on your computer, you probably have form templates similar to those mentioned here; these are named Invoice.dot, Purchase Order.dot, and Weekly Time Sheet.dot. You can use these templates with Word 97, but Word has to convert the WordBasic macros they contain. There's more information about this in "Making a Calculation Happen" later in this chapter. ■

All three templates are protected. In order to see what's behind them, you must unprotect them (as explained earlier).

One of the most interesting and useful features of these form templates is that they illustrate the use of macros. Even if you're not a macro expert, you can use these macros in your own forms. You'll understand why macros are so important when you read about forms that include automatically calculated fields in the next section of this chapter. See Chapters 29 through 33 for additional information about macros.

Part
II

Ch
4

The sample forms also illustrate how you can provide help text that appears in the status bar while a user works with a form.

Calculated Fields in a Form

Many forms contain calculated values. For example, invoice and purchase-order forms usually contain spaces for quantity, price per unit, and extension; the extension amount is calculated by multiplying the quantity by the price per unit. Calculations such as these can be made automatically in electronically displayed forms. The three examples of form templates on the Office CD-ROM contain calculations.

You'll get a useful insight into forms that contain calculations by creating a document based on one of these templates and entering information on the form. As you do so, notice the help text in the status bar.

Before you can construct forms of this type yourself, you need to understand some basic principles.

Getting Behind the Invoice Template   To explore the Invoice template, open that template (the template itself, not a document based on it). As provided, the template is protected, so you can't see what's behind it. Choose Tools, Unprotect Document to unprotect the document. Also, make sure the Forms toolbar is displayed. Figure 4.9 shows the top part of the invoice form.

FIG. 4.9

The Invoice template contains several instructive elements.

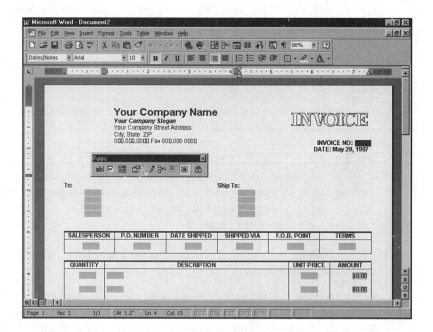

The following are some points you should notice about the form template:

- Gray bars in many places indicate the presence of fields—places where a specific type of information is displayed or entered. If you don't see the gray blocks on your screen, click the Form Field Shading button in the Forms toolbar.

- The word INVOICE at the top-right is a picture object. Double-click the object to open it in a picture-editing window.

- The gray block at the right of INVOICE NO: is a text form field (there's more information about text form fields in the next section "Specifying Form Fields"). To confirm that it is a form field, click within the field and press Shift+F9. The gray block is replaced by {FORMTEXT}. Press Shift+F9 again to go back to the gray block.

- The gray block at the right of DATE: is a date field. To confirm this, click the field and press Shift+F9. The gray bar is replaced by {date \@ "MMMM d, yyyy"}. This shows the field is indeed a date field that displays a date in a specific format.

The lower part of the form consists of a table with four columns. The top row of the table consists of column headings. Below that are seven rows for data. Let's look in detail at the fields in the top data row.

Select the Quantity field in that row. When you do so, the Form Field Options button in the Forms toolbar becomes enabled. Click that button to display the Text Form Field Options dialog box shown in Figure 4.10.

FIG. 4.10

The Text Form Field Options dialog box is where you control how each form field displays data and where you specify any macro that runs when the field receives or loses the focus.

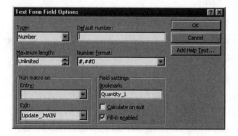

N O T E The Text Form Field Options dialog box title bar contains the familiar question mark button. You normally use this button to activate the mouse pointer that allows you to get help about any item in a dialog box. This functionality hasn't been incorporated into the Text Form Field Options dialog box. The only help you receive is No Help topic is associated with this item. ■

Select each of the fields in the first data row in turn and examine the Text Form Field Options dialog box. Now we'll look at that dialog box in detail.

Specifying Form Fields The top part of the Text Form Field Options dialog box specifies the type of data that can be entered into the field, and how it is displayed or printed.

The Type drop-down list box provides a choice of six types. These types are used as follows:

- *Regular Text.* Any text can be entered into the field. The text is left-aligned within the field. Regular Text is the default type.
- *Number.* Only numbers (together with thousands and decimal separators) can be entered in the field. The numbers are right-aligned within the field.
- *Date.* The intention, apparently, is to use this type for fields that can only accept dates. However, other types of data are accepted by the field. Perhaps a subsequent Word update will correct this problem.
- *Current Date.* This type of field displays the current date.
- *Current Time.* This type of field displays the current time.
- *Calculation.* The data in this field is automatically calculated from data in other fields.

The Maximum Length box is used to specify the maximum number of characters that can be entered into the box. The default is `Unlimited`; you can replace the default with a specific number.

The box to the right of the Type box is labeled `Default Text`, `Default Number`, `Default Date`, or `Expression` depending on the selected type. In this box, enter whatever should appear in the field by default. Usually, this box is left empty. This box is disabled if you select Current Date or Current Time as the type. If you select the Calculation type, an equals sign appears in the box ready for you to define the calculation. Defining the calculation is explained subsequently in the section "Calculating a Value."

The list box to the right of the Maximum Length box is where you can select the format in which data is to be displayed in the field. When you open the list, you see various formats that are appropriate for the selected type.

The bottom-left part of the dialog box is where you can select macros. When you open the Entry list, you see the names of all macros that are accessible from the current template. These are all macros within the template itself, all macros in the Normal template, and all macros within any other templates that are temporarily global. Choose any macro that should run when the field receives the focus.

When you open the Exit list, you see the same list of macros. Choose any macro that should run when the field loses the focus.

The bottom-right part of the dialog box is where you control the field's settings (properties). The Bookmark field allows you to provide an identifying name for the field. Word automatically provides names for fields. When you use macros that refer to fields, it's sometimes necessary to replace the automatically assigned names with others. To replace the name Word suggests, just delete the suggested name and replace it with another.

The Calculate On Exit check box is apparently intended to provide a means to display a calculated value when a Calculate-type field loses the focus. This functionality is not implemented in the current version of Word.

The Fill-In Enabled check box is checked for Regular Text, Number, and Date field types. It is disabled for Current Date, Current Time, and Calculation fields. In the case of a Regular Text, Number, or Date field, you can remove the check mark. In that case, the default value for that field cannot be changed.

The Add Help Text button provides access to a dialog box in which you can provide online help to the form user, as described in the section "Providing Help on Forms" later in this chapter.

Calculating a Value   If you've followed along so far, you have a basic understanding of how to create a form that contains various fields, including a Calculation field. Now, we have to consider how to make the calculation actually happen.

Let's start with a form that contains a table with headings Quantity, Description, Unit Price, and Amount. Under these headings there are several rows. In each row, the Quantity field is of type Number, the Description field is of type Regular Text, the Unit Price field is of type Number, and the Amount field is of type Calculation.

The question at this stage is: How do you define the calculation? The answer: In much the same way that you do in an Excel worksheet.

Word considers a table to have rows numbered consecutively, starting with row 1, and columns to be identified alphabetically, starting with column A. The first row of the table consists of column headings, so the first data row is row 2. Specific fields in the table are designated by the column letter followed by the row number.

In the first data row, the Quantity field is A2 and the Unit Price field is C2. Just as you do in Excel, you can use the cell addresses to access the data in those cells. The value to be calculated in the Amount field is expressed as =PRODUCT(A2,C2). Likewise, the value to be calculated in the second data row is expressed as =PRODUCT(A3,C3).

N O T E   Although you may have assigned bookmarks to cells, you cannot use these bookmark names in calculations. In calculations, you must use cell addresses. Unlike in Excel, Word cell addresses are always absolute (never relative). ▪

▶ **See** "Linking to Other Web Pages or Internet Resources," **p. 786**

Unfortunately, this isn't the whole story. If you create a form with calculated values expressed like this, anyone who uses the form will have a problem. The calculations defined in the table don't actually occur until the user selects a calculated cell in the table and presses F9. I don't think you would be very proud of yourself in creating a table that imposed this on the table users! What you have to do is to provide a macro that runs automatically to make the calculation occur. More about this in a moment.

The preceding description mentioned only one of the functions that can be used in calculations: Product. Table 4.2 contains a complete list of available functions.

Part

II

Ch

4

Table 4.2   Functions for Calculated Fields

Function	Value Returned
ABS(x)	The positive value of the number or formula x, regardless of whether x is actually positive or negative.
AND(x,y)	True (1) if x and y are both true (1). Otherwise false (0).
AVERAGE( )	The average of a list of values.
COUNT( )	The number of items in a list.
DEFINED(x)	True (1) if x is defined. Otherwise false (0).
FALSE	False (0).
IF(x,y,z)	y if x is true (1 or "True"). z if x is false (0 or "False").
INT(x)	The digits to the left of the decimal place in x.
MAX( )	The maximum value in a list.
MIN( )	The minimum value in a list.
MOD(x,y)	The remainder resulting from dividing x by y (y is a whole number).
NOT(x)	True (1) if x is false (0); false (0) if x is true (1).
OR(x,y)	True (1) if x or y (or both) is true (1). False (0) if x and y are both false (0).
PRODUCT(x,y)	The result of multiplying x by y.
ROUND(x,y)	The value of x rounded to y decimal places.
SIGN(x)	1 if x is positive or zero; -1 if x is negative.
SUM( )	The sum of a list of values.
TRUE	True (1).

In addition to formulas, you can use the following operators in a calculation: +, –, *, /, %, ^, =, <, <=, >, >=, <>.

TIP By default, references are to cells within a single table. To refer to cells in a different table, identify that table with a bookmark such as RefData.

The function {=Product(A1,B3)} refers to cells within its own table. The function {=Product(RefData A1,B3)} refers to cells in the table bookmarked RefData.

Making a Calculation Happen   At last we get to the glory of macros! Macros make it possible for calculations in a form to occur automatically. The form template Invoice.dot that's on the Office 97 CD-ROM illustrates how this can be done.

The first row in the second table in Invoice.dot contains column titles. Rows 2 through 8 are where the user supplies data. If you select the cells in Row 2 one at a time and examine each cell's Text Form Field options, you can see what's behind each cell. Don't forget to choose Tools, Unprotect Document so that the Form Field Options button on the Forms toolbar is enabled. Notice that:

- The first cell is type Number, has the bookmark Quantity_1, and the macro Update_.Main is specified to run on Exit.
- The second cell is type Regular Text, has the bookmark Description_1, and has no macro specified.
- The third cell is type Number, has the bookmark Price_1, and the macro Update_.Main is specified to run on Exit.
- The fourth cell is type Calculation, has the bookmark Amount_1, and has no macro specified.

The macro Update_.Main causes the calculation in the fourth cell to occur and the result of the calculation to be displayed in that cell. Thus, whenever a user changes the quantity or unit price and presses Tab to leave the cell, the corresponding amount changes automatically. The macro also calculates the Subtotal and Total values.

One of the neat tricks in this macro is that it can be used for any row in the table. The bookmarks for the cells in the first data row all end in _1, those in the second row with _2, and so on. The macro detects which row the user is on, and automatically uses the appropriate bookmarks for that row.

With the Invoice.dot template open, you can see the macro by choosing Tools, Macro, Macros and then in the Macros dialog box, choosing Update_.Main and clicking Edit. If you're at all familiar with Word macros, you shouldn't have too much difficulty in following how this macro works. Otherwise, refer to Chapters 29 through 33 of this book for information about macros.

You can copy this macro into similar forms that you design so that they, too, automatically calculate values. When doing so, you must either use the same bookmarks or modify the macro to refer to your bookmarks.

Here's a final piece of information about using macros in forms. While you can specify a macro to run on Entry or on Exit for any type of field, Run Macro on Exit has no effect for Calculation fields. That's one of the reasons the Invoice.dot template runs the Update_.Main macro on Exit from the Quantity and Unit Price fields, both of which are of type Number.

N O T E Versions of Word prior to Word 97 used WordBasic as a macro language. Although Word 97's macro language is Visual Basic for Applications (VBA), it can run WordBasic macros by converting each statement into a VBA property. The macro in Invoice.dot is a converted WordBasic macro, not a true VBA macro. ▪

Part

II

Ch

4

More Form Elements

When a form asks for a first name, last name, address, and the like, you have to provide a space for respondents to insert words. In other cases, such as when the respondent can only answer Yes or No, it's better to provide *check boxes*. Where a respondent can choose one or more responses from a list, you should provide a *list box* on the form. Check boxes and list boxes make it easy for users to make choices.

Adding Check Boxes   To add a check box, place the insertion point where you want the check box to be and then click the Check Box Form Field button on the Forms toolbar. To set options for a check box, select the box and then click the Form Field Options button on the Forms toolbar to display the Check Box Form Field Options dialog box shown in Figure 4.11.

FIG. 4.11

Use the Check Box Form Field Options dialog box to set check box options.

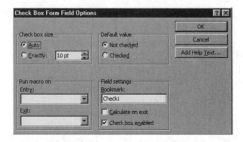

The settings available in this box are similar to those for text fields already described, and don't require any further explanation.

After you've added a check box to a form template, don't forget to protect the template. If you don't protect it, a user who creates a new document based on the template won't be able to add or remove a check mark in the box.

Adding Drop-Down List Boxes   To add a drop-down list box, place the insertion point where you want the drop-down list box to be and then click the Drop-Down Form Field button on the Forms toolbar. To set options for a drop-down list box, select the box and then click the Form Field Options button on the Forms toolbar to display the Drop-Down Form Field Options dialog box shown in Figure 4.12.

FIG. 4.12

Use the Drop-Down Form Field Options dialog box to set drop-down list box options.

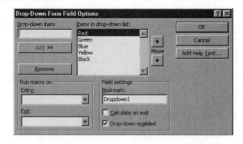

Again, many of the settings available in this box are similar to those for text fields already described, and don't require any further explanation. However, you may appreciate some information about creating items to be shown in the drop-down list. Simply enter items one at a time in the Drop-Down Item box, and click Add to move each item into the list. After you've done so, you can change the order of items by selecting an item and clicking the Move buttons. To delete an item from the list, select that item and click Remove.

N O T E   The first item in the list is displayed on the form when a user opens a document based on the form template. ■

There's no way to edit items in the list. If you need to change an item, you must remove it and then replace it with a new item.

After you've added a drop-down list box to a form template, don't forget to protect the template. If you don't protect it, a user who creates a new document based on the template won't be able to open the list.

Providing Help on Forms

It's easy to provide help for form users. You can provide brief help messages that always appear in the status bar at the bottom of the form window, or more lengthy help messages (up to 255 characters) that appear in a pop-up message box when the user presses F1.

The Text Form Field Options dialog box (as well as the options dialog boxes for check boxes and drop-down list boxes) all have an Add Help Text button. Click this button to display the Form Field Help Text dialog box with the Status Bar tab selected, as shown in Figure 4.13.

FIG. 4.13

Use the Form Field Help Text dialog box to select or enter help text that appears in the status bar.

By default, the None option is selected. If you want (though I can't think why you would), you can choose help messages from the AutoText entries you've saved. Generally, you'll want to select Type Your Own and then type the appropriate help text in the text box. The text you provide here appears automatically in the status bar while the user enters data into the form.

To provide more lengthy help messages, choose the Help Key (F1) tab of the dialog box. This tab is identical in appearance to the Status Bar tab. You can provide messages consisting of up to 255 characters that will appear in pop-up boxes when the user presses F1.

As always, protect the form template after you've added help text, and then save it.

Part

II

Ch

4

Using a Form

Despite all the talk about "the paperless office" (and the millions of dollars spent in attempts to create one), the fact is most people work with paper documents. To satisfy these people, you'll have to print many of your forms, have people write their responses and send the completed form back to you, and then transcribe each form into a database. The concept is simple; the implementation is tedious.

If you're creating a form for computer users who share LAN or workgroup access, after designing and protecting your form save it as a template on a disk to which everyone has access. Instruct users to create a new document based on the template, complete the form on their computers, and save the completed form in a specific place on the LAN.

You can also create a form to use on a Web page, but detailed treatment of this is beyond the scope of this chapter. Sample forms of this type are available in the Web Page Wizard that's supplied with Office 97. To use the Web Page Wizard, choose File, New to display the New dialog box, and choose the Web Pages tab. In that tab, choose Web Page Wizard. This wizard guides you through creating three kinds of forms on Web pages: Feedback, Registration, and Survey. For more information about creating Web documents, refer to Chapter 38, "Creating Web Documents." ●

CHAPTER 5

Power Tools

Following on from Chapter 3, this chapter provides more suggestions about how you can take advantage of the power that's built into Word.

You probably already use some of the buttons on the Standard and Formatting toolbars that Word displays. But toolbars don't stop there. Word has many more than these two toolbars, and you can create your own. Clicking a button on a toolbar can save you from having to open dialog boxes and make choices.

No lengthy document is complete without a table of contents and an index. You learn in this chapter how Word can help you with what otherwise can be the very tedious tasks of creating tables of contents and indexes. You'll also learn how to make cross references (and hyperlinks) from one place to another in a document.

Do you find yourself doing repetitive tasks in Word? How about doing the task just once and then automatically repeating what you did? That's what macros are for. Read about these types of macros in this chapter. ■

Create custom toolbars that contain buttons you need to use

You can also modify the toolbars supplied with Word.

Create tables of contents, tables of figures, and similar tables automatically

If you apply appropriate styles to headings and subheadings, Word can create tables automatically.

Use Document Map to review a document's structure

Click the Document Map button to see the structure of a document and easily move from place to place.

Create cross-references and hyperlinks automatically

Cross references and hyperlinks keep track of the pages that a reader can refer to.

Provide your readers with the convenience of indexes

It can help you provide your readers with the indexes they need to locate material in your document.

Use macros to simplify your work

Save yourself time by recording a sequence of keystrokes and choices made with mouse clicks as a macro.

Powerful Toolbars

Toolbars contain buttons that provide quick access to much of Word's functionality, as well as drop-down lists from which you can make choices. You can modify the toolbars supplied with Word, and you can create custom toolbars.

Displaying Toolbars

When you first open Word, only the Standard and Formatting toolbars are displayed, but Word contains many others, three of which were mentioned in the "Forms Provided with Office" section of Chapter 4. To see a list of most of the available toolbars shown in Figure 5.1, choose View, Toolbars.

FIG. 5.1

The Toolbar list shows most of the toolbars supplied with Word. Those toolbars that are currently displayed are checked.

Some toolbars not shown in this list are available only when you're working in specific areas of Word. For example, the Mail Merge toolbar is available only when you are working with Mail Merge. See Chapter 6 for information about Mail Merge.

 TIP   If the list on your system doesn't contain all the toolbars listed in Figure 5.1, that's probably because some Word components aren't installed on your system.

The presence of a check mark in the check box at the left of a toolbar's name indicates that toolbar is displayed. Click any toolbar name to hide a displayed toolbar or to display a hidden one. The menu and list of toolbars disappear whenever you click a toolbar name.

 TIP   A faster way to display or hide several toolbars is to choose Customize at the bottom of the list of toolbars. Then, in the Customize dialog box, you can display and hide any combination of toolbars. See "Creating a Custom Toolbar" later in this chapter for more information about the Customize dialog box.

If you're not already familiar with all the toolbars, I suggest you open them all and make a mental note of what they contain. Figure 5.2 shows most of Word's toolbars.

FIG. 5.2
This screen shows most of Word's toolbars. They are shown floating within the document pane.

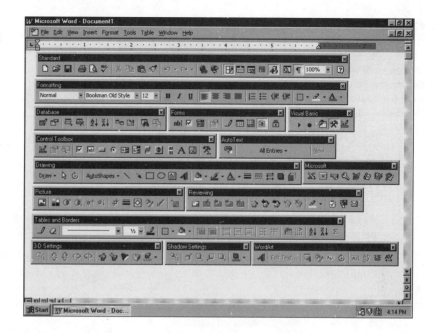

When using Word, display only the toolbars you actually need so that you have as much space as possible to work on your document. Normally, you need only the Standard and Formatting toolbars and one, or at the most two, of the other toolbars. Each toolbar can be "docked" at the top, bottom, left, or right edge of the window, or it can be shown floating within the document pane. As shown in Figure 5.2, floating toolbars have title bars that contain their names.

Some of the techniques you can use with toolbars are:

- Drag the two narrow vertical bars at the extreme left end of a horizontally docked toolbar, or at the extreme top end of a vertically docked toolbar, to convert the toolbar to floating.

- Drag the title bar of a floating toolbar to move that toolbar.

- Double-click the title bar of a floating toolbar to dock that toolbar in its most recent docked position.

- Right-click any toolbar to display a list of all toolbars (the same list that's displayed when you choose View, Toolbars).

- Drag one of the borders of a floating toolbar to change its shape.

- Click the Close button at the right end of a floating toolbar's title bar to hide that toolbar.

Creating a Custom Toolbar

To begin creating a custom toolbar, choose View, Toolbars and then at the bottom of the list of toolbars, choose Customize to display the Customize dialog box shown in Figure 5.3.

Part
II

Ch
5

FIG. 5.3

The Toolbars tab of the Customize dialog box shows a list of available toolbars that includes some not included in the shortcut list of toolbars.

As mentioned in the previous section, you can use this dialog box to display and hide any combination of toolbars.

To create a new custom toolbar, click New to display the New Toolbar dialog box shown in Figure 5.4.

FIG. 5.4

Here you give the new toolbar a name and choose where the toolbar will be stored.

Replace the name Word proposes with a suitably descriptive name.

You can choose to save the new toolbar in the template on which the open document is based—in the Normal template or in the document itself. Where you save the new toolbar affects which documents have access to it:

- If you save the toolbar in the template on which the open document is based, that document and all other documents based on the same templates have access to the toolbar.

- If you save the toolbar in the Normal template, all documents have access to the toolbar.

- If you save the toolbar in the open document, only that document has access to the toolbar.

Open the Make Toolbar Available To drop-down list to choose where you want to save the toolbar. By default, Word proposes to save the new toolbar in the Normal template; normally, it's better to save a toolbar in the template on which the open document is based, rather than in the Normal template. When you click OK, the dialog box disappears and the new toolbar, just wide enough for one button, appears. The name of the new toolbar appears at the bottom of the list of toolbars in the Customize dialog box.

Now that you have a custom toolbar, the Rename and Delete buttons in the Customize dialog box are enabled. Word lets you rename and delete custom toolbars, but not the supplied toolbars.

To add a command button to the new toolbar, choose the Commands tab of the Customize dialog box, choose from the list of command categories, and then drag a command from the list of commands into the toolbar. Each time you drag a command into the toolbar, the width of the toolbar automatically increases to accommodate the new button. To add one of Word's built-in menus to the toolbar, choose Built-In Menus from the list of categories, and then drag a menu name from the Commands list into the toolbar.

To delete a button from a toolbar, hold down Alt while you drag the button off the toolbar.

You can use the techniques described in the previous two paragraphs to add buttons to, and delete buttons from, the toolbars supplied with Word. After you've made any changes to a supplied toolbar, you can restore it to its original form by selecting that toolbar in the Customize dialog box and clicking Reset. You cannot reset a custom toolbar in this way.

TROUBLESHOOTING

If the Word toolbars you see on your computer are different from those shown in this chapter, that's because someone has made changes. To get the standard toolbars back, choose View, Toolbars, Customize. In the Customize dialog box, select the toolbar you want to reset and click Reset. Word asks you to confirm that you want to reset the toolbar as it's defined in the template you're currently using. Click OK to reset the toolbar. Repeat this process for each of the toolbars you want to reset.

▶ **See** "Basing a Document on a Template," **p. 63**

Part
II

Ch
5

Creating Tables of Contents and Similar Tables

Long documents such as books, reports, theses, and the like usually have a table of contents as part of their front matter (the pages that come before the first chapter). These documents may also contain a table of figures, a table of equations, and other tables that list specific content material. Each table consists of a list of headings or titles and the page number on which those headings or titles appear.

Word provides an easy way for you to create a table of contents and similar tables. In addition, Word provides powerful tools you can use to create more specialized tables, but using these involves some considerable effort. Whether you choose the easy way, or the more powerful tools, Word automatically keeps track of page numbers so that the final tables have correct page numbers for each item, no matter how many changes you make to the document.

After you've created a table of contents, you can use that table to move quickly to any heading in your document. Just point to the page number in the table and click.

The following sections refer specifically to an ordinary table of contents that lists headings and subheadings throughout a document. Subsequent sections deal with other types of tables.

Identifying Headings

The first step in creating a table of contents is to identify the headings and subheadings it should contain. The easiest way to do this is to assign a specific style to each level of heading. All templates include paragraph styles named Heading 1, Heading 2, Heading 3, and so on that are intended for this purpose. Assign the Heading 1 style to principal headings such as chapter titles; assign the Heading 2 style to main section headings; assign the Heading 3 style to section subheadings, and so on. After you've done this, Word can automatically create a table of contents.

You don't have to use the Heading styles provided with Word. You can, of course, modify these styles (as explained in the "Modifying an Existing Style" section in Chapter 4), or you can create you own paragraph styles with whatever names you choose. All that matters is that you are consistent in applying styles to each level of heading in your document, and you don't use these styles for anything other than headings.

TIP I recommend using the Heading styles, rather than creating styles with different names. This is because Document Map, described in the "Mapping a Document" section later in this chapter, only uses the Heading styles. Another reason for staying with Heading styles is that you can use shortcut keys to change a heading level; press Alt+Shift+← to promote a heading (such as from Heading Level 1 to Heading Level 2), or press Alt+Shift+→ to demote a headings (such as from Heading Level 2 to Heading Level 1). You can't use these shortcut keys if you use styles with other names for your headings.

If you want the table of contents to contain the exact wording of the headings in the document, use the method of identifying headings described in the previous two paragraphs. But what if you want the wording in the table of contents to differ from the headings in your document? You have to do more work in this case. Instead of applying specific styles to headings throughout the document, you have to mark those places in the document that are referred to in the table of contents by inserting TC field codes into the document.

Suppose an actual heading in your document is "Calibrating the Model A-456-B Optometer for Optimum Precision." You've decided to restrict the entries in your table of contents to a single line, so you need to summarize this heading. Here's how you do so:

1. Select the entire text of the heading as it appears in the document, and press Alt+Shift+O to display the Mark Table of Contents Entry dialog box shown in Figure 5.5. If the text you selected is long, as in this example, the Entry box shows only the last few words of the selected text. You can press Home to see the beginning of the selected text.

2. Change the text in the Entry box to the text as you want it to appear in the table of contents (such as **Calibrating the Optometer**).

3. Leave the Table Identifier unchanged as C for a table of contents.

4. Select the appropriate heading level in the Level box.

5. Click Mark to insert a TC field code into the document. You'll see the actual field code inserted after the selected text. At this time, you can add another TC field code at the same position. When you've finished, click Close to close the dialog box.

FIG. 5.5

Use this dialog box to customize a table of contents item.

NOTE   You can find detailed information about TC field codes in the Word help topic "Tables of Contents, Field Codes." ▓

You can mark headings throughout your document in this way. However, if only some of the headings require modification in this way, you can identify all the others by applying a style, as described previously. Word can create a table of contents based on a document that contains some headings identified by styles and other headings marked by TC field codes.

Creating a Table of Contents

After identifying headings (with styles) or marking headings (with field codes) throughout the document, you can create the actual table of contents. Place the insertion point at the position in the document where you want the table of contents to be, and choose Insert, Index and Tables to display the Index and Tables dialog box. Choose the Table of Contents tab shown in Figure 5.6.

Part

II

Ch

5

FIG. 5.6

The Table of Contents tab of the Index and Tables dialog box is where you specify what's to be in the table of contents.

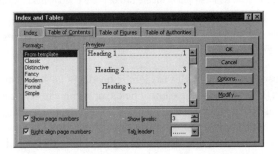

Word offers seven formats for tables of contents; you can see what these look like by selecting them one at a time in the Formats list and looking at the Preview pane. The From Template format uses the TOC 1, TOC 2, TOC 3, and so on styles for the various levels of entries in the table of contents. Choose the one you want to use.

TIP You can easily modify the format of a table of contents by choosing From Template and modifying the default TOC styles. Click Modify in the Index and Tables dialog box to display the Style dialog box with the TOC styles available for modifying.

If you've applied Word's Heading styles to the headings and subheadings in your document, just click OK and wait a few seconds for Word to create and display the table of contents with three levels of headings displayed. To display more or less than three levels of headings, change the number in the Show Levels box before clicking OK. You also have the option of showing leader dots or not between the last letter of the heading text and the page number.

If you've used styles other than the Heading styles for headings in the document, click Options in the Index and Tables dialog box. The Table of Contents Options dialog box shown in Figure 5.7 lists all the available paragraph styles and shows the table of contents level associated with the those styles. By default, Heading 1 style is shown for TOC Level 1, Heading 2 style for TOC level 2, and so on. Delete the TOC level numbers from those styles you haven't used for headings, and enter TOC level numbers for those styles you have used.

FIG. 5.7

In this dialog box, mark the TOC level numbers for the styles you've used for headings.

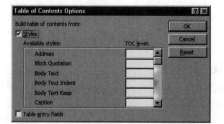

N O T E Word lets you mark two or more styles with the same TOC level number. This can occasionally be useful, such as when you combine two or more documents in which different style names are used for headings. It can also cause problems; for example, if you accidentally mark some styles with TOC level numbers and those styles are used for text other than headings, your table of contents will contain unwanted items. ■

By default, Word uses paragraph styles to identify headings for inclusion in the table of contents. Alternatively, Word can use table entry fields, or it can use styles and table entry fields to identify text for a table of contents. The Table of Contents Options dialog box, shown previously, contains two check boxes named Styles and Table Entry Fields. By default, the Styles check box is checked, meaning that Word uses styles to identify text for inclusion in the table of contents. You can uncheck Styles and check Table Entry Fields to make Word use only table entry fields, or you can check both boxes to make Word use styles and table entry fields.

 TIP Here's a little-known tip about tables of contents: You can use a table of contents to move quickly to any heading in a document. After you've created a table of contents, move the mouse pointer onto a page number in the table. With the mouse in the position where the pointer changes to a pointing finger, click. Word jumps immediately to the heading you chose.

Creating a Table of Contents for a Multi-File Document

In the case of short documents, it's usual to create the table of contents as part of the document the table refers to. However, in the case of a long document that consists of several files, you have to create the table of contents as a separate file so that it can include headings from all the document files. Here's how:

1. Create a new document. Display hidden text by clicking the Show/Hide button in the Standard toolbar, and turn on the display of field codes by pressing Alt+F9.

2. Choose Insert, Field to display the Field dialog box shown in Figure 5.8. In the Categories list, choose Index and Tables; in the Field Names list, choose RD. The Description section near the bottom of the dialog box tells you what the RD field is used for.

FIG. 5.8

Use this dialog box to identify a document to be included in the table of contents.

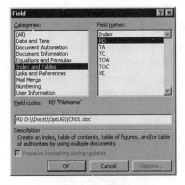

3. In the Field Code box, after RD and a space, type the fully qualified file name of the first document to be included in the table of contents.

N O T E The fully qualified file name must have double backslashes, as shown in Figure 5.8. If the folder or file names contain spaces, the entire folder or file name must be enclosed within double quotation marks. ■

4. Repeat steps 2 and 3 for each additional document to be included in the table of contents.

5. Create the actual table of contents in the manner described in "Creating a Table of Contents" earlier in this chapter.

Updating a Table of Contents

Although Word doesn't automatically update a table of contents when you make changes to a document, updating is only a few keystrokes away. Because a table of contents is, in fact, a field, you update it in the same way that you update any other field. Place the insertion point anywhere within the table of contents and press F9 to display the Update Table of Contents dialog box shown in Figure 5.9.

FIG. 5.9

Choose whether you want to update page numbers only, or to update the entire table of contents.

T I P To make sure you always print the current table of contents, choose Tool, Options and then select the Print tab. In the Printing Options section, check the Update Fields check box. Subsequently, Word always updates the table of contents (as well as other fields such as PAGE and DATE) whenever you print the document.

Creating Tables of Figures and Other Tables

Creating tables of equations, tables of figures, tables of tables, and other types of tables requires no special techniques. As with tables of contents, the items you want to show in the table must be identified either by a specific character style or by table entry fields. To create these types of tables, select the Table of Figures tab in the Index and Tables dialog box shown in Figure 5.10.

FIG. 5.10

In this dialog box, choose the type of table and its format.

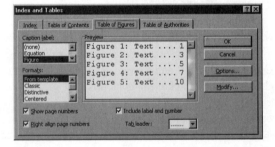

Click Options to display the Table of Figures dialog box in which you choose whether you want to create the table based on a style (and, if so, which one), table entry fields, or both. If you are using table entry fields, you must also select a table identifier character (Word suggests F for tables of figures).

You can use this method to create as many additional tables as you need. The Table of Authorities tab in the Index and Tables dialog box makes it easy for you to add a properly formatted table of authorities to your doctoral thesis.

Mapping a Document

Sometimes I get the impression that new features added to an updated version of an application are solutions looking for a problem, rather that useful new capabilities. Document mapping isn't like that—it's a very useful new feature in Word 97 for anyone who works with long documents. Unfortunately, you have to play by its rules. Specifically, you must apply Word's Heading styles to all the headings and subheadings in your document.

At any time while you're working with a document (in which you've applied Word's heading styles to your headings and subheadings), you can click the Document Map button in the Standard toolbar (the first button to the left of the Show/Hide button) to split your screen into the two panes shown in Figure 5.11.

FIG. 5.11

After you click Document Map, your Word window has two panes. The pane on the right shows the current document. The pane on the left shows the documents headings.

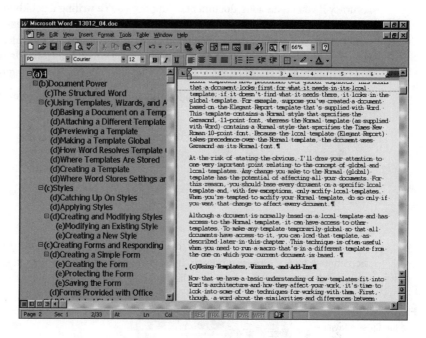

N O T E If your document doesn't contain Heading styles, Word tries to guess which paragraphs in your document are headings. Frankly, this doesn't work. You must use Heading styles if you want to use Document Map. ■

The document map is somewhat similar to the Outline view of a document. You can expand and collapse headings to show whatever granularity you need. When you click any heading in the left pane, the corresponding part of the document is shown in the right pane. Try it, and you'll wonder how you ever lived without it.

 If you're writing for publication, your publisher may require styles that have names different from Word Heading styles. Unfortunately, this means that you can't use Word's Document Map feature. To overcome this problem, create the document with Word's standard Heading styles and, only when you are ready to submit your work to the publisher, use Replace to change the Heading styles into those your publisher requires.

Part

II

Ch

5

After you've finished using Document Map, click the Document Map button **again** to return to the normal view of your document.

Cross-Referencing and Hyperlinks

Word's automatic cross-referencing feature is a great time-saver and a valuable contribution to accuracy if you create long documents. Suppose you're writing a cookbook that includes the recipe for Eggs Benedict. That recipe includes a reference to Hollandaise sauce. You may well want to help your reader find information about Hollandaise sauce by including the phrase see page 152. But how do you keep track of the page on which the Hollandaise sauce reference will eventually appear? Word makes it easy: Use either cross-referencing or hyperlinks.

Cross-referencing involves two steps: Identify the items to be cross-referenced, and create the references.

The items to be cross-referenced can be identified as:

- Numbered items
- Headings
- Bookmarks
- Footnotes

- Endnotes
- Equations
- Figures
- Tables

To make a reference to an item, type the introduction text such as **see** (including a space), and then choose Insert, Cross-reference. In the Cross-reference dialog box, shown in Figure 5.12, open the drop-down Reference Type list and choose the type of reference you want to make.

FIG. 5.12

Use the Cross-reference dialog box to specify the type of cross reference you want to make.

The choices in the Cross-reference dialog box vary according to the type of cross reference. For example, if you choose Bookmark as the Reference Type, a list box shows all the bookmarks in your document so that you can choose the one you want. Open the Insert Reference To drop-down list to choose how you want the reference to appear in your text: As Text, As a Page Number, and so on.

If you're preparing a document to be printed, remove the check mark from the Insert as Hyperlink check box. However, if you're preparing a document to be viewed on-screen, leave this box checked so that readers can simply click the reference to jump to the appropriate place in the document.

Creating an Index

Every nonfiction book that's worth buying contains an index. You can expect to use the index of a book to find the place in the book where a subject of interest is covered. Readers of any long document you create have the right to an index they can use to quickly find whatever information they're looking for.

The problem is that the person who creates the index has to list the subject and relate it to the words the author used when writing about the subject. For example, suppose you are creating index for a cookbook that contains a recipe for Pollo Alla Cacciatora (Chicken in the Hunter Style). What reference should you make to this recipe in the index? Should it be "Pollo Alla Cacciatora," "Chicken, Italian Style," "Chicken in Tomato Sauce," "Hunter's Chicken," or something else?

There's no right answer to this question. You can't possibly list all the possible words a reader might look for to find information about a particular subject. If you did, the index would occupy more pages than the subject matter of the document you're indexing.

What Is Indexing?

Indexing is an art—it's not mechanical. Although Word can help you create an index, it can't create an index automatically in the same way that it creates a table of contents. If you need to be convinced that there's a lot more to creating a good index than you might initially think, glance through the 47 pages about indexing in *The Chicago Manual of Style*, published by the University of Chicago Press. The comment in that book "Indexing requires decision making of a far higher order than computers are yet capable of," is something to consider. Nevertheless, Word can provide valuable help in creating an index.

The process of creating an index consists of five principal stages:

1. Mark the places in the document to which the index should refer. For each place, designate the text to occur in the index. This is the stage that requires decision-making and detailed knowledge of the document and its subject matter.
2. Create the index. This is the part that Word does for you.
3. Examine the index carefully and mark any incorrect or missing entries.
4. Revise the index markings in the document to correct problems you noticed in step 3.
5. Re-create the index.

Be forewarned: You'll have to repeat steps 4 and 5 several times. The next few sections looks at steps 1 and 2 in detail.

Marking the Document

Word marks items to be indexed by inserting XE field codes into the document. You normally don't see these field codes, but you can reveal them by clicking the Show/Hide button in the Standard toolbar.

Part
II

Ch
5

Word provides two ways for you to mark items to be indexed:

- Create a table (Word calls it a *concordance*) that contains words and phrases to be indexed, together with the index text for each. After you've done this, Word can search the document and insert the appropriate XE field code wherever the words and phrases you've listed occur.

- Separately identify each place in the document by manually inserting the appropriate XE field code.

The first is the quick and dirty way. Yes, it does allow you to create an index quickly, but it's not likely to result in an index that readers find useful. The second is the way to create a good index. The problem with the first way is that text within the document may talk about an idea without using any specific word or phrase. For example, a book about cooking might contain some information about grilling. You should probably refer to that section from several places in the index, including barbecue, even though the word barbecue might not appear in the section.

Because a concordance isn't likely to create a useful index, we'll deal here only with manually inserting XE field codes in the document to be indexed.

TIP Even though the concordance method of creating an index isn't likely to create a satisfactory index, some people like to make a first cut at an index in this way, then go back through the document to make corrections and add to the XE field codes Word automatically inserted.

To insert an XE field code in the document, place the insertion point immediately before or after the text to which you want the index entry to refer; then press Alt+Shift+X to display the Mark Index Entry dialog box shown in Figure 5.13.

FIG. 5.13

Use this dialog box to define the index entry.

N O T E Don't insert the XE field code between the letters of a word; if you do so, you won't subsequently be able to use the Find command to find that word. For example, if your document contains the word cat and you place an XE field code within the word, your document will actually contain something like c{ XE "animal" }at; Word won't be able to find cat. For the same reason, don't insert an XE field code anywhere within a phrase you're likely to want to search for. ∎

Type the Main Entry for the index reference and, where appropriate, the Subentry. Of the three options offered, Word suggests the default Current Page, which is normally what you want. Click Mark to insert the XE field code. Quite often, you want more than one index entry for the same place in the document. For this reason, the dialog box stays open after you've inserted the field code so that you can insert more XE field codes at the same place.

TIP While you work, keep an updated list of the main entries and subentries you provide. By doing so, you can easily make sure that you consistently name subsequent items to be indexed. If you don't do this, you'll inevitably create index entry items that should be the same but are slightly different. Be particularly careful about consistently using the singular or the plural for index entries (I suggest you use the singular unless the entry refers specifically to a plural item). Be consistent with capitalization; the *Chicago Manual of Style* recommends capitalizing main entries but not subentries.

After you insert an XE field code, you probably won't see it in your document. To show the field, click Show/Hide in the Standard toolbar. Then you'll see a field code such as one of the following:

```
{ XE "Grilling" }
```

```
{ XE "Grilling:Barbecue" }
```

The first XE field code marks an index entry that has only a main entry (Grilling); the second marks an index entry that has a main entry (Grilling) and a subentry (Barbecue). Notice that the main entry and the subentry are separated by a colon.

Insert XE field codes for each place in the document that's to be referenced in the index. This is a time-consuming but necessary process.

TIP People usually leave indexing until after they've completed the document. While you're writing the document and have each subject clearly in mind, it's a good idea to make a note of index entries as they come to mind. Consider marking index entries while you write (if you subsequently change your mind, you can easily modify those entries).

Part

II

Ch

5

Instead of referring to a specific page, you may want an index entry to refer to a range of pages. You can do this by first identifying the range of pages with a bookmark. To do so, select the range of pages, choose Insert, Bookmark and use the Bookmark dialog box to enter a book-mark name. After you've done this, press Alt+Shift+X to display the Mark Index Entry dialog box. In the Options section, choose Page Range Bookmark, and then select the appropriate bookmark from the list of bookmarks. The index Word subsequently creates refers to the range of pages on which the bookmarked text appears.

Creating the Index

After you've inserted XE field codes at every place in the document that's to be indexed, the rest is easy. Place the insertion point where you want the index to start and choose Insert, Index and Tables to display the Index and Tables dialog box. If necessary, choose the Index tab, shown in Figure 5.14.

FIG. 5.14

The Index tab of the Index and Tables dialog box is where you specify the format of the index.

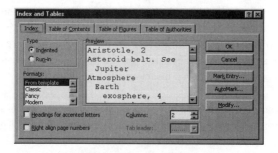

Make your choices among the options in this dialog box and wait a few seconds for the index to appear. Although you see the actual index on your screen, Word actually inserts an Index field code, such as:

```
{ INDEX \c "2" }
```

in the document. You can see this field code by placing the insertion point anywhere within the document and pressing Shift+F9. Press Shift+F9 again to go back to displaying the actual index.

> **N O T E** The \c switch in the Index field code tells Word to create an index formatted in more than one column; the number in quotes specifies the actual number of columns, two in this case. Word can create indexes with up to four columns. ∎

As already mentioned, you should carefully examine your first attempt at an index for a document, and note any places that require modification. Then go back to the document, make whatever changes are necessary to the XE field codes, and re-create the index.

> **T I P** Word lets you make changes to the actual index, but it's not a good practice to do so because any changes you make like this will be lost the next time you update the index. Always make changes to the XE field codes within the document and then update the index.

Modifying *XE* and *Index* Fields

Word provides many ways for you to tailor indexes to suit your specific needs. In addition to the choices offered in the Mark Index Entry dialog box and the Index and Tables dialog box, you can manually add a variety of switches to the XE and Index field codes. To see what switches are available, open Word Help and choose Contents; in the Contents list, choose Reference Information, Field Types and Switches. There you can find information for:

- Field Codes: XE (Index Entry) Field
- Field Codes: Index Field

The following section about creating multiple indexes contains one example of using switches.

Creating Multiple Indexes

While most publications have a single index, some have two or more indexes. For example, a history book may contain an index of events, an index of people, and an index of places.

The \f switch is the essence of multiple indexes. In XE and Index fields, \f is followed by a single alphabetic character enclosed within double quotation marks. By default, if an XE or Index field doesn't have an \f switch, the field behaves as if it had the switch \f"i".

What does this mean? The answer to this question can be summarized as follows:

■ All XE fields that don't have an \f switch, or have an \f"i" switch, are included in Index fields that don't have an \f or \f"i" switch.

■ All XE fields that have an \f"x" switch are included only in Index fields that have an \f"x" switch (here, "x" represents any alphabetic character other than "i").

Coming back, now, to the original example of a document that has separate indexes for events, people, and places, you can identify all the event references with one switch (such as \f"e"), all the people references with another switch (such as \f"p"), and all the place references with yet another switch (such as \f"l"). Then you can create three separate Index fields, each with one of these switches.

Creating and Using Macros

In the old days (only a few years ago), a macro was simply a recorded sequence of keystrokes. Now, a macro can be a sophisticated program written in Visual Basic for Applications (VBA). In this chapter, we'll consider only simple macros that replicate a sequence of keystrokes. Chapters 30 through 34 contain information about more complex macros.

A *macro* is really a program—a sequence of instructions your computer can follow. Unlike other programs, a macro is not a separate file: It's stored in a template or within an individual Word document.

Part II

Ch 5

N O T E Earlier versions of Word could only save a macro within a template. ■

Recording and Running a Macro

The simplest type of macro lets you reduce the amount of work you have to do. Here's an example: Suppose you have a document in which you want to make some important words large and bold. One way you could do so would be to locate each word to be bolded, select the entire word, press Ctrl+B to bold the selected text, and press Ctrl+] to increase the font size by one point. That's quite a lot of work if you're dealing with a long document. You could save yourself time by creating a macro that automates the process. Here's how:

1. Place the insertion point at the beginning of the first word to be enlarged and bolded.

2. Choose Tools, Macro, Record New Macro to display the Record Macro dialog box shown in Figure 5.15.

FIG. 5.15
Use the Record Macro
dialog box to define the
macro and where you
want it to be saved.

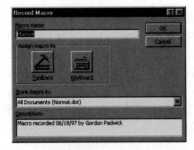

3. Enter a name (such as **Bolder**) for the new macro, and choose where you want the macro to be saved (in the Normal template, in the template on which the document is based, or within the document itself). If you want, change the description Word supplied automatically to something more appropriate.

4. Click Keyboard to display the Customize Keyboard dialog box. In this dialog box, choose a shortcut key (such as Alt+Shift+B) for the macro and click Assign to assign that shortcut to the macro. Then click Close to close the dialog box.

5. Soon after you click Close, Word displays the small Macro toolbar that contains two buttons: Stop Recording and Pause Recording. Ignore that toolbar for the present.

6. Press Ctrl+Shift+→ to select the word to the right of the insertion point.

7. Press Ctrl+B to make the selected word bold.

8. Press Ctrl+] to increase the font size.

9. Click Stop Recording in the Macro toolbar.

That completes recording the macro.

To check the macro operation, place the insertion point at the beginning of another word in the document and press Alt+Shift+B (the shortcut you assigned to the macro). The word to the right of the insertion point should now be bold and in a larger font. Now you can easily make any other words bold and large.

Examining and Editing a Macro

To examine a macro, choose Tools, Macro, Macros to display the Macros dialog box that lists all the macros currently available—those in the open document, in the template on which the open document is based, and in the Normal template.

Select the macro you want to examine, and then click Edit. Word displays the NewMacros (Code) dialog box shown in Figure 5.16.

What you're seeing here is a subprocedure that contains some VBA code. You can clearly see that the subprocedure contains three parts:

```
Selection.MoveRight Unit:=wdWord, Count:=1, Extend:=wdExtend
```

extends the selection from the insertion point to the end of a word.

```
Selection.Font.Bold = wdToggle
```

changes the selected text from Roman to bold or from bold to Roman.

```
Selection.Font.Grow
```

increases the size of the font by 1 point.

FIG. 5.16

The NewMacros (Code) dialog box shows what's in the selected macro.

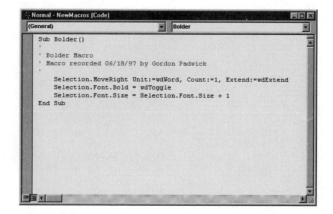

You can edit the VBA code in the NewMacros (Code) dialog box. Of course, the changes you make must result in valid VBA code, otherwise your macro won't run. You can make simple changes to a macro without knowing much about VBA code. For example, suppose you want to change the macro so that it enlarges a word's text without making the text bold. That's simple: Just delete the second line of the code. Or suppose you want to enlarge the text by 2 points. That's also simple: Just repeat the third line in the code.

 An easy way to effectively delete a line of code in a macro is to insert a single quotation mark at the beginning of the line. This has the effect of changing a line of code into a comment—text that Word doesn't regard as VBA code.

After you've made a change to a macro, choose File, Close and Return to Microsoft Word to close the NewMacros (Code) dialog box and return to your document where you can try out the changed macro.

At this stage, the changes to the macro are in memory, not saved to disk. If, when you created the macro, you chose to save it as part of the document, it's saved whenever you save the document. However, if you chose to save the macro within a template, you must save the template in order to save the macro. Word always prompts you to save a template whenever there's a possibility you might lose changes to a macro.

Many macros contain much more complex code than described here. Chapters 30–34 contain detailed information about macros and VBA code. ●

Part
II

Ch
5

CHAPTER 6

Advanced Mail Merge

Word contains very versatile capabilities for creating documents, such as form letters, that are based on a pattern. These documents contain text, graphics, and so on that appear in every document in a set, and other elements, such as people's names and addresses, that are different in each document. Traditionally, this type of capability is known as *Mail Merge* because it's most often used to create form letters ready for mailing. However, the capability can be used for many other purposes, such as creating price lists that are tailored for different localities.

Read this chapter to gain a good understanding of how you can use Word to create documents based on a pattern. You'll learn how to include data from databases, spreadsheets, and address lists in your documents. You'll also learn how to insert various Word fields into a document to control what's included in, or excluded from, documents.

As a final bonus in this chapter, you'll learn how to send documents created by Mail Merge directly as e-mail or electronic faxes. ▪

Understand how Mail Merge works

The first part of this chapter provides a basic understanding of main documents and data sources, the fundamental components of Mail Merge.

Use existing documents and data to create merge documents

You can easily convert a Word document into a Mail Merge main document and insert merge fields into it so that it can use information from an existing database, spreadsheet, or address book.

Select and order information in your data source

It's quite simple to select specific information from a data source and use that information in an order you choose.

Choose the text you want to include in your merge documents

By using Word fields, you can be selective about the text that appears in your merge documents.

Send your merge documents by ordinary mail, e-mail, or fax

You can use Mail Merge to print envelopes or labels, or you can automatically send your merge documents by e-mail or electronic fax.

What Is Mail Merge?

Mail Merge is the Word capability you can use to create form letters and address envelopes, as well as print labels and create catalogs and lists.

When you write form letters, memos, or other documents to send to various people, it's often necessary to tailor each copy to suit the needs, interests, prejudices, and whatever of each person. If only two or three people are involved, it doesn't take much effort to make a few copies of an original document and then manually edit each of them. But what if two or three hundred people are involved? That's where Word's Mail Merge can save you an enormous amount of time.

With Mail Merge, you can create form letters that have conditional text—text that's included in some letters but not in others. You can also create catalogs and price lists that contain different information (such as prices and warranty statements) according to the locality to which they're sent.

To use Mail Merge, you create two documents: the main document and the data source. Then you merge the two together to create individualized merge documents.

Mail Merge documents range from very simple to very complex. To get started, let's consider one of the simplest—a reminder about bringing a contribution to an office potluck. Figure 6.1 shows an example of such a memo.

FIG. 6.1

Here's an example of a short memo created by Mail Merge.

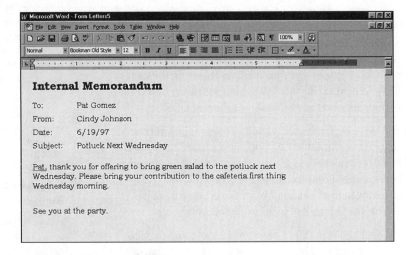

Notice that the memo contains three items that are specific to each person who will receive the memo: first name (used twice in the memo), last name, and the item that person has promised to bring to the potluck.

The Main Document

The main document contains everything that's to be included in all the merge documents. Every item that's unique to each document is represented by a *placeholder* (Word calls it a *field code*). The memo shown in Figure 6.1 has three field codes: <<FirstName>>, <<LastName>>, and <<Item>>.

> **N O T E** I've shown the field names enclosed within chevrons, because that's the way they appear in Word documents. You don't type the chevrons—Word displays them automatically when you place field codes in the main document. ■

Figure 6.2 shows the Mail Merge main document from which the merge document shown in Figure 6.1 was created.

FIG. 6.2

The main document contains the text that's included in all the merge documents and field codes representing the text that's unique to each merge document.

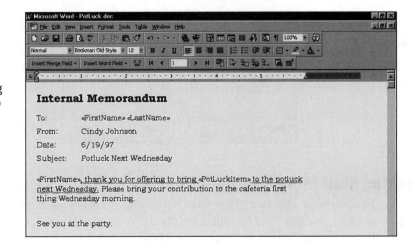

The Data Source

A *data source* is a list of values to be substituted for the field codes in the main document. One of the simplest data sources is a Word table, such as that shown in Figure 6.3. This table contains three columns, one for each of the field codes in the main document. The first row of the table contains the names of the field codes; each of the following rows contains information for one merge document.

Instead of using a Word table for the data source, you can use data that already exists in spreadsheets, databases, and address books.

Merging a Main Document with a Data Source

After you've created a main document and specified a data source, just give Word the command to merge the two together. Word can create a file of all documents for you to review, print individual documents, send individual documents by e-mail, fax individual documents, print envelopes, or print mailing labels.

FIG. 6.3

Mail Merge creates one merge document for each row of information in the data source table.

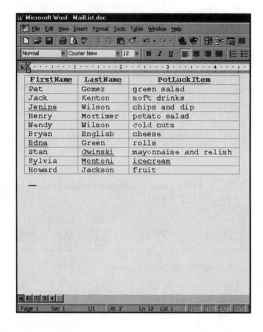

Making Mail Merge Happen

Now you know what Mail Merge does, but how do you make it all happen? For a simple example, open a new Word document and choose Tools, Mail Merge to open the Mail Merge Helper Wizard. You can see its first dialog box in Figure 6.4.

FIG. 6.4

The Mail Merge Helper Wizard leads you through the three steps of creating Mail Merge documents.

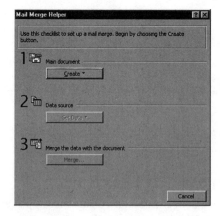

Here's a quick rundown of how you use the wizard—I'll assume you're creating a form letter from scratch and don't already have a main document or data source:

1. Click Create. The wizard offers you a choice among Form Letters, Mailing Labels, Envelopes, and Catalog. Choose Form Letters.

2. The wizard wants to know whether you already have a draft of the main document in the active window, or whether you want to create a new main document. Click New Main Document.

3. Now the wizard wants to know about your data source. Click Get Data. The wizard offers you a choice among Create Data Source, Open Data Source, Use Address Book, and Header Options. Choose Create Data Source. The wizard now leads you through the process of creating a Word table as your data source.

4. The wizard displays the Create Data Source dialog box in which you can choose any of 13 predefined field names, and in which you can name your own fields. Follow the instructions in the dialog box to create a data source that contains the fields you need.

N O T E Field names contain up to 44 characters, the first of which must be a letter. Subsequent characters may be letters, numbers, or the underscore character. ■

5. When you click OK to indicate you've finished defining fields, the wizard displays a Save As dialog box. Name the data source and save it as a Word file. Now, you can go ahead with adding data to the data source, or you can create the main document—it doesn't matter which you do first.

6. Click Edit Data Source. The wizard displays the Data Form dialog box in which you enter data for the first form letter. After you've completed the data for the first letter, click Add New and then add data for the next form letter. Continue in this way until you have entered data for several letters—you don't have to finalize the data at this time.

N O T E The data in each field can contain up to 40 characters. ■

7. Click OK to indicate that you've finished, at least for the time being, entering data. The wizard opens a new Word document with the Mail Merge toolbar displayed, as shown in Figure 6.5. Now you're ready to create the main document.

Part
II

Ch

6

FIG. 6.5

The Mail Merge toolbar, shown here immediately below the Formatting toolbar, contains 15 buttons that help you create merge documents.

The main document contains three types of elements:

- Items that appear in every copy of the letter, including characters you type, as well as imported, embedded, and linked items.
- Field codes that indicate where data from your data source should be placed.
- Word fields that control actions that happen during the merge process, such as deciding which paragraphs to include.

For the moment, we'll deal only with the first two types of elements.

Start typing the main document just as you would type any other Word document. When you come to a place where data from the data source should appear, click Insert Merge Field in the Mail Merge toolbar to display a list of fields in your data source. Choose the one you want; the field name, enclosed by chevrons, appears in the document.

 TIP   If, instead of a field name enclosed by chevrons, you see something like { MERGEFIELD FirstName }, just press Alt+F9 to see the field name enclosed in chevrons. The section "Using Word Fields in a Main Document" later in this chapter contains more information on this subject.

Continue creating the main document in this way until you've entered all the common elements and placed field codes where they need to be. Remember to insert a space between field codes if you want the resulting form letter to have a space between the text that replaces the field codes, such as between the FirstName and LastName field codes. The completed Mail Merge main document looks something like the one in Figure 6.2.

Now you can see what the individual merge documents will look like. Click the Check for Errors button in the Mail Merge toolbar (the sixth button from the right). Word offers you the choice to:

- Simulate the merge and report errors in a new document.
- Complete the merge, pausing to report each error as it occurs.
- Complete the merge without pausing, reporting errors in a new document.

The second of these, which is normally what you want to use, is the default. Click OK to proceed. If there are no errors, Word displays all your form letters in one document, with a section break separating each letter from the next.

Finally, to print the merge documents, click the Merge to Printer button in the Mail Merge toolbar.

That covers the basics of using Mail Merge—all you need to know for creating simple form letters. The remainder of this chapter deals with more sophisticated matters.

 TROUBLESHOOTING

You may see a message telling you that your data source is a Mail Merge main document. This occurs when you have your data source document selected when you choose Tools, Mail Merge. To solve this problem, close the message box and open the data source document again. Choose Tools, Mail Merge and then choose Create. Finally, click Restore to Normal Word Document, then save and close the data source.

Using an Existing Document as a Mail Merge Main Document

You won't always want to create a main document and data source from scratch; quite often you'll already have a document you want to convert to a Mail Merge main document, as well as a database, spreadsheet, or address list to use as a data source.

Preparing an Existing Document

Suppose you've already written a letter and now you decide to use Mail Merge to personalize that letter for several individual people—the annual Christmas letter you send to family and friends is a good candidate. Examine the existing letter, and make sure any elements that need to be personalized are clearly marked. Although it's not necessary, it's sometimes helpful to replace these elements with something that won't actually occur in the final letters—I use $$$$$. For example, if the original letter started with Dear John, you would replace this with Dear $$$$$.

Before continuing, you should have your data source ready. If you don't already have a data source, refer to the section "Creating a Data Source" later in this chapter.

Placing Field Codes in the Main Document

Open the document you've prepared to use as the main document, and choose Tools, Mail Merge to display the Mail Merge Helper Wizard. Choose Create, Form Letters, and then Active Window to tell the wizard you intend to use the existing document.

In the Mail Merge Helper, choose Get Data, Open Data Source. In the Open Data Source dialog box, navigate to the existing data source, select it, and choose Open. The wizard automatically adds the Mail Merge toolbar to the Word document and reminds you that there are no merge fields in the main document. Click Edit Main Document to continue.

Now you're ready to add field codes into the main document. Move the insertion point to where you want to put the first field code, click Insert Merge Field in the Mail Merge toolbar, and choose a field code from the list. Continue through the main document, inserting field codes wherever necessary. If you previously marked every place where field codes are needed, you can find them easily. When you've finished, click Check for Errors in the Mail Merge toolbar to see the merge documents.

Part
II

Ch
6

Creating a Data Source

There are many ways in which you can create a data source. The following sections describe some of these.

N O T E   By default, Mail Merge creates one merge document (letter or other item) for each record in the data source, and creates them in the order of the records in the data source. As explained in "Selecting Records in a Data Source" later in this chapter, you can select only certain records from the data source, and you can change the order in which Mail Merge uses those records. ▇

Using a Word Table as a Data Source

When you use the Mail Merge Wizard to create a main document from scratch and choose Get Data, Create Data Source, the wizard guides you through a series of steps that creates a Word table. Instead of following this process, you can create a Word table separately, or use an existing Word table.

I'm not going to go into a lot of detail about creating a Word table here, but I'll provide a few hints. A Word table used as a Mail Merge data source has one column for each field code that's to be inserted into the main document. Usually, the top row of the table contains the names of the field codes (but this isn't necessary, as I'll explain soon); other rows of the table contain the data that replaces each field code, with one row for each merge document. Don't be concerned about column widths and the way words wrap within columns of the table. Make sure there are no spaces, text, or blank lines above the table, and that there are no blank rows anywhere in the table.

T I P   Unlike a Word table created by the Mail Merge Wizard, a table you create this way can contain field code names longer than 44 characters. Also, field code names can contain spaces (Word automatically changes each space in field code names to an underscore character when the table is accessed as a Mail Merge data source).

Save the table as a separate Word document. If you're using a table that already exists within a document, copy just the table into a separate document.

By default, Mail Merge assumes the top row of a Word table used as a data source contains the names of field codes—this row is known as the *header row*. However, you can use a table that doesn't have a header row; to do so, you must have a separate *header file*—a table with only one record that contains the field code names. The columns of this table must, of course, contain the field code names in the same order as the field code values in the data source table.

N O T E   If several people use the same table as a data source, they might prefer that the table does not have a header row. Then they are free to use whatever names they like for field codes in their master documents. ▇

To use a Word table that has a header row as a data source, choose Get Data, Open Data Source in the Mail Merge Wizard, as previously explained. If the Word table doesn't have a header row, you have to identify the header file before you identify the data source:

1. Choose Get Data, Header Options, Open.
2. In the Open Header Source dialog box, select the header file and click Open.
3. Choose Get Data, Open Data Source, select the data source file, and click Open.

This process relates the columns in your data source table to the columns in the one-row header file.

Using an Access Table as a Data Source

The steps involved in using an Access table are quite similar to those for a Word table. In the Mail Merge Helper, choose Get Data, Open Data Source. At the bottom of the Open Data Source dialog box, open the Files of Type list and select MS Access Databases (*.mdb), navigate to find the Access file, select that file, and choose Open. After a few seconds' delay, the Microsoft Access dialog box opens, displaying a list of tables in the selected file. Choose the table you want to use, and click OK.

In the Mail Merge main document, when you click Insert Merge Field in the Mail Merge toolbar, you see a list of the field names in the Access table. You can insert these field names as field codes in the main document.

Using an Excel Worksheet as a Data Source

Whereas an Access file contains tables, an Excel file contains worksheets and ranges. Unless the data source you want to use occupies an entire worksheet, you should identify the data source as a named range in the worksheet. Also, you should note whether the top row of the named range contains column names; if not, you need to create a separate header file, as explained in the previous section "Using a Word Table."

When you tell Mail Merge you want to use an Excel file as a data source, you can choose from a list that includes the entire worksheet and all the named ranges within that worksheet.

Using Other Types of Data Sources

You can use virtually any source of organized data in a computer-readable file as a data source for Mail Merge. The Open Data Source dialog box offers a choice among:

- Word Documents
- Rich Text Format
- Text Files
- MS Access Databases
- MS Excel Worksheets
- MS Query Files
- dBASE Files
- MS FoxPro Files
- All Files

You can also use an Outlook Address Book as a data source, though that's not included in the Open Data Source list because Mail Merge uses a different process to access data in Outlook, as described in the subsequent section "Using an Outlook Address Book as a Data Source."

Part
II

Ch
6

N O T E By installing the appropriate file converters that are supplied with Office, you can also use data in many other formats, including:

- Other versions of Word (older versions of Word for Windows, as well as Macintosh and DOS versions)
- Older versions of Excel
- WordPerfect (Windows and DOS)
- Lotus 1-2-3 versions 2.x–4.x

Also, by installing ODBC drivers (several of which are supplied with Office), you can use data in many other database formats.

If you don't have the converters or drivers necessary to access data in a specific format, you might find that one of the other Office applications can translate data into a format suitable for Mail Merge. For example, Access can convert data in a Paradox file into an Access table; Excel can convert data from a Quattro Pro spreadsheet into an Excel workbook. ▆

Using an Outlook Address Book as a Data Source

You can use an address book created for use with Microsoft Exchange Server, Outlook, or Schedule+ 7.0 contact lists (or similar address lists created with a MAPI-compatible messaging system) as a data source. To illustrate how this works, we'll use an Outlook address book.

In the Mail Merge Wizard, choose Get Data, Use Address Book. The wizard displays the Use Address Book dialog box shown in Figure 6.6.

FIG. 6.6

The Use Address Book dialog box offers a choice of address books.

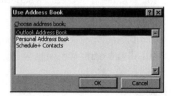

Choose Outlook Address Book to use that as a data source. Almost immediately, you see the Choose Profile dialog box. Choose the profile that accesses the address book you want to use. There's a short delay while Word converts the address book into a format suitable for Mail Merge. Subsequently, when you click Insert Mail Merge in the Mail Merge toolbar, you see a list of all the fields available in an Outlook address book. You can insert any of these fields as field codes in your Mail Merge main document.

Selecting and Ordering Records in a Data Source

The preceding sections of this chapter have assumed that you want to create form letters addressed to everyone listed in a data source, and you want Mail Merge to create those letters in the order of the data source records. It's likely, though, that you'll often want to create letters for only some of the people listed in the data source, and that you want Mail Merge to create those letters in specific order—sorted in postal code order ready for mailing. You can do this in two ways:

- Create a customized data source. If your data source is in Access or Excel, you can easily extract the records you need and place them in an appropriate order for use in your Mail Merge.

- Use the facilities within Mail Merge to choose and order the records you want to use.

For most purposes, I prefer the first alternative. However, because this is a chapter about Mail Merge, I'll ignore that and focus on the second. Mail Merge lets you select records, sort records, or do both.

Selecting Records in a Data Source

Create a Mail Merge main document in one of the ways previously described in this chapter, then click Mail Merge Helper in the Mail Merge toolbar. Now click the Query Options button in the Mail Merge Helper dialog box to display the Query Options dialog box with the Filter Records tab selected, as shown in Figure 6.7.

FIG. 6.7
Use this dialog box to filter the records in the data source.

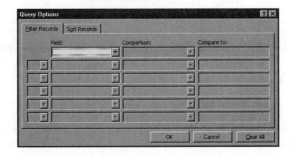

To illustrate how you can filter records, suppose the data source you've selected contains people's names and addresses, and you want to use only records for those people with the last name of Smith who live in California.

When the Query Options dialog box first appears, only one box is enabled—the Field box in the top row. Open that box's drop-down list to show the names of all the fields in the data source, then choose the first field name you want to use. In this case, choose the LastName field.

As soon as you make the choice, the adjoining Comparison field becomes enabled with Equal To displayed—this is the comparison you want in this case. Also, the adjoining Compare To field becomes enabled. Type the last name you want to compare each record in the data source to—**Smith**.

Now you can enter another comparison in the second row. Choose HomeState for the field name, Equal to for the comparison, and then type **CA** for the Compare To field. After you've done so, your Query Options dialog box should look like that in Figure 6.8.

Part
II

Ch
6

FIG. 6.8
This Query Options dialog box will filter the data source to find only those records in which the LastName field contains Smith and the HomeState field contains CA.

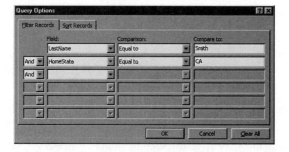

Click OK to tell Mail Merge to merge the main document with the filtered data source.

You can define up to six comparisons, each of which can use one of the following conditions:

- Equal to
- Not equal to
- Less than
- Greater than
- Less than or equal to
- Greater than or equal to
- Is blank
- Is not blank

The first comparison is always used. The second comparison can start with either And or Or. If it starts with And, only data source records that satisfy both conditions pass through the filter; if it starts with Or, data source records that satisfy either the first or the second condition pass. The third through sixth comparisons, if used, can also be combined with the preceding conditions by And or Or.

N O T E   As you might expect, when fields contain alphanumeric information (any value that is not entirely numeric), comparisons are made on the basis of the ASCII values of the alphabetic characters. ■

Sorting Records in a Data Source

By default, merging uses records in the order that those records occur in the data source. You can, if you like, change this order based on up to three fields.

Open the Query Options dialog box, as described in the preceding section, and choose the Sort Records tab shown in Figure 6.9.

Start by opening the Sort By list and choosing the first field on which you want to sort; choose either Ascending or Descending sort order. If necessary, you can select two more fields.

Using Word Fields in a Main Document

You can add a great deal of flexibility to Mail Merge by using Word fields. You can use these fields for such purposes as selectively adding information to merge documents and controlling how data is merged.

To insert a Word field into a Mail Merge main document, click Insert Word Field in the Mail Merge toolbar to see the drop-down list shown in Figure 6.10.

FIG. 6.9

The sort specification shown here creates merge documents sorted first by postal code, then by last name, and then by first name.

FIG. 6.10

Any of the nine Word fields shown in this list can be inserted into a Mail Merge main document.

N O T E Three additional fields, described later in this section, are available by choosing Insert, Field. ■

Table 6.1 provides a brief explanation of the available Word fields. The field names used in the Field dialog box and in the Mail Merge toolbar drop-down list are slightly different.

Table 6.1 Available Word Fields

Field Name (Field Dialog Box)	Field Name (Mail Merge Toolbar)	Purpose
Ask	Ask	Provides a value for a bookmark that applies to all merge documents or to individual merge documents.
Compare		Compares one value with another. Returns 1 if the comparison is true, 0 if it is false. The comparison can be used in an IF statement.
Database		Inserts the results of a database query in a Word table.
Fill-in	Fill-in	Provides customized text that applies to all merge documents or to individual merge documents.

Part

II

Ch

6

continues

Table 6.1 Continued

Field Name (Field Dialog Box)	Field Name (Mail Merge Toolbar)	Purpose
IF	If...Then...Else	Choose between two items of text depending on the value of a data source field or bookmark.
MergeField		Inserts the value of a data source field.
MergeRec	Merge Record	Inserts into merge documents a number corresponding to the sequence number of the sorted data source record.
MergeSeq	Merge Sequence	Inserts into merge documents the sequential number of successfully merged documents.
Next	Next Record	Go unconditionally to the next record in the data source.
NextIf	Next Record If	Go to the next record in the data source if a specified condition is true.
Set	Set Bookmark	Assigns text to a bookmark.
SkipIf	Skip Record If	Skips the current data source record if a specified condition is true.

The following sections provide an introduction to Word fields. You can find additional information and examples in Word's online Help.

 TIP By default, Word fields are not displayed in Mail Merge main documents. In order to see Word fields, you must either:

- Press Alt+F9. After you do so, all field codes are displayed in detail for the current document.
- Choose Tools, Options, View. Then check Field Codes. After you do so, all field codes are displayed in detail for all Word documents.

Including Alternative Text in Merge Documents

You can use the IF Word field to include some text or some other text in each merge document, or to include or omit text, depending on the value in one or more data source fields.

Let's consider a simple example. Suppose you're preparing an invitation to a company-sponsored event for which company employees can purchase tickets for $5, while non-employees must pay $10. Your data source contains an Employee field that contains Yes for employees and No (or anything else) for non-employees. You want the invitation to employees to contain the phrase ...admission is $5., whereas the invitation to non-employees should contain the phrase ...admission is $10..

In the Mail Merge main document, start the phrase with the words admission is $, insert an IF field, and then complete the phrase with a period (.).

Here's how it's done:

1. At the appropriate place in the Mail Merge main document, type **admission is $**.
2. In the Mail Merge toolbar, open the Insert Word Field list and choose If...Then...Else.... Word displays the Insert Word Field: IF dialog box shown in Figure 6.11.

FIG. 6.11

Use this dialog box to define the IF field.

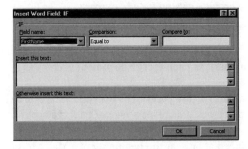

3. Open the Field Name list and choose Employee.
4. Leave the Comparison box with the default Equal To.
5. Type **Yes** in the Compare To box.
6. Type **5** in the Insert this Text box.
7. Type **10** in the Otherwise Insert this Text box.
8. Click OK to close the dialog box and return to the Mail Merge main document.
9. Type **.** to end the phrase with a period.

If you have previously chosen to display field codes (by pressing Alt+F9 or by enabling field codes in the Options, View dialog box), you'll see the IF field as shown in Figure 6.12.

FIG. 6.12

This is how the completed IF Word field appears in the Mail Merge main document.

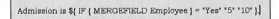

Admission is ${ IF { MERGEFIELD Employee } = "Yes" "5" "10" }|

When you subsequently create the merge documents, those documents based on data source records for which the Employee field contains Yes will contain 5; documents based on all other records will contain 10.

N O T E When you want to include text if the condition is true, but otherwise omit that text, leave the Otherwise Insert this Text box empty. ■

Selecting Alternative Phrases Interactively

Instead of using the value of a data source field to select the text to appear in each merge document, you can make the choice at the time Word creates each merge document. Suppose, for example, your data source doesn't contain an Employee field, but you still want to tell some people that the price of a ticket is $5 and tell other people it is $10. You can do this by using a bookmark instead of the value of a data source field in the IF statement. There are two separate steps:

- Use an ASK field to provide a value for a bookmark.
- Use an IF field to select the text.

Inserting the ASK Field   An *ASK field* creates a bookmark and provides an opportunity to assign a value to that bookmark as each merge document is created.

> **N O T E**   A *bookmark* is a name given to a position in a Word document, or to a value that's available behind the scenes. If you're a programmer, think of a bookmark as a variable. ■

An ASK field is usually placed at or near the beginning of a Mail Merge main document, so move the insertion point to the beginning of the document. Open the Insert Word Field drop-down list and choose ASK to display the Insert Word Field: ASK dialog box shown in Figure 6.13.

FIG. 6.13

Use this dialog box to provide a name for the bookmark, and also the prompt that's displayed when you merge the main document with the data source.

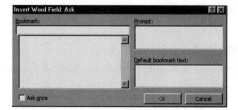

Enter a name for the bookmark in the Bookmark box. If you've previously created bookmarks in the document, you'll see their names in the list box underneath the Bookmark box. The name you enter must be different from the names of any existing bookmarks. An appropriate name in this case is **BkmkEmployee**.

The Prompt box is where you enter the prompt that appears on the screen as each merge document is created. Type something like **Employee: Yes or No?** in the Prompt box.

If there's a default value for the bookmark, enter it in the Default Bookmark Text box. In this case, you might type **No**. Figure 6.14 shows the dialog box with the suggested entries completed.

When you click OK, Word shows a sample of the message box you'll see when you create merge documents. Click OK to return to the Mail Merge main document in which you see the ASK field (providing you have previously chosen to display fields). The ASK field in your document will look something like:

```
{ ASK BkmkEmployee "Employee: Yes or No?" \d "No" }
```

in which the \d merely indicates that the quoted text that follows is the default response. For detailed information about the format of this field, choose Help, Contents and Index, and then double-click Reference Information. Double-click Field Types and Switches, and then double-click Field Codes: Ask Field to display the Field codes: Ask field topic.

FIG. 6.14

Here's the Insert Word Field: Ask dialog box with a typical prompt and default bookmark text entered.

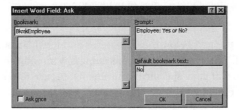

N O T E At the bottom-left corner of the Insert Word Field: Ask dialog box, there's a check box labeled Ask Once. By default this box is unchecked. When that's the case, Word asks you for a value for the bookmark as each merge document is created; the value you provide is available only while that merge document is being created.

If you check the Ask Once box, Word asks for a value for the bookmark only when the first merge document is created; the value you provide is available while the current and all subsequent merge documents are being created. ▮

Inserting the IF Field   Now find the place in the main document where you want the IF field to insert text, and place the insertion point there.

In this case, it's not a good idea to create an IF field by choosing from the Insert Word Field drop-down list. That's because the Insert Word Field: IF dialog box only lets you choose among the fields in your data source; it doesn't allow you to choose a bookmark. Instead, go to the Word menu bar and choose Insert Field to display the Field dialog box shown in Figure 6.15.

FIG. 6.15

Use the Field dialog box to insert an IF field.

Part

II

Ch

6

N O T E   You can create an IF field by choosing from the Insert Word Field drop-down box and temporarily choosing one of the available fields from the data source. Then, after inserting the IF field in the main document, you can edit it to replace the temporary field name with the name of the bookmark. ▇

In the Categories list, choose Mail Merge to display the list of field names shown in Figure 6.15. Notice that this list contains more types of fields than are available in the Insert Word Field drop-down list.

Choose IF and notice that the text below the Categories and Field Names lists summarizes the syntax of the IF statement. The text box below this summary already contains IF; you have to complete this statement to suit your specific requirements. Figure 6.16 shows the dialog box with the completed IF statement.

FIG. 6.16

Here is the IF statement that provides "5" if the bookmark value is Yes, or "10" if the bookmark value is anything else.

N O T E   Be careful about where you use quotes in an IF statement. The conditional value for the bookmark is not enclosed within quotes. The text provided if the condition is true is enclosed within quotes, as is the text provided if the condition is not true. ▇

Providing Values for the Bookmark   After you've completed the Mail Merge main document, or at least the part that contains the ASK and IF statements, you can run a trial merge by clicking the Check for Errors button in the Mail Merge toolbar. The merge process begins to create the first merge document and displays the message box shown in Figure 6.17.

FIG. 6.17

This message box shows the prompt and the default response you entered in the ASK statement.

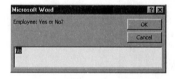

If the default No is the appropriate response, click OK. Otherwise, enter **Yes** and click OK.

When you click OK, Word enters the response as the value for the bookmark in that merge document, and then starts to merge the second document. Again, you choose whether to accept the default response or enter a different one. Proceed in this manner to merge the remaining documents.

 T I P You only get one chance to provide a value for the bookmark. Once you click OK, Word moves to the next document. See the section "Merging to a New Document" for information about correcting errors.

Filling in Text

Although being able to choose between two words or phrases is often all you need, there are times when you need much more flexibility. You might, for example, want to be able to insert some personalized text into each form letter. You can use the FILL-IN field to do so.

In the Mail Merge main document, place the insertion point where you want to be able to insert personalized text. Open the Insert Word Field drop-down list box and choose Fill-In. Word displays the Insert Word Field: Fill-In dialog box shown in Figure 6.18.

FIG. 6.18
Use this dialog box to mark the place where you can insert personalized text into each merge document.

Enter a prompt such as **Insert personalized text here** in the Prompt box. If there's some text you want to use in most merge documents, you can enter that in the Default Fill-In Text box. When you click OK, Word displays a sample of the message box you'll see for each merge document. Click OK again to return the Mail Merge main document with the Fill-In field displayed.

N O T E   Like ASK, the Insert Word Field: Fill-In dialog box contains an Ask Once check box. ▪

Part
II

Ch
6

Subsequently, as Word creates merge documents, merging pauses at each document to allow you to add personalized text.

Printing and Distributing Form Letters

The preceding sections of this chapter have covered many, but by no means all, of the aspects of creating a Mail Merge main document and providing a data source for it. In those sections, we frequently used the Check for Errors button on the Mail Merge toolbar to see the results of our work on the screen. But this doesn't produce merge documents you can send to people. Now we turn to the process of actually producing merge documents.

Printing Directly

If you have a very simple Mail Merge main document (and great confidence in your work), you can go directly to printing your merge documents. Click the Merge to Printer button on the Mail Merge toolbar and you'll see the familiar Windows Print dialog box. You know how to use that! If you have ASK or FILL-IN fields in the main document, printing will pause to allow you to provide the necessary information.

Chances are, though, that you'd like to save a few trees by reviewing the merge documents, or at least some of them, before you commit to printing.

Merging to a New Document

To review what the merge documents will look like before you print them, click Merge to New Document in the Mail Merge toolbar. The merge process pauses whenever necessary to allow you to provide information in response to ASK and FILL-IN fields. On completion, you can review all the merge documents on-screen. This is particularly useful if you want to review your responses to ASK fields. Whatever action Word took as a result of your responses is shown in the merge documents. If you did make a mistake, you can edit individual documents instead of going back through the entire process of responding to every document (and making different errors).

Once you are satisfied that all the merge documents are correct, you can print this document just like any other Word document.

 T I P After you've printed the merge documents, save the merged file until you've checked the printed pages. Even your eagle eye might have missed one or two errors when you reviewed the file on-screen. If you do spot an error at this time, you can correct it in the saved file and reprint just that page. Only when you've finally sent the printed pages on their way should you delete the merge file.

Distributing by Conventional Mail

So far in this chapter we've concentrated on creating form letters. After you've created those letters, you need to print envelopes or labels if you intend to send the letters by snail mail.

You can use Mail Merge to print envelopes and labels in much the same way that you print form letters. Open a new Word document, open the Mail Merge Helper Wizard, choose Create, and then either Mailing Labels or Envelopes. From there, the process is similar to that of creating a simple form letter. Just follow the instructions provided by the Mail Merge Helper.

Distributing by E-Mail or Fax

Instead of going through the time-consuming procedure of printing documents, printing envelopes or labels, inserting pages into envelopes, sealing envelopes, attaching stamps, and taking the pile of envelopes to the mail box, perhaps you should use e-mail or fax. Sounds like a time-saver. Unfortunately, sending Mail Merge documents by e-mail or fax is by no means as straightforward as I'd like it to be.

Let's suppose you have created a Mail Merge main document and you have provided a data source that has e-mail and fax address fields. Here's what you do:

1. Display the Mail Merge main document and then click the Mail Merge Helper button on the Mail Merge toolbar to open the Mail Merge Helper dialog box. Choose Query Options to display the Query Options dialog box with the Filter Records tab selected.

2. Open the Field drop-down list in the top row and choose the field that contains e-mail or fax numbers.

3. Open the Comparison drop-down list, and choose Is Not Blank. Leave the Compare To field empty and click OK.

4. In the Mail Merge Helper dialog box, click Merge. Then in the Merge dialog box, open the Merge To drop-down list, as shown in Figure 6.19.

FIG. 6.19

Use the Merge dialog box to choose Electronic Mail or Electronic Fax.

5. If in step 2 you chose a field that contains e-mail addresses, choose Electronic Mail from the list. Alternatively, if you chose a field that contains fax numbers, choose Electronic Fax from the list.

6. Click Setup to display the Merge to Setup dialog box, shown in Figure 6.20. Open the Data Field with Mail/Fax Address drop-down list and, once again, choose the field that contains the e-mail or fax address (as appropriate). Click OK to return to the Merge dialog box.

FIG. 6.20

Choose the data source field that contains the e-mail or fax address and, optionally, provide a subject line for your messages.

Part
II

Ch
6

7. In the Merge dialog box, click Merge to open your e-mail or fax application (such as Outlook).

What happens from here depends on your e-mail or fax application. If you're using Outlook, for example, and you have two or more e-mail or fax addresses for people you're sending to, you can choose which of the available addresses to use for each person. After you've made those choices, Outlook places the messages in its Outbox and sends them in the normal manner.

That's the process. It works, but I hope future versions of Word and Outlook will make it simpler to use. ●

Microsoft Excel

7   Advanced Templates   131

8   Advanced Work with Charts   149

9   Using Ranges   167

10   Advanced Work with Formulas   185

11   Using Worksheet Functions   209

12   Using Lists   233

13   Pivot Tables   251

14   Connecting to Access Databases   273

15   Analyzing Data   303

16   Using the Solver   323

Advanced Templates

▬ **Use templates**

Open new workbooks that all start with the same structure and data.

▬ **Create templates**

Examine design considerations for worksheets and charts.

▬ **Use the Template Wizard with Data Tracking**

Learn how to store information entered in workbooks based on a template in a single database or summary workbook.

You can save Excel workbooks in several different formats—in workbook format, of course, and in different text formats and as dBASE and 1-2-3 files. Another format is the *template* format. When you save a workbook as a template, new Excel workbooks can be based on that template.

When you open a workbook based on a template, all the information in the template migrates to the new workbook. That information isn't limited to data: It includes characteristics such as cell and worksheet formats, and custom controls such as toolbar buttons, formulas, defined names, and so on.

For the stand-alone user, the template is a convenience. It saves you time when you need to repeatedly create forms such as invoices.

In a networked environment, where a template can be shared by many users, it's still a convenience. But the template can then become a useful control mechanism. For example, when 100 sales representatives submit monthly expense reports, it's certainly useful for all those reports to have an identical structure. That makes the process of rolling up all the data into a single report quicker and more accurate.

Templates also help you manage the data more effectively. They provide an automated mechanism that you can use to coalesce, in a single file, data sprayed through hundreds or thousands of workbooks either on a single hard disk or across a network. ■

Using Templates

Several situations call for using templates. Periodically, you might need to create a report that has specific formatting characteristics and formulas. Each time you create the report from its template, only the data and the results of the formulas change.

If you base the report on a template, you need to provide the new data, but that's all. The template provides the report with the necessary formats, formulas, objects such as text boxes and custom buttons, print areas, and so on. And if you set things up properly, it's even possible to arrange for the template to obtain the data from another source such as an Access database or other Excel workbooks.

Or you might need to provide other users with a standard form. Suppose that your firm has several branch locations that need to submit monthly inventory reports to the main location. Each report is an Excel worksheet, and the reports must have a particular structure so that the main location can consolidate the reports properly. This sort of situation is perfect for a template. It's particularly well-suited to a networked environment where you can store the template in a shared folder that's accessible to all branch locations.

Or you might need to create forms such as invoices on a regular basis. Using a template with the structure you want makes it easy to create new invoices. But you can also arrange for the template to store the invoice data in a database as you enter the information. Later, you use the database to display a summary report of all invoices, this month's invoices, the invoices for a particular customer, unpaid invoices—whatever subset you want. The process is discussed in this chapter's section on the Template Wizard.

Opening Workbooks Based on Templates

I have a client who designed a workbook for use by other companies to enter technical information about their products. After the design work was completed, he saved the workbook as a template and was disconcerted to find that it didn't work as he expected. He thought that the user could open the template itself, either using File, Open or by double-clicking the template's icon on the Windows desktop. He expected that Excel then would create a new workbook based on the template, and change the .xlt (a template) file name extension to .xls (a workbook). He also expected Excel to increment an index that would identify the new workbook as a new instance of workbooks based on that template: for example, Product1.xls, Product2.xls, and so on.

Now these were reasonable expectations. Other kinds of templates work in exactly that way. But it's not how Excel templates work. (Not, at least, by default. If you're skilled at writing code in Visual Basic for Applications, or *VBA*, you could arrange for all that to occur.)

Instead of opening the template itself, you open a new Excel workbook and specify that it's to be based on a template. Choose File, New, or click the New button on the Standard toolbar. If there are templates stored in particular locations on your disk, the New dialog box shown in Figure 7.1 appears.

FIG. 7.1

To open a new workbook that's not based on a template, choose the Workbook icon.

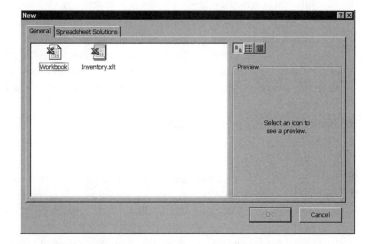

Either double-click a template, or select it and choose OK. When you do so, Excel opens a new workbook and applies to it all the settings, formats, and contents it finds in the template. No file name extension is used—Excel does not add the .xls extension to a workbook until you save it for the first time. The new workbook's name is that of the template, plus an index that identifies the workbook among the *open* workbooks based on that template.

For example, suppose that you open a workbook based on a template named Inventory.xlt. The first workbook you open is named Inventory1. If you leave Inventory1 open and open another workbook based on Inventory.xlt, the second workbook is named Inventory2.

But if you close Inventory1 and then open another workbook based on Inventory.xlt, the new workbook will also be named Inventory1. It's the names of the open workbooks that control the index assigned to new workbooks.

What You Can Store in Templates

Some workbook characteristics that can be defined in templates are obvious: formats, reports labels, and so on. Some are not so obvious. Here's a list of the elements that you might typically include in a template:

- Formatting elements such as cell number formats, column widths, background colors, and cell styles.
- Worksheets, chart sheets, and VBA objects such as modules. A workbook based on the template has the same sheets, with the same sheet names, that are in the template. As mentioned later in this list, you can set certain workbook options in the template. For example, you might have three sheets in the template, and use Tools, Options to set

Part

III

Ch

7

Number of Sheets in New Workbook to 5. The workbook named Inventory1, based on the template, will have the three sheets found in the template. But with Inventory1 open, if you then open a new workbook that is *not* based on the template, it will have five sheets.

■ Formulas that recalculate based on new data entered by the user.

■ Numeric data. In practice, it's unusual to include numbers in a template—that's the information that you typically want the template's user to provide. But if the template contains many formulas that all use the same constant value (for example, the Life argument to the DB financial function), you might decide to put that constant in some cell. Later, if it's necessary to modify the constant, you just replace it in the cell and re-save the template.

■ Named ranges and print area settings.

■ Labels such as header rows for lists, print titles, and headers and footers for printed output.

■ Tools that make the new workbook easier to use, or that automate certain tasks. You might want to put some VBA procedures into new workbooks; then, it's considerate to include a custom toolbar with buttons that run the procedures. You can also save controls such as list boxes and option buttons on a template's worksheets. Even hyperlinks can be saved in a template (however, you need to take special care establishing the path to the hyperlink's target when you place one in a *shared* template file).

■ Drawing objects such as text boxes and arrows that you might use to provide instructions to the user.

■ The protected status of different worksheet areas. If a worksheet is protected and certain cells are unlocked, only those cells will be available to a user who opens a workbook based on the template.

■ Options in the Tools, Options dialog box that pertain to calculation settings and that define which objects, such as row and column headers, appear in the active window.

Two other elements that you might save in a template can be based on external data sources such as existing Excel workbooks or external databases. These two elements are *pivot tables* and *external data ranges*.

Suppose that, using the methods described in Chapter 13, you use Microsoft Query to create a pivot table based on an external data source. If you then save the workbook with the pivot table as a template, new workbooks based on that template also contain the pivot table. If the data in the external data source have changed since you last viewed the pivot table, you can update the pivot table by choosing Data, Refresh Data. The procedures for creating and refreshing an external data range are analogous to those used for a pivot table.

The Excel documentation refers to templates that are connected to external data sources as *report templates*. It's a little misleading to give them a special name, though: They're just templates that happen to have some additional information about where to find the data source and what to do with it.

▶ **See** "What's a List?" **p. 234**

▶ **See** "Creating Pivot Tables from External Sources," **p. 255**

Finding Templates

Office 97 ships with three pre-designed templates for use with Excel: an invoice template, a purchase order template, and an expenses template. If you choose to install these templates when you run the Office Setup routine, the New dialog box appears when you choose File, New as shown in Figure 7.2.

FIG. 7.2
Excel templates supplied with Office 97 appear on the Spreadsheet Solutions tab.

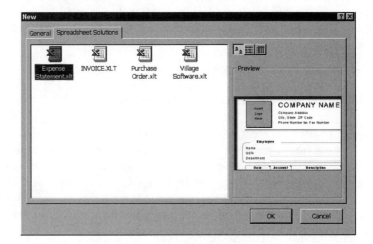

Notice in Figure 7.2 that there is also a Village Software.xlt template. This fully functioned template eases the task of ordering products from Village Software.

If you need a template for an invoice, a purchase order, or an expense report in a hurry, one of the supplied templates is an adequate choice. But if you have the time to design your own, do so. The supplied templates are driven by macros that you cannot modify—they're saved as password-protected add-ins, which are not editable—and if you need to make any major change to the templates, then it's likely that the macros will not run as intended.

N O T E The Office 97 CD contains additional Excel templates in the Valupack\Template\Excel path. They are stored in Excel 5.0/95 format. There is a timecard, sales quote, change request, loan, lease, personal budget, and a business planner template. The business planner contains a sample income statement, balance sheet, and cash flow sheet. ■

The important point about Figure 7.2 is the tabs on the New dialog box. The tabs on the dialog box correspond to folders in the path that Excel follows to get to templates. This path is largely dependent on the location choices you made when you installed Office 97, but a typical one is:

C:\Program Files\Microsoft Office\Templates

Part
III

Ch
7

Because the Templates folder itself contains a Spreadsheet Solutions folder with the supplied invoice, purchase order, and expense report templates, the Spreadsheet Solutions folder's name appears as a tab in the New dialog box.

When you save your own templates, you of course choose their location on the disk. If you create a new folder under Templates and put at least one template in it, a new tab with that folder's name is added to the dialog box. This is a useful way to organize your own templates, and to make them easily available to other users in a shared environment.

If you want *all* new workbooks that you open to have certain characteristics, put those characteristics in a template and save the template with the name **Book.xlt** in your Excel startup folder. The default Excel startup folder is named Xlstart, and is usually found inside the Office folder.

You can also put the Book.xlt default template in an alternate startup folder. Define this folder by choosing Tools, Options, and clicking the General tab. Type its path and name in the Alternate Startup File Location edit box, and choose OK.

T I P If you're a frequent user of VBA, you probably have preferences about the options that are available. One of these, Option Explicit, can be invoked by default. From the Visual Basic Editor (VBE), choose Tools, Options; click the Editor tab; and select the Require Variable Declaration check box. You cannot similarly require, for example, Option Base or Option Compare. To set these and other options automatically, start the VBE and insert a module. Type in that module the options (and their settings) that you want, exit the VBE, and save the workbook as a template. Now, new workbooks based on the template will contain a module that carries your option settings.

You might also want to create a template for worksheets that you insert into a workbook that's already open. To do so, follow the same procedure as you do for saving a default Book.xlt workbook template, but save it as **Sheet.xlt**. If you put more than one worksheet into Sheet.xlt, choosing Insert, Worksheet puts that number of new worksheets into an open workbook.

Of course, you might run into problems with sheet names when you use a worksheet template. Suppose that a worksheet in Sheet.xlt is named Sheet1, and that your open workbook also has a sheet named Sheet1. The worksheet that's inserted will automatically be named Sheet1(2) to distinguish it from Sheet1. If you want it to have a different name, you will have to rename it manually.

If you used the PivotTable Show Pages command in Excel 95 in combination with a Sheet.xlt template, you're used to seeing the new pages follow the settings in the template. This does not occur in Excel 97.

Creating Templates

In one sense, creating a template is extremely simple. After you've designed it, just choose File, Save As. In the Save as Type drop-down list, choose Template (*.xlt). Navigate to the location where you want to save the template, and choose Save.

> **CAUTION**
>
> Be sure to use the drop-down list to specify the .xlt extension—if you just type it yourself in the File Name edit box, Excel will not save it as a template.

Of course, that's deceptively simple advice. The hard part, after all, is the template's design.

Designing a Worksheet Template

As an example of designing the elements in a template, Figure 7.3 shows a template that I use to keep track of how I use my working time.

FIG. 7.3

This template is meant to mimic the appearance of a dialog box.

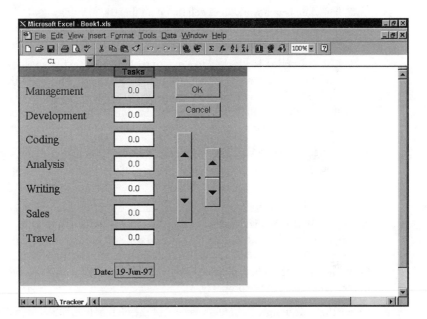

The template in the figure is a legacy from Excel 95. I wanted to be able to control the appearance of its elements—for example, the formatting of the labels. But in Excel 95, you did not have control of properties such as fonts, background colors, and foreground colors in a true dialog box, so it was desirable to design a template that looks like a dialog box. When a new workbook is opened and based on the template, it works much like a dialog box. The important elements are these:

- No row or column headers. Use Tools, Options and click the View tab. Then clear the Row & Column Headers check box. The next three options are accessed from the same View tab.
- No gridlines. Clear the Gridlines check box.
- Neither a horizontal nor a vertical scroll bar. Clear the Horizontal Scroll Bar and the Vertical Scroll Bar check boxes.

- No sheet tabs. Clear the Sheet Tabs check box.

- Each label (Management, Development, and so on) is actually on a text box that's fit to the size of the cell beneath. The associated "edit boxes" are also text boxes, similarly fit to cells. The rationale for the text boxes is explained next.

- The background color of the pseudo dialog box is set to gray, following the convention used by actual dialog boxes.

- When clicked, the two spinners control the values in the text boxes. A spinner's incremental value must be an integer. Therefore, the VBA procedure that's attached to the smaller spinner divides its value by 10. Then, it concatenates that fractional value to the larger spinner's integer value and displays the result in a text box.

- The date is in a worksheet cell that contains the formula =NOW(), and formatted as d-mmm-yy. When a workbook based on the template is opened, the formula evaluates to display the current date.

- The OK button is attached to a macro that puts the text box values in cells and saves the workbook. The Cancel button is attached to a macro that closes the workbook without saving it. The Cancel macro sets Application.DisplayAlerts to False before closing the workbook, and then back to True. So doing suppresses the standard Save the workbook? warning that Excel displays when you close a changed, unsaved workbook.

The rationale for using text boxes for the labels and to stand in for edit boxes is two-fold. First, you cannot place an edit box on a worksheet—only on an Excel 95 dialog sheet or an Excel 97 user form.

Second, worksheet cells do not respond to clicks by running an assigned macro, whereas text boxes can. When the user clicks a text box—either a label or a pseudo edit box—a macro changes the color of both the label's font and the edit box's background, to indicate which pair is selected. The macro that responds to a click on a text box sets the value of the spinners to the value currently in the edit box. The macro determines which text box called it by means of the Application.Caller property.

Notice that this template contains several of the elements mentioned in the section "Using Templates:" formats, a worksheet, VBA modules, formulas, controls, and window options (objects such as scroll bars and sheet tabs belong to the window, not to the worksheet).

With the added functionality of Excel 97 user forms, you might think that this template is no longer needed. For example, VBA lets you set the font and color characteristics of controls on user forms.

But I continue to use it for several reasons. I'm used to it. I like it. There's no place on it to enter the time it would take to convert it to an Excel 97 user form. And, by means of Data Tracking, it automatically moves the data that I enter into an Access database. You'll find information on setting up that capability in this chapter's final section, "Using the Template Wizard with Data Tracking."

Designing a Chart Template

After you have created a chart, it's possible to save its design and formatting elements in a template. You can then set that template as the default chart type that Excel will use when you create a new chart.

To create a chart template, first create a sample chart. Then, choose Chart, Chart Type; click the Custom Types tab; and choose User-Defined. Figure 7.4 shows the dialog box that appears.

FIG. 7.4

After you choose the User-Defined option button, the active chart appears in the Sample box.

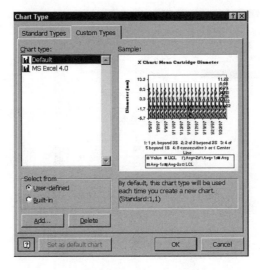

Note that two other chart types—the current default chart format and one that uses Excel 4.0 formatting—appear in the Chart Type list box. At this point, do not select either of those types. If you do, the active chart disappears from the Sample box and you will not be able to get it back without canceling out of the dialog box.

1. Click the Add button. The Add Custom Chart Type dialog box appears, as shown in Figure 7.5.

FIG. 7.5

Provide a name and description here to make the template easier to use.

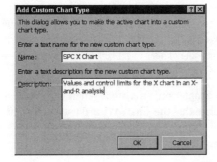

2. Using the Name edit box, assign a name to the new custom chart type. You should also type a description of the chart type in the Description edit box. After you save the chart type as a defined custom type, you are not able to add or alter a description.

3. Choose OK to save the chart as a defined custom chart type.

Figure 7.6 shows the appearance of the Custom Types tab after you have added a custom chart type.

FIG. 7.6

The name and description of your custom chart type are displayed in the Custom Types tab.

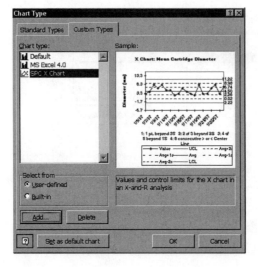

If you now click the Set as Default Chart button, Excel (after verifying your intent with a message box) sets the selected chart as its default for new charts. You need not then use the Custom Types tab in the Chart Wizard's first step to specify your custom chart type. Whatever built-in chart type (Line, Bar, Pie, Area, and so on) forms the basis for your custom chart type is selected when the Chart Wizard starts. When it creates a new chart, Excel uses any custom formatting that you have added to the basic built-in chart.

CAUTION

Although your custom chart is the default, the user can still create a chart based on a different built-in chart type. Any formats that you used in your custom chart type will be used in combination with the structure of the built-in type that the user selects. Your formats might not work well with a different built-in chart type.

What's this material doing in a chapter on templates? When you create a custom chart type, you're actually creating a template that the Chart Wizard uses to format new charts. The template is not stored in a standard .xlt template file, but in a file named Xlusrgal.xls (short for Excel User Gallery) in the Office folder.

If you want to alter some aspect of the chart template that you have created, you can do so by opening the Xlusrgal.xls file, finding the sheet tab that corresponds to the name you gave the chart type, and activating that sheet. Then, select some aspect of the chart (an axis, perhaps, or the chart title) and modify it as you would any other—usually, by means of the Format menu.

The built-in custom chart types are found in Xl8galry.xls, which is also in the Office folder.

Using the Template Wizard with Data Tracking

If you saw just the name `Template Wizard` as it appears in the Data menu, you might well think that it's a wizard that helps you design a template. It doesn't.

This wizard does save a normal Excel workbook as an .xlt template file, but its primary purpose is to automate the entry of data from a workbook based on the template into some other storage medium, such as an ODBC (Open Database Connectivity) database or another Excel workbook.

The idea is that you might want to enable yourself and other users to enter data in a convenient place. That place could be a Data Form, or a template-based workbook with instructions on how to enter data.

▶ **See** "Using a Data Form with Lists," **p. 248**

When the user finishes entering the data and saves the workbook, the information is automatically stored not only in the workbook but also in the database. The aim is to make data entry convenient, and to make the data storage (and the summary of the data) efficient.

Installing the Template Wizard

The Template Wizard is an add-in, so you must choose to install it during the Office 97 Setup procedure:

1. In Setup, choose the Microsoft Excel option and click Change Option. Then, choose the Add-ins option and again choose Change Option.

2. Select the Template Wizard with Data Tracking check box and choose OK.

3. Before leaving Setup, choose the Data Access option in the same dialog box where you chose the Microsoft Excel option. Choose Change Option and click the Database Drivers option.

4. Choose Change Option again. You will see a list of database drivers, including one for Microsoft Access, dBASE, Excel, Microsoft SQL Server, and Text and HTML. Select the check boxes associated with any one or more of these drivers, and choose as many OK buttons as necessary to complete Setup.

Start Excel, and choose Tools, Add-Ins. If Setup completed correctly, you will find Template Wizard with Data Tracking in the Add-Ins Available list box. Ensure that its check box is selected, and choose OK.

When the wizard's check box is selected, the Template Wizard item appears in the Data menu. You can now use the wizard to set up the template.

Part
III

Ch
7

Choosing a Database Driver

Before moving on to the actual use of the Template Wizard, it's useful to consider which database driver you want to use. Suppose that you chose to install both the Microsoft Access and the Excel database drivers. Later, when you actually use the Template Wizard, you have an opportunity to select either the Access or the Excel driver.

N O T E You need to have Microsoft Access installed in order to create an Access database by means of the Template Wizard. You also need Access itself to be present if you want to examine or manage the data. However, after the database has been created, you do not need to have Access installed if all you want to do is store data by means of the template. ■

Unless you have some special reason to use the Access driver, you should usually choose the Excel driver. The reason is that the most valuable characteristic of a true database is its relational capability. It has multiple tables. Data such as lengthy text labels need to be stored only once each. Short IDs that identify those labels are stored many times. This often results in dramatic savings in storage space.

But the Template Wizard does not take advantage of the relational capability. Suppose that you have created a template by means of the Template Wizard, and have chosen an Access database as the place to store new data. You have opened a new workbook based on the template, entered the necessary information, and are ready to save the new record. When you do so, the entire record is written to one and only one table in the Access database.

The record contains a customer name such as:

> Minnewawa Minnesota Portcullis Factory

These 38 characters become part of the database record, and are part of each record that you subsequently enter for that particular customer. The record does not contain an ID such as 23 which could uniquely identify the customer.

Therefore, much of the strength of a relational database is lost. And in that case, you might as well direct the data to an Excel workbook, where you have access to Excel's data analysis, summary, and charting capabilities.

On the other hand, suppose that you have taken the trouble to set up your Excel template with a list box. Using the Forms toolbar, you place the list box on the worksheet and assign it a cell link (right-click the list box, choose Format Control from the shortcut menu, and click the Control tab). The cell link contains the list box's index value of the customer name, rather than the name itself.

Users could then choose customers from the list box, instead of typing a full customer name each time. And you would use the Template Wizard to arrange the delivery of the numeric value in the cell link, rather than the customer name itself, to the Access database driver. So doing would set the stage for leveraging the database's relational capability.

So, there's a tradeoff of effort for efficiency. If you anticipate collecting large amounts of data, if you're willing to do the extra work in Excel of assigning brief IDs to lengthy labels, and if you want to arrange the necessary lookups and links in Access, then by all means use the Access driver.

Otherwise, use the Excel driver. That way, when you open the workbook that stores all the data records, you can immediately start using Excel's tools and functions to analyze the data.

And no, I don't really think that anyone is still making portcullises. Not in Minnesota, anyway.

Setting Up the Template

Suppose that you have created an Excel workbook that you will use to enter and print invoice data. An example is shown in Figure 7.7.

FIG. 7.7
The invoice form is set up for ease of data entry and for appropriate appearance when it's printed.

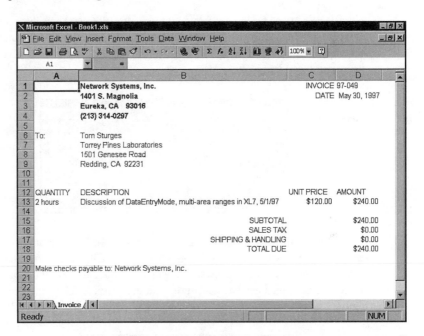

Once you have designed the format that you want, save it as a workbook—not as a template. The Template Wizard will save the .xlt file for you when it sets up the required connectivity information.

Structuring the Template　After saving the workbook, and with the workbook still active, choose Data, Template Wizard. The dialog box shown in Figure 7.8 appears.

The name of the workbook that is active when you start the Template Wizard appears in the dialog box's drop-down list. Verify that it is the workbook you want to use as the basis for the template, and if necessary use the drop-down list to choose another workbook; when you do so, that workbook is activated.

Part
III

Ch

7

FIG. 7.8

The names of any open workbooks are in the drop-down list.

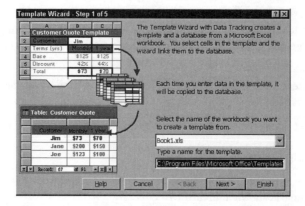

In the Type a Name for the Template edit box, drag across the visible path and name. When you reach the final backslash, you can enter a particular file name. If you want to use the active workbook's name for the template as well, just skip this step and click Next to go to step 2 of the wizard (see Figure 7.9).

FIG. 7.9

Select a database driver in step 2.

After selecting the driver you want to use, as discussed in the prior section, you need to indicate whether you want the wizard to establish a new database or to add data to an existing database. If the latter, click Browse to navigate to that database; if the former, type the path to and the name of the new database in the edit box. Then, click Next. The dialog box shown in Figure 7.10 appears.

FIG. 7.10

Use step 3 of the Template Wizard to identify the location of the data and the associated labels.

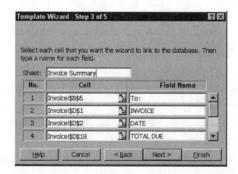

In step 3, type a name for the database table that will contain the data—or, if in step 2 you chose to store the data in an Excel workbook, the name you type will be that of a worksheet in that workbook.

The grid in the third step is where you indicate the location, in the template and in the template-based workbooks, of the data that will be stored. Click the cell that contains the first data value; its address appears in the Cell box for grid row 1. Then, click under Field Name in the same row of the grid.

What then appears in the associated Field Name box depends on how you have set up the worksheet. In Figure 7.10, notice that the label INVOICE appears in cell C1, to the left of the invoice number 97-049 on the worksheet. If there is a label in the same row and to the left of the data cell, Excel supplies that label as a default field name. If you have set up the data as a list, with header labels in the top row of the list, Excel supplies the header label as a field name.

If there is no label in the same row or same column, you will need to type a field name in the dialog box's grid.

In either case (label in the same column and above, or label in the same row and to the left), you can overwrite the default label with another. It's usually best, though, to accept the default label. That way, you'll find it easier to determine the correspondence between fields in the database and data in the worksheet.

This step highlights the reason to use a template for the process of data entry. As new data are entered and collected in the database or worksheet, it's important that the information always be entered in the same location. The use of a template that establishes the worksheet's layout helps ensure that the data will always be found in the same locations.

After you have finished specifying the location of data and the field names, click Next to display the wizard's fourth step, shown in Figure 7.11.

FIG. 7.11

Step 4 gives you a chance to add data from existing workbooks to the database.

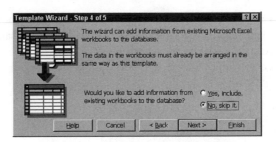

Suppose that you had been creating invoices using the same layout as in the current worksheet for some time, but had not yet arranged to collect the data in a central location. In that case, you would likely want to add the information in those existing workbooks to the database, and step 4 is where you decide to do that.

As Figure 7.11 shows (note the instruction The data in the workbooks must already be arranged in the same way as this template.), the identical layout is necessary. If you are familiar with data consolidation in Excel, you know that you can choose to consolidate by

Part
III

Ch
7

position or by category. To *consolidate by position* is to combine data that occupy the same addresses on different worksheets. To *consolidate by category* is to combine data that have identical labels—not necessarily the same addresses—on different worksheets.

You can think of the Template Wizard as similar to consolidation by position. The addresses occupied by identical fields in different workbooks must themselves be identical. The Template Wizard does not support the labeling approach used in consolidation by category.

If you do have existing data laid out in the required fashion, you can choose the Yes, Include option button; otherwise, choose the No, Skip It option button. Choosing Yes, Include and then clicking Next displays the dialog box shown in Figure 7.12.

FIG. 7.12

Although the dialog box contains different controls, the Template Wizard considers it to be part of step 4.

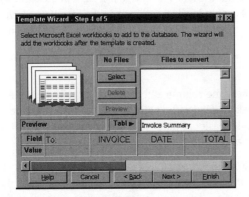

When you click the Select button, you will see a dialog box that is identical (except for its name) to the File, Open dialog box. Use it to navigate to the locations of the workbooks whose data you want to include in the database. As you locate them, select their names and then choose Open. Each file is added to the Files to Convert list.

To preview a file, select it in the Files to Convert list and click the Preview button. The point, of course, is to enable you to verify that a file really does conform to the same cell addresses as in the template you are creating. If you add a few files, preview them; if you find that one or more have a layout that's even slightly wrong as to cell addresses, you can click Remove to take them off the list.

Step 5 appears when you click Next (see Figure 7.13).

You should note somewhere the summary information—the name and location of the template and of the Excel or database file that collects new data—for later reference.

Once you click Finish, the database or Excel workbook that will store the data is created, and the workbook that was active when you started the Template Wizard is saved as a template with the .xlt file extension.

Entering New Data Based on the Template   When you subsequently open a new workbook based on the template, enter data, and choose either File, Close or File, Save, you see the dialog box shown in Figure 7.14.

FIG. 7.13

If you have installed Outlook or Exchange, you can automatically route new workbooks based on the template to addresses in the Personal Address Book.

FIG. 7.14

At this point, you can choose whether or not to add the data in the new workbook to the database.

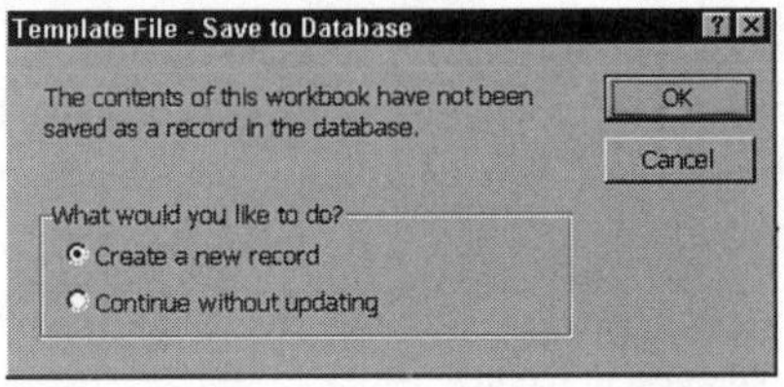

Use the dialog box shown in Figure 7.14 to save the new data in the database (choose Create a New Record) or to omit the record from the database (choose Continue Without Updating).

The General tab on the dialog box that appears when you choose Tools, Options contains a Macro Virus Protection check box. If the check box is selected, Excel displays a warning message when you open a workbook that contains macros. You can choose to enable the macros, disable them, or to stop opening the workbook.

Suppose that you have saved a workbook based on the template, and have chosen Create a New Record when you did so. If you later open that workbook, and if the Macro Virus Protection check box is selected, you will see the message that warns you about existing macros.

That's a little disconcerting, but the reason is that the template you created puts macros into new workbooks that are based on it. These macros help maintain the relationship between the workbook and the database. (The macro sheet's `Visible` property is `xlVeryHidden`, so you can't unhide it using Format, Sheet, Unhide. You would need to use VBA to change its `Visible` property and display it.)

The dialog box shown in Figure 7.14 gets an additional option button if you re-open a workbook that was based on the template and change any data. The additional option button is Update the Existing Record. Select it and click OK to modify the existing record in the database with the new information.

Part

III

Ch

7

TROUBLESHOOTING

If you click Finish in the Template Wizard, you might see a message that an Access database couldn't be created. Check first to see that you have Access installed. If you do, check the labels in the workbook you're using to create the template. If you want to create an Access database, the labels in the workbook must conform to Access naming rules. So, your labels should *not* contain a period (.), and exclamation point (!), an accent grave ('), square brackets ([]), or leading spaces. You should also keep labels shorter than 64 characters—the shorter, the better—and unique with respect to one another.

N O T E   The "links" referred to in steps 1, 3, and 5 of the Template Wizard are not links in the usual sense; they are not the same as, say, setting cell A1 in Book1 equal to cell A1 in Book2. Changing a value in one of the workbooks whose data are stored in the database does not result in an immediate change of value in the database.

Instead, if you change a value in an existing workbook based on the template, the macros take over. They change the value stored in the database to the new value. ■

Advanced Work with Charts

Chart axes and scales

The implications of the values' scale of measurement for the chart type that you choose.

Dealing with data labels

Conveniently attach uncharted data labels to charted data points.

Creating special effects in charts

Use your knowledge of scales and axes to bring about completely new types of charts.

Excel 97 has 14 different types of basic charts. In addition, there are 20 custom chart types; mostly, these are cosmetic variations on the basic charts.

It's easy to conclude from glancing at the Chart Wizard's example of each chart type that you're limited to what's shown there. That's not the case—and if it were, Excel's applicability would be severely limited. Virtually every profession, every specialty, and every scientific discipline has its own set of special chart formats. These formats convey particular information to other members of that profession or discipline. If only for credibility, it's important to be able to create charts that conform to your colleagues' expectations.

Don't be concerned about creating a special type of chart in Excel. The one you're after might not be one of the basic or custom types, but if you understand how different chart types manage their data series and their axes, then you're well on your way to designing whatever you're after. This chapter begins with that topic. ■

Understanding Chart Axes and Scales of Measurement

The axes on your chart and the scales that the axes use to display the data are closely related to the nature of the data that you chart. Additionally, the way that Excel places the data series on the chart is closely related to how you have placed the data on the worksheet.

Using a Category and a Value Axis

Suppose that you want to examine the payroll for three departments: Sales, Finance, and Manufacturing. You have available information on each department's headcount and its payroll budget.

One of your variables is Department, and it is a *category* variable. In the absence of any other information about each department, there is no quantitative scale to distinguish among them. Contrast that Department variable with, say, Payroll. A Payroll value of $100,000 is not only larger than a value of $50,000, but it is obviously and exactly twice as large. You can't make similar statements about the relationships between the values of a Department variable, such as the value *Sales* and the value *Marketing*.

Your payroll and headcount variables are *continuous*. By examining any two headcount values, you can tell which is larger. The distinction—whether you can make a quantitative comparison of two different values—has important implications for the way you chart data.

Every Excel chart type has at least two axes. Most chart types have, in Excel's terminology, a *category* axis and a *value* axis. For example, a Column chart's horizontal axis is the category axis and its vertical axis is the value axis. If you were going to chart Payroll by Department on a Column chart, you would put Department on the horizontal, category axis, and Payroll on the vertical, value axis (see Figure 8.1).

Excel terms the values that are charted on the category axis as the *X (Category) Axis Labels*. The values on the value axis are termed *Values*. The actual data points—the columns on a Column chart, the bars on a Bar chart, and so on—are termed *data markers*.

N O T E The term *value axis* is, by the way, a little misleading. Categories such as Sales and Marketing are values, after all. They're arbitrary categories, but they're values nevertheless. If I were King, I'd have named it a *continuous* axis instead. ▪

If, on the other hand, you wanted to chart Payroll and Department on a Bar chart, the orientation would be different. A Bar chart's vertical axis is the category axis and its horizontal axis is the value axis (see Figure 8.2). That's the only difference between the two chart types: A Bar chart is just a Column chart turned on its side. The choice between the two types of chart is often—*not* always, as you will see—just a matter of personal preference, and whether there's more vertical than horizontal space available for the chart.

FIG. 8.1

The departments are equally spaced along the horizontal category axis.

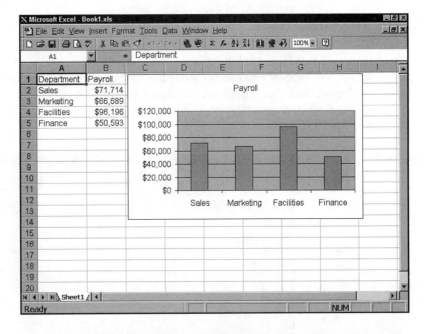

FIG. 8.2

A Bar chart's vertical axis, which is a category axis, spaces each department as does the Column chart's horizontal axis.

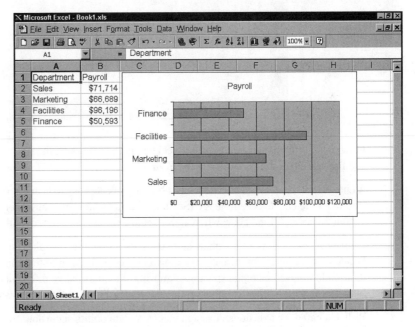

Consider a Pie chart. It has a category axis, represented by the different slices, and a value axis, represented by the size of each slice. A Pie chart gives you a slightly different perspective than Bar or Column charts. If you want to consider total headcount as 100 percent, the Pie chart does a good job of showing each Department's contribution to the total.

Using Two Value Axes

The XY (Scatter) chart is fundamentally different from other chart types because it has *two* value axes (see Figure 8.3). If you want to examine the relationship between Headcount and Payroll, the XY (Scatter) chart is the one to use. You anticipate that generally the higher the headcount, the higher the payroll. A category axis won't show you that relationship because it doesn't distinguish quantitatively among different values—it just shows them in the order that they appear on the worksheet.

FIG. 8.3

Notice that both the horizontal and vertical axes space the values according to their magnitude.

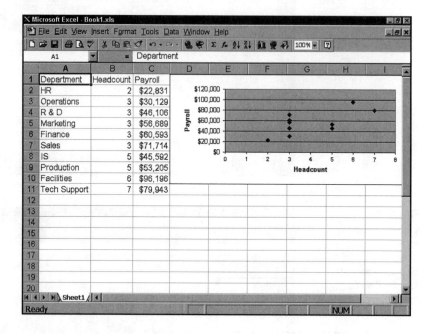

For a chart that has two value axes, Excel terms the values on the horizontal axis the *X Values* and the values on the vertical axis the *Y Values*.

A Line chart, like a Column chart, has a horizontal category axis and a vertical value axis. Because Line charts resemble XY (Scatter) charts so closely, many users get themselves into trouble by using a Line chart when an XY (Scatter) chart is needed, and vice versa.

Figure 8.4 shows how a Line chart and an XY (Scatter) chart would display Payroll and Headcount. Compare the two charts shown in Figure 8.4, and notice that the Line chart gives the Headcount values equal spacing—ignoring the quantitative differences between the values. In contrast, the XY (Scatter) chart reflects the magnitude of the values on its horizontal axis.

Well, if a category axis doesn't assign values to data points according to their numeric magnitude, what values does it assign to them? A category axis assigns the first category a value of 1, the second category a value of 2, and so on. In other words, the value of a category is its ordinal position with respect to the other values. And that, of course, is a function of each data point's placement on the worksheet.

FIG. 8.4

Although both charts use the same source data, the horizontal axis spacing and the trend- lines are different.

XY(Scatter) chart —

Line chart —

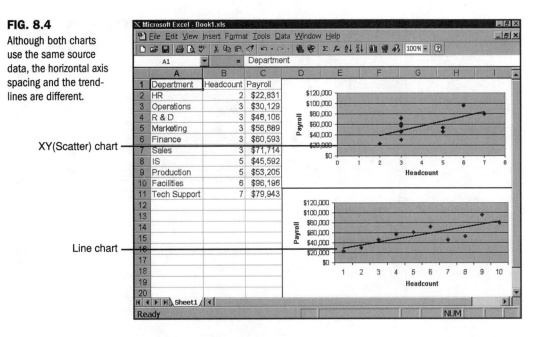

In any chart, a trendline depends on the relationship between the sets of values on the two axes. In the XY (Scatter) chart, the trendline depends on the relationship between the actual values of Headcount and Payroll.

But in the Line chart, the trendline depends on the relationship between the actual values of headcount and the ordinal value (1, 2, 3...) of each payroll measurement. Unless you're sure that you want to trend a continuous variable against a series of equally spaced integers, use an XY (Scatter) chart for your trendlines.

There's a major exception to the general rule about how Excel treats values on a category axis. When the category values are formatted as dates on the worksheet, Excel 97 adjusts the scale of the category axis accordingly (see Figure 8.5).

You will find that the same effect occurs in other chart types when you place values formatted in date units on the category axis. That format causes Excel to use the actual date values on the category scale instead of their ordinal values.

Another chart type, new in Excel 97, is the *Bubble chart*. In a sense, a Bubble chart has three value axes. It is like an XY (Scatter) chart because both the horizontal and vertical axes are value axes. In addition, the size of the chart's bubbles, the third axis, can represent some third continuous variable.

Suppose that you wanted to chart information about sales transactions; in particular, you're interested in the relationship between product revenue and product cost for each sale. It's quite possible that there are multiple instances of sales with identical revenues and costs.

FIG. 8.5

The Line chart spaces the date values properly on the category axis.

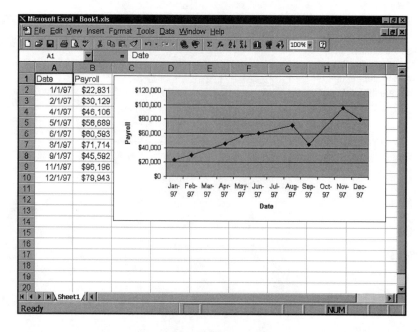

You would want some visual indicator of the number of times a pairing of a specific revenue value and a specific cost value occurs. The size of the bubbles can be that indicator. Figure 8.6 shows the proper layout of the data and the resulting Bubble chart.

FIG. 8.6

The larger the bubble, the greater the value in column C.

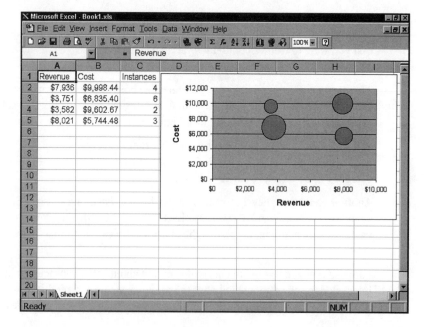

You can always adjust the role of the different data series after you've created the initial chart, but Excel by default uses the values in the rightmost column to size the bubbles.

Putting Two Data Series on the Same Axis

Suppose that you have two different ranges of values that you want to chart against the same category labels—or, in the case of an XY (Scatter) or a Bubble chart, two sets of Y values that you want to chart with one set of X values. Figure 8.7 shows this situation.

FIG. 8.7

By offsetting one set of Y values, you can arrange for two charted data series.

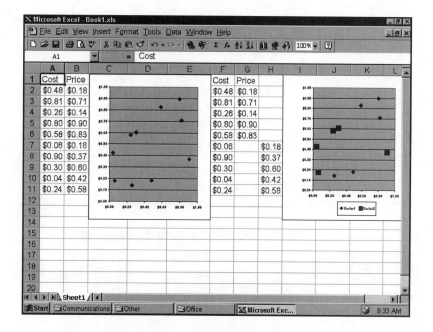

In Figure 8.7, the chart on the left displays the values in A2:B11. The chart on the right displays the values in F2:H11. Notice that Excel treats the values in B2:B11 as one data series.

In contrast, Excel treats the values in G2:G6 and G7:G11 as two separate data series. The result is that, in the chart on the right, you can see in two dimensions the separation between the two data series.

Another way to obtain the effect shown in Figure 8.7, one that you use after creating the initial chart, involves copying and pasting. You begin by creating the chart with the data in A2:B6. When the chart is complete, select A7:B11, and choose Edit, Copy. Select the chart, and choose Edit, Paste Special. Because you are pasting into a chart rather than into a worksheet, a different Paste Special dialog box appears, as shown in Figure 8.8.

You could also select the new range and drag it by its border into the chart. You then see the Paste Special dialog box shown in Figure 8.8. Extending a charted range by dragging the Range Finder handle always adds new points to the charted series; using the Range Finder does not add a new series to the chart.

FIG. 8.8

The Paste Special dialog box gives you choices as to how the chart will show the new data.

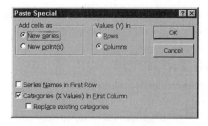

Choose to add the data as a New Series. If you choose to add the data as New Points, the existing data series is simply extended. Select the Categories (X Values) in First Column check box. When you do so, and when New Series is selected, the Replace Existing Categories check box becomes enabled. Do not select it unless you have a special reason for doing so.

When you select the Replace Existing Categories check box, the data points that are already in the chart are given the same X values as the new data points that you are pasting. While there are some situations that call for this, they're unusual.

After you click OK, the chart will appear as does the rightmost chart in Figure 8.7.

The Chart Wizard's Series tab is yet another way to manipulate a chart's data series. You get to that tab at the wizard's second step, or after the chart is created by choosing Chart, Source Data. In either case, click the Series tab. The dialog box shown in Figure 8.9 appears.

FIG. 8.9

Use the Series tab options to add new data or rearrange existing series.

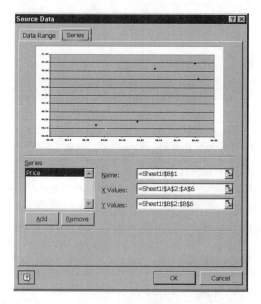

In the present example, you would begin by clicking the Add button to add a new series to the chart. Click the X Values reference edit box and drag through A7:A11, and then click the Y Values edit box and drag through B7:B11. After you choose OK, the chart includes A2:B6 as the first data series, and A7:B11 as the second data series.

Part
III

Ch
8

TROUBLESHOOTING

Say you create a chart and then select a new data range and drag it into the chart. But the chart just added the range as new points, and you didn't see the Paste Special dialog box. This can happen when you repeatedly add and delete a range from a chart. To force the display of the Paste Special dialog box, drag the new range into the chart by a right click instead of a left click on the range's border.

Dealing with Data Labels

The tick mark labels on a chart's axes are the usual way to tell what each data marker represents. A Column chart that shows monthly expenses per department would usually show each department's name on the horizontal category axis. Figure 8.10 shows an example.

FIG. 8.10
This unadorned column chart provides basic information about departmental expenses.

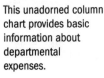

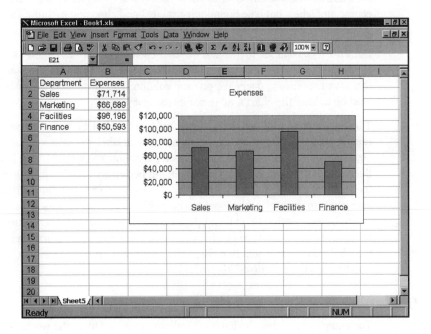

At times, though, you need to display additional information that better identifies each data marker. For example:

■ The relative height of each column makes it easy to compare departments as to their operating expenses. But to determine the actual expense figure itself, you need to refer to the value axis. It can be useful to display the expense value along with the data marker.

■ Purely for formatting reasons, you might want to modify the horizontal axis to gain space in a report. You would select the horizontal axis; choose Format, Selected Axis; click the Patterns tab; and set Tick Mark Labels to None. Then, display each department's name as a label on its own column marker.

Showing Values and Showing Labels

Excel makes it very easy to put the two types of data labels on a chart. To label each column with the actual expense value, you would select the chart and choose Chart, Chart Options. Select the Data Labels tab and choose to Show Value.

To label each column with the department's name, you would choose to Show Label instead of Show Value. (In the case of data labels, Excel terms the category axis value a *label*.)If the chart type is one that has a category and a value axis, such as a Column or Bar chart, you have the choice just described: You can choose to Show Labels or Show Values in the data labels. If the chart type is, say, an XY (Scatter) in which there is no category axis, you have the same choice, but choosing to Show Labels shows the horizontal axis values (which are, of course, not labels but true quantitative values) and choosing to Show Values shows the vertical axis values.

But what if you wanted to indicate whether each department's expenses for the current year are greater or less than its expenses for the prior year? To do so, you would like to show a label that says Increase or Decrease on each column. The problem is that Increase and Decrease exist on neither the chart's value nor its category axis.

There are many situations in which you want to attach data labels, but you want neither the category label nor the value axis value as the data label. Perhaps you have created an XY (Scatter) chart of staff salaries and length of employment. You would like to label each point with the name of the associated staff member, but because you didn't include employees' names in the chart, you can't attach their names as labels. The usual solution to this problem is to attach data labels to the series, choosing to show either Labels or Values. When the labels have been created, select each label in turn by clicking it. The selected label's value—which is actually text, regardless of the type of label you chose—appears in the Formula Bar. Type new text for the label into the Formula Bar; when you then press Enter, the new text appears in the selected data label on the chart (see Figure 8.11).

Designing the User Interface

The entry of data labels by hand is a tedious solution. Often, the worksheet already has a range of values that you did not include in the chart and that you want to use for the data labels. Why re-type them? A better solution is to write a VBA procedure to loop through the data points in the series, read the values from the worksheet, and write the values to the data labels. Following Figure 8.12 are instructions for creating the procedure:

1. With the workbook that contains the chart's data open, choose Tools, Macro, Visual Basic Editor.

FIG. 8.11

Unless you type a new value for a data label, the label's value is linked to the chart's source data.

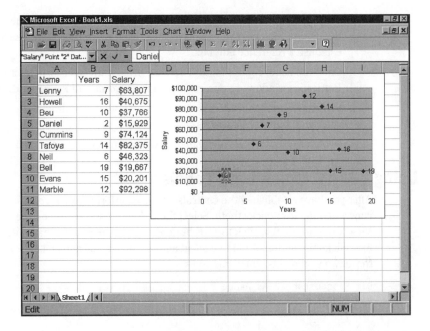

FIG. 8.12

VBA in Office 97 makes use of User Forms instead of the dialog sheets supported in earlier versions.

Reference Edit box ⎯

Properties window ⎯

Label control ⎯
Command Button control ⎯
RefEdit control ⎯

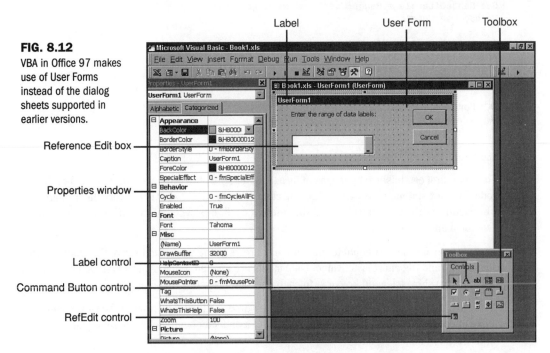

2. Choose Insert, UserForm. The screen now appears much as is shown in Figure 8.12. If you do not see the Toolbox, choose View, Toolbox.

3. Click the RefEdit control in the Toolbox. When you now move the mouse pointer across the user form, it changes to a crosshair. Hold down the left mouse button and drag to establish a reference edit box.

4. Click the Label control in the Toolbox. Drag in the user form to create a label. In the Properties window, enter a caption such as **Enter the range of data labels**.

5. Click the CommandButton control in the Toolbox and drag in the user form to create a command button. Change its caption to OK.

6. Repeat step 5 to create a command button with a Cancel caption.

Using VBA to Attach Data Labels

After you have established the controls on the user form, you need to supply the VBA code that runs when the user clicks them. Select the OK command button on the user form, and choose View, Code (or double-click the OK button) in order to create a macro that will run when the user clicks the button. A module sheet appears with a Sub and an End Sub statement. Between those two statements, enter this code:

```
Dim RangeOfLabels As Range
Dim CountLabels As Integer
Dim i As Integer

Set RangeOfLabels = Range(UserForm1.RefEdit1.Text)
Unload UserForm1

CountLabels = RangeOfLabels.Rows.Count
ActiveSheet.ChartObjects(1).Activate
With ActiveChart.SeriesCollection(1)
    .ApplyDataLabels Type:=xlDataLabelsShowLabel, _
        LegendKey:=False
    For i = 1 To CountLabels
      .Points(i).DataLabel.Text = _
      RangeOfLabels.Offset(i - 1, 0).Resize(1, 1)
    Next i
End With
```

This code first establishes, by means of its Dim statements, the three variables needed in the code. The Set statement assigns to the object variable RangeOfLabels the worksheet range whose address the user has placed in the reference edit box. The Unload statement closes the user form and releases the memory it uses.

Then, CountLabels is set equal to the number of rows in the worksheet range that contains the data labels, and the chart is activated. Data labels are applied to the chart's first data series, and the option to show a legend key next to each data label is set to False.

A For-Next loop is then entered. It loops as many times as there are rows in the worksheet range of data labels. During each loop, the text of a data label in the chart is set equal to a value in the range of data labels.

Part
III

Ch
8

N O T E Although compact, this code is fairly sophisticated. It uses techniques such as a `With` block, an object variable, a loop, and range offsets that change each time the loop executes. If you're unfamiliar with any of these, refer to Part VII of this book, particularly Chapter 31, "Building Forms and Dialog Boxes," on forms and Chapter 32, "VBA Programming." ■

In the same way that you establish the code given for the user form's OK button, you should attach a subroutine such as this:

```
Private Sub CommandButton2_Click()
End
End Sub
```

for the Cancel button. The `End` statement causes the VBA code to stop executing and returns control to the user.

As noted, the code samples given in this section run when the user clicks a button on the user form. One more item is needed: a way to get the user form on the screen. After establishing the user form, choose Insert, Module to get a blank module sheet. Enter just these three lines of code:

```
Sub AttachLabels()
UserForm1.Show
End Sub
```

(Your user form is already named `UserForm1`, unless you have used a VBA project that already has a user form in it.)

Choose File, Save to save the active workbook (including the VBA project, its form, and modules). Then choose File, Close and Return to Microsoft Excel. Now, whenever you want to attach data labels to a chart, choose Tools, Macro, Macros and select AttachLabels from the Macro Name list box. The user form appears as shown in Figure 8.13.

Extending the VBA Code

The VBA code given in this section is a bare set of bones. As you gain experience with user forms and VBA, here are some enhancements that you would want to consider:

■ Put a custom button on a worksheet toolbar. Assign the subroutine `AttachLabels` to the custom button, so that it's more convenient to run the macro.

■ Give the user form a caption such as `Attach Data Labels to Chart`.

■ Force the user to begin by selecting the chart and the data series that will get the data labels. So doing extends the functionality of the code to situations in which there is more than one chart on the active worksheet and more than one data series in the chart.

■ Include a check to verify that the number of data points in the charted data series is the same as the number of labels in the worksheet range. Display a warning message and terminate the procedure if the two numbers aren't the same.

■ The code given here requires that the range of labels on the worksheet consist of one column and some number of rows. You could also allow for the situation in which the labels are in one row and some number of columns.

FIG. 8.13

Drag across the range of labels, and then choose OK to put them into the chart as data labels. The chart is shown with the data labels already inserted.

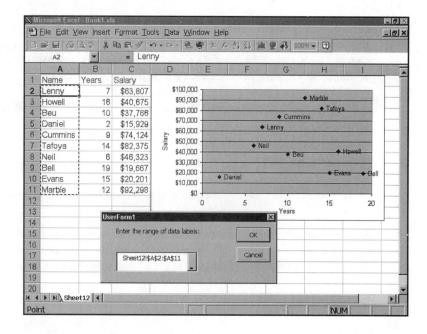

Creating Special Effects in Charts

This chapter's first section, which discussed chart axes and scales of measurement, warned you about some of the unintended consequences of putting a continuous variable on a chart's category axis. But if you have an intended consequence in mind, a category axis can be exactly the right place for a continuous variable.

For example, consider the chart shown in Figure 8.14. The chart in Figure 8.14 is a *probability plot*, often used in quality control situations. You might never have a reason to create a probability plot, but this section will examine its structure closely. The intent is not to inform you about the esoterica of probability plots, but to communicate a sense of how you can manipulate different aspects of charts to achieve effects that aren't built in.

Notice first the scale of the chart's vertical axis. The tick mark labels are evenly spaced as to the distances between them, but not as to their numeric values. Toward the top and the bottom of the vertical axis, the values indicated by the tick mark labels are more spread out; the closer you get to the center of the axis, around the 50.00% tick mark label, the values are squeezed closer together. This arrangement is typical of probability plots, and for years the users of such plots had to purchase special paper with the chart's vertical axis pre-printed for them.

Defining the Vertical Axis

Using an Excel Bar chart makes it possible to arrange the vertical axis as shown in Figure 8.14. A Bar chart, as discussed at the beginning of the chapter, treats the values on its vertical axis as category labels and the values on its horizontal axis as quantitative. If in Figure 8.14 the vertical axis were a value axis, as in a Column or XY (Scatter) chart, the values would be spaced according to their relative magnitude. This situation is shown in Figure 8.15.

FIG. 8.14
It may not look like it, but this is a Bar chart.

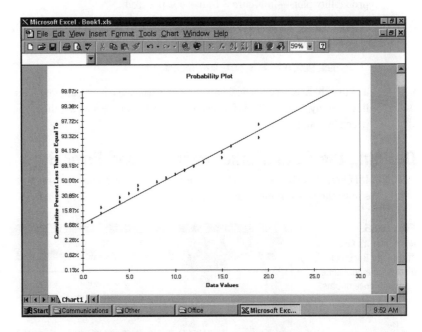

FIG. 8.15
The data in Figure 8.14 shown in an XY (Scatter) chart.

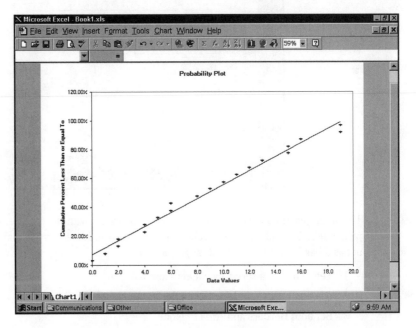

Notice the difference between Figures 8.14 and 8.15. The tick mark labels in Figure 8.15 are now spaced according to their relative magnitude, and the "squeezed" effect—required by probability plots—in Figure 8.14 has disappeared.

But the squeezing is easily accomplished with a category axis. You just create a sequence of values such as this one:

99%, 98%, 95%, 80%, 50%, 20%, 5%, 2%, 1%

and use them on the vertical category axis. Because it's a category axis, Excel spaces the quantities evenly, so that the difference between 1% and 2% appears the same as the difference between 50% and 80%.

Defining the Data Marker Patterns and Error Bars

If Figure 8.14 shows a Bar chart, where are the bars? They're there, just invisible. Figure 8.16 shows the chart immediately after it's been created.

FIG. 8.16

Right after it's first drawn, the Bar chart displays the data series as a sequence of bars.

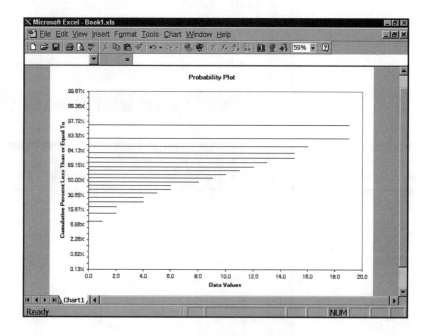

The arrangement shown in Figure 8.16 isn't consistent with the requirements of a probability plot, which demands that each data point be shown as some sort of small marker such as a dot, not as a bar. To get rid of the bars, you would:

1. Select the data series by clicking any bar.
2. Choose Format, Selected Data Series, and click the Patterns tab.
3. Set both Borders and Area to None.

The result is to remove everything in the chart's plot area. This gets rid of the bars, but of course the chart needs to indicate their location in some way.

One such way would be to attach data labels to each invisible bar. But there's a drawback to data labels. Recall that this chapter's section on Data Labels presented a VBA subroutine that attaches data labels to a chart by means of a For-Next loop. Such a loop is, of course, much faster than entering data labels manually, one by one.

But what if you have a very large number of points in the data series? The probability plot, for example, contains 600 data points. When a For-Next loop in VBA claims more and more of the computer's resources—as it does when it adds data labels—the loop slows with each additional iteration. On a P100, it can take as long as a minute to loop through 600 data points in a chart and attach a data label to each one.

This problem is more painful when, as in the case of the probability plot, it doesn't matter what the data label shows. For example, each data label could contain an "x" because all that's necessary is to show that the point exists on the chart; recall that the Bar chart's normal data markers, its bars, have been rendered invisible by setting their areas and borders to None.

Using Error Bars Instead of Data Labels

To avoid taking a full minute to attach data labels, use Error Bars instead. To do so:

1. Select the data series. Usually, you do so by clicking the series, but that's hard to do if it's invisible. To select an invisible data series, click on any visible chart component (an axis, for example) and then use the keyboard arrow keys to move from component to component until you have selected the data series. You can tell that you have it when you see its SERIES formula in the Formula Bar and its name in the Name Box.

2. Choose Format, Selected Data Series and click the Y Error Bars tab.

3. Choose either Plus or Minus error bars.

4. Choose the Fixed Value option button, enter 0 as the error amount in the edit box to the right of Fixed Value, and choose OK.

You could, of course, attach the error bars prior to making the chart's default bars invisible. But recommending that sequence would have removed the opportunity to tell you how to select an invisible data series.

Excel attaches the error bar to each data point in the series *very* quickly—so fast that you probably won't be able to see it happening. With the zero-value error bars, your chart now has a visible indicator of the location of each data point, using neither data markers nor data labels.

The intent of this section is not to show you how to create probability plots—although you will find that material useful if you are involved in any sort of quality control situation. The important point is that there is practical value to an awareness of the different properties of the axes in different types of charts.

Were you a quality control specialist, it might take a while before it occurred to you that the route to creating a probability plot in Excel begins with creating a Bar chart. But if you start your planning by thinking about the nature of the axes that are required, rather than about the default appearance of each available type of chart, you would be much closer to the solution. ●

Using Ranges

A *range* in Excel is a group of worksheet cells. Typically, the cells in the range are contiguous, forming a rectangular area of some number of rows by some number of columns—for example, C3:H6. A range need not conform to that shape. It could consist of C3:C10 and E3:E10, omitting column D. Or it could include row 3 and row 5, omitting row 4. It could even consist of a few widely scattered cells, such as B5, G24, and Z10.

But ranges such as these would be idiosyncratic, defined for some special and perhaps insidious purpose. Usually, you find yourself working with ranges that include contiguous rows and columns.

Using ranges properly is absolutely essential to efficient use of the Excel application. Chapters 10 and 11 show you how to take advantage of ranges in formulas, functions, and charts. But before you can make efficient use of ranges in those contexts, you need to know how to establish them.

An astonishingly large percentage of otherwise competent Excel users neither understand nor make full use of ranges. This chapter goes into the details of range establishment. ■

■ **Referring to ranges with reference operators**

Identify a range of cells, the combination of multiple ranges, or the intersection (the overlap) of multiple ranges.

■ **Understanding multiple selections**

Simultaneously select more than one range, and distinguish between adjacent and contiguous selections.

■ **Naming ranges**

Make ranges and formulas easier to work with by giving names to the ranges.

■ **Selecting, moving, and copying ranges quickly**

Use shortcut menus to speed up your work.

■ **Working with 3-D ranges**

Extend the reach of a range to cover multiple worksheets.

Referring to Ranges with Reference Operators

In this expression:

```
=A1 + B1
```

the plus sign is an *operator*. Besides all the arithmetic, logical, and text operators in Excel, there are three *reference* operators for ranges: the range operator, the union operator, and the intersection operator.

The *range operator* is the colon. You're used to referring to ranges such as D1 through G8 by expressions such as D1:G8. Formally, the colon establishes a range reference by encompassing all worksheet cells between and including the two named cells.

The *union operator* is the comma. This operator is implied when you make a multiple selection by selecting one range, holding down Ctrl, and selecting another range. Suppose that your multiple selection is A1:B2 and D1:E2. Used in a formula, usually with a function such as SUM, this multiple selection is represented as:

```
=SUM(A1:B2,D1:E2)
```

In many cases, including this SUM example, the comma's role as a separator of arguments to the function has the same effect as its role as a union operator. In other cases, such as this FREQUENCY example:

```
=FREQUENCY(A1:A20,B1:B4)
```

the comma acts solely as a separator of arguments. In the context of functions, the comma's role as argument separator takes precedence over its role as union operator.

The *intersection operator* is the single space. It returns the value in a cell where two ranges intersect. Figure 9.1 shows two such intersections.

In Figure 9.1, this formula in cell B11:

```
=B5:M5 D3:D7
```

returns the value in cell D5, the one cell that the two ranges have in common—where they intersect. This formula, array-entered in two cells:

```
=B4:M5 E3:E7
```

returns the values in cells E4 and E5. You will learn more about array formulas in Chapter 10. And as you will see in this chapter's section on named ranges, formulas that use intersection operators are best used when their arguments are range names instead of cell references.

▶ **See** "Using Array Formulas," **p. 188**

FIG. 9.1

Intersections can consist of one cell or of multiple cells.

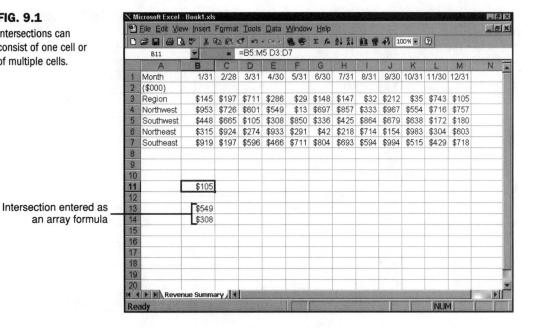

Intersection entered as an array formula

Understanding Multiple Selections

As mentioned in the prior section, you select two ranges by selecting the first (say, A1:B2), holding down Ctrl, and then selecting the second (say, D3:G5). Together, these two selected ranges are termed a *multiple selection*. Multiple selections come in different flavors, defined by whether they are *contiguous* and whether they are *adjacent*. Although people frequently use these two terms as though they were synonymous, they are not.

When you select two or more ranges that do not fully touch each other, the ranges are *non-contiguous*. Two contiguous and two non-contiguous ranges appear in Figure 9.2.

The ranges in A1:B3 and C1:D3 are contiguous. They touch at a column border, and occupy the same rows along that border. The ranges in F1:H2 and F3:H4 are contiguous. They touch at the row border and occupy the same columns along that border.

The ranges A9:B11 and D9:E11 are non-contiguous. They are separated by column C. F14:H15 and E16:G17 are non-contiguous. Although not separated by a row, they do not occupy the same columns along their row boundary.

In contrast, adjacent ranges occupy the same rows or columns; they may or may not be contiguous. Non-adjacent ranges are always non-contiguous, but they also occupy different rows or columns. Some examples appear in Figure 9.3.

FIG. 9.2

Contiguous ranges touch at all points along their boundaries.

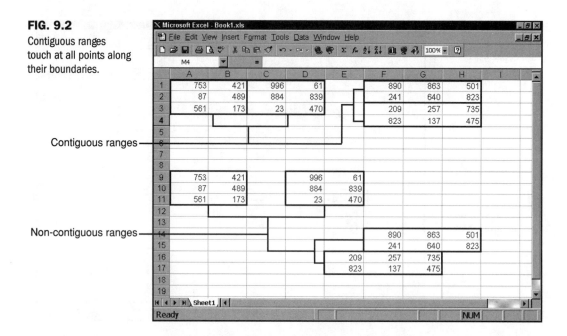

Contiguous ranges

Non-contiguous ranges

FIG. 9.3

Adjacent ranges might or might not touch at all points along their boundaries.

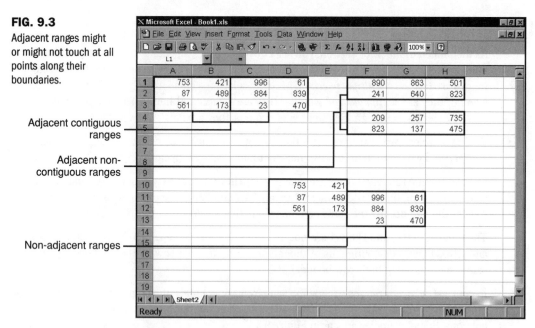

Adjacent contiguous ranges

Adjacent non-contiguous ranges

Non-adjacent ranges

The ranges in A1:B3 and C1:D3 are adjacent: They occupy the same rows. It happens that they are also contiguous, because they touch at each row along their column boundary.

The ranges in F1:H2 and F4:H5 are adjacent: They occupy the same rows. They are non-contiguous, because they do not touch at each row.

D10:E12 and F11:G13 are not adjacent: They do not occupy the same rows. Ranges that are not adjacent cannot be contiguous.

Is this just semantics? No, there's a functional difference. Suppose that you selected F1:H2 and F4:H5—adjacent ranges—and chose Edit, Copy. You could now select some other cell and choose Edit, Paste.

But if you chose D10:E12 and F11:G13—non-adjacent ranges—and chose Edit, Copy, you would get the error message That command cannot be used on multiple selections. This is a misleading message. If you couldn't use Copy on multiple selections, then you couldn't use it on F1:H2 and F4:H5. You cannot copy *non-adjacent* multiple selections.

There's a useful aspect to copying and pasting an adjacent multiple selection, shown in Figure 9.4. Suppose that you made the multiple adjacent selection A1:C2 and A4:C5. After making the selection, you choose Edit, Copy, then select A8 and choose Edit, Paste. The intervening row is removed, and the paste goes into A8:C11.

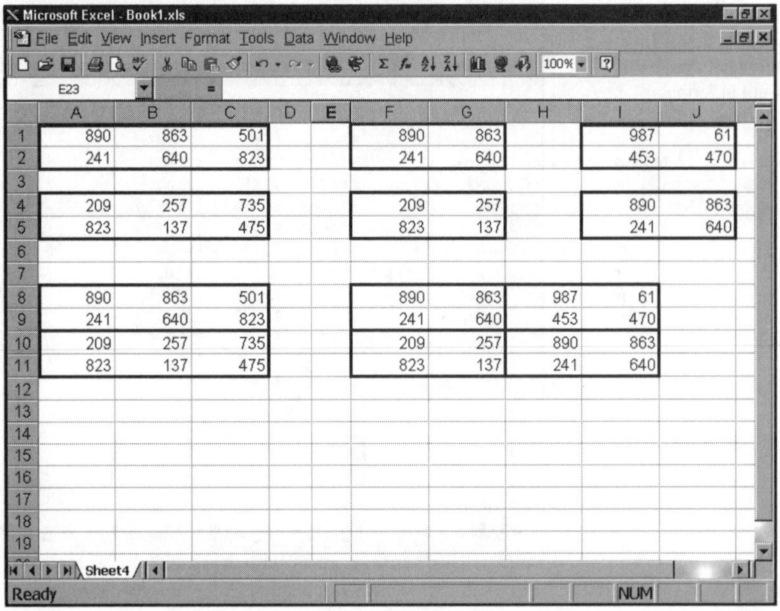

Part III
Ch 9

FIG. 9.4

Excel removes intervening rows and columns when it pastes a multiple adjacent selection.

This effect is also shown in Figure 9.4 for the ranges F1:G2, I1:J2, F4:G5, and I4:J5. Copied as a multiple selection and pasted starting at F8, both the intervening row 3 and the intervening column H are ignored in the paste.

TIP Keep this tip in mind when you are looking for a way to reduce the size of a worksheet. Many users lay out worksheets using empty columns and empty rows as separators. While they are sometimes necessary for the purpose of formatting reports, these separators add to the file size by pushing used rows down and used columns over. You might want to reduce the file size, or you might want to copy the information elsewhere without taking the empty rows and columns along with the data.

Naming Ranges

As you will see, you can assign a name to a range. That name has two important properties:

- The name itself—for example, Revenues or Dates
- What the name refers to—the cell references to the range that's represented by the name

Figure 9.5 shows two examples.

FIG. 9.5

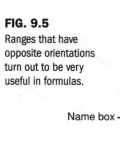

Ranges that have opposite orientations turn out to be very useful in formulas.

Name box ⎯

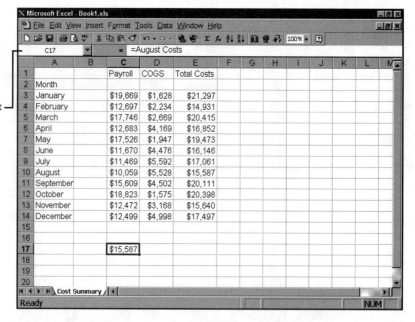

The worksheet range E3:E14 has been given the name Costs. The name is Costs; Costs refers to E3:E14.

The worksheet range C10:E10 has been given the name August. The name is August; August refers to C10:E10.

As you will see in Chapter 12, this particular setup lends itself to formulas that are self-documenting, such as this one:

`=August Costs`

There are several ways to assign a name to a range. For example, to name the range August shown in Figure 9.5, you might:

- Select C10:E10, and choose Insert, Name, Define. Type **August** in the Names in Workbook edit box. The Refers To edit box is filled in by default with the address of the range that you began by selecting.
- Select the range, click the Name box (see Figure 9.5), and type the name **August**.
- On the worksheet, type the range's name in a cell directly above or immediately left of the range. Select the range, including the cell with the name, and choose Insert, Name, Create. Fill the Top Row or Left Column check box, or both check boxes, and click OK.

There are other ways to define range names, and there are subtle differences among the three methods mentioned here. Chapter 10 discusses some of these differences. For now, simply be aware that you have at your disposal several ways to name ranges.

Now that you've gone to the trouble of naming the range, how do you benefit? Here are just a few of the ways:

- You named a range as Revenues. In some cell outside that range, enter

    =SUM(Revenues)

    to get the total of the values in the range. (If you see that you would cause a circular reference by entering the formula within the range itself, then you understand this material.) Or you gave a range the name ProductSold. In a range of cells, enter as an array formula:

    =FREQUENCY(ProductSold, ProductSold)

    to get a count of each unique value in ProductSold.

- Click the Name box. Select from the drop-down list the name of a range that you've already defined and press Enter, or double-click the name. The range that the name refers to is immediately selected.
- Enter many formulas, each of which uses the name Revenues in some way. Later, it becomes necessary to add another value to Revenues. So, just re-define the reference of the Revenues range. All the formulas recalculate to take account of the new value.
- Feel free to forget a range's name. If you need it in a formula, start typing the formula. When you reach the point that you need the range name, choose Insert, Name, Paste, and select the name from the list. (You can also get to the name from the Name box.) This also helps you avoid mis-keying.
- Suppose that you have established several range names. Before doing that, you had already entered formulas that refer to those ranges by means of cell references. Now, select the formulas and choose Insert, Name, Apply. The range names replace their associated cell references in the formulas.

  ▶ **See** "Using Array Formulas," **p. 188**
  ▶ **See** "Using Lists in Formulas," **p. 242**

Part III

Ch 9

Selecting, Moving, and Copying Ranges Quickly

Excel provides almost 90 keyboard shortcuts just for editing and moving data around. Nobody knows them all, much less uses them all.

We each have our own particular, preferred ways to get around in a worksheet. The way that we develop a set of worksheet navigation methods is usually haphazard—issues such as our routine tasks, how we structure worksheets, and pure accident determine the ones we use.

No one knows for sure how many Excel users routinely employ Ctrl+Shift+| to select cells that differ from the comparison cell in the same row as the active cell in each column. Almost certainly, the number of such users is both positive and non-vast.

As to ranges, though, there are just a few keyboard shortcuts and mouse actions that are widely applicable. For example, every user needs to be able to select a range and get to the end of a range.

Selecting Ranges

When the range you're interested in is completely visible on the screen, it's best to use the mouse along with the keyboard. You select the cell in the upper-left corner of the range, hold down the Shift key, and select the cell in the range's lower-right corner. Of course, you can also just drag from the upper-left to the lower-right with the mouse pointer as you hold down the mouse button.

This sequence highlights the entire range. Suppose, though, that the range you're interested in isn't entirely visible on your screen, *and that it contains data*. You can quickly select the entire region using Ctrl+*. (A normal 101 keyboard has an asterisk on the numeric keypad. If your keyboard doesn't have that asterisk, you can use Ctrl+Shift+8, because a Shift+8 is an asterisk.) Figure 9.6 shows some examples of regions, which are different from ranges.

In Figure 9.6, the range A1:B4 is a region. You can select any cell in that range and press Ctrl+* to select A1:B4. Cell B4 would be part of the region because it is diagonally contiguous to cell A3.

In contrast, if you selected cell D6 and pressed Ctrl+*, only D6 would be selected. There is no cell containing data that is contiguous to D6.

But if you began by selecting C5 and pressed Ctrl+*, the range A1:D6 would be selected. D6 contains data and is diagonally contiguous to C5. The same is true of B4. And because A3 is diagonally contiguous to B4, A1:A3 is also selected.

Cell G5 would never be part of the region, because there are at least two empty cells between it and any other cell that contains data.

So Ctrl+* helps you select a range of data that constitutes a region. Various cells in the region can be empty, and they will still be selected. The full region, of course, need not be visible on the screen.

FIG. 9.6

A region is a range of the cells that contain data and that are touching.

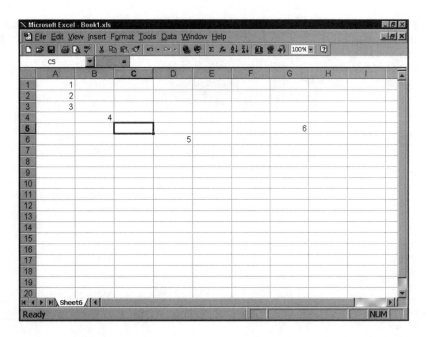

What about selecting data in a single row or a single column? Again, when the entire set of cells you want to select is visible, it's easy to select them all by means of clicking the first cell, holding down Shift, and clicking the last cell.

But if they're not all visible, you use the combination of the Ctrl key and one of the keyboard's arrow keys (see Figure 9.7).

Suppose that you're in cell A2 and you want to get to the final date in column A. Use Ctrl+↓. Assuming that no cell between A2 and A120 is empty, but that A121 is empty, Ctrl+↓ takes you to A120.

Similarly, you might be in B1 and you want to get to the final, rightmost value in row 1. If all cells between B1 and Z1 contain data, Ctrl+→ takes you to Z1.

N O T E　The combination of Ctrl and a direction key does not select a range, but simply selects the last value that Excel encounters. To select A2:A120, starting from A2 and assuming that each cell in A2:A120 contains data, Ctrl+Shift+↓ selects that entire range. Ctrl+Shift+→ would select B1:Z1, under the same sort of assumption. ■

In words, the Ctrl key in combination with the direction key means "find the final non-empty cell in this direction." The Shift key, used in combination with the Ctrl and direction keys, means "select the starting cell, all the intervening cells, and the final non-empty cell in this direction."

FIG. 9.7
The column of dates extends down to A120. The row of products extends to Z1.

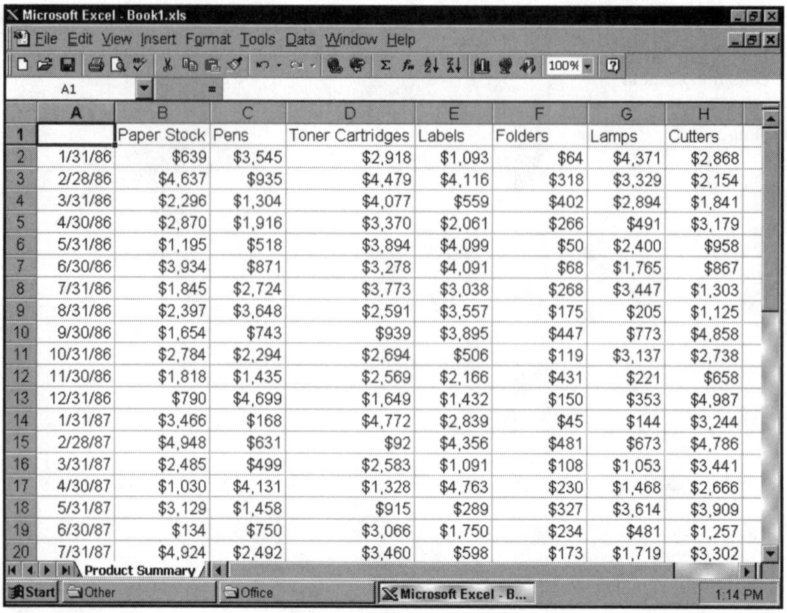

	A	B	C	D	E	F	G	H
1		Paper Stock	Pens	Toner Cartridges	Labels	Folders	Lamps	Cutters
2	1/31/86	$639	$3,545	$2,918	$1,093	$64	$4,371	$2,868
3	2/28/86	$4,637	$935	$4,479	$4,116	$318	$3,329	$2,154
4	3/31/86	$2,296	$1,304	$4,077	$559	$402	$2,894	$1,841
5	4/30/86	$2,870	$1,916	$3,370	$2,061	$266	$491	$3,179
6	5/31/86	$1,195	$518	$3,894	$4,099	$50	$2,400	$958
7	6/30/86	$3,934	$871	$3,278	$4,091	$68	$1,765	$867
8	7/31/86	$1,845	$2,724	$3,773	$3,038	$268	$3,447	$1,303
9	8/31/86	$2,397	$3,648	$2,591	$3,557	$175	$205	$1,125
10	9/30/86	$1,654	$743	$939	$3,895	$447	$773	$4,858
11	10/31/86	$2,784	$2,294	$2,694	$506	$119	$3,137	$2,738
12	11/30/86	$1,818	$1,435	$2,569	$2,166	$431	$221	$658
13	12/31/86	$790	$4,699	$1,649	$1,432	$150	$353	$4,987
14	1/31/87	$3,466	$168	$4,772	$2,839	$45	$144	$3,244
15	2/28/87	$4,948	$631	$92	$4,356	$481	$673	$4,786
16	3/31/87	$2,485	$499	$2,583	$1,091	$108	$1,053	$3,441
17	4/30/87	$1,030	$4,131	$1,328	$4,763	$230	$1,468	$2,666
18	5/31/87	$3,129	$1,458	$915	$289	$327	$3,614	$3,909
19	6/30/87	$134	$750	$3,066	$1,750	$234	$481	$1,257
20	7/31/87	$4,924	$2,492	$3,460	$598	$173	$1,719	$3,302

Copying and Moving Ranges

When you have selected a range, it's often because you want to copy or move it elsewhere. There are a few special tools you can use to speed things up.

You're doubtless familiar with moving a range by putting the mouse pointer on its border, pressing the left mouse button, and dragging the mouse pointer to another location. This sequence emulates the effect of choosing Edit, Cut; selecting another cell; and choosing Edit, Paste.

You can do this only if you allow cell drag-and-drop. To do so, choose Tools, Options and select the Edit tab. Then, select the Allow Cell Drag and Drop check box. To protect yourself against the accidental loss of existing data in the destination range, select the Alert Before Overwriting Cells check box. (The default is that both of these check boxes are checked.)

But suppose you click the right mouse button instead of the left mouse button when the pointer is on a range border. Then, when you drag the range to a new location, a shortcut menu appears when you release the button (see Figure 9.8).

N O T E   You can't drag the border of a multiple selection, because a multiple selection does not have a border to drag. For the same reason, you can't get to the shortcut menu by dragging a multiple selection's border. ■

FIG. 9.8

One shortcut menu encompasses a variety of worksheet menu sequences.

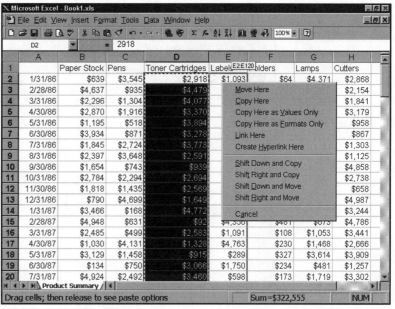

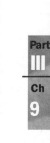

Notice that the shortcut menu enables you to:

- *Move Here*. This has the same effect as choosing Edit, Cut and then Edit, Paste.

- *Copy Here*. This has the same effect as choosing Edit, Copy and then Edit, Paste.

- *Copy Here as Values Only*. This has the same effect as Edit, Copy and then Edit, Paste Special, Values. It is a convenient way to convert formulas to values. Just right-click the range border, drag it one column or row in some direction, and then drag it back to its original location. When you choose the Copy Here as Values Only item from the shortcut menu, Excel converts the formulas in the range to values.

- *Copy Here as Formats Only*. This has the same effect as using the Format Painter: The formats of the cells in the originally selected range are copied to the new range.

- *Link Here*. This creates one or more reference formulas. Suppose you began by selecting cell A1. When you right-click, drag, and choose Link Here, Excel inserts the absolute reference formula =$A$1. But if you begin by selecting A1:A2, Link Here inserts the relative reference formulas =A1 and =A2.

- *Create Hyperlink Here*. If the workbook has not yet been saved, this shortcut menu item has no effect. If the workbook has been saved, it creates a hyperlink to the upper-left cell in the range that you began by selecting. The hyperlink *exists* in each cell in the range that you have dragged to, but it *references* the range's upper-left cell only (see Figure 9.9). You can alter the target's reference by right-clicking the hyperlink, choosing Hyperlink from the shortcut menu, and selecting Edit Hyperlink from the cascading menu.

FIG. 9.9

Although the hyperlink's target spans several cells, the hyperlink takes the user to the target's upper-left cell only.

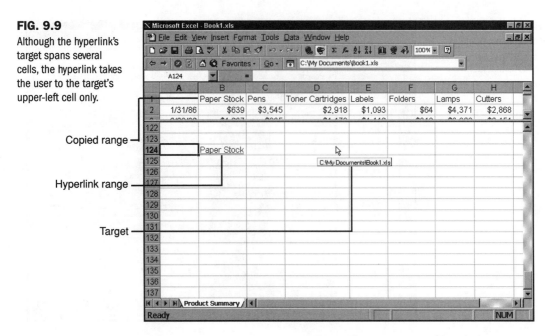

Copied range

Hyperlink range

Target

Some discussion of inserting ranges is necessary before continuing with the items in the short-cut menu that appears when you right-click and drag a range's border. Suppose that you copy or cut a range of cells, and then select a cell in a non-blank range. This situation is shown in Figure 9.10.

FIG. 9.10

A simple Paste overwrites the information in the destination range.

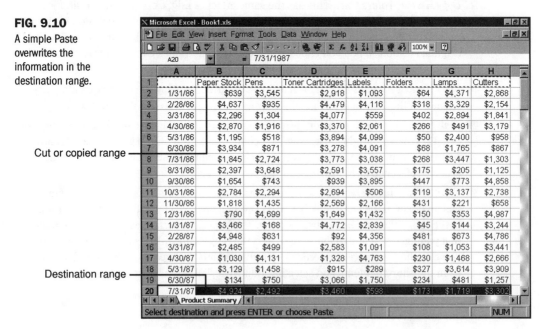

Cut or copied range

Destination range

If you now choose Edit, Paste, the cells in the destination range are replaced with information from the cut or copied range. But if instead you choose Insert, Copied Cells (or Insert, Cut Cells), then you can arrange for cells in the destination range to shift right or down. This makes room for the cut or copied range without the loss of existing information (see Figure 9.11).

FIG. 9.11

Choosing to insert cut or copied cells moves existing information in the destination out of the way.

Cut or Copied range

Destination range

Down-shifted cells

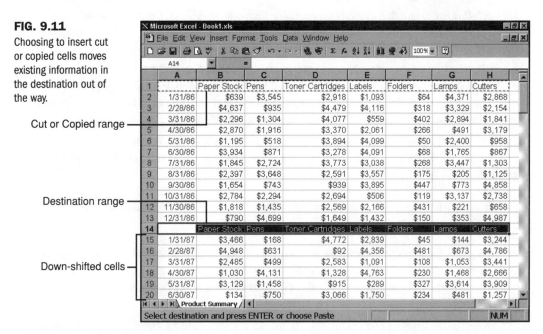

After you choose Insert, Copied (or Cut) Cells, an Insert Paste dialog box appears, allowing you to choose between shifting cells right and shifting cells down.

This technique has broad applicability. You might use it to insert monthly data between quarterly data in an existing report. For example, you could copy data for January through March, and Insert Paste that information onto the existing range for Quarters 2 through 4, shifting that range down or right as necessary. Or you could use it to insert data into the proper location in a sorted list, rather than pasting the data to the end of the list and then resorting.

These processes—cutting or copying before pasting, shifting cells right or shifting them down—are included in the range drag shortcut menu (refer to Figure 9.8):

- *Shift Down and Copy.* This has the same effect as choosing Edit, Copy; then Insert, Copied Cells; and selecting Shift Cells Down in the Insert Paste dialog box.
- *Shift Right and Copy.* This has the same effect as choosing Edit, Copy; then Insert, Copied Cells; and selecting Shift Cells Right in the Insert Paste dialog box.
- *Shift Down and Move.* This has the same effect as choosing Edit, Cut; then Insert, Cut Cells; and selecting Shift Cells Down in the Insert Paste dialog box.

Part

III

Ch

9

■ *Shift Right and Move.* This has the same effect as choosing Edit, Cut; then Insert, Cut Cells; and selecting Shift Cells Right in the Insert Paste dialog box.

Working with 3-D Ranges

A *3-D range* is one that extends across more than one worksheet. Consider the selection A1:B2 on Sheet1, and A1:B2 on Sheet2, and A1:B2 on Sheet3, and so on. This is a 3-D range, covering the same set of rows and columns across multiple worksheets.

Suppose that your workbook contains three worksheets. You establish a 3-D range by making a normal range selection on Sheet1. Then, hold down Ctrl and click the sheet tabs for Sheet2 and Sheet3. When you do so, each sheet tab becomes selected as you click it—although its sheet does not become visible. In effect, you're making a multiple selection across worksheets.

The sequence need not be precisely as described in the prior paragraph. You could begin by holding down Ctrl and clicking the sheet tabs, and then selecting the range of interest on the visible sheet.

NOTE If you can't see the sheet tabs, choose Tools, Options; select the View tab; and select the Sheet Tabs check box. ■

To select a subset of the sheets in the workbook, you can also hold down the Shift key as you click the tab of the final contiguous sheet that you want to select. For example, if you have four sheets in the workbook, you select sheets 1–3 by clicking Sheet1's tab, holding down Shift, and clicking Sheet3's tab.

A quick way to select all the sheets in the workbook is to right-click any sheet tab and choose Select All Sheets from the shortcut menu. The act of selecting more than one sheet is also termed *grouping* sheets; you can use the same shortcut menu to ungroup the selection.

Modifying the Characteristics of 3-D Ranges

Once you have made a 3-D selection, most operations that you perform on the visible portion of the selection also take place in the remainder of the selection (see Figure 9.12).

In Figure 9.12, each sheet in the multiple selection is shown in a different window. Entering the value **January** in cell A1 of the active sheet causes the same value to appear in cell A1 of the remaining sheets in the 3-D range.

Selecting a Currency format for the selected range on the active sheet assigns that format to the same range on the remaining sheets. Inserting new row in the range on the active sheet inserts a new row in the remaining sheets.

Entering a formula in the 3-D range causes that formula to appear on the remaining selected sheets. If the formula uses cells on the active sheet as its arguments, the formulas on the remaining sheets use the same cell references—but because those cells might have different values on the different sheets, the results of the formulas might also be different.

FIG. 9.12

Set the values or formats of the 3-D range or insert rows and columns by performing the operation on the active sheet only.

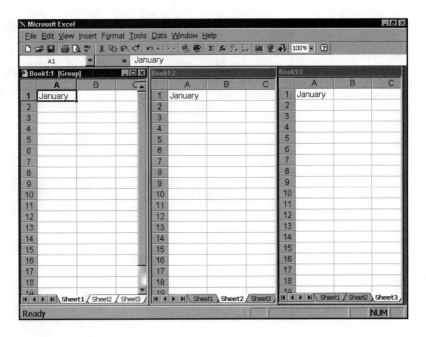

Part

III

Ch

9

Using 3-D Ranges in Formulas

It's likely that the most common and effective use of a 3-D range is to consolidate information from multiple worksheets into one consolidation range on a single sheet. Just as you use single-sheet named ranges in formulas, you can also use 3-D ranges in formulas to roll up information across multiple sheets. Figure 9.13 shows an example.

Each worksheet in the workbook has the same layout—that is, the Sales figure for modems in January is in cell B2 in the Oregon worksheet, and it's found in the same location in the Washington worksheet. This makes it very easy to define and use a 3-D range named JanuaryModems. To define the name:

1. From any worksheet in the workbook, choose Insert, Name, Define.

2. In the Names in Workbook edit box, type **JanuaryModems**.

3. Click the Refers To edit box. Click the sheet tab for the Oregon worksheet, hold down the Shift key, and click the Washington worksheet tab.

4. Click in cell B2 of the active worksheet, and choose OK.

The Refers To edit box now contains:

=Oregon:Washington!$B$2

as the reference for the 3-D range named JanuaryModems. You then obtain the sum of sales for modems in January across the 3-D range by means of:

=SUM(JanuaryModems)

FIG. 9.13

Consider using 3-D ranges whenever you consolidate information, such as department budgets or regional sales, into a single range.

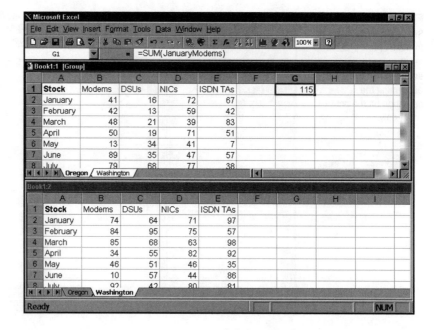

Notice the use of the range operator between the sheet names in the 3-D reference. Its effect is analogous to its effect in an ordinary cell reference—that is, it specifies everything between and including the two named worksheets.

Now suppose that you want to insert a new worksheet for Colorado, laid out similarly to the Oregon and Washington worksheets. If you insert the Colorado sheet between the Oregon sheet and the Washington sheet, the 3-D reference automatically captures the Colorado sheet. The range named `JanuaryModems` refers to:

`=Oregon:Washington!$B$2`

and the colon specifies the inclusion of every sheet in the workbook, between and including Oregon and Washington.

When the worksheets in a 3-D range are *not* laid out identically, you might not be able to use the 3-D range as named previously. Suppose that on the Oregon worksheet, modem sales in January were in cell B2, but were in cell C3 on the Washington worksheet. Then, to get their sum, you'd need to use:

`=SUM(Oregon!B2,Washington!C3)`

You could define the 3-D range name `JanuaryModems` as referring to:

`=Oregon!B2,Washington!C3`

but then Excel is unable to evaluate that range name when it's used in a function. This formula, for example:

`=SUM(JanuaryModems)`

returns the #VALUE! error value when the name refers to different cells on the comprising worksheets.

There are a couple of other restrictions on the use of 3-D references. You cannot use them as arguments to array formulas (see Chapter 10), nor can you use them as arguments to a formula that contains an implicit intersection. For example, if the name SalesTotal refers to A1:A10 on one sheet only, then this single-cell formula:

```
=.5*SalesTotal
```

returns a valid result when it's entered in some cell in rows 1–10. The intersection of the row where the formula is entered with the column of values in SalesTotal is implicit in the formula (so, this sort of formula uses what's termed an *implicit intersection*).

But if SalesTotal is a named 3-D range covering more than one worksheet, the formula fails and again returns #VALUE!.

Whether the range that you've named exists on one sheet or is a 3-D reference, the main value of the name is its use in formulas. Chapter 10 shows you the best ways to profit from the small amount of effort required to name a range.

TROUBLESHOOTING

If nothing happens when you try to create a hyperlink by right-clicking and dragging, make sure that you have saved the workbook before you try to create a hyperlink in it.

It's also possible that you've created the hyperlink, but can't see it. When you create a hyperlink by right-click and drag, the cell containing the hyperlink might contain no value and thus appear empty. Right-click the cell and choose Hyperlink, Select Hyperlink. Or, select a contiguous cell and use an arrow key to move into the hyperlink's cell. Then type some value or label to make the hyperlink overt. Best is to start by typing a label in the cell; put a hyperlink in the cell only after it has a label.

CHAPTER 10

Advanced Work with Formulas

The heart of any spreadsheet application such as Excel, as you doubtless know, is the evaluation of formulas. What made the very first spreadsheet a killer app was its ability to automatically update calculated values based on new inputs to formulas.

Formulas go much further than simple sums and differences. You use different types of cell referencing to make it easier to extend formulas. A special kind of formula, the *array formula*, returns results that are otherwise very difficult to obtain. Some formulas establish links to other worksheets or workbooks. Any of these formulas can result in different kinds of errors—errors that you can fix if you know their meaning and how to repair them. ▪

Referencing cells

Learn how to use absolute, relative, and mixed references to achieve different results.

Using array formulas

Find out how to present an array, rather than a single value, to a worksheet function.

Naming formulas

Make your formulas easier to use and understand by giving them meaningful names.

Linking formulas

Establish links within and between workbooks, and track down phantom links.

Auditing formulas

Find a formula's precedents and a cell's dependents, and locate invalid data.

Referencing Cells

The simplest kind of formula that you can use in Excel is along these lines:

```
= 10 + 5
```

Of course, the simpler the formula, the less useful it is, and so you normally use formulas such as this one:

```
= A1 + B1
```

where the formula refers to values found in cells A1 and B1. The way that you choose to express these cell references controls how the formula behaves when you copy it to another location.

Absolute References

Suppose that instead of entering this formula:

```
= A1 + B1
```

you entered this one:

```
= $A$1 + $B$1
```

Both formulas return the same result—if cell A1 contains the value 10, and B1 contains 5, then both formulas return 15. But the dollar signs in the second formula make its cell references *absolute*. That is, if you copied that formula and pasted it to a different cell, the formula would remain unchanged. The effect is the same if you drag the cell's fill handle (the black square at the cell's lower-right corner): No adjustment to the cell references.

The basic notion is that the cell references with dollar signs are fixed, or absolute; they do not change when you copy the formula.

Most people use the *A1* reference style in their worksheets. This reference style causes Excel to refer to columns by a letter and to rows by a number. At times, it's handy to use the *R1C1* reference style, which causes Excel to refer to both rows and columns by numbers. For example, you might want to set a VBA range object variable using the `Cells(RowNumber, ColumnNumber)` syntax. That's a lot easier to do if, on the worksheet, you see a number at the head of a column, instead of trying to figure out the number of column EH.

You select the A1 or the R1C1 reference style by choosing Tools, Options and clicking the General tab. Then, choose the R1C1 style by selecting its check box, or the A1 style by clearing it. If you choose the R1C1 reference style, an absolute reference formula that adds the value in cell A1 to that in B1 appears as:

```
=R1C1+R1C2
```

Relative References

In contrast, cell references without dollar signs are *relative references*. Suppose that you enter this formula:

```
= A1 + B1
```

in cell A3. If you now copied cell A3 and pasted it to cell C3—two columns to the right—the cell references would adjust, so that the formula in C3 would be:

```
= C1 + D1
```

That is, as the formula moves, so do its references. The references are *relative* to the cell where the formula exists. As entered in cell A3, the reference to cell A1 is to a cell that's two rows up from and in the same column as the formula itself. When you copy the formula two columns to the right, into cell C3, the reference to A1 becomes a reference to C1. The reference is relative to the location of the formula.

If you use the R1C1 style, Excel depicts the relative reference as:

```
=R[-2]C+R[-2]C[1]
```

That is, the value found two rows up in the same column, plus the value found two rows up and one column to the right.

It's important to understand that Excel adjusts cell references only when you copy a cell, or when you autofill by dragging the cell's fill handle. If, instead of using Edit, Copy you use Edit, Cut, relative cell references remain the same when you Edit, Paste into another cell.

Mixed References

You can mix absolute with relative references in the same formula. Here's a simple example:

```
= A$1 + B$1
```

In the formula, the column references are relative, and the row references are absolute. If you copy and paste the formula into a cell to the right or left, the column references will adjust accordingly. But if you copy and paste it into another row, the absolute row references will not adjust. So, if you enter the formula into cell D1 and then copy it into cell E2, the formula in cell E2 becomes:

```
= B$1 + C$1
```

Here's a slightly more complicated example:

```
= $A$1 + B$1
```

If you enter this formula in cell C3, and then copy it to cell D3, it becomes:

```
= $A$1 + C$1
```

The absolute column reference $A does not change, but the relative reference to column B adjusts to column C. No matter where you copy the formula, both absolute row references remain the same.

Mixed references become really valuable in formulas that use functions. For example, the formula:

```
= SUM($A$1:B$1)
```

uses Excel's SUM() function to return the total of the values in cells A1 and B1. Suppose that you enter the formula in cell B2, and then copy and paste it into cells C2 and D2. Cell C2 would then contain:

= SUM($A$1:C$1)

and cell D2 would contain:

= SUM($A$1:D$1)

This is a useful way to obtain a series of running totals whose start point is always the same cell, but whose end point depends on how far they're copied. You might use this technique to obtain, for example, a running total of revenue by month.

> **TIP** It's inconvenient to use the mouse pointer to insert and delete dollar signs. It's far easier to highlight a cell reference in the Formula Bar by dragging across the reference and then pressing the F4 key repeatedly. This cycles the reference among both absolute, mixed (relative column and absolute row), mixed (relative row and absolute column), and both relative.

Using Array Formulas

An *array formula* is a special kind of formula, one that either returns an array of values or that takes an array as an argument (an *argument* is what the formula operates on; in = A1 + B1, both A1 and B1 are the formula's arguments).

Key to understanding array formulas are two concepts:

- When you want to use a formula in multiple cells, and each of those cells should display a different value, use an array formula.
- When you want to supply an array as an argument to a function that doesn't normally expect one, use an array formula.

Using Functions that Return Arrays

Some of Excel's functions require that you use them in array formulas. For example, the statistical function LINEST() returns an array of values to the worksheet, five rows high and two or more columns wide. To use LINEST() properly, you need to follow this sequence:

1. Select a range such as F1:G5. This range, with more than one column and up to five rows, conforms to the requirements of the LINEST() function.

2. Type the formula in the Formula Bar. It might be:

   =LINEST(A1:A20,B1:C20,,TRUE)

3. Hold down the Ctrl and Shift keys, and as you are holding them down press Enter. This is called *array-entering* the formula.

After you have followed these steps, you will notice that:

- The cells in the range you selected before entering the formula now contain different values.
- The formula as shown in the Formula Bar is surrounded by curly braces.

The curly braces around the formula indicate that Excel has treated the formula as an array formula. Do not type the braces yourself—if you do, Excel treats the formula as a text entry.

Most of the functions that require you to array-enter them are used specifically for matrix algebra and statistical analysis. But one matrix algebra function, TRANSPOSE(), has broad applicability. Figure 10.1 shows an example.

FIG. 10.1

Use TRANSPOSE() to reorient a range's rows and columns.

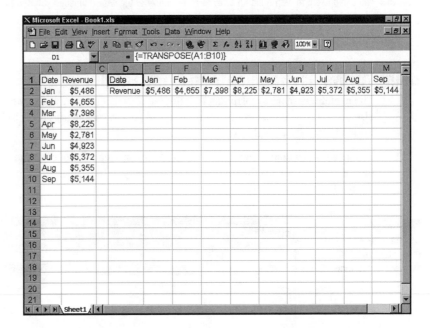

There are many good reasons to show each month in a different row, as in A1:B10 of Figure 10.1. Worksheets have more rows than columns, and you might have too many data points to put each month in a different column. Perhaps more likely, you have used Excel to open a text file that's created by a different application—one that orients the data with each month in a different row.

But formal reports normally show each month in a different column: We're used to seeing dates progress from left to right. This orientation is also shown in Figure 10.1 in cells D1:M2. One way to reorient the data is to select A1:B10; choose Edit, Copy; select cell D1; choose Edit, Paste Special; select the Transpose check box; and click OK.

But this method pastes values. What if the data in A1:B10 changed? You'd want the information in D1:M2 also to change. So, use the TRANSPOSE() function in an array formula:

1. Select cells D1:M2.

2. In the Formula Bar, type:

   =TRANSPOSE(A1:B10)

3. Press Ctrl+Shift+Enter.

Now, if you need to change a value in A1:B10, that change is reflected in D1:M2. Notice that Excel has added the curly braces around the formula. Also notice that each value in the array formula's range is different, even though you entered only one formula.

 Prior to Excel 97, Excel's Function Wizard (now termed *Paste Function*) did not support array formulas. You could use it to help build an array formula, but after the wizard finished you had to re-enter the formula with Ctrl+Shift+Enter. In Excel 97, though, you can hold down Ctrl+Shift as you click the Paste Function's OK button to complete the array formula.

Using Arrays as Arguments to Array Formulas

The usefulness of array formulas isn't limited to returning arrays to a worksheet range. You also use array formulas when you want to use an array as an argument to a function that normally expects a single value.

Suppose that you have a worksheet range that contains a list of customers, and a corresponding range that contains the number of hours that you have worked for each customer (see Figure 10.2).

FIG. 10.2

Use an array formula to create a conditional sum.

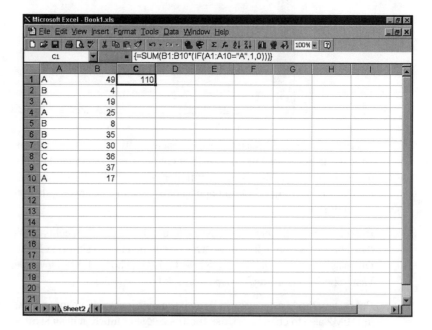

You'd like to get the total number of hours that you have worked for customer A. To do so, array-enter this formula:

```
{=SUM(B1:B10*(IF(A1:A10="A",1,0)))}
```

As shown in cell C1 of Figure 10.2, this formula returns 110. What is it up to?

A useful way to understand an array formula is to break it up into its components. After you have array-entered the formula, drag across this portion in the Formula Bar:

```
IF(A1:A10="A",1,0)
```

When you have highlighted this component, press the F9 key. Doing so causes Excel to evaluate the highlighted portion of the formula and display the result. In this case, the result is:

```
{1;0;1;1;0;0;0;0;0;1}
```

The IF function in the formula specifies that when a value in A1:A10 is an "A", return 1; otherwise, return 0. When evaluated, the IF returns an array of 1s and 0s.

Once it has the 1s and 0s, the formula multiples that array by the values in B1:B10. A value in B1:B10 multiplied by 1 returns that value; a value in B1:B10 multiplied by 0 returns zero. To see the result, drag across this portion in the Formula Bar:

```
B1:B10*(IF(A1:A10="A",1,0))
```

and press the F9 key. The result is:

```
{49;0;19;25;0;0;0;0;0;17}
```

This array contains the number of hours you worked if the associated client is "A", and zero otherwise. Finally, starting the array formula with the SUM function returns the sum of the values in the array—110 total hours worked for client A.

Why is it necessary to array-enter the formula? Because the IF function does not normally expect to receive an array as an argument. Pressing Ctrl+Shift+Enter, instead of just Enter, causes Excel to evaluate the entire array, perform the multiplication and summation, and return the complete result in cell C1.

> **N O T E** If you examine the partial results of an array formula by highlighting and pressing F9, be sure to finish by pressing Esc or clicking the Cancel button on the Formula Bar. Otherwise, Excel saves the formula with the displayed values instead of with the function that creates the values. ■

Using Array Constants

Usually, you supply a range of cells as an argument to an array formula. At times, though, it can be handy to supply an array of constant values.

Suppose that you need to obtain the day of the week today, one year from today and two years from today. The WEEKDAY() function helps you do that. The default version of this function returns a 1 for Sunday through a 7 for Saturday. Here's how to get the results you're after:

Part III

Ch 10

1. Select a range of cells consisting of one row and three columns.

2. Array-enter this formula in the selected range:

   `{=WEEKDAY(TODAY()+{0,365,730})}`

   to return three numbers between 1 and 7, representing particular days of the week: today, 365 days hence and 730 days hence.

3. To get the names of the days instead of their numbers, array-enter this formula in the same range:

   `{=TEXT(WxEEKDAY(TODAY()+{0,365,730}),"dddd")}`

The results are shown in cells A1:C2 of Figure 10.3.

FIG. 10.3

Use array constants when the formula's arguments won't change.

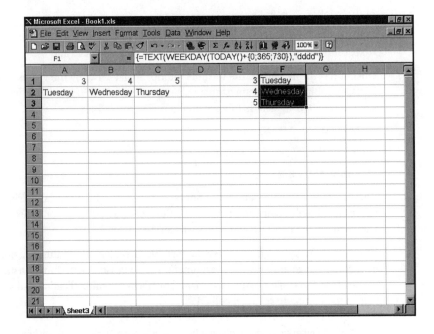

The array of constants in the formula is `{0,365,730}`. By array-entering the formula in three contiguous cells that are in the same row, you add first 0, then 365, then 730 to today's date. The WEEKDAY() function converts the resulting dates to weekday numbers. Finally, surrounding the formula with the TEXT function and a name-of-day format converts the weekday numbers to weekday names.

The commas in the array of constants cause Excel to create an array in one row. If you want an array in one column, use semicolons instead of commas. For example, cells E1:E3 in Figure 10.3 use this array formula:

`{=WEEKDAY(TODAY()+{0;365;730})}`

and cells F1:F3 use this array formula:

`{=TEXT(WEEKDAY(TODAY()+{0;365;730}),"dddd")}`

Notice that the only difference between the formulas in A1:C2 and those in E1:F3 is that commas are used in A1:C2 while semicolons are used in E1:F3.

This technique is also useful when you want to re-create on a worksheet the values represented by a chart trendline. Suppose that you insert a second-order polynomial trendline in an XY (Scatter) chart. You're satisfied with the result, and you want to put the predicted trendline values on the worksheet. One way would be to display the trendline's equation on the chart, and then to retype it into a range of worksheet cells. That's nuts. Here's a better way.

Let your XY chart's x-values be in A1:A20 and its y-values in B1:B20. To get the values implied by the trendline into your worksheet, select a range such as D1:D20 and array-enter this formula (see Figure 10.4):

`{=TREND(B1:B20,A1:A20^{1,2})}`

Part
III

Ch
10

FIG. 10.4

Use the array constant {1,2} to raise an array of values to the first and second powers.

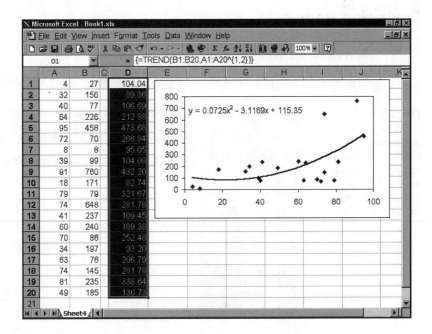

A second-order polynomial trendline predicts y-values from the original x-values and from the square of the x-values. You replicate the trendline on the worksheet by using the TREND() function. But you also need to tell the TREND() function to use the x-values raised to the first power (the original x-values) as well as the x-values raised to the second power (the squares of the x-values).

You do this in the TREND() function by means of the array constant {1,2}. The array formula raises the values in A1:A20 to the first, then the second power, and predicts new y-values from the resulting arrays.

TIP When you have entered an array formula into a range of cells, you cannot change those cells without first removing the array formula. Suppose you've entered an array formula in A1:C3. You now cannot make a new entry in cell C3 without removing the array formula. You cannot delete row 1, 2, or 3, or column A, B, or C. You cannot insert a new row between rows 1 and 3, or a new column between columns A and C.

Naming Formulas

Names are a powerful tool in Excel. By giving a range of cells in a worksheet a name, you make it easier to reference that range. By assigning a name to constant values, you make your worksheet more self-documenting. And, by assigning a name to a formula, you save time when you need to use the formula repeatedly—as well as the time spent correcting errors made when you mis-key the formula.

Reviewing Names

There are two principal methods of creating names: by means of the Name menu item in the Insert menu, and by means of the Name Box.

Suppose that a worksheet contains revenues by month, as shown in Figure 10.5.

FIG. 10.5

Giving the name Revenues to the highlighted range means that you can use the name in formulas instead of the actual cell addresses.

Name Box

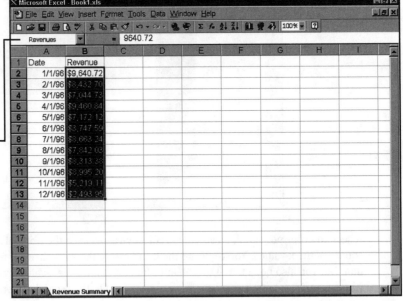

After selecting the range B2:B13 so that it is highlighted as shown in Figure 10.5, do one of two things:

- Click the Name Box and type **Revenues**. Then, press Enter. The name `Revenues` remains in the Name Box, as shown.

- Choose Insert, Name, Define. Notice that the Refers To edit box already contains the cell address of the highlighted range. Type **Revenues** in the Names in Workbook edit box, and click OK.

Now, instead of entering in a cell a formula such as this one:

`=SUM(B2:B13)`

which in itself tells you nothing about the intent of the formula, you enter:

> **=SUM(Revenues)**

which makes the meaning of the formula's result immediately apparent.

It's easy to define so many names that it becomes difficult to remember them. If so, paste the name instead of typing it:

1. Enter whatever formula or function you want, without referring to the name; rather, use an open parenthesis. For example:

   > **=AVERAGE(**

2. Choose Insert, Name, Paste. From the list of defined names, select the name that you want to use, and click OK. Then, supply a closing parenthesis and press Enter. The resulting formula is:

   `=AVERAGE(Revenues)`

The Name Box makes it easy to select a range that you have given a name. Just click the Name Box to display a drop-down list of available names, and click the name that you want. The full range that it refers to is immediately selected.

TIP The Name Box is also a convenient way to name or rename custom controls on a worksheet. After using the Forms toolbar to create, say, a check box on the sheet, right-click the check box. Its default name appears in the Name Box. Rename the control by clicking the Name Box, typing a new name, and pressing Enter.

Understanding Sheet-Level and Workbook-Level Names

There are two broad classes of names: *sheet-level* (also termed *local* names), and *workbook-level* (also termed *global* names). Sheet-level names have these characteristics:

- The name, when defined, begins with the name of the sheet it belongs to—for example, Sheet1!Revenues.

- Unqualified by its sheet name, the name is accessible from the sheet where it is defined, but only from that sheet.

Part
III

Ch
10

Suppose that you highlight B1:B12 on Sheet1; choose Insert, Name, Define; and type the name **Sheet1!Revenues** into the Names in Workbook edit box. Now, if Sheet1 is the active sheet, you can enter:

`=SUM(Revenues)`

to obtain the sum of the values in B1:B12. Notice that although the sheet portion of the name is missing in the formula, it is implicit: When you refer to the name on its "home" sheet, you need not use the sheet portion of the name.

But if you entered the same formula on Sheet2, it would return the `#NAME!` error value. Excel cannot interpret a sheet-level name when you use it on a different sheet. Instead, you would have to enter:

`=SUM(Sheet1!Revenues)`

to obtain the proper result anywhere other than on Sheet1.

There is much merit in this approach. You might want to keep monthly revenues on different worksheets, each of which represents a different fiscal year. The worksheets might be named FY1995, FY1996, and FY1997. Then, you might define a sheet-level name on each worksheet: a FY1995!Revenues, a FY1996!Revenues, a FY1997!Revenues, and so on.

In contrast, workbook-level names do not have a sheet name as part of the name. If you choose Insert, Name, Define to define the name Revenues as referring to B1:B12 on Sheet1, you can use that name anywhere in the workbook. However, you cannot have more than one workbook-level name of Revenues (or of any other name). *You* might know which one you mean, but Excel wouldn't.

After you have defined a sheet-level name, it shows up in the Define Name dialog box differently than it did in versions of Excel that precede Excel 97. The name `Sheet1!Revenues` appears in the list box with `Revenues` at the left margin and `Sheet1` at the right margin.

N O T E It is sometimes necessary to use the name of the workbook when you use a workbook-level name. For example, if you want to use the workbook-level name Revenues defined for Book1.xls in a chart's `SERIES` formula, you would have to use Book1.xls!Revenues. ■

  T I P The Name Box displays only workbook-level range names.

Naming Formulas

When you create a formula that you use repeatedly, it is convenient to give that formula a name, just as you give a name to a cell or range of cells. Then, when you want to use the formula, you just type its name into the Formula Bar, preceded by an equal sign, and press Enter. This is far more sane than retyping a complicated formula over and over.

Suppose that you have a list of customers in A1:A100, dates when they paid you in B1:B100, and payment amounts in C1:C100. The range A1:A100 is named `Customers`, B1:B100 is named `PaymentDate`, and C1:C100 is named `PaymentAmount`.

You want to know the total amount that the customer named David Smith has paid you. One way would be to enter this array formula:

`{=SUM(IF(Customers="David Smith",PaymentAmount,0))}`

The name `Customers` refers to an array of values: those in A1:A100. Because the `IF()` function does not normally expect to receive an array as an argument, it's necessary to array-enter the formula.

The `IF()` function returns an array consisting of values in the `PaymentAmount` range when the associated value in `Customers` equals `"David Smith"` and zero otherwise. The `SUM()` function returns the total of this array: David Smith's payment amounts, and zeros for all the other customers. This total, of course, is the sum of David Smith's payments. The result is shown in Figure 10.6.

Part
III

Ch
10

FIG. 10.6

The actual ranges used in the array formulas extend from row 1 through row 100.

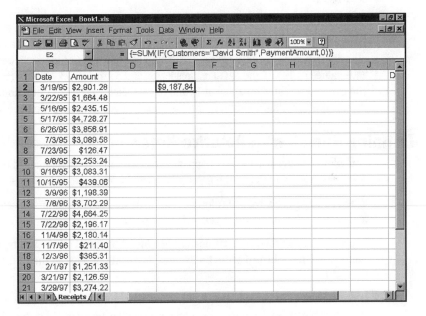

Every time that you wanted to check a particular customer's total payments, you could array-enter the formula as it's given above. But if you give the formula a name such as `TotalPayment`, you could just enter:

`=TotalPayment`

in, say, E1, when D1 contains the name of the customer whose payments you want to total. You need not array-enter the formula—when entered in a single cell, a named array formula does not need the Ctrl+Shift.

Here's the sequence to name and use the formula:

1. Choose Insert, Name, Define.
2. In the Names in Workbook box, type **TotalPayment**.
3. In the Refers To box, type:

   =SUM(IF(Customers=$D$1,PaymentAmount,0))

4. Click OK.

Now, enter any name in your customer list in cell D1. When you want the total of the payments a customer has made, select any cell on the worksheet and enter the named formula:

`=TotalPayment`

The formula returns the total of the payments made by the customer whose name is in cell $D$1.

It happens that you can dispense with the IF() function in the `TotalPayment` formula. This is equivalent:

`=SUM((Customers=D1)*PaymentAmount)`

Here, the fragment `(Customers=D1)` returns an array of TRUE and FALSE values. When you multiply that array by `PaymentAmount`, which is an array of numeric values, Excel treats the TRUE values as 1s and the FALSE values as 0s, and so the effect of the formula is the same as if you explicitly created an array of 1s and 0s by means of the IF() function. You can verify this in the usual way by highlighting in the Formula Bar and pressing the F9 key.

Defining Names with Relative References

You might wonder what would happen if you entered a relative, instead of an absolute, cell reference when you define the name as a formula. Well, magic happens.

When you use a relative cell reference in the definition of a name, the cell reference is *relative to whatever cell is active when you define the name.*

Suppose that you select cell B1 and choose Insert, Name, Define. You type the name **SameRowOneColumnLeft** in the Names in Workbook box. In the Refers To box, you type **=A1**.

If you click cell A1 instead of typing it, Excel automatically supplies the dollar signs, making the reference `=$A$1`. To make the reference relative, you can either type it yourself, delete the dollar signs that Excel supplies, or highlight the reference in the box and press the F4 key.

Suppose now that you have the value `"Anderson"` in cell A1. When you select cell B1 and enter **=SameRowOneColumnLeft**, the value that's in the same row, one column to the left of B1, appears in B1—that is, `"Anderson"`.

If you now select cell F10 and enter **=SameRowOneColumnLeft**, whatever value is in cell E10 appears in F10. Excel evaluates the formula in terms of whatever cell is active when you enter it.

Back to the formula named `TotalPayment`. Recall that column A contains customer names, column B contains payment dates, and column C contains payment amounts. If you now select cell D1 and define the name `TotalPayment` as:

```
=SUM(IF(Customers=A1,PaymentAmount,0))
```

then the formula uses the value found in the same row, three columns to the left, regardless of where on the worksheet you enter the formula.

Suppose that you're idly scanning this listing of customers and payments, and you happen to notice the name Frank Jacobs in cell A67. You wonder briefly how much Mr. Jacobs has ever paid you. You select cell D67 (same row, three columns to the right, as the value `"Frank Jacobs"` in A67) and enter this formula:

```
=TotalPayment
```

Your formula finds the name in the same row, three columns to the left, compares it to all the names in the `Customers` range, and returns the total of the payments for any instance of `"Frank Jacobs"` in the `Customers` range (see Figure 10.7).

Part III

Ch 10

FIG. 10.7
When you define a name as a formula with relative references, the formula's results depend on where you enter the formula's name.

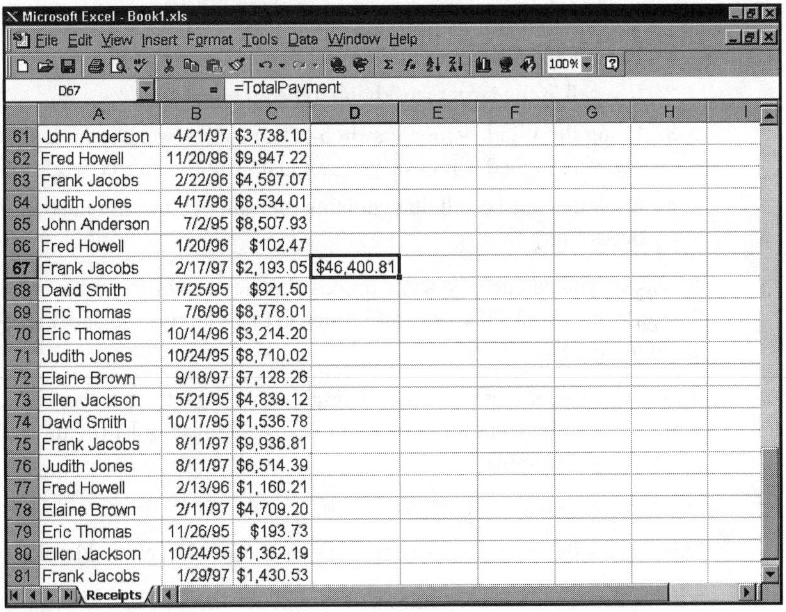

This is much easier than trying to remember the proper syntax for the formula. As a bonus, if you have trouble remembering even the formula's name, you can paste it to a cell by choosing Insert, Name, Paste. Excel supplies the equal sign for you.

Linking Formulas

Any advanced, real-world use of Excel involves multiple worksheets and workbooks. Budget rollups combine information from department budgets, usually found in different workbooks. Analyses of national sales grab data from regional workbooks. Quality analyses look to workbooks that contain manufacturing data, others that contain customer service and warranty information, and yet others that detail the purchase of raw materials.

Whatever the application, the accuracy and the timeliness of the summary depends on its linkages to the details. You normally want live—not static—links between a budget rollup and departmental budgets. When Wally in Information Systems finally gets canned, you want to show the change to salary accruals in both the IS budget and the company budget—and you want this update to happen automatically. You manage this, of course, with links.

Linking Separate Workbooks

It's convenient to term the workbook that contains the linking formula as the *target*, and to term the workbook that the formula points to as the *source*. The fastest way to create a link between the source and target workbooks is as follows:

1. Have both workbooks open, and the target workbook active.

2. In a cell in the target workbook, type an equal sign.

3. Using the Window menu, switch to the source workbook. If you have the two workbooks showing in tiled windows, you can just click the source workbook's window.

4. Click the source cell that contains the value you want to use in the target workbook, and press Enter.

Of course, you can use the same process between a source and a target worksheet that are in the same workbook. The only difference is that you use the sheet tabs instead of the Window menu to get to the source.

If you want something more than a single value from the source, you just drag across the source range that you want. For example, to get into Book1 the total of some values in Book2, you'd use this formula:

=SUM([Book2.xls]Sheet1!$A$1:$A$10)

Excel terms this sort of reference—one to another Excel workbook—an *external reference*.

If the source range is noncontiguous, you'd use the Ctrl key to help you select more than one range. The resulting formula might look like this:

=SUM([Book2.xls]Sheet1!$A$1:$A$5,[Book2.xls]Sheet1!$E$1:$E$5)

Notice the .xls extension in the workbook names. Its presence indicates that the workbooks have already been saved. When you open a new workbook—Book3, perhaps—it has no extension until you save it.

Suppose that you create a linking formula between two unsaved workbooks, with Book1 as the target and Book2 as the source. The linking formula might be:

```
=[Book2]Sheet1!$A$1
```

Now, if you choose File, Save with Book1 active, Excel displays a message asking if you want to save Book1 with references to unsaved documents. In this case, of course, the unsaved document is Book2. Your options are OK and Cancel.

If you choose OK, Book1 is saved as Book1.xls, with its reference to Book2. Subsequently, you save Book2 as Book2.xls. Later, when you open Book1.xls, it looks for Book2 in order to update the link. But, even if Book2.xls is open, Book1.xls can't find it; it's looking for Book2 without the extension.

So, unless you're just experimenting, be sure to save source workbooks *before* saving target workbooks.

The Long and Winding Link

By dint of native intelligence, 10 years of experience, and a head of thick, glossy hair, you've been named National Sales Manager. It's time to review your company's sales performance for the past 12 months.

You open National Sales.xls and are confronted by the message that the workbook contains links; do you want to update them? You choose Yes.

Excel now looks into two workbooks named Region1.xls and Region2.xls, which are the source workbooks for the external references in National Sales.xls. Excel updates the linked formulas with the current information in the source workbooks. You print the national sales report, carry it personally to your company's CEO, and leave for the golf course.

This national sales managing is so easy you could mail it in. It seems to be mainly a matter of opening workbooks and having good hair.

What you don't realize is that you're about to be fired. Region1.xls and Region2.xls themselves contain links to other workbooks: Ohio Sales.xls, Iowa Sales.xls, Illinois Sales.xls, and other Midwestern states that begin with vowels. These state sales workbooks were recently updated with new information, but since then no one has opened Region1.xls and Region2.xls. If the regional workbooks had been opened, their links to the state workbooks would have been updated with the new state sales data.

Because the regional workbooks weren't opened, they still have old data; your National Sales.xls workbook updated its links with old information.

When Excel refreshes links, it goes no further than the workbook referenced in the linking formula. The eventual target might be several workbooks away, but Excel stops at the target specified in the link. When Excel checks a value in, say, Region1.xls, it doesn't check whether that value is itself a link to yet another workbook.

The lesson is that you should take one of these precautions:

- Ensure that your links go no further than one workbook away. This is usually impractical, but National Sales Managers who still have their jobs do it all the time.
- Include cell notes that remind you to open and update intermediate workbooks before opening the eventual target workbook.
- Automate the process with a VBA procedure.

Understanding links is no substitute for having good hair, but it helps.

Troubleshooting Links

It occasionally happens that an external reference's source disappears. When this occurs, it's usually because the reference contains a link to a workbook that's been deleted or moved to another location.

Suppose that you are working with an income statement in an Excel worksheet, and that one of its cells links to another workbook named 1997 Sales.xls. When you open the workbook that contains the income statement, Excel might display a message that asks whether you want to update this workbook with changes made to the other workbook.

 TIP To suppress this message, choose Tools, Options; click the Edit tab; and clear the Ask to Update Automatic Links check box.

If, for some reason, Excel cannot locate 1997 Sales.xls, it displays a File Not Found dialog box. From this dialog box, you can navigate to its new location. But what if someone has completely deleted the workbook? You can't navigate to a nonexistent workbook.

It's often easy to fix this problem in a small, simple workbook. You just locate the cell with the linking formula and edit it as necessary. Perhaps the workbook originally named 1997 Sales.xls has merely been renamed—then, you'd adjust the external reference in the linking formula. Or, it may be feasible to convert the formula to a constant value.

But in a large, complicated workbook, the problem can be serious. There are many possible locations for the linking formula, and finding it can be tedious. That Excel does not tell you the location of the link's target complicates the problem enormously. Here's how to resolve it more quickly.

Select in turn each worksheet in the workbook that contains the link that Excel cannot resolve. Choose Edit, Find. In the Find What edit box, enter an exclamation point (!), make sure that the Find Entire Cells Only check box is cleared, and that Formulas is selected in the Look In drop-down box. Then, click Find Next. Excel searches the worksheet for formulas that contain exclamation points.

An external reference uses an exclamation point to separate the name of the linked workbook from the name of the linked worksheet. Therefore, when Excel finds an exclamation point in a formula, it's likely that you've located an external reference. Check that the reference is still valid.

If you cannot find the reference with this method, open any charts in the workbook. Select each data series contained in the chart and look in the Formula Bar to see whether the data series refers to a range in a different workbook.

Another place to look is in custom controls such as buttons and scroll bars. Right-click the control and choose Format Control to check the object's control options. A scroll bar might, for example, have a cell link to another workbook.

Finally, you should check whether any defined names contain references to external workbooks. This is not simply a matter of using Insert, Name, Define to locate names in the workbook. Hidden names do not appear in the Names in Workbook combo box, nor does a name that has somehow become corrupted.

Instead, put this VBA subroutine into a module and run it with a blank worksheet active:

```
Sub ListNames()
Dim oName As Name
Dim i As Integer
Dim TempRefersTo As String
i = 1
For Each oName In ThisWorkbook.Names
    TempRefersTo = "'" & oName.RefersTo & "'"
    Cells(i, 1) = i
    Cells(i, 2) = oName.Name
    Cells(i, 3) = TempRefersTo
    i = i + 1
Next oName
End Sub
```

This subroutine writes to your worksheet the index number of each defined name (i), the name's Name (that is, the value you'd normally find in the Names in Workbook combo box), and what the name refers to. The latter value is stored as a string in the variable TempRefersTo. Then, when the sub writes TempRefersTo to a worksheet, it does so as a string rather than as a reference. This prevents the sub from writing error values such as #REF! when a Refers To points to a cell that doesn't exist. For example, if the Refers To points to a relative reference five columns left, it would return #REF! when it appeared in column C.

When the sub has completed, look in column C of the active worksheet to see whether any names refer to a workbook that has been moved or that no longer exists.

Auditing Formulas

Over time, a workbook can become more and more complex. This is particularly true of workbooks used for finance and accounting purposes; the ongoing growth and diversification of a business is mirrored by the growth and diversification of its financial records. When more data and categories of data are added, structures that were originally kept on one worksheet are given their own sheets, or even their own workbooks. Formulas that once were simple become sophisticated as further refinements are made. As new accountants and analysts join the business, the labor is divided among them, and so are the workbooks.

Eventually, this process results in formulas that refer to multiple cells and ranges—references that, through linking, point to locations two and even three or more workbooks away from the referencing formulas.

Inevitably, someone makes a mistake, causing one of these complicated formulas to return an erroneous result. Then begins the laborious process of tracing the references used in the formula to their destinations, checking at each intermediate point until the problem is found and corrected.

Excel has some tools that can help. They don't make a difficult process easy, but they add visual elements to the worksheet that help you determine where you need to look for problems.

Using Excel Tracers

Consider a formula on a worksheet that returns the sum of two values that are found on the same worksheet. As shown in Figure 10.8, Excel can point you to the locations of those two values.

FIG. 10.8

The tracer arrows point from the formula to the formula's cell references.

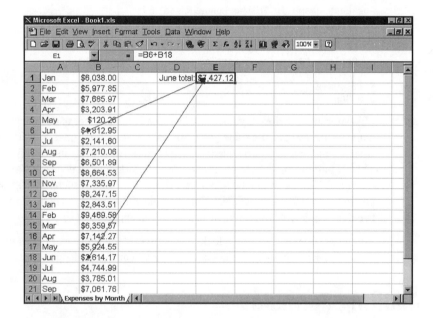

The arrows shown in Figure 10.8 are called *tracers*, or *tracer arrows*. They extend from the cell containing the formula—called the *dependent cell*—to the cells containing the formula's references—called the *precedent cells*. To display these arrows on the worksheet, select the dependent cell and choose Tools, Auditing, Trace Precedents.

If the cell does contain one or more references to precedent cells, tracers appear on the worksheet that visually connect the dependent cell to its precedent cells.

What if some of the precedents are found on a different worksheet, or in a different workbook? Then, the tracers look different. Figure 10.9 shows a tracer from a dependent cell to a precedent on the same worksheet, and to precedents found elsewhere.

FIG. 10.9

A tracer that ends in a worksheet icon indicates that precedents can be found off the active worksheet.

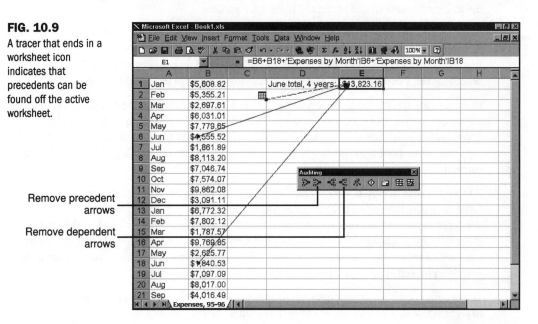

Remove precedent arrows

Remove dependent arrows

If you now double-click the tracer arrow that ends with a worksheet icon (see Figure 10.9), the Go To dialog box appears with the location of the off-sheet precedents.

To activate an off-sheet precedent cell, select that cell in the list box and click OK. Excel activates the proper worksheet and selects its precedent cell, opening its workbook if necessary to do so.

In practice, it's quite possible that you will not have reached the end of the line when you select an off-sheet precedent. That precedent might itself depend on a reference in yet another workbook. So, while tracer arrows can make it easier to track down the source of an error, they don't do it on your behalf. The difficulty of the tracing process is entirely a function of the complexity of the structures you have created.

Once you have located a precedent cell that contains an error, you can make the necessary correction, and any formulas that depend on that precedent cell will update automatically. It's wise to choose Tools, Options; select the Calculation tab; and check to see whether the Manual option button is selected. If it is, set Calculation to Automatic, or click Calc Now, or press the F9 key to ensure that your correction migrates through any open workbooks.

When you want to remove any tracer arrows that you have added to a worksheet, choose Tools, Auditing, Remove All Arrows. You cannot selectively remove any particular tracer arrow. If you have created tracers for more than one dependent cell, you cannot selectively remove the tracers for one cell and retain the tracers for another.

Tracing Dependents

Just as you use tracers to locate a dependent cell's precedents, you use them to locate a precedent cell's dependents. However, your reason to do so is usually different.

In most cases, the reason to trace a dependent cell's precedents is to locate and correct the source of an error. But once you've corrected the error in the precedent cell, any and all dependent cells automatically update to reflect the correction (unless, as noted in the preceding section, you have set Calculation to manual; then, you should use Calc Now to enforce the correction).

If there are cells in closed workbooks that depend on the formula that you corrected, their formulas will update when you open their workbooks. Although Excel is able to locate precedent cells in closed workbooks, it is unable to locate *dependent* cells in closed workbooks. (Excel, smart as it is, can't tell that there's a closed workbook on some file server that contains a cell with a reference to an open workbook.) Therefore, there is seldom a good reason to go searching for cells that depend on a precedent that you have corrected.

You usually search for dependent cells to see what effect a change in a precedent cell might have. Suppose that you decide to convert the values in an inventory worksheet from counts of units to counts of thousands of units. This change will make the monthly inventory report easier to read—of course, you will add a notation to the report that says something like "Quantities shown in thousands" or, in a header row, "(000)".

However, any cells that depend on these values must be adjusted to take account of this change in the scale of measurement. An income statement, for example, would usually display a valuation of inventory, and this value might depend on formulas that refer to your count of units in stock.

Making a drastic change like this obliges you to check its possible impact elsewhere. To do so, first make sure that any workbooks containing dependent formulas are open—again, Excel cannot do this on your behalf.

Then, select the precedent cell and choose Tools, Auditing, Trace Dependents. Tracers that point to dependent cells appear on the active worksheet. You can now select or go to those cells and note any changes you need to make there, so as to take into account the change you have in mind for the precedent cell.

 TIP   If you have traced both precedents and dependents on the same worksheet, you can remove the precedent tracers and keep the dependent tracers—or, you can remove the dependent tracers and keep the precedent tracers. To do so, use the Auditing toolbar (refer to Figure 10.9) by choosing Tools, Auditing, Show Auditing Toolbar. This toolbar has a Remove Precedent Arrows button and a Remove Dependent Arrows button. You cannot accomplish this by means of the Worksheet menu.

Tracing Invalid Data

Excel 97 has a new feature pertaining to the validation of data. For any cell or range of cells, you can set rules that limit what can be entered into a cell. For example, you might decide to restrict user input to date or time values, or text only, or integers only.

Suppose that you routinely import data from a text file into a worksheet. Your experience with this file tells you that in some cases it supplies values that Excel treats as text. However, you want to ensure that Excel treats all the incoming values as numeric.

You can combine data validation with validation arrows to locate text values that come from the text file. After you have opened the text file and completed the Text Import Wizard, take these steps:

1. Select the entire worksheet by clicking the Select All button (immediately to the left of column A's column heading and immediately above row 1's row heading).
2. Choose Data, Validation. In the Allow drop-down list, select Decimal.
3. In the Minimum edit box, type a very small number, such as **-1E200** (-1 followed by 200 zeros).
4. In the Maximum edit box, type a very large number, such as **1E200**, and choose OK.
5. Choose Tools, Auditing, Show Auditing Toolbar.
6. With the Auditing toolbar visible, click the Circle Invalid Data button.

As shown in Figure 10.10, Excel draws a circle around any cells that contain text—that is, any values that do not conform to your validation rule that all data must be numbers that fall between -1E200 and 1E200. You can now easily find those cells and change them to numeric values.

FIG. 10.10
Validation rules display alerts only for the entry of new data. To find existing data that violate new validation rules, use validation circles.

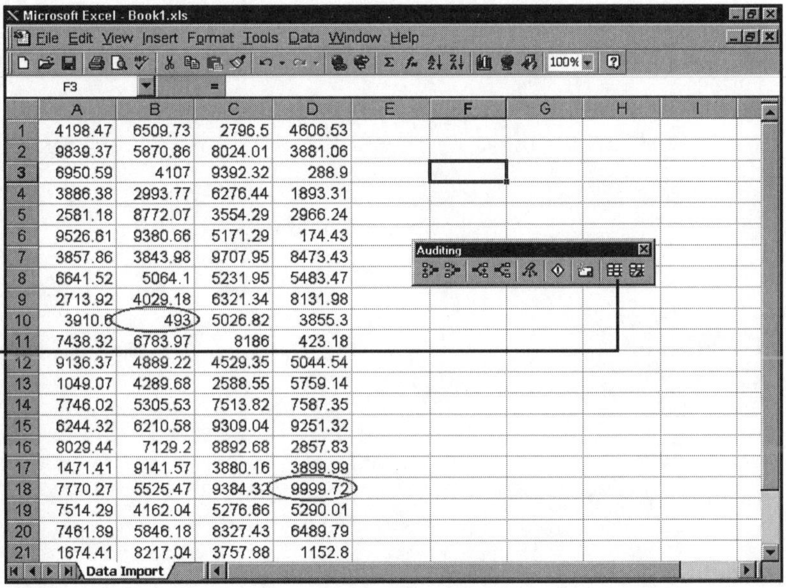

Circle Invalid Data button

CAUTION

If you have established validation rules for an entire worksheet, be careful when you audit the data for violations of the rules. Before clicking the Circle Invalid Data button, select only the range of cells that you want to check. It can take Excel a very long time—even with a P200—to check the entire worksheet for violations, and it could appear as though the application has hung.

CHAPTER 11

Using Worksheet Functions

▬ **Lookup and Reference functions**

Learn how to use functions in charts that update automatically when you put new data into a worksheet, and how to use them to extend array formulas.

▬ **Statistical functions**

Find out how to create normal curves on charts as a point of comparison for your data, and how to tell what kind of trendline you should use on your charts.

▬ **Financial functions**

Use NPV and IRR to help you make investment decisions.

▬ **Excel 4.0 functions**

Dress up old macro functions in new clothing to get results that would otherwise require VBA.

Excel 97 supplies 329 built-in worksheet functions. Most books about Excel give you a list of the function names arranged by category, along with a one- or two-sentence description of the purpose of each function. Such a list is little more than the Paste Function committed to paper.

The reason, of course, is that a full discussion of each of the 329 worksheet functions would make a book too long to publish. To make this book publishable, and yet provide you with more information about the functions than you usually get, this chapter does some very specific picking and choosing. It discusses only a few of the functions that are available to you, but it does so using some contexts and usages that you might not have seen before. ▬

Lookup and Reference Functions

At first glance, some of Excel's Lookup and Reference functions appear to have limited usefulness. How often are you going to want to use ROW to store in a cell the row number where a range starts? When you can just look at it, why would you want to use INDEX(MyRange,4,6,1,1) to store in a cell the value in the fourth row, sixth column of MyRange?

Although these functions can be helpful when used for their apparent purpose, it's when you start to use and combine them in creative ways that they get really valuable. In particular, they enable you to create array formulas that return results that are otherwise very difficult to obtain.

Using *OFFSET* in Charts

A common complaint about Excel charts goes like this: "Once I've charted a data series, I'd like it to update automatically when I add new data to the worksheet. I wish I didn't have to re-create the chart, or edit the data series, when I add a new row of data to the charted range."

If you use some imagination along with the OFFSET function, you can arrange to have your chart update automatically as you add new data to the worksheet. Suppose that you've created a line chart of the values in A1:A10. When you select the data series in the chart, here's what appears in the Formula Bar:

=SERIES(,,Sheet1!$A$1:$A$10,1)

Notice that the SERIES formula uses cell references, and that they're absolute. Given that setup, there's no way that the chart can update when you add new data. What you need is a chart series reference that is sensitive to new data. The solution involves using named ranges in combination with the OFFSET and COUNTA functions.

OFFSET takes one range or cell as an argument, and returns another range or cell, offset from the first one. Its other arguments specify how far to offset from the first range, and the dimensions of the result. For example:

=OFFSET($A$1,3,5,2,4)

returns the values in the range $F$4:$I$5. As offset from $A$1, this range is three rows down, five columns right, two rows high, and four columns wide. Because the offset range contains more than one cell, the formula would be array-entered in a two-row by four-column range.

You can make the number of rows returned by OFFSET depend on the number of values in a range of cells. You do so by using the COUNTA function, which returns the number of cells in a range that are not empty. Assuming that each cell in the range $A$5:$A$10 contains a value, and the rest of column A is empty:

=COUNTA($A:$A)

returns 6. (Notice that its cell references do not use rows. This is how you refer to a complete column.) So this formula:

```
=OFFSET($A$1,3,5,COUNTA($A:$A),4)
```

returns the values in a range that, vis-à-vis $A$1, is three rows down, five columns right, four columns wide, and with as many rows as there are values in column A.

As you saw in Chapter 10, "Advanced Work with Formulas," you can define names that refer to formulas. Suppose that your active sheet is Sheet1, and you choose Insert, Name, Define to define the name Sheet1!DataToChart. Then, type this into the Refers To box:

```
=OFFSET($A$1,0,0,COUNTA($A:$A),1)
```

Now, open your chart, click the charted series, and replace this SERIES formula:

```
=SERIES(,,Sheet1!$A$1:$A$10,1)
```

with this one:

```
=SERIES(,,Sheet1!DataToChart,1)
```

Now, when you insert a new value in column A, the name DataToChart recalculates to take account of the new count of values in column A. The chart reevaluates what DataToChart refers to, and automatically redraws the charted series.

N O T E Be sure you don't have any stray values in the column you're charting. If your intention is to chart A1:A10, but you have an extra value in A10, then COUNTA($A:$A) will return 11 instead of 10. ■

Part
III

Ch
11

Using *INDEX* in Array Formulas

Both OFFSET and INDEX return a value in a range. The main difference between the two functions is that you normally use OFFSET to refer to a range that's removed from OFFSET's own range argument. In contrast, you use INDEX to refer to its own range argument. Both functions can return an array of values when you use them in array formulas.

INDEX becomes particularly useful when you use it with an array that's not visible on the worksheet. Suppose that the range A2:A100 contains the names of products, and that B2:B100 contains the revenue from each product. You update the revenue figures monthly, and would like cell D1 to contain the name of the product that has the greatest revenue.

Begin by naming the range of product names as Products and the range of revenue values as Revenues. This is so that you can move those ranges around on the worksheet if you want, without wreaking havoc with formulas that refer to the ranges.

Then, enter this formula in D1:

```
=INDEX(Products,MATCH(MAX(Revenues),Revenues,0))
```

The result is shown in Figure 11.1.

FIG. 11.1

You could achieve the same result with a data filter, but it would not recalculate automatically.

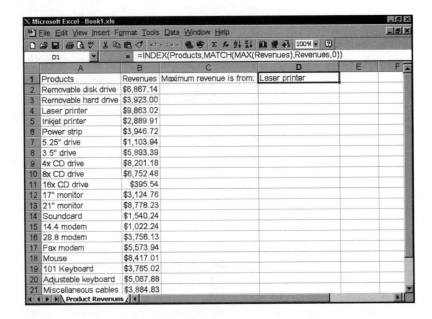

Because the formula occupies a single cell, and because the functions it uses expect to receive arrays as arguments, it's not necessary to array-enter the formula.

Work from the inside out. In the Formula Bar, highlight MAX(Revenues) and press F9. You see 9863.02, which is the largest value in the Revenues range. Press Esc to get the full formula back, and highlight MATCH(MAX(Revenues),Revenues,0). You see 3, which is the row within Revenues that matches the first instance of 9863.02, the result of the MAX function.

Be sure you see that 3 is not necessarily the worksheet row that contains the value 9863.02; rather, it's the instance in Revenues that matches 9863.02. This means that the Products range and the Revenues range could start in different worksheet rows, and the formula would return the same result.

Once the formula has arrived at the number 3 for the Revenues row that contains the maximum revenue value, INDEX takes over. At this point, the formula evaluates to INDEX(Products,3). This is the third row within the Products range, or Laser printer.

If you change the values in the Revenues range, the formula automatically recalculates to locate the product that now has the maximum Revenue value.

Using *COLUMN* or *ROW* to Create a Sequence of Numbers

Both COLUMN and ROW can be used in array formulas when you need to get a sequence of numbers. For example, if you enter this formula in some cell:

```
=ROW(A1:A5)
```

you'll see the number 1 in that cell. But if you click in the Formula Bar and press F9, you'll see this:

```
={1;2;3;4;5}
```

Cool, maybe, but are there practical applications? Yes indeed. Suppose that you have a list of people's names, and you want to extract their last names from that list. It might first occur to you to use this formula on the name George Washington in cell A1:

```
=RIGHT(A1,LEN(A1)-FIND(" ",A1))
```

You're looking for the last name, so you want some number of characters at the right of the string. The FIND function locates the first space in the name—with George Washington that is 7, the 7th character in the string. Subtract 7 from the length of the string (17 characters) to get 10. Return the 10 rightmost characters, or Washington.

Perfect! You have the names of the subsequent Presidents in A2:A42, so you drag your formula down into B2, B3…and in B6 you find that it returns not Adams but Quincy Adams. Unfortunately, the FIND function returns the first instance of a space, which comes between John and Quincy. What you need is a way to find the *last* instance of a space within a name. To do so, array-enter this formula in, say, B1:

```
=RIGHT(A1,MATCH(" ",MID(A1,LEN(A1)+1-ROW($A$1:$A$17),1),0)-1)
```

Again, working from the inside out, ROW($A$1:$A$17) returns this array, no matter where you use the function:

```
{1;2;3;4;5;6;7;8;9;10;11;12;13;14;15;16;17}
```

The length of the string in A1, plus 1, is 18, so this component:

```
LEN(A1)+1-ROW($A$1:$A$17)
```

returns this array:

```
{17;16;15;14;13;12;11;10;9;8;7;6;5;4;3;2;1}
```

Getting close. To get to the last instance of a space in the name, this array of descending values is needed. Notice that the first value in the array is 17, the length of the string in A1. This is why the formula adds 1 to the length of that string; otherwise, the first value in the array would be 16.

Expanding one level farther, this component:

```
MID(A1,LEN(A1)+1-ROW($A$1:$A$17),1)
```

returns this array:

```
{"n";"o";"t";"g";"n";"i";"h";"s";"a";"W";" ";"e";"g";"r";"o";"e";"G"}
```

which is, of course, the letters in George Washington in reverse order. Using the array of descending values, the MID function returns the 17th, then the 16th, the 15th… letter in the string.

Now, use MATCH to locate the first instance of a space in the array of reversed characters. (You can't use FIND because it won't accept an array as an argument.) When MATCH finds that, it has found the final instance of a space in the original string. Here, that location is 11. To complete the formula, subtract 1 from 11 to get rid of the space itself, and return the 10 rightmost characters—Washington.

The result is shown in Figure 11.2.

FIG. 11.2
You could now sort the entire range on last name.

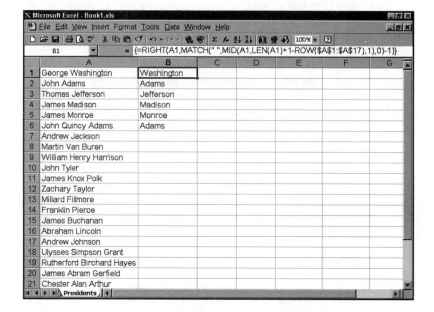

The same formula finds the final instance of a space in John Quincy Adams to return Adams. In order to keep manageable the size of the arrays as they appear here, the formula uses ROW($A$1:$A$17). An array of 17 values isn't long enough to deal with, say, William Henry Harrison. You could instead use, say, ROW($A$1:$A$50). But the next section discusses a better approach.

Using *INDIRECT* to Assemble Cell References

Normally, the INDIRECT function takes as its argument a cell that contains another reference. For example, if A1 contains "C1" and C1 contains "Value in C1", then =INDIRECT(A1) returns "Value in C1". Note that A1 must contain a cell reference *as text*.

Dull of me, I suppose, but I've never understood why anyone would need to do that. However, INDIRECT has a useful role to play in the problem of finding last names. Keep in mind that INDIRECT expects to be evaluating a text value.

Suppose that in the present example, you entered:

```
=INDIRECT("C1")
```

In that case, INDIRECT would still return "Value in C1". So INDIRECT can evaluate cell references given as text values. Suppose that you array-enter this formula:

```
=ROW(INDIRECT("1:17"))
```

in a range consisting of one column and 17 rows. It returns 1, 2, 3…17. Assuming that `George Washington` is in cell A1, this array formula:

```
=ROW(INDIRECT("1:" & LEN(A1)))
```

returns the same 17 values. You use the length of each name itself to create the array of descending values. So the formula becomes:

```
=RIGHT(A1,MATCH(" ",MID(A1,LEN(A1)+1-ROW(INDIRECT("1:"&LEN(A1))),1),0)-1)
```

Using `INDIRECT` with the length of the name ensures that you have an array large enough to get at all the characters in each name—and no larger. As you copy the formula from B1 down to B42, the `LEN(A1)` within the `INDIRECT` function changes to use the length of A2, A3, and so on.

Okay, if you apply this formula to `Martin Van Buren`, you get `Buren`. But people always forget him anyway.

Using *MATCH* and *VLOOKUP* on Multiple Columns

Both `MATCH` and `VLOOKUP` return information about a value found in an array. The key distinction between the two functions is that `VLOOKUP` returns a value from the array, while `MATCH` returns a value's location in an array.

Consider the array and functions shown in Figure 11.3.

FIG. 11.3
`MATCH` returns the row 10. `VLOOKUP` returns the associated value $6,752.48.

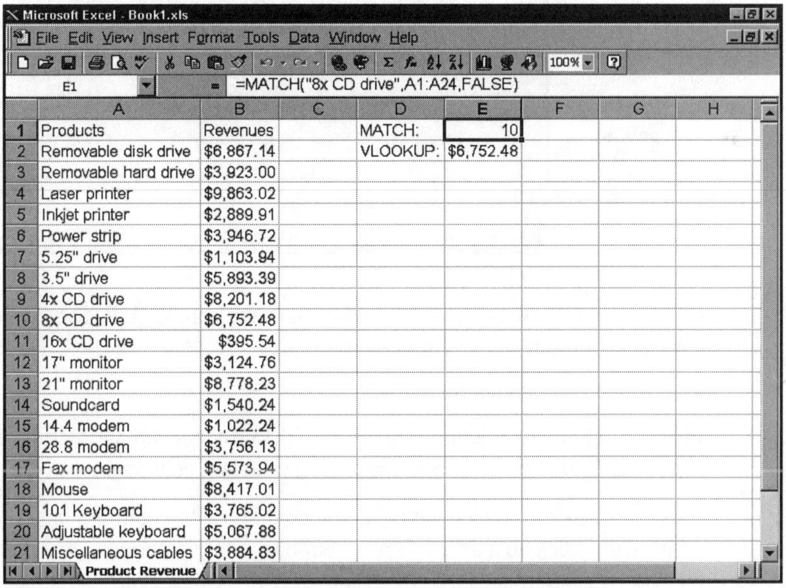

Microsoft Excel - Book1.xls

E1 =MATCH("8x CD drive",A1:A24,FALSE)

	A	B	C	D	E
1	Products	Revenues		MATCH:	10
2	Removable disk drive	$6,867.14		VLOOKUP:	$6,752.48
3	Removable hard drive	$3,923.00			
4	Laser printer	$9,863.02			
5	Inkjet printer	$2,889.91			
6	Power strip	$3,946.72			
7	5.25" drive	$1,103.94			
8	3.5" drive	$5,893.39			
9	4x CD drive	$8,201.18			
10	8x CD drive	$6,752.48			
11	16x CD drive	$395.54			
12	17" monitor	$3,124.76			
13	21" monitor	$8,778.23			
14	Soundcard	$1,540.24			
15	14.4 modem	$1,022.24			
16	28.8 modem	$3,756.13			
17	Fax modem	$5,573.94			
18	Mouse	$8,417.01			
19	101 Keyboard	$3,765.02			
20	Adjustable keyboard	$5,067.88			
21	Miscellaneous cables	$3,884.83			

Product Revenue

Cell E1 uses the MATCH function in this way:

```
=MATCH("8x CD drive",A1:A24,FALSE)
```

Cell E2 uses VLOOKUP in this way:

```
=VLOOKUP("8x CD drive",A1:B24,2,FALSE)
```

In each case, the final argument (FALSE) to the function specifies that it is to find in the array an exact match to the first argument. When an exact match is required, the array need not be sorted.

This is fine when you have unique values in the lookup column. But what if it's a combination of two or more columns that, taken together, result in unique values? Figure 11.4 gives an example.

FIG. 11.4

It's only by combining the Product with the Region that you get a unique value.

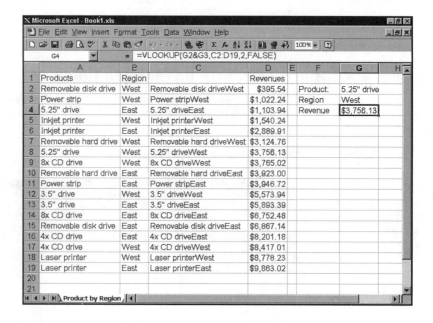

One possible solution is to concatenate the values in A2:A19. The concatenation appears in column C of Figure 11.4. That way, you can use VLOOKUP on the concatenated values:

```
=VLOOKUP(G2&G3,C2:D19,2,FALSE)
```

In Figure 11.4, this function returns $3,756.13. By concatenating the values in columns A and B, you obtain the unique combinations of values in column C.

This can make the worksheet ugly. You could hide the column, but an alternative solution that uses MATCH relies on a defined name. Suppose that you choose Insert, Name, Define to create the name ProductAndRegion, referring to:

```
=$A$2:$A$19 & $B$2:$B$19
```

This name performs the concatenation of columns A and B in the name, not in the worksheet, so as to keep the worksheet itself a little cleaner. Now, using the MATCH function in combination with INDEX,

```
=INDEX(D2:D19,MATCH(G2&G3,ProductAndRegion,0))
```

returns the same value of $3,756.13. MATCH returns the row in the defined name that contains the combination of the Product and the Region, and then INDEX looks in that row in column D. The concatenation shown in column C of Figure 11.4 need not exist on the worksheet.

Why use INDEX and MATCH in this case, instead of VLOOKUP? Because VLOOKUP requires an array with two columns: one to contain the lookup values, and one to contain the values that VLOOKUP returns. But, as defined, the name ProductAndRegion refers to a one-column array of lookup values. So, use MATCH to find the correct combination of Product and Region, and INDEX to get to the proper row in Revenues.

Statistical Functions

Please be careful when you use Excel's statistical functions to help make real-world decisions. Because Excel's help documentation is not intended as a textbook, you can't expect much guidance there. Without the appropriate theoretical background or the advice of a statistician, it's all too easy to go wrong.

Part
III

Ch
11

Nothing against Excel's statistical functions: Within the generous limits to arithmetic accuracy that are imposed by a PC's chip architecture, these functions are quite accurate. The problem is in knowing when it's appropriate to use one of the functions and when it's not.

For example, Excel's help documentation for t-tests says that you use them to test whether the average values of two groups are different. It does not tell you that it would be misleading to use three t-tests to analyze the differences in the average values of three or more groups. The probabilities returned by the three t-tests would be inaccurate, because you would have violated one of the assumptions underlying the mathematics of the t-test. With three or more groups, you should use analysis of variance (ANOVA).

Similarly, Excel's trendlines and the worksheet functions LINEST and TREND make it easy to force a regression equation's constant (the intercept) to zero. When they notice that doing so normally increases the regression's R^2, users often choose that option. They do not realize that so doing reparameterizes the sums of squares, which are no longer centered on the mean of the y-values. And then they're in trouble. If you're going to consult a statistician for guidance, choose a good one. Excel's Analysis ToolPak contains a tool named t-Test: Two Sample Assuming Unequal Variances. On the Internet, I have found people who are actually teaching statistics at universities but who do not realize that this tool adjusts the t-test's degrees of freedom. Nor do they realize that it is *supposed* to do so. This information is usually discussed toward the end of an introductory course in inferential statistics, and yet two assistant professors of statistics did not know it. Be careful who you listen to, and question authority.

Charting Normal Curves Using *NORMDIST* and *FREQUENCY*

Statistical process control and quality improvement projects often need to know whether a set of observations at least roughly follows a normal distribution—that is, the famous (recently, infamous) bell curve. There are various statistical tests that return a probability that a set of numbers are normally distributed. Excel's CHIDIST function is useful in this context, if all you need is the numeric probability.

But nothing beats a visual analysis. It's usually informative to look at a chart that overlays actual observations onto a normal curve. This section describes one way to do that.

Suppose that your observations are in E1:E21, with a header row that contains a label such as Observations in E1 (see Figure 11.5).

In F1, enter:

=AVERAGE(E2:E21)

and in F2, enter:

=STDEV(E2:E21)

Now, set up the x-values for the chart. In cell A1, enter the value **-3**. With A1 selected, choose Edit, Fill, Series. In the Series dialog box, choose Series in Columns, Type Linear, and set Stop Value to 3. Set Step Value to .1. This creates 61 values; if you choose a Step Value of .01, you'll get a smoother curve, but you're also dealing with 601 values.

In B1, enter:

=$F$1+(A1*$F$2)

and copy and paste the formula into B2:B61. This rescales the values in A1:A61 to have the mean and standard deviation of your actual observations.

Select C1:C61, and array-enter:

{=FREQUENCY(E2:E21,B1:B61)}

The FREQUENCY function takes two arguments: what Excel calls its *data array* and its *bins array*. The function's purpose is to count the number of values in the data array that are between any two values in the bins array.

TIP   You can use the same range for FREQUENCY's data array and its bins array. If you do so, you obtain a count of each unique value in that range.

Assume that exactly two of the values in the data array are 1, and assume that two consecutive values in the bin array are .88 and 1.14. In that case, the function would return the number 2 (there are two values) at the row in the bin array that contains 1.14. The two data values of 1 are between .88 and 1.14 (see Figure 11.5).

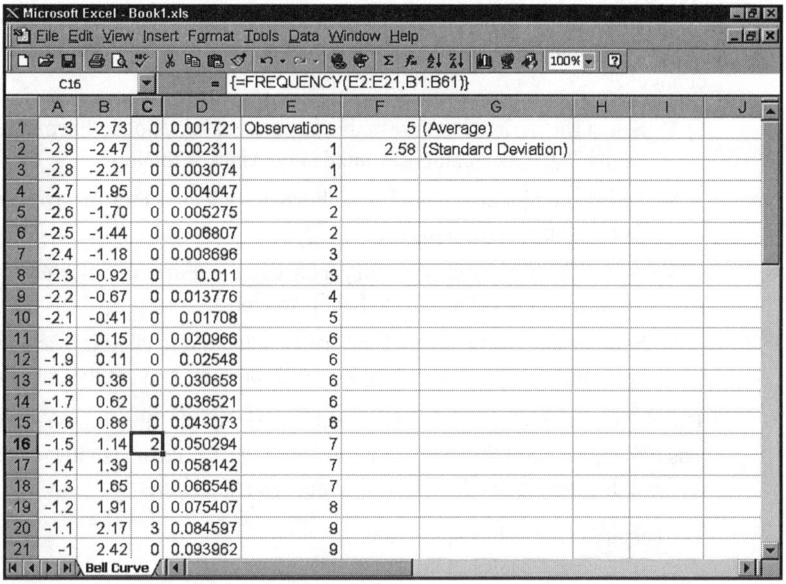

	A	B	C	D	E	F	G
1	-3	-2.73	0	0.001721	Observations	5	(Average)
2	-2.9	-2.47	0	0.002311	1	2.58	(Standard Deviation)
3	-2.8	-2.21	0	0.003074	1		
4	-2.7	-1.95	0	0.004047	2		
5	-2.6	-1.70	0	0.005275	2		
6	-2.5	-1.44	0	0.006807	2		
7	-2.4	-1.18	0	0.008696	3		
8	-2.3	-0.92	0	0.011	3		
9	-2.2	-0.67	0	0.013776	4		
10	-2.1	-0.41	0	0.01708	5		
11	-2	-0.15	0	0.020966	6		
12	-1.9	0.11	0	0.02548	6		
13	-1.8	0.36	0	0.030658	6		
14	-1.7	0.62	0	0.036521	6		
15	-1.6	0.88	0	0.043073	6		
16	-1.5	1.14	2	0.050294	7		
17	-1.4	1.39	0	0.058142	7		
18	-1.3	1.65	0	0.066546	7		
19	-1.2	1.91	0	0.075407	8		
20	-1.1	2.17	3	0.084597	9		
21	-1	2.42	0	0.093962	9		

FIG. 11.5
Cell C16 contains the number of values in E2:E21 that are between the values in B15:B16.

In cell D1, enter this formula:

```
=NORMDIST(B1,$F$1,$F$2,FALSE)
```

and copy and paste it into D2:D61. The `NORMDIST` statistical function returns the height of the normal curve—a chart's y-values—at each of the values in B1:B61—a chart's x-values. The second and third arguments are the mean and the standard deviation of the observations in E2:E21.

There are two reasons to use `NORMDIST` instead of the simpler `NORMSDIST` function:

- You are not dealing with standard z scores in B1:B61.
- `NORMSDIST` does not provide the choice between the cumulative density and point estimate version (using `FALSE` as `NORMDIST`'s fourth argument gives the point estimate).

Create the chart. Select B1:D61 and use the Chart Wizard to create a combination chart. In the Chart Wizard's first step, click the Custom Types tab, and choose Line–Column on 2 Axes in the Chart Type list box.

In the wizard's second step, click the Series tab. You should see the worksheet name and `B$1:$B$61` in the Values edit box. If not, select a different series in the Series list box. Drag across the full reference in the Values box and choose Edit. Click in the Category (X) Axis Labels edit box, and choose Paste. Then, click the Remove button to remove that range as a data series.

In the wizard's third and fourth steps, choose any options that you want. Because there are only two data series, and because they are formatted differently, it usually makes sense to clear the Legend tab's Show Legend check box.

When the wizard has created the chart, you have your actual counts overlaid on a normal curve. It's a matter of personal preference, but you might consider making these format changes:

- Select the series that shows the normal curve. Choose Format, Selected Data Series to set its Patterns as Line Automatic and Marker to None.

- Select the plot area and choose Format, Selected Plot Area to set its Patterns as Border Automatic and Area to None.

- Select the horizontal, category axis. Choose Format, Selected Axis to set its Patterns for Tick Marks and Tick Mark Labels to None.

- Select each visible column in turn (you'll need to click it twice, slowly, to select a specific column). Choose Format, Selected Data Point and set its Data Label to Show Label.

The reason for the last two points in this list is that the chart does not line up the horizontal axis tick mark labels with each column such that you can visually associate each column with its label. It's best instead to show the label as a data label.

The result is shown in Figure 11.6.

FIG. 11.6

You can now visually assess how well your data approximate a normal distribution.

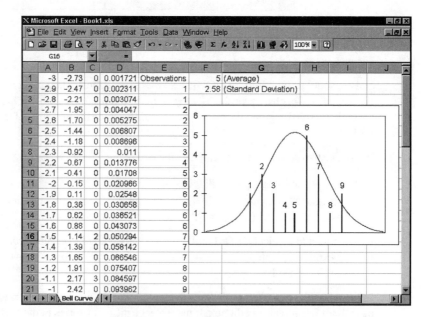

Using *LINEST* and *FDIST* to Evaluate Polynomial Trendlines

Sometimes computer programs make things too easy for their users' own good. An example in Excel is a polynomial trendline in a chart.

Suppose that you are responsible for the operation and maintenance of a medium-sized fleet of delivery vans. You are interested in the relationship between a van's average miles per gallon (mpg) and the number of times per month that the van gets any sort of maintenance.

On a worksheet, you enter data on mpg and frequency of maintenance for 20 vans. To examine the relationship visually, you create an XY chart and see that there appears to be a relationship between the two variables. Curious, you insert a linear trendline and use the Trendline Options tab to display the R^2 value on the chart. You get an R^2 value of 0.216.

Idly, you wonder if a polynomial trendline would fit the data better. So you change the linear trendline to a polynomial with an order of 2. R^2 increases a little. Hmmm. What about order 3 or order 4? You increase the order of the trendline and at order 4; R^2 has climbed all the way to 0.348 (see Figure 11.7).

FIG. 11.7

As you increase the order of the polynomial trendline, the R^2 almost always increases.

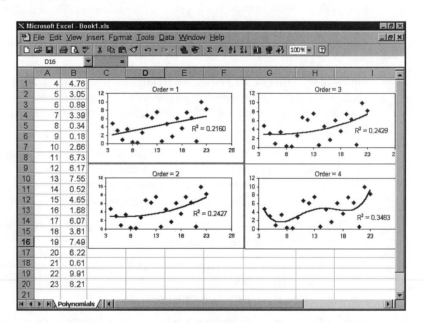

What do you learn from this data snooping? When you increase the order of a trendline, you are increasing the exponent of the charted x-values. A linear trendline shows the best fit regression line of the y-values (here, mpg) against the x-values (here, frequency of maintenance). A second-order polynomial trendline regresses the y-values against the combination of the x-values and the square of the x-values, and so on; a fourth-order trendline regresses the y-values against the combination of the x-values, and the x-values squared, and cubed, and raised to the fourth power. You can remind yourself of this by using the trendline option that shows the equation on the chart.

Understanding R^2 and Best Fit   The larger an R^2 value, the stronger the relationship between the y-values and the x-values. In fact, you interpret an R^2 as the proportion of variability in the y-values that can be predicted from the x-values. So, in your experiment, an R^2 of 0.216 means that 21.6 percent of the variance in mpg can be predicted from frequency of maintenance—the linear trendline. You interpret your fourth-order R^2 as meaning that 34.8 percent of the variability in mpg can be predicted by the combination of the x-values themselves—the x-values squared, cubed, and raised to the fourth power.

While all of this is true, it is also extremely misleading, and the reason is found in the phrase "best fit." All Excel trendlines, except Moving Average, are regression lines, and regression lines are lines of best fit. The math that underlies regression analysis has one goal: to minimize the squared differences between the actual y-values and the predicted y-values (hence the term *least squares*).

In deriving the equation that provides this best fit, regression analysis relies heavily on the correlations among the individual x-variables and y-variables. It treats these correlations as though they were error-free, but in practice they never are. There is always some amount of sampling and measurement error due to chance circumstances. Because regression analysis seeks the best fit, it relentlessly fits not only the accurate part of the observations but their inaccurate part as well. This biases R^2 upward.

Choosing the Order of the Polynomial Trendline   Every time you throw, willy-nilly, another variable into the equation (which is what you do when you increase the order of the trendline), you add another opportunity for the equation to capitalize on chance and spuriously inflate the R^2 value.

There are various ways to protect yourself against this. The best is always to have a good theoretical reason to increase the order of the trendline. But in the process of theory-development, which is what you're doing when you first investigate the relationship between mpg and maintenance frequency, you don't yet have a mature theory to rely on.

Another way is to increase substantially the number of observations. Often, though, this is either too expensive or simply impossible.

A reasonable solution (not as good as basing your decision on your theory or increasing sample size, but still reasonable) is to run a statistical test on the *change* in R^2 that occurs as you increase the order of the polynomial trendline.

Excel's LINEST worksheet function is both a basic and powerful means of analyzing regression. When you set its fourth argument to TRUE and array-enter it in a range of five rows, it returns several statistics that are fundamental to evaluating the regression. In particular, the first column, third row of the array contains the R^2 value. So this formula:

```
=INDEX(B1:B20,A1:A20^{1,2,3,4},,TRUE)
```

returns the R^2 for the regression of the values in B1:B20 on the values in A1:A20 raised to the 1st, 2nd, 3rd and 4th powers. And this formula:

```
=INDEX(B1:B20,A1:A20^{1,2,3},,TRUE
```

returns the R^2 for B1:B20 on A1:A20 raised to the 1st, 2nd, and 3rd powers. By subtracting the second R^2 from the first, you obtain the change in R^2 attributable to changing the trendline from a third-order polynomial to a fourth-order polynomial (see Figure 11.8).

FIG. 11.8

Notice that the R^2 values are the same as those shown for the trendlines in Figure 11.7.

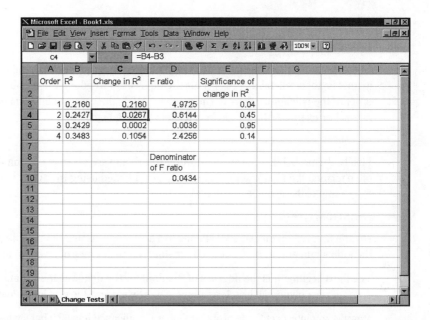

After obtaining R^2 for each of the four trendlines, calculate the difference from one to the next by simple subtraction. The change in R^2 for the first-order, or linear, trendline is the same as its R^2 itself: A "zero-order" polynomial trendline would predict no values, and would therefore have an R^2 of zero.

As noted previously, R^2 is the proportion of predictable variability. Therefore, $1-R^2$ is the proportion of unpredictable variability. When you divide each proportion by a quantity called *degrees of freedom*, you obtain an expression of the predictable and the unpredictable variance (these are the variance due to regression and the residual variance, with their unit of measurement rescaled).

Then, by taking the ratio of the predictable to the unpredictable variance, you can judge how large the predictable variance is relative to the unpredictable variance. There is a statistical test, the *F test*, that evaluates ratios of variances and returns an associated probability. The smaller this probability, the more likely that the relationship between the two variances will stand up if you repeat the experiment. Put another way, the smaller this probability, the more likely that the change in R^2 is due more to something real than to capitalizing on chance.

Creating the Statistical Test Here's how to translate all this theory into practice. Referring to Figure 11.8, the values in column B contain the R^2 values obtained from INDEX and LINEST for the different polynomials. For example:

```
=INDEX(B1:B20,A1:A20^{1,2,3},,TRUE)
```

Column C contains the change in R^2 from one polynomial to the next, obtained by B4-B3, B5-B4, and B6-B5. Column D contains the ratios of the variances, also termed *F ratios*. Each ratio's numerator is its associated change in R^2. It happens that the degrees of freedom for these changes in R^2 is 1, and dividing the R^2 change by 1 is just the R^2 change itself.

Part III

Ch 11

The denominator of each F ratio is in cell D10. It is obtained by:

```
=(1-B6)/(20-4-1)
```

where `(1-B6)` is the same as `(1-R²)` for the fourth-order polynomial: the proportion of variability that is not predictable. `(20-4-1)` is the degrees of freedom: the number of y-values, less the order of the polynomial, less 1. The value in D10 is the correct denominator for all four F ratios. For example, the F ratio in cell D4 is obtained by:

```
=C4/$D$10
```

Finally, the probabilities associated with each F ratio are given in column E. The probability, often termed the *significance* of the F ratio, is obtained using the FDIST worksheet function. For example, the formula in cell E3 is:

```
=FDIST(D3,1,20-4-1)
```

FDIST's first argument is the F ratio itself. The second argument is the degrees of freedom for the ratio's numerator. As mentioned previously, the degrees of freedom for a change in R^2 is 1.

The third argument is the degrees of freedom for the denominator. That is, observations less order of the polynomial less 1, or `(20-4-1)`—the same value employed in cell D10.

How do you interpret these probabilities or significance levels? That's where you have to apply your judgment. The significance for the first-order, linear trendline is 0.04. That means that if you repeated this experiment 100 times, and if there were no relationship between frequency of maintenance and mpg, you would obtain an F ratio as large as 4.97 four times (0.04 * 100 = 4). So, 4.97 is a fairly unlikely F ratio if there's no relationship.

In contrast, consider the change in R^2 for the second-order polynomial. Its significance is .45. If you repeated the experiment 100 times, in 45 of them you would get a change in R^2 as large as 0.0267 (.45 * 100 = 45), even if there were no relationship between mpg and the square of frequency of maintenance.

Evaluating the Statistical Test   Many people would regard a significance level of 0.04 as important. They would believe that it is not rational to regard this experiment as one of the four out of 100 where an R^2 of 0.216 would be obtained by chance, when in fact there was no relationship. They would believe that it is more rational to believe that a relationship exists.

And many people would regard a significance level of 0.14 for the change in R^2 from the third- to the fourth-order polynomial as marginally important at best, or even unimportant. When you can get a change in R^2 as large as 0.1054 14 times out of 100 purely by chance, they would prefer to regard this experiment as one of those chance 14, and would not employ a fourth-order polynomial.

So, you have to exercise your judgment. If you believe that the probability analysis means that only the linear component is important, back off your second-, third-, and fourth-order polynomials and stick with the linear trendline.

It may seem like a lot of work, compared to clicking a spinner in the Trendline dialog box. But doing the spadework keeps some geek statistician from pointing at your chart and giggling at you.

Financial Functions

Most Excel users are familiar with some of its financial functions. There is a cluster of financial functions—RATE, PV, FV, NPER, and PMT—that work together to describe how you might pay for a house or a car. If you've ever purchased anything with a bank loan, you're familiar with the results of these functions and how they depend on one another.

It's when you encounter functions that address investment decisions and capital budgeting that things start to get complicated. In that context, two valuable functions are *net present value (NPV)* and *internal rate of return (IRR)*.

Using Net Present Value to Evaluate an Investment

The notion of *Net Present Value (NPV)*, which you calculate using Excel's NPV function, is a powerful one. It tells you the value of an investment at some point in the future. In the process of calculating this value, it takes into account both the initial investment and the cash flow earned from the investment (this is the *net* part of NPV).

NPV also takes into account the time value of money: the fact that the value of a dollar bill today is smaller at some future time (the *present value* part of NPV).

Suppose that you have $200 hanging around. You know that you don't want to just sit on it; a few years from now, it will buy much less than it can buy today. You know of an extremely generous bank that will pay you 10 percent annual compound interest if you deposit your $200 with them for five years. At the end of that period, how much has your $200 grown? This formula returns the value of your bank account after one year:

```
=1.1 * 200
```

If you entered that in A2, you could enter this in B2:

```
=1.1 * A2
```

and drag it to C2:E2. At the end of five years, cell E2 shows you that your account has grown to $322.10. If you do the algebra, you'll see that you could calculate the same end result using just one formula:

```
=1.1^5 * 200
```

If you entered the numbers 1 through 5 in A1:E1, you could get your account balance at the end of each year by entering this formula in A2:

```
=(1.1 ^ A1) * 200
```

and dragging it through B2:E2.

A bank account, of course, isn't the only way you could use your $200. You could also spend it on equipment that would help you manufacture goods to sell. Over a five-year period, you would realize a net income from selling those goods. You estimate your annual revenue and cost of goods sold to arrive at the net income during each year, as shown in Figure 11.9.

FIG. 11.9

Early on, your net income is negative; you have to subtract expenses such as the cost of goods sold from the revenues.

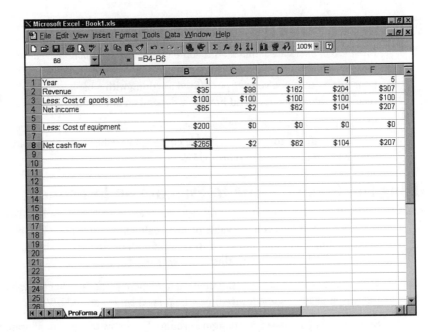

An adjustment to net income is still needed. You need to subtract the cost of the equipment incurred in year 1. Once you've done that, you have an estimated net cash flow for each year.

When you spend the $200 on equipment, though, you're foregoing the 10 percent interest you could earn at the bank. So, to get a more accurate picture of how much you're making from selling goods made by the equipment, you adjust the net cash flow by this factor:

=(1+$B$10)^B1

As shown in Figure 11.10, this formula is entered in cell B11 and copied into C11:F11. (Notice that this formula is equivalent to the one used earlier to calculate the bank account interest.) The value in cell B10 is the interest rate you could earn at the bank. The resulting values in B11:F11 are termed the *discount factors*.

Then, to arrive at a cash flow estimate that takes into account the interest earnings you forego, you divide the net cash flow by the discount factors. The results are in B13:F13 in Figure 11.10. They tell you the value of your cash flow, discounted by the value of an alternative use of your original $200 capital.

So, given this discounted cash flow, how long does it take for your equipment investment to become profitable? During the first two years, you're still in the red; you start showing a profit in the third year, but these profits are used to recoup your original investment. Figure 11.10 shows that you get back into the black in year 5.

The formula in cell B15 is:

=SUM($B$13:B$13)

FIG. 11.10

Because your cumulative discounted cash flow turns positive in Year 5, the *payback period* is five years.

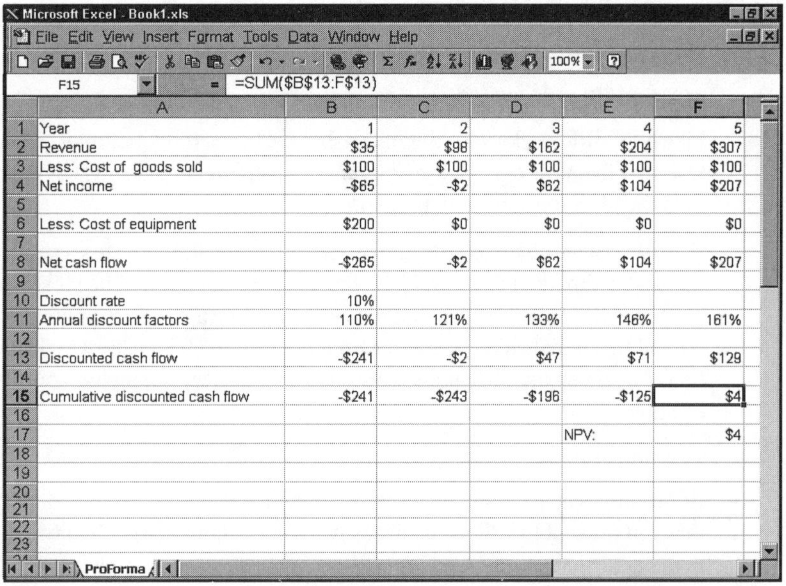

The formula is dragged through C15:F15. Notice that the formula makes use of a mixed reference, as discussed in Chapter 10, to create a running total.

After all that work, you arrive at the value in cell F15, which is $4. It is the NPV of your equipment investment at the end of five years. To get there, you took into account the revenues and the cost of goods sold, the cost incurred to obtain the equipment, and the value of an alternative use of your capital. Because you're foregoing that alternative use, you decrease the value of the net cash flow each year—you *discount* the net cash flow—by the earnings rate of the alternative investment.

Is there an easier way to calculate that $4 NPV? Yes. Cell F17 in Figure 11.10 contains the NPV function:

```
=NPV(B10,B8:F8)
```

The NPV function takes as its arguments the discount factor (in this example, 10 percent) and the net cash flow (in Figure 11.10, cells B8:F8).

Using Internal Rate of Return to Evaluate NPV

The *internal rate of return (IRR)* of an investment helps you compare the net discounted cash flow to the discount rate.

The example in the previous section resulted in an NPV of $4 at the end of the fifth year. This means that the investment in the equipment eventually performs better than the alternative investment—$4 better at the end of the fifth year.

You can convert this result to a rate: that is, a figure in the same metric as the discount rate. Using the data and the cell references in Figure 11.10, enter:

```
=IRR(B8:F8)
```

Like NPV, IRR works with the net cash flow. Here, the function would return 10.49 percent. Over the five-year period, the equipment investment performs slightly better (0.49 percent) than the discount rate of 10 percent.

IRR uses an iterative algorithm to arrive at its result. It iterates a maximum of 20 times to get to the best estimate of the IRR. If the function doesn't get this best estimate by the 20th iteration, it returns the #NUM! error value. IRR starts out by assuming an initial value of 10 percent. Should this initial value be too far from an eventual best estimate, IRR could run out of iterations. So, if you use IRR and get #NUM!, you could try supplying your own estimate. For example:

```
=IRR(NetCashFlowRange, .2)
```

IRR requires at least one negative and one positive value to return a valid result. If the array that you present to IRR as its first argument contains fewer than two values, or if all the values in the array have the same sign, IRR will return #NUM!. Supplying your own estimate does no good in these cases.

Another way to conceptualize the IRR is that IRR is the discount rate that would result in an NPV of zero (see Figure 11.11).

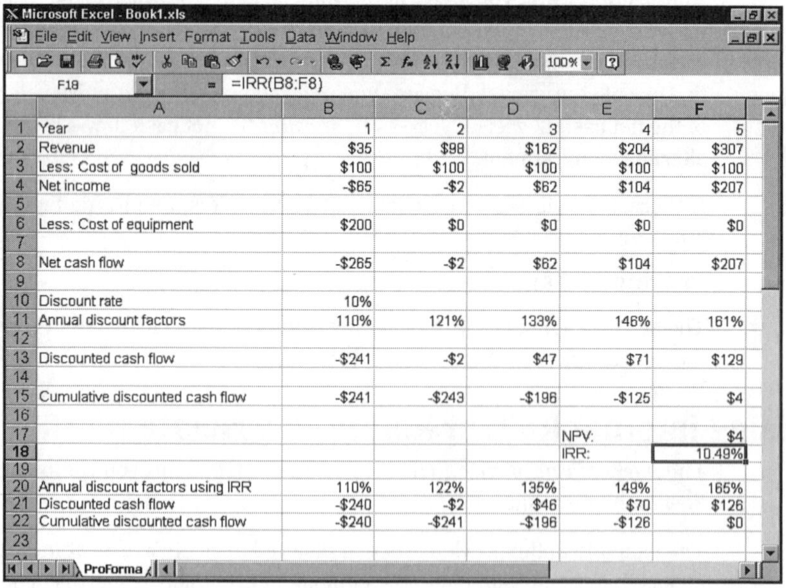

FIG. 11.11

Given the net cash flow in B8:F8, the IRR results in a net present value of zero.

	A	B	C	D	E	F
1	Year	1	2	3	4	5
2	Revenue	$35	$98	$162	$204	$307
3	Less: Cost of goods sold	$100	$100	$100	$100	$100
4	Net income	-$65	-$2	$62	$104	$207
5						
6	Less: Cost of equipment	$200	$0	$0	$0	$0
7						
8	Net cash flow	-$265	-$2	$62	$104	$207
9						
10	Discount rate	10%				
11	Annual discount factors	110%	121%	133%	146%	161%
12						
13	Discounted cash flow	-$241	-$2	$47	$71	$129
14						
15	Cumulative discounted cash flow	-$241	-$243	-$196	-$125	$4
16						
17					NPV:	$4
18					IRR:	10.49%
19						
20	Annual discount factors using IRR	110%	122%	135%	149%	165%
21	Discounted cash flow	-$240	-$2	$46	$70	$126
22	Cumulative discounted cash flow	-$240	-$241	-$196	-$126	$0
23						

The annual discount factors shown in B20:F20 use 10.49 percent, the IRR in F18, instead of the 10 percent discount rate used in the NPV calculation. The net cash flow is adjusted by the new discount factors to return a new discounted cash flow in B21:F21. Finally, the cumulative discounted cash flow is shown in B22:F22; discounting a net cash flow by its own internal rate of return results in zero.

Profitability Indexes

What if you had several different ways that you could use your capital of $200 to create income? If each investment is fairly sensible, it's quite possible that they have similar NPVs. But you might have one opportunity that requires your entire $200, and another that requires only $120.

If the two investments have identical NPVs, how do you choose between the two? There might, of course, be strategic reasons to prefer one investment to the other. If not, a *profitability index* can help put the choices into perspective. Figure 11.12 shows two examples.

FIG. 11.12

The profitability index helps to distinguish between two projects with the same NPV.

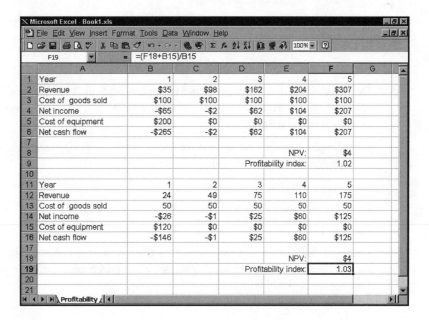

The profitability index in cell F9 uses this formula:

`=(F8+B5)/B5`

In other words, add the initial investment to the NPV, and divide the result by the initial investment. An analogous formula is used to obtain the profitability index in cell F19. The higher the profitability index, which removes the effect of the amount of the initial investment from the comparison, the more attractive the investment.

Excel 4.0 Functions

If your experience with Excel goes back as far as version 4.0 or earlier, you may be familiar with its old macro language. This language was obscure, and was so specific to Excel that knowledge of the language did not generalize to any other application.

VBA changed that. With VBA, Excel users get a language that is built on the familiar BASIC and Visual Basic programming languages. With Office 97, the VBA model is exposed across all Office applications—so, if you can use VBA in Excel, all you need to program in VBA for Access is to know the Access object model.

But something was lost in the translation. There are some version 4.0 macro functions that were handy. Fortunately, while you can't use them directly in a worksheet, you can still use them in names.

Compared to VBA, these functions are still obscure. It's much easier to enter, in VBA:

```
PathName = ActiveWorkbook.Path
```

to return the path of a saved workbook, than to use the version 4.0 macro function:

```
Get.Document(2)
```

where the function's argument, 2, specifies that it is to return the document's path.

On the other hand, if you're going to use `ActiveWorkbook.Path`, you need to use VBA. By using `Get.Document(2)` in a name, you return the path directly to the worksheet without opening the Visual Basic Editor.

For example, suppose that you choose Insert, Name, Define to create the name `WhereAmI`. In the Refers To edit box, you enter:

```
= Get.Document(2)
```

Then, in some worksheet cell, you enter:

```
=WhereAmI
```

If the workbook has been saved—and thus has a path—the cell would contain the full path to the workbook, omitting the final backslash. If the workbook were in the My Documents folder, then `WhereAmI` would return:

```
C:\My Documents
```

Some other ways that you might use the `Get.Document` macro function are shown in Figure 11.13.

Consider row 3 in the figure. The macro function used is `GET.DOCUMENT(10)`. The name `LastRow` has been defined as referring to:

```
=GET.DOCUMENT(10)
```

FIG. 11.13
You could not otherwise
display these results
without resorting to
VBA.

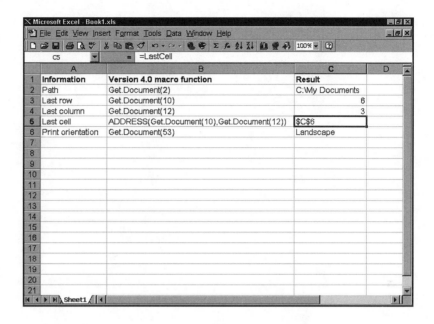

This formula:

`=LastRow`

has been entered in cell C3, and returns 6, which is the last used row in the worksheet.

Notice that you can use version 4.0 macro functions as arguments to regular worksheet functions. For example, ADDRESS takes a row number and a column number as its arguments, and by default returns an A1-style reference. So, to show the worksheet's last used cell, you could define the name LastCell as referring to:

`=ADDRESS(Get.Document(10),Get.Document(12))`

In Figure 11.13, cell C5 contains:

`=LastCell`

There are many such arguments to Get.Document that you can use. Another version 4.0 macro function is Get.Cell. Depending on the argument that you use with Get.Cell, you can obtain such information as its number format, or whether the cell is locked.

You need to have access to a list of these functions and their arguments. The Office 97 and Excel 97 Help documentation does not contain a listing. You can find the list in Excel 95's Help by looking up Equivalent Excel 4.0 Macro Functions in the Help index.

Used in names, these functions do not automatically recalculate. To make sure that a formula such as =LastCell, which uses version 4.0 macro functions, is returning current information, click it in the Formula Bar and press Enter. ●

Part

III

Ch

11

CHAPTER 12

Using Lists

When you enter information into a new worksheet, you're designing it. Whether you have some eventual report format in mind, or you're just sticking in some values that you want to add up, you're giving structure to the framework provided by a new sheet.

And you have great leeway within that framework. A worksheet has no inherent requirements for data placement. Nothing stops you from entering 1996 sales in row 1 and 1997 sales in row 2. Or, you can enter 1996 sales in column A and 1997 sales in column B if that's your preference. On a really bad day, you might decide to vent your spleen by entering 1996 sales in A1 and 1997 sales in IV65536.

But when it comes time to *use* the data—to analyze it, to summarize it, to forecast from it, to chart it—things come home to roost. The choices you make early on begin to make subsequent tasks easy or exacting, quick or laborious. If you keep in mind from the outset the eventual layout requirements that you'll have to meet, you'll save yourself a lot of headaches.

You can meet virtually all these layout requirements if you organize your data in lists. The term *list* has a very specific meaning in Excel. A list has a particular orientation and structure. It's also quite intuitive.

Lists make formulas, functions, charts, filters, names, and labels easier to use. They make it possible to create pivot

What's a list?

The technical and structural requirements are contrasted with the logical requirements.

Filtering lists

This chapter shows you how to view only the records that you're interested in.

Using a data form with lists

Data forms make it easy to edit a list's contents, to navigate through the list, and to view subsets of a list's records.

tables and data forms, and to tightly couple worksheets with external databases. This chapter discusses how to structure lists most effectively, and how to use their relationship to names and labels in the context of actually using the data. ■

What's a List?

A list is a set of contiguous worksheet cells with these characteristics:

■ Each column contains values or formulas that represent the same concept. For example, a column in a list might contain 1996, 1997, and 1998, while another column in the same list might contain the annual revenue for each year. Other terms for the columns in a list are *field* and *variable*.

■ The first, topmost row in the list contains a label for each column. This row is often termed a *header row*. For example, the header row's first column might contain the label Year and its second column might contain the label Revenue.

■ Each subsequent row in the list contains *records*, or observations, or instances such that the values in each column go together. Continuing the example, the value 1996 for the year and the revenue amount for that year are in the same row.

It's important to distinguish between ranges that are lists in a technical sense—that is, they conform structurally to the definition of a list—and lists that both have the correct formal structure *and* are laid out effectively. Figure 12.1 shows several worksheet ranges. Only one of them contains both the technical structure and appropriate layout that make it a true list.

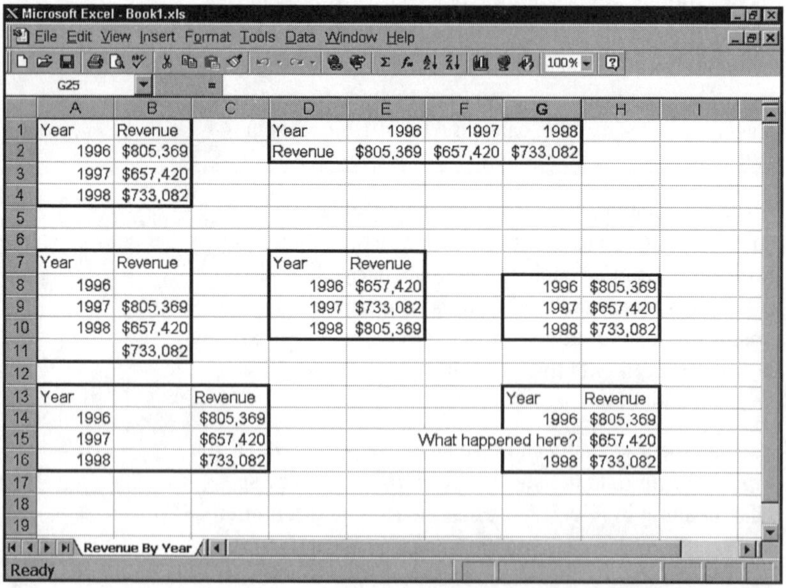

FIG. 12.1

Lists have a very specific structure, but it's a structure that's easy to use.

Of the seven ranges shown in Figure 12.1:

- Cells A1:B4 constitute a list. There's a header row with the labels Year and Revenue. The values in each column describe the same concept. Each row contains values that belong together that, taken together, describe the same record.

- Cells D1:G2 do not constitute a list. Although their layout is sensible and useful, the labels occupy the first column instead of the first row. And each record occupies a separate column instead of a separate row.

- Cells A7:B11 contain a list in the technical sense only. The revenues for each year are offset by a row from the year they belong to. When it comes time to use the range in a chart, pivot table, or formula, you'll start running into problems because the rows are misaligned. While empty cells are allowed in lists' records, misalignment within records is a logical flaw in the structure.

- Again, the range D7:E10 is a list in the technical sense only. But given the accuracy of the data in A1:B4, D7:E10 is wrong because each year's revenue is not in the same row as its year's value. Keeping each record's values in the same row is an important logical characteristic of a list.

- The range G8:H10 is technically a list. But Excel would treat its first row as headers. If you tried to use the range in a data form, or as a data source for a pivot table, or if you applied a filter, Excel would treat 1996 and $805,369 as header row labels rather than values.

- Cells A13:C16 are discontiguous—there's an empty column in there. You could not use the range A13:C13 as a pivot table's data source.

- Cells G13:H16 conform to the technical structure of a list. But using the list in any sort of analysis will create problems because there's a comment instead of a year in G15. Good design calls for the value 1997 in G15, perhaps with the existing comment included as a cell note.

There is in theory at least one good reason to structure each of the ranges in Figure 12.1 as shown. In reports, for example, our eyes like to see time-series data proceed from left to right, so D1:G2 could well be the proper layout in a report. But it isn't a list.

Or, cells B9:B11 might be projections that are associated with each year in A8:A10. On a chart, you might want to offset each projection from its year, so you begin by shifting the dollar amounts down by one row. Structurally, it's a list. Whether it's a list in the logical sense depends on the user's intent.

A little thought tells you why lists are oriented with records occupying their own rows, and with variables occupying their own columns. In Excel 97, a worksheet has 256 columns and 65,536 rows. It's normal for data sets to have more records than variables. If the records in a list each occupied a different column, you'd be limited to 256 records. If you have as many as 65,536 records or more, shame on you: You should be storing them in an Access database.

Filtering Lists

In practice, you usually work with data sets that are more extensive than shown in Figure 12.1. A more typical situation is shown in Figure 12.2.

FIG. 12.2
A list such as this lends itself to filtering and maintenance with data forms, pivot tables, and so on.

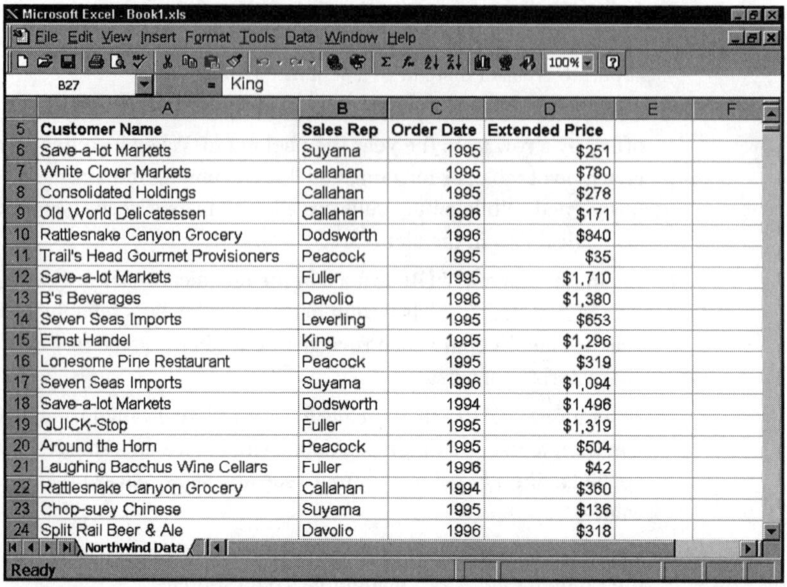

	A	B	C	D	E	F
5	Customer Name	Sales Rep	Order Date	Extended Price		
6	Save-a-lot Markets	Suyama	1995	$251		
7	White Clover Markets	Callahan	1995	$780		
8	Consolidated Holdings	Callahan	1995	$278		
9	Old World Delicatessen	Callahan	1996	$171		
10	Rattlesnake Canyon Grocery	Dodsworth	1996	$840		
11	Trail's Head Gourmet Provisioners	Peacock	1995	$35		
12	Save-a-lot Markets	Fuller	1995	$1,710		
13	B's Beverages	Davolio	1996	$1,380		
14	Seven Seas Imports	Leverling	1995	$653		
15	Ernst Handel	King	1995	$1,296		
16	Lonesome Pine Restaurant	Peacock	1995	$319		
17	Seven Seas Imports	Suyama	1996	$1,094		
18	Save-a-lot Markets	Dodsworth	1994	$1,496		
19	QUICK-Stop	Fuller	1995	$1,319		
20	Around the Horn	Peacock	1995	$504		
21	Laughing Bacchus Wine Cellars	Fuller	1996	$42		
22	Rattlesnake Canyon Grocery	Callahan	1994	$360		
23	Chop-suey Chinese	Suyama	1995	$136		
24	Split Rail Beer & Ale	Davolio	1996	$318		

The data in Figure 12.2 are fundamentally different from the data in Figure 12.1. In Figure 12.1, there was a simple, one-to-one correspondence between each year and each revenue figure. In Figure 12.2, there are multiple identical observations in the fields—for example, several records for the sales rep named Callahan, together covering three different years and four different customers.

Because the data are organized in lists, it becomes easy to work with and analyze this very complex data set.

Filtering Lists with AutoFilter

Suppose that you wanted to quickly find the top 10 sales in the data set. Just select any cell in the list and choose Data, Filter, AutoFilter. Excel inserts a drop-down list in each column in the list's header row. You use that drop-down list to display some subset of the list.

For example, you might want to view the 10 records in the list that have the highest Extended Price. You click the drop-down arrow in cell D1 and select Top Ten. When you do so, AutoFilter displays the information as shown in Figure 12.3.

Figure 12.3 shows the top 10 order amounts. Because the list contains multiple columns, you also see the name of the customer, sales rep, and year that's associated with each of those 10 orders. The remaining rows in the list are still there. They are just temporarily hidden until you change the criteria, or until you again choose Data, Filter, AutoFilter to remove the existing filter.

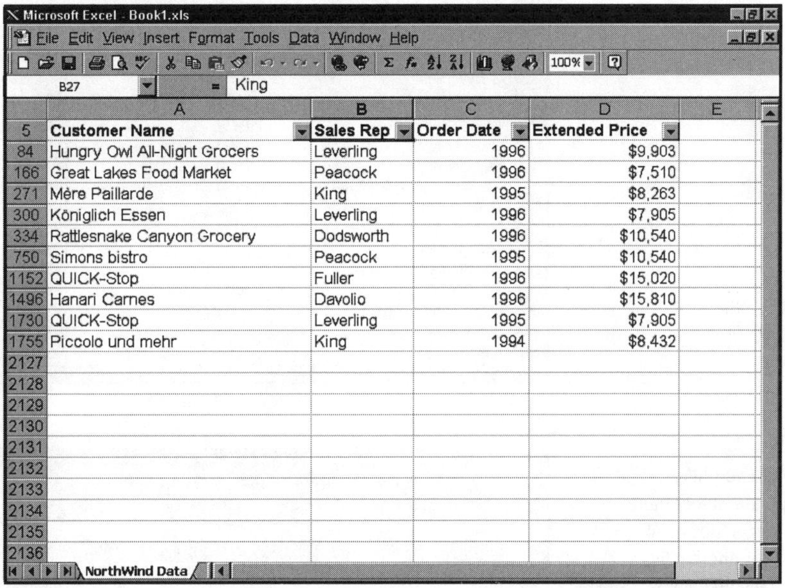

	Customer Name	Sales Rep	Order Date	Extended Price
84	Hungry Owl All-Night Grocers	Leverling	1996	$9,903
166	Great Lakes Food Market	Peacock	1996	$7,510
271	Mère Paillarde	King	1995	$8,263
300	Königlich Essen	Leverling	1996	$7,905
334	Rattlesnake Canyon Grocery	Dodsworth	1996	$10,540
750	Simons bistro	Peacock	1995	$10,540
1152	QUICK-Stop	Fuller	1996	$15,020
1496	Hanari Carnes	Davolio	1996	$15,810
1730	QUICK-Stop	Leverling	1995	$7,905
1755	Piccolo und mehr	King	1994	$8,432

FIG. 12.3 Although the AutoFilter offers a Top Ten option, you can use it to call for some other number of extreme records.

If, in the AutoFilter's dialog box, you had chosen to display the Top Ten percent instead of the Top Ten items, you would see 212 rows because the full list contains 2,120 rows.

Your interest might center on a particular sales rep, customer, or year instead of on the Top Ten sales amounts. Then, you could use the drop-down list for Sales Rep, and select (say) King to view all of King's records, as in Figure 12.4.

The multi-column list structure lets you string out filters as though they were connected by logical ANDs. In Figure 12.5, the filter on Extended Price is set to Top Ten items, and the filter for Sales Rep is set to King. This displays the two records for King that are among the Top Ten Extended Price items.

What if you wanted to see the Top Ten Extended Price items that belong either to King *or* to Dodsworth? Set up a Custom criterion. Use the drop-down list for the Sales Rep column, choose Custom, and complete the resulting dialog box as shown in Figure 12.6.

To re-display an entire list, choose All in any drop-down list where you have established a filter.

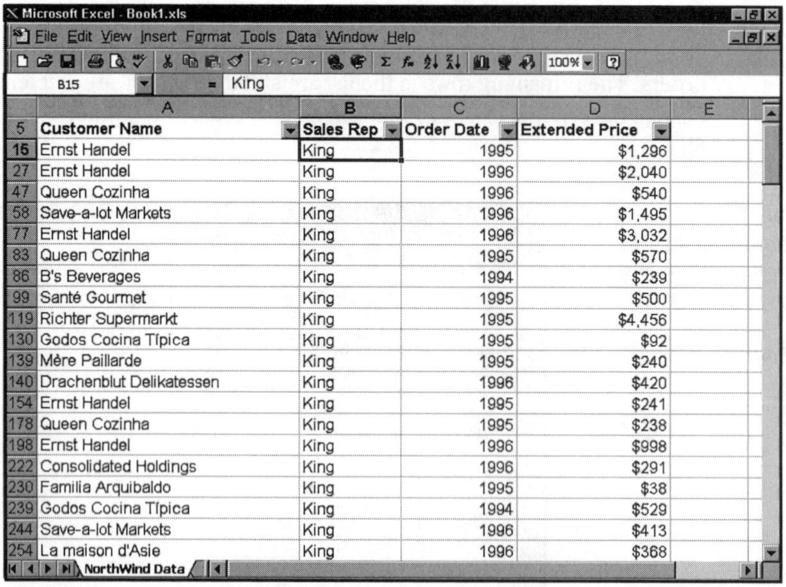

FIG. 12.4

When a filter is being used, the color of its drop-down arrow is blue. This helps you identify which filter(s) you are using.

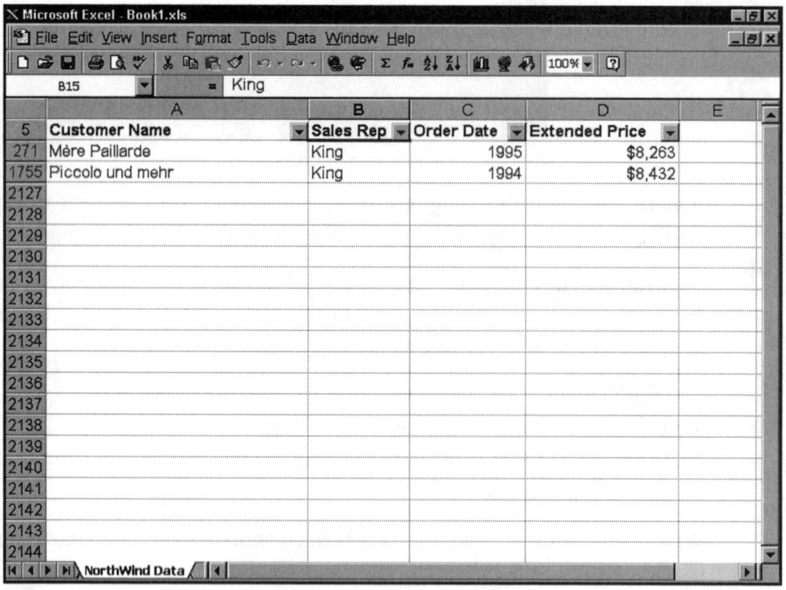

5	Customer Name	Sales Rep	Order Date	Extended Price
15	Ernst Handel	King	1995	$1,296
27	Ernst Handel	King	1996	$2,040
47	Queen Cozinha	King	1996	$540
58	Save-a-lot Markets	King	1996	$1,495
77	Ernst Handel	King	1996	$3,032
83	Queen Cozinha	King	1995	$570
86	B's Beverages	King	1994	$239
99	Santé Gourmet	King	1995	$500
119	Richter Supermarkt	King	1995	$4,456
130	Godos Cocina Típica	King	1995	$92
139	Mère Paillarde	King	1995	$240
140	Drachenblut Delikatessen	King	1996	$420
154	Ernst Handel	King	1995	$241
178	Queen Cozinha	King	1995	$238
198	Ernst Handel	King	1996	$998
222	Consolidated Holdings	King	1996	$291
230	Familia Arquibaldo	King	1995	$38
239	Godos Cocina Típica	King	1994	$529
244	Save-a-lot Markets	King	1996	$413
254	La maison d'Asie	King	1996	$368

FIG. 12.5

When you have applied one or more filters, choosing All for yet another filter means all records that meet the criteria for existing filters.

5	Customer Name	Sales Rep	Order Date	Extended Price
271	Mère Paillarde	King	1995	$8,263
1755	Piccolo und mehr	King	1994	$8,432

Be sure to recognize how easy all of this is. You begin by selecting any cell in columns A through D, and choose Data, Filter, AutoFilter. Excel automatically determines where to put the drop-down lists and where to find the records. It automatically puts the available choices into each drop-down list.

FIG. 12.6
A custom AutoFilter criterion can include one or two criteria, connected by an AND or an OR.

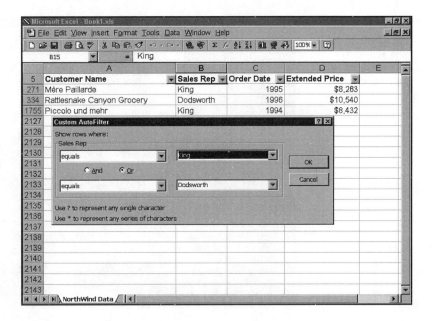

The reason that all this is so easy is that you began by structuring the data as a list: a header row, variables in columns, and records in rows.

Filtering Lists with Advanced Filter

The term *Advanced Filter* tends to put some users off. While you can do more things with Advanced Filter, it need be no more complicated than AutoFilter. The tradeoff for Advanced Filter's additional functionality is that you must supply a little more information.

Suppose that, given the list used in the preceding section, you wanted to see the Top Ten sales for King, Dodsworth, and Fuller: Perhaps those three sales reps together constitute a sales region.

If you're keeping in mind the worksheet design issues discussed at the beginning of this chapter, the first thing that should occur to you is that you should have included a Region column in your list. But because you didn't, and because lists lend themselves to ad hoc analysis, you decide to filter on a Sales Rep name.

Using AutoFilter, you run into a snag. A custom AutoFilter enables you to combine no more than two criteria for a given column. Using the dialog box shown in Figure 12.6, you could limit filtered records to two of the sales reps you're interested in—but not to three sales reps.

An Advanced Filter gives you more flexibility, but you have to do a little setup first. See the layout in Figure 12.7.

Part
III

Ch
12

FIG. 12.7

To use Advanced Filter criteria, you need to include an additional range. Here, that range is A1:D4.

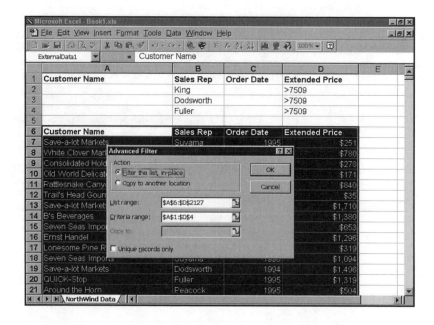

The range A1:D4 is called the *criteria range*. The criteria range always has, as its first row, the same labels as are in the header row of the list you want to filter. (An exception to this rule is a computed criterion; information on setting up a computed criterion appears later in this section.) Subsequent rows in the criteria range contain the criteria themselves. In Figure 12.7, the Sales Rep criteria contain the names of the sales reps that you want to display.

The Extended Price criteria are each > 7509. From the earlier work done with the AutoFilter, it's known that the smallest sale in the Top Ten is $7,510. Notice that this criterion is entered in each of the range's rows. This causes the criterion to apply to each of the sales rep criteria. Entering > **7509** in just one of the rows would cause the criterion to be associated only with the sales rep criterion that's in the same row.

Rows in a criteria range are treated as though they represented logical ORs, so the criterion for sales reps becomes King OR Dodsworth OR Fuller.

Columns in a criteria range are treated as though they represented logical ANDs. Therefore, a formulaic translation of the full criteria range in Figure 12.7 is:

```
=AND(OR(Sales Rep = King, Sales Rep = Dodsworth,
   Sales Rep = Fuller),Extended Price > 7509)
```

There are two further important points about the layout of the criteria range:

■ The criteria range is placed *above* the list that is filtered. Suppose that you placed the criteria range in rows that are shared by the list. If you choose Filter the List, In-Place, Advanced Filter hides the rows that do not meet the criteria. Then, the rows that contain the criteria could be hidden and you wouldn't be able to see or modify the criteria until you removed the filter. (The filter would still work, though.)

■ There is at least one blank row between the last row of the criteria range and the top row of the list. Suppose that the two ranges were to abut one another. Then, when you selected some cell in the list and started Advanced Filter, Excel would treat the criteria range as though it were part of the list itself.

TIP After you have created the criteria range, use the Name Box to name it Criteria (select the range, click in the Name Box, and type **Criteria**). Then, when you start Advanced Filter, the address of the criteria range automatically appears in the dialog box along with that of the list.

To apply an Advanced Filter, choose Data, Filter, Advanced Filter. To remove it, choose Data, Filter, Show All.

Earlier, this section suggested that from your prior work with AutoFilter, you already knew that $7,510 is the smallest of the Top Ten Extended Prices. That suggestion is a little disingenuous. More likely, you'd use a computed criterion as shown in Figure 12.8.

FIG. 12.8

Unlike value criteria, a computed criterion has no label.

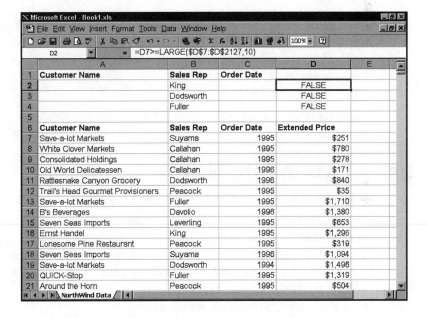

The criteria > 7509 in Figure 12.7 have been removed in Figure 12.8. Cells D2:D4 each contain this formula:

`=D7>=LARGE($D$7:$D$2127,10)`

The formula has these important characteristics:

■ The computed criteria do not have a label. If you provide a label, as you do for value criteria and as is done in Figure 12.7, all records are hidden.

■ The formula tests cell D7. More generally, a computed criterion tests against the row occupied by the first record in the column.

- The formula makes use of the LARGE worksheet function. Because it uses 10 as an argument to the function, it returns the 10th largest value in the range that contains Extended Price. Of course, if you were interested in the 10 smallest values, you could use SMALL instead of LARGE. Or, if you wanted the 50 largest values, you would replace 10 in the formula with 50.

- The range that's evaluated by LARGE uses absolute references. Relative references (such as D7:D2127) are reevaluated in the formula as the Advanced Filter hides nonqualifying rows. When this happens, the LARGE function returns unexpected results because it's constantly evaluating different ranges of values.

Notice that the Advanced Filter dialog box shown in Figure 12.7 has a couple of other options. If you choose to copy the list to another location and fill the Unique Records Only check box, you can obtain a separate listing of the unique values in the list. In this case, you probably would not want to include any criteria at all. The "other location" that you copy to *must* be on the same worksheet as the list itself.

CAUTION

Be careful when you copy unique values to another location. If you already have values or formulas in the other location's column(s), no matter how far down they are in the column, they will be overwritten. Excel does not warn you that this is about to occur.

Again, list structures make possible this kind of relatively sophisticated analysis. The next section shows how lists have implications for the use of natural language formulas.

Using Lists in Formulas

In the past, you've probably seen formulas such as this one:

```
=August Sales
```

There's a lot packed into that formula. What's particularly useful about it is that it's self-documenting. Provided that the person who entered it was in his right mind, the formula tells you that the value it returns is the sales figure for August. If, in contrast, you were confronted with this formula:

```
=INDEX(SALES(MATCH("August",MONTHS,0),1))
```

you'd probably spend a minute or so determining the meaning of the value it returns.

Worse is:

```
=INDEX(SALES(MATCH(A1,MONTHS,0),1))
```

where there isn't even a month name to give you a clue to the purpose of the formula.

To arrange for the formula to be self-documenting, someone had to:

- Define a range name, August, which refers to some address such as $H$2:$H$13.

- Define another range name, Sales, which refers to an address such as $B$2:$M$2. The two ranges, August and Sales, must share at least one cell.

- Use the intersection operator—a blank space—between the two range names in the formula. This causes Excel to return the value in the cell where the two ranges intersect. (If there is no such cell—if the two ranges do not intersect—then a formula using the intersection operator returns the #NULL! error value.)

Creating Natural Language Formulas from Lists

Microsoft claims its market research shows that only around 10 percent of Excel users know how to define range names and use them in formulas. In an effort to make formulas such as = August Sales easier to create, Excel 97 offers the ability to use not only names but labels in formulas. When they use labels, these formulas are termed *natural language formulas*.

Historical note and commentary: Microsoft has a track record of introducing products and product enhancements that just aren't very good at first. But if you stick around long enough, you find that Microsoft makes them better and better until it gets them right. Sometimes they become dead solid perfect.

An example is the Excel version 4 Crosstabs facility. It wasn't even native to the Excel application, but was supplied as an add-in. It was clumsy and underfeatured. Version 5 introduced pivot tables as a replacement for and enhancement to Crosstabs. Since then, pivot tables have become one of the most powerful data summary and analysis tools available in the entire Excel application.

Perhaps the evolution of natural language formulas will follow the same path as was followed by pivot tables. The idea is certainly an elegant one. But the current incarnation's execution of the idea is, well, incomplete. Natural language formulas are discussed in this chapter, not as a recommendation that you routinely use them, but to give you a possible preview of subsequent releases of Excel. You will also find it useful to understand what you're dealing with when you encounter natural language formulas on someone else's worksheet. Nevertheless, there's meat here, carnivores (see Figure 12.9).

Part

III

Ch

12

The table in Figure 12.9 is much like a list. It has a header row and data in columns—in fact, you could use it as a list for purposes of filtering, sorting, creating a pivot table, and so on. But the table has not only a header row of labels but a column of labels as well, and the formulas make use of both sets of labels.

Examine the formulas shown in F3:F8. Their results appear in G3:G8. None of these formulas refer to defined names, as they would have had to do in prior versions of Excel. In effect, Excel interprets a label in a natural language formula as though it were a range name.

Consider the formula shown in cell F3, = Jul Profit. It returns the value shown in cell G3, $41,027. In the table that occupies A1:D13, the intersection of the Jul row and the Profit column contains $41,027. The formula in F4, =SUM(Expenses), returns $181,056, just as shown in cell C15.

FIG. 12.9

The formulas refer not to names but to labels.

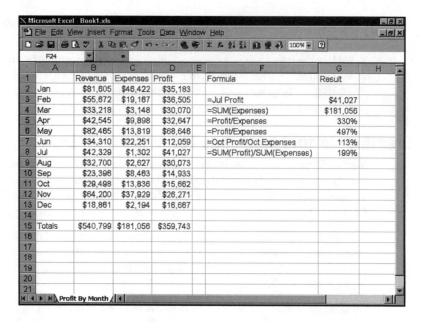

The formula in F5, =Profit/Expenses, is a different matter. It returns 330%. Which Profit? Which Expenses? That's determined by the row in which the formula is entered. As entered in row 5, it's the ratio of April Profit to April Expenses, because data for April is in row 5. As entered in row 6, it returns 497%, the ratio of May Profit to May Expenses.

To specify a particular ratio of Profit to Expenses, it's necessary to specify the month label you're interested in. The formula in G7, =Oct Profit/Oct Expenses, returns 113% no matter where you enter it. The formula specifies both the required row (Oct) and the required columns (Profit and Expenses).

Finally, the formula in G8, =SUM(Profit)/SUM(Expenses), returns 199%. This demonstrates that you can combine multiple instances of functions that refer to labels in a natural language formula.

Now this is very handy, especially in the unlikely event that you're one of the 90 percent of Excel users who have no clue about range names. But things start to break down when you don't have both row and column labels (see Figure 12.10).

In Figure 12.10, the label January is adjacent to two sets of values: two below it, and two to the right. There are also three cells with borders. Each of these cells contains this formula:

=SUM(January)

The three instances of the formula are identical, but they return different results. Cell C3 returns the sum of 9 and 6, values that are found to the right of the label. Cell E6 returns the sum of 7 and 6, values that are found below the label. And cell F7 returns the sum of 7, 6, and 13—where 13 itself represents the sum of January.

FIG. 12.10

The formula returns a different result, depending on its placement.

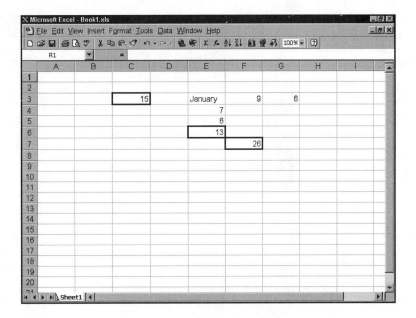

Suppose that you selected cell F7; chose Edit, Copy; then selected cell H1 and chose Edit, Paste. The result would be a #NAME! error in cell H1. Natural language formulas that do not evaluate intersections do not paste well.

The lesson is that if your worksheet doesn't have labels in rows and columns that intersect, beware of the use of natural language formulas. Rely instead on defined range names.

A range can be defined with the same name as a label. In Figure 12.11, the range D2:D9 is defined with the name Kansas, and D6 has the defined name May. Kansas also exists as a label in cell B1, and May exists as a label in cell A6.

The formula in cell G2 is = May Kansas. Using the traditional range intersection, it returns 25, the value in cell D6.

In cell G3 is the natural language formula = May Kansas. It returns 19, the intersection of the label Kansas in column B and the label May. The single quote marks in the formula are used to distinguish the defined names from the (identical) labels.

T I P The conventions that are used for labels in natural language formulas resemble those for defined names—for example, a label cannot resemble a cell address, and begins with a letter, backslash, or underscore, but not a number.

You might well decide that you want to protect yourself against natural language formulas. If so, choose Tools, Options and click the Calculation tab. Clear the Accept Labels in Formulas check box. When you do so, you are warned that Excel will replace the labels with cell references—you can cancel the operation if you want.

Part

III

Ch

12

FIG. 12.11

A range name takes precedence over an identical label.

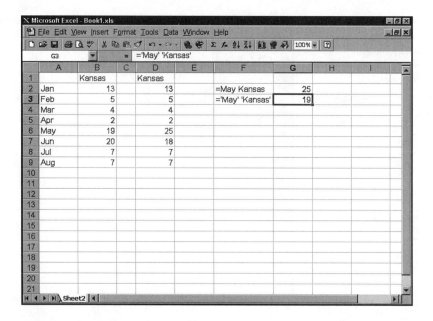

Using the Database Functions with Lists

Lists have more uses in formulas than simply to provide labels for natural languages formulas. There are, for example, the Database functions such as DAVERAGE and DSUM. These functions allow you to specify a range of criteria, exactly as you do for Advanced Filter. The results these functions return are based on those records that meet the criteria you have set up. Figure 12.12 gives an example.

The value in cell E5 in Figure 12.12 is $9,078. This is the average value of the Extended Price variable for the three records shown. An Advanced Filter has been applied to the data range. But the Advanced Filter could be removed, and the DAVERAGE function would return the same result. The results of the filter are shown in the figure so that you can compare them to the results of the DAVERAGE function.

Notice the arguments to the function as shown in the Formula Bar. The data in the list were retrieved from the sample NorthWind Access database by means of Data, Get External Data. When the data were returned from the database, the range that they occupy was automatically named ExternalData1. This becomes the name of the list, and it is used as the first argument to the DAVERAGE function. (Subsequent queries would name the ranges occupied by the data as ExternalData2, ExternalData3, and so on. The Get External Data menu item is available if you have installed Microsoft Query during the Office setup procedure.)

This chapter's section on filtering lists recommended that you give the name Criteria to the range that contains your criteria for Advanced Filter. If you do so, then the Criteria Range edit box in the Advanced Filter dialog box is automatically filled with the criteria range's address. A side benefit of naming this range is that you can use the name Criteria as a Database function's third argument. It is used in the DAVERAGE function in Figure 12.12.

FIG. 12.12

Using a Database function enables you to apply selection criteria.

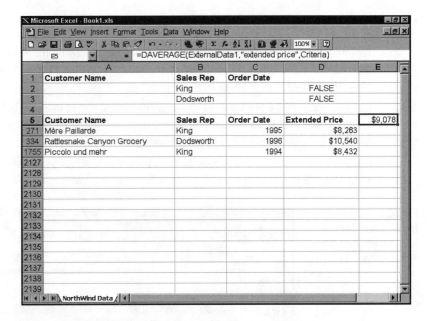

The second argument to DAVERAGE is Extended Price, and it's here that the list structure works to your advantage. The second argument to any Database function can be a label in a list's header row. You could, instead, use the actual cell reference of D6:D2126. But the formula would not then be self-documenting, and face it: It's a pain to select 2,100 rows just to get their address into a formula.

Other Database functions that you might find use for include the following. In each case, you can employ a criteria range to restrict the records that are evaluated. If the list column is Extended Price, then:

- DSUM returns the total of Extended Price.

- DMAX and DMIN return the largest and smallest values of Extended Price.

- DCOUNT returns the number of numeric values in Extended Price. DCOUNTA returns the number of nonblank (thus, both numeric and text) values in Extended Price.

- DSTDEV, DSTDEVP, DVAR, and DVARP return measures of the variability of the values in Extended Price.

- DPRODUCT returns the product of all the selected values in Extended Price.

- DGET returns the value of Extended Price for a single record if the criteria identify a single record. If more than one record meet the criteria, DGET returns the #NUM! error value.

Part
III

Ch
12

Using a Data Form with Lists

It's often more convenient to change records in a list directly on the worksheet. There, you can add records at the end of the list or, by inserting a row, partway through the list. You can delete records by clearing or deleting rows.

But especially if a list is a long one, it can be more efficient to use a *Data Form*. To use it sensibly, the Data Form requires that you have structured your data as a list—that is, a header row and contiguous columns with records in their rows.

Given a list structure, it's very easy to use a Data Form: Select any cell in the list and choose Data, Form. Excel constructs and displays the form, as shown in Figure 12.13.

FIG. 12.13

The Data Form uses the list's header row to label its edit boxes.

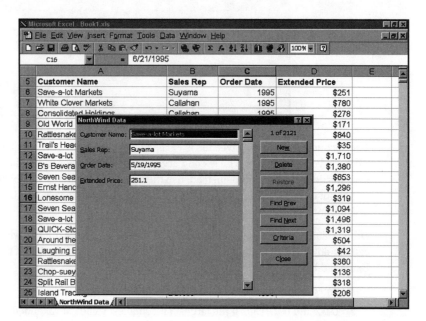

The Data Form has several useful aspects:

- The Data Form is titled according to the name of the active worksheet.
- The number of the current record and the total record count appear at the top-right corner of the form.
- Each field in the list has an edit box labeled according to the values in the list's header row. Edit box labels are supplied with hot keys. You can enter values, but not formulas, in the edit boxes.
- The scroll bar lets you move up and down in the list's records.
- Click the New button to add a record at the bottom of the list.

- Click the Delete button to delete the record showing in the Data Form from the list. The cells that comprise the record are deleted—not simply cleared—from the list. Note that it's the cells that are deleted, not the row that they occupy.

- The Restore button becomes enabled when you have made a change to any of a record's values. If you click Restore, the changes you have made are undone. Restore does not undo changes after you have pressed Enter or moved to another record, and Restore does not recover a deleted record.

- The Find Prev and Find Next buttons move you up and down in the list. When you use either one to leave the current record, any changes you have made are ignored.

Use the Criteria button in the Data Form to establish one or more selection criteria (see Figure 12.14).

FIG. 12.14

Restrict the records available to the Data Form by entering selection criteria.

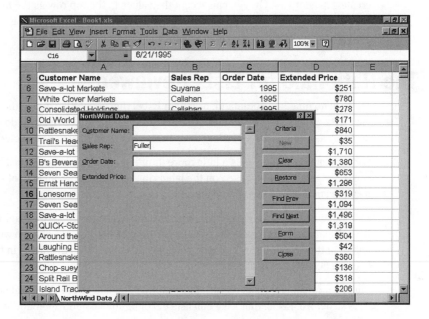

The criteria entered in Figure 12.14 cause the Data Form to display only records for which the Sales Rep field equals Fuller. You can, of course, enter more than one criterion so as to further restrict the record set. Multiple criteria require that a record meet all the criteria that you establish.

Computed criteria are also allowed. For example, you could enter **>9000** in the Extended Price box to restrict the records to those with an Extended Price greater than $9,000.

You can also enter partial criteria. Entering **F** in the Customer Name edit box returns any record where the Customer field begins with F. Criteria are not case-sensitive.

Click Clear to remove any criteria that you have entered, or Restore to undo any changes you have made to the criteria.

When you finish entering criteria, click the Form, the Find Next, or the Find Prev button to return to Form view and continue working with the records. The criteria are not in effect immediately: That is, the record you see when you return to Form view might not meet the criteria that you established. When you move to another record, however, the selection is based on the criteria you entered.

N O T E   Note that Data Validation does not work in conjunction with Data Form. And if you have a filter in place for the list, the filter has no effect on the selection of the records that are displayed in the Data Form. ▧

A Data Form does not absolutely require that you have text labels in the list's top row. If you do not, Data Form displays a message to that effect, and you can then cancel the operation and create a header row. Or, you can accept the values in the top row as the header row. But in this case, the top row probably constitutes an actual record. If you let Data Form treat that first record as a header row, you won't be able to edit or delete that record.

The Rationale for Lists Reviewed

There is no function, command, or tool in Excel that absolutely demands that you structure your data as a list. But many tasks become much more effective if you do so. These tasks often begin by assuming that a header row is present in the data you've selected.

Sorting data, for example, is a little more intuitive when the range to sort has a header row. You can select the sort keys based on the labels in the header row, instead of selecting column headers such as Column A or Column C.

Exporting and importing data from Excel to Access is much more straightforward when you have organized your data in lists. It's easier to work with the associated wizards when you can tell them that the first row in the data is a header row. Then, the labels in the header row become field names in the Access database.

Furthermore, many tasks require that your data be laid out in ways that are consistent with a list's structure. Recall that a list consists of contiguous columns—it does not include an empty column. If you try to create a pivot table based on a range with an empty column, the method fails. A header row with text labels is not required, but if you don't have one, then the pivot table is likely to treat the first actual record as though it contained field names. ●

Pivot Tables

When Excel included pivot tables as a new feature in version 5, it added a capability of extraordinary power and flexibility. If you use Excel for something more than a repository of information—if you use it to analyze data at all—then you need to become familiar with pivot tables.

Defining essential terms

Understand the relationships among lists, fields, and items.

Creating pivot tables from external sources

Base pivot tables on databases such as those created by Microsoft Access.

Using calculated fields and items

Learn how to add calculations to your pivot table after the fact.

Pivot tables enable you to create analyses such as these:

■ Total revenues by Product and Region, with a subtotal for each Product (across Regions) and for each Region (across Products).

■ Summarize revenues by Product and Region as a percentage of each Region's revenue, of each Product's revenue, and as a percentage of total Revenue.

■ Quickly rearrange the layout of a pivot table, showing each Product in a separate row and each Region in a different column, instead of the other way around.

■ Change the data that underlie the pivot table and quickly show the result of that change in the pivot table itself.

Pivot tables can return analyses that are much more sophisticated and subtle than the ones mentioned here. But even if you never use pivot tables to do anything more complex than break down Revenue by Product and Region, you will have added something powerful and flexible to your bag of tricks. ■

Defining Essential Terms

There's some special terminology that clarifies the discussion of pivot tables. Figure 13.1 shows a pivot table on the right, and its source data range on the left.

FIG. 13.1
The major components of a pivot table.

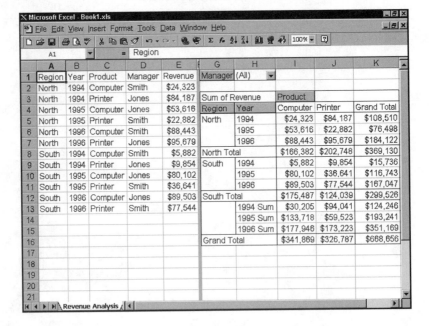

Notice the correspondence between the components in the pivot table and the data in its data source:

- Each column, or *list*, in columns A through E corresponds to a *field* in the pivot table. In Figure 13.1, the lists in columns A and B correspond to the pivot table's Row fields. The list in column C corresponds to the pivot table's Column field, and the list in column D corresponds to the pivot table's Page field. Each list's header becomes the name of the corresponding pivot table field.

- The information in the pivot table's Data field summarizes the information in column E's list. Here, the pivot table displays the sum of E2:E13 for each combination of values in A2:D13. Each cell in the pivot table's Data field is termed a *subtotal*, but this is a little misleading. The Data field can also display an average, a standard deviation, a count, and so on. Whatever it displays, the cells in the Data field are termed *subtotals*.

- Each different value in a list in columns A through D corresponds to an *item* in the pivot table's Row, Column, and Page fields. The value "North" in column A's list corresponds to the "North" item in the pivot table's Row field.

- Notice the subtotals for Year at the bottom of the pivot table. These are subtotals across Region: That is, the $30,205 value for 1994 adds $24,323 for North to $5,882 for South. These are termed *block subtotals*, and they are not provided automatically when you create the pivot table. You can create a block subtotal for the innermost row or column field only. (Suppose that Product were another Row field instead of a Column field, and that the table displayed Year within Product within Region. You could create a block subtotal for Year, but not for Product.)

- The shaded buttons that contain the field names are *pivot table buttons*. You can click-and-drag them on the pivot table itself to pivot the table. For example, you could drag the Year button to the right of the Product button; doing so would change Year from a Row field to a Column field. You can also double-click a pivot table button to customize the characteristics of that field.

You create the pivot table by selecting any cell in the source data range (in Figure 13.1, that's A1:E13). Then, choose Data, PivotTable Report and follow the PivotTable Wizard's four steps. For a basic pivot table, you typically just accept the wizard's defaults.

The only action required of you is to drag buttons where you want them in the wizard's third step. This establishes which fields you want as Row, Column, Page, and Data fields. The only field that's absolutely necessary is the Data field (see Figure 13.2).

The way that you want a pivot table to look—thus, the set of analyses that the pivot table can display—is completely dependent on how you set up the pivot table's source data range. The same data that are shown in Figure 13.1 are also shown in Figure 13.3.

Part
III

Ch
13

FIG. 13.2

Drag the field buttons at the right edge of the dialog box into one of the four field areas. You can put more than one field button into each field area.

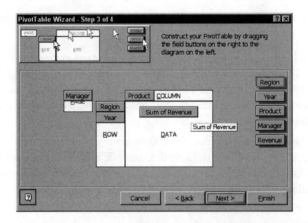

FIG. 13.3

This layout does not lend itself to creating a pivot table.

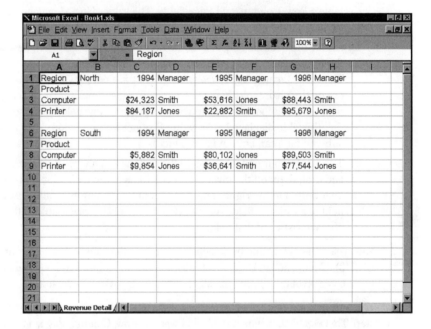

Although the data in Figure 13.3 are the same as in Figure 13.1, you could not create a pivot table using the layout in Figure 13.3. You need—and Figure 13.3 does not show—a list with a header row for each pivot table field, containing each value that will become an item in the pivot table field, in the same row as the value that is summarized in the pivot table's Data field. Contrast the layouts in Figures 13.1 and 13.3: Only the data in Figure 13.1 are organized properly to act as a pivot table's source data range.

There's one particularly important component of a pivot table that you can't see in the figures—or, for that matter, in the workbook itself. That's the pivot table's *cache*.

When you create a pivot table, Excel caches the data. You can neither view nor manipulate the cache directly, but it is the cache that makes a pivot table so flexible. You can drag buttons around, suppress and create subtotals, hide or display items, re-sort values in the table, and so on. When you do so, Excel simply looks to the data cache to recalculate the pivot table's values and rearrange its structure, in response to the changes you've made.

There's a tradeoff, though. You might expect the pivot table to respond immediately if you change anything in the pivot table's source data range. Excel does not meet this expectation. If you make a change to the source data, you must first refresh the pivot table's cache before the change will appear in the pivot table. To refresh the cache, select any part of the pivot table. Then, either click the red exclamation point on the Pivot Table toolbar, or choose Data, Refresh Data. You can also choose Refresh Data from a shortcut menu if you right-click somewhere in the pivot table.

We're all so used to seeing Excel recalculate formulas automatically when we change the cells on which the formulas depend, that it's disconcerting at first to have to refresh the cache. It's a little like having to choose Tools, Options, Calculate Now each time you change a cell value.

But as usual, you get something back. The fact that the data exist in the pivot table's cache means that you can delete the pivot table's source data. After creating the table, just clear the source range if you want, or delete the source data cells. Because the cache maintains the data, you can manipulate the table any way you want and still see accurate values.

If at some future time you want to bring the source data back, just double-click the cell that represents the pivot table's Grand Total row and its Grand Total column. In Figure 13.1, this is cell K16. Excel inserts a new worksheet and writes the data in the cache into the new worksheet, preserving the source data's original layout. This process is termed *drilldown*.

 TIP If you try to retrieve data from the cache in this way and it doesn't work, you probably need to set the drilldown option. Select some portion of the pivot table and choose Data, PivotTable Report. In step 4 of the wizard, choose the Options button and fill the Enable Drilldown check box. You can also click PivotTable on the PivotTable toolbar, or right-click the pivot table and choose Options from the shortcut menu.

Part
III

Ch
13

Creating Pivot Tables from External Sources

You have probably noticed, and perhaps used, the External Data Source option in the PivotTable Wizard's first step. If you choose that option, a variety of data sources are available to you, including:

Access	SQL Server	Excel
dBASE and FoxPro	Text and HTML	

The available sources depend on the options selected when you ran Setup for Office 97. To modify the list of drivers, run Setup and follow Data Access to Database Drivers.

The beauty of using a true database (one created using Access, dBASE, or FoxPro) is that it is virtually guaranteed to have a structure that's consistent with a pivot table's requirements. These databases have records and fields. Conceptually, a database's records correspond to the entries in a worksheet's list. A database's fields are analogous to different lists on a worksheet. Therefore, using an external data source, there's no need to worry about structuring Excel lists in such a fashion as to support a pivot table.

Furthermore, a relational database can store truly enormous amounts of data—amounts that would choke an Excel workbook—in a relatively small amount of space. I have a client who has three Excel workbooks that together occupy more than 13M of disk space. The client uses the workbooks to maintain several years' worth of financial data and associated formulas.

But for the purpose of analyzing all that information via pivot tables, the client uses Access. The 13M worth of Excel data is replicated in an Access database that occupies only 3M. When the client wants to summarize the data with a pivot table, he first refreshes the pivot table's cache from the Access database. During the refresh operation, the information travels from Access to Excel as fast as bad news.

In Chapter 14, "Connecting to Access Databases," you learn how Data Access Objects (DAO) can make this kind of data acquisition occur so quickly. But DAO requires the use of VBA, and it requires that you have at least a nodding acquaintance with Structured Query Language (SQL).

In contrast, if you choose the External Data Source option in the PivotTable Wizard's first step, you are guided through a process that sets up the connection between a pivot table and an external database. You need know neither VBA nor SQL: Instead, much of the coding is done on your behalf, and you define the connection by pointing, clicking, and dragging things around. The remainder of this section takes you on a guided tour.

Defining the Data Source

When you choose External Data Source in the PivotTable Wizard, you first see a different version of the wizard's second step. In addition to the usual Next, Back, and Cancel buttons is the Get Data button, shown in Figure 13.4.

If you do not see the Choose Data Source dialog box after clicking Get Data in the PivotTable Wizard's second step, you probably have not installed Microsoft Query. Run Office Setup again to install it. Otherwise, you can select an existing data source, or select New Data Source. Assuming that you select New Data Source, clicking OK brings up the Create New Data Source dialog box shown in Figure 13.5.

Begin by naming the new data source. In Figure 13.5, it is named Northwind. Because the Northwind sample database that accompanies Office 97 is an Access database, Microsoft Access Driver (.mdb) is chosen from the Select a Driver drop-down list. After you choose a driver, the Connect button is enabled. Clicking that button displays the ODBC Microsoft Office 97 Setup dialog box (see Figure 13.6).

FIG. 13.4

Choosing External Data Source in the wizard's first step displays a different version of its second step. When you then choose Get Data, the Choose Data Source dialog box appears.

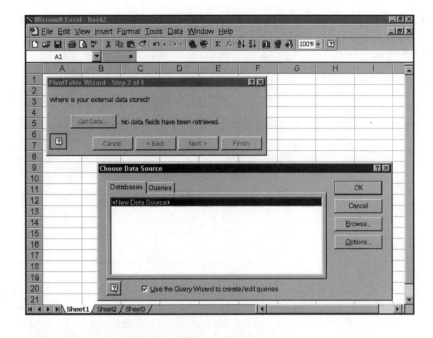

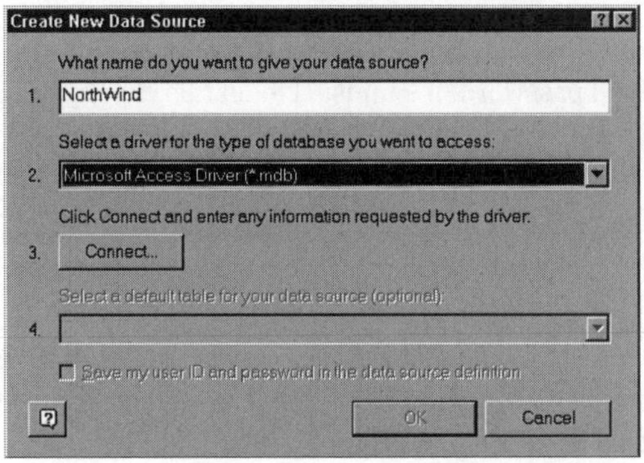

FIG. 13.5

The data source you create here will subsequently appear in the Choose Data Source dialog box.

There is a wide variety of selections you can make from the ODBC Microsoft Access 97 Setup dialog box. For example, use the Advanced button to set values for parameters such as the login name and password to use when making the connection to the database. Or, choose Compact to squeeze excess, unneeded space out of an Access database.

But if all you want to do is establish the data source for a pivot table, use the Select button to browse to the location of the database file. In this example, that's the Northwind sample database, which is usually stored in Program Files\Microsoft Office\Office\Samples.

NOTE If this process appears to hang after you have selected a database, another user may already have the database open. You will have to exit or wait until the database has been released. You might also see an error message that the database is exclusively locked. Again, this usually means that someone else is using the database and you will have to wait until it's available. ■

Part
III

Ch
13

FIG. 13.6

In most cases, all you need do in the ODBC Microsoft Access 97 Setup dialog box is select the database by browsing to its location.

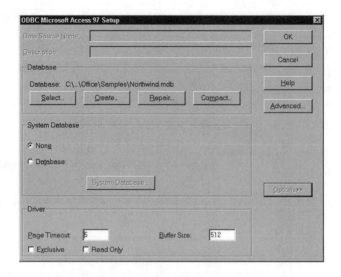

As shown in Figure 13.6, once you see at least the partial path to the database and the database name in the Database group box, choose OK to return to the Create New Data Source dialog box. If you want, you can use the drop-down box in item 4 to specify a table in the database that will be used by default when you actually connect to the database.

At this point, the Create New Data Source dialog box enables a check box that allows you to save your user name and password. It's unusual to fill this check box. All the information that you've been supplying—the type of driver to use, the name and location of the database, and possibly the name of a table to open by default—is stored in a data source definition file. This file's format is simple ASCII, and it can be read by anyone who has a text editor that's no more sophisticated than Notepad. Filling this check box adds a password to the ASCII file, so it's no longer public.

If there's no one else around to snoop for the password, why are you using one? Who are you protecting the database from? Yourself? Okay, there are some circumstances that might cause you to fill the check box. But it's a stretch.

When you click OK in the Create New Data Source dialog box, you return to the Choose Data Source dialog box, which now contains the name of the new data source that you just created. If necessary, select that name and choose OK. What happens next depends on whether you filled the check box labeled Use the Query Wizard to Create/Edit Queries.

Using the Query Wizard

If you filled the Query Wizard check box in the Choose Data Source dialog box, you next see the Query Wizard's Choose Columns dialog box, shown in Figure 13.7.

The Available Tables and Columns list box shows the tables in the database you selected. Each table has a plus symbol beside its name: Click the plus symbol to display the names of the table's available columns. Select one or more tables, or one or more columns within a table, and click the right-arrow button to move columns into the Columns in Your Query list box.

FIG. 13.7
You can also choose to use the Query Wizard if you want to edit the definition of an existing data source.

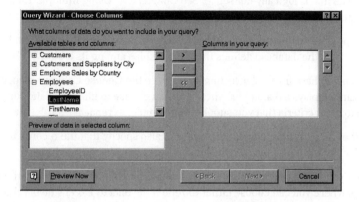

Once you have moved at least one column into the list box, use the left-arrow button to move columns back out of the list. This is a convenient way to select all but a few columns from a given table; move the entire table into the list box, then remove the unwanted columns.

N O T E Don't get lost in these steps. Keep in mind your eventual purpose: to create a pivot table using data from a database that's external to Excel. Also, keep in mind that you're in the process of defining what information to pull into the pivot table. When you've done this once for a given pivot table, the information you're specifying here is saved with the pivot table. Thereafter, clicking the Refresh button is all you need to do to perform an update. ■

The Query Wizard refers to "columns." These columns are fields in the database's tables. When you select a column, you're selecting a database field that might eventually become a field in the pivot table. Bearing that in mind, be sure to choose any columns that you want to include as pivot table fields.

This process also may require that you be familiar with the structure of the database. Suppose that, using the Northwind database, you'd like to know how much each employee has sold to each customer. You select the column named CompanyName from the Customers table, LastName from the Employees table, and ExtendedPrice from the Order Details Extended table. Your intent is to create a pivot table that shows the customer's name as the Row field, employee's name as the Column field, and extended price as the Data field.

The problem is that these tables do not have any fields in common. The Order Details Extended table has no information about which employee sold the order, nor does it have any information about which company made the purchase.

If you set up a situation like this, the Query Wizard gives up. It shrugs its shoulders, tells you that it can't join the tables you chose, and turns control over to you. It displays the Query window (see the next section for information about the Query window) and leaves it to you to fix things up.

Part

III

Ch

13

At this point, you must either cancel out of the process, modify the selection you've made, or use the selection as it stands. The selection might be syntactically legitimate, but return a set of records that is logically nonsense. See Chapter 21, "Using Multiple Tables," for information about querying from tables that are not joined.

The point is that to make effective use of queries on more than one database table, you need to know how the database defines the relationships among its tables.

When you have finished selecting columns in the Choose Columns step, click Next. The Query Wizard displays a dialog box where you can choose to filter the data, suppressing records that fail to meet criteria that you supply (for example, ExtendedPrice > 100).

In the Query Wizard's third step, you can also specify that the records be returned in a sorted order (for example, sorted by CompanyName in ascending order).

After you have specified any sorts that you want, click Next to display the Query Wizard's final step, where you can choose either to return the data to Excel's PivotTable Wizard, or to view the results of the query. Choosing to view the query's results displays the Query window. Using this window is discussed in the next section.

Using the Query Window

Recall that you invoke the Query Wizard by filling the check box in the Choose Data Source dialog box (refer to Figure 13.4). If you did not fill this check box, or if you choose to view query results in the Query Wizard's final step, you see the Query window as shown in Figure 13.8.

FIG. 13.8

The Query window displays the chosen tables and their joins, as well as the records and fields that result.

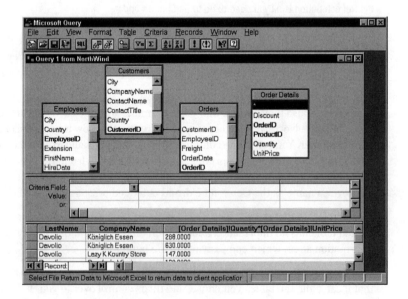

So, in the process of defining a pivot table's external data source, you have two ways to view the Query window. You can get there indirectly, by way of the Query Wizard, which you use to set up the information in the Query window for you. Or you can get to the Query window directly from the Choose Data Source dialog box, by clearing the Query Wizard check box. In that case, the Query window includes no tables, filters, or sorts—you're working with a blank slate.

Once you're familiar with the Query window, you'll probably want to go to it directly: It's a little faster to work there than it is to step through the Query Wizard. If you've done much work in Access, you're probably familiar with this window. It's similar to the window you see when you define a new query in Access's Design view.

In Figure 13.8, the Query window already has some tables and fields defined, so the records returned by the query are also visible. Notice these aspects:

- The window has three panes: The top one is the Table pane, the middle one is the Criteria pane, and the bottom one is the Data pane.

- The tables have arrows connecting them. This means that the tables have fields in common. The tables are joined to one another by means of these common fields. You can add more tables by choosing Table, Add Tables.

- The fields that are returned by the query appear in the Data pane. You can add additional fields by dragging a field from a table into an empty column in the first row of the Data pane.

- You can create or modify existing criteria in the Criteria pane. However, there is no Sort By row, as there is in Access's query design. To specify or modify a sort, choose Records, Sort.

- You can create calculated fields using the Query window (but not in the Query Wizard). To do so, click the first row of an empty column in the Data pane, and type an expression. (Do *not* begin the expression with an equal sign: So doing violates the syntax rules.)

In Figure 13.8, there is a calculated expression that multiplies Quantity by UnitPrice to return the extended price for each record. To create that expression, or a similar one, click in a blank cell in the first row of the Data pane and type:

```
[Order Details]!Quantity*[Order Details]!UnitPrice
```

Notice that you must specify the name of the tables that contain the fields involved in the calculation; here, that name is [Order Details]. Square brackets are required when a table's name contains a special character such as a blank space.

When you use the Query window to create a calculated field, the name of the field by default becomes the expression itself. Most likely, you do not want a pivot table field whose name is, for example:

```
[Order Details]!Quantity*[Order Details]!UnitPrice
```

Part
III

Ch
13

If you want to name the field as, say, Extended Price, select the field in the Data pane and choose Records, Edit Column. Type **Extended Price** in the Column Heading edit box and click OK.

TIP You can also rename fields in the context of the pivot table. Right-click a cell in the field that you want to rename, and choose Field from the shortcut menu. Type the name that you want the pivot table to show in the Name edit box. The difference between renaming a field in Query and renaming it in the pivot table is that in Query, you actually give the field a new name. In the pivot table, you're just changing the label—the source field retains its existing name.

When you have made any modifications you want, choose File, Return Data to Microsoft Excel, or click the Return Data button. When you do so, you are (finally!) returned to the second step of the PivotTable Wizard. You now continue as usual by defining the Row, Column, Page, and Data fields for the pivot table.

The resulting pivot table appears in Figure 13.9.

FIG. 13.9

This pivot table results from the query shown in Figure 13.8. The data source is the database itself, and therefore does not appear in the workbook.

Sum of Extended Price	LastName					
CompanyName	Buchanan	Callahan	Davolio	Dodsworth	Fuller	King
Alfreds Futterkiste			$1,342			
Ana Trujillo Emparedados y helados						
Antonio Moreno Taquería			$957			$2
Around the Horn		$899	$2,932	$5,167		
Berglunds snabbköp	$2,130	$4,120	$6,785	$5,465	$613	
Blauer See Delikatessen		$464		$1,632		
Blondel pére et fils	$1,420	$660		$2,040	$1,176	
Bólido Comidas preparadas				$280		
Bon app'	$510	$2,286	$4,253	$2,172	$2,032	
Bottom-Dollar Markets			$1,888	$1,209	$5,436	
B's Beverages			$1,500	$140	$1,328	
Cactus Comidas para llevar		$531		$13	$477	
Centro comercial Moctezuma						
Chop-suey Chinese	$625		$2,312			$
Comércio Mineiro		$2,169	$108		$406	
Consolidated Holdings		$632			$156	
Die Wandernde Kuh		$3,469	$695		$1,615	$
Drachenblut Delikatessen		$1,692	$1,118			
Du monde entier			$269		$63	$

It's important to realize that you need to go through these steps only once. After you have defined the pivot table's data source, that information stays with the pivot table. Pivot tables have a property named `SourceData`, and if you're really interested, you can use VBA to view this property. Invoking the `SourceData` property with VBA returns a read-only variant. To see it, use code such as this:

```
Sub ShowSourceData()
Dim SD As Variant
```

```
SD = ThisWorkbook.Sheets(1).PivotTables(1).SourceData
For i = LBound(SD) To UBound(SD)
   Sheets(2).Cells(i, 1) = SD(i)
Next i
End Sub
```

There are usually nonprinting characters in the resulting cells. Use Excel's CLEAN() function on the cells to remove those characters and view their contents more conveniently.

Because the source data definition stays with the pivot table, you can refresh the pivot table's cache at any time by means of Data, Refresh Data. (You can usually refresh a pivot table's cache from an external data source even if someone else is using the database.) You would do so if you knew or suspected that the data in the database had changed.

Therefore, once a pivot table has been created, and so long as you don't need to modify some aspect of the data source, there's no need to use either the Query Wizard or the Query window again. (However, you would need to modify the data source definition if you change the location of the database, find that you want to add tables or fields, or if you want to make some other change to the existing definition. Usually, you do so by creating a new pivot table with a new data source definition.)

Furthermore, you can create new pivot tables based on the one that you have already created. To do so, choose Another Pivot Table in the PivotTable Wizard's first step. The new pivot table is based on the existing pivot table's cache. Therefore, the new pivot table uses the same data source as does the old one, and you refresh both pivot tables in the same way.

Page Fields and External Data Sources

It's rare, but it can happen that you build a pivot table that's based on a database so huge that you encounter memory problems when you originally retrieve the data, or when you refresh the pivot table's cache.

If you're willing to work temporarily with only a subset of the data, you can arrange to return information from the database on a Page field item basis. That is, you set an option that causes only the data associated with a given Page field item to come back from the data source. You determine which item will be retrieved by selecting that item from the Page field's drop-down list.

To set this option, double-click the Page field's button in the pivot table to display the PivotTable Field dialog box, and click the Advanced button. In the resulting PivotTable Field Advanced Options dialog box, select the Query External Data Source as You Select Each Page Field Item option button (see Figure 13.10).

The Page field options shown in Figure 13.10 are available only when the pivot table's data source is an external one. When you choose to retrieve data for all Page field items, the entire pivot table is refreshed in one step. When you choose to retrieve data one Page field item at a time, less memory is required—but to effect a complete refresh of the pivot table, you must step through each Page field item in turn. And Microsoft Query remains open, so as to respond immediately to your selection of different Page field items: This consumes some of the memory that you're trying to conserve.

Part
III

Ch
13

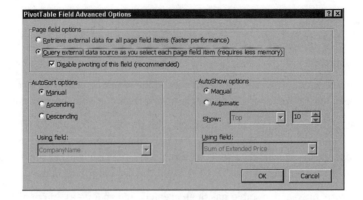

Furthermore, every time you select a different Page field item, the data are refreshed—even if
no changes to the data source have occurred. So, selecting item A, then item B, then item A
again results in three separate refreshes. Also, the usual (All) Page field item disappears from
the drop-down list, and you can no longer use Show Pages to write each Page field item's data
to a separate worksheet.

Notice in Figure 13.10 the Disable Pivoting of this Field (Recommended) check box. When
filled, this check box prevents the user from moving the selected Page field out of the Page
area. If you clear the check box and move the Page field, you cancel the effect of choosing to
retrieve data one Page item at a time.

On the topic of Page fields, Excel 97 gives you a new way to arrange them in the pivot table.
When you use more than one Page field simultaneously, prior versions stacked the fields' drop-
down lists atop one another. In Excel 97, you can string the Page fields out horizontally, as
shown in Figure 13.11.

The arrangement of the Page field drop-down lists in Figure 13.11 trades rows for columns:
Fewer rows but more columns are used. Because the Page fields are side by side instead of
stacked, you can see which Manager item is selected when you invoke the Year field's drop-
down list. If they were stacked, the Year's drop-down list would hide the selected item in the
Manager field.

To get this set up for Page fields, use the PivotTable Options dialog box. Open this dialog box
in the PivotTable Wizard's final step, or from the PivotTable drop-down list on the PivotTable
toolbar, or by right-clicking any cell in the pivot table. The dialog box is shown in Figure 13.12.

In the Page Layout drop-down list, select Over, Then Down. This aligns the Page fields as
shown in Figure 13.11. Of course, the option has a noticeable effect only when there are at
least two Page fields showing.

Choosing Over, Then Down instead of Down, Then Over has no functional results—the choice
is entirely a matter of appearance and convenience.

FIG. 13.11
Arranging the Page fields as shown can save space on the worksheet, and can make it more convenient to use their drop-down lists.

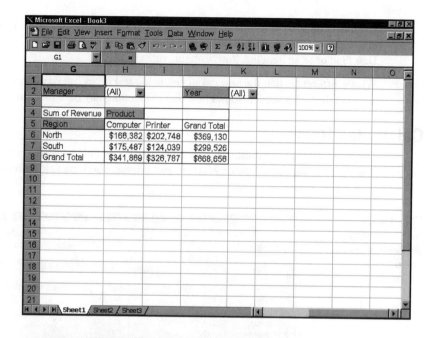

FIG. 13.12
Several new options are available in Excel 97 pivot tables.

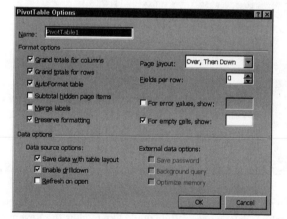

Using Calculated Fields and Items

Among Excel 97's new features are calculated fields and items in pivot tables. If you're an experienced user of pivot tables, this might not seem like big news: After all, you've always been able to use calculated values in pivot tables. For example, suppose that cell C1 contains:

```
=A1-B1
```

and that cell C1 is part of the range of data used to build the pivot table. If so, then the difference between the values in A1 and B1 is going to show up somewhere in the pivot table—in a Data field or as an item in a Row, Column, or Page field.

What's different is that the new calculated fields and items can be defined *after* the table has been created. This section shows how that distinction may have functional value.

Calculated Items

Suppose that you have created a pivot table with a Row field named Product. This Row field has four items: Computer, Monitor, Modem, and Printer. The Data field is Revenue. The pivot table is shown in Figure 13.13.

FIG. 13.13

The pivot table sums the Revenue for each product.

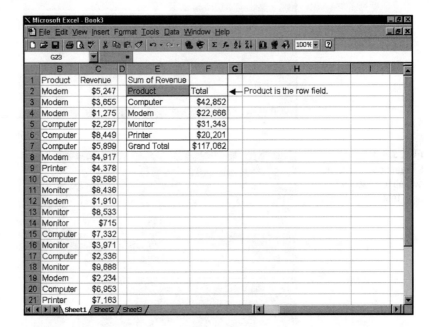

After creating the pivot table, you realize that you could have done a better job of planning the structure of the table's data source. While you'd like to view the Revenue associated with each product, you'd also like to contrast the Revenue due to the Computer product with the Revenue for all the other Products—call them Peripherals.

If you'd thought ahead, you could have arranged to have an additional field called Product Type, with just two items: Computer and Peripherals. Then, by including both Product and Product Type when you created the pivot table, you could switch back and forth between the two as Row fields. The pivot table in Figure 13.13 also appears in Figure 13.14, with Product Type as the Row field.

Or, also shown in Figure 13.14, you could display the Product and Product Type fields simultaneously.

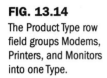

FIG. 13.14
The Product Type row field groups Modems, Printers, and Monitors into one Type.

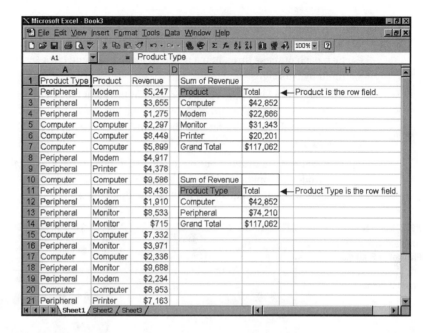

But that's wishful thinking. You didn't plan ahead and you want to see Computer compared to Peripherals right now. So, follow these steps to create a calculated item:

1. In the pivot table, click the Product field button to select it and its existing items.

2. Either right-click the Product field button to display its shortcut menu, or click the PivotTable drop-down list on the PivotTable toolbar.

3. Choose Formulas, Calculated Item. The Insert Calculated Item dialog box appears (see Figure 13.15).

FIG. 13.15
The items that appear in the Items list box depend on which field you have selected in the Fields list box.

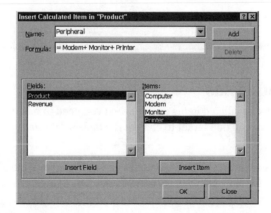

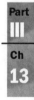

Part
III

Ch
13

4. If necessary, select Product in the Fields list box.

5. In the Name box, type **Peripheral**.

6. In the Formula box, type **=Modem + Monitor + Printer**. Or, type = and then click in turn each of these three items in the Items list box and click Insert Item, separating them by plus signs.

7. Choose OK to insert the calculated item in the pivot table. Figure 13.16 shows the pivot table at this point in the process. Notice that you have duplicated information: Modem, Monitor, and Printer, along with their sum in Peripheral, so the Grand Total is too high, due to including their revenues twice.

8. Double-click the Product button to obtain the PivotTable Field dialog box. Use it to hide the Modem, Monitor, and Printer items. Figure 13.16 also shows the pivot table as it appears when you choose OK to close the dialog box.

FIG. 13.16

You can now use the PivotTable Field dialog box to hide individual Product items.

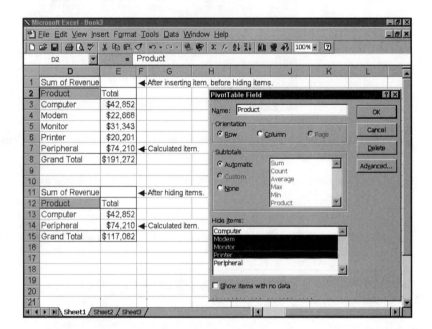

Creating Calculated Fields

The best reason to use calculated items occurs when you need to make a change to an existing pivot table, but you don't want to change the table's data source. The same is true of a calculated field.

Figure 13.17 shows a data range in columns A, B, and C. You create the pivot table from these data, with Product as the Row field and with Price and Cost as the Data fields. After creating the pivot table, you realize that you'd also like to see product margin.

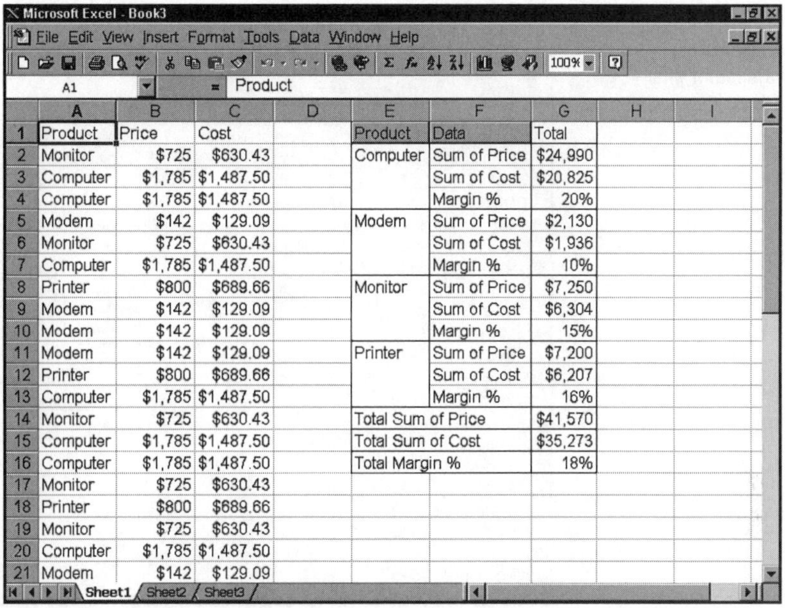

FIG. 13.17

A calculated field appears in the pivot table's Data area.

Using the PivotTable toolbar or by right-clicking a field button, choose Formulas, Calculated Field. In the Insert Calculated Field dialog box, you create a new field named Margin and set its formula to:

```
=(Price - Cost) / Cost
```

After formatting the new Margin field as Percent, the pivot table appears as shown in Figure 13.17. Notice that the calculated Margin is the ratio of the Sum of Price, less the Sum of Cost, divided by the Sum of Cost. This is the also the result that you get if you apply the formula to individual records in the underlying data range. The formula, as applied to the Sums, returns the same result as it does when applied to the individual records.

Figure 13.18 shows that this is not always true.

In Figure 13.18, your data consist of a Product, its Price, and Quantity sold. After creating the pivot table that sums Quantity, you would like to see Extended Price for each Product. So, you add Price to the pivot table and create a calculated field named Extended Price. Its formula is:

```
= Price * Quantity
```

The result is as shown in the second pivot table in Figure 13.18.

Those Extended Price values are a little high. The calculated field takes the sum of price and the sum of quantity, and multiplies their totals. It does not multiply Price times Quantity, and sum the products, which is what you would want for Extended Price.

Part
III

Ch
13

FIG. 13.18

Calculated fields do not always return what you're looking for.

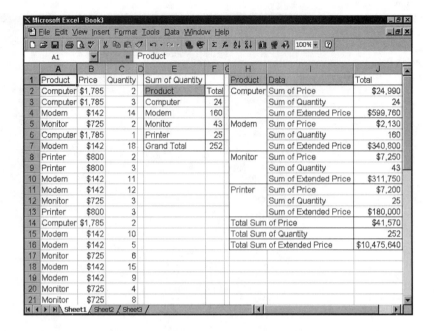

In order to get the result you're after by means of a calculated field, you'd have to rearrange the underlying data. It should have one row for each sale of a given product (as it stands, each row represents several sales of a given product). Then, the resulting pivot table would automatically provide Extended Price.

As the data range is actually laid out, you need to calculate Extended Price outside the pivot table. For each row in the underlying data range, you should calculate the product of Quantity and Price. Then, include that column in the pivot table as a Data field.

Limitations to Calculated Fields and Items

There are plenty of limitations to calculated fields and items. For example, you can't use custom subtotals to show the Data field as an average, standard deviation, or variance when you have created a calculated item. However, you could create a formula for a calculated item that does this for you. You might define a West Region Average item whose formula is:

```
= (California + Oregon + Washington)/3
```

Again, though, it's much more sensible to include a Region field in the pivot table's data range and create a custom subtotal for that field.

Other limitations include:

■ You can't use an item from one field as part of the formula for a calculated item in another field.

■ You can't use a Data field in a formula for a calculated item.

■ A calculated field cannot be used as a Row, Column, or Page field; it must be a Data field.

Given these limitations, you can derive a general rule for calculated fields and items. If you find yourself using them, you could profitably spend more time thinking about the structure of the pivot table's data source. ●

Connecting to Access Databases

The Microsoft Office Professional suite includes the Access database application. If you have a large amount of data, you should consider storing and maintaining the data in Access rather than in Excel. This is because Access is optimized for data storage and retrieval; it performs both these functions with much greater efficiency than does Excel.

In contrast, Excel is optimized for data analysis and reporting. When it comes time to summarize the data, find relationships, or display the data in a chart, Excel is the better choice.

When you use Access for data storage and Excel for analysis, you get the best of both applications. The only remaining issue is arranging to make the Access data available to Excel. You'll find the best way to do that described in this chapter. ■

Why use a relational database?

Learn how to understand situations that call for using a database for data storage and Excel for data analysis.

Creating a pivot table using VBA and DAO

Use Data Access Objects (DAO) efficiently to return data to Excel.

Modifying Access databases from Excel

Use DAO in the Excel context to control a database.

A sample application

Accommodate users who are familiar with Excel but not with Access.

Why Use a Relational Database?

Consider a situation in which you have many different products, each of which you can describe in a variety of ways. Each product has some number of instances in your inventory. Each product has dollar amounts that describe its contribution to your revenue, its contribution to your cost of goods sold, its current valuation, and so on.

Any of your products might have a very long name, such as "Rosewood Dining Table With Dropleaves." In an Excel workbook, it might be necessary to store that product name several times: once in the inventory count worksheet, once in a contribution margin analysis, once in a product sales summary, once in an accounts payable worksheet—you get the idea. You find your Excel workbooks storing product names that are as long as 50 characters many times. And if you have 500 such products, the situation quickly starts to get out of control.

I have seen a firm with not 500, but more than 700 products, each of which could have a name longer than 50 characters, trying to store all its domestic and international revenue information in a single Excel workbook. The workbook occupied nearly 4M on the firm's disks. It was taking the analysts almost a minute just to open the workbook and calculate all the formulas, even on P200 computers. They were having trouble closing their books in a timely fashion at the end of each quarter. They were starting to use Word to update their resumes.

That workbook was stuffed full of lengthy, repetitive information, and they should have been using Access to store the data. This firm could have—and eventually did—store each product name *once* in an Access database. An integer code that represented each product name was stored many times: once for domestic revenue, once for international revenue, once for unit sales, and so on. Storing 700 integer values instead of 700 50-character text values saved the firm an enormous amount of disk space (not, though, before some of those resumes had been circulated).

Now, when it comes time to analyze the data in Excel, Access looks up the text name of each product according to its integer code, and sends the text name to Excel along with its associated financial information. While there is a tradeoff in processing time for disk space, the tradeoff usually works in favor of the user—and that's the fundamental idea behind a relational database.

N O T E   The material in this chapter relies heavily on both DAO and VBA. If you are unfamiliar with either one, consider deferring this chapter until you have examined the book's chapters on Access (Part IV) and VBA (Part VII). ■

Connecting Excel and Access

Office has several ways to move data between Access and Excel. Some ways are legacies from earlier versions of Office and have been kept both for the user's convenience and for backwards compatibility. The available methods include:

■ *Pivot tables.* Using the PivotTable Wizard, you can specify that the data come from an external data source. Choosing this option requires that you have the Microsoft Query add-in installed, along with the necessary database drivers. The connection is a one-way street: You cannot directly move Excel data to Access via pivot tables.

- *Microsoft Query.* To use Query, you must install the XLQUERY.xla add-in into Excel. Using Query, you can retrieve data from an external database into Excel, and also update the database. Nevertheless, Query's functionality and speed are restricted.

- *Access Links.* Again, this requires installing an add-in, ACCLINK.xla. Once installed, the add-in puts menu items into the Data menu; these items enable you to create a form or report based on data in an Access database, and to send data from Excel to an Access database. Again, the speed and functionality are restricted.

- *The XLODBC.xla add-in.* This add-in has more power and functionality than either Query or Access Links. If you are developing Excel capabilities that must be compatible all the way back to Excel version 5, consider using XLODBC.xla. It gives your VBA code access to several different database connectivity functions, although nowhere near as many as does DAO. XLODBC.xla does not add any functionality to Excel's menu structures.

- *DAO (Data Access Objects).* Use DAO in situations where Excel 95 and 97 only are involved. DAO is the fastest, most powerful method to connect Excel and Access (or any other ODBC-compliant database). DAO lets your VBA code interact directly with the Microsoft Jet database engine. Using DAO, you have access to a wide variety of functions, and your queries execute surprisingly fast.

This chapter shows you how to use DAO to get data in and out of Access and Excel.

> **N O T E** Much of the material in this chapter makes reference to controlling Access. This is to keep the language straightforward. Sometimes, when you take some action or execute a line of VBA code, you're actually using Access; other times, you're actually using the Jet database engine. Because the distinction is usually transparent, this chapter refers to Access in each case. ■

Installing DAO

Before you can use DAO, you must install it from your Office CD. In the Office Setup routine, select the Data Access check box in the Options list box. Click Change Option, and if necessary, select the Data Access Objects for Visual Basic check box. Then, complete the Setup installation.

After you have installed DAO from Office Setup, you also need to make it available to your VBA code. After starting Excel, press Alt+F11, or choose Tools, Macro, Visual Basic Editor to open the VBE. Choose Tools, References, and select the check box for Microsoft DAO 3.5 Object Library.

Now, any VBA code that you write in the active project has access to DAO objects, methods, and properties. For example, you can now declare object variables in your VBA code that refer to database objects:

```
Dim DatabaseToOpen As Database
Dim DataToRetrieve As Recordset
```

Part
III

Ch
14

and subsequently make use of any of these objects' properties and methods. Furthermore, you can make use of methods in the Excel VBA object model that require DAO, such as the `Range` object's `CopyFromRecordset` method.

Creating a Pivot Table Using VBA and DAO

To repeat: Installing DAO makes no changes to the usual Excel user interface. DAO is a collection of objects that, when installed, are available to your VBA code. If you're not yet comfortable with VBA, you might want to defer reading the rest of this chapter until you have studied this book's section on VBA.

Otherwise, here's an approach to retrieving data from an Access database into an Excel pivot table.

Setting Up the Access Structures

It's often best to point Excel at an Access query, rather than at an Access table. There are several reasons:

- A query can easily pull records from more than one table.
- A query can have built-in criteria, so that you retrieve a subset of records that meet the criteria you have defined.
- A query can obtain a subset of fields from a table, so that you retrieve only those fields that you want for the pivot table.
- A query can return totals across groups of records that have the same value on some field—for example, Department or Product.
- A query can include calculated fields (for example, `TotalCost = Quantity * UnitCost`). While you can have calculated fields in pivot tables in Excel 97, you might find it more convenient to let Access do the calculation and return the result to Excel. The result is returned as a value, not as a formula.

Suppose that you have set up four tables and associated relationships in an Access database, as shown in Figure 14.1.

The tables (and the data in the tables) shown in Figure 14.1 are taken from the NorthWind sample database that accompanies Access. The rationale for their structure is that each record in Order Details represents the sale of some Product by some Employee. When you want to look at an analysis of product sales by employee, you want to see the name of the product and the name of the employee.

However, the fact that you want to see these names in an analysis does not mean that the database must store the name of the employee and the name of the product along with each recorded sale in the database. Instead, you store codes that represent the names along with each sale. When it comes time to view a report, Access looks up the name that's associated with the code and returns the name. This makes for much more efficient data storage.

FIG. 14.1

The relationships between the tables enable a query to retrieve records properly from the correct tables.

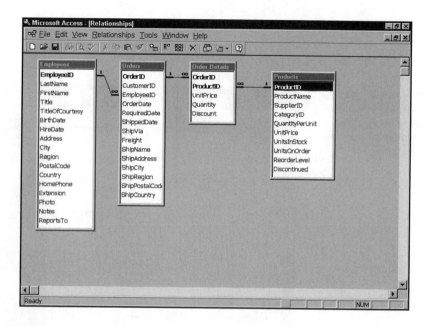

The associations between the codes and the names are implied by the arrows between the tables in Figure 14.1. In words: "For each record in Order Details, return LastName from Employees, based on EmployeeID (getting to Employees via Orders). Also return ProductName from Products, based on ProductID."

Given this structure and the relationships among the tables, you create a query as shown in Figure 14.2.

FIG. 14.2

The query specifies that only certain fields from the tables should be returned.

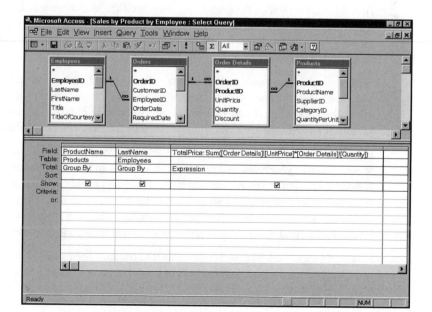

Part
III

Ch
14

Figure 14.2 displays the design of the query, which is named Sales By Product By Employee. The first few records returned by the query are shown in Figure 14.3. You switch from Design view to Datasheet view by choosing View, Datasheet View.

FIG. 14.3

In Datasheet view, this query displays the data found in one field from each table.

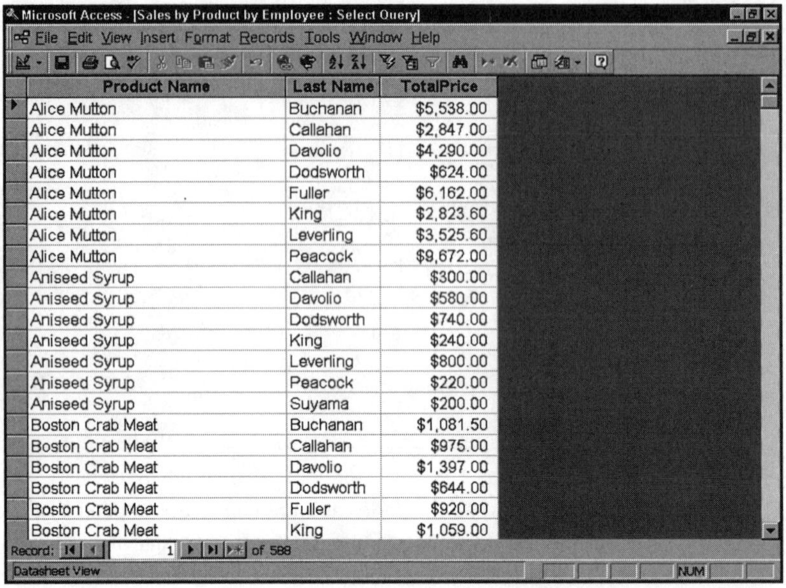

Product Name	Last Name	TotalPrice
Alice Mutton	Buchanan	$5,538.00
Alice Mutton	Callahan	$2,847.00
Alice Mutton	Davolio	$4,290.00
Alice Mutton	Dodsworth	$624.00
Alice Mutton	Fuller	$6,162.00
Alice Mutton	King	$2,823.60
Alice Mutton	Leverling	$3,525.60
Alice Mutton	Peacock	$9,672.00
Aniseed Syrup	Callahan	$300.00
Aniseed Syrup	Davolio	$580.00
Aniseed Syrup	Dodsworth	$740.00
Aniseed Syrup	King	$240.00
Aniseed Syrup	Leverling	$800.00
Aniseed Syrup	Peacock	$220.00
Aniseed Syrup	Suyama	$200.00
Boston Crab Meat	Buchanan	$1,081.50
Boston Crab Meat	Callahan	$975.00
Boston Crab Meat	Davolio	$1,397.00
Boston Crab Meat	Dodsworth	$644.00
Boston Crab Meat	Fuller	$920.00
Boston Crab Meat	King	$1,059.00

These are the records, and the fields for each record, that the query will return to Excel in preparation for setting up the pivot table.

The tables, their relationships, and the query itself are all that's needed to bring the data, properly arranged to create a pivot table, into Excel. In practice, however, an Excel user normally wants to be able to return the results of more than one query, so as to do more than just one analysis.

Suppose that a user wanted to break down sales by both Employee and Product, and also by both Employee and Year—that is, the year in which each employee made sales. In that case, it would be easy enough to add Year to the query shown in Figures 14.2 and 14.3. Then, to perform each analysis, the user can simply rearrange the fields in the resulting pivot table.

But suppose that you wanted to enable the user also to create a pivot table that shows number of employees by year hired and country of residence. In that case, the unit of analysis is not the individual sale, but the individual employee. While you could add HireDate and Country to the sales query, to do so would be wasteful. You don't need to know the hire date and country for each employee for each sale—just for each employee. So, you create another query, named Employee By HireDate by Country, that returns one record for each employee.

Finally, it's useful to set up an Access table that contains the names of the queries. The VBA code that creates the pivot tables needs to know the names of the Access queries in order to retrieve the data. One way to accomplish this would be to hard-code the query names into VBA.

But to specify the query names in the code makes things very rigid—whenever you wanted to create another query, you'd have to include the name of the new query in the VBA code. By establishing an Access table with the query names, all you need to do is put a new query's name into the table. Then, when it's time to get the data into Excel, the VBA code starts by looking in the table with the query names to find out which queries to use.

The table with the query names can also provide VBA with information about how to structure the pivot tables by including the name of the pivot table's data field, row field, column field and page field. Of course, the user can rearrange the pivot table's structure after VBA has created it.

The design of the table, named QueryNames, is shown in Figure 14.4, and its records are shown in Figure 14.5.

FIG. 14.4
The QueryNames table brings together information about which queries to execute and how to structure the pivot tables.

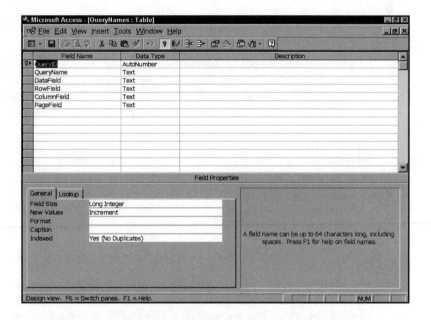

FIG. 14.5
Each query is associated with information about how to use the fields in its pivot table.

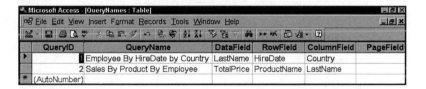

With these queries and tables established, it's time to develop the VBA code and the user interface.

The VBA code that returns data from the database and creates the pivot tables consists of four subroutines:

- Sub Driver() opens the database, calls the other subroutines, and performs a few housekeeping tasks.
- Sub GetQueryNames() obtains the names of the queries that will return the data from the database.
- Sub DialogHandler() modifies a user form so that the user can select which queries should be executed.
- Sub ImportData() gets the data from each query and creates a pivot table to display that data.

Recall that, before this code can be run, a reference to the DAO object library must be established in the module that contains the code.

The *Driver* Subroutine

Prior to the start of the Driver subroutine, options that require the declaration of variables (Option Explicit) and that establish the base of declared arrays (Option Base 1) are set, and a user-defined data type is declared. The data type, named QueryType, declares an element for each of the fields in the Access database's QueryNames table. These preliminary statements are as follows:

```
Option Explicit
Option Base 1

Type QueryType
    QueryName As String
    DataField As String
    RowField As String
    ColumnField As String
    PageField As String
End Type
```

The Driver subroutine then begins. It makes use of DAO's Database object to declare a variable, DatabaseToOpen, that represents the Access database itself. Driver also declares a few other variables, including QueryArray(). This array is of type QueryType, so that each row in the array will have the five elements declared in QueryType's Type statement.

```
Sub Driver()
Dim DatabaseToOpen As Database
Dim DatabaseName As String
Dim QueryArray() As QueryType
Dim i As Integer
Dim AllQueries As Boolean
```

Driver then displays a built-in dialog box that enables the user to browse to the location of the database. The file types that the dialog box displays are restricted to files that have an .mdb extension. This extension identifies Microsoft Access databases.

You could hard-code the path to and the name of the Access database into your VBA code. Doing so has three drawbacks:

- The location of the database might change.
- The name of the database might change.
- You might want the user to be able to choose among several databases that have similar structures but different data.

For these reasons, it's usually best to force the user to browse to and choose the database.

If the user clicks the Cancel key in the built-in dialog box, it returns the string value `"False"`. In that case, the VBA code stops processing. In prior versions of Excel, the return value was the Boolean `FALSE`; this is a change in Excel 97. It's just a flesh wound, though: If you need to allow for both Excel 95 and Excel 97, you can include a version test in your code. For example:

```
If Left(Application.Version, 1) = "8" Then
```

After the user has located the database and closed the dialog box, the `OpenDatabase` method sets the object variable `DatabaseToOpen` to represent the database itself. This method applies to a workspace object; the default workspace is assumed when, as here, it isn't supplied explicitly.

```
DatabaseName = Application.GetOpenFilename("Access files (*.mdb),*.mdb")
If DatabaseName = "False" Then
    End
End If
```

```
Set DatabaseToOpen = OpenDatabase(DatabaseName)
```

The next two statements pass control to the subroutines named `GetQueryNames` and `DialogHandler`. Along with control of the processing, the variables named `QueryArray()`, `DatabaseToOpen`, and `AllQueries` are passed. These subroutines are discussed in the next two sections.

```
GetQueryNames QueryArray(), DatabaseToOpen
DialogHandler QueryArray(), AllQueries
```

When control has returned from these subroutines, `Driver` freezes the screen to speed up processing and to avoid annoying the user with unnecessary screen updating. A new workbook that will contain the pivot tables is opened, and a new worksheet named ScratchSheet is added to that workbook. ScratchSheet will temporarily contain the data returned from the database.

```
Application.ScreenUpdating = False
Workbooks.Add
Sheets.Add
ActiveSheet.Name = "ScratchSheet"
```

The heart of the code now starts. The subroutines `GetQueryNames` and `DialogHandler` have populated `QueryArray` with information about the queries in the database: There is one row in `QueryArray` for each query that should be executed. Each query is tested against an associated checkbox control in a user form named `QueryDialog`. If the user has selected properly arranged to create a pivot tablet that checkbox, the subroutine named `ImportData` executes, pulls the data for that query into ScratchSheet, and creates a pivot table. If the user did not select that checkbox, the associated query is skipped.

Part
III

Ch

14

N O T E Notice that the index for the checkbox controls is (i-1), not i. Even with Option Base
1 set in the VBA code, the user form controls are by default indexed beginning with
zero. ◼

For the user's convenience, there is also a checkbox control that, when selected, means that
the user wants all the queries executed. Selecting that checkbox sets the Boolean variable
AllQueries to TRUE.

```
For i = 1 To UBound(QueryArray)
    If VBAProject.QueryDialog.Controls(i - 1).Value = True Or AllQueries Then
        ImportData DatabaseToOpen, QueryArray(i)
    End If
Next i
```

After the final query has executed and the final pivot table has been created, Driver cleans
things up by closing the database, deleting ScratchSheet from the workbook, and unfreezing
the screen.

Excel by default displays a warning message when a worksheet is about to be deleted. Because
you want unconditionally to delete ScratchSheet, the DisplayAlerts property is temporarily
set to False, and is then returned to True after ScratchSheet has been deleted.

```
DatabaseToOpen.Close
Application.DisplayAlerts = False
Sheets("ScratchSheet").Delete
Application.DisplayAlerts = True
Application.ScreenUpdating = True
End Sub
```

The *GetQueryNames* Subroutine

Here's a closer look at the GetQueryNames subroutine. The statement that declares the sub
includes its arguments in parentheses following the name of the sub. Notice that the variable
type for each argument is specified. Failing to specify the types causes them to default to the
Variant type.

The sub then declares several variables. One, QueryRecordSet, is declared as a recordset.
A *recordset* is an object that represents the records found in a table, or the records that are
returned by a query. In this case, the records will be those found in the table QueryNames: the
name of each query, which field will be the pivot table's data field, which field its row field, and
so on.

Also notice that TemporaryQueryArray is declared as type Variant. This is a condition of the
method, GetRows, that will populate TemporaryQueryArray. Although it will be an array, it must
not be declared as an array—it will become an array as a consequence of using the GetRows
method.

```
Sub GetQueryNames(QueryArray() As QueryType, DatabaseToOpen As Database)
Dim i As Integer
Dim QueryRecordSet As Recordset
```

```
Dim TemporaryQueryArray As Variant
Dim QueryCount As Integer
```

After declaring the variables, `QueryRecordSet` is set to the records contained in the table `QueryNames`, by means of the `OpenRecordset` method. The recordset type is specified as `dbOpenDynaset`, because `dbOpenDynaset` is capable of dealing with fields from more than one table or query. Using `dbOpenDynaset` allows for the possibility that the query names and the field names might exist in different locations (in this example, however, they are all in one table).

To get a count of the number of queries identified in the `QueryNames` table, the `MoveLast` method is used. Doing so fully populates the recordset so that the number of records can be counted. This method slows down performance, so you shouldn't use it unless absolutely necessary. It's necessary in this case because a count of the number of records is needed as an argument to the `GetRows` method.

```
Set QueryRecordSet = DatabaseToOpen.OpenRecordset(Name:="QueryNames",
Type:=dbOpenDynaset)
With QueryRecordSet
   .MoveLast
   QueryCount = .RecordCount
   .MoveFirst
End With
```

The data in `QueryRecordSet`, which represents the records in the `QueryNames` table, are now assigned to the `Variant` named `TemporaryQueryArray` by means of the `GetRows` method. `GetRows` requires assignment to a `Variant`. Because of limitations to the amount of data that can be contained in a `Variant` array, the `GetRows` method should not be used on recordsets that contain large amounts of data.

The array that contains the results of `GetRows` has one column for each record in the recordset, and one row for each field in the recordset. The array's dimensions have a lower bound of zero, and its first ("zero-th") row contains the record number. This orientation is often inconvenient conceptually, so the array's contents are rearranged and moved into `QueryArray` (which has lower bounds of 1, due to `Option Base 1`):

```
TemporaryQueryArray = QueryRecordSet.GetRows(QueryCount)

ReDim QueryArray(UBound(TemporaryQueryArray, 2) + 1)

For i = 0 To UBound(TemporaryQueryArray, 2)
   With QueryArray(i + 1)
     On Error Resume Next
     .QueryName = TemporaryQueryArray(1, i)
     .DataField = TemporaryQueryArray(2, i)
     .RowField = TemporaryQueryArray(3, i)
     .ColumnField = TemporaryQueryArray(4, i)
     .PageField = TemporaryQueryArray(5, i)
   End With
Next i
```

Finally, `GetQueryNames` releases some memory by erasing the temporary array and setting the `QueryRecordSet` object variable to `Nothing`. When the subroutine has finished, `QueryArray` has

Part

III

Ch

14

been populated with information about the names of the existing queries, and how the queries' fields should be used in pivot tables. The newly populated QueryArray is then returned to the Driver subroutine.

```
Erase TemporaryQueryArray
Set QueryRecordSet = Nothing
End Sub
```

Once the Driver sub knows which queries to execute, it passes control to Sub DialogHandler. This subroutine displays the names of the queries to the user, giving a chance for the user to select only a subset of the available queries or to select all of them.

The *DialogHandler* Subroutine

The GetQueryNames subroutine works with a user form named QueryDialog. This user form must be customized according to the results of GetQueryNames. In Design view, the user form appears as shown in Figure 14.6.

FIG. 14.6

In Design view, all controls in a user form are visible—regardless of how their Visible properties are set.

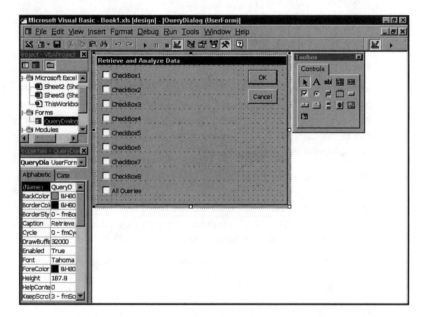

The user form contains nine checkboxes. The first eight are reserved for the names of the queries that were obtained by GetQueryNames. The ninth checkbox is reserved as a means for the user to select all defined queries.

The general flow of DialogHandler is as follows:

1. Step through QueryArray. For each query found there, set certain properties of an associated checkbox on the user form.

2. Set any remaining checkboxes on the user form such that their `Visible` property and `Enabled` property are both `False`. If the checkboxes aren't needed to represent queries, why leave them there to clutter up the form?

3. Show the user form.

Here are the specifics. Begin by looping through `QueryArray`, at each step giving a checkbox a caption that is a query's name. Also, make sure that the checkbox is visible and enabled, and that it's cleared (`.Value = 0`). Recall that by default, the controls on a user form have a zero base, but `QueryArray` is 1-based: therefore, 1 is added to the loop's control variable `i` when it's used to identify a record in `QueryArray`.

```
Sub DialogHandler(QueryArray() As QueryType, AllQueries As Boolean)

Dim i As Integer

With VBAProject.QueryDialog
    For i = 0 To UBound(QueryArray) - 1
        With .Controls(i)
            .Caption = QueryArray(i + 1).QueryName
            .Visible = True
            .Enabled = True
            .Value = 0
        End With
    Next i
```

N O T E In earlier versions, dialog sheets were used instead of user forms. Dialog sheets had various collections: checkboxes, edit boxes, spinners, and so on. This was convenient. In Excel 97, user forms do not have these collections, and you must specify a particular control by its index or its name. This is inconvenient. Fortunately, Excel 97 still recognizes, as hidden objects, dialog sheets created in earlier versions, as well as their collections and members of the collections. ■

N O T E If you adapt this code to your own purposes, it would be wise to include an error trap to prevent the number of queries from exceeding the number of checkboxes. To avoid further complications in this code, the error trap is omitted here. ■

Then, make the remaining checkboxes both invisible and disabled, up to the third-last control (the last three controls are the `AllQueries` checkbox, the OK button, and the Cancel button). As a nod to the obsessive-compulsive, ensure that the AllQueries checkbox is visible and enabled. Finally, show the user form, end the subroutine, and return control to `Sub Driver`. (Notice the use of the nested `With` structure in `With .Controls("AllQueries")`.)

```
    For i = UBound(QueryArray) To .Controls.Count - 3
        .Controls(i).Visible = False
        .Controls(i).Enabled = False
    Next i
    With .Controls("AllQueries")
        .Visible = True
        .Enabled = True
    End With
```

Part
III

Ch
14

```
    .Show

    If .Controls("AllQueries").Value = xlOn Then
        AllQueries = True
    End If
End With

End Sub
```

Recall that the `Driver` subroutine loops through the user form's checkboxes. When a checkbox has been filled (or if `AllQueries` is `True`), `Driver` calls `ImportData`, the fourth and final subroutine, with information about that query as an argument.

Figure 14.7 shows the user form as it might actually appear to the user.

FIG. 14.7
At runtime, VBA displays only as many check-boxes as there are available queries.

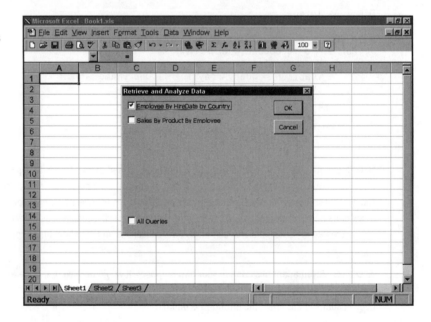

The *ImportData* Subroutine

Here's the code that actually returns data to Excel and creates the pivot tables. As arguments, the subroutine takes the database itself and information about the current query. Just as in `GetQueryNames`, a recordset that will contain the records from the query is declared:

```
Sub ImportData(DatabaseToOpen As Database, QueryData As QueryType)

Dim RecordSetName As Recordset
Dim OutputRange As Range
Dim icols As Integer
Dim lrecs As Long
Dim i As Integer, j As Integer
Dim FieldNameArray() As String
Dim FromWhere As String
```

With the variables declared, the recordset is opened. The pivot table will require that each field that's returned have a header row, so `FieldNameArray` is redimensioned and then populated with the names of each field.

```
Set RecordSetName = DatabaseToOpen.OpenRecordset _
    (QueryData.QueryName, dbOpenDynaset)
icols = RecordSetName.Fields.Count

ReDim FieldNameArray(icols)

For i = 1 To icols
    FieldNameArray(i) = RecordSetName.Fields(i - 1).Name
Next i
```

The variable `icols` contains the number of fields available from the current query: This is also the number of columns in the range to be occupied by the data returned from the database. The code can get the number of rows in that range by counting the number of records, `lrecs`, in the recordset. Strictly, the code doesn't need to know these two values in order to obtain the data. But `icols` and `lrecs` will come in handy when it's time to create the pivot table.

N O T E   You might want to include a check on `lrecs` in your code. The approach to retrieving data that's discussed here pulls records first into an Excel worksheet, and then creates the pivot table by using the worksheet range as the data source. If you try to pull more than 65,536 records into a worksheet, you'll run out of rows and the procedure will fail. ■

```
RecordSetName.MoveLast
lrecs = RecordSetName.RecordCount
RecordSetName.MoveFirst
```

It's now time to actually return the data from the database. The data will be written to ScratchSheet, into the range named `OutputRange`. The act of writing the data is accomplished by means of the `CopyFromRecordset` method of the `Range` object. This method takes as its argument the name of the recordset. The range's `Offset` method is used to put the data into the range starting at its second row; the first row will contain the field names.

```
Sheets("ScratchSheet").Activate
Set OutputRange = Range(Cells(1, 1), Cells(lrecs + 1, icols))
OutputRange.Offset(1, 0).CopyFromRecordset RecordSetName
OutputRange.Offset(0, 0).Resize(1, OutputRange.Columns.Count) = FieldNameArray
```

(The subroutine's code could stop right here if all you want to do is return the data from the database.)

With the data from the database in ScratchSheet, a new worksheet is added to contain the pivot table. The worksheet is named according to the current query's name. A string, `FromWhere`, is assigned the source of the data. Here, it's ScratchSheet, an exclamation point, and the address of `OutputRange` using R1C1 reference style (as required by the `PivotTableWizard` method of the `Sheet` object).

Then, the `PivotTableWizard` method is invoked to actually create the pivot table. The `DataField` element in `QueryData` identifies the field that's to be used as the pivot table's data field:

Part III
Ch 14

```
Sheets.Add
With ActiveSheet
   .Name = QueryData.QueryName
   FromWhere = OutputRange.Parent.Name & "!" _
      & OutputRange.Address(ReferenceStyle:=xlR1C1)
   .PivotTableWizard SourceType:=xlDatabase, SourceData:=FromWhere, _
      TableName:=QueryData.QueryName

   .PivotTables(QueryData.QueryName).PivotFields _
      (QueryData.DataField).Orientation = xlDataField
```

The `RowField`, `ColumnField`, and `PageField` elements of `QueryData` are checked. If they contain something other than a null string, they are used as pivot table fields. The `AddToTable` argument is used for the column and row fields; else, control fields that have already been added would be removed from the pivot table.

```
If QueryData.RowField <> "" Then
   .PivotTables(QueryData.QueryName).AddFields _
      RowFields:=QueryData.RowField
End If

If QueryData.ColumnField <> "" Then
   .PivotTables(QueryData.QueryName).AddFields _
      ColumnFields:=QueryData.ColumnField, _
AddToTable:=True
   End If

If QueryData.PageField <> "" Then
   .PivotTables(QueryData.QueryName).AddFields _
      PageFields:=QueryData.PageField, _
AddToTable:=True
   End If
End With
```

Finally, `OutputRange` is cleared in preparation for data from another query, and control is returned to the `Driver` subroutine:

```
OutputRange.Clear
End Sub
```

Because the pivot table saves the underlying data in its cache, it's not necessary to retain the actual records and fields that were returned from the database. You can always retrieve the original data from the cache by double-clicking the cell in the pivot table that represents the intersection of the grand total for columns and the grand total for rows.

Figure 14.8 shows what `OutputRange` looks like after it has been filled by means of the `CopyFromRecordset` method.

At times, you might need to replace data in `OutputRange`. For example, your query might return values that have been set by checkboxes in an Access form. These appear in the worksheet as TRUE (checked) and FALSE (not checked). Especially for use in a pivot table, you might want to replace TRUE with 1 and FALSE with zero. For example:

```
OutputRange.Replace What:="TRUE", Replacement:="1", LookAt:=xlWhole, _
   SearchOrder:=xlByRows, MatchCase:=True
```

FIG. 14.8

OutputRange contains the raw data returned from the query. If you need to replace any data, this is the place to do it.

	A	B	C	D	E	F	G
1	ProductName	LastName	TotalPrice				
2	Alice Mutton	Buchanan	5538				
3	Alice Mutton	Callahan	2847				
4	Alice Mutton	Davolio	4290				
5	Alice Mutton	Dodsworth	624				
6	Alice Mutton	Fuller	6162				
7	Alice Mutton	King	2823.6				
8	Alice Mutton	Leverling	3525.6				
9	Alice Mutton	Peacock	9672				
10	Aniseed Syrup	Callahan	300				
11	Aniseed Syrup	Davolio	580				
12	Aniseed Syrup	Dodsworth	740				
13	Aniseed Syrup	King	240				
14	Aniseed Syrup	Leverling	800				
15	Aniseed Syrup	Peacock	220				
16	Aniseed Syrup	Suyama	200				
17	Boston Crab Meat	Buchanan	1081.5				
18	Boston Crab Meat	Callahan	975				
19	Boston Crab Meat	Davolio	1397				
20	Boston Crab Meat	Dodsworth	644				

Figure 14.9 shows the pivot table created from the Sales By Product By Employee query.

FIG. 14.9

The pivot table conforms to the field definitions contained in its query. At this point, you can use the PivotTable Wizard interactively to customize the pivot table's appearance.

	A	B	C	D	E	F
1	Sum of TotalPrice	LastName				
2	ProductName	Buchanan	Callahan	Davolio	Dodsworth	Fuller	Kin
3	Alice Mutton	5538	2847	4290	624	6162	
4	Aniseed Syrup		300	580	740		
5	Boston Crab Meat	1081.5	975	1397	644	920	
6	Camembert Pierrot	4896	2951.2	9125.6	1496	6324	
7	Carnarvon Tigers		3312.5	5037.5	3250	6750	
8	Chai	936	1072.8	1278	630	1620	
9	Chang	1064	1254	3952	494	1235	
10	Chartreuse verte	1656	1350	2019.6	180	1440	
11	Chef Anton's Cajun Seasoning	264	1320	132		1188	
12	Chef Anton's Gumbo Mix		864.25	1105			
13	Chocolade			229.5			
14	Côte de Blaye	8432		23978.5	15019.5	26086.5	
15	Escargots de Bourgogne	556.5	795	742		318	
16	Filo Mix		282.8	413	308	700	
17	Fløtemysost	1307.2	1204	5852.3	1247	451.5	
18	Geitost	155	75	104	37.5	255	
19	Genen Shouyu			155		775	
20	Gnocchi di nonna Alice	1824	2014	4636		4339.6	

The table QueryNames contains the name of each query and the correspondence between pivot table's fields and recordset's fields. But it could also contain other information about how to structure the pivot table. For example, QueryNames could have a field named DataFormat

Part
III

Ch
14

that contains, as a string, the format that you want to use for the pivot table's data field (as an example, for currency, `"$#,##0"`).

Be sure to compare this method, which uses DAO, of returning data from a database with one that uses the PivotTable Wizard interactively to invoke Microsoft Query. You will find DAO to be considerably faster. The drawback to this method is that the number of records you can return is limited to 65,536, unless you arrange for the 65,536th and subsequent records to occupy row 1 in new columns.

Modifying Access Databases from Excel

What about going the other direction—that is, sending queries or other information to Access while you're in Excel?

Most of the additional speed you get from the code discussed in the prior section is due to using DAO. But a little bit of the acceleration is due to the fact that the queries already existed in compiled form in the Access database. At times—particularly on an ad hoc basis—you might want to trade in that tiny increment in speed for the added flexibility of defining queries in Excel/VBA, and sending them to Access for execution.

This comes at a cost, though. Working in Access, you are able to define queries by clicking and dragging with your mouse. You can create a relationship between two tables by dragging a field in one table to a field in another table. Later, when you add these tables to a query, the existing relationship is retained. Behind the scenes, Access automatically generates the Structured Query Language (SQL) statement that really defines the linkage.

You can't do that clicking and dragging in the context of Excel. You need to know enough about the structure of the database, and enough about SQL, to write the SQL statement yourself. Figure 14.10 shows a fairly simple example.

Working within Access, here's all you need to do to create this query:

1. On the Queries tab, choose New. Add the Products table and the Order Details table. If Access can find a linkage between the tables on the basis of field names, it creates that linkage.
2. Define a field named TotalPrice. Use the Expression Builder to set the field equal to the product of UnitPrice and Quantity.
3. Drag the Product Name field into the query grid's Field row.
4. Click the Totals button. The Product Name field defaults to Group By. In the TotalPrice field, use the drop-down list to select Sum.
5. In the Sort row, choose Descending for TotalPrice.

That's it, and it's almost entirely menu- or button-driven. In contrast, here's the resulting SQL statement:

```
SELECT Sum([Order Details]![UnitPrice]*[Order Details]![Quantity]) _
    AS TotalPrice, Products.ProductName
FROM [Order Details] INNER JOIN Products _
    ON [Order Details].ProductID = Products.ProductID
GROUP BY Products.ProductName
ORDER BY Sum([Order Details]![UnitPrice]*[Order Details]![Quantity]) DESC;
```

FIG. 14.10

This query contains just two tables and one calculated field.

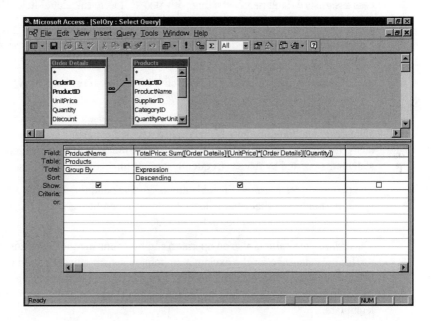

Okay, it's more complicated than clicking and dragging. And you should usually perform operations such as creating tables and queries, establishing relationships, and (definitely) designing forms or reports from within Access.

But if you are designing a VBA application for interactive use, you will want to provide the user with different options for viewing the data. Often, there will be enough options that it makes more sense to let VBA assemble the SQL statement and then pass it to Access, rather than trying to anticipate all possible combinations and saving an Access query for each combination.

To get you started, here's an English language translation of the SQL statement shown previously.

The *SELECT* Statement

The SELECT statement specifies which fields the query is to return, including the locations of the fields. In the example:

```
SELECT Sum([Order Details]![UnitPrice]*[Order Details]![Quantity]) _
    AS TotalPrice, Products.ProductName
```

there are two fields to return. One field is a calculated field: the result of multiplying UnitPrice by Quantity (both found in the Order Details table), and summing the result. The records to

Part
III

Ch

14

be summed are chosen by their value in whatever the query groups by—here, the GROUP BY clause specifies that the grouping variable is ProductName.

The fields are returned in the order in which the SELECT clause names them.

A calculated field is often given an *alias*, determined by the AS keyword. Without an alias, Access assigns a default name, starting with "EXPR", to the calculated field. Here, the completed calculation is returned from the query with the alias TotalPrice.

Notice the syntax used in selecting fields. Here's another legitimate version of the same SELECT statement:

```
SELECT Sum([Order Details]!UnitPrice*[Order Details]!Quantity) _
   AS TotalPrice, Products.ProductName
```

Notice that the name of the Order Details table is enclosed in square brackets, while its field names are not. You must supply square brackets when a name contains a space or a special character such as an underscore. Otherwise, the brackets are not needed. You'll find that SQL statements created by Access frequently contain unnecessary brackets.

The period, or *dot*, between the table name Products and the field name ProductName is the *dot operator*. It indicates that what follows the dot is a member of what precedes the dot. The ProductName field is a member of the Products table.

The *exclamation point* is also an operator, and functions in much the same way as the dot operator. It's normal usage for the exclamation point to separate user-defined objects and for the dot operator to separate objects, methods, and properties in the Access object model. However, this usage isn't fully consistent. For example, this version of the example SELECT clause is legitimate:

```
SELECT Sum([Order Details].UnitPrice*[Order Details].Quantity) _
   AS TotalPrice, Products!ProductName
```

Notice that, compared to the prior versions, an exclamation point has replaced the dot and a dot has replaced the exclamation points.

Finally, the SELECT keyword specifies that this is—make sure you're sitting down first—a Select query. It returns records. It doesn't delete or add records; it doesn't make a new table. It just returns records.

The *FROM* Clause

The FROM clause names the tables or queries that contain the data to be returned. As in the example, it may also specify the criteria that are used to match rows in record sources:

```
FROM [Order Details] INNER JOIN Products _
   ON [Order Details].ProductID = Products.ProductID
```

The INNER JOIN keyword specifies how records in Order Details are to be matched with records in Products. The linking field is ProductID: Only those records in each table that have matching values for ProductID are returned. (See Chapter 21, "Using Multiple Tables," for information about other kinds of joins.) So, the query does not return Products records that aren't in Order Details, nor does it return Order Details records that aren't in Products.

The ON keyword indicates which field in each table is used in the link between the tables. Although in this case the two fields have the same name, ProductID, they can have different names.

The *GROUP BY* Clause

If you don't want any grouping levels in the data the query returns, you don't need a GROUP BY clause. The example query uses this clause:

```
GROUP BY Products.ProductName
```

to summarize the data by ProductName. The SELECT clause calls for Access to return two fields: ProductName and TotalPrice, a calculated sum. Without the GROUP BY clause, the query results in an error message. The SUM function in the SELECT statement implies that all fields named in the SELECT statement must either be arguments to a function or be included in a GROUP BY clause. The only way to eliminate the GROUP BY clause in this example would be to remove ProductName from the SELECT statement. Then, the query would return one value only: the sum of TotalPrice across all records.

The *ORDER BY* Clause

The ORDER BY clause:

```
ORDER BY Sum([Order Details]![UnitPrice]*[Order Details]![Quantity]) DESC;
```

just specifies that the rows returned by the query are sorted according to the calculated field. The DESC keyword specifies descending order; ascending order would be specified by ASC. You normally use ORDER BY, if at all, as the final clause in a SELECT statement.

Sending SQL to Access

Once you've defined the SQL, you need to supply it to Access, and to do so you need to use VBA. Compared to the code used to create a pivot table, this is simple. Keep in mind, though, that because the code uses DAO objects, it's necessary to establish a reference to the DAO object library.

```
Option Explicit
Option Base 1

Sub GetData()
Dim DatabaseToOpen As Database
Dim DatabaseName As String
Dim SelectQuery As QueryDef
Dim RecordSetName As Recordset
Dim OutputRange As Range
Dim SelectString As String, FromString As String, _
    GroupByString As String, OrderByString As String
Dim FullString As String
```

After declaring the necessary variables, the SQL for the SELECT statement is assembled. The sample code does so by establishing a different string for each clause, and then concatenating the strings into a single SELECT statement. This is just to make things clearer: you could construct a single SELECT without going through separate string assignments.

```
SelectString = "SELECT Sum([Order Details]!UnitPrice*" _
    & "[Order Details]!Quantity) " _
    & "AS TotalPrice, Products.ProductName "
FromString = "FROM [Order Details] INNER JOIN Products ON " _
    & "[Order Details].ProductID = Products.ProductID "
GroupByString = "GROUP BY Products.ProductName "
OrderByString = "ORDER BY Sum([Order Details]!UnitPrice*" _
    & "[Order Details]!Quantity) DESC;"

FullString = SelectString & FromString & GroupByString & OrderByString
```

N O T E The ampersand in the block of code is the *concatenation operator*. It joins two strings. For example, "100% " & "Not Guilty." becomes "100% Not Guilty.". ■

The variable FullString now contains the entire SELECT statement that will be passed to Access. The next task is to open the database:

```
DatabaseName = Application.GetOpenFilename("Access files (*.mdb),*.mdb")
If DatabaseName = "False" Then
    End
End If
.
Set DatabaseToOpen = OpenDatabase(DatabaseName)
```

With the database opened, the code next creates a query by means of the Database object's CreateQueryDef method. This is the same as the action of inserting a new query from within Access:

```
Set SelectQuery = DatabaseToOpen.CreateQueryDef _
    (Name:="SelQry", sqltext:=FullString)
```

If you try to create a new query that has the same name as an existing query, a runtime error occurs. (One good solution is to create a temporary query. This process is discussed in the next section.) Assuming that its query name is a new one, the CreateQueryDef method results in a query that stays in the database: It's a persistent object. So you must be careful, when using the approach described here, that you do not supply a query name that already exists in the database.

The remaining code is similar to that used in the pivot table subroutines. An output range is established, and a recordset is created by using the new query. The recordset is returned to an Excel worksheet by using the CopyFromRecordset method. The database is closed, a little formatting is applied, and the subroutine ends:

```
Set RecordSetName = DatabaseToOpen.OpenRecordset("SelQry", dbOpenDynaset)
Set OutputRange = Cells(1, 1)
OutputRange.CopyFromRecordset RecordSetName
DatabaseToOpen.Close
```

```
Columns("A:A").NumberFormat = "$#,##0.00"
Columns("A:B").EntireColumn.AutoFit
End Sub
```

The results are shown in Figure 14.11.

FIG. 14.11

These data are returned from an Access database without ever actually having to use Access.

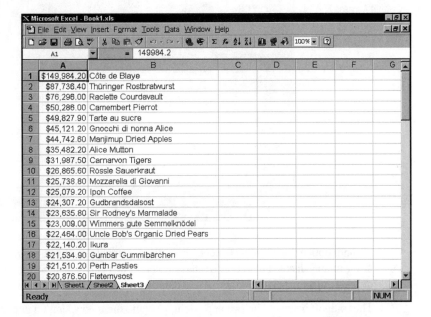

The definition of the query that was created, and that persists in the Access database, is shown in Figure 14.12.

Creating Temporary Queries

You can prevent a query definition from persisting—from staying in the database and thus preventing another instance of a query with the same name—by creating a temporary query. This requires only a small change to the code described in the prior section. Instead of these two statements:

```
Set SelectQuery = DatabaseToOpen.CreateQueryDef _
    (Name:="SelQry", sqltext:=FullString)
Set RecordSetName = DatabaseToOpen.OpenRecordset _
    ("SelQry", dbOpenDynaset)
```

you use these two statements:

```
Set SelectQuery = DatabaseToOpen.CreateQueryDef _
    (Name:="", sqltext:=FullString)
Set RecordSetName = SelectQuery.OpenRecordset(dbOpenDynaset)
```

Notice first that, in the `CreateQueryDef` method, the `Name` argument is assigned a null string. This prevents the query from being saved with the database.

Part

III

Ch

14

FIG. 14.12

The query created by means of VBA is exactly the same as if it had been created interactively within Access.

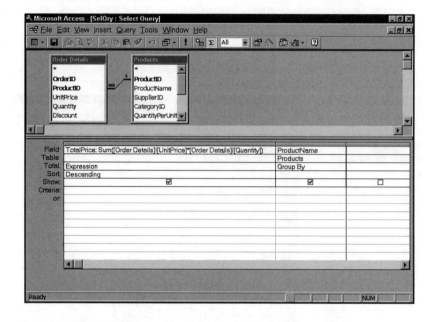

Second, notice that the OpenRecordSet method is applied to the QueryDef object named SelectQuery, instead of to the Database object. The OpenRecordSet method applies to a variety of DAO objects, including queries and databases.

The tradeoff between the two approaches—name the query, don't name the query—is:

- You can't save a new query with the same name as an existing query. Name a query when you won't redefine it, but will use it to retrieve data that has changed.

- Ipso facto—you can't save a temporary query at all. Create a temporary query when you want to query a database repeatedly with different sets of conditions.

A Sample Application

This section describes a sample application of using DAO objects in combination with a simple user interface, so that the user can select the fields to retrieve from a database.

The user interface, consisting of checkboxes that identify the fields available in each of three tables, is shown in Figure 14.13.

When the button labeled Retrieve Now is clicked, a subroutine named RetrieveNow() is run. The basic flow of the subroutine is as follows:

1. Loop through the checkboxes, looking for those that are selected. During the loop, extend a SELECT statement to include the associated table name and its chosen fields.

2. Also during the loop, put the names of the chosen tables into an array.

3. Loop through the array of table names, and assign a FROM statement on the basis of the chosen tables.

4. Submit the resulting SELECT statement to Access and return the data to a new worksheet.

FIG. 14.13
With this interface, the user can check the fields to obtain from the database, and then click the command button to retrieve the data.

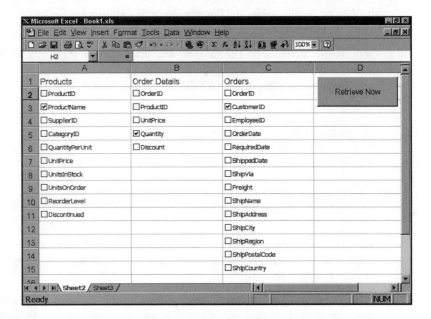

The RetrieveNow() subroutine begins as usual with the declaration of the necessary variables:

```
Sub RetrieveNow()

Dim i As Integer
Dim SelectString As String
Dim FromString As String
Dim FullString As String
Dim TableName As String
Dim TablesUsed(3) As String
Dim TableCounter As Byte
Dim DatabaseToOpen As Database
Dim DatabaseName As String
Dim SelectQuery As QueryDef
Dim RecordSetName As Recordset
Dim OutputRange As Range
```

The loop builds on the SELECT statement by adding a field name to SelectString whenever it encounters a selected checkbox. But the statement must begin with the SELECT keyword, so initialize SelectString:

```
SelectString = "SELECT "
```

Then, loop through the 29 checkboxes. A selected checkbox has a value of 1, so when the loop encounters a checkbox with that value, it starts to record information:

Part
III

Ch

14

```
For i = 1 To 29
    With ActiveSheet.CheckBoxes(i)
        If .Value = 1 Then
```

There are 10 checkboxes associated with fields from the Products table, five checkboxes for the [Order Details] table, and the remaining checkboxes are for the Orders table.

The current value of i, the loop's control variable, is used to determine which table is involved at the loop's current step. The TableName variable will be used to qualify the fields' names, so it is assigned the name of the table plus either the dot or exclamation point operator. Then, the TablesUsed array is populated with the table name, with no operator.

```
If i < 11 Then
    TableName = "Products."
    TablesUsed(1) = "Products"
ElseIf i < 16 Then
    TableName = "[Order Details]!"
    TablesUsed(2) = "[Order Details]"
Else
    TableName = "Orders."
    TablesUsed(3) = "Orders"
End If
```

The SelectString variable is extended to capture the table name and operator, and the field name. The field name itself is used in the checkbox's caption, which you retrieve by its Characters.Text property.

When the loop begins, SelectString equals "SELECT ". If the loop finds that the checkbox for, say, ProductID is selected, the following assignment statement would cause SelectString to become "SELECT Products.ProductID, ":

```
            SelectString = SelectString & TableName _
                & .Characters.Text & ", "
    End If
        End With
Next i
```

When the loop completes, SelectString contains the names of the tables and the fields that the user selected with the checkboxes. Also, TablesUsed() contains the names of each table that is required.

If the user did not select any checkboxes before clicking the Retrieve Now button, the original value of SelectString has not been changed. In that case, end processing. Otherwise, remove the final comma and space at the end of SelectString:

```
If SelectString = "SELECT " Then Exit Sub
SelectString = Left(SelectString, Len(SelectString) - 2)
```

Now, find out how many tables are involved. This information is needed to build the FROM statement:

```
TableCounter = 0
For i = 1 To 3
    If TablesUsed(i) <> "" Then TableCounter = TableCounter + 1
Next i
```

If there is only one table involved—the user clicked checkboxes for fields that belong to one table only— the FROM statement is very simple:

```
Select Case TableCounter
    Case 1
        For i = 1 To 3
            If TablesUsed(i) <> "" Then _
                FromString = " FROM " & TablesUsed(i)
Next i
```

When only one table was selected, the code loops through TablesUsed() to get the table's name, and appends the name to the FROM keyword. Note the space before FROM in the assignment statement. This is eventually to separate the final character in SelectString from the keyword FROM.

When two tables are needed, the FROM syntax is more complex. It's necessary to know the name of the join key that links the two tables. An IF-ELSEIF-ELSE structure is used to uniquely identify the two required tables, and the FROM string is hard-coded on that basis:

```
Case 2
    If TablesUsed(1) <> "" And TablesUsed(2) <> "" Then
        FromString = " FROM Products INNER JOIN [Order Details] " _
            & "ON Products.ProductID = [Order Details].ProductID"
    ElseIf TablesUsed(2) <> "" And TablesUsed(3) <> "" Then
        FromString = " FROM Orders INNER JOIN [Order Details] " _
            & "ON Orders.OrderID = [Order Details].OrderID"
    Else
        FromString = " FROM Orders INNER JOIN " _
            & "(Products INNER JOIN [Order Details] ON " _
            & "Products.ProductID = [Order Details].ProductID) " _
            & "ON Orders.OrderID = [Order Details].OrderID;"
    End If
```

Notice the assignment statement following the Else condition. The user has chosen fields that require the Products table and the Orders table. These two tables have no common link. Instead, it's necessary to link them through their links to Order Details. Working from the inside of the FROM clause out, first join Products to Order Details using ProductID. This returns a row for each instance where the link's value is the same in both tables. Then, join those rows to the Orders table, using OrderID as the join key.

When all three tables are needed, only one FROM clause is necessary. Again, the Products and the Orders tables are linked by invoking each table's key on Order Details:

```
    Case 3
        FromString = " FROM Products INNER JOIN (Orders INNER JOIN " _
            & "[Order Details] ON Orders.OrderID = [Order Details].OrderID)" _
            & " ON Products.ProductID = [Order Details].ProductID;"
End Select
```

Finally, FromString is concatenated to SelectString, the database is opened, and the query is passed as a temporary query—that is, one with no query name. This ensures that the query does not persist in the database, so the user can retrieve data repeatedly without creating a query that already exists. A new worksheet is added, and the data returned to it using the CopyFromRecordset method.

Part
III

Ch
14

```
FullString = SelectString & FromString

DatabaseName = Application.GetOpenFilename("Access files (*.mdb),*.mdb")
If DatabaseName = "False" Then
    End
End If

Set DatabaseToOpen = OpenDatabase(DatabaseName)
Set SelectQuery = DatabaseToOpen.CreateQueryDef(Name:="", _
    sqltext:=FullString)
Set RecordSetName = SelectQuery.OpenRecordset(dbOpenDynaset)
Sheets.Add
Set OutputRange = Cells(1, 1)
OutputRange.CopyFromRecordset RecordSetName
DatabaseToOpen.Close

End Sub
```

This probably seems like a lot of code to support a simple Select query. But if the user selects only one checkbox for each of the three tables, there are 700 possible combinations of fields that might be returned. If the user selects more than one checkbox from any table, the number of possible combinations of queries quickly climbs into the hundreds of thousands. As simple as the query is, it is also extremely flexible. And the user need not know how to use Excel's Access Links add-in or the Query add-in. All that's needed is to check the boxes that correspond to the desired fields.

The user interface could include additional functionality, of course. Listboxes could be supplied, to create a GROUP BY and an ORDER BY clause based on the fields chosen from the listboxes.

While it would be possible to supply a means by which the user can create calculated fields, such as the TotalPrice field discussed in the prior section, it is probably better to create those fields explicitly in the database's tables. A customized calculation facility would be more flexible, but it would also have to allow for all possible numeric fields, for all possible arithmetic operators, and for as many fields in an expression as the user might want to include.

This chapter has focused on passing select queries to Access. You can also pass other types of queries, such as update queries, append queries, and delete queries, to the database. The general method is much the same. Using VBA:

1. Assemble the required SQL code.
2. Open the database.
3. Set the QueryDef object so that it contains the SQL code.
4. Establish a recordset object by means of the QueryDef.
5. Use one of the recordset's methods such as AddNew or Delete, or an assignment statement to change a field value. Then, invoke the Update method.

However, it's usually *much* easier to accomplish these tasks from within the Access application. Only in very specific circumstances—for example, users are unfamiliar or uncomfortable with

Access, but you need to enable them to do more than just return data to Excel—should you consider building other kinds of queries into an Excel/VBA application.

The select query is advantageous in the Excel context because it plays to Excel's strengths: sophisticated analysis and attractive display of data. And it plays to a relational database's strengths: the efficient storage and retrieval of information. ●

CHAPTER 15

Analyzing Data

▬ **Creating and managing scenarios**

Enter different sets of inputs and retrieve them quickly to examine their effects on the outputs.

▬ **Using Goal Seek**

Backtrack to a necessary input value by specifying a desired output value.

▬ **Using the ATP's Exponential Smoothing tool**

Forecast future values from known inputs.

As noted in Chapter 14, "Connecting to Access Databases," Excel's principal strength is the display and analysis of data. By creating formulas and using functions that treat your data in certain ways, you reach conclusions about such matters as the strength of a business, the relationships between environmental variables and public health, whether a manufacturing process is staying within its specifications, and how best to allocate resources among competing projects.

The notion of *changing the inputs* is central to all such analyses. Whether you examine the effect of changing inventory valuation on a company's balance sheet, the reduction of airborne particulates on the incidence of respiratory ailments, an increase in the thickness of a glaze on the quality of a ceramic tile, or a reduction in advertising budgets on sales, you focus on changing an input and recalculating a result.

In addition to functions that return different results in response to different inputs, Excel gives you tools that make it easier and more efficient to manage the changing of the inputs. Two of these tools are the Scenario Manager and Goal Seek.

Excel also works with the Analysis ToolPak, or ATP, an add-in that you install during Office setup. The ATP is a collection of tools that automate the data analysis tasks you would otherwise have to complete manually.

This chapter details the use of the tools that make changing the inputs more efficient. ▬

Creating and Managing Scenarios

A *scenario* is nothing more than a group of values that are associated with certain worksheet cells. By storing the values in a scenario, instead of in the cells themselves, you are able to:

■ Change the cells' values on the worksheet, and subsequently recall the values that you stored in the scenario.

■ Define several scenarios, each with a different set of values for the cells. Then, switch between the scenarios to see their different effects on dependent formulas, one scenario at a time.

■ Summarize multiple scenarios, including the resulting values of dependent formulas, in a report or in a pivot table.

■ Employ various scenario management tools, such as tracking changes that have been made to scenarios and merging scenarios from different worksheets into one location.

Chapter 11 described the meaning and use of the NPV (Net Present Value) function by means of an analysis of cash flows from an investment. That analysis is repeated here in Figure 15.1.

FIG. 15.1
The NPV for the investment depends on various assumptions, including the sales dollar amounts and the discount factor.

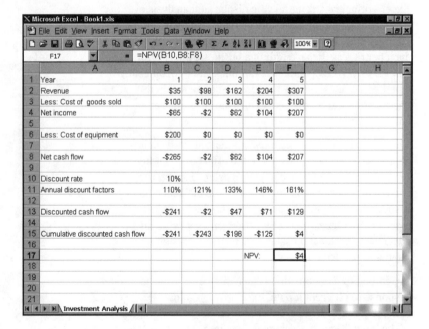

Suppose that you wanted to check the NPV of this investment opportunity under different conditions—for example, with a different discount factor, or with different projections for annual sales. The Scenario Manager is an ideal tool for this sort of analysis.

Establishing a Scenario

Begin with the existing values shown previously in Figure 15.1. Perhaps they represent a best guess; an apt name for a scenario that uses the existing values would then be Best Guess. Working with the data as shown in Figure 15.1, here's how to set up the scenario.

Select cells B2:F2. Hold down Ctrl and click cell B10 to add it to your selection. Choose Tools, Scenarios. The dialog box shown in Figure 15.2 appears.

FIG. 15.2

Until at least one scenario is defined on the active worksheet, you can only Close the dialog box, Add a scenario, or Merge other scenarios.

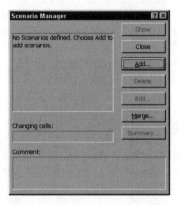

Choose Add to create a new scenario. When you do so, the Add Scenario dialog box appears as shown in Figure 15.3.

FIG. 15.3

If you choose to protect or to hide a scenario, you must then choose Tools, Protection, Protect Sheet, and check Scenarios.

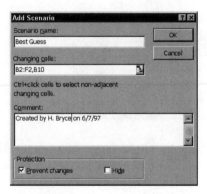

In the Scenario Name edit box, enter a descriptive name such as Best Guess. When you later retrieve a scenario, you select it by means of the name you give it here.

Because you began by selecting B2:F2 and B10, these cell references appear in the Changing Cells edit box. You can use this edit box to modify your choice of cells.

The term *changing cells* is a little obscure. They are the cells whose values are saved in the scenario. Because the values of the cells can, and usually do, change when you switch from scenario to scenario, they are called *changing cells*. For consistency, if nothing else, this term is also used by the Goal Seek tool (discussed in the next section of this chapter) and by the Solver tool.

▶ **See** "Specifying the Changing Cells," **p. 326**

Enter any comment you want in the Comment edit box. However, it's a good idea to keep the default comment, consisting of your name and the date you create the scenario. This information is handy when you later need to manage multiple scenarios.

Protecting a scenario makes it impossible to modify the values of its changing cells after you have finished defining it. You and other users can view the scenario, but cannot modify it. Hiding a scenario prevents anyone from viewing it—and, therefore, from modifying it. However, neither of these choices has any effect until the worksheet that contains the scenario has been protected, perhaps with a password. To modify the changing cells in a protected scenario, or to view a hidden scenario, first unprotect its worksheet by means of Tools, Protection, Unprotect Sheet.

> **CAUTION**
>
> Early releases of Excel 97 contained a bug that crashed Excel if the user attempted to show a hidden scenario. Unless you're sure that you have a version with a fix, do not attempt to Show a hidden scenario that is the only scenario in a protected worksheet.

When you have finished entering information in the Add Scenario dialog box, choose OK. The Scenario Values dialog box appears as shown in Figure 15.4.

FIG. 15.4

If you have identified more than five changing cells, use the scroll bar to display them.

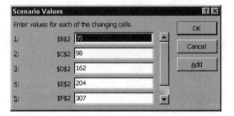

Usually, you accept the values shown for the changing cells in the Scenario Values dialog box, but if you want to change any of them this is the place to do it. Choosing Add takes you back to the Scenario Name dialog box, where you can add more changing cells to the scenario. Choosing OK returns you to the Add Scenario dialog box.

You might now define another scenario named something such as Worst Case. This scenario would probably reduce the assumed revenues in B2:F2 to very pessimistic values, and it might also increase the discount factor in B10 so that competing investment alternatives become more attractive.

A Best Case scenario would use revenue projections obtained from the company's sales force, and a discount factor based on prevailing interest rates paid on checking accounts.

Once the alternate scenarios are defined, it's very easy to switch between them. A Worst Case scenario appears in Figure 15.5; contrast it with Figure 15.1. Notice in particular the effect on the NPV in cell F17: It recalculates from $4 in the Best Guess scenario to -$34 in the Worst Case.

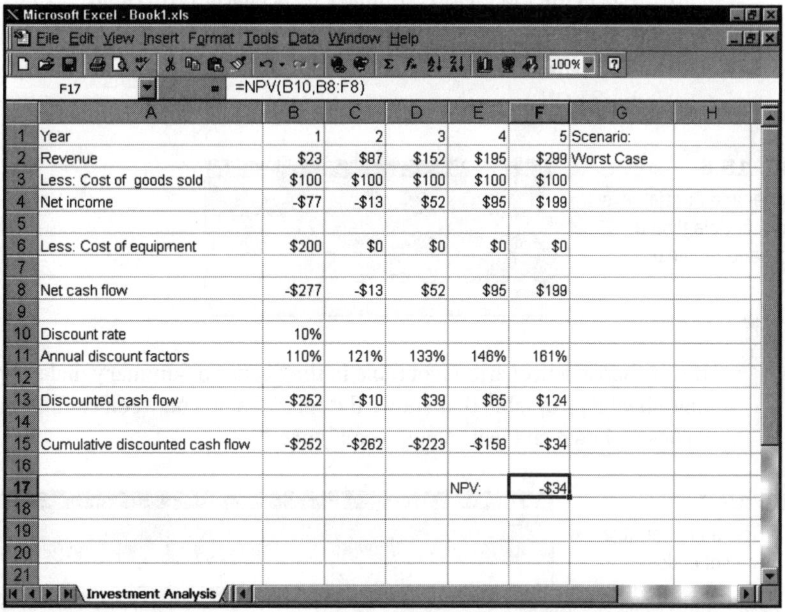

	A	B	C	D	E	F	G	H
1	Year	1	2	3	4	5	Scenario:	
2	Revenue	$23	$87	$152	$195	$299	Worst Case	
3	Less: Cost of goods sold	$100	$100	$100	$100	$100		
4	Net income	-$77	-$13	$52	$95	$199		
5								
6	Less: Cost of equipment	$200	$0	$0	$0	$0		
7								
8	Net cash flow	-$277	-$13	$52	$95	$199		
9								
10	Discount rate	10%						
11	Annual discount factors	110%	121%	133%	146%	161%		
12								
13	Discounted cash flow	-$252	-$10	$39	$65	$124		
14								
15	Cumulative discounted cash flow	-$252	-$262	-$223	-$158	-$34		
16								
17					NPV:	-$34		
18								
19								
20								
21								

FIG. 15.5
Notice that the name of the scenario appears in cell G2: It is included as one of the Changing Cells. This helps keep track of which scenario is in use.

To use a particular scenario, choose Tools, Scenarios. From the Scenarios list box, click a defined scenario name and choose Show. The values for the changing cells that are associated with that scenario are placed into their worksheet cells and the dependent formulas recalculate accordingly. You must then choose the Close button on the Scenarios dialog box to remove the scenario from the screen.

Summarizing Scenarios

One of the ideas behind scenarios is that they enable you to change several values on a worksheet in one stroke. Because the alternate values of the changing cells are stored in scenarios, they are out of the way, yet immediately accessible.

Without scenarios, it would be necessary to store all the information shown in Figure 15.5 three times, each time using a different set of values for the changing cells. You might then store the results of using each set of values on a different worksheet. This is a wasteful and inconvenient way to store and switch between different sets of input assumptions.

Although the scenario approach has obvious benefits, the drawback is that you can't view the results of all defined scenarios simultaneously. To do so, create a scenario summary:

1. With a worksheet active that contains scenarios, choose Tools, Scenarios to open the Scenario Manager dialog box.

2. Choose Summary. When you do so, the Scenario Summary dialog box appears, as shown in Figure 15.6.

3. Select either Scenario Summary or Scenario PivotTable.

4. Verify, and modify if necessary, the cells that Excel proposes to use as result cells. The *result cells* are those containing formulas that depend on the changing cells. Then choose OK.

FIG. 15.6

A Scenario PivotTable is more flexible than a Scenario Summary.

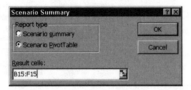

If you choose a Scenario PivotTable in the Scenario Summary dialog box, Excel creates on a new sheet a pivot table that shows the relationships between each scenario's changing cell values and its result cell values (see Figure 15.7).

FIG. 15.7

In a Scenario PivotTable, you can set options such as number formats only after the pivot table has been created.

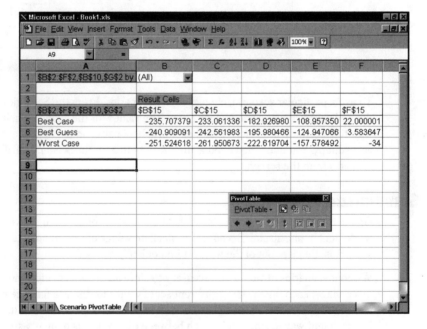

Notice the following aspects of the pivot table shown in Figure 15.7:

- The result cells are shown as items in the Column field.
- Each scenario is shown as a different item in the Row field. The collective address of the changing cells is used as the Row field's name.
- The original number formats in the pivot table's data source are not preserved in the pivot table itself.

Another aspect of the pivot table, although not visible in Figure 15.7, is that each result cell is a different Data field. The creator of each scenario is a different item in the Page field. And, if your different scenarios use different sets of changing cells, each set of changing cells is represented in a different Row field. Each Row field then has its own set of items.

You can, as usual, use the controls on the PivotTable toolbar to modify the pivot table's layout and format so that it's easier to interpret and use. However, you cannot refresh the pivot table's data cache. If your scenarios change, you need to create a new Scenario PivotTable to summarize their results correctly.

If you prefer to create a Scenario Summary, choose that option in the Scenario Summary dialog box. An example of the resulting report appears in Figure 15.8.

FIG. 15.8
Use the Outline buttons to group or ungroup levels of the Scenario Summary.

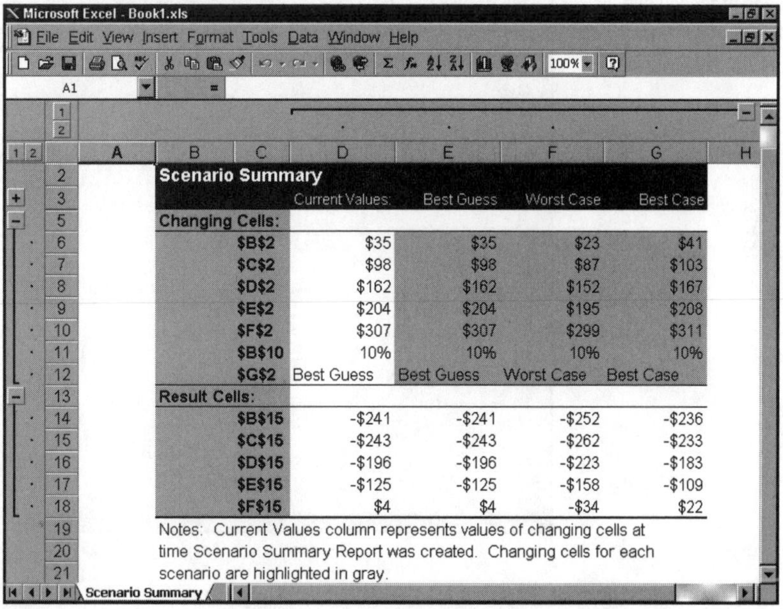

	Current Values:	Best Guess	Worst Case	Best Case
Scenario Summary				
Changing Cells:				
$B$2	$35	$35	$23	$41
$C$2	$98	$98	$87	$103
$D$2	$162	$162	$152	$167
$E$2	$204	$204	$195	$208
$F$2	$307	$307	$299	$311
$B$10	10%	10%	10%	10%
$G$2	Best Guess	Best Guess	Worst Case	Best Case
Result Cells:				
$B$15	-$241	-$241	-$252	-$236
$C$15	-$243	-$243	-$262	-$233
$D$15	-$196	-$196	-$223	-$183
$E$15	-$125	-$125	-$158	-$109
$F$15	$4	$4	-$34	$22

Notes: Current Values column represents values of changing cells at time Scenario Summary Report was created. Changing cells for each scenario are highlighted in gray.

Using either the Scenario Summary or the Scenario PivotTable, you can judge the sensitivity of the result cells to changes in the input assumptions—that is, in the changing cells.

You can also use this information to evaluate how well you have specified the values of the changing cells. For example, if you find a wildly aberrant result cell for a particular scenario, that's a good clue that the changing cells for that scenario have unrealistic values. One way to obtain a more realistic value for a changing cell is to use Goal Seek.

Using Goal Seek

The fundamental approach taken by any spreadsheet application is to apply input values to formulas: You supply an input value and a formula, and the application supplies the result of the formula.

Goal Seek turns this sequence around. By using Goal Seek, you specify the formula and its result, and request that Excel supply the input value.

Suppose that you have $1,000, and you wonder how long it would take to turn it into $1,200 at a 6 percent compound annual interest rate. You enter the necessary information into a worksheet as shown in Figure 15.9.

FIG. 15.9

Finding a value by means of the Tedious, or Untutored, method.

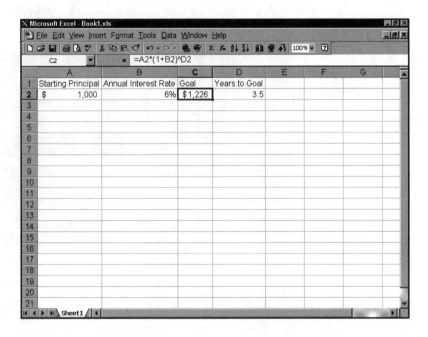

Cell A2 contains the $1,000 value that you have at present, B2 contains the 6 percent interest rate, and D2 contains your guess as to the length of time needed to earn $200 in interest. Cell C2 contains the formula:

=A2*(1+B2)^D2

This formula returns the result of earning 6 percent on an original investment of $1,000 for as many years as are entered in cell D2. If you're unfamiliar with Goal Seek, try out different values in D2 until you close in on $1,200 in cell C2.

It's a lot faster and usually more accurate to use Goal Seek. See Figure 15.10.

FIG. 15.10

Finding a value efficiently by means of Goal Seek.

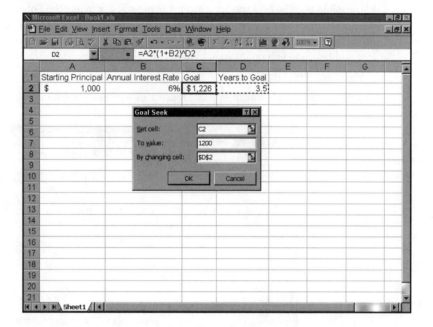

1. Select C2, and choose Tools, Goal Seek. In the Goal Seek dialog box, C2 already appears in the Set Cell edit box.

2. In the To Value edit box, type **1200**, the goal—or end result—that you want to achieve.

3. In the By Changing Cell edit box, enter **D2**, the cell containing the value that you want to adjust in order to reach the goal you've specified.

Goal Seek then iterates through different values in cell D2 until cell C2 contains the value of 1200.

For some formulas, Goal Seek might encounter difficulty in reaching the solution that you specify. For example, if you were to specify -1200, instead of 1200, in step 3 above, Goal Seek would be unable to reach a solution.

Sometimes, though, Goal Seek just needs to work longer than its defaults allow in order to solve the problem you set it. You can change these defaults by choosing Tools, Options, and selecting the Calculation tab. Increase the value shown in the Maximum Iterations edit box.

Goal Seek is more valuable when given more complicated problems to solve. Consider the investment analysis discussed in "Establishing a Scenario" earlier in the chapter. The Best Guess scenario resulted in an NPV of $4, achieved during the fifth year of the investment.

In other words, the break-even point—the date when you have recouped the original investment and subsequent expenses—occurs during Year 5.

What if you needed to break even during Year 4? One way to do so would be to increase your revenues during the first four years. How much of an increase would you need?

It's possible that the best way to answer this question is to use the Solver, which is covered in detail in Chapter 16. One reason is that Goal Seek lets you specify one changing cell only, while the Solver lets you specify multiple changing cells. However, there's a way to use Goal Seek on this problem, and you might want to do so for a preliminary analysis or because it's desirable to change only one cell.

Refer to Figure 15.11, which repeats Figure 15.1 for your convenience.

FIG. 15.11
The goal is to break even during Year 4 instead of Year 5.

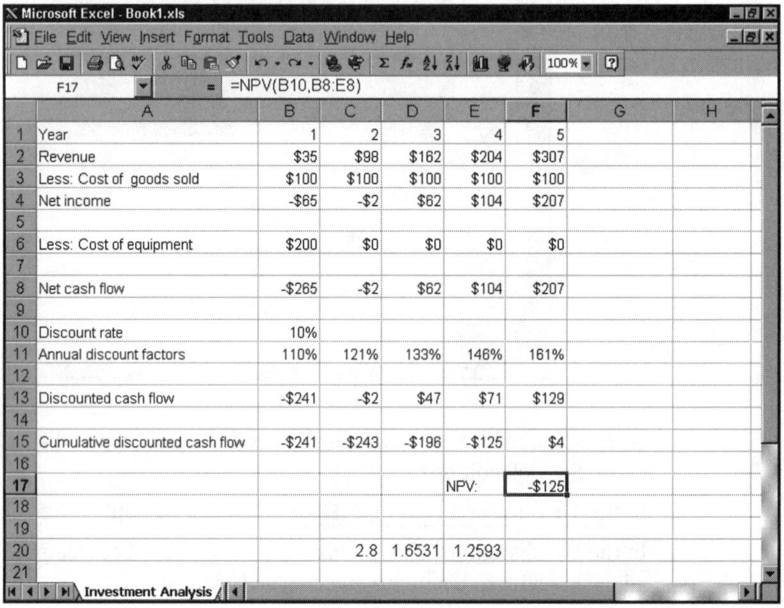

	A	B	C	D	E	F	G	H
1	Year	1	2	3	4	5		
2	Revenue	$35	$98	$162	$204	$307		
3	Less: Cost of goods sold	$100	$100	$100	$100	$100		
4	Net income	-$65	-$2	$62	$104	$207		
5								
6	Less: Cost of equipment	$200	$0	$0	$0	$0		
7								
8	Net cash flow	-$265	-$2	$62	$104	$207		
9								
10	Discount rate	10%						
11	Annual discount factors	110%	121%	133%	146%	161%		
12								
13	Discounted cash flow	-$241	-$2	$47	$71	$129		
14								
15	Cumulative discounted cash flow	-$241	-$243	-$196	-$125	$4		
16								
17					NPV:	-$125		
18								
19								
20			2.8	1.6531	1.2593			
21								

Then, take these steps:

1. Change the NPV formula in cell F17 to:

   =NPV(B10,B8:E8)

   Doing so calculates the NPV as of the end of Year 4, resulting in -$125.
2. In cell C20, type **=C2/B2**.
3. Drag this formula from C20 into D20:E20. In C20:E20, you now have the ratios of the second, third, and fourth years' revenue to that of each prior year.
4. Select C20:E20. Choose Edit, Copy, and then choose Edit, Paste Special, Values to convert the formulas to values.

5. In cell C2, enter **=B2*C20**.
6. Drag the formula in C2 into D2:E2. This gives you the original revenue estimates in C2:E2, but as formulas instead of values. Each of these formulas is now based, in part and indirectly, on the value in cell B2.
7. Select cell F17, which contains the NPV function. Choose Tools, Goal Seek.
8. The Set Cell edit box contains F17. In the To Value edit box, enter **0**. In combination with the NPV function's arguments, this specifies an NPV of $0—the break-even point—during Year 4.
9. In the By Changing Cell edit box, enter **B2**, and choose OK.

Goal Seek now iterates through values in B2. As it does so, the formulas in C2:E2 recalculate in response. And the NPV function in F17 eventually reaches $0. See Figure 15.12.

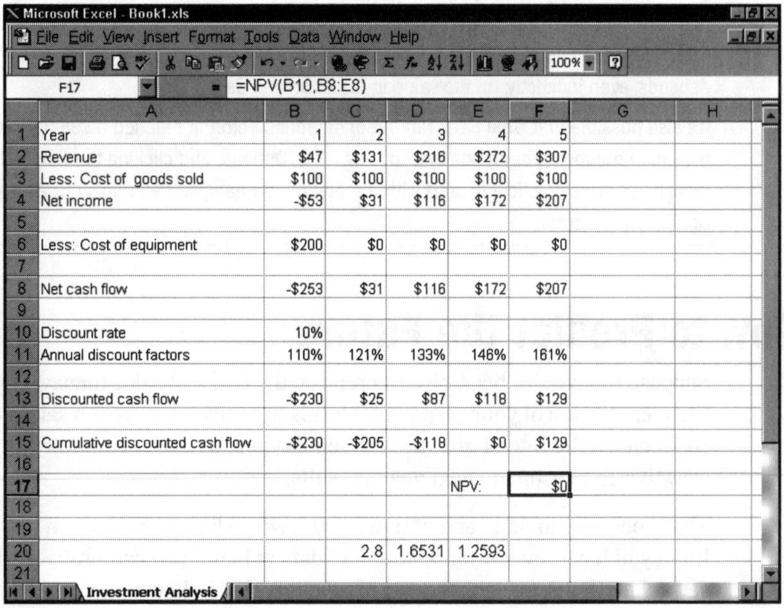

	A	B	C	D	E	F	G	H
1	Year	1	2	3	4	5		
2	Revenue	$47	$131	$216	$272	$307		
3	Less: Cost of goods sold	$100	$100	$100	$100	$100		
4	Net income	-$53	$31	$116	$172	$207		
5								
6	Less: Cost of equipment	$200	$0	$0	$0	$0		
7								
8	Net cash flow	-$253	$31	$116	$172	$207		
9								
10	Discount rate	10%						
11	Annual discount factors	110%	121%	133%	146%	161%		
12								
13	Discounted cash flow	-$230	$25	$87	$118	$129		
14								
15	Cumulative discounted cash flow	-$230	-$205	-$118	$0	$129		
16								
17					NPV:	$0		
18								
19								
20			2.8	1.6531	1.2593			
21								

FIG. 15.12
The values in B2:E2 are required to bring about a break-even point in Year 4.

It is probable that the Solver would return a different result. By constraining cells C2:E2 to maintain particular ratios to B2, you make it possible for Goal Seek to solve this problem. In contrast, the Solver can reach a solution without those constraints, because it can change more than just one cell.

But that's not necessarily a virtue. It's possible—even probable—that you would want the projected revenues to take on a specific growth rate, such as an annual 10 percent increase. You would edit the formulas in C2:E2 accordingly: For example, C2 might equal 1.1 * B2, D2 might equal 1.1 * C2, and E2 might equal 1.1 * D2.

Something such as this is likely to occur if you obtain revenue estimates from the sales force. Given a choice between spending time with a customer and spending time making sales projections, a good sales rep will opt for the former every time. The result is that sales forecasts are frequently a straight-line guess based on the prior year's actuals.

In that case, you would not want the Solver to change cells C2:E2. You would want to change the first year's revenue only, and, in that case, you might just as well use Goal Seek.

Of course, neither Goal Seek nor the Solver is able to change actual sales results. That's up to the sales force, the marketplace, and your product line. But this technique can tell you what the sales results need to be in order to reach break-even during different years.

TROUBLESHOOTING

Goal Seek may stop and say it has not found a solution. This problem is most frequently caused by mis-specifying the Changing Cell. If the Set Cell's formula is not dependent on the Changing Cell, then Goal Seek could iterate forever and not change the Set Cell's value. Make sure that the Set Cell depends, even indirectly, on the value in the Changing Cell.

It's also possible that Goal Seek ran out of iterations before it reached a solution. You can change the maximum number of iterations by choosing Tools, Options, and clicking the Calculation tab. Often, though, it's more practical to start with a value in the Changing Cell that's closer to the one you expect Goal Seek to return.

How to Predict the Future

Suppose that you've been hired to replace the national sales manager who was fired back in Chapter 10. One of your responsibilities is to project next year's sales revenue. To do so, you could check the rate of growth between last year's results and this year's, and apply that growth rate to estimate next year's results.

That's one way to do it, and at times you have so little to go on that you have no other option. But if you have several years' worth of data at hand, you can probably do better. Excel provides several methods, such as the TREND function, that help you forecast ahead from a baseline of data.

It's not a good idea to use functions such as TREND and GROWTH, or chart trendlines that have forecast options, unless you're certain that you understand their underlying assumptions and that your data meet those assumptions. Even then, these regression-based approaches can be the wrong ones to use.

Office 97 has an Excel add-in, the Analysis ToolPak (ATP), that provides a tool it calls Exponential Smoothing. This is a pretentious term for a fairly simple technique that's very similar to a moving average. Using it along with a reasonable amount of data can give you an objective forecast of the next, as yet unobserved, value in a series. And its assumptions are nowhere near as restrictive and sensitive as those used in regression approaches.

To use the ATP's tools, you must have installed the add-in during Office 97 setup; it's found in the Add-Ins component when you're specifying Excel options. After installing the ATP during Office setup, you must also install it in Excel. Choose Tools, Add-ins and ensure that the Analysis ToolPak check box is selected. When it is, you will find a Data Analysis item in Excel's Tools menu. Selecting that item is how you get to the Exponential Smoothing tool.

Before actually using the tool, though, you need a baseline of data.

Setting Up the Baseline

This section has used the term *baseline* twice, rather loosely. In the context of forecasting, it means a series of observations in a time sequence: for example, 1986 sales, 1987 sales…1996 sales.

A useful baseline has a few additional characteristics:

- *No missing data.* You shouldn't try to use a baseline of data that includes all years from 1986 through 1996 except 1990.

- *Each time period should be equally long.* Don't intersperse, say, the average of three days' worth of data with other observations that are all daily. Slight deviations, such as 31 days in January versus 28 days in February, are permitted.

- *The observations all come from the same point in a time period.* For example, if your data include monthly observations, then all observations should be as of the end of the month, or halfway through, or on the first of the month. Avoid getting data from January 1, February 15, March 7, and so on.

That's about it for assumptions. Contrasted with the laundry list of assumptions needed for a valid regression model, it doesn't seem too onerous.

Making use of the list structure that's so handy in Excel, your baseline might look like the one shown in Figure 15.13.

Creating the Forecast

Once you've set up your data as shown in Figure 15.13, you're ready to make the forecast. To do so, take these steps:

1. Choose Tools, Data Analysis. Click Exponential Smoothing and choose OK.

2. The dialog box shown in Figure 15.14 appears. Referring to the data ranges shown in Figure 15.13, enter **$B$1:$B$22** as the Input Range, type **.7** as the Damping Factor, and select the Labels check box.

3. As the Output Range, choose an empty worksheet cell with a blank area below and to its right. Select the Chart Output check box, and choose OK.

The results appear in Figure 15.15.

Although the Exponential Smoothing tool has finished, you do not yet have a forecast for the next period. Select cell C22 and use its fill handle to copy it down into C23. The resulting value is the first forecast after the end of the baseline.

FIG. 15.13

The data comply with the requirements for a valid baseline.

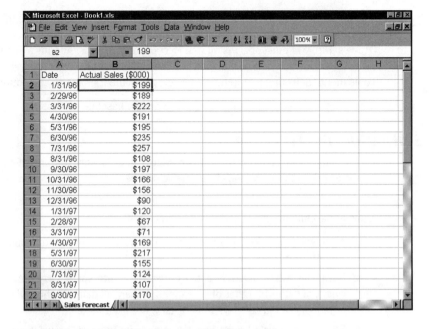

FIG. 15.14

Although the dialog box displays New Worksheet Ply and New Workbook as options, they are disabled in Exponential Smoothing.

Then select cell C23 and drag it by its border into the chart, so that the chart's forecast series includes the new forecast.

Understanding the Forecast

The fundamental idea behind smoothing is that each forecast is comprised of two components: the prior forecast, and the error in the prior forecast.

The error component is just the difference between the prior observation and the prior forecast. It's used to adjust the new forecast in a direction that would have improved the accuracy of the old forecast. This is where the *smoothing constant* (which is related to the *damping factor* in the Exponential Smoothing dialog box) comes into play. Excel uses its value as part of the adjustment to the prior forecast.

FIG. 15.15

The forecasts appear both in the chart and in cells C2:C22.

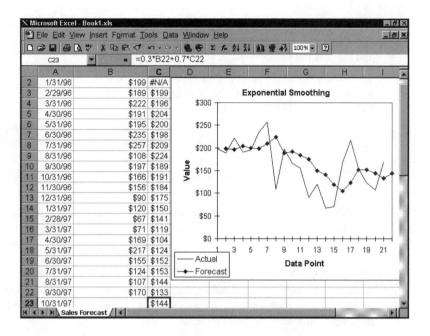

Suppose that, in January, you forecast sales of $16,000 for February. At the end of February, you find that your sales were only $10,000. The error was $6,000. Using a smoothing constant of .3, your forecast for March would be:

```
= Prior Forecast + (Smoothing Constant * Error)
= 16000 + (.3 * (10000-16000))
= 16000 - 2000
= 14000
```

Notice that the adjustment to the prior forecast is negative. In making the new forecast, the prior forecast of $16,000 is reduced by $2,000 because $16,000 was an overestimate.

If, on the other hand, you forecast sales of $10,000 for February, but had sales of $16,000, then the forecast for March would be:

```
= 10000 + (.3 * (16000-10000))
= 10000 + 2000
= 12000
```

In this case, the adjustment to the prior forecast is positive. In making the new forecast, the prior forecast of $10,000 is increased by $2,000 because $10,000 was an underestimate.

In each case, smoothing "pulls" the new forecast in the direction that would have improved the prior forecast. The amount of pull—the smoothing constant—in the prior two examples is .3.

A little algebra shows how the equations given above turn into the equations used by Excel. Given that y[t] is a forecast of the series at time t, that Y[t] is an observation made at time t, and that a is the smoothing constant:

```
y[t+1] = y[t] + a * (Y[t] - y[t])
y[t+1] = y[t] + a * Y[t] - a * y[t]
y[t+1] = a * Y[t] + (1 - a) * y[t]
```

The quantity (1 - a) in the third equation is what Excel calls the *damping factor*. The damping factor is always 1 minus the smoothing constant, so it doesn't matter which one you specify. The prior discussion focused on the smoothing constant because it clarifies the definitional aspects of smoothing. Choosing a damping factor of .7 in the Exponential Smoothing dialog box results in a smoothing constant of .3.

The third equation is what you get on your worksheet after you have run the Exponential Smoothing tool. For example, in Figure 15.15, the forecast for 11/30/96 uses this formula:

```
=0.3*B11+0.7*C11
```

The prior observation (or Y[t]) is in cell B11. The prior forecast (or y[t]) is in cell C11. The analysis in Figure 15.15 used a damping factor of .7, and therefore a smoothing constant of .3. So, in words, the new forecast is the smoothing constant times the prior observation, plus the damping factor times the prior forecast.

Why might exponential smoothing be superior to some other method such as a TREND function or (equivalently) a linear trendline on a chart? The reason has to do with recency. Using smoothing, the greatest influence on a new forecast is the prior observation: directly via the smoothing constant, and indirectly via the error associated with the prior forecast.

In contrast, a regression-based forecast places equal weight on all the values in the baseline so as to create the regression equation. That means that an observation taken 20 years ago has as much influence on the regression equation as one taken last year. That approach might or might not be appropriate.

Suppose that you are tracking and forecasting inventory levels. Last month you made a major purchase of raw materials to take advantage of relatively low pricing from your suppliers. Does it make sense to forecast inventory for next month by giving equal weight to the inventory level two years ago and to the inventory level last month? Probably not. By using smoothing, you give more weight to recent observations and less weight to older observations.

Smoothing doesn't throw out those older observations. Each forecast is based in part on the prior forecast, which itself was based on the prior observation. You can backtrack in a similar fashion all the way to the beginning of the baseline. The very first observation has an effect on each subsequent forecast. It's just that for a given forecast, the older the observation the smaller its effect.

Most regression approaches require that you use some other variable—for example, the value of the year or month itself, or the ordinal value of each observation in the baseline—as the equation's x-values. (An exception is an autoregressive model, which regresses each value onto prior values.) With smoothing, you're always forecasting from the baseline itself.

But there are plenty of drawbacks to smoothing. One is that you're limited to a one-step-ahead forecast: That is, you can't forecast farther than one time period into the future because you run out of prior observations. With regression, you can always add another x-value and compute the resulting y-value. There are other drawbacks that are more theoretical in nature; if you're interested, you should consult an intermediate-level text on forecasting.

Choosing the Damping Factor

The Excel Help documentation suggests that you use a smoothing constant of .2 to .3, resulting in a damping factor of .7 to .8. This is a reasonable suggestion, but it's just a rule of thumb. The documentation also notes correctly that the larger the smoothing constant, the more closely the forecast tracks the actual baseline. The smaller the smoothing constant, the less the forecast tracks "noise" in the baseline—but the more slowly it responds to real changes in the baseline.

One good way to select the damping factor—and, thus, the smoothing constant—is to use the one that minimizes the *square* of the forecast errors. This approach uses the Solver to identify the best damping factor.

NOTE Don't worry if you're not familiar with the Solver. Chapter 16 discusses it in detail, and this section's use of the tool is very basic. ■

The Solver is used instead of Goal Seek because Goal Seek requires that you specify a particular value as its goal. The problem of minimizing the square of the forecast errors requires finding some unknown minimum value—because it's unknown, you can't specify it beforehand. In contrast, the Solver lets you search for a minimum, a maximum, or a specified value.

Begin by entering the formula whose result the Solver will minimize. As shown in Figure 15.16, enter this formula in cell D1:

=SUMXMY2(B3:B22,C3:C22)

The SUMXMY2 function takes the difference between each value in B3:B22 and the corresponding value in C3:C22, squares the difference, and returns the sum of the squared differences. It's this amount that the Solver will minimize.

Then, take these steps:

1. In cell F1, type **.3**.
2. In cell F2, type = **1 - F1**. F1 and F2 now contain starting values for the smoothing constant and the damping factor, respectively.
3. Select cell C4, and enter **=$F$1*B3+$F$2*C3**. (Notice the absolute referencing for cells $F$1 and $F$2.)
4. Copy the new formula in C4 and paste it through C5:C23. You have now replaced the actual values for the smoothing constant and the damping factor with cell references. The purpose is to enable the formulas to recalculate as the Solver iterates through different values for the smoothing constant.

5. Select cell D1 and choose Tools, Solver (if you do not see the Solver in the Tools menu, refer to Chapter 16 for instructions on installing it). Cell D1 appears in the Set Target Cell edit box. See Figure 15.17.
6. Choose the Min option button. In the By Changing Cells edit box, enter **F1**.
7. Click the Add button. In the Add Constraint dialog box (see Figure 15.18), enter **F1** as the Cell Reference, >= as the operator, and **0.0** as the Constraint. Choose the Add button to add that constraint. When you do so, the edit boxes clear.

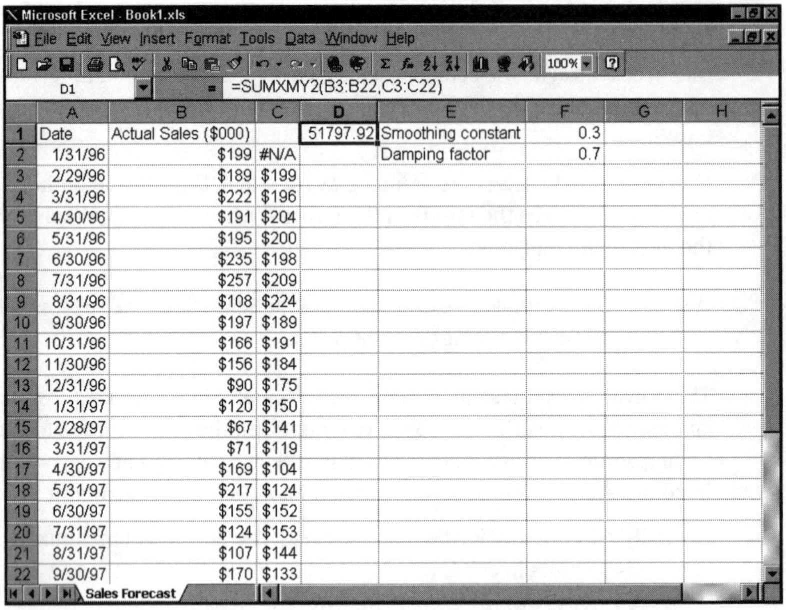

	A	B	C	D	E	F	G	H
1	Date	Actual Sales ($000)		51797.92	Smoothing constant	0.3		
2	1/31/96	$199	#N/A		Damping factor	0.7		
3	2/29/96	$189	$199					
4	3/31/96	$222	$196					
5	4/30/96	$191	$204					
6	5/31/96	$195	$200					
7	6/30/96	$235	$198					
8	7/31/96	$257	$209					
9	8/31/96	$108	$224					
10	9/30/96	$197	$189					
11	10/31/96	$166	$191					
12	11/30/96	$156	$184					
13	12/31/96	$90	$175					
14	1/31/97	$120	$150					
15	2/28/97	$67	$141					
16	3/31/97	$71	$119					
17	4/30/97	$169	$104					
18	5/31/97	$217	$124					
19	6/30/97	$155	$152					
20	7/31/97	$124	$153					
21	8/31/97	$107	$144					
22	9/30/97	$170	$133					

FIG. 15.16
After the Exponential Smoothing tool has returned forecasts, replace the actual values in the formulas with cell references.

8. Enter **F1** as the Cell Reference, <= as the operator, and **1.0** as the Constraint.
9. You have now established a range of possible values, 0.0 to 1.0, for the smoothing constant. Choose OK to close the Add Constraint dialog box and return to the Solver dialog box.
10. Choose Solve. The Solver iterates through different values for F1 (the smoothing constant) until it finds the value that results in the smallest result in D1 (the sum of the squared forecast errors).

When it reaches a solution, the Solver notifies you and you then have the choice of keeping its solution or restoring the original values.

Given the target that you called for, the solution that the Solver reaches will be the one that minimizes the sum of the squared forecast errors. By this criterion, you have reached the best forecast for the next time period at the end of the baseline.

▶ **See** "Setting the Solver Parameters," **p. 324**

FIG. 15.17

There are only four options you need to set in the Solver dialog box to complete this analysis.

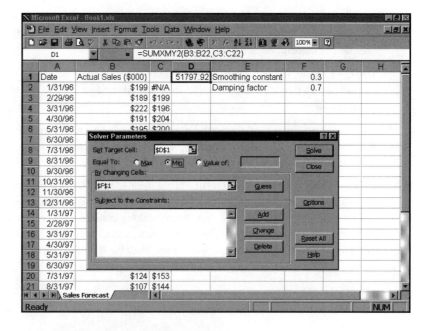

FIG. 15.18

By adding constraints, you set limits to the possible solutions that the Solver can reach.

Dealing with Autocorrelation

All baselines have a characteristic called autocorrelation. If the autocorrelation in the baseline is large, the Solver won't be of much help in finding the best smoothing constant.

The *autocorrelation* is the correlation between each point in the baseline and the next point. For the data in Figure 15.17, you estimate the autocorrelation by entering in some blank cell:

=ABS(CORREL(B2:B21,B3:B22))

Using the ABS function with the CORREL function returns the absolute value of the correlation. The result must be between 0.0 and 1.0, due to the way that a correlation and an absolute value are defined. If the result is at all large—say, greater than 0.5—then there's substantial autocorrelation in the baseline data.

In that case, using the Solver to determine the best smoothing constant would often result in a value of 1.0, which is equivalent to a damping factor of 0.0. This means that the best forecast is identical to the prior observation. The forecast would track too much noise and not enough signal.

If you do encounter a situation like this, subtract each observation, starting with the second one, from its prior observation. This is called *first-differencing*, and its effect is almost always to remove the autocorrelation from the data.

Use the Exponential Smoothing tool, and subsequently the Solver, with this differenced series instead of with the original series. The differenced series will have one observation fewer than the original.

Once you have completed the analysis, replace the differenced series with the original. The forecast values recalculate accordingly, and you will now have your forecasts in their original scale of measurement.

This section has explored the use of a fairly simple tool, Exponential Smoothing, to forecast a new value from a baseline of values. Once the initial forecast is complete, you can use the Solver to find the optimum value for the smoothing constant and, perforce, the damping factor. This use of the Solver just scratches the surface, and Chapter 16 goes into detail on how you can use the Solver to develop more complex models. ●

Using the Solver

At the end of Chapter 15, "Analyzing Data," you saw a brief introduction to using the Solver. There, it was pointed out that the Solver resembles the Goal Seek command: Both backtrack to a precedent value that satisfies a dependent value that you specify. But the Solver also differs from the Goal Seek command: You can specify only one precedent in Goal Seek, whereas the Solver can accommodate many precedents.

In addition, the Solver lets you set conditions, or *constraints*, on the solution—that is, you use the Solver to specify that certain values and formulas must satisfy your conditions before a solution is judged to be acceptable. ■

Setting the Solver parameters

Learn how to structure a worksheet to represent a business model and how to specify the inputs, the constraints, and the result that you are seeking. You'll also see how to use scenarios to manage different Solver solutions effectively and how to interpret different Solver reports.

Controlling the Solver's actions

Decide which cells the Solver should alter and which ones it should leave alone. You'll find that there are both syntactic and logical reasons to choose the changing cells with care.

Setting the Solver's options

Understand the effects that different calculation options have, both on the solution that the Solver reaches and on the way it goes about finding the solution.

Setting the Solver Parameters

The Solver is an add-in supplied with Office 97, so you must install it specifically before you can use it. To do so, start the Office 97 Setup routine. In Setup's first option dialog box, select Excel and choose Change Option. In the Excel options section, select Add-ins and choose Change Option. In the Add-ins dialog box, select the Solver check box, and click OK until Setup finishes the installation process.

After the Office 97 Setup routine has finished, verify that Solver is an item in the Tools menu. If you do not see it there, choose Tools, Add-Ins and select the Solver Add-In check box in the Add-Ins Available list.

The steps and the considerations involved in defining the problem for the Solver are described in the next three sections.

Structuring the Problem for the Solver

Suppose that you are a publisher who is considering the publication of a new book on a suite of software applications named Cubicle 97. The shelf life of such books is fairly short, because the product line must keep current with new software releases. Given the short shelf life, your decision is an important one: You will incur significant costs in development, printing and binding, marketing, and getting the book through the distribution channel.

You sit down with your Excel worksheet and start to input some timelines, costs, and revenue projections. After a few minutes, you come up with the rough estimates shown in Figure 16.1.

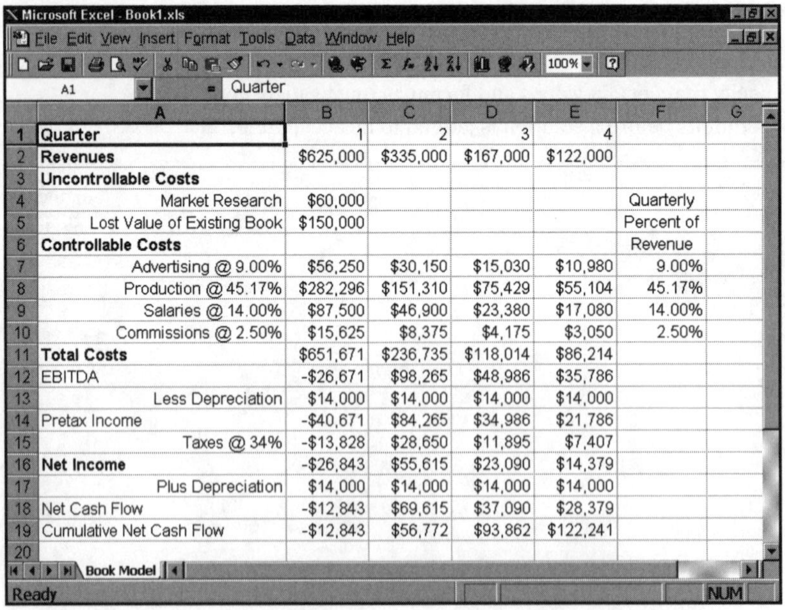

FIG. 16.1
The eventual goal is to optimize the cumulative net cash flow at the end of the fourth quarter.

	A	B	C	D	E	F	G
1	Quarter	1	2	3	4		
2	Revenues	$625,000	$335,000	$167,000	$122,000		
3	Uncontrollable Costs						
4	Market Research	$60,000				Quarterly	
5	Lost Value of Existing Book	$150,000				Percent of	
6	Controllable Costs					Revenue	
7	Advertising @ 9.00%	$56,250	$30,150	$15,030	$10,980	9.00%	
8	Production @ 45.17%	$282,296	$151,310	$75,429	$55,104	45.17%	
9	Salaries @ 14.00%	$87,500	$46,900	$23,380	$17,080	14.00%	
10	Commissions @ 2.50%	$15,625	$8,375	$4,175	$3,050	2.50%	
11	Total Costs	$651,671	$236,735	$118,014	$86,214		
12	EBITDA	-$26,671	$98,265	$48,986	$35,786		
13	Less Depreciation	$14,000	$14,000	$14,000	$14,000		
14	Pretax Income	-$40,671	$84,265	$34,986	$21,786		
15	Taxes @ 34%	-$13,828	$28,650	$11,895	$7,407		
16	Net Income	-$26,843	$55,615	$23,090	$14,379		
17	Plus Depreciation	$14,000	$14,000	$14,000	$14,000		
18	Net Cash Flow	-$12,843	$69,615	$37,090	$28,379		
19	Cumulative Net Cash Flow	-$12,843	$56,772	$93,862	$122,241		
20							

Your estimates are educated guesses. Some of them are based on solid empirical information, such as the costs associated with salaries and taxes. Some are based on nothing more quantifiable than your own current sense of the market. And some blend real data such as sales of earlier books with guesses: for example, how aggressively the manufacturer will market the new software release.

Using these data sources, you arrive at the estimates in Figure 16.1. There are, of course, many costs that the firm will incur that are not shown, but the ones in the figure are those that are relevant to the business decision.

Specifying the Target Cell

The revenues and costs flow through the model you have set up to result in a cumulative cash flow, net of the relevant costs, of $76,458 in cell E19. Your first reaction on seeing this figure is that it is an inadequate return on the costs you will incur. You believe that to make the decision to go ahead with the book worthwhile, that value must be at least $300,000.

You decide to make cell E19 the Solver's Target Cell. When you choose Tools, Solver, the Solver dialog box appears as shown in Figure 16.2.

FIG. 16.2

Although the Solver can handle many Changing Cells, it solves for just one Target Cell.

If you selected cell E19 prior to starting the Solver, its address would appear in the Set Target Cell reference edit box. Otherwise, drag across whatever address appears there and click in cell E19.

As with the Goal Seek command, the target cell that you specify for the Solver must contain a formula. Otherwise, if that cell contains a value, the Solver could change the values of other cells repeatedly and the target's value would never change.

In the Solver example at the end of Chapter 15, the goal was to minimize a particular value, and the Min option button was chosen. In this example, you are seeking a particular value—so, choose the Value Of option button and type **300000** in the associated edit box.

Each of the choices you make is capable of causing the Solver to fail, and one of the most important concerns setting the goal for the target cell. When the Min option was chosen in Chapter 15's example, it was possible to arrive at a minimum value. The target cell contained a formula that totalled the squares of other values. Because of the way that the second power of a value is defined, a square can never be a negative value.

Because zero is a true minimum possible value for any square (and thus is a true minimum for the total of a set of squared values), it is possible for the Solver to find a minimum target value.

Not so in the present example. If you were, perversely, to set the target value for the cumulative net cash flow to a minimum, you would make it impossible for the Solver to reach a solution. Any one of several outcomes is possible:

- The Solver might return a message that it could not find a feasible solution.
- You might see a message that an internal error had occurred, or that the Solver ran out of memory.
- The Solver might exceed the number of permissible iterations.
- Exceptionally, the Solver might find a minimum value that's legal but completely ridiculous—for example, a negative $184,538,962.

Similarly, if you specified a maximum value for cell E19, the Solver could just keep on increasing the Revenue values in B2:E2 until it encountered some error condition.

So, before you specify a target cell goal for the Solver to find, make sure that the formulas on the worksheet will support the goal you specify.

Specifying the Changing Cells

In the model shown in Figure 16.1, there are many cells that are precedent to the result in cell E19, the final cumulative net cash flow.

The Revenue values in B2:E2 and the percentages in F7:F10, though, are the real drivers. Various cost figures (Advertising, Salaries, Production, and Commissions) are completely dependent upon the revenue amounts and the associated percentages. For example, the cost of advertising during the first quarter is $56,250, or 9 percent of the revenue value of $625,000.

These costs are controllable. It's possible for you to make decisions about, for example, the advertising budget that will raise or lower its quarterly costs. Because they actually are under your control, the percentages that drive these costs are good candidates for Changing Cells.

By Changing Cells, the Solver means values that it can adjust in order to reach the goal that you specify for the Target Cell. Just because the Solver can change them, though, doesn't mean that it necessarily will do so. Several factors determine whether the Solver will change the value of a particular cell as it searches for a solution.

For example, you might establish a constraint (see the next section for information on Constraints) that establishes very narrow bounds on the values a Changing Cell can take on. The Solver might not change that cell's value if so doing has a negligible impact on the Target Cell value.

Or it might be that some other Changing Cell has such a strong relationship to the Target Cell's value that the Solver reaches its target before it has even gotten around to changing some other cell by more than a very small amount.

The point is that it occasionally takes some experimenting before you reach the right mix of values, formulas, and constraints. If the Solver makes a huge change in one Changing Cell and leaves another completely alone—and if this isn't what you want—you'll have to make some adjustments to the Constraints, to the formulas, or both.

Two costs, that of market research and that of the lost value of the existing book, are constant values. Your market research firm will charge a fixed fee of $60,000, and you know that you still have $150,000 worth of the existing book on Cubicle 95 in your inventory. While you could use the Solver to alter these two values in pursuit of a higher cash flow, to do so would be irrelevant. In the Solver, you have control over those values, but in reality you do not—so they are poor candidates for Changing Cells.

Just because you can't control these costs, though, doesn't mean that they don't belong in the model. They have an effect on the Target Cell both in reality and in the model, and so they remain on the worksheet as actual costs.

Both the controllable and the uncontrollable costs, along with taxes, investment dollars, and depreciation, are subtracted from the revenue figures to reach eventual net cash flow figures. The cumulative net cash flows are just the running total of the net cash flows.

You decide that you want Solver to modify the percentages that, along with the estimated revenues, determine the controllable costs. You note, though, that even if each of those costs dropped moderately you would still not have reached your goal of $300,000 cumulative net cash flow at the end of the fourth quarter. You can't reduce the costs too far or there would be no resources left available to produce the book.

Given the irreducible impact of the controllable costs on the cash flow, all that's left to adjust are the revenue estimates. So you decide to let the Solver change them, as well as the cost percentages, as it searches for the target.

In the Solver dialog box, click the By Changing Cells reference edit box, and drag across cells B2:E2 to capture the revenue estimates. Then, press Ctrl and drag across F7:F10 to capture the cost percentages. The dialog box, with both the Target Cell and the Changing Cells identified, now appears as shown in Figure 16.3.

Instead of specifying the Changing Cells yourself, you could have left the By Changing Cells reference edit box empty and chosen the Guess button. If you do so, the Solver does its best to determine which cells are precedent to the Target Cell. In the process of doing its best, the Solver can set up a situation in which too many cells, or the wrong cells, are identified as Changing Cells. With the model set up as in this example, using the Guess button would return this range of Changing Cells:

$B$13:$E$13,$B$4:$B$5,$B$2:$E$2,$F$7:$F$10

That range uses some cells unnecessarily. As discussed previously, the market research and lost inventory costs in B4 and B5 should not enter the analysis, because they aren't under your control. When you can't change these costs in reality, why allow the Solver to change them in the worksheet model?

FIG. 16.3

You still need to set some Constraints in order to keep the Solver from assigning un-realistic values to the Changing Cells.

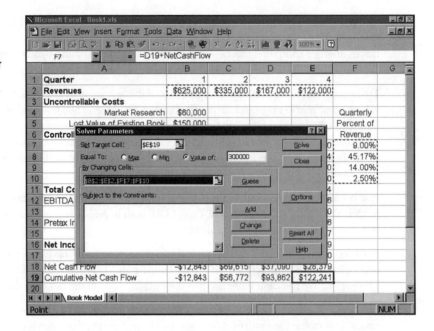

And by specifying the estimated revenues in B2:E2 and the percentages of revenues in F7:F10, you completely specify all the other controllable costs: advertising, production, salaries, and commissions. To arrange for the Solver to change, say, advertising costs in B7:E7 would be redundant.

Suppose that you identified the advertising costs in B7:E7 as Changing Cells, in addition to the estimated revenues in B2:E2 and the cost percentages in F7:F10. Apart from the redundancy and inefficiency of doing so, you do not want the Solver to alter B7:E7. Those cells contain formulas. When the Solver changes a cell, it changes its value. If a cell starts out with a formula, the Solver replaces the formula with the value that helps get to the target. Then, you've lost your formulas.

Occasionally, and with a very simple model, you might find it convenient to use the Guess button. But be aware that when you do so you relinquish control of the model, and Solver's best guess for the Changing Cells might well be different from what you intend.

Specifying the Constraints

To turn the Solver loose on the model as specified in Figure 16.3 would be to tell the bull where the china shop is. It might decide to turn the cost percentages in F7:F10 into negative values. This would change the costs from reductions to the revenue into contributions to the revenue (that is, subtracting a negative $30,000 from a positive $100,000 results in $130,000). So, you still need to provide some boundaries, or *constraints*, for the Solver to use as it modifies the values in the Changing Cells.

Begin by clicking the Add button. The Add Constraint dialog box appears as shown in Figure 16.4.

FIG. 16.4
The drop-down list of available operators appears when you click the drop-down arrow.

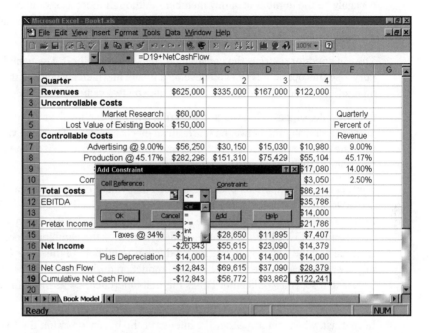

To add a constraint to the model, click the Cell Reference box, and then click a cell in the worksheet. This is the cell whose value the Solver will constrain. Click the drop-down arrow to choose from among the available operators; as shown in Figure 16.4, you can choose from three comparison operators and two special operators (int and bin).

If you choose one of the comparison operators (less than or equal to, equal to, and greater than or equal to), then you also specify in the Constraint box a number, a cell reference, or a formula that returns a number.

For example, you might decide to prevent the Solver from reducing the value 9 percent in cell F7 below 5 percent. You would do so if you believed that you could not allow advertising costs to fall below 5 percent of estimated revenue without jeopardizing the marketing effort. You would choose >= as the comparison operator. Then, in the Constraint box, you could enter:

- The number **.05**
- The address of some worksheet cell that contains the number .05
- The address of a cell that contains a formula whose result is .05
- The formula **0.1/2**

Any one of these, in combination with the >= operator, prevents the Solver from setting the associated cost percentage to a value lower than 5 percent.

The int operator restricts the constrained cell's value to an integer. For example, if you were using the Solver to establish a family budget, one of the values in the model would almost certainly be the number of family members. Although there are some circumstances in which it seems desirable to have a fractional number of children, it's unrealistic and you should constrain that value to take on only integer values.

The bin operator restricts the constrained cell's value to 1 or 0: The term *bin* is short for *binary*. Use this operator when you develop a model in which a value is either present or absent, on or off, or some other situation that can take on two values only.

For example, suppose that you are analyzing a model that involves switching logic—perhaps to predict the mean time between failures in an electric system. Then, the value that represents the state of the switch should be 1 or 0, and you would constrain it to one of those two values by means of the bin operator.

If you choose a comparison operator, the cell that you're constraining can be anywhere on the active worksheet. It need not be one of the Changing Cells that you have identified. In the example model, cell B8 contains the total production costs for the first quarter. It is not one of the Changing Cells, but it is completely determined by the combination of the first quarter Revenue and the cost percentage for Production—and both of these *are* Changing Cells. You might want to make sure that the cost of production during the first quarter does not exceed $300,000. If so, you would enter **B8** as the Cell Reference, **<=** as the comparison operator, and **300000** as the Constraint.

In contrast, when you use either the integer or the binary operator, the Cell Reference edit box must contain one of the Changing Cells. Neither operator is legal with a cell outside the range of Changing Cells, even if that cell changes value during the process of reaching a solution.

In either case, the Solver fills in the Constraint edit box for you, displaying integer if you choose int, and binary if you choose bin.

After specifying a constraint, click Add in the Add Constraint dialog box. The constraint is added to the list of constraints in the Solver dialog box, and the edit boxes in the Add Constraint dialog box are cleared. Continue until you have added all the constraints you want, and click OK. If you have finished adding constraints but the edit boxes have been cleared because you clicked OK, just click Cancel. Both the OK and the Cancel button return you to the Solver dialog box, with the constraints identified in the Subject to the Constraints list box.

For the current example, suppose that you choose to keep the advertising, production, salaries, and commission cost percentages from falling below 7, 40, 10, and 2 percent, respectively. When you return to the Solver dialog box it appears as shown in Figure 16.5.

You now have a chance to change your mind about a constraint. To remove any constraint, click it in the list box and choose Delete. Or if you want to modify a constraint, click it and choose Change to display the Change Constraint dialog box. The Change Constraint dialog box is identical to the Add Constraint dialog box. There, you can change the Cell Reference, the operator, and the Constraint value itself.

FIG. 16.5

The constraints you
specify in the Add
Constraint dialog box
are listed in the Subject
to the Constraints list
box.

N O T E Long-time users of the Solver know that it has been dangerous to identify a named cell or
range as a constraint, because the Solver returns an error message if the user tries to
change that constraint. This bug appears to have been removed from the Office 97 version of the
Solver. ■

Using the Solution

After identifying the Target Cell, Changing Cells, and Constraints, you are ready for Solver to
find a solution. When you click the Solve button, the Solver tries different values in the Changing Cells until it reaches the target value that you specified. You can watch the Solver's
progress in the status bar, where it displays information about the current trial solution.

If the Solver reaches a solution that conforms to the target value and that complies with the
constraints you specified, you see the dialog box shown in Figure 16.6.

FIG. 16.6

You might choose to
Restore Original Values
if you don't want to lose
them.

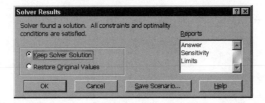

You will want to be careful at this point. Suppose that you choose Keep Solver Solution. If you
do, the new values for the Changing Cells stay on the worksheet, and you will have lost their
original values. Keeping in mind that the Solver puts values only—not formulas—in the Changing Cells as it seeks a solution, notice that any formulas or values that were in the Changing
Cells when you started the Solver will be lost.

For this reason among others, it's a good idea to create a scenario, perhaps named Initial Values, before you start the Solver (see Chapter 15 for information on creating and managing
scenarios). If you do so, you can retrieve the original values—not formulas: scenarios don't
save formulas—that were in the Changing Cells whenever you want.

Notice that one of the options shown in Figure 16.6 is to Save Scenario. If you choose that
option, the Solver displays a dialog box where you can type a name for the scenario. After you

enter the name and click OK, the Solver creates a scenario for you and returns to the Solver dialog box. The Changing Cells that you specified for the Solver are used as the Changing Cells for the scenario.

Taking this approach means that you can later use the Scenario Manager to switch back and forth between a scenario that uses the original values for the Changing Cells and scenarios created by the Solver that represent different solutions—some that use different target values, some that use different Changing Cells, and some that use different sets of constraints. Be sure to give each scenario a descriptive name, so that you can tell how it differs from other scenarios.

The solution returned by the Solver for the current example is shown in Figure 16.7. The solution is based on the target of $300,000 for the cumulative net cash flow at the end of the fourth quarter, on the revenue estimates and cost percentages that were identified as the Changing Cells, and on the constraints that were specified, as shown in Figure 16.5.

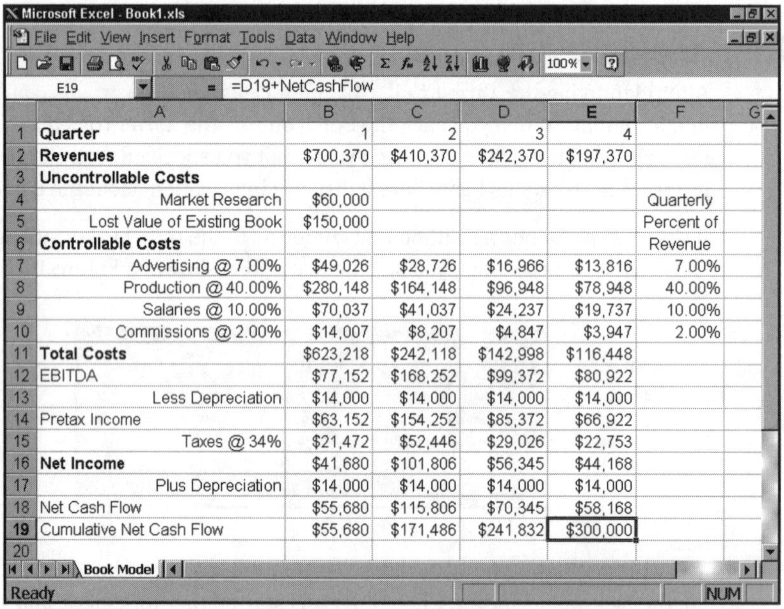

FIG. 16.7

You always need to evaluate a Solver solution in terms of reality: Does it pass the giggle test?

	A	B	C	D	E	F
	E19		=D19+NetCashFlow			
1	Quarter	1	2	3	4	
2	Revenues	$700,370	$410,370	$242,370	$197,370	
3	Uncontrollable Costs					
4	Market Research	$60,000				Quarterly
5	Lost Value of Existing Book	$150,000				Percent of
6	Controllable Costs					Revenue
7	Advertising @ 7.00%	$49,026	$28,726	$16,966	$13,816	7.00%
8	Production @ 40.00%	$280,148	$164,148	$96,948	$78,948	40.00%
9	Salaries @ 10.00%	$70,037	$41,037	$24,237	$19,737	10.00%
10	Commissions @ 2.00%	$14,007	$8,207	$4,847	$3,947	2.00%
11	Total Costs	$623,218	$242,118	$142,998	$116,448	
12	EBITDA	$77,152	$168,252	$99,372	$80,922	
13	Less Depreciation	$14,000	$14,000	$14,000	$14,000	
14	Pretax Income	$63,152	$154,252	$85,372	$66,922	
15	Taxes @ 34%	$21,472	$52,446	$29,026	$22,753	
16	Net Income	$41,680	$101,806	$56,345	$44,168	
17	Plus Depreciation	$14,000	$14,000	$14,000	$14,000	
18	Net Cash Flow	$55,680	$115,806	$70,345	$58,168	
19	Cumulative Net Cash Flow	$55,680	$171,486	$241,832	$300,000	
20						

Examining the solution might suggest to you that you shouldn't publish the book. In order to return a final cumulative net cash flow of $300,000, the Solver had to simultaneously increase the estimated revenues and decrease the percentages for the cost categories.

The model suggests, then, that in order to reach your target, you would have to reduce the advertising budget, presumably bringing the book to the attention of a smaller audience. You would have to reduce the production budget, possibly binding the book in a less attractive cover or cutting some other cost that would make the book less marketable. And you would have to reduce the salary budget, assigning fewer editors to the development process.

Any one of these actions could make it more difficult to sell the book to book stores, thus reducing the potential revenue. But the Solver's solution also suggests that you need higher revenues than you initially estimated in order to reach the target. Therefore, you might well decide that it would be a bad decision to publish the book.

Equally, you might decide to go ahead with it. Suppose that you started out with initial values that were very conservative as to estimated revenues and very pessimistic as to cost percentages. You could now evaluate the Solver's solution and judge whether it's realistic.

Given the conservative initial revenue estimates, are those suggested by the Solver attainable? Given the pessimistic cost percentages, are those suggested by the Solver feasible? If so, you might decide in favor of publishing the book. All depends on how you regard the initial values that you supplied. A blind acceptance of the Solver's results changes artificial intelligence into artificial stupidity.

This section has warned you about allowing the Solver to overwrite the initial values for the Changing Cells with the values that bring about your target result. While you can make your life easier by saving in Scenarios both your initial values and the values that are returned by the Solver, you can make things easier yet by keeping each Changing Cell as simple as possible.

Consider the cost percentages in the current example. Each one was set out separately, in cells F7:F10. The percentages are used in the quarterly cost formulas; for example, the formula in cell B7 is:

=$F$7*B2

which multiplies the advertising cost percentage by the first quarter's revenue estimate.

You could, of course, specify cell B7 (and, for that matter, the remainder of the cells in B7:E9) as one of the Changing Cells. But if you do so, the Solver replaces the formulas with values. You then lose the ability to modify the cells by changing either a revenue estimate or a cost percentage. Furthermore, you lose the entire logic of the model, which implies that expenses and revenues are directly related.

Therefore, whenever possible, you should set up the worksheet such that the Changing Cells contain values that are used by formulas. These formulas, in turn, control the value in the Target Cell.

This approach is followed in the example worksheet. The Changing Cells each contain a single value, one that is easy to recapture by means of the Scenario Manager, and no violence is done to the intermediate formulas in B7:E18.

▶ **See** "Creating and Managing Scenarios," **p. 304**

Understanding the Solver's Reports

When the Solver reports that it has found a solution, you can direct the Solver to create three additional reports: an Answer report, a Sensitivity report, and a Limits report (refer to Figure 16.6). Choose any or all reports by clicking them in the list box. When you then choose OK, the Solver creates a new worksheet for each report. The first portion of the Answer report is shown in Figure 16.8.

Part III
Ch
16

FIG. 16.8

The Solver uses the terms *Changing Cells* and *Adjustable Cells* interchangeably.

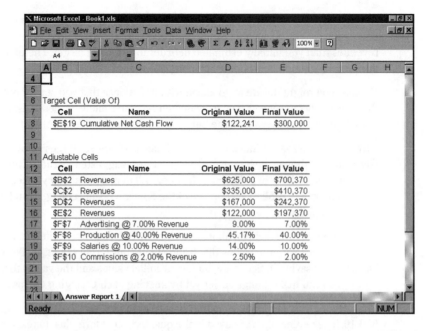

The Answer report is a convenient way to view information about the initial and the final values for the Target Cell and the Changing Cells. Below that information there is a section on the constraints that you specified (see Figure 16.9).

FIG. 16.9

The Cell Values in the Constraints section of the Answer report are their final values.

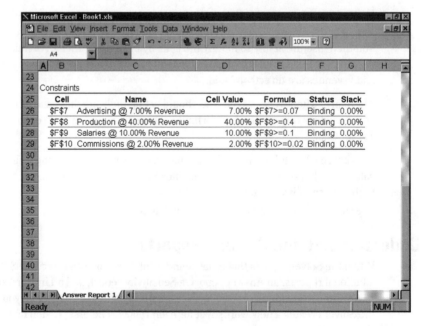

The Constraints section identifies the constrained cells, their final values, and the constraint that you established for each. It also shows whether or not the final value for the constrained cell equals the bound for the constraint, and the difference between the two. *Binding* means that the solution value is at the constraint's bound; *Not Binding* means that it is not at its bound.

The Slack value is the absolute value of the difference between the final value of the constrained cell and the constraint's bound. You can use this information to judge whether or not the constraints that you established are too rigorous.

Suppose that instead of adjusting the Commissions percentage to 2.00 percent, the Solver had reached its solution without changing the initial 2.50 percent. Then, the slack value for Commissions would be 0.50 percent: the difference between the solution value of 2.50 percent and the constraint bound of 2.00 percent.

The Limits report is shown in Figure 16.10.

Part

III

Ch

16

FIG. 16.10

The Limits report displays information about the Target Cell value for each constraint's upper and lower limits.

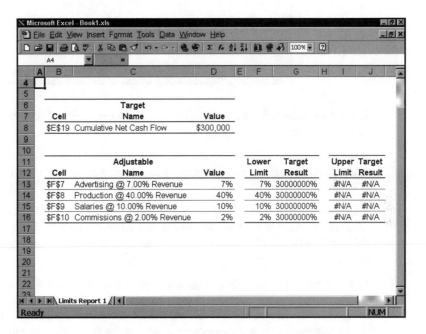

Notice in Figure 16.10 that you can evaluate the target value (labeled `Target Result`) associated with each constraint's lower and upper limits. If a constraint was not given one limit or the other, the Limits report displays `#N/A` as the Target Result.

Notice also that the Limits report erroneously uses the cell format for the constraint cell as the format for the Target Result. For example, the advertising cost percentage is formatted as a percent; the Target Result associated with that constraint is also formatted as a percent.

The Solver's Sensitivity report for this example appears in Figure 16.11.

FIG. 16.11

When a solution satisfies the specified target value and the constraints, the reduced gradient is zero.

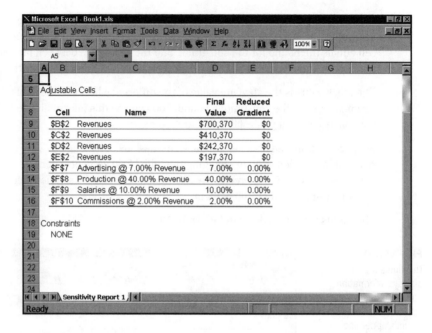

You will see a Constraints section in the Sensitivity report only if you have constrained cells that are not among the Changing Cells.

If, in the Solver Options dialog box, you choose Assume Linear Model (see the next section for information about the linearity options), you will see a Sensitivity report that resembles the one in Figure 16.12.

A full discussion of the material in the Sensitivity report shown in Figure 16.12 is beyond the scope of this chapter. You can, however, derive information about the amount of variability allowed for different Changing Cells and constraints from the sensitivity report for a linear model.

However, some understanding of the gradients that are mentioned in Figure 16.11 is useful if you want to manipulate the Solver options described in the next section. The Solver works by substituting new values in the Changing Cells and observing the effect—both the direction and the magnitude—of those changes on the value of the Target Cell. In a formal mathematical sense, the value of the Target Cell is said to be a function of the Changing Cells.

The Solver finds the first derivative of that function; the first derivative measures the rate of change of the function in response to modifications in the Changing Cell values. In a case such as the current example where there is more than one Changing Cell, there is not just one derivative but several partial derivatives, each measuring the rate of change in the function as a result of modifying the value in each Changing Cell.

FIG. 16.12
Linear models result in a richer Sensitivity report.

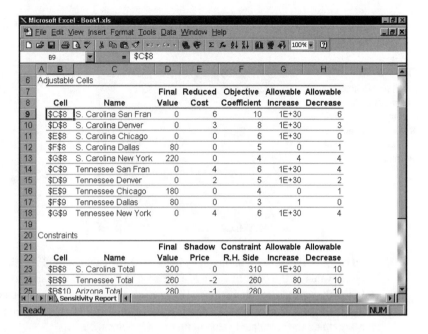

That set of partial derivatives is called the *gradient* of the function, and the partial derivatives associated with a particular Changing Cell constitute a *partial gradient*. At the point in the solution process that the Solver has found values that result in the target value you specified, the partial gradient for each Changing Cell equals zero. This is shown in the Reduced gradient column on the Sensitivity report for a problem that does not assume a linear model.

How this process is affected by Solver options you might choose is described in the next section.

Setting the Solver's Options

Choosing the Options button on the main Solver dialog box displays the dialog box shown in Figure 16.13.

In many cases, there is no need to even look at these options, much less change them. On occasion, though, you will find it necessary to make some adjustments.

Controlling the Precision

The default value of 100 for both the number of seconds and the number of iterations that the Solver uses is fairly generous. But for a very complicated problem, and especially when a nonlinear model is involved, the Solver might return to the Solver Results dialog box with a message that it could not find a solution. If it seemed to you that the Solver took a long time before it displayed the Solver Results dialog box, you might try increasing the Max Time and Iterations values. So doing gives the Solver more opportunity to converge precisely on the target value that you specified. The maximum permissible value for Max Time and for Iterations is 32,767.

FIG. 16.13

The Solver Options dialog box enables you to control the amount of work the Solver does, and how it goes about reaching a solution.

You can give the Solver a mulligan by increasing the value in the Precision edit box. When the Solver evaluates the current value of a constrained cell or of the target cell, it does so in terms of the value of the Precision option. The precision value must be between 0 and 1. If you change the precision to, say, .95, you are saying that a difference between a specified constraint or target and the calculated value of up to .95 is acceptable.

The Tolerance option is another way of saying "close enough." It applies only to models that have constraints using the int operator—in other words, there is at least one cell that you have constrained to be an integer. When a constrained cell cannot take a fractional value—when that cell is constrained to integer values only—it might not be possible to reach the exact value that you specified for the Target Cell. By increasing the Tolerance to, say, 10 percent, you indicate that a solution as much as 10 percent higher or lower than your target value is acceptable.

Suppose that you have $100,000 to spend on the purchase of several cars. You have set up a model that Solver will use to arrive at an average purchase price of $17,000. One of the constraints is the number of cars to purchase. You cannot purchase a fractional number of cars, so you constrain that cell to integer values.

But to arrive at an average purchase price of $17,000 on a total purchase of $100,000, you must purchase 5.88 cars. That conflicts with the integer constraint. Therefore, set the Tolerance to 15 percent, allowing a result somewhere between 85 and 115 percent of $17,000. So doing enables an average purchase price based on either five or six cars—both integer values.

The Convergence option comes into play when the Solver is nearing a solution. The Solver continually examines the most recent five solutions it has calculated as it varies the values in the Changing Cells. If 1 plus the ratio of the amount of change—not the values themselves, but the change in values—from solution to solution is less than the Convergence value, for five consecutive solutions, the Solver concludes that it's not going to get any closer to your target value. Make the Convergence more precise by providing a smaller number, any fractional value between 0 and 1.

Defining the Search

The Solver Options dialog box also lets you establish some control over how the Solver will go about seeking a solution to the problem you set it.

If you check the Assume Linear Model check box, you make a fundamental change in how the Solver goes about evaluating the problem. Recall from the prior section "Understanding the Solver's Reports" that the Solver proceeds by modifying values in the Changing Cells and by observing the resulting differences in the function's gradient.

You prevent this from occurring by assuming a linear model. With a linear model, the Solver can simply calculate a linear equation that fits different Changing Cell values to Target Cell values. In effect, the Solver backtracks from a specified solution to a set of requisite Changing Cell values by means of that equation. This speeds up the solution process dramatically, because it's not necessary to evaluate a series of trial solutions.

If there is no exponentiation in any of the Changing Cells, in the Target Cell, or (more typically) in any of the formulas that come between the Changing Cells and the Target Cell, then it's quite possible that the model is a linear one.

It can happen, though, that there is nonlinearity in the model, not immediately apparent to you, that's induced by the relationships among the Changing Cells, and between the Changing Cells and the Target Cell. If so, you may be setting the Solver an impossible task by telling it to assume a linear model. You might get an error message that the conditions for a linear solution aren't met. Or it's possible that the Solver will return the correct solution to the wrong problem.

While a nonlinear search is slower, in a time when many users are running Excel with processors whose clock speed exceeds 200MHz, you can probably afford to assume a nonlinear model. If your model turns out to be linear, its linearity is unlikely to make a difference in the solution.

So, when the difference in solution time is a matter of a few seconds and when you're likely to obtain the same result, it's sensible to leave the Assume Linear Model check box in its default cleared state.

It can help to select the Use Automatic Scaling check box when the scale of measurement of the Changing Cells and that of the Target or Constraint cells are very different. In this chapter's example, the Changing Cells use both percentages (to derive costs) and hundreds of thousands of dollars (to represent revenue estimates). The automatic scaling option can speed up calculation in this and similar situations.

The Assume Non-Negative option is a good shortcut when you have Changing Cells that should not be assigned negative values. In the current example, if you were willing for any cost percentage to be zero but not negative, you could dispense with the Constraints and select the Assume Non-Negative check box instead.

It can be useful to select the Show Iteration Results check box. Doing so causes the Solver to pause after each iteration. This gives you an opportunity to examine the current values of the

Changing Cells and the Target Cell and to save the current solution as a scenario. Subsequently examining the differences among the temporary solutions can give you some insight into the relationships among the Changing Cells and the Target Cell.

Influencing the Calculations

When the Solver establishes a gradient of partial derivatives, it extrapolates from that gradient to choose the next set of values that it will assign to the Changing Cells. It can do that on either a linear or a nonlinear basis. If you keep the default value, Tangent, for Estimates, the Solver lays a straight line that's tangential to the gradient. It then extrapolates along that line to reach the next set of values it will try for the Changing Cells.

If you choose Quadratic instead of Tangent, the Solver lays a curve against the gradient. In nonlinear problems, this can speed up performance, because it's not necessary repeatedly to create straight-line tangents to extrapolate to the next set of Changing Cell values. Again, though, because of the speed of today's microprocessors, the option will usually be irrelevant to you.

When the Solver is in the midst of evaluating a current solution and trying to figure out the next set of Changing Cell values it should try, it does so by altering each Changing Cell slightly, and keeping track of the combined effect on the rate of change, the derivative, of the Target Cell value. This is how the default option for Derivatives, Forward Differencing, works.

If you choose Central Differencing, the Solver makes two estimates at each iteration, instead of just one. It does this by selecting values for the Changing Cells that cause the two estimates to lie in different directions along the gradient from the current estimate. This results in more accurate calculations at each step—but it also results in more calculations.

The choice between the Newton (actually, quasi-Newton) and the Conjugate methods is abstruse. *Very* briefly, the Newton method calculates analytic derivatives at each iteration. The conjugate gradient method constructs each iteration's estimate by means of a minimization procedure. It takes longer per iteration, and requires more iterations, than the Newton method. You'll usually do fine by accepting the default Newton option.

TROUBLESHOOTING

When you choose Tools, Solver, you might see the message Solver: An unexpected internal error occurred, or available memory was exhausted.. If you do, make sure that no control on the worksheet, such as a list box or check box, is active when you start the Solver. Suppose that you click some item in a list box on the worksheet and immediately choose Tools, Solver. You *may* see that error message. But if after selecting the list box item you click some worksheet cell before choosing Tools, Solver, you will not see the error message. The word *may* is used here because the controls that you place on a worksheet by means of the Forms toolbar do not cause this error message. The controls that you place on the worksheet by means of the Control Toolbox do cause it.

If you use the Solver on a data set and get one solution, another colleague may use the Solver on the data set and get a different solution. Most often, this occurs when two users have some Solver option set differently. But it can happen even when both users have set the Solver options identically. Very small differences in the starting values of the Changing Cells can exert an apparently disproportionate influence on the results returned by the Solver. Try copying the starting values from one user's worksheet to the other user's worksheet, and then running the Solver again.

If you set the constraint for a range of cells to `integer`, when the Solver finished you might find that the cells weren't integers. The Solver comes as close as it can to integer values for integer-constrained cells. It can happen, though, that slight variances from the integer value occur. When this happens, the variances tend to be beyond the tenth decimal place—for example, instead of 3, the Solver returns `3.000000000594`. For most purposes this is close enough. But if not, use the TRUNC function on the Changing Cells in question, copy the results, and paste them as values over the original Changing Cells. Then, compare the new value for the Target Cell with the one that the Solver returned.

Part

III

Ch

16

Microsoft Access

17 Creating Access Tables   345

18 Working with Data   367

19 Querying Data   389

20 Database Reports   413

21 Using Multiple Tables   433

22 Macros   445

CHAPTER 17

Creating Access Tables

The first step to using Microsoft Access is creating a database, but the most important step is creating the tables. Every database is made up of tables. Tables store the data that make that database useful.

Access provides several methods for creating tables, all of which are covered in this chapter. Each has its strengths and weaknesses. Review them carefully and choose the one that best suits your situation. ■

Create a new table

Build tables quickly and easily using a variety of methods.

Working with data types

Data comes in many different forms. Each data type presents unique opportunities and limitations.

Working with field properties

Field properties affect the way that Access data is collected and displayed.

Modifying a table

Tables are not static entities. Their design needs to change as quickly as their purpose.

Working with relationships

Tables can have relationships to other tables in a database. These relationships can be specifically defined.

Creating a New Table

Create a new table by opening a database window, selecting the Tables page, and clicking the New button. As mentioned, tables can be created using several different methods. A view can be used to create the table from the available data or data design. Tables from other databases can be used to create new tables, or the Table Wizard can create a new table using your input. These methods are presented by Access in the New Table dialog box, shown in Figure 17.1:

FIG. 17.1

You must choose a method to use when creating a new table.

- *Datasheet view* builds a table by collecting the data that will be contained within the table. One column is created for each column of values. Values from each column are used to determine the column's data type and formatting. This view creates tables from organized data without heavy emphasis on table design.

- *Design view* creates a new table using a definition of data types for columns. The definition determines how the data will be entered, stored, and displayed. Information can also be provided that performs validation tests on data, provides default values, and documents the purpose of the data. This view creates tables from a table design— regardless of the existence or nonexistence of any data.

- *Table Wizard* creates a new table from an existing table design. The Table Wizard offers a choice of commonly used table designs for business or personal use. After choosing a design, the table can be customized to suit a more specific purpose. New users can use the Table Wizard to quickly create useful tables, and experienced users can use the wizard to create tables with a standard design.

- *Import Table* copies the design and data from a table contained in another database into the current Access database. The table can be an Access database or any other type of database that Access can read data from. This action creates a new table from an existing table's design and copies all of the existing table's data to the new table. Any changes made to the new table are not reflected in the table used to create it.

- *Link Table* copies the design of a table contained in another database. Again, the table can be an Access table or any other type of database that Access can connect to. While this action creates a definition for a table, the table cannot hold any data. Instead, it is a reference or pointer to the table that was used to create it. Any changes made to the data displayed for the new table are made directly to the table that was used to create it.

The following sections contain more detailed information as to the actual procedures for creating tables with the different methods.

Creating a Table with Datasheet View

Tables created using Datasheet view are created from organized data. That is, the data is available in a form that is very close to how the new table will store it (see Figure 17.2). Written records or paper forms, such as a customer list or invoices, could easily contain data that is organized as it will be stored in a database table. The majority of the table design is completed, and there is no need to build a definition of the table's columns before entering the data.

> **CAUTION**
>
> Well-organized data doesn't always translate into a well-designed table. Review the data to determine how it fits into the database and make any necessary adjustments.

Part **IV** Ch **17**

FIG. 17.2
Well-organized data can make table design very easy or even unnecessary.

First Name	Last Name	State
Scott	Warner	AZ
Sandy	Cooper	NV
Mary	Stroud	OH
Ronald	Warner	IN
Rhonda	Schultz	FL

After choosing Datasheet view in the New Table dialog box, enter your data into the datasheet. Each column corresponds to a field in the table, and each row is a record. Fields do not have data types until the table is saved. When the table is saved, Access assigns each field a data type based on the information contained in that field. You can change the data type in Design view after the table is saved. Figure 17.3 shows Datasheet view with the data from Figure 17.2.

FIG. 17.3
Enter data into Datasheet view just as you would enter data into a spreadsheet.

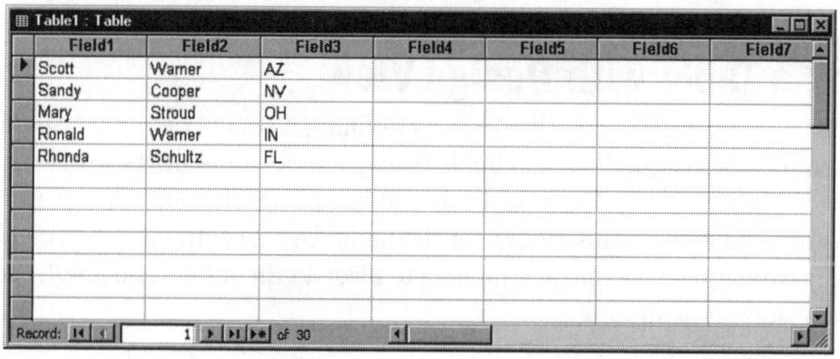

Field1	Field2	Field3	Field4	Field5	Field6	Field7
Scott	Warner	AZ				
Sandy	Cooper	NV				
Mary	Stroud	OH				
Ronald	Warner	IN				
Rhonda	Schultz	FL				

After you have entered the data, save the table. First, Access prompts you for a table name. Then, Access opens another dialog box to inform you that no primary key has been defined for the table (see Figure 17.4). This makes sense because Datasheet view doesn't have you build a definition for the table; you just enter the data. Click the Yes button in the dialog box to have Access create a primary key field for your table. The new field is added to the beginning of the table, as shown in Figure 17.5. It automatically generates a new unique number for each new record.

> **N O T E** You are not required to let Access create a primary key field for you. The data you entered into the datasheet may already contain one or more fields that should act as the primary key for the table. If this is the case, click the No button in the Primary Key dialog box and define your primary key in Design view. ■

FIG. 17.4

Access can create a primary key field, or you can designate an existing field as the primary key.

 T I P You can change the field names by double-clicking the field header, which is labeled Field1, Field2, Field3... by default, and typing a new name.

FIG. 17.5

A saved table has data types defined for its fields and may have a primary key defined.

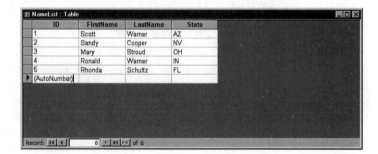

Creating a Table with Design View

Tables are created in Design view by defining a set of columns, or fields, for the table. A data type is assigned to each field. The data type limits the type of information that can be placed into the field. Each field can also have a description. One or more fields can also be designated as the primary key for the table. Use Design view to create tables when you have only a design for a table and no data to place in the table. This might be the case if the table is to store appointments.

> **CAUTION**
>
> It's not necessary to have any data available to create a table in Design view. However, test data can help identify which data types should be used and eliminate the need for changes later.

After choosing Design view in the New Table dialog box, enter your field names into Design view. In addition to the field name, enter a data type and description for each field. A primary key is assigned by right-clicking the field(s) and choosing Primary Key from the pop-up menu. Figure 17.6 shows how the table created using Datasheet view would look if it were created with Design view.

 T I P Field descriptions make it easier for others to use and maintain a table. Descriptions are also very helpful when documenting an entire database.

FIG. 17.6

Design view works with the definition of the table and is not concerned with any specific data.

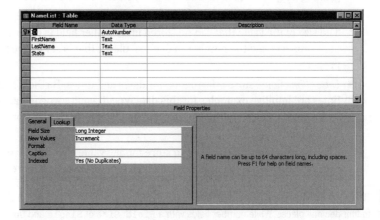

Design view has many data types to choose from. Data types are discussed in detail in the section "Using Data Types." Each field has a set of properties that determines the behavior of that field. The properties vary according to the data type for that field. These properties are discussed in the section "Working with Field Properties."

Working with Data Types After naming a column, you must assign a data type. This data type determines what type of information you can enter into a specific column. This feature separates Access from other Office products in that it helps to guarantee the integrity of a set of data. As an example, an integer data type will not allow decimal points to be entered—or letters for that matter. Date/Time columns understand how many days are in each month, including leap years. By carefully selecting a data type, a user can provide safeguards against bad data input.

To select a data type, simply choose the appropriate selection from the drop-down list box; they are as follows:

- The *Text* data type contains text or combinations of text and a number up to 255 characters in length. With no real constraints on this type of field, the user can enter just about anything in this field. Names and descriptions are the most common entries for this data type.

Part
IV

Ch
17

Use the Text data type to store phone numbers, ZIP codes, and social security numbers. While these values are normally made up entirely of numbers, they should never have any mathematical calculations performed on them. In addition, such values may start with 0, which is not permissible in a numeric data type.

- *Memo* fields are used for large pieces of text. This data type can grow as large as 65,535 characters, more text than any of us will ever type into a database. Use this data type sparingly; Access does not allow sorting on this data type, and prevents the user from printing a report sorted alphabetically by a memo field's contents.

- *Number* fields can store only numeric values. No text can be stored in a Number field. The size of the value that can be stored in a number field is determined by the `Field Size` property and the number of decimal places that is set by the `Decimal Places` property.

- *Date/Time* fields store information for dates and times. Birthdates and appointment times are intuitive examples for this data type. If you're worried about year 2000 capability in Access, you shouldn't be. Access' Date/Time fields can store values for the years 100 through 9999.

- The *Currency* data type is used to store money values. Not surprisingly, the currency data type is really just a numeric data type that understands currency symbols.

 The Currency data type can be used for a field that requires many calculations involving data with one to four decimal places. While number fields with a `Field Size` of `Single` and `Double` require floating-point calculation, the Currency data type uses a faster fixed-point calculation.

- The *AutoNumber* data type generates a unique sequential number, incremented by 1, for each new record in a table. Fields of this data type cannot be updated. This feature is especially useful when defining the primary key of a table.

- The *Yes/No* data type holds a value of either Yes or No. This data type is what mathematicians call a *Boolean value*, meaning it must have one of two values.

> **CAUTION**
>
> Only use the Yes/No data type when you are absolutely sure the field can be described with a Yes or No. This can be difficult as we are often forced to deal with an UNKNOWN answer. As an example, an Employee table might contain a Gender column to indicate the gender of employees. A Yes could indicate one sex, while a No could indicate the other. But what will the company do when it does not yet know the gender of the employee? For whatever reason, the answer was omitted from the employee's application. Suddenly, a third value is necessary in this table, making a Yes/No data type a bad choice.

- The *OLE Object* data type links or embeds an object, such as a document or spreadsheet, in an Access database. If you are looking to store employees' pictures or Microsoft Word resumes, choose this data type. This data type has a size limit of 1G and cannot be used to sort data.

▶ **See** "Linking and Embedding," **p. 39**

▶ **See** "Understanding Linking and Embedding," **p. 40**

■ The *Hyperlink* data type is used to store links to intranet/Internet sites. As an example, a company might store employees' home page links in the database. Hyperlink fields cannot be used to sort data.

N O T E A hyperlink address can have up to three parts:

- The displaytext is the text that appears in a field or control. It is essentially the title of the Web address specified in the address and subaddress. This part is optional.

- The address is the path to a file (UNC path) or page (URL). This part is required unless the subaddress points to an object contained within the current database.

- The subaddress is a location within the file or page. This part is optional.

Each of these parts can contain up to 2,048 characters. The easiest way to insert a hyperlink address in a field or control is to click Hyperlink on the Insert menu. ■

▶ **See** "Adding Hyperlinks," **p. 752**

■ The *Lookup Wizard* creates a field that allows you to choose a value from another table or from a list of values that you supply, by using a list box or combo box. Start the Lookup Wizard by choosing this data type for a field. Figure 17.7 shows the first step of the Lookup Wizard, where you choose to get values from another table or supply them yourself. After you complete the wizard, Access selects a data type for the field based on the values provided to the wizard.

Part
IV

Ch
17

FIG. 17.7
The Lookup Wizard makes it easy to present choices for a field's value.

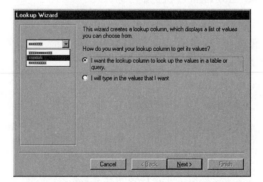

Working with Field Properties   Data types control the type of information that is stored in each field. However, Access fields are capable of much more intelligent behavior than simply storing data. They can enforce business rules, display input masks, insert default values, and more. A field's advanced behavior is controlled by the field's properties.

Field properties are displayed in the lower portion of the Design view as shown in **Figure** 17.8. The properties for a field will vary with the data type. Each data type has a different set of properties that it uses, but the properties are all drawn from these possibilities:

Field Size	Default Value
New Values	Validation Rule
Format	Validation Text
Decimal Places	Required
Input Mask	Indexed
Caption	Allow Zero Length

FIG. 17.8

A brief explanation of the selected property is displayed to the right of the properties list.

Field Size The *Field Size* can be used to specify the maximum length for Text, Number, and AutoNumber fields. This property also sets the precision, or accuracy, of Number and AutoNumber fields. Text fields are given a field size ranging from 0–255, which is the number of characters that can be in the field. Table 17.1 shows the possible values for the Field Size property of Number and AutoNumber fields.

Table 17.1 Number Field Size Property Settings

Setting	Numeric Range	Decimal Precision
Byte	0 through 255	None
Integer	–32,768 through 32,767	None
Long Integer	–2,147,483,648 through 2,147,483,647	None
Single	–3.402823E38 through –1.401298E–45 for negative values, 1.401298E–45 through 3.402823E38 for positive values	7
Double	–1.79769313486231E308 through –4.94065645841247E–324 for negative values, 1.79769313486231E308 through 4.94065645841247E–324 for positive values	15
Replication ID	Globally unique identifier (GUID), used for replication	N/A

TIP The `Field Size` property for the Text data type can be very handy when working with specific types of information, such as phone numbers. In the case of a phone number, you can define the field as Text with a `Field Size` of 14, using the format (212) 555-1212. In this way, no additional characters can be entered into the phone number field. An input mask can be used to format input data.

New Values The `New Values` property determines how the AutoNumber field generates values. This property can be set to `Increment` or `Random`. AutoNumber generates unique sequential numbers, incremented by 1, when set to `Increment` and generates unique random numbers when set to `Random`. `Increment` is the default setting and should be used most of the time. `Random` should only be used when a database is being replicated to multiple sites.

Format The `Format` property of a field indicates the way data will be displayed to the user. Text and Memo fields will normally appear as-is, but Numbers and Date/Times can be displayed with a variety of useful formatting options. As an example, Date/Times can be formatted as General, Long, Medium, or Short. A Long Date will appear as Wednesday, January 01, 1997, while a Short Date will appear as simply 1/1/97. Numbers can also be formatted easily, including the ability to use commas as thousands separators (Standard) or without commas (Fixed). In addition, numbers can be formatted as Currency, Percent, or Scientific depending upon the user's needs. Finally, Yes/No fields can be formatted to show Yes/No, True/False, or On/Off.

NOTE In addition to the Format properties that are predefined for data types, you can create custom formats for your own needs. The Access help file contains more information on custom formats. ▪

Decimal Places The `Decimal Places` property affects how many decimal places are used when displaying a number. It does not affect the way that a number is stored in the table. This property is set to `Auto` by default and can also be set to a specific number from 0 through 15. If this property is set to `Auto`, the `Format` property setting is used to determine the number of decimal places displayed. Otherwise, the number that this property is set to determines the number of digits displayed to the right of the decimal place, and the `Format` property setting determines how digits are displayed to the left of the decimal place.

Input Mask The `Input Mask` property is used to control the values that can be entered into the field. As a result, data entry is more accurate and usually easier to perform. A classic example of an Input Mask is a telephone number. You may want a telephone number to always be entered in the form (###) ###-####. An Input Mask can force a user to enter the data in this form by using special characters the control what can be input into each space of the field. These special characters are explained in Table 17.2. Non-control characters are called *literal characters*. Literal characters display "literally" as the character that they are.

Table 17.2 *Input Mask* Property Setting's Special Characters

Character	Description
0	Number 0 to 9, no spaces allowed.
9	Number 0 to 9, spaces allowed.
#	Number 0 to 9, spaces allowed, + and – sign.
L	Letter A to Z, entry required.
?	Letter A to Z, entry optional.
A	Letter or number, entry required.
a	Letter or number, entry optional.
&	Any character, entry required.
C	Any character, entry optional.
. , : ; - /	Decimal placeholder and thousand, date, and time separators.
<	Converts all characters to lowercase.
>	Converts all characters to uppercase.
!	Causes display to be from right to left, characters fill in left to right; this character can appear anywhere in the mask.
\	Causes following character to display as its literal character (\A displays as A).

T I P Use the Input Mask Wizard to quickly create complicated input mask criteria. Start the Input Mask Wizard by clicking the button next to the Input Mask property.

The Input Mask can contain as many as three sections, separated from each other by a semi-colon. Table 17.3 explains the three sections.

Table 17.3 *Input Mask* Property Setting's Sections

Section	Description	Example
First	The actual input mask.	(000) 000-0000
Second	Specifies if literal display characters should be stored or just the entered characters.	0 to store literals 1 or blank to not store
Third	Specifies character to indicate the position of the cursor.	" " "?"

NOTE If you leave the third section of the Input Mask property blank, the underscore character (_) is used. ■

Caption The Caption property determines the default text used for the description of a control that is bound to the field. For example, if a text box is placed on a form for a field with a caption of My Caption, that text will be placed on the form next to the control. Figure 17.9 illustrates this point. If the field is viewed in a datasheet, the caption is used as the column heading.

NOTE The field name is used when the Caption property is blank. ■

FIG. 17.9
Captions are used to make identifying a field easier.

Default Value The Default Value property is exactly what its name implies. All new records will contain a field's default value. This is especially helpful for fields with predictable results. For example, if most of your customers come from Arizona, you could make Arizona the default value for a state field. You would simply change the value for customers from a different state.

 Automate the entry of a Date/Time field by using a function in the default value. Set the Default Value to **=Now** to capture the time a record was entered. Without requiring user entry, Access automatically fills in this field with the current date and time for every new record.

Validation Rule and Validation Text The Validation Rule property is a logic check that Access applies to a field before allowing a new record to be entered. This check is in addition to the limits placed on a field by its data type. These rules can be customized for each field, allowing the database designer to implement both simple and complex business rules with ease. Typically, these rules belong to one of two categories, although they can become far more complex. These categories are absolute comparison and relative comparison.

Absolute comparison checks the contents of the field to ensure it passes a predefined, fixed logic check. For example, the rule >0 guarantees that any new value must be greater than 0. Similarly, the rule Between 0 and 100 ensures that a new value, in this case a percentage, cannot be negative and cannot be greater than 100. Note that most Access expressions can be used in validation rules.

NOTE Access doesn't normally allow a Null value. Add Is Null to a Validation Rule to allow a Null value. For example, <> 8 Or Is Null allows all values not equal to 8, including null values. If you are going to allow null values, make sure the Required property is set to No. ■

Relative comparison checks one field's contents in a record against another field's contents in the same record. For example, an Appointments table might contain a field for Start Time and End Time. Obviously, the End Time would have to fall after the Start Time of the appointment. To prevent this problem, the user could enter **[Start time]<[End Time]** as a validation rule.

The `Validation Text` property is the message that Access displays when the user violates a Validation Rule during data entry. Validation Rules can be up to 2,048 characters long, but Validation Text can only be up to 255 characters. Using the previous example, the Validation Text might be `A meeting must start before it ends..`

Required and Allow Zero Length   The `Required` property determines if a value is required in a field. This property has two possible values—`Yes` and `No`. `No` is the default value. A value must be entered into a field if the property is set to `Yes`. Fields do not require a value if there `Required` property is set to `No`.

The `Allow Zero Length` property determines if a zero-length string (`""`) can be stored in the field. This property applies only to Text, Memo, and Hyperlink fields. The `Allow Zero Length` property works independently of the `Required` property. The `Required` property determines only if Null values are allowed. If the `Allow Zero Length` property is set to `Yes`, a zero-length string is allowed regardless of the `Required` property.

> **CAUTION**
>
> While the `Required` and `Allow Zero Length` properties operate independently of each other, different combinations of the two do result in different behavior. However, the behavior is predictable when taking each property's effect into consideration.

Indexed   The `Indexed` property sets a single-field index. Indexes speed up queries that access indexed fields, as well as sorting and grouping operations. For example, if you index a field that contains values for last names, operations that use that field to sort or group are performed faster. Table 17.4 shows the possible values for the Indexed property. `No` is the default setting.

Table 17.4   *Indexed* Property Settings

Setting	Description
`No`	No index
`Yes (Duplicates OK)`	Index that allows duplicates
`Yes (No Duplicates)`	Index that doesn't allow duplicates

Create as many indexes as necessary. Indexes are created when the table is saved, and are automatically updated. Add or delete indexes at any time in Table Design view. However, Memo, Hyperlink, and OLE Object fields cannot be indexed.

N O T E   If the primary key for a table is a single field, Access will automatically set the Indexed
property for that field to Yes (No Duplicates). ■

Set multiple-field indexes in the Indexes window. Choose Indexes from the View menu to open
the Indexes window. Single-field indexes added in the Indexes window cause the Indexed
property for the field to be set to Yes.

Working with Table Properties   Like columns, tables also have properties. A table's properties describe the table and affect the way the table behaves. Figure 17.10 shows the Table
Properties dialog box. The properties for tables are as follows:

FIG. 17.10

All tables have the
same number and
type of properties.

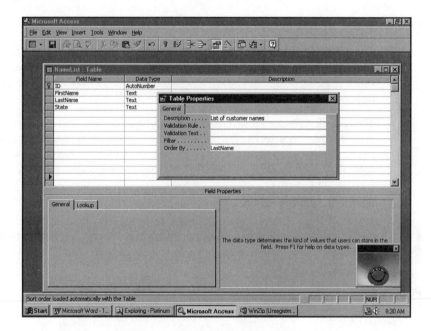

Part

IV

Ch

17

■ The Description property is, as the name suggests, a description of the table. It can
contain up to 255 characters. A table's description is displayed in the Description column
in the Details view of the Database window. Access displays the connection information
for a linked table in the Description property.

■ The Validation Rule property is nearly identical to the field-level Validation Rule
property, the difference being that this rule can apply to the entire table.

CAUTION

Tables can change over time. Fields might be added, deleted, or their data type changed. Defining Validation
Rules at the table level can make it more difficult to make these type of changes.

■ The Validation Text property is the text that displays when a new record fails a
Validation Rule.

- The Filter property allows the user to specify a subset of records to be displayed when the filter is applied. A filter is a WHERE clause without the WHERE keyword. For example, a Filter property value of Code = 1 displays only records with a Code value of 1—when the filter is applied. This property can also be changed using the Filter By Form window or the Advanced Filter/Sort window.

- The Order By property specifies how records in the table are sorted. It is a string expression consisting of the name of the field(s) that the records are to be sorted by. Separate multiple fields names with a comma. Records are sorted in ascending order by default. Type **DESC** at the end of the Order By property to force the sort to be arranged in descending order.

Creating a Table with the Table Wizard

After choosing the Table Wizard in the New Table dialog box, the first dialog box of the Table Wizard appears. The Table Wizard automatically creates a table from input that you supply in a series of dialog boxes. As shown in Figure 17.11, the Table Wizard lists a series of predefined table designs.

The table designs are broken into two categories: Business and Personal. Choose one of those two categories by selecting one of the radio buttons located near the bottom of the first screen. Each category lists a different set of tables in the far-left list box. Choose a table to display the fields that are most-often used in that table. Then use the arrow buttons to choose which fields you would like to use in your table. After making your selections, click the Next button to continue to the next dialog box.

 T I P Fields can be added from different tables, and tables from different categories can be used. If a field name doesn't make any sense in your table, rename it by clicking the Rename Field button.

FIG. 17.11
The Table Wizard breaks table designs into business and personal categories.

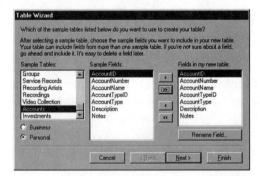

The next Table Wizard dialog box lets you decide to have Access set a primary key or to allow you to determine the primary key. Figure 17.12 shows that in addition to the Yes or No choice involving the primary key, you need to supply a name for your table.

FIG. 17.12

You can set the primary key or the Table Wizard can.

Figure 17.13 shows the Table Wizard dialog box that lets you choose a column to act as the primary key. In addition to choosing a column, you must select a method for providing the primary key's value. Access can use the AutoNumber data type to automatically generate a unique number for each new record, or the user can provide either a number or any combination of letters or numbers.

FIG. 17.13

The Table Wizard gives you several options for defining your primary key.

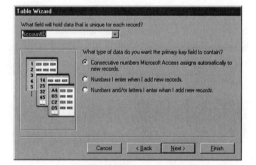

N O T E If you click the Finish button at any time, the Table Wizard closes and generates a new table using the information gathered to that point. ■

After completing the primary key settings, the Table Wizard prompts you for information about how this new table relates to the other tables in the database. Not all tables have relationships with other tables. In fact, it's possible that there are no other tables in the database yet. Make your changes, if any, to the relationships defined in the Table Wizard dialog box shown in Figure 17.14. See "Working with Relationships" in this chapter for more information about relationships.

The final Table Wizard dialog box, shown in Figure 17.15, presents three choices of action that can be performed after the table is created:

- The table can be opened in Design view and possibly modified.
- The table can be opened as a datasheet. This allows you to edit the table data directly.

■ The Table Wizard can generate a data-entry form to be used with this table. In addition, you can select the check box at the bottom of the dialog box to view help on working with the table after it is created.

FIG. 17.14
The Table Wizard can create relationships between existing tables.

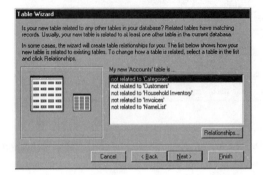

After your choice is made and the table is generated, the option you chose in the last dialog box is carried out.

TIP Use the Table Wizard to create tables that follow the same standards, such as naming conventions. The tables can be modified later to suit your specific needs by using Design view. See the section "Modifying a Table" later in this chapter.

FIG. 17.15
The Table Wizard can even create a data-entry form for the new table.

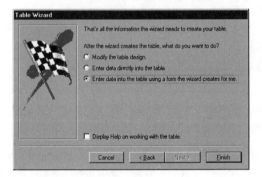

Creating a Table by Importing a Table

Tables can be imported for several reasons. If the table is contained in a sophisticated SQL database, you may want it in Access format to take it with you while traveling. Also, you may be converting all of your databases to Access.

After choosing Import Table in the New Table dialog box, the Import dialog box appears. The Import dialog box is basically an Open File dialog box. Find the file you want to import and select it in the dialog box. Click the Import button to actually import the file into the Access database. Table 17.5 shows the types of data sources that can be imported into an Access database.

Table 17.5   Data Sources that Can Be Imported

Data Source	Version or Format Supported
Microsoft Access	All versions
Microsoft FoxPro	2.x and 3.0
dBASE	III, III+, IV, and 5
Paradox	3.x, 4.x, and 5.0
MS Excel spreadsheets	3.0, 4.0, 5.0, 7.0/95, and 8.0/97
Lotus 1-2-3 spreadsheets	.wks, .wk1, .wk3, and .wk4
Delimited text files	ANSI text files with values separated by commas, tabs, or other characters
Fixed-width text files	ANSI text files with field values placed at specific intervals
HTML	1.0 (if a list) 2.0, 3.x (if a table or list)
SQL tables and other	Supported ODBC drivers ODBC data sources

ON THE WEB

For a list of supported ODBC drivers, search the Access Web site at

http://www.microsoft.com/access

Once imported, a table is just like all other Access tables. An imported table maintains no relationship with the table that it was imported from. None of the changes made to the new table are reflected in the table that was used to create it.

Creating a Table by Linking a Table

Linking a table can be used to access existing databases in other formats. This method can also be used to connect to large SQL databases so that you can use the Access interface to work with them.

After choosing Link Table in the New Table dialog box, the Link dialog box appears. The Link dialog box is basically an Open File dialog box. Find the file that you want to link to and select it in the dialog box. Click the Link button to build the link to the file. Table 17.6 shows the types of data sources that can be linked to an Access database.

Table 17.6   Data Sources that Can Be Linked

Data Source	Version or Format Supported
Microsoft Access	All versions
dBASE	III, III+, IV, and 5
Paradox	3.x, 4.x, and 5.0
MS Excel spreadsheets	3.0, 4.0, 5.0, 7.0/95, and 8.0/97
Lotus 1-2-3 spreadsheets	.wks, .wk1, .wk3, and .wk4 (read-only)
Delimited text files	ANSI text files with values separated by commas, tabs, or other characters
Fixed-width text files	ANSI text files with field values placed at specific intervals
HTML	1.0 (if a list) 2.0, 3.x (if a table or list)
SQL tables and other	Supported ODBC drivers ODBC data sources

A linked table is similar to other Access tables, but it does have some limitations. A linked table maintains a direct relationship with the source table. The data and table definition is contained in the source table and cannot be modified from Access. However, certain properties that affect how the data is displayed can be changed, such as:

Format   Input Mask

Decimal Places   Caption

 T I P   While most table properties are not usable for linked tables, some of those same properties can be set for controls that are used to manipulate the data on a form. For example, the `Default Value`, `Validation Rule`, and `Validation Text` properties can be set for a control to limit the data being entered into a linked table through that form.

Modifying a Table

Now that you know all the different ways to create a table and have created a table, you might find that you need to modify the table. You will draw heavily on the lessons you learned in the section "Creating a Table with Design View."

It is not necessarily the end of the design process after a table is created. Changes may need to be made for one reason or another. For instance, the type of data that is stored in a field might change or a field might not be needed any more. Whatever the reason for it, changes are made to a table using Design view. Several types of changes are common when modifying a table:

■ Renaming a field is accomplished by changing the Field Name in the Design View window. In addition, the description can be changed in the same manner—for example, if you needed to change a field name from PhoneNumber to WorkPhone to differentiate between different phone numbers.

■ Adding a new field is accomplished by selecting the row before the point where you want to insert a row and then choosing Rows from the Insert menu—for example, if you discover that you need to add a MaidenName field to your Employees table.

 Right-click a field to open a pop-up menu that can be used to add and delete rows to the table.

■ Deleting a field is accomplished by selecting the row you want to delete and then selecting Delete Rows from the Edit menu—for example, if there is a field that you discover you will not be using or accidentally created.

■ Rearranging fields is accomplished by selecting the row you want to move and dragging it to the new desired location within the table—for example, if you find that entering data directly into a table is more convenient when the LastName field is before the FirstName field.

■ Changing a field's data type is accomplished by selecting a new data type for that field— for example, if you initially created the SocialSecurityNumber field as a numeric field and now you want it to be a character field.

CAUTION

Changing a data type or the size of a field can result in the loss of all or some of the data stored in that field. If the data cannot be stored in the new data type, it is lost; if the data is too long for the new field size, it is truncated.

■ Changing a field's properties is accomplished by entering or selecting new values for the properties—for example, if you want to change the Caption property of a field to make it more appropriate.

TROUBLESHOOTING

To store character values in a Number field, change the data type of the field to allow the use of characters as well as numbers.

If you need to change a data type and you know that the change will force you to lose data, make a backup of the data and use it to restore the lost values.

If you find out later that your primary key cannot uniquely identify records in a table, create a new field in the table using the AutoNumber data type and designate that field as the primary key.

Working with Relationships

Tables in a database can be related to one another. A field in one table can be related to the primary key field of another table. The fields must have matching data types. Relationships should be defined using the Relationships window. Once they are defined, relationships can help to guarantee the accuracy of data and improve the performance of a database. A relationship is referred to as a *join* when it is used to retrieve data from both tables. There are two types of joins:

- *Inner joins* occur when there is a matching record on each side of the relationship. For example, a Customer ID in an Invoice table should always have a matching record in the Customer table.

- *Outer joins* occur when there are unmatched records on at least one side of the relationship. Using the previous example, this would mean that Customer IDs existed in the Invoice table that did not correspond to a record in the Customer table.

Choose Tools, Relationships to open the Relationships window, which is shown in Figure 17.16. Use the Relationships menu to hide and show tables and relationships. After you have added the tables that you want to create a relationship for, simply drag the join field from the parent table to the corresponding join field in the child.

FIG. 17.16

Relationships are created quickly and easily using drag and drop.

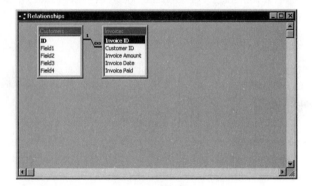

Access displays the Relationships dialog box, shown in Figure 17.17, to let you modify the properties of the new relationship. You can display this dialog box for any relationship by double-clicking the line that represents the relationship. The Enforce Referential Integrity property ensures that a relationship has a matching entry between the parent and child table. When this property is selected, it is not possible to enter a value into the join field of the child table unless there is a matching value in the join field of the parent table. That is where the name comes from.

FIG. 17.17
Relationships have their
own set of properties.

N O T E Relationships should always be defined, and referential integrity should always be used in databases. ■

Select the Cascade Update Related Fields option to ensure that a change in the join field of a relationship will automatically alter the corresponding records in the child table. This feature is rarely used, but it is a time-saver when it is. The Cascade Delete Related Fields option removes records from a child table when the corresponding record in the parent table is deleted. If this option is not selected, but Enforce Referential Integrity is selected, you will not be able to delete a record that has child records.

> **CAUTION**
> When the Cascade Delete Related Records option is selected, all of the children records are automatically deleted when the parent record is deleted. Otherwise, you are prompted that you cannot delete the parent record because there are records related to it.

The Join Type button is used to select the type of join used for the relationship. An inner join is used by default. Click the Create button to save the relationship after you have made all of your changes in the Relationships dialog box. A line is drawn between the two fields that represents the relationship.

At this point, you can create tables in Access and define the properties of these tables to make them work for you. In addition, you should have a good knowledge about how relationships work in Access. ●

Part
IV

Ch
17

CHAPTER 18

Working with Data

In Chapter 17, you learned how to set up the framework of your database using Access' tables. In this chapter, you'll explore various ways to create and manipulate the actual data in your database.

The data for your database can come from a variety of sources; however, you'll usually find that your data is one of two general types: data from an existing source on a computer system (such as an old database) or data that comes from a non-computer source (such as "hard" copies of information). Obviously, existing data in computer form is much easier to work with, mainly because it does not require all that typing. With Access, however, you will find the flexibility to work with various data sources.

In this chapter, we will explore various data sources and how to get that data into your Access database. ■

Import and link data

This section shows you how to use data from existing databases into your database.

Add and edit new data

Here you will learn about the two most common ways to enter original data: the Datasheet (or Table) view method, and the Form view method.

Sort data

Explore the various ways to sort your Access database.

Filter data

View only certain portions of your database by filtering and "hiding" data that does not meet your filter criteria.

Importing and Linking Data

Many times, you will discover that the data you need for your Access database already exists in some other database. For example, your organization may have an older Paradox database, or there may be data in an Excel spreadsheet that you want to use in your database. Access supports a variety of data formats and allows you to *import* or *link* that data to your database.

Importing versus Linking

At the outset, you need to decide if you want to import or link the data. Here's the difference.

When you import data, you actually retrieve the data from the source location and create a new copy of the data within your Access database. You can then manipulate, update, and otherwise change the data without affecting the data at the source. This can be useful (and perhaps necessary) if you do not have the authority to change the source data, or if you simply want to keep the source data intact. The main thing to remember with importing is that once the data is imported, changes you make in your new copy will not change the data in the original source data.

Linking data allows you to use the source data directly in your database. With linking, you do not create a new copy of the data, but simply use the original data. If you have update rights in the original data, you can also change the original data source directly from your Access database.

Deciding whether to link or import data is an important first consideration. Generally, if the data you need in the source is not likely to change, or if you just want a "snapshot" of the data, importing is probably the best bet. (Likewise, you may have only "one-time" access to the data, such as purchased mailing lists, in which case importing is the way to go.)

On the other hand, if the data source is constantly being updated in the original program or location, and if having up-to-date versions is important for your database applications, linking may be best.

If either choice seems equally acceptable, keep in mind that Access works much faster on its own tables than on linked data; so when in doubt, import.

Working with Other Data Sources

Access 97 allows you to import or link data from a variety of sources, including:

- Other Access databases: versions 1.x, 2.0, 7.0 (95), and 8.0 (97)
- Microsoft Excel
- dBASE III, III+, IV, and 5
- FoxPro
- Paradox
- ODBC databases (with an appropriately configured ODBC driver)

- HTML tables and lists
- Lotus 1-2-3 files

N O T E Not all of the import and link drivers are automatically installed when you install Access 97. Most notably, the drivers for Paradox and Lotus 1-2-3 are not included in the Setup, but they are available through the Office 97 ValuPack. If you need data from these sources, be sure and load the drivers from the ValuPack on the CD-ROM, or obtain these drivers from Microsoft's Web sites. (To access the information on the Web, use the Help menu in Access 97 and choose Microsoft on the Web and Free Stuff.) ▪

How to Import or Link Data

Now that you've located compatible data and decided that you want to link or import that data, here's how you do it. The exact steps vary somewhat depending on the location and type of data you are importing or linking, but this listing gives you the general steps (note that the steps are almost identical whether you are linking or importing, except for step 2):

1. Open the database where you will use the imported or linked data. Make sure the Database window is visible. Figure 18.1 shows the Database window of the Access sample Northwind Database.

FIG. 18.1

Before importing or linking data, be sure the database you want to use is open and the Database window is visible.

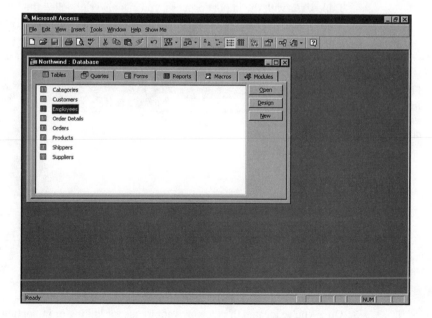

2. If you are going to import data, choose File, Get External Data, Import. (You can also right-click anywhere on the Database window and choose Import, or you can click the New button on the database table window, then use the Import Table option.)

You will then see the familiar file selection window, like the one in Figure 18.2. Using this window, you can choose the type of data you want to import by using the Files of Type drop-down box, then locate the specific file containing the data you want to import. (Here, we have selected Microsoft Access and several files appear.)

FIG. 18.2
This is an Import dialog box for selecting the file you want to import.

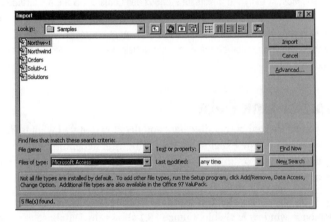

If you are going to link data, the process is similar. Choose File, Get External Data, Link Tables. (As with the import process, you can also right-click the title area of the database window and choose Link Tables, or click the New button on the Tables window and double-click the Link Table option in the New dialog box.) Select the location of the data file, the type of data, and the specific file from the Link dialog box shown in Figure 18.3.

FIG. 18.3
The Link dialog box is similar to the Import dialog box.

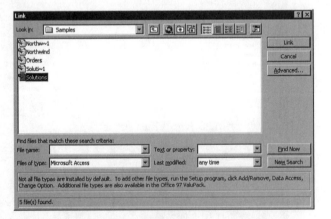

3. Once you've located the file you want to use for linking or importing, select the file, then click the Link (or Import) button on the dialog box. (Or, you can simply double-click the file name.)

4. Respond to any further dialog boxes that appear, such as this one in Figure 18.4, which appears when we double-clicked the Northwind file in the Link dialog box.

From the box shown in Figure 18.4, choose the table of data you want to link (or import, if you have been importing data) and click OK.

FIG. 18.4

From this dialog box, we can select the specific data we want to link to from the selected file.

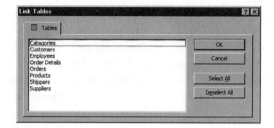

5. Access creates the linked data entry in the Database table window. (Here, because we used a table with the same name, Access added the number "1" to the name to create a new linked table called Categories1 as shown in Figure 18.5.)

FIG. 18.5

You can see the new linked table in the updated Database table window.

Linked table

Note that Access uses a different icon to represent linked tables. As shown in Figure 18.5, those icons have a small arrow to the left of the symbol, indicating the link.

 In the examples used here, we have created duplicate copies of the same data within the Northwind sample database, a procedure that you may actually use from time to time. As with most other file names in Windows 95, you can right-click the table name and choose Rename to use a different name for the newly created duplicate data file, if you don't care for the "1" extension added by Access. You can use this technique to rename any object in Access 97.

Using Linked or Imported Data

Once you have imported data from another source, you can use that data just as if it had been originally created in Access.

Linked data, on the other hand, can be restricted in use depending on a variety of factors, including the type of data, the location, your rights to the data, and so on. While you cannot add, delete, or change the fields of a linked data table, you can change some properties of the table using Design view from the Tables menu. For more information about changing table properties, see Chapter 17, "Creating Access Tables."

Part
IV

Ch
18

TROUBLESHOOTING

From time to time, the source file containing linked data may be moved to a new location. Because Access stores the information about the "link" to your data along with the table in your database, if the source is moved the program won't find the data. You can fix this problem by using Access' Linked Table Manager. Choose Tools, Add-Ins, and select Linked Table Manager. If you installed this option at Setup, a list of linked tables will appear, and you can use the check boxes to select the tables you want to update. Click OK, and the Table Manager will present a dialog box that allows you to select the new location of the linked table.

Note that the Linked Table Manager cannot help you if the linked data is deleted or the table has been completely renamed. In those cases, you will generally have to delete the link and start over with a new link.

Adding and Editing Original Data

In the previous sections, you learned how to import data from existing data sources. In this section, we'll take a look at adding and editing data directly into a table.

Datasheet View and Form View

You can add, edit, and delete individual data records from Access tables using either of two formats, or *views*: Datasheet view or Form view. In Datasheet view, the program displays a number of records on the screen at one time in a table format. By clicking the Open button in the Tables window with the Customers table highlighted, you can see (as in Figure 18.6) the Northwind Customers table in Datasheet view.

Using Form view, Access displays the records one at a time in a format that you design for those records. To see an example of Form view, click the Forms tab in the Northwind database window, highlight the Customers form, and click Open (see Figure 18.7).

Creating Forms

If you want to view data in Form view, you need to create forms for the data tables you want to view in that form. Creating custom forms can be quite an art form; the intricacies of form design is beyond the scope of this chapter. For more information about form design, refer to Que's *Special Edition Using Microsoft Access 97*.

Fortunately, Access has a nice feature that allows you to quickly create basic forms if you prefer Form view but don't want to do a lot of work. To use this feature, highlight the table (or query) for which you want a form, and click the drop-down arrow next to the New Object button (the next-to-last button on the Database toolbar).

From the list that appears, choose AutoForm and Access will create a simple form for you.

FIG. 18.6

Datasheet view shows several records in a table at one time. From here, you can edit, add, or delete records.

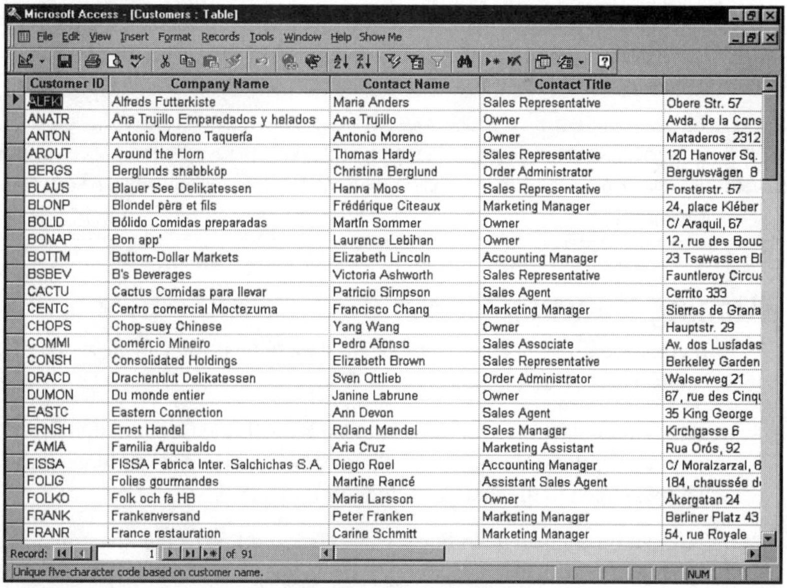

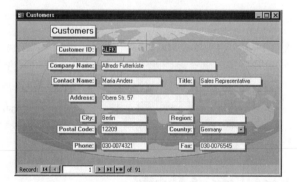

FIG. 18.7

Form view shows one record at a time, and is sometimes easier for users because it is similar to using paper forms.

For example, if you highlight the Customers table in the Northwind Database window, then use the AutoForm feature, you will get a form like the one shown in Figure 18.8.

FIG. 18.8

This simple form was created by Access using the Customers table and the AutoForm feature.

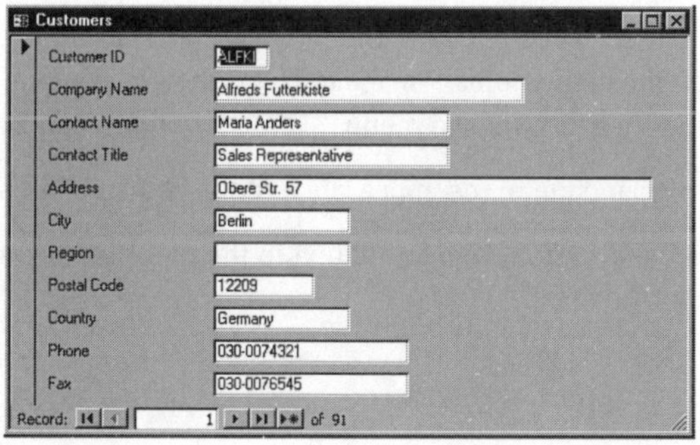

You can also add a little more artistic appeal to your simple forms by choosing Form from the same drop-down toolbar and then using one of the three AutoForm custom options such as AutoForm: Columnar, AutoForm: Tabular, or AutoForm: Datasheet.

 TIP Once you have created your simple form, don't forget to save the form when you close it so you can use it later. All of the forms you have saved can be viewed by clicking the Forms tab in the Database window.

Switching Between Views

If you have created a form for certain data tables, you can view that data in either Form or Datasheet view at any time.

To open the data in Datasheet view, click the Tables tab and double-click the table you want to view, or highlight the table and click Open. You can also right-click the table and choose Open. This will open to the view depicted in Figure 18.6.

To open the same data in Form view, click the Forms tab and double-click the form you want to open. Just like Datasheet view, you can also select the form you want to use and click the Open button, or right-click the form and use Open. This will open to the form view as shown in Figure 18.7.

When you are in Form view, you can quickly switch over to Datasheet view by using the View toolbar button, which is the first button on the left of the main Access toolbar. When you click this button in Form view, you can then choose between Datasheet view, Form view, or Design view.

N O T E Form view is *not* available from the View drop-down button if you originally opened the table in Datasheet view. However, Design view is always available. (Design view is not used to manipulate data—it is simply used for working on the form itself.) ■

Changing Datasheet View—A Hybrid

If you need to see several records at one time but aren't crazy about the plain "vanilla" Datasheet view, you can customize Datasheet view. To do this, open the table in that view, then use the Formatting (Datasheet) toolbar.

Normally when you are in Datasheet view, the Formatting (Datasheet) toolbar is visible; if it's not, simply right-click the main toolbar (while in Datasheet View mode) and click the Formatting toolbar, or use the View drop-down menu's Toolbar option to do the same thing.

Using this toolbar, you can change the appearance of the datasheet in several ways, including:

- Change the font and/or font size for all text in the datasheet by using the Font and/or Font Size drop-down lists.

- Underline, italicize, and/or boldface all text by clicking the appropriate button on the toolbar.

- Change the background color of the sheet by clicking the drop-down arrow next to the Fill/Back Color button and choose your favorite color. You change the foreground (text) and gridline colors in the same way by using the appropriate drop-down arrow.

- You can customize the gridlines or hide them altogether by using the drop-down arrows next to the Gridlines and the Special Effects buttons. (You should experiment with various combinations to get the look you want, as not all grid effects are available with the various hide/show combinations.)

- You can adjust the width of any column to its widest visible data element or column header with just a double-click. Move the mouse pointer between two column selectors (the header row containing the names of the fields) to the right of the column you want to adjust. When the mouse pointer is directly over the separating line, it changes to a vertical bar. Double-click the mouse, and the column adjusts wider or narrower to just display the widest visible data element or field name.

In Figures 18.9, you can see a sample of a Datasheet view.

FIG. 18.10

This is the standard Datasheet view.

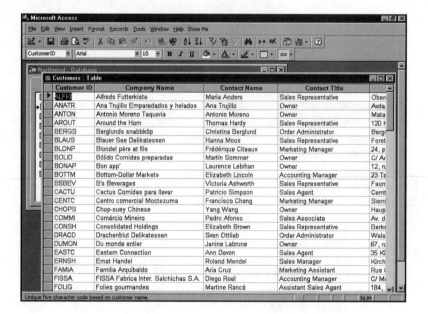

Moving Around the Data

Now that you have seen the two views used to view data, you will next want to move around within your database. Navigating from record to record in a form or a datasheet is simple. Using the navigation buttons at the bottom of the Form or Datasheet window or by choosing

Edit, Go To, you can go to the First, Last, Next, or Previous records. You can also select New Record to move to a blank form in Form view or to a new record line in Datasheet view. The navigation buttons and the Edit, Go To options are both shown in Figure 18.10.

FIG. 18.10

The navigation buttons at the bottom of the screen duplicate the functions of the Edit, Go To options.

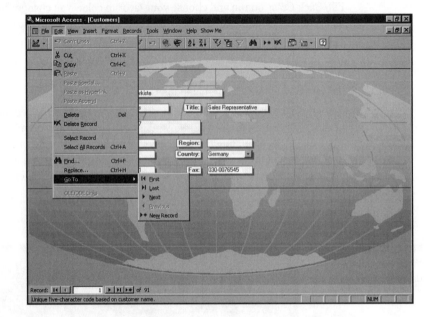

In Datasheet view, you can also use the scroll bars (if visible) to scroll the data records. Use the vertical scroll bar on the right side of the screen to scroll up and down records. You can scroll through the various columns in Datasheet view by using the horizontal scroll bar at the bottom of the window.

 If your Datasheet view contains more columns than you can view at one time, you may encounter a problem with critical columns scrolling off the left side of the screen. To correct this problem, you can freeze one or more columns so that they always stay on the screen.

To accomplish this, simply select the column(s) you want to freeze, and choose Freeze Columns from the Format drop-down menu, or right-click at the top of the column and choose Freeze. With these columns frozen, the other columns will scroll off the left, but leave the frozen columns always visible. You can unfreeze the columns by choosing Format, Unfreeze All Columns. (Also, if the column(s) you freeze are not already the leftmost on the screen, Access will move the column(s) to the left side of the datasheet.)

Adding Data

Once you have learned how to manipulate the data views and move around the data in your tables, adding data is a straightforward process. Simply move to a blank record in either Datasheet or Form view and type the contents of each field for which you want to add data.

For example, in Form view, click the New Record navigation button and type the information you want to put in the first field, as shown in Figure 18.11.

FIG. 18.11

Here is a new record in the Northwind database with only the first field completed.

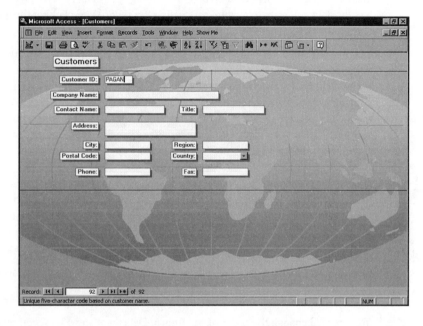

Next, press Tab or Enter to move to the next field, or, if you want to skip around, click the next field you want to fill in. Access will save your new record when you move to another record. If you made mistakes (such as leaving a critical field blank), Access will not let you leave the new record until you have corrected the error or confirmed that you want to leave.

Figure 18.12 shows the same partially completed record in Datasheet view.

FIG. 18.12

Datasheet view contains a partially completed new record. Note the small "pencil" icon, which reminds you that this record has not yet been saved.

Pencil icon

> **N O T E** A note if you are a hard-core spreadsheet user: In Access, there is no need to insert a record between any other records. As you will see later in this chapter in the section "Sorting Data," Access sorts the records any time you ask it to; therefore, you just place new records into the table using the New Record feature described and "sort it out later." ■

Editing Data in a Table

With a few minor things to keep in mind, editing data in an Access table is simple. Simply se-lect the data you want to change by locating the record and clicking the appropriate field, and use your text editing skills to change the information.

There is one matter to keep in mind, though: When you are in a particular field, you may be in edit mode or navigation mode. If you used the keyboard to reach a particular field, that field's entire contents are selected instantly. If you begin to type at that moment, you will delete the contents selected and insert new data. On the other hand, if you jumped to a field by clicking the mouse, you are in edit mode and the cursor will blink at the insertion point. Typing now will simply insert new data without deleting the previous contents. To switch back and forth from the edit and navigation modes, use the F2 key to toggle.

TIP Most of your Windows-style word-processing editing features work while editing records in Access. However, there are a few extras that can come in handy. For instance, you can use the "ditto" marks (Ctrl+") to copy the data from the same field in the preceding record. This can be a big time-saver if several records contain similar data. Also, the Ctrl+; combination inserts the current date. If a field has a preassigned default value, pressing the combination of Ctrl+Alt+spacebar will insert that value.

For more editing keys and other data-entry information, view the subtopics under Data Entry in the Help menu index.

You can also change the order of columns in Datasheet view. To accomplish this, use the mouse pointer to drag and drop the column in the desired location. (Frozen columns cannot be dragged.)

Rearranging the columns (as opposed to freezing) might be desirable for several reasons: the nature of the presentation of the data, or performing multi-column sorts (described in the upcoming section "Sorting Data").

Deleting Data

From time to time, you will need to delete data from your database. To do so, simply select the record you want to delete, then choose Edit, Delete Record, or, after moving to the record, press Ctrl+–. Access will then delete the current record after confirming that this is what you want to do. You can also delete data by pressing the Delete key after selecting the record you want to delete, or by selecting the row where the record is located and right-clicking that row, then selecting Delete Record. If you make a mistake, you can use the Undo feature to correct it.

Likewise, you can select several records for deletion (in Datasheet view) by clicking the first record, then dragging over the records you want to delete.

Sorting Data

Once you have all of your data imported, linked, or entered into your database, the real power of Access begins to kick in. You can now sort and filter your data.

Sorting data, as the name implies, means putting the data records in your table in some type of order, such as ascending or descending order, based upon the number in one of the table's fields.

Simple Sorts

The most common of all sorts is the *alphabetic* (or *alpha*) *sort*. Alpha sorts can be either ascending (A to Z) or descending (Z to A).

In Figure 18.13, we see the first of several records in the Northwind Customer table as they probably appear on your system (if you loaded the sample database). It's easy to see they are sorted alphabetically by the Customer ID field. (Note that we have used the column freezing technique discussed earlier in this chapter to freeze the Customer ID field and scrolled over so that the Country field is right beside it.)

FIG. 18.13

These records have been sorted in an ascending alphabetic sort by Customer ID.

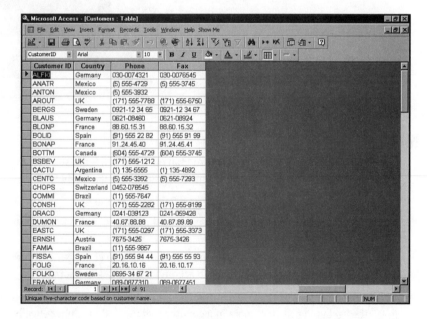

What if we wanted to view our list sorted so that all the customers in a particular country appeared adjacent to each other? This is a simple ascending (or descending) alphabetic sort. Here are the steps:

1. Open the Customer table in the Database window in Datasheet view.
2. Click the Country field so that this column is highlighted.

3. Click the Sort Ascending or Sort Descending toolbar button, or make the same selection by choosing Records, Sort, Sort Ascending (or Sort Descending). You can also right-click the column and make the same selections.

Figure 18.14 contains the result.

FIG. 18.14

This is the same list sorted in ascending alphabetical order, but this time by the Country field.

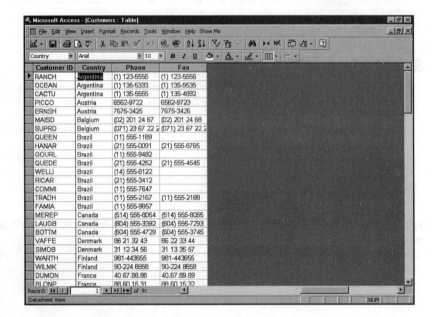

Multiple Sorts

You can also perform sorts on more than one field at a time, sometimes called a "sort within a sort." However, there are several limiting factors to keep in mind:

- Access will only sort on *adjacent* fields (or columns).
- The sort is performed on the leftmost column of fields first, and then the next to the right, and so on.
- Because of the first two items, you may have to change the order of one or more of the columns in your datasheet to accomplish the desired sort.

In the next sort, we want to arrange the Northwind customers alphabetically first by country (thus grouping all customers in a country together), then alphabetically by Customer ID within each country. (Note in Figure 18.14 that this is *not* the case, as we only sorted by country, not Customer ID.)

To accomplish this, we do the following:

1. Unfreeze the Customer ID column, if you still have it frozen.

2. Using the mouse pointer, drag and drop the Customer ID so that it is *to the right of, and adjacent to* the Country field column.

3. Click the Country column, then Shift-click the Customer ID column so that both columns are selected.

4. Click the Sort Ascending toolbar button.

Note the difference between the result here (see Figure 18.15) and the result in the preceding example.

FIG. 18.15

Here we have sorted the data first by Country, then by Customer ID by moving the columns so they are in that order and then sorting on both columns at the same time.

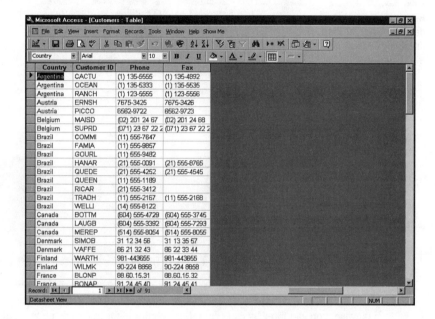

This type of "sort within a sort" is particularly useful, for instance, where you have a large list of names with several people having the same last name (as in a telephone book).

 Sorts can also be performed in Form view in much the same manner; however, we have used Datasheet view so that the results are more immediately apparent.

To remove the effect of the sort, choose Records, Remove Filter/Sort. This will return the records to their original order—that is, unsorted. (You can also right-click anywhere on the sheet and use Remove Filter/Sort.)

Data Filtering

Filtering data is the process by which you locate and isolate one or more records that you want to view and hide the rest of the data. For instance, using the previous examples, you might want to view *only* those customers within a particular country and (temporarily) hide all the rest. A filter is the way to accomplish this goal.

Simple Filters To apply a filter to the Northwind Customer data so that only customers from Germany are seen, simply go to the Customer table and click Open. Move over to the Country column and click a record with the data record "Germany" filled in. Next, use the Filter by Selection toolbar button or choose Record, Filter, By Selection.

The result is a list of only those Customers with locations in Germany, as shown in Figure 18.16.

FIG. 18.16

Here is the Northwind database of customers filtered by Germany in the Country field.

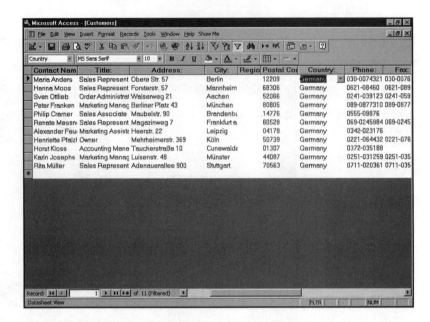

Likewise, you can filter by *excluding* the selection—for instance, by excluding all the customers in Germany to produce a list of only those customers in countries other than the selected criteria. (Don't forget to use Remove Filter/Sort before moving on.)

Just as you can apply the filter in Datasheet view, you can filter in Form view, though you have to look carefully to see the results. To see this work, click the Forms tab and open the Customers form. Next, click the Country field and, again, click the Filter by Selection button.

This time, the result is in Figure 18.17.

You have to look carefully at the bottom of the form to notice that the notation `Filtered` has been added near the navigation buttons and that the number of records has changed to 11 as a result of the filter. (Again, don't forget to remove the filter before leaving the form.)

You can apply a "filter within a filter" or, in other words, further filter your data by first applying a filter (as we did earlier) and then applying another filter (a selection or exclusion) to the newly filtered list. You can continue this process as many times as needed (or until you run out of data that meets the filter criteria).

FIG. 18.17
Here is a filtered Form view using Germany as the Filter Selection.

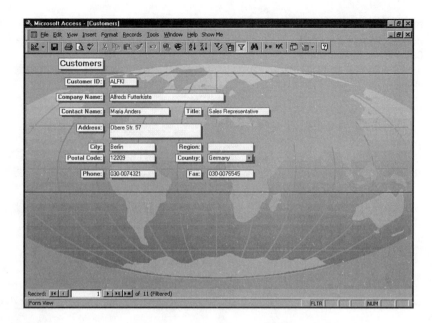

More Complex Filtering Your filter criteria need not be an entire field value; you can filter by a portion of a record, or by using Access' new Filter by Input feature, you can select filter criteria using *wild cards* and *masks*. For instance, you can use the wild card * symbol to search for all records starting with the letter P by entering **P***, or all the names in a list that begin with the letters A–F by using the symbol **<G** as the criteria.

Filtering by User Input In Figure 18.18, we have right-clicked the Customer table in the Customer ID field, and we have filled in less than C by using <C in the Filter For box.

And Figure 18.19 contains the result of this process.

Filtering by Form If you prefer, you can create *form filters* by choosing Records, Filter, Filter by Form. A blank filter form will appear, along with a revised toolbar and new tabs near the bottom of the form. To begin creating the filter form, first click one of the fields and use the drop-down box to select the criteria the record must contain to pass the filter. You can select more than one criteria in the initial form; the criteria are considered *And criteria*. In other words, a record must match the criteria in *all* of the fields to pass the filter. In Figure 18.20, we have used the Country field and used "Germany" as the criteria, *and* we have used the City field and selected "Berlin" as the criteria. Thus, in order to pass this stage of the filter, the record must contain *both* Germany and Berlin.

Part
IV
Ch
18

FIG. 18.18

By right-clicking the Customer table, you can use the Filter For (input) feature.

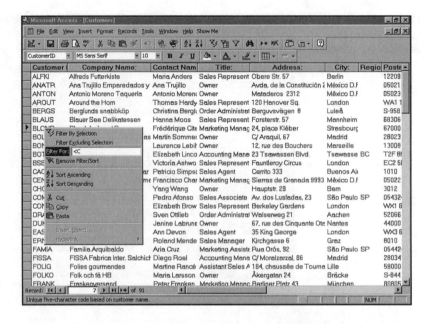

FIG. 18.19

Here is the result of the Filter For search using <C.

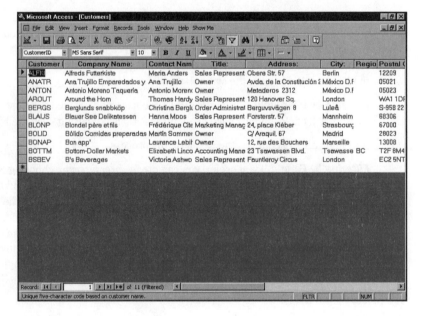

FIG. 18.20

Using the Filter by Form feature, we have selected "Germany" and "Berlin" as search criteria in the first stage of the filter.

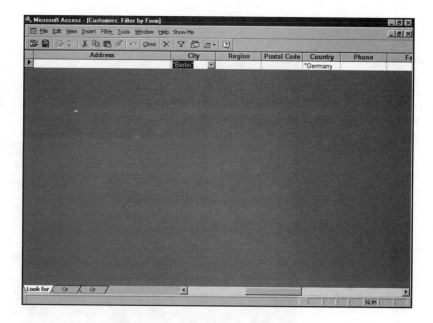

Note that the Form window has tabs near the bottom of the screen. Now, we want, *in addition* to all of the customers in Berlin, Germany, all of the customers in Austria, this time without regard to city. We accomplish this by clicking the first Or tab, clicking the Country field, and finally, selecting Austria from the list, as shown in Figure 18.21.

FIG. 18.21

Here we have used the Or tab to include customers from Austria in our filter form.

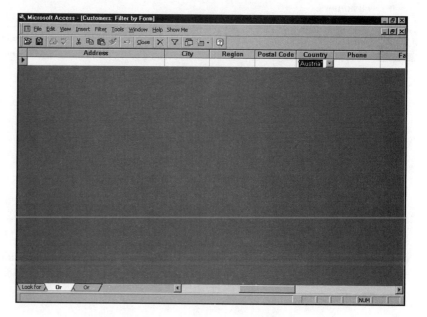

Finally, we click the Apply Filter toolbar button and obtain the results, shown in Figure 18.22.

FIG. 18.22
Here are all the
customers in either
Berlin, Germany, or any
city in Austria.

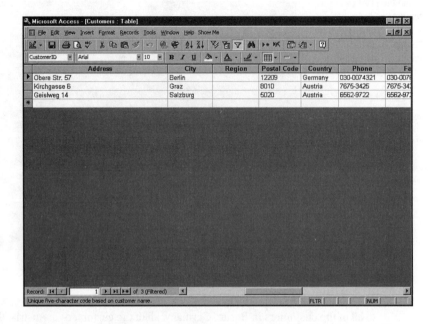

You will recall from previous examples that there were a total of 11 customers in all of Germany, and here we have filtered down to one German customer in Berlin, *plus* the two Austrian customers.

If you design a particularly complex filter form and plan to use it frequently, you should use the File menu's Save as Query feature and save the filter as a query. (See Chapter 19, "Querying Data," for more information on creating queries.)

Advanced Filters and Sorts   Using the Advanced Filter/Sorts feature of Access, you can perform many of the features described in the preceding sections all at one time from a single window.

To launch this feature, be sure your table is open, then choose Records, Filter, Advanced Filter/Sort. A window similar to Figure 18.23 will appear.

This Advanced Filter/Sort window contains the "leftover" criteria from our latest filter. From here, you can add to the grid any field(s) that you want to specify sort order or filter criteria for.

For instance, to specify a sort order for the Customer ID field, double-click the Customer ID field in the box in the upper-left corner; that field is added to a new column in the grid. Next, click the row labeled Sort and choose Ascending. Now the filter looks like Figure 18.24.

FIG. 18.23

From the Advanced Filter/Sort window, you can perform several filter and sort functions at once.

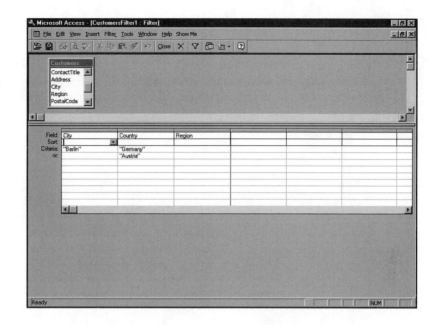

 TIP You can also drag and drop fields from the box in the upper-left corner to the desired column in the grid. This is useful for inserting a field between multiple columns already loaded into the grid.

FIG. 18.24

Here you can add additional sort or filter criteria, such as an ascending Customer ID sort.

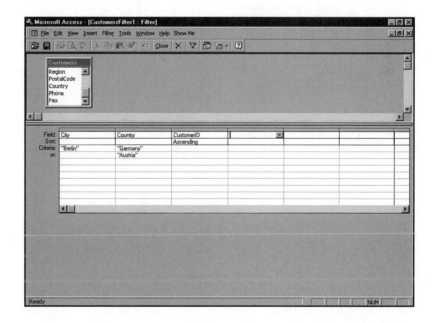

Finally, you can save the filter as a query by choosing File, Save As and then apply the filter by choosing Filter, Apply Filter/Sort or clicking the Apply Filter toolbar button.

By using a combination of logical operators (less than, greater than, between, and so on), exact criteria matches, and sorts, you can create complex filters. For more information about this process, see Chapter 19 and also refer to Que's *Special Edition Using Microsoft Access 97.* ●

Querying Data

Databases store large amounts of information. Taken all at once, this information can be overwhelming. A single table can contain millions of records, and a database can contain many tables. The size of a database can make it difficult to retrieve meaningful information.

Queries are used to retrieve subsets of data. These subsets are more manageable chunks of data that normally contain only information relevant to a particular task. In addition to retrieving a subset of a single table, queries can also combine the information of several tables together and perform calculations on data. ■

Create a query

Create queries that retrieve only the subset of information that you are interested in.

Use criteria

Criteria can be used to customize a query. Each time the query is run, the user is prompted to supply the criteria.

Use calculations

Calculations can be used to extract summary data and perform operations on table data.

Work with query results

Queries return a result set that contains a subset of the records in a table or tables.

Use action queries

Action queries allow you to use a query's result set to perform an action on a table, such as creating or updating a table.

Creating a Query

Although all of the data in a database may be useful, different groups of data are useful to different groups of people—possibly at different times. The challenge is to provide the right information to the right people in a timely manner. Queries are used to pinpoint specific information in a database.

A query acts like a question that is presented to the database. For example, you might want to know which of your customers are from Mexico. To find out which customers are from Mexico, you ask the database that question by putting it into the form of a query. The database gives you an answer in the form of query results.

NOTE   Query results are often referred to as a *dynaset*, meaning that it is a dynamic, or virtual, set of records. The results are dynamic because they depend on the data that is contained in the underlying table(s). ■

Dynasets returned by a query can be treated as if they were a table. A dynaset is presented in a datasheet, just like tables are. Records can be sorted and data can be modified. Any change made to the data is made directly to the table that the data was drawn from. A dynaset ceases to exist when the datasheet is closed. The data is retrieved again the next time the query is run. Changes made to the data in the interim are reflected in the new query results.

Open a database window and click the Queries tab to work with queries. Click the New button to create a new query. The New Query dialog box appears (see Figure 19.1). Queries can be created using one of the following options:

- Design view
- Simple Query Wizard
- Crosstab Query Wizard
- Find Duplicates Query Wizard
- Find Unmatched Query Wizard

Basic select queries are created using either Design view or the Simple Query Wizard. These two methods are discussed in the "Creating a Query with the Design View" and "Creating a Query with the Simple Query Wizard" sections in this chapter. In addition to the methods for creating simple queries, the New Query dialog box, which is shown in Figure 19.1, has several other options. Choose an option and click the OK button, or double-click an option to select it and continue.

Creating a Query with the Design View

At this point, you should know what queries are used for and how to start creating one. After choosing Design view in the New Query dialog box, the Show Table dialog box appears. This is where you choose which tables and/or queries will be used in the query. So, if you wanted information about customers and their orders, you would select those two tables. Add tables by selecting them and clicking the Add button. Tables can also be added by double-clicking them. Click the Close button after you add the tables you need.

FIG. 19.1
Most queries are created using either Design view or the Simple Query Wizard.

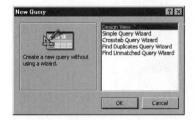

Queries are written in *Structured Query Language*, or *SQL*. However, Access doesn't require you to know SQL. Instead, it lets you *Query By Example*, which is referred to as *QBE*. As its name promises, QBE lets you provide examples of what you want. You can drag and drop the fields you want to view and provide criteria that limits the data that is returned by the query. Figure 19.2 shows the Design view. The grid at the bottom is where the QBE information is placed.

FIG. 19.2
Query By Example allows you to write complex queries with no knowledge of SQL.

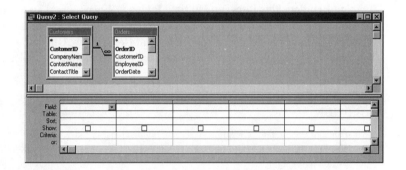

The following sections discuss the actions that can be performed in Design view.

Adding and Removing Tables or Queries   A query needs to change as quickly as the information needs of the people who use the query. This might require that tables or queries be added or removed from a query. For example, if you need a query that returns a list of orders which have not been filled to also include the customer name and phone number for that order, you will have to include the Customer table in the query.

To add a table or query, choose Show Table from the Query menu. The Show Table dialog box lets you choose from a list of tables, queries, or both. Click the tab of the list you want to view. In Figure 19.3, the Show Table dialog box lists the queries in the current database.

Select the tables and/or queries that you want added to the query. Then, click the Add button to add the selected objects to the query. Finally, click the Close button to exit the Show Table dialog box. Any time that multiple tables or queries are used, they must have a relationship or join defined between them. This relationship can be defined for the entire database or just for the purpose of the query.

FIG. 19.3

Queries can be used as the source table(s) for other queries.

TIP Tables and queries can also be added to the query Design view using drag and drop. Simply select a table or query in the database window and drag it to the upper part of the query's Design view.

To remove a table or query, select the table or query in Design view that you want to remove. Click anywhere on the table or query to select it. Then, press the Delete key and the object is removed from the query. Any fields from the removed table or query that were being used in the query is removed from the query's field list.

Defining Relationships Between Multiple Tables   When more than one table or query is used in a query, a relationship must be defined that somehow connects the two sets of data. If a relationship is already defined, it will show up in Design view. Otherwise, you must define one. The relationship tells Access how to present the data from multiple tables as a single set of data.

> **CAUTION**
>
> A relationship should almost always exist between tables that are being used in combination for a query. If a relationship is not defined, it may be a sign that either one needs to be or that the section of the database needs to be redesigned.

To join two tables or queries, click a field name in one table and drag it to a matching field in the other table. Figure 19.4 shows this action. The fields should be of the same data type and contain similar data. Now, the query's result set will only contain records from the two tables where the joined fields' values are equal.

FIG. 19.4

Tables are joined by connecting their similar fields.

The relationship is an inner join by default. You can change the relationship to an outer join by using the Join Properties dialog box, which is shown in Figure 19.5. Double-click the line that represents the relationship to open the Join Properties dialog box. An outer join selects all the records from one table or query and only those records from the other table where the joined fields are equal.

FIG. 19.5
The join properties of relationships can be changed for a query.

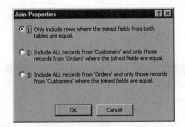

To delete a join between two tables, click the relationship line for the relationship that you want to delete. The line appears bold when selected. Then, press the Delete key and the relationship is gone.

N O T E Relationships that are deleted within a query only affect two tables' relationship within that query. If they had a relationship defined for the database, it still exists. ▪

▶ **See** "Working with Relationships," **p. 364**

▶ **See** "Exploring Multiple Table Relational Types," **p. 434**

Working with Fields   After you have added all of the tables and queries needed to perform your query, it is time to start working with the fields contained in those tables. Some fields will be displayed in the query results, but most probably will not. Usually, a limited number of the fields are retrieved, but only what's necessary. The limited number makes it easier to use the information retrieved and will improve the speed of queries, especially on large databases. Over time, you may have to perform the following tasks with fields:

- Add a field
- Remove a field
- Move a field
- Insert a field between other fields
- Show or hide a field in the query results

The following sections discuss each of the actions that can be performed on fields in a query.

Adding a Field   Simply adding tables to a query doesn't return any data when the query is run. You must specify which fields of data that you want retrieved. These fields are added to the query. Fields from different tables can be added. The relationship between the tables takes care of matching the records.

N O T E Newly-added fields can displace fields that were already in the query. In other words, a field can be added in between fields that were previously added to the query. ▪

Part
IV

Ch
19

To add a field to a query, find the table or query that contains the field(s) you need in the top part of Design view. If the table or query is not there, add it to the view using the Show Table dialog box. Select the field(s) that you want to add to the query—multiple fields are selected simultaneously by holding down the Shift or Ctrl key—and drag them to the grid at the bottom of Design view. This action is shown in Figure 19.6.

FIG. 19.6

Fields in the query are listed in the grid at the bottom of Design view.

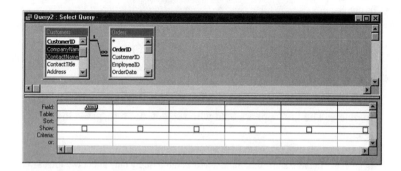

Fields can be added to a query's Design view using two other methods:

- Double-click a field to immediately add it to the query.
- Select the field in the Field row of the grid at the bottom of Design view.

Removing a Field   Queries can be used over and over. Eventually, they may need to be changed. New fields might need to be added, and other fields might need to be removed. For example, a query that retrieves data used to prove that you are complying with a law or government regulation would become unnecessary if the regulation were done away with.

To remove a field from a query, find the field in the design grid at the bottom of Design view. Select the field by clicking the thin gray bar at the top of the column that it is listed in, as shown in Figure 19.7. Then, press the Delete key to remove the field from the query.

FIG. 19.7

Selected columns take on a highlighted appearance.

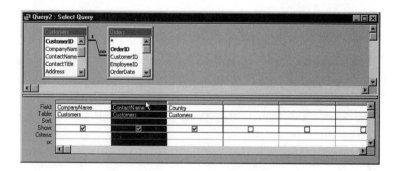

TIP You can select several columns to delete more than one field at a time. While contiguous columns can be selected by either dragging the mouse pointer over them or using the Shift key, noncontiguous columns can be selected using the Ctrl key.

Moving a Field Fields are displayed in the query results in the order they appear in the design grid. If the order of the fields is important, you may occasionally need to move a field to a different position in the design grid.

To move a field(s), select the appropriate column or columns. Click the column selector of one of the columns. The *column selector* is the thin gray bar at the top of the column. Then drag the column or columns to the new location. Figure 19.8 shows two columns being dragged to a new location. The field that is displaced and all fields to the right of it move to the right to make room.

FIG. 19.8

An outline of a small box just below the cursor indicates that columns are being moved.

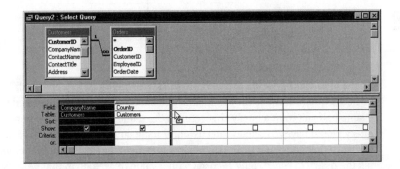

Changing a Field Name Fields in a query can be renamed to better describe the data that are contained in the field. Changing a field name in the design grid changes the column heading in the query's Datasheet view. For example, a field that contains phone numbers and would normally have a column heading of Phone can be given a new heading of Work Phone. This is particularly useful when working with calculated fields. Unless you enter a name for calculated fields, Access assigns names such as Expr1 or SumOfOrder Amount.

The new name will be used when controls are bound to the field in the query. However, controls that were bound to the field before the change continue to use the same field name. None of these changes affect the underlying table that the data is being drawn from.

NOTE Changing a field's name in the design grid has no effect in the query results' Datasheet view if the source table's Caption property has been set. So, if you're changing the field name specifically for datasheet columns, or label captions in forms and reports, it is better to set the Caption property of the source table. ▪

To change a field name, place the cursor at the beginning of the field name in the design grid. Then enter the new field name followed by a colon. Figure 19.9 shows a renamed field name. The colon separates the field name to be used as the label in the query's Datasheet view from the name of the field that the data is contained in. If Access has already assigned a field name (Expr1 or Expr2, and so on), replace only the name. Do not change the expression after the colon.

FIG. 19.9

Spaces can be used when renaming fields in a query.

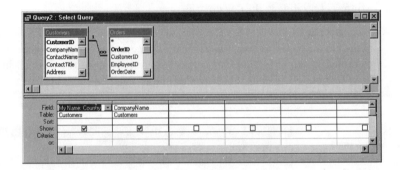

Showing or Hiding Fields in Query Results Sometimes, a query contains fields that need to be in the query because they help limit the data that is retrieved or used to sort the data. For example, if you want a query that returns the names of all the customers from Mexico, that query would have to contain the customer name and customer country fields. You don't want to display the data from the customer country field, but you have to include it so that you can tell the query to return only records with a value of Mexico in that field. By choosing to hide the column, it is not displayed in the query's Datasheet view.

To show or hide a field in a query, check or uncheck the Show check box in the design grid for that field. If the check box is checked, the field is included in the query's Datasheet view; if it is not checked, the field is not included. Figure 19.10 shows the example of retrieving only customer names for all customers from Mexico. See the section "Using Criteria" later in this chapter for more information on limiting the data that is retrieved.

FIG. 19.10

A field in a query isn't necessarily displayed in the query's Datasheet view.

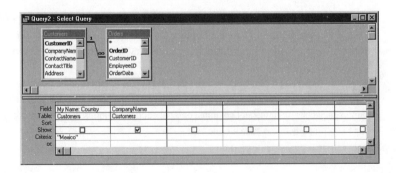

N O T E Access moves all hidden fields to the columns on the far right of the design grid when a query is closed. ■

Changing Column Widths Field names can be lengthy, and it may be difficult to identify them in the design grid. Part of the name might be cut off, leaving only the first section of the field name showing. You can change the width of the column so that you can read the entire field name. Changing the column widths in the design grid has no effect on the columns in the query's Datasheet view.

To change the width of a column in the design grid, move the cursor over the right edge of the column until the cursor changes to a double-sided arrow. Then click and drag the side of the column to the desired width. Select multiple columns to resize more than one column at a time. Figure 19.11 shows two columns being resized.

FIG. 19.11
Resize columns to make field names easier to read in the design grid.

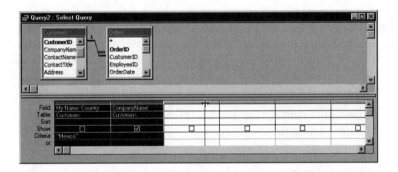

 TIP Double-click a column with the double-sided arrow to change the column width to match the width of the field name.

Using Criteria *Criteria* are used to restrict the data that a query retrieves. For example, you may only want a query to display products from a certain category or customers from a certain region. Most queries use criteria to limit the data that is returned. The sections that follow discuss different aspects of using criteria.

Setting or Changing Criteria Criteria are set in the design grid of the Design view. There is a row for criteria in the grid. The criteria is placed in the column of the field that the criteria acts upon. So, criteria that limit the country a customer could come from would be in the customer country field's column.

To specify criteria for a field, place the cursor in that field's Criteria cell. Type the criteria into the cell. Figure 19.12 shows simple criteria that force the query to only return customers from Mexico. Remember, you're using QBE, and the text you typed into the Criteria cell is the example that the records must follow to be included in the query's results. Criteria can be entered for more than one field.

FIG. 19.12

Criteria can simply be text values.

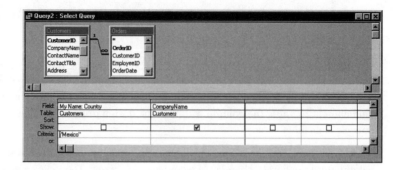

N O T E Values specified for the criteria of fields from linked tables are case-sensitive. ■

In the previous example, the criteria was very simple. It was just a text value that the field needed to match to be included in the query results. However, criteria are often defined in a more complex expression. The expression is made up of identifiers and operators. Identifiers and operators are discussed in the next section, "Using Identifiers and Operators."

Using Identifiers and Operators Identifiers are used in expressions to refer to the value of a field. For example, [Customers]![Country] is an identifier that refers to the value of the Country field in the Customers table.

An *operator* is a symbol or word that indicates that an action needs to be performed on an element of an expression. A less-than sign (<) and the word Or are both operators. Access has several classes of operators, including arithmetic, comparison, concatenation, and logical operators. Table 19.1 shows these operators and which class they belong to.

Table 19.1   Classes of Operators

Operator	Class	Description
-	Arithmetic	Subtracts one value from another.
*	Arithmetic	Multiplies two values together.
/	Arithmetic	Divides one value by another.
\	Arithmetic	Divides two values and returns an integer.
^	Arithmetic	Raises a value by a specified power.
+	Arithmetic	Adds two values together.
Mod	Arithmetic	Divides two values and returns the remainder.
<	Comparison	Less than
<=	Comparison	Less than or equal to
<>	Comparison	Not equal to

Operator	Class	Description
=	Comparison	Equal to
>	Comparison	Greater than
>=	Comparison	Greater than or equal to
Between	Comparison	Between FirstValue and SecondValue.
&	Concatenation	Puts text together ('M' & 'e' = 'Me').
And	Logical	Both values must be true.
Eqv	Logical	Logical equivalence on two values.
Imp	Logical	Logical implication on two values.
Not	Logical	Value is not equivalent to comparison value.
Or	Logical	Either value can be true.
Xor	Logical	Logical exclusion on two values.

TIP Consult the Access help file for tables that show how the complex logical operators evaluate values.

Sometimes, you are only concerned with partially meeting criteria. You use wildcard characters as placeholders for other characters when this is the case. For example, you might want to find all values that start with Tr. As long as the value starts with those two characters, you want it in the query's result set. Using wildcard operators can accomplish this. Use wildcard characters with text data types. At times, they can be used with other data types, such as dates, but it could be inaccurate and unpredictable because of regional settings. Table 19.2 shows the wildcard operators.

Part IV
Ch 19

Table 19.2   Wildcard Operators

Character	Usage	Example
*	Matches any characters.	wh* finds what and why.
?	Matches any single alphabetic character.	b?ll finds ball and bill.
[ ]	Matches any single character within the brackets.	B[ae]ll finds ball and bell but not bill.
!	Matches any character not in the brackets.	b[!ae]ll finds bill and bull but not bell.

continues

Table 19.2   Continued

Character	Usage	Example
-	Matches any one of a range of characters; the range must be specified in ascending order.	b[a-c]d finds bad, bbd, and bcd.
#	Matches any number.	1#3 finds 103 and 123.

N O T E   When using wildcard characters to search for characters that are used as wildcard characters, enclose the item you're searching for in brackets. For example, to search for a question mark, type **[?]**. ■

Using Expressions and Compound Criteria   Expressions can be used to better control the data that is returned by a query. Using different operators makes criteria more powerful. Instead of giving example values, text fragments and formulas can be used to determine which data should be retrieved.

You can enter an expression directly into the Criteria cell of a field, or you can use the Expression Builder. The *Expression Builder* is similar to a wizard, except it only has one window. To use the Expression Builder, place the cursor in the cell that you want to build an expression for and click the Build button on the toolbar. Use the Expression Builder to build your expression. Click the OK button to place the expression you've built into the active cell. Figure 19.13 shows the Expression Builder.

FIG. 19.13

Use the buttons and other items of the Expression Builder to complete your expressions.

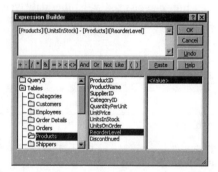

Additional criteria can be defined for the same field or different fields. Access combines expressions for the same field using the Or operator and combines expressions for different fields using the And operator.

N O T E   If expressions are in different rows of the design grid, Access uses the Or operator to combine them. Records which meet criteria in any of the cells will be retrieved. ■

To insert a criteria row, click the row that is below where you want the new row to appear. Then, choose Rows from the Insert menu. A new row is inserted above the previously selected row. Click anywhere in a row and choose Delete Rows from the Edit menu to delete a criteria row.

Specifying a Sort Order for the Query Results   Queries return a subset of data to make it easier to find information, but they can still return large amounts of data. Sorting the data can make it easier to find the information that you need. For example, you could sort a query by customer's company name. Then, you can quickly scan sections of the query to find customers.

To specify a sort order for query results, arrange the fields from left to right in the order that you would like them sorted. For example, to sort on the Country field first and then on the CompanyName field, the Country field must be to the left of the CompanyName field in the grid. Figure 19.14 illustrates this point. Then choose the type of sorting that you would like done from the drop-down list box in the Sort cell.

FIG. 19.14

Fields are sorted from left to right in the design grid.

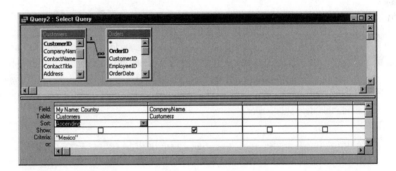

Performing Calculations on Data   You can perform calculations in a query using either predefined calculations or custom calculations. Predefined calculations, called *totals*, compute the following amounts for groups of records or for all the records combined in the query:

- Sum
- Average
- Count
- Minimum

- Maximum
- Standard deviation
- Variance

Custom calculations perform calculations on each record using data from one or more fields. A new calculated field must be created in the design grid for this type of calculation. Regardless of how they were derived, calculated values can serve one of the following purposes:

- Calculations can be part of a query's result set.
- Calculations can act as criteria for the query.
- Calculations can update data from an update query.

The following sections cover calculations in greater detail.

Part

IV

Ch

19

Numeric Calculations and Text Concatenation   Adding, subtracting, and dividing fields in Access is easy. To achieve this result, simply type the name for the new column, a colon, and the calculation; for example,

```
Total Cost: [UnitPrice]*[Quantity]
```

In this example, our query results will contain a field called `Total Cost`. If other fields in the query were called `UnitPrice` or `Quantity`, the table name would also have to be used in the identifier. To perform mathematical operations, use the following syntax:

Operator	Example
Addition uses the + symbol	`Price Increase: [Price]+1.19`
Subtraction uses the × symbol	`Discounted Price: [Price]-1.19`
Multiplication uses the * symbol	`Total Cost: [UnitPrice]*[Quantity]`
Division uses the / symbol	`NewColumn:[Sales]/[Price]`
Power uses the ^ symbol	`Squared Price: [Price]^2`

TIP   To perform certain pieces of an equation before others, enclose the segments in parentheses: `[Sales]*([Price]-[Discount])`. This is especially important if you are using both the addition and multiplication operands in the same expression. As a predictable rule, Access will perform multiplication and division before it performs addition and subtraction. The use of parentheses will override this default behavior.

Columns in calculated expressions can be built to reflect very complex calculations. Operands can be used several times, as can individual columns. As an example, average price per unit sold would be constructed as:

```
AveragePrice: [Sales]*[Price]/[Sales]
```

CAUTION

Be extremely careful if you are including potential null values in your equations. Access treats an expression containing a null value as a null, not a zero. That means 3 + null = null. For example, if Price were accidentally left null in some Purchase records, any calculations using the Price field would return a null value.

In addition to using numeric fields in expressions, we can also use non-numeric (text) fields. Typically, this is called *concatenation*. A good rule of database design is to store data at its most detailed level. For George Patton, that means you would store Last Name and First Name separately. However, you might want query results to contain his full name, and you might also want the query sorted by last name. To achieve this, we use the concatenation operator (&).

Note that concatenation is a very literal process and will not intuitively place spaces or parentheses in logical places. The formatting is entirely up to you. For example, Patton's name would be rebuilt with the syntax:

```
FullName:[LastName] & ', ' & [FirstName]
```

The resulting name appears as Patton, George.

Built-In Functions In addition to creating our own expressions, Access features a wide set of functions and tools to allow us to create more complex and useful expressions. While the list contains literally dozens of functions, we will limit our focus here to several of the ones considered invaluable by many Access users. Of course, using these functions is as easy as placing them in the field section of your query definition, exactly as we built our own expressions.

- The Now function returns the current date and time.

- The CurrentUser function returns the login ID of the user running the query.

- The Trim function truncates leading and trailing spaces.

- The Mid function provides us with a means to extract pieces of fields, provided they are textual. For example, you might want to query just the first three digits of Social Security Number. To achieve this effect, we must know three pieces of information: field name, starting position of the desired information, and length of the desired information. Having already stated we are interested in the first three characters of Social Security Number, building the expression is easy:

  ```
  StartSSN: Mid([Social Security Number],1,3)
  ```

- The Ucase function makes all characters uppercase.

- The Lcase function makes all characters lowercase.

- The IIF function is a special kind of IF statement that can be an invaluable tool, especially if you have fallen victim to the problem of using nulls in calculated expressions. The idea behind the IIF function is that it will return one of two possible values in the query results, depending upon criteria that we provide. For example, the IIF function can look at a field and determine if its value is null. If so, IIF can return a 0; otherwise, IIF can return the field value.

- The DateAdd function is a simple and easy way to both add and subtract Date/Time information. For example, you may want to ensure that you drink all your wine within 90 days of purchasing it.

Setting Query Properties Queries have properties that you can set. Click anywhere in Query Design view outside the design grid and the field lists, and then click the Properties button on the toolbar. The Query Properties dialog box appears (see Figure 19.15).

FIG. 19.15

Queries are objects and have properties that help define them.

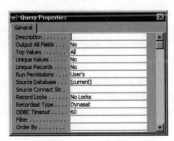

Part

IV

Ch

19

TIP If you need more space to enter or edit a property setting, press Shift+F2 to open the Zoom box.

Type a setting or expression in the property box to set that property. If an arrow appears in the property box, click the arrow and then choose value from the list that appears. Click the Build button, if it appears next to the property box, to display a builder. The properties for a query are the following:

- The Description property enables you to document the purpose of the query. Descriptions can be up to 255 characters.

- The Output All Fields property forces every column in the underlying tables to appear in the query results. It is helpful during the testing stages of a query to ensure that you are getting back the appropriate records. After testing, however, you should consider setting this property to No and having Access return only the fields necessary for your specific business question.

- The Top Values property limits the number of values that are returned. A specific number or a percentage can be used. For example, a query could retrieve the top 20 values or the top 5 percent of all values in a field.

- The Unique Values and Unique Records properties determine whether or not you get only unique rows for a query. This can be an extremely powerful tool for determining the various entries in any specific field. To see only unique combinations of records, set the Unique Values property to Yes. Note that by doing so, Unique Records is automatically set to No.

- The Run Permissions property is used in a multiuser environment. Various individuals, including the database owner, may own queries. This flag determines which set of permissions to use when running the query—the owner's or the user's. Most often, you should leave this flag set to User's.

- The Record Locks property locks data that is retrieved in a query. Unless you have an extremely compelling reason, leave this property set to No Locks.

- The Recordset Type property is helpful for some, as they claim to achieve greater performance through its manipulation. For the fastest query results, set this property to Snapshot, although doing so will prevent you from being able to edit the underlying data. The Dynaset options allow you alter the underlying data based on specific criteria. For the most flexibility in altering data, choose Dynaset (Inconsistent Updates). For the middle ground, leave this property set to Dynaset.

- The ODBC Timeout property determines the number of seconds that Access will wait before providing you an error message if your query doesn't work. You may want to increase this number if you are working with large tables and complex queries. Otherwise, the default of 60 seconds is a reasonable one.

- The Filter property allows you to use a predefined filter with a query. To do so, simply type the appropriate filter in the provided space. Note, however, that this capability does not provide you with functionality that Access queries do not inherently already have. Most people choose to use straight criteria to apply their filters within a query definition.

- The Order By property provides you with another way to do something Access queries already do—in this case, sort data. To use this property, simply type the Sort Order into the provided space. Again, however, you are probably better off using the Sort functionality provided in the query definition screen.

- The Max Records property prevents you from returning too many rows from a query—in this case, an ODBC data source. To use this property, simply type the maximum number of records you want to see in your query results and rerun the query. Use this property carefully, however, as it will potentially eliminate legitimate records in your query result.

Modifying the SQL Statement Directly   Access uses a Query By Example interface to shield you from the complexities of SQL. However, you may be more comfortable using SQL. If that's the case, it is possible to directly edit the SQL statement.

To view the SQL statement, choose SQL View from the View menu. The SQL statement that is equivalent to what you created in Design view is displayed. Figure 19.16 shows an SQL statement. Make your changes to the SQL statement. Choose Design View from the View menu to see the effect of your changes.

FIG. 19.16

SQL can be used while working in Access.

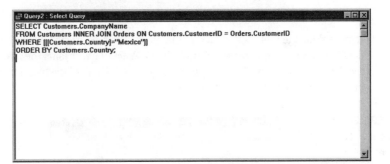

TROUBLESHOOTING

To insert an entirely new column into the design grid, click anywhere in the column to the left of which you want to add a new column. Then, choose Columns from the Insert menu.

If the data you need for a query is stored in a different Access database—or even a different type of database—link the table(s) that you need from their individual databases. Then you can use the linked tables in your query.

To clear the design grid, choose Clear Grid from the Edit menu.

Creating a Query with the Simple Query Wizard

The Simple Query Wizard can be used to quickly create basic select queries. New users should find this feature helpful while trying to learn, but experienced users can also take advantage of this wizard. Queries created using the wizard are similar because they are all created using the same logic. This creates a standard that can be followed for all queries.

Part
IV

Ch
19

After choosing the Simple Query Wizard in the New Query dialog box, the first dialog box of the Simple Query Wizard appears. The Simple Query Wizard automatically creates a query using your input, which you supply in a series of dialog boxes. As shown in Figure 19.17, the Simple Query Wizard lets you choose fields to include in the query from tables and other queries.

FIG. 19.17

The Query Wizard lets you choose the fields to be included in the query.

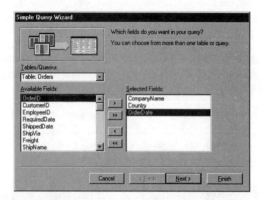

If more than one table is included in the query, the next wizard dialog box asks you to choose a detail or summary query (see Figure 19.18). A *detail query* joins the two tables and lists all of the data from them, while a *summary query* would list all of the data for one table and summary information about the data in the other.

FIG. 19.18

A query can list information in its entirety or summarize it.

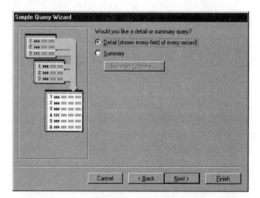

Figure 19.19 shows the Summary Options dialog box. This dialog box lets you determine what summary values need to be calculated and for which fields.

The final dialog box, shown in Figure 19.20, lets you name the query. You can also choose to open the query and view the information that it retrieves or open the query in Design mode. If you need any additional help, click the Display Help check box at the bottom of the dialog box. When it is checked, the wizard opens the help file for queries after generating your new query.

FIG. 19.19
Different calculations can be used to generate summary information.

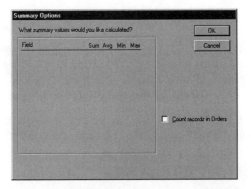

FIG. 19.20
Single-table queries can be created in two steps using the wizard.

Using Action Queries

An *action query* is a special type of query that lets you change the field values in your records. For example, you can change a unit price field to increase all prices by 25 percent, or delete the information from the records of terminated employees.

When you create any query, Access creates it as a select query automatically. You can specify a different type from the Query Design menu. From this menu, you can choose from several different types of action queries:

- Make-Table Query—from specified records in a query
- Update Query—in a group of records
- Append Query—from one table to another
- Delete Query—from a table or group of tables

Like select queries, action queries create a dynaset you can view in a datasheet. To see the dynaset, you simply click the Datasheet button on the toolbar. Unlike select queries, action queries perform an action, such as creating a table; to perform that action, click the Run button on the toolbar.

> **CAUTION**
> Because action queries perform a specific task, many times that can be an unintended destructive task. Make sure you view the changes that the action query will make before you run the action query. Verify afterward that they made the changes you anticipated.

In addition to specifying the fields and criteria of an action query, you must specify an action-specific property—Delete Where/From, Update To, Append To, and New Table Name.

Deleting Records with Action Queries

Delete queries have the ability to wipe out records from tables permanently and irreversibly. Like other action queries, delete queries act upon a group of records on the basis of scoping criteria.

> **N O T E**   A delete action query can work with multiple tables to delete records; however, you must define the relationship between the tables in the Relationships Builder, check the Enforce Referential Integrity option, and check the Cascade Delete Related Records option for the join between tables. ■

To create a delete query for all employees who have been terminated, perform the following steps:

1. Create a new query using the Employees table.
2. Choose Delete Query from the Query menu.
3. Select the Notes field from the Employees table.
4. Specify the criterion **Terminated** in the Notes field. See the Delete Query Design window in Figure 19.21. The only field that must appear in this delete query is the first field, Notes.

FIG. 19.21
The delete query's QBE pane lets you choose which records to delete.

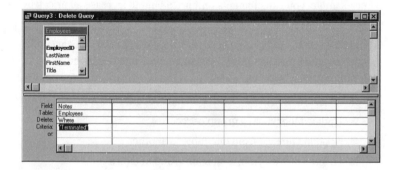

5. Go to the datasheet and verify that only records specifying Terminated are there.
6. Return to the Design window, and click the Run button on the toolbar (choose Query, Run). Access will display a message dialog box warning you that you are about to delete X number of rows from the table.

CAUTION

Remember that delete queries remove entire records, not just the data in a specific field.

7. Click the Yes button to complete the query. The records are removed from the table.

After completing the delete query, you can check your results by clicking the Datasheet button on the toolbar. If the query ran as it should, there will be no records in the datasheet.

Updating Records with Action Queries

Suppose that all employees working in Scottsdale are going to start reporting to Mr. Smith. To create this query, you work with the Employees table.

You could probably update each record in the table individually by using a form or a datasheet. However, using a select query dynaset to make these changes takes a very long time. The method is not only very time-consuming but also inefficient. As always, this method can produce numerous typing errors as you enter the new text into fields—which requires more work in the future.

This type of situation is best handled with an *update action query* to make the changes in just one operation. You will save time and eliminate potential typos from manual edits.

NOTE Because action queries are irreversible, you can performs the following steps to create a safe query:

1. Create a select query. View the data you want to update by clicking the Datasheet button.

2. Convert the select query to an update query. Run the update query after you are satisfied that it will affect only the records you want to affect. ■

Creating a Select Query The first step in making an update query is to create a select query. In this situation, the query is for all employees working in Scottsdale. Complete the following steps:

1. Create a new query using the Employees table.

2. Select the City and the ReportsTo fields from the Employees table.

3. Specify a criterion of **Scottsdale** in the City field (see Figure 19.22).

4. Examine the datasheet to make sure that it has only the records you want to change. Return to the design surface when finished.

The dynaset will show only the records for employees in the Scottsdale area. Now you can convert the select query you created to an update query.

Converting the Select Query After you create a select query and verify the selection of records, it's time to create the update query. To convert the select query to an update query, complete the following steps:

1. Choose Update Query from the Query Type button on the toolbar (or choose Update Query from the Query menu).

Part

IV

Ch

19

FIG. 19.22

Provide example data to limit the query's results.

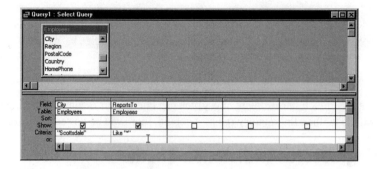

2. Enter **Mr. Smith** in the Update To cell of ReportsTo.

> **TIP** You can change more than one field at a time by filling in the Update To cell of any field you want to change.

3. Click the Run button on the toolbar (or choose Query, Run).

4. Click the Yes button to complete the query and update the records. If you select No, the procedure will stop and no records will be updated.

After you complete the update query, you should always check your results to make sure the query ran correctly. Change the update query back to a select query and review the changes in the datasheet.

Appending Records with Action Queries

An *append query* attaches or adds records to a specified table. The table you want to add records to must already exist. You can append records to a table in the same database or in another Access database.

When working with append queries, keep in mind the following information:

- If the table you are appending records to has a primary key field, the records you add cannot have Null values or duplicate primary key values. If they do, Access will not append the records.

- If you add records to another database table, you must know the location and name of the database.

- If you use the asterisk (*) field in a QBE row, you cannot also use individual fields from the same table. Access assumes that you are trying to add field contents twice to the same record and will not append the records.

- If you append records with an AutoNumber field (an Access-specified primary key), do not include the AutoNumber field if the table you are appending to also has the field and record contents.

After you complete the append table queries, make sure you verify your results.

Making Tables with Action Queries

You can use an action query to create new tables based on scoping criteria. To make a new table, you create a *make-table query*.

A new publishing company has approached you for a mailing list of employees at your store who also are considered customers of your store. This company wants to send your employees under the age of 25 who shop at the store the first issue of a new women's magazine. The publishing company plans to create mailing labels and send the first issue of the magazine.

You decide to create a make-table query for all customer employees under the age of 25. Complete the following steps to create the query:

1. Create a new query using the Customers and Employees tables.
2. Select Make-Table Query from the Query Type button on the toolbar to display the Make Table dialog box (see Figure 19.23).

FIG. 19.23
The Make Table dialog box prompts you for a table name.

3. Type **Customer Employee Magazine** in the Table Name field and click the OK button.
4. Select the fields from the Customer table (ContactName, Address, and City). Select BirthDate from the Employees table.
5. Specify the criteria >#7/7/92# in the BirthDate field. The Query Design window should look similar to Figure 19.24.

FIG. 19.24
Several tables can be combined to create a new table.

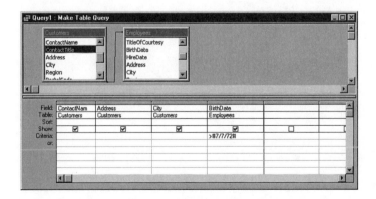

6. Click the Datasheet View button on the view the dynaset.
7. Make sure that the dynaset has only the records you specified.

Part
IV

Ch

19

8. Click the Design button to switch back to Query Design view.

9. Deselect the Show property of the field BirthDate. You do not want to copy this field to the new table because you do not need the information. By deselecting a field with a criteria set, you can base the scoping criteria on fields that will not be copied to the new table.

10. Click the Run button on the toolbar (or choose Query, Run).

11. Click the Yes button to complete the query and make the new table. (If you select No, then the procedure is stopped and no records are copied.)

After you complete the make-table query, you should check your results. You can do so by opening the new *Customer Employee Magazine*, which has been added to the database container. ●

CHAPTER 20

Database Reports

In previous chapters, you've learned how to create your own Access database, import or input data, and query the data. In this chapter, you will explore various ways to output your data in reports.

Access reports are especially useful for providing organized data to end users in a user-friendly format. In this chapter, we will look at a variety of ways to lay out and create reports. ■

Create reports

Get an overview of Access reports and how they are created.

Create AutoReports

Learn the "quick and easy" way to create simple but effective reports.

Use Report Wizard and create mailing labels

Explore Access' more sophisticated wizards that help you create reports and mailing labels tailored to your own needs.

Customize reports

Take a brief look at some of the more complex and sophisticated design tools available to help you create custom reports.

Publish your reports

Once your report is complete, you will want others to see it; explore how to publish your report in HTML for use on the Internet or via e-mail, and learn other ways to get your report out to those who need it.

Creating Reports

Before you create *any* type of report, you should carefully consider several priorities:

■ Who will use the report?

■ What will they use it for?

■ What data (both fields and records) need to be included and which need to be excluded?

■ What types of tables, forms, and queries do I have in my database?

■ Do I really need a report (output) or do I need a form (for input)?

■ What types of reports are the end users already using to obtain this information, and will my new report improve on them (or at least not be any worse)?

■ Have I talked to the people who will use the report to find out what *they* want?

Once you have carefully planned your report by considering all the important factors, you are ready to start work on your report.

Creating Reports with AutoReport

If you want a *really* quick and easy report, for example, to quickly produce a plain listing of certain data, or maybe just to help you get started deciding what kind of report you might eventually want to use, consider using Access' AutoReport feature.

AutoReport is really a wizard with no (or very few) user options. Using AutoReport, you can create columnar (or vertical) reports and tabular reports. Figures 20.1 and 20.2 show examples of each, using the Northwind sample database.

FIG. 20.1

A columnar (or vertical) report created with the AutoReport feature.

The columnar format of AutoReport allows you to pick a table from which this special wizard places each field on a separate line with the field label printed to the left.

Figure 20.2 provides the same information as Figure 20.1, but this time using the AutoReport Tabular feature. If you have just a few fields and you want to put as much as you can on a single page quickly, you may find this layout useful.

FIG. 20.2

An AutoReport-created tabular report.

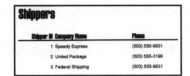

Creating an AutoReport Columnar Report

Using AutoReport is fairly simple. To create a columnar report using AutoReport, first open the database for which you want the report, then follow these steps:

 You can use AutoReport from anywhere in the Access database—you do not necessarily have to be in the Reports tab.

1. Choose Insert, Reports to access the New Report dialog box as shown in Figure 20.3. (You can also use the New Object toolbar button.)

FIG. 20.3

From the New Report dialog box, you can select AutoReport: Columnar option.

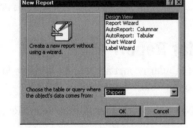

2. From this panel, choose AutoReport: Columnar.
3. Using the drop-down box at the bottom, select the table from which you want the report.
4. Click OK, and the AutoReport: Columnar Wizard creates a simple report for you, as shown in Figure 20.4.

From here, you can use the Design View toolbar button and many other report editing features, which are described in more detail later in this chapter, to customize your report. You can also use the File menu to save the report with a file name.

Part
IV

Ch
20

FIG. 20.4

This report is a preview of the report created using AutoReport: Columnar.

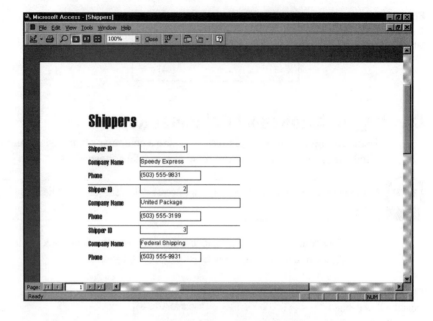

Creating an AutoReport Tabular Report

The steps for creating an AutoReport tabular report are similar to those for a columnar report. (Again, be sure you have a database open before beginning.)

1. Using the Insert menu or the New Object toolbar button, select Reports to access the New Report dialog box.

2. This time, choose AutoReport: Tabular, as shown in Figure 20.5.

FIG. 20.5

This time, the AutoReport: Tabular option is selected.

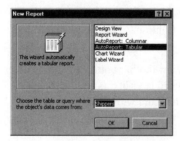

3. Again, using the drop-down box at the bottom, select the table from which you want to create the report.

4. Click OK, and the AutoReport: Tabular Wizard creates the report for you, as shown in Figure 20.6.

FIG. 20.6

From this point, you can customize the report, edit the layout, and so on.

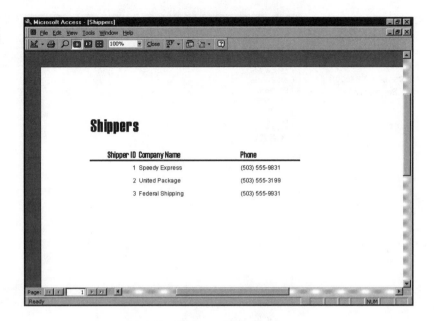

Shippers

Shipper ID	Company Name	Phone
1	Speedy Express	(503) 555-9831
2	United Package	(503) 555-3199
3	Federal Shipping	(503) 555-9931

As you can see, using the AutoReport features is an easy way to get started creating reports, or to create "final" versions of simple reports. If you need (or simply want) a bit more control over the design of your report, move on to the next section on the Access Reports Wizard.

Using the Access Reports Wizard

As is true with many Office 97 applications, using the wizards in Access 97 can be a quick and easy way to create a useful report. In this section, we'll take a look at several types of reports the Access wizards can help you create, showing some samples of each. (In later sections, we'll look at the more "manual" ways of creating reports, such as using the Design View method.)

If you have used wizards in any other Office 97 applications, the Reports Wizards will look familiar. The exact procedures you use will depend on what you want your report to look like, the data you want it to contain, and so on. Here are the general steps for creating a report using the Reports Wizard:

Part

IV

Ch

20

1. To use an existing table, open your database and click the Tables tab. Select the table name you want to use by highlighting it.

   If you want your report to include a filter or sort that is associated with the table, open the table in Datasheet view and be sure the filter or sort is in place. If so, the report will automatically include the sort or filter. Figure 20.7 shows the Northwind database Tables tab with the Suppliers table highlighted.

2. If you want to use an existing query to create your report, click the Queries tab and highlight the query you want to use. (You can also open the query in Datasheet view.)

3. In this example, we will use the Suppliers table for our report. Using the New Object toolbar button, shown in Figure 20.8 (or using the Insert menu), select Report.

FIG. 20.7

The Tables tab of the Northwind sample database is used to create a sample report in the Report Wizard.

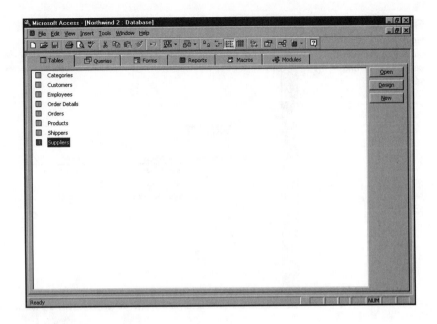

FIG. 20.8

Use the New Object toolbar button to access the New Report dialog box. (Notice that the New Object icon changes as items from that drop-down list are used.)

4. This time, highlight Report Wizard. Notice that the table you selected is already in the drop-down box, as shown in Figure 20.9.

Now we reach the heart of the Report Wizard. Notice that you can in this wizard—unlike in the AutoReport feature—change your mind about the table or query you want to use by changing the selection in the Tables/Queries drop-down list box. Figure 20.10 shows what the Report Wizard dialog box looks like before any selections or other changes have been made.

5. Select the fields you want to include in your report. To add one field at a time, use the > button; to add all the available fields, use the >> button. Similarly, to remove fields one at time from those you have selected, use the < button; to remove all of them at once, use the << button. In Figure 20.11, we have added a few fields, one at a time, for our report.

FIG. 20.9
Notice this time we will use the Report Wizard. Also notice that the table you highlighted is already in the box at the bottom.

FIG. 20.10
The Report Wizard dialog box gives you choices about the table or query you want to use and which fields you want in your report.

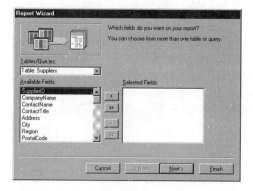

FIG. 20.11
Use the dialog box to pick and choose the fields you need for your report.

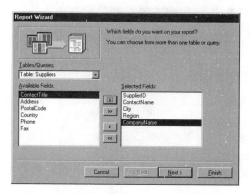

6. Once you have selected your fields, click Next to move to the next series of wizard options. The first possible option to appear (if it is needed) is the Grouping Levels options box. From here, you can group your report by additional levels. For instance, you might want to group your company's supplier by region so that users of the report can tell at a glance which suppliers are located in the various regions. In Figure 20.12, we have done exactly that.

To choose the grouping field, either double-click the field, or highlight the field and click the > button. (If you choose more than one grouping, you can move the grouping levels up and down using the Priority buttons.) Also, once you have chosen to use groupings, the Grouping Options button becomes active and you can click it to select the interval you want for your grouping.

FIG. 20.12

Using the Grouping feature, we have chosen to use the Region field to group our suppliers.

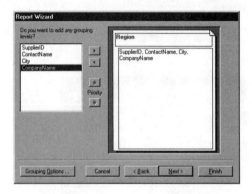

7. Once you have the groupings to your liking, click Next to move to the Sort Order and Summary Information screen. In our case, we have decided to sort the report in alphabetical order by the suppliers' company names, as shown in Figure 20.13.

FIG. 20.13

Use this screen to sort your report by up to four different fields.

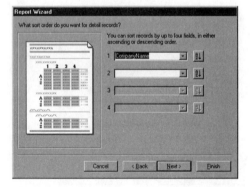

Notice that this box did not have the Summary Options button, as there were no numeric fields. If your report has numeric fields, the box will look like the one in Figure 20.14.

If you click this button, a typical Summary Options box appears, which looks like Figure 20.15.

8. Once you have your sorts and summaries selected, click Next to access the Report Wizard layout dialog box. Notice that the box will be different depending on whether you have selected groupings or not. If, as we did, you have groupings, your box will look like the one in Figure 20.16.

FIG. 20.14

This dialog box has the Summary Options box available because we have selected numeric fields for our report.

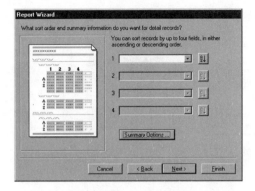

FIG. 20.15

Access this dialog box by clicking the Summary Options button, when available. There will be summary options for each numeric field in your report.

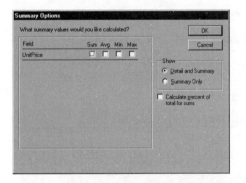

FIG. 20.16

Use this dialog box for choosing layouts for a grouped report.

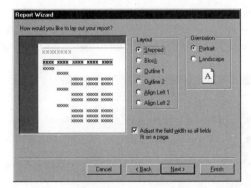

If you do not have groupings, your box will look more like Figure 20.17.

In either event, select the available style you want and click Next.

9. Experiment with the available styles, as shown in Figure 20.18; choose the ones you want and click Next.

FIG. 20.17
This is the dialog box for layouts of non-grouped reports.

FIG. 20.18
This box displays the available report styles. The preview window is useful for deciding which one you like the best.

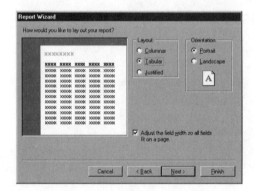

10. Notice the suggested title and make any changes you want. (Keep in mind that this title will be used for the report title, the report name within the database file, and the report caption.) Click Finish (see Figure 20.19), and the wizard will create your report.

FIG. 20.19
When all of the settings are correct, click Finish on this dialog box to complete your report.

When Access has completed the report, it will appear in Print Preview, as shown in Figure 20.20.

FIG. 20.20

This is our completed sample report in Print Preview mode. From here, you can perform a variety of functions on the report.

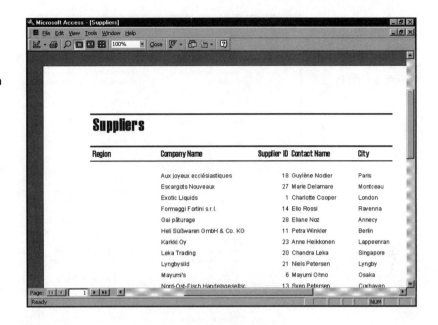

From this view, you can do several things with your report, including:

- *View the report in a variety of formats.* You can use Design or Layout Preview views to make changes to your report. In addition, you can choose to view one or several pages of the report on the screen at one time by using the Multiple Pages, One Page, or Two Pages toolbar buttons.

- *Print the report.* You will probably want to print your new creation so that you can provide hard copies to certain users. Use the normal Windows printing functions (for instance, File, Print, or the Print toolbar button) to print your report. You can see a printed version of our sample report in Figure 20.21; notice the Region groupings for those suppliers listed in particular regions.

- *Send the report to another Office application.* Using the OfficeLinks toolbar button, you can send the report to Word or Excel for use in those applications.

- *Publish the report in HTML format.* See the section later in this chapter "Publishing Reports" for details on using this feature.

- *Send the report via your mail system.* To send your report via your e-mail system, choose File, Send. Select the format you want and follow the instructions for sending your report.

Part
IV

Ch
20

FIG. 20.21
The printed version of our two-page sample report of the Northwind Suppliers, grouped by region.

Suppliers			

Region	Company Name	Supplier ID Contact Name	City
	Aux joyeux ecclésiastiques	18 Guylène Nodier	Paris
	Escargots Nouveaux	27 Marie Delamare	Montceau
	Exotic Liquids	1 Charlotte C̄ oper	London
	Formaggi Fortini s.r.l.	14 Elio Rossi	Ravenna
	Gai pâturage	28 Eliane N̄	Annecy
	Heli Süßwaren GmbH & Co. KG	11 Petra Winkler	Berlin
	Karkki Oy	23 Anne Heikkonen	Lappeenran
	Leka Trading	20 Chandra Leka	Singapore
	Lyngbysild	21 Niels Petersen	Lyngby
	Mayumi's	6 Mayumi Ohno	Osaka
	Nord-Ost-Fisch Handelsgesellsc	13 Sven Petersen	Cuxhaven
	Norske Meierier	15 Beate Vileid	Sandvika
	Pasta Buttini s.r.l.	26 Giovanni Giudici	Salerno
	PB Knäckebröd AB	9 Lars Peterson	Göteborg
	Plusspar Lebensmittelgroßmärkt	12 Martin Bein	Frankfurt
	Refrescos Americanas LTDA	10 Carlos Diaz	São Paulo
	Specialty Biscuits, Ltd.	8 Peter Wilson	Manchester
	Svensk Sjöföda AB	17 Michael Björn	Stockholm
	Tokyo Traders	4 Yoshi Nagase	Tokyo
	Zaanse Snoepfabriek	22 Dirk Luchte	Zaandam
Asturias			
	Cooperativa de Quesos 'Las Ca	5 Antonio del Valle Saave	Oviedo
LA			
	New Orleans Cajun Delights	2 Shelley Burke	New Orlean
MA			
	New England Seafood Cannery	19 Robb Merchant	Boston
MI			
	Grandma Kelly's Homestead	3 Regina Murphy	Ann Arbor
NSW			
	G'day, Mate	24 Wendy Mackenzie	Sydney

Region	Company Name	Supplier ID Contact Name	City
OR			
	Bigfoot Breweries	16 Cheryl Saylor	Bend
Québec			
	Forêts d'érables	29 Chantal Goulet	Ste-Hyacint
	Ma Maison	25 Jean-Guy Lauzon	Montréal
Victoria			
	Pavlova, Ltd.	7 Ian Devling	Melbourne

Creating Mailing Labels

A specialized type of Access Report Wizard is the *Mailing Label Wizard*. This type of report allows you to print standard Avery-type mailing labels and further allows you to customize the layout of your labels and perform other functions, such as sorting your label list.

TROUBLESHOOTING

If you use labels other than Avery, you may be able to save some time in designing your label reports by contacting the supplier or manufacturer of your labels. Often, even non-standard size labels have an "Avery equivalent," and you can use this setting to avoid having to design your label reports from scratch.

Creating mailing labels is similar to using the Report Wizard, only with several fewer steps. Again, be sure the appropriate database is open, then start from the database window with a table or query highlighted. (You can also start in the Reports window of your database and select New.)

Click the New Object toolbar button and select Report. This time, click the Label Wizard in the New Report dialog box, as shown in Figure 20.22.

FIG. 20.22

The New Report dialog box shows the Label Wizard highlighted and Customers in the table box.

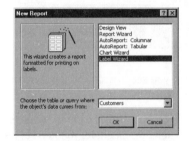

Choose the appropriate label format from the lists that appear (see Figure 20.23), or use the Customize button if your organization uses some other type of labels.

FIG. 20.23

Select your label size, or create your own custom-sized label layout.

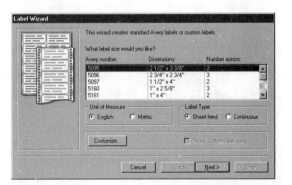

After you have selected your label type, click Next to select the font and font size you want, along with color and other options.

When you have completed that process, click Next to access the layout dialog box. From here, you can select the fields that you want to use on your labels. In Figure 20.24, you can see a typical label layout. Notice that the Prototype label is sized to fit the labels you have chosen; therefore, if you can't seem to fit all the fields you want on your label, it's because the label will not hold all the data.

TIP   If your label does not seem large enough to hold all the fields you want to use, try going back and reducing the font size. You can also eliminate some unnecessary fields to make the others fit.

Part
IV

Ch
20

FIG. 20.24
Select the fields you need and move them around to get the label look you want.

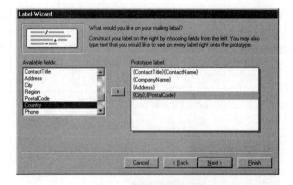

The Prototype label is set up in a "what you see is what you get" format—therefore, be sure your fields appear exactly as you want your labels to appear, such as in Figure 20.24.

Notice that you can move around the Prototype with the cursor or the direction keys. Also, you can type directly on to the Prototype where, for example, you need to insert characters, such as a comma between the City and the PostalCode fields.

Click Next to move to the sort dialog box. If you want your label report sorted, choose the field and sort order as shown in Figure 20.25.

FIG. 20.25
You can sort your labels from this dialog box.

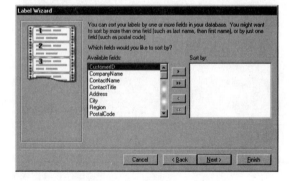

Click Next again and select a title for your label report, or accept the default value. Click Finish and Access will create your label report (see Figure 20.26).

 Don't forget to send the report to the correct printer and load the appropriate labels before printing, especially if you have a long list of records to print!

FIG. 20.26

This is the completed label report. You are now ready to print the report on mailing labels.

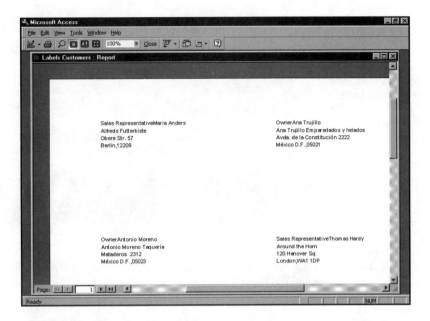

Customizing Reports

In the previous sections of this chapter, we have seen how Access' features can help you create very nice looking reports, especially those reports that are typical for most organizations.

However, at times you might need to modify the standard reports created by the wizards, or to create a report completely from scratch. In that case, Access provides a variety of powerful tools to help you create your reports.

N O T E Creating custom reports is almost identical to creating custom forms. Therefore, if you are already familiar with that process, creating reports will be much easier. ■

While the intricacies of creating complex custom forms is beyond the scope of this book, a basic familiarity with some of the design tools may prove useful. For more information about form design, refer to Que's *Special Edition Using Microsoft Access 97*.

Figure 20.27 shows some of the available tools for our Suppliers sample report, this time opened in Design view.

As with most layout applications, you can perform a variety of sophisticated functions on the layout of your report. For example, you can drag and drop the field headings to new locations; change the font, font size, color, and other attributes of the labels; and generally redesign the report layout to suit your needs and taste.

Part
IV

Ch
20

FIG. 20.27

This is a report in Design view. From here, you can see and experiment with some of the sophisticated design tools available in Access 97.

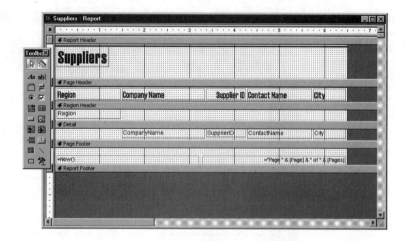

You can also use the AutoFormat feature to apply predefined styles to your report. To use AutoFormat, use the Format menu and choose AutoFormat. You can now select a style to apply to your report.

 TIP You can also customize the AutoFormats, so that when you use the Reports Wizards, the styles available to you are those you have customized from here.

If you want to apply individual styles to only certain areas of your report, you can select only those "controls" that you want to apply styles to. You select the controls you want to work with by using Select Objects in the toolbox. Select the Select Objects tool in the toolbox using the mouse, and then click any object in the report with the mouse or tool. Multiple objects can be selected by holding down the Shift key, dragging the tool over several controls, or dragging the tool along the left or top borders to "sweep" a group of controls. Then, you can apply those styles you want only to the selected controls.

For example, in Figure 20.27, you can select the Region header and apply a style only to that control.

All of the functions that were available in the wizards are also, of course, available in Design view. For instance, Figure 20.28 shows the Grouping and Sorting functions as they appear in Design view. To access these features, use the View menu and select Sorting and Grouping.

Notice that this figure contains the "left-over" sorts and groups from our previous examples.

The possibilities while using Design view to create custom reports are almost endless. Try it out a bit yourself to get the hang of it.

 TIP If you are new to customizing reports, you should start with a report created with a wizard or AutoFormat just to ensure that the basic building blocks of your report are present.

FIG. 20.28

This is how you sort and group in Design view.

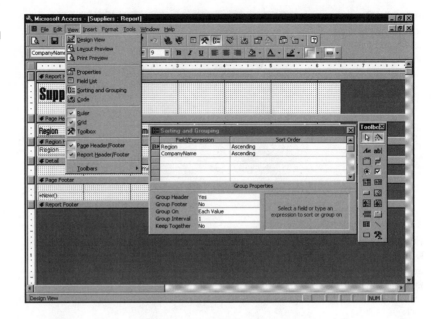

Publishing Reports

Once you have created a report, you will want to make that report available to other users. Of course, those users who have direct access to the database can simply call up the report (as you do) on their own workstation, assuming they have the appropriate authorization. However, for those who do not have that access, you will want to transmit (or publish) that report in some format.

Of course, you can publish the report by printing hard copies and distributing them. But today, it's often appreciated if you distribute reports in electronic format. To help you publish your report, Access 97 has several tools that you will want to explore.

Publishing Reports in HTML

One of the most popular formats today is *HTML (HyperText Markup Language)*, which is used extensively on the Internet, especially the World Wide Web. Publishing your report in HTML is now easy with Access 97, as it includes a Publish to the Web Wizard.

To access the Publish to the Web Wizard, simply open your report (optional) and select Save as HTML from the File drop-down menu. The startup screen in Figure 20.29 appears.

As with other wizards, simply provide the called-for information and click Next. Here we click Next to access the screen shown in Figure 20.30.

Part

IV

Ch

20

FIG. 20.29

Access now has an easy-to-use Publish to the Web Wizard.

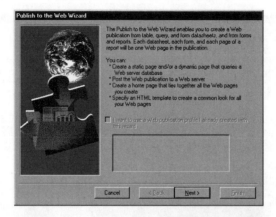

FIG. 20.30

From this dialog box, we can select the items we want to publish.

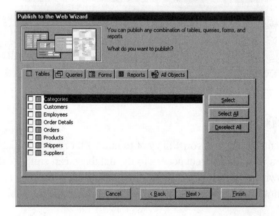

Use this dialog box to select the objects you want to publish in HTML. Use the check boxes and tabs to select as many as you need—or you can choose to publish all objects in the database by selecting the appropriate box.

If you have a pre-existing HTML template that you want to use, use the dialog box shown in Figure 20.31 to select it. If not, simply click Next.

The next several screens (not shown) simply walk you through the steps of creating an HTML document by asking several questions about the type of document you want and where you want to store it. At the end, Access creates your HTML format report.

Publishing Reports on E-Mail

You can also quickly and easily send another user a copy of your report via e-mail by choosing Send from the File menu to access this dialog box (see Figure 20.32).

FIG. 20.31

Use this dialog box to select your previously created HTML templates.

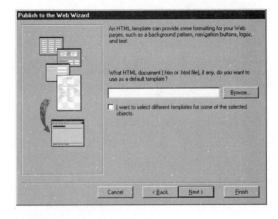

FIG. 20.32

This dialog box is accessed via the File, Send option.

We will select HTML again, though you could use any of the appropriate formats. Again, you will be asked for an HTML template, which you can supply if you have one. If not, don't worry—just click OK and Access will create the document for you. Finally, it will place the document, ready to go, into your e-mail system. (In Figure 20.33, the system is Microsoft Outlook e-mail.)

FIG. 20.33

Here, Access has reformatted the report (both pages) into HTML and placed it as an attachment ready to be sent via e-mail.

The report is ready to be sent zipping through the e-mail ether. ●

CHAPTER 21

Using Multiple Tables

Access 97 databases enable you to separate the data in your database into tables that contain fields of data of a similar type or group—for example, names, credit information, purchasing history, medical history, and more. Each of these various categories of data has a corresponding table in a relational database.

Combining the data from these multiple tables inside an Access database and the linking of the tables is the topic of this chapter. ■

Exploring multiple table relational types

Learn the three basic types of relational databases and explore examples of each.

Table relationships

Find out how you can link tables together in Access 97.

Multiple table queries

Explore the use of queries that are created from multiple tables.

Multiple table forms

Learn how to create and use forms that are based on multiple tables.

Multiple table reports

Explore reports that are based upon multiple tables.

Exploring Multiple Table Relational Types

Generally, tables in a database should contain only fields about one topic. (This is referred to as being *imperial*.) For example, a Customer table should contain the fields that are associated with customers (Name, Address, Customer type, and so on), and a Salesperson table should contain fields like Salesperson name, Employee Number, Department, and so on. While both sets of fields could function in one table, the table would be sloppy and hard to maintain.

The best way to create a database is to separate data (fields) into tables where they are associated only with other fields that relate to a particular topic. The term *relational database* refers to a database with multiple tables wherein each relate to a particular subject or topic.

This section explores the three basic types of relational databases. Each model is presented and explored.

One-to-Many Model

A one-to-many relationship is the most common type of relationship. In a one-to-many relationship, a record in Table A can have many matching records in Table B, but a record in Table B has only one matching record in Table A.

Figure 21.1 shows a one-to-many relationship in the Microsoft Access Relationship Editor.

FIG. 21.1

The one-to-many model is by far the most common relational database model.

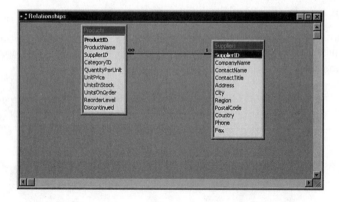

In this example, each one of the Suppliers (One) can have multiple Products (Many). This would follow the real-life relationship between a supplier and the inventory. One supplier may provide several products in the inventory.

In Access, a one-to-many relationship is created if only one of the related fields is a primary key or has a unique index. The link in this example is created with the SupplierID field (which is a field in both tables) and the primary key in the Suppliers table. It is not necessary for the fields in both tables to be named the same. Also notice that in Access the link line between the two tables has a "1" and infinity symbol. These symbols indicate which table is on which end of the one-to-many relationship.

Many-to-Many Model

A many-to-many relationship is really two one-to-many relationships with a third table. In a many-to-many relationship, a record in Table A can have many matching records in Table B, and a record in Table B can have many matching records in Table A. This type of relationship is only possible by defining a *junction table* whose primary key consists of two fields: the key fields from both Tables A and B. Figure 21.2 shows an example of this type of relationship.

FIG. 21.2

The Order Details is the junction table.

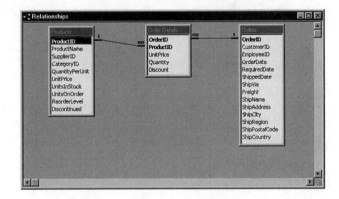

In this example, the Orders and the Products tables have a many-to-many relationship that's defined by creating two one-to-many relationships to the Order Details table. Each record in the Orders table can have many matching records in the Order Details table. This is because each order (one record in the Orders table) will have multiple products sold (each represented by a record in the Order Details table).

In turn, each record in the Products table can have many matching records in the Order Details table. This is because each product item (one record in the Products Table) will be sold more than once (assuming there is more than one in the inventory), so each product item will have many matching records in the Order Details table.

One-to-One Model

A one-to-one model dictates that each record in Table A can have only one matching record in Table B, and each record in Table B can have only one matching record in Table A. Figure 21.3 is an illustration of this type of relationship. A one-to-one relationship is created if both of the related fields are primary keys or have unique indexes.

This type of relationship is not very common, because most information related in this way would be in one table. However, one might use this one-to-one relationship model to divide a table for security reasons as in our example. The client fields that are sensitive such as credit limit, discount, and so on are stored in a separate table named Client Private. This enables you to password-protect the Client Private table and keep prying eyes out. The client fields that are not sensitive are stored in another table. This table (Clients) can be accessed by anyone for purposes of mailing labels and the like.

Part

IV

Ch

21

FIG. 21.3

The information on the clients is divided into two tables.

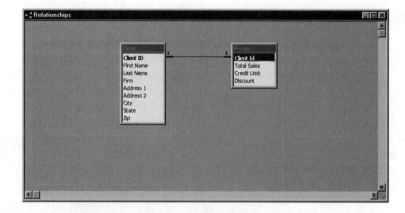

Another reason to use this type of relationship model would be to divide a very large table into two tables. Sometimes when tables contain many fields, dividing the overloaded tables into separate tables enhances database performance.

Table Relationships

In Access, table relationships are created, modified, and viewed in the Relationships window. In this section, we will create each of the previously mentioned relationship types.

Because one-to-many relationships are the most popular, we will create one in the first example in this section. To create any relationship, you must first open the Relationships window by selecting Relationships from the Tools menu. Figure 21.3 shows the open Relationships window.

In this example, we will add both the databases shown in the Show Table dialog box in Figure 21.4. Because our employees in the Employee table work in various departments that are represented in the Department table, we will link the two tables together. At this point, we drag the field Department Name from the Department table and drop it on the Department field in the Employees table. Figure 21.5 shows the resulting window.

FIG. 21.4

If there are no previous relationships in your database, the Show Table dialog box pops up when you first enter the Relationships window.

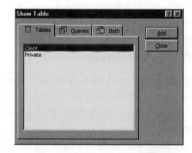

FIG. 21.5

The Relationship Editor pops up after you drag and drop the field.

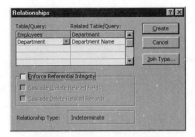

Now select the Enforce Referential Integrity box and click Create. A one-to-many relationship has been created. Figure 21.6 shows how the relationships between these two tables look.

FIG. 21.6

Notice that the line in between the tables shows the type of join that has been created.

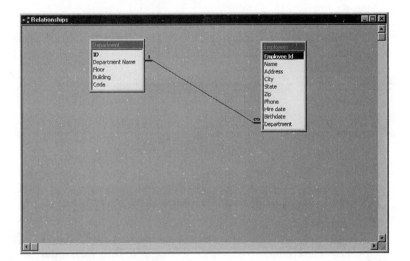

N O T E In this example, we checked the Enforce Referential Integrity box. *Referential Integrity* is a system of rules that is particular to Access. This system of rules is used to ensure that relationships between records in related tables are valid, and that you don't accidentally delete or change related data in the database. This means that if a value is entered on the many side of the enforced relationship without an existing, corresponding value on the one side, Access will prevent the record from being updated or added.

Also, if a related value in a record is modified or deleted from the one side of the relationship and Cascade Updates or Deletes has been selected, any related records on the many side will be modified or deleted, respectively. ▇

Creating a many-to-many relationship requires the use of a junction table. The classic example of this is the Order and Product tables with an Order Details table acting as the junction table. Figure 21.7 shows the Relationships window with the three tables unlinked.

Part
IV

Ch
21

FIG. 21.7

At this point, you link the Orders and the Products tables to the Order Details table.

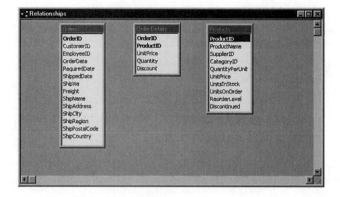

The first step to create this many-to-many link is to link the OrderID field. Drag the OrderID field from the Orders table to the OrderID field in the Order Details table. Figure 21.8 shows the setting that you would use in this link.

FIG. 21.8

Here are the appropriate settings for a join of this type.

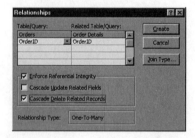

The next step is to create the link between the Products table and the junction table (Order Details). The Product ID field is the linking field. Drag the ProductID field from the Products table to the ProductID field in the Order Details. Figure 21.9 shows the settings for this join.

FIG. 21.9

This many-to-many link also uses Referential Integrity.

Now a many-to-many relationship exists between the Orders and Products tables. Remember that in the junction table, both of the fields that are linked to the other tables must be indexed. Figures 21.10 and 21.11 show the field settings for the OrderID and the ProductID fields in the Order Details table, respectively.

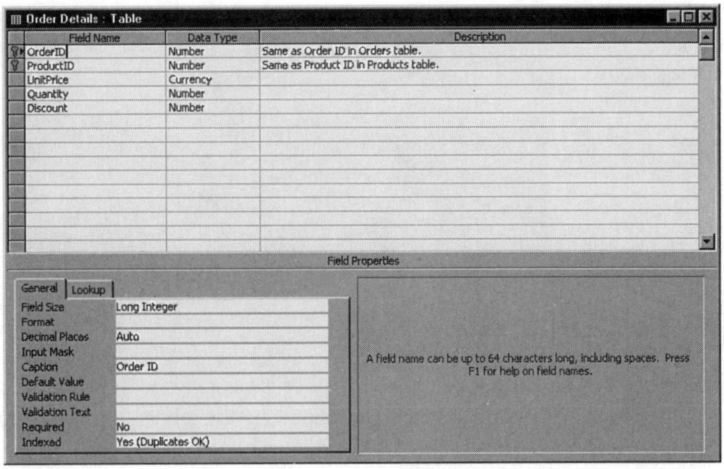

FIG. 21.10

These are the settings for the OrderID field.

FIG. 21.11

And these are the settings for the ProductID field.

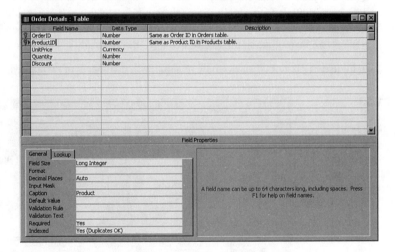

Notice in Figures 21.10 and 21.11 that both fields are designated as Primary keys. This is done automatically when Access realizes that the table is a junction table.

The final type of join that we are going to explore in this section is the one-to-one relationship. To create a one-to-one join between two tables, we will drag the Client ID field from the Client table onto the Client ID field in the Client Private table. Figure 21.12 shows the settings for this join.

This one-to-one join enables you to separate the information on the clients into two categories: public and private. The private table can be password-protected to prevent unauthorized access.

FIG. 21.12

Check the Enforce
Referential Integrity box
for this one-to-one join.

Multiple Table Queries

Another way tables can be linked together is via a *query*. By adding more than one table to a
query, you can create a powerful link between the tables. In this section, we explore some
queries where multiple tables are used.

Queries create table-like dynasets that can be treated like tables. *Dynasets* combine fields and
data from multiple forms into a single dynamic spreadsheet. It is considered *dynamic* because
any changes made to the data in a dynaset are reflected in the corresponding table. Forms and
reports can be built upon these multiple table queries rather than upon the tables themselves.

In Figure 21.13, notice an example of a query that consists of two tables.

FIG. 21.13

When two or more
tables are used in a
query, Access will
automatically display
any existing relation-
ships between the
tables.

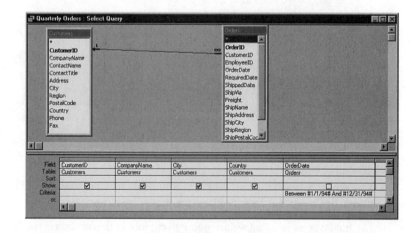

When two or more tables are used in a query, data from any table can be selected or filtered
based on selection criteria from any of the other tables. In the previous example, the
OrderDate field from the orders table has the following selection criterion:

```
Between #1/1/94# And #12/31/94#
```

This selection criterion will filter the data that both tables will produce in the query to the
orders that fall between the dates specified. This is how using multiple tables in a query
enables you to create powerful database queries.

In the next example, we will look at a larger multiple table query. Figure 21.14 shows a query with six tables used to bring data from the various tables together to create an invoice.

FIG. 21.14
Some multiple table queries are used just to bring related data together from various tables with no selection criteria.

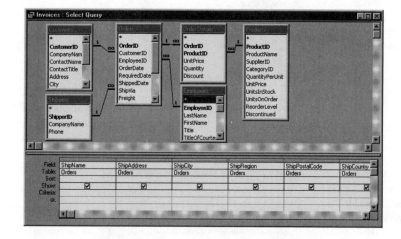

This query brings the necessary fields from all six tables together so a form or a report could be built. The relationships that exist between the tables create the selection criteria. If no relationships exist, they must be added manually to the query, or the data from the different tables will not be matched correctly. For example, the CustomerID field links the Orders and the Customers tables together so that for each record in the query the correct customer and order are together.

Multiple Table Forms

If your design doesn't call for a query to bring fields from multiple tables together for the purpose of building a form, you can add fields from multiple tables to your form. When you create a form, Access will ask you for a form or a query from which to build the form. Figure 21.15 shows this New Form dialog box.

FIG. 21.15
There is no ability from this dialog box to initially base your form off of multiple tables.

Part
IV

Ch
21

As a matter of practice, you should select the table or query that has the majority of the fields that you are planning to use. After the form is created, you can add fields from other tables via the Expression Builder. Figure 21.16 shows the basic form with a text box field being created.

FIG. 21.16

Adding a text box and assigning the control source to field in another table is a way of linking that information to this form.

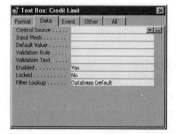

In the Control Source property field, click the ... button to display the Expression Builder, which enables you to select a field from any table in the database. Figure 21.17 shows the Expression Builder listing the fields from another table in this example database.

FIG. 21.17

The Expression Builder assigns the field to the text box's Control Source field.

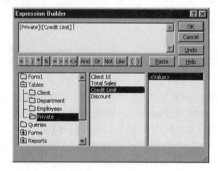

Because the tables in this example are linked with a one-to-one relationship, the link with Referential Integrity will keep the Credit Limit field in sync with the other fields in our form.

Because forms are widely used for input purposes, forms based on multiple tables can be used to input data across multiple tables. For example, if you have a form designed to input basic client information into a client database, you could add some additional fields from another table and instantly add greater functionality to the existing form. Now this one form is used to enter data in two tables, cutting data entry time and possibly eliminating the need for another input form.

Multiple Table Reports

The method of using multiple tables in reports is the same as in forms (assuming, of course, that you are not basing the report on a query). Figure 21.18 shows the dialog box that you use to choose the table or query to base your report on.

After you have based your report on a table and you have created its basic layout, you create a field on your report and assign its control source to the desired table and field via the Expression Builder.

Figure 21.19 shows the Credit Limit field in the report after a control source has been assigned.

FIG. 21.18

As in with forms, you can only select one table from this dialog box.

FIG. 21.19

The Expression Builder assigns the field and table to the control source of the field on the report.

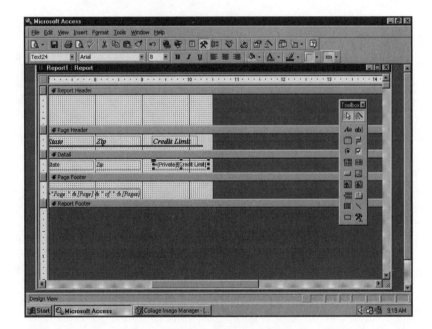

As in forms, the link between the tables keeps the data in sync. This is assuming that the link uses Referential Integrity.

Using multiple tables in reports enables you to create reports that "pull" data together for comparison purposes. In relational databases, data is stored into various tables organizing it into topics. For example, in a client database the following tables may be created:

Name:	Name and address information
Financial:	Financial and credit information
History:	Purchasing history

A multiple table report that collects data from all three of these tables can provide useful management reports.

Relational databases offer you the ability to correctly divide the data in your database into tables. Building these multiple tables and the relationships between them is a very important part of database development. ●

CHAPTER 22

Macros

Create and modify macros

This section discusses the creation of macros and the use of conditions within macros. Additionally, it covers the use of macro names.

Refer to controls from within macros

Learn about the proper syntax in referring to controls within the body of a macro.

Use macros in forms and reports

Explore ways to initiate a macro from within a form and a report.

This chapter explores the use of macros in Access 97. After you've set up your tables, forms, and reports, you may want to automate your database or create a custom action for a control. There are two ways of accomplishing automation or custom actions: VBA procedures and macros. Deciding which to use depends on several variables. In the majority of situations, you will find that macros are quicker to build and require less debugging than VBA procedures.

Macros can handle the simpler operations or control actions, and VBA procedures are used to handle the more advanced operations or control actions. Macros are a lot easier to build than VBA procedures. VBA procedures require the typing of commands and variables in a very accurate manner. Macros, on the other hand, let you create actions by clicking the desired action from a drop-down list. However, in addition to their power limitations, there's also the fact that macros execute much more slowly than VBA procedures.

The next section of this chapter shows you how to create and modify macros in this point-and-click manner. It will also give you a better idea of the capabilities and limitations of macros. ■

Creating and Modifying Access Macros

Before we talk about the actual steps in creating or modifying an Access macro, let's discuss what a macro is and how it works. A *macro* is a set of actions that perform operations, such as opening a form, assigning a value to a field, performing a query, and so on. In a sense, macros are actually little programs performing a series of instructions one after the other. With macros, it is important to remember that each instruction (called an *action*) is executed from the top to bottom, one at a time. So, the order in which you create the instructions will affect the outcome of the macro.

Understanding Macro Sheets

Macros are created and modified from a screen called a *macro sheet*. To get to a macro sheet, you select the Macro tab from the database window then select New. A macro sheet (as shown in Figure 22.1) is a table-like screen where you select the steps of the macro.

FIG. 22.1

The default macro sheet has an Action column and a Comment column.

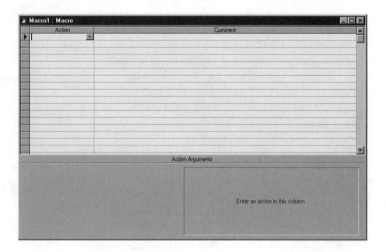

The default macro screen has two columns (later in this chapter in the section "Adding Conditions to Your Macro" you'll see other columns that are sometimes used on the macro sheet). The first default column is called the Action column. In this column, you use the drop-down list to select the actions you want the macro to take. Table 22.1 shows a list of all the possible actions.

Table 22.1   Access 97 Macro Actions

Action	What It Does
AddMenu	Creates a new menu on a custom menu bar.
ApplyFilter	Applies a filter to a table, form, or report to show only certain records.

Action	What It Does
Beep	Causes the computer to beep. Plays the default sound set in the Control Panel.
CancelEvent	Cancels the event that caused the macro to execute.
Close	Closes the specified form or window.
CopyObject	Copies an object to a different database or to a new location within the current database.
DeleteObject	Deletes specified object.
Echo	Shows or hides the results of each step in a macro on the screen.
FindNext	Repeats the previous FindRecord operation.
FindRecord	Finds the record that matches the entered criteria.
GoToControl	Moves the focus to the specified control.
GoToPage	Moves the cursor to the specified page in a multi-page form.
GoToRecord	Moves the focus to the specified record.
Hourglass	Temporarily transforms the mouse cursor to an hourglass to indicate that the macro is running.
Maximize	Maximizes the current window.
Minimize	Minimizes the current window.
MoveSize	Resizes or moves the active window to your specifications.
MsgBox	Displays a message on the screen in a message box.
OpenForm	Opens a specified form.
OpenModule	Opens a Visual Basic module. Modules contain VB procedures.
OpenQuery	Opens a query.
OpenReport	Opens a report. You can specify Print Preview or Print with this action.
OpenTable	Opens the specified table.
OutputTo	Exports data to specified format.
PrintOut	Prints the specified table, form, report, or query.
Quit	Closes Access. Not just the current database, but the whole program.
Rename	Renames the specified object.
RepaintObject	Updates the screen on the specified object.

continues

Table 22.1   Continued

Action	What It Does
Requery	Re-executes the query that is underlying the specified object.
Restore	Returns a minimized or maximized object to its original size.
RunApp	Starts another application and runs it in the foreground.
RunCode	Executes the specified VB function.
RunCommand	Executes the specified menu command.
RunMacro	Runs another macro.
RunSQL	Executes a specified SQL statement.
Save	Saves to disk the specified object.
SelectObject	Selects (or gives focus to) the specified object.
SendKeys	Sends keystokes to a specified program or to Access.
SendObject	Sends the specified object in an e-mail message.
SetMenuItem	Sets the appearance of a menu item as grayed or checked.
SetValue	Sets the value of a control, field, or property.
SetWarnings	Enables you to hide or display all warning boxes.
ShowAllRecords	Removes an applied filter (refer to the ApplyFilter action).
ShowToolBar	Shows or hides a specified toolbar.
StopAllMacros	Stops all macros that are currently running.
StopMacro	Stops the current macro.
TransferDatabase	Imports or exports data in another database.
TransferSpreadsheet	Imports or exports data in a specified spreadsheet.
TransferText	Imports or exports text from a text file.

The other default column is the Comment column. This is an optional field. However, I would strongly urge you to use it. Commenting each action of your macro helps in the following ways:

- *Other users can understand what you are doing in your macro.* If you work in a environment where others may be using the database that you are creating or modifying, it will be very helpful for them to see what you are doing or attempting to do in your macro. With each action commented, anyone can read the "plain English" definition of each action and instantly understand the operations being performed by the macro.

- *Comments are a memory jog when you go back to modify old macros.* When you edit a macro that you created a year ago, comments will help you to remember the purpose of each step in the macro.

■ *When you are designing larger macros, comments help you keep your brain on track*. For example, if you have a macro that uses a series of eight SetValue actions, it's just a lot easier to look at the Comment column to find the particular action you're looking for than to click each action and look at the arguments.

In addition to the two default columns, there is another very important area of the macro sheet that you'll use extensively in creating and modifying macros. This is the *argument area*. Each action you specify in an Access macro will have at least one or two arguments. In Figure 22.2, you can see that after we select the OpenReport action, a list of arguments appears in the bottom-left corner of the macro sheet.

FIG. 22.2

Arguments appear in the bottom-left corner of the macro sheet; context-sensitive help text appears in the bottom-right corner.

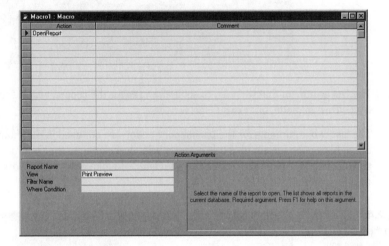

In the case of the OpenReport action, the arguments include Report Name (which report to open), View (whether to print the report or print preview the report), Filter Name (which filter to apply, if any), and Where Condition (an optional SQL Where statement that can be included).

This list of action arguments changes depending on the action that is specified. Notice in Figure 22.3 that the arguments for the SetValue action are different from the arguments that we just looked at in the OpenReport action.

Now, let's walk through the creation process of a typical macro.

Creating a Macro

Let's create a macro that opens a sales report in Print Preview. To start, click the Macros tab in the Database window, and then click the New button. This opens the blank macro sheet (refer to Figure 22.1).

Next, choose the OpenReport action from the Action column. After you have selected the action from the drop-down list, you have to set the arguments for the OpenReport action. The Report Name should be set to Sales Report.

Part

IV

Ch

22

FIG. 22.3

Arguments change depending on the action selected.

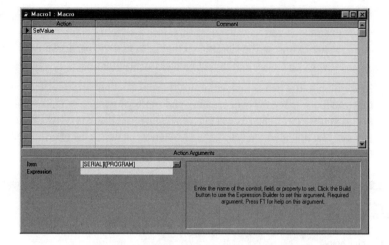

The last argument that we need to set is the View for the report, which can be Print (the default), Design mode, or Print Preview.

The last two arguments for the OpenReport action are not used in our example, so we will skip them. It's a good idea to give this action a brief description in the Comment column (it only takes a second, and you might be thankful later). Just jot down a few words in plain English (see Figure 22.4).

FIG. 22.4

Get into the habit of commenting even your small, one-action macros.

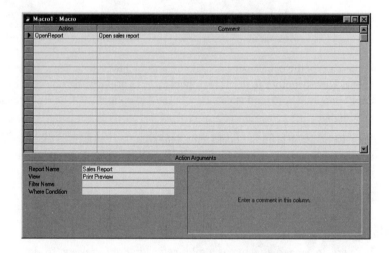

Now the macro is ready to be saved; just close the macro sheet window and you'll be prompted for a name. Of course, you'll want a name that's more descriptive than the default name that Access offers (Macro1, Macro2, Macro3, and so on). The name will appear in the Macros section of the Database window as shown in Figure 22.5.

FIG. 22.5

The name Print Preview Sales Report is a bit more descriptive than anything Access has to offer.

You'll also find the macro name wherever a macro can be used to automate a control. Figure 22.6 shows the macro list that appears when you select the On Click event for a command button.

FIG. 22.6

Check it out—the new macro is listed under the [Event Procedure] option.

It's finished. And you didn't have to type in any arguments or complicated code. In fact, the only typing that occurred was when the comment was entered.

Adding Conditions

Another column you might see on the macro sheet is the *Condition column*. This is where you control whether or not a macro action actually executes in a macro. Without any conditions, a macro executes every action, but you can specify conditions that limit the statements a macro executes.

To activate the Condition column, choose View, Condition. You can enable this column even if you have already begun working on a macro. Figure 22.11 shows the macro sheet with the Condition column activated. Notice that the Condition column always appears to the left of the Action column.

Here's a useful example of a condition. In a database that's used to create invoices for a mail-order cactus business located in Texas, sales tax is only due from customers who are also from Texas.

The following table shows the fields in the database that are important in creating this macro:

[State]	The customer's state
[SalesTaxRate]	The sales tax rate

The first step is to set the value of the [*SalesTaxRate*] field to 0, because we don't want to charge sales tax to Texas residents. Notice that in Figure 22.7 the SetValue action is on a macro sheet that has the Condition column activated.

FIG. 22.7

Start by setting the value of the sales tax to 0 percent.

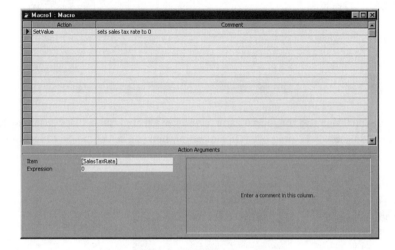

Now, take care of the customers from Texas. In Figure 22.8, notice that in the Condition column of the second SetValue action the expression is [*State*] = "TX". This means the second SetValue action will only execute when the expression [*State*] = "TX" is true.

FIG. 22.8

Condition expressions must evaluate as being either true or false.

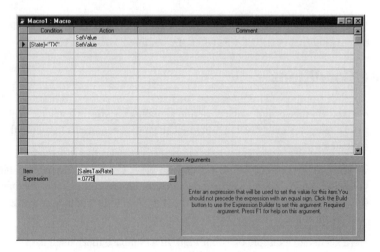

Close and save the macro, and be sure to run it before any invoice total is created. Because this macro changes the value of a field, the change might not be picked up if it is executed after the invoice total is calculated on the form. See "Using Macros in Forms and Reports" later in this chapter to learn about the placement of macros in forms.

Assigning Macro Names

The other option column in a macro sheet is the *Macro Name column*. Figure 22.9 shows a macro sheet with the Macro Name column and the Condition column activated.

FIG. 22.9

The Macro Name column will always appear as the leftmost column.

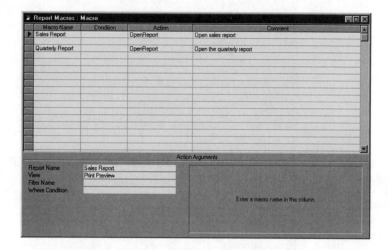

The Macro Name column enables you to group macros together (activate it by choosing View, Macro Names). As you can imagine, a large database with many forms and reports would have dozens of macros. If each of these macros had its own macro name, the list of macros would be overwhelming. To avoid macro-shock, group the macros together. The Macro Name column lets you create one macro sheet that contains all macros for a form. Each macro has its own Macro Name on the macro sheet, but you can save the macro sheet under its own name. With macro names in use, the macro still executes top to bottom. However, the macro begins on the same line as the macro name and ends at the next macro name or an empty line in the macro sheet.

For example, you can create a macro sheet that contains all the macros that run under a form. Figure 22.10 shows a form named Report Menu, with command buttons that produce the various reports.

With a total of six macros behind the buttons on this form, we will create a macro sheet called Report Menu that contains six macro names that correspond to the six report producing buttons on the form. Figure 22.11 shows the completed macro sheet with the six macro names.

The macro sheet is saved and named "Report Menu" because it contains all the macros for that form. The macro names in the macro sheet follow the format:

```
macro sheet name.macro name
```

For example, `Report Menu.CustList`.

Figure 22.12 shows how this naming convention looks in the `Click On` event of a command button.

FIG. 22.10
Each button on this form has a macro defined in the Click On event.

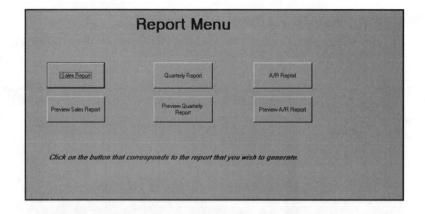

FIG. 22.11
Each button on the Report Menu form refers to one of the macro names on this Report Menu macro sheet.

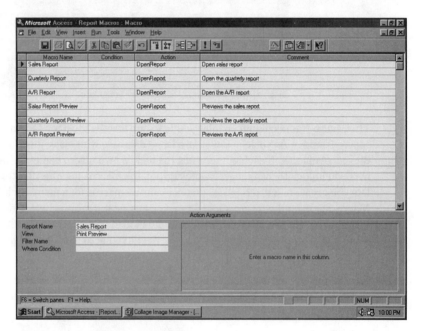

FIG. 22.12
The macro names appear in the drop-down list.

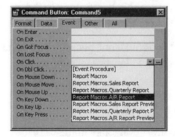

This is a great way to stay organized, for yourself or anyone else who works with your macros.

Manipulating Rows in the Macro Sheet

The macro sheet is a lot like a datasheet, and it has the ability to add, delete, and move rows of actions. In Figure 22.13, notice that the left edge of the sheet offers you a way to select rows.

FIG. 22.13

When you're working in a macro sheet, you can select rows of actions to delete or move.

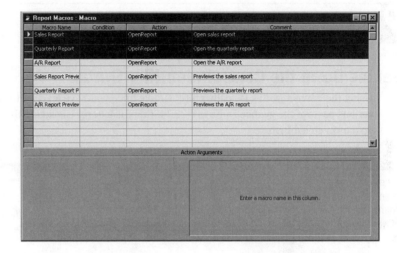

Select a row (or multiple rows) and then perform the function you need: Delete by pressing the Delete key, insert rows by pressing the Insert key, or move rows by dragging and dropping them to their new position on the macro sheet.

CAUTION

Unlike a datasheet, the changes you make aren't saved until you specifically save the macro again. This is an important difference to keep in mind when editing macros.

Referring to Controls from Within Macros

You'll probably find yourself using the SetValue action more than any other. You can use it to assign a value to a field on a form, and when you're working with forms, you have to refer to the control on the form in the correct manner. If you don't, weird things can happen.

For example, if your macro opens a form, you might think of that newly opened form as the current form (it probably even has the focus to reinforce your thinking). Well, your logic is fine, but Access doesn't use the same logic. Access thinks that the form that launched that macro is the current form, and doesn't even care which form has the focus. So if you make an assignment with the SetValue action and you use a reference to the current form, you have to understand the Access definition of current form. Refer to the one Access wants to call current or your macro might crash (or, at best, values will be assigned incorrectly).

Another thing to keep in mind when assigning values to multiple forms is that the form you refer to in a control must be open. The only sure-fire way to take care of this is to open the form in your macro before the SetValue action.

 If you don't want forms popping up on the screen and confusing your database users, you can set the visible property of the form to No when you're opening them in your macro.

Breaking Down the Control Identifier Syntax

Using the correct syntax is really pretty simple once you have learned the meaning of the various parts of the syntax. In Figure 22.14, there is a SetValue action that refers to a Date field on a form called Invoice.

FIG. 22.14

Using the correct syntax in referring to a control on a form is the trickiest part of working with macros.

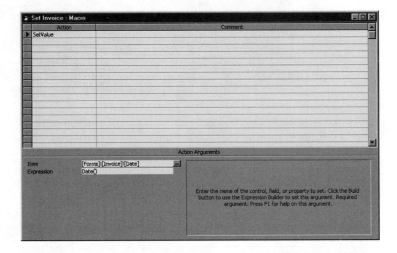

Let's break apart the syntax used in the following control reference that was used in Figure 22.14:

[Forms]![Invoice]![Date]

Name	Description
[Forms]	The form list in the current database
[Invoice]	The name of the form that houses the control we want to reference
[Date]	The control that we want to change the value of

The ! that appears between the different parts of the control reference indicates that the part that follows is a user-defined item. In this case, the form and the control are user-created.

So, to refer to a control called Report Date on a report called AR, you would use the following syntax:

[Reports]![AR]![Report Date]

Now that the syntax is established, let's look at a shortcut.

Using the Expression Builder

Access 97 has a utility that helps you build the correct syntax when you are creating a control reference. You can start the Expression Builder by clicking the Build button next to an argument field. Figure 22.15 shows the Expression Builder, which launches as a result of clicking the Build button next to the Item field.

FIG. 22.15

The Expression Builder can be found throughout Access.

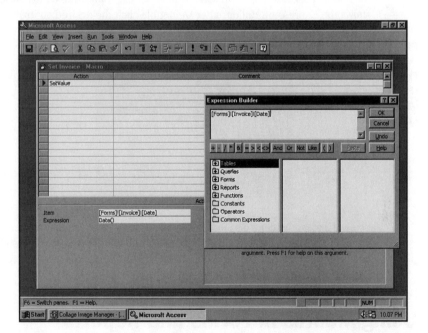

The top pane in the Expression Builder is where the expression or control reference is built. The bottom-left pane has a list of the various components of the database. As you select a component—for example, the plus sign in front of Forms—a tree expands to show you either the loaded forms or all the forms in the database. In Figure 22.16, we selected the Report Menu form and the bottom middle pane of the Expression Builder shows a list of controls on that form.

FIG. 22.16
The bottom middle pane of the Expression Builder lists all the controls for the selected form.

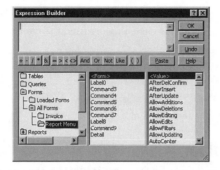

If we were assigning a value (using the `SetValue` action in the macro that launched the Expression Builder) to the `Label0` control on this form, we would double-click the `Label0` control in the middle pane and the Expression Builder would "build" the control reference. Figure 22.17 shows the Expression Builder after we double-click the desired control.

FIG. 22.17
The top pane in the Expression Builder shows the correct control reference to the `Label0` control.

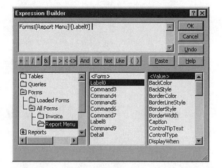

You can accept the control reference by clicking OK, and the control reference appears in the argument field that launched the Expression Builder. The Expression Builder can help you build the correct control reference, and it returns you, as does the macro builder, back to the simpler world of point and click.

Using Macros in Forms and Reports

A macro doesn't do anything if it is never launched. In this section, you'll find some examples of using macros in forms and reports.

Generally, an *event* triggers the launch of a macro. Picking the correct event to launch your macro can make all the difference between your database application working or not.

To launch a macro with a command button on a form, you create a *button*. Access 97 automatically launches the Command Button Wizard, if Control Wizards are turned on (see Figure 22.18).

FIG. 22.18

Choose a category and an action in this dialog box.

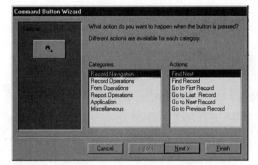

To assign a macro to a control button, follow these steps:

1. Select Miscellaneous from Categories.
2. Select Run Macro from Actions.
3. Press Next; the next wizard screen appears.
4. Select a macro name. (Figure 22.19 shows a list of macros.)
5. Press Next; the next wizard screen appears.
6. Select a text or picture, and press Next (the next wizard screen appears).
7. Name the button.
8. Press Finish.

FIG. 22.19

Select the macro you want to assign to the button.

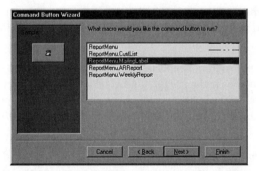

The macro will be launched when a user clicks the button. Understandably, this is a very popular way to launch a macro, because a user just has to decide when a function or process should take place. This makes sense when the process is printing reports or opening forms.

However, there are going to be times when you don't want the user to decide when to launch a function or process. For example, in the macro that checked to see if a customer was from Texas or not, it would be foolish to let a user decide whether to run the process. It's far better to run it from an event that is automated.

Luckily, you can assign the Sales Tax macro to a control on the invoice form. Figure 22.20 shows the On Exit event of the Zip Code control with the Sales Tax macro being assigned.

FIG. 22.20

The On Exit event executes when the control loses the focus.

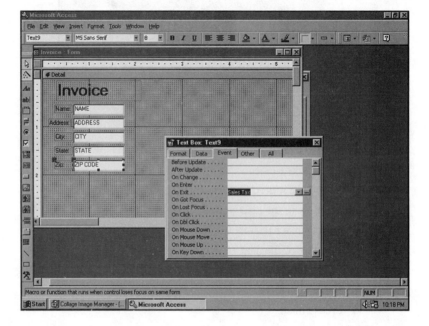

With the macro assigned to the last field in the customer information area of our invoice form, the macro is launched and the appropriate sales tax is assigned without any participation from the user.

You can also launch a macro from a report event. In the example, when the invoice report runs, the user has to load invoices in the printer. It's a good idea to remind the user with a message box, so you avoid the chance of printing invoices on checks or plain paper that might be in the printer. Figure 22.21 shows the properties for an invoice report to which such a macro can be assigned.

To build this macro, click the Builder button and select the Macro Builder (which is a blank macro sheet). Set the action to MsgBox and enter the message in the argument field (see Figure 22.22).

Close the macro sheet to assign the macro to the On Open event of the Invoice report.

Building macros "on-the-fly" is a practical way of creating macros. However, they may not be very organized when you are finished building your database. So, if you're creating a large database that will have lots of macros, it's better to create your tables, forms, and reports first, and then create and assign your macros.

FIG. 22.21

The list of the possible events for a report.

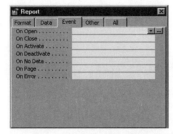

FIG. 22.22

Use the MsgBox action to display a Message Box on the screen.

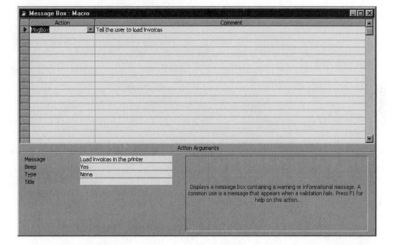

Microsoft Outlook

23   Customizing Views   465

24   Integrating the Outlook Elements   493

25   More Power with Exchange Server   513

CHAPTER 23

Customizing Views

The way information displays in any of the Outlook Information Viewers (the display of a folder's contents) is totally configurable, and the choices for structuring views are enormous. The ability to realign information is important when you need to set priorities, create reports, or just get your daily work done.

You can use these features to establish permanent views of any folder, including folders you create for yourself or those you'll share with other users.

In this chapter, we'll look at some of the permutations and combinations available as you arrange data, fields, and other elements in an Information Viewer for a folder. ■

Sort the items

You can sort, subsort, and continue to subsort using the displayed fields or undisplayed fields. There's a rich variety of elements to choose from as you arrange the items in your viewer.

Group the items

Grouping lets you sort and then group the sorted items according to criteria you set. This is extremely useful when seemingly unconnected items have a common thread.

Filter the items

Use the elements attached to items to set up a display that acts as a report.

Change or add to the built-in views

You can change any of the views that are preconfigured for a folder's Information Viewer, or add your own design as a new built-in view.

Create and manipulate folders

Create your own folders, design the views, and move items into them.

Create custom fields

Invent fields to display information not available in any defined field for the folder.

Understanding the Elements of a View

A *view* is a method of displaying items; the Information Viewer for each of the Outlook folders has a set of standard views that are available on the toolbar. In addition, you can design your own view for a quick look at items under special conditions, and you can name and save any view you design.

All views have several things in common:

- A *view type*, which is the form of a view. There are five view types: Table, Timeline, Card, Day/Week/Month, and Icon.
- *Fields*, which are the containers for data. Fields have labels and contain data specific to that label.
- An *order of display*, which can range from random to a carefully ordered scheme that is sorted on multiple levels.
- *Display attributes* such as fonts, font sizes, and color.

By now you should have seen the standard default views for the Information Viewer for each of the Outlook folders, so it's unnecessary to go over the elementary intelligence. We'll start by manipulating the views using the Sort, Group, Group by Box, and Filter features in Outlook. Then we'll examine ways to change the contents and options for the views in the Current View box on the toolbar.

The most important thing to know about configuring the display of items in an Outlook Information Viewer is that your configuration changes apply only to the current folder and the current view for that folder. This gives you a great deal of power to configure Outlook exactly as you need it.

Sorting the View

You can sort items that are displayed in a Table, Card, or Icon view (the date-related views, Timeline, and Day/Week/Month cannot be sorted). You'll find that most of the time you'll use Table view when you want to sort.

 In a multi-column Table view, if some columns are not wide enough to display the entire contents of a line, just move your pointer to the right separator line on the column heading bar. When the pointer changes to a double-headed arrow, double-click. This is faster than dragging the separator bar. In fact, double-clicking the separator bar for any column changes the column width to the size necessary to accommodate the widest item in the column. You cannot change the width of columns that contain icons.

Sorting by Displayed Columns

The quickest sort maneuver is to click a column heading. The table sorts by that column. Click again to reverse the order.

To subsort by another column, hold down the Shift key and click the second column. To reverse the sort order of any column included in a multi-column sort, use the Shift key (clicking without the Shift key will sort the table by that column alone).

N O T E The Information Viewer for each Outlook folder has its own default sort criteria for Table view:

- Contacts Sort by File As
- Inbox Sorts by Received Date (Last Date First)
- Tasks Has No Default Sort Criteria
- Journal Sorts by Date (Last Date First)
- Calendar Sorts by Date (First Date First)
- Deleted Items sorts by Received Date (last date first) and defines Received Date as the date the item was placed in the Deleted Items folder. ■

Sorting by Any Available Field

There are many more fields attached to an item than are displayed on the viewer. You can sort by any of them with the Sort dialog box that you get to via the Sort command on the View menu. When the Sort dialog box appears, it displays the current sorting scheme (see Figure 23.1).

FIG. 23.1
Change the default sort field and add subsorts with the Sort dialog box.

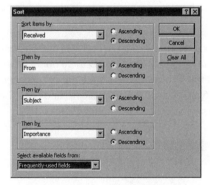

Use the drop-down lists to select fields for sorting or subsorting. The fields that display in the dialog box are from the set of fields named Frequently-Used, but you can choose any other field set from the Select box at the bottom of the dialog box.

Part
V

Ch
23

N O T E   Outlook provides a great many fields for the various items, and there is a set of fields most frequently used (named the Frequently-Used set). You can use other field sets to add less frequently used fields to your selection list. Most of the field sets are connected to a particular Outlook folder (for instance, document fields, task fields, and so on). Each field set also includes the fields that were selected for the Frequently-Used set. However, you'll find that many of the fields not included in the Frequently-Used set are available only if you're connected to a network that uses Microsoft Exchange Server. See Chapter 25, "More Power with Exchange Server," for information about using Outlook with Exchange Server. ■

Creating a New View from the Sort Scheme

There are some sort schemes that seem so important and useful that you'll want to use them constantly. You can do that by replacing an existing view's sort with your own, or by modifying an existing view and giving it a name so you can return to it whenever necessary.

One of the best examples of this, in my opinion, is the way Outlook handles Contacts. For any number of valid reasons, people need to sort this list by City, State, or even Zip Code ("Hey Sam, I need to know which regional reps are assigned to which customer contacts to invite them to the reception at the convention, so print me the list sorted by state").

You can't. At least not using the standard tools. You cannot click a column on any of the views available in the Contacts Information Viewer to sort by City, State, or Zip. If you bring up the Sort dialog box, you cannot find City, State, or Zip in the Frequently-Used set of fields. You're fooled for a minute by the possibilities you sense in a view named Location, but it turns out that Outlook means "country."

By default, in all Contacts views, Outlook sees an address as one discrete unit and combines all the address information into that unit. City, State, and Zip do not exist as individual entities. However, the information is on the Contact card, broken out properly (which means you can find a way to get to it). To satisfy your curiosity, open a card and click the Address button. Then take a look at the Check Address dialog box (see Figure 23.2).

FIG. 23.2

Finding fields that don't exist in the standard views is both frustrating and encouraging.

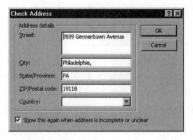

You can create your own view with the fields that you need to sort the items more efficiently. If you don't particularly need the Contacts database sorted this way, there might be some other missing ingredient in another Outlook folder—the steps you take to remedy this are the same:

1. Bring up the Sort dialog box from the View menu.

2. Create your sort scheme. When you get to a sort that requires an unavailable field, choose the appropriate field set from the Select box at the bottom of the dialog box.

   The field set you select is not global for the dialog box. You can select a different field set for each level of the sort (see Figure 23.3). This is a very powerful feature.

FIG. 23.3
Each of the sort fields are from different field sets.

3. Choose OK when you have finished establishing your sort criteria. For each field you've used that is absent from the view, you are given an opportunity to add it to the view (which is usually a good idea).

The display changes to include the new sort fields and is sorted according to your scheme. You can view or print it as you need to.

TROUBLESHOOTING

When you add fields to a view, you can end up with a display that is almost impossible to read. The new fields are columns, which will probably make the Information Viewer so crowded that you'll have to use the scroll bars to navigate through all the columns. The reduction in efficiency and productivity can be severe.

The first thing to try is to close up all the column widths. This is, at best, a semi-solution because you probably won't be able to see enough of the data in any column to make sense of it. (Remember that the real efficiency in an Information Viewer is the at-a-glance information you receive. Having to stretch the columns and reduce them again every time you have to see a data item kills all of that productivity.) You can get rid of columns you aren't using; instructions for that (along with other information about designing your own displays) are found in the section "Designing Folder Views" later in this chapter.

Once you've created your new view, you have to make a decision about its future:

■ You can discard it once used if you think you won't need the same configuration again.

■ You can save it with a new name for future use.

■ You can save it as a new configuration of the original view you used to build it (take this route only if you feel the original view isn't useful).

To make the choice, choose any other view from the Current View drop-down list on the toolbar. As soon as you make this move to change views, Outlook presents those choices to you (see Figure 23.4).

FIG. 23.4

After you've finished the work, you can make it permanent.

If you decide to save the new view with its own name, choose a name that reflects the contents (as a reminder to yourself) and specify its use (see Figure 23.5).

FIG. 23.5

An explicit name will be helpful when you look at the drop-down list a month from now.

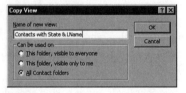

Now that the view is saved, you can sort it any way you need to and use it the same way you use the built-in views.

A Few Things to Remember About Sorting

- The fields available for use change according to the Outlook folder you're working on.

- A field does not have to be displayed on the Information Viewer to be used as a sort field. However, if you do select a field that isn't displayed, Outlook asks if you want to show it. Answer Yes to create a new column for the field.

- If you're sorting the Inbox and the Subject field is part of your sorting scheme, the prefixes in the Subject field (RE: for replies and FW: for forwarded mail) are not used during the sort—only the text in the field is used.

- To clear the sort scheme, choose Clear All in the Sort dialog box. The items don't rearrange themselves, but any items added thereafter are displayed in a "first come, first served" basis.

- When you sort a view, your sorting scheme remains in effect until you sort that view again. The sort survives a shutdown and restart of Outlook.

Grouping the View

Grouping adds another dimension to sorting in that Outlook provides some additional display elements. When you group items, the sorting scheme you design displays along with headings for each sort level. A *grouped display* is, in effect, an outline. It can be expanded and collapsed (by clicking the plus and minus symbols) to give you control over the number and level of headings you see at any time (see Figure 23.6). Grouping is only available for Table and Timeline views.

Part
V
Ch
23

FIG. 23.6

The sorted items are grouped, and there's a heading for each group and subgroup.

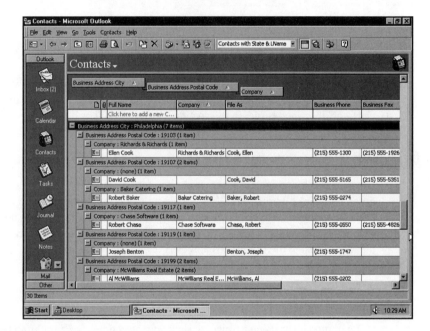

Check out the area over the column headings, where the fields used to sort and subsort are represented graphically with buttons:

- Hold down the Shift key and click any button to reverse the sort order for that field.
- Drag a field to the left or right to change the grouping order.
- Drag a column heading up to add it to the sort for the grouped items. The placement (left to right) indicates its sorting level.

Grouping is facilitated through the Group By command on the View menu (see Figure 23.7).

The Group By dialog box works similarly to the Sort dialog box. One important difference is the presence of a check box for each group that indicates whether or not you want to show the field in the view (which means a missing column would be added and an existing column deleted).

FIG. 23.7
Group items to sort
them with headings that
proclaim what they have
in common.

After you've grouped the items in a view and moved to the Current View box to change the
view, Outlook offers the same options—the three choices for changing or discarding your new
view—as described earlier in the section "Sorting the View."

Applying Group by Box

Group by Box is a graphical shortcut method for achieving grouping. It's a way to sort and
group items in an Information Viewer by employing graphical tools and using only the fields
available in the current display. When the groups are formed, however, none of the groups are
expanded, and you only see the titles, which look like gray boxes (hence the name). Click the
plus signs next to the titles to expand the boxes and see the items. Like grouping, Group by
Box is available for Table and Timeline views.

To use this feature, click the Group by Box button on the toolbar (or choose Group by Box
from the View menu):

1. Immediately, using a graceful, slick animated process, the column heading bar slides
   downward to create a space between it and the banner at the top of the Information
   Viewer. A note appears in the new space, instructing you to drag a column header to the
   space in order to group the items by that column's field (see Figure 23.8).

2. As soon as you begin to drag the column header you want to use for the first (or only)
   level of grouping, two facing arrows appear in the space to guide you. They're red—
   you can't miss them—and they want you to drop the column between the arrows (see
   Figure 23.9).

3. Release the mouse button; the items are grouped by the field you chose (see Figure
   23.10).

Each box has a label indicating the field name, the selected data for that field, and the number
of items included in the group. You can expand the group or drag another column heading up
to create a subgroup.

FIG. 23.8
Outlook has opened a space so you can use the drag-it-yourself method of creating groups.

Space created by Outlook—

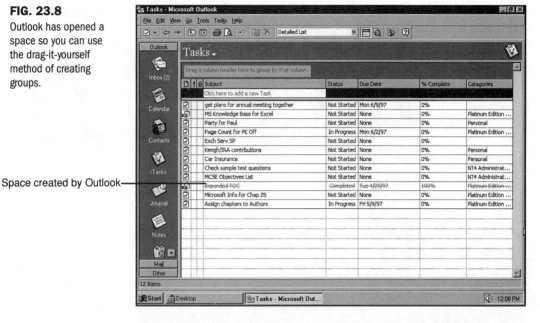

FIG. 23.9
Head for the arrows with the field of choice.

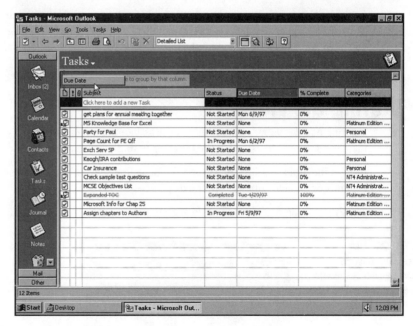

FIG. 23.10

The items are grouped by boxes as soon as you create a grouping field.

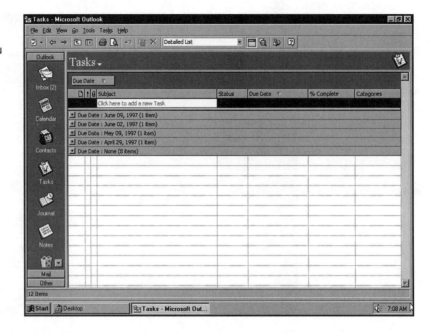

Group by Box is efficient (as long as the only fields you need are the ones that are displayed), because as soon as the grouping is accomplished, it's very easy to move to exactly the group you need and expand it. Scrolling through a series of boxes is easier than scrolling through lots and lots of data.

Filtering the View

Filtering a folder view is the same process as filtering a database when you need reports. You merely set criteria to establish the basis for letting data through the filter.

As with the other manipulations for an Information Viewer, you can filter based on displayed columns or on fields not used in the display.

The Filter dialog box is reached through the View menu (see Figure 23.11).

FIG. 23.11

It's easy to create a simple filter by checking against text in the available fields.

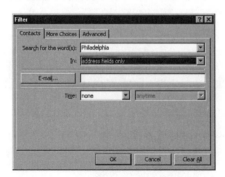

The More Choices tab is essentially for creating Read/Unread, Attachment/No Attachment filters for the Inbox, but there is also an opportunity to filter on categories (which is more global and can be applied to all the Outlook folders).

The real power is in the parameters available on the Advanced box, which lets you build a list of criteria. Start by selecting a field—every field in the system is available (see Figure 23.12).

FIG. 23.12

The choices are enormous, but they're broken down by category to make it easier to hunt for the field you need.

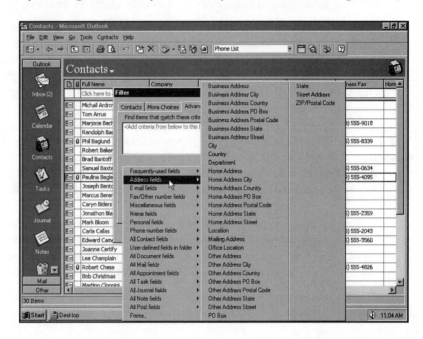

 T I P You can also use any custom fields you've created in the Advanced tab. Information about creating custom fields is found later in this chapter.

After you've selected the field, specify a condition and a value. The conditions that are available are specific to the selected field, and the value depends upon the conditions (some conditions are specific Boolean choices such as exist or not exist, and no value is needed). When you have established the criteria for the filter, add it to the list (see Figure 23.13).

FIG. 23.13

Do you think sales will increase if I send birthday cards to customers?

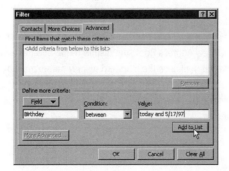

Repeat the process to narrow the criteria as much as you need to:

- The filter that's applied is for all the criteria you set. The criteria list is examined, and filtering is applied from top to bottom. The longer the list, the longer the process takes.

- You can make your filter more flexible by applying different conditions to the same field, or by applying different values to the same conditions. In effect, you build an OR filter.

When your list is complete, choose OK to apply the filter. The items that matched your criteria are displayed, and you can proceed with whatever manipulation you'd planned for them. For instance, in the example used here, I could select all the names in the filtered display, drag them to the Inbox, and automatically create e-mail that says "Happy birthday." Probably not the same task you'd apply, but the functions work the same for more important business procedures.

If you've established a list of criteria in the Advanced tab and the list of displayed items seems shorter than you think it should be, redisplay the Filter dialog box (which is configured to reflect filters applied to the currently displayed Information Viewer). Go to the Advanced tab and highlight the criteria item you think may be responsible for overfiltering. Choose Remove, then choose OK to reprocess the filter.

When you display a filtered list, the words `Filter Applied` appear at the bottom of the Outlook Bar and on the banner of the Information Viewer. This is also true for those built-in views that are filtered. The Inbox, for instance, has a number of built-in filtered views (Unread Messages, Last Seven Days, and so on), as do the Tasks, Journal, and Calendar folders.

Turn off the filter by displaying the Filter dialog box and choosing Clear All.

TROUBLESHOOTING

It's nerve-wracking when you know there are items that match your criteria, but they don't show up in the display after the filter is processed. This occurs most often when searching the Inbox for specific messages, using the To or From fields in the header as part of the criteria. Here's the trouble—the filter is looking for an exact match, and the header does not necessarily have the text you think it does. Remember that your address book doesn't show the e-mail addresses; it shows display names. The fields available in the Filter dialog box are designed to let you click and pick recipients, using an Address Book, so that only display names are available. You cannot filter for real e-mail addresses. Therefore, any external mail that uses real e-mail addresses in the To or From field won't be picked up during the Filter process.

I've solved this problem by entering an e-mail address as a display name in my Address Book when I enter a new Internet Mail address. In my Address Book, the display name and the e-mail address are identical for those items, while internal mail uses the standard display name/mailbox convention formats. If you're connected to Exchange Server, make sure the administrator uses this approach for the Global Address Book. This is one of those problems you have to plan ahead for; it's too late by the time you need to use the Filter function.

Finding Items Anywhere in Outlook

If you use Filter to locate items in order to view them to gain quick information, try Find instead. It's often a better choice for the task. Find gives you more than just the capacity to set criteria and match the items against it:

- You can save the search criteria for any Find process in order to use it again later.
- When you installed Outlook, the Find program on your Start menu was updated to include a submenu item for Outlook. This means you can find information in your Outlook folders even when Outlook isn't running.

Part
V
Ch
23

Use the Find icon on the toolbar, or choose Find from the Tools menu. When the dialog box appears, you can specify the basic parameters for the search:

1. In the Look For box, choose the item type you need (notice that the list offers more than Outlook items—you can search for files).
2. When you select the item type, Outlook automatically chooses a logical location for the search. You can change the location or specify multiple locations by choosing Browse. Then select all the folders you want to include in the search from the Select Folder(s) dialog box (see Figure 23.14). You can also indicate whether or not you want subfolders searched.

FIG. 23.14

Choose all the folders that should be searched for the items you require.

3. Select parameters for the Find operation on the first tab (which is named to match the type of item in the current folder).
4. Use the More Choices tab to narrow the criteria (this tab also changes its options to match the item type).
5. Use the Advanced tab to narrow the search options even more (see the previous discussion on the Advanced tab for the Filter dialog box).
6. Choose Find Now to begin the search. The more narrow you made the specifications, the longer the process takes. The results are displayed below the Find dialog box.

When the results are displayed, you can treat the results window as a mini Information Viewer. Right-click any column heading to see the choices for sorting, grouping, or otherwise manipulating the window (see Figure 23.15). You can also manipulate the individual items—right-click to choose a command from the shortcut menu.

FIG. 23.15

The display window can be manipulated to make using your search results more productive.

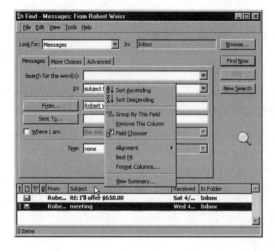

If you want to save the Find parameters, choose Save Search from the File menu. Select a folder and name the search. Searches are saved with an .oss extension (Office Saved Searches).

To use this search again, open Find, then choose Open Search from the File menu. You can also delete the saved search by deleting it when the Open dialog box appears.

Working with Folders

All of Outlook is based on folders. When you display items, the Information Viewer is really a view of the items contained in a folder. The icons on the Outlook Bar represent folders, and different folder icons appear depending on the current Outlook Bar group (Outlook, Mail, or Other):

■ The Folder List icon on the toolbar toggles the folder display off and on.

■ When the folder display is off, the folder name on the banner of the Information Viewer has a down arrow which you can click to see a temporary display of the folder hierarchy—click again to toggle the display off.

 The Outlook folder list is larger, and the type of manipulation you can perform on folders is more extensive if you're connected to Microsoft Exchange Server. Information about using some of those enhanced features is found in Chapter 25, "More Power with Exchange Server."

Adding Folders

As you use Outlook and the standard Outlook folders become crowded, you'll find it's productive to add folders to your Outlook system. You can use them to aggregate items that have some common bond.

The quickest way to add a folder is to decide which folder will be the parent to the new folder and start from there. If you want the new folder at the same hierarchical level as the Outlook folders, use the Personal Folders container as the parent:

1. Right-click the Parent folder and choose Create Subfolder.
2. In the Create New Folder dialog box, enter a name for the folder.

   You can also enter a description for this folder (but if you name the folder specifically enough, you probably won't need a description). The default parent folder (the one you clicked to start this process) is highlighted automatically, but you can select any folder as the parent.
3. Specify whether you want a shortcut icon for this folder on the Outlook Bar.

 TIP Having icons for folders on the Outlook Bar is convenient, but don't overdo it, or else you'll find yourself scrolling so much to find the appropriate icon that you've lost some of the enhanced productivity the icon should have brought you. Personally, a practice I've found useful is to create folders for major projects (usually under the Tasks folder) and place shortcut icons for them on the Outlook Bar. I tend to use that folder a great deal while I'm busy with the project. When the project ends, I delete the shortcut icon, but not the folder.

Moving Items to Folders

Any item in Outlook can be moved to any other Outlook folder (including the folders you've created). Select the item (or multiple items) and click the Move to Folder icon on the toolbar. A drop-down list appears, showing the folders that have already been used as targets for moving items, as well as a Move to Folder command. Until you've moved items around a bit, the drop-down list may not contain the target folder you need, so choose Move to Folder to display the Move Items dialog box (see Figure 23.16). Then select the target folder for the items you want to move.

FIG. 23.16
A click of the mouse transfers an item, or multiple items, into another folder.

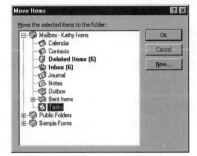

Part **V**

Ch **23**

CAUTION

While dragging is the easy way to move items while you're working in the operating system, or in most Windows applications, it doesn't work in Outlook. Because of the way the folders and features interact with each other, Outlook provides special functions for dragging items, and those functions do not include the normal move or copy procedures. Do not drag items from an Information Viewer to a folder; use the Move to Folder command. Information about the interrelationship features for Outlook folders is in Chapter 24, "Integrating the Outlook Elements."

Archiving Folders

Outlook folders can be *archived*, removing the items of a certain age (which you specify) and transferring them to an archive file (that's file, not folder). In effect, archiving is exporting. By default, all the archived items are placed in that file; there are not separate files for each folder. Archiving can be automatic or manual, depending upon the method that makes you feel most comfortable.

You can protect any individual item from the AutoArchive process by selecting Do Not AutoArchive on the item's Properties dialog box (open the item and choose Properties from the File menu).

By default, automatic archiving is turned on for the system, and most of the Outlook folders have default AutoArchive options set. The folders and the age of the items that are AutoArchived are:

- The Tasks folder, for six-month-old items
- The Journal folder, for six-month-old items
- The Calendar folder, for six-month-old items
- Sent Items, for two-month-old items
- Deleted Items, for two-month-old items

You can change the settings for any of those folders and add AutoArchive settings to other folders, including any you've created.

 The one folder you can't AutoArchive is the Contacts folder. Because there is rarely activity against any item (unless you have a lot of contacts who constantly change phone numbers or addresses), all the items within it would expire and be included in the first AutoArchive. As contacts become obsolete, delete them and they'll be archived from the Deleted Items folder.

Configure AutoArchive   To set or change AutoArchive schedules, use any of several methods to go to the Properties dialog box for the folder:

- Right-click the folder's icon on the Outlook Bar and choose Properties.
- Right-click the banner of the folder's Information Viewer and choose Properties.
- Right-click the folder itself (if Folder view is active) and choose Properties.

Move to the AutoArchive tab (see Figure 23.17).

FIG. 23.17

Establish AutoArchive settings or change the current settings with the Properties dialog box for any Outlook folder.

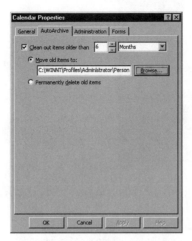

When you create a new Outlook folder, AutoArchive is not turned on; even if the parent folder does have AutoArchiving turned on. There are preconfigured settings, but they are grayed out until you select AutoArchive as an option. By default, new folders are set for AutoArchiving every three months:

1. To turn on AutoArchive (automatic cleaning out of old items), select the Clean Out Items check box. Then specify a number and a unit of measurement (Months, Weeks, or Days).

2. Once you've established the fact that you want to clean out the folder, you must choose the method; select Move Old Items To for archiving, or Permanently Delete Old Items if you don't care about archiving.

3. If you like, you can change the location and name of the archive file for this folder.

Run AutoArchive   AutoArchive activity takes place during the launch of Outlook, at the interval established in the AutoArchive tab of the Options dialog box (Tools menu). By default, this interval is set for 14 days.

The folders are checked and a message is displayed if AutoArchiving is due. You can opt to let it proceed or cancel it.

The date used to decide if an item should be archived is not necessarily the obvious one, such as the received date for a message or the date attached to an appointment. Instead, the last modification date is checked (from the operating system properties for the item). And, tasks are not archived if they are not marked as completed, regardless of their age.

Archive Manually   You can choose Archive from the File menu to archive one or all folders whenever you think it's appropriate (see Figure 23.18).

FIG. 23.18

Clean house whenever you need to.

Select options on the Archive dialog box according to your own priorities. You cannot archive a folder without archiving its child folders.

 TIP If you decide you always prefer to archive manually, turn off the AutoArchive option in the Outlook Options dialog box. If the decision to archive manually affects one particular folder (that gets crowded fast and you get tired of scrolling through the items), turn off AutoArchive for that folder.

Restore Archived Items   Oops, you need some items back—they were archived by mistake. Or, there's some other reason you need to look at older items. Restoring archives is simply a matter of importing the archive file into your Outlook system:

1. Choose Import and Export from the File menu.

2. The Import and Export Wizard launches (see Figure 23.19). Choose Import from a Personal Folder File.

FIG. 23.19

The archive file is a .pst file that you have to import to regain the items in it.

3. Follow the wizard instructions to import the archive file.

Designing Folder Views

You can design your own view for the Information Viewer of any folder you create, or for any existing Outlook folder. There are many ways to accomplish this, and this section covers just a few of the options. Once you understand what has to be done, it will be easy to design and implement a view.

You can add or remove fields in Table or Card view. For a table, fields are columns; for a card, fields are labeled boxes:

■ You can create a view from an existing view by creating a sorting or filtering scheme and saving it under a new view name, or by simply adding fields to an existing view and naming the new view. We've covered these methods earlier in this chapter.

■ You can create a view from scratch.

Creating a View from an Existing View

If you *do* create a view by adding fields, you are also adding columns, so it's likely you have a very crowded Information Viewer. It's probably a good idea to remove some of the columns from that view.

Or perhaps you just want to add or delete columns from an existing view in order to create a view that gives you specific information. There are a number of ways to do this, and a number of dialog boxes that exist for that purpose.

Here are some of the quick methods for creating a new view from an existing one:

■ To delete a column in Table view, right-click its column heading and choose Remove this Column.

■ To add, delete, or change the order of existing columns in Table view, right-click any column heading and choose View Summary. When the View Summary dialog box appears, choose Fields (see Figure 23.20). You can select fields to add or remove, or you can change the order of display. Incidentally, you can get to the same Show Fields dialog box by choosing Show Fields from the View menu.

FIG. 23.20

Add, remove, or change the order of fields/columns in a view.

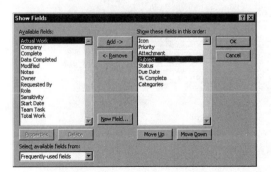

■ To add fields in Table view, choose Field Chooser from the View menu. When the Field Chooser dialog box appears (see Figure 23.21), drag the field you need to the column header row.

FIG. 23.21

The Field Chooser displays all the unused fields.

After you complete the process, save the view with a new name when the Save View Settings dialog box appears. You can, of course, create a sort scheme, filter the items, or group them before saving the new view.

If you plan to make more comprehensive changes, you may find it easier to work with the Define Views dialog box (see Figure 23.22), which is available from the View menu.

FIG. 23.22

All of the existing views for the current folder are available in the Define Views dialog box.

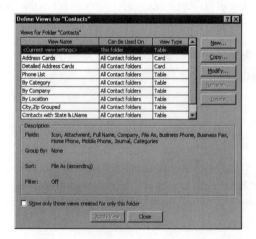

You can select any existing view and modify it. When you select the view, the dialog box displays the current settings for Fields, Groups, Sort, and Filter. Choosing Modify brings up the View Summary dialog box, discussed earlier in the chapter. If you change your mind, use the Reset button to put the view back the way it was.

If you want to build a new view based on an existing view, choose Copy. The Copy View dialog box asks you to give the new view a name and to select its availability:

Part
V

Ch
23

- Available in the current folder, visible to any user
- Available in the current folder, visible only to you
- Available in all child folders of the current folder

Then just make the changes you need to create a new view

Creating a New View from Scratch

The Define Views dialog box also provides a way to create an entirely new view, building it from the ground up:

1. Choose New to begin the process. The Create a New View dialog box requests a name, type, and availability information (see Figure 23.23).

FIG. 23.23

Start building your new view by specifying the basic information.

2. Choose OK to bring up the View Summary dialog box.
3. Select the Fields, Groups, Sorts, and Filters you need for your new view.

The new view appears on the drop-down list of the Current View box on the toolbar. Just as with a built-in view, you can sort it, group it, filter it, and so on.

Creating New Fields

There are several cogent reasons for creating a new field. You might want to enter information in an item but there's no current field for it. Or, perhaps you need a field in an Information Viewer that combines information from two existing fields (and you don't want two columns). You can also create fields that are based on a formula you invent:

- Fields can be created for any Table or Card view.
- Fields you create can only be used in the current folder (you have to create them again if you want a similar field in a different folder).

> **N O T E** While the field exists for the folder, by default it appears only on the view that was current when you created the field. To add the field to other views in the same folder, move to the new view and choose Show Fields from the View menu. Instead of Frequently-Used fields, use the User-Defined Fields in Folder field to find your new field. Or, choose Field Chooser from the View menu, move to User-Defined Fields in Folder, and drag the field to the column header row. ■

Creating a Simple Field

A *simple field* is a field that will hold data that matches the information you need. You need only create it; there are no special steps for formulas or other manipulations. Start in the Show Fields dialog box (from the View menu):

1. Choose New to display the New Field dialog box (see Figure 23.24), and enter a name for this field.

FIG. 23.24

The field name is the label that appears on the form; make it descriptive so users know exactly what information you want entered.

2. Use the drop-down list in the Type field to select a field type.
3. If the field type you select has a variety of choices for formats, choose the appropriate one in the Format box.
4. Choosing OK places your new field in the Show Fields dialog box, and everything proceeds as if you had just added a field to the display.

   Use the Current Fields box on the toolbar to force the Save View Settings dialog box to appear. You can add this field to the current view or create a new view for it.

Using a Simple Field in a Form

Once you create a field for simple data, the view will never have any data in that field if it isn't entered when the original item is created. In order to enter data, you must put the field into the blank form. Except for blank Contact forms, this involves creating a form. The Outlook Contact form has a tab named All Fields. Move to that tab and select User-Defined Fields in this Folder from the drop-down list. When your field appears, enter the data.

For Tasks or Calendar (probably the only folders for which you'll find it necessary to add your own fields), move to the folder for which you've created the new simple field and open a blank form:

1. Choose Design Outlook Form from the Tools menu to see the Design version of the form.

2. Move to a blank tab, which causes the Field Chooser to display. Use the drop-down list at the top of the Field Chooser to select User-Defined Fields in Folder as the field set.

3. Drag the simple field to the tab and place it attractively and tastefully on the page (see Figure 23.25).

Part V Ch 23

FIG. 23.25

The Design version of a form is for tweaking.

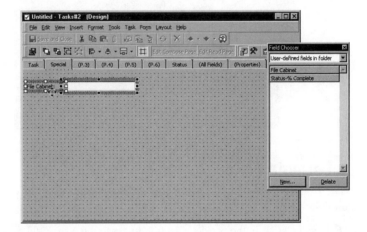

4. Choose Rename Page from the Form menu and give this tab a name (the default name of p.2 isn't terribly useful).

5. Click the Publish Form As button on the toolbar and give this form a name. Then choose Publish In from the Publish Form As dialog box.

6. Place this form in a Forms Library or in a Folder Library:

   - Select Forms Library and then choose Personal Forms to store this form in your mailbox for your own personal use.

   - Select Forms Library and store the form in the Organization Forms Library if you are connected to Microsoft Exchange Server and want the form to be available to all users in the organization.

   - Select Folder Forms Library and choose the appropriate Outlook folder for this form. Personally, I think this is the best choice, so consider this the recommendation and the rest of this section continues as if you made this choice.

7. When you return to the Publish Form As dialog box, choose Publish. Then close the Form and answer Yes to the query "Do you want to save changes?".

The form is installed in the folder you chose. In order to take advantage of the new form, you must use it for creating items instead of the form that appears when you click the New button on the toolbar. Use the menu to the left of the Help menu (which changes its name depending on the current folder) and select the form from the bottom of the menu (see Figure 23.26).

FIG. 23.26
Your new form works just like the original Outlook form.

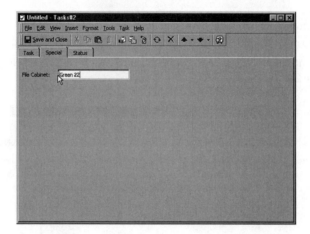

Creating a Formula Field

A *formula field* works by taking existing data and manipulating it, then displaying the results in the new field:

1. Follow the steps in the previous section to get to the New Field dialog box and name the field.

2. Choose Formula for the field type. The last field changes its label from `Format` to `Formula`.

3. You can enter the formula directly into the Formula field, but it's much easier to choose Edit and move to the Formula Field dialog box.

4. Choose Function to select a function for your formula by category.

5. When the function is inserted into the Formula field (see Figure 23.27), substitute arguments within the formula syntax. Unless you have all of the possibilities memorized, you should press F1, then select the function you're working with to see a list of named arguments, along with syntax instructions.

6. Use the Field button to choose any field that is used in the formula (or insert the field name in square brackets).

Close all the dialog boxes by clicking OK, and the new field, displaying the results of the formula, is on the Information Viewer. For example, in Figure 23.28 I used the formula `DateDiff("d",[Sent],Now())`. To display the length of time between the day, I sent a message and the current date.

FIG. 23.27
The formula can be entered with a click of the mouse, then the arguments must be inserted.

FIG. 23.28
This formula is used to determine how long it's been since I sent the message.

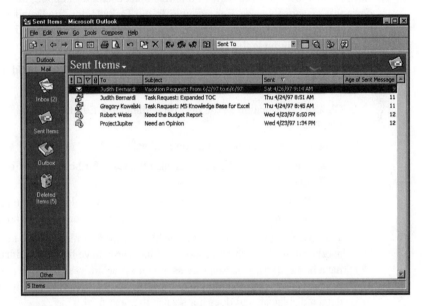

If an error displays, it could mean either that the field that supplies data has none, or that there is something wrong with the formula. If every item displays an error, the odds are the problem is with the formula (although you really could have used a field that nobody bothered to fill out).

Check the field first, then, if necessary, edit your formula:

1. Return to the Show Fields dialog box and remove the field from the displayed field list (removing it returns it to the Available Fields list).

2. Select the field in the Available Fields list and choose Properties to display the formula field.

3. Figure out what is wrong and do it again.

 Depending on the contents of the formula field, you may want to change its appearance in the column. For instance, if the field displays numbers, it's easier to read them if they're right-aligned. To change the alignment, right-click the column heading and choose Alignment from the shortcut menu.

CAUTION
You cannot sort, group, or filter on a formula field.

Creating a Combination Field

A *combination field* takes data from multiple fields and displays it in one column (for Table view) or on a row (for Card view). I find this most useful for keeping the number of columns down to a manageable size. For example, in the Tasks folder, the Detailed List view shows both the status and the percentage of the task that is complete. Combining these related items mean I had one less column in the view.

To establish a combination field, follow the steps to get to the New Field dialog box, then name that field:

1. Choose Combination as the field type, then click Edit to open the Combination Formula Field dialog box.
2. Choose the method of combining field values:
   - Choose Joining Fields to display the value for both fields. For this task, it's the appropriate choice.
   - Choose Showing Only the First Non-Empty Field when you are building a combination field that is looking for data from one field or another.

   This is useful for data that might be in one field for one item and in another field for another item. For example, some Contact cards have business addresses and others have home addresses. Regardless, you need an address in order to send snailmail or packages. The combination field searches in the order you specify, and as soon as it finds data, it displays it and does not search the next field.
3. Click the Field button and choose a field category, then choose the field for the first field in your combination formula. Repeat to add all the fields you need.
4. Click OK until you're back at the view, looking at your new column.

If you used a combination field to replace multiple existing columns, delete the two columns you replaced (or else there isn't much point to your work).

CAUTION
You cannot sort, group, or filter on a combination field.

ON THE WEB

Helpful hints about displaying information in Outlook are available on the Internet by selecting Outlook articles at:

http://www.mpicrosoft.com/kb/

CHAPTER 24

Integrating the Outlook Elements

All of the Outlook elements get along extremely well—they're well suited, well matched, and interact with each other perfectly. Outlook is a model family of interconnected individual units.

It's extremely easy to bring any two Outlook elements together. In fact, most of the time your mouse can do the work.

Each folder in Outlook knows its place, knows the type of item it wants, and automatically welcomes a foreign type of item by converting it.

This chapter covers all the automatic, semi-automatic, and manual ways to merge items from disparate elements. ■

Dragging objects between Outlook elements

You can drag an item from one folder to another and autocreate a new item in the target folder.

Use journal entries to track your work

You can link items to journals in order to keep track of what you've done, with whom, to whom, why, where, and how.

Report by category across all folders

Use categories to link items in different folders to generate global information.

Dragging Objects Between Outlook Elements

You can drag an object from one Outlook folder to another in order to autocreate a new object. The new object matches the item type of the target folder. There are many permutations and combinations available with that statement, and this section covers a number of them.

The beginning of this section is all about dragging e-mail messages to various Outlook folders, because that's the most common interaction for most users. The arrival of a new message frequently kicks off a task, announces an appointment, requires a journal entry, or has some other impact beyond the text of the message. (Of course, those commonly sent messages about personal lunch plans are an exception and rarely require any further action.)

After discussing the effects of dragging messages to Outlook folders, we'll briefly go over some of the other permutations available.

Some Tips About Dragging Objects

There are a few things to know that will make your life easier as you begin to integrate the various Outlook folders by dragging items among them:

- You can drag multiple items from one folder to another, but only one new item will be created.

- If you use the right mouse button to drag an item to a folder, a shortcut menu offers choices about the way the new item is configured.

- If you choose to make the original item an attachment in the new item, you will be increasing the size of the new item.

- If you begin dragging an item and realize the target folder shortcut is not currently visible on the Outlook Bar (perhaps the Mail icons are visible and you need the Contacts shortcut icon), drag toward the appropriate button (Outlook, Mail, or Other) at the top or bottom of the Outlook Bar. As soon as your pointer is over the button, the Outlook Bar changes to reveal those icons. Then continue to drag to the right target icon.

- If you begin dragging and the icon you need is not available because it is above or below the current visible portion of the Outlook Bar, drag toward the scroll arrow. As soon as your mouse is over the scroll arrow, the display will scroll and the target icon will be visible.

- If you change your mind after you've begun a dragging operation, just press the Esc key. The operation stops immediately.

Create a Task from an E-mail Message

If you examine the items in your Inbox, you'll see that a great deal of your e-mail is more than simple information. The text or subject line of many of your messages implies an inherent task. When you see text such as:

```
Please submit the budget
```
```
I'd like that report by next Tuesday
```

`You've been put in charge of the company picnic`

the message is the kick-off for a task.

Drag a Message to the Tasks Folder   Instead of moving to the Tasks folder and starting a new item, let Outlook do the preliminary work for you. Drag the message from the viewer to the Tasks icon in the Outlook Bar. A new task form opens, and the subject is filled in by copying the subject text from the message (see Figure 24.1).

FIG. 24.1

Putting the contents of the message into the text box of the Task form means that all of the available information about this task is recorded for you.

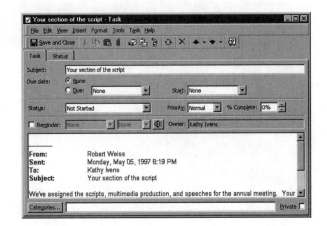

However, you have all the freedom in the world to change the information:

- If you want, edit the text in the Subject field. Remember that the Tasks window can be sorted or grouped by that text, so you may want to use a format that makes it more useful for that purpose.
- Remove or edit as much of the message text as you think necessary.
- Use the fields in the form to set a due date, configure a reminder, and add any other pertinent information available at this time.

Drag Multiple Messages to the Task Folder   If you have multiple messages about the same topic, you can select all the messages and drag them to the Tasks icon. However, only one task is created, regardless of the number of messages you drag.

When the new task is autocreated, all of the messages are in the text box. The subject line, however, remains blank (even if the Subject field of all the messages used the exact same text).

Right-Drag a Message to the Task Folder for More Options   You have more choices about the way the new task is established if you right-drag the message to the Tasks icon. The choices on the shortcut menu give you some flexibility in setting up the task (see Figure 24.2):

- *Copy Here as Task with Text.* Inserts the text of the message into the text box of the task (the same as left-dragging the message to the Tasks icon).
- *Copy Here as Task with Shortcut.* Places a shortcut to the message in the text box of the new task. Open the shortcut to open the original message.

- *Copy Here as Task with Attachment.* Creates a copy of the message and places that copy into the new task as an attachment. As with all attachments, double-clicking its icon opens the item. This is a full copy of the message so the task item gets much larger in file size than a normal task.

- *Move Here as Task with Attachment.* Removes the message from the Inbox and places it in the task as an attachment.

FIG. 24.2

Set up the new task with your own options by right-dragging.

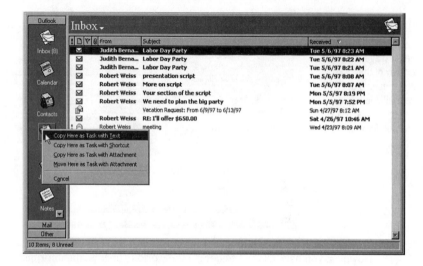

Create an Appointment from a Message

If an e-mail message includes text that involves a meeting (either one you should attend or one you should set up), you can autocreate an appointment by dragging the message to the Calendar icon.

A new appointment form opens with the subject line filled in to match the text of the message subject. The message is placed in the text box of the appointment form.

Everything else, however, has to be entered or edited. The meeting date defaults to the current date (Outlook cannot read the text that refers to a meeting date and figure out that the date and time should be placed in the appropriate fields automatically, although it would be nice).

The options for right-dragging, and dragging multiple messages, are the same as for creating a task.

Create a Contact from a Message

When you drag a message to the Contact icon on the Outlook Bar, a new contact form opens (see Figure 24.3).

The Full Name field is filled in automatically, using the text in the message From field. The E-mail address field is filled in automatically, also using text in the message From field. Usually one or the other of these will have to be changed in the contact form. Also, the File As field is filled in with the appropriate format (usually last name first, but you can change that in the Properties for your address book).

FIG. 24.3

The information in the message header is used to fill in fields, and the message itself is placed in the text box of the contact form.

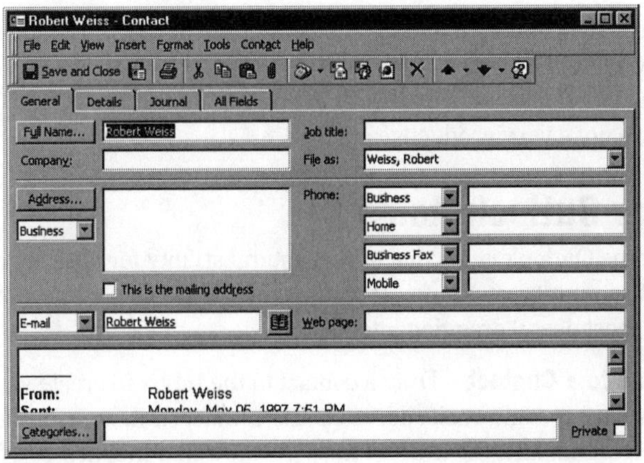

CAUTION

If you drag multiple messages to the Contacts icon, the contact form appears with no information filled in (although the text box on the form receives all the messages). Even if both messages were from the same person, the form is totally blank. Of course, it doesn't make sense to drag multiple messages to the Contacts icon, but in case you were curious about what would happen, I'm pointing it out.

Create a Journal Entry from a Message

One of the most efficient autocreate actions occurs when you drag a message to the Journal icon. A journal entry is automatically created with all the important information about this event (see Figure 24.4).

FIG. 24.4

Your journal has an entry reflecting the fact that you received this message.

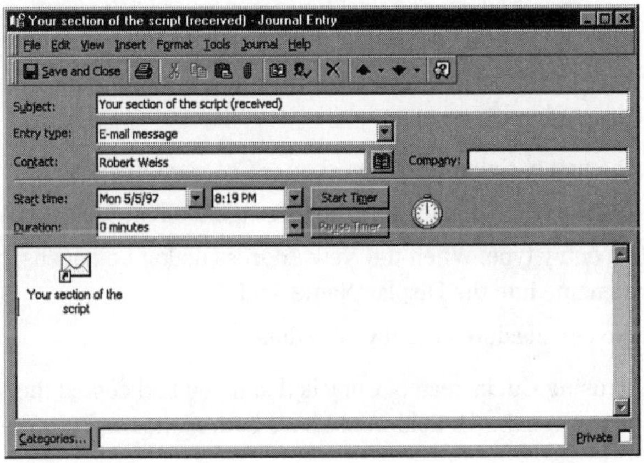

You may want to change the text in the subject line to make it more succinct, or to match it with other entries about the same subject. This generally makes sorting and filtering the journal entries easier.

If you drag multiple entries to the Journal icon, none of the information is transferred to the entry form (although shortcuts for all the messages are placed in the text box). This is true even if all the messages are from the same person and carry the same text in the Subject field. Therefore, it's not a very productive idea.

Dragging Other Outlook Items

There are some Outlook items that have a natural affinity for togetherness. Dragging one to the folder of another creates a new item that marries them. This section gives an overview of some of the most useful dragging interactions.

Create E-Mail to a Contact   Drag a contact to the Inbox to create an e-mail message. If the contact does not have an e-mail address in the contact card, an information dialog box appears to inform you of that fact. Click OK to keep going. When the message form opens, the contact's name is in the To field (see Figure 24.5).

FIG. 24.5

Create an instant e-mail message to a contact.

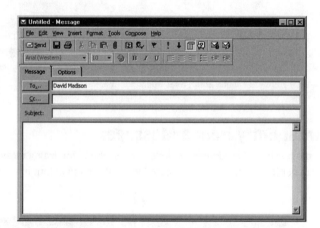

You'll either have to replace the name with an e-mail address, or, better still, add this name to your e-mail address book:

1. Select the name, right-click, then choose Cut from the shortcut menu.
2. Click the Address Book icon on the message toolbar, then choose New.
3. Select an entry type. When the New Address dialog box opens, press Ctrl+V to put the contact's name into the Display Name field.
4. Fill in the e-mail address, and you're done.

The reason for using Cut instead of Copy is that if you had copied the name, when you returned to the message the To field would have both names and you'd have to delete one.

You can do the same thing if you've already changed the contact's name to an e-mail address on the message form. Just reverse the Paste action—copy it to the e-mail address box and then enter a display name.

Turn Any Item into a Note   Outlook Notes are useful, clever, fun, and easy to use. One of the quickest ways to create a note is to drag an Outlook item to the Notes icon. Regardless of the item type, a text-only version of the information in the original item is created as a note (see Figure 24.6).

FIG. 24.6

Notes are created for messages, tasks, and contact cards for fast access to information when I'm working on a project.

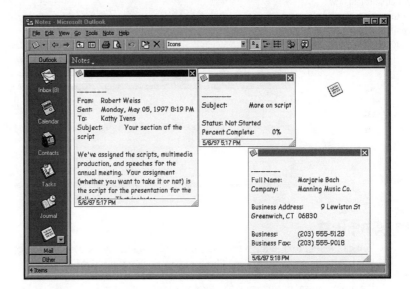

Part

V

Ch

24

TROUBLESHOOTING

After dragging many messages, contact cards, and tasks to the Notes icon to create all sorts of handy reminders, you open the Notes folder and have no idea what any of those notes are about—there are no titles under them.

You're not going crazy; that happens because for some reason, if you don't create the note yourself, Outlook doesn't read the first sentence of text in order to use it as the note's title. That means the only way to figure out what the note is about is to open it and read it. It also means that in order to find a specific note, you have to open all the notes until you get to the right one (like kissing all the frogs to find a prince). If you have a lot of untitled notes in your Notes folder, you could spend a great deal of time doing this, ruining any productivity this feature was supposed to bring to you (doesn't do much for your mood, either).

While there's no snappy-quick way to fix this, there is a solution that isn't terribly onerous. Open the note, place the insertion point at the top of the note, and type something that reveals the contents of the note. When you close the note, the text you entered becomes its title.

Send a Note as a Message   When you create a note for yourself as a reminder (perhaps to jot down some specific facts you don't want to forget, or to document some casual conversation that is important), you can e-mail the information to somebody else.

Drag a note to the Inbox icon to open a message form. The note's title is the subject, and the text box is filled in with the complete contents of the note (see Figure 24.7).

FIG. 24.7

The recipient can now drag this message to his Notes folder and his Contacts folder.

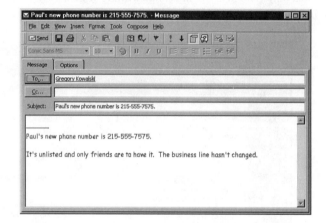

Dragging Text

You can select text in any Outlook item and drag the selection to a folder icon on the Outlook Bar to autocreate a new item. The text can be from any field.

It's most common, however, to use comments or notes from the text box of an item—you can select it and use it as the basis of a new item. For example, notes on an appointment form can be dragged to the Tasks folder. Your note is placed in the text box of the new task, and you can enter all the other necessary information (see Figure 24.8).

FIG. 24.8

My notes for a conference call appointment kicked off a task.

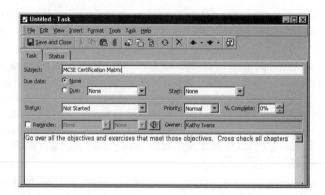

Dragging Items Outside of Outlook

You can also drag Outlook items to containers outside the application. This is most useful for tasks and contacts. You can drag a task to the desktop, and then as you perform the work connected to the task, you can track what you've accomplished. Likewise, dragging a contact card to the desktop means you can enter items in the Journal tab as you perform work connected to this contact.

The target can be any folders on the Outlook Bar (use the Other button first to access those folders), any folder on the desktop, or the desktop itself (see Figure 24.9).

FIG. 24.9

Move an Outlook item to the desktop for permanent access to it.

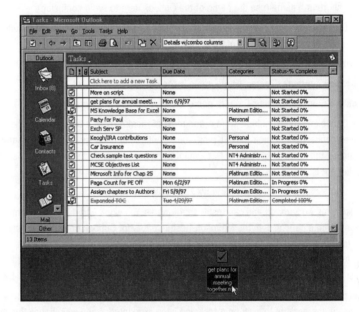

Part

V

Ch

24

When you drag an Outlook object outside the Outlook system, you can open it even when Outlook isn't running. Double-click the object's icon to open it in order to view it or make changes.

In fact, Outlook does launch in the background but it presents only the object's form, not the entire application. If you have configured multiple profiles, you will have to choose one just as if you were launching Outlook before the item opens. When you close the item (either by using Save and Close or just closing the form's window), you see the familiar Please Wait While Microsoft Outlook Exits information dialog box.

TROUBLESHOOTING

When you open the item you've placed outside the Outlook system and make changes, the next time you use Outlook you find the original item does not reflect the changes. You clicked the Save and Close button, so why don't you see the item in its current state? It's a bug. That's my opinion, not Microsoft's.

continues

continued

Microsoft calls it a *design plan*. However, there is a workaround. Isn't it nice when there's a workaround for a design plan? Workarounds are usually reserved for bugs.

The workaround involves creating a shortcut, which I find easiest to do from the desktop (later you can move the shortcut to any folder you want):

1. Right-click a blank spot on the desktop and choose New. Then choose Shortcut.

2. When the Create Shortcut dialog box appears, enter text in the Command Line box.

3. After you have entered the appropriate text in the Command Line box, choose Next and give this shortcut a name (use the name of the Outlook item to avoid confusion).

If the Outlook item is filed as a single word (usually that means a task, it would be unusual to have a single name contact), enter one of the following:

outlook:tasks/~name, where *name* is the name of the task

outlook:contacts/~name, where *name* is the name of the contact

outlook:calendar/~name, where *name* is the title of the appointment

If the Outlook item has multiple words (and most of them do), it's a bit more complicated because it requires concentration when you're typing. You have to fill in each space with the characters **%20**. For instance, if the name of the task is Get Annual Budget Information, the syntax for the command line of the shortcut is:

outlook:tasks/~Get%20Annual%20Budget%20Information

I've used this workaround and can testify that it works. You won't find it in any documentation, Microsoft white papers, or in the Microsoft Resource Kits for Outlook or your operating system. You'll have to take my word for it that this works. If you find the idea of a desktop shortcut useful, you might want to write to Microsoft and suggest it build in shortcuts for Outlook items (add a PS to your letter and suggest it link the Briefcase to Outlook items, too, which would be an extremely handy feature).

If you perform these steps, the shortcut will be a true shortcut, and you won't have to keep the Outlook window on the desktop to work on a task and keep it updated. When you change the shortcut, the original item reflects the changes.

Keeping Journal Entries

Outlook has a robust set of features as a *Personal Information Manager (PIM)*. Unlike many other PIMs, Outlook can be configured to keep a journal of some significant events on an automatic basis, saving you the trouble of opening an item or a file and entering text to indicate your latest actions. Most users find that keeping a journal on anything that is connected to a contact is the most useful application of this feature. That means when you look at a contact card, you know everything you did that's connected to that contact.

Journal entries can appear in the Journal folder, on the Journal tab of a contact card, or both.

Any e-mail item can be kept in a journal automatically, as can any telephone call initiated by autodialing through a contact card. You cannot autocreate a journal entry for a task or an appointment, but if you are connected to Microsoft Exchange Server, any task or meeting requests are eligible for autocreation.

On the semi-automatic side, any existing item can be kept in a journal by dragging it to the Journal folder.

Manual journal entries are, of course, a simple matter of opening a journal and recording an event, conversation, your thoughts, or even a couplet of poetry, if you like.

Documents created by any other Office 97 application are also automatically placed in a journal. Notice that I did not say "can be;" by default, they are. And you might want to turn that feature off—open your Journal folder and see how long the list is (check it with the Entry List view, not the Last Seven Days view, to get a real picture). Every document you created in any Office 97 application is listed.

Setting Journal Options

The first thing to do is configure Outlook to make automatic journal entries for the things that are important to you. This is accomplished via the Journal tab of the Options dialog box, which is opened from the Tools menu (see Figure 24.10).

FIG. 24.10

The first time you access this dialog box, all of the applications are selected, and none of the autorecord options are selected.

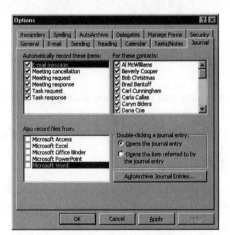

Application Options   Personally, I begin by removing all the check marks next to the Office applications. I figure if I want to keep a journal for a letter or spreadsheet, I'll do it myself; with the default settings, the list gets ridiculously long. Every time you create, open, close, or save any document in any selected application, there's a journal entry. I've never been able to figure out why anyone needs that information. Decide which office applications you have installed that you need to keep journal entries on.

Item Options   Except for an e-mail message, the items listed as being available for automatic recording are only accessible if you are running Microsoft Exchange Server. Select the ones you want, then select the contacts for whom you want to keep a journal. If you select e-mail messages, both sent and received messages are kept in a journal for every selected contact.

Contact Options   The list of contacts displayed in the Options dialog box is linked to the individual contact cards. If you select a contact in this list, a corresponding check mark appears in the contact card on the Journal tab (see Figure 24.11). If you turn on automatic journal entries on the contact card, a check mark appears in this dialog box. Removing the check mark from either place removes it from both.

FIG. 24.11

You can turn on the automatic journal feature for a contact from the contact card as well as the Options dialog box.

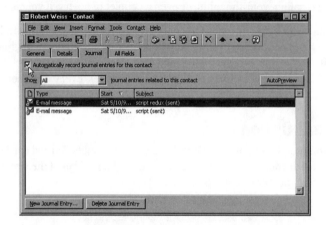

Journal Entry Options   Select an option for the action that occurs when you double-click a journal entry in the Journal folder:

- You can open the journal entry and read it, then open the item it refers to if you need to do so.
- You can open the item referred to in the journal entry and skip the entry itself.

Using Automatic Journal Entries

Automatic journal entries such as e-mail messages (both sent and received) are actually recorded in two places: the Journal folder and the Journal tab of the associated contact card.

> **CAUTION**
>
> Automatic journal entries for contacts only work for those contacts in your Outlook Contacts folder. If you create subfolders in order to separate your contacts according to some sorting scheme, you cannot take advantage of automatic journal entries for any contacts in a subfolder.

Add E-Mail Correspondents to the Contacts Folder   If you have e-mail in your Inbox from people who are not in your Contacts folder, you can add them quickly. Open the message and right-click the sender's name. Then choose Add to Contacts. A new contact card opens with the sender's name filled in. Just fill in the rest of the information. Don't forget to go to the Journal tab and select Automatically Record Journal Entries.

Automatic journal activity starts at that point; previously received messages are not posted to the journal. However, you can drag any messages from this contact to the Journal icon on the Outlook Bar. When you do, the message is also automatically placed on the Journal tab of the contact's card.

Set Up Contacts in an Address Book   To take advantage of the automatic e-mail journal entries for sending mail, make sure your contacts are available in an address book. That means you have to establish an address book for your contacts (unless you want to add all your contacts to the Personal Address Book, which is something I'm certainly too lazy to do).

This is a two-step process: First you must set up the service that provides address books from Outlook folders; then you must add the specific folders you want to use to your list of address books.

Part
V

Ch
24

If it wasn't established during Setup, add Outlook Address Book as a service:

1. Open the Services dialog box from the Tools menu.
2. On the Services tab, choose Add. When the list of available services displays, select Outlook Address Book.

   The service begins after you exit and return to Outlook.

Now make your Contacts folder the Outlook Address Book:

1. Right-click the Contacts icon on the Outlook Bar or the Contacts Folder from the folder display.
2. Choose Properties and move to the Outlook Address Book tab.
3. Select Show this Folder as an E-Mail Address Book.
4. Fill in the Name for this address book (the default name, **Contacts**, is probably as good a descriptive name as any).

To check that your new address book is installed as an Outlook Address Book, return to the Services dialog box and select the Outlook Address Book service. Choose Properties and make sure your address book is listed. Incidentally, you can remove an address book from that Properties dialog box, but to add one you have to go to the Properties of the folder you want to add.

Use the Contacts Address Book   Once you've added an address book for your contacts, sending e-mail to them is easier, and that process is recorded automatically.

When you want to send e-mail to a contact, open the address book from the message form (click To:). Click the arrow to reveal the drop-down list in the Show Names text box (see Figure 24.12). Then choose Contacts from the list of Outlook Address Books.

FIG. 24.12

The address books available to you vary depending on the services installed in Outlook. This computer has a Global Address List because Exchange Server is installed.

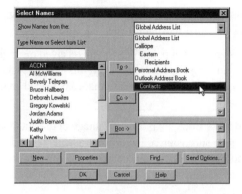

The Contacts list appears in the Select Names dialog box, and you can see a list of contacts from your Contacts folder (see Figure 24.13).

FIG. 24.13

Use the Contacts address list the same way you use your Personal Address list.

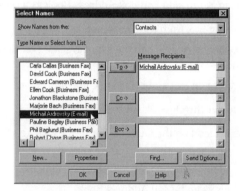

TROUBLESHOOTING

You might notice one of three things that causes you alarm when you open the Contacts Address list:

- You can't find a specific contact in the Contacts Address list.

- The list obviously has fewer names than the Contacts folder.

- Some names that are listed indicate there's a fax number instead of an e-mail address.

Don't panic; neither you nor Outlook made an error when the Contacts Address Book was created. Only those contacts for whom you entered an e-mail address or a fax number on the contact card are displayed. The e-mail address takes priority, so if you entered both, the listing reflects the fact that an e-mail address is present. (The fax number is there so you can also use this address book to fax directly from an application.)

If you add data for either field to an existing contact card, that contact will thereafter appear in the address book listing.

If the listing shows only a fax number for a contact and you know the e-mail address, you can enter it right from the address book—you don't have to go back to the contact card. Select the contact and choose Properties. Move to the FAX-Address tab and enter the e-mail address (clean up the display name at the same time). The information is not written back to the contact card; if you also need it there, be sure to add it.

Outlook permits you to enter a name directly into the To, Cc, or Bcc field of a message without opening an address book. However, the name is checked against address books. If the name is not found in an address book, it is checked to ensure it is a valid e-mail address format. That doesn't mean the address is correct; it just means you formatted it properly. So, it's much better to have Outlook check against a known e-mail address to ensure that you're message is properly addressed.

Adding the Contacts Address Book to the list of available address books does not automatically include it in the address checking routine. You have to do that manually:

1. Choose Services from the Tools menu and move to the Addressing tab. The list of address books for checking names includes the Personal Address Book (and the Global Address List, if you're connected to Microsoft Exchange Server).

2. Choose Add to see the Add Address List dialog box, which should include the Contacts Address Book. Select it and choose Add.

Hereafter, whenever you enter a display name into the addressing part of the message header, the name will also be checked against this address book.

Drag to Create a Journal Entry

You can create a journal entry out of any existing item by dragging it to the Journal folder.

For instance, if you wanted to keep a journal entry for a meeting you had, drag it to the Journal folder. A Journal Entry form opens with most of the information filled in (see Figure 24.14). You'll probably want to add notes about the item to refresh your memory later.

FIG. 24.14
Keep a journal entry for any significant meeting by dragging it to the Journal folder.

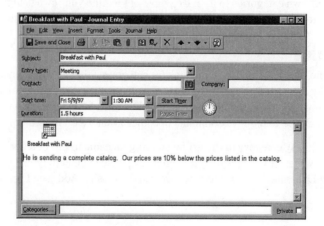

Part V

Ch 24

Manually Create a Journal Entry

You can create your own journal entries for contact cards (on the Journal tab) or directly into the Journal folder.

To add a journal entry to a contact card, open the appropriate contact card and move to the Journal tab. Choose New Journal Entry to bring up a blank form and fill in the information. The journal entry is also written to the Journal folder and exists in both places.

To add a new entry to the Journal folder, move to the folder and open a blank Journal Entry form. Enter notes about conversations, thoughts, ideas, or whatever you want to add to your journal.

There is a field for Contacts on the Journal Entry form, with an icon for the address book. Click the icon and select your Personal Address Book (or the Global Address Book, if you are connected to Exchange Server). Choose a contact. The journal entry is written to the contact card as well as the Journal folder.

Notice the specifics in the preceding paragraph. In order to duplicate the journal entry on the contact card, you cannot use your Contacts Address Book—it won't work. This is a bug. There two possible workarounds for this bug:

- Make all journal entries that involve contacts from the Journal tab of the contact card.
- Copy or import your Contact list to your Personal Address Book.

Use Categories to Connect Items

Categories are words or phrases you can use to build relationships between items, even if the items are of different types and reside in different folders. You can attach a category to any item except an e-mail message.

You can type a word or phrase into the Category box on an item, but it's much better to select a category from the list. Even though Outlook has supplied a Master Category List, you are free to add your own categories to it. In fact, most of the time your own categories serve better because they are named for specific projects or other meaningful events.

Add Categories

There is no discrete function in Outlook for categories; that is, you cannot find any menu item specifically aimed at working with categories, unconnected with an item. Instead, you must move to any folder that contains items and select one of the items (don't open it, just select it). At that point, the Categories command becomes available on the Edit menu.

You can add any category to the list by entering its name in the Categories dialog box. You can enter a new Master Category (by definition, available to all item types) by choosing Master Category List, entering the category name, and choosing Add (see Figure 24.15).

FIG. 24.15

Enter a new category for an item, or a new Master Category for all items.

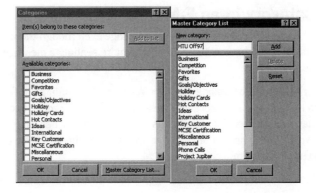

 You can open any item and click Categories on the item form and get to the same place.

CAUTION

If you select an item in a list just to be able to get to the Categories function, the process of adding a category also places that new category on the item. If that's not what you meant to do, open the item and delete the category.

Assigning Categories

There are several methods for assigning categories to items, and you'll probably use all of them at one time or another, depending on the circumstances at the moment:

■ When you create a new item, click the Categories button and select a category from the list.

■ Select an item (or multiple items) from the displayed list and choose Categories from the Edit menu. Click the appropriate category to place a check mark in the check box. All the selected items are assigned to that category.

■ Select an item (or multiple items) and choose Categories from the Edit menu. Add a new category. The selected items are assigned to the new category.

 You can also open an item and type a word or phrase directly into its Categories field. If your typing is accurate and it matches an existing category, the link is made. If you enter a new category (one that doesn't exist in the Category list), the item is assigned to that category. If you want to assign other items to the same category, you either have to add that category to the list or remember to type it the same way every time (the former is a better plan, of course).

You can assign multiple categories to the same item. If you are entering categories directly instead of using the list, separate the categories with a comma.

Assigning a Category to an E-Mail Message

You can, in fact, add a category to an e-mail message even though there is no category field on the message form. This can be useful when you're sending a message or when you've received one.

Use Categories When Composing E-Mail   When you're sending a message, you can add a category so that later you can sort sent messages by that category. If your recipient uses Outlook, you may want the receiver to add this category to his or her list (probably because the message involves some project or event that you believe should have a category in the recipient's Outlook system):

1. While you're composing the message, choose Categories from the Edit menu.

2. Choose a category from the list or enter a new one.

3. Avoid panic, confusion, or saying "Huh, what?" out loud when you see absolutely no indication of a category anywhere on this message—it doesn't show up anywhere.

After you send the message, open it in the Sent Items folder and move to the Options tab. The Categories field has magically appeared, and the category you assigned is filled in. In fact, open any item in the Sent Items folder and you find the Categories field.

Use Categories for Received Messages   If a category was added to a message you receive, you can see the category on the Options tab of the received message. If that category does not exist in your system, choosing Categories from the Edit menu while the message is open displays a list that includes this category with a parenthetical note that the category is not included in the Master Category List. You can add the category to the Master List if you want.

If you receive messages that did not have a category added by the sender, but you want to track messages by category, move to the Options tab of the received message and add a category to the Categories field.

View Items by Category

All of the folders in your Outlook system, except the Mail folders, have a built-in view named By Category. When you select this view, the items are displayed in grouped boxes sorted by category. Click the plus sign next to any box to expand it and see the items within it (see Figure 24.16).

Using the By Category view lets you take a quick look at anything you're tracking by category, such as a project, an event, or just the divisions you've created for your workload:

- Any item that has multiple categories is listed under each of those categories. There is still only one item—it is just displayed more than once. If you open any item that appears twice and make changes to it, you will see those changes in all the other iterations of that item within the view.

- You can drag an item from one category box to another to add the target category to the item (see Figure 24.17).

FIG. 24.16

Notice that the task named Registry Changes is listed twice, indicating multiple categories for that task.

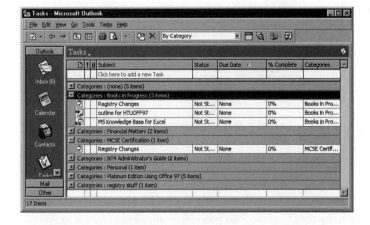

FIG. 24.17

Drag an item to a category box to add that category to the item.

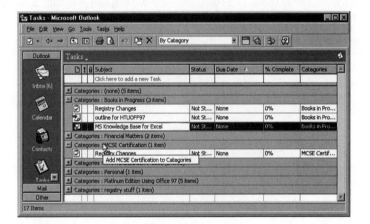

Find All Items Connected to a Category

The categories that appear in your Categories list are global; they exist across all Outlook folders. Every Categories field in every item points to the same Categories list. This makes it easy to find items across all the Outlook folders, so you can gather anything and everything connected to a category. You'll find this extremely useful if you use categories to track projects.

To put together all the Outlook items connected to the same category (see Figure 24.18), click the Find Items icon on the toolbar of any viewer:

1. In the Look For field, choose Any type of Outlook item.

2. Move to the More Choices tab and click Categories, then choose the category you want to report on. You can choose more than one category.

3. If you aren't looking for a complete list of items in this category, you can narrow the search with the criteria available in the Find dialog box.

FIG. 24.18

Use Find to bring
together all the Outlook
items in a category.

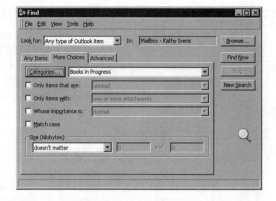

When the results of the Find process are displayed at the bottom of the dialog box, you can
sort them, group them, add columns to the display, and generally treat the display as if it were
a folder view.

It's a good idea to save the search so that the next time you want to see the items for this category you
don't have to rebuild the Find dialog box. Just choose Save Search from the File menu. When you want
to use the search criteria again, choose Open from the File menu.

CHAPTER 25

More Power with Exchange Server

If you're using Outlook on a network that runs Microsoft Exchange Server, there's a great deal of additional power you can tap into. Outlook takes advantage of the interconnectivity available through Exchange Server to add features and functions well beyond those in a standard Outlook setup.

In this chapter, we'll discuss some of the innovative and productive tools you can access through Exchange Server. ■

Apply rules to mail handling

You can put your mailbox on autopilot by setting up rules that give Outlook the power to act automatically under conditions that you specify.

Use e-mail to poll

If you need answers from other users on any subject, it's easy to design an e-mail message that has buttons your recipients can click to indicate their responses. Then Outlook will collect and tabulate the answers.

Set delivery options for mail

Get notification of mail delivery, control the delivery time, and create expiration dates for the e-mail you compose.

Assign projects and tasks to other users

When you're in charge of a project or a task, you can use Outlook's Task Assignments feature to send the work to another user. Outlook has all the necessary tools to track progress and get reports.

Use public folders to distribute mail and forms

Use system-wide folders that other users can open in order to see your message, form, or document.

E-Mail Features

With the addition of Microsoft Exchange Server, the e-mail features in Outlook multiply many times over. The power is apparent as soon as you compose your first e-mail message, because there are more options than are available to Outlook users who don't have Exchange Server. In this section, we'll explain how to apply a few of Outlook's most interesting and productive features to your e-mail tasks.

Managing Your Mailbox with Rules

When you return to the office after a business trip or vacation, the contents of your mailbox can be overwhelming. Sometimes you find several messages from the same person who has become impatient with your lack of response. Or, worse, some deadline was missed while you were unaware of the contents of your mailbox. You can avoid all that aggravation with Outlook's *Out of Office Assistant*, which will let people know what's going on and direct the mail to specific people (and solutions) in your absence.

Even when you are in the office, there's probably a great deal of mail you don't really have to deal with directly—it could be handled on an automatic basis or delegated to another person. With the Outlook Inbox Assistant, you can set up self-propelled responses, or you can establish a delegate who gets the appropriate mail from your mailbox and then performs any resulting necessary tasks.

The configuration process for all this automatic processing of messages is quite simple; you establish criteria and actions. The messages that meet the criteria fire up the actions. Outlook calls this combination of conditions and actions *rules*.

Using the Out of Office Assistant

When you're going to be away from the office (really away, not traveling for a day or two and dialing in for your mail), you can use the Out of Office Assistant to act in your absence. The Out of Office Assistant is on the Tools menu, and you have to be connected to the Windows NT server for Exchange Server in order to use it (if you're not connected, the choice is dimmed). The Out of Office Assistant dialog box offers two choices for handling mail, and you can use either or both of them (see Figure 25.1):

- You can send an AutoReply to everyone who sends you mail while you're out.
- You can use a variety of automatic actions to process mail.

Whether you use one or both of these choices, you don't have to re-invent the wheel every time you go away. Once you establish your settings, it takes only a simple click of the mouse to tell Outlook you're out of the office to put them into effect.

Send an AutoReply The AutoReply feature is easy—just enter text. A message containing your text is sent one time to each person who sends e-mail while you're away. (That means if somebody absolutely inundates you with e-mail, you won't be able to return the favor with the

AutoReply option; the sender gets one notification only.) Incidentally, it's a good idea to indicate a return date in your text if you know when you'll be back. It's a better idea to indicate a date that's really a day or two after your return if you need some time to catch up before people expect answers from you.

FIG. 25.1
Use the Out of Office Assistant to let people know you're away or to automate e-mail message handling.

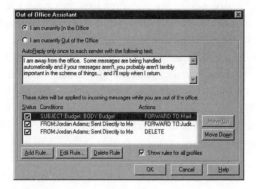

Use Rules to Process Mail The most productive way to handle your mail is to process those items that need attention while you're absent. Use the Rules section of the Out of Office Assistant to establish the conditions under which mail is processed and to specify the actions involved in processing.

Before you start, there are a couple of things to keep in mind:

- The only mail you can process is the mail that arrives in your server-based mailbox.
- If you are going to create actions that result in your mail being transferred into folders so it can be handled by delegated users, you must give those users folder permissions that are adequate to take care of the tasks you want performed.

To create a rule, choose Add Rule to get to the Edit Rule dialog box (see Figure 25.2). If the choices seem almost overwhelming, it's because they are, but it isn't difficult to get the concept and the choices under control and use the enormous variety of options to suit your needs:

FIG. 25.2
Establish criteria, then direct Outlook to take specific actions when messages meet the criteria.

■ *From*. For specifying senders, if that is a condition you want to set. You can enter as many names as you like, separating them with semicolons. The semicolon is the same as an OR operator.

If you type in the names, be sure to use the Check Names button to certify that each name exists in the address book (an underline indicates a successful match). Most of the time it's faster to click the From button to display the address list, then double-click your way through the list to select names.

■ *Sent To*. For specifying names of recipients for any message which is also received by you. You can also stipulate whether you're on the To list or the Cc list (or both). You can combine this field with the From field to narrow the criteria, but most of the time you'll find you'll use one or the other.

Leave Sent To blank and select Sent Directly to Me or Copied to Me or both to embrace a wider set of messages. If you've placed names in the From field, of course, that narrows your criteria.

■ *Subject*. The place to enter a word or phrase that triggers a match if it appears in the Subject field of a message. It's more efficient to use a word or two instead of a complete phrase in case the sender uses slightly different wording.

Using Subject as the only field in your criteria is frequently sufficient; combining it with other fields narrows the criteria substantially.

T I P   Some organizations have protocols about phrasing the subject for certain important company topics. If this is in effect, using the Subject field as part of the criteria for processing messages is extremely efficient. If you have the power to do so, you might want to set up such a system for significant topics, such as budget, personnel issues, and so on. It's useful for more than just the Out of Office Assistant; it makes sorting the contents of the Inbox by Subject more accurate.

■ *Message Body*. Offers the same opportunity for text matching as the Subject field (except, of course, the body of the message is searched for the match). You can enter multiple words or phrases and separate them with a semicolon (which acts as an OR operator).

Using one or more of the these fields is going to satisfy all the conditions you need most of the time. But if you need to narrow your selection even more, choose Advanced to display the Advanced dialog box (see Figure 25.3) where the following criteria are available:

■ *Size (Kilobytes)*. Message size range (which I've never used and never even been able to imagine the circumstances under which I would, but perhaps I just haven't had the right situation occur).

■ *Received*. Received dates range (useful if you're going to be away for an extended period and you know when to expect that important notice about your raise and you've appointed a delegate to receive the paperwork and fill out the form).

■ *Only Items with Attachments*.

■ *Importance and Sensitivity*. Messages that carry specific priority and sensitivity options.

FIG. 25.3
Once you've established basic conditions, narrow them further by applying additional yardsticks.

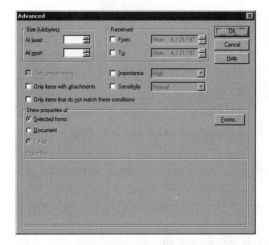

■ *Show Properties Of.* If the message is a form, or a document is attached, you can opt to examine the properties in order to qualify or disqualify the message. The most common conditions would be the author's name, the subject, or perhaps the keywords. This only works if senders actually fill in the properties of documents or forms (not the norm for many organizations).

■ *Only Items That Do Not Match These Conditions.* You can select this option after you've made the other choices. It is a way to set up your criteria to exclude rather than include. For example, use this check box to get only those items without attachments, or that fall outside the date range you've entered.

N O T E Sensitivity is another one of those nifty features of Outlook that is available only with Exchange Server. You can mark a message with a sensitivity level: Private, Personal, or Confidential. If you send someone a message that is marked for a sensitivity level, the recipient can prevent others from seeing it when delegated users are given access to the recipient's mailbox. In addition, a Private message cannot be modified, even by the recipient, if it is sent on. Of course, the recipient also has to be using Outlook on an Exchange Server system to use the Sensitivity feature. ■

Select the Action to Perform on the Mail After you've selected the criteria you need, it's time to tell Outlook what to do when there's a match. The bottom half of the Edit Rule dialog box displays the choices:

■ *Alert With.* Issues an alert you can design. Select the check box to activate the Action button, then click it to configure the alert for audio, video, or both (see Figure 25.4).

N O T E Of course, the idea of an alert seems a bit incongruous for an Out of Office configuration (who would see or hear it?), but I guess if somebody uses your computer while you're away, you can leave instructions about an alert-producing message (don't forget to give the appropriate permissions for the resulting assignment). ■

Part
V

Ch
25

FIG. 25.4

Make a noise, flash a message—the e-mail you've been waiting for has arrived.

- *Delete*. Moves the message to the Deleted Items folder.

- *Move To*. Lets you choose a folder to receive the message. This is usually combined with permissions given to other users for the target folder so the contents of the message can be read and subsequent actions taken.

- *Copy To*. The same as Move To (except obviously a copy of the message remains in the Inbox).

- *Forward*. Forwards the message to a user of your choice (click the To button to see the address books and choose a user). Messages marked `Private` are not forwarded.

- *Reply With*. When selected, makes the Template button available. Click it to open a blank message window and fill in the message body with the text you want to send in response to this received e-mail. You can add recipients and attach files if you like. Use Save and Close when you have finished the reply.

- *Custom*. When selected, gives access to a drop-down list of custom features outside of Outlook. Click the one you need for this rule.

  Items are added to the Custom list by programmers, and the custom application is hooked to this category. The routine must be written in C. Once it's installed, you can choose it and it will run when the selection criteria fires it.

You can continue to make as many rules as you think you'll need, and each rule can have as many permutations and combinations as you can devise. The possibilities are close to endless.

Add, edit, and delete rules at will—then, before you leave the office for an extended period, make the last task you perform that of clicking the I Am Currently Out of the Office radio button. All rules go into effect and stay active until you return and select I Am Currently In the Office to turn them off.

 As a suggestion, you might want to have the text in the AutoReply indicate that you're out of the office and tell the sender that if the message is urgent and it has to be waiting for you when you return, the Subject field should say SAVE or URGENT. Then establish an action that processes messages with that subject text (perhaps moving them to a folder you've established for this purpose). Also establish an action that deletes all messages lacking that subject text. When you return, your mailbox isn't filled with messages.

Using the Inbox Assistant

Even when you are in the office, there are features available in Outlook that give you opportunities to automate the way e-mail messages are handled. This, of course, frees up your time so you can improve your golf game or take longer lunches.

The Inbox Assistant provides a scope of options similar to the Out of Office Assistant, letting you create rules that Outlook uses to auto-process your e-mail. Access the Inbox Assistant from the Tools menu to get started (see Figure 25.5).

FIG. 25.5

Autoprocessing messages makes e-mail easier to handle.

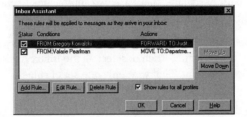

The only differences between setting up rules in the Out of Office Assistant and the Inbox Assistant are:

Part

V

Ch

25

- The Inbox Assistant has no radio button to make it active or inactive (although you can deselect specific rules at will).
- The Inbox Assistant has no AutoReply choice.

Using the Inbox Assistant means you can automatically move e-mail to a logical location, saving the time and energy it would take to relocate the messages manually. The target locations might be folders (messages about projects can move to folders created for those projects) or mailboxes belonging to other users (messages about meetings can be automatically forwarded to the person who schedules your calendar).

Things to Watch For   If you use identical criteria followed by different actions (a "first do this, then do that" scenario), make sure the rules are listed in the proper order in the Assistant dialog box. Rules are acted upon in the order in which they appear on the list. For instance, if you have a rule that says certain messages should be forwarded to someone else, and you don't want to find a copy of the message in your Inbox when you return, you can create a rule for the same circumstances with Delete as the action. Use the Move Up and Move Down buttons on the dialog box to place the Delete action after the Forward action.

If there is a problem with the actions you specify (the actions cannot be performed for some reason), the dialog box listing displays a red X next to the troublesome rule. Choose Edit Rule to examine and fix your configuration.

If you want to turn off a rule (as opposed to deleting it), check the box in the Status column to deselect it.

If you use both Inbox Assistant and Out of Office Assistant, be aware that the Inbox Assistant is processed first, then the Out of Office Assistant is processed. There is no exclusive precedence; everything fires. That means if the Inbox Assistant forwards all messages from Moby Dick to Captain Ahab, and the Out of Office Assistant forwards all messages from Moby Dick to Jonas Inwhale, both events will occur. If the Inbox Assistant deletes messages that meet certain criteria and the same criteria in the Out of Office Assistant result in a message being forwarded, the latter event will not occur because the message will not be there when the Out of Office Assistant rules are processed.

If you're planning to use both Assistants, there are two approaches to choose from that make sure you don't end up with problems:

- When setting up the Out of Office Assistant, repeat the Inbox Assistant rules that you want to maintain in your absence, then deselect all the Inbox Assistant rules when you turn on Out of Office Assistant. That way, only one set of rules is processed and everything is covered.

- When you turn on the Out of Office Assistant, turn off (deselect) any conflicts in Inbox Assistant. The trouble with this approach is that if you have complex rules with compound actions, you may miss a conflict that moves or deletes a message that should have been processed in the Out of Office Assistant.

Of course, these tips are unnecessary if you are extremely careful in your logic when setting up rules and never devise any rules that conflict.

Voting

It's not a straw poll for the next presidential election, nor is it a way to determine the popularity quotients of employees ("Who's the best looking guy in the purchasing department?"). *Voting* is a method of offering mail recipients a multiple choice question and then tabulating the results. Most organizations have a real need for this, for example when:

- Managers try to arrange recurring meetings (Is 9 A.M. better than afternoons? Are Mondays better than Thursdays?).

- Department heads try to get a headstart on determining possible results of a proposition that's being considered.

- Other projects benefit from the ability to tabulate answers to questions.

Creating a Voting Message   You start with a normal e-mail message. Almost always, the recipient is a distribution list, or at least a group of individual recipients (there is little point in polling one person). Enter the subject, a short message explaining what the question is, and move to the Options tab of the message window and select Use Voting Buttons (see Figure 25.6). Then choose one of the built-in button selections.

If the built-in buttons don't suffice, you can invent your own:

1. Select Use Voting Buttons to activate the default buttons.

2. Highlight the button text and delete the entry.

3. Enter your own button names, separating each button with a semicolon (see Figure 25.7).

FIG. 25.6

Turn on voting and choose the buttons you need.

FIG. 25.7

Create the voting buttons you need to fit the situation.

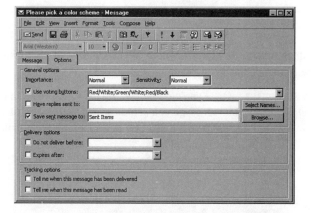

Part

V

Ch

25

Buttons you create aren't saved in the system; the next time you use Voting and look at the drop-down list, only the original three built-in buttons are displayed.

Responding to a Voting Message   When you receive and open a message that involves voting, the buttons provide the mechanism for replying. Don't click the Reply icon on the toolbar; merely click the button that represents your vote. The buttons are just below the toolbar and they look like toolbar buttons (see Figure 25.8).

As soon as you vote, an informational dialog box appears confirming your vote and giving you a chance to change your mind (see Figure 25.9). When you're sure of your vote and ready to have it recorded, send it and then close the message window.

FIG. 25.8
Voting kicks off the
Reply process.

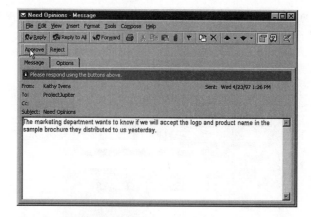

FIG. 25.9
Tell Outlook to send the
response when you're
sure you've picked the
correct choice.

Later, if you don't remember how you voted, you can view your response in your Sent Items
folder. The Subject field includes your vote.

Tracking the Responses   Once you've sent a voting message, you can track the responses as
they arrive. Open the original message you sent in which you asked the recipients to vote (it's
probably in your Sent Items folder). It has a new tab: Tracking (see Figure 25.10).

FIG. 25.10
The first response is in
and you're one-up for
approval.

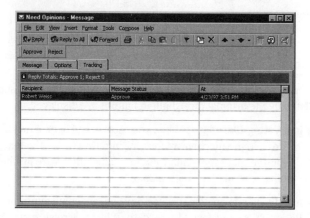

The individual responses are listed, and the totals display above them.

If you need to create reports, copy and paste the grid from the Tracking tab and move the data
to a document or a spreadsheet (where the grid will maintain its columns and rows).

Tracking Mail

When people don't respond to e-mail messages, it's annoying at best and interferes with productivity at worst. There's nothing more frustrating than being put on hold because you need an answer from someone before you can proceed to the next step. When you finally contact the person by telephone or with a follow up e-mail message, you sometimes hear, "I never got the message." That's hard to believe. E-mail systems don't fail that often, especially without bouncing the mail, along with an error message. Those people are either ignoring your message or they're too fast with the Delete key.

Outlook and Exchange Server work together to help you track mail so you know for sure what happens after you click that Send button. (That ought to keep people throughout your organization on their toes.) You can use this feature to learn when mail is delivered or, even more powerful, to learn when it was read (or both).

Requesting Tracking Information   There are a number of different schemes offered by Outlook for this feature. The default arrangement is:

- Tracking is enabled on a message-by-message basis.
- Notification is sent to your Inbox as soon as the information is available.

Let's play this out with an example. If you are sending a message to another user on your Exchange Server system and you want to know that the message arrived without incident, and you also want to know that the recipient read the message, it requires only a couple of mouse clicks to set that up:

1. Fill out the message header and enter the text of your message.
2. Move to the Options tab and select the Tracking option(s) you need (see Figure 25.11).

Part

V

Ch

25

FIG. 25.11

If it's not enough to learn that the message has reached the recipient's mailbox, tell Outlook you want to know when the recipient saw the message.

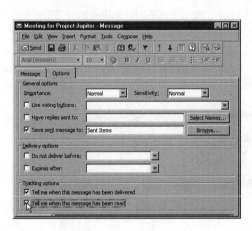

3. Send the message. Wait. Do some work.

    Within a few minutes, a message appears in your Inbox indicating the e-mail has been delivered (see Figure 25.12).

FIG. 25.12
When Exchange Server
delivers the message,
you receive a note
indicating a successful
delivery.

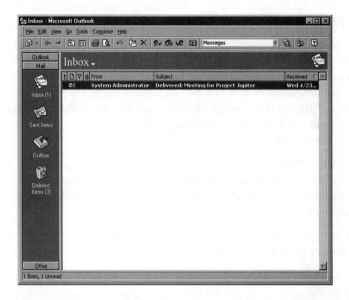

N O T E The message delivery is quick if you and the recipient are connected by network cable or
an open telephone line. If your organization has multiple locations and e-mail is delivered
by dialing out periodically, you won't get notification immediately; you'll have to wait until the next time
the servers exchange information. Remember that basically there are two mail deliveries being made—
your notification is just another piece of e-mail to the system. ■

When the recipient opens the message, notification of that event is sent to you. Instead of saying `Delivered:` followed by the subject text, this notification says `Read:` followed by the subject
text.

You can delete the notification messages without losing track of the date and time the recipient
read the message. Just find the original message (which should be in the Sent Items folder
unless you changed the defaults) and check the Tracking tab (see Figure 25.13).

FIG. 25.13
You know exactly when
the recipient opened the
message to read it.

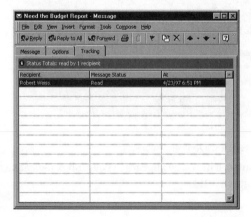

The Tracking tab logs only the Read: activity (because the message must have been received in order to be read). This method, however, is not foolproof; it is only an indication that the message was opened. Outlook does not have a function that permits the software to peer through the monitor and see if the recipient did indeed read the message. Okay, that's picky and it's probably safe to assume that the message was read.

Incidentally, the recipient knows that the message has tracking turned on but doesn't learn about it until after the message is open. A glance at the Options tab reveals the presence of the tracking check marks.

 T I P If tracking is important, you should create a folder for messages that have tracking tabs and use the Move to Folder icon to transfer the original message from the Sent Items folder. (I made mine a subfolder under the Sent Items folder and placed a shortcut to it on the Outlook Bar for easy access.) This prevents the need to scroll through the Sent Items folder looking for the message when you do need to verify the delivery. It also means you can clean house periodically by deleting messages from the Sent Items folder without the risk of losing the information.

Changing the Options for Tracking There are a couple of options you can set for Outlook's tracking capacity. You can configure Outlook to delete the notification messages that arrive in your Inbox automatically. Open the Options dialog box from the Tools menu and move to the E-mail tab. Select Delete Receipts and Blank Responses After Processing. The information is still entered in the Tracking tab of the original message.

You can also set tracking as the default option. Use the Sending tab of the Options dialog box and turn on tracking for delivery or reading or both. If you do set tracking as the default, you can deselect it for any individual message on the Options tab.

Specifying Delivery Options

Another Outlook feature available to users of Exchange Server is the ability to hold back delivery of a message until a specified date and time.

In addition, you can create an expiration date and time for a message, making it unavailable to the recipient after that.

Both of these features are invoked from the Options tab of the message.

Redirecting Replies

Also available on the Options tab of a message is the ability to redirect any replies to the message. Click the Select Names button and choose the user who will receive any responses to the message. This is extremely useful in any situation in which you are requesting information and there is another user responsible for keeping track of that information.

Part
V
Ch
25

Additional Power for Tasks

The Tasks features in Outlook are powerful and productive, but they gain more of both assets when used on an Exchange Server system.

With Exchange Server, you can assign tasks to other users and continue to track the progress of a task automatically. This is especially useful when there's a large project at hand, because keeping track of who is doing which part of the project and tracking each person's progress can be daunting.

How Task Assignments Work

It's worthwhile to spend a moment or two looking at task assignments conceptually, because the implementation can involve so many different permutations and combinations. Later in this section, we'll go over the steps for assigning tasks, which are quite straightforward.

Task Ownership   One important concept in assigning tasks is ownership. The owner of a task has three important characteristics:

- Only the current owner of a task can make changes to the basic configuration of that task.

- The owner of a task can assign it to another user, who becomes the new owner.

- Any user who ever owned a task receives automatic updates on the status of the task.

The person who creates a task owns it first. This is a permanent ownership until it is relinquished by assigning the task to another user.

When an owner sends an assignment request to a user, that action strips the owner of ownership. The recipient of the task assignment request becomes the owner immediately.

When a user receives a task assignment, that user is a temporary owner. The temporary ownership is changed when:

- The temporary owner accepts the task, in which case he or she becomes the permanent owner.

- The temporary owner refuses the task, in which case ownership returns to the last permanent owner (the user who assigned it).

- The temporary owner assigns the task, which means he or she accepted permanent ownership and then immediately gave it up.

The important element in the last scenario is that there was permanent owner status for the user, albeit for a very short period of time, which entitles that user to receive updates on the task just like all permanent owners in the history of the task.

> **N O T E**   As a task moves through a variety of owners, changes to the task's configuration can only be made by the current owner. If a task assignment is made and the temporary owner has not yet decided what to do with the task, during that period of temporary ownership, the undecided

user is the current owner and can make changes to the task. When the task is accepted, returned, or reassigned, it contains the changed configuration. ▇

Task Updates   When an owner assigns a task, he or she relinquishes all owner rights to change the configuration. However, all previous permanent owners of a task can keep a copy of the task in their Task folder. If they do so, changes to the task (configuration and status) are sent to that copy so whenever a previous permanent owner views the task, it is an updated view. It is, however, a read-only view.

A previous owner can opt to delete the task and give up the right to receive automatic updates ("out of sight, out of mind" is sometimes a good management philosophy).

T I P   If you created the task and are therefore the first permanent owner, you should probably keep a copy of the task in your Task folder. If, however, you were one of a chain of permanent owners and reassigned the task to another user, it's probably not necessary for you to continue to track the progress of the task.

Tracking Multiple Owners   An important concept to remember is that you can only receive tracking information from a single owner. If you assign a task to multiple users, automatic updates are not an option. This usually occurs when the task is quite large, and it makes sense to assign the task to multiple users.

However, as an owner/creator, it's not a good idea to give up the automatic updating feature—there's probably somebody to whom you have to report.

I've found a solution to this problem that works well. First, there is the obvious solution of creating as many discrete tasks as you need and assigning each task to a specific user. Even if that user reassigns the task, you continue to get updates. However, the tasks and updates are in your Task folder as individual entities, and after you've done this a few times, it's hard to remember which of the tasks belong together (and started out as one task).

My solution is to use the Outlook Categories feature to simulate a project. Then I create individual tasks for the project and assign them. There is no real concept of "project" in Outlook; it's an artificial device I use to make sure I keep related tasks bundled.

Here's how to make this work:

1. Create the first task for the project.
2. When you have completed the configuration of the task, click the Categories button on the Task window to display the Categories list.
3. Enter a new category, using the name you want to assign to this project (see Figure 25.14). Then choose Add to List and OK.

The new category is part of the Outlook category list and is available system-wide. Thereafter, assign this category to every individual task you create. Notify others who are creating tasks connected to this project to do the same.

Part

V

Ch

25

FIG. 25.14
Add a category to the
Outlook Category list
in order to create a
project.

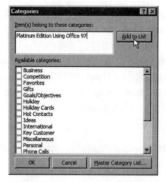

In your Tasks viewer, group your tasks by category; the display will resemble a project listing
(see Figure 25.15). As you assign tasks, you can sub-group by owner for even more efficiency.

FIG. 25.15
Group tasks by
categories to emulate
project reporting.

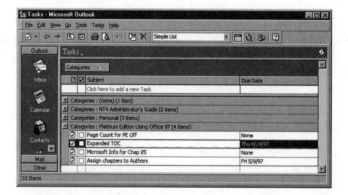

Once a category is in the system, it's available to other Outlook functions such as Contacts and
Calendar. Assign the project category to those items whenever you're working on something related to
this project. You can print reports that look at all Outlook functions by category, which gives you an
enormously powerful way to track major projects.

Assigning Tasks

Tasks are assigned via *Task Requests*, the Outlook term for a message that invites a user to
accept a task assignment from you. You can assign a task as part of the process of creating one,
or you can assign an existing task.

To create and assign a task at the same time, choose New Task Request from the Tasks menu
(the command is also available under File, New, but that's the long way). A Task Request window opens (see Figure 25.16) that looks like a combination of a task window and a message
window:

FIG. 25.16

A Task Request is an e-mail message with task information.

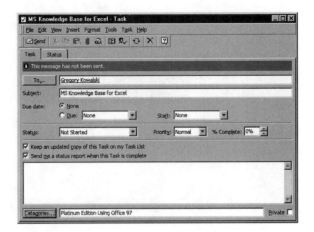

1. Click To and choose a user from the address list.

2. Fill out the Subject, Due Date, and any other configuration information you have at this time.

3. As needed, use the choices for keeping an updated copy of the task and receiving a status report when the task is complete.

4. If the task is part of a project, select the appropriate category.

5. Choose Send to assign the task.

The task is on your task list, and the Task icon has a hand in addition to the normal Clipboard icon, indicating the task is assigned. You no longer own this task.

To assign an existing task, open the task and click the Assign Task button on the toolbar (it looks like the assigned task icon, a hand under a clipboard). A Task Request window opens so you can send the message to the user of your choice.

Accepting Task Assignments

Because a Task Request is really an e-mail message, when you receive one it shows up in your Inbox (see Figure 25.17).

The minute the task is in your Inbox, you are the temporary owner. Open the message to choose whether or not you want to keep the task. The toolbar on the message window has buttons for accepting and declining the assignment (see Figure 25.18).

You have several options available:

- Accept the request by clicking the Accept button on the toolbar.

    If you want to enter a comment for the sender, when the confirming dialog box appears, choose Edit the Response. Enter your comment in the message window and then choose Send.

Part

V

Ch

25

FIG. 25.17

A Task Request in the Inbox is recognizable by the icon.

FIG. 25.18

The message window is specifically designed for accepting or declining the task request.

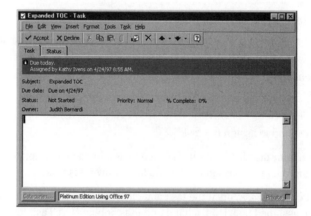

- Decline the Request by clicking the Decline button on the toolbar.

  You can use the same method to enter a comment as described for accepting the request.

- Assign the task to someone else by clicking the Assign Task button on the toolbar and proceeding as described. You can choose to receive updates and notification of completion.

If you accept the task, it is placed on your Task List, and you work on it as if you were working on a task of your own invention. As you work on the task, the previous owner is sent updates (choosing Save and Close triggers the update).

Meanwhile, back at the ranch....

The user who assigned the task receives the e-mail notification of the acceptance or rejection. If the task is accepted, the assigning user can open the task from his or her task list and see the current status.

Using Public Folders with Outlook

Public folders, a Microsoft Exchange Server feature, provide a quick, productive method for organizing information and making it available to other users. Besides placing documents and forms in public folders (the most frequently applied use), you can move Outlook items in and out of these system-wide containers.

Explaining how to set up and use public folders is beyond the scope of this book, but give some thought to the power of public folders and how you can avail yourself of those services with Outlook, for example:

- Public folders can be established as bulletin boards to centralize discussion about tasks, projects, and contacts.
- Create a local folder for a project and include all the contacts, meetings, and tasks connected to the project. Then copy that folder to a public folder so the information is available to all users. They can copy the folder to their local Outlook system.
- Keep a running To Do list in a public folder.

Depending on the nature of your work and the way you use Outlook, you'll think of many more uses for public folders.

Using Public Folders for Outlook Features

It's a good idea to create public folders for major projects that you are tracking with the Outlook Tasks feature. And, Outlook calendar items that affect a large number of users (company-wide events or department-wide events) are good candidates for public folders.

N O T E   To create a public folder, you must have the necessary administrative permissions. To access a public folder, you must have permissions equal to the task you want to perform in the folder (read, create, edit, and so on). If you are the administrator for your Microsoft Exchange Server system or have administrative powers, be sure that all the Outlook users get the appropriate permissions for their use of the folders you create. It might be a good idea to give users who frequently supervise large projects the right to create public folders. ■

One of the most productive things you can do with a public folder you expect to be using a great deal is place a shortcut to it on your Outlook Bar. Just display the folder list, right-click the public folder you need, and choose Add to Outlook Bar from the shortcut menu.

Add an Outlook Item to a Public Folder   You can place an Outlook item into a public folder. You'll probably use this commonly for large projects (assuming a public folder has been established for the project).

The easiest way to accomplish this is to drag the item from its Viewer window to the public folder:

1. Display the folders by clicking the Folder List button on the Outlook toolbar.
2. Right-drag the Outlook item to the appropriate folder.

3. Release the mouse button and choose the move or copy command you need (see Figure 25.19):

FIG. 25.19

Create a public folder posting of an Outlook item to share it with users all over the system.

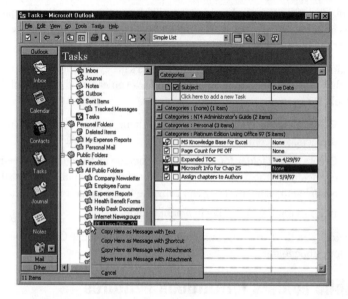

- *Copy Here as Message with Text.* Post a message in the public folder with the information about the Outlook item displayed as text.

- *Copy Here as Message with Shortcut.* Post a message that has a shortcut icon to the Outlook item.

- *Copy Here as Message with Attachment.* Post a message that has the item included as an attachment.

- *Move Here as Message with Attachment.* Remove the item from the Viewer and place it in the public folder.

 If you create a public folder for an Outlook item that shouldn't be available to the Global User List, set permissions by user to include only those users who are permitted to know about the item. If you created an e-mail distribution list for these users, select it when you add permissions to the folder to avoid having to give each user permissions individually.

Use an Outlook Item in a Public Folder   Once an Outlook item is in a public folder, anyone with access to that public folder can view it. In addition (depending on the type of item), there are several other manipulations available:

- ■ *Move the item to a local folder.* Open the public folder and right-drag the item to the appropriate shortcut on the Outlook Bar. Choose the menu command you want (Copy, Move, with other choices depending on the type of item).

- *Respond to the item.* Open the item and add information or comments, then choose Post Reply to place your contribution into the public folder.

- *Open the attachment or shortcut in the item.* If the item was placed in the public folder as an attachment or a shortcut as part of the posting, once it's opened you can manipulate it as you would any other item. Save it, move it, or copy it.

Public folders and Outlook items are a natural combination. Once you get used to using public folders, you'll find yourself distributing e-mail, contact information, task information, and journals via public folders.

Designing Outlook Forms

All of the functionality of Outlook is based on forms: the message form, task form, and so forth. In addition to these built-in forms, you can create your own forms for special needs. Outlook provides a Forms Designer and even has some sample forms you can play with to nudge your creative thinking.

Installing the Sample Forms

If you want to use the sample forms, open the ValuPack directory on your Office 97 CD-ROM (they're not transferred to your hard drive during installation), and follow these steps:

1. Expand the ValuPack folder and move to \Template\Outlook.
2. Double-click Outlfrms.exe to launch the installation program for Outlook forms.
3. Specify the target folder on your local drive (usually the default choice is appropriate).

The forms are installed to your local drive.

T I P If you used My Computer to get to the forms on the CD-ROM, there are a number of folder windows open by the time you get to the forms installation file. Here's a tip: Hold down the Shift key when you close the top window, and all the windows will close automatically.

After the forms are installed, you have to set up a folder for them in your Outlook window:

1. Choose Open Special Folder, Personal Folder from the File menu.
2. Move to the folder you specified during the installation.
3. Open forms.pst.

If your folders aren't displayed, use the Folder List button to add the folders panel to your Outlook window. A new folder named Sample Forms is displayed (see Figure 25.20).

Using the Forms

To use the forms, select the sample form you need in the folders pane, then open the Compose menu and select the form you need (the message in the right panel is not the form, it's just a message about the form). When the form opens, fill it in and post it or send it (see Figure 25.21).

FIG. 25.20

The sample forms in the folder are messages that have instructions about using the forms.

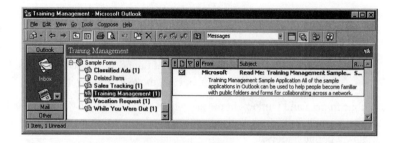

FIG. 25.21

This standard form has choices built in for the category.

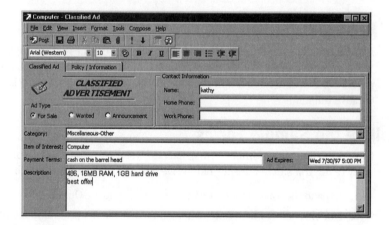

Most of the forms are designed to be posted to public folders (note the Post button on the toolbar instead of a Send button). Any item in a public folder can be opened by other users, who can post a reply.

However, when you installed the sample forms, they were placed on your local hard drive, which means the folder in which they reside is like a personal folder. After you filled out the form and saved it or posted it, it remained in the local folder. Therefore, you need to move your filled-out form to a public folder:

1. Select the filled-in form and click the Move to Folder button on the toolbar.

2. Choose an appropriate folder from the list of All Public Folders.

3. If there isn't a public folder that fits the occasion, you can choose New to create one if you have the necessary permissions (if you don't, ask the Exchange Server administrator to give you the rights you need).

4. When you choose OK on the Move Item To dialog box, your filled-out form is sent to the public folder where the whole organization can see it.

Anyone who sees the form can post a reply to the public folder, so check the folder occasionally to see if there's a response. A user could also opt to use the Reply function, which means the response is sent to your Inbox.

Modifying and Customizing the Forms

You can change any of the sample forms to fit your own needs. While it is beyond the scope of this book to present a detailed set of instructions for all the options available for Outlook forms, an overview should be sufficient to get you started with some experimental forays into the world of customization:

1. Highlight the form in the Folders pane, then choose it from the Compose menu to open the form (see Figure 25.22).

FIG. 25.22

Open a sample form to use it as the basis of a new form.

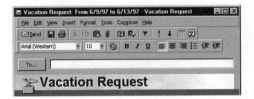

2. From the Tools menu on the form's menu bar, select Design Outlook Form. The form changes to display its design format (see Figure 25.23).

FIG. 25.23

Every element in a sample form is available for modification.

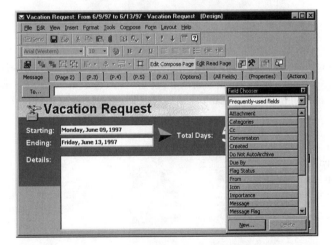

3. The Field Chooser box opens by default, but if it's in your way you should close it. When you need it again, click the Field Chooser button on the toolbar. (See the section "Using the Field Chooser" later in this chapter).

4. Click any element (text, text box, icon, and so on) to edit it. An edit box with sizing handles appears around the element. You can change the size, change any label text, and use the buttons on the toolbar to format text, group graphics, or align the elements.

   You can also right-click an element and choose actions from the shortcut menu. These actions include Edit (for text elements) as well as an opportunity to change the order in which the element appears on the form.

N O T E When you first open the design format page, the Compose page is displayed. This is the page users see when they ask for a form, and it is where they compose a message in the form. Use the Edit Read Page button on the toolbar to design the page seen by users who receive the form. ■

Use the Properties of the Form's Elements You can also change an element by working directly with its properties. For example, right-click a label element and choose Properties from the shortcut menu to see information similar to that shown in Figure 25.24.

FIG. 25.24

The Properties dialog box for a caption shows its configuration, and you can make any changes you like.

The properties for an element other than text are concerned with the way the element is used. For example, the box in which users fill out the start and end dates for their vacation schedule has information in the Value tab of the Properties dialog box (see Figure 25.25).

FIG. 25.25

You can change the format of the date and the initial value of the field.

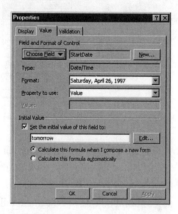

Use the Control Toolbox You can build additional elements on the page or on additional pages, which appear as tabs in the message form (such as the Options tab on an e-mail message form) by using the tools available in the Control Toolbox. Choose Control Toolbox from the Form menu and use the tools to create new elements (see Figure 25.26).

FIG. 25.26

List boxes, buttons, scroll bars, check boxes—just pick what you need.

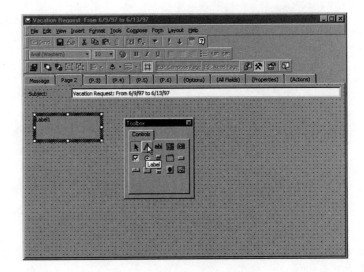

Use the Field Chooser You can add a field to any page by opening the Field Chooser and dragging the name of the field to the appropriate position on the page (see Figure 25.27). The field's label and the box that holds text are automatically sized for you, but you can use the sizing handles to change the dimensions.

FIG. 25.27

To satisfy company policy, this vacation request needed a Cc field in order to send a copy to the department head.

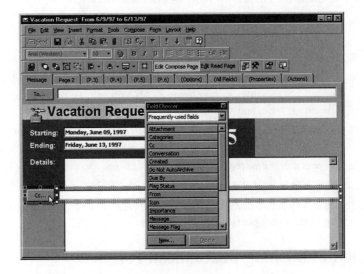

Add a Page If you need additional information that doesn't fit on the Message page or isn't suitable for the Message page, add elements and fields, then choose Rename Page from the Form menu (see Figure 25.28).

FIG. 25.28

For this form, additional fields are placed on a new page.

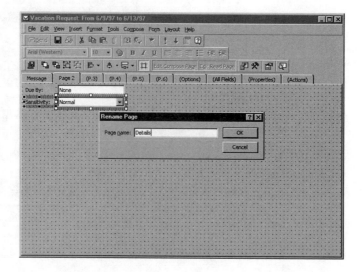

Name the page (actually, you're naming the tab). Do not use the names Message, Options, or Tracking because those are part of the standard tab names for Outlook forms. The moment you add an element to a page, that page exists in the form.

Enable and Disable Actions   Move to the Actions page (tab) to see the actions that are enabled for this form. The actions have specific characteristics:

- *Each action has a name.* Reply, Reply to All, and Forward are the most familiar action names.

- *Each action has a form type that displays.* For instance, Reply opens a message form.

- *There is an addressing scheme for the form.* This determines the address fields in the header. For example, if you choose Reply, you will see the standard e-mail address fields (To, Subject, Cc, and so on).

- *There is a layout setup for entering responses.* There may or may not be a duplication of the original message text, and if there is, its formatting (alignment) can be determined.

- *There is a prefix for the Subject field.* This means a word or phrase is added at the beginning of the subject field in the format Prefix : Original Subject Text.

Double-click any action to display its properties and make changes (including enable/disable), according to your own plans for this form (see Figure 25.29).

Saving and Publishing Customized Forms

After your new form is complete, you must save it for future use. There are several mechanisms available for saving a new form, and the choices determine how you want the form to be used.

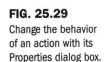

FIG. 25.29

Change the behavior of an action with its Properties dialog box.

Save the Form as an E-Mail Form for Your Own Use   The simplest way to save the new form is to choose Save from the File menu or click the Save icon on the toolbar. The form is saved in the open folder (the folder on your local drive which was the target for the installation of forms).

Move to the Properties tab of the Form Design window to change the name of the form if you don't want to replace the existing form. You can use this form anytime you like by selecting it when you're sending e-mail.

Save the Form as a File   You can save the form as a file in order to use it in an application. Choose Save As from the File menu, then name the form and select a file type that works with the application you plan to use (Choose Among Text, RTF, Outlook Template, and Message Format).

You can share this file with others by e-mailing it to them.

Save the Form as a New Form for All Users   If you want to make this form available to all users, you must save it in a forms library:

1. Choose Publish Form As from the File menu.

2. In the Publish Form As dialog box (see Figure 25.30), enter a name for the form.

FIG. 25.30

Publish a form to make it a new Outlook form.

3. By default, the form is published in the Personal Forms folder, which is on your local drive. To publish it in a system-wide library, choose Publish In on the Publish Form As dialog box (see Figure 25.31).

Part V

Ch

25

FIG. 25.31

Publish the form in a public location to make it available to all the users on your Exchange Server system.

4. Choose a target location according to the way you expect the form to be accessed by users:

   - Keep the default Forms Library selection but change the library to Organizational Forms, which is a server-based library. This makes the form available to any user with permissions for the library.

   - Select Folder Forms Library and then choose the public folder that this form will be used in. The form will be available to any user accessing that public folder.

5. Choose OK to return to the Publish Form As dialog box, where the new location is displayed. Choose Publish to complete the process.

The most common, and most convenient, way to publish a form that needs no response (announcements, catalogs, and so on) is to place it in the system Organization Forms Library.

The best place for a form that requires user responses is an appropriate public folder. All public folders have form libraries attached to them (although until you create a form, the library for each public folder is empty), and your form is added to the folder's library. It is listed on the Compose menu, and any user who accesses the folder can choose it.

TROUBLESHOOTING

There are two common problems faced by users who want to publish forms to the Organization Forms Library. The first is that the Organization Forms Library is not listed on the Publish In dialog box. The second is that if the library is available, the system refuses to let the user place the form in the library because of insufficient permissions. Both problems are solved by the administrator of Exchange Server.

The Organization Forms Library is not created during the installation of Exchange Server, so the administrator must perform the task post-installation. This is performed at the server using the Exchange Server Administrator program. When the Administrator window opens, move to the Folders\System Folders container and follow these steps:

1. Select the Eforms Registry container and choose Forms Administrator from the Tools menu.

2. In the Organization Forms dialog box, choose New. Then enter the Library folder name **Organization Forms** and choose the language (most likely English).

3. Choose OK to return to the Organization Form dialog box and choose Permissions. By default, all users in the organization are given Reviewer permissions, giving them the ability to read items (that permission level also makes the folder and its contents visible).

4. Select the users who should have permission to post forms to the library and give them Owner permissions.

If you want to add or change permissions later, use the Permissions button on the General tab of the Organization Forms Properties dialog box.

Note that the Help files for Exchange Server indicate a path for the Organization Forms Library that is incorrect (it is shown one level too high). If you follow the instructions in this section, the container is created properly, and all forms posted to it are available to all users.

If you are a user who received an insufficient permission level error message, ask the administrator to give you temporary Owner permissions so you can install your form.

Once a form is installed in the Organization Form library, any user can access it by choosing New, Choose Form from the File menu (or by choosing Chose Form from the menu immediately to the left of the Help menu in an Information Window—that menu item changes its name depending on the current folder).

More Power with Exchange Server Forms

Exchange Server also has a forms designer, and it is much more powerful than the Outlook feature. With Exchange Server, you can design forms and then write programs that distribute the forms, collect them, place the returned information in a database, perform calculations, issue reports, and accomplish lots of other maneuvers.

Exchange Server cannot use forms you designed in Outlook, but Outlook can use any forms you create in Exchange Server.

Check the Exchange Server documentation to learn how to use the powerful forms program. ●

Microsoft PowerPoint

26 Working with Objects   545

27 Creating a Slide Show   563

28 Creating Multimedia Presentations   585

CHAPTER 26

Working with Objects

Manipulate objects

Use multiple shapes and art work and arrange or animate them in a variety of dramatic and effective ways.

Link and embed objects

Insert objects that originated in another application; linking provides a way to keep data current.

The last thing you want to do is stand up in front of an audience and present a long series of text slides. Think about it for a moment. Huh, what? Oh, sorry—I dozed off.

Add a variety of object types to your slides and manipulate them to keep the audience awake, to emphasize particular points, to inject humor, and to make your slide show as professional as possible.

One thing that enhances the professional look of your work is the manner in which you present objects on a slide. Using them well, making them serve a purpose, can make a big difference.

PowerPoint provides a robust assortment of maneuvers to exploit the advantages in using graphics and presenting text. This chapter covers some of the procedures you'll find useful. There's not a lot of basic "how to do it" in this chapter (you probably already know how to do it); instead, there are overview explanations of the available features including how and where they work. ■

Manipulating Objects

The variety of shapes available in PowerPoint is enough to provide all the graphic interest you need in a slide. Shapes can be twisted, bent, stretched, and condensed, giving you the opportunity to have plenty of graphics without repeating yourself.

Besides shapes, there are plenty of other objects available for graphic interest, including clip art, pictures, and animation. All of these objects can be put together to accommodate any imaginative scheme you invent.

And, of course, there is an almost unlimited number of ways to present text; in PowerPoint, text is just another object.

You also can stack or group objects to create interesting graphic effects, and then position them exactly the way you need them.

Stacking Objects

If you have more than one object on a slide, technically you have a stack. Each object you add is theoretically sitting on a layer, with each new object on top of the previous object (see Figure 26.1). You just don't notice it until objects overlap. When there is no overlapping, the layers and the order of the stack (from front to back) are transparent to the user and therefore irrelevant.

FIG. 26.1
For the three objects on this slide, the order in which they were inserted determines the stack layers.

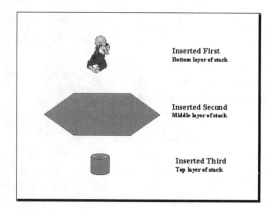

If an individual object is moved anywhere on the slide, (even to a position that overlaps with another object), it does so within its own layer (see Figure 26.2).

Because of this, it's possible to "lose" an object. If you move too fast when you drag and you release the mouse over an object on a higher plane in the stack, the original object disappears behind it.

You can move objects from layer to layer within the stack. The easiest way to do this is to right-click the object and choose Order from the shortcut menu. Then choose the movement that's appropriate:

- Bring to Front moves the object to the top layer of the stack.
- Send to Back moves the object to the bottom layer of the stack.
- Bring Forward moves the object one layer higher in the stack.
- Send Backward moves the object one layer lower in the stack.

FIG. 26.2

Objects that are moved stay in their own stack layer.

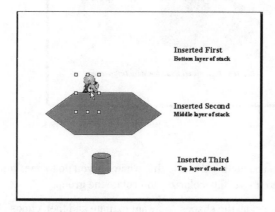

If you've lost the object so you can't select it in order to move it, you can move the object that's on top of it back a layer. Or, use the Tab key to move through all the objects in the slide. When you get to the hidden object (see Figure 26.3), right-click the object and choose Order, Bring Forward to move it forward.

FIG. 26.3

When you see the sizing handles, you know you've found the hidden object.

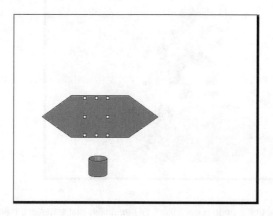

Stacking objects is a good way to create an interesting visual element for your presentation. You can combine different types of graphics, perhaps placing a clip art file on top of a shape, to make your point (see Figure 26.4).

FIG. 26.4
Merging shapes with clip art is an easy way to build a stack of objects for an effective graphic.

Grouping Objects

Grouping objects means uniting them so that whatever you do to one, you do to all. Some of the things you can do are move, flip, colorize, and rotate the group.

To group shapes, select all the shapes you want to unite and then choose Draw, Group from the Drawing toolbar. Remember that PowerPoint expects the Shift key instead of the Ctrl key when you select multiple objects. The sizing handles for each individual object disappear and new ones appear for the group (see Figure 26.5).

FIG. 26.5
Multiple objects become one object when you group them.

> **N O T E**   Having said that a group is one object, I'll now qualify that statement. If any element in the group is an AutoShape, you can change the AutoShape as if it were still an individual object. Just select the group; choose Draw, Change AutoShape; and select a new shape. Be careful: If you have multiple AutoShapes in the group and each one is a different shape, this command changes all the AutoShapes to the newly selected one. ■

You can also create nested groups:

- Select one or more individual objects and select an existing group, then create a new group.
- Select two or more groups and create a new group.

You can nest groups as deeply as necessary, except that if you have to change anything in one of the first groups, you'll have a lot of ungrouping to do. Be sure each element is exactly the way you want it before you create the next group.

Changing an Element in a Group

If you want to make changes to any element in a group, you have to ungroup, make the changes, then regroup:

1. Right-click the group, then choose Grouping, Ungroup. Each element in the group displays its frame and sizing handles (see Figure 26.6).

FIG. 26.6
The sizing handles for each individual element in the group are displayed when you ungroup.

New Employee Benefits

Day Care Available For
All Employees

See Your Department Head for More Information

2. Click outside the graphics to clear the individual frames, and then click the element or elements you want to manipulate.
3. When you have completed your tweaking, right-click any element from the original group and then choose Grouping, Regroup.

PowerPoint remembers the elements in the group and uses that information when you apply the Regroup command. If, while you were working ungrouped, you added another element, regrouping will fail to include it. You must regroup, then select both the group and the new element and group the new combination (or create an entirely new group).

If your group is nested and the element you want to change is further down, you must keep ungrouping until you get where you need to be. Then regroup your way back to the top.

Rotating Objects

There are a variety of ways to rotate objects, and your choice depends not only on the specific rotation you need, but also on how steady you are with a mouse.

Most of the time, rotating means moving the object clockwise or counterclockwise, but you can also *flip* an object (which is like picking up the object, turning it over, and setting it back down in the same place).

Graphics are not the only objects you can rotate; text boxes can also be manipulated in this manner. That means you can take a title text box and run it along a side, or create any other interesting and attention-attracting device for your text.

 T I P   It's probably not a good idea to flip text boxes unless you provide cushions for the moment your audience has to do headstands to read your text.

Rotating an object requires only that you select it and then make a choice from the Rotate or Flip submenu on the Draw menu:

- Choose Free Rotate to rotate the object manually. You can click the Free Rotate button on the Drawing toolbar for faster access to this function.
- Choose Rotate Left to rotate the object 90 degrees in a counterclockwise direction.
- Choose Rotate Right to rotate the object 90 degrees in a clockwise direction.
- Choose Flip Horizontal to turn the object over from left to right.
- Choose Flip Vertical to turn the object over from top to bottom.

If you elect to rotate the object yourself with the Free Rotate function, the object displays rotation handles instead of sizing handles, and your mouse pointer displays a rotation arrow (see Figure 26.7).

FIG. 26.7
Drag the rotation handle to turn the object.

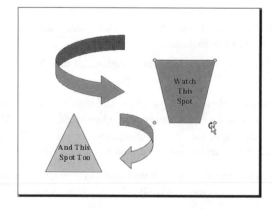

You can automate the free rotation function a bit by holding down the Shift key as you move the rotation button. This forces the rotation to proceed in 15-degree increments. That way, if you want to rotate the object about 20 degrees, you only have to control the mouse for a small movement after you've taken advantage of the 15-degree movement.

When you rotate a graphical object that has text in it, the results differ depending upon the way text was added (see Figure 26.8):

- If the text is a result of a text box placed on the object, the text does not rotate with the object.
- If the text was entered directly on the object, the text rotates with the object (see the section "Placing Text on AutoShapes" later in this chapter).

FIG. 26.8
Text boxes have to be rotated individually; direct text entries follow along with the object's rotation.

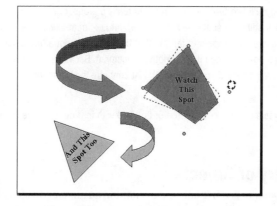

Objects that are not original PowerPoint objects cannot be rotated without some tinkering, and some cannot be rotated under any circumstances. Most clip art, for instance, seems not to be able to be manipulated in this way (except there's usually a way to tinker with it to permit rotation). If you select clip art and find that the commands on the Rotate or Flip submenu are grayed out, the object cannot currently be rotated. Here's the way to fix this:

1. Right-click the clip art and choose Grouping. If Ungroup is available on the submenu, it means this clip art can be disassembled. Choose Ungroup, and the clip art figure displays each object in the group (see Figure 26.9).
2. Right-click anywhere in the clip art and choose Grouping, Regroup (if Regroup is grayed out, choose Group). Now the Rotate commands are available for this clip art.

The fact is, when you ungroup and regroup clip art, you convert the object into a Microsoft Office drawing.

FIG. 26.9
Individual frames are displayed when you ungroup a clip art object.

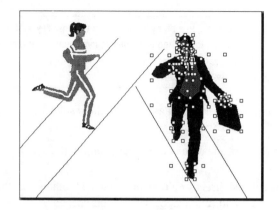

> **N O T E**   Sometimes you'll find that the clip art is not really a group, or at least was not assembled as a group. It still can usually be broken down into element-like components, so it acts like a group. A warning message may appear to tell you that this clip art is not a true group, and if you ungroup it you'll lose any links between it and another document. Because it's probably the case that this object isn't linked (you'd know if you'd linked it), just continue the operation. ■

> **N O T E**   Bitmap objects cannot be converted or tinkered with in order to rotate them. ■

Animating the Entry of Objects

In PowerPoint, *animation* doesn't only mean running an animated video clip; it means you can animate the way every element of your slide shows up on your slide. This not only gives you a way to make your slides more interesting and attention-getting, but it also gives you the power to control the order in which information is imparted. For example, you could present a slide with three bullet items and count on the audience to inspect each item with equal attention, or you could slide the bullet list onto the slide one line at a time. The latter technique certainly ensures that your audience gives full attention to each of the important points on your slide.

As with almost everything in PowerPoint, you have a number of choices for performing the animation functions.

Animation Effects Toolbar   One of the quickest ways to create simple animation is to choose one of the effects in the Animation Effects toolbar. Select an object on the slide and click the Animation Effects button on the Formatting toolbar. The Animation Effects toolbar appears, displaying text animation choices if you've selected a text object (see Figure 26.10), or graphics animation choices if you've selected a graphic element (see Figure 26.11). Most of these animations use sound effects in addition to moving the object onto the slide in some creative fashion. The Animation Effects toolbar also has an icon for Custom Animation (discussed later in this chapter in the section "Custom Animation").

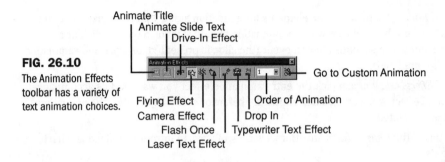

FIG. 26.10

The Animation Effects toolbar has a variety of text animation choices.

Animate Title
Animate Slide Text
Drive-In Effect
Go to Custom Animation
Flying Effect
Camera Effect
Flash Once
Laser Text Effect
Order of Animation
Drop In
Typewriter Text Effect

FIG. 26.11

For graphics, there are fewer choices on the Animation Effects toolbar.

Flying Effect   Camera Effect
Drive-In Effect   Flash Once

You can create multiple animations for your slide with this toolbar:

1. Select an object, then select an effect from the Animation Effects toolbar.

2. Select a different object on the slide, then a new (or the same) effect. The animation order number displays in the Animation Effects toolbar so you know when this animation will play back.

3. Continue to select objects to create a series of animations, choosing them in the order in which you want them to appear on your slide.

4. Choose Animation Preview from the Slide Show menu to see what the effects look like (and sound like).

An annoying problem with the Animation Effects toolbar is that there is no Preview tool. You have to open the Slide Show menu and choose Animation Preview (there's no keyboard combination for quick access to that command), and the animation is presented in a small window.

Preset Animations   Another quick method for animating an object is to select the object you want to animate and make a selection from the list of Preset Animations available on the Slide Show menu. Like the Animation Effects toolbar, there are different choices depending upon the type of object.

Custom Animation   Click the Custom Animation button on the Animation Effects toolbar to display the Custom Animation dialog box to create, edit, or remove animation. If you've used the Animation Effects toolbar, or chosen a Preset Animation from the Slide Show menu, you'll see it in the dialog box (see Figure 26.12). Otherwise, the blank dialog box awaits your creative instructions.

You can use the Custom Animation dialog box to build some fairly elaborate animation routines for each element in the slide:

Part
VI

Ch
26

■ Use the *Timing tab* to select the elements for animation along with their order of entry animation, and then indicate whether animation should start on a mouse click or a specific number of seconds after an event (the slide is presented, or a previous animation effect is completed).

■ On the *Effects tab*, you can pick the entry animation effect you want and its accompanying sound effect. You can also determine the behavior of the object after the animation effect is completed.

■ For a chart, the *Chart Effects tab* offers a variety of ways to introduce individual chart elements.

■ The *Play Settings tab* is where you determine the animation for movies, sounds, or OLE objects.

FIG. 26.12
The Custom Animation dialog box is the place to design and preview complex animation effects.

N O T E   If you are planning to use two Whoosh sound effects in a row, be warned that the resulting effect sounds like a sneeze. ■

Working with Text Objects

You cannot be quite as aggressive in your manipulation plans when it comes to text, because you have to worry about readability.

In fact, the issue of entering text isn't always as simple and straightforward as it might seem—PowerPoint has some rules and conventions that might not be obvious and can therefore make text entry a bit frustrating. This section is an overview of the PowerPoint approach to text entry and manipulation.

There are three ways to add text to a slide:

■ Enter text into a placeholder.

■ Create a text box and enter text in it.

■ Enter text directly onto a graphic element.

Placeholders   Most of the placeholders in the standard designs available in PowerPoint present text placeholders for title slides or titles of slides that contain bullet items.

You don't have to restrict yourself to a text placeholder if you decide text would be appropriate somewhere else. The process of entering text in a placeholder for any object type turns it into a text placeholder.

The important thing about using placeholders is to enter the appropriate amount of text and use the appropriate language (chatty prose doesn't work for a slide title).

Text Boxes   The way the text in a text box behaves depends on how you insert a text box on the slide:

- Click the Text Box tool, then click to place the text box on the slide. Begin entering text, and as you type, the box widens to accept the text. The text does not wrap.

- Click the Text Box tool, then drag to position the text box on the slide. As you enter text, the text wraps in order to keep the width of the box you dragged. The box deepens as you continue to enter text.

- Place a text box on an AutoShape, using either method mentioned.

Once you have the text box, you can change it into an AutoShape if you feel you need to add more interest to it or draw attention to the text:

1. Select the text box, then choose Draw, Change AutoShape.

2. Choose a category, then choose a shape.

3. It appears as if nothing has changed. That's because you have a clear shape on a clear background. Select the object and fill it with color (see Figure 26.13).

FIG. 26.13
Even thought you can't tell it at a glance, both of these text boxes have been changed to the same AutoShape.

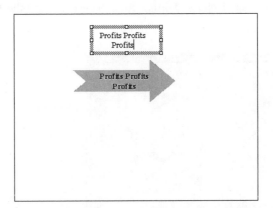

Part
VI

Ch
26

Placing Text on AutoShapes   You can place text on any AutoShape (except lines, connectors, or free form drawings) simply by selecting the object and typing. This is an extremely effective use of AutoShapes as well as a great way to draw attention to text. Just select the AutoShape object and start typing:

- The text is automatically centered by default.

- The text will not wrap; it will spill beyond the borders of the AutoShape. You can press Enter to move to the next line, but it's better to manipulate the text to force it to wrap (discussed next).

- The text is an inherent part of the shape and will move with the shape when the shape is rotated, flipped, moved, grouped, or so on.

You can manipulate the text that's on an AutoShape to make it behave a bit more like text in a text box. Select the AutoShape object, which now shows the same type of crosshatch selection frame as a text box (see Figure 26.14). (Normally, AutoShapes show only the sizing handles when you select them.)

FIG. 26.14

An AutoShape with text displays a text box frame when you select it.

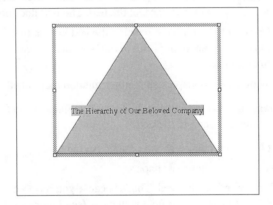

The Hierarchy of Our Beloved Company

With the AutoShape selected, choose Format, AutoShape and select the Text Box tab (see Figure 26.15).

FIG. 26.15

The text on an AutoShape can be manipulated in the Format AutoShape dialog box.

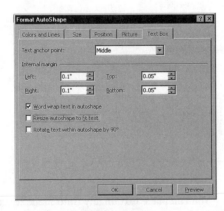

The following options appear on the Text Box tab:

- Choose the Text Anchor Point for placement of the text in the AutoShape (top, middle, bottom, and so on).

- Set the Left, Right, Top, and Bottom margins (the space between text and the edge of the AutoShape).

- Select Word Wrap Text in AutoShape if you want the text to wrap within the AutoShape.

- Select Resize AutoShape to Fit Text to make the graphic large enough to hold the text as it's currently formatted.

- Select Rotate Text to move the text 90 degrees in a clockwise direction.

TROUBLESHOOTING

There are several annoying problems that can arise when you are trying to manipulate text in an AutoShape and almost all of them are the result of the current state of the Resize AutoShape selection on the Format AutoShape dialog box. To solve the following problems, make sure the Resize AutoShape option is either selected or deselected as described here:

- If entering margin changes has no effect—select it.

- If positioning text doesn't work—deselect it.

- If you can't reduce the size of the shape to match your own taste—deselect it (selecting Word Wrap will probably make the object look better).

- If the AutoShape grows when you place additional text on it—deselect it.

Also consider the effect that selecting Word Wrap has on some of these problems. That's frequently a quick way to make the text narrow enough to avoid selecting Resize AutoShape in order to make text fit in a shape.

Working with WordArt

It's quite possible that you have two different WordArt programs to use while you are working in PowerPoint. The WordArt that launches from the Drawing toolbar is a PowerPoint tool that gives you access to the fun and creativity available in WordArt. In addition, there's probably a copy of Microsoft WordArt 3.0 available on your system through the installation of other Microsoft applications (Publisher or various versions of Office). You can use either or both.

There are some differences between the way the two operate when you create and manipulate a WordArt object.

The PowerPoint WordArt Tool   Click the WordArt tool on the PowerPoint Drawing toolbar to create a WordArt object. This method starts with a display of the WordArt Gallery (see Figure 26.16).

When you select a WordArt style and click OK, the Edit WordArt Text dialog box opens so you can insert the text you want for this WordArt object. Notice that the dialog box has a small formatting toolbar. You can change the font or the font size, and you can add bold and italic attributes to the text.

FIG. 26.16
The WordArt Gallery shows the available shapes for WordArt text objects.

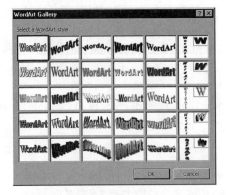

As soon as you click OK in the dialog box, the object is placed on the slide.

- Use the sizing handles to resize the object.
- Drag the object to move it.
- Rotate or flip the object with the Draw menu.
- Change the color with the Fill Color tool on the Drawing toolbar.
- Add, remove, or change the shadow with the Shadow tool on the Drawing toolbar.
- Add a 3-D effect with the 3-D tool on the Drawing toolbar.

When the object appears on the slide, you should also see the WordArt toolbar (see Figure 26.17). If you don't see the toolbar, right-click the WordArt object and choose Show WordArt Toolbar from the shortcut menu.

FIG. 26.17
The WordArt toolbar is available whenever the WordArt object is in Edit mode.

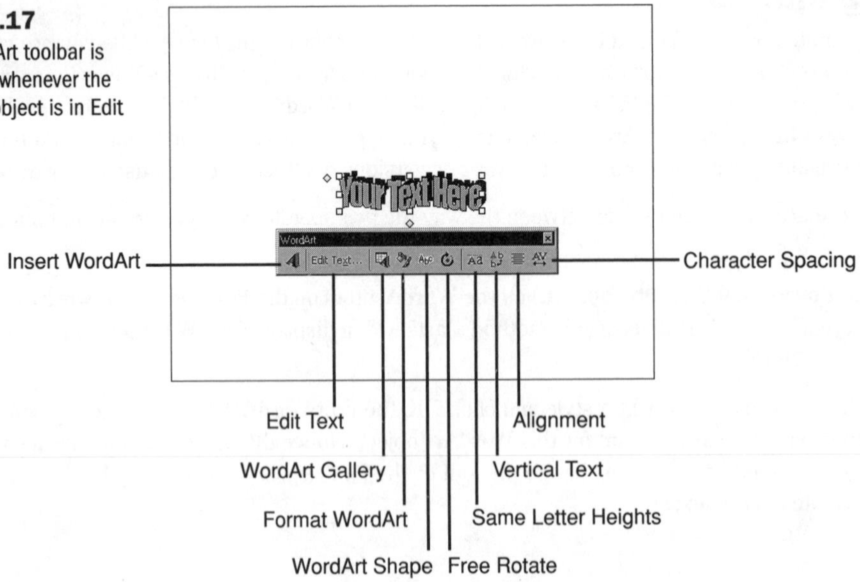

Insert WordArt ——————

—————— Character Spacing

Edit Text

Alignment

WordArt Gallery

Vertical Text

Format WordArt

Same Letter Heights

WordArt Shape   Free Rotate

WordArt Software   To launch Microsoft WordArt, open the Insert menu and choose Object. Scroll through the list of object types to find Microsoft WordArt (you may have either Version 2.0 or 3.0). If it's not there, you most likely haven't installed software that included the program and you can move right along to the next topic in this chapter. If it is there, open it to examine the differences between this program and the WordArt tool in PowerPoint.

When you insert your text, there are not any tools available on the dialog box. You merely enter the word(s) you want to use, update the display, and close the text box. The object is in Text Edit mode, indicated by the crosshatch frame that appears. In this mode, the PowerPoint toolbars are replaced with the WordArt application toolbar (see Figure 26.18). All the tools you need are there.

FIG. 26.18
The application toolbar provides all the tools in one place.

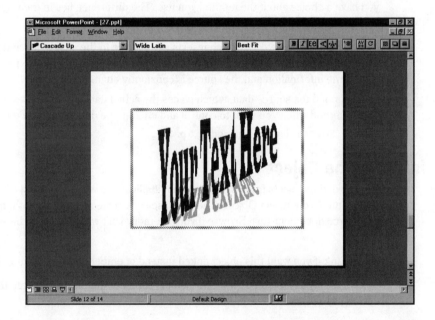

There are two separate edit modes for a WordArt object that is created with Microsoft WordArt 3.0: *Text Edit* and *Object Edit*.

Double-click the object to go to Text Edit mode (refer to Figure 26.18), where you can manipulate the contents of the object. You are really using the Microsoft WordArt application in this mode. Incidentally, Edit mode lacks right-click functions.

Single-click the object for Object Edit mode, which allows you to resize and move the object. You are working in PowerPoint, and the shortcut menu is available. However, the full PowerPoint Drawing toolbar is not available—this is a semi-embedded object from another application. You cannot, for instance, use the Rotate menu commands but must go to Text Edit mode and use the WordArt Special Effects dialog box.

Part
VI

Ch
26

Personally, I find that if I just want to insert a word or phrase for a little attention-getting technique, the PowerPoint WordArt tool is far easier. The WordArt object choices in the Gallery are already in full color, contain shadow effects, and have been poured into some of the interesting shapes. If I want something designed a bit more elaborately that has to fit some grand plan for my slide or the presentation, the controls I gain by using Microsoft WordArt are usually worth the extra work.

Linking and Embedding Objects

You can place existing objects from other applications into your PowerPoint presentation, and you have a choice about the method you use. The difference lies in the way the source data is treated:

■ Link the source data, which inserts a reference to the source file and its location into your presentation. Use this method when the presentation has to present actual, real-time information and the source is constantly changing.

■ Embed the source data, which places the actual data into your presentation. Use this method when you want to control and change the data from the PowerPoint end.

▶ **See** "Linking and Embedding," **p. 39**

Inserting the Object

Insert existing objects from OLE-compliant applications with the Object command on the Insert menu. In the Insert Object dialog box, select Create from File and then enter the path to the source document (use Browse if your memory isn't what it used to be—mine certainly isn't).

Select Link if you want this object linked instead of embedded (embedding is the default).

Select Display as Icon if you want an icon to represent the object (activate the icon by double-clicking it).

N O T E You can use icons only if you run your presentation from a computer. ■

Converting Objects

There are a variety of reasons to convert an embedded or linked object from its original state to a new state. You may no longer care about a link to an object, you may not need to edit the object in its original associated application, or you may just need to convert an icon to the object it represents (or the other way around).

Convert an Object to PowerPoint   To convert any embedded or linked object to a PowerPoint object, just ungroup it. Select the object and use the shortcut menu or the PowerPoint Draw menu and choose Ungroup. Then choose Regroup or Group (depending on which is available—it varies by object type).

Once an object is converted to a PowerPoint object, your manipulation of it is limited to those features provided in PowerPoint.

Convert Between Icons and Objects   You can convert an icon to its object, or vice versa, without disturbing any links or associated software connections. Select the icon or object, then choose *<object name>* Object from the Edit menu. The name of this menu option changes depending on the object—for instance, if the object is an Excel worksheet, the menu item may be Worksheet Object or Linked Worksheet Object. You may also have a Chart Object, a Document Object, a Linked Document Object, and so on.

When the dialog box opens, select or deselect the Display as Icon option.

Manipulating Linked and Embedded Objects

The way you work with an object in your presentation depends on how you inserted it (whether the object is linked or embedded).

Embedded Objects   Embedded objects are edited within their source applications. Double-click the embedded object to launch the application and display the object in the editing window. Some applications open an application window for editing, while others may not open a separate window but instead provide their tools and commands within the PowerPoint window.

- It's not unusual to run into some memory problems when you open an embedded object, especially if you keep several applications open all the time.

- If you've ungrouped (and regrouped) an object, double-clicking does not launch its original associated application. It is now a PowerPoint object and cannot be edited. You'll have to open the application and start all over again.

Linked Objects   There are a number of configuration items attached to a linked object, and you can update the configuration in addition to updating the data for the linked object.

To manipulate and configure the link, choose Edit, Links (you don't have to select the object). The Links dialog box displays all the links in the current presentation (see Figure 26.19). Select the linked object you want to reconfigure:

- If the source file has moved, choose Change Source and indicate the new path.

- To edit the original document in the source application (and automatically update the data link), choose Open Source.

- To update the data, choose Update Now.

- To change the way the object is updated, select Automatic or Manual.

- To disassociate the object from the original object (creating an embedded object), choose Break Link.

Part
VI

Ch
26

 TIP   If you receive an error message when you try to update or edit a link and the configuration information in the Links dialog box is correct, somebody else may be accessing the file. Either wait for that person to finish or do something aggressive to make the other user close the file (depending on how much of a hurry you're in).

FIG. 26.19

All the information related to the linked object is available for viewing or changing.

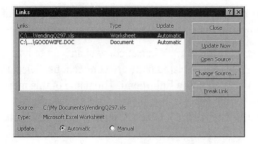

TROUBLESHOOTING

Sometimes an embedded or linked document is cropped when it is inserted into PowerPoint. After going back to the original document, changing font sizes and margins, and making other changes, the problem persists. It's very annoying (and embarrassingly obvious to the audience) if the object is a Word document because the text doesn't make much sense if the last couple of words on every line aren't there, or if only a part of the last column in a Word table is showing.

The reason for the cropping problem is the fact that you're working in a slide format. The largest area available to an object is 6×9 inches. If you have a slide format that includes a title text box, a border, or anything else that occupies any part of the slide, there is even less room available for the embedded or linked document. PowerPoint does not adjust font size or word wrap; it crops. In addition, PowerPoint objects have no margins (or a margin of 0 inches if you prefer to think of it that way).

Here's the cure: Let PowerPoint build the embedded object. For example, if you have a Word document you want to insert, open Word, select it, and copy it to the Clipboard. Then choose Insert, Object. Instead of selecting Create from File (the way you'd normally insert an existing object), choose Create New and select Microsoft Word as the object type. Paste the document into the window (which is configured for PowerPoint).

CHAPTER 27

Creating a Slide Show

The alternative to using overhead transparencies or slides in a live presentation is to create a slide show. It's a bit more work, but in certain situations it can be more effective (and in other situations, such as unattended presentations, it's the only choice).

The difference in equipment is that for a slide show you need a computer, with or without a human presenter. For a presentation involving overhead slides, you need a slide projector and a live presenter.

In this chapter, you'll learn how to turn a standard presentation (the one where you use slides or overhead transparencies and you have to talk a lot) into a show. ■

Timing slide shows

Set the length of time a slide is displayed. The duration depends on the contents, the effects (for instance, sound), or prerecorded narration.

Using transitions

There are plenty of clever animated ways to change slides or to bring the elements onto a slide one at a time.

Self-running shows

You can design a slide show that runs without benefit of any human interference.

Slide shows for the Internet

Designing an interactive or self-running Internet presentation gets your message out to the world.

Using notes and handouts

Use notes for your own participation in a show, and use handouts so the audience doesn't leave without a reminder of your presentation.

Understanding Slide Shows

A *slide show* is a pre-assembled series of slides, sometimes accompanied by sound or narration (or both) that is run on a computer.

The audience views the computer output, and the way that's accomplished can vary:

- The audience can view a show run from an unattended computer attached to a projection device.

- The audience can view a show run from a computer attached to a projection device, with a live presenter providing the narration.

- The audience can view a show run from an unattended computer in a trade show booth or kiosk.

- The audience can view a show run from a computer by huddling around the computer and watching the monitor (with or without a presenter).

- The audience can view a show over their computers via a conference hookup (your computer is the source of the display).

- The audience can view a show by dialing into the Internet and watching it on your Web page (or on the company intranet).

The common thread is the use of a computer for playing or viewing the show.

Timing Your Slide Show

First of all, you don't really have to set timings for a slide show; you can sit in front of the computer that's displaying the show and advance through your presentation manually. In fact, there are times when that's desirable, such as a presentation where questions are entertained as each slide displays. (Even when the audience has no opportunity to effect the length of time a slide displays, if you're a power freak you might like to maintain control of the slide show.) If either of those scenarios fit your situation, go away—move on to the next section of this chapter, "Setting Slide Transitions."

In any other situation, however, a timed show is slicker and more professional. And, for unattended presentations such as an exhibit booth or the Internet, timing is an essential element.

Timing merely means setting a length of time that an individual slide is displayed. There are a couple of ways to approach specifying that time:

- Manually set the duration for each individual slide by specifying a number of seconds for that slide, using the slide show dialog box.

- Rehearse the narration (just sit there and talk to yourself, out loud) and notify PowerPoint each time you finish the narration for an individual slide. PowerPoint will track the duration between each notification and apply that timing.

Regardless of the method, you can continue to fine-tune and tweak the timing until it's absolutely perfect.

Even if you're not a power freak, you'll probably be relieved to know that with an automatically timed show, you don't have to give up control of the show. You can tell PowerPoint to advance a slide when its time is up, or when you click the mouse (whichever comes first). This method also works well if the show is self-running and you want the viewer to have a choice about waiting for the next slide to appear, or forcing it to appear.

Setting Timings Manually

You can establish a specific timing for one slide, for a group of slides, or even specify the same duration for every slide in the show:

1. Display the first slide in the PowerPoint window, or select it in Slide Sorter view. You can select multiple slides in Slide Sorter view (remember that PowerPoint uses the Shift key for multiple selection instead of the Ctrl key).

2. Choose Slide Show, Slide Transition (see Figure 27.1), select the automatic choice, then specify the number of seconds you want to display this slide.

 If you are in Slide Sorter view, you can right-click any slide and choose Slide Transition from the shortcut menu.

FIG. 27.1
Indicate the method of advancing this slide, and specify the number of seconds to wait for the advance.

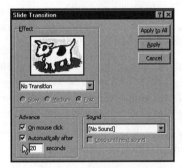

3. Deselect the On Mouse Click option if you want locked-in timing. If you leave the option selected, you can advance the slide with the mouse at any point before the timed duration is reached.

4. Choose Apply to apply the specifications to the selected slide(s). Choose Apply to All if you want to use this timing for all the slides in your slide show.

 While a slide show is running, you have access to a right-click shortcut that has a Next command for advancing to the next slide. If you want to advance slides manually and you will be using the mouse for something else during the show, deselect both items in the Advance section of the Slide Transition dialog box. This puts the only mouse control for advancing a slide on the shortcut menu.

Repeat these steps for each slide or group of slides in your slide show. As you enter the information for each slide, its timing displays in Slide Sorter view (see Figure 27.2).

FIG. 27.2

The first three slides for this slide show are configured and display their duration.

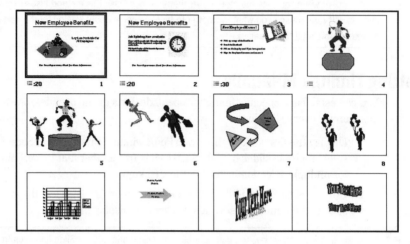

Setting Timings Automatically

Get your script (don't forget your ad lib jokes), clear your throat, and get ready. You're going to read the narration to yourself and tell PowerPoint "advance now" at each appropriate place. Here are a couple of tips for making this easier and more effective:

- When you write your script, indicate the point at which you want to advance to the next slide. Use text in parentheses—such as (advance to slide #2)—or find some other way to make the fact that the slide needs advancing separate from the narration. You don't want to read "slide 2 here" out loud to the audience.

- When you write your script, use phonetic spelling as much as possible to avoid stumbling over difficult words, technical terms, or names.

N O T E Phonetic spelling is an accepted method of speech writing. It's most commonly used for the TelePrompter scripts your local newscaster reads. In fact, at most television stations, the phonetic spelling is an absolute rule. For example, TelePrompter copy frequently reads "the press conference is scheduled for seven ay em." If it weren't typed in that manner, there's a perceived risk in the news business that the newscaster would say "the press conference is scheduled for seven ay period em period." Of course, this may be more indicative of the attitude of newsroom production personnel than it is a true assessment of newscaster literacy levels. ■

- During the process, read the speech out loud, not to yourself. In fact, use the same voice volume you plan to use at the presentation. You may think you read at the same speed when you mumble or speak softly, but you don't. Don't forget to pause for laughter and applause.

Now that you understand the basics, you can begin auto-timing your slide show:

1. Choose Slide Show, Rehearse Timings. The first slide appears in rehearsal mode, and the clock starts ticking (see Figure 27.3).

FIG. 27.3

The Rehearsal dialog box counts the seconds as you practice your speech.

2. When you finish reciting your narration for this slide, click the Advance button (or press Enter) to move to the next slide.

   If you have already animated the way the elements are placed on any slide (flying text, drop-in graphics, and so on), each click triggers the next animation instead of the next slide. Be sure to note that fact in your script so you know when you are advancing the animation, as opposed to advancing to the next slide.

3. Continue the process until you are finished with your entire presentation.

After the last slide has been timed, an information dialog box is displayed to tell you the total time for your presentation, and inquires whether you want to record these times and use them for viewing your presentation. If you want to redo everything, answer No and start the rehearsal process again.

If you say Yes, you are asked whether you want to see the times in Slide Sorter view. If you do, all the slides in your presentation are displayed with their duration times (individual times for each animation on a slide are not noted).

The Rehearsal dialog box provides information and functions:

■ The digital box in the upper-right corner counts the duration of the current slide. Every time you advance to a new slide, it resets to 00:00:00.

■ If you click during the timing of a slide that has animated actions, you are setting the timing for each animation action. The digital counter does not reset until all the actions are complete and you move to the next slide.

■ The digital read out in the upper-left corner is the accumulated time for your slide show.

■ The Repeat button resets the timing for the current slide so you can re-time it.

■ The center button pauses the timing (in case you lose your place, the phone rings, or you have to sneeze or something).

Setting Slide Transitions

You don't have to move from slide to slide with a quick switch; you can have a special effects transition between slides. This provides visual interest, attracts attention, and keeps the audience awake:

1. In Slide Sorter view, select the slide(s) you want to advance with special effect. Then choose Slide Show, Slide Transition.

2. Choose an operation from the Effect drop-down list in the Slide Transition dialog box (see Figure 27.4).

FIG. 27.4
Choose something special for this slide's first appearance in your slide show.

3. Choose a speed for the effect.

4. If you want, add a sound effect.

5. Choose Apply to attach this effect to your selected slide(s). Choose Apply to All to make this the global choice for all slides in your slide show.

The effect is used when the slide is first revealed (see Figure 27.5). Any animation attached to elements within the slide remains as originally configured.

FIG. 27.5
Vertical blinds open to reveal this slide.

When a slide is configured for animation, a small arrow appears under it in Slide Sorter view.

This is one of those places where it is very easy to get into trouble. There is nothing more annoying than a slide show that is too busy. You might as well flash a slide that says "I'm an amateur and I love to click all the special effects buttons."

If a slide contains a lot of element animation and the last element is added late in the slide's on-screen life, keep the next slide's entry simple.

Don't mismatch sound effects and video effects—the sound of a laser gun makes no sense behind a lazy, graceful movement.

Don't wait until the entry animation is complete before beginning the narration—an audience that has to sit and watch an effect instead of learning about the upcoming slide knows you're trying to show off your animation effects.

Running the Slide Show

You'll probably find you want to run your slide show a number of times before its debut in front of an audience. You'll want to tweak it, change it, and perfect it. There are a number of features that help you accomplish this.

To run your slide show, select the first slide and click the Slide Show icon at the bottom of the PowerPoint window, or choose Slide Show, View Show.

Press Esc at any point to stop the slide show from running.

Testing the Timing

The first thing you should do is test the timing of the slides with your narration. Read your script as the slide show runs and make notes about the slides that have to be advanced at a later or earlier time, or about animated slides that have to bring their elements in faster or slower.

You'll probably find that without having to worry about clicking to set the timing (as you did when you rehearsed timing), your narration speed changes a bit. Now you can make adjustments to fine tune the slide show.

Adjusting Slide Advances

You'll probably find that some slides have to move along faster so the next slide can display, and other slides have moved on before you finish your narration about their contents. So, you'll want to make the necessary adjustments.

The fastest way to do this is move to Slide Sorter view and right-click each slide you want to change, then choose Slide Transition from the shortcut menu. Change the time and choose Apply. The new transition time is noted below the slide.

To test the timing, select the slide you changed (in Slide Sorter view) and click the Slide Show icon. The slide show runs from that slide forward, so you don't have to wait for it in order to test it against your narration.

Adjusting Slide Animation

Matching your narration to the animated movement of the slide's elements can be tricky. You may have to tighten or loosen the times between the appearance of each element. To do this, bring the slide into the PowerPoint window:

1. Select the text or graphic you want to change.
2. Choose Slide Show, Custom Animation (see Figure 27.6).

FIG. 27.6

Change the timing for a slide element that pops in, flys in, or otherwise makes a dramatic appearance.

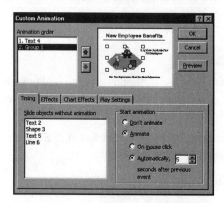

3. Make sure the element is selected in the Animation Order box, then change the automatic start time. You are changing the interval between the previous event (either a previous animation on this slide, or the advancement from the previous slide to this slide) and the current event.
4. Select and alter any other animated elements on this slide, if necessary. Then choose OK.

Don't bother with the Preview button; it only shows the animation effect and pays no heed to any timing specifications you've entered.

 When there are several animated effects for a single slide, I've often found it easier to adjust the script rather than try to fine-tune the animation. Adjusting the time for each element's entry can be like adjusting a wobbling three-legged table.

Metering a Manual Presentation

Sometimes, after you've created a well-timed script, you decide to give your presentation manually, clicking the mouse for each slide change. This could occur because a slide show is planned for an audience that will be asking questions during the presentation, or because you will verbally add some information that is not reflected on your slides.

While you're running your slide show, you can display a meter on your screen in order to keep yourself on schedule. You can watch your progress slide by slide, as the meter shows you whether you are running ahead of, or behind, the timing for each slide. This prevents the inclination to run on and on, making your presentation too long (and therefore, probably boring).

To display the meter, start the slide show, right-click when the show starts, and choose Slide Meter from the shortcut menu. When the Slide Meter appears (see Figure 27.7), it measures your manual progress against the preset timings:

FIG. 27.7
Stay close to your
perfect target times
with the Slide Meter.

- The top digital readout is the elapsed time of the currently displayed slide.
- The bottom digit readout is the elapsed time of the slide show.
- The progress bar between the digital displays is the comparison of your current progress with the timed show, with a color key for quick comprehension.
- If the bar is green, it means you are close to the pre-timed parameters.
- If the bar is yellow, it means you are missing your target times a bit—check the black indicator to see if you're erring on the side of speed or slowness.
- If the bar is red, it means you are missing your target times by a lot—check the black indicator to see if you're erring on the side of speed or slowness.

If you're presenting the slide show over a conference setup, the other participants will not see the meter. In any other situation, the meter shows on the presentation screen (which means unless you want the world to know you're off your timing marks, you should only use this feature for conferences).

Running the Show for an Audience

When everything is just perfect and you're ready to let others see your presentation, it's time to establish the configuration for running your slide show. This is accomplished with the Set Up Show dialog box, available on the Slide Show menu (see Figure 27.8).

There are three methods offered for running your presentation, with some configuration options for each of those methods: Presented by a Speaker, Browsed by an Individual, and Browsed at a Kiosk.

In this section, we'll discuss the first two options; the Kiosk presentations should always be self-running and is covered in the next section of this chapter, "Creating Self-Running Shows."

FIG. 27.8

What is the setting and who is the audience for your slide show?

Presented by a Speaker   A show that is presented by a speaker is one in which the presentation runs full screen and the speaker usually has some controls over the pace of the show. Most of the time, it's a good idea to have your computer hooked up to a large-screen output device (you can rent these from any audio-visual company, and there are usually half-day, full-day, and weekly rates). Depending upon the occasion, the audience, or any other circumstances, you may want to establish some additional configuration settings:

■ Select Show Without Animation if you just want to show the slides and discuss them. When you're presenting a show to an audience who wants to discuss the topics (or ask questions), this provides a more matter-of-fact ambiance for the presentation.

■ You can choose to present all the slides in your presentation, or any group of contiguous slides.

■ Decide whether you want to advance the slides Manually or Using Timings. If you are presenting your show to an audience that will be discussing the slides, the manual approach is best.

Using Two Computers   You can also present your slide show using two computers. I've found this especially useful when I take the show to an audience instead of having the audience come to me. I can prepare my show on a portable computer, then hook it to a large computer (with a very large screen) at the presentation site. This offers some additional advantages, because I can use the mouse, PowerPoint commands, and other features without having them appear on the computer that the audience is watching.

To accomplish this, you need a null-modem cable that connects to a serial port on each computer. PowerPoint must be installed on the viewing computer. You also need to tell PowerPoint about your plans (on both computers), so that the special features available for a two-computer presentation are available:

1. Choose Slide Show, View on Two Screens on the first computer you want to configure to bring up the View on Two Screens dialog box (see Figure 27.9).

FIG. 27.9

Identify each computer to use the Two Screens feature in PowerPoint. If this is my computer, I'll select Audience when I configure the viewing computer.

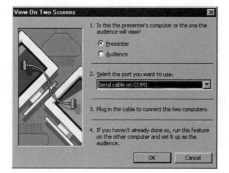

2. Choose the appropriate serial port for this computer.

3. Move to the other computer, open PowerPoint, and configure it.

When you run your presentation, you can control the show from your computer without giving away the behind-the-scenes secrets, because your tools don't display on the computer the audience watches. You can use the Slide Meter, the Slide Navigator (explained next), and display your speaker notes and keep it all to yourself.

Using the Slide Navigator   When you're presenting your slide show, live and in person, before an audience who wants to discuss, question, or argue about the information you're presenting, it's sometimes helpful to move to a specific topic to resolve the discussion. The Slide Navigator lets you move to any slide in your show at any moment. While the slide show is running, right-click to see the slide show shortcut menu commands. Choose Go, then choose Slide Navigator (see Figure 27.10).

FIG. 27.10

Move quickly to another slide when necessary— notice that the Slide Navigator reminds you which slide you're on now so you can return.

If any slides are hidden, the Slide Navigator displays the slide number in parentheses.

If you've hidden slides and decide at the last moment you want to show a hidden slide, when you are on the slide immediately before the hidden slide choose Go, Hidden Slide from the shortcut menu. The command is only available if the next slide is a hidden one.

Browsed by an Individual   This form of presenting your slide show is usually performed for connected audiences, over a network or the Internet. These are also called *conference* *presentations*. This is not the same as an Internet presentation (covered later in this chapter in the section "Creating Presentations for the Internet") which is a slide show designed to be seen by people who dial into your Web site.

Individuals who are dialed into a conference (or connected by cable on your network) use PowerPoint's Presentation Conference Wizard on the Tools menu. Each viewer sees the show in a PowerPoint window and can use the PowerPoint pen to draw notes on slides (seen by all participants).

However, as the presenter, the tools you use to manipulate the show's progress are not seen by the audience.

N O T E The Presentation Conference Wizard is an easy-to-follow Wizard that sets up a presentation conference for either the presenter or the participant. Each step is designed to configure your computer and PowerPoint for your role in the conference. The only trick is to make sure that if you are the presenter you do not click the Finish button until all the other (participant) computers have clicked the button on their wizards. When the presenter chooses Finish, the conference begins. ■

Creating Self-Running Shows

Most of the self-running slide shows you prepare will be for booths at exhibits, conventions, and other places where you want to present information and don't want to worry about having a live presenter there. (PowerPoint calls these places *kiosks*.) However, don't limit yourself to these special marketing events for self-running slide shows; I've helped clients prepare employee information shows and set them up in the company cafeteria. Some of them have been interactive, which is a great way to get feedback.

In addition, presentations for the Internet must, of course, be self-running. (See the section "Creating Presentations for the Internet" later in this chapter):

- A self-running presentation starts all over again after it's finished.
- You can establish a self-running presentation so that it runs totally by itself, using automatic timings.
- You can also configure a self-running presentation that uses viewer input—for example, the viewer clicks the mouse to advance slides.
- You can also configure the show so that the viewer has no control over the advancing of slides, but does have an opportunity to jump to specific slides by clicking hyperlinks.
- You can configure a self-running presentation to start over if a user-advanced slide has been displayed for more than five minutes (which probably means the viewer has walked away from the presentation).
- You can create commands and other controls that viewers can use to move around the show (selecting from a Table of Contents, for example) or to respond to questions by filling in information.

You will, of course, have to add narration or some sort of sound track to your presentation because you won't be there to recite the audio portion. If the slides are self-explanatory and don't require additional elucidation, you should have music, sound effects, or both to make your presentation more professional.

Configuring a Self-Running Presentation

The first thing you must do to make your presentation self-running is confirm that all the necessary slide configuration options are present:

- Slides must have automatic timings attached (just glance at the slides in Slide Sorter view to make sure each slide has a time noted).

- You cannot have any slides with icons or links if you don't permit user input.

To establish your slide show as a self-running presentation, open that presentation in PowerPoint and choose Slide Show, Set Up Show. When the Set Up Show dialog box appears (see Figure 27.11), choose Browsed at a Kiosk. This automatically forces the Loop Continuously option, which cannot be changed.

FIG. 27.11

The Browsed at a Kiosk option is the equivalent of self-running a slide show.

By default, all the slides are selected, but you can choose any group of contiguous slides. This lets you build extremely large presentations, divide them into sections, and then choose particular sections for any self-running slide show you want to present.

Adding Action Buttons

For interactive viewing, you can place buttons on your slides to give the viewer some control over the manner in which your presentation is seen. With the appropriate slide in the PowerPoint window, choose Slide Show, Action Buttons (see Figure 27.12).

Click the Action Button you need, then click the slide and drag to make the button the size you desire. When you release the mouse, the Action Settings dialog box displays so you can configure your button (see Figure 27.13).

Part
VI

Ch
27

FIG. 27.12

Your audience can navigate the presentation with action buttons you supply.

FIG. 27.13

Configure the response for the Action Buttons you insert in your slide show.

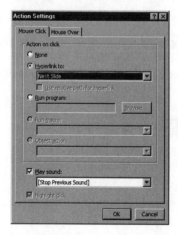

You are really establishing a hyperlink with the action buttons. In this case, because the action button is a forward arrow, I linked to the next slide. There are some commonly used buttons for slide shows that I took advantage of:

- For all slides except the first one, I also added a Home button which links to the first slide, and a Previous button which links to the previous slide.

- All slides have a button to Exit the presentation.

- For all slides except the last one, I added an End button which links to the last slide, and a Next button which links to the next slide.

You can also configure a sound effect for the action, including stopping an existing sound that may be playing behind the current slide.

The dialog box gives you a choice of launching the action with a click, or merely a mouse passing over the button. For most of the Action Buttons, it would be unconventional (and therefore confusing) to kick off an action with a pass-over.

There are Action Buttons for launching a program, opening a document, moving to another slide show, and so on. There is also a custom button you can use to design your own action. When you do, you can choose an available action for this button from the dialog box.

When the buttons are placed on the slide, you can add text directly on the button, or add a text box on the button or below it. Figure 27.14 shows a slide that has action buttons configured in a variety of ways.

FIG. 27.14

Do not attempt this as a design—it's far too ugly, but it shows some methods for labeling action buttons.

Adding Actions to Slide Elements

You can use the same choices that are available for Action Buttons on other elements of a slide. Choose the element and right-click, then choose Action Settings from the shortcut menu.

I find this feature very useful for a number of tasks. For example, in a slide that refers to a document, the viewer can open the document (see Figure 27.15).

Sometimes I use a graphic to cross-reference another slide, as illustrated in Figure 27.16.

FIG. 27.15

Clicking the graphic of the manual opens a text copy of the manual.

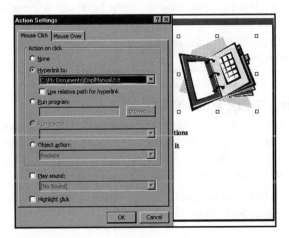

FIG. 27.16
Use Action Settings to let a viewer move directly to a slide that has information you're referring to.

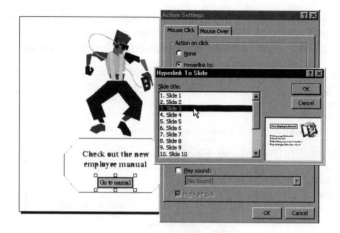

Then, of course, I insert an Action Button in the target slide to let the viewer return to the source slide. (There is a pre-configured action for Last Slide Viewed.)

The ability to include interactive actions makes your presentation a powerful source of information.

Build ActiveX Controls with Visual Basic

If you're comfortable using Visual Basic, you can set up controls via icons in your slide show that viewers can use to kick off actions you build in. These are called *ActiveX Controls*, and they are really Visual Basic programs. You can use existing controls, build your own controls, or build macros onto existing controls to expand their functions. Then just place an icon on a slide, and a click of the mouse launches the action you connect to that icon.

To add an ActiveX Control to your presentation, display the Control Toolbox toolbar (right-click an existing toolbar and choose Control Toolbox). Choose a control and place it on a slide. Right-click and choose the control from the shortcut menu (it's named for the type of control you chose), and then choose Edit from the submenu.

When the Microsoft Visual Basic application window opens, your control is in the application window and you can begin programming it.

Starting a Self-Running Presentation

There are several choices for launching a self-running slide show, and you can choose the one that's appropriate for the setting. Remember that you can use a self-running presentation for any site, not just a kiosk. In fact, I've found it handy for presentations at which I was present but chose not to act as a presenter.

You can start your slide show by launching PowerPoint, opening the file, and clicking the Slide Show icon (or choosing Slide Show, View Show).

If you're going to present your show inside PowerPoint, it's quicker to create a desktop short-cut for each presentation file. Double-clicking the shortcut opens PowerPoint with that presentation in the PowerPoint window.

For both of these techniques, when you stop the presentation, you return to the PowerPoint window.

Instead, you can make your self-running presentation independent of the PowerPoint window. It opens as a running show, and when you close it you are not in the PowerPoint application. This is accomplished by saving the file as a show instead of a PowerPoint document file:

1. With the self-running presentation in the PowerPoint window, choose File, Save As.
2. In the Save as Type list box, choose PowerPoint Show.
3. By default, your presentation keeps the same name, but the extension changes to .PPS (PowerPoint Show). You can change the file name if you like.

Once your PowerPoint presentation is saved as a show, you can double-click it in Explorer to launch the show just as if you had opened PowerPoint and gone through all the keystrokes or mouse clicks necessary to open the file and run the slide show. PowerPoint runs in the background to present the show, and when you exit the show you are returned to Explorer.

Create a desktop shortcut for this .PPS file to make it even more convenient. When the show ends, you're returned to the desktop.

 I frequently take self-running presentations to sites away from the office, and I've found a way to make the whole event look more professional. I've made my portable computer look like a traveling PowerPoint presentation tool. I created a desktop folder named Presentations, and all my .PPS files are in it. I open the folder and maximize it, then double-click the show I want to run. Viewers never see my desktop.

Creating Presentations for the Internet

If you have a Web site, you can put a self-running presentation on the site to sell, explain, or otherwise talk about your product or service.

There are two ways to prepare a presentation for Internet viewing:

- Use the AutoContent Wizard to create a presentation specifically designed for Internet viewing. Save it as an HTML document.
- Use an existing presentation and save it in HTML format.

When you choose Internet as the way the presentation will be used in the AutoContent Wizard, everything the wizard does is pre-configured for Internet use. Graphics are ready for hyper-links; there are lots of graphics, and you can use any graphic as a menu choice that jumps to a document or another slide (see Figure 27.17).

FIG. 27.17
An Internet presentation is graphic-heavy and relies on hyperlinks.

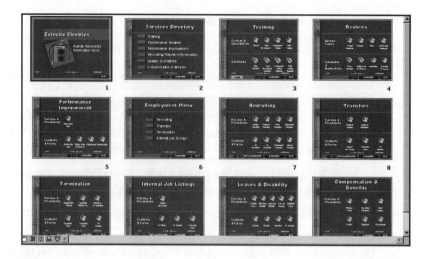

If you choose to design your own presentation, create one from scratch, or have one you created with a different AutoContent type, you can still use it on the Internet—just save it as an HTML document.

Using the PowerPoint Internet Assistant

When you choose File, Save as HTML, the PowerPoint Internet Assistant appears to walk you through the process of preparing your slide show for the Internet (see Figure 27.18).

FIG. 27.18
The Internet Assistant helps you customize your presentation so it works well on the World Wide Web.

The Internet Assistant is a wizard, and like all wizards it asks questions and moves on in response to your answers.

If your presentation was originally prepared for the Internet by the AutoContent Wizard, the process is quite easy (and short). If, however, you are using an existing presentation that was designed to be shown with a presenter, or as a self-running show from your computer, the Internet Assistant has a little more work to do.

Defining a Layout   Your existing layout will be changed to a layout more suitable for the Web (see Figure 27.19).

FIG. 27.19
Choose the Web layout style you prefer, and the Internet Assistant will reconfigure your presentation to match it.

Nothing is etched in stone here; this is still your presentation, and you can make changes to it even after you have finished preparing it for the Web (or after it's been on your Web site for a while).

Configuring Graphics   Because graphics are such an enormous consideration for the Web, you'll be asked to pick a graphics format:

- *GIF (Graphics Interchange Format)* is the default choice, which probably is the best bet due to the fact that all browsers can handle it.

- *JPEG (Joint Photographic Experts Group)* is available if you feel you want to use a compressed file format.

- *PowerPoint Animation* is the third choice, and if the Web viewer does not have the PowerPoint Animation Player, he/she will be prompted to download it.

You will also be asked to configure your graphics for a specific resolution (remember that computers are downward-compatible in this regard) and to choose the width of the graphics (a fourth of the screen, half the screen, and so on).

 For information about getting the Animation Player add-in for yourself, choose Help, Microsoft on the Web, Product News.

Creating an Information Page   An *information page* is configured so that it can point to your Web home page, present an e-mail address, and display any other information you want the viewer to see. In addition, you can establish a download button so the viewer can download your presentation for later viewing. (There's also a way to build an option to download Microsoft Internet Explorer.)

Choosing Colors and Buttons   The buttons, pages, and text in your presentation can use the default colors for your browser, or you can create an original color scheme. You also must decide on a button style (or opt for plain text).

Setting the File Location   The Internet Assistant creates an HTML document folder for this presentation, usually in the My Documents folder. You can decide on the path at this time (the folder's name is determined by the name of your presentation, but you can change it later).

Saving the Conversion Settings Information Before the Internet Assistant performs the conversion, you have an opportunity to name it and save all the settings you decided upon so you can use them again. It's a good idea because it means all your Internet presentations will have a consistent look.

Once you have answered all the questions, the conversion begins, one slide at a time. When it is complete, each slide is an HTML document, each graphic is a GIF file (if that was your choice), and there are other documents in the folder that are needed to have your show run on the Web.

For a quick check, open Explorer and look at the folder (see Figure 27.20).

FIG. 27.20

Your presentation is a group of Internet documents after you convert it for Internet viewing.

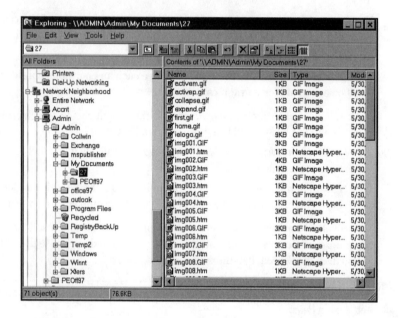

You might want to double-click one of the HTML files, which should launch your browser and put that page in the browser window (see Figure 27.21).

When you've checked the conversions and you're sure everything is just dandy, put this presentation on your Web site.

FIG. 27.21

There's the hyperlink I built to the text document for this graphic—I can tell because my pointer changed to a hand.

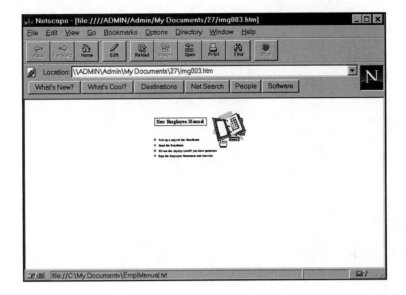

CHAPTER 28

Creating Multimedia Presentations

Multimedia, when applied to computer presentations, means the presence of video that moves (animation) and sound. It's a dynamic way to present your message, and the only requirement is that the presentation must be displayed with a computer instead of slides on an overhead projector. With or without a live presenter, a multimedia presentation is usually an extremely effective way to get information to an audience.

This chapter covers the planning, creation, and execution of multimedia shows using PowerPoint. ■

Understanding multimedia

A professional approach makes all the difference. There are effective ways to marry audio and video, and then there are ways to do it wrong and watch your audience OD on all your fancy effects.

Using video clips

Add video clips to your presentation for dynamic effects and to give the audience detailed information.

Using sound clips

Insert sound effects and sound tracks to make a presentation slick and professional.

Understanding Multimedia

To create good multimedia shows, you have to be aware of the essentials that make a show good. When you're using PowerPoint to build your multimedia presentation, your problem is a bit more complex: You have to understand the ramifications of using computers to present your show, and you have to understand how and why multimedia works well as a presentation technique.

Technical Considerations

Think Pentium. Even a fast 486 with a MHz rate equal to a Pentium machine isn't going to give you the performance you need. Get the fastest Pentium processor you can afford. Jumpy jerky video is tacky.

RAM is also important, and 32M is the minimum (regardless of Microsoft's claim that the requirement is 16M).

Get a good video card, with memory optimized for multimedia performance. Video is getting more complicated to buy because there are more choices.

For instance, video RAM comes in several flavors and, from slow to fast, here are the choices:

- *DRAM (Dynamic RAM)* is common and inexpensive. It's slow because the video data must be refreshed constantly and also because DRAM cannot read while it is being written to.
- *EDO (Extended Data Out) RAM* is a bit faster than DRAM because memory writing can be accomplished separately.
- *VRAM (Video RAM)* is able to write data to memory at the same time that images are being written to the screen.
- *MDRAM (Multibank DRAM)* is specifically designed for graphics applications. The chips contain individual small memory banks that draw the screen faster than VRAM.
- *SGRAM (Synchronous Graphics RAM)* is used on high-end video cards and is extremely fast.

The fact is that the memory on a video controller is really more helpful for keeping up the refresh speed when you want to display more colors and/or use high resolution.

For real performance in multimedia, you need to think about a *graphics accelerator*. This is a chip that is mounted on the video card in addition to memory. It's a video coprocessor, and it offloads the video duties from the computer's processor. The coprocessor is designed and built for video duties, and handles them with an enormous amount of efficiency. (Did you know that your computer can spend a third of its time or more just redrawing your screen?)

Graphic accelerators also come in varying configurations. The width of the data path makes a substantial difference, of course, and you can find 64-bit and 128-bit cards. And, there are cards with video acceleration which means functions for full-motion video are built into the chips. These cards are generally marked MPEG-1 compatible, and they're worth the extra money if you're going to be serious about multimedia. (There are other accelerator configurations for video controllers, but there's no particular point in turning this chapter into a full lesson on video.)

Be sure to buy a monitor that takes advantage of all the features of your expensive video card. A multisync monitor should be considered a necessity. A good sound card and good speakers are also a necessity. And last but certainly not least, make sure you have plenty of hard drive space; multimedia files are disk hogs.

TIP If you travel to other sites to show presentations, invest in a portable computer with all the bells and whistles you need. And invest in a good projection system (you can rent them by the day in most cities). Take it from me, trusting the equipment that's waiting for you at the remote site is frequently a disappointing experience—even though you're told "no problem" when you explain your needs. Never believe anyone who says "no problem."

Presentation Considerations

"The busier it is, the better it is" is a prevailing multimedia philosophy, and approaching your show design with that philosophy is like hanging a neon sign over your show that says "amateur."

The way you put audio and video together is very important, and there are some guidelines you can follow to make sure your presentation is as professional as possible.

First, let's define *audio*: It's any sound, including narration, sound effects, music, or natural sound (people speaking in a movie, for instance). You can have more than one audio element at the same time—in fact, that's usually preferable. Music mixed with narration, or sound effects mixed with music, work well.

Video and audio usually complement each other, each adding its own dimension. But sometimes they should match instead of being separate. The best way to decide about the audio-video relationship is to think about what you see and hear when you watch television.

On the hour, local stations identify themselves. Usually you'll see video that has the station's call letters and the channel number. And it's rare to hear audio that matches, more often it's "eight-alarm fire, film at 11" or some other promotional announcement. This is a two-fer; the station gets to send one message on video and a different message on audio—and all in the space of less than four seconds. The television jargon for this is *shared I.D.* Sometimes they do it the other way around, and you see a picture of a fire with the logo for the evening news on the video, while the announcer intones "This is Channel 5, WWWW-TV".

However, when you see station identification video for a network (as opposed to your local station that is affiliated with that network), the audio and video usually match. For example, you'll see the CBS eye and hear "This is CBS." The networks run *non-shared I.D.* announcements, and when you see one it means that the next thing you see will be a commercial from your local station instead of a commercial that's being run nationally over the network. The non-shared I.D. is a secret signal to the local stations that says "Okay, wake up in the control room; the next two-minute commercial break belongs to you so you can earn money."

As the closing credits for a show roll, you'll usually hear two different audio tracks. One is the music that is built into the show's tape, and it's designed to run under the closing credits (usually it's the show's theme song). The other audio is a voice track, and it usually promotes the next show coming up: "Stay tuned for more adventure on the Leave It to Indiana Jones Show."

This all works because neither the audio nor the video needs reinforcement; each can stand alone. It's a great way to get double impact.

There are times, though, when audio and video must match. For example, it's annoying when you're watching a football game and a superimposed note is on the screen saying "3rd and 4" while the announcer says "Okay, folks, it's 3rd and 5, so we're expecting a screen pass." This happens when announcers don't obey the rules about looking at the monitor that's been provided for them so they know what the producer is putting on the air (and it happens a lot because few announcers follow the rule about watching the monitor; they prefer to look at the field and guess the yardage themselves). Back in the truck (football games are produced from mobile studios in trucks), the producer screams and swigs anti-ulcer medication.

Another instance in which audio and video match is during the weather report on your local news. While you're looking at artwork that shows the expected high temperatures for the next five days, you expect the weather person to announce the same numbers you're seeing.

So, in television the standard practice is to get a two-fer except for those times when very specific, exact information (especially if it involves numbers) is being presented. You'll do well to follow the same guidelines as you create your multimedia presentation.

And, the most important thing is to start with a good script, where everything is noted precisely. Mark the script with every video change, every sound effect, every music mix, and the narration (whether you're presenting the narration live or pre-recording it).

Getting the Best Out of Video and Audio

If your presentation is designed and created to instruct the audience, there are some established guidelines to keep in mind as you insert objects into the slides you'll use.

There's an accepted philosophy in teaching that you can assist the learning process if you understand the way most people retain information. The pecking order is:

- Hands-on learning works best and the information is retained the longest.
- Information presented to the eye usually is absorbed more accurately than information presented to the ear.
- Audio works better if there are memorable video clues accompanying the information presented in the audio.

Hands-on learning is difficult to achieve with a computer presentation, even if it is interactive. That's real classroom work.

Combining video and audio effectively can make a real difference in the way your information is absorbed and retained by the audience.

For information presented on static slides (as opposed to movie clips), make sure your narration, sound effects, or music is designed to help the audience retain what they see.

For example, suppose you have statistics that show the growth of a product's sales over the past five years. Is it important for the audience to remember the exact numbers? Or is it important for the audience to understand the excitement of this growth? The answer is probably the latter, so you might want to consider having the statistics on the audio (or in your live narration) and use video that enhances your point, perhaps using one of these techniques:

- Show charts that illustrate the growth.
- Show a bullet list with each line referring to the growth in some dynamic way ("Another booming year—sales up 25%").
- Show a cartoon that illustrates booming growth.
- Show animated video that gives the impression of good news, growth, or both.

 TIP Whatever you do, don't show the statistics and read them at the same time; that's *droning*, and it's a quick way to dull the senses of the audience.

On the other hand, there are times when it's important for the audience to learn the specifics, such as a training course. In that case, audio and video should reinforce each other more specifically. For example, if you want to teach your audience how to install a computer peripheral, as you recite the steps you must make sure each slide (or video) is specifically aimed at matching the narration. You shouldn't use the video to create a mood; you must use the video to reinforce the lesson.

Using Video Clips

Video is everything that shows on the screen, including text, clip art, pictures, and movies. In this section, we'll talk about *movies*—video that moves.

You can use any video file that's written for Windows, which means file names with extensions of .MOV and .AVI. There are some included in the Office 97 Clip Art Gallery, and you can obtain others through a host of sources including the Internet.

Video from the Clip Art Gallery

The easiest way to add a video clip is to grab one from the Clip Art Gallery that comes with Office 97. To do this, you probably need to have your Office 97 CD in the CD drive from which you installed Office. The normal installation processes do not transfer the movie files to your hard drive:

1. Choose Insert, Movies and Sounds, then choose Movie from Gallery from the submenu. The Microsoft Clip Gallery opens with the Videos tab in the foreground.

2. Select a video clip that looks promising and choose Play. A window opens to play the video, then closes when the file is finished (see Figure 28.1).

FIG. 28.1

Use the Play button to see what the video clips look like before you decide which one you want to use.

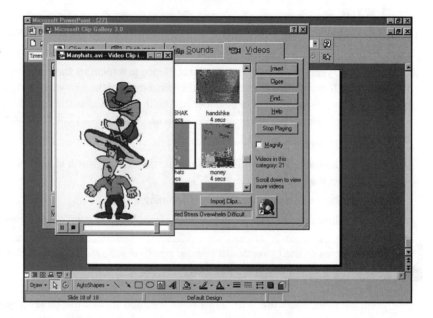

3. When you find the video you want to use, select it and choose Insert.

Video from Other Sources

You can use any .AVI or .MOV file you've managed to get your hands on. Then use these steps to add it to your presentation:

1. Choose Insert, Object, and when the Insert Object dialog box appears, select Create from File (see Figure 28.2).

FIG. 28.2

Choose a file from your hard drive to insert in the slide.

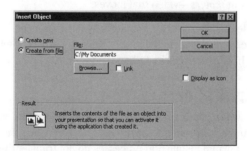

2. Enter the path and file name (or choose Browse and find the file).

3. If you want a generic icon to appear on your slide instead of the picture, select Display as Icon (see Figure 28.3).

FIG. 28.3
The two objects on this slide are for the same video clip, but one is displayed as an icon.

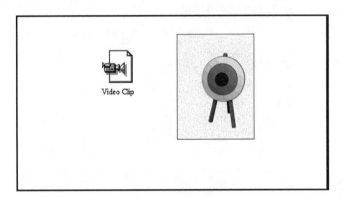

When the file is inserted on the slide, double-click to test it.

TROUBLESHOOTING

There's a problem with PowerPoint 97 that I've been unable to resolve (or get a fix for): You cannot embed large video clips (and because most video clips are fairly large, that really means you can't embed any video clips). I prefer to embed everything in my PowerPoint presentations, even though it makes the PowerPoint file enormous. I prefer it to linking because I don't have to worry about having all the original video files available on my hard drive or having access to the CD.

By default, PowerPoint is supposed to embed files that are less than 100K (unless you specify Link when you insert the object), and link files greater than that size. You can change the maximum size in the General tab of the Options dialog box (on the Tools menu). Most video clips are larger than 100K, so if you want to embed them you have to raise the maximum to at least 600K.

That process doesn't work for video files; PowerPoint ignores the new ceiling and continues to link them (it does work for sound files).

As a workaround, I transfer the video files from the Clip Gallery on the CD to my hard drive, then insert them as objects instead of choosing the Insert option that's tied to the Clip Art Gallery. This way, if I take my presentation somewhere else I don't have to carry the CD with me.

In fact, even when I insert files from my hard drive, I move those files into the PowerPoint directory before I insert them. Having linked video files in the same directory as your PowerPoint presentation makes everything run faster (but not as fast as if they were embedded—aargh).

Editing Video

You can edit a video clip by right-clicking it and choosing Open Video Clip Object. This opens the Microsoft Media Player, where you can configure the following options:

■ Choose Edit, Options to bring up the Options dialog box (see Figure 28.4). The options are self-explanatory (or you can right-click any of them and ask What's This?).

FIG. 28.4

Choose the options you need for this video clip.

■ Choose Edit, Selection to change the length of the video clip by skipping some of the beginning or stopping before the end (see Figure 28.5).

FIG. 28.5

This video has been stopped about halfway through because nothing much happens after that point.

If your presentation requires a specific length to match narration or sound effects, you can enter the appropriate numbers in the Set Selection dialog box.

However, if you're changing the length because you don't like something in the beginning or the end of the video, determine the start and stop points in the Media Player window by following these steps:

1. To change the starting point, play the video and click the Start Selection button at the point where you want to begin showing the video (see Figure 28.6).

FIG. 28.6
Use the Start Selection button to mark the spot for the beginning of the video playback.

2. To change the ending point, play the video and click the End Selection button at the point you want the video to stop playing.

3. Choose Edit, Selection to see the timings, then make small changes to fine-tune the playback.

TIP To start all over again, choose Edit, Selection and click None to clear the selection times.

To save your changes choose File, Update. To return to PowerPoint, choose File, Exit & Return.

Configuring the Playback Action

Use the Action Settings dialog box (right-click the video object and choose Action Settings) to configure the method for playing this video during your presentation (see Figure 28.7). You can choose Play when you click the mouse or when you pass the mouse over the object.

Part
VI

Ch

28

FIG. 28.7
A whooshing sound will
play and the video will
run when the object is
clicked during the
presentation.

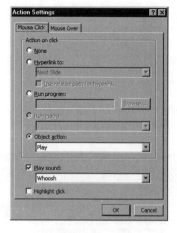

During playback, click anywhere within the object's frame to start the video clip.

Configuring the Playback Animation

You can use the Custom Animation settings instead of (or in addition to) the Action settings.
Right-click the object and choose Custom Animation from the shortcut menu. In the Custom
Animation dialog box, move to the Effects tab and specify the effects you want to use on the
video clip (see Figure 28.8).

FIG. 28.8
You can configure
animation actions
for this video and any
other object on the
same slide.

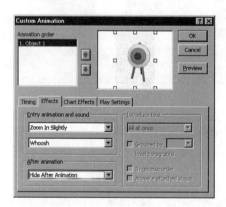

Move to the Play Settings tab where you can choose to Play the action automatically (instead
of using the Playback Animation dialog box settings which involve a mouse). This is necessary
for self-running presentations, but you might want to automate your clips even if you're
running the presentation yourself.

Using Audio Clips

Sound effects and music can usually do more to emphasize video than the narration does. You can use sound effects to draw attention to information, and you can use music to create a mood and also give consistency to a section of your presentation. When the music changes, the information changes (or, think of it the other way around).

Think of the movies you see, very few of which are devoid of music. Music is used to set the mood, to tell you when to expect a dire twist in the plot, to let you know that the current scene is light and it's okay to be amused, and to perform lots of other chores (it's slicker to change the music than to have an announcer say "And now for something completely different…" or "Meanwhile, back at the ranch…").

You can find sound files in the Clip Art Gallery that is part of Office 97, in your operating system directory, and on the Internet.

If the size of the sound file is less than the maximum size for embedded objects (check Tools, Options), the sound is embedded in your presentation and you don't have to worry about having the original file on hand.

You can edit sound files in the same way you edit video files.

Using Sound from the Clip Art Gallery

Office 97 provides a number of sound files in the Clip Art Gallery. Usually these files aren't transferred to your hard drive during installation, so you must have the Office 97 CD in its drive in order to use the Gallery.

With the slide you want to add audio to in the PowerPoint window, choose Insert, Movies and Sounds, then choose Sound from Gallery from the submenu. The Clip Art Gallery opens with the Sounds tab in the foreground (see Figure 28.9).

FIG. 28.9
Select a sound file and choose Play to hear it before you decide whether you want to use it.

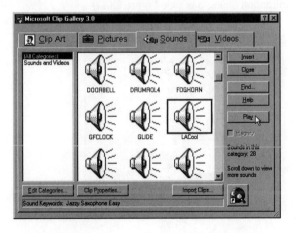

Part
VI
Ch
28

Insert the sound file and move its icon to a convenient (or innocuous) position on the slide.

Using Sound from Other Sources

To insert a sound file from a source other than the Clip Art Gallery, choose Insert, Object and when the Insert Object dialog box appears, select Create from File.

Enter the path and file name of the sound file you need, or choose Browse to select it from the Browse dialog box.

Configuring the Sound Playback

Now that the sound is attached to a slide, you can determine the way it plays back. Your decisions should depend upon the type of sound file (sound effects or music) and the audio it is accompanying.

As an example, let's configure sound for a slide that has two sound clips attached. The first sound file is a sound effect; the second is music. You can see the two icons in Figure 28.10.

FIG. 28.10

The icon in the left corner is for a music file; the one in the right corner is a sound effect.

Right-click any object on the slide and choose Custom Animation, then move to the Timing tab of the Custom Animation dialog box (see Figure 28.11).

FIG. 28.11

The order of animation for all the objects on the slide can be configured in the Custom Animation dialog box.

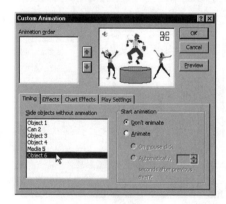

In this case, the sound effects will play first as the slide appears, then the music will start. To find the sound effects slide, click the objects listed in the dialog box, and watch the insert. When sizing handles appear on the object you want to configure, you can begin the configuration for that object with these steps:

1. Choose Animate, then select On Mouse Click or Automatically. You can use the mouse click if you're controlling the slide show, but if this presentation will be self-running, you must choose automatic animation.

2. Move to the Effects tab, where you can set Entry animation effects (the way the object enters the slide). Because this is a sound file, there's no entry, so choose No Effect.

3. On the Play Settings tab, fill out the Object Action field by choosing Play. It's also a good idea to select Hide While Not Playing because there's no particular reason to have your audience look at the icon for a sound file.

4. Choose OK to close the dialog box, then click Slide Show view to run your slide show starting with this slide. If the sound effect plays properly, you can move on. If you don't like the effect or something occurred you didn't expect, go back and fill in the configuration options again.

5. Right-click any object and choose Custom Animation to return to the dialog box and configure the music clip. Choose the correct object and select Animate (in this case, because the music must start right after the sound effect, choose Automatically and specify one second after the previous event).

6. On the Play Settings tab (see Figure 28.12), select Play Using Animation Order. Then select the other options depending on your plan for the slide show.

FIG. 28.12
In this case, the slide show continues while the music plays, and the music continues to play through two slides.

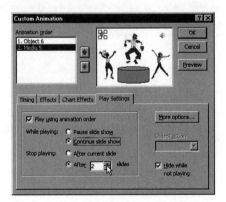

7. Choose OK and run the slide show again to test this combination of sounds.

Now that your audio is configured, you can animate other objects on the slide (see Figure 28.13).

FIG. 28.13
The dancing man falls
into the slide along with
the sound effect, then
the music starts.

From here, move to the other slides in the presentation and animate them, add music, or add video.

 If the music file is long enough, you might want to extend it through a number of slides (or the whole slide show). Remember that you can *loop* the audio file, which means regardless of its length it will continue to play because when it ends it starts all over again.

Visual Basic for Applications

29   Using VBA Macros   601

30   Working with Application Objects   617

31   Building Forms and Dialog Boxes   633

32   VBA Programming   657

33   Using VB Script   683

CHAPTER 29

Using VBA Macros

Microsoft Office 97 is the first office suite to include the powerful Visual Basic programming language as a macro builder for each application. Visual Basic for Applications (VBA) is a subset of the full Visual Basic programming environment which millions of programmers around the world use to quickly build a variety of powerful applications. Before Office 97, Microsoft included scripting capabilities such as WordBasic to allow you to manipulate and automate functions within Word or various macro building tools in the other Office applications. By introducing the programming power of Visual Basic to the whole suite, Office 97 can be used as an easy way to create custom intranet applications without the heavy coding involved in other solutions.

While you may never have used Visual Basic or even WordBasic, your programming capabilities and functions are present in all Office 97 applications. If you feel somewhat intimidated by the mention of the word "programming," don't worry. Programming VBA applications can be very easy for simple tasks, but can be extended to build more complex applications. ■

Record a macro

You learn to record a VBA macro in Excel and see where it's stored. Using the macro recorder is one of the best ways to learn VBA because the recorder writes the basic code for you!

Edit a macro

Once you've recorded a macro, you can edit it just like any VBA program. I show you how to make some changes to the code so a simple macro can be turned into a piece of a complete application.

Create a custom toolbar for a macro

Once a macro has been created, adding a custom toolbar will let you integrate the macro into your application environment. Users of your solution can simply click your custom icon to activate the macro.

Executing a macro

You can create your document so a VBA macro is executed using a toolbar button, a key combination, or an automatic event activation. You learn how to use each of these techniques to execute your VBA routine.

Creating a Macro

It is possible that you have not used a macro in any of your Office documents. A *macro* provides an easy way to automate tasks that could become too repetitive or which may require many steps. To create your first macro, it may be helpful to let the Office application do the initial work for you so you can review the VBA code that is produced. To do this, we can create a macro by letting the application record our keystrokes and commands. Later in this chapter, we'll cover the VBA macro-editing environment in more depth. So for now, let's just make a quick macro to see the code that is produced.

In this example, we will use Word to create a simple macro that inserts your name and address into your document. To start, open a new Word document and choose Tools, Macros, Record New Macro. You'll see a dialog box like the one shown in Figure 29.1.

Start by naming the macro. In this case, let's call the macro **Signature**. The Signature macro can be started by a toolbar button or by a keystroke combination (whichever you prefer). Let's assign the macro to a toolbar button. However, before we click the Toolbars button to start creating our macro, it is a good idea to assign this macro only to this particular document. By default, macros you create will be saved into the template from which you created the new document. For this exercise, let's just create the macro in this particular document rather than add it to the template.

To change the location where the macro will be stored, select the Store Macro In drop-down menu and choose Document1 (document) as shown in Figure 29.1.

FIG. 29.1

Macros can be stored in templates or individual documents depending on the functions that the macro serves.

After you have selected the option to save the macro in the current document, click the Toolbars button. The Customize dialog box will appear (see Figure 29.2), which enables you to modify the toolbar icon.

For now, just click the Close button and we'll come back to the toolbar customization after we've created the macro. As soon as you close the dialog box, the mouse pointer changes to an arrow with a tape attached to it as shown in Figure 29.3. Additionally, you will have a "floating" macro recording toolbar that will allow you to pause or stop the macro recording session.

FIG. 29.2

The Customize dialog box allows you to configure the appearance of the toolbar button for a macro.

FIG. 29.3

The mouse pointer changes to indicate that you are now in "record" mode for the macro.

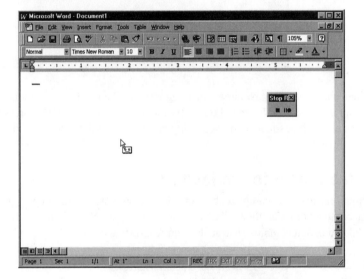

At this point, we can begin assigning keystrokes, font changes, paragraph styles, and other formatting options to the macro. Begin typing your name and address in a format that you might use to address an envelope.

N O T E Don't panic about a typo. If you make an error and backspace over the text to retype it, the macro recorder will capture the mistake and the keystrokes you used to fix it. ■

After you've completed the text of your name and address, change the font size of your name to 20-point Courier. While recording a macro, you can't simply drag the mouse pointer over the text to select it. You have to position the cursor in front of the first character of your name using the arrow keys and then while holding down the Shift key, press the right arrow until your entire name is highlighted, as shown in Figure 29.4.

FIG. 29.4
Selecting text while recording a macro must be done without the help of the mouse.

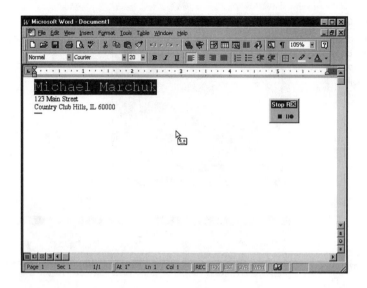

Then change the font by either selecting 20-point Courier from the toolbar or by using the menu bar to choose Format, Font. After the font has been changed, press the Stop Recording button (the little square) on the floating macro recording toolbar (which is labeled `Stop Recording`).

Adding the Macro to the Toolbar

Now your macro is complete, but you cannot access it from the toolbar just yet. To assign the macro to a button on the toolbar, choose Tools, Customize. Figure 29.5 shows the Customize dialog box that contains all available commands that can be added to a button on the toolbar.

FIG. 29.5
The newly created macro can be added to the toolbar using the Customize dialog box.

Scroll down the Categories list and select Macros. The Commands pane next to the list shows the name of the new macro we just recorded (along with the names of other macros, if applicable). The name is displayed as `Project.NewMacros.Signature`, which indicates that the `Signature` command is a macro that was created for this document.

To add the macro to a toolbar, simply click and drag the command name up to the toolbar area. You'll notice that a bold "I" beam pointer (see Figure 29.6) indicates where the new button will be placed. Also, you can tell when you are allowed to drop the new button by the indicator that appears just under the mouse pointer. In Figure 29.6, the indicator shows a plus sign, which means that the button can be dropped here. An "X" would indicate that the button couldn't be dropped yet. You can place the macro toolbar button anywhere within the toolbar area, but for this example, we'll add the button to the end of the first toolbar.

Part

VII

Ch

29

 TIP If you want to remove a macro toolbar button, or any toolbar button for that matter, click and drag the button onto the open document. The mouse indicator will show an "X" as you do so. When you drop the button, it will be removed from the toolbar. You can add and remove toolbar buttons only while the Customize dialog box is displayed.

Once you've added the new toolbar button, you'll notice that it shows up as a text-only button. This option can be changed once the button has been dropped on the toolbar. Within the Customize dialog box, new buttons will appear after you drop the macro button on the toolbar. The Modify Selection button contains several options that can alter the display properties of the macro toolbar button.

FIG. 29.6

The macro button can be placed in a toolbar using the Customize dialog box and displayed as either text or an icon.

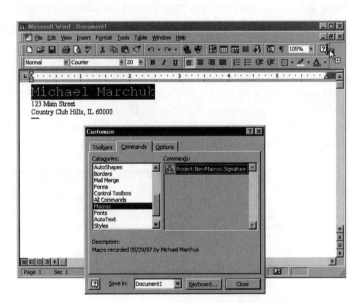

Changing the Appearance of the Toolbar

The default icon and text for a macro are rather bland. If you do not use a document with a macro very often, even you might be confused as to the meaning or usage of a toolbar button with a name like Project.NewMacro.blahblahblah.

To change the appearance of the macro button, choose one of the button styles from the Modify Selection pop-up list. If you want to match the icon look of the Office 97 toolbar, choose the Default Style option. This will create a small icon that represents the macro in the toolbar.

To change the picture on the icon, click the Modify Selection button again and select the Edit Button Image option to manually edit the icon bitmap, or select the Change Button Image option to pick an icon from a group of predefined images.

If none of the stock icon images fit your needs, you can choose Edit Button Image from the Modify Selection pop-up menu. This option provides a complete icon bitmap editor, if you have a lot of creativity and time to create your own images.

The final modification for the macro toolbar button should be done to ease the identification of the button. As you move the mouse over any standard toolbar button, the button will display a *ToolTip* (also known as a *ScreenTip* or *ControlTip*) which identifies the function of that button. For instance, the "B" icon in the toolbar produces the "Bold" ToolTip that informs you about the meaning and usage for the button. To change the ToolTip text for the new macro button, click the Modify Selection button in the Customize dialog box and edit the text in the Name field to indicate the text that you want displayed. Make sure that this text is informative, especially if the icon image you have chosen may not have any specific meaning. The text stored in the Name field is also displayed when the Text of a toolbar button is shown.

After you have finished changing the options for the macro's toolbar button, the final step in the process is testing the macro. Make sure you test your macro under several circumstances, because the macro you recorded may not operate the same way in all situations. For example, if the Signature macro that we created in this section is used in an empty document, the results seem to be just as we would expect. When you click the macro button, the name and address text you recorded in the macro are displayed. However, if you are in a situation where other formatting is already in place, the results may not be as you expected. Figure 29.7 shows how the Signature macro can produce different results depending on the paragraph formatting.

FIG. 29.7

A macro can produce different results depending on the circumstances in which it is used.

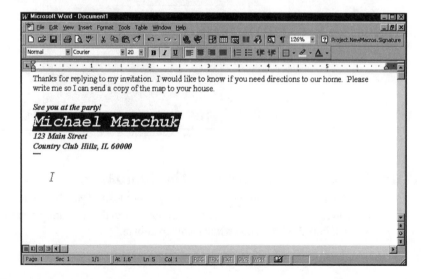

So what do you do after you have recorded a macro that doesn't perform exactly what you want it to do? You edit the macro.

Part
VII

Ch
29

Editing a Macro in VBA

If you are creating a macro from scratch or just fixing one you recorded, the VBA macro editor provides an extensive programming environment to get the job done. If you have never used Visual Basic before and do not consider yourself a programmer, then this environment may appear to be a little overwhelming (see Figure 29.8). However, don't worry; we'll just look at a small segment of the VBA programming environment in this section. If you want to really get into developing some heavy-duty macros or building customized applications, you'll want to check out Chapter 31, "Building Forms and Dialog Boxes," and Chapter 32, "VBA Programming."

FIG. 29.8

The VBA development environment provides a great deal of flexibility and power, so don't be intimidated if you're new to programming.

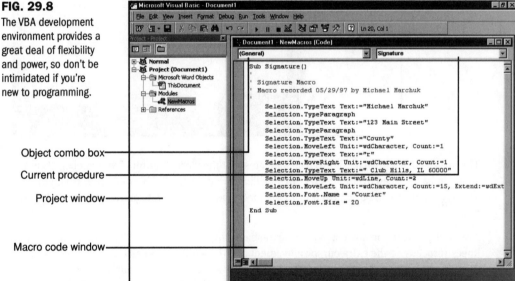

Object combo box

Current procedure

Project window

Macro code window

Because we're just going to cover editing a recorded macro, it might be helpful to have a brief overview of the VBA development environment. First, you will notice that the macro code itself is only a small portion of the overall environment. Remember, this is a subset of Visual Basic, so there are many optional components which can be used to build complex applications.

The other parts of the VBA programming environment provide access to the overall project and other macros or code modules which have been written as part of an application. Again, because our macro is the only code contained in this document and template, we have very little to see in terms of a large number of macro code functions that may be stored in a document. The rest of this section will assume that you are just going to make small changes to a recorded macro, and not develop any fancy application code.

By looking at Figure 29.9, you will see a sample macro which contains a few extra keystrokes that were captured while recording the new macro. The extra keystrokes are used to correct a typing mistake made while recording the macro.

FIG. 29.9

While recording a macro, several extra keystrokes were captured trying to correct a typographical error.

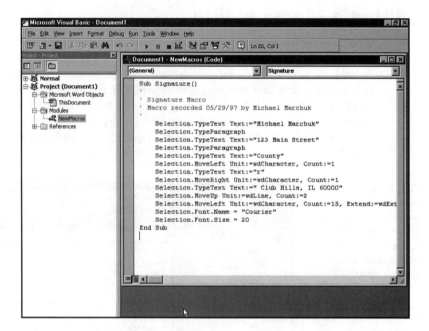

The macro code shown in Figure 29.9 indicates that the word "Country" was spelled "County" and then backspaced over to correct the spelling by adding an "r" between the "t" and the "y." This typing error can be removed from the macro because it is not relevant and will take extra time to process.

Now, this particular mistake is not so earth-shattering and shouldn't bring your computer to its knees (processing the extra cursor movement and the additional keystroke isn't that big a deal). However, in a situation where a thousand rows of an Excel spreadsheet are being manipulated, the extra processing time may become significant and may impact other work being performed. In any case, this example is to show you the process of editing the macro to correct any mistakes which may have crept into the macro during its recording.

To edit a macro, choose Tools, Macro, Visual Basic Editor or press Alt+F11. The VBA programming environment will be loaded. The project frame on the left side of the window shows all of the items contained within the project. The macro is located in the Modules section of the project within the NewMacros object. Open the folder by double-clicking the Modules icon. Now open the macro code window by double-clicking the macro item.

The macro code which is displayed takes on many of the characteristics of Visual Basic code. Again, if you are not familiar with Visual Basic or have only passing experience with WordBasic or other scripting languages, this may look very unfamiliar. To ease any possible distress over the syntax and usage of the VBA language, it will be helpful to have a brief overview of VBA. If you are an experienced Visual Basic programmer or WordBasic user, however, you'll want to skip the next section and instead review Chapter 32, "VBA Programming," which covers the VBA environment in much greater depth.

Macro Subroutines

The functionality of a macro, the code that executes and does the work, is contained within a code segment called a *subroutine*. Because programmers don't like to type more than they have to, the word *subroutine* is shortened to *sub*. A subroutine is simply a segment of code which can be called from a larger application to do something within the application.

For example, our Signature macro is called by the Word application to type our name and address. Subroutines can perform very complex operations and call other subroutines to complete their functionality. Programming macros can be very powerful, yet if they become too complex, their operations can be sometimes slightly confusing when the code is examined. To make the code more straightforward, you can break an operation into several subroutines called by a central macro. Depending on your needs for macros, you can get pretty creative with VBA.

Some subroutines return values when they are complete. For example, it is possible that you have a mortgage payment calculation that you are using within a mortgage pre-qualification document. Instead of running a subroutine that types the payment, you may want the code to return the value of the payment so you can use it within another subroutine. This kind of code segment is called a *function*. Functions return values to the subroutines which called them, instead of simply performing a preset action within the code. Because our Signature macro code isn't returning any values, it is simply a subroutine and not a function.

Anatomy of a Subroutine

Subroutines have a defined structure which allows you to see what happens within the code. In the case of our Signature macro, the subroutine is named `Signature()`. The parentheses after the `Signature` name indicate that there is no additional information being given to the subroutine when it starts. Consider this example:

```
Sub Age_Calculator(DateBorn as Date)
  'Calculates someone's age based on
  'her birth date.
  ...
End Sub
```

You will notice that the parentheses now include the statement `DateBorn as Date`. What this is telling the application is that there will be information being sent to this subroutine. The subroutine should call that information `DateBorn` and the `DateBorn` information should be treated as a `Date`.

The `DateBorn` name for the information being used is called a *variable*. Variables are another way that data can be manipulated within a subroutine. In this case, the `DateBorn` variable will be used in a mathematical function to calculate someone's age based on the date she was born.

If you are following everything at this point, you may have figured out that this code could also be written as a function which could return the age back to the calling function.

At the bottom of the subroutine shown, you'll notice that the End Sub statement finalizes the code. This allows the application to contain any variable information or other actions within this particular subroutine. If the document contains other macros, they would show up as other subroutines as shown in Figure 29.10.

FIG. 29.10

Multiple macros are displayed as many subroutines within a document's module section.

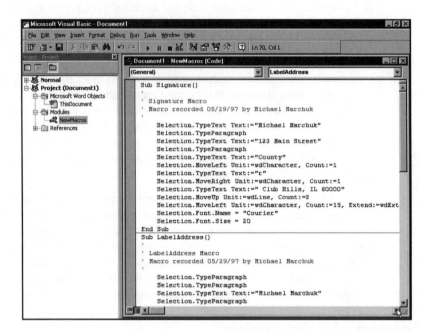

```
Sub Signature()
'
' Signature Macro
' Macro recorded 05/29/97 by Michael Marchuk
'
    Selection.TypeText Text:="Michael Marchuk"
    Selection.TypeParagraph
    Selection.TypeText Text:="123 Main Street"
    Selection.TypeParagraph
    Selection.TypeText Text:="County"
    Selection.MoveLeft Unit:=wdCharacter, Count:=1
    Selection.TypeText Text:="r"
    Selection.MoveRight Unit:=wdCharacter, Count:=1
    Selection.TypeText Text:=" Club Hills, IL 60000"
    Selection.MoveUp Unit:=wdLine, Count:=2
    Selection.MoveLeft Unit:=wdCharacter, Count:=15, Extend:=wdExt
    Selection.Font.Name = "Courier"
    Selection.Font.Size = 20
End Sub
Sub LabelAddress()
'
' LabelAddress Macro
' Macro recorded 05/29/97 by Michael Marchuk
'
    Selection.TypeParagraph
    Selection.TypeParagraph
    Selection.TypeText Text:="Michael Marchuk"
    Selection.TypeParagraph
```

Class Objects

If you aren't a programmer, the term *object-oriented* probably doesn't mean much to you. What the programming term means is that code and variables can have certain attributes and properties which can be used to define something or change the way something works. In the Signature macro code that we have created, there are several examples of object methods which are being used. As you look at Figure 29.11, you'll see that the Selection object is used to perform an action on the document. In this case, the action, or *method* as it is called within VBA, includes both typing text and moving the cursor.

By looking at the macro code, you'll see that the Selection object has a few methods which are used to type our address. The first method is the TypeText method. Without going into the gory details of how to use each and every function within VBA, it may be helpful to show the basic structure of an object method.

FIG. 29.11

The Signature macro uses objects and methods to perform its actions.

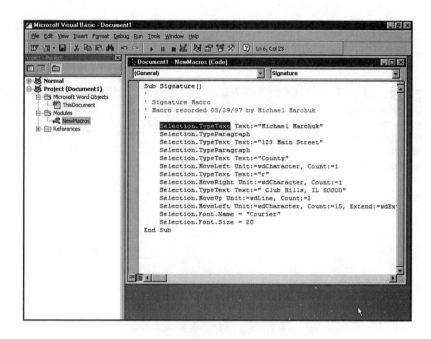

In general, objects are identified first with the method or property that is being addressed, following a period. In reviewing the code example in Figure 29.11, the object is `Selection` and the method is `TypeText`. The method of `TypeText` requires additional input—namely, the text that is to be typed. This information is specified after the object by adding the `Text` property and the value which should be used (in this case, the text of the address).

If a method requires more information to complete the task, multiple properties can be assigned by separating each property with a comma. Notice the `Selection.MoveLeft` method assigns a `Unit` property and a `Count` property.

Try not to get hung up on the specifics of the usage. At this point, just absorb the fundamentals of the structure so that you can be more familiar with the usage as you go further.

Modifying VBA Code

Now that you've got a handle on the structure of the macro code, you may want to venture forth and make some changes to see what happens. In this case, our Signature macro has some extra keystrokes which were recorded when we fixed a typing mistake in our address. At this point, you should be able to see where the macro code is typing the address information using the `Selection.TypeText` method as shown in Figure 29.12. Let's fix our macro by removing the editing keystrokes and correcting the typing mistake within the code.

To do this, you'll need to identify the line which is doing the majority of the typing. Click the line which contains the `Selection.TypeText` code and correct the typing mistake. Then remove the other `Selection` method lines which are simply there to move the cursor around and type the additional characters. You'll want to leave the final `Selection` method, which instructs the application to insert a carriage return paragraph ending. Your final code should resemble Figure 29.12.

FIG. 29.12

The corrected Signature macro does not contain any extra cursor movements or keystrokes.

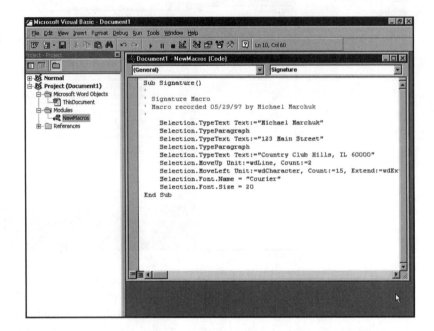

Now that we have corrected our Signature code, let's move on to see how we can activate the code within our documents.

Executing Macros

Macro functions are not much use if they stay dormant within an application. There are several ways in which to activate a macro within your document. These activation methods include:

- Pressing a key combination
- Clicking a toolbar button
- Auto-activation on a document opening or closing

We've already shown you how to create a toolbar button that will run your macro. The other two methods will be covered in this section so that you may choose the method which makes the most sense for your macro needs. Keep in mind that you may have macros that are activated by each of these methods contained within the same document. Additionally, macros can be activated by more than one method.

Keyboard Macro Execution

One of the most traditional methods of executing a macro is that of a key combination. Word processors from days gone by used this method to activate macros since there wasn't any other way to do so. In this case, a macro can be assigned a particular combination of keystrokes which, when pressed, will identify to the application that a macro should be run.

For example, we can assign our Signature macro to be executed when the Alt key and the S key are pressed. To do this, open the Customize dialog box by choosing Tools, Customize.

Because we want to assign a key combination to activate this macro, click the Keyboard button. This will display the Customize Keyboard dialog box (see Figure 29.13) which will allow us to type a keyboard combination for this macro.

FIG. 29.13

The Customize Keyboard dialog box allows a key combination to be assigned to the macro.

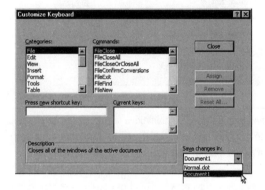

Select the document name from the Save Changes In drop-down list; that is where the Signature macro is stored. Notice that the Customize Keyboard dialog box also contains a Categories list and a Commands list. By scrolling down the categories, you will see the Macros option. Selecting Macros from the Categories list will cause the Commands list to change to a Macros list (see Figure 29.14) that displays our Signature macro.

FIG. 29.14

Select the Signature macro from the Macros list to assign a key combination.

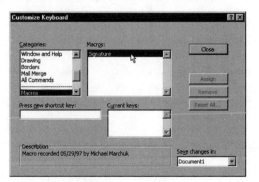

Click the Press New Shortcut Key text box. Then press the key combination that you want to assign to execute the macro. In this case, we want the Alt+S combination to be assigned. After pressing Alt+S, the keyboard shortcut text box indicates the combination we selected, and a message below the shortcut (see Figure 29.15) indicates what functions are already assigned to that combination. In this case, no other functions have been assigned to the Alt+S combination.

FIG. 29.15

If the key combination is being used by another macro, the Customize Keyboard dialog box will indicate what command is in conflict.

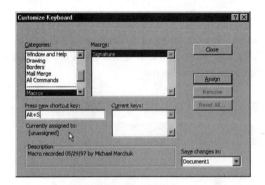

 You may be surprised to find that many key combinations are already assigned through the Office application suite. Try not to reassign a pre-existing key combination or those who use your document may get undesirable results when making changes.

Once you've found a key combination which is not conflicting, you can click the Assign button to specify that functionality. Click Close (twice) and try out your new key combination.

Auto-Execution of Macros

One of the powerful functions of Office is the ability to execute a macro when a particular function has occurred, such as when a document is loaded or closed. This functionality has been exploited by viruses which can do damage by executing embedded VBA applications that delete files or perform other malicious activities.

> **CAUTION**
>
> Many antivirus applications will search for auto-executing macros. Additionally, Word will warn a user when a document contains an auto-executing macro. If you include this type of functionality, make sure you inform your users so that they will not become alarmed when they see a warning message.

To automatically execute a macro, you need to do some VBA programming. First, open up the Visual Basic Editor by choosing Tools, Macro, Visual Basic Editor or by pressing Alt+F11. Then double-click the ThisDocument object within the project frame. This will open the code window which shows the document methods. Select the right-hand drop-down list from the code window toolbar. This will have the three Document methods of New, Open, and Close. If you want a macro to execute when someone opens your document, select the Open method. You will then see an empty subroutine like the one shown in Figure 29.16.

FIG. 29.16

The code window in the Visual Basic Editor allows you to add an auto-execute macro command.

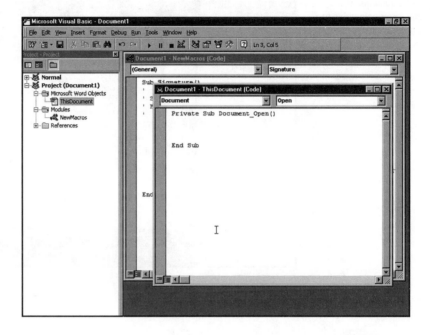

 T I P Test your macro using a key combination or toolbar button before creating an auto-execute macro. This will allow you to verify the operation of the macro before allowing it to auto-execute.

To initiate the macro during the open process, we need to insert the command to call the macro subroutine. If we had a VBA macro named DisplayWelcomeScreen that showed a dialog box when the document was opened, we could place this code into the Open event. To do this, place the name of the macro into the Open subroutine as shown in Figure 29.17.

In the code, you may have noticed that certain lines that begin with an apostrophe (') appear to be written in English. They are! The apostrophe (') command is a comment keyword that makes invisible to VBA all the text on the line that follows it. You can put comments in English to describe what the code is doing.

Commenting your code is strongly recommended as it allows you to understand what is happening when you look at the code days, weeks, or months later. You can also use comments to describe the use of variables so other people can use functions that you've created.

Auto-execute macros are typically used with forms and dialog boxes that are built for a more complex application. You can read more about forms and dialog box usage in Chapter 31, "Building Forms and Dialog Boxes." Simple macros can also be built which auto-execute for a purpose such as saving the file as a new name on opening, before any changes are made to the file.

FIG. 29.17

Enter the macro subroutine name into the Open subroutine to call the macro when the document is opened.

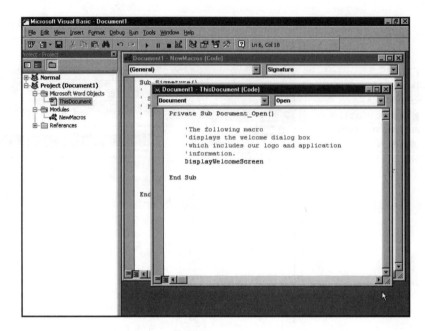

CHAPTER 30

Working with Application Objects

The key to programming in Visual Basic for Applications is understanding how to use the various pieces of built-in functionality that each of the Office applications provides. Each application in the Office suite has a central Application object that can be used to manipulate all of the other objects contained within that program. In Excel, for example, the Application object can be used to Open a new workbook or switch between documents.

This chapter explores application objects which provide this functionality and outlines the various object models for the Office applications. All of the objects of an Office application are structured like a tree, starting a top root object and branching into all of the objects lower in the object model. The Application object is the root object in all of these object models. ■

Overview of application objects

An object model is organized like an organizational chart or tree diagram. The Application object is the root of the tree. Learn how an Office application is structured around this object.

Use application objects to provide VBA functionality

Learn how to manipulate Excel and Word by using VBA programming to access their object models. You will add code to call VBA procedures and activate on the occurrence of VBA events.

Use common application objects in various Office programs

All of the Office applications are defined with object models. Some of the objects in Excel, Word, PowerPoint, and Access are described. You'll also see how to manipulate the Office Assistant through VBA.

Application Object Overview

In order to understand programming VBA applications, you need to know how to use the built-in functions that Office applications provide. For example, when building a VBA application which accepts data input from a form and then graphs a chart based on that data, there is no point in developing code which calculates the graphics needed to display the data in a chart. You can simply use the charting object within Excel to provide the type of chart you need. Not only will the chart look good, but you can build your application quickly and with less code.

Let's examine the parts of a simplified object model which describes the objects within an application. This example object model will show you the general format that most object models will follow. An application's object model tends to look something like a company's organizational chart. At the top of the object model is the application under which all objects reside. Figure 30.1 shows object model for Word.

FIG. 30.1

Object models group functionality into a hierarchy.

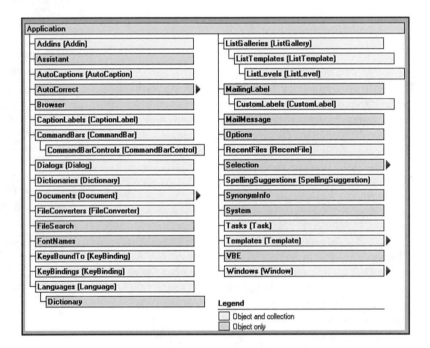

Don't let the number of objects you see in Figure 30.1 discourage you. Using these objects is easy and makes pretty good sense. Objects are grouped together in a collection which provides an easy way to understand what the object is doing in relationship to the other objects in the collection.

For example, let's take a very small subset of the Word application object model (shown in Figure 30.2) and see how objects fit together. You'll notice that the Word application object sits at the top of the model. Under the Word object is the Documents object which contains the Words object and the Paragraphs object. The Words and Paragraphs objects are known as a *collection* because they are under the larger Documents object. Each of these objects then have various properties and methods which can be used to build a particular set of functionality into your VBA application.

FIG. 30.2

Object collections are subordinate to a higher-level object.

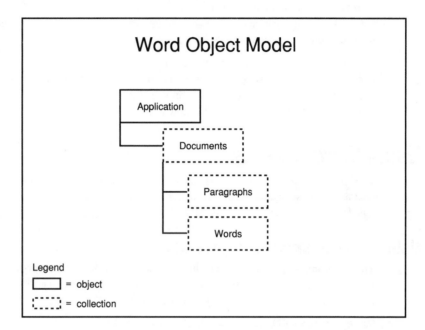

Each object within a collection may be manipulated either individually or as part of the collection. This allows you to build powerful functions with very little coding effort. You can address either very small portions of the application object to achieve a high level of control, or make sweeping changes rapidly by addressing the larger object collection. For example, you could change the font of a particular character in a Word document, or italicize the entire document, depending on your VBA application needs.

Manipulating Objects

Objects have *methods* and *properties* which can be modified to suit your application's needs. Methods are actions which cause the object to do something while properties are characteristics of an object. The methods and properties of an object are linked to the object using a dotted notation. For example, the method Application.Calculate in Excel recalculates the spreadsheet.

Properties for a particular object may require a great deal of specification if the property is for a deeply subordinated object. For example, the property setting to alter the heading style of your current document within Word to italics would be

```
ActiveDocument.Styles(wdStyleHeading2).Font.Italic = True.
```

Part

VII

Ch

30

Manipulating objects within various Office applications takes some time to get used to, especially if you are new to VBA programming. The best way to understand the objects and their functionality is by using the Office application and learning what object controls the functionality that you want to incorporate into your VBA application. Object models differ between the various Office applications. So the remaining portion of this chapter will allow you to explore some of the more popular objects within each Office application.

The following sections that contain descriptions of the various Office objects is certainly not comprehensive, because there have been entire books written about these objects and their use. The descriptions are meant to begin your familiarization with the various objects that are available, and to provide examples of how to use a few of the more popular objects.

Using Word Objects

The Word Application object has many object collections which center around the active document and selections within the document. The most frequently used collections are detailed in this section with some examples of how they are used within a VBA application.

Using the *Documents* Object Collection

The Documents object collection includes a variety of objects which provide a number of properties, methods, and events. However, the Documents collection has only a few properties and methods. For example, you can open a document with the statement

```
Documents.Open FileName:="C:\My Documents\Sales.doc"
```

and then save the document with

```
Documents.Save NoPrompt:=True, OriginalFormat:=wdOriginalDocumentFormat
```

or close the document with

```
Documents("Sales.doc").Close SaveChanges:=wdDoNotSaveChanges
```

The Documents collection can be used to load a particular document based on someone's input into a form within your VBA application. Form creation is covered in depth in Chapter 31, "Building Forms and Dialog Boxes."

Using the *Document* Object Properties

The Document object contains many properties which can be addressed for any document within the collection or for the currently active document. When you are referencing the document which is active, then the syntax ActiveDocument can be used rather than explicitly identifying Documents("Sales.doc"). In the examples shown in this section, the ActiveDocument syntax will be used.

 TIP When you have many documents open at once, it may be best to explicitly identify the document whose property you want to use. This will prevent your application from providing incorrect information or even destroying data in a document which may have been mistakenly activated.

PageSetup   The PageSetup property also has a collection of properties which allow your VBA application to modify various page attributes affecting the entire document. For example,

```
ActiveDocument.PageSetup.RightMargin = InchesToPoints(1)
```

changes the right margin to one inch for the whole document.

Path   The Path property identifies the directory from which the document was loaded. In a networked environment, you may want to use this property to alert users that copy a document to a local drive that they may not have the most recent changes.

```
If ActiveDocument.Path <> "Q:\BUDGET\FY98" Then
      MsgBox ("You are using a local copy of this document!")
End If
```

TROUBLESHOOTING

Paths are often difficult to manage from VBA because of their constantly changing nature. The user may move a document or rename a directory which will alter the path. The network drive may also be mounted as E: instead of D:. Here are a few techniques for dealing with paths:

- *Check the path of the Application object.* The Application object itself has a Path property. You can use this property to determine the location of another document in relation to the Application itself.

- *Use the Mid$ function to take a path string apart.* The Mid$ function can be passed a string as well as a beginning and length parameter. You can use this function in conjunction with the InStr$ function (which locates a particular string within a string) to determine each directory level or drive designation within a Path property.

- *Use the relative directory commands.* Most Path properties support the use of relative directory functions. These include the single dot (.\mydir\myfile.txt) command to activate the current directory, and the double dot (..\mypicts\myfile2.gif) to move one directory up in the hierarchy. You can use these commands to specify relative paths, allowing you to move an entire directory without rewriting the path code.

ReadOnly   The ReadOnly property can be used to determine whether or not your VBA application can save changes to the active document. This is a good way to catch errors before they happen in your VBA application.

```
If ActiveDocument.ReadOnly = True Then MsgBox("Changes cannot be saved.")
```

Saved   Your VBA application can check the Saved property to see whether any changes have been made since the last time it was saved. This property is useful when your application is controlling the data entry into a form and you want to ensure that all information in a particular section is saved before moving on to prevent data loss.

```
If ActiveDocument.Saved = False Then ActiveDocument.Save
```

SaveFormat   When your VBA application requires interaction with other applications such as WordPerfect or your application reads in data from external applications, you may want to

Part
VII

Ch
30

check the file format and convert the document to a native format. A code sample which checks the format might look like:

```
If ActiveDocument.SaveFormat <> wdFormatDocument Then
    ActiveDocument.SaveAs FileFormat:=wdFormatDocument
End If
```

Because Word supports a great number of document types, you can check the individual format type using the values in Table 30.1.

Table 30.1   Word Document Types

Document Type	Format Code
Word Native Document	wdFormatDocument
DOS Text	wdFormatDOSText
DOS Text with Line Breaks	wdFormatDOSTextLineBreaks
Rich Text Format	wdFormatRTF
Word Document Template	wdFormatTemplate
Plain Text	wdFormatText
Plain Text with Line Breaks	wdFormatTextLineBreaks
Unicode Text	wdFormatUnicodeText

Using the *Document* Object Methods

Interacting with documents within Word requires using Document object methods. This section will outline some of the more commonly used Document methods and provide examples of when you might want to make use of that method in your VBA applications.

Activate   The Activate method is useful for applications which use many documents for data entry, documentation, or application instructions. This property allows your VBA application to bring a particular open document to the foreground to be viewed or edited.

```
Documents("Instructions.doc").Activate
```

CheckGrammar and CheckSpelling   The CheckGrammar and CheckSpelling methods are very useful because they initiate the grammar- or spell-checking routines within Word. This might be used in a VBA application where the document is saved to an archive area or is routed via e-mail to others within your organization. In this case, either of these methods may be invoked prior to saving or sending the document. The syntax for these methods is simple:

```
ActiveDocument.CheckGrammar
```

```
ActiveDocument.CheckSpelling
```

Open, Close, Save, and SaveAs   The Open, Close, Save, and SaveAs properties allow your VBA application to manage the documents which it uses. These methods will probably be frequently used in your VBA applications.

```
Documents.Open FileName:="C:\MyFiles\MyDoc.doc"
```

```
ActiveDocument.Close
```

```
ActiveDocument.Save
```

```
ActiveDocument.SaveAs FileName:="Sales.rtf", FileFormat:=wdFormatRTF
```

SendMail   Your VBA application may interact with your local Microsoft Exchange mail server to distribute documents to others within your organization. The SendMail method allows you VBA application to initiate the process of sending a document via e-mail.

```
Options.SendMailAttach = True
ActiveDocument.SendMail
```

The code example also shows how to specify that the document is to be sent as an attachment to the mail message. If Options.SendMailAttach was not included, the default option would be to send the document as the text portion of the message. Depending on your application and the mail client that recipients of the document will be using, you may want to send the document one way or the other.

Using the *Document* Object Events

The macro virus writers have capitalized on the Document object event triggers to wreak havoc with Word macros. The same events can, however, be used in productive ways. Unfortunately, your VBA application may set off virus-protection software alarms or warning dialog boxes within Word when particular events (like opening or closing a document) are used. So be cautious when implementing this type of functionality within your VBA application because a casual user may mistake your productive VBA code for a malicious virus before it even does any work.

Open   This is where the infamous Concept virus did its work. Many virus programs disable the Open event macros. If you choose to implement the Open event as a trigger for your VBA application, make sure that you understand that some users may disable the functionality which is placed within the Open event code.

```
Private Sub Document_Open()
    MsgBox "Please contact Herb Schlonskins " + _
        "before making changes to this document."
End Sub
```

Close   The Close event can be used to make a copy of the document to a public or archive area on the network or to a local storage area on the user's hard drive. To implement this type of functionality, you may want to either prompt the user for a location to save the copy of the file or to inform the user that a copy is being saved elsewhere.

Part

VII

Ch

30

```
Private Sub Document_Close()
    ActiveDocument.Save
    ActiveDocument.SaveAs "\\NetworkServer\DocumentArchive\" _
        & ActiveDocument.Name
End Sub
```

Font Selection   The Font Selection property provides an easy way for your application to change the font characteristics of a particular selection of text within the document.

```
Selection.Font.Name = "Arial"
Selection.Font.Size = 12
Selection.Font.Bold = True
```

Using *Selection* Methods

Once a user has selected text, or if your VBA application selects text within a document, your code can make use of the many Selection methods. These methods provide a great deal of flexibility to manipulate text needed.

The Copy, Cut, and Paste methods for the Selection object move the selected text to the Windows Clipboard where it can be used by other applications or by your VBA application. Recall that the Cut method will remove the text and place it in the Clipboard while the Copy method does not remove the text from the original location. One example of this could be to move data from one document to another.

```
Selection.Copy
Documents.Activate("Finance3Q.doc")
Selection.Paste
```

Using Excel Objects

Excel lends itself very well to VBA programming because the main purpose for most worksheets is "number crunching." Building a VBA application which manipulates ranges of cells or provides enhanced data entry makes use of the vast array of properties, methods, and events that Excel objects have to offer. This section will cover some of these objects and provide examples of how those objects can be used within a VBA application.

Using the *Workbooks* Object Collection

The Workbooks object collection includes the objects associated with an Excel workbook. The Workbooks collection has a few properties, methods, and events which you might use within your VBA application.

Using *Workbook Count* Property   The Count property can be used to see how many workbooks are opened within Excel. This might be useful if your VBA application loads a large or complex workbook and you want to ensure that there are no other workbooks opened which could be using needed memory resources.

```
If Workbooks.Count > 1 Then
        MsgBox ("Please close all workbooks before using this workbook.")
End If
```

Using the *Workbooks* Collection Methods   Of the handful of Workbooks methods, you may only need to use a few. The Add, Open, and Close methods provide access to file operations which your VBA application can use.

The Add method will create a blank workbook. This method can accept optional parameters which aid in creating a new workbook from an existing workbook's template.

```
Workbooks.Add "c:\data\financial\expenses.xls"
```

The Open method also accepts several parameters which are used to indicate any special needs that the workbook has, like passwords or link updates. The example shows an Open statement which includes a password-protected workbook.

```
Workbooks.Open("c:\data\budget\FY98.XLS","MagicWord")
```

When you have completed updates to a workbook, your application can use the Close method.

```
Workbooks.Close("FY98.XLS")
```

Using the *Workbook* Object Properties and Methods

The few Workbook object properties and methods which you might use in a VBA application are outlined here. The ReadOnly and Saved properties provide your VBA application with information related to the status of the active workbook. The ReadOnly property returns a True value if the workbook was opened as read-only. The Saved property returns true if there were no changes made to the active workbook, thus the open workbook is the same as the saved copy.

```
If ActiveWorkbook.ReadOnly = True and ActiveWorkbook.Saved = False Then
  ActiveWorkbook.SaveAs fileName:="NewWorkbook.xls"
End If
```

The Activate method can be used to switch to another open workbook.

```
Workbook("FY98.XLS").Activate
```

The Close, Save, and SaveAs methods allow your VBA application to apply the changes made in the active workbook by saving them to disk. The Close method includes an optional parameter which can specify whether to save the changes made to the workbook.

```
Workbook("FY98.XLS").Close(True)
Workbook("FY98.XLS").Save
ActiveWorkbook.SaveAs("FY98 Revised.XLS")
```

The Workbook object also supports events such as SheetCalculate which is triggered when a particular worksheet is recalculated, and an Open event which allows your application to modify workbook properties when the workbook is opened. There are several other events which can be used, but most of these will probably not find there way into your initial VBA applications.

Part
VII

Ch
30

Using the *Worksheets* Object Collection

The Worksheets collection is made up of all of the worksheet objects within a workbook. This is somewhat different than the Sheets collection which covers dialog sheets and chart sheets in addition to worksheets.

The Worksheets collection provides a few properties and methods which you may use in your VBA applications. One property which is used often when building applications that add worksheets to a workbook is the Count property. The Count property returns then number of worksheets within the collection.

```
If Worksheets.Count < 12 Then
     Worksheets.Add After:=Worksheets(Worksheets.Count)
End If
```

The Add property which is shown in the previous example provides several options for adding new worksheets to a workbook. These options are expressed by appending a parameter and value after the Add command. For example, you can choose to add a worksheet before or after a particular worksheet, add more than one worksheet, or add a different type of worksheet. The following example shows how to add two worksheets ahead of the current collection of worksheets:

```
Worksheets.Add Before:=Sheets(1), Count:=2
```

Using *Worksheet* Object Properties

The Worksheet object is part of the Worksheets collection and the Sheets collection. Each worksheet can be identified by using its name as shown in the worksheet's tab or by referencing the index number of the worksheet's position in the workbook. For instance, if you wanted to reference the third worksheet within the collection which was named Third Quarter, you could either reference it as ActiveWorkbook.Worksheets(3) or ActiveWorkbook.Worksheets("Third Quarter").

 T I P If your application has a predefined naming scheme for multiple worksheets within a workbook (South, MidWest, and so on), you may want to reference the worksheet by name so that you will not have any trouble debugging the VBA code which might simply reference Worksheets(5).

The Name property will assist you in creating worksheets which have useful names. When you create a worksheet in Excel, by default the name is simply Sheet followed by a number which is based on how many sheets you have added to the workbook. Unfortunately, this does not provide the user with any additional assistance when using your application. By using the Name property, you can set the name which appears in the workbook tab to identify the active worksheet. For example, you could use Worksheets(2).Name = "MidWest".

The Visible property may be used to hide a worksheet from the user's view. You might want to use this as part of a larger VBA application which makes use of various worksheets at different times or based on different conditions. This way, the user does not see the alternate worksheets for data entry unless your VBA applications allows them to be visible. The `Visible` property has a syntax like this:

```
Worksheets(3).Visible = False
```

There are a few worksheet methods which will be used often in your VBA application. These include methods to manually calculate the worksheet, delete a worksheet, or copy a worksheet. The syntax for each of these methods are shown here:

```
ActiveWorksheet.Calculate
```

```
ActiveWorksheet.Copy
```

```
ActiveWorksheet.Delete
```

The `Copy` method also allows you to specify where the copy of the current worksheet should be placed. You can choose either `Before` or `After` options to identify where the copy of the worksheet will be placed within the workbook. For example, the following code indicates that the new copy should be placed after the fourth worksheet in the workbook:

```
ActiveWorksheet.Copy After:=Worksheets(4)
```

Using the *Range* Object

The `Range` object provides a way for you to manipulate a range of cells within an Excel spreadsheet. The `Range` object is very powerful and will most likely be used in all of your Excel VBA programming.

The `Range` object can be used to specify a range of cells which can be:

- A single cell such as Range("R32") or Range("C18:D55")
- A named range such as Range("Third Quarter Totals")
- The current cell, or active cell, which is specified as `ActiveCell.ActiveCell`

Using the *Range* Object Properties   The major `Range` object properties which you may use within your application include the `Address`, `Cells`, and `Formula` properties. These properties will provide you with information about the currently selected range or the named range within the active worksheet.

The `Address` property has several options which provide different types of returned addressing. For example, if you wanted the absolute address of the range, you would specify the address like this:

```
ActiveCell.Address(RowAbsolute:=True, ColumnAbsolute:=True)
```

The message box in Figure 30.3 shows how the `Address` property returns information based on the `ActiveCell` code shown here.

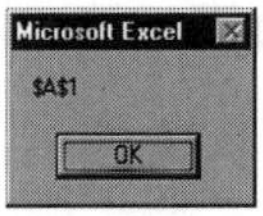

FIG. 30.3

The Address property can be used to identify the currently active cell within the worksheet.

The Cells property is most often used to reference a cell which is relative to a specific range. By choosing to include the optional Row and Column references, you can specify a cell in relation to its position within an identified Range object. For example, if you had a named range which started at cell B100, you could reference cell D102 by including the following code:

```
ActiveCell.Cells(2,2).Activate
ActiveCell.Value="Here I am!"
```

The Formula property allows your application to provide additional functionality by setting a particular cell's formula. Most commonly, this would be to total a column's values using the SUM formula. The following example shows how the Formula property can be used to SUM a column of data:

```
Range("B100").Formula = "=SUM(B1:B99)"
```

N O T E   Notice that the Formula property is used as if you are typing in the formula. You'll need to quote the formula and provide the same syntax (the equal sign before the formula) for this to work as you expect it to. ■

Using *Range* Object Methods   The Range object has several methods which you will find to be useful as you develop your VBA applications within Excel. These methods include Activate, Clear, Copy, PasteSpecial, and Sort.

The Activate method simply tells Excel to put the focus on the cell which is currently specified. For example:

```
Range("B100").Activate
```

The Clear method can be used to erase the contents of the specified range. This method erases both formatting and formulas. For example:

```
Worksheets("Third Quarter").Range("A1:G37").Clear
```

The Copy method provides a mechanism to copy the contents of the specified range on to the Clipboard. This is most often used with the PasteSpecial method which places the Clipboard contents back into the active worksheet. The following example copies a range and pastes it back into the active worksheet at a different location:

```
ActiveSheet.Range("B100:D100").Copy
ActiveSheet.Range("H200:J200").PasteSpecial
```

The Sort method provides a way to sort a range of values within the worksheet. The following example shows how to sort the values with two sort keys.

```
ActiveSheet.Range("A1:C20").Sort Key1:=ActiveSheet.Range("A1"), _
        Key2:=ActiveSheet.Range("B1")
```

N O T E The Sort method has too many optional parameters to list here. You should review the various options within the Excel VBA help file to find the sort method which will suit your needs best. ■

Using Access Objects

Microsoft Access contains a somewhat different object environment from the other Office products. The Access object model is made up of two objects which are used for different purposes. First, the Access Application object is used to control the forms, reports, and modules of the VBA applications you write for Access, while the *Data Access Object (DAO)* is used to control the data manipulation within the databases themselves.

The Application object within Access provides a mechanism for creating forms-based applications, custom reports, or special data-manipulation modules. Chapter 22, "Macros," provides a good overview for developing VBA applications using the Access Application object.

The DAO provides the mechanisms for working with the databases within Access. The DAO and data manipulation objects are covered in Chapter 18, "Working with Data."

Using PowerPoint Objects

PowerPoint objects are focused on the slides which are contained within the show. You can manipulate the transitions, shapes, and text on each of the slides using VBA code in your application. Because PowerPoint already includes a great deal of preset transitions and effects, you may want to explore these options before building a VBA application which duplicates the functionality. However, if you are building an interactive presentation or need to tailor a whole set of presentations for a particular audience, you may want to write a VBA application which modifies the city name in a set of presentations to reflect the city you will be presenting in.

Presentation

The Presentation object identifies the presentation which contains the slides of the material being presented. The Presentation object includes methods such as Open, Close, and Save which provide the ability to manipulate the presentation file. For example,

```
Presentations.Open Filename:="C:\DATA\PPTFILES\NETWORK.PPT"
```

opens the NETWORK PowerPoint presentation file.

Slides

The Slides object provides properties and methods which identify individual slides as well as the text, shapes, and charts on the slide. Some of the more generally used methods for the

Slides object include the Add and Delete methods. For example, you can add a slide using the following code:

```
ActivePresentation.Slides.Add(Index:=2, Layout:=ppLayoutText)
```

There are many other PowerPoint objects with a great deal of properties and methods. You should reference the VBA help file for PowerPoint to check the details on using VBA to control or modify PowerPoint presentations.

Using Office Assistant Objects

The Office Assistant is a great way to add fun help or instruction to your VBA application. By using the Office Assistant, your VBA application cannot only provide the help that is necessary, but also provide a polished look of a professional application.

From within VBA, you can reference one of the Office Assistant characters by creating code to specify the assistant you want to use. The following code indicates that the HoverBot character should be used to display the help in your VBA program.

```
Dim MyAssistant As Assistant
Set MyAssistant = Assistant
MyAssistant.FileName = "Hoverbot.act"
```

N O T E   Make sure your assistant file is either in the same directory path of your document or explicitly specify the location. In the example, the Hoverbot.act is assumed to be in the same directory as the document that contains this VBA code. If you do not specify a particular assistant, the ClippIt character is used by default. ■

The fun for the Office Assistant comes from making the assistant react or animate during a particular situation. Therefore, you'll want to add code to your application that provides changes to the character based on the your program's activity. For example, to alert the user, you may want to set the following code:

```
MyAssistant.Animation = msoAnimationGetAttentionMajor
```

This code will change the assistant to show the GetAttentionMajor animation. There are many Animation property values which can be used. These properties are shown in Table 30.2.

Table 30.2   Animation Property Values

Property Name	Contains Continuous Animation
MsoAnimationAppear	Yes
MsoAnimationBeginSpeaking	Yes
MsoAnimationCharacterSuccessMajor	Yes
MsoAnimationCheckingSomething	No

Property Name	Contains Continuous Animation
MsoAnimationDisappear	Yes
MsoAnimationEmptyTrash	Yes
MsoAnimationGestureDown	Yes
MsoAnimationGestureLeft	Yes
MsoAnimationGestureRight	Yes
MsoAnimationGestureUp	Yes
MsoAnimationGetArtsy	No
MsoAnimationGetAttentionMajor	Yes
MsoAnimationGetAttentionMinor	Yes
MsoAnimationGetTechy	No
MsoAnimationGetWizardy	Yes
MsoAnimationGoodbye	Yes
MsoAnimationGreeting	Yes
MsoAnimationIdle	Yes
MsoAnimationListensToComputer	Yes
MsoAnimationLookDown	Yes
MsoAnimationLookDownLeft	Yes
MsoAnimationLookDownRight	Yes
MsoAnimationLookLeft	Yes
MsoAnimationLookRight	Yes
MsoAnimationLookUp	Yes
MsoAnimationLookUpLeft	Yes
MsoAnimationLookUpRight	Yes
MsoAnimationPrinting	Yes
MsoAnimationSaving	No
MsoAnimationSearching	No
MsoAnimationSendingMail	Yes
MsoAnimationThinking	No
MsoAnimationWorkingAtSomething	No
MsoAnimationWritingNotingSomething	No

You can use the Balloon object to display help when the user needs it. By creating the Balloon object and assigning properties such as Heading, Text, Label, and Button, you can control how the user sees the balloon help to display information.

For example, you could code the following VBA statements which provide a pop-up help balloon:

```
Dim MyAssistant as Assistant
Dim MyBalloon as Balloon
Set MyAssistant as Assistant
Set MyBalloon as MyAssistant.NewBalloon
MyAssistant.Animation = msoAnimationThinking
With NewBalloon
        .Heading="About Tires"
        .Text = "Your tires are important; learn how you can make them last
➥longer."
        .Labels(1).Text = "Proper Inflation Techniques"
        .Labels(2).Text = "Using Protective Coatings"
        .Labels(3).Text = "Driving Smart"
End With
NewBalloon.Show
```

There are many creative ways for you to express the help within your VBA application. The Office Assistant makes it easier to provide this help and add a little fun to your program. ●

CHAPTER 31

Building Forms and Dialog Boxes

Welcome to the incredible world of Visual Basic programming. There is no other single skill that you can master to leverage the power available in all of the Office applications.

By programming Visual Basic for Applications (VBA), you can extend the capabilities of any of myriad of applications that support the development environment. These include all of the Office applications (excluding Outlook which uses VB Script, a subset of VBA), Visio, and AutoCAD. The number of supporting applications is increasing every day.

This chapter will provide an introduction to creating VBA solutions in the Office applications through the use of forms and dialog boxes. You'll enter some VBA code which will be briefly explained. Don't worry if you don't understand all of the code that you type. In the next chapter, we will fully introduce the VBA language itself and how to program in it. By first learning the environment that VBA programs are created within, learning the actual programming will come much more easily. ■

Create user forms

You'll begin by creating a form (a window) in the VBA environment that is stored in the file of the application.

Manage the VBA programming environment

The VBA environment, including the Project Explorer and various other windows, allows you to manage all of the various pieces that make up your final VBA application.

Controls—ActiveX and OCX

The strength of the VBA technology is its ability to access controls, from the text box or command button to graphing and dialog controls.

Communicate between an Excel sheet and a form

After you've created a complete VBA form, you can create a button on an Excel sheet to activate the form.

Create a form in PowerPoint

The VBA environment is identical across the Office applications PowerPoint, Excel, Word, and Access. You'll create a simple application in PowerPoint that demonstrates all of the same skills used in all office applications.

Beginning with an Excel Macro

You have already created some macros to control an application. The macro recorder stores all of its operations in VBA code. The VBA code for a particular macro is readily available and may be called by any VBA routine. A macro may also *be called* by another VBA program.

We will begin by using Excel to construct a form that activates a macro that you'll record. We can then augment the functions of the macro so it will become a complete VBA routine.

Begin by loading Excel with an empty document. Choose Tools, Macro, Record New Macro. When asked for a name of the macro, enter the name **myMacro**.

The macro begins recording. We want to click three different cells and enter three numbers. Begin by clicking a cell and entering a number. Click another cell and enter a number. Finally, click a third cell and enter a number (see Figure 31.1). Click the Stop button to stop recording the macro.

FIG. 31.1

The screen shows Excel after clicking three different cells and entering a number into each cell.

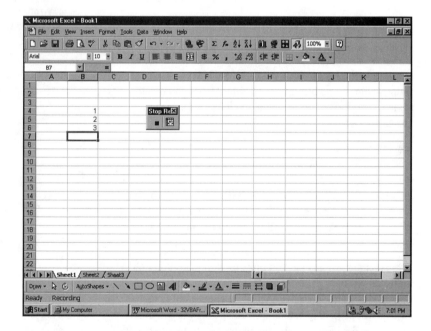

You now have a macro that selects three specific cells and enters a number into each. The macro is stored in a *module* in the Excel file. In a VBA project, a module stores VBA code that does not have any visible component. A form or window, for example, has a visual component, while a module stores only code.

Let's take a look at the VBA code of the macro we recorded. Bring up the Visual Basic Editor (VBE) with either the keyboard shortcut (Alt+F11) or by choosing Tools, Macro, Visual Basic Editor (see Figure 31.2).

If you look at the taskbar of your Windows operating system, you'll see that the Excel application has not disappeared. Instead, the Microsoft Visual Basic Editor has been added as an extra tab. You can switch between the Excel application and the editing environment very quickly.

Part
VII
Ch
31

FIG. 31.2

The Visual Basic Editor displays the current project.

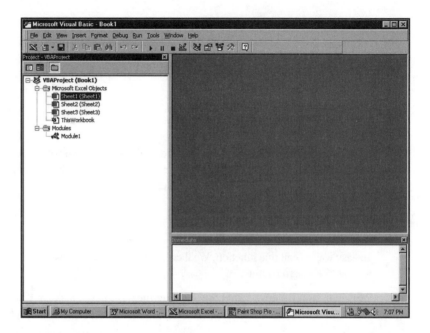

In the left pane is the VBA Project Explorer that displays all of the current pieces contained in this project. The Microsoft Excel Objects show all of the sheets that are part of the document. Below these objects is a folder named Modules. If you expand this folder, you will see the module named Module1. This is the module where your macro is stored.

Double-click this module item, and a code window will open and show the source code for the macro. You should already be familiar with the macro system from past chapters. We're going to modify the macro to demonstrate activating the macro from controls on a form.

Let's modify the code that currently enters specific numbers into the cells of the worksheet so that those numbers are instead randomly generated. In the code, you should see three statements that set the values of particular cells equal (=) to the values you typed. We're going to use the random (RND) VBA command to place a random value in the cells instead of the entered numbers. To do this, we simply have to replace the number on the right side of the equal sign with the command RND.

Modify the macro code so that RND is a statement that replaces the three numeric values that currently set the FormulaR1C1 property. When you're finished, your code should look something like the code shown here:

```
Sub myMacro()
'
' myMacro Macro
' Macro recorded 6/15/97 by Dan Rahmel
'

'
    Range("B4").Select
    ActiveCell.FormulaR1C1 = Rnd
    Range("B5").Select
    ActiveCell.FormulaR1C1 = Rnd
    Range("B6").Select
    ActiveCell.FormulaR1C1 = Rnd
    Range("B7").Select
End Sub
```

Now if you execute this macro, the selected cells will be filled with a random number between the value of 0 and 1. To test this new macro, click the Excel application in the taskbar and run the macro by choosing Tools, Macro, Macros.

Adding a Form to the Project

Now that we have a macro that will visibly change the values stored in these cells, we need an easy way to call this function. We'll create a form window that has a command button that will call the macro routine.

Return to the VBA environment by clicking the VBE in the taskbar. Choose Insert, UserForm. This option will insert a form window into your current project and display it.

You should notice a few changes to the environment when you selected this option. First, a new form named UserForm1 appeared in the document window. A window titled Toolbox should have appeared to float above your document. Also, in the Project menu in the left pane, you should see an added folder named Forms. Within the Forms folder, you will see your first form that is labeled UserForm1.

We need to place a command button control on the form that will activate our macro. The window that is labeled Toolbox is your Control Toolbox palette. It contains all of the controls that are currently available for use in this project. If you move the mouse cursor over the palette and pause over the various icons, you will see that the name of the control appears as a ScreenTip.

Click the control icon that is labeled CommandButton. Draw a command button on the form by clicking and dragging. The newly created control should be labeled CommandButton1 and appear similar to the one shown in Figure 31.3.

Before we add any code to this control, we'll want to name the control. All code that relates to this control as well as any other routines that need to access it will call it by name. Therefore, it is good to name the control something descriptive to make your code more readable and understandable.

FIG. 31.3

The form contains the newly created command button control.

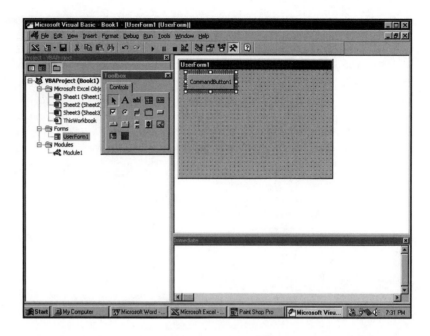

Naming any new control is often a good habit to get into. If you were to leave naming the control until later in the project, you would then have to make several changes to your VBA code. Often this is too much trouble and therefore never gets done, creating a situation of generically named controls and code which references them that is difficult to understand.

Adopting the habit of naming controls as soon as they are created is a practice that will benefit you increasingly as you do more programming.

In order to change the name of the control, we need to modify the control's *properties*. Each control has a number of properties that affect how that control appears and functions.

To change the properties of the object, you need to use the Properties window. Under the View menu, select the Properties Window option and the window should be displayed under the Project Explorer pane.

The Properties window will display the properties of whatever form or control is currently selected. Since we have just drawn the command button, its properties should be showing in the window. If it wasn't selected, simply clicking the control would make its properties the ones shown in the window.

If you double-click one of the properties, the current value is selected. Typing will then replace this value with the newly typed characters. We need to change the (Name) property which is the first property on the list. Double-click the (Name) property and set it to **cmdmyMacro**. Then set the Caption property to Set Values. Changes to these properties should now be reflected in both the properties listing and the control itself (see Figure 31.4).

FIG. 31.4

The command button reflects the changes made in the Properties window.

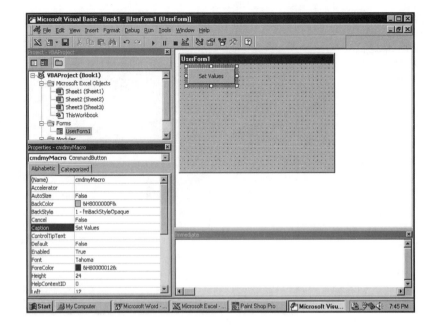

Adding Code to the Command Button

You now have a form and a command button, but they don't do anything. By adding code to the command button, you'll be able to have it execute the earlier macro to change the values in the Excel cells.

To get to the code for any control, you double-click the control on the form. Double-click the command button, and the display of the form should be replaced by the code window.

This code window is the same type that you used earlier to modify the macro code. This time, the `Click` event for the command button is being displayed. The VBA system operates by responding to a number of events. These events may be user-generated (such as the user clicking the command button) or system-generated (such as the control being painted on the screen).

In this case, we are looking at the code that is activated when the user clicks the command button. You can see the event starts with the keywords `Private Sub` which is short for a *private subroutine*. This is followed by the control name, an underscore, and the name of the event. The line that follows this definition is blank. That's because no code is executed when the command button is clicked!

We need to enter code into the `cmdMyMacro_Click` subroutine for the `Click` event. The `Call` keyword can be used to activate our macro. Type the `Call` keyword followed by the name of your macro so your code reads like this:

```
Private Sub cmdmyMacro_Click()
    Call myMacro
End Sub
```

Okay, you're ready to go. Let's execute this form to see how the routine works. Under the Run menu, select the Run Sub/UserForm option or press the F5 key (which is the keyboard shortcut) to begin the execution.

Your user form should appear floating over your current Excel sheet. Click the button; you should see the numbers on the sheet change to random values. Click the button multiple times. You've completed your first VBA form.

To return to the VBA environment, click the Close box. This will automatically halt execution of the form. We're now going to use the form to input values that are entered into the sheet.

Adding Text Box Controls to Our Form

Now we want to add three text box controls to the form so we can demonstrate passing information from the form into the cells of the spreadsheet. On the Toolbox palette, select the TextBox control. Draw a text box on the form that is large enough to allow a user to type in a numeric value.

Repeat this process until you have three text box controls on the form. Set the (Name) property on the first control to txtValue1. Name the other two controls txtValue2 and txtValue3. Your form should now look approximately like the one shown in Figure 31.5.

FIG. 31.5
The form now has three text box controls on it named txtValue1, txtValue2, and txtValue3.

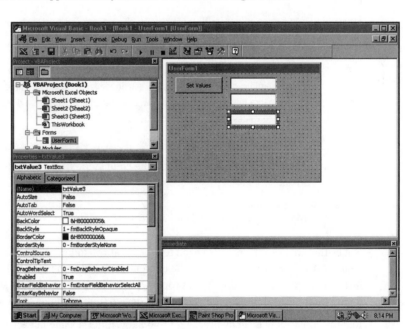

Now that we have our text boxes, we need to modify the code in the macro to accept values that are passed to it and store them in the necessary cells. Double-click the Module1 item again in the Project Explorer window.

The open and closed parentheses () that appear right after the name of the macro indicate that this routine accepts no values passed to it. We need to change the routine so it will accept the three values that we are going to read from the text box controls on the form.

We also need to change the command on the right side of the equal sign to set the cells to equal the passed values rather than random numbers. Change the code to reflect the necessary changes so it appears like this code:

```
Sub myMacro(tempVal1, tempVal2, tempVal3)
'
' myMacro Macro
' Macro recorded 6/15/97 by Dan Rahmel
'

    '
    Range("B4").Select
    ActiveCell.FormulaR1C1 = tempVal1
    Range("B5").Select
    ActiveCell.FormulaR1C1 = tempVal2
    Range("B6").Select
    ActiveCell.FormulaR1C1 = tempVal3
    Range("B7").Select
End Sub
```

Now we need to change the calling routine in the command button to pass the three values we need from the form to the macro.

N O T E   A macro that can be executed from the Macro window in Excel cannot accept any parameters. Therefore, the myMacro routine will no longer appear in the Macro window. If you still need to call the macro routine from this window, create a small routine that doesn't accept any values, yet passes three values to the myMacro routine. ▓

To return to the macro code, double-click the UserForm1 item in the Project Explorer. Then double-click the command button. Modify the code in the Click event to pass the values stored in the text boxes:

```
Private Sub cmdmyMacro_Click()
    Call myMacro(txtValue1.Value, txtValue2.Value, txtValue3.Value)
End Sub
```

Notice that we used the name of each text box control, followed by a dot(.) command, followed by the Value keyword. This passes the current setting stored in the Value property of each text box control. You can find the Value property in the Properties window and even set it at design time. When the form is run, the value set at design time becomes the default value displayed.

Run the application again by pressing the F5 key. Enter a value in each of the text boxes and click the command button (see Figure 31.6). The values will be transferred to the cells in the spreadsheet!

FIG. 31.6

Setting the text box controls to values and clicking the command button enters the values into the sheet.

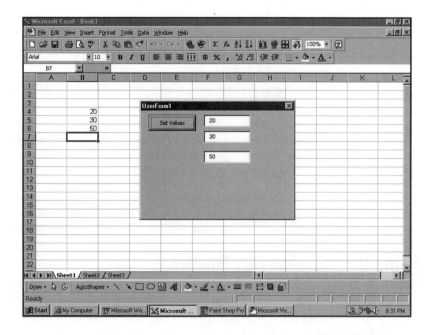

This demonstration has been a simple example of using a form for input to modify Excel. Instead of directly placing the values in the cells, we could have done calculations on them. Or we could have read the values that were already stored in each cell and processed the numbers for placement in another cell. Because you can access any of the information stored on the spreadsheet and store any information to the sheet, a simple form could bloom into a complete application solution.

Using Other Controls

In this project, we have only used the CommandButton control and the TextBox control. VBA includes a number of useful controls that you will find yourself using in most of your projects. Let's take a look at some of the other controls available to you for creating an application within VBA:

- *ComboBox*. This control provides a drop-down list of available items. This control is most commonly used for lists of options such as the font and font size combo boxes in the toolbars of Microsoft Word, Excel, and other applications.

- *ListBox*. The ListBox control displays a list of items from which the user can choose. Unlike the ComboBox that allows only a single item selection, the ListBox shows as many values as screen space allocated to it. This allows for multiple selections.

- *CheckBox*. The very common check box in most Option dialog boxes is available for use on your VBA forms for ON/OFF option selections.

- *Radio button*. When the user needs to select among a few options (such as the Calculation settings in the Excel Options dialog box), multiple radio buttons may be used. When placed on a form or within a frame control, selecting one option automatically deselects all other radio buttons.

■ *Frame.* The frame is used to separate controls on a form and also to group them. Controls placed within a frame such as radio buttons don't directly interact with other radio buttons on the form or in other frames. Also, all controls placed within a frame are moved together when the frame is moved.

■ *Tab control.* Common to Options dialog boxes, the Tab control allows many controls to be placed on a form, but only the controls on the currently selected tab are displayed. This allows you to maximize the available screen space while still keeping related options within a single form.

Controls may also be added to the Control Toolbox that have been installed in the system. Clicking the right mouse button of the Toolbox provides the option to add additional controls. We will discuss this option is greater detail in "Control Toolbox Palette" later in the chapter.

Using the Message Box Function

So far, we've called the routine that we created by recording a macro. VBA has a number of routines (called *functions*) built into the system. One of these, a function called MsgBox, will display a number of different dialog boxes depending on the functions that are passed to it.

A *dialog box* is a window that's explicit purpose is to get information from the user. The Options window that is available in each of the Office applications is an example of a dialog box. It will not let the user continue working on the document until either the OK or Cancel button is pressed. It suspends the program operation because the information you supply will directly affect how the program functions.

The MsgBox function provides a much simpler variety of dialog box. It provides the common dialog boxes that simply require the user to click yes or no or click the OK button. The dialog box that prompts you Do you want to save the changes you made to Filename? in the Office applications is a good example of the type of dialog box that can be generated by the MsgBox function.

MsgBox can display a dialog box of one of four types, each with different buttons: OK, OK/Cancel, Yes/No, and Yes/No/Cancel. There are four parameters that are passed to MsgBox: the type of the dialog box, the icon to be displayed, the title of the displayed window, and the message.

Let's modify three new buttons on our form. Draw the button and name them cmdAlert, cmdInfo, and cmdSaveAs. Set the Caption property for the buttons to Alert, Info, and Save As. Figure 31.7 shows the command buttons when they've been placed on the form.

In each of the click events, add the necessary code; you can switch between the form window and the code windows by using the Window menu:

```
Private Sub cmdAlert_Click()
    result = MsgBox("You are about to experience a meltdown! Shut down now?", _
        vbYesNo + vbCritical, "MeltDown alert")
End Sub

Private Sub cmdInfo_Click()
    result = MsgBox("Hello world", vbOKOnly + vbInformation, "Hello Message")
End Sub

Private Sub cmdSaveAs_Click()
    result = MsgBox("You have made changes. Save changes before quitting?", _
        vbYesNoCancel + vbQuestion, "Save?")
End Sub
```

FIG. 31.7

Three command buttons are placed on the form, and each one will show a different message box when clicked.

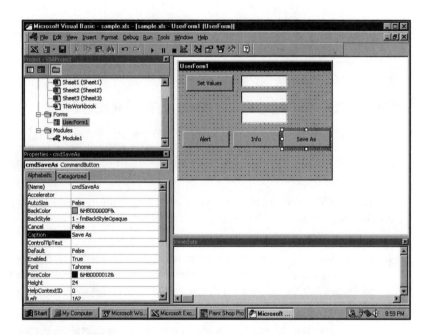

If you execute the form now and click each of the buttons, a different dialog box will be displayed for each. In Chapter 32, "VBA Programming," we will directly explain exactly how the MsgBox function receives these values to vary its display.

TROUBLESHOOTING

In all of the previous code, we've used the MsgBox command as a routine that returns a value. You can use MsgBox as a procedure that doesn't return a value as well. If you try to use the command in this way, you will get an error:

MsgBox("Hello")

continues

continued

Only a function that returns a value can be enclosed within parentheses. Therefore, you have a couple of choices:

- You can just create a variable to hold the value and never access the variable:

```
trashVar = MsgBox("Hello")
```

- You can use the `Call` command to place a call. This command allows using the parentheses to surround parameters:

```
Call MsgBox("Hello")
```

- You can eliminate the parentheses and simply place a space between the routine name and the first parameter:

```
MsgBox "Hello"
```

Using any of these methods will prevent you from this error.

Activating the Form from the Sheet

We've been running our window from within the VBA environment, but this is often not an option for users. You may want to hide your code so the users of your application do not accidentally damage it, or because they simply wouldn't be sophisticated enough to execute the form on their own.

We can add a command button to an Excel sheet that can automatically activate our form so the user merely clicks the button to access the functions we have added.

We will need to draw a command button on our form. Select the main Microsoft Excel tab on the taskbar or close the VBE to return to the Excel worksheets. If you click the right mouse button in a blank area of the Excel toolbar, a context menu should show you all of the available toolbars. Click the Control Toolbox option to display this toolbar.

It will appear as either a floating window or become added to the current toolbars at the top of the window. You can see the command button on this palette. Select the control and draw a button directly onto your spreadsheet.

Right-click the newly created control and select the Properties option to display the Properties window. Change the `(Name)` property to `cmdShowForm` and the `Caption` property to `Show Form` (see Figure 31.8).

Now we need to add the necessary code to show our form. Double-click the cmdShowForm button; the VBE should appear with the button's `Click` event code shown in the window. In the event, enter the following code:

```
UserForm1.Show
```

This code calls the `Show` routine on our form (which is named UserForm1) that will display the window. Return to the Excel environment.

FIG. 31.8

The Excel sheet now has a command button that will activate our form.

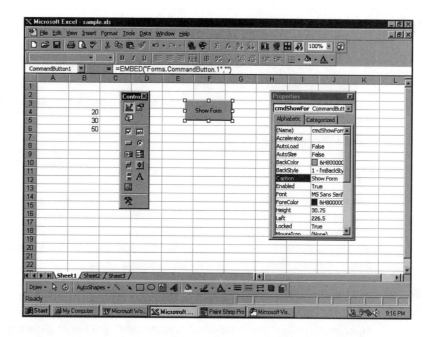

In the top-left corner of the Control Toolbox, you will see an icon that contains a ruler, a pencil, and an angle. Note that this icon appears depressed. This indicates we are currently in the form's Design mode. If you move the mouse cursor over the command button on our Excel sheet, you will notice that you cannot click the button. In Design mode, clicking a control allows you to move or resize the control. However, it does not execute the attached VBA code.

Click the Design Mode icon, and you will see that is no longer depressed. You can now click the button, and it will show the form.

Click the command button now, and the window will appear. Set some values and click the Set Values button. You can see that it operates in the same manner as it previously did. There is one difference you will notice when you close the form—you are not returned to the VBA development environment! Because the window is activated from the spreadsheet, it returns control there when it is closed.

Changing a window into a dialog box is easy. Remember how we said that dialog boxes stop all program interaction until they are dismissed with the OK or Cancel button? Any window can be made to do this by simply adding a parameter following the Show command.

Bring up the code for the command button again. Simply add the number 1 at the end of the Show command like this:

```
UserForm1.Show 1
```

Now when you click the button to activate the window, clicking anywhere else on the screen until the window is closed simply makes the machine beep.

Input Box Function

Visual Basic also provides an additional function for dialog boxes called the InputBox function. The input box displays a dialog box that prompts the user for input and returns the value to the program.

Create another button on the form, name it cmdInput, and set the Caption property to Input. In the Click event of the button, enter the following code:

```
Private Sub cmdInput_Click()
    tempName = InputBox("Please enter your first and last name:", "User name")
    result = MsgBox("Welcome " + tempName, vbInformation, "Welcome")
End Sub
```

Now when you click this button, you will be asked for your name. After you have entered your name and clicked the OK button, a message box will welcome you by name. The InputBox function is extremely useful for quickly getting parameters that don't need a complete form or text box control for input. You can even set the InputBox function to jump to a particular place in your program's help file if the user presses the F1 key.

In most commercial programs, there is a help file (.HLP) that contains information about the program. You will need some special programs to compile a help file. Creating and compiling this HLP file is slightly complicated and may be too difficult to create if you're just beginning to program VBA.

However, you do want to provide help to your users if you're going to distribute your application. There is a property available on most controls called the ControlTipText property. You can place text in this property that is displayed when the user places the cursor over the control (just like the icons on the Office toolbars).

You can also program the Office Assistant to help your users. We'll give an example of programming the Assistant in the next chapter, Chapter 32, "VBA Programming."

Exploring the Parts of VBA Environment

When you select the Visual Basic Editor option, you actually expose much more than a simple text editor. The VBA environment includes windows, palettes, and a menu bar. Most of the VBA windows are shown as panes within the entire screen window. You can, however, select them so they appear as separate windows.

The most critical windows in the VBA environment include the Project Explorer, the Properties window, the Control Toolbox palette, the Immediate window, and the Object Browser. Using this variety of windows, you can develop an entire solution for use by you or an entire organization.

Project Explorer Window

All of the pieces of a form are displayed in the Project Explorer window. The Project Explorer works essentially like the File Explorer that you are already accustomed to using. Clicking the plus sign (+) on the left of a folder will expand the folder in the Explorer window.

Included in any project can be five different types of folders:

Application objects	Class modules	Modules
Forms	References	

A project will only show these folders if they contain one of more of the objects they store. For example, the Forms folder won't appear until a form is added to the file.

N O T E   Application objects are specific to the application that is executing. For example, Microsoft Word Objects are included in any Word VBA solutions and include the documents contained within the file. There are Word objects, Excel objects, and Access objects. PowerPoint does not include any native objects that are stored within the project. ■

Any user forms that are inserted into the project appear in the Forms folder. Forms cannot be copied from one file to another. You must select the Export option to save the file to an FRM file that can be imported into a different project.

The Modules folder contains all of the code modules present in a project. The *Class Modules* are code that is used to create your own objects. You won't create any Class Module code until you have a much better grasp of programming and use of the VBA system.

Properties Window

The Properties window displays all of the properties of the currently selected control or form. You can change any of the properties by selecting the row that contains the intended property and then typing the new value you want.

Some properties are limited to a certain number of options. These properties feature a combo box list that allows you to select from a list to select them.

Other properties such as the color properties and the file-based properties have special forms featured that will provide an extra dialog box or pop-up window for selecting the appropriate value. For example, double-clicking the BackColor property of the form or many controls will display a color palette of available colors.

N O T E   Not all properties for an object are available in the Properties window. There are properties that may be set at design time, and these appear in the Properties window. Properties not available until runtime will not appear in the list, yet are available. Consult the online help files or your reference manuals to determine all of the properties of a given control or object. ■

Control Toolbox Palette

The Control Toolbox palette displays all of the controls currently available for use on the form. The controls we have already described such as the combo box, text box, list box, and more are available by default. However, Office has even more controls available for use within your project.

Right-clicking within the Toolbox window will let you add additional controls. Extra controls are included with your Office Setup and are also available for purchase. For example, a wide variety of commercial controls are available that do everything from image and multimedia manipulation controls to Gantt chart controls.

Immediate Window

So far, all of the code we've created have been attached to a button or other control. What if you want to test a single command? The Immediate window in the VBA environment allows you to enter a command and have it execute immediately.

At the bottom of the screen in your VBA environment, you should see a pane that is labeled Immediate. If this window pane is not visible, you can make it visible by choosing View, Immediate Window.

Click in the window and you will see the cursor flashing. You can enter many of the Visual Basic commands into this area, and the VBA environment will automatically execute the entered code. The Immediate window only allows you to enter a single line of code for execution. When you press the Enter key on a line of text, the VBA engine will attempt to execute the code that it finds there.

N O T E Not all Visual Basic commands will execute in the Immediate window. Most commands, such as commands that handle events or dimension variables, cannot be used. For example, these commands will return an error stating they cannot be used in the Immediate window:

```
Dim joe as Object
```

or

```
Dim x
```

When you encounter this error, attempt to do the operation with another command. The `Dim x` command creates a variable (explained in the next chapter) named *x*. A command that simply sets the value of the variable will execute fine and have the same final result. For example:

```
x=5
```

Printing Numbers To begin using the Immediate window, we can use the `Print` command to display numbers to the screen. The simplest use of the `Print` command is simply typing it into the Immediate window followed by a number like:

```
print 2
```

The output of the Immediate window can be formatted using commas. If you separate printing several values with commas, they can all print on the same line. For example:

```
print 2,6,8
```

This code will print the three numbers with about an inch of space between them. The `print` command is just one example of a Visual Basic command in the Immediate window. How about the `MsgBox` function that we used earlier? Enter this code in the window:

```
MsgBox "Hello"
```

Did you run it? The Message Box dialog box should have appeared and waited for you to click the OK button before returning to the VBA environment.

Unlike a word processor or text editor, pressing the Enter key in the middle of a line of code does not split the text into two parts, one on each line. The Enter key instead accepts the entire line for execution. This prevents you from splitting a line in half and generating an error because of incomplete code.

Although you can only enter a single line of code for execution, you can enter multiple commands on a line. The colon (:) command can be used to separate several commands.

We briefly explained using loops in programs to repeat a number of program commands. However, you need to start the loop with the For command, include the loop code, and end the loop with a next command. By using the colon, we can include this entire structure on a single line. Enter the following line in the Immediate window to print 12 numbers:

```
for i = 1 to 12 : print i : next
```

As soon as you press the Return key, the window should have printed the numbers 1 through 12, one number per line.

Using the Immediate window allows you to test code much more easily. The immediate results that are generated allow you to quickly attempt many different ways of reaching a solution without having to edit and re-execute an entire program every time.

Object Browser

All of the Office applications are controllable through VBA. You've already controlled Excel in the application that we created in order to set the values of particular cells. What you may not have realized was that you were accessing Excel objects. An *object* is a re-usable data structure that holds information and the code routines that control the information. For example, an Excel sheet is an object. If you add a sheet to an Excel workbook (which is also an object), two objects are contained within the document. Everything in the Office applications down to the cells in Excel, the slides in PowerPoint, the tables in Access, and the text in Word are stored as objects.

How objects work and their definition will be covered in much more depth in the next chapter. The VBA environment includes a window called the Object Browser that lets you examine and search the object collections of any registered object models. Choosing View, Object Browser or pressing the F2 key will display the Object Browser as shown in Figure 31.9.

The combo box on the top left of the object browser defaults to <All Libraries>. You can select this combo box to display only the objects for the application you are executing. If you're in Excel, you can select the Excel listing to view only the Excel objects.

Common Dialog Boxes

In the VBA environment, you've already seen two dialog boxes that are available through functions. Microsoft has included other common dialog boxes such as the Open, Save, Print, Color (see Figure 31.10), and Font dialog boxes in an ActiveX/OCX Control with the Office system.

FIG. 31.9

The Object Browser will display the objects for registered object models.

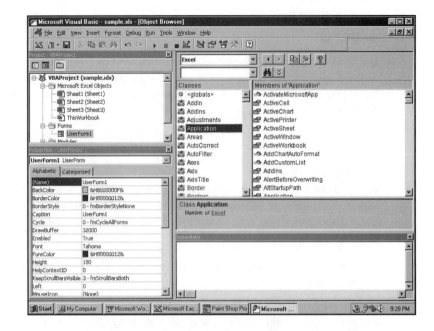

FIG. 31.10

The Color dialog box is only one of the common dialog boxes included in the Common Dialog control.

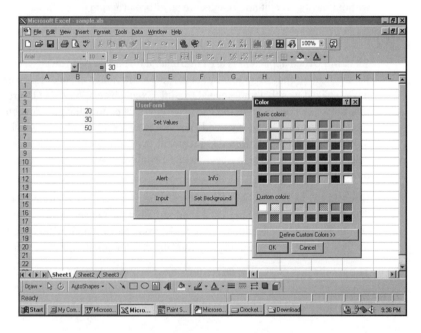

To use these dialog boxes, you need to add an additional control to the current Control Toolbox. If you closed the Excel project we created earlier, open it again and make sure that the form is showing. You should have the Control Toolbox showing on the screen.

Move the mouse cursor into the empty region at the bottom of the Toolbox. Right-click this area and select the Additional Controls option. You will be presented with a dialog box containing all of the controls that are available on your system.

N O T E As you do more development, you may increasingly hear the terms *OCX*, *OLE Customer Control*, and *ActiveX Control* used interchangeably. When components were first created back when Visual Basic was at version 3.0 and VBA didn't exist, they were known as *Visual Basic eXtensions* or *VBXs*. Microsoft updated the specifications so they could be used in any language and called them *OLE Custom Controls*, *OLE Extensions*, or *OCXs*. There were both 16-bit versions (Windows 3.1 and Windows for Workgroups) and 32-bit versions (Windows 95 and Windows NT) of OCX Controls.

The birth of the Internet and the widespread acceptance of 32-bit operating systems made Microsoft update the OLE control specification. Partially marketing and partially technical, ActiveX Controls were born. A 32-bit OCX and an ActiveX Control are essentially identical. Typically, controls labeled ActiveX Controls are smaller because they are intended to be distributed over the Web. ■

Some of the ActiveX/OCX Controls displayed in this list within the dialog box are not available for programming, but were installed and are used explicitly by a particular application. If you scroll down the list, you should find an entry that says Microsoft Common Dialog Control, Version 5. Click the check box to the left of this control to add the control to you project.

You should see another icon added to your Control Toolbox palette. Click this icon and draw the control on your current form. It doesn't matter the size or location of the control. When you released the mouse button, you will see an icon on your form. This icon will be invisible when you run this program. The Common Dialog control is a non-visible control.

The (Name) property on the Common Dialog control is automatically created as CommonDialog1. We have no need to change this default.

Setting the background color of the current cell is as easy as setting the color value. Each cell object has a variety of properties just like some of the properties that we've been changing on our form objects.

We're going to use the Color dialog box to select a color that will set the background color of the currently selected cell in the Excel spreadsheet. Add another command button to the form. Set the (Name) property to cmdSelectColor and the Caption property to Set Background Color.

Double-click the command button and enter the following code into the Click event of the button. This code activates the routine in the Common Dialog control called ShowColorDialog. This routine will display the control and allow the user to select a background color for the cell. When the user selects a color and clicks the OK button, our code sets the color of the cell B4 to the color property of the selected Common Dialog.

```
Private Sub cmdSetColor_Click()
    ' Display the Color dialog
    CommonDialog1.ShowColor
    ' Select the B4 cell
    Range("B4").Select
```

```
        ' Set the color to the setting the user selected
        Selection.Interior.Color = CommonDialog1.Color
        ' Make the pattern solid
        Selection.Interior.Pattern = xlSolid
End Sub
```

In addition to setting the color, we should also set the pattern to solid so the color is shown clearly. Return to the Excel spreadsheet and click the button to show our window. Click the Set Background button and try selecting a color. The currently selected cell should fill with the color you've chosen as soon as you click the OK button.

 In all of the code we've used so far, we've accessed cells by using the Range object. You can also set the range dynamically using the Cells object. For example, to set the value of the second row of the first column to 10, you could use the statement:

```
ActiveSheet.Cells(2, 1).Value = "10"
```

Using numbers to reference cells allows you to access a number of cells easily with a loop.

Form Layout Considerations

Now that we have created a sample application within Excel, you may want to begin you own projects. When building new forms, there are a number of considerations that should be given thought. How do I want the form to appear? To behave? In what order should the user be able to tab around the form? How should the controls look on the form?

The VBA environment gives you the power to determine what your application will look like. The following sections will describe some of the features included with VBA so you can make you application the best.

Form Properties

To make an attractive and useful application, the form becomes a crucial part of the user experience. Each form has a number of properties that govern its appearance and behavior. Some of these properties, such as the (Name) property and the Caption property, are found on most controls, but the form control features a few properties that are special to it.

A form may contain scroll bars to allow movement around a large document or image. The Scrollbar properties allow you to set the type of scroll bars (Vertical, Horizontal, or both) and how they react within the window.

The Picture property for a form displays any picture in bitmap (BMP), JPEG (JPG), GIF, Windows Metafile (WMF, EMF), or Icon (ICO, CUR) file format. The picture becomes part of the background of the form. Just as an example, click this property and you will see a button with three dots appear to the right of the entry. Click this button and you will be presented with a file selection dialog box.

Move into the Windows directory and select the Carved Stone.BMP file. When you click the OK button, this small image should appear in the center of the form. Any controls will appear to sit on top of the bitmap.

The `PictureSizeMode` property defaults to 0—`frmPictureSizeModeClip`. If you change this property to 1—`frmPictureSizeModeStretch`—the picture should stretch to the size of the form. Change the property back to 0 so the bitmap appears in the center of the form again.

The `PictureAlignment` property allows you to move the bitmap to a corner of the form. This property defaults to displaying the picture in the center of the form.

If you want the picture to appear as a complete background to the form, set the `Picture Tiling` property to `True`. The bitmap will be tiled across the entire form background.

N O T E Background textures can dramatically add to the attractiveness of a form. However, they can also be the worst thing you could do to a user.

You might choose a texture that makes the text or information presented on the form difficult or impossible to read. Tiling the picture may also slow down the redraw on older machines. Make sure you think about your users and their needs before adding a feature that merely "looks good." ■

The `Startup Position` property allows you to set the position of the form on the screen. For example, you can set the property so the form will be automatically centered in relation to the screen.

Setting the Tab Order of Controls

In most programs, if you have multiple controls such as text boxes that appear on a form, pressing the Tab key advances the cursor to the next control, and pressing Shift+Tab moves backwards one control. VBA forms operate in the same way and use the Tab key to navigate the form.

Changing the cursor location is known as *changing the focus*. Whichever control currently has the focus is sent all of the user keystrokes. Controls include properties to determine the order of controls on the form.

The `TabStop` property determines whether the focus can be placed on a control by pressing the Tab key. This property defaults to `True`.

The `TabIndex` property is automatically set for each control as it is added to the form. You can renumber these index properties to set the order to whatever you need. The control that has a `TabIndex` property of zero (0) is the first control to receive the focus when the form is shown. Each control follows this first control numerically.

If you change the `TabIndex` property on one control, the other `TabIndex` values are automatically renumbered. For example, you might have a form with four text box controls (0, 1, 2, and 3). If you were to set the property of a control with a current index of 3 to the value of 0, the original control with the zero value would become 1 and so on for all of the controls on the form.

Aligning and Sizing Controls

Laying out a form is never an easy task. The form should comply with typical user interface standards. Controls that affect common feature areas should be grouped together. Tab indexes should be set so a user can easily move through the form filling out the proper information.

Making the form look good is also an important decision. Earlier we set the `Picture` property on one of the forms to give it a background texture. The VBA environment provides a number of features that aid you in constructing attractive and balanced forms.

Aligning multiple controls is often difficult to do by hand. The Alignment options allow you to select multiple controls and have VBA align them for you. Under the Format menu, alignment options include Align Lefts, Align Centers, Align Rights, Tops, Middles, Bottoms.

To allow for layout control, objects have an order within the form. Sometimes a control may appear to cover up another control. Under the Arrange Buttons submenu on the Format menu, you can send and bring controls in the order just like you normally would in a drawing program.

Controls may be made to fit the size of the grid. Fitting them to the grid makes producing common shapes, sizes, and boundaries much simpler process.

One of the most useful operations is the Make Controls the Same Size command. This allows you to ensure that all of your buttons or text fields are consistent on the form.

There are other layout features such as horizontal and vertical spacing, arrangement of controls, and grouping that even further expand you abilities to simplify and cultivate your form.

PowerPoint Creations

Now that you've seen the creation of a form in Excel, let's create another sample within PowerPoint so you can apply your understanding to any of the Office applications.

You don't have to record a macro to start adding VBA programs to a file. The Visual Basic Editor is available to any document and allows you to insert your own modules.

Execute the PowerPoint application and start with a blank presentation. Bring up the VBE (Alt+F11). Choose Insert, Module. This will insert a new module where we will create a macro by hand.

There is a programming structure called a *loop* (covered in the "Using Multiple Commands" section of Chapter 32, "VBA Programming") which will repeat a block of commands multiple times. For example, if you wanted to create five slides, you could enter five commands, each creating a new slide. However, if you used this technique for all things you had to do multiple times, you would generate a tremendous amount of code. It also limits your ability to decide, while the program is running, how many new slides you want.

A loop repeats a block of commands based on a number that can be set while the program is running. This number can even be input by the user.

The cursor should be present in the code window. Enter the following code to create a new macro named Macro1. By entering the opening line with the Sub keyword and the closing line with the End Sub keyword, a macro will be created.

```
Sub Macro1()
    For I = 1 To 10
        ' Add a new slide and record the number in the slideNum variable
        slideNum = ActivePresentation.Slides.Add(Index:=1, _
            Layout:=ppLayoutText).SlideIndex
' Jump to the new slide
        ActiveWindow.View.GotoSlide slideNum
        ' Select the bullets rectangle
        ActiveWindow.Selection.SlideRange.Shapes("Rectangle 3").Select
        ' Select the text within this shape
        ActiveWindow.Selection.ShapeRange.TextFrame.TextRange.Select
        ' Set the text to our string.
        ActiveWindow.Selection.TextRange.Text = "Apples" + _
            Chr$(13) + "Oranges" + Chr$(13) + "Insert #" + Str(I)
Next
End Sub
```

This macro will add 10 slides to the current presentation and set the text to reflect pre-programmed values. If you execute this macro from within PowerPoint, the slides will be inserted into the presentation.

N O T E   In the code, you may notice there are lines that start with the apostrophe (') symbol that contain what looks like plain English. It is! The apostrophe is known as a *comment keyword*. Any text that appears after the apostrophe is ignored by VBA until a new line is begun.

When you enter this sample code, you can omit typing the comments into the program and it will not affect the functioning. However, it is often a good idea to enter the comments anyway because they provide instructions that stay with the program. ■

This application that uses VBA within PowerPoint is not very useful as it is coded, but now you can modify it for other needs. Do you need a presentation where every third slide contains a certain format? You can easily create such an application by changing the code. Do you want to insert a particular picture such as your logo on every third slide? Once again, with simple modifications this application is possible.

Given the VBA environment, the easiest way to create applications of this type is to simply record a macro of the action that you need to perform. Then cut the relevant code and paste it in the framework of a working application such as the one we've just constructed. This method will speed development without requiring you to know everything about the particular Office application.

Related Sources

VBA is a broad technology. Much information regarding it can be found in magazines. Many of the best sources are available on the Internet:

- The Microsoft Office Developer forum (**www.microsoft.com/officedev/**) features numerous resources for VBA developers.

- An excellent book on the subject of VBA is *Special Edition Using Visual Basic for Applications 5* (ISBN 0-7897-0959-7) by Que that discusses everything from simple VBA to advanced concepts such as the Win32API. I keep this handy on my desk for VBA information.

- For professional developers, there is a Office 97, Developer Edition. This edition includes a stand-alone runtime for Access applications, Visual Sourcesafe source code control, the Replication Manager, Setup Wizard, and additional ActiveX Controls (including FTP, HTTP, and Gopher).

- Office VBA Central (**www.coherentdata.com/officevba**) contains information about VBA and sample source code.

- Ask the VB Pro (**www.inquiry.com/techtips/thevbpro**) has an excellent Q&A section that provides many details regarding VBA and Visual Basic.

- The fantastic Visio drawing program includes VBA and also supports Binder functionality. The Visio Web site (**www.visio.com**) includes resources and information about programming VBA in Visio.

CHAPTER 32

VBA Programming

You've seen a little VBA code in the previous chapter and some of it was explained. In this chapter, we will cover more detail about coding in VBA to create any solutions that you might need.

Explaining an entire programming language is not something that can be done in a single chapter. We'll cover all of the basic programming concepts and build a couple of applications. You should then have the foundation to continue learning Visual Basic. ■

Simple programming in the Immediate window

You will test many of the programming structures and concepts that make VBA powerful in the Immediate window for instant feedback.

Details on program structures such as If...Then

All of the most common programming structures supported in VBA such as If...Then, Do While...Loop, and so on will be demonstrated.

Control the Office Assistant

By creating a form with command buttons on it, you will be able to control the Office Assistant and make it say and do what you want.

Control the Excel application from Word

Through the use of objects, you will control Excel to create a document from within the VBA system in Word.

Create a Word VBA macro

A miniature contact form can be automatically inserted and formatted into your Word document at the press of a key.

Starting VBA Programming

In the previous chapter, we introduced the Immediate window that allowed you to directly enter commands and have them execute. This window is one of the most wonderful tools to help you learn how to program. You receive immediate feedback to let you know if you did something right or need to modify it slightly.

This is what programming is all about—test and retest. Learning to program is essentially overcoming your fear that you might break something. If you have an idea, try it. When it doesn't work, tinker with it until it does. You won't do any damage to the machine. VBA does an excellent job of shielding you even from crashing the system, so please experiment.

Let's begin with a concept crucial to all programming—variables. *Variables* are places in the computer's memory that store values. Imagine an Excel cell that you can place numbers or characters into. If you name this cell and make it invisible, you essentially have a variable.

We'll be doing most of our experimenting in Microsoft Word, so open it now. Create a new blank document—it doesn't matter what type. Move to the Visual Basic Editor by pressing Alt+F11.

In the Project Explorer window, you will see the first project is labeled Normal. This is the Normal template for Word. You can add functions and forms to the normal document that will be available to all documents. Right now, we're going to be using the Immediate window so we don't need to add anything to either project.

If the Immediate window is not visible, select the Immediate Window option under the View menu or press Ctrl+G. Click in the window titled Immediate, type the following, and press Enter:

```
print 5
```

Like in the previous chapter, the number 5 should have printed in the window. Now we're going to create a variable to hold the number 5. Our variable will be called x. Type into the window:

```
x = 5
```

Now try typing the command `print x`. The `print` command will print the value that is store in the x variable. Now let's add 5 to the value already stored in x. We need to set the variable x equal to the old value of x plus the number five, like this:

```
x = x + 5
```

If you print the variable x, you will see that the value is incremented by 5. You can use the same method to multiply (*), divide (/), or subtract (–) values from the number stored in the x variable. To multiply the value by 50, type:

```
x = x * 50
```

You can verify that the multiplication occurred by printing the value of x. In addition to the basic four mathematical operators, VBA includes several others for more advanced calculations. See the "Using Mathematical Operators" section in this chapter.

Numbers aren't the only values that can be placed within variables. You can also enter strings of characters. For example, type the following into the Immediate window:

```
myString = "My number:"
print myString
```

This code will set the variable `myString` to equal the characters within the double quotes (`""`). VBA will also convert a number to a string automatically if the situation requires it. You can use the concatenation operator (+) which combines two strings to print the string followed by the numeric value:

```
print myString + x
```

You should see a single string labeling the number and displaying the current value of x.

N O T E   The names of variables can be just about any length (up to 255 characters), but there are restrictions on the characters that may be used within a name. Variable names must contain alphanumeric characters but may not include any spaces nor most of the symbols such as the exclamation point (!), the parentheses (()), and quotes (""). You also cannot use existent Visual Basic keywords as the name of a variable. For example, you cannot have a variable named `Beep` which is the name of a VB command.

You may use the underscore (_) character within a variable name, and many programmers use this character in place of a space character which is not allowed. For example:

my_String = 5 ■

Now that you understand variables, you are halfway to creating a complete program. Programs are essentially only the process of executing commands that manipulate variables. Blocks or sequences of commands are what actually make up a program routine, which is the other half of programming.

Using Multiple Commands

We briefly described the structure of a loop in the last chapter. A loop will repeatedly execute one or more commands for a specified number of times.

If we needed to print the numbers 1 through 10 in the Immediate window, we could create 10 `print` statements. A much better idea is to place a single `print` statement in a loop which cycles 10 times. The loop uses a structure that has a `For` command that specifies the beginning of the loop and a `Next` command that marks the end. Any commands between `For` and `Next` will be executed until the loop is completed.

Let's create a loop to print 10 numbers into the Immediate window. You did this in the last chapter but may not have understood it. Every loop needs a variable that is incremented after every cycle to keep track of how many cycles remain. We'll call our variable `loopvar`. Type the following code into the Immediate window:

```
for loopvar = 1 to 10 : print loopvar : next
```

The numbers 1 through 10 will appear in the Immediate window. You can make the loop count from any number to any other number. You can even make the loop count backwards, but you must use the Step command. To make the loop count backwards from 5:

```
for loopvar = 5 to 1 Step -1 : print loopvar : next
```

T I P   For the Immediate window, the colon (:) command is essential because only one line of execution is possible. However, in normal programs, use the : command only when necessary. It makes code difficult to read and comment.

In a complete program, the colon command is most often used only for setting multiple variables. Use your best judgment and understand that putting more commands on the same line does not result in faster execution.

We have the beginning of a simple program, but this Immediate window program disappears as soon as it is executed. If we create this code within a subroutine, it can become part of a permanent program.

Creating a Subroutine

In order to place code into a program, we must have either a code module, a class module, or a form. Because the routine that we're going to create doesn't require any buttons or other user interface elements, we'll create a code module.

Make sure you're in the Visual Basic Editor. In the Project Explorer, you should see a project labeled Project (Document1). This project contains all of the forms and code modules associated with the document file.

Click the Project (Document1) line item so this project is selected. Choose Insert, Module. This will insert a code module into the document where we can place a new subroutine.

Before you inserted the code module, the Procedure option on the Insert menu was dimmed. A *procedure* is another name for a routine. Now that you have added a code module to the project, you can insert procedures. Choose Insert, Procedure to show the Add Procedure dialog box.

We'll name our new procedure myLoop. Type **myLoop** into the Name text box and click the OK button. A procedure will be created within the code module, and your screen should look approximately like the one shown in Figure 32.1.

We were very limited to the code we could enter in the Immediate window, but with a subroutine we have a great deal more flexibility. Let's expand the loop so it accepts user input as to the number of repetitions.

Also, it is good programming practice to define what types of variables are being used. We will explain variable typing in more depth later in the "Creating Variables" section, but the practice involves telling VBA exactly what type of information will be stored in a particular variable. For example, if you wanted a variable named myName to hold a string of characters, you can define it explicitly as a string. If you would try to enter a number into the variable, an error would occur.

FIG. 32.1

The module window shows the new myLoop subroutine that has been inserted.

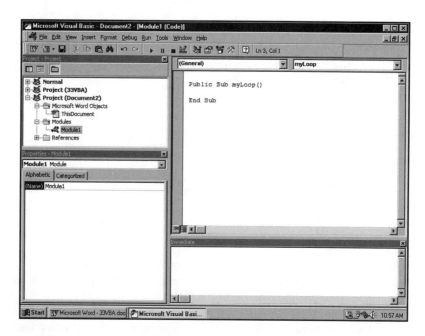

You might be wondering why you would bother to set the variable type when not defining the type seems so much more flexible. There are two main reasons to set a variable type: *bug prevention* and *speed*.

If you type a variable named myVar as an Integer, you cannot place a string within it. Because the name myVar is not descriptive, you may forget that you've already used it somewhere else and try to use it again. Or you might forget the variable's particular use. A variable type is defined using the Dim keyword. Explicitly creating a variable and setting the type also becomes a visible marker—you have a place in the code where the variable is set. The error generated by the variable's misuse can alert you to a subtle problem that might otherwise take hours to find.

Variables that are typed also execute at nearly twice the speed of variables that do not have a defined type. In a mathematical routine that repeats a loop several thousand times, the speed increase can be substantial.

N O T E If you don't explicitly state a variable type, then the type defaults to a variant. A *variant* can switch from type to type in an instant. The code x=5 could be followed by a line that states x="joe" without any error occurring. A variant can accept any type of data that is presented to it. ▪

We will create a subroutine that prints numbers to the Immediate window based on the number of repetitions the user has specified. Enter the text so your subroutine matches the following code:

```
Public Sub myLoop()
    ' Define and type the three variables we'll be using
    Dim userStr As String
    Dim userNum As Integer
    Dim loopVar As Integer

    ' Get the user to input a string of how many loops
    userStr = InputBox("How many cycles?", "Loop number")
    ' Convert the string to a number
    userNum = Val(userStr)
    ' Did the user enter a valid number?
    If userNum > 0 Then
        ' Repeat print for the input number
        For loopVar = 1 To userNum
            Debug.Print loopVar
        Next
    End If
End Sub
```

While you are entering the code, you might notice that as you enter some of the text, such as Dim userNum as and press the space bar, a pop-up list of options automatically appears. This is one of the fantastic new features of VBA 5 that helps you automatically complete a function definition or a command. For the Dim command, the pop-up provides a list of possible variable types you can define. You can use the arrow keys to select one and then press the Tab key to allow VBA to automatically complete the selection. Pressing the Esc key will make the list disappear.

From the Immediate window, you can type either the command **Call myLoop** or simply type the subroutine name **myLoop**. When calling procedure, the Call command is optional and, if missing, is implicit. The input box then asks you to enter a number for the cycles through the loop (see Figure 32.2).

FIG. 32.2

The Loop Number dialog box is waiting for the user to click OK after he entered the number 8.

Type a number and click the OK button. The Immediate window displays the number of values you requested. Execute the procedure again (by typing its name in the window), and this time enter text in the box or click the Cancel button. No items were printed in the window.

Why? Let's take a look at the code. We've added a number of items that make the routine more like a regular program. You can see in the first three lines we use the Dim command to set up the variables and specify their exact type.

The InputBox function returns a string. Therefore, we needed a string to accept the number the user entered. But you don't want a string—you need a number to determine the repetitions. In the next line, we use the Val() function to convert the value stored in the string into a number.

Next, we use the If...Then programming construct to determine if the number entered was greater than zero. If the user entered characters or clicked the Cancel button, the userNum would be set to zero. Only if the value is greater than zero does the code within the If...Then statement execute.

After the user has entered a proper number, the loop begins to print the numbers by calling the Print routine in the Immediate window.

> **N O T E** The previous loop differs slightly from the code you used in the Immediate window. When you placed the For...Next loop in the subroutine, you needed to add the word **Debug** before the Print statements. This made the command call the Print routine on the Debug window object.
>
> In the past, the Immediate window could only be used when debugging code and, up until Visual Basic 4, was called the *Debug window*. You may still see it referred to as the Debug window in some documentation. This is the historical reason for the Immediate window to be labeled Debug when it is called from code. ▪

You should now have a basic grasp of how programming in VBA works. Before we continue constructing programs, we need to cover some of the essential principles of programming.

Part

VII

Ch

32

Using Procedures and Functions

You've created a routine using the Sub...End Sub keyword tags. In programming, there are many different ways to refer to the same routines. Some common terms include *subroutines*, *routines*, *procedures*, *functions*, and *methods*.

Although most of these terms are used interchangeably, the two keywords that have specific meaning are *function* and *method*. A function is any routine that returns a value. For example, a mathematical function called Abs() might be passed a negative number and return an absolute value of that number. A function always returns a value, even if that value is a Null value. The InputBox() routine is an example of a function. It returns whatever string the user inputs into the dialog box.

> **N O T E** One of the most difficult concepts for a beginner to grasp is the value of a Null. A *null value* is not a zero value. Rather, it indicates that nothing is stored in the variable at the present time. The null value is most useful because it doesn't take up any memory.
>
> For example, you might have a string named myString that can accept a string up to 3,000 characters long. If the string is empty, it still contains a " " value. If this string is not variable in length, then this empty string takes up all 3K of memory! However, a null value indicates nothing is stored in the field, so no memory is used.
>
> Null values are used most frequently in databases. Empty fields that take up space, multiplied over thousands of records, can make a database unwieldy. With null values, only fields that actually contain information take up storage space. ▪

A method is a routine that is specific to a particular object. In the myLoop() procedure you created previously, you called the Print routine of the Debug window object to print the numbers. The Print routine is really known as the Print method. Objects are an important concept that you will run into throughout your programming life, so it's important to understand the basics that make up an object.

Understanding Objects

In the past, programming languages have been called *procedural languages* because they execute procedures that interact with variables. Most of the programming we've done so far has been exactly this type. Variables are created somewhere in the programming environment. Functions and procedures are created to manipulate these values. However, the routines and the variables are not bound together.

When the variables and the routines that relate to those variables are held within a single self-contained structure, it is known as an *object*. Variables within an object are known as *properties*. Procedures and functions within an object are known as *methods* (as described earlier).

You may be thinking, "Didn't we set properties for the form and the command buttons in the last chapter?" Yes, because forms and controls are objects. When you used the command UserForm1.Show, you were activating the Show method on the UserForm1 object. Pretty simple, isn't it? We have a few more important concepts for you to master before you can truly understand objects.

Binding the variables and the routines makes managing programs simpler, but this is not truly why objects are so powerful. They are powerful because once you create a self-contained object, it can be duplicated as many times as you want. For example, when you create a new document in Word, you're really creating a new object of a document object.

To continue the description of how objects work, we're going to use the metaphor of building a house to help you understand two key concepts: *classes* and *instances*. When we need to build a house, we need a blueprint to know how the house is constructed. Once we have the blueprint, we can construct many houses that are exactly the same from the blueprint. We can then decorate the inside of the houses to make them different.

A class is like a blueprint. Multiple object instances can be created from a class. The process of creating an instance is known as *instantiating*. Let's return to our example of a Microsoft Word document. Word has an object class built into the program. When you want a new document, a document instance is built from the class. You then add text to the object instance, like the decorations added to a house.

The term *object* is used to refer to both an object instance and an object class. What is actually meant depends on the context of the use. For example, if you're going to create a new Word object, you are not likely to mean that you're going to construct your own Word blueprint. Instead, you're going to create an object instance from the Word blueprint.

In the previous chapter, we mentioned that there are three primary type of items that can be added to a project: forms, modules, and class modules. Now you can understand that a class module is just like a module that you have used so far, except it is used to create a class from which object instances can be created. Creating a class module is beyond the scope of this book. For complete information on this aspect, see the book *Using VBA 5* listed in the "Related Sources" section.

Objects may be large or small. Most of the object classes you create will most likely be small. A large class is most often defined by a team of programmers. However, you may create a large object instance. All of the Office applications can be treated as objects. Therefore, you can create an object instance of the entire PowerPoint application. We'll create an instance of Excel later to demonstrate how VBA can be used to create an Excel document from within Word.

Using *If...Then...Else* Statements

In the sample procedure we created earlier, we used an If…Then statement to determine whether the string entered by the user contained any numbers. The If…Then statement allows you to execute programmed commands only if certain conditions are met. You can also add a block of code to execute if the conditions weren't met.

We've modified the code from the routine a little to add a message box notifying the user that a correct number wasn't entered. The following code demonstrates the If…Then…Else construct:

```
If userNum > 0 Then
        ' Repeat print for the input number
        For loopVar = 1 To userNum
            Debug.Print loopVar
        Next
Else
        Result = MsgBox("You didn't enter a valid number", _
            vbInformation, "No number.")
End If
```

The structure begins with the If keyword. This is followed by the conditional expression. In this case, we're testing the condition to determine if userNum > 0. If this condition is true, the value of True is sent to the If statement. We can do more than one evaluation within the conditional expression. To make sure the number entered was greater than zero but less than 10, we could use the statement:

```
If userNum > 0 And userNum < 10 Then
```

The And statement requires both of the conditions to be true in order to execute the Then expression. There are also commands such as Or and Nor to link multiple conditions.

Followed by the condition is the Then keyword. Anything that comes after this keyword is executed if the condition is True until Visual Basic encounters one of the other structure commands such as Else, ElseIf, or End If.

If the condition is not True, execution jumps directly to the Else command and begins execution of commands that follow it. A variation of the else command is the ElseIf command that requires another conditional expression. The ElseIf then executes if this expression returns a True.

The entire If...Then structure is completed by an End If command. Whether any Else or Else If commands are used, an If structure always ends in an End If.

If...Then statements can also be placed within If...Then statements. Likewise, loops can be placed within loops. These structures are called *nested structures*.

Using *Do While...Loop* and *Do...Until*

You now know how to create a loop and use the If...Then statements for conditional execution. How about a loop that executes while a condition is True or Until a condition is True?

The Do...While structure will continue executing while the condition returns a True value. To loop while i is less than 10, we could use a routine like:

```
Public Sub myWhile()
    Dim i As Integer

    Do While i < 10
        Debug.Print i
        i = i + 2
    Loop
End Sub
```

The Do...Until structure operates the same way, except it executes while a condition is False and stops when the condition is True. For example:

```
Public Sub myUntil()
    Dim i As Integer

    Do Until i > 10
        Beep
        i = i + 2
    Loop
End Sub
```

This loop uses the Beep command which beeps the speaker until the conditional expression i > 10 returns the value True. As you do more programming, you will find increasing uses for these conditional loop structures.

Using the Debugger

As we stated at the beginning of the chapter, debugging is essentially the key to good programming. Only very rarely will you get it right the first time. Much more commonly, you will try over and over, making slight changes with each repetition.

Luckily, one of VBA's strongest features is its debugging capabilities. You can set variable watches that stop execution when a particular value is reached, you can set break points in your code, and you can always use the Immediate window to test code and values.

The best way to learn the debugger is to use it. Therefore, let's begin by creating an error in our subroutine. In a very common situation that generates an error, a variable accidentally is set to zero. Then another calculation uses the variable as a divisor, causing a `Divide by zero` error. Right before the line with the `If...Then` statement, insert this code:

```
divisor = 0
userNum = userNum / divisor
```

Now execute the routine by typing **myLoop** into the Immediate window. Type a number into the loop dialog box and click the OK button. An error dialog box will appear stating that there is a `Divide by zero` error. You then have two options—you can end the execution, or enter the debugger. Click the Debug button to pause execution and debug the code.

The window displays your code with a yellow highlight on the line that caused the error (see Figure 32.3). You can begin execution again at any time by pressing the F5 key. In this case, the condition that caused the error would still be in place, so you would be confronted by the same error dialog box.

Part VII

Ch 32

FIG. 32.3

The debugger is activated and shows the point at which execution has halted.

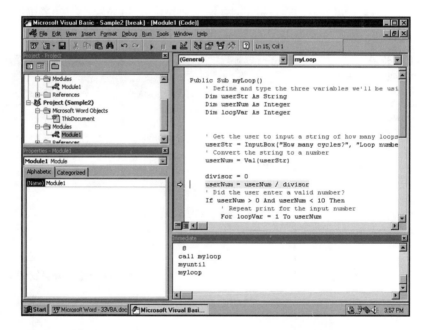

In addition to the highlighting on the line, there is also an arrow in the gray region to the left of the code that shows the current stop point. The Immediate window is still active, so type the following code to determine what value the divisor variable contains:

```
print divisor
```

It's set to zero, just as we set it in the line before. We need to change this value. First, let's place a variable watch on it. A watch will constantly display the value contained in the variable. This allows you to step through the code watching changes made to the variables.

First, we must show the Watch window. Choose View, Watch Window. The window will probably initially squeeze the Immediate window over so that it is too small to be usable. Click the border that separates the two windows and drag it until both are about equal horizontally.

Choose Debug, Add Watch. The Add Watch dialog box will appear that allows you to specify aspects of the watch. In the Expression text box, type **divisor** and click the OK button.

In the Watch window, you should see a column that is titled Expression. The variable named divisor should appear in this column. In the Value column next to it, you should see the number zero.

We'll now change the value of divisor and the Watch window will be instantly updated. Click the Immediate window and enter the following:

```
divisor = 1
```

As soon as you press the Enter key, you will see the Value of the variable in the Watch window update (see Figure 32.4).

FIG. 32.4
The Watch window on the right shows the new value of divisor that was entered into the Immediate window on the left.

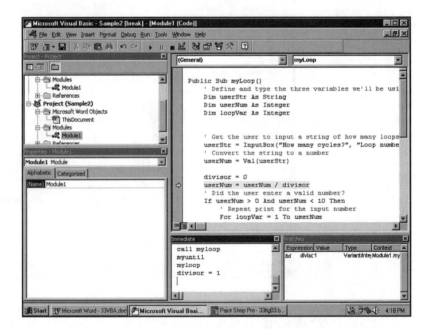

Using the Step Feature

Now if you ran the program, it would execute properly. However, let's take this opportunity to show another aspect of the debugger—*stepping*. We'll need to add another watch expression to make our examination worthwhile. Choose Debug, Add Watch and enter **loopVar** in the Expression text box. The loopvar should appear as the second variable in the Watch window.

If you select the Debug menu, you will see three step commands: Step Into, Step Over, and Step Out. The Step Into command you will use frequently. It executes the current line of code and stops at the next. Step Over and Step Out are for calls to other procedures.

Our routine doesn't call any procedures that we've constructed. If it did, choosing the Step Into option when the current line had a call to another procedure, the debugger would enter that procedure and stop at the first line. The Step Over command keeps you within the same procedure. If you accidentally stepped into a procedure that you didn't need to debug, the Step Out feature brings you out of the procedure without having to step through each line of code.

Select the Step Into command either from the Debug menu or using the F8 key on the keyboard. This time, the code line executed without generating a Divide by zero error. Use the Step Into command several more times so you can see how it works. As the loop is executed, you will be able to see how the loopVar variable increments with each pass through the loop.

Press the F5 key to continue execution without having to step through each line. Before we continue, let's set a breakpoint in the code.

Setting Breakpoints

What if you don't have an error that stops execution, but merely returns the wrong value or doesn't do what you want? You can set a breakpoint anywhere in the code that will stop execution and allow you to examine variables, single-step through the routine, or perform any other operation that is standard in the debugging mode.

Click in the source code so the cursor is flashing on the line you want execution to pause. How about on the line that calls the InputBox function? Under the Debug menu, select the Toggle Breakpoint option. You could have also pressed the F9 key or clicked the gray region to the left of the desired line.

The line should now be highlighted in red and have a small red circle in the gray region to the left (see Figure 32.5). If you execute the program now, it will stop before the line that the breakpoint is set on will execute.

At this point, you can use the Immediate window to test or modify the values of any variables. If you want to examine the execution from this point, the stepping options will let you individually watch the execution of each statement. Additional breakpoints may also be set while execution is paused. You can begin execution again by pressing the F5 key.

Note that breakpoints are not saved with the file or project. Therefore, any breakpoints that you set are lost when you close the VBA document.

Creating Variables

You've learned how to create variables both implicitly by setting a variable name to a particular value as well as explicitly using the Dim command. We haven't yet covered the various types of variables that may be created using the Dim...As command.

FIG. 32.5

The breakpoint is set on the InputBox line and will stop execution before the dialog box is shown.

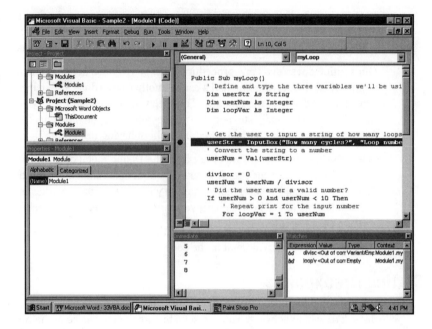

In the routine we created, we used two types of variables: the variable length string and the integer. Also available are:

Byte	Boolean
Long	Currency
Single	Double
Date	String * length (for fixed-length strings)
Object	Variant user-defined type

Right now you don't have to know all of these types, but if you're aware they are available, examining other people's code will be less confusing.

Additionally, the Dim statement can be used to define an array. An *array* is a structure that holds a number of similar elements that may be referenced by an index number. For example, if I needed to reference the different types of ice cream flavors in my program, I could create an array to hold their names. My routine might look like this:

```
Public Sub myArray()
    ' Create an array to hold three values
    Dim myFlavors(3) As String

    ' Define the strings in the array
    myFlavors(0) = "Vanilla"
    myFlavors(1) = "Chocolate"
    myFlavors(2) = "Strawberry"
```

```
      ' Print each ice cream flavor
      For i = 0 To 2
          Debug.Print myFlavors(i)
      Next
End Sub
```

This procedure creates an array of strings which are then set to the various flavors of ice cream. The For...Next loop prints the name of each flavor.

Once an array is defined, you can resize the array without losing the data it already contains. This is done using the ReDim command with the new amount of elements. To expand the number of available flavors, we can use code like:

```
ReDim myFlavors(10) As String
```

This code will make the array hold 10 items while preserving the three values that are currently entered.

Using Other Mathematical Operators

In addition to the standard math operators, VBA includes the caret (^) operator (for exponents), the Modulus (Mod) operator (for remainders), and numerous financial functions.

To calculate the value of 2 to the fifth power, in the Immediate window type:

```
print 2^5
```

The Modula operator can return the remainder if two numbers were divided. For example, dividing 57 by 10 would result in the remainder of 7. Type the following into the Immediate window:

```
print 57 Mod 10
```

The Modulus operator is particularly useful for calculations that require a particular limit such as 360 degrees. You can use a command like x Mod 360 to return the value of a variable named x that is limited to be within the range of 0 to 360.

VBA also includes such functions as FV, Nper, Rate, and so on to calculate loan amounts, annuities schedules, and the like. In the VBA help file, search for **Financial functions** for a complete list of the functions and their operation.

Including Disk Functions

VBA also allows you to read and write files to the disk. Although this cannot replace the use of a database for information storage, you can store simple text very easily.

Our first example program will open a text file for writing using the Open command. The Open command has a For operator to specify what the file will be opened to do. In this case, we'll use the Output keyword to make VBA write to a file. You can then specify a file reference number for output. All reads and writes occur by using this reference number. Insert a procedure named myFileWrite and enter the following code:

```
Public Sub myFileWrite()
    ' Open a test file for writing
    Open "test.txt" For Output As #1
        ' Output 3 lines
        Print #1, "Hello"
        Print #1, "This is a test"
        Print #1, "of VBA disk access."
    ' Close file
    Close #1
End Sub
```

This routine will open a file named test.txt and write three lines of text into the file. Execute this routine by typing its name in the Immediate window. Once you've executed the routine, the text file will have been created for use by the next routine.

Next, we'll create a routine to read all of the text in a file and output it line-by-line to the Immediate window. Add this procedure to the current module and then execute it:

```
Public Sub myFileRead()
    ' Open test file to read
    Open "test.txt" For Input As #1
        ' Keep loading until End-Of-File is reached
        Do While Not EOF(1)
            ' Read a single line
            Input #1, a$
            ' Print line to the Immediate window
            Debug.Print a$
        Loop
    ' Close the file
    Close #1
End Sub
```

Instead of opening the file for output, this procedure used the Input keyword. The EOF() function is used to test whether the end-of-file has been reached. Notice that we must pass the file reference number to the EOF() routine. We also use the Not operator that turns a True value into a False and vice versa.

Rather than using the Not option with a Do While loop, we could have simply used the Do Until command. Remember that these two conditional loops operate exactly opposite to each other in terms of how they evaluate the conditional expression.

CAUTION

Whenever you include file read/write capabilities in an application, it can be dangerous for others to use on their system. You may accidentally write over an identically named file or read a file that is private. Therefore, be careful to test any code that uses disk functions, and limit the number of people who will be using it to individuals who understand what file access will actually occur.

Selecting Events

In the last chapter, you added a number of pieces of code to event procedures such as the Click event for the button. Each form and control on a form have a number of common events.

Basic form events include the Paint event when the form paints the window, the Load event which activates when the form is loaded, and the Unload event when the form is unloaded from memory.

To select the events for a particular object, double-click the object on the form. This will display the code for the particular object. Look at the two combo boxes that appear at the top of the form—the left combo displays the name of the currently selected object while the right combo displays the current event that is being shown in the window.

If you click the combo box that appears in the top-right corner of the window, you will see a list of all of the events associated with the object (see Figure 32.6). Clicking any of these events will show you the code associated with it. When there is actually code stored in an event, it appears in a bold font on the combo box list.

Part
VII

Ch
32

FIG. 32.6

The right combo box that is currently expanded shows all of the events for the object selected in the left combo box.

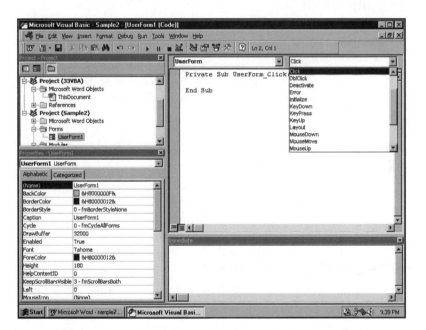

Accessing Databases

One of the most important technologies available to VBA and Visual Basic programmers is the database access functions. Known as *Data Access Objects (DAO)*, you can add, edit, or manipulate any database supported by ISAM drivers (Access, FoxPro, dBASE, Paradox, Excel) as well as ODBC support (nearly every available database). The topic, however, is far too broad to even introduce in this chapter.

We suggest you purchase a book that focuses on database systems. There are some listed in the "Related Sources" section. You can also examine one of the database examples included with Microsoft Access.

> **N O T E** Visual Basic, VBA, and Microsoft Access all share the same database engine known as the *Jet engine*. That means that any database created with one of these technologies is accessible to all. Therefore, if you learn about programming the Access database engine, all of the code and files are instantly usable by the VBA and VB environments. ∎

Programming with Objects

You may have heard of *object-oriented programming* or *OOP* in books and magazines. When you are programming with VBA, you are most often accessing objects that make up the Office system. Learning how objects are used is critical to programming for the future.

Creating Objects

When we covered classes and objects in an earlier section, we explained that we wouldn't be showing you how to create your own class. However, you can easily create instances from objects that already exist.

A new instance of an object class can be created using the New keyword. This keyword may be used either during the Dim stage of the variable creation:

```
Dim newInstance As New UserForm1
```

or when you're using the Set keyword to place a reference to the object within a variable:

```
Set newInstance = New UserForm1
```

These methods are typically for classes that are contained within the VBA environment. When you need to go outside the VBA objects and instantiate (create in memory) objects that are stored on the system as ActiveX Controls or ActiveX DLLs, you must use either the CreateObject() or GetObject() functions.

Accessing the Excel Object

One of the strengths of VBA is the integration into every Office application. By using the VBA language, you can control one of the Office applications from another.

You can write a program to take one piece of data from one program and insert it directly into the document of another. To demonstrate this capability, let's create a procedure that creates a new Excel workbook, sets the name of the worksheet, stores a number of random values in the sheet, and saves the file. The great thing about this routine is all of the control is done from within Word!

Insert a new procedure in Word and enter the following code:

```
Public Sub CreateExcel()
    ' Create the Excel object
    Set AppXL = CreateObject("Excel.Application")
    ' Create the reference to the Application object
    Set xl = AppXL.Application
    ' Add a workbook
    xl.Workbooks.Add
    ' Create reference to the Active sheet
    Set ws = xl.ActiveSheet
    With ws
        ' The title of the sheet
        .Name = "VBASheet"
        ' Set the first cell
        .Cells(1, 1).Value = "VBA Test"
        ' The loop to place random values
        For i = 1 To 10
            .Cells(i + 2, 2).Value = Rnd
        Next
    End With
    ' Save the file to the C drive
    xl.ActiveWorkbook.SaveAs "C:\VBA.xls"
    ' Close the file
    xl.ActiveWorkbook.Close
    ' Clear object references
    Set ws = Nothing: Set xl = Nothing: Set AppXL = Nothing
End Sub
```

When you execute this procedure, it will store an Excel file named VBA.xls in the root directory of the C: drive. When you open the file in Excel, it will appear like the worksheet in Figure 32.7.

FIG. 32.7
This worksheet was created entirely through automation by creating and controlling the Excel object in Word.

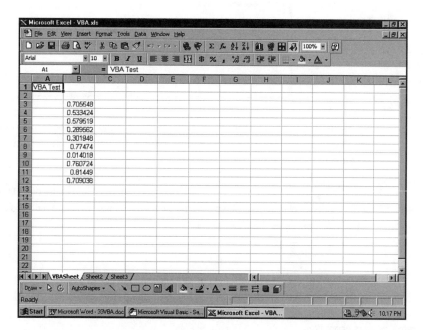

Part VII
Ch 32

You may see a number of unfamiliar references within the source code. These are not VBA commands, but consist of calls to Excel object methods and setting of Excel properties.

For example, the SaveAs method was called in the line:

```
xl.ActiveWorkbook.SaveAs "C:\VBA.xls"
```

The method was passed the parameter of a string that contained the desired file name. All of the objects for a particular application (such as Excel, Access, and so on) are contained within the application's *object model*. The object model shows all of the objects, properties, and methods and how they relate to each other.

In the help files, each Office application contains a hyperlinked object model diagram (see Figure 32.8). Clicking the individual objects presents information about the objects and their methods and properties.

FIG. 32.8

The Outlook object model diagram as found in the Outlook help file.

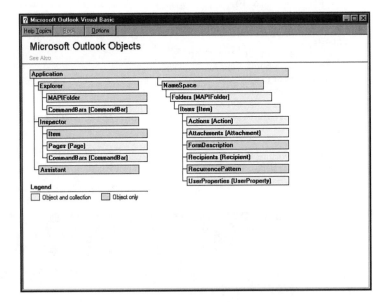

By navigating the object model, you can create new spreadsheets in Excel, add slides in PowerPoint, read paragraphs of text from a Word document, add a contact in Outlook, or create a new report in Access.

TIP   Help files that contain the object model are not installed by default. They are part of the application-specific programming help file. You can install them using the Setup program or follow the instructions in the "Help from Visual Basic" section.

TROUBLESHOOTING

Using an Office application through VBA can sometimes cause almost invisible problems. For example, if you call the saving routines and provide a path and file name that is already taken, the Office application will halt and request feedback on how to proceed.

This type of halt or other execution error can stop your application from functioning smoothly. To troubleshoot errors such as this:

- *Make the application visible.* When you create an instance of an Office application, it is invisible by default. You can set the `Visible` property on the `Application` object to make it appear in the taskbar.

- *Provide progress indicators within your application.* Many times, a user has a problem and calls you to correct it. If you have good status indicators, you can ask the user to tell you the current status. By knowing where execution stopped, it will be much easier to diagnose where the error occurred.

- *Check for errors when objects are created.* When you create an instance of an object (such as a worksheet or new document), an error code will be returned if the object could not be created. Check to make sure objects are valid before you use them.

Creating a Simple Application in Word

Even within Word, you can create functions that you have always needed. If you insert these routines into the Normal template file (Normal.dot), they will be available to every document. You can even assign a key code to automatically execute the code when a particular key has been pressed.

In this example, executing the routine takes two input strings: one for the contact name, and the second for the description of the call. It then formats this information along with the current date and time, and inserts a formatted table into your existing Word document.

Enter the following code into a code module. If you insert the module into the project labeled Normal in the Project Explorer, it will be available to all documents:

```
Sub myContact()
    Dim contactName As String
    Dim desc$

    contactName = InputBox("Enter contact name", "Contact Name")
    If contactName <> "" Then

        desc = InputBox("Enter description of call", "Call Description")
        If desc = "" Then
            Exit Sub
        End If
        ActiveDocument.Tables.Add Range:=Selection.Range, _
            NumRows:=2, NumColumns:=4
With Selection
```

```
                      .TypeText Text:="Date"
                      .MoveRight Unit:=wdCell
                      .TypeText Text:="Time"
                      .MoveRight Unit:=wdCell
                      .TypeText Text:="Contact"
                      .MoveRight Unit:=wdCell
                      .TypeText Text:="Description"
                      .MoveRight Unit:=wdCell
                      .TypeText Text:=Date
                      .MoveRight Unit:=wdCell
                      .TypeText Text:=Time
                      .MoveRight Unit:=wdCell
                      .TypeText Text:=contactName
                      .MoveRight Unit:=wdCell
                      .TypeText Text:=desc
                      .Tables(1).Select
                      .Tables(1).AutoFormat Format:=wdTableFormatSimple1, _
                      ApplyBorders :=True, ApplyShading:=True, _
                      ApplyFont:=True, ApplyColor:=True, __
                      ApplyHeadingRows:=True, ApplyLastRow:=False, _
                      ApplyFirstColumn:=True, _ ApplyLastColumn:=False, _
                      AutoFit:=True
                      .MoveDown Unit:=wdLine, Count:=1
                      ' Enter a blank line
                      .TypeParagraph
                  End With
          End If
    End Sub
```

If you assign the module to a macro key (such as Ctrl+Shift+? which is available), it can conveniently enter the table right at your existing cursor location. We've inserted a few sample contacts within our Word document to demonstrate (see Figure 32.9).

FIG. 32.9

Using the myContact routine, several contact tables have been automatically inserted and formatted in the current document.

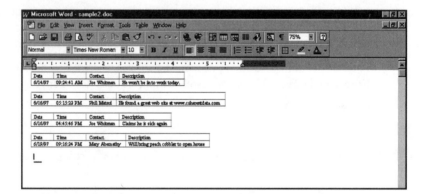

Programming the Office Assistant

You have already seen VBA code that reads and writes files, displays dialog boxes, activates forms, creates Excel and Word documents, and a host of other things. Did you know that you can control the Office Assistant from within a VBA program?

For online help, the Office Assistant can greatly aid when you give your application to someone else. How many times have you sent a colleague a complicated spreadsheet, knowing he would be calling you for an explanation of how each part works? The Office Assistant can provide instant information for the most common questions in a friendly manner.

Create a new form and draw seven command buttons on the form (see Figure 32.10). Name the four direction buttons cmdLeft, cmdRight, cmdUp, and cmdDown. For the other three buttons, you must name them according to their function: cmdIdle, cmdThinking, and cmdBalloon.

FIG. 32.10

The Office Assistant is being controlled by the buttons on the form. It is presenting options after the Balloon button was pressed.

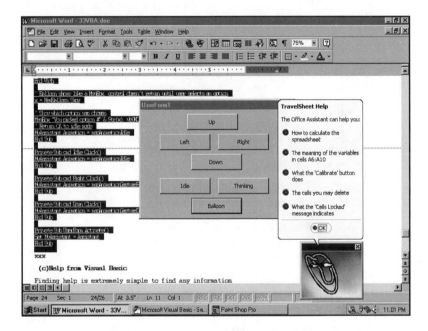

After all of the buttons have been created, you're ready to enter the necessary code. First, the form needs a variable that is accessible from any control. Set the left combo box to read (General) and the right box to read (Declarations). Enter the following line:

```
Dim MyAssistant As Assistant
```

This creates a variable to hold the reference to the Assistant. Now enter the rest of the event code into each button on the form. The code will make the Assistant take a different action when each is clicked.

```
Private Sub cmdThinking_Click()
MyAssistant.Animation = msoAnimationThinking
End Sub

Private Sub cmdLeft_Click()
MyAssistant.Animation = msoAnimationGestureLeft
End Sub
```

Part
VII

Ch
32

```vba
Private Sub cmdUp_Click()
MyAssistant.Animation = msoAnimationGestureUp
End Sub

Private Sub cmdBalloon_Click()
Dim x As Integer
Set NewBalloon = MyAssistant.NewBalloon
MyAssistant.Animation = msoAnimationSearching
' Set list of items to be displayed by the OA
With NewBalloon
.Heading = "TravelSheet Help"
.Text = "The Office Assistant can help you:"
' Each balloon can have up to 5 labels, these are set to buttons
.Labels(1).Text = "How to calculate the spreadsheet"
.Labels(2).Text = "The meaning of the variables in cells A6:A10"
.Labels(3).Text = "What the 'Calibrate' button does"
.Labels(4).Text = "The cells you may delete"
.Labels(5).Text = "What the 'Cells Locked' message indicates"
End With

' Balloon shows like a MsgBox, control doesn't
' return until user selects an option
x = NewBalloon.Show

' Show which option was chosen
MsgBox "You picked option #" & Str(x), _
      vbOKOnly + vbInformation, "Your Selection"
' Return OA to idle mode
MyAssistant.Animation = msoAnimationIdle
End Sub

Private Sub cmdIdle_Click()
MyAssistant.Animation = msoAnimationIdle
End Sub

Private Sub cmdRight_Click()
MyAssistant.Animation = msoAnimationGestureRight
End Sub

Private Sub cmdDown_Click()
MyAssistant.Animation = msoAnimationGestureDown
End Sub

Private Sub UserForm_Activate()
    Set MyAssistant = Assistant
    MyAssistant.Visible = True
End Sub
```

Once you execute the form, you will be able to control the Assistant with the command buttons. Imagine using the Assistant as a way to inform your users about a new feature of your spreadsheet or guide a user through a PowerPoint demo. Of course, the most common use will be to provide help for users who do not understand how to use a particular feature.

Getting Help from Visual Basic

For VBA, learning is best done by experimenting. Often, though, you might not know what a particular command or function does. Finding help is extremely simple to find, thanks to the online help provided with VBA. Put the cursor on the keyword or function that you'd like help on and press the F1 key. This will show the help that directly relates to that keyword or function.

Additionally, you can get information on all of the controls on the Control palette. Click one of the tools. Now press the F1 key. The context that relates to that tool will be displayed.

Part

VII

Ch

32

N O T E Most of the VBA help files are not installed by default when you install Office. When you press the F1 key, if you get an error, it will tell you which file it needs. You can do any of the following:

- Insert the CD-ROM—which makes future accesses look to the CD-ROM.
- Re-execute the Setup program for Office and use the Add/Remove Components to add the files.
- Copy the help files from the CD-ROM to the proper directory on your hard disk.

For example, if you try to get VBA commands help from Microsoft Word, it will tell you that the language reference file is missing from a particular directory (write down the file and path). You can go to the CD-ROM, search for the file (veenlr3.hlp), and determine that it is located in the folder \OS\MSAPPS\VBA. Simply copy the file to the directory that is requested in the missing file dialog box. ■

Differences Between Visual Basic and VBA

Now that you have a fairly good understanding of how VBA works, do you want to move to the full Visual Basic programming system? To answer this question, you have to decide what you're trying to do with your programming.

Both Visual Basic and VBA work from the same command set. This means that the languages themselves are identical. All of your code is directly compatible.

The objects you reference, however, may be very different. In Visual Basic, of course, you don't have the built-in Excel functions. In Excel, many of the components that ship with Visual Basic are not included with Excel. Here is a short list of the most noticeable items that are included with Visual Basic that are typically not present in a VBA system:

- The ability to create stand-alone applications. Visual Basic can compile standard EXE files. VBA, with the exception of the Access runtime, cannot be run without the hosting application itself being present on the user's machine.
- Visual Basic includes a Setup Wizard that will construct install disks to install a program build in VB onto another person's machine. This install will contain all of the EXE, DLL, and other files required for correct functioning.

- You can use VB to create ActiveX Controls that can be used within the Office applications or even over the Internet.

- To install an application over the Internet, ActiveX documents can be created in VB. These can be placed on a Web page; when the user clicks the link, the entire application can be automatically downloaded and installed to the user's machine.

- The ability to create ActiveX DLLs which can be used in any OLE Automation environment. This includes use on Active Server Pages, with DCOM, and through the Microsoft Transaction Server.

- The Remote Data Objects (RDO) provide a fast and effective bridge to ODBC drivers. Although ODBC can be accessed through DAO, this tends to create a great deal of overhead and limits flexibility. RDO provides a very close-to-the-driver translation.

- In addition to DCOM, Visual Basic provides a Remote Automation Manager that allows objects to be instantiated and executed from machine to remote machine.

- Compilation for speed. Visual Basic allows a program to be compiled into machine code for quick execution. For mathematically intense projects or ones that require extensive loops, the code may execute up to 20 times faster.

Of all these reasons, the most prominent is the ability to provide stand-alone applications. If distribution of your application requires the user to have Excel or PowerPoint installed on his machine, this limits your potential audience.

Related Sources

VBA can be learned by experimentation, although it would take a great deal of time. You are far better off by beginning with the examples in this chapter and the last and then buying a book specific to the language:

- As we did in the last chapter, we recommend *Special Edition Using Visual Basic for Applications 5* (ISBN 0-7897-0959-7) by Que for learning more about VBA. It addresses the language itself in depth as well as its application with the various Office applications.

- For beginners, the best place to get answers to specific questions is a local Visual Basic user's group.

- There are a number of newsgroups on the Internet relevant to Visual Basic. Check out the **comp.language** section for those most applicable to your needs.

- If you begin doing more advanced database and client/server work, check out Client/Server Central (**www.coherentdata.com/cscentral**) for information on everything from database to object systems.

- For Visual Basic database development, get *Database Developer's Guide with Visual Basic* by Roger Jennings. It is a large book and covers all of the primary concepts dealing with database design and creation.

- To learn more about Visual Basic, the book I co-authored *Teach Yourself...Visual Basic 5* (ISBN 1-55828-547-4) tells you how to build VB programs, ActiveX Controls, object-oriented programs, and more.

CHAPTER 33

Using VB Script

VB Script is a subset of the Visual Basic language. Although missing some of the commands available in Visual Basic and VBA, VB Script is built for transportability. This means that the language can be easily used in a variety of environments from groupware to Web browsers to server applications. It is also constructed for security and easy self-containment. When code is automatically transported and executed remotely (such as VB Script on a Web page), there is no virus or data loss danger to the machine that is executing it. ■

Overview of VB Script

The VB Script language is a subset of the VBA language. Most of the VBA commands that aren't present in VB Script directly relate to portability and security issues.

Create a custom Outlook form with VB Script

You'll create a custom VB Script program and manipulate some of the fields in the Microsoft Outlook Contact form.

Navigate the Outlook object model with VB Script

Use VB Script code to create new contacts, set appointments, or most anything you can do by hand in Outlook.

Add VB Script to your Web pages

Use VB Script in your Web pages to execute on the visitor's Web browser.

Use VB Script to run Personal Web Server

You can use Microsoft's free Personal Web Server to create server-side content.

VB Script Overview

VB Script is currently used in Microsoft Outlook (for programming forms), Internet Explorer (for Web scripts), and the Active Server Platform (for executing programs on the Web server). With the next major release of Windows, VB Script will be integrated into the operating system.

VB Script is available on a wide variety of machines, primarily through the IE application. The following platforms currently support VB Script:

> Windows 95 and Windows NT (Alpha, MIPS, PowerPC)
>
> Windows 3.1 and Windows for Workgroups (16-bit Windows)
>
> Macintosh

VB Script soon will be ported to UNIX for Sun, Hewlett-Packard, Digital, and IBM. This means that your VB Script skills have broad applicability.

Netscape claims that ActiveX Controls can be run within Netscape Communicator. First, this does not include a VB Script implementation. Also, it is not a direct solution, but instead requires an additional technology known as *JavaBeans* for indirect access. There is however a plug-in to allow Netscape to run both VB Script and ActiveX controls (see the "Related Sources" section at the end of this chapter).

In this chapter, you will learn how to use VB Script in your Outlook applications and with IE, and to create a dynamically constructed Web page. Since you've been introduced to programming in VBA in the last few chapters, learning VB Script will be easy for you.

VB Script versus VBA

The most noticeable difference between VB Script and VBA is not the language itself at all, but rather the context of implementation. VBA uses the single common environment with forms, dialog boxes, code modules, and so on. Therefore, VBA programs, whether they are written in Word, Excel, PowerPoint, or the complete Visual Basic environment, all appear similar. Not so with VB Script. The development environments themselves look nothing alike and the way in which the VB Script is activated varies dramatically.

When using VB Script with Outlook, the VB Script Editor is used to write your code (see Figure 33.1). Code is linked to individual forms. The code is directly related to the form that it resides upon. Most of the VB Script code you will use in Outlook will manipulate the Outlook object model which is not present in the other scripting environments.

For VB Script used within Web browsers, the ActiveX Control Pad application (see Figure 33.2) is used to allow insertion of ActiveX Controls and preprogrammed availability of VB Script events. The Control Pad's Script Wizard will provide all of the standard event programming structures. Microsoft Window's Notepad application is also commonly used to create HTML pages with embedded VB Script.

FIG. 33.1

The Outlook VB Script programming environment is a simple text editor.

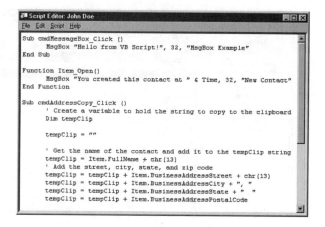

FIG. 33.2

The ActiveX Control Pad can be used to insert VB Script code into a Web page.

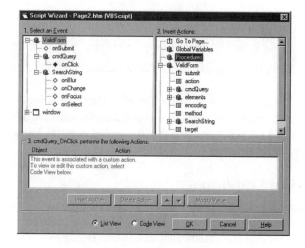

Part
VII

Ch
33

Most Active Server Pages developers will use the Visual InterDev application (see Figure 33.3) to create their server-based VB Script code. Visual InterDev will do simple HTML syntax checking and also allows the use of *design-time ActiveX controls* that automatically create VB Script code for tasks such as database access and table generation. Design-time controls function essentially like the wizards you find in other Office applications.

You can see that the broad range of development environments can be challenging when creating your VB Script code. The debugging environments also are different in these implementations. When VB Script is used within Internet Explorer, there is an integrated debugger available. In Outlook, a run-time debugger is provided instead. Active Server Pages returns errors as HTML pages. Debugging code for each of these environments provides different challenges.

FIG. 33.3

The Visual InterDev application will be used for much of the Active Server Page construction.

However, keep in mind that each environment uses *exactly* the same VB Script engine to execute your code. Therefore, there will be no special implementation or compatibility problems. Once you've learned VB Script on any one of these platforms, the knowledge is immediately usable on any of the other ones.

Understanding the Language

The VB Script language contains commands that are identical to those in VBA. Since VB Script is a subset of VBA, some commands are missing. Most noticeable are the lack of variable data typing and the file access commands. Eliminating data typing simplifies the VB Script and implementation issues. File access restriction is required for security.

The features that are missing from VBA can be roughly divided into two categories: completely missing and partially missing. Completely missing features essentially means that the whole category is missing from VB Script. Partially missing, in contrast, is simply missing particular aspects of a category of commands. For example, even though the Date and Time commands are missing, the Now command can be used to retrieve and format the information for similar solutions.

Features that are completely missing include:

- *Data types.* You cannot set a variable to a particular type such as Integer or String. All variables are of the type variant so they change their type as they are assigned a value.
- *Constants.* Except for five basic constants defined later in this section, there are no constants supported in VB Script—just variables. Therefore, statements that use

constants in example VBA files will often have to be translated to their numeric equivalent before they will execute. There is no `Const` command.

■ *User-defined types*. You cannot use the `Type` command to create your own data structures.

■ *File access commands*. Any commands that access the file system (such as `Open #1`, `Read`, and so on) do not exist in VB Script. By eliminating access to a client machine's file system, the scripts are far more secure.

■ *Printer object*. Absence of the `Printer` object limits printing options to the features of the hosting application.

■ *Financial functions*. None of the financial functions present in VBA are usable, including the `IIF` command.

■ *Declare statements*. No Dynamically Linked Libraries (DLLs) can be activated from VB Script.

■ *DDE functions*. Functions that access DDE clients and servers have not been included. DDE is a technology that is being phased out in favor of the more advanced OLE technology.

■ *Conditional compiling functions*. The statements `#Const, #If...Then...#Else...` are used by the Visual Basic compiler to include or exclude code from the program. These conditions are determined at compile time before execution has begun.

Features that are partially missing include the following:

■ *Date and time commands*. Although certain data and time functions are not supported (such as `Date()` and `Time()`), a majority including `DateSerial()`, `DateValue()`, `TimeSerial()`, `TimeValue()`, `Now()`, `Year()`, `Month()`, `Day()`, `Weekday()`, `Hour()`, `Minute()`, and `Second()` functions are available.

■ *String commands*. Almost all commands to handle strings are supported with the exceptions of the `Lset()`, `Rset()`, `Mid()`, and `StrConv()` functions. Fixed-length strings aren't supported either.

■ *Conditional flow keywords*. The most important missing commands include the `With...End With` structure and most of the error-checking keywords. Also, because neither line numbers nor line labels are provided, all of the `Goto` and `Gosub` commands have been omitted.

■ *Named arguments*. Although you can pass variables between routines, you cannot use named arguments as you can in VBA. You must instead rely on the argument's order to pass them correctly.

■ *Object manipulation*. The `TypeOf` command that lets you conditionally check if the particular object in a certain class type is not included.

■ *Option statements*. The commands `Deftype`, `Option Base`, `Option Compare`, and `Option Private` are not available. `Option Explicit` is included in VB Script.

■ *On Error commands*. Only the `On Error Resume Next` is supported, so complete error trapping is not available.

Part
VII

Ch
33

■ *Clipboard object.* The `Clipboard` object is not accessible as it is in VBA. However, you can use objects to copy to the Clipboard as you'll see later in the chapter in the "Creating an Effective VB Script Function" section.

Although some of the features normally available in Visual Basic are not implemented, there are often workaround processes to achieve the same result. Using a little inventiveness, we can perform most of the same operations that would traditionally be available as a VB keyword.

VB Script also does not allow direct access to the Clipboard. The `Clipboard` object is not contained in the engine for standard manipulation. However, there are ways around this limitation. Our Outlook example later (in the section "Creating an Effective VB Script Function") will show how you can use other controls (such as the `Text` control) to find and implement functions that are missing from the VB Script environment.

Although constants aren't supported in VB Script as a general rule, five built-in constants are available:

Empty	True	Null
Nothing	False	

Many people wonder why VB Script has so few constants. Constants are often very specialized (such as `BarChartType` for an Excel chart). Because VB Script code must be transportable, the constants that it supports must be available everywhere. To include a large library of constants would make VB Script much larger and wouldn't add much to its usability.

CAUTION

Sample Microsoft code often contains a great number of named constants which won't run correctly in VB Script. This happens because much of the code is ported from VBA. The values of constants can almost always be found in the Help files and substituted in the source. If you find sample VB Script code that will not execute correctly, check for constants that might not exist in the code.

The fact that there are no data types presents special challenges to a programmer or designer. If you pass the incorrect type to an object method, for example, an error may be returned.

To solve this problem, VB Script retains all of the `Is` testing functions provided in VBA. For example, the `IsString()` function could be used to determine if the variable contains a string before it is passed to another routine. Also available are the following:

IsEmpty()	IsDate()	IsNull()
IsNumeric()	IsArray()	IsObject()

Use these functions to determine the type of value held in the variable.

Defining variables is nearly the same as the commands used in VBA. As we've mentioned, there are no strictly typed variables is VB Script. Therefore, although you use the `Dim` keyword to create the variables, the `As` keyword does not exist.

Although a variable type cannot be set with a keyword, you can explicitly force the variable into a type using the conversion functions. The CBool, CByte, CDate, CDbl, CInt, CLong, CSng, and CStr functions can be used to convert a value to an explicit type. For example, we can make sure the variable contained in myVar is a string:

```
myVar = CStr(myVar)
```

Even if you use these conversion functions, the variable type can be redefined instantly by the next function. Therefore, use this technique with care.

For arrays, the Dim command is used as it normally would be. Redimensioning arrays is done in the same way it is when using VBA with the Redim keyword. The Redim keyword preserves data stored within the array if the array size is increased. If decreased, the currently stored data is truncated to fit the new array size.

Because there are no type definitions within VB Script, passing parameters is also different from VBA. The Parameter list of a function does not have As keyword. For example, in VBA a function definition might look like:

```
Function myFunc(myVar As Integer) As String
```

This function would accept an integer variable and return a string variable. Because VB Script does not include an As keyword, the same function would appear as:

```
Function myFunc(myVar)
```

The passed argument would be of variant type as would the returned result.

In VB Script, the Date and Time functions are limited. The Date data type is not supported. Additionally, the Date, Time, and Timer functions are not available. However, the following functions can be used to achieve most of the same results:

DateSerial	Month
DateValue	Day
TimeSerial	Weekday
TimeValue	Hour
Now	Minute
Year	Second

Natively, VB Script has no way of accessing the printer. Therefore, to print anything, you will have to rely on the object model available in the hosting environment.

N O T E Many of the environments that support VB Script also support JavaScript (with the notable exception of Outlook). Microsoft has created a scripting engine called the *ActiveX Scripting environment*. Many different languages can be plugged into this engine, and Microsoft includes both VB Script and their version of JavaScript (known as *JScript*) in the standard implementation. Check the environment where you'll be using VB Script for these options. ■

Scoping Variables

Because of VB Script's various implementations, the scope of the available variables differs greatly. For example, an application might require global variables that multiple routines need to access. In Outlook, variables can only be scoped within a form. Therefore, to pass a variable between multiple forms would require some type of patchwork approach. You might define a new field in the contact list that could be used to store such a variable.

When you use VB Script in IE, you may keep variables at the page level. By using the <SCRIPT> tag, you can place variables that can be read and modified by any routine on the form.

Using the Unicode Standard

Because VB Script is meant to be a standard language even for international programming (especially on global Web pages), there are functions included in VB Script to convert Unicode that are missing from VBA.

On personal computers in the past, the standard system for storing characters used a system called *ASCII* (pronounced "as-key"). The ASCII system used a single byte (8 bits) for each character. In memory, 1K of RAM represents 1,024 bytes, allowing 1,024 characters to be stored in 1K of RAM.

All characters are stored as numbers. The ASCII system stored numbers between 0 and 255, which was plenty for the upper- and lowercase Roman alphabet, numerals, and special characters (such as the exclamation point and the comma). However, great difficulties arose when other alphabets were required (such as Japanese). The Unicode standard uses a 32-bit value for every character and therefore can represent more than 65,000 different characters. As computers become increasingly international, they are moving toward the Unicode standard.

Since VB Script will be used in both international groupware functions and global Internet Web pages, VB Script includes the mechanisms to use Unicode. The AscW function can be used to convert an ASCII value to the equivalent Unicode notation. Unicode is supported primarily on the Windows NT operating system.

Activating Events

In Visual Basic and VBA, the event methods were implemented in a standard fashion. VB Script, however, has a variety of different event models. Outlook activates events in much the same way that VBA has in the past. However, the development environment shows the event code along with other procedural code in a single window.

Web browsers, on the other hand, include their event activation routines within other HTML code. Some of the events are even renamed (GotFocus becomes Enter) for compatibility with JavaScript. Active Server Pages uses a third model where events are generated through objects stored on the server.

Therefore, when programming VB Script, pay attention to the environment that it is running on. Because each event model is different, the code may appear in vastly different forms.

In the last chapter, we described the basic unit of measurement for graphics, known as the *twip*. Unlike with VB and VBA, measurement in VB Script is expressed in *points*, not twips.

Trapping Errors

The lack of implicit error checking through `On Error Goto` routines requires VB Script programs to be more aware of possible errors. Explicit checking for errors is required because there is no error trapping routine. Therefore, make sure you include these routines in critical points such as database access.

The `Err` object can be used to determine if an error occurred. This object works the same way that it traditionally has in VBA, although the number of returned error codes is fewer. The following are trappable errors:

Error Code	Description
0	No error detected
5	Invalid procedure call
6	Overflow
9	Subscript out of range
11	Division by zero
35	Sub, Function, or Property not defined
91	Object variable not set
92	For loop not initialized

You might notice that the error numbers are identical to VBA errors. Therefore, you can even prototype error-checking routines in VBA for later transplanting into the VB Script environment.

Part
VII

Ch
33

Using Objects

There are two ways of creating an object: using the Class or the ClassID. The Class will be familiar to you as this is the model you typically use in VBA. The Class is the English name for the object. For example, you can create an Excel object using the `CreateObject` function:

```
myObject = CreateObject("Excel.Application")
```

The argument passed to the `CreateObject` function is the name of the Class. However, many VB Script implementations require the ClassID to be used. For example, to use an animated control on a Web page, the code might look like:

```
<OBJECT ID="AniPushButton1" WIDTH=100 HEIGHT=51
        CLASSID="CLSID:F72CC885-5ADC-101B-A56C-00AA003668DC">
```

The ClassID that you see is a unique identifier of the particular object on the system. The ClassID is given to the object at the time when the company that created it did its final compile.

The ClassID is used in place of the Class itself to minimize the possibility that the wrong object is used. In our Excel example, if the user who executed the code had an old version of Excel or a different application that was named Excel, execution could cause problems or errors because an object would be accessed that was different than our original intention.

Because the ClassID is unique for each original compile, even different versions of the same application would have different ClassIDs. Obviously you cannot easily remember the ClassID of an object. Tools such as Visual InterDev and ActiveX Control Pad will insert the ClassID for you.

Instantiating objects in VB Script is accomplished differently than in VBA. In VBA, creating a new instance of an object is done with the New command in the Dim statement. For example:

```
Dim myNewObject as New Object
```

Because there is no As keyword in VB Script, it uses a technique called *late-binding*. This means that the object is not bound to the object variable until the program is running. New objects are created using the Set keyword—for example:

```
Set myNewObject = New Object
```

This creates the new instance of the object as it is setting the reference to the variable.

Outlook and VB Script

Outlook is quickly becoming the standard Personal Information Manager in use. You may be using Outlook already for all of your contact management and scheduling needs. It can be used as either a stand-alone application or in conjunction with an Exchange server (as you've already discovered in previous chapters). Outlook can be customized through preferences and menu items, but its true flexibility lies in its ability to create custom forms that contain VB Script code.

VB Script will let you add any type of programming to an Outlook application. Would you like to add your own custom field that is filled in every time you create a new contact? Would you like to write a program that automatically creates a "Merry Christmas" e-mail to everyone that worked for XYZ Corp.? These applications and much more are possible when you create your own custom solution in Outlook.

At this point, you should already be familiar with Outlook. Before we begin adding VB Script code, we must first create a custom form. Unlike VBA where code can simply be placed in a code module to be called from any routine, all VB Script must be directly connected to a form.

To create a form, you must base it on one of the current templates. That means it is best to choose a form that already closely matches whatever application you want to build. For example, if you want to build routines that use names in the address book, it would be best to begin from a Contact form. For an e-mail-based solution, the Message form would be the best choice.

Creating a Simple VB Script Form

Let's begin creating a new form. In Outlook, choose File, New. We're going to base our example on the Contact form because later we will make a function that pulls values from the Contact database. Therefore, choose Contact from the New submenu.

Now that the form has been created, we'll need to add code to one of the tabs. Right now, you probably only see four tabs (General, Details, Journal, and All Fields). We want to add a tab that will hold a couple of buttons.

Choose Tools, Design Outlook Form. You should now see all 11 general tabs included with the form.

See how the tabs for certain pages have parentheses that surround the tab name? This is an indicator that these tabs are normally invisible when the form is visible.

We want to make the (P. 2) tab visible, so first click this tab. Choose Form, Display This Page. The parentheses should disappear from the tab title. The tab is now visible from the form in general mode.

Choose Form, Rename Page and name the page VB Script. We'll put all of our controls and scripts on this page like we added controls and code to the forms in Chapter 32.

▶ **See** "Programming the Office Assistant," **p. 678**

In Chapter 32, we started demonstrating forms by using a simple command button control that displayed a message box. We'll make this our first example here too so you can see the similarities with the VBA environment.

The Control Toolbox is not automatically displayed in Design mode. Therefore, right-click the form and then choose Control Toolbox. You should now see the toolbox floating above the window. Select the CommandButton icon.

Draw a CommandButton on the form. Your form should look something like the one shown in Figure 33.4.

Right-click the command button and select Properties. Set the Name property to cmdMessageBox and the Caption property to ShowMessage. Click the OK button to accept these changes.

N O T E It is a good idea, as mentioned in Chapter 32, to name your controls right when they are created. Programmers have a tendency to wait to set the Name property, and soon there is a great deal of code that is written to access the generic button name such as CommandButton1. To ensure that the code is most readable, it is a good habit to simply name the control when it is first created. ■

Adding VB Script code is not as simple as in a VBA system. In VBA, you simply double-clicked the control and the code window appeared for the proper event. In VB Script, you have to explicitly enter the code window; choose Form, View Code.

FIG. 33.4

The Outlook VB Script programming environ- ment is a simple text editor.

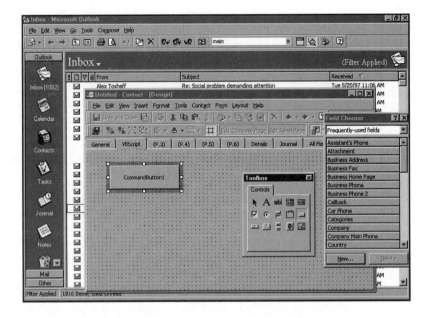

We're going to begin by placing a simple button on one of the tabs that shows a message box. We've used this command already in VBA so it will be familiar to you. By duplicating this same function, you can see the relation between the two development languages.

The development environment that is included with Outlook is not as robust as the one you've become accustomed to when doing VBA programming. Outlook provides a simple text editor to enter VB Script code.

To give you the best idea of how Outlook can be used, let's create a simple function in VB Script that is activated when you click a command button.

You are now presented with a Script Editor window. The Script Editor works like any simple text editor such as Notepad. The Script Editor does not provide all of the advanced editing features such as color-coded text and autocompletion, which are available in VBA. However, your VB Scripts will most likely not be as long or as intensive as those you will create with VBA, so advanced editing is not as critical.

In a moment, I will show you how to insert the event codes using the Events Wizard included with the Script Editor. For now, type in all of the code shown in the listing, including the Sub...End Sub keywords. In the Script Editor window, enter the code:

```
Sub cmdMessageBox_Click ()
    MsgBox "Hello from VB Script!", 32, "MsgBox Example"
End Sub
```

Close the Script Editor window. You will not be asked to save the code before you execute the form because like Microsoft Access, you can instantly switch between the Design and Execu- tion modes. Only when the form is closed will you be prompted to save it.

After you've closed the Script Window, choose Tools, Design Outlook Form. You used this option before to enter Design mode. The option works like a toggle between Design and Execution mode.

The button should be displayed on the form; clicking it produces the message box similar to the one we created in VBA. You can see the similarities between VBA and VB Script, with the primary difference being the environments used to create each.

Now let's further extend this example by reacting to events that are generated by the system rather than the user. Enter the Design mode again and bring up the Script Editor window.

Make sure the cursor is flashing after your current event code. The Events Wizard will insert code at the position of the cursor.

You might have noticed that there is a Run option under the Script menu. This Run command works very much like the Run command in the VBA environment. If you select the Run command, the current text in the window will gray and it will appear as if nothing is happening. In reality, all of the code you have in the script window right now only executes when specific events occur. Because none of the events will occur until Outlook is in Execution mode, nothing will happen.

However, if you leave code outside of the event subroutines, it will execute when the Run command is selected. If you started the Run operation, use the Stop command to halt execution. Now copy the MsgBox line of code and place it outside any of the events. Selecting the Run command will display the Message Box instantly as shown in Figure 33.5.

FIG. 33.5
The MsgBox command executes outside of any event code.

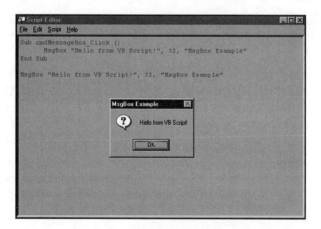

This is a good way to do syntax checking on small pieces of code. Temporarily copy the code out of a procedure and run the program. Any errors in the code will halt execution. Stop execution now and delete the extra MsgBox code so the script appears as it was before we did our Run experiment.

Choose Script, Event to display a dialog box showing you all of the events available to this current form. These events include the following:

Open	ReplyAll	Read
Forward	Write	PropertyChange
Close	CustomPropertyChange	Send
CustomAction	Reply	

Each of these events activate your routines when the event occurs. Most of these events are activated when the user manipulates an Outlook message.

N O T E   You may notice that there is no Click event listed in this Events box for buttons or other controls. The events listed are the ones that apply to the entire form. The Click event is not generally used for the form itself. ∎

For now, we're interested in the Open event. The Open event is activated when the form is originally opened. We're going to use this event to display a welcome dialog box. Click the Add button to insert the Open event in the Script window.

This time we'll create a message box that notifies the user of the time the contact was created. Enter the message box line so your code matches the code shown here:

```
Function Item_Open()
    MsgBox "You opened this contact at " & Time, 32, "New Contact"
End Function
```

Now we'll save this form and create a new contact so you can see it in action. Close the Script Editor window. Choose File, Publish Form As, and then enter the name **VB Script** and click the Publish button.

Your form is saved and can be used any time you create a new contact. Close the Open window now and when asked if you want to save changes, click the No button. This Save Changes dialog box is not asking if you want to save changes to the design form, but if you want the actual contact information (such as name, address, and so on) saved on the new form. We didn't enter any information; therefore, a No answer does not lose any data.

If you select the Contacts menu, you'll notice a new option has been added as the last entry on the menu. It should read "New VBScript" to indicate the form that we just created. If you select this option, your screen should display the message box that we created in VB Script (see Figure 33.6).

FIG. 33.6

After the option New VB Script is selected, the Open event is activated to display our message box.

Click the OK button to display the form. You'll notice that the VBScript tag is present and the button that we placed on it is active.

Creating an Effective VB Script Function

The VB Script programs that we've worked on so far have been very simple, just to provide you with examples of how VB Script is entered into the environment. Let's create a really useful function that copies the current contact information to the Clipboard.

We can create a button that will copy the Name, Company, and Address fields into the Clipboard so they can be pasted into a word processor or text editor. This can be useful when you need to write a letter to a contact and you don't want to retype the address or copy multiple fields.

Enter the Design mode again. Using the Control Toolbox, create another command button on the form. Set the Name property to cmdAddressCopy and the Caption to Copy Contact Address. Also add a text box control that you will name txtCopy and set the Caption to Copy Address.

Because the text field will need to hold the entire name and address of the current contact, we should set the text control to support multiple lines of text. Right-click the control and select the Advanced properties. This properties window should be very similar to the one in VBA. Set the MultiLine property to True. Now the control will display the text broken by carriage returns (ASCII value 13) on sequential lines.

View the code window. Notice that unlike VBA where all of the procedures for the different controls are separated, VB Script contains all the script for all of the code related to the form in a single text window. Unfortunately, you cannot print from this window so any code must be copied to a text editor such as Notepad to print it.

Now enter the following code. This routine will be activated when the user clicks the cmdAddressCopy command button.

```
Sub cmdAddressCopy_Click ()
       ' Create a variable to hold the string to copy to the Clipboard
       Dim tempClip

       ' Create string to store our concatenated address
       tempClip = ""

       ' Get the name of the contact and add it to the tempClip string
       tempClip = Item.FullName + chr(13)
       ' Add the street, city, state, and zip code
       tempClip = tempClip + Item.BusinessAddressStreet + chr(13)
       tempClip = tempClip + Item.BusinessAddressCity + ", "
       tempClip = tempClip + Item.BusinessAddressState + "   "
       tempClip = tempClip + Item.BusinessAddressPostalCode

       ' Create object reference to the Inspector object
       set MyItem = Item.GetInspector
       ' Get the collection of all of the user tab pages
       Set pgs = MyItem.ModifiedFormPages
```

```
    ' Get our page that we named VBScript
    Set pg = pgs("VBScript")
    ' Create reference to all of the controls on this page
    Set ctls = pg.Controls
    ' Create a reference to the text box control - txtCopy
    Set ctl = ctls("txtCopy")
    ' Set the Text property to the string we created
    ctl.Text = tempClip
    ' Select the current text that we just placed in the Text property
    ctl.SelStart = 0
    ctl.SelLength = 32000
    ' Execute Copy method to move selected text to the Clipboard
    ctl.Copy
End Sub
```

To publish this form, choose File, Publish Form. You can name the form VB Script. For more information on publishing forms, refer to Chapter 25.

In Chapter 25, you learn how to place a form on a public Exchange server for common use. The form that you modified can not only contain additional fields that you add, but also contain all of the VB Script code. The code itself is stored with each form.

CAUTION

Security for macros is automatically placed at a high setting to ensure that VB Script does not commonly download and execute on a person's machine without him being made aware that it is doing so. Unfortunately, this warning appears every time a form with a piece of VB Script code is loaded by Outlook. Check the Outlook manual for instructions on overriding this function.

Before you turn off the security, however, make sure that your exchange system is secure. If people can freely place executable code within forms, a villain could create a VB Script that could do anything from deleting contact or schedule data to copying this private data somewhere for later retrieval.

Now that you've had a little experience using VB Script, let's cover some background material so that as you become more proficient, you'll be able to know exactly what you can and can't do.

Remember when we said that the advantage of VB Script over VBA was its ability to be portable? For this reason, VB Script does not include any commands that require it to interact with the base system. Primarily, VB Script is missing all file operation commands. You wouldn't want a VB Script to be able to download into your browser and access or delete your files.

 Microsoft has created an accepted way to supplement any features missing from VB Script. VB Script can access components; therefore, missing functions can be added via components. For example, when using Microsoft's Web server technology known as Active Server Pages, you need to be able to access files. VB Script includes no file commands, so to the Active Server Page platform, Microsoft has added a `FileSystem` object. A VB Script program can simply call this object which has routines for file read and writes.

Outlook Object Model

The Outlook object model allows you to access most of Outlook to modify fields, control forms, or nearly anything else that is possible through manual intervention. You can even create new forms with some simple code shown here:

```
Sub CreatemyItem()
' Create a reference to the main Outlook Application object
    Set objOutlook = CreateObject("Outlook.Application")
    ' Execute the CreateItem method to create a new message
    Set myItem = objOutlook.CreateItem(0)
End Sub
```

As we've stated earlier, you cannot use constants in VB Script. Therefore, the CreateItem method requires the numeric type of new item to be passed. In Table 33.1, you'll see the values of all of the items that may be created in Outlook.

Table 33.1 Outlook Object Types

Item Name	Constant	Numeric Code
Mail message	olMailItem	0
Appointment	olAppointmentItem	1
Contact	olContactItem	2
Task	olTaskItem	3
Journal entry	olJournalItem	4
Note	olNoteItem	5

N O T E Although a description of the Outlook model is beyond the scope of this book, you can find the object model in the online help. Note that the only way to access the VB Script help is to have the Scripting window open, otherwise Outlook will access the traditional help file. ■

In Figure 33.7, you can see the hierarchy. You can access this object model by searching in the index for **object hierarchy** and then selecting the **Microsoft Outlook Objects** topic.

Using VB Script in a Web Browser

VB Script can be used within a Web page to provide client-side computing. Currently, the Microsoft Internet Explorer supports VB Script, but a plug-in for Netscape Navigator is also available (see the "Related Sources" section).

Let's use the ActiveX Control Pad to insert the code into an HTML page. You can use the Notepad text editor if you'd like, but the Control Pad allows you to insert VB Script events and automatically tracks script code.

Part
VII

Ch
33

FIG. 33.7
The Outlook object model in the help file allows you to click objects to gain information about them.

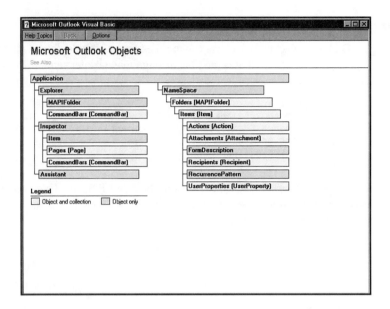

ON THE WEB

The ActiveX Control Pad is available for free download on the Microsoft Web site at:

http://www.microsoft.com/workshop/author/cpad/

If you're going to be doing a fair amount of VB Script coding for Web pages, we highly recommend this excellent free utility.

We are going to create a VB Script program that runs within IE and changes a greeting that is displayed when the page is viewed. If the time is before noon, Good morning is displayed. Good afternoon and Good evening are each displayed at the appropriate time.

Execute the Control Pad application, and you should be presented with a blank HTML file. The cursor should automatically appear between the Body tags to begin inserting code.

You need to insert a global variable called 'myGreeting' that will be used by the greeting procedure. Select the Script Wizard option under the Tools menu. If you click the right mouse button on the Global Variables item in the right window pane, a context menu should appear as shown in Figure 33.8. Click the New Global Variable option.

You should be presented with a dialog box where you can enter the variable name. Type **myGreeting** and click the OK button. In the right pane, the Global Variables item should now have a plus (+) sign that indicates it contains a variable. Click the plus to expand the options, and you should see your variable. Click the OK button on the window to accept this script.

The header of the HTML document should now show the creation of your variable. Now add the code shown here and save it to the disk. When you load this into your browser, you will be greeted with the appropriate message for the time the page is being accessed.

FIG. 33.8

The context menu allows you to create a global variable for the HTML page.

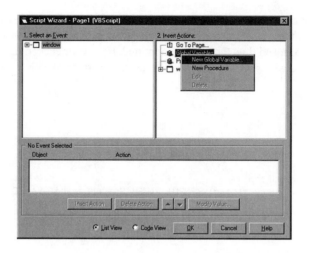

```
<HTML>
<HEAD>
<TITLE>VB Script Greeting</TITLE>
    <SCRIPT LANGUAGE="VBScript">
<!--
dim myGreeting

Sub PrintGreeting()
    ' Determine what greeting should be shown and write to HTML
    If Hour(time) < 12 then
        myGreeting = "Good morning.<P>"
    ElseIf Hour(time) < 17 then
        myGreeting = "Good afternoon.<P>"
    Else
        myGreeting = "Good evening.<P>"
    End If
    Document.Write myGreeting
End Sub

' Execute the routine to insert proper text
PrintGreeting
-->
 </SCRIPT>
</HEAD>
<BODY>
<H1>This VB Script is running on the browser.</H1>
</BODY>
</HTML>
```

The customization available from VB Script can really add good effects to your Web pages. However, most scripts are used for more practical purposes. The most prevalent use of VB Script so far is to validate information prior to submitting it to a server. For example, in a form that you require the address to be filled out, the user might accidentally leave the field blank. Instead of submitting the form and having the server do all of the processing before returning an error, you can create a VB Script to check the data on the form before it is submitted.

Part
VII

Ch
33

The VB Script code shown here demonstrates this capability. It provides a simple query text box and makes sure that the user entered a query string. If the text has been entered, a message box is shown and then the form is submitted. If the user clicked the Start Query button without entering a query, a warning box is presented and the form is not submitted.

```
<HTML>
<HEAD>
<TITLE>Data Validation</TITLE>
</HEAD>
<BODY>
<H1>Data Validation with VB Script</H1>

<FORM NAME="ValidForm">
        Enter query string: <INPUT NAME="SearchString" VALUE="" MAXLENGTH="50"
SIZE=50>
        <INPUT TYPE="BUTTON" VALUE="Start Query"  NAME="cmdQuery">
</FORM>

<SCRIPT LANGUAGE="VBScript">
Sub cmdQuery_OnClick
    ' Create variable to hold object reference to the HTML Form
    Dim curForm
    ' Create reference to form
    Set curForm=Document.ValidForm
    ' Check value to determine whether it's blank
    If RTrim(curForm.SearchString.Value)="" then
        MsgBox "Please enter a query value.", 16, "No query string found"
    Else
        MsgBox "Starting Query...", 32, "Query OK."
        curForm.Submit
    End if
End Sub
</SCRIPT>

</BODY>
</HTML>
```

This code should provide an excellent example of using VB Script to add a great deal of value to a Web page.

TIP If you're saving HTML files using the Notepad application, make sure that the file type that is selected in the Save dialog box is set to the All Files selection. Otherwise, Notepad adds the TXT extension to any extension you've added. Therefore, test.htm becomes test.htm.txt.

Now that you've had some experience with writing VB Script, look on the Web for the numerous available examples. Realize that when VB Script calls a method within IE, it defaults to using the IE object. Therefore in some sample code, what appears to be VB Script commands that are unfamiliar to you may in fact be methods of the IE object.

Note that in IE, several of the event functions have been renamed for compatibility with JavaScript. The two most apparent examples are the GotFocus which is renamed as the Enter event and the LostFocus event which is renamed Exit.

TROUBLESHOOTING

Creating VB Script code that functions properly can be a tedious process. If you can't quite get a piece of code working correctly:

- *Check the source in the browser.* Many times, you will make changes to your code and be unable to understand why it doesn't seem to change the results. Very often, you've simply forgotten to click the Reload button to load your new changes. Choose View, Source to make sure your new code is being executed.

- *Try with other browser versions.* Many times a user has a problem that you cannot duplicate. Be sure to test your VB Script code on different browser versions and platforms. In my experience, execution between the Windows and Macintosh platforms is nearly the same, but errors still occur. Make sure you test the application on several browsers.

- *Use the Script Debugger.* Microsoft has a free Script Debugger that will install within your IE browser. Tracking down errors with a complete debugging environment dramatically simplifies coding.

Using VB Script with Active Server Pages

Now that you've created an HTML file that contains VB Script, you know how a Web browser that supports VB Script can execute your code. But what if you need to cater to users who are using Netscape Navigator or some other browser that doesn't natively support VB Script? What if you need to store information entered into an HTML form into a database on your Web server? You can use VB Script!

Microsoft has created a technology known as *Active Server Pages (ASP)*, which can execute processes on your Web server. The ASP technology is included as part of both Internet Information Server (IIS) and Personal Web Server (PWS).

If you're running a professional Web server, you'll want to use IIS. But did you know that you can set up a Web server on your personal machine that can be accessed by anyone else that is hooked up to your LAN? Personal Web Server is freely available from Microsoft. It is also included with every copy of FrontPage. Any Windows 95 or Windows NT machine may become a Web server.

You could set up your own Web pages, create a Web application that accepts input and enters the data into a Microsoft Access database, or generate custom content based on the user. All of this is possible with PWS combined with VB Script.

ASP is a part of the Web server that processes files that have an .ASP extension. The ASP files can contain any scripting language supported by the ActiveX Scripting engine (which includes both VB Script and JScript). The code in the ASP file is executed and may generate pure HTML that is sent to the user's browser.

To use this wonderful technology, simply install IIS or PWS. Whatever folder that is going to hold the ASP file must have Execute privileges which tell the Web server that code may be executed in files contained within the folder. See the Web server documentation for information about setting privileges. We'll create a simple example program that executes a loop in VB Script and generates an HTML Web page.

> **CAUTION**
>
> Make sure that any folder in which you place an important ASP file has Execute privileges. If there are no execute privileges on the directory, when the user accesses the file (for example, by typing **www.mycompany. com/myfile.asp**) through a Web browser, the file type will not be recognized and the user will be able to download the file. If you have VB Script code in your ASP file that accesses your server database, the downloaded file can download the file that contains your user name and password, making your system completely insecure.

In this example, we're going to use the Visual InterDev program to create our VB Script because it has a great deal of added functionality when creating ASP files. However, the following code may be entered into the Notepad text editor and saved in the appropriate directory.

When you install PWS or IIS, the demo application called Adventure Works should be automatically installed. We want to save our file to the AdvWorks folder which has already been set to have Execute privileges. Use the Find Files or Folders option under the Start menu to locate the AdvWorks folder. With Personal Web Server, the folder is usually located at C:\WebShare\ ASPSamp\AdvWorks (see Figure 33.9).

```
<%@ LANGUAGE="VBSCRIPT" %>

<HTML>
<HEAD>
<META NAME="GENERATOR" Content="Microsoft Visual InterDev 1.0">
<META HTTP-EQUIV="Content-Type" content="text/html; charset=iso-8859-1">
<TITLE>VB Script Loops</TITLE>
</HEAD>
<BODY>
<H1>Demonstration of VB Script loops</H1>

<% for I=1 to 5 %>
    HTML Hello #<% = I %> <P>
<% Next %>

<% for I=1 to 5
    Response.Write "Write Hello #" + CStr(I) + "<P>"
Next %>

</BODY>
</HTML>
```

Save the file to a folder.

FIG. 33.9

The Visual InterDev environment with our ASP file.

In Figure 33.10, you can see the page as it appears once the Web browser accesses the ASP file. You can see that the file is executing on the server because the two loops have created the HTML source and sent it to the browser.

FIG. 33.10

The Netscape browser showing the Web page dynamically generated with the VB Script code.

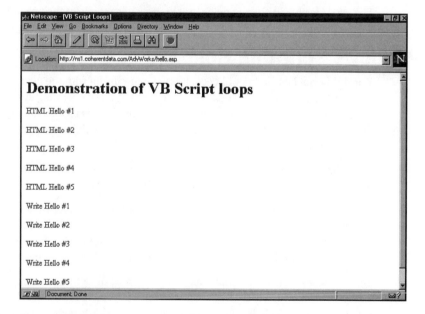

You might notice that this figure shows Netscape Navigator displaying the file. Navigator does not natively support VB Script. Because the script is executing on the Web server, simple HTML code is all that is broadcast to the browser. If you do a view source of the page, it should look like the code shown here. Notice that there is no VB Script here.

```
<HTML>
<HEAD>
<META NAME="GENERATOR" Content="Microsoft Visual InterDev 1.0">
<META HTTP-EQUIV="Content-Type" content="text/html; charset=iso-8859-1">
<TITLE>VB Script Loops</TITLE>
</HEAD>
<BODY>
<H1>Demonstration of VB Script loops</H1>
        HTML Hello #1 <P>
        HTML Hello #2 <P>
        HTML Hello #3 <P>
        HTML Hello #4 <P>
        HTML Hello #5 <P>
Write Hello #1<P>Write Hello #2<P>Write Hello #3<P>Write Hello #4<P>Write Hello
#5<P>

</BODY>
</HTML>
```

Further description of the VB Script implementation within ASP is beyond the scope of this book. The ASP technology has an entire object model to manipulate Web interaction including forms, database access, banner advertisement, cookies, and more. For further information, see the "Related Sources" section at the end of this chapter.

This ASP file should show you one more powerful example of the use of VB Script.

Windows Scripting Host

Your VB Script knowledge will become even more useful with the next revision of both Windows and Windows NT. The next version of both of these operating systems will include the scripting engine built into the operating system itself. This new technology is called *Windows Scripting Host* and will allow you to use any ActiveX Scripting language (including VB Script and JScript) to execute scripts that can control the machine.

VB Script can then be used to map a network drive, launch an application, activate a network printer, or even search the network for machines or data.

Desktop scripting files are supported via the Windows Scripting Host engine. In the past the MS-DOS world used batch files (BAT files such as AUTOEXEC.BAT); now many of these same types of applications can be performed in windows using WSH. The power to control the entire machine that is available to VB Script programmers will be incredible.

To execute a script on a machine that has script hosting active, you simply execute the CSCRIPT.EXE, which is the key command line executable for the WSH. The command-line parameter simply includes the path and the file name of the script to be executed.

Related Sources

The Internet is one of the best places to find additional information on using VB Script:

- The first place to visit on the Web is the Microsoft VB Script site (**www.microsoft.com/vbscript**) that contains the latest information, upgrades, and developments concerning the VB Script language.

- Microsoft has placed the complete online handbook of all VB Script commands (**www.microsoft.com/vbscript/us/vbslang/vbstoc.htm**).

- If you have Netscape Navigator users who need to access VB Script and ActiveX, NCompass Labs (**www.ncompasslabs.com**) sells a Netscape plug-in called ScriptActive. It will execute ActiveX and VB Script in Netscape Navigator, including compatibility with Netscape Communicator.

- The Ask the Active Platform Pro (**http://www.inquiry.com/vbscentral**) is an excellent resource of common questions regarding VB Script and ActiveX.

- The Client/Server Central (**www.coherentdata.com/cscentral**) Web site has information on using VB Script in professional solutions. Most information focuses on using VB Script with Active Server Pages.

Part
VII

Ch
33

Microsoft Publisher

34 Manipulating Objects 711

35 Adding Publisher's Special Elements 729

36 Publishing to the Web 747

37 An Overview of Other Small Business Edition Applications 761

CHAPTER 34

Manipulating Objects

For publishing brochures, booklets, newsletters, or other standard publications, Publisher offers lots of advantages over a word processor. The preconfigured layouts and the built-in publishing functions make Publisher an easy-to-use assistant for professional-looking documents.

Every object in your publication, from text to complicated graphics, can be moved, nudged, arranged, or otherwise manipulated to give you a slick professional look.

Text boxes, which are objects, are probably the most important part of your publication, because in the end it's the information or story that counts. Everything else—all the other objects—are enhancements you use to improve clarity, draw attention, or provide amusement. ■

Flowing text between text boxes

Long articles that spill across pages can be linked so the reader can follow the story to the correct next page.

Group and ungroup objects

Objects that are touching, overlaid, or spaced exactly as they are needed can be manipulated as a group so you don't lose their relative placement.

Wrap text

You can have body text wrap around a graphic frame, or around a graphic image, even if it's irregularly shaped.

Manipulating Text

If your article or story doesn't fit within its column or page, you continue it on another page. As you type, when the text box, column, or page fills, another page is not started automatically (as with your word processor). There is no more space allotted to hold your additional text, yet you can continue to type. No error messages appear, no scroll bar is presented to give you access to your text, and, in fact, you cannot see what you are typing. You have entered Publisher's text la-la land.

Actually, of course, the text is there; it's just tucked away in its own private hiding place, a storage area. Publisher sends a message when you've begun to use the storage area by changing the icon on the Connect button at the bottom of the frame. As long as your text fits inside the frame, there's a diamond on the Connect button. When you enter the storage area, the symbol on the Connect button changes to three dots.

If you don't want to enlarge the frame (or you can't because there isn't room on the page), you must move the stored text to another frame or page. If you've already established multiple pages that have text boxes or columns set up in your publication, you've saved yourself a step here. If not, you must create the space for your overflow text.

Adding Pages

If you have to add pages to your publication, there are a couple of approaches to use.

To add a new page at the end of your publication, move to the last page and click the Next Page arrow in the lower-left corner of the window. Publisher will ask if you are trying to add another page—click OK to confirm that you are. Then use the Text tool to put a text box on that page.

If you want to add a new page within the document, move to the page immediately before or after this new page and choose Page from the Insert menu (or press Ctrl+Shift+N). The Insert Page dialog box appears (see Figure 34.1) so you can configure this new page:

FIG. 34.1

The Insert Page dialog box lets you insert a new page and configure it for text at the same time.

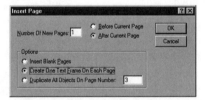

- Specify the number of new pages you want to add, and whether they are to be placed before or after the current page.
- If you want to design the elements for the page yourself, choose to insert a blank page.
- If you are planning to fill this new page with text, choose to create a text frame on the page—the text frame will fill the page.
- If your publication is already designed for columns, text boxes that share the page with other elements, or any other design you've invented, you can replicate one of the pages.

If your publication is designed as a booklet, you have to work in even numbers of pages; frequently your view of your work is the Two-Page Spread view. When you use the Insert command in that view, the Insert Page dialog box looks a bit different (see Figure 34.2).

FIG. 34.2

Publisher assumes you'll add two pages at a time when you work with two-page spreads.

The fact is, you don't have to add two pages at a time, or any multiple of two. Sometimes that would be inconvenient, or destroy your plan for the publication's total look. However, if you add only one page, you must find another location within your publication to add it.

Flowing Text into a New Frame

Now that you have the two magic ingredients—extra text and an empty text frame—you can put them together. Just click the Connect button (the one with the three dots). Your pointer turns into a pitcher (it's holding the extra text, of course), and you can move to the target text frame and click anywhere in the frame to empty the pitcher contents into it. If there are three dots on the Connect button of this target frame, repeat the process until all the extra text has found a home.

You can also fill the pitcher first and create the page afterward. The pointer remains a pitcher while you take all the necessary steps. Click anywhere outside your publication to get your pointer back; the text is placed back into the overflow area, and you can return to the Connect button to fetch it later.

Even though the text is split among pages and frames, it is linked. If you go to any of the frames and select all the text (using Ctrl+A), then make formatting changes (font, font size, attributes, and so on), the changes are reflected in the text throughout all the frames. In fact, if you select all the text in any one frame (using Ctrl+A) and delete it (thinking you're deleting those paragraphs), you delete the entire story.

When text frames are linked, the Connect button changes to a link and a Frame Jump button helps between the connected frames. In fact, if a text frame is in the middle of several linked frames, there will be two Frame Jump buttons: one indicating the previous frame, the other pointing to the next frame. You can use the Frame Jump buttons to move around any particular story. Of course, these indicators are only visible when you select the frame.

You can also disconnect frames, and reconnect the overflow text to a different frame. Perhaps the amount of text changed because of edits and you can use a smaller frame for the overflow text. Or, perhaps you put the text in a small frame and now you want to add text, and would prefer to find a larger frame rather than having another overflow frame.

Part
VIII

Ch
34

To disconnect frames, start with the first (prior, earlier) of the two frames that will be disconnected. This does not necessarily mean the first frame of the story, because you may have more than two frames for that story. Click the Connect button and immediately the link breaks, the text that is cut adrift is sent back into the overflow section (la-la land), and your cursor turns into a pitcher. Find or create a new frame and click to pour the text into it and establish this new connection.

It rarely all works perfectly, with text sliding gracefully into frames looking like a professional publication, so there are some devices you can use to make up for deficiencies.

Perfecting Text Appearance

When you let text flow into additional frames, there are a number of things that can go wrong. I'm not talking about technical problems or error messages—I'm talking about appearance. There are adjustments you can make that will give you a slicker, more professional look for your publication.

If the last text frame has very little text, try one of these techniques to eliminate the need for the frame:

- Reduce the margins in the preceding frame(s).
- Enlarge the preceding frame(s).
- Reduce the font size.
- Eliminate some of the text.

Reverse the solutions if the last frame is more than half filled and you want to try to fill it out.

Another very large problem is widow and orphan control, an important publishing concept that Publisher fails to provide a tool for (although your word processor probably does). A *widow* is the last line of a paragraph that is also the first line of a new column or page. An *orphan* is the first line of a paragraph that is also the last line of a column or page. Check any newspapers, magazines, and books you might have at hand; you will rarely see this layout error. Without a Publisher tool to rewrap text or change the break points for columns or pages, you must apply the text-manipulating techniques listed here.

Adding a Continued Notice

One way to set up a publication is to treat it like a book, where the stories start on the first page and then flow to each additional page. That's easy to set up; it's easy to pour your text into each succeeding page.

But often you'll be creating publications that are more like newspapers or newsletters, where stories start on the first page but might continue on any page in the publication. In this case, it's a good idea to let the reader know which page to turn to in order to finish reading the story.

After your story is tucked neatly into connected frames, Publisher can add the appropriate references for you. There are two separate messages available:

■ Continued On, with the page number of the next frame. This message becomes the last line of the frame.

■ Continued From, with the page number of the previous frame. This message becomes the first line of the frame.

To insert the Continued message, move to any connected frame and right-click. Choose Text Frame Properties from the shortcut menu and then select Continued On, Continued From (or both, if the current frame is in the middle of a series of connected frames). See Figure 34.3.

FIG. 34.3

Choose a Continued message and let Publisher fill in the page number references automatically.

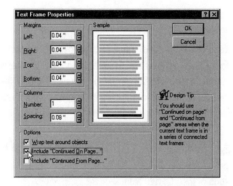

The text appears in the appropriate place, which is the end of the frame for Continued On (see Figure 34.4), or at the top of the frame for Continued From.

FIG. 34.4

The Continued message is placed in the correct spot on your frame—notice that the Style box on the toolbar reflects the style for this feature.

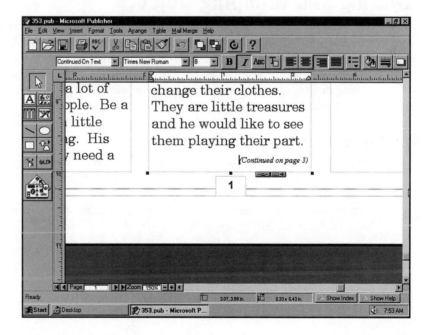

(Continued on page 3)

You can select the message and make changes if you like. You can change the text, font, font size, or attributes.

If you make changes and decide they are so perfect that you want all your Continued notices to look exactly like your new design, select the text and click the Continued style in the Style box on the toolbar. Then press Enter. The Change or Apply Style dialog box appears and offers the choice of changing the style to match your design, or returning the text to its original formatting.

TROUBLESHOOTING

If you play around with the formatting of a Continued notice and accidentally delete the page number reference (which is very easy to do, believe me), you can fix it easily. Place your insertion point where the page number reference goes, and choose Page Numbers from the Insert menu. Instead of inserting the current page number, Publisher inserts the correct page number for the linked frame. This works because when you are working inside a Continued Text style, Publisher is designed to insert the referenced link.

Incidentally, you can take advantage of this feature if you want to change the wording of the Continued notice. For example, you could alter the Continued text so it says `Please turn to page X for more`, replacing the X with the results of Insert, Page Numbers.

Layering and Grouping Objects

Objects in your publication can be moved, manipulated, and positioned in order to provide special effects and attention-grabbing graphics. You can layer objects, placing them one atop another, or overlapping them, in order to make one effective graphic out of several elements. You can also group objects, taking multiple elements that have been arranged together and treating them as one unit so that when you manipulate that unit, all the elements participate in the manipulation.

Arranging the Layers of Objects

Every object you place on a page is on its own plane and has its own layer. The first object you place is on the bottom layer, the next is one layer higher, and so on. Most of the time, objects occupy their own section of the page so you can't tell which layer they are on (and it doesn't matter). Sometimes, however, objects overlap and then the layer assigned to each object becomes important (see Figure 34.5).

In addition, you can stack objects one atop another and take advantage of layering. In this case, manipulating the level of the layer becomes extremely important (see Figure 34.6).

To change the layer on which an object sits, select it and then choose the appropriate command from the Arrange menu: Bring to Front, Bring Closer, Send Farther, or Send to Back.

FIG. 34.5
The order in which you placed objects on the page determines the layer level, and it doesn't always work properly when you overlap the objects.

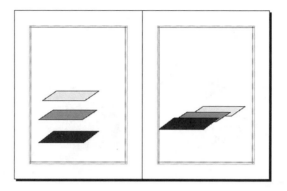

FIG. 34.6
You can arrange the order of layers to create a viable graphic from a group of elements.

You can change the layer of multiple objects at one time by selecting them while pressing the Shift key. The objects retain their layer relationships to each other, but move as a group to change their relationship to the other objects on the page.

CAUTION
Any object you place on the background page is always furthest back and cannot be moved forward.

Layering Text Boxes

When you work with text boxes, the layering is just as important, but the effect you want to end up with is usually different than the look you're going for when you layer graphic shapes.

Most of the time, you want text to wrap around a graphic object or to be layered on top of it in a way that makes the combined objects look as if they are one object—the text is part of the graphic.

If you're layering a text box to place it on top of a graphic (after you move the text box forward to make it closer to the top layer than the graphic object), it's frequently a good idea to make the text box object transparent by selecting it and pressing Ctrl+T (see Figure 34.7).

FIG. 34.7
When you place a text box object on top of another object, you can make it transparent if you want it to look like an integral part of the object behind it.

You might also want to have the text in your text box wrap around a graphic element. Accomplishing this is a simple matter of dragging the graphic onto the text box, except:

- The graphic must be on a layer that is further forward than the text.
- The text box must be configured to wrap around graphic objects.

Look at Figure 34.8 to see the possibilities. Starting on the top of the left page and moving clockwise:

FIG. 34.8
The layer occupied by each element determines the way they look when they overlap.

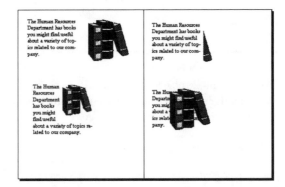

- The original two elements are side by side; the graphic element was placed on the page before the text element (so the graphic element is on the bottom layer).
- The graphic element has been dragged to the text element. Because it is on a lower layer, it is automatically placed behind the text (not the desired intent).
- The graphic element has been brought forward (using Arrange, Bring Closer; or Arrange, Bring to Front). It sits on top of the graphic element.
- The graphic element is on top of the text element and Text Wrap is turned on. See the section "Wrapping Text" later in this chapter for more details about text wrapping.

You could also, of course, move the text frame backwards instead of bringing the graphic element forward in order to change the layers.

Grouping Objects

Grouping objects is a method of connecting them and treating multiple objects as one object. There are a variety of reasons for grouping objects:

- All of the objects in the group have to be moved, and it is easier to move them as a group than to move each one individually.
- All of the objects in the group have to be resized, and the proportions among them must remain the same.
- All of the objects in the group need to be rotated to the same degree, and it is easier to do one rotation than multiple individual rotations.
- The objects in the group are distanced from each other very precisely, and if any object moves, all must move to keep those distances intact.

And there are probably more reasons you can come up with as you work on your own publications.

Creating a Group

The first thing you must do before manipulating the elements as a group is to create the group.

If all the elements are contiguous, the easiest way is to click the Selection tool and then drag a line around the elements you want to include. When you release the mouse, the group is formed (see Figure 34.9).

FIG. 34.9
Drag the mouse to form a box around a group of elements.

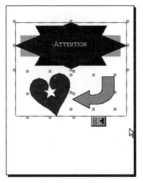

Part
VIII

Ch
34

The group is created automatically. Click the Group button on the lower-right side of the group box. The two parts of the Group button join together to form the permanent group. You can always ungroup by clicking the Group button again (the two parts of the button will separate).

 TIP If you grouped the items to perform a specific manipulation and then will have no further use for the group, you do not have to make it a permanent group. Just don't click the Group button.

If the elements aren't contiguous or won't fit neatly into a rectangle, click each element you want to include in the group while holding down the Shift key. When you release the mouse, you can see your group (see Figure 34.10). Click the button to make the group permanent if you need to.

FIG. 34.10
The group displays sizing handles for the elements included in it.

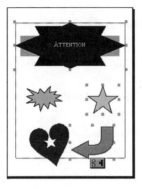

Even though there may be a rectangle surrounding more elements than the ones you included, there are no sizing handles showing on the excluded elements. And, as you manipulate the group, you'll see that only the selected elements go along for the ride (see Figure 34.11).

FIG. 34.11
When the group moves, you can see that unselected elements stay behind.

You can move, resize, and rotate the group at will, as seen in Figure 34.12.

FIG. 34.12
Each element in the group moves proportionately when you manipulate the group.

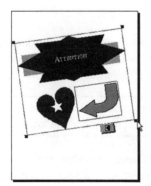

You can select an individual element in the group and change its color, border, or text (for a text element) without changing any other element in the group.

N O T E Some elements (graphics from the Design Gallery, some clip art) actually are groups. You can treat them as individual elements when you are creating a group because you can nest groups. You could also create your own set of groups for nested groups. ■

Aligning and Nudging Objects

One of the tools Publisher provides to help you gain a professional look for your publications is *layout guides*. These are lines that appear on your screen (but don't print), and they provide reference points you can use to make your pages and elements consistent. In fact, you can force the elements on your page to line up with them.

Another tool related to alignment is *object alignment*, which means you can line up multiple objects on the same page so there's a pattern. There's nothing worse than using your eye to line things up, and then the printed version shows that the middle object of the three you lined up so carefully is just a smidgen below the other two.

Nudging is a technique of moving an object in itsy-bitsy steps to its absolutely perfect position on the page. Unless you have an abnormally steady hand with a mouse, it's pretty much impossible to do this manually, so Publisher has provided a tool.

Configuring Layout Guides

Layout guides let you arrange all the elements of your pages into consistent columns and rows, giving your publication a slick professional look. When you establish layout guides they are global, but you can change the guides for any individual page using the page-only guides called *ruler guides*.

To establish layout guides for your publication, choose Layout Guides from the Arrange menu. In the Layout Guides dialog box (see Figure 34.13), configure the publication:

Part
VIII

Ch
34

FIG. 34.13
Margin guides and grid guides are configured with the Layout Guides dialog box.

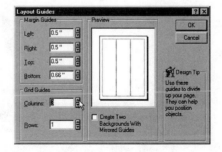

1. Set the margin guides, which appear pink in your document.
2. Set the number of columns and rows you want to use for layout. These lines appear blue as you work.

3. Select Create Two Backgrounds with Mirrored Guides to establish mirror images for the left and right pages if your publication is a booklet.

N O T E   Mirroring the page layouts for facing pages is absolutely essential for booklets or books. And don't forget to allow room for the binding of the book: If you need a half-inch for binding (or even for staples), add that amount to the margin on the binding side of the page. In publishing jargon, that space is called a *gutter*. And, as long as I'm passing along jargon, the right page is called *recto*, and the left is called *verso*. ▪

Configuring Ruler Guides

If an individual page in your publication will contain a lot of elements or some special arrangement of elements, you can ensure an orderly arrangement by putting ruler guides on that page. Then, just line up all the stuff to those guides.

You create ruler guides by using the rulers on your Publisher window (guess that's how they got the name). Horizontal guides start with the top ruler, and vertical guides start with ruler on the left side of the Publisher window. Ruler guides are quite easy to create; just do this:

1. Hold down the Shift key and move your mouse over the horizontal or vertical ruler until the pointer changes to a double arrow (technically, it's called an *adjust pointer*).

2. Drag to the point on your page where you need a guide (see Figure 34.14).

FIG. 34.14

Drop a ruler line at any point on the page you think you might need to line up objects.

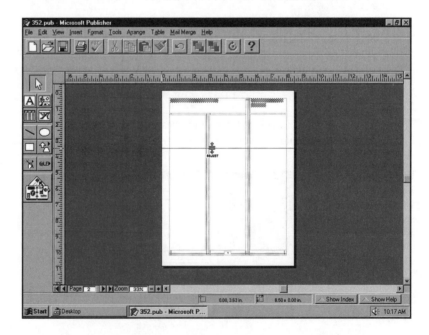

When the guide is in place, it appears as a green line on your screen. Time for a color reminder: Green is ruler guide; pink is margin guide; and blue is layout guide.

To remove the guides, hold down Shift and put the pointer over the guide you want to get rid of. When the pointer changes to the adjust pointer, drag the guide back onto the ruler you used to create it (or drag it off the page and on to a blank spot in the Publisher window).

Snapping Objects

You can tell Publisher to make those guides you've established act in a very aggressive manner. Whenever an object gets near a guide, it will reach out and grab the object, then yank it in so it touches the guide line. The term for this activity is *snap to* (nicknamed *snapping*).

The downside of this is that if you do invoke snapping, whenever you put an element near a guide, it's going to keep going and snuggle up to that guide.

But there's more available in snapping than just snapping to your guides:

- You can snap to objects, which means as you drag an object near another object, the static object reaches out and snaps the moving object to itself.
- You can snap to ruler marks, which means that if you drag an object near a marking on the ruler (which is divided into eighths of an inch) the object will snap to the nearest exact measurement line on the ruler.

Snapping is a boolean option and you can turn it on and off for each type of snapping by using the Tools menu. All three types of Snap To commands are available on the menu; just click to select (or deselect) the snapping you need (a check mark indicates the feature is on).

When Snap To is enabled, using it is a breeze. To snap an object to a guide:

1. Select the object and move the pointer to the place on the object where the pointer turns into the Mover.
2. Drag the object toward the guide you want to use. When you are almost at the guide, the edge of the object snaps into place along the guide line.

Use the same technique to snap to a ruler mark or another object. You can snap multiple items by selecting them with the Shift key.

If you know you want to snap to a guide, it's best to have only that Snap To command enabled so you won't accidentally snap to a ruler mark or an object. In fact, if you're lining up elements using Snap To, select only the Snap To option you need for that maneuver.

 TIP If all three of the Snap To commands are enabled, there's a pecking order: Guide, Object, Ruler Mark.

Part
VIII
Ch
34

Lining Up Objects

You can also make the objects on a page neater by making sure objects are lined up with each other (not the same as snapping objects to objects). This is a way to effect a pleasing, professional arrangement for those objects that should not be placed along layout guides.

To line objects up so they look as if they're arranged properly on the page (instead of haphazardly dropped there), select the objects you want to manipulate. You can use the Shift key to select them, or draw a box around them if they are contiguous. Then create a relationship between or among the elements that looks slick and professional:

1. With the objects grouped, choose Line Up Objects from the Arrange menu. This displays the Line Up Objects dialog box (see Figure 34.15).

FIG. 34.15
Line up the objects to form a graphic relationship among them.

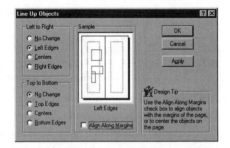

2. Choose an alignment that is Left to Right or Top to Bottom.

3. Choose the point on each object that you want to use as the reference point for lining up (for example, Left Edges).

4. If you want to align the objects along the margin in addition to the inter-object alignment, select Align Along Margins.

If you have multiple rows and columns of objects, you can perform several processes in order to line up the columns, then the rows, each in different ways. For example, in Figure 34.16, the objects in the left column are lined up on their right edges, and the objects in the right column are lined up on their left edges. The rows are lined up along the centers of the objects.

FIG. 34.16
These objects are lined up to each other to make the page easy to read.

Nudging Objects

Sometimes objects don't have to be perfectly aligned or against margins. You might want them almost touching, just off center, or one a tad higher than the other.

Using a mouse can be nerve-wracking when you're making small adjustments. You overshoot, then you try to inch back and go too far. You get the object pretty much exactly where you want it and then decide to try one more step, just one more little move. The object moves too far and then you can't get it back to the exact place where it was when you thought it looked pretty good.

Don't worry, be happy. Here's the trick: Select the object, then hold down the Alt key while you use the cursor arrows to nudge it along.

Perfection is easy when you have the right tools, isn't it?

Wrapping Text

When you insert a graphic (a picture or WordArt) into the body of a story, most of the time you'll want the text to wrap around the graphic. That's the normal, professional way to do things.

It's not quite so simple, however, because you have some decisions to make (decisions always seem to complicate matters). There are three ways to wrap text around a graphic:

- Wrap the text around the graphic frame.
- Wrap the text around the graphic, ignoring the frame.
- Wrap the text around the graphic by moving text around the graphic to meet every irregularity in the shape.

Wrapping Around Frames

By default, when you place a graphic (a picture or WordArt) on top of text, the text wraps around the frame of the graphic (see Figure 34.17).

FIG. 34.17
When you look at the text around these graphics, it's easy to see that it wraps around the frames of the graphics.

This isn't a bad approach; certainly the text is easy to follow and the graphics stand out nicely. Nothing muddy about it. However, there is always all that extra white space around the picture—it is, of course, the space occupied by the picture's frame.

You can fine-tune the text wrap a bit, either by resizing the frame or by cropping the picture.

Depending on the picture or its shape, you can frequently tighten up the white space that represents the frame by resizing the frame on one or two sides.

You can also try cropping the picture. *Cropping* removes part of a picture, leaving behind only the part you want (or feel is important). To crop a picture:

1. Select the picture.
2. Click the Crop Picture icon on the Format toolbar.
3. Place the pointer over a sizing handle—it changes to a cropping symbol.
4. Drag to form a box over the picture that includes only the portion of the picture you want to keep.
5. Click the Crop Picture icon again to restore your normal mouse pointer.

Cropping doesn't work with all pictures, only with those that can stand to have some of the picture disappear without losing the effect. Pictures that are round or square in aspect don't crop well, but a picture of a man with a tall feather in his cap can usually survive a crop that gets rid of the top portion of the feather.

Wrapping Around the Picture

You can wrap text around the picture, ignoring the frame, to create a tighter wrap (see Figure 34.18). Just right-click the graphic frame and click the Wrap Text to Picture button on the Format toolbar (or choose Object Frame Properties from the shortcut menu and select Picture Only).

FIG. 34.18
When the frame is ignored, the text wrap follows the shape of the picture.

Your Text Here

 Sometimes you might find that the text wraps a little too closely to the picture when you eliminate the frame. To loosen things up a bit, go back to the Object Frame Properties dialog box and create some white space around the picture by setting a margin.

Wrapping with Customized Settings

For a nifty look, you can wrap text around a graphic figure in a manner that duplicates the shape of the figure. This won't be terribly effective with a circle of course, but if the picture is irregular, it's sometimes interesting to try to match the text wrap to the irregularities.

To accomplish this, you must have already opted to wrap text around the picture instead of the frame:

1. Select the picture.

2. Note that the Crop Picture icon on the Format toolbar has changed to the Edit Irregular Wrap icon. Click that icon. A sizing handle is placed at every point on the picture that there is a twist or turn in the shape. Press F9 to zoom in for a better view (see Figure 34.19).

FIG. 34.19

Sizing handles indicate each variation of the edge of the picture.

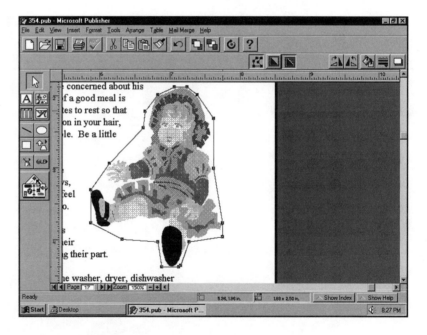

3. When your pointer is over one of the sizing handles, it changes to an adjust pointer. Move the sizing handle, and the text wrap will follow.

4. If you want to adjust the text wrap at a place where there is no sizing handle, create one by holding down Ctrl. When the pointer changes to an add pointer, click to lay down a new sizing handle. Then drag it to adjust the text wrap.

You can also drag a sizing handle away from the picture, which increases the white space between the picture and the text. This is an effective way to emphasize the irregularity of the graphic shape. ●

CHAPTER 35

Adding Publisher's Special Elements

Publisher provides a number of special features and tools that make your publication look slick and professional. You don't have to know a lot about graphic design to add professional graphic designs to your work. ■

The Design Gallery

Insert ready-made design elements into your publication without having to spend time or money on graphic artists.

The Page Wizards

Insert and configure special elements like coupons, ads, and other useful mini-pages when you need them.

Linking and embedding document objects

Distribute your publication as a computer document instead of hard copy so you can use sound and video clips.

Using the Design Gallery

Publisher's Design Gallery is like a commercial art museum, housing a collection of professionally designed graphic elements you can add to your publication.

The graphic elements are in a variety of types, including:

- Ornamental artwork that is designed to draw attention to an element on the page (or just to fill space in an attractive manner if you have such a need).

- Headlines that have backgrounds, borders, multiple graphic elements, and everything else you could think of (except the text) to produce an eye-catching headline.

- Attention Getters that give a slick look to any text you want to use to draw the attention of your reader.

- Sidebars that provide predesigned boxes you can use for text you want to highlight outside the main body of your story or article.

- Pull Quotes that offer fancy boxes you can use when you want to pull a line from a story and place it on the page to attract attention to the story.

- Titles that are really fancy elements you can place behind and around your title text.

- Web graphics to use on those publications that aren't printed on paper.

- Reply Forms for those items below the dashed line, making it easy to print credit card information forms or other elements that the reader fills out and returns.

- Table of Contents backgrounds and borders to make that boring listing more artistic.

Inserting Gallery Objects

Open the Design Gallery by clicking its icon on the Publisher toolbar (see Figure 35.1).

FIG. 35.1
Choose some fancy doo-dads to make your publication slick and professional.

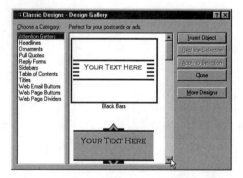

Choose a category, then scroll through the graphics to find the one you want to use. Then double-click it to place it on your page. When you look at it, you're quite likely to find it's a *group*—a collection of shapes (some with a text box) cleverly put together to form an attractive graphic (see Figure 35.2).

FIG. 35.2
Ungrouping this graphic reveals the individual parts.

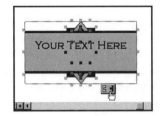

Many of the grouped graphics have text boxes within the group (the hint is you'll see Your Text Here), and you add your text by replacing the placeholder text.

Some, however (especially titles), do not contain text boxes but instead use WordArt for the text. Your clue is that when you click the title area, your pointer does not turn into an I-beam (the standard "ready-to-edit" signal from Windows), but instead you see a Move pointer indicating a graphic element. Double-click to change the text in the WordArt graphic, using the standard WordArt functions.

Altering Gallery Objects

Ungrouping any gallery object gives you the opportunity to tweak, fine-tune, or otherwise change it to match your own style. In fact, you have full freedom to mess it up, which happens often because few of us have the graphic skills and taste of the professional artists who inspired the original objects. If you really go too far, delete the graphic and reinsert it.

When you begin to manipulate the ungrouped object, you'll frequently discover that the graphic has nested groups. When you click an ungrouped element, you may see another connection button indicating this element is itself a group (see Figure 35.3).

FIG. 35.3
You have to drill down to ungroup a nested group when you want to manipulate the elements.

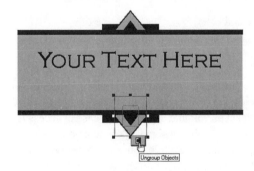

Each element in a gallery graphic can be treated as if it were an element you created, and you can flip, rotate, colorize, move, and resize it. The text can be formatted in the same manner as any other text in your publication, and you can change the font, font size, attributes, alignment, and color.

Part

VIII

Ch

35

Visiting Other Galleries

By default, you work in the Classic Designs Gallery when you open the Design Gallery. There are several additional galleries available to you, each specializing in its own art style (see Figure 35.4). As you visit them, you'll find that some have additional types of graphics (backgrounds and other generic design elements). Choose More Designs on the Design Gallery dialog box to choose another gallery to visit.

FIG. 35.4

From top to bottom, these graphics came from the Jazz, Modern, and Plain Galleries.

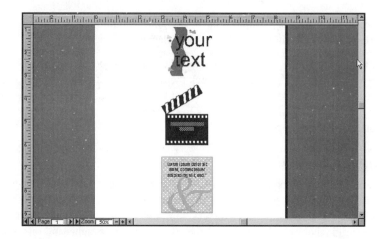

Creating Your Own Gallery

You can open a new wing of the Design Gallery to hold your own objects, making them available to you whenever you need them. Those objects can be:

- Objects you've created
- Objects you've inserted from the Design Gallery
- Design Gallery objects you've modified

What actually happens is that you create a design set for the current publication (the various gallery choices such as Classic, Plain, and so on are design sets). You can put as many design elements into this design set as you like. Incidentally, ease of access is one good reason to add objects that you've inserted from the Design Gallery to a new design set for the publication. If you're using the object (perhaps it's a title you want to use on multiple pages), you don't have to open the Design Gallery—find the right design set, and then find the graphic.

To create your own design set:

1. Select the graphic you want to add to the design set.
2. Open the Design Gallery, then choose More Designs. The drop-down menu has two additional choices at the bottom:

- Designs for the current publication (the menu choice actually has the name of the current publication)
- Add Selection to Design Gallery

3. Choose Add Selection to Design Gallery. A dialog box asks you to confirm that you want to start a new design set (and reminds you that you cannot add objects to the current Publisher design set).

4. Choose Yes to bring up the Adding an Object dialog box (see Figure 35.5).

FIG. 35.5

Assign a name and a category to your object so you can place it in your new design set.

5. Give the object a name and then choose a name for a category you want to create for this design set (name your categories in a way that makes sense for you; there's no real rule about it).

6. Choose OK to move to the Create New Category dialog box, where you enter a description of this new category.

7. Choose OK when you have entered the description and you are returned to the Design Gallery dialog box.

The Design Gallery title bar indicates you are in the design set for your publication, which has one category and one item in that category. This design set is available whenever you work on this publication. (It's available when you're working on other publications also as described later in this section.)

You can choose other objects from your publication and add them to your design set by following the previous steps. As you add categories, they become available on the Category list so you can select one when you're using a category you've already established (instead of creating a new category).

T I P

If you've inserted a graphic from the Design Gallery into your publication and you think you'll be using it multiple times, put it in the publication's design set so you don't have to hunt for it throughout the Design Gallery. Even better, if you've manipulated and changed a graphic that originally came from the Design Gallery, make sure you put it into your design set (all that work and creativity means you'll show it off by using it over and over).

Part
VIII

Ch
35

Hereafter, whenever you load this publication, the design set is accessible in the Design Gallery.

To reach the design set when you are working in the publication attached to it, open the Design Gallery and choose More Designs. The bottom of the menu will display the name of your current publication design set. Select it and choose the graphic you want to place into the publication.

To reach the design set when you're working in another publication:

1. Open the Design Gallery and choose More Designs.

2. Choose Other Designs from the drop-down list.

3. From the Other Designs dialog box (see Figure 35.6), choose the publication that has the design set you want to use.

FIG. 35.6

Select the publication that has the needed design set attached to it.

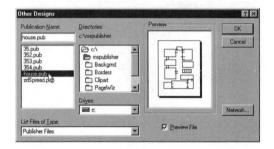

4. Double-click the file name for the publication that has the desired design set. The Design Gallery displays the design set (you are not opening the publication, just its design set).

N O T E   There's a small problem with this system in that you cannot tell by looking at the Other Designs dialog box whether or not a publication has a design set attached. And, of course, you can't tell which designs are in a design set even if your memory is good enough to know which publications have design sets. There is no easy solution to this problem. I've tried keeping a chart, which I can never find on my desk; Post-It notes, which lose their stickiness so they fall on the floor and become trash; and several courses in improving my memory. Nothing worked; I was constantly opening one file after another.

When the time came that I was using my publication designs often, I came up with a solution that works, but it is a bit onerous. I keep one publication that is nothing but my favorite designs. If I change a graphic or invent one for another publication, I immediately open my special publication, head for the last publication I was working on (I can remember that much), and open its design set. I insert the new design into my graphics publication, close it, and go back to work on the original publication. Then, whenever I need one of my own designs, there's only one file name I have to remember. ■

Using the Special Elements PageWizard

Apart from the main Publisher PageWizard that helps you through the design and planning of a publication, there's a PageWizard tool on the Publisher toolbar. It's a PageWizard you use in publications that are already in progress.

The PageWizard tool is designed to help you place any of these special elements into your publication:

- Calendar
- Coupon
- Ad
- Logo

Just click the appropriate element from the menu list to bring up the PageWizard, which walks you through the process (exactly what a Microsoft wizard is supposed to do).

Creating a Calendar

Newsletters, brochures, and other publications frequently need some form of a calendar to provide details about events. Creating an appropriate calendar is easy, because the PageWizard does most of the work:

1. Click Calendar in the PageWizard menu list, then drag a rectangle on your page to lay out the position for the calendar. You can adjust the size and position later, so it's not all that important to be precise.

2. When you release the mouse button, the Calendar PageWizard Design Assistant opens (see Figure 35.7), and you must choose a style for your calendar. Click Next after you've made your selection.

FIG. 35.7
Start with a style that matches your publication or your personality.

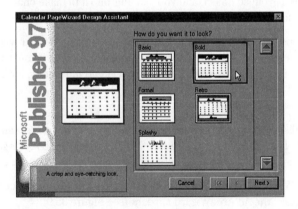

3. Answer the PageWizard's questions, choosing Next as you pass each milestone. The answers you give determine whether your calendar will have a picture, and will print the dates in boxes designed to have plenty of space to write notes to yourself.

4. Choose the year and the month for this calendar, then continue to make choices about other details.

5. Choose Create It when the PageWizard announces that all the questions have been answered.

6. After a few seconds, the PageWizard finishes its work and asks if you want step-by-step help as you finish up the design of the calendar. Select Yes or No depending on your mood or your sense of adventure. If you opt for help, the Help system opens in the Publisher window with the appropriate help topics available.

The calendar is on the page (see Figure 35.8), ready for you to add any finishing touches you think are necessary.

FIG. 35.8
The calendar appears on the page and is usable as-is, but most of us can't help tinkering a bit.

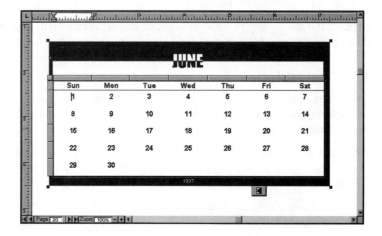

The calendar is a grouped object, and you can ungroup it to make changes to any individual element (don't forget to regroup it).

The gray buttons that appear across the top and sides of the calendar when you select it are row and column selectors. Click one to select its row or column if you want to change anything (you might want to format the columns for the weekend differently, for instance).

Creating an Ad

If you use Publisher to create a newsletter, it's quite possible you have an occasion to insert an advertisement. That could mean you're creating an ad for somebody or some company that is buying space in your newsletter, or you're running an ad to promote an event.

Click the PageWizard tool, choose Ad, and drag across the page to place the ad. When you release the mouse, the Ad AreaWizard appears (see Figure 35.9).

Make selections as needed, choosing Next to move on. If you like, the wizard will even suggest phrases for your ad.

The finished ad is placed on the page, ready for you to customize it with your own text (see Figure 35.10).

FIG. 35.9
Choose an ad type that fits your purpose.

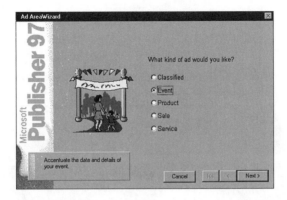

FIG. 35.10
To complete the ad, insert the appropriate information in the placeholders.

Almost invariably, the ad (like the other special elements) is a grouped object. Some of the changes you have to make do not require that you ungroup the object, because the individual elements are accessible while grouping is in place. Other changes, such as manipulating the basic design of an element, do require ungrouping.

It is not necessary to ungroup the object to insert graphics or text in the placeholder frames. Using the ad seen in Figure 35.10, let's customize this object (different ads or ad designs may require different procedures of course).

Click the graphic (in this case, it's a car), and a red line outlines its frame, indicating it can be manipulated while in the group. Right-click and choose Insert Clip Art from the shortcut menu, then select a graphic you like better.

Click the Date, Time, and Location placeholder to display its frame. In this case, the mouse pointer is a Move pointer, indicating this is not a text box but a graphic (WordArt is a safe guess). Double-click the element to open WordArt and make the appropriate changes to the text. You can also change the graphic look by changing the shape, font, or anything else.

Part
VIII

Ch

Click the telephone number at the bottom of the ad. The mouse pointer changes to a Drag pointer, indicating this is a text box. Click the text and use standard procedures to make changes. It might be easier if you press F9 to zoom in on the text.

When you've finished, the ad has all the correct information (see Figure 35.11).

FIG. 35.11
The information is correct, but I really don't like the way the graphic art looks.

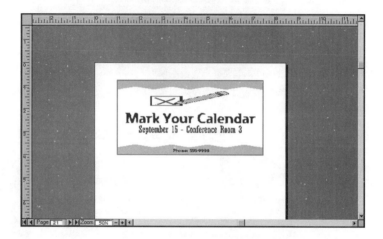

When you replace clip art, if the new art is not in the same aspect ratio as the original art, the replacement doesn't work properly (as in this case, where the new art work looks terrible, as if it's been squished). You can either insert a different piece of artwork that fits the aspect ratio or change the shape of the frame to make the artwork look better.

If you want to change the shape of the frame, you must ungroup the object.

When you ungroup an object, you see the individual sizing handles for each element. They are grayed out, however, and you must click the element you want to manipulate in order to work with it. Don't forget to regroup when you are finished—drag a rectangle around the elements and then click the Group button that appears when you release the mouse.

Make a decision based on your time, skill, and fussiness levels.

TROUBLESHOOTING

When you change any of the basic elements in a grouped object, especially size, there's a domino effect, and you can find yourself in a lot of trouble. Changing a horizontal frame to a more vertical aspect in order to use a particular piece of clip art usually means the new shape and size overlaps another existing element. Change or move that element, and you're likely to bump into another element or a border. As a result, sometimes the more you tinker, the worse it gets.

To prevent getting into so much trouble that you have to start all over again (a real pain if you've already gone to the trouble of inserting text in placeholder frames), take a one-step-at-a-time approach, and save between steps. Save your publication before you start tinkering, and each time you make a change save again. Make one change at a time. The first change that causes you a real headache is the point at which you should close the publication without saving and open it again to the last saved revision.

Creating a Coupon

Coupons are great incentives, and they don't have to be money-back coupons. You can use coupons to get people to sign up for volunteer work, join a committee, or respond to any other type of request. Coupons are also a good way to get information from people; just have them fill out the appropriate lines and return the coupon (much easier than having them call you).

Click the PageWizard tool and choose Coupon from the menu to bring up the Coupon Page Wizard Design Assistant. Answer the questions and make your selections, then tweak the finished object to make it perfect.

Coupons offer a wide variety of configuration options. If you think of a coupon as a vehicle for collecting information (in addition to the typical uses of a coupon), you can use those options to define a really useful element for your publication. The configuration can include check boxes, expiration dates, mailing addresses, and other useful items.

Creating a Logo

The *Logo PageWizard* is a robust design assistant that offers so many permutations and combinations of graphics, layout, and text that it's impossible to explain them adequately. You'll be amazed at the things you can do with this feature.

The choices are almost overwhelming, and they begin when you click the PageWizard tool and choose Logo from the menu. The Logo PageWizard Design Assistant appears (see Figure 35.12) and your decision-making begins.

FIG. 35.12
Logo designs for company recognition or brand recognition are easily created with the help of this wizard.

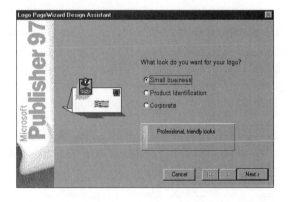

As you go through the wizard, you'll be able to choose graphics, tag lines (the text that always appears with the logo), and other important elements that go into the design of a logo. You can substitute your company initials for artwork (instead of a graphic image) if you think it will be effective (or it fits the advice of your marketing expert).

Inserting Special Objects

There are some wonderfully clever and creative additions you can make to your publication, but they only work if you're going to distribute your masterpiece via a computer. That means anything from providing a copy of it to another user for his or her machine, to sending the publication to the Internet. These additions are sound and video clips, elements that printers cannot produce. In Publisher, sound and video clips are part of the Clip Gallery. The process is similar to adding clip art.

N O T E   The important thing to bear in mind as you're having all this fun creating an electronic publication is that adding sound and video swells the size of the publication document immensely. On the other hand, the size of today's hard drives may not make that such a problem. If you want to ship the file to a reader (on disk or over a modem), be reassured that compressing these files (for instance, with WinZip) makes an enormous difference—there is plenty of "air" in a large publication file so it zips down to a small percentage of its original size. ■

In order to send a file so the recipient can read your publication on a computer, the reader has to have Publisher installed.

You can also save your publication as a Web document, and it can be read by anyone with a browser (see Chapter 36, "Publishing to the Web," for more information).

Inserting a Sound Clip

You can put a sound clip into your publication so your electronic readers can hear the music, sound effect, or other sound that enhances the story they're reading:

1. Click the Picture tool and drag a rectangle on the page to hold the clip.
2. Right-click the rectangle and choose Insert Clip Art from the shortcut menu.
3. When the Microsoft Clip Gallery appears, move to the Sounds tab (see Figure 35.13).
4. Scroll through the clips to find one with a name that sounds as if it might be just what you're looking for. Select that object and choose Play to hear it. When you find the right one, double-click it (or choose Insert from the dialog box).

T I P   When you select a sound object, the bottom of the dialog box displays the keywords associated with that object. Most of the time, those keywords include descriptive terminology that describes the type of sound. For example, if you see the keywords `Lazy Easy Listen`, you probably won't use the clip in a story about blood and gore.

When the sound clip is inserted, an icon appears in the picture frame you prepared for it. You can move and resize the frame, color the object, and generally treat the icon and frame as you would a graphic.

FIG. 35.13
Find the built-in sound clips in the Microsoft Clip Gallery.

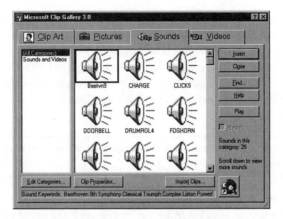

Double-clicking the icon plays the sound clip. The sound file is actually embedded in the publication and travels with it. The original sound file does not have to be accessible when the recipient of your publication wants to play the sound.

It's important to understand that fact: The sound clip is embedded. Most of the time, you have to insert your Office 97 CD to fetch the sound clip (unless you installed Office with the option to transfer everything in the Clip Gallery to your hard drive, which is not recommended). It's not necessary for the recipient to have installed the sound files on the local hard drive, or to have the Office CD accessible.

Inserting Other Sound Files

You can also embed sound files that aren't in the Clip Gallery using any other sound files you have available. To accomplish this, do the following:

1. Insert a picture frame, then right-click it and choose Insert Object from the shortcut menu.
2. When the Insert Object dialog box opens (see Figure 35.14), select Create from File.

FIG. 35.14
Embed an existing file into your document with the Insert Object dialog box.

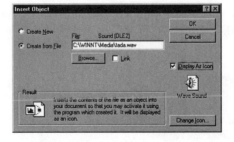

3. Enter the path to the file you want to embed, or click Browse to find it.
4. Select Display as Icon, then choose OK to insert this sound object into your publication.

The file is embedded—the reader does not have to have the file locally. However, the reader does have to have the software to play that file. For .WAV files, you can take it for granted that the sound will play back, but if you use other sound files (files with extensions of .MID or .RMI for example), the reader will have to have a system configured to handle that sound file type. Of course, you can add a note to that effect within the publication, or insert a short note in the picture frame, under the icon (perhaps something like **This file requires the MS Media Player**).

 T I P You can change the icon for an embedded object by choosing Change Icon and making a selection from the available icons.

If you have the software and equipment to record sound files, you can narrate or add comments to your electronic publication. After you've recorded and saved the sound file, insert it as an object as described earlier.

Editing Sound Files

Once a sound file has been embedded, right-click the icon to see the shortcut menu, and you'll notice that a menu choice has been added for this file.

Edit Clips from the Clip Gallery   A sound clip from the Clip Gallery has a shortcut menu item, *Sound (OLE2) Object*, with a submenu that includes Play, Edit, Open, and Convert. You can make changes to the sound clip by choosing Edit from the submenu, which opens the Microsoft Sound Recorder.

If the clip is exactly the musical accompaniment you want but is too long, you can shorten it. Before you do, however, you need to decide whether you want to shorten the clip by stopping it when the required amount of time has expired, or starting the clip at some point past the beginning so that it gets to the end in the required time.

To start the sound clip at the beginning and stop it when the allotted time has expired, follow these steps:

1. Click Play and keep an eye on the Position display on the left side of the dialog box.

2. When the duration of the music is near the allotted time and the music has an obvious place to stop (not in the middle of a musical passage; pick a pause), click Stop (see Figure 35.15).

FIG. 35.15

If you need 30 seconds of music, you might have to live with a bit more or less to avoid a tasteless sudden end to your selection.

3. Choose Edit, Delete After Current Position, which eliminates everything past your stopping point. You'll be asked to confirm that you want to delete all the data after that position.

4. Choose File, Exit & Return to *<the name of your publication>*.

The embedded selection is now shorter, which is a nice thing to do for the recipient of this publication because there's no way to stop an embedded sound clip once you've double-clicked it.

If you plan on starting the selection at some point that gets you to the end in the required amount of time, you'll have to do the math, which means you have to get hold of your calculator, or find a pencil and paper (if you still remember how to add and subtract with a pencil). Then do the following:

1. The total length of the sound clip is displayed on the right side of the Sound Object dialog box. Subtract from that number the time you want to allot for this clip to play. The result is the position at which the clip must start.

2. Click Play and keep an eye on the number of elapsed seconds displayed on the left side of the dialog box.

3. When there is a break in the music at the correct number of seconds (listen for a place that would work as a good starting point for the clip), click Stop (see Figure 35.16).

FIG. 35.16
Starting a clip in the middle lets you play it for the allotted time and still hear the dynamic ending.

4. Choose Edit, Delete Before Current Position (you'll be asked to confirm the deletion).

5. Choose File, Exit & Return to *<name of your publication>*.

Edit Other Sound Files   Sound files that did not come from the Clip Gallery have the shortcut menu item *Media Clip Object*, with the same submenu choices. Choose Edit to manipulate them.

Many sound files are associated with Microsoft Media Player (.MID files and .RMI files, for example), so that's usually the application that opens when you want to edit the file (see Figure 35.17).

FIG. 35.17
The Media Player has controls for playback options.

Part
VIII

Ch
35

With the Media Player, you can establish configuration options for playback.

Choose Edit, Options to bring up the Options dialog box so you can configure the environment when the sound file is played back (see Figure 35.18).

FIG. 35.18

Establish playback configuration in the Options dialog box.

You can make the choices you want, but there are a couple that you should pay careful attention to:

- Select Control Bar on Playback to make sure the Media Player's Control Bar window opens when the sound file is double-clicked. If the Control Bar isn't available, the reader has no way to stop the music until it's over, and because some music files can play for many minutes, that's not very nice. The Control Bar that appears during playback is not the same one that was launched when you chose to edit the file—it is missing the menu bar.

- Select Play in Client Document so that when the sound file icon is double-clicked, the music file is loaded. Otherwise, the Media Player opens and the reader has to load the file.

- If you opt for Auto Repeat, the sound file will play over and over and over until the reader stops it. Do not select this option unless you also select the Control Bar on Playback option so the poor person can stop the performance (in case he doesn't know to right-click and use the shortcut menu to get to the Media Player).

To change the length of the selection, do the following:

1. Choose a starting point and click the Start Selection button.
2. Choose an ending point and click the End Selection button. (Listen to the music as you do this so you end up with a section of music that you like from beginning and end.)
3. Choose Edit, Selection to see that the Set Selection dialog box has recorded your choices (see Figure 35.19), and choose OK.

FIG. 35.19

You can change the length of music files that are too long.

4. Choose File, Exit & Return to *<name of publication>*, confirming the changes when asked.

T I P When the Set Selection dialog box appears, you can tweak the selection a bit by changing the numbers. For example, if you think you ended the selection a bit abruptly, add a couple of seconds to the end time.

Inserting a Video Clip

Like sound enhancements, video adds a slick touch to your electronic publication. The process is similar to adding sound clips:

1. Create a picture frame, then right-click it to bring up the shortcut menu. Choose Insert Clip Art.

2. When the Clip Gallery opens, move to the Videos tab and find the video you want to insert (see Figure 35.20). Double-click its icon.

FIG. 35.20

The video files in the Clip Gallery display the icon that appears in your publication, and the length of the video playback.

3. Resize the picture frame so it is large enough to see the video properly.

Double-clicking the video icon starts the playback as long as the reader has the software to run the file—for example, MS Media Player for .AVI files.

You aren't limited to using the video clips in the Clip Gallery; you can also embed a video file from your own collection. Use the same procedure described earlier for embedding audio clips.

You can edit the video clip in the same manner as editing an audio clip. ●

Part
VIII

Ch
35

Publishing to the Web

Publisher is designed to make it easy to distribute your publication via the Internet. You can build a publication from the ground up with the Web in mind, or you can convert an existing publication into an electronic document.

This chapter covers the features available in Publisher for Web publications. ■

Create a Web publication

From the first step, plan and design a publication that the world can read over the Internet.

Check and preview a Web publication

Before you send your publication to your Web site, you can use Publisher's tools to make sure everything works as it should.

Convert a publication to a Web document

You can take an existing document from paper to the Web, with plenty of assistance from Publisher for each step you need to invoke.

Creating a Web Publication

Publisher has built-in features and tools for creating documents that are published to the Internet instead of paper. You can use preconfigured layouts, or work one page at a time; either way, your goal of producing a professional-looking Web document is easy to accomplish.

To start a Web publication from scratch (as opposed to converting an existing publication, which is covered later in this chapter in the section "Converting Publisher Documents for the Web"), you can choose between two methods:

- Use the Web Page Design Assistant to have the PageWizard provide a layout that's perfect for the Web.

- Build your own publication, a page at a time, using the Web page layout available in Publisher.

Using the Web Site PageWizard

The Publisher Web Site PageWizard is, like all wizards, a step-at-a-time approach to building a full, multipage Web publication. Choose File, Create New Publication and choose Web Site from the PageWizard (see Figure 36.1).

FIG. 36.1

The PageWizard has pre-defined Web publications you can use to make everything easier.

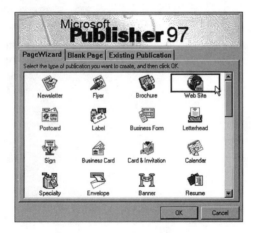

As with all wizards, using this feature is a matter of answering questions and making choices. You'll choose a layout style, button/icon styles, and so on. The permutations and combinations are immense (too many to discuss effectively), but there are some choices you should be prepared for so you don't have to make hasty decisions. For instance, if you're creating a multiple-page Web document, the wizard asks questions about your plans for those pages (see Figure 36.2).

If you chose a personal Web site instead of a business site, the choices offered would be different, of course. And, remember that regardless of your responses, nothing is etched in stone—you can change the text and graphics to make any page suitable for a different type of information.

FIG. 36.2
What type of information would you like to have on your company's Web site?

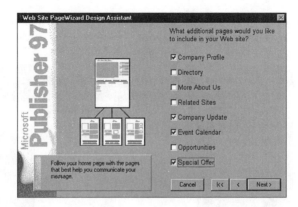

Personalizing the Layout   When the PageWizard has all your answers, your Web pages are created. Placeholders await your own creativity as you insert your text and pictures (see Figure 36.3).

FIG. 36.3
Replace the placeholder graphics and text to start building your own Web publication.

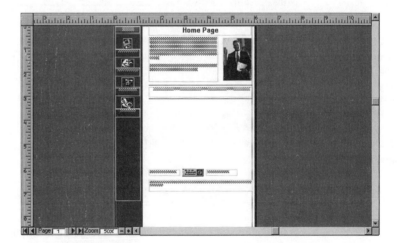

Your home page is the logical place to start:

- Create an opening message.
- Build hyperlinks for the icons, as well as for the special text that's established for hyperlinks.
- Replace the graphics with your own pictures or art work.

Begin with an opening message and then use other parts of the page for any important or timely information (see Figure 36.4).

Checking the Hyperlinks   Publisher has created the additional pages of your publication, and icons and text are ready for hyperlinks.

Right-click an icon or one of the hypertext entries and choose Hyperlink to bring up the Hyperlink dialog box (see Figure 36.5).

FIG. 36.4

Your home page is the first thing readers see— make sure you let them know what you're all about.

FIG. 36.5

You can make changes to your hyperlink as you like, using any of the other available options.

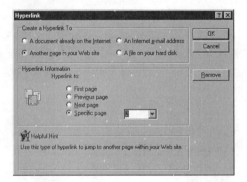

The dialog box is preconfigured to match the icon or hypertext entry you're working on (that's the beauty of letting the PageWizard do the work for you).

Move through all the pages of your publication, adding text, changing graphics, and checking the hyperlinks. You can add pages, but be sure to redo your hyperlinks to accommodate the new pages.

Checking the Publication   When you are finished, you should run the Design Checker, which checks for hyperlinks, file downloading efficiency, and other Web issues. You should also launch a test run. See the section "Running the Design Checker" later in this chapter for details about performing these steps.

T I P If you use the standard layout and format provided by the PageWizard, and don't add pages or make other major revisions, the odds of having serious Internet-related problems, such as graphics that don't display properly, are greatly diminished.

Using Blank Web Pages

The other method of creating a Web publication from scratch is to use the Web page as a template as you build your document.

Choose File, Create New Publication, then go to the Blank Page tab of the Publisher opening window and choose Web Page. In effect, you'll be designing a page at a time, using the Web page features available in Publisher.

You build each page, then add the next page, in the same manner you create a publication that will be printed on paper. However, there are special considerations you have to bear in mind because you are printing to the Web, and this section covers those concepts.

Understanding Text on a Web Page   The word *text* has a very narrow definition when you're publishing to the World Wide Web. If you print to paper, text can mean any group of characters that spell words or list numbers. It doesn't matter how the text got there—it can be read. WordArt, text on top of a graphic shape, text that's enclosed in a fancy border—whatever shape it's in, it's text. The printer just prints the pictures and characters, and readers read the text.

On the Web, however, you don't hand out the hard copies of your publication the way you do with a printed publication. The publication has to appear on a reader's screen, and may even occasionally be downloaded. The Internet handles text faster and more easily than it handles graphics, so you'll want to make sure that text is really text and is treated as text.

When you're creating a publication for the Web, if you add any graphic element to text, it is no longer treated as text—it's a graphic. It takes longer to load on the screen, and it takes longer to download.

The following text is considered a graphic in a Web publication:

- WordArt
- Text with border art
- Text in a frame that has a pattern fill
- Text in a frame that has a gradient fill
- Text in any table
- Text that has been rotated
- Text that is wrapped around any object
- Text that overlaps any other object

Understanding Graphic Regions   Whenever there is any overlap of objects on a Web page, the objects automatically become a graphic, and the rectangular area that is needed to enclose both of the objects is called a *graphic region* (see Figure 36.6). *Graphic* is the operative term here, because even if the two objects are plain text boxes—since they overlap and form a graphic region—the text is treated as a graphic.

FIG. 36.6
An imaginary line that would enclose both objects forms the graphic region, which is always treated as a graphic object on the Web.

However, because you chose a Web blank page to create your publication, the Publisher Web features are in effect, and you're warned about the consequences of letting your text boxes overlap even the slightest bit (see Figure 36.7).

FIG. 36.7
Publisher knows the rules for Web publications and keeps you alert by warning you when you might inadvertently blunder.

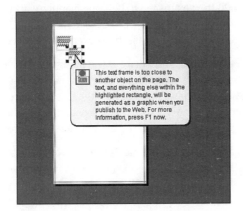

Adding Web Graphics   If you're designing for the Web, there are some conventions you should pay attention to, especially those that deal with special graphics that users expect to see on the Web, such as buttons and page dividers.

The Design Gallery has three Web graphics available for you to place on your Web pages: Web e-mail buttons, Web page buttons, and Web page dividers, all of which are present in Figure 36.8.

Adding Hyperlinks   You can place a hyperlink in any object in your publication. In fact, you can place a hyperlink on a specific part of an object.

The following hyperlink targets are available on the Hyperlink dialog box:

- A document already on the Internet, which requires the address of that target document. This is usually in the form **http://www.url/<_document_>.html**.
- An Internet e-mail address.
- Another page in your Web site, which could be the first, previous, next, or a specific page.
- A file on your hard disk, which requires the path and file name. The file can be on your local drive, on a connected computer on your network, or on a server.

FIG. 36.8

The Web graphics in the Design Gallery are available in all of the default design sets.

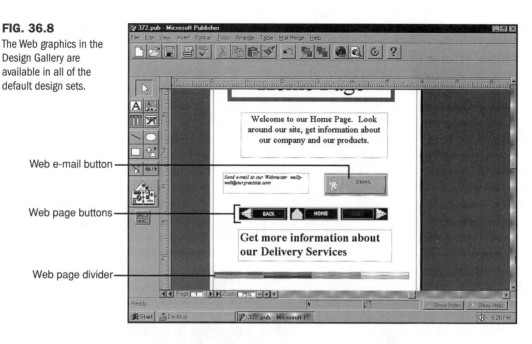

Web e-mail button

Web page buttons

Web page divider

To insert a hyperlink in a graphic object, right-click it, and choose Hyperlink to display the Hyperlink dialog box (see Figure 36.9).

FIG. 36.9

I need a hyperlink to an e-mail address for the e-mail button I inserted from the Design Gallery.

To insert a hyperlink in text, select the text, right-click and choose Hyperlink from the shortcut menu. The Web page buttons in the Design Gallery are actually text boxes in a graphic shape. You must select the text, then hyperlink to the appropriate page.

To insert a hyperlink in one place of a graphic instead of the entire graphic, use the *Picture Hot Spot tool*. This is a handy device that appears on the Publisher toolbar when you are working on a Web page. Click the tool, then drag a small rectangle on the spot of the graphic you want to use for the hyperlink. When you release the mouse, the Hyperlink dialog box appears and you can specify the target.

> **T I P**   Don't worry if the hot spot doesn't seem very visible while you're working in Publisher (there's a pale
> outline only). When your publication is on the Web, the mouse pointer changes to a hand (the
> traditional hyperlink signal) when it is inside the area of the rectangle.

Figure 36.10 shows one way to use hot spots. There are four hot spots on the map (three in the United States and one on the other side of the Atlantic). When the reader clicks any hot spot, he is sent to a page related to that hot spot. For example, clicking the hot spot on the Western side of the United States causes a jump to the page on Delivery Information for Western United States. There are pages for each of the hot spots on the map.

FIG. 36.10
Use a hot spot to pinpoint a part of a graphic for a hyperlink.

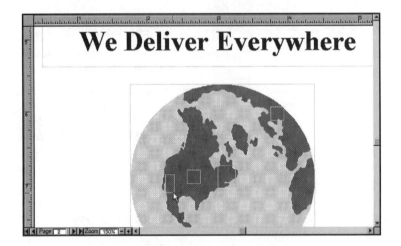

Changing Text Hyperlink Colors   It's traditional on the Web to have text hyperlinks display in a different color, and to have that color change once the hyperlink has been clicked. This is how people know which hyperlinks they've followed and which are still unvisited links. To establish this for your text hyperlinks, do the following:

1. Choose Format, Background and Text Colors.

2. When the Background and Text Colors dialog box opens, move to the Custom tab (see Figure 36.11).

3. You can also add Texture to the background of your Web page. Choose Browse and select a picture (see Figure 36.12).

Changes made to colors for text hyperlinks don't affect (and are not affected by) other text color changes you make in your publication.

FIG. 36.11
Choose the colors you want to use to highlight text hyperlinks.

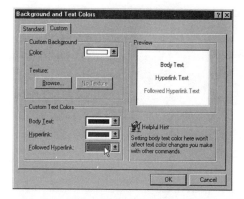

FIG. 36.12
A textured background can add zip to your Web page.

Publishing Web Pages

Before you place your publication on your Web site, you have to check every aspect of it. How does it look; is it readable? Are there hyperlinks that don't work? What other problems are there?

Publisher has a tool that can take a careful, critical look at your publication and point out problems. This tool, called *Design Checker*, can be used for paper publications as well as Web publications.

Running the Design Checker

To run the Design Checker, choose it from the Tools menu. The first dialog box asks if you want to check all the pages or just specific pages. It's best, the first time you check your publication, to check all pages. Click the Options button to see the Options dialog box (see Figure 36.13), which lists the problems the Design Checker is capable of looking for. There's rarely a reason to deselect any of them, unless you've been checking, fixing, checking, fixing, and now have reached the point where you know there could only be specific problems left.

When the Design Checker finds a problem it notifies you, and offers one or more solutions (see Figure 36.14).

FIG. 36.13
The Design Checker has a way to check for problems you probably never even thought of.

FIG. 36.14
The Design Checker has identified a problem and has a number of suggestions for fixing it.

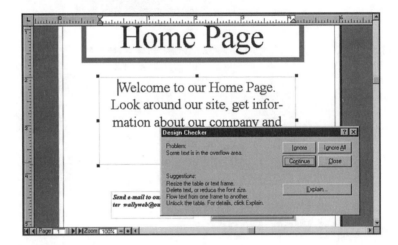

You have several choices for attending to each problem that's presented:

- Move to the page and fix the problem.

- Choose Ignore to do nothing about the problem and have Design Checker continue its work.

- Choose Ignore All to tell Design Checker not to notify you of any other occurrences of this particular problem.

- Choose Continue to move on to the next problem after you have fixed this one.

- Choose Close if you want to exit the Design Checker and work on your publication before running it again.

- Choose Explain to learn more about the problem, and to see suggestions for fixing it (see Figure 36.15). Click the icon next to a suggestion to see step-by-step procedures for implementing the solution.

Most of the time, you should either fix things yourself or use the Explain button to guide you through a solution. Go into the publication and make whatever changes are necessary. Don't close the Design Checker. Then return to the dialog box and choose Continue.

FIG. 36.15
Possible solutions for
this problem are
displayed in the Help
system.

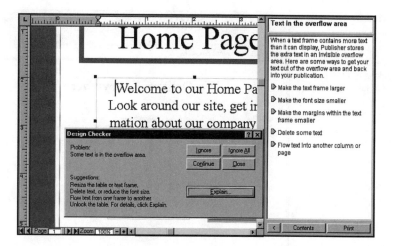

 TIP One of the common problems the Design Checker finds is that clip art is not in the same proportion as its original file. That's usually because you've tweaked the frame to make it fit better, and most of the time this doesn't really affect the look of the clip art. It's almost always perfectly safe to choose Ignore or Ignore All when this problem is brought to your attention.

When the Design Checker finishes checking a Web publication, it asks if you want to check the download times for the pages in your publication. It's a good idea to respond Yes. If a particular page (usually with large complicated graphics, for instance) is found to be a potential problem for Web readers by being so large that the download time is annoying, you'll be notified. You should try to make the page less complicated.

After the Design Checker has completed its work and you've made the appropriate changes, save the publication.

Previewing the Publication

The next step is to see what the publication will look like on the Web. Choose File, Preview Web Site to carry out this test. Your Internet browser opens and your pages are in the window (see Figure 36.16).

Move through the pages, clicking every hyperlink in sight (take notes about problems; you cannot make changes when you're working in your browser). When you're finished, you are returned to the Publisher window, and a Preview Troubleshooter is displayed so you can get advice about any problems you found.

Putting Your Publication on the Web Site

Publishing to the Web is really not much more than copying your publication to your Web server. You also have the option of publishing to a local subdirectory and moving it to the Web after that.

FIG. 36.16

The mouse pointer turns into a hand when it's on the hot spot—and clicking it moved me to the right page. Hooray!

During the process of publishing to your Web site, the title of your Web site (on the title bar of the browser window) takes the name of the publication when you move the publication to the Web. All your pages are converted to HTML, and your home page takes the name INDEX.HTML.

TROUBLESHOOTING

There are some Internet Service Providers who do not use the convention of naming home pages INDEX.HTML. If such an ISP is handling your Web pages, you must change the name of the home page file. Because Publisher does not have a page-naming command, you must use the Web Site Properties command on the File menu to open a dialog box to effect this change. When the Web Site Properties dialog box is displayed, enter the required Home Page File Name and File Name Extension (these are two separate fields in the dialog box).

To publish directly to your Web site, choose File, Publish to Web. If the Web Publishing Wizard is installed on your computer, move through the wizard to upload the files. If the Web Publishing Wizard is not installed, a dialog box appears that offers to download the software for you. Answer Yes to open your browser and begin the download.

If you're not ready to upload to the Web, you can publish to a directory (folder) on your computer; choose File, Publish Web Site to Folder. The Select a Folder dialog box opens with a default selection (see Figure 36.17).

Choose New Folder to create a folder for the publication, or choose Network to put the folder on any connected computer.

FIG. 36.17
Store your Web publi-
cations locally and
upload them whenever
you want.

When you publish to a folder, all the same processes take place (page conversion to HTML files, graphics conversion to GIF images).

Converting Publisher Documents for the Web

If you've produced a super publication and think it should be shared with the world on your Web site, you can convert it. There are lots of details to attend to, but there's also lots of help from Publisher.

N O T E Be aware that there are very few printed publications that make a successful transition to the Web. The two media are quite different, and your work should be created with one or the other in mind. In fact, sometimes even if you do have the world's greatest publication, you should think about re-creating it with the Web Design Assistant instead of converting it. However, if you're determined to do this, this section gives you an overview of the process. ▨

Open the publication you want to convert (if it's already open, save it to make sure you have all your changes saved). Then choose Create Web Site from Current Publication.

The first thing that appears is an offer from Publisher to run the Design Checker—you must say Yes. The Design Checker will look for all the things expected in a Web publication (and will find none of them). This works as a blueprint for you as you add the elements you need and clean up the elements that won't work.

You will have to place hyperlinks throughout your document. Even if you only use Next and Previous buttons, your Web readers need a way to move through the publication.

You will want to insert buttons (or you can use any graphic shape) to move people to specific articles or features in your publication. Don't forget to insert a button at the target side to take them back where they started.

When you finish converting your publication, save it under a new name; do not replace your original masterpiece. ●

CHAPTER 37

An Overview of Other Small Business Edition Applications

Small Business Financial Manager

The SBFM is a software application that works with Excel to manipulate the data in your accounting software. You can design "what-if" scenarios, make financial decisions, and print customized reports.

AutoMap Streets Plus

Use this clever software to track the locations of customers, offices, family or friends.

The Office 97 SBE contains three interesting applications that are not included in the Standard or Professional editions: Microsoft Publisher, Small Business Financial Manager, and AutoMap Streets Plus. This book has chapters covering Microsoft Publisher, and we've included instructions for using the other two in the CD you received with this book.

This chapter discusses Small Business Financial Manager and AutoMap in brief, highlighting the features and giving some information about what you need to do in order to get the most out of the software. Detailed information about using these software applications is contained on the CD that's part of this book. ■

Understanding SBFM

No matter how robust your accounting software is, or how creative you can be in structuring your own reports, the database that holds your financial information isn't the right tool for creating scenarios. You cannot change data in your accounting system just to see what will happen.

Besides scenarios, detailed specialized reports may be difficult to obtain from your accounting data. Many of the accounting programs favored by small businesses do not have full report writing features, so it can be difficult to get exactly the data you want to see and compare.

The Small Business Financial Manager was designed to help you get more information from your accounting data. You don't do your bookkeeping entries into SBFM; you continue to use your accounting software and bring the data into SBFM.

The Small Business Financial Manager is not software in the way we usually think of that terminology. When the installation is finished, there's no menu item, no icon, nothing to click to launch this software. The software is an add-in for Excel.

SBFM sits between Excel and your accounting software, using its features to create documents that take advantage of both of those entities.

Built into the SBFM program are preconfigured, complicated Excel structures: scenarios and solvers. Using SBFM means never having to construct these functions yourself.

Excel and SBFM

The Small Business Financial Manager is an add-in to Excel, and you can tell when it's been added to Excel because there are two differences in your Excel window: a new menu item, Accounting, is on the menu bar; and an item called Financial Manager Help Topics is on the Help menu.

If those elements don't exist, and you know you installed the SBFM software (it's hard to forget something like that), you just have to activate it. Choose Tools, Add-Ins and place a check mark in the box next to SBFM (see Figure 37.1). In a second or two, Excel and SBFM connect.

FIG. 37.1

Enable and disable the Small Business Financial Manger with the Add-Ins dialog box.

When Excel and SBFM retrieve your accounting data, they create a duplicate of the data they find and use that duplicate for all the work that's done. Original data is not touched. Make sure your accountant understands that—accountants get extremely nervous when business people announce they're manipulating data.

Because most accounting software packages are databases, when the data is brought in, it's kept in a database format (in fact, a Microsoft Access .mdb file). SBFM understands databases generically, and specifically knows the database structure of the supported accounting software.

Supported Accounting Software

As of the time of this writing, the following accounting software applications are supported by SBFM:

- Simply Accounting for Windows v3.0 (U.S. and Canada) and 4.0 (Canada)
- ACCPAC Plus Accounting for DOS v6.1a
- DacEasy Accounting for DOS v5.0
- Great Plains Accounting for DOS v8.0, 8.1, and 8.2
- One-Write Plus for DOS v4.03
- Peachtree Complete Accounting for DOS v8.0
- Peachtree for Windows v3.0 and 3.5
- Peachtree Complete Accounting for Windows v4.0
- Timeline MV Analyst/Server v2.3, 2.4, and 2.5*
- QuickBooks for Windows v3.1 and 4.0
- Platinum Series for DOS and Windows v4.1 and 4.4*
- BusinessWorks for Windows v9.0
- M*A*S 90 Evolution/2 for DOS v1.51

Additional software may have been added to the list by the time you read this, and you can call Microsoft at 800-426-9400 to find out whether your package is now supported (or will be).

Configuring Your Accounting Software

The following criteria must be met by your accounting software setup:

- You must use accrual accounting instead of cash-based.
- You must be set up for 12 periods, but SBFM supports non-calendar fiscal years.

In addition, SBFM has a system that uses numbers for account tracking, and that system is available in the supported packages. That doesn't mean you used it when you set up your accounting software, and if that's the case, SBFM has a feature that will remap your accounts after you've imported the data. Here's an overview of the approach used by SBFM:

1110 Cash and cash equivalents

1111 Credit card receipts

1121 Accounts receivable

1122 Allowance for bad debts

1130 Inventory

1190 Other current assets

1211 Property, plant, and equipment

1212 Accumulated depreciation

1290 Other non–current assets

2110 Accounts payable

2120 Short-term debt

2130 Credit cards payable

2190 Other current liabilities

2210 Long-term debt

2240 Other non–current liabilities

3100 Equity

3200 Retained earnings

3999 Revenue/ expense clearing

4000 Net sales

5000 Cost of sales

6100 Amortization and depreciation expense

6200 Bad debt expense

6300 Officer compensation

6400 Interest expense

6500 Operating expense

7100 Non–Operating income

7200 Non–Operating expense

8000 Income taxes

Specific Software Considerations

Having had experience with almost all of the accounting packages supported by SBFM, I can point out some considerations you should be aware of. Incidentally, some of these packages have different (more robust) features in other versions—these comments are directed at the specific version supported by SBFM.

ACCPAC Plus for DOS   A/R invoicing doesn't post or track product information, so you won't be able to get SBFM reports on a by-product basis.

DacEasy   There isn't any posting (or any other detail-saving interaction) between the G/L and sales. No sales reports are available through SBFM.

Great Plains   The Chart of Accounts does not have a retained earnings account. That figure is computed and must be entered manually at year end in order to close the year. SBFM does not perform calculations on G/L reports so no equity information will be available.

Also, remapping accounts is necessary because Great Plains puts division/department information in the front of the account numbering scheme.

Peachtree for DOS   Be careful about importing data (or updating the import) so that you perform your work in SBFM before you close a period. This software deletes details during closing.

If you want to use SBFM features on sales figures, you'll have to configure Peachtree's Invoicing and Order Entry modules to provide the information. By default, Peachtree does not send the G/L information about entries from A/R invoicing or Order Entry. Make sure you choose to create G/L entries during invoicing (then go to the G/L and use Transfer Summary Journals).

Platinum for Windows 4.02   This software is designed for small business and has only a G/L. No sales reports are available from SBFM.

QuickBooks   This software maintains information it doesn't use when producing its reports, and does not give users an opportunity to customize reports. For example, sales with tax information separated out, sales reports by customer (only available if there's a product on the invoice), and other anomalies. However, the information is available (it's posted separately) and SBFM finds it. As a result, reports from SBFM may not match the line totals of reports generated from the software.

Simply Accounting for Windows   This software doesn't post or track information about product sales (although it is entered during invoicing and everything is calculated properly at that time).

Other Supported Accounting Software   My experience with Business Works and MAS90 is that most of the reports SBFM produces are already available in the software (MAS90, for example, has a cash flow report and even has a field for cash flow type in the account setup). The SBFM scenarios, however, can't be reproduced by the software.

Understanding What Data Is Imported

There may be some preliminary procedures that you'll need to perform before you can import your data. And, depending upon the way you've configured your accounting software, there may be some parts of SBFM you cannot use.

If you don't post module information to the General Ledger in detail, you won't be able to use SBFM reports that analyze that data.

In addition to G/L posting data, the following data is also imported from the G/L (if it's included in your accounting software and defined in your accounting data):

- Chart of accounts information
- Posted G/L transactions with detail

N O T E Note that if your accounting system keeps budget information in the G/L it will not be imported. ▥

Beginning balances are imported for each General Ledger account that is part of the Balance Sheet (Income Statement accounts always start with a zero opening balance, of course). If there is no beginning balance in your data (either because it's the first year you have used the software and you haven't entered the beginning balances yet, or your software doesn't maintain this information), zero is assumed.

SBFM imports some invoice information (from the A/R side) if it is present in your accounting data:

- Customers
- Products
- Quantities sold
- Detail invoice amounts
- Salespersons

Inventory information such as beginning and ending stock balances is not imported.

SBFM Built-In Reports

The SBFM Report Wizard offers to create reports, some of which you may not be able to get from your accounting software (for instance, few of the software packages supported can produce a real cash flow report—and most accounting firms charge quite a bit to produce one).

The available reports include:

- *Balance Sheet*. Standard, with prior year comparisons, with scenarios.
- *Cash Flow*. Period and YTD comparisons, rolling 12-period trend, rolling 12-period trend with projections, 1 period with scenarios, YTD with scenarios.
- *Income Statement*. Period and YTD comparisons, rolling 12-period trend, rolling 12-period trend with projections, rolling four-quarter trend, FY by period, FY by period with projections, FY by Qtr, FY by Qtr with projections, 1 period with scenarios.
- *Ratios*. Rolling 12-period trend for ratio reports, including the standard solvency, operational efficiency, and profitability reports (but not leverage ratios).
- *Sales Analysis*. Customer, totals, product, region, salesperson (showing revenue, Cost Of Sales, and/or gross profit).
- *Changes in Stockholders' Equity*. One period activity, YTD activity.
- *Trial Balance*. One period and YTD with comparisons, TB with scenarios (includes the net change for each account).

Don't forget to do an update import before producing any report.

Scenarios

What-if scenarios are extremely powerful and this is where SBFM can be a real help in planning and decision making. Before you use the data from your accounting software, take advantage of the tutorials available in SBFM.

I used the tutorials to build some very complicated scenarios, and each step was quite easy (of course, I needed an accountant to help me interpret some of the results).

One of the most useful scenarios you'll find in SBFM is the buy-versus-lease analysis (it's also one of the most complicated to build in a spreadsheet program or to perform manually). You plug in the data and get back information that helps you decide whether to use cash on hand, take a loan, or lease when you need a capital item.

There's a sample company included with SBFM that makes practicing and tutorials easy.

Part VIII

Ch

37

Understanding AutoMap Streets Plus

There are quite a few useful business tasks you can perform in AutoMap Plus, but sometimes I just have fun with it. This section is an overview of some of the features in AutoMap Streets Plus—all the detailed information about using the software and getting the most out of it for your business is on the CD that comes with this book.

After installation, launching the software sends a jazzy tune your way as the opening screen appears (see Figure 37.2).

FIG. 37.2
The AutoMap opening screen and menu choices give an indication of all the things you can do with this software.

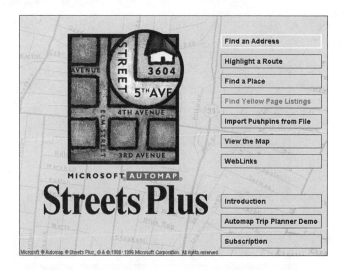

Most people head right for the "find an address" function, using some familiar landmark such as a home address, a relative's home, or perhaps a favorite restaurant. After you fill in the address, along with a city and state, a map appears with a pointer to the address (see Figure 37.3).

FIG. 37.3

You can add your own comments to the information that AutoMap provides.

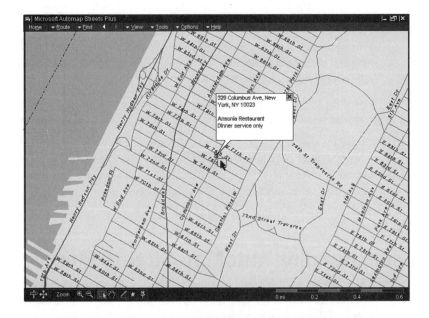

Click the pushpin to see points of interest around this address. You can move the distance slider to indicate how far you're willing to travel to get there (see Figure 37.4).

FIG. 37.4

For this address, setting a distance of five miles should provide plenty of points of interest.

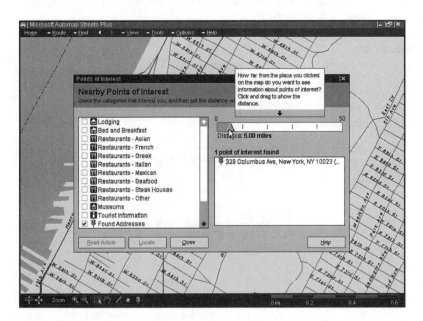

As long as you're in the neighborhood, why not add your own pushpins to anyplace nearby? Click the pushpin tool (it's on the bottom of the map) and click the location. When the Pushpin Properties dialog box appears (see Figure 37.5), choose the features you want to use.

FIG. 37.5

Your own pushpins can be attached to information as short as a name, or as long as a detailed note.

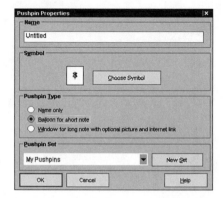

If you have a customer listing or any other address list that exists as a text file, you can bring it into AutoMap and turn it into pushpins that pop up at you whenever you open a map (well, a map that includes an address from your mailing list).

Then, you can view your pushpins and get a graphic view of where your friends or customers are.

Be aware that there are lots of neighborhoods that don't exist in this software. As all of us played with AutoMap to find our own houses, there were many places we couldn't find. ●

Office 97 on the Internet

38   Creating Web Documents   773

39   Publishing to the Net   789

40   Understanding ActiveX   801

41   Publishing Web Sites with FrontPage 97   813

42   Making Your Web Sites Interactive   833

CHAPTER 38

Creating Web Documents

If you've used Microsoft's Assistants of old, or any other HTML editor for that matter, you'll appreciate the HTML support built into Office 97. Word has many dedicated HTML editors beat from the get-go. It supports a large portion of the latest HTML 3.2 standard. You can create tables or add inline images, for example. And the best part is that a person who is familiar with Word can create fabulous Web pages without learning the complicated tag language or even learning how to use a dedicated HTML editor such as Microsoft FrontPage.

In this chapter, you learn how to use Word to convert your existing documents into Web pages and how to create new Web pages using Word. This chapter doesn't assume that you know anything at all about HTML. It does assume that you have a basic knowledge of how the Internet works, however. It also presumes that you know how to use a Web browser and understand what a URL (Uniform Resource Locator) is. If not, you might want to take a look at some of Que's Internet books, such as *Special Edition Using the Internet*, Fourth Edition or even *Using the Internet*, Third Edition, a lighter introduction to the Internet than the Special Edition. ∎

Learn enough HTML to create your own Web pages

With Office, you don't have to know a lick of HTML in order to create great Web pages. You'll better understand how Web pages work, however, if you learn a few basics.

Convert your existing documents to HTML

Instead of starting a Web page from scratch, convert your existing documents to HTML. You can save any Office document as a Web page; then, you can edit that Web page in Word.

Create professional-looking Web pages with Word

Word has many full-blown HTML editors beat. It supports just about every HTML feature you'll ever need for creating impressive Web pages.

Learn the key differences in the HTML editor mode

Word works just a bit differently when you're editing a Web page than it does when you're editing a DOC file. This chapter points those differences out so you can get up-to-speed fast.

Understanding How HTML Works

You store Web pages in HTML files that are plain-text files. You can easily create or read an HTML file with any text editor—Notepad, for example. An HTML file is a combination of the content you're publishing and the specialized formatting you apply to the content. Everything you see on a Web page, including the special formatting, is represented as text within the HTML file. In that respect, HTML is much like RTF (rich-text files), only HTML is much easier to decipher.

By no means will you be able to create Web pages by hand after reading this section. If you're really interested in doing so, take a look at Que's *Special Edition Using HTML 3.2*, Third Edition. What you will be able to do is understand the HTML files that Word generates. You'll also understand why certain features work the way they do when you're editing a Web page.

NOTE One myth that I must debunk is that HTML is a programming language: HTML is *not* a programming language. I've frequently heard people describe themselves as "HTML programmers." Nonsense. *Programming* implies creating complicated applications that are procedural in nature. You learn how to work with extremely complicated constructs, algorithms, application programming interfaces, and so on. On the other hand, HTML is nothing more than a handful of keywords that specify how a document looks in combination with the contents of the document itself. ■

HTML Is a Markup Language

HTML is a language of sorts that specifies how a document looks. Call it a *tag* or *markup* language, if you want to sound like you know what you're doing. You change the format of a document by adding a tag to it that specifies exactly how you want the text to look. All HTML tags begin with an opening bracket (<) and end with a closing bracket (>). For example, the tag that makes text italic is the <I> tag. The tag that makes text bold is the <B> tag.

Both tags are *containers* because they enclose their contents. That is, you mark the beginning of the content with a tag like <B> and the ending of the content with the corresponding closing tag, </B>. Note that the closing tag begins with the forward slash (/); otherwise, it looks the same as the opening tag. You can insert text within a container, as well as additional HTML tags. To make this container concept clearer, take a look at the following example, which shows you a sentence that contains a bolded word. The <B> tag turns on bold characters, and the closing </B> turns off bold characters.

```
This sentence contains a <B>bolded</B> word.
```

Other HTML tags are not containers. They're tags that just insert a special element into the Web page or perform a specialized function within the Web page. For example, you use the <LI> tag to add a line to a bulleted list or the <BR> tag to add a line break. In either case, you don't use a closing tag to mark the end of the block.

TIP A common convention among HTML folks is to refer to a container tag by its opening name, and infer the use of its closing counterpart. For example, if I told you to use the <B> tag, you should automatically infer that you use the `</B>` tag to close the container. It's up to you to know which tags are containers and which aren't.

Many HTML tags also accept parameters called *attributes*. You use an attribute to provide additional information to the Web browser about how you want to apply a tag. If you add a tag to your Web page that creates a table, for example, you'd also use attributes to specify how many rows and columns you want in the table. Attributes are names to which you assign a value using the equal sign (=). For example, to create a link to an HTML file, you'd assign the URL of the HTML file to the HREF attribute, like this:

```
HREF=example.htm
```

You put this assignment within the opening and closing brackets of the `<A>` tag (don't put attributes in closing tags):

```
<A HREF=example.htm>
```

 Anytime that a value contains spaces, you must enclose the value within quotation marks (single or double). For example, `<A HREF="My Web Page.htm">`.

Every Web Page Follows a Basic Structure

Every HTML file follows the same basic structure. Each file begins with the `<HTML>` tag and ends with the closing `</HTML>` tag. Within the `<HTML>` container, you have two additional containers: `<HEAD>` and `<BODY>`. The `<HEAD>` container specifies title information for the Web page, while `<BODY>` contains the actual contents of the Web page. Within the `<HEAD>` container, you'll find one more container that specifies the title of the Web page as the user sees it in the Web browser's title bar: `<TITLE>`.

The following code shows you an example of a complete HTML file. In fact, you can save this code to an HTML file on your computer and then use it as a template. Note that the contents of each container are indented a couple of spaces so that you can easily see the structure of the document. Most times, you put an entire container on a single line when it's a simple container like `<TITLE>` and when it's brief.

```
<HTML>
<HEAD>
<TITLE>An Example of a Complete HTML File</TITLE>
</HEAD>
<BODY>
The actual content of the Web page goes in this container.
</BODY>
</HTML>
```

TIP While you're experimenting with HTML, you can leave out most of the tags described in this section. Most Web browsers correctly display a Web page that doesn't contain the <HEAD>, <TITLE>, or <BODY> tags.

Most HTML Tags Specify Formatting

A majority of the HTML tags that you'll use specify how a portion of the document looks in the Web browser. You can change how the text looks or indent a block of text, for example.

Much like Word, HTML has two different types of formatting: *character* and *paragraph*. You're quite used to using both character and paragraph formatting in Word, as you use both every time you create a Word document. When you choose Heading Level 1 from Word's list of styles, for instance, you're applying a paragraph format. When you click Bold in the Formatting toolbar, you're applying a character format.

N O T E *Physical* formatting specifies exactly how you want text to look. Bold, italic, and small caps are examples of physical formats. HTML also supports *logical* formatting. Logical formatting specifies what a block of text represents, such as emphasized text or a heading, and then lets the user's Web browser determine how best to display that type of text. Whenever possible, stick to logical formatting so you can let the Web browser make all the hard decisions and make sure that the Web page looks as good as possible in every Web browser that might display it. ■

Character Formatting   Character formatting includes tags like <B>, which bolds text, and <I>, which italicizes text. Table 38.1 shows you some of the character formatting tags supported by HTML 3.2. Every tag in this table is a container, which means that you must use the corresponding closing tag to turn off that bit of formatting.

Table 38.1   HTML 3.2 Character Formatting Tags

Tag	Type	Makes the Text:
<B>	Physical	Bold
<BIG>	Logical	Larger
<CODE>	Logical	A code sample
<EM>	Logical	Emphasized (usually italic)
<FONT>	Physical	Use a specific style, size, color
<I>	Physical	Italic
<PLAINTEXT>	Logical	Fixed width
<S>	Physical	Strikethrough
<SAMP>	Logical	Sample text
<SMALL>	Logical	Smaller

Tag	Type	Makes the Text:
<STRIKE>	Physical	Strikethrough
<STRONG>	Logical	Emphasized (usually bold)
<SUB>	Physical	Subscript
<SUP>	Physical	Superscript
<TT>	Logical	Teletype
<U>	Physical	Underlined
<VAR>	Logical	A placeholder
<XMP>	Logical	Example text

Part
IX
Ch
38

N O T E When a Web browser displays an HTML file, it collapses all of the white space in the document. Thus, if you insert three spaces between two words, the Web browser only displays a single space. If you add three blank lines between two lines of text in the text file, the Web browser replaces all of the blank lines with a single space and breaks the text at the right-hand edge of the window. ■

Paragraph Formatting   Paragraph formatting includes tags like <P>, which marks a normal paragraph, <H1>, which marks a level one heading, and <LI>, which marks a list item. Table 38.2 lists most of the paragraph formatting tags that HTML 3.2 supports. All of the tags in this table are containers, except for <LI>, so you must end the paragraph with the corresponding closing tag.

Table 38.2 HTML 3.2 Paragraph Formatting Tags

Tag	Formats the Paragraph As:
<ADDRESS>	A mailing address
<BLOCKQUOTE>	A block quote
<CITE>	A citation
<H1>...<H6>	A heading (levels 1 to 6)
<LI>	An entry in a list
<OL>	An ordered list (use with <LI>)
<P>	A normal paragraph
<PRE>	Unformatted text (keeps white space)
<UL>	An unordered list (use with <LI>)

Other Tags Perform Specialized Functions

The remaining HTML tags perform some sort of specialized function. The <A> tag adds a link to the Web page, for example. The <HR> tag adds a horizontal line (rule) at the location you insert it. See Table 38.3 for a list of some of these HTML tags. This table also indicates whether or not a tag is a container.

Table 38.3   HTML 3.2 Specialized Tags

Tag	Container	Description
<A>	Yes	Adds a link.
<APPLET>	No	Inserts a Java applet.
 	No	Breaks the line at that location.
<EMBED>	Yes	Embeds a multimedia file.
<FORM>	Yes	Creates a form.
<FRAME>	Yes	Creates a framed Web page.
<HR>	No	Adds a horizontal line (rule).
<IMG>	No	Inserts an image.
<OBJECT>	Yes	Inserts an ActiveX Control.
<PARAM>	No	Passes parameters to a control.
<SCRIPT>	Yes	Embeds a script in the Web page.
<STYLE>	Yes	Creates a style sheet for the page.

TIP To see these tags in action, open a Web page in Internet Explorer and choose View, Source from the main menu.

Converting Existing Documents to HTML Documents

Reuse the documents you've already created. If you work in an office environment, you've undoubtedly created dozens if not hundreds of documents. Many of these documents are ripe for your Internet or intranet Web site. For example, if you have a corporate mission statement that you created in Word, put it on your intranet so the employees can see it. If you publish financial statements that you create in Excel, you can publish those as a Web page, too. An individual resume created in Word is also a document you might want to publish on the Internet.

Expect to lose some of your formatting when you convert an Office document to HTML. HTML just doesn't support the complete range of formatting that Word or Excel does. HTML doesn't have a formatting tag that you can use to create hanging indents, for example. Thus, when you save a document that has paragraphs formatted as hanging indents, they look more like block quotes than hanging indents. You can easily clean up a converted document, though, by opening the Web page in Word and reformatting it using the HTML-specific commands that Word provides.

N O T E It's possible you didn't install Office's HTML authoring tools when you first ran the Setup program—particularly because they aren't part of the typical install. Check the Options list in Office's Setup program and see if the Web Page Authoring (HTML) option is checked. If so, you've installed the tools. If not, check it and click Continue to install the HTML authoring tools. ▪

Word Documents

Word documents are by far the most straightforward type of document to convert to HTML. Open a document and choose File, Save as HTML from Word's main menu. Provide the file name and close the dialog box. Word will give you a warning that says you're going to lose any special formatting. Dismiss the warning, and Word saves the document in your new HTML file. You won't lose the original version of the document, but you might lose any changes you made since the last time you saved it. Word immediately opens the HTML file so you can edit it using Word's specialized HTML commands.

 After you convert a document to HTML, all of the menu options and dialog boxes change to reflect only those commands that make sense in HTML. Take a look at the Insert menu, for example, and you'll see several new menu options such as Horizontal Line and Background Sound.

TROUBLESHOOTING

If you convert a document to HTML before you save any recent changes, you'll lose those changes in the original document. You will find all of your changes in the HTML version of the document, however. To add those changes back to the original document, cut and paste them from the HTML version to the original version, then reformat the text as necessary.

Excel Spreadsheets

When you convert an Excel spreadsheet to HTML, Excel saves the data as a table. You can save the table in a new HTML file, or you can add it to an existing HTML file. Because converting an Excel spreadsheet to HTML isn't as straightforward as converting a Word document, Excel provides the Internet Assistant Wizard to guide you through the steps:

1. Select the range of cells that you want to convert to HTML. Remember that a Web browser provides a very limited canvas so you want to keep the number of columns you select down to a minimum, while it doesn't matter how many rows you select.

2. Choose File, Save as HTML from Excel's main menu. You see the dialog box in Figure 38.1. Click Add to add additional ranges to the list.

FIG. 38.1

Sort the list by clicking the up- and down-arrow buttons. The order of the list determines which tables appear first in the Web page.

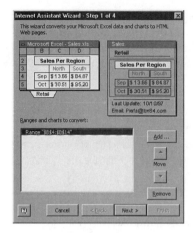

3. When you're satisfied with your choices, click Next. Choose to create a new HTML file with the ranges you selected as its only contents, or to insert the data into an existing HTML file. Click Next.

4. If you chose to create a new HTML file, provide the header information that Excel requests and click Next.

   If you chose to add your table to an existing HTML file, provide the path of the HTML file. Add the marker **<!--##Table##-->** to the HTML file at the location where you want Excel to insert the table as shown in Figure 38.2; click Next.

FIG. 38.2

Use a text editor, not Word, to add this marker to the HTML file. Word substitutes character codes for the left and right brackets; thus, Excel won't find the marker.

Marker

5. Provide the file name of the new HTML file and close the dialog box. If you inserted the tables into an existing HTML file and provided a different file name, your original HTML file remains unchanged.

 TIP After you've converted a range in a spreadsheet to HTML, you can open that HTML file in Word to dress up the table with colors and other specialized formatting.

PowerPoint Presentations

When you convert a presentation to HTML, PowerPoint creates an HTML file for each slide in the show. It also creates a variety of other HTML files for things like an information page or presentation outline. Like Excel, PowerPoint provides a wizard to guide you through the process of converting a presentation to HTML:

1. Choose File, Save as HTML from PowerPoint's main menu. You see the Save as HTML dialog box in Figure 38.3, which describes each of the steps (lots of them). Click Next.

FIG. 38.3
Each of the major steps shown in this dialog box contains a number of substeps.

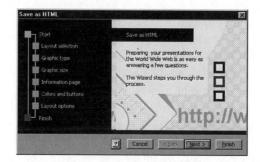

2. Choose an existing layout or create a new layout. You name a layout after you fill in all of the dialog boxes in the wizard. Thus, the first time you save a presentation as an HTML file, you won't see any layouts in the list. If you choose an existing layout, PowerPoint prefills all of the dialog boxes with the values you provided in that layout. Click Next.

3. Choose whether you want to use a simple page layout or frames. Use frames if you want to have a table of contents on the left-hand frame as well as navigation buttons in the top frame of the window. Click Next.

4. Choose the image file format that you want to use. GIF files are the norm on the Internet, while JPEG files provide more compression than GIF files. If you choose to use the PowerPoint Animation Player, PowerPoint creates a Web page that embeds an ActiveX Control that plays existing PowerPoint presentations, as opposed to converting the presentation to multiple HTML files. If in doubt, choose the GIF image format. Click Next.

5. Choose the resolution of the monitor that you anticipate the presentation to be viewed on. If you're publishing your presentation to the Internet, don't assume that the user will have anything more than a 640×480 resolution screen. If you're converting your presentation to HTML for your own purposes, choose the resolution at which you'll be showing the presentation. Click Next.

6. Provide the contact information requested. PowerPoint will create an additional HTML file that provides information about how to contact you. Definitely provide this information if you're publishing the presentation to the Internet so people know how to get in contact with you via Internet mail. Click Next.

7. Change the colors that your presentation will use. You can change the background, text, and link colors. You can also choose to make buttons transparent. If you don't change any colors, the user will see the browser's default colors or the colors he configured in the browser's preferences. Click Next.

8. Choose the style of button that you want to use. If your presentation will be part of a larger Web site, try to choose a button style that comes as close as possible to the buttons used on other Web pages. In this way, the whole Web site looks a bit more consistent. If you didn't create a framed version of the presentation, the next dialog box asks you to select the position at which you want the buttons. Click Next.

9. Specify whether or not you want to include your slide notes in the HTML files. If you're going to show your presentation using the HTML files, don't do so, as your audience will see your notes (not always a good thing). Click Next.

10. Provide the name of the folder to which you want PowerPoint to save your presentation. PowerPoint will create a subfolder for your presentation that has the same name as the presentation's file.

11. Move to the next dialog box and close it to save the presentation to disk. PowerPoint asks you for a layout name so that you can reuse all of the settings you just made. Type a name, and close the dialog box. Within the presentation's subfolder, you find an HTML file for each slide and a handful of image files.

12. Open the first page of your presentation in the Web browser to start the presentation. You find the first page in the file called index.htm. Figure 38.4 shows what a presentation looks like in Internet Explorer. It also indicates the buttons you can use to move around the presentation.

N O T E   PowerPoint saves each slide as a complete image file that it embeds into a Web page. That is, it doesn't actually add HTML tags to the Web page for each element on the slide. Thus, the images it creates might be fairly large. You'll notice as well that the presentation text has severe jagged edges, and some of the clip art is hard to decipher. ▩

Publisher Documents

Publisher provides many more HTML publishing capabilities than the other Office applications. You can use Publisher to publish a Web page with the same ease with which you create designer publications. In fact, it does such a remarkable job of converting a document to HTML that you might not even notice a difference between the Web page and the original. That's because it saves portions of the document that might not work well in HTML as images that it displays in the Web page. In particular, it saves any overlapped text areas as an image so that it preserves your formatting.

Publisher provides two different ways to convert a publication to HTML. You can change the file type to HTML in the Save As dialog box, but you'd lose most of the formatting and all of the images. The best way to convert a publication to HTML is to "publish" it to your computer:

FIG. 38.4

The quality of a Power-Point presentation that's converted to HTML is very poor compared to the original version. If you find it unsatisfactory, use the PowerPoint Animation Player described in step 4.

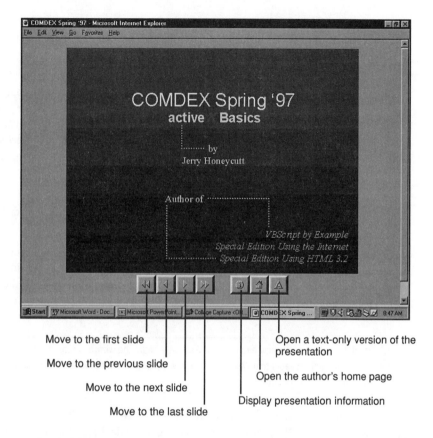

Move to the first slide

Move to the previous slide

Move to the next slide

Move to the last slide

Open a text-only version of the presentation

Open the author's home page

Display presentation information

1. With an existing Publisher document open, choose Create Web Site from Current Publication from Publisher's main menu. The phrase *Create Web Site* is a bit misleading as the only thing Publisher does is create a copy of the document that you can convert to an HTML file.

2. Publisher asks you if you want to run the Design Checker before converting the publication to HTML. The Design Checker checks the suitability of your document as a Web page. For example, it checks the download time of the page's images to make sure that they'll download quickly. Run the Design Checker if you want.

3. After you run the Design Checker, Publisher creates a copy of the document in the Publisher window. It's an untitled document.

4. Choose File, Publish Web Site to Folder. Select a folder in the Select a Folder dialog box and close it. Publisher saves the document as an HTML file and saves each image in the document as a separate graphics file.

N O T E Publisher uses the Web Publishing Wizard, which you learn about in the next chapter, "Publishing to the Net," to upload your Web pages to the Internet. You can choose File, Publish to Web from Publisher's main menu to access the Web Publishing Wizard, or you can use the wizard as described in the next chapter. ■

▶ **See** "Publishing with the Web Publishing Wizard," **p. 794**

Creating HTML Documents with Microsoft Word

You're already very familiar with how to use Word. You know how to apply character and paragraph formats. You know how to add tables to your document. Because you do know Word so well, and you use the same basic commands to create a Web page that you use to create a DOC file, I'm not going to try to teach you those commands all over again. Instead, I'll show you how those features differ while you're editing a Web page.

Creating a New Web Page

You create a new Web page like you create any other document in Word. Choose the Blank Web Page template under the Web Pages tab in the New dialog box.

You can also use the Web Page Wizard that you find in the Web Pages tab of the New dialog box. It gives you the choice of 11 different types of Web pages in combination with eight different Web page styles. Select the type of Web page you want to create in the first page of the wizard and the style on the second page. When you close the wizard, it creates the Web page as a new untitled HTML file that you can change and save to your computer's disk.

 TIP   Word allows you to preview each type of Web page while the wizard is running. When you select a Web page type, Word creates that Web page in a new window. Move the wizard's window out of the way so you can get a full view of the Web page.

After you create a new Web page, you need to give it a title. The title you provide is what the user sees in the Web browser's title bar. Choose File, Properties from the main menu to display the Properties dialog box shown in Figure 38.5, fill in the title, and close the dialog box.

FIG. 38.5
Click More to display the Properties dialog box that you're used to seeing with normal Word documents.

Adding Text to Your Web Page

You add text to your Web page as you'd normally add text to any document. However, those of you who rely on lots of tabs, spaces, and line breaks for formatting will be a bit shocked when you open the Web page in a browser. All Web browsers collapse whitespace down to a single space. If you insert three spaces in the document, the Web browser displays only a single space. If you insert tabs into the document, the Web browser again displays only a single space.

The biggest difference you find when editing a Web page is how the formatting commands work. When you open a Web page in Word, the menus, toolbars, and dialog boxes all change to reflect the features that apply to HTML documents. For example, the Font dialog box only lets you apply character formatting that is directly supported by the tags described in Table 38.1. Thus, the dialog boxes are much slimmer as you don't have nearly as many formatting options available.

Applying Character Formats   You have three different places to look to for changing character formatting. Select the block of text, and use one of the following means to apply a character format to it:

- Choose Format, Font to apply any of HTML's physical styles shown in Figure 38.6. You can also change the font's style, size, and color, too.

FIG. 38.6

You only apply physical character formatting using this dialog box. Use the Style list in the Formatting toolbar to apply logical character formatting.

- Choose Format, Case to change the case of the selected text.
- Choose one of the logical character formats in the Formatting toolbar's Style list. The items in this list roughly correspond to the logical formats described in Table 38.1.

N O T E   When editing a Web page, the Formatting toolbar contains two new buttons: Increase Font Size and Decrease Font Size. Each of these buttons changes the size of the font relative to the size of the surrounding text. ■

   You can add HTML tags of your own design to a Web page you build in Word. Use the HTML Markup style in the Formatting toolbar's Style list. Word copies anything that you format using this style directly to the HTML file directly. Make sure that you click the Show/Hide Paragraph Marks button in the Formatting toolbar so that you can see any HTML tags you add to the Web page.

Applying Paragraph Styles   While editing a Web page, Word limits your choice of paragraph styles to the choices that make sense in HTML. This corresponds to those tags shown in Table 38.2. Choose a paragraph style from the Formatting toolbar's Style list in order to apply it.

Part
IX

Ch
38

You won't find entries in the Style list for centering a paragraph or creating a list. For those styles, use the Formatting toolbar. You can left-align, center, or right-align a block of text using the toolbar, for example. You can also create a numbered or bulleted list using the Formatting toolbar.

 Click Web Page Preview in Word's Standard toolbar to preview your Web page in your Web browser. That'll give you a better idea of what your Web page is going to look like when you publish it.

Inserting Pictures into Your Web Page

You must use plenty of text in your Web page in order to communicate your message; but, nothing adds pizzazz to a Web page like graphical images. Images break up long, monotonous blocks of text, providing a place for the reader to rest his eyes. You must also remember the old saying that a picture is worth a thousand words; it's true.

You can link your Web page to an image, but that's not the best thing to do. A Web browser opens a linked image in the browser window when the user clicks the link. The image then occupies the entire browser window. Thus, the user can't see the image in relation to the surrounding text.

The better way to add images to your Web page is to add the image inline with the surrounding text. Adding an image to an HTML document works the same as adding an image to a DOC file: Choose Insert, Picture from Word's main menu; choose Clipart or From File; choose an image; and close the dialog box.

 You can align an inline image using the Formatting toolbar. If you left- or right-align an image, the surrounding text wraps around the exposed edge of the image.

Linking to Other Web Pages or Internet Resources

One of the best things you can do for the people who visit your Web page is to provide links to other Web pages. In fact, the links you add to your Web page are absolutely the only way that users can move from one page to another on your Web site. You'll also want to link your Web pages to related sites on the Internet. For example, if you publish a Web page that describes a great new product your company is producing, you might want to link that Web page to some of the periodicals that have given the product great reviews.

A link has two different parts. The part that you see on the Web page is called an *anchor*. It can be text or an image. The part that tells the Web browser the address of the Internet resource to open when the user clicks the link is called the *URL reference*. A URL reference to a file on the same computer is also known as a *relative reference*. An *absolute reference* is a URL that specifies the complete URL, including the protocol, host name, and path.

To add a link, highlight the text or image that you want to use as the anchor. Then, click the Insert Hyperlink button in Word's Standard toolbar to display the Insert Hyperlink dialog box.

Provide the URL reference of the link and close the dialog box. You'll notice that a text anchor is now underlined or a graphical anchor now has a border around it.

N O T E Word prefills the list of addresses in the Insert Hyperlink dialog box with the list of addresses from your Web browser's address bar. Thus, you don't have to retype the URL if you've recently visited the Web page to which you're linking; just select it from the list. ■

T I P Adding a link to an Office presentation or spreadsheet works exactly the same way as it does in Word. Select the anchor, click the Insert Hyperlink button in the toolbar, provide the URL, and close the dialog box.

Formatting Content with Tables

For the most part, editing tables in a Web page works like editing tables in a DOC file. You use the exact same menu options to insert a table, change a table's properties, and so on. The resulting dialog boxes are different, however, to account for the limitations in HTML:

■ The Table Properties dialog box shown in Figure 38.7 contains settings that let you choose how text wraps around a table, how much space you want between the table and surrounding text, the color of the table, and the space between individual columns.

FIG. 38.7
If you don't want to wrap text around a table, but you do want to align it, select the entire table and use the Formatting toolbar to left-align, center, or right-align it.

■ The Cell Properties dialog box contains settings that let you choose how content is aligned within the cell, the color of the cell, and the size of the cell. Note that Word doesn't let you specify the full range of values that HTML allows for the size attribute. You can't specify the size of a cell as a percentage of the table size, for example.

■ The Borders dialog box contains settings that let you specify whether or not you want a border around the table and the size of the border.

CHAPTER 39

Publishing to the Net

In order to make your Web pages available to the rest of the world, you must publish them. There's a bit more to publishing your Web site than just uploading the files, though. Publishing your Web site starts with how you organize your files on your own computer while you're authoring them.

Then, once you're satisfied with each Web page, you upload it to your service provider's Web server using that same organization. Don't forget testing, either. You should test your Web pages before and after you publish them to make sure that everything works correctly. Otherwise, you might suffer severe embarrassment when a user sends you a mail message about all the broken links and missing images he found on your Web site. ■

Stage your Web pages on your own computer

Learn how to manage your Web site's files on your own computer. By choosing a good organization, you'll never lose track of the files that belong with each Web page.

Find a good home for your site

If you don't yet have an Internet service provider, you need one in order to publish your Web site. You also need a handful of information from your ISP before you can upload your HTML files.

Check your Web pages before you upload them

Don't even bother publishing your Web pages if you haven't yet checked them for errors. This chapter recommends four simple things to check so that you don't embarrass yourself.

Publish your files with the Web Publishing Wizard

Office comes with the Web Publishing Wizard, which you can use to easily upload all of your Web site's files to the Web server.

Verify your Web site with an online test tool

Doctor HTML is one of the premier online test tools that'll verify everything from the links in your Web pages to the time required to download a Web page on a 14.4K modem.

Managing Your HTML Files

You want to organize the files in your Web site so that they follow the structure of the Web pages themselves. Use the hierarchical structure of the file system. If you think about your Web site for a moment, you'll realize that it probably has a very hierarchical structure, like an outline. Create a folder structure on your disk that reflects this organization.

For example, if your Web site is organized similar to Figure 39.1, you might create a folder structure that looks like Figure 39.2. Note how the home page is in the root folder, while each Web page to which the home page is linked has a folder directly underneath the home page. All of the files required by a Web page (graphics, sounds, controls, and so on) are stored in the folder with the home page so you can keep an accurate inventory of the files on which the Web page is dependent.

FIG. 39.1

Keep your Web pages simple and organized hierarchically so that users can more easily navigate your Web site.

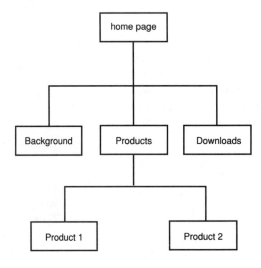

FIG. 39.2

If you link to a Web page from multiple places, don't duplicate the folder for that Web page; just refer to the first occurrence of it.

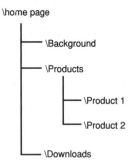

Mirroring (or Staging) Your Web Site Locally

If you're not using one of the Web site management programs such as Microsoft FrontPage, you'll want to keep a copy of your Web site on your local hard drive—regardless of your Web site's folder structure. In fact, you should edit those files locally, and then upload them to the Web site when they're ready. In doing so, you always know that the files on your local disk are the one-and-only master copy of your Web site. This process is called *staging* by most Web authors.

When working with the files on your local disk, you can use one of the Windows built-in file utilities to organize them:

Utility	Description
Explorer	Windows 95 and Windows NT provide Explorer, which is very similar to File Manager but makes working with files as documents much easier.
File Manager	All versions of Windows, including Windows 95, provide File Manager. In Windows 95, choose Run from the Start menu, type **WINFILE.EXE**, and press Enter.

Part
IX

Ch
39

> **CAUTION**
>
> In order to mirror your Web site locally, you must use folder and file names that are valid on both your workstation and the Web server. Note that you can use an FTP client to automatically convert file extensions from one form to another when you upload your HTML files. For example, an FTP client will automatically convert files with the HTM extension to the HTML extension when you upload them.

Creating Relative References

Relative references are URLs that are relative to the URL of the containing HTML document. *Absolute references* are URLs that contain the complete protocol, host, and path. For example, **next/page.htm** is a relative reference, whereas **http://www.myserver.com/next/page.htm** is an absolute reference.

You should always use relative references when linking to a resource on your own Web site. The reason is simple: If you change servers or you move your Web site to another folder, you have to change all of the absolute references. If you're using a tool such as FrontPage, these would be fixed for you automatically. Because you're managing your files manually, you have to actually change each reference within each file. Relative references assure that if you simply move the entire folder structure of your Web site from one location to another, you don't have to change each reference.

Launching Related Files

Make sure you have the appropriate programs associated with the files to which a Web page is dependent. By doing so, you can easily launch those files while you're exploring the Web site's files. For example, if you're exploring your Web site, you might want to take a look at a graphics file or play a sound file.

Windows 95 users have it made. You can view most graphics formats using QuickView, which is provided with Windows 95. You can also launch most video and sound files using the Media Player.

 T I P If you don't have a program associated with a particular type of file, such as JPG, you can probably view that type of file in your Web browser.

Finding a Home for Your Web Pages

If you don't currently have an Internet account, you can't publish your Web. In most cases, you'll find several ISPs from which to choose. When shopping for an ISP, make sure that a certain amount of Web space comes with your account. If not, or if they try to charge you extra for Web space, move on to another ISP.

If you do have an Internet account, double-check to make sure that you have Web space available. You can check your ISP's home page or you can ring the support line (most ISPs don't like these types of calls, though).

Your ISP is probably using UNIX. This is important for five reasons:

- You'll probably use FTP (File Transfer Protocol) to upload your Web to the Web server.
- You'll probably use your PPP user name and password to access the FTP server. Your PPP user name is the name you type when you first log onto the ISP.
- You'll probably upload your Web to the path **\public_html**.
- You'll probably give your home page the file name **index.html**.
- You'll probably browse your Web at **http://*www.isp.com*/~*name***, where ***www. isp.com*** is the host name of your ISP's Web server and ***name*** is the user name you use to log onto the ISP (your PPP user name).

Just to make sure, though, you should verify each of these items with your ISP. That is, you need to make sure you know the FTP address to which you'll upload files, the user name and password you'll use to access the FTP server, and the URL you'll use to browse your Web.

Checking Your Web on Your Own Computer

There is little sense in publishing your Web pages if you're missing files or the Web pages don't work correctly. Double-checking each Web page beforehand saves you a lot of aggravation and embarrassment.

Word doesn't provide many tools for automatically finding broken links or checking the design of your Web page. You can use Publisher's Design Checker to check the download time of your Web page, but that's about it. If you're sharp, however, you'll learn how to recognize the signs that something is amiss. Thus, before you publish a Web page, check for the top four errors that authors usually make.

Check the Layout in Netscape Navigator

One of the biggest problems you'll find with your Web pages is that a Web page that looks good in Internet Explorer might not look terrific in Netscape Navigator. Just because you're a die-hard Internet Explorer fan doesn't mean you should abandon all those folks who use Netscape Navigator, particularly because there are so many of them. Browse your Web site in Netscape Navigator to make sure it looks like you expected. You might even browse your Web site in the previous version of each Web browser, too, so you can make sure it's backward compatible.

One of the biggest culprits is tables. In some cases, Internet Explorer displays tables differently than Navigator. Thus, if nothing else, check every Web page that contains a table. If it doesn't look quite right, work with the column widths until it does.

ON THE WEB

You can download an evaluation copy of Netscape Navigator at

http://www.netscape.com

Part
IX

Ch
39

Browse to Find Broken Links

Office won't tell you that a link is broken. It can't, because it assumes any link you create might point to Internet resources that are available while you're editing a Web page. Thus, you should browse your Web in Internet Explorer and click each link. If you do find a broken link, you can easily fix it in Office by putting the insertion point anywhere within the link and clicking the Insert Hyperlink button in the Formatting toolbar.

N O T E You can also use Word to browse your Web pages. Click the Web Toolbar button in Word's Standard toolbar, and you'll see a toolbar that looks very similar to Internet Explorer's toolbar, including the Back, Forward, Stop, Refresh, and Favorites buttons. To open a URL, type it in the Address field you see in the toolbar. ▪

Verify that Each Image File Exists

The example in Figure 39.3 is pretty obvious. You can see that this Web page refers to an image file that doesn't exist because it leaves a huge blank spot at the top of the Web page. In some cases, images are more subtle and you should check each Web page carefully in your Web browser for the image icon as shown in the figure.

Double-Check All Custom HTML Tags

Be wary of any custom HTML tag that you add to your Web page. To view a custom HTML tag, click the Show/Hide Paragraph Marks icon in Word's Standard toolbar. Then, look for any text that's formatted using the HTML Markup style. Each case represents an HTML tag that Word doesn't understand. There are two cases where this tag will pop up. First, you might have inserted your own bit of custom HTML into the Web page. Second, if you used a template or borrowed a Web page from another source, the author might have used HTML tags that Word doesn't understand.

FIG. 39.3
Double-check every Web page on your Web site and make sure you don't see the dreaded image icon.

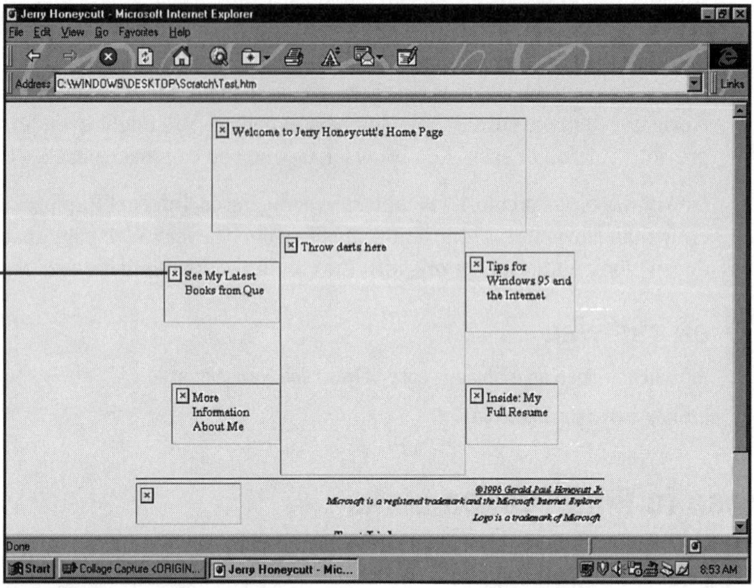

Image icon ———

Publishing with the Web Publishing Wizard

In order for you to let other people on the Internet visit your Web pages, you have to publish those pages so users can get access to them. To do so, you post your Web pages to your ISP's Web server in a folder that they've set aside for your account. Typically, most ISPs make a few megabytes of Web space available to each Internet account they host. As well, with most ISPs, you use FTP to upload Web pages into a \public_html folder on the Web server.

You can publish your pages the hard way, using an FTP client such as WS_FTP, or you can use the Web Publishing Wizard to publish your Web pages to the Internet. You find the wizard on your Office CD-ROM in \VALUPACK\WEBPOST\WEBPOST.EXE. To install the wizard, double-click this file and follow the instructions you see on the screen. Note that the setup program doesn't give you a choice as to where it installs the wizard.

N O T E   Some service providers won't let you upload your Web pages yourself. They require that you e-mail them the files, and they post them to the Web server. In cases like these, a service provider might charge a small fee for posting your Web pages. Thus, talk to your service provider if the instructions that follow don't work. ■

Once the wizard is installed, you can use it to publish your Web pages:

1. Start the Web Publishing Wizard, and you see the first dialog box, which is a brief introduction. Click Next.

2. Select folders and files that you want to publish to the Web. Make sure that you select any image files, ActiveX Controls, HTML layouts, and so on that you want to publish with the HTML file. Click Next.

3. Select an existing Web server from the drop-down list, click Next, and go to step 14 of these instructions. Alternatively, click New to create a new entry in the list. If you're publishing to an ISP, you'll need to add that service provider to this list.

4. Type a name that describes your Web server and select your ISP from the list. If your ISP isn't in the list of service providers, select <Other Internet Provider> so that you can add them. Click Next.

5. Type the URL of your home page in the space provided. This is the URL that you use to browse your home page, which probably looks something like **http://www.server. com/~*username***. Click Next.

6. Choose to access the Internet via your LAN (or proxy server), or via Dial-Up Networking. If you chose Dial-Up Networking, select your ISP's connection from the drop-down list. Click Next.

7. The Web Publishing Wizard tells you that it's ready to verify the information you provided. Click Next, and it'll do just that.

8. If the Web Publishing Wizard is able to upload your Web pages given the information you provided, you can skip to step 14 of these instructions. Otherwise, the Web Publishing Wizard needs just a bit more information from you. Dismiss the dialog box that tells you that the wizard can't post your files.

9. Choose the protocol that you use to upload files to the Web server. In most cases, you should select FTP as this is the protocol used with UNIX Web servers. Click Next.

10. Provide the user name and password for your Web server. This is probably the same name and password that you use to log onto your ISP in the first place. Remember that your user name and password is case-sensitive. Click Next.

11. Provide the host name of the FTP server that you upload your Web pages to. This is probably the same host name as your Web server. Click Next.

12. Provide the relative path to which you want to upload your Web pages and the URL of your home page. Note that if your service provider uses UNIX Web servers, the relative path should probably be \public_html.

13. The Web Publishing Wizard once again tells you that it's ready to verify the information you provided. Click Next.

14. The Web Publishing Wizard is now ready to upload your files to the Internet. Close the dialog box, and it'll do just that. The Web Publishing Wizard doesn't provide you with status information so you won't know how far along it is in the process until you see the dialog box telling you that it's finished. Dismiss this dialog box, and the Web Publishing Wizard will close.

Part
IX

Ch
39

N O T E   If you've checked everything before you uploaded your Web, you probably won't encounter many problems. If you're organizing your files in different folders and used different names on the server than you did on your computer, you might be missing images or have broken links in one or more Web pages. Thus, open each Web page in your Web, and make sure that you see every image and that every link works as planned. ■

Validating Your Web Pages Online

In the world of software development, programs are built in essentially three phases: design, programming, and testing. The purpose of each phase is self-explanatory.

When building Web pages, you probably work with the same sort of phases. You design your Web pages, even if you just make a mental note of the document's general layout before you begin working on it. Then you implement the Web pages using Word or another editor. Last, you test your Web pages to make sure they work as you planned and that they're correct.

Doctor HTML is a verification service that analyzes the contents of a Web page. It makes that last phase, testing, much easier to do. For example, you can use it to spell-check a Web page, verify the syntax of the HTML in a Web page, or even check a Web page for broken links. You can also use Doctor HTML to verify your entire Web site, but Web site verification is a commercial service to which you must subscribe.

Doctor HTML isn't a program that you download onto your computer before using. It's a service that you access on the Web at **http://www2.imagiware.com/RxHTML**. Click Single Page Analysis in the left frame and you'll see the Web page shown in Figure 39.4. Table 39.1 describes each test shown in the figure.

FIG. 39.4
You can order all tests by selecting Do All Tests or order individual tests by selecting Select from List Below.

Click to start test ————

Type the URL ————

Select to order individual tests ————

Select the tests you want to order ————

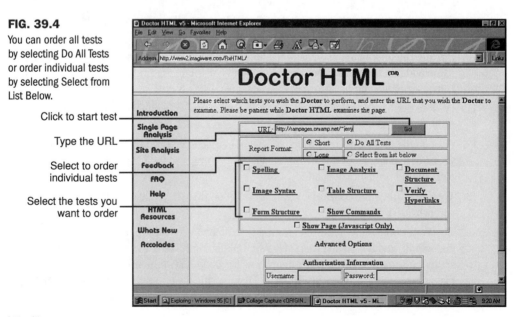

Table 39.1 Doctor HTML Tests

Test	Description
Spelling	Removes the tags and accented text from the HTML file and scans it for spelling errors.
Image Analysis	Loads all the images to which the HTML file are linked. It then determines the bandwidth required by each image and reports any images that require excessive download time. Doctor HTML also reports the size of and number of colors in each image.
Document Structure	Tests the structure of the HTML file, including unclosed HTML tags.
Image Syntax	Makes sure you're using the HEIGHT, WIDTH, and ALT attributes within the IMG tag. These attributes give the browser hints that help it load the HTML document faster.
Table Structure	Checks the structure of each table in the HTML document. It looks for any unclosed TR, TH, and TD tags.
Verify Hyperlinks	Reports each invalid link contained in your HTML file. Just because Doctor HTML reports a link as being "dead" doesn't mean that the link is invalid; the server may be running slowly.
Form Structure	Verifies the structure of each form in the HTML file. It only looks at INPUT tags.
Show Commands	Displays an indented list of HTML commands that shows the structure of your HTML document.

Part
IX

Ch
39

Type the URL of the Web page you want to verify in the URL field. If you want to specify the individual tests you want to run, choose Select from List Below, select each test, and then click Go. Figure 39.5 shows the results of the tests I performed on my home page.

Verifying Links Within a Web Page

One of the best uses for Doctor HTML is to verify the links contained in your Web page. Type the URL of your Web page in URL, choose Long, choose Select from List Below, and select Verify Hyperlinks from the list of tests to run. You'll see output similar to Figure 39.6. The table lists each link found in the Web page. For each link, it identifies the link's URL; the type, size, and change date of the file to which the link points; the line numbers on which the link is used; and any additional comments regarding the link.

N O T E Doctor HTML doesn't verify the links contained within imagemaps. ▪

FIG. 39.5
Doctor HTML's output is easy to read.

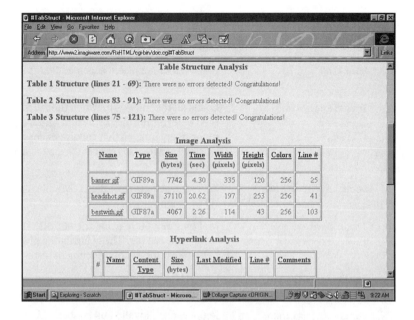

FIG. 39.6
Doctor HTML only lists those links for which it finds warnings or errors.

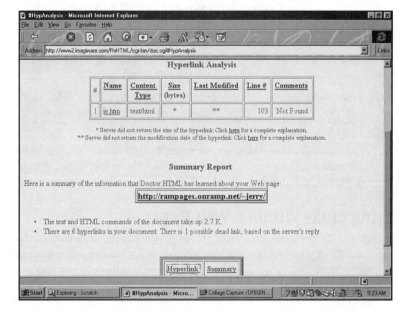

Checking the Performance of Your Images

One of the biggest complaints heard from some users is the time required to download Web pages that contain a lot of images. You can get a realistic view of how long a typical user will spend downloading your Web page by using Doctor HTML to check the download time for each image on the page. Type the URL of your Web page in URL, choose Long, choose Select from List Below, and select Image Analysis from the list of tests to run. You'll see results similar to Figure 39.7. The most important column to note is the Time column, which indicates how long the image takes to download using a 14.4K modem.

FIG. 39.7
The summary, at the bottom of the results, indicates the total download time for all of the images on the Web page.

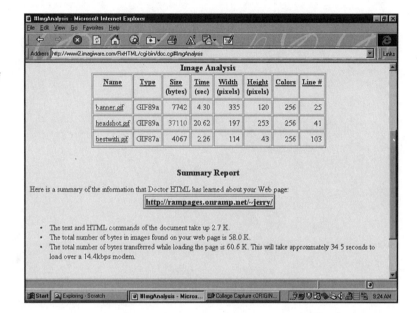

Part
IX

Ch
39

CHAPTER 40

Understanding ActiveX

A lot of people are wandering around mumbling something like "ActiveX—what is ActiveX?" Nobody knows for sure. You can check in day to day with Microsoft to see what's the latest definition of ActiveX, but you'll soon tire of doing that.

ActiveX is a big umbrella that Microsoft uses to encompass all of its Internet-related technology. It's not a product. It includes technologies that programmers can use to build Internet-enabled applications, products that end users can use to access the Internet, and technologies that content developers can use to build terrific Web sites.

One of the most exciting ActiveX technologies is *ActiveX Controls*. These controls let you add diverse functionality to your Web site by inserting a control right in the Web page. You can insert a control that pops open a menu, for example, or you can insert a control that performs a query on a database and displays the result. There are thousands of controls available; you need only find one to fit your needs. ■

Add ActiveX Controls using the <OBJECT> tag

You can add ActiveX Controls to your Web page using the <OBJECT> and <PARAM> tags. These are simple HTML tags that associate an object with your Web page.

Associate scripts with the objects on a Web page

Once you've added an ActiveX Control to the Web page, you'll want to associate scripts with it so that you can control it.

Work with ActiveX Control using the Control Pad

The ActiveX Control Pad makes short work of adding ActiveX Controls to your Web page. You can use it to set a control's properties or to even write scripts using the Script Wizard.

Control your Web page's layout

You use the ActiveX HTML Layout Control to maintain complete two-dimensional control over the format of your Web page.

TIP ActiveX is another example of a buzz word gone awry. Microsoft serfs don't pronounce the X in ActiveX. It's silent. Instead of saying active-x-controls, for example, say active-controls.

Manually Working with ActiveX Controls

Microsoft provides a basic collection of ActiveX Controls with Internet Explorer. You need only install Internet Explorer to get them. However, Microsoft packages some controls only with the complete installation of Internet Explorer, while providing other controls through its ActiveX Gallery Web site at **http://www.microsoft.com/activex/gallery**. Each control you find on this Web site has a page that shows you a demo and provides instructions for using it. In some cases, controls on this Web site are commercially available, so you must pay for them.

Once you've found a control that you want to use, you should download it onto your computer and place it in the same folder as your Web page. That way, you don't have to turn flips in order to specify to Internet Explorer where to find the control. After downloading the control, you need to insert it in your Web page using the <OBJECT> tag and possible associated scripts with it.

Inserting Controls with the *<OBJECT>* Tag

You use the <OBJECT> tag to insert a control into your Web page. The <OBJECT> tag identifies the control you're using. When the Web browser opens your Web page, it takes note of the control in the <OBJECT> tag and checks to see if the user already has it installed. If not, the browser downloads the control and installs it on the user's computer per the instructions you give it in the <OBJECT> tag. You also give the control a unique name so that you can control it with scripts: JavaScript or VBScript.

TIP If you're using Word to build your Web page, you can type the HTML described in this section directly into the page, then format it using the HTML Markup style you find in the style list.

In its simplest form, the <OBJECT> tag looks similar to the following:

```
<OBJECT
       CLASSID="clsid:1A771020-A28E-11CF-8510-00AA003B6C7E"
       ID=Track1
       WIDTH=400
       HEIGHT=2
       ALIGN=left>
  <IMG SRC="noobject.gif">
  <PARAM NAME="Image" VALUE="image.gif">
</OBJECT>
```

The CLASSID attribute uniquely identifies, on the user's computer, the control you're using. The control's CLASSID is the number that Windows uses to identify that control. You can think of the CLASSID as a name that is guaranteed to be unique. In this case, I'm using the View Tracker control. You use the id attribute to identify the control so that you can associate scripts with it. width, height, and align work the same as with other types of tags; they specify the size and location of the control on the Web page. You can add the CODEBASE attribute to the <OBJECT> tag to specify the URL of the control on the Web server. This helps the Web browser find the control if it's not already installed on the user's computer.

The <OBJECT> tag provides a way out for those browsers that don't support it. Browsers that do support the <OBJECT> tag ignore anything between <OBJECT> and </OBJECT> that isn't a PARAM tag (you learn about this in the next section). Browsers that don't support the <OBJECT> tag will ignore it and the PARAM tags, and use the content sandwiched between the <OBJECT> and </OBJECT> tags instead. In this case, if the user's Web browser supports the <OBJECT> tag, she sees the View Tracker control inserted into her Web page. Otherwise, she sees an IMAGE.GIF image inserted using the IMG tag.

> **N O T E** Some sources refer to the content sandwiched between the <OBJECT> and </OBJECT> tags as the *apology section*, as in, "I'm sorry you don't support this object; here, try these tags instead." You can also refer to this content as *alternative content* and still sound smart. ∎

 T I P Search the Windows 95 or Windows NT Registry for a CLASSID to find the entry that defines the control. Doing so, you can actually track down the control's file.

Setting a Control's Properties with the *PARAM* Tag

You will need to set the properties of the ActiveX Controls you put on the Web page to control its appearance or functionality. For example, you need to give the Stock Ticker control the URL of the text file it should use for data. You need to provide the Label control the text it should display. The only way to know for sure which properties each control requires is to check in the control's documentation. You can also use the ActiveX Control Pad to set a control's properties, as described in "Introducing the ActiveX Control Pad" later in this chapter.

So how do you set these properties? You use the <PARAM> tag to assign a value to a named property within the control. This works very much like Visual Basic property sheets. Note that the <PARAM> tag has no closing </PARAM> tag. This tag has many attributes, but you frequently need to use only the NAME and VALUE attributes:

```
<PARAM NAME=ENABLED VALUE=TRUE>
```

In this case, the value that you're setting is called ENABLED, and the value you're setting it to is TRUE.

The following is an example of inserting an ActiveX Control. The CLASSID attribute specifies the Popup Menu control, and each <PARAM> tag adds a menu item to the menu.

```
<OBJECT
        ID=iemenu1
        CLASSID="clsid:0482B100-739C-11CF-A3A9-00A0C9034920"
        WIDTH=1
        HEIGHT=1
        ALIGN=left
```

Part

IX

Ch

40

```
        HSPACE=0
        VSPACE=0
  >
  <PARAM NAME="Menuitem[0]" VALUE="First Choice">
  <PARAM NAME="Menuitem[1]" VALUE="Second Choice">
  <PARAM NAME="Menuitem[2]" VALUE="Third Choice">
  <PARAM NAME="Menuitem[3]" VALUE="Fourth Choice">
  <PARAM NAME="Menuitem[4]" VALUE="Fifth Choice">
</OBJECT>
```

Connecting Controls to Scripts

Now, we're getting to the meat of the matter. You learned how to insert ActiveX Controls into your Web page using the <OBJECT> tag. Now you need to learn how to interact with those controls using a scripting language. In the sections that follow, you learn how to handle the events that are triggered by a control. You also learn how to get and set a control's properties from your scripts. Incidentally, the scripting language of choice is VBScript for these examples. The JavaScript versions of these examples aren't much different, however.

ActiveX Controls act like and quack like the elements on a form. You interact with each ActiveX Control's properties, methods, and events in exactly the same way in which you interact with a form's elements. You handle a control's events when the control needs attention, you call a control's methods, and you get and set the control's properties.

Handling an Event   In a Web page, an object causes events in response to the messages the object receives from Windows. When you click inside of an object, Windows sends a message to the object telling it that you clicked the mouse. In turn, the object causes a click event, and the browser looks for a special script procedure or function called an *event-procedure* to handle that event.

You can use a couple of different methods of handling events for forms and elements (event-procedures, inline event-handlers, and so on), but there's really only one way to handle an ActiveX Control's events: using the FOR/EVENT attributes of the SCRIPT tag.

The FOR and EVENT attributes let you associate a script with any named object in the HTML file and any event for that object. Take a look at the following:

```
<SCRIPT LANGUAGE="VBScript" FOR="btnButton" EVENT="Click">
<!--
 window.alert( "Ouch! You clicked on me." )
-->
</SCRIPT>
<OBJECT ID="btnButton" WIDTH=96 HEIGHT=32
        CLASSID="CLSID:D7053240-CE69-11CD-A777-00DD01143C57">
        <PARAM NAME="Caption" VALUE="Click Me">
        <PARAM NAME="Size" VALUE="2540;847">
</OBJECT>
```

This defines a button (with an ID of btnButton) that executes the script when the user clicks it. Take a look at the <SCRIPT> tag. It contains the FOR and EVENT attributes that define the object and event associated with that script. FOR="btnButton" EVENT="Click" says that when an object named btnButton triggers the Click event, every statement in this script is executed.

The HTML comment tags keep older browsers from displaying the script as content on the Web page.

Some events pass arguments to the event handlers. How do you handle arguments when you're handling the event using the FOR/EVENT syntax? Like the following:

```
<SCRIPT LANGUAGE="JavaScript" FOR="btnButton"
    ➥EVENT="MouseMove(shift, button, x, y)">
```

The enclosed script can then use any of the parameters passed to it by the MouseMove event.

TIP Once you've specified a language in your HTML file, you don't need to do it again. Your browser defaults to the most recently used language used in the HTML file. You can put <SCRIPT LANGUAGE= "VBScript"></SCRIPT> at the very beginning of your HTML file one time and forget about it. The rest of the scripts in your file will use VBScript.

You just saw the Click event. ActiveX Controls support a wide variety of other events. The only way to know for sure which events a control supports is to consult the control's documentation or the ActiveX Control Pad's documentation.

N O T E Often, the easiest way to see the events, properties, and methods that an ActiveX Control supports is to insert the Control into a Web page using the ActiveX Control Pad, and pop open the Script Wizard. The Script Wizard lists all of the control's events in the left pane. It lists all of the control's properties and methods in the right pane. ■

Changing an Object's Properties Many objects let the user input data. For example, the user can choose an item from a list, type text in an edit box, or click a check box. What good are objects if you can't get and set their value? Not much. You read the value of most elements using the object's value property in an assignment or logical expression. The following example assigns the text that the user typed into the txtTextBox control to a variable called str. The next example compares the text that the user typed into the txtTextBox with the word "Howdy."

```
str = txtTextBox.value
If txtTextBox.value = "Howdy" Then
```

You can also set the value of an element by assigning a string to the element's value, as follows:

```
txtTextBox.value = "New Contents of the Text Box"
```

The value property is the default property for most ActiveX Controls that accept user input. Thus, you can use the control's value in an expression without explicitly using the value property, such as:

```
alert txtTextBox
txtTextBox = "New Contents of the Text Box"
```

Introducing the ActiveX Control Pad

There is certainly a better way to add ActiveX Controls to your Web page: Use the ActiveX Control Pad. The *ActiveX Control Pad* is a free product from Microsoft that makes short work of adding controls to a Web page. You get it through the Microsoft's Site Builder Workshop at **HTTP://WWW.MICROSOFT.COM/WORKSHOP/AUTHOR/CPAD/**. Figure 40.1 shows you the Control Pad's HTML editor with an HTML file in it.

FIG. 40.1

The editor window shows you only the contents of your HTML. Save the file to disk and open it in your Web browser to preview what the Web page looks like.

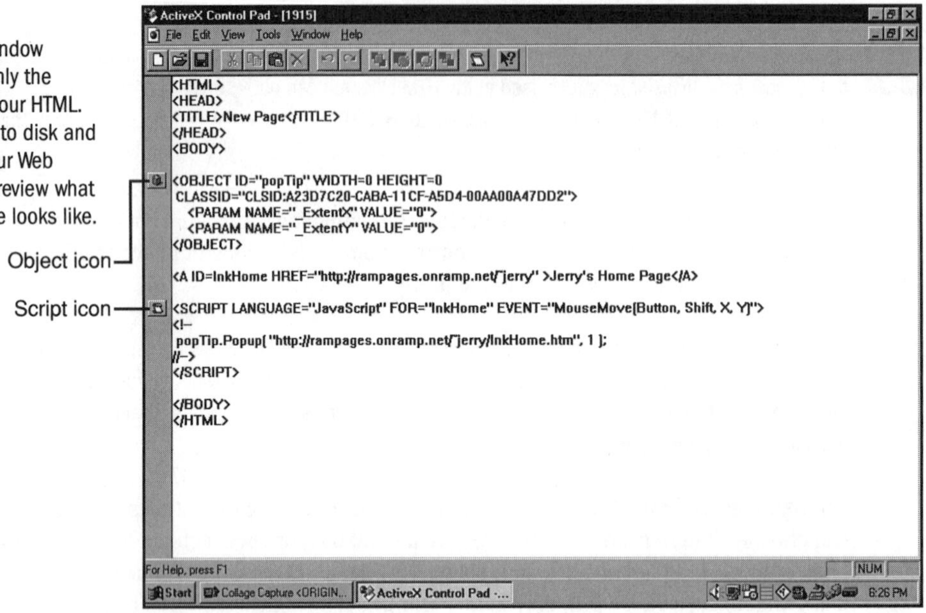

Object icon —
Script icon —

 The Control Pad uses VBScript by default. If you want to use JScript, you need to set it up to do so. Choose Tools, Options, Script from the main menu, and select JavaScript. The Script Wizard will now generate JScript language scripts instead of VBScript language scripts.

The HTML file you see in Figure 40.1 contains an object. You click the Object icon next to it in order to change the properties of that object. You click the Script icon, next to the script shown in the figure, to change the script using the Script Wizard.

You can type any text you like in the editor window. You can add forms to the file, for example. You can also add everyday text and tags, such as headings, lists, and so on. If you're really into punishment, you can add objects to your HTML by typing them in the editor window. Considering the features you will learn in the next section, you are strongly discouraged from doing the preceding steps.

Placing Objects into Your HTML File

Position your mouse pointer to the point at which you want to insert an object, and right-click. Choose Insert ActiveX Control, and you'll see a dialog box similar to the one shown in Figure 40.2. The Insert ActiveX Control dialog box lets you pick one of the many controls that are available on your computer.

FIG. 40.2

Not all of the controls shown in this list will work within a Web page.

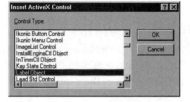

Select one of the controls in the list and close it. The Control Pad then opens the Object Editor and property sheet for the control, as shown in Figure 40.3. You can change each of the control's properties using the property sheet shown in the figure. You can also adjust the size of the control by grabbing one of its handles in the Object Editor and dragging it. When you close both windows, Control Pad saves your changes to the HTML file.

FIG. 40.3

Select a property, change its value at the top of the property sheet, and click Apply to save your changes.

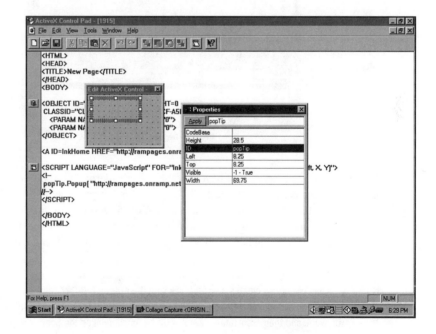

Part
IX
Ch
40

Using a control in this manner is called using it at *design time*. You're designing how the control is going to look on your Web page. The user uses the control at *run-time*, because all he is doing is using a page built with that control. Many controls require that you have a license to use them at design time. The controls you see in this chapter do not require a license, however, because they all come with Internet Explorer.

 You can change the control's properties in the HTML (<PARAM> tags) using the Control Pad's text editor. The next time you open that control's property sheet, the property sheet will reflect any changes you made.

Editing Scripts Using the Control Pad's Script Wizard

The Script Wizard provides two different ways you can edit scripts: List view and Code view. List view is a bit easier to use. Click the Script Wizard button in the toolbar to open the Script Wizard. Then click the List View button at the bottom of the window. See the window shown in Figure 40.4.

FIG. 40.4

In most cases, the List view is all you ever need to create exciting Web pages.

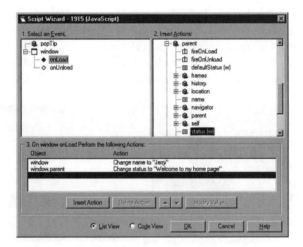

You associate an object's event with another object's methods and properties. Select an event on the left-hand pane of the wizard. Choose a method or property in the right-hand pane. When you click the Insert Action button, the Script Wizard prompts you for the value of the property or for any parameters you want to pass to a method. You can rearrange the order of the actions in the bottom pane of the Script Wizard. Close the Script Wizard, and it'll add your script to the HTML file.

N O T E The Control Pad creates a script block with the FOR and EVENT tags for each event that you handle. Alternatively, you can write a VBScript or JScript function that handles an event the way you want, and then associate an event with the function using the Script Wizard. ■

If you're more comfortable with the traditional programmer view of life (optimistic about everything), you can use the Script Wizard's Code view (see Figure 40.5). This works just like List view, except that you don't see a list of associated events and actions in the bottom pane. You see the actual code the Script Wizard creates instead. Click the Script Wizard button in the toolbar to open the Script Wizard. Then click the Code View button at the bottom of the window, add your script, and close the Script Wizard.

FIG. 40.5

You have to use Code view if you want to use compound statements such as If in your scripts.

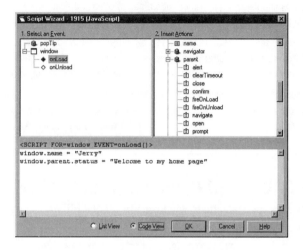

 TIP Keep your Web browser running with the Web page you're working on open in it. Then, you can save the changes, flip to the browser, and refresh the Web page to see your changes while you're working in Control Pad.

Controlling Page Layout with the HTML Layout Control

Microsoft created the ActiveX HTML Layout control to give you precise two-dimensional control over the layout of your Web page. You can place an object at a specific coordinate, for example. You can also overlap objects and make parts of some objects transparent so that objects in the background show through.

The HTML Layout control is similar to all the other objects you've seen in this chapter. You insert the HTML Layout control into your Web page using the <OBJECT> tag.

The HTML Layout control is a container. This is the primary concept you need to understand about this object. It's an object you put in your Web page that can contain other objects. Think of the HTML Layout control as a form. It works just like forms you create in Visual Basic. You drop an HTML Layout control on the Web page, and then you can arrange objects within it in any way you like.

W3C to the Rescue

In the meantime, W3C (World Wide Web Consortium) is developing a standard for HTML that will give you complete control over how you position objects in a Web page. You will be able to specify the exact horizontal (x) and vertical (y) position (coordinates) of each object on a Web page. Until its release, use the HTML Layout control.

You should know that the HTML Layout control is a temporary solution. It will go away eventually. Thus, when the W3C defines their standard, and browsers such as Internet Explorer and Netscape support it, you will not need to use the HTML Layout control to have 2-D placement of objects.

Microsoft has committed to providing a utility that you can use to convert your ActiveX HTML Layout control layouts to the new HTML standard for 2-D layouts when that standard becomes available. You can get more information about this standard at **http://www.w3.org/pub/WWW/TR/WD-layout.html**.

Inserting the HTML Layout Control into an HTML File

A layout has two components. First, you insert the actual HTML Layout control in your Web page using the `<OBJECT>` and `<PARAM>` tags. This tag looks similar to the following:

```
<OBJECT CLASSID="CLSID:812AE312-8B8E-11CF-93C8-00AA00C08FDF"
  ID="example" STYLE="LEFT:0;TOP:0">
  <PARAM NAME="ALXPATH" REF VALUE="file:example.alx">
</OBJECT>
```

The other component is the layout itself. You store a layout in a separate text file that has the ALX file extension. The ALXPATH property that you see in the previous example tells the HTML Layout control where to find this file. You can set this property to any valid URL, including a Web server. You do have to copy the ALX file onto the Web server with all of your other files. You learn more about the contents of the ALX file later in this chapter.

You don't have to insert the `<OBJECT>` tag or create the ALX file by hand, since the ActiveX Control Pad does it automatically. To add the HTML Layout control, right-click the location where you want to add the control and choose Insert HTML Layout. The Control Pad will ask you for a file name. Type the name of the ALX file and close the dialog box.

Editing the Layout

After you have inserted an HTML Layout control into your Web page, you can open it for editing. This allows you to place other ActiveX objects inside the HTML Layout control. Click the Layout button (in the margin next to the HTML Layout control), and the Control Pad opens the layout in the Layout Editor, as shown in Figure 40.6.

The Layout Editor lets you drag controls from the toolbox to the layout. Then you can re-arrange the controls, write event handlers for controls, and so on. When you close the Layout Editor, the Control Pad saves your layout to the ALX file.

FIG. 40.6

The Layout Editor is very similar to VBScript's Form Editor.

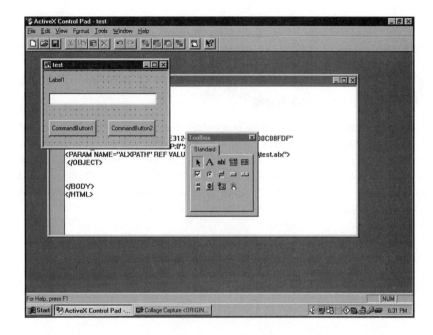

Adding Controls to a Layout   You drag a control from the toolbox and drop it on the layout in the Layout Editor. Once you've added a control to the layout, you can change its properties using the control's property sheet. You can also resize the control by dragging its handles.

 You can create control templates in the Layout Editor. Create a new page in the toolbox, right-click a tab, and choose New Page. Drag a control from your layout onto the new page. You can then use this template at any time by dragging it onto a layout.

Adding Scripts to Your Layout   You can add scripts to a layout just as you would add scripts to an HTML file. You use these scripts to handle the events fired by the objects in the layout. Click the Script Wizard button in the Control Pad's toolbar. In this case, the Script Wizard works exactly as you learned earlier in this chapter.

N O T E   ActiveX Controls that you put on an HTML Layout control have many more events, properties, and methods than the ActiveX Controls you use directly on the Web page. Also, when you open the Script Wizard in an HTML Layout control, you don't see the events, properties, and methods for ActiveX Controls on your Web page or the browser's object model. ▪

Changing a Layout's Tab Order   When you create a form using the HTML Layout control, the user can't tab between each field if you have not set up the tab behavior for each field. First, double-click each control in the layout, and set the TabStop property to True and TabKeyBehavior to False (if the control supports it). Then, change the TabIndex property for each control in the layout. Set TabIndex to 0 for the first control in the tab order. Set TabIndex to 1 for the next control in the tab order, and so on.

Part
IX

Ch
40

TIP You can leave the property sheet open all the time. When you select a different object on the layout, the property sheet changes to the one for that object.

TROUBLESHOOTING

You need to make sure that you consider older browsers who don't support ActiveX Controls or scripting. Provide alternative content for each <OBJECT> tag that you insert into your Web page. That is, in addition to include <PARAM> tags within the <OBJECT> container, include plain HTML tags that other browsers will display when they don't understand the <OBJECT> or <PARAM> tags. Also, surround the scripts you put in a <SCRIPT> tag with the beginning and ending HTML comment tags (<!-- and --s>) so that older browsers don't display the scripts as content.

CHAPTER 41

Publishing Web Sites with FrontPage 97

In other chapters of this book, you have seen how many components of Microsoft Office 97 can be used to publish HTML (HyperText Markup Language) Web pages. These HTML pages can be published directly to a Web site, either on the World Wide Web or on your office, organization, or community intranet.

There are limitations to creating Web pages using the HTML publishing features of Office programs. You will lose some of your page formatting when you convert your reports, documents, spreadsheets, presentations, and graphs to HTML using Office applications. And it is difficult to integrate HTML pages into a coherent Web site without a program designed to do just that. These limitations are addressed by integrating Microsoft FrontPage 97 into the mix. ■

Create Web sites with FrontPage 97 Explorer and your Web server

The main Office 97 applications allow you to save your documents, spreadsheets, reports, and presentations as HTML format Web pages.

Import files into your Web site in FrontPage 97 Explorer

The FrontPage Explorer is where you can easily import documents and graphics, and integrate them into a Web site with a coherent style and theme.

Polish Web page layout in the FrontPage 97 Editor

HTML documents generated in Office 97 applications lose some of their formatting. You can touch up page layout in the FrontPage Editor, and make changes to content and format as well.

Edit graphic image properties in the FrontPage 97 Editor

You can edit graphics in the FrontPage Editor by resizing and reshaping them, making background colors transparent, placing beveled frames behind them, and changing the graphic file format. Even more sophisticated editing could be done with FrontPage 97's companion program, Image Composer.

From Web Pages to Web Sites

FrontPage 97 enables you to add the following to your Web pages:

- The capability to define a Web site theme embracing many HTML pages
- More control over page layout and format
- More control of graphic images
- Easier publishing to intranet servers and the World Wide Web
- The capability to collect data input from visitors in forms

Office 97 applications include powerful capability for saving files as HTML files. There's no need to duplicate that effort when you organize a Web site using FrontPage 97. The HTML files, as well as the graphic image files generated by Office 97 documents, can be easily imported into FrontPage 97 for additional touching up.

Figure 41.1 shows the hardcopy of a document in Microsoft Word. That document incorporates some of Word's powerful publishing features including a floating image with wraparound text.

FIG. 41.1
Word document before conversion to HTML—note the graphic figure with wrap-around text.

In Figure 41.2, this same Word document has been published as an HTML document, and is being viewed with Internet Explorer 3.0, a Web browser. Word did a decent job of publishing the document to HTML. All the text survived well, as did the text formatting. You will notice, however, that not all the formatting translated well. The text no longer wraps around the figure, which has been moved.

FIG. 41.2
A Word document saved to HTML and viewed with Internet Explorer 3.0. Some of the layout attributes have been lost in the conversion. These can be restored and touched up in FrontPage 97.

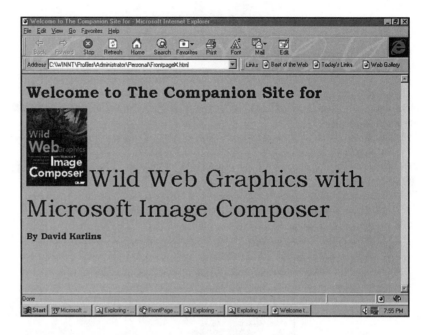

When you save Word documents, Publisher publications, Excel spreadsheets and graphs, PowerPoint presentations, and Access reports as HTML files, you will be impressed at how well Office 97 converts all the elements of your publications to Web pages. You will also note significant format problems that you will want to touch up with a Web page editor. In this chapter, you will touch up Web pages generated in Office 97 applications. Figure 41.3 shows the same Web page as the one displayed in Figure 41.2. FrontPage 97 has been used to wrap text around the image, to create a page background and to touch up the text formatting.

You will also find that FrontPage 97 makes it easy to publish your Web pages to your intranet or the World Wide Web. You will learn to use FrontPage 97's Explorer to send large numbers of files to a Web server.

In Chapter 42, "Making Your Web Site Interactive," you will see how FrontPage 97 can do much more than edit Web pages. You'll use FrontPage 97 to create input forms in your Web site, and collect data from visitors. And you will see how FrontPage 97's WebBots can make your Web site interactive.

In the course of creating a Web site with FrontPage 97, you may want to review the specific methods for publishing Office 97 documents as HTML files that are found in each of the sections of this book. Chapter 38, "Creating Web Documents," provides a useful introduction to HTML, and an outline for publishing Office documents to HTML.

FrontPage 97 is actually two programs rolled into one. The two main components are the Editor and the FrontPage 97 Explorer (not to be confused with the Windows Explorer or Internet Explorer). FrontPage also comes with Web servers, including the Personal Web Server. The Web servers bundled with FrontPage are not necessary if you are already connected to a Web

server, either on your intranet or on the World Wide Web. If you do not have a Web site from
an Internet Service Provider (ISP), your own Internet site, or a Web on an intranet, you should
install and use the Personal Web Server.

▶ **See** "Converting Existing Documents to HTML Documents," **p. 778**

FIG. 41.3

Text now wraps around
the image, and
FrontPage has been
used to add additional
text, graphics, and
formatting.

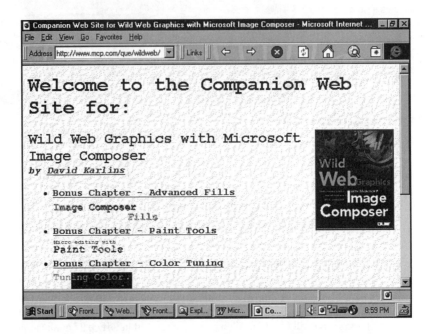

Letting FrontPage Explorer Coordinate Your Web Site

The FrontPage 97 Explorer acts like an office manager in a busy office, carefully filing and
tracking all the different components of a Web site. A *Web site* is a collection of files. It can
include HTML Web pages, image files, and possibly other files including programs that allow
the Web site to interact with visitors. While you will not spend a lot of time working in the
Explorer module of FrontPage 97, it is the pivotal element of making FrontPage 97 much more
than a Web page editor.

When it comes time to publish (transport) your Web site components to a Web server, the
FrontPage 97 Explorer handles this task for you as well. And finally, the FrontPage Explorer
not only acts as a file manager for your site, but it performs interior decorator tasks as well!

The FrontPage 97 Editor and the FrontPage 97 Explorer are inseparable if you want to really
use what FrontPage 97 can do. The FrontPage 97 Editor by itself can publish text and images
as HTML and Web-compatible graphics files. But you can also do most of this using the main
Office 97 programs. What makes FrontPage 97 special is the way the editor and FrontPage 97
Explorer interact to allow you to include interactive programs in your Web site.

A Quick Look at the FrontPage 97 Editor

The second main module of FrontPage 97 is the FrontPage 97 Editor. The FrontPage 97 Editor is…an editor! It looks much like the Word or Publisher environments, and allows you to edit text and graphics, as well as place interactive Web site programs on a Web page.

Most of this chapter will focus on using the FrontPage Editor. And this is the where you will do most of your work creating your Web site. Once you have gathered the elements of your Web site in the FrontPage 97 Explorer, the editor is where you will format, design, and even create Web pages.

The FrontPage Editor does not have as powerful word processing capabilities as Word. Spreadsheets created in Excel are easily published directly to HTML pages. You can create tables in the FrontPage Editor, but that is a complicated process beyond the realm of this book. Reports generated in Access and Excel graphs are easily converted into HTML pages in those programs. The modules in this book that address individual Office applications offer detailed advice on how to transform your documents to HTML. In short, you can take advantage of your Office 97 skills to do much of the work that can be done in the FrontPage 97 Editor.

If you decide that you would rather use the FrontPage Editor to create HTML pages, you will find a basic introduction to that process in this chapter (See the section "Editing and Formatting Text in FrontPage 97 Editor"). For a more detailed examination of the FrontPage Editor, you will want to choose from the large collection of available FrontPage 97 books. Que's *FrontPage 97 6-in-1* is a comprehensive exploration of the FrontPage Editor, Explorer, Image Composer, servers, and design techniques.

Web Pages, Servers, and Web Sites

If you are not connected to a Web server, you should install the Personal Web Server that comes with FrontPage on your own computer. FrontPage 97 is a Web server. If you already have access to a Web server, either on the Internet or on your intranet, you can use that server. This software installs on your computer and allows you to test all Web site features, even without a connection to a professional Web server. Without being connected to a server, you will not be able to test the interactive features of your Web site, like search boxes and input forms.

In order for the FrontPage 97 Editor and the FrontPage 97 Explorer to work together, you must save your FrontPage 97 Web site to a Web server. A *Web server* is a program installed on a computer that allows Web pages to be accessed by Web browsers.

If you are already connected to an intranet with a Web server installed, you will need to ask your Web administrator to install FrontPage 97 extensions on that server before you can use it to publish your FrontPage 97 Web site. These extensions are available free for all popular Web servers at Microsoft's Web site: **http://www.microsoft.com**.

If your office network is running on the Microsoft NT4 network operating system, you received a free Web server from Microsoft called the *Internet Information Server (IIS)*. With IIS, your local NT4 network can function as an intranet, where you can publish and visit Web sites.

Part

IX

Ch

41

Dozens of ISPs will sell you space on their FrontPage 97-ready Web servers. You can find lists of these providers at Microsoft's Web site as well.

ON THE WEB

The list is currently posted at:

http://microsoft.saltmine.com/frontpage/wpp/list/

If you don't have access to any type of Web server, that's no problem. If you purchase FrontPage 97, you will get the Personal Web Server, a program that installs directly on your stand-alone computer. The Personal Web Server isn't powerful enough to connect your computer to a network, or to the World Wide Web. But it will let you run your Web site on your own computer, and test it with an Internet browser like Internet Explorer or Netscape Navigator.

Installing and maintaining FrontPage 97 extensions on Web servers is beyond the scope of this book. Advanced FrontPage 97 books discuss using FrontPage 97 with Web servers. Que's *FrontPage 97 6-in-1* includes a module on Web servers.

From Office Documents to FrontPage 97 Web Sites

FrontPage 97 allows you to create and publish integrated Web sites that combine many files. Some of the Office 97 programs, notably PowerPoint, do a helpful job of organizing all the Web files you will need into a directory when you save them to your computer, or to another Web site. That's part of the process of organizing files into a Web site. Beyond that, FrontPage 97 will handle the whole process of making sure that every file associated with your Web site gets transferred to whatever Web server your site ends up on.

Because FrontPage 97 takes responsibility for all the elements of your Web site—HTML pages, graphics files, and interactive programs—you need to start work in FrontPage 97 Explorer.

When you start FrontPage 97, you will see the FrontPage 97 Explorer. The first step in working with FrontPage 97 is to create or open a FrontPage 97 Web in the Explorer. The FrontPage 97 Explorer can only have one Web open at a time.

In order to save a Web, you need to have a server running. If you have installed the Microsoft Personal Web server, that server program will open when you start FrontPage. During the FrontPage 97 installation process, you are given the option of installing the Personal Web Server, naming it, and giving yourself a password. With this information, you can use the Personal Web Server to save and test FrontPage 97 Webs.

Managing Web Sites with FrontPage 97 Explorer

Here's what you need to convert HTML documents created in Office into a FrontPage 97 Web site:

1. Install Microsoft FrontPage 97—available with a Bonus Pack that includes the Personal Web Server, Internet Explorer, and a graphics program called Microsoft Image Composer. If you are not connected to a Web server already, install the Personal Web Server.

 TIP PowerPoint is one good source of graphic images. FrontPage 97 comes with Image Composer, a graphics package specifically designed for creating *Web* graphics. For a complete exploration of Image Composer, see Que's *Wild Web Graphics with Microsoft Image Composer*.

2. Create Web site components using Office 97 programs.

That's it! If you have FrontPage 97, and you have created HTML pages, and optionally Web graphics using Office, you are ready to put together an impressive, interactive Web site in FrontPage 97.

Once you start FrontPage 97, you can import all the Web files you created in Office via the FrontPage 97 Explorer.

Importing Web Site Components

You can import Web pages and other elements of your Web site into the FrontPage 97 Explorer. You can also import elements using the FrontPage 97 Editor, but if you are organizing your site from components already created in Office, the FrontPage 97 Explorer is the best way to import files.

When you start FrontPage 97, you will see the Explorer module, and you will be prompted to open or create a Web site. Even if you already have Web pages, you will want to create (or open) a Web site. The site is the form that FrontPage 97 uses to organize all the related files that you want to publish to your intranet or the World Wide Web. If you already have a Web site, and you are adding files to it, click the Open Existing FrontPage 97 Web radio button, and click OK in the Getting Started with Microsoft FrontPage 97 dialog box. If you are starting from scratch, choose the Blank FrontPage 97 Web dialog box.

If you have already created FrontPage 97 Webs, the most recent will appear as an option button option in the Getting Started with Microsoft FrontPage 97 dialog box. You can choose that option button to quickly reopen the last Web you worked on.

Part
IX

Ch
41

N O T E The two other options in the Create a New FrontPage 97 Web area of the Getting Started with Microsoft FrontPage 97 dialog box allow you to create a Web from a template or import a Web. If you are combining Office 97 files with this quick FrontPage 97 tutorial, you won't need those options. Creating FrontPage 97 Web sites from templates is explored in detail in Que's *FrontPage 97 6-in-1* book. ▨

If you elect to create a new Web, you'll be prompted for a server and the Name of New FrontPage 97 Web. The server will be the server to which you are publishing your Web site. If you have installed the Personal Web Server and not given it a name, you can enter default in the Web Server or File Location area of the Normal Web Template dialog box. The name you enter must not have any spaces, and you should avoid symbols as well.

When you have named your Web site and identified your server, choose OK in the Normal Web Template dialog box.

Once you name your Web site, or elect to open an existing site, you'll be prompted for a passcode to access your server. If you are using a Web site, the network or ISP administrator needs to provide you with a passcode to access the Web server. If you are using the Personal Web Server, you will use the password you defined when you installed FrontPage 97.

N O T E   If you forgot your FrontPage 97 Server password, you can reinstall FrontPage 97 and assign a new password. ▓

Many Ways to Explore Your Web Site

As soon as you enter a password, you will create or open a FrontPage 97 Web in the FrontPage 97 Explorer. The FrontPage 97 Explorer can be viewed in two views. Figure 41.4 shows the Folders view.

FIG. 41.4

FrontPage 97 Explorer— the Folders view is selected.

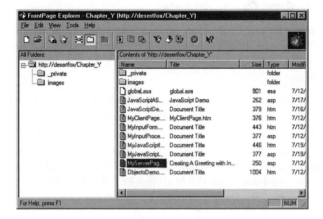

The views are:

- ▓ *Folders*. Displays your Web site files organized into folders.
- ▓ *Hyperlinks*. Displays existing links to and from a selected Web site page or component. Pages are selected from the frame on the left side of the Hyperlink Status view. Figure 41.5 shows a selected page Hyperlink Status.

The essential views for working on your Web site are the Folders view and the Hyperlink view. You can identify hyperlinks that need to be tested or fixed by looking at the list of links and files generated when you click Hyperlink Status in the Views column of the FrontPage Explorer.

FIG. 41.5
FrontPage 97 Explorer—
Hyperlink view shows
links between files in
the Web site.

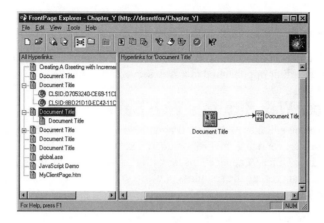

Importing Files

You can import files into your FrontPage Web site with any of the views selected in the FrontPage Explorer. However, it will be easier to keep track of your imported files if you selected the Folders view before you start the process.

Regardless of which view you have selected, you can import files into the FrontPage 97 Explorer by following these steps:

1. Select File, Import from the FrontPage 97 Explorer menu bar.
2. Click the Add File button in the Import File to FrontPage 97 Web dialog box.
3. Navigate to the folder that contains your file(s) in the Add File to Import List dialog box.
4. Select the file(s) that you want to import into your Web site (see Figure 41.6).

 TIP FrontPage 97 Explorer fully supports Windows drag and drop. You can just drag a file into the FrontPage Explorer from other applications.

FIG. 41.6
You can select files to import in the Add File to Import List dialog box. The selected files are added to your Web site and will be shown in the FrontPage Explorer Folders view.

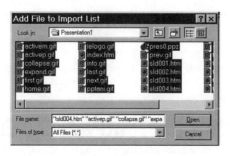

Part
IX

Ch

41

5. Click Open in the Add File to Import List dialog box. You can repeat this process to add additional files to the Import File to FrontPage 97 Web dialog box.

6. When you have added all the files you want to import, click the OK button in the Import Files to FrontPage 97 Web dialog box.

The files you import into your Web in the FrontPage 97 Explorer can be edited in the FrontPage 97 Editor or published to a Web server.

Publishing Your Web Site to a Web Server

Even before you edit files in the FrontPage 97 Editor, you can publish your Web site to a different Web server using the FrontPage 97 Explorer. If you have wrestled with the Connection Wizards in Office 97 applications, or with the upload instructions you get from an ISP, you will really appreciate the seamless publishing process from FrontPage 97 to a FrontPage 97-enabled Web server.

If you have created your Web site using the Personal Web Server, you can publish it to an intranet server or a site on the World Wide Web using the FrontPage 97 Explorer. The steps are:

1. Select File, Publish FrontPage Web from the FrontPage 97 Explorer dialog box.

2. Click the More Webs button in the Publish dialog box.

N O T E   When you publish your site to a Web, you will choose that destination from a list that appears in the Publish dialog box. However, if your target Web site is not listed, you can always click the More Webs button and define a new target for your site. ■

3. The Please Specify the Location drop-down box will have your current Web server as the default. Enter the URL of the server to which you are publishing (copying) your Web site.

N O T E   The Secure Connection Required (SSL) check box is used when you are publishing your Web to a secure Web server. Your Web administrator will notify you if your server falls into that category. Secure Web servers provide protection against unauthorized viewing of data. ■

4. Your site will take some time to copy to the destination server. When the files are successfully copied, you'll choose OK, saying that your Web has been successfully copied.

The capability to copy Webs to Web servers is one of the big advantages of the FrontPage 97 Explorer.

Editing Web Pages in the FrontPage 97 Editor

Every Office 97 program comes with powerful Web publishing capability. Excel spreadsheets can be published as HTML Web pages. Excel graphs are saved as Web-compatible *.GIF format files. PowerPoint presentations can be saved as HTML pages with built-in navigation links. Word and Publisher have powerful Web page features, and even Access reports can be saved as Web pages.

All this is very helpful, and you'll find as you touch up and tweak Web pages in FrontPage 97 that the Web-publishing features in Office applications save a lot of time and work. Word and Publisher, for example, do a very faithful job of translating text formatting into HTML code, so that the formatting you define in your document appears in Web pages just as you created it.

Nevertheless, it's still the case that if you want professional-quality Web pages, you will need to do some work on the Web pages that are generated by Office applications. In the FrontPage 97 Editor, you can touch up text content and format, add Web page backgrounds and clip art, arrange page layout, and create text and graphic hyperlinks.

Editing and Formatting Text in FrontPage 97 Editor

You can open any HTML file in the FrontPage 97 Editor by double-clicking that file in the FrontPage 97 Explorer. If you have many files in your Web site, you can organize them by clicking the column heading in the FrontPage 97 Explorer—Name, Title, Size, Type, Modified Date, or Column. Clicking a column heading alphabetizes the list of files by that column (or sorts by value in the case of Date and File Size).

N O T E You can also open other types of files, like graphic images or Office 97 files, from the FrontPage 97 Editor. To do this, you have an application program installed and associated with that type of file. This is controlled by selecting Tools, Options from the FrontPage 97 menu bar, and clicking the Configure Editors tab in the Options dialog box. ■

HTML files have an HTM file name extension in the FrontPage 97 Explorer. Once you double-click an HTML file in the FrontPage 97 Editor, you automatically launch the FrontPage 97 Editor and open that file.

The FrontPage 97 Editor window looks similar to the Word or Publisher environments. You will recognize many of the buttons in the toolbar as being identical to those in Office applications—like the New, Open, Cut, Copy, and Paste buttons. You'll also recognize many of the buttons in the FrontPage 97 Editor Format toolbar. You know how to point to tools and read ScreenTips to learn about buttons you don't recognize.

There is one element of the FrontPage 97 Format toolbar that looks the same, but functions differently than it does in Word and Publisher. That is the Change Style drop-down list. Unlike styles in Word and Publisher, HTML styles cannot be redefined, and do not play the same helpful role they do in hardcopy publishing programs.

You will also note the Text Color button in the FrontPage 97 Editor Format toolbar. The Text Color feature is more central in formatting text in Web sites than it is when creating documents intended to be printed. While many printers and copiers are still limited to one color, the vast majority of Web browsers and monitors are color, and you will want to take that into account in defining text format.

You may be somewhat confused by the appearance of Web pages when you open them in the FrontPage 97 Editor. Office 97 applications place HTML code in some of the Web pages they generate that is not necessary in FrontPage 97. This superfluous code appears in the FrontPage 97 Editor as small yellow squares with < ! > marks in them. You can view this HTML code by double-clicking one of these small yellow icons. Figure 41.7 shows some HTML code in the HTML Markup window that appears when one of these yellow icons is selected. These HTML comments will not be visible when visitors see your page in a Web browser-like Internet Explorer.

FIG. 41.7

HTML code can be viewed or edited in the FrontPage 97 Editor by clicking the HTML tab.

You can edit text content and format using the same editing techniques you use in Word and Publisher. You can add text by clicking with your mouse to place the insertion point and typing. You can delete by selecting text and pressing the Delete key on your keyboard. You can cut, copy, and paste text (or graphics) using the editing buttons on the Standard toolbar.

You can make text larger or smaller in the FrontPage 97 Editor by selecting the text and clicking the Increase Text Size or Decrease Text Size buttons in the Formatting toolbar. Figure 41.8 shows text being made larger.

FIG. 41.8

You can use the Increase Text Size button to enlarge selected text.

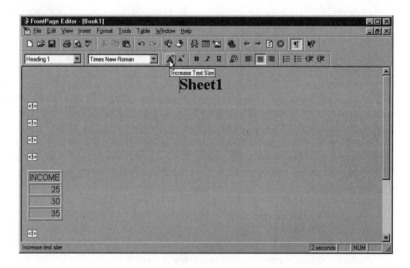

You can assign fonts to selected text by using the Change Fonts drop-down list. However, if you use fonts besides Times Roman or Courier, the appearance to your visitors is determined by whether they have matching fonts on their own computers. If not, the fonts will be converted by the visitor's browser into the closest matching font that is available.

HTML files do not allow the same paragraph formatting options available in Word and Publisher. You cannot define paragraph spacing—all paragraphs have a line of space between them. You can, however, press Ctrl+Enter to create a forced line break within a paragraph that will be single spaced.

You can indent (or outdent) paragraphs using the Increase Indent and Decrease Indent buttons in the Formatting toolbar. You can also assign bullets or numbering to paragraphs using the Bulleted List and Numbered List buttons in the toolbar. The other available paragraph format tools enable you to Left Align, Center, or Right Align selected paragraphs.

The Spell Check button in the Standard toolbar launches a spell checker very similar to the one you worked with in Office 97. It's a good idea to spell-check the text of imported documents if you have edited them in FrontPage 97.

If you are going to be doing extensive formatting in the FrontPage 97 Editor, it might be worthwhile to invest in a full-fledged FrontPage 97 book like Que's *FrontPage 97 6-in-1*. Defining and editing tables, complex lists, and special text attributes like scrolling and blinking text are beyond the scope of this book. However, for basic editing and formatting, your Office 97 skills will take you a long way.

Working with Images in FrontPage 97 Editor

You can assign important attributes to images in FrontPage 97. Those attributes are available from the Image toolbar that appears on the bottom of the FrontPage window when you click an image in the FrontPage 97 Editor.

Table 41.1 describes the buttons on the Image toolbar.

Table 41.1 FrontPage 97 Image Tools

Image Tool	Button Name	What It Does
	Select	Selects an image.
	Rectangle	Assigns rectangular hotspot.
	Circle	Assigns circular hotspot.
	Polygon	Assigns polygonal (oddly shaped) hotspot.
	Highlight hotspots	Highlights assigned hotspots.
	Make Transparent	Makes a selected image color transparent.

Part
IX
Ch
41

The first five buttons in the Image toolbar relate to assigning hyperlinks to that image. Those features are touched on briefly later in this chapter in the section "Creating Text and Graphic Hyperlinks."

The Transparency button allows you to make one background color in an image invisible. Some Web graphic images created in Office cannot be changed to transparent images in FrontPage 97. However, many images can have a background color removed by clicking the Make Transparent tool, and then clicking the color in the image which you want to make disappear.

N O T E A full discussion of the image editing tools in FrontPage 97 is beyond the scope of this book, but feel free to experiment with them. You can always undo changes to an image by clicking the Reset button in the Image toolbar, *as long as you have not saved your Web page or click the Resample button.* ■

CAUTION

When you save your Web page, you will be prompted to save changes to embedded graphic images on that page. After you OK the Save Embedded Files dialog box, you cannot revert to your original image in FrontPage. Your only option is to import the original into your Web again and replace the edited image.

Assigning Other Image Attributes

There are important image attributes that are not available in the Image toolbar. You can assign interlacing, alternate text, and text wrapping. *Interlacing* allows your image to "fade in," so that visitors to your Web site can see a vague version of the image before the file completely downloads. Alignment enables you to wrap text around an image. Alternate Text defines text that displays for visitors whose browsers do not display graphics, and that displays when visitors move their cursor over an image. Alternate text also displays while an image is loading.

You can also edit image size in the FrontPage 97 Editor. To edit graphic image attributes:

1. Right-click the graphic image in the FrontPage 97 Editor and select Image Properties.

2. Use the General tab of the Image Properties dialog box to choose graphic image format (GIF or JPEG), interlacing (available only with GIF format), transparency, and alternate text (in the Text area).

3. Use the Appearance tab in the Image Properties dialog box to define image alignment. This tab also enables you to define Border Thickness, Horizontal Spacing, and Vertical Spacing around an image in pixels (the tiny dots that make up a monitor image).

   You can define image size in pixels or percent (of the screen) in the Appearance tab of the Image Properties dialog box. However, it is easier to define image size by clicking and dragging corner or side handles on the image itself in the FrontPage 97 Editor.

N O T E A brief note on image formats: Web browsers can interpret images in two graphic file formats, GIF and JPEG, also referred to as JPG. GIF files allow interlacing and transparency, while JPEG files do not. A thorough discussion of Web graphic file formats can be found in many Web graphics and FrontPage 97 books. In general, you can simply use the GIF file format for Web graphics. ■

To resize images in the FrontPage 97 Editor, follow these steps:

1. Click the image to select it. Eight small handles appear on the corners and sides.
2. Click and drag a corner handle to resize the image without changing the proportions of the image, as shown in Figure 41.9.
3. Click and drag on a side, top, or bottom handle to resize and reshape an image.
4. Save the Web page using File, Save, or by clicking the Save button in the FrontPage 97 Editor menu bar. You will be prompted to resave the image.

FIG. 41.9

Resizing an image in the FrontPage Editor.

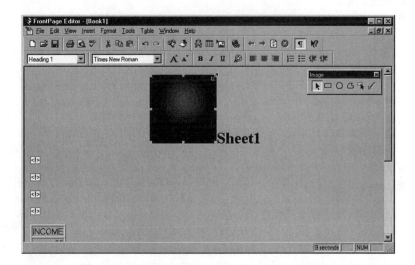

Adding Backgrounds, Clip Art, and Icons

You can enhance your Web page by adding background, clip art, and other icons in the FrontPage 97 Editor.

To change background color or image:

1. Right-click anywhere in the FrontPage 97 Editor, and select Page Properties from the shortcut menu.
2. Choose the Background tab of the Page Properties dialog box.
3. Use the Background pop-up list to choose an alternate background color for your Web page. Avoid colors that will clash with or cover up your text.

4. Use the Background Image check box to assign a background pattern to your Web page. You can use any graphic image as a background. The image will be tiled (copies placed side-by-side) to fill the whole page.

5. Some backgrounds fill the left edge of the Web page with an image, and work best with a margin assigned to the page. You can assign a top or right page margin in Margin tab of the Page Properties dialog box.

6. When you have defined page background (and margin if you like), choose OK in the Page Properties dialog box.

Figure 41.10 shows a Web page with the GrayWeave background.

FIG. 41.10

A Web Page in the FrontPage Explorer with a background image and a left margin.

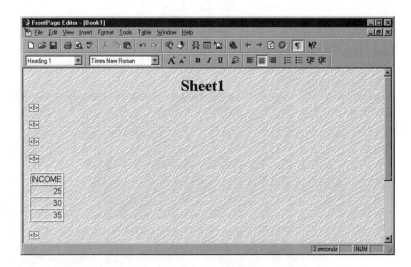

You can add images to your Web site using FrontPage 97's collection of clip art. Select Insert, Clipart from the FrontPage 97 Editor menu bar. When you have selected an image, OK the Image dialog box.

Another option for placing images on your Web page is to copy images directly from Office 97 applications into the FrontPage 97 Editor. When you save your Web page, you can save these embedded images as part of the Web site.

Creating Text and Graphic Hyperlinks

There are many Web page attributes that can be assigned in the FrontPage 97 Editor, but one of the most important is defining *hyperlinks*—links to other objects on an intranet or the World Wide Web. When a visitor clicks a hyperlink in your Web page, he or she jumps to the target of that link.

The easiest way to place a text hyperlink in FrontPage 97 is to simply type a Web address. That address can be a Web page, starting with **http://**, or an e-mail address starting with **mailto:**.

Typing text that starts with **http://** or **mailto:** automatically creates a hyperlink when you press the spacebar or press Enter.

Figure 41.11 shows a Web site address typed into the FrontPage 97 Editor. The underlined display indicates that this text is hyperlinked.

FIG. 41.11

The underline indicates that it is a hyperlink.

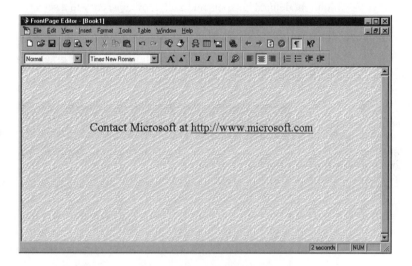

You can also assign hyperlinks to text or graphics. Here's how:

1. Select the text or graphic image to which you will assign a hyperlink.

2. Click the Create or Edit Hyperlink button in the Standard toolbar.

3. If you are creating a link to a Web page in your current Web site, double-click the target Web page in the list that appears in the Create (or Edit) Hyperlink dialog box.

4. If you are defining a link to another site on the World Wide Web, enter that URL (location) in the URL area, or click the Use Your Web Browser to Select a Page button and navigate to the target page in the World Wide Web.

N O T E You can use the other icons in the Create (or Edit) Hyperlinks dialog box to define links to files on your local dive, an e-mail address, or a new Web page that you design in FrontPage. A full discussion of types of Internet locations is beyond the scope of this chapter. ■

5. When you have defined your hyperlink, OK the Create (or Edit) Hyperlink dialog box.

Defining Image Maps

Image maps are Web graphics that have more than one hyperlink. You can assign image map hotspots using the Image toolbar that appears when you select an image.

Part

IX

Ch

41

To create an image map:

1. Click an image to which you will assign hotspot links to other Web locations.

2. The Image toolbar appears with the Select tool depressed by default. The three shaped tools (Rectangle, Circle, and Polygon) are used to define hotspots. The remaining tools highlight defined hotspots and assign transparency to a selected color. In many cases, the Rectangle tool will be the best choice for defining hotspots. Circular hotspots can be defined using the Circle tool. The Polygon tool is reserved for quite complex hotspots.

   Click the appropriate tool, and draw a hotspot on your graphic image, as shown in Figure 41.12.

FIG. 41.12
Define an image map hotspot using the Rectangle tool.

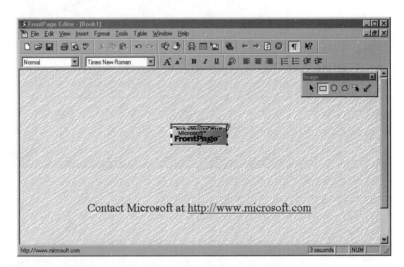

3. As soon as you release the mouse button, the Create Hyperlink dialog box appears. Define a hyperlink using the same procedures covered in the previous section in this book.

Saving and Testing Your Web Site

When you save a Web page, you will be prompted to save any changes you have made to images on that page. If your images were not originally saved to a Web-compatible format like GIF, FrontPage 97 will convert them to GIF files.

Saving any document frequently is always a good idea. Saving FrontPage 97 Web pages takes on special importance, because embedded images are saved as well.

You can get a good idea of how your Web page will look in the FrontPage 97 Editor. You can even test hyperlinks in the FrontPage 97 Editor by holding down your Ctrl key and clicking hyperlinked text or images. Figure 41.13 shows a hyperlink being selected in the FrontPage

Editor. You can also test hyperlinks by viewing your Web page in Preview mode—by clicking the Preview tab in the FrontPage Editor. In the Preview tab, you can test hyperlinks by clicking them.

FIG. 41.13
Check a hyperlink in the FrontPage Editor Preview tab. The target URL is tested for status.

Still, to really test your Web page, you want to see it in a browser. FrontPage 97 is bundled with Internet Explorer, one of the two most popular Web browsers. During the installation process, you can elect to install IE along with FrontPage 97.

You can view your Web page in your system's default Web browser by choosing File, Preview in Browser from the FrontPage 97 Editor menu, or by clicking the Preview in Browser button in the Standard toolbar.

Save your work before you preview your page. Only changes that have been saved to the Web site will be reflected in your browser.

After you save your Web page and view it in your browser, you can return to FrontPage 97 to touch up your page.

When you close and save all open pages in FrontPage 97, changes are all recorded and organized in the FrontPage 97 Explorer. You can then close the Explorer, and there is no need to save the Web site.

Part
IX
Ch
41

TROUBLESHOOTING

You can verify that your hyperlinks are current and working in the FrontPage Explorer. Select Tools, Verify Hyperlinks in the FrontPage Explorer menu. The FrontPage Editor will test all your hyperlinks, and list those whose links are broken.

CHAPTER 42

Making Your Web Site Interactive

You can use the Web pages and Web page elements you create in Office by combining them with the additional Web muscle of FrontPage. You will work with the FrontPage Explorer to import your Web site files, and the FrontPage Editor to fine-tune your Web pages. ■

Timestamp your Web pages

Visitors may be curious when your Web site was last updated. FrontPage 97 will automatically post a message with that information on your Web page.

Generate tables of contents

FrontPage 97 will generate and automatically update a table of contents for your Web site that includes hyperlinks to all the pages in your site.

Search engines let visitors find information quickly

You can define search boxes with FrontPage 97, with the option of displaying the size, date, and relevance of located Web pages in your site.

Get input from visitors

Use Input Forms for surveys, customer support, or sales. FrontPage 97 lets you direct input data to e-mail, HTML Web pages, or even reports that can be opened and edited using Office 97 applications.

Creating Interactive Web Sites

The FrontPage 97 Explorer is a powerful tool for organizing, orchestrating, and coordinating Web sites. And the FrontPage 97 Editor allows you to touch up, edit, and format Web pages you created by saving Office 97 documents as HTML files. But there is much more to FrontPage 97.

FrontPage 97's most powerful features are those that allow you to create an interactive Web site. Interactive Web sites change in relation to input from visitors. This interaction can be as simple as a navigation button changing its look when a visitor moves his or her cursor over the button. Or, interactivity can take the form of visitors submitting comments to a Web site that are immediately published for other visitors to share.

Interactivity on Web sites is possible without FrontPage 97, but it requires programming in Java, Perl, JavaScript, CGI, and other programming languages that are not the kind of thing even a programmer picks up in a weekend. Even for an advanced Office 97 user, it is much easier to add interactivity to your Web site with FrontPage than it is to wrestle with the latest Web-compatible programming language.

Figure 42.1 shows a Web page with several interactive components:

- Search capability.
- A line informing the user the last time the page was updated.
- An updated table of contents with the date that the site was updated

This chapter will cover the process of placing all these interactive elements in your Web site, as well as other interactive components.

FIG. 42.1

FrontPage helps you create an interactive Web page. This one has a search tool, an up-dated table of contents, and a message telling visitors when the site was last updated.

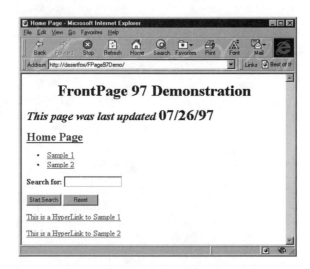

Later in this chapter, you will learn to create input forms like the one in Figure 42.2. Input forms collect data from visitors.

FIG. 42.2

An input form lets you get information from visitors. This one includes radio buttons, check boxes, drop-down lists, and input areas.

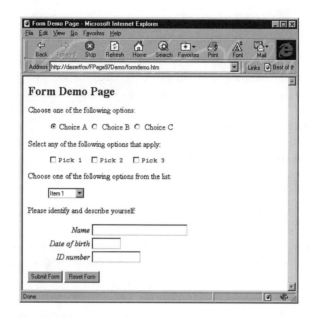

Timestamping Your Page

Timestamps let your visitors know when the Web page was last changed. You insert a timestamp in the FrontPage Explorer simply by placing your cursor where the timestamp is to appear, and choosing Insert, Timestamp from the FrontPage Editor menu bar. Figure 42.3 shows the Timestamp Properties dialog box that appears when you insert a timestamp. The Timestamp Properties dialog includes two display choices and two format choices—you can define how you want to display your timestamp, and how you want the timestamp to be updated.

FIG. 42.3

Select timestamp options to display the date and time the page was updated.

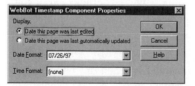

If you choose the Date This Page Was Last Edited radio button, your timestamp will display the date that you manually made changes to your site. If you choose the Date This Page Was Last Automatically Updated radio button, the timestamp will indicate the date automatic changes were made to the page. For example, if you place a table of contents on your Web page, and that table of contents has been updated, the second radio button option will reflect that change, but the first one will not.

Part
IX

Ch
42

The other choices in the Timestamp Properties dialog box are pretty simple—you can elect to display either the date the page was updated, the time, or both. And the two drop-down lists let you choose a format for displaying date (and time, if you elect to display it).

You can place a timestamp anywhere in a Web page that is open in the FrontPage Editor. A timestamp does not need to simply take the form of "this page was last updated...." For example, in Figure 42.1, the embedded timestamp is integrated with a table of contents that also updates whenever the Web site is updated.

Generating a Current Table of Contents

FrontPage 97 will generate a table of contents that lets visitors see the contents of your entire Web site.

To insert a table of contents, follow these steps:

1. Place your cursor in the FrontPage Editor at the spot in your Web page where you want to insert the table of contents. Often this is done at the beginning or the end of a site's home page.

2. Select Insert, Table of Contents from the FrontPage 97 menu bar.

3. Enter an URL, or browse to one, to define a Starting Point of Table. You can leave this at the default, which will be the site's home page. Leaving the URL set to the Web site home page will include all Web pages in the table of contents. If your Web site is organized into subfolders, you can elect to only display select folders.

4. Choose whether or not to display an automatically generated title for your Table of Contents. If you select None from the Heading Size drop-down list, you can still add a heading for the table of contents in the body of the Web page.

5. Click the Show Each Page Only Once check box to list each page one time only. If you deselect this check box, you may get multiple listings of a single page if there are several hyperlinks to that page.

6. Click the Show Pages with No Incoming Hyperlinks *only* if you want to send visitors to pages in your Web site to which there are no links running back to the site home page. If you have pages on your Web site that are not open to the public, do not select this check box.

7. Select the Recompute table of contents When Any Other Page Is Edited if you want the table to automatically regenerate when new pages are added (or old ones are deleted). This is a very handy option, as it keeps your Table of Contents updated automatically.

8. When you have made your choices from the Table of Contents Properties dialog box, choose OK. You will only see the actual contents of your Web site when you view your Web site using an online browser.

N O T E   The Preview Tab of the FrontPage Editor will hide codes and formatting marks that are not visible in a browser. However, you cannot use the Preview tab to test most interactive features. Active buttons don't act "active" in the Preview tab; the table of contents does not display site contents; and so on. ■

Adding a Search Engine to a Web Page

FrontPage 97 will allow you to create search engines that let visitors search your entire Web site. The way the Search box works is that visitors enter some characters (letters, numbers, or symbols)—usually words—and FrontPage's search engine will find pages in the Web site that contain all or most of the characters. After you place a search box in your Web site, visitors can use it to find pages that are relevant to topics they are looking for. The search engine then gives visitors a list of pages, listed in order of relevancy.

You can define the way search engine results are displayed. Figure 42.4 shows the results of a search, displaying the Document Title, Date, File Size, and Score of each of the found Web pages. Only the Document title need be displayed; the other three columns are optional. But the form of Search Result display is defined by the Web site designer (you), not the visitor.

FIG. 42.4

Search results are shown with details. Visitors see when the date pages were created, the size of the page, and a score that tells them how relevant the page is to the topic they are searching for.

To create a Search box:

1. Place your cursor in the FrontPage Editor where you want to insert the Search Box in the Web page.

2. Select Insert, Active Elements, Search from the FrontPage menu bar.

3. You are likely to be happy with the default settings in the Search Form Properties tab of the Search Form Properties dialog box. Or, you can redefine the name of the on-screen label by entering text in the Label for Input area. You can resize the button in the Width in Characters area, and rename the button in the Label for "Start Search" Button area. And you can rename the Reset button in the Label for "Clear" Button area.

Part

IX

Ch

42

4. The Search Results tab is where you define the form of the report table that displays search results. Use the check boxes to display (or not display) Score, File Date, and File Size. Leave the entry in the Word List to Search at All, as it is in the default dialog box. If you want to hide pages from visitors searching your site, move them into the _Private folder in the FrontPage 97 Explorer.

5. When you have defined the Search box and the format that results will display in—as shown in Figure 42.5—choose OK in the Search Form Properties dialog box.

FIG. 42.5

Define the properties of a Search box.

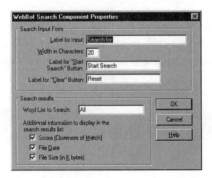

Designing Input Forms

Input forms are a powerful form of collecting and sharing information over the Web. Without any programming or database expertise, Office 97 users can use FrontPage 97 to collect and organize data from site visitors.

Can't you collect information from visitors through e-mail? Yes, you can. But e-mail is totally unstructured, and the information you get is completely defined by the person sending you the message. When you define input forms, you can collect exactly the data you are looking for. And you can send that data to a file that can be opened by any Office 97 application.

Creating Input Forms

You can collect input in a variety of forms in your Web site: radio buttons, check boxes, one-line text boxes, drop-down menus, and scrolling text boxes. Radio buttons are grouped, and a visitor must select one and only one radio button in a group. Check boxes can be selected or not. Drop-down menus allow visitors to pick from a multiple choice of options. One-line and scrolling text boxes allow for free-form input.

All input form fields are organized into forms. As soon as you define an input form field—any of the five types discussed previously—a form is defined in the FrontPage Editor, and Submit and Reset buttons are placed in the form.

All the data collected by form fields within an input form is saved to the same target file. The section later in this chapter "Collecting Data from Input Forms" shows you how to assign target files.

Figure 42.6 shows an input form with five different types of input fields. The form is enclosed with dotted lines. All form fields must be within a form in order for input to be processed.

FIG. 42.6

Defining a form in
FrontPage Editor.
The form has radio
buttons, check boxes,
a drop-down list, and
a one-line text box.

Radio buttons ——

Check boxes ——

Drop-down menu ——

One-line text box ——

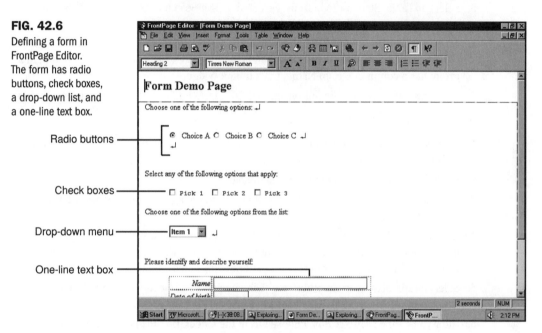

Different types of form fields have different parameters and options. Each Form Field dialog box has a Tab Order area, where you can define the order that this field is accessed by visitors who press the Tab key to move from one form field to another.

All form fields all must be within an input form—which will be delineated by dotted lines. If you attempt to create a new form field outside an existing input form, a new input form will be generated with Submit and Reset buttons.

Any type of form field can be placed on a Web page using the Forms toolbar in the FrontPage Editor. You can view the Forms toolbar by selecting View, Forms Toolbar from the FrontPage 97 menu bar. You can also insert a form field by choosing Insert, Form Field.

To insert radio buttons:

1. Place your cursor in the FrontPage Editor at the location you will create an input form. If you want to include your radio button input fields in an existing form, place your cursor within the existing form.

2. Click the Radio button in the Forms toolbar.

3. Enter a label so the visitor knows what it is she is selecting with the radio button.

4. Double-click the inserted Radio button and enter a Group Name and a Value. The Group Name encompasses all radio buttons that together comprise a multiple choice. Visitors will only be able to select one of any group of radio buttons. The Value will display in reports generated by visitor input.

5. Select an Initial State radio button—Selected or Not Selected. Only one radio button in a group can have an initial state of being selected.

6. After you have created one radio button, copy it to create more choices. Edit the cloned radio buttons by double-clicking them and changing the values so each radio button in a group has a common Group Name, but a unique Value.

7. After you define each radio button, choose OK in the Radio Button Properties dialog box.

To insert check boxes:

1. Place your cursor in the FrontPage Editor at the location you will create an input form, or within an existing input form.

2. Click the Check Box tool in the Forms toolbar.

3. Enter a label so visitors know what it is they are checking or not checking with the Check Box.

4. Double-click the inserted Check Box and enter a Name and a Value. The Name is a unique field name that identifies the nature of the input when input results are generated. The Value will display in reports generated by visitor input.

5. Select an Initial State radio button for each check box—Selected or Not Selected. Any check box can be selected or not selected.

6. After you define a Check Box, choose OK in the Check Box Properties dialog box.

To insert drop-down menus:

1. Place your cursor in the FrontPage Editor at the location you will create a drop-down menu, or within an existing input form.

2. Click the Check Box tool in the Forms Toolbar.

3. Enter a label so visitors know what it is they are choosing from the drop-down menu.

4. Double-click the inserted Drop-Down Menu field, and click the Add button in the Drop-Down Menu Properties dialog box. The Add Choice dialog box allows you to enter selections to be made by the visitor filling out the form. If you like, you can click the Specify Value check box, and then enter a value for each choice. For example, if a visitor chooses "I brush my teeth 3 times a day," the value of that choice (that will be sent to a report) can be "3."

5. Choose OK in the Add Choice dialog box when you have finished defining a menu choice. Continue to add choices as needed. You can double-click a line in the Choice area of the Drop-Down Menu Properties dialog box to edit choices.

Both one-line and scrolling input boxes allow visitors to enter text. Scrolling input boxes allow unlimited entry, while one-line input boxes are limited to one line of text.

You can create these input fields the same way you insert other form fields. You can assign field Names to each of these input boxes. Normally, you won't assign an Initial Value to a text box. If you do, it will appear as a default entry which can be erased when visitors enter text.

N O T E All form field property boxes have Validate buttons that allow advanced FrontPage 97 users to establish validation criteria for input. These validation criteria are tricky to define and are the province of advanced FrontPage 97 books. ■

Use FrontPage 97 Templates

One easy way to create a Web page is to take advantage of the many template Web pages available in the FrontPage Editor. To create a new Web page, select File, New from the FrontPage Editor menu bar.

The New dialog box has dozens of page templates. You can see a preview of what the page will look like by clicking one of the pages in the list. Figure 42.7 shows a Four Column Page (centered) template selected and previewed.

FIG. 42.7
Preview a Web page template. The four-column layout is displayed in the Preview area on the right of the dialog box.

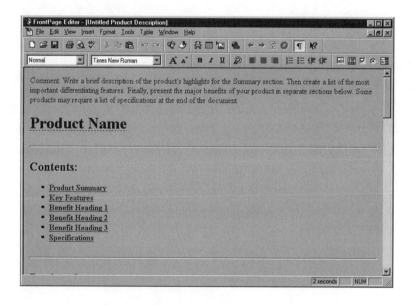

Template Web pages use features beyond the scope of this book, like using tables to create a column text look. You can incorporate these advanced features into your Web site by borrowing from FrontPage 97's list of templates.

Part
IX

Ch
42

You can create even more complex Web pages by clicking the Frames tab in the New dialog box. With the templates available in the Frames tab, you can create Web pages that combine more than one Web page in a browser.

More FrontPage 97

There is a large FrontPage 97 support community you can go to for additional help with FrontPage 97. Que has FrontPage books available for every level of user.

ON THE WEB

You can find a list of FrontPage support resources at the Unauthorized FrontPage Support Site:

http://infomatique.iol.ie:8080/dave

You can also get information on FrontPage at the Microsoft FrontPage site. The URL is:

http://www.microsoft.com/frontpage/

Office 97 Power User Reference
for Windows 95

43 Windows Navigation Basics   845

44 Managing Files   881

45 Adding New Hardware to Windows 95   935

46 Controlling Printers   961

47 Installing, Running, and Uninstalling Windows
Applications   993

48 Backing Up and Protecting Your Data   1015

CHAPTER 43

Windows Navigation Basics

What you learn in this and the next chapter will help you operate Windows and any Windows application. This chapter describes the parts of the Windows screen, how to start Windows and applications, and reveals numerous productivity tips.

This chapter also briefly introduces Windows Explorer (which Chapter 44, "Managing Files," covers in more detail). ■

Techniques for starting and quitting Windows

Explanations of the different ways to start and shut down Windows 95.

How to run programs automatically at startup

If you launch the same program every time you start your day, why not let Windows 95 launch it for you?

How to start programs with different Windows properties

Learn to configure your system's environment so programs with special requirements get exactly what they need to run productively.

How to create shortcuts for starting programs and opening documents

Learn how to skip the menu system by getting where you want to go directly from the desktop.

How to use Explorer and My Computer to start applications

Can't find a program on the menu? Here's another way to click and launch applications.

How to manage Windows when a program fails

Don't turn off the computer; Windows 95 has features to help you unfreeze your system.

Starting and Quitting Windows

After you install Windows, you can start Windows simply by turning on your computer. In most cases, computers start directly into Windows 95. If your computer requires a real-mode (16-bit) driver, you might see a DOS-like text screen as the drivers load. (Windows 95 has many new drivers, but real-mode drivers might be required for hardware that does not have a Windows 95 32-bit driver. These real-mode drivers are the ones used by Windows 3.x or DOS.) Also, if your Windows has multiple configurations installed—for example to work with different hardware configurations—then a text screen prompts you to choose between the configurations. After you make your choice, Windows starts.

 T I P   For a faster startup, press the Esc key during startup of Windows 95 to bypass the Windows 95 logo. To permanently bypass the logo, use Notepad or WordPad to edit the MSDOS.SYS file. Add LOGO=0 to the Options section. To see the logo on startup, just change the 0 to 1.

When Windows starts, it may display a dialog box that contains your name and a space for you to enter your password. Windows uses the name and the password from the login dialog box for several purposes:

- Windows uses the name to match it against a User Profile so that when users log in, the system displays the desktop and the software settings they configured.

- If the computer is connected to a network, Windows logs you into the network using the name as the network username and the password to enforce network security. (If the computer is connected to a network, an additional field will be displayed in the dialog box for the Domain or server name.)

N O T E   If you are not using the login dialog box to enter a network password or to load custom settings, then you might as well avoid seeing it each time you start Windows. To prevent the login dialog box from appearing, follow this procedure:

1. Right-click Network Neighborhood, then click Properties.
2. Click the Configuration tab, then choose Windows Logon from the Primary Network Logon pull-down list. Click OK.
3. Click No when Windows prompts to restart the computer.
4. Open the Start menu and choose Settings, Control Panel to open the Control Panel.
5. Double-click the Passwords icon.
6. Choose the Change Passwords tab, then click the Change Windows Password button. Click OK, then enter a blank password. ■

After login is complete, the Windows 95 desktop is displayed, with the My Computer, Recycle Bin, and Network Neighborhood icons. You might also see the My Briefcase icon and shortcut icons created by prior users. The *taskbar* usually appears at the bottom of the screen.

If you share a computer with others, you must restart to use your customized features. Windows 95 saves desktop and network settings by name (in profile files with the extension .PWL). Shut down with the Close All Programs and Log On as a Different User? option (see Figure 43.1).

Part

X

Ch

43

FIG. 43.1

Windows enables you to shut down the computer, restart the computer, restart the computer in MS-DOS mode, or close all applications and log on with another user ID.

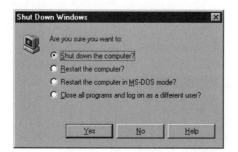

N O T E   The taskbar might not appear at the bottom of the screen as shown throughout this book. It can be moved or hidden. If hidden, it appears as a very thin line at the edge of a screen. To display the taskbar, move the pointer to the edge of the screen where the taskbar resides. ■

   When you initially run Windows, it displays a Welcome to Windows 95 screen. People usually disable this by clearing the check box on this Welcome dialog box. If you ever want to rerun the Welcome screen, click Start, Run, and type Welcome in the edit box and click OK.

   If there are multiple desktop profiles on your Windows 95 system (either because there are multiple users or because you've created different desktops for different configurations), sometimes you can't tell which desktop you're using currently. To know who and where you are at all times, create a folder for the desktop for every profile. Name the folder to indicate the login name—for example, "This is Mary's Desktop." If you do this for each configuration, a glance at this empty folder's title will let you know which desktop you are currently working on. If you want, you could place a text file in the folder that enumerates the settings for this desktop profile.

Running Applications at Startup

You can customize programs to start automatically when Windows starts. You can even specify whether the program starts in a maximized or normal window.

Running Programs or Documents on Startup   To specify the programs or documents you want to run at startup, create a shortcut to the program or document in the Windows\Start Menu\Programs\Startup folder. When a document is in the Startup folder, Windows starts the document's program, then loads the document.

T I P If you want folders to open on your desktop when Windows starts, create shortcuts to the folders, then drag the shortcuts into the Startup folder. Set the shortcut's properties so the folder opens minimized to keep the desktop uncluttered.

To specify programs or documents that you want Windows to run at startup, follow these steps:

1. Right-click in a gray area between buttons on the taskbar, then click Properties.
2. Select the Start Menu Programs tab (see Figure 43.2).

FIG. 43.2
Use the Start Menu Programs page to specify programs to run at startup.

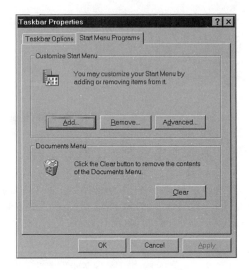

3. Choose Add, then click Browse.
4. Select the program you want to add to the Startup folder, then click Open (or double-click the program).
5. Click Next.
6. Select the Startup folder, then click Next.
7. Accept the default title for the program or type a new title in the Select a Name for the Shortcut text box. The name you enter appears in the Startup menu.
8. Click Finish.
9. Repeat steps 3 through 8 to add more programs to the Startup folder, or choose OK if you are finished adding programs.

N O T E   If you frequently change the programs or documents that you want to run on startup, make the Startup folder accessible as a shortcut on the desktop so you can drag shortcuts to program or document files in and out of it. Don't drag the actual program or document file to the Startup folder because you might delete the actual file during later changes to the Startup folder. Creating shortcuts is described in the section "Using Shortcut Icons on the Desktop" later in this chapter. ■

To bypass the Startup group during Windows startup—preventing the objects in the Startup group from opening—hold down the Shift key while Windows is starting (after you enter your logon user name and password). Release the Shift key after the desktop appears.

To remove a program or document from the Startup folder, follow these steps:

1. Choose Remove on the Start Menu Programs dialog box.
2. Double-click the Startup folder.
3. Select the program you want to remove and choose Remove.
4. Choose Close.

You can also delete the shortcut from the Windows\Start Menu\Programs\Startup folder.

Controlling the Window in Which Startup Programs Appear   After specifying that a program run at startup, you must choose to have the program run maximized, in a normal window, or as a button on the taskbar (minimized).

To control how a program appears on startup, follow these steps:

1. Add the program to the Startup folder, as described in the previous section "Running Programs and Documents on Startup." (If you manually drag a file into the Startup folder, use a right-drag and create a shortcut rather than leaving the actual file in the Startup folder.)
2. Open the Startup folder in either My Computer or Explorer. The Startup folder is located in Windows\Start Menu\Programs\Startup.
3. Right-click the program object, then choose Properties.
4. Select the Shortcut tab.
5. Select one of the three options, Normal Window, Minimized, or Maximized, from the Run drop-down list (see Figure 43.3).
6. Choose OK.

TROUBLESHOOTING

After putting some applications in the Startup folder so they would run on startup, Windows might fail to start correctly. Check to see if the applications in the Startup folder are causing the problem by holding down the Shift key as Windows starts. This prevents applications in Startup from starting. If Windows starts correctly, then a problem exists with one of the applications. Remove all the applications from the folder, then put each back, one at a time, until you find the offending application.

FIG. 43.3
Use the Shortcut
Properties page to
configure how Word for
Windows will run on
startup.

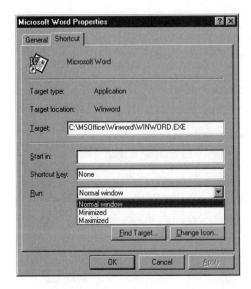

Starting Windows After Technical Problems Occur

If you have trouble starting Windows, there are a number of paths you can take to continue
working with Windows and to troubleshoot the problem so it doesn't recur.

ScanDisk Automatically Checks for Disk Errors   A new feature in the OSR2 release of Windows 95 is that if you have to shut down Windows abnormally then ScanDisk automatically
runs when you reboot. If, for example, you are forced to use the Ctrl+Alt+Delete key sequence
to shut down, ScanDisk will automatically check your hard disk for damaged files before Windows 95 restarts. Or, if someone turns off your computer without shutting down Windows,
ScanDisk runs when you start up your computer again. This assures that if there are any
damaged files on your hard disk, they will be detected by ScanDisk.

Using the Startup Disk   During the installation of Windows 95 there was an opportunity to
create a startup disk. If you didn't take advantage of the opportunity, you should have created a
startup disk once you configured your system. Then, if you have trouble starting Windows, you
can use the startup disk to start your computer. For example, if Windows becomes corrupted
by a virus, you can still retrieve undamaged data from your hard drive before you reformat the
drive and reinstall Windows. Always make multiple startup disks and test them to make sure
they give you access to your hard drive and CD-ROM drive.

If you have a startup disk and you cannot get Windows to run, you can boot from the startup
disk and copy data off the hard drive or copy missing files back on the hard drive that may be
needed by Windows. If you have modified the startup disk for CD-ROM access, you will have
access to your CD-ROM drive so you can reinstall Windows.

CAUTION

If you didn't create the startup disk during installation or have misplaced the disk, you can create one after Windows is installed. Make sure to do so now, before you need the disk.

To create a startup disk, follow these steps:

1. Open the Start menu and choose Settings, Control Panel.
2. Double-click the Add/Remove Programs button.
3. Click the Startup Disk tab (see Figure 43.4).

FIG. 43.4
Use the Startup Disk Properties Page to create a startup disk or to update an existing startup disk after you've made changes to your system.

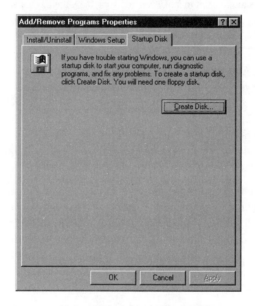

4. Insert a disk in drive A. The contents of this disk will be deleted.
5. Choose Create Disk and follow the instructions as they appear on-screen.

   To create the startup disk, you must have your original Windows program disks (or CD-ROM) since the Startup Disk boot files are copied from the source disks to be sure of their integrity.

6. Click OK.

Make at least two copies of your startup disk. Keep one accessible and the other in a safe location.

CAUTION

A startup disk created for a FAT16 version of Windows 95 will not give you access to the data on a hard drive formatted for FAT32 under Windows 95 OSR2. If your computer uses FAT32 created with OSR2, then you must create your startup disk from this system.

To use the startup disk, insert it in the disk drive and reboot the computer. Read the next section, "Starting Windows in an Alternate Startup Mode," for instructions on diagnosing and correcting problems.

 Label the startup disk and write-protect it to make sure it's going to be there when you need it and to prevent anyone from using it. Make two copies of your startup disk, one for your office and one for the vault.

Starting Windows in an Alternate Startup Mode   If the computer has difficulty starting, you will want to start Windows in one of its diagnostic modes. In most troubleshooting situations, you will want to start in *safe mode*. In safe mode, Windows uses basic default settings that restart Windows with minimal functionality. For example, if you install the wrong driver for a new monitor, you might not be able to see the Windows display when you restart Windows. In this case, restarting Windows in safe mode enables you to see the display so you can use the Control Panel or the Device Manager to correct problems.

The default safe mode settings use a generic VGA monitor driver, the standard Microsoft mouse driver, and the minimum device drivers necessary to start Windows. When you start Windows with the default settings, you cannot access CD-ROM drives, printers, modems, or other external hardware devices. One of the safe modes allows networking.

To start Windows in a different mode, follow these steps:

1. Turn on the computer.
2. As soon as you see the message Starting Windows on your monitor, press F8 to display the Windows 95 Startup Menu. This menu displays choices for different starting modes.

CAUTION

You need fast reflexes to boot into safe mode. If you press F8 before the Starting Windows message appears, it won't work because the keypress won't be noticed by Windows. If you wait longer than a second or so after the message appears, it's too late, so you'll have to shut the computer off and try again, and perhaps again and again until you get it timed properly. Incidentally, if you have dual boot choices, you have to select Windows 95 before all of this occurs.

The Microsoft Windows 95 Startup Menu offers choices that reflect the configuration of your system. You may see some or all of the following choices:

- Normal
- Logged (\BOOTLOG.TXT)
- Safe mode
- Safe mode with network support
- Step-by-step confirmation
- Command prompt only
- Safe mode command prompt only
- Previous version of MS-DOS

3. Type the selection number for the mode in which you want to start, then press Enter.

To skip the Windows 95 Startup Menu and start directly in a mode, start your computer and press one of the key combinations in the following table when the message Starting Windows appears.

TIP Windows 95 automatically starts in safe mode if you restart Windows 95 after it has failed to start successfully.

Operating Mode	Key Combination	Actions
Windows 95 in safe mode without networking	F5	Loads HIMEM.SYS and IFSHLP.SYS, loads DoubleSpace or DriveSpace if present, then runs Windows 95 WIN.COM. Starts in safe mode.
Windows 95 in safe mode with minimum of network functions	F6	Loads HIMEM.SYS and IFSHLP.SYS. Processes the Registry, loads COMMAND.COM, loads Double-Space or DriveSpace if present, runs Windows 95 WIN.COM, loads net drivers, and runs NETSTART.BAT.
DOS 7.0 without disk compression	Ctrl+F5	Loads COMMAND.COM.
DOS 7.0 with disk compression	Shift+F5	Loads COMMAND.COM, and loads DoubleSpace or DriveSpace if present.

A message informs you that Windows is running in safe mode and that some of your devices might not be available. The words Safe mode appear at each corner of the screen.

Understanding How Windows Achieves Safe Mode   Windows boots to safe mode using settings that enable most computers to run their basic system. The following steps describe what Windows does as it boots in safe mode:

1. Bypasses the Registry, AUTOEXEC.BAT, and CONFIG.SYS files.

2. Loads HIMEM.SYS without processing command line switches.

3. Loads IFSHLP.SYS.

4. Loads path information from the MSDOS.SYS file.

5. If Windows 95 files are available, then Windows executes from the command

   ```
   Win /D:m
   ```

   to boot into safe mode.

   If Windows 95 files are unavailable, then COMMAND.COM executes leaving the system in DOS mode.

6. If Windows booted correctly, then it looks for the Windows\SYSTEM.CB file. The SYSTEM.CB file loads virtual device drivers. If it cannot be found, a clean copy of SYSTEM.CB is created, which loads the following virtual device drivers:

mouse=*vmouse	device=*vcache	device=*biosxlat
device=*configmg	device=*vcond	device=*vmcpd
device=*vwin32	device=*int13	device=*vkd
device=*vfbackup	device=*vxdldr	device=*vdd
device=*vshare	device=*vdef	device=*ebios
device=*vcomm	device=*dynapage	device=*vtdapi
device=*ifsmgr	device=*reboot	device=*vmpoll
device=*ios	device=*vsd	woafont=dosapp.fon
device=*vfat		device=*parity

7. The SYSTEM.CB file is discarded and WIN.COM loads Windows. Windows 95 then uses the original Registry settings, SYSTEM.INI and WIN.INI files. This process effectively disables all the protected mode devices.

8. Finally, Windows 95 resizes the desktop to standard VGA, 640×480 resolution with 16 colors.

Troubleshooting in Safe Mode

Running in safe mode enables you to check and change device drivers that might be causing a problem or failing to work. For example, if you selected an incorrect video device driver, Windows 95 might fail on restart and leave you in safe mode.

If you suspect an incorrect video driver, follow these steps:

1. Right-click the desktop and choose Properties.

2. Select the Settings tab.

3. Click Change Display Type to display the Change Display Type dialog box in which you can check or change the Monitor or Adapter type. Click the appropriate Change button to select a different monitor or adapter using the Select Device dialog box.

4. Select Show All Devices from the Manufacturers list, then choose the right device from the Models list. If you're having serious problems or aren't sure about your hardware, choose the Standard device from each list (which will work with almost any hardware).

5. If you're changing a device, you'll need the original Windows 95 disks (or CD-ROM) or a disk from the hardware manufacturer in order to transfer the correct drivers. The drivers for the Standard devices are installed as part of your Windows 95 system.

If you suspect other hardware problems, see Chapter 45, "Adding New Hardware to Windows 95," for information on hardware troubleshooting.

Using a BOOTLOG.TXT to Troubleshoot Failures

Test for failure in loading device drivers by following the procedure mentioned in the earlier section "Starting Windows in an Alternate Startup Mode" and selecting 2. Logged (\BOOTLOG.TXT). This will attempt to start a normal load of Windows 95. During the loading of Windows, each action is recorded in the file BOOTLOG.TXT. This file is in the root directory of the boot disk.

If Windows fails to load, restart in Windows safe mode or DOS mode and read BOOTLOG.TXT by typing the command type **bootlog.txt|more** at a command prompt. This is a hidden file so you will not see it in a directory listing, but you can type it out.

BOOTLOG.TXT lists successful and failed actions as it loads devices. For example, you may see the following lines among the many lines in the file:

```
Loading Device = C:\WINDOWS\HIMEM.SYS
LoadSuccess = C:\WINDOWS\HIMEM.SYS
Loading Vxd = VCOMM
LoadSuccess = VCOMM
Loading Vxd = msmouse.vxd
LoadSuccess = msmouse.vxd
SYSCRITINIT = VCACHE
SYSCRITINITSUCCESS = VCACHE
DEVICEINIT = PAGEFILE
DEVICEINITSUCCESS = PAGEFILE
Dynamic load device netbeui.vxd
Dynamic init device NETBUI
Dynamic load success netbeui.vxd
Dynamic init success NETBUI
```

If a process failed, the word FAILED appears instead of SUCCESS. That means you either have a missing or bad driver, or for some reason Windows 95 can't load it.

Incidentally, in the preceeding list, Vxd means virtual device drivers and the references to NETBUI indicate network protocols that have to be loaded if the configuration included the installation of them.

Using Step-by-Step Mode to Interactively Test Startup

Interactively test each action in the boot process by following the procedure mentioned in the earlier section "Starting Windows in an Alternate Startup Mode" and selecting

4. `Step-by-Step Confirmation`. Each action will be displayed on-screen. You must type a **Y** (Yes) or **N** (No) for each action. You can boot Windows 95 but bypass suspect drivers by responding with **N**.

Frequently Used Troubleshooting Techniques

Windows 95 is far more stable than previous versions of Windows. However, if you face startup problems, the following sections describe some of the more frequently used troubleshooting tips.

Missing Files Message on Startup   If during startup you receive the error message `Bad or missing` *filename* and the file is a SYS file, then check the spelling and path names in CONFIG.SYS and check the existence of the file. Any device drivers that refer to the drive containing Windows should be moved to the beginning of CONFIG.SYS so files on the drive can be accessed.

If a system file is corrupt or missing, Windows might not run or operate. In that case, you will probably have to run the Windows 95 Setup and choose the option to reinstall in order to replace missing files.

Lost or Failed System Registry Files   Windows 95 stores user customization information as well as system and application information in Registry files that are required for operation. If the files are corrupt or lost, Windows 95 will attempt to recover on its own.

Windows 95 makes backup copies of SYSTEM.DAT and USER.DAT, which are stored with the extension DA0. If SYSTEM.DAT fails, Windows uses the backup SYSTEM.DA0. If Windows starts and displays the Registry Problem dialog box, then click the Restore From Backup and Restart button to restore both Registry files from their DA0 backups. If both SYSTEM.DAT and SYSTEM.DA0 files are missing, the Registry will not be restored. In that case, you need to copy backup copies of SYSTEM.DAT and USER.DAT back to the Windows folder. If you do not have backup copies, reinstall Windows.

Suspected Hardware Problem   If Windows cannot recognize certain installed devices, it will cause problems. Restart Windows in safe mode if it is not running, and make safety copies of your CONFIG.SYS and the device driver files referenced by CONFIG.SYS. These files may be useful for restoring your system to its previous configuration.

Use the Device Manager, as described in Chapter 45, "Adding New Hardware to Windows 95," to see if the device has conflicts. If the device has memory, IRQ, or SCSI port conflicts, try changing these values so they don't conflict with other devices. If you cannot resolve conflicts, use the Device Manager to remove the device, then reinstall the device using the Add New Hardware program found in the Control Panel. Chapter 45 discusses the Add New Hardware program.

Checking the Failure of Compression, Partitioning, and Hard Disk Operation   Some computers are configured to use compression software, or have a partitioned hard drive (especially if the partitioning was for multiple operating systems), or use special drivers for the hard disk in order to access all the available space on a large disk (for instance, drivers for large IDE drives in computers that don't have enhanced IDE controllers). These schemes can complicate attempts to remedy boot problems.

Real-mode drivers may have been required for the correct operation of some software programs such as compression and partition utilities as well as the operation of hardware such as hard disk drives. To check if a real-mode driver is required and if it is loaded during Windows 95 startup, go into an alternate startup mode by pressing F8 during startup and choose Step-by-Step Confirmation. Press Y to confirm each device driver as it loads. Watch for drivers that fail to load. When this occurs, check for missing files. If all drivers load, then compare the list of loaded device drivers to the device drivers that you think might be needed by your system.

Troubleshooting a Failure to Boot into MS-DOS   You will have trouble if you attempt to dual-boot into MS-DOS if the MS-DOS files are missing or are a version earlier than 5.0. The message Previous MS-DOS files not found will appear. If you need to start using an earlier version of MS-DOS, use a startup disk. When using an earlier version, drivers such as DBLSPACE.SYS might not be available.

Incorrect Application Starts on Startup   First, open the Windows\Start Menu\Programs\ Startup folder and see if the shortcuts there are the same as the programs you want to start. Delete shortcuts for programs you do not want to start.

Programs that start when Windows starts but do not appear in the Startup folder might be incorrect entries in the Registry. To check that the Registry points to the Startup folder as the folder containing the startup files, open the Start menu and choose Run, type **Regedit**, and choose OK. Choose Edit, Find and search for the Key "Shell Folders." You want to find the following key:

HKey_Current_User\Software\Microsoft\Windows\CurrentVersion\Explorer\Shell Folders

In the right pane, the Startup value should be *Windows*\Start Menu\Program\Startup. *Windows* is the drive and folder of the Windows 95 files. If the Startup folder is incorrect, double-click Startup and edit the Startup folder path in the Value Data edit box.

Restarting and Reinstalling from Your Startup Disk

If Windows 95 fails to boot and you can't get alternative boot modes such as fail safe to run, then you might need to start using the startup disk you made. After booting from the startup disk, you will be in DOS mode. You can copy important files or reinstall Windows 95 from this mode. If you did not make a startup disk, you might be able to use one from another Windows 95 computer to access your system. The startup disks must use the same file allocation system, either FAT16 or FAT32.

If you need to access a CD-ROM drive or a drive with compression installed, you will need to create an AUTOEXEC.BAT and CONFIG.SYS file on your startup disk that loads the appropriate drivers. Don't forget that any driver or file loaded by either AUTOEXEC.BAT or CONFIG.SYS has to exist on the disk.

To start your computer using the startup disk, turn off your system, insert the startup disk, and turn your system back on. Your computer will start in DOS mode.

N O T E   If the boot from drive A process doesn't work and your computer goes directly to drive C to boot, you'll have to check your system setup and make sure it's configured for a drive boot sequence of A, C. Getting into the CMOS setup varies depending upon the manufacturer of your BIOS. ■

Before reinstalling Windows 95, create backup copies of the SYSTEM.DAT and USER.DAT files. After reinstalling, you can restore these files to regain access to applications and user customization. SYSTEM.DAT and USER.DAT are hidden system files.

After reinstalling Windows, make backup copies of the default SYSTEM.DAT and USER.DAT files created by the reinstalled Windows. If you continue to have a problem, then copy your original two files back to the Windows folder. Restore their Hidden, System, and Read Only attributes by opening Explorer, right-clicking the file name, choosing Properties, and checking these attributes.

Using the Start Menu

The Start menu, which you access by clicking the Start button on the taskbar, is the starting place for many of the tasks you will accomplish in Windows. From the Start menu, you can open your programs, customize the look and feel of Windows, find files and folders, get Help, and shut down your computer (see Figure 43.5).

FIG. 43.5
Click the Start button for access to programs, resources, and recently used documents.

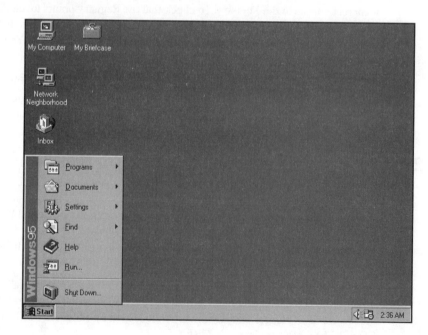

When you install Windows software the installation program places a shortcut to each program on a submenu that appears off of the Start menu. You can open the program simply by selecting it from a menu (see Figure 43.6).

FIG. 43.6

You can select the program you want to start from one of the menus that cascades from the Start menu. Here the user is starting WordPad.

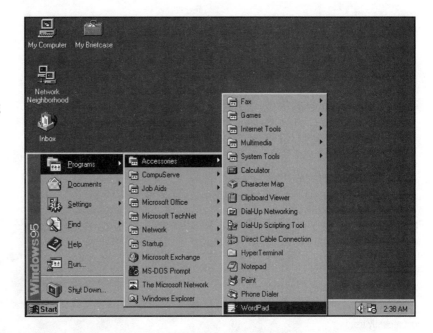

N O T E If you are upgrading from an older version of Windows to Windows 95, the Group windows that appeared in the Program Manager will become submenus that appear off of Programs in the Start menu. ■

 To display the taskbar and open the Start menu, even when the taskbar is hidden, press Ctrl+Esc.

Starting a Program from the Start Menu

To start a program from the Start menu, click the Start button, then click the program, if it appears at the top of the menu, or click Program. Click the program you want to start. To find the program you want, you might have to move through a series of submenus. You also can press Ctrl+Esc and use arrow keys to select a program, then press Enter.

If you have customized the taskbar, you might not see the taskbar and Start button on screen. If the Auto Hide feature is enabled, the taskbar resizes itself to a thin line at the edge of the screen. It may be difficult to locate this line if the taskbar has been moved to a screen edge other than its default position at the bottom of the screen. To display the taskbar and Start button, move the pointer to the edge of the screen where it is stored. Or, press Ctrl+Esc to display the taskbar and open the Start menu. (Press Esc to close the Start menu and keep the taskbar displayed.)

Buttons on the taskbar tell you which programs are open. Click a button to open or activate a program window. Learn more about switching between programs later in this chapter in the section "Using the Taskbar to Switch Between Programs."

N O T E   Usually, you should find the program you want to open in one of the Start menu's sub-menus. When you install Windows, the installation program looks for all your applications and puts each in one of the menus. If, however, you can't find your program in the Start menus, you can add a program or folder to the Start menu. ▓

Starting a Document from the Start Menu

After you click the Start button, you will notice a Documents command in the Start menu. When you choose this command, the Documents submenu appears with a listing of the files you have worked on recently (see Figure 43.7). Notice that only 32-bit Windows 95 programs display their documents on the most recently used list. Older 16-bit programs do not display documents in the list.

FIG. 43.7

The Document menu maintains a list of the documents you have worked with most recently so you can quickly reopen your most recently used documents.

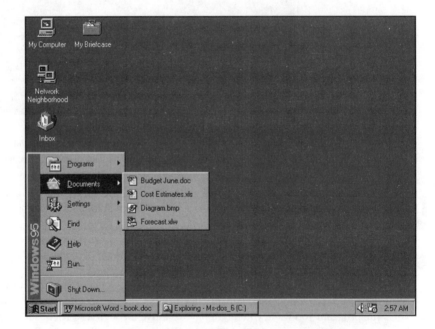

N O T E   The reason for that is that it's the software that is placing documents on the list, not the operating system. The software application takes advantage of the operating system's features by calling on Windows to display the name of the document. ▓

To open a document in this list, simply click it. Windows then automatically starts the associated application, if it is not already running, and opens the document.

After a while, the listing in the Documents menu can become quite long and contain documents you no longer are working with. To clear the list, open the Start menu and choose Settings, Taskbar. Select the Start Menu Programs tab on the Taskbar Properties sheet and choose the Clear button (see Figure 43.8). Click OK to close the Taskbar Properties sheet.

FIG. 43.8

Click Clear on the Start Menu Programs page to clear out your document list so you don't have to wade through a long list of documents.

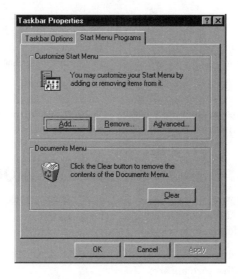

 If you often want to pare down your most frequently used documents list, create a shortcut on your desktop that points to the Windows\Recent folder. Double-clicking this folder will show you shortcuts to all the documents on the most recently used list. You can selectively delete documents you want off the list.

Using the Taskbar to Switch Between Programs

The taskbar is one of the most important and innovative features in Windows 95, making everything a lot easier than it was in previous versions of Windows. And, beyond ease of use, there are plenty of power and enhanced productivity levels available in the taskbar once you become more experienced and begin to customize them.

 If you can't see the full name of a program and document on a crowded taskbar, just pause the mouse pointer over the taskbar button and the full name will show in a ToolTip label.

If you work with a lot of open applications, your screen can become cluttered with many open windows. Rather than clutter the screen with several open windows, you can reduce the applications you're not using currently to buttons on the taskbar. As more buttons appear on the taskbar, the other buttons shrink to make room. To activate an application, you simply click its button on the taskbar. Figure 43.9 shows a taskbar with several buttons. To close an application from the taskbar, just right-click and choose Close.

FIG. 43.9
Use the taskbar to temporarily store applications while you're not using them.

TIP When the task bar gets crowded, it's usually easier to make it larger so you can see everything (rather than letting the buttons get so small you're not sure what they represent). You can drag the edge of the taskbar to resize it just as you can drag a window. Once it's larger, the buttons expand so you can read them.

To reduce an application to a button on the taskbar, click the Minimize button. To reactivate an application, click its button in the taskbar.

Using the Power of Shortcuts and Desktop Icons

Shortcuts are one of Windows 95's most powerful new features. You see shortcuts as icons with a small curved arrow at the icon's lower-left corner. They are actually pointers to a program, document, disk, folder, or other object such as a printer.

The flexibility of working with shortcuts is more amazing the more you work with them. Some of the things you can do with shortcuts are:

■ Start programs, open documents, or open folders

■ Drag and drop documents onto printer or fax shortcuts

■ Double-click shortcuts to Backup or Defragmenting tools to run them with settings you specify

■ Open documents directly to a specific location

■ Run DOS batch files that run DOS or Windows applications

■ Display a file in different folders or drives without creating multiple copies of the file

■ Link to the World Wide Web

■ Send shortcuts to other Windows users as embedded objects within a document

N O T E If you don't need (or want) to see those little curved arrows on shortcuts to remind you that a shortcut is a pointer, you can eliminate them:

1. Choose Run from the Start menu and enter REGEDIT in the Open text box. Choose OK.

2. In the Registry Editor window, click the plus sign next to the HKEY_CLASSES_ROOT folder.

3. Find the folder named lnkfile and select it to display its contents in the right pane.

4. In the right pane, right-click the IsShortcut item and choose Rename.

5. When the name is highlighted, use your arrow keys to move to the beginning of the name. Insert a letter (any letter) at the beginning of the name (for example, if you use

an x, the name will be xlsShortcut). Press Enter or click anywhere outside the name to complete the process.

6. Repeat the process in the folder named piffile (which eliminates the arrow in DOS shortcuts, including the shortcut to the MS-DOS prompt that is a must for every desktop).

Be aware that this action will give you no visual distinction between a shortcut and a program. ▪

Creating Shortcuts to Programs or Documents

To create a shortcut on your desktop for a program or document, follow these steps:

1. Using Explorer or My Computer, locate the program for which you want to create a shortcut. Position Explorer or My Computer window so you can see a portion of the desktop.

   See Chapter 44, "Managing Files," to learn how to use Explorer and My Computer for browsing files and folders.

2. Right-drag the file onto the desktop, then release the right mouse button.

3. Choose Create Shortcut(s) Here to create the shortcut.

If the document to which you created a shortcut is associated (or registered) with a program, you can start the program and open the document by double-clicking its shortcut.

Create a shortcut on the desktop to a program or document without opening Explorer or My Computer by right-clicking the desktop. Choose New, Shortcut to open a shortcut wizard. In the Wizard's first dialog box, choose Browse and select the program or document file to which you want a shortcut. Choose Next and edit the label for the shortcut. Finally, choose Finish.

N O T E If you're creating a shortcut for a program file, you don't have to right-drag the file object from Explorer or My Computer and then choose to place the shortcut from the right-drag menu. Windows 95 is smart enough to know that you're not moving an executable; you're making a shortcut. A simple left drag will accomplish the feat for program files.

The left drag technique does not work for batch files. If you want to create a shortcut for an executable with a .BAT extension, you must use the right-drag method. ▪

TROUBLESHOOTING

Double-clicking a shortcut icon no longer opens the document or program. What might have happened is that the file to which the shortcut pointed was moved or deleted. To correct this problem, you can either delete and then re-create the shortcut, or you can correct its Properties sheet. To delete the shortcut icon, right-click the icon, then choose Delete. Choose Yes when asked to confirm the deletion. Re-create the shortcut with the methods described in this section. To fix a shortcut to a file that has moved, right-click the icon, then choose Properties. Click the Shortcut tab. Check the file and path name in the Target box. They might be wrong. To find the file, click the Find Target button. This opens a window in My Computer to the file if it is found. If it cannot be found, you can search in My Computer for the correct file and path name.

Using Shortcut Icons on the Desktop

To start a program, you simply double-click its shortcut. If you don't like using menus to start your programs, you might prefer using shortcuts. A drawback to this method, however, is that to access the shortcut icons, your desktop must be visible. If a program is maximized, you cannot see the shortcuts. See the section "Accessing the Desktop" later in this chapter.

To open a document, double-click its shortcut. If the document's program is running, it will activate and open the document. If the program is not running, the program will start, then open the document. A document must be associated with a program for this to occur automatically. Normally, file associating or registration occurs during program installation.

Creating Shortcuts to Frequently Used Folders

Use shortcuts to folders as time savers. A shortcut to a folder into which you frequently move files can save you time moving files. A shortcut folder on the desktop also can help organize your desktop. Within the desktop shortcut folder, you can drag and drop the program and document shortcut icons you use. When you want to use one of these stored shortcuts, just double-click the folder shortcut.

If you frequently move files from Explorer into a specific folder, make a shortcut to that folder on the desktop. Now you can drag files from Explorer and drop them onto the folder shortcut. The shortcut acts like a tunnel, guiding the files into the real folder.

To make a shortcut that points to a folder using Explorer or My Computer, follow these steps:

1. Open Explorer or My Computer to display the folder from which you want to create a shortcut.
2. Right-drag the folder from either the right or left pane onto the desktop.
3. Choose Create Shortcut(s) Here.

TROUBLESHOOTING

After creating a shortcut to a folder, the folder doesn't appear to exist in Explorer or My Computer, but it does exist on the desktop. What has happened is that, in the process of right-dragging the folder onto the desktop, you accidentally chose the Move Here command instead of Create Shortcut(s) Here. Your folder still exists, but it is now located in the Windows\Desktop folder. To move it back to its original location, open Explorer and left-drag the folder from the Windows\Desktop folder back to the location where you want it.

Editing a Shortcut Name and Deleting Shortcuts

If you want to modify the name that appears under the icon, click the name once to select it. Then click the text and pause the mouse pointer. The pointer changes to an I-beam. You can press Delete to delete the name or click the I-beam where you want the insertion point. After you edit the name, press Enter or click a blank spot on the desktop.

To delete a shortcut, highlight it and press the Delete key (or right-click the shortcut and choose Delete). Choose Yes when the confirmation dialog box appears.

 TIP You can arrange icons on the desktop by right-clicking the desktop, then choosing the Arrange Icons command. You are given alternative ways of arranging them.

CAUTION

Be careful when deleting shortcuts from the desktop. When you delete a shortcut for a file, you delete only the shortcut, not the file. However, when you delete an icon that represents a file, you delete the file. Icons that appear with a small arrow at a lower corner are shortcuts. They can safely be deleted. Shortcuts that are deleted are sent to the Recycle Bin so you can retrieve them if you've deleted something by mistake.

Setting the Properties for a Shortcut Icon

You can change how a shortcut icon acts and how it appears by opening its Properties sheet and changing its properties. On the Properties sheet, you can find information such as when a shortcut was created. You also can make a variety of changes, such as the following:

- Change the file that the shortcut opens.
- Make an application start in a folder you specify.
- Add a shortcut key that activates the shortcut.
- Indicate whether you want the document or application to run minimized, maximized, or in a window.
- Change the icon used for a shortcut.

To display the Properties sheet and set the properties for a shortcut icon, follow these steps:

1. Right-click the shortcut icon.
2. Click Properties to display the General page of the Shortcut Properties sheet (see Figure 43.10).

   On the General page, you can read where the LNK file for the shortcut is stored, as well as when it was created, modified, and last used. You also can change its file attributes.
3. Click the Shortcut tab to see the Shortcut page (see Figure 43.11).

   At the top of the page, you can read the type of shortcut it is and the folder in which it is located. In the figure, the shortcut is to Explorer application in the Windows folder.
4. If you want a different file to start from the shortcut, type the folder and file name in the Target text box.

   If you are unsure of the location, click Find Target to open the My Computer window in which you can look for the file and folder you want. After you find the folder and file, close the My Computer windows and type the name in the Target text box.

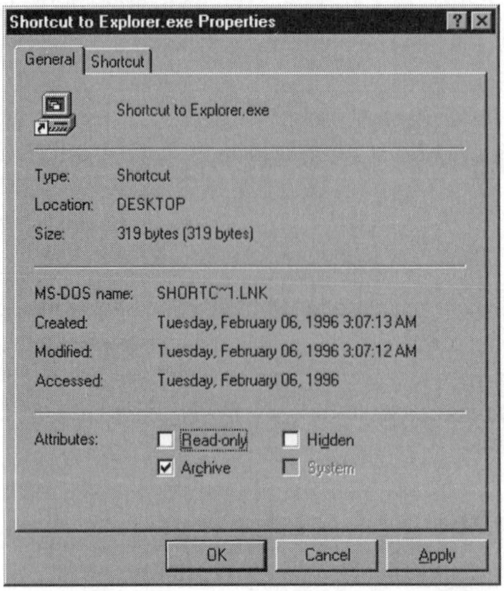

FIG. 43.10

The General page shows you file information about the shortcut icon.

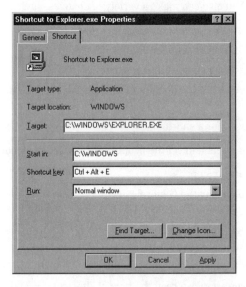

5. To specify a folder that contains the file or files necessary for operation, enter the drive and folders in the Start In text box.

6. To specify a shortcut key that will activate this shortcut icon, type the key you want as the shortcut key in the Shortcut Key text box. The key must be a letter or a number. You cannot use Esc, Enter, Tab, the space bar, Print Screen, or Backspace. To clear the Shortcut Key text box, select the text box and press the space bar.

   To use this shortcut key, you press Ctrl+Alt and the key you indicated. Shortcut keys you enter take precedence over other access keys in Windows.

FIG. 43.11

The Shortcut page enables you to specify the file, startup folder, shortcut key, and icon used by a shortcut.

T I P You can press a shortcut's key combination to run the shortcut's program or document even when
another program is active.

7. To specify the type of window in which the application or document will run, choose
Normal Window, Minimized, or Maximized from the Run drop-down list.

8. To change the icon displayed for the shortcut, click Change Icon to display the Change
Icon dialog box (see Figure 43.12).

The Change Icon dialog box displays a list of icons stored in files with the extensions
EXE, DLL, and ICO.

FIG. 43.12
You can select the icon
you want for your
shortcut.

9. Select the icon you want and choose OK.

10. Click the OK button to make your changes and close the Shortcut Properties sheet.
Click Apply to make your changes and keep the Shortcut Properties sheet open for more
changes.

N O T E When selecting icons for a shortcut, you don't have to restrict yourself to the icons in the
file the shortcut points to. You can select an icon from any other DLL, EXE, or ICO file. To see
other icon files in the Change Icon dialog box, click the Browse button. ▪

 T I P You can find icons in the Windows 95 file Windows\Subsystem\SHELL32.DLL. There are additional
files hidden in the same folder in the files PIFMGR.DLL and COOL.DLL. If you still have access to
Windows 3.x files, you can use Windows\PROGMAN.EXE and Windows\MORICONS.DLL.

Opening Programs and Documents
from Explorer or My Computer

Windows Explorer is an application that comes with Windows 95. Explorer is similar to the
earlier Windows versions' File Manager, but is much more powerful. You can use Explorer to
view the files and folders on your computer; move, copy, rename, and delete files and folders;
and perform other file-management tasks. You also can start programs and open documents

from Explorer. My Computer is similar to Explorer. The main difference between them is that, unlike the Explorer window, the My Computer window does not enable you to view the overall structure of or relationships among all your computer's resources. Typically, when you use My Computer, you view the contents of one folder at a time.

Using Explorer to Start Programs and Open Documents

You can use Explorer to find any file on your computer. After you find the file, you also can use Explorer to start the program or open the document. If the file is a program file, you can start the program by double-clicking the file in Explorer. If the file is a document, you can start its associated application and open the document simultaneously. If the application is already running, Windows opens the document in that application.

Figure 43.13 shows the Explorer window displaying files in Detail view. Look at the Type column in the right pane of Explorer to see the file type.

FIG. 43.13
Explorer window displays all of your computer's resources, including folders and files.

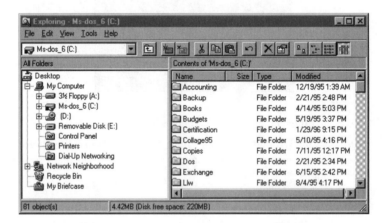

TROUBLESHOOTING

Double-clicking a file in Explorer doesn't immediately open the file. The Open With dialog box displays asking which program should be used to open the file. Windows does not recognize the application used to open the document you double-clicked. Windows displays the Open With dialog box so you can select the application to open. Windows records this application so it can open the same application the next time you double-click this type of document.

Many users prefer to organize their documents in the Explorer folders, which are named by category. Rather than work in a program such as Word to open files, they leave Explorer open. When they want to open a document, they open the appropriate folder in Explorer and double-click the document's file.

Using My Computer to Start Programs and Open Documents

The first time you start Windows, you see an icon called My Computer on your desktop. If you double-click this icon, the My Computer window appears (see Figure 43.14). You can use My Computer to view your computer's resources, including folders and files. Figure 43.15 shows a window of folders that displays after double-clicking the C: drive icon.

FIG. 43.14
The My Computer window is an all-encompassing view of the folders and objects in your computer.

FIG. 43.15
Double-click a folder to display its contents.

After you open a window for a folder so you can view its contents, you can start a program or open a document by double-clicking its file. New users and Macintosh users find this window simpler and less confusing than the Explorer window shown in Figure 43.13.

Working from Your Desktop

The desktop is a convenient location for storing frequently used folders and shortcuts. Some computer users do the majority of their work directly from the desktop and rarely use the Start menu or Explorer.

Reduce the chance of deleting important files and folders by putting only shortcuts to files and folders on your desktop. If you put the actual files and folders directly on the desktop, you could delete them when they are selected by pressing the Delete key.

Create custom desktops for each person who uses Windows. A custom desktop can include desktop preferences, customized Start menus, and distinct shortcut icons. Use the Password program found in the Control Panel to enable custom desktops.

Making a Desktop Folder to Hold Other Shortcuts

Keeping folders on the desktop is an efficient way of storing shortcuts so your desktop doesn't become cluttered. To clear your desk of icons, just drag and drop shortcut icons into the folder. When you want to use one of the shortcut icons, double-click the folder and, when the folder opens, double-click the program or document icon.

A folder on the desktop does not have to point to a folder you have created in Explorer. To create a folder directly on your desktop, right-click the desktop, then choose New, Folder. A folder appears on the desktop with its name selected so you can type a new name.

Folders on the desktop are actually folders that are in the Windows\Desktop folder. You can see these folders and manipulate them like any other folder by opening Explorer or My Computer and displaying the Windows\Desktop folder.

Accessing the Desktop

It can be difficult to get to the desktop when it is covered with open program windows. Some users go through long, difficult processes to make their desktops accessible. Some magazines have listed complex methods that modify the Registry so the desktop appears on the Start menu. Or you can go through a laborious method of creating shortcuts that duplicate everything on the desktop and placing it on the Start menu. There are some very easy solutions to making the desktop accessible.

Creating a Shortcut to the Desktop   To customize your system so items on the desktop are available in the taskbar, follow these steps:

1. Double-click My Computer.
2. If the toolbar is not visible, choose View, Toolbar.
3. Pull down the Different Folder list from the toolbar, scroll to the top, and choose Desktop. This displays the full contents of the desktop in the folder window.
4. Choose View, Arrange Icons, Auto Arrange to arrange icons in this folder that is now a miniature desktop.
5. Choose View, Toolbar to remove the toolbar from the folder. The folder should now look like Figure 43.16.
6. Leave the folder open on the desktop or minimize it to the taskbar.

FIG. 43.16

Create a Desktop folder and keep it on your taskbar for quick access to the desktop.

Part

X

Ch

43

The desktop folder you just created shows everything the desktop would. If you are using a mouse, drag to the screen edge where the taskbar is and click the Desktop button to display it. If you are using a keyboard, press Alt+Tab until the Desktop folder is selected. Leave the Desktop folder on the taskbar when you shut down Windows and it will be there when you restart.

 To put the desktop on the Start menu, drag the folder you just created to the Start button. This will place the Desktop on the top of the Start menu.

 If you use the Microsoft Natural keyboard, notice that it has a Windows key—the keycap looks like the Windows logo. To minimize all program windows so the desktop is accessible, press Windows+M. This gives you quick desktop access. To restore minimized programs to their windows, press Shift+ WINDOWS+M.

 If you have many windows open, you can minimize them by right-clicking the taskbar, and choosing Minimize All Windows. To restore the minimized windows, right-click the taskbar and choose Undo Minimize All.

Using Shortcuts and Icons on the Desktop

If you want to select an icon, just click it. To select it and display the shortcut menu, right-click the icon. Double-clicking a program icon opens the program if it is running or activates it if it is already running. Double-clicking a document opens the document's program if necessary and loads the document. When you double-click a folder icon, the folder opens with its last used settings.

Select multiple adjacent icons on the desktop by clicking the first icon, holding down the Shift key, and clicking the last icon in the adjacent group.

Select multiple non-adjacent icons on the desktop by clicking the first icon, then holding the Ctrl key as you click additional icons. To remove icons from a selected group, hold the Ctrl key as you click an icon that is currently selected.

Select multiple icons on a desktop to delete, copy, or move them at the same time. Figure 43.17 shows a rectangular group of icons selected by dragging the mouse. To select a group of icons that are in a rectangular area of the desktop, click at one corner of a rectangle that would enclose the icons, then drag to the opposite corner of the rectangle. An enclosing rectangle appears as you drag. When you release the mouse button, all icons in the rectangle are selected. Add or remove icons from the selection by clicking icons while holding the Ctrl key.

Deselect all icons on the rectangle by clicking the desktop.

FIG. 43.17

Drag across multiple icons to select them.

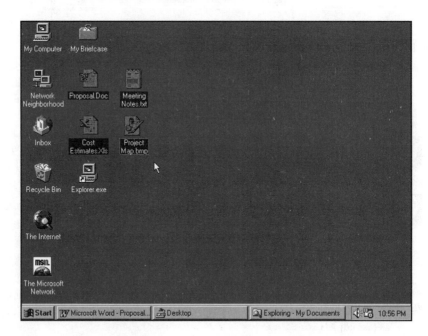

Arranging Icons on Your Desktop

After you create folders on your desktop in which to store shortcuts and icons, you will want to arrange the icons on your desktop. To arrange icons (except for the system icons like My Computer and Network Neighborhood), right-click the desktop, then click one of the following commands in the shortcut menu:

Command	Action
Arrange Icons	
by Name	Arrange icons in alphabetical order except for system icons.
by Type	Arrange icons grouped by type except for system icons.
by Size	Arrange icons by file size except for system icons.
by Date	Arrange icons by creation date.

continues

continued

Command	Action
Auto Arrange	Command toggles on or off. When the command is on, icons snap back to fill the left side of the desktop and align on the invisible grid.
Line Up Icons	Align icons on an invisible grid in their current order.

You might work better if you arrange icons on your desktop so they are grouped in different areas. To group icons anywhere on-screen, make sure the Arrange Icons, Auto Arrange command is turned off. When it is turned off, you can drag desktop icons into any position. Figure 43.18 shows icons arranged in groups.

 TIP After arranging icons on your desktop, you can get them to align—but not move significantly out of your arrangement—by right-clicking the desktop, and choosing Line Up Icons.

FIG. 43.18
Turn off Auto Arrange so you can drag icons into groups.

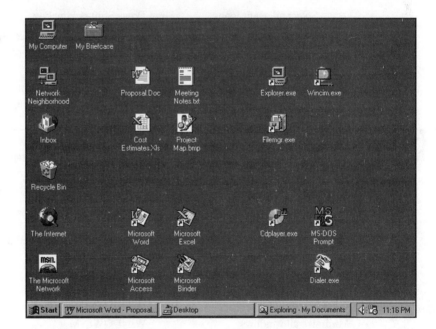

Change the vertical and horizontal spacing of the grid on which icons position themselves by right-clicking the desktop, choosing Properties, and selecting the Appearance tab.

Working on Your Desktop with the Keyboard

If your mouse fails at an important time or you're trapped in a cramped airline seat, you know how important it is to know a few important Windows keystroke commands. One set of important keystroke commands is the one used to work on the desktop.

To activate or select icons on the desktop by keyboard, follow these steps:

1. Minimize or move program windows so you can see the desktop icons you want to work with. Press Alt+Spacebar to activate the program's control menu so you can minimize or move the application.

2. Press Ctrl+Esc or the Windows button to activate the shortcut menu, then press Esc to remove the menu, and select the Start button.

   At this point, each press of the Tab key will cycle the focus from the Start button, to the taskbar, and to the desktop.

3. Press Tab to activate the taskbar. (Move between task buttons with the arrow keys.)

4. Press Tab again to activate the desktop. Use the keystrokes in the following table to select or activate desktop icons.

Action	Do This...
Select an icon	Press arrow keys
Select adjacent icons	Press Shift+arrow key
Select non-adjacent icons	Select first icon, then press Ctrl+arrow to next icon to select, then press Ctrl+Spacebar to select it
Activate an icon	Select the icon, press Enter
Delete an icon	Select the icon, press Delete

If you work long hours at the keyboard, seriously consider buying a Microsoft Natural keyboard or other ergonomic keyboard that places keys at a less stressful angle. Use a wrist rest to keep your wrists straight. I can attest to the fact that tendonitis and carpal tunnel syndrome can seriously affect your quality of life—not just your career. Take care of the problem before you even notice the symptoms.

If you use the Microsoft Natural keyboard with Windows 95, you can use a number of shortcut keys that are faster than using the mouse. The Windows key referenced in the table is the key on the Microsoft Natural keyboard that has the Windows logo.

Action	Keystroke
Display the Run dialog box	WINDOWS+R
Minimize all windows	WINDOWS+M
Undo minimize windows	Shift+WINDOWS+M
Help	WINDOWS+F1
Display the Windows Explorer	WINDOWS+E
Display Find:Computer	Ctrl+WINDOWS+F
Cycle through taskbar buttons	WINDOWS+Tab
Display System Properties sheet	WINDOWS+Break

Changing Settings and Properties with the Right Mouse Button

One important Windows concept is that most *objects* that you see on-screen have *properties* related to them. Objects that display a properties sheet are such items as desktop icons, shortcuts, files, the desktop, and the taskbar. Properties displayed in the properties sheet can include such characteristics as an object's appearance and behavior.

You can change some properties, but others are *read only*—you can view them, but cannot change them.

You can experiment to find the properties of objects on the desktop, in Explorer, in My Computer, and in most Windows 95 applications. To see an object's properties, point to the object and click the right mouse button (that is, you *right-click* the object). A Properties sheet displays, or a context menu displays a Properties command. For example, you can place the pointer's tip on most objects, such as the desktop or a file, and then click the right mouse button. From the context menu that appears, select the Properties command.

N O T E   Don't be afraid to experiment when you look for properties. To discover how you can customize Windows, right-click files, taskbars, and so on. If you do not want to change the object's properties, press the Esc key or click the Cancel button in the Properties sheet that appears. ■

To see the properties that you can change on the desktop, right-click the desktop and then choose the Properties command. The Display Properties sheet shown in Figure 43.19 appears. In this dialog box, you can change the display's background, color, and screen saver, and display adapter settings. Click the Cancel button to remove the dialog box without making changes.

Using the Send To Command for Frequent Operations

Microsoft included the Send To command on many shortcut menus; it is a real time-saver and is one of the most powerful, customizable features in Windows 95. Figure 43.20 shows the Send To command after right-clicking a file. The Send To command appears when you right-click files in Explorer, in folder windows, or on the desktop.

At first, the Send To command appears to be a simple little device to make it easy to send documents to a printer, fax, e-mail, Briefcase, or disk. That in itself is very useful, but Send To can do a lot more.

FIG. 43.19

Right-click the desktop and then choose Properties to see the desktop properties. The Screen Saver page, shown here, enables you to choose a screen saver.

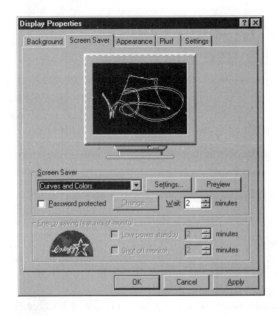

FIG. 43.20

Use Send To as a shortcut for dragging an object to a target.

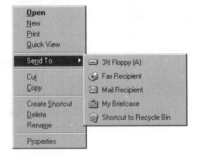

When you learn how to customize Send To, you can add items to the Send To menu to give it greater functionality. Some of the custom things you can have Send To do are:

- Send documents to the same printer using different printer setups
- Send documents to local or network folders or disks
- Move a file or folder to the desktop
- Send batch or SYS files to Notepad for editing
- Send documents to applications that start with unique parameters

To perform an operation on a document with Send To, display the document icon or shortcut you want to work on. The document might be on the desktop, in a folder window, or in Explorer. Right-click the document icon, then choose Send To. A submenu appears giving you locations where you can send the document. The default locations on Send To for Windows with a full install are:

Floppy (A:)   Mail Recipient

FAX Recipient   My Briefcase

Shortcut to Recycle Bin

Arranging Windows from the Taskbar

There are times when you want to quickly arrange a few applications on your desktop so that you can compare documents, drag and drop between documents, and so forth. Manually moving and resizing each Window is a tedious job, so Windows 95 has a few shortcuts that can make this type of work easier.

 TIP When the taskbar has a lot of application buttons, the titles may be too truncated to read. Pause the pointer over a button to see a ToolTip label.

First, you can make your desktop easier to work on by minimizing all applications so they appear as buttons on the taskbar. To do this quickly, right-click an area between buttons on the taskbar. When the shortcut menu appears, click Minimize All Windows. To restore minimized applications, right-click in a clear area of the taskbar and choose Undo Minimize All. If you have the Microsoft Natural Keyboard, minimize applications by pressing WINDOWS+M. Restore minimized applications by pressing Shift+WINDOWS+M.

N O T E The Minimize All Windows command does not work on applications that are currently displaying a dialog box. ■

If you want to compare documents in two or three applications, minimize all applications except the two or three you want to work with and then right-click a gray area of the taskbar. When the shortcut menu appears click either Tile Horizontally or Tile Vertically. Your applications will appear in adjacent windows that fill the screen as shown in Figure 43.21.

If you want to be able to quickly see all the application title bars so that you can click title bars to switch between many application windows, right-click in the gray area of the taskbar. When the shortcut menu appears, click Cascade. The windows will arrange as shown in Figure 43.22.

Managing Windows After an Application Failure

Windows 95 significantly improves upon previous versions of Windows when it comes to how failed or misbehaving applications are handled. Windows 95 continuously polls the applications to see if they are running and responding. When an application fails to respond, Windows 95 displays the Not Responding dialog box. In this dialog box, you can click the End Task button to close the application. You lose all changes to data in the application since the last time you saved. Click Cancel to return to the application.

FIG. 43.21

Tiling application windows horizontally or vertically makes it easy to compare documents or to drag and drop contents.

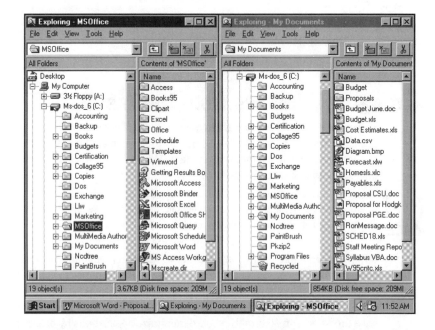

FIG. 43.22

Cascading application windows overlays them so that you can see each title bar. It is then easy to move among windows by clicking the title bars.

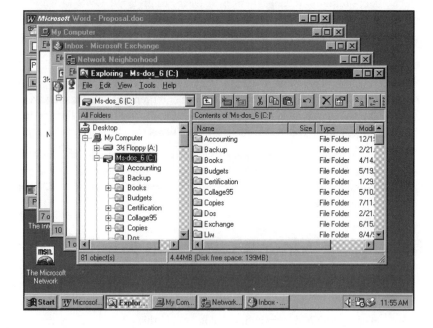

If the application misuses memory or has a fatal error that causes the application to crash, other applications in Windows usually will not be involved. When an application fails to respond—for example, clicks or keystrokes get no response—press Ctrl+Alt+Delete to display the Close Program dialog box.

The application that has trouble will show the phrase [Not responding]. To continue working in Windows on your other applications, you must shut down this application. Select the application and click End Task. If you click Shut Down or press Ctrl+Alt+Delete again, all applications and Windows 95 will shut down. ●

Part

X

Ch

43

CHAPTER 44

Managing Files

To gain the most from Windows 95, it is essential that you learn how to efficiently work with and manage files.

The first part of this chapter explains how to use the Windows Explorer to work with and manage the files on your computer. You also learn how to carry out many file management tasks using My Computer. The later part of the chapter describes how you can customize Explorer, synchronize files between different computers, and associate new document files with an application. ∎

How to use the Explorer and folder windows from My Computer to manage files and folders

In addition to managing files and folders, this chapter contains many tips and some undocumented tricks that will improve your productivity.

Manage the Recycle Bin so you can undelete files

Learn how to restore deleted files or permanently delete files.

View and change file attributes

Using the Windows Explorer, change hidden, system, read-only file attributes. It's also easy to specify that Windows Explorer or My Computer hide files that are not EXE or documents.

Learn to synchronize files between laptop and desktop computers

The Briefcase enables you to synchronize files between two computers.

How to use Explorer on a network

The Windows Explorer and My Computer show you what resources are shared across the network.

Understanding Files and Folders

If you are familiar with the MS-DOS/Windows system for organizing files, a folder is analogous to a directory, and a folder within a folder is analogous to a subdirectory of a directory. If you like to think hierarchically, you can continue to visualize the organization of your files in exactly the same way you did with DOS and earlier versions of Windows. The only difference is that instead of directories and subdirectories, you have folders and folders within folders. And, as you see in the next section, you can view the hierarchical arrangement of your folders using Explorer.

 Should you misplace a file, use the Find command (Start, Find, Files or Folders) to search for the file by name, type, date saved, or content.

This capability to have folders within folders enables you to refine your filing system, categorizing your files in a way that makes it easy for you to locate a file even if you haven't used it for a long time. If you prefer to use the folder metaphor, you will want to use folder windows created from My Computer.

 Folder windows opened in My Computer view are like single-pane Explorer windows—the right pane which contains a hierarchical structure is not shown in folder windows. Many of the tips and techniques described in the Explorer section of this chapter also work in folder windows.

Using Windows Explorer to View Files and Folders

With Windows Explorer, you can view the hierarchical arrangement of the folders on your computer, and you can look into each folder to see what files are stored there. You also can use Windows Explorer to reorganize and manage your files and folders. You can create new folders; move and copy files from one folder to another, to a floppy disk, or to another computer (if you are on a network); rename and delete files and folders; and perform other file management tasks.

 The File Manager used in Windows 3.x is still available in Windows 95. Open the file WINFILE.EXE located in the Windows folder to see the new File Manager. Be careful, the File Manager does not support long file names. If you use it, you will lose long file names you have created with Windows 95 applications or the Windows Explorer. It takes some getting used to, but once you learn a few Explorer tips described in this chapter, you'll see that Explorer is a much more powerful file management tool.

To open the Windows Explorer, right-click Start, then choose Explore. The Explorer also can be found in Programs in the Start menu or by right-clicking My Computer. Figure 44.1 shows the Explorer with the left pane showing system resources and the right pane showing the folders in the local C: drive.

FIG. 44.1

Use Windows Explorer to view the files and folders on your computer. This view shows the Windows Explorer with large icons and a toolbar.

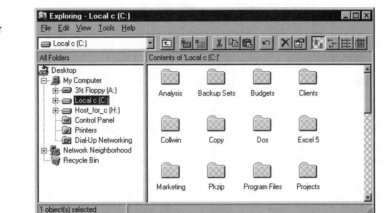

 You'll use Windows Explorer frequently to work with your files and folders. If you need to open Windows Explorer to display frequently used folders, create Explorer shortcuts that open Explorer to these folders. Make these shortcuts quickly accessible by adding them to the Start menu.

Viewing Your Computer's Resources

The Windows Explorer window is divided into two panes (refer to Figure 44.1). Move between different panes in Explorer by pressing the Tab key. The left pane displays a hierarchical view of the organization of the folders on your computer. At the top of the hierarchy is the Desktop icon. This represents all the hard disks and resources available to your computer. Just beneath desktop is My Computer, represented by an icon of a computer. Under My Computer are listed all the resources on your computer. These resources include floppy drives and local hard drives. Three special folders—Fonts, Control Panel, and Printers—are used for managing the fonts and printers on your computer and for customizing your computer's settings.

Two other folders that are branches of the Desktop icon are *Network Neighborhood* and the *Recycle Bin.* Network Neighborhood appears on your desktop if you installed a network client. Open this folder to browse the computers in your workgroup or on your entire network. The Recycle Bin temporarily holds files when you delete them from a folder, so you have the opportunity to recover them if you change your mind. Depending on the resources on your computer, you may see other folders displayed underneath My Computer. If you have a CD-ROM drive or a removable media drive installed on your computer, for example, you will see their icons under My Computer, too. You may also see an icon for the *Briefcase* folder. The Briefcase is a special folder used for working on the same files at two locations and keeping them synchronized.

> **N O T E** If you have specific network drives mapped, they will appear under My Computer in
> alphabetical order following your local hard drives. Otherwise, you can browse your network
> resources using the Network Neighborhood icon. ■

Just beneath the menu bar is the toolbar. If the toolbar is not displayed, choose View, Toolbar
to see it. You can use the drop-down list at the left end of the toolbar to open the main folders in
the Desktop and My Computer folders. This drop-down list shows all the drives on your computer, including network drives. If you scroll through the list, you'll also find your Control
Panel, Briefcase (if installed), Printers (if installed), Network Neighborhood, and Recycle Bin
at the bottom of the list. This list also displays the folder hierarchy of the currently open folder,
as shown in Figure 44.2. You can, for example, quickly select the Recycle Bin folder without
having to scroll to the bottom of the list in the left pane of the Explorer. To select from the list,
click the down arrow next to the text box and click the folder you want to open.

FIG. 44.2

The folders in the
hierarchy above the
current folder (Apps) are
shown in addition to the
list of drives and other
main resources. The rest
of the folder hierarchy is
collapsed for quick
access.

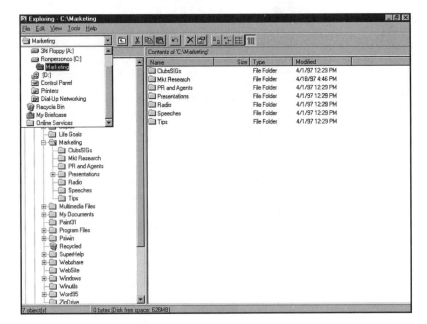

Browsing the Contents of a Folder

The right pane of the Explorer window displays the contents of whatever folder is selected in
the left pane. If you select the Local C: drive under My Computer, for example, you see a list of
all the resources on your computer, including the floppy and hard drives (see Figure 44.3). To
display the contents of your hard disk, click its icon in the left pane. To see the contents of a
folder, select the folder on the left and its contents are listed on the right. You can select a
folder by clicking it with the mouse or by using the up- and down-arrow keys on the keyboard.

TIP You can open a specific folder without wading through the Explorer hierarchy by selecting Tools, Go To. Enter the path of the folder you want to open and then click OK.

You can expand and collapse the hierarchical view to display more or less detail. If a plus sign (+) appears next to an icon in the left pane of Explorer, additional folders are within this folder. To display these folders, click the plus sign (or double-click the folder). All the folders within this folder are displayed. Some of these folders, in turn, may have folders within them, which you can view using the same procedure. To hide the folders within a folder, click the minus sign (–) next to the folder (or double-click the folder). By collapsing and expanding the display of folders, you can view as much or as little detail as you want. Figure 44.3 shows an expanded view of the Local C: drive folder, which is collapsed in Figure 44.1. Notice that some of the folders on the C drive have plus signs next to them, indicating that they contain additional folders.

Part

X

Ch

44

FIG. 44.3
An expanded view of
the Local C: drive in the
My Computer folder,
showing its folders.

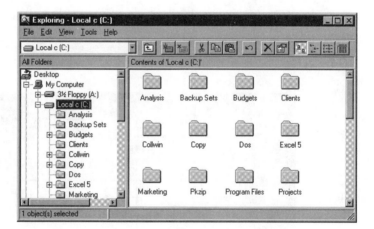

Understanding the File Icons in Windows

Windows uses various icons to represent folders and different types of files. In Figure 44.4, folders within the Windows folder are represented with a folder icon. You can quickly display the contents of a folder within a folder by double-clicking its icon in the right pane of the Explorer. The easiest way to redisplay the original folder is to click the Up One Level button on the toolbar. The Up One Level button is a picture of a folder with an up arrow in it. You also can redisplay the contents of the original folder by clicking its icon in the left pane of the window.

NOTE Icons that have a small curved arrow in the lower-left corner are shortcut icons. They are pointers to the actual file and folders that may be located in another folder. ■

In addition to folders, many types of files can appear in the list of contents. Each type is represented by its own icon. Calendar files, for example, are represented by a calendar icon, and

Help files have their own special icon, as shown in Figure 44.5. These icons are helpful for visually associating a file with its program. You can, for example, readily distinguish a file created in the Calendar program from a file created in Paint. You can open a file in its program by double-clicking the file's icon in Explorer.

FIG. 44.4
Folder icons in the right pane of the Explorer represent folders within the folder selected in the left pane.

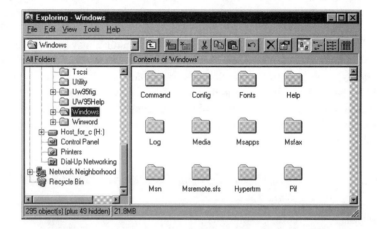

FIG. 44.5
Different icons are used to represent different file types.

You may need to update the display of files and folders in the right pane of the Explorer. If you are viewing the contents of a floppy disk, for example, and you switch disks, you won't see the contents of the new disk unless you *refresh* the window. To refresh the window, click the icon for the folder you want to refresh, in this case the icon for the floppy drive, in the left pane of the Explorer. You also can refresh by choosing View, Refresh or by pressing the F5 key.

Using My Computer to Manage Files

New users of Windows may prefer to use My Computer to work with their files. My Computer is a folder on your desktop containing all the resources on your computer. When you first open My Computer by double-clicking its icon on the desktop, the My Computer window displays an icon representing each of the resources on your computer, as shown in Figure 44.6. Notice that the folder window opened from My Computer is the right pane from the Explorer window.

Part
X

Ch
44

FIG. 44.6
The My Computer window is another way to view the files and folders on your computer.

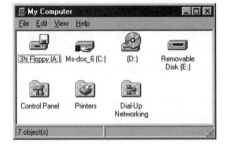

To look at the contents of a resource, double-click the appropriate folder. To view the folders on your hard drive, for example, double-click the hard disk icon. A new window opens, displaying the folders on your hard drive (see Figure 44.7). You can continue browsing through the folders on your computer by double-clicking any folder whose contents you want to view.

FIG. 44.7
You can browse through the folders in My Computer by double-clicking the folders whose contents you want to see.

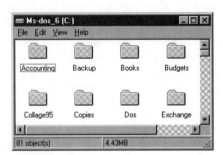

As you open new windows in My Computer to view the contents of the different folders, you won't really have a sense of the hierarchical organization of the folders the way you do in Explorer. In Explorer, you always have a map of the organization of your folders in the left pane. With My Computer, it is more difficult to visualize the hierarchical structure of your folders. If you don't think hierarchically, this may be a relief, as you may prefer to simply think of folders inside other folders that you open one-by-one. You can move back through a series of opened folders by clicking the Up One Level button in the toolbar. This is a handy way to retrace your steps.

Move up one level in a folder window by pressing the Backspace key or clicking the Up One Level button on the toolbar.

If you find it annoying to end up with layer upon layer of folder windows as you open the folders on your computer, you can choose to have the contents of a newly opened folder replace the current contents of the My Computer window, instead of opening a new window. Choose View, Options and select the Browse Folders by Using a Single Window option. Now when you open a new folder, the folder's contents replace the contents of the current window. You can still use the Up One Level button to move back through a series of folders that you have opened.

If Windows 95 currently uses a single window to display the contents of folders you open, but you want a new window to open when you open a folder, hold down the Ctrl key as you double-click a folder. Conversely, if Windows 95 is currently opening a new window when you open a folder but you want to use a single window and replace its contents with the contents of the new folder, hold down the Ctrl key as you double-click a folder.

 If you have opened a trail of new single-pane folder windows, you can close them all by holding the Shift key as you click the Close button (X), at the top-right corner of the window.

 If you prefer to run your programs from a folder rather than from the Start, Programs menu, here's a shortcut for making a program folder: Double-click the file PROGRAMS.GRP in the Windows folder. This opens a folder window showing a folder for each submenu off the Start, Programs submenu. Minimize this folder so it's always accessible on your taskbar.

You can perform virtually all the file management tasks in My Computer that you can in Explorer. To manage your files in My Computer, use the same techniques described throughout this chapter. You can use either the menus or the mouse to open, move, copy, rename, delete, and preview your files. You can drag-and-drop files from one folder window to another. And all the shortcuts accessible with the right mouse button in the Explorer also can be used in My Computer. The display options described for customizing Explorer work exactly the same way in My Computer as well.

As you work with Windows 95, you can decide whether you prefer to use Explorer or My Computer to manage your files. You may find a combination of the two approaches works best for you. Because the commands are identical in both, you can move back and forth between the two with ease. Whichever approach you take, you will undoubtedly come to appreciate how easy it is to manage your files in Windows.

Managing Your Files and Folders

Explorer is an essential tool for managing the files and folders on your computer. You can use the Explorer to create new folders, move folders from one location to another, copy and move files from one folder to another, and even move files from one disk drive to another. You also can use the Explorer to delete and rename files and folders.

Selecting Files and Folders

To select a file or folder, click it. If another file in the right pane of the Windows Explorer is already selected, you can use the up- and down-arrow keys on the keyboard. The selected file is highlighted.

To select multiple files at once, click the first file, and then hold down the Ctrl key and click each additional file you want to select. To deselect a file, continue holding down the Ctrl key and click a second time on the file. To quickly select a group of contiguous files, select the first file in the group, hold down the Shift key, and select the last file in the group. All the files between the first and last file will also be selected.

If files are in one of the icon views, you can select a group of contiguous files by dragging a box around the group of files with the mouse.

If your files are arranged free form, you may find it convenient to select groups of files by dragging a rectangle around them using the pointer. Figure 44.8 shows how you can click and drag a rectangle around multiple icons. All the icons within the rectangle will be selected. Once they are selected, you can deselect or select additional files by holding down Ctrl and clicking icons.

FIG. 44.8

Drag a rectangle around the group of file icons you want to select.

You also can select multiple files with the keyboard. To select multiple adjacent files, select the first file by tabbing into the right pane, then press and hold down the Shift key while moving to the last file by pressing the arrow key. To select non-adjacent files, select the first file, hold down the Ctrl key, use the arrow keys to move to the next file to be selected, and press the space bar. While you continue to hold down the Ctrl key, move to each file you want to select and press the space bar. To deselect a file and retain the other selections, hold down the Ctrl key, use the arrow key to move to the file, and press the space bar.

To select all the files and folders displayed in the right pane, choose Edit, Select All (or press Ctrl+A). If you want to select all but a few of the files and folders in the right pane, select the files and folders you don't want to select; then choose Edit, Invert Selection.

To cancel the selections you have made, simply select another file or folder, using either the mouse or the keyboard.

Renaming Files

To rename a file, click the file name, pause, then click the file name again. The name will be selected and the pointer changes to an I-beam to indicate you can edit the text underneath. Click the pointer in the name where you want the insertion point and rename the file. To undo your edits, press Esc. To accept your edits, press Enter or click another file.

Renaming Multiple Files

Unlike MS-DOS or Windows 3.x, the Explorer has no facility for renaming multiple file names with a single command. However, you can preserve long file names while renaming multiple files by going to a DOS window and using the RENAME command to rename multiple files.

> **CAUTION**
>
> Using the Windows 3.x or Windows 95 File Manager to rename one or more files converts the long file names for those files into their 8.3 equivalents.

To rename long file names in multiple files using MS-DOS, follow this procedure:

1. Click Start, then Programs, MS-DOS Prompt to open an MS-DOS window.

2. At the DOS prompt, type **CD *pathname*** to switch to the directory containing the files you want to rename.

3. Type **REN *originalname.ext newname.ext***. If the *originalname* or *newname* are long file names or include spaces, then enclose the name and extension in quotes. Press Enter.

When you use the DIR command to see the file names in a DOS window, remember that file names using 8.3 format will be on the left and long file names will be on the right of the listing.

The following list of file names will be used as examples:

Jun Forcast 01.Xls	Aug Forcast 05.Xls
Jul Forcast 12.Xls	Sep Forcast 07.Xls

To correct the spelling of "forecast," use the ? wild card to match against any single letter in that character position. Use the MS-DOS command line:

```
rename "??? forcast ??.xls" "??? forecast??.xls"
```

This renames the files to:

Aug forecast05.xls	Jul forecast12.xls
Sep forecast09.xls	Jun forecast01.xls

Match against any number of characters by using the * wild card, even within the quotes needed for long file names. For example, the MS-DOS command line:

```
rename "??? Forcast???.*" "??? Forcast.xls"
```

renames the original collection of files to:

Jun Forcast.xls	Sep Forcast.xls
Jul Forcast.xls	Aug Forcast.xls

Creating New Folders

You can use Windows Explorer to create new folders.

 TIP Create a new folder by right-clicking in the blank area of the right pane in Explorer. Choose New, Folder. Type a name for the folder and press Enter. In Windows 95 applications that use the common Save As dialog box, you can create new folders using this same process before you save a file.

To create a new folder, follow these steps:

1. Select the folder in the left pane of Windows Explorer in which you want to create a new folder.

2. Choose File, New, Folder.

   A new folder appears in the right pane of the Explorer, ready for you to type in a name.

3. Type a name for the folder and press Enter.

Folders can use long names just like files. Folder names can be up to 255 characters and can include spaces. Folders can't use these characters:

\ ? : " < > |

Moving and Copying Files and Folders

Moving and copying files and folders is an essential file-management task. Using the Explorer and the mouse, you can quickly move and copy files and folders without ever touching the keyboard.

You can use two approaches for moving and copying files and folders. You can either use the Cut or Copy commands or use the mouse to drag-and-drop the files.

To move or copy files using the menu, follow these steps:

1. Select the files or folders you want to move in the right pane of the Windows Explorer.

2. Perform one of the following actions:

   - To cut the file so it can be moved, choose Edit, Cut; right-click, choose Cut; press Ctrl+X; or click the Cut button on the toolbar.

- To copy the file so a duplicate can be made, choose Edit, Copy; right-click, then choose Copy; press Ctrl+C; or click the Copy button on the toolbar.

3. In either pane of the Explorer, select the folder in which you want to paste the cut or copied file, then follow one of these methods. To paste the file, choose Edit, Paste; right-click, then choose Paste; press Ctrl+V; or click the Paste button on the toolbar.

To move or copy files using the drag-and-drop method, follow these steps:

1. Select the files or folders you want to move in the right pane of the Windows Explorer.

2. If the folder to which you want to move the selected items is not visible in the left pane of the Explorer, use the scroll bar to scroll it into view. If you need to display a subfolder, click the + sign next to the folder containing the subfolder.

3. To move the selected items, drag the selected items to the new folder in the left pane of the Explorer.

   Or, to copy the selected items, hold down the Ctrl key and drag the selected items to the new folder in the left pane of the Explorer. A plus sign (+) appears beneath the mouse pointer when you hold down the Ctrl key, indicating that you are copying the files.

   Make sure that the correct folder is highlighted before you release the mouse button.

Drag and drop selected items on the destination folder with the right mouse button. When the shortcut menu appears, click Move Here to move items or Copy Here to copy items to the new location.

If you attempt to drag-and-drop a program file to a new folder, Windows creates a shortcut for that program in the new location. This is to prevent you from inadvertently moving a program file from its original folder. When you attempt to drag a program file, an arrow appears beneath the mouse pointer, indicating that you are about to create a shortcut for that program.

To quickly move selected items to a floppy disk, click the selected items with the right mouse button. Click Send To and then click the disk drive to which you want to send the selected files. Add other drives or folders to the Send To menu through customization.

N O T E If you routinely copy or move files to particular folders or a disk drive, you can create a shortcut for the folder or drive on your desktop. Then you can quickly drag-and-drop files onto the shortcut icon instead of having to scroll to the folder or drive in Explorer. To create a shortcut for a folder (or drive), select the folder (or drive) in the Explorer, drag it with the right mouse button onto your desktop, and release the mouse button. Choose the Create Shortcut(s) Here command. You can now drag-and-drop files onto this shortcut icon to copy or move files to this folder (or drive). ■

Copying Disks

At times, you may want to make an exact copy of an entire floppy disk. This is easy to do in either Explorer or My Computer.

You can copy from one floppy disk to another using the same drive, but both disks must have the same storage capacity. The disk you copy onto will be erased in the process.

To copy a disk, follow these steps:

1. Insert the floppy disk you want to copy.
2. Right-click the disk in My Computer or in the left pane of the Explorer window.
3. Choose Copy Disk from the shortcut menu. This opens the Copy Disk dialog box shown in Figure 44.9.

FIG. 44.9
The Copy Disk dialog box shows the selected drives for the copy operation

If you have only one drive of this size, that drive will be highlighted for both the Copy From and Copy To areas of the dialog box. If you have another drive of this same size, it will be listed, as well, and you can select it to copy from drive to drive.

4. Choose Start.
5. If you are using the same drive for the master and the copy, you will be prompted to switch floppy disks when necessary.
6. When the disk is duplicated, you can copy another disk by choosing Start, or choose Close if you are done.

Copying disks is much faster in Windows 95 than in prior versions of Windows. This is due to the addition of a high-speed floppy driver. If you frequently copy disks, you will notice the speed improvement.

Deleting Files and Folders

Windows now has a folder called the Recycle Bin, where deleted files are temporarily stored. The Recycle Bin empties on a rolling basis with the oldest files in the Recycle Bin actually being removed to make room for more recently deleted files. You can restore files from the Recycle Bin if you change your mind or accidentally delete a file.

If you realize right away that you have accidentally deleted a file or folder, choose Edit, Undo Delete to restore the files. Press F5 to refresh the file listing and see the restored file or folder.

To delete a file or folder, follow these steps:

1. Select the file or folder you want to delete.

   You can select multiple files or folders using the techniques described in "Selecting Files and Folders" earlier in this chapter.

2. Click the selection with the right mouse button and click Delete; choose File, Delete (or press the Delete key or click the Delete button on the toolbar); or drag and drop the file onto the Recycle Bin icon on the desktop.

 TIP To change whether a confirmation is required to delete a file, right-click the Recycle Bin, choose Properties, and select Display Delete Confirmation Dialog.

3. Click Yes when the Confirm File Delete dialog box appears (see Figure 44.10). Or click No if you want to cancel the file deletion.

   If you are deleting multiple files, Explorer displays the Confirm Multiple File Delete dialog box.

CAUTION

If you delete a folder, you also delete all the files and folders contained in that folder. The Confirm Folder Delete dialog box reminds you of this. Be aware of what you are doing before you delete a folder.

You also should be careful not to accidentally delete a program file. If you attempt to delete a program file, the Confirm File Delete message box warns you that you are about to delete a program. Click No if you don't mean to delete the program, but other selected files will be deleted. Click Cancel to stop all deletions.

FIG. 44.10
The Confirm File Delete dialog box gives you a chance to check your decision before deleting a file.

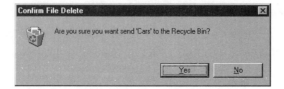

CAUTION

Files deleted from the MS-DOS prompt, or from a disk or network drive, are not saved to the Recycle Bin. If you delete them, they are gone. You can use utilities such as Norton Utilities for Windows 95 from Symantec to give a broader range of undelete capabilities.

 TIP Permanently delete files without sending them to the Recycle Bin by holding down the Shift key as you delete them.

When deleting some files, you may see a message warning you that the file is a system, hidden, or read-only file. System files are files needed by Windows 95 to operate correctly and should not be deleted. Hidden and read-only files may be needed for certain programs to work correctly, or they may just be files that you have protected with these attributes to prevent accidental deletion. Before deleting any of these file types, you should be certain that your system does not need them to operate correctly.

Restoring Deleted Files

Part

X

Ch

44

You can open the Recycle Bin folder just as you do any other folder and select a file and restore it to its original location. You also can move or copy files from the Recycle Bin to a new location, in the same way you learned how to move and copy files from other folders.

To restore a deleted file or folder, follow these steps:

1. Double-click the Recycle Bin icon on the desktop to open the Recycle Bin window, as shown in Figure 44.11.

2. Select the file or files you want to restore.

   You can use the techniques described in the earlier section, "Selecting Files and Folders," to select multiple files.

3. Click the selected files with the right mouse button and click Restore, or choose File, Restore.

   The files are restored in the folders from which they were deleted. If the folder that a file came from has been deleted, the folder also is restored.

FIG. 44.11

Select files to restore in the Recycle Bin.

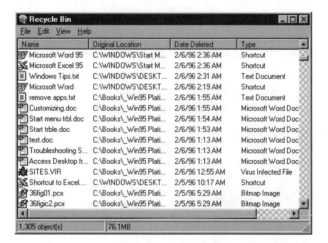

You also can restore a file to a different folder than the one it was deleted from. Open the Recycle Bin folder in Explorer, select the files you want to restore, and use one of the techniques discussed earlier in this chapter to move the file where you want it.

Emptying the Recycle Bin   Periodically, you may want to empty the Recycle Bin to free up space on your hard disk. To empty the Recycle Bin, follow one of these procedures:

- If the Recycle Bin is already open, choose File, Empty Recycle Bin.
- Click the Recycle Bin icon on the desktop with the right mouse button and click Empty Recycle Bin.

Once you have emptied the Recycle Bin, you can no longer recover the deleted files and folders that were stored there.

You also can delete selected files from the Recycle Bin. To delete selected files from the Recycle Bin, follow these steps:

1. Open the Recycle Bin and select the files you want to delete.
2. Click the selected files with the right mouse button and click Delete.
3. Choose Yes to confirm the deletion.

> **CAUTION**
>
> The Recycle Bin can be a lifesaver if you accidentally delete a critical file. But don't forget to delete confidential files from the Recycle Bin so that others can't retrieve them.

Changing the Size of the Recycle Bin   You might prefer having more free disk space rather than storing a large history of deleted files. If so, you can change the amount of disk space used for the Recycle Bin.

To change the size of the Recycle Bin, follow these steps:

1. Right-click the Recycle Bin icon on the desktop or in the Explorer and click Properties. The Recycle Bin Properties sheet appears, as shown in Figure 44.12.

FIG. 44.12

Change the size of the Recycle Bin on the Recycle Bin Properties sheet.

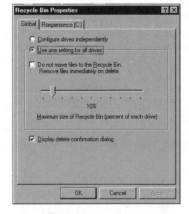

2. Select the Configure Drives Independently option if you want to change the Recycle Bin size separately for each drive.

   Or, select the use One Setting for All Drives option if you want to use the same size Recycle Bin for all drives.

3. Drag the slider to change the maximum size of the Recycle Bin as a percentage of the total disk size.

4. Click OK.

Part

X

Ch

44

Deleting Without Using the Recycle Bin   If you don't want to use up disk space storing deleted files, you can tell Windows to purge all files when they are deleted instead of storing them in the Recycle Bin. To purge all files when deleted, follow these steps:

1. Right-click the Recycle Bin icon on the desktop or in Explorer and click Properties.

2. Select the Purge Files Immediately on Delete option.

3. Click OK.

When you select this option and delete a file, the Confirm File Delete dialog box warns you that the file will not be moved to the Recycle Bin.

N O T E   You can turn off the confirmation message for the Recycle Bin, by deselecting the Display Delete Confirmation Dialog check box on the Recycle Bin Properties sheet. ■

Previewing a Document with Quick View

As you manage the files on your computer, you may want to look at the contents of a file before you make decisions about opening, moving, copying, deleting, and backing up the file. It can be very tedious and time-consuming to open each file in the program that created the file. Windows has a tool called *Quick View* for previewing many types of files without having to open the original program. You can access Quick View from the Explorer or from any folder window.

N O T E   A worthwhile product to add to your toolkit is Quick View Plus from the people who wrote Quick View for Microsoft. Quick View Plus extends the Quick View that comes with Windows. It works with over 200 file formats from Windows, DOS, and Macintosh applications. It works with Microsoft Exchange so you can view e-mail and their attachments no matter what their source. It replaces the Quick View command on the context menu so it's easy to access. Quick View Plus sets its viewing screen side-by-side with Explorer so the two act almost like one program. Quick View Plus also enables you to find documents, print, and copy. And Quick View Plus is inexpensive. For more information or trial software, contact:

Inso Corporation
401 North Wabash, Suite 600
Chicago, IL 60611
Phone: (312) 329-0700
Web: **http://www.inso.com** ■

TIP Preview documents by right-clicking the file and choosing Quick View.

To preview a file using Quick View, follow these steps:

1. Select the file you want to preview.

2. Choose File, Quick View. The Quick View item does not appear on the menu if the file type you select does not have a viewer installed.

   Or, click the selected file with the right mouse button and click Quick View.

   Or, drag the file into an existing Quick View window.

   The Quick View window opens, displaying the contents of the file, as shown in Figure 44.13.

You can scroll through the document using the scroll bars or keyboard. If you decide you want to edit the file, choose File, Open File for Editing (or click the Open File for Editing button at the left end of the toolbar).

 TIP If you want to compare the contents of two files, you should have a new window opened for each file.

FIG. 44.13
Quickly preview the contents of many types of files using Quick View.

Open file for editing
Increase font size
Decrease font size
Replace window

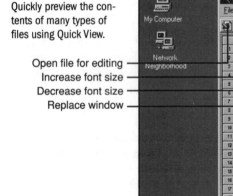
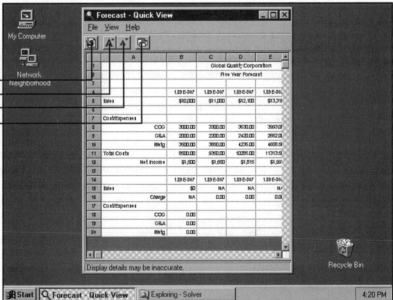

By default, Quick View opens a new window for each file. If this default has been changed, or you need to change it back, choose View and look at the menu. If a check mark appears next to Replace Window in Quick View, choose that option to deselect it and have a new window opened for each file. If you want the contents of the current Quick View window to be replaced when you select a new file for previewing, choose View, Replace Window to select this option. You can use the Replace Window button on the toolbar to activate and deactivate this option.

When you first open Quick View, you see a portion of the page of your document. To view whole pages, choose View, Page View. A check mark appears next to the command when it is activated. When you are in Page view, you can click the arrows in the upper-right corner of the page to scroll through the document. To return to viewing portions of a page, choose the command again.

When you are in Page View, you can rotate the display to preview the file in landscape orientation by choosing View, Landscape. Choose the command again to return to portrait orientation.

You also can change the font and font size used in the display by choosing View, Font and selecting a new font or size. To quickly increase or decrease the font size, click the Increase Font Size or Decrease Font Size tools on the toolbar. When you change the font and font size, it affects only the display in Quick View and does not alter the original file. It's handy to be able to increase the font size if you can't easily read the contents of the file, especially when you are in Page view.

To exit Quick View, choose File, Exit, or double-click the Quick View icon at the left end of the title bar.

Viewing and Changing the Properties of a File or Folder

In Windows, it is easy to check the properties of a selected file or folder. You can find out the type of a file; the location and size of the selected item; the MS-DOS name; and when the file or folder was created, last modified, and last accessed. Each file and folder on a disk also has a set of *attributes,* or descriptive characteristics. Attributes describe whether the file has been backed up, is a Windows system file, is hidden from normal viewing, or can be read but not written over. With Windows Explorer, you can display these attributes and change them.

To display the properties of a particular file or folder, follow these steps:

1. In Explorer (or any folder), select the file or folder whose properties you want to check.

2. Right-click and choose Properties, or choose File, Properties. Windows opens a Properties sheet (see Figure 44.14).

3. View the file or folder's properties.

4. If you want, change the attributes for the file or folder, as described in the following table:

Attribute	Description
Read Only	Sets the R or Read-Only attribute, which prevents a file or folder from being changed or erased. Set this attribute for a file or folder when you want to prevent someone from accidentally changing a master template or erasing a file that is critical to system operation.

continues

Part

X

Ch

44

continued

Attribute	Description
Archive	Sets the A or Archive attribute. Marks with an A any file that has changed since being backed up using certain backup programs, including Backup, which comes with Windows. If no A appears, the file has not changed since you backed it up.
Hidden	Sets the H or Hidden attribute, which prevents files from displaying in the Explorer and My Computer.
System	Sets the S or System attribute, which prevents files from displaying. System files are files that your computer requires to operate. Deleting a system file could prevent your computer from working. Folders cannot have the System attribute set.

   5. Click OK.

FIG. 44.14

You can check the
properties of a file or
folder on its Properties
sheet.

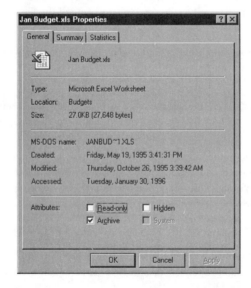

> **CAUTION**
>
> Read-only files can still be deleted from within Explorer. You will see one additional warning dialog box prompting you if you attempt to delete a read-only file. So, setting this attribute does not entirely protect a read-only file from deletion.

N O T E   If you want to reduce the odds of accidentally changing or erasing a file, set the attributes
to Read-Only and Hidden or System. But remember that Read-Only and System files

require only one additional confirmation to delete. So be careful when confirming the message that prompts you when deleting files.

To display files with the Hidden or System attribute, choose View, Options. Click the View tab and select the Show All Files option. Now hidden and system files are displayed in the list of files. You can carry out these steps in either Explorer or My Computer. ■

Opening a Document from the Explorer

You can open documents directly from Explorer. In fact, if you like to think in terms of opening documents rather than opening programs and then opening documents, you can use Explorer as your primary interface with your computer, doing all your viewing, opening, and printing of files from Explorer.

To open a document from Explorer, the file type for that document must be registered with a program in order for Windows to know what application to use to open and print the document. Windows automatically registers file types when you install an application.

To open a document in Explorer, double-click the file icon in Explorer or in a folder window. Explorer starts the program for the file and opens the file. If the program is already running and it works with a multidocument interface, then the document loads into the program.

Opening an Unrecognized File Type   If Windows does not recognize the file type of the file you double-click, it displays the Open With dialog box shown in Figure 44.15. This dialog box enables you to tell Windows which application should be used to open the file. Choose the program you want to open the file from the Choose the Program list. If you want the program to always be used to open a file of this type, make sure the Always Use this Program to Open this File check box is selected.

FIG. 44.15
Double-clicking a file that is not recognized produces the Open With dialog box so you can tell Windows which program to use to open the file.

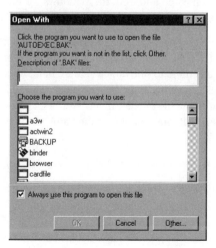

You may want to open a file with a program different than the program it has an association with. To do that, hold the Shift key as you right-click the file. Choose Open With, and then choose the program with which you want to open the file.

Printing Files

You can send files directly to the printer from Explorer. When you print with Explorer, you send the file to the default printer. To change the default printer, use Control Panel.

To print a file with Explorer, the file must be registered with a program. To print a file using Explorer, follow these steps:

1. Open the folder that contains the file or files you want to print.
2. Select the file or files you want to print.
3. Choose File, Print.

   If you have created a shortcut for your printer on your desktop, drag and drop the selected file or files onto the Printer icon on the desktop.

 Quickly print files by right-clicking the file, choosing Send To, and then selecting the printer. To add a printer to the Send To menu, right-drag a printer icon from the Printer folder in My Computer into the Windows\SendTo folder. Choose Create Shortcut(s) Here.

Finding Files

If you are familiar with the Search command from the Windows 3.1 File Manager, you should be impressed by the new features added for finding files in Windows 95.

The Find tool enables you to look for a specific file or group of related files by name and location. When searching by name, it's no longer necessary to use "wild cards" to specify your search, although you can still use them to fine-tune a search. In addition to this improvement, you can search by date modified, file type, and size. The most powerful new feature allows you to search by the text contained in the file or files. If you ever need to look for a file and you can remember a key word or phrase in it, but don't know the name of the file, this will be a real time-saver.

To find a file or group of related files, follow these steps:

1. Open the Start menu, choose Find, and then choose Files or Folders.

   Or, in Explorer, choose Tools, Find, Files or Folders or right-click in the left pane and choose Find, Files or Folders. The Find dialog box appears (see Figure 44.16).
2. Type an entry in the Named text box.

   If you know the name of the file, type it in the text box. If you don't know the complete name of the file, just type whatever portion of file name you do know. Windows 95 will find all files that have these characters anywhere in the name.

You also can use wild cards to look for all files of a particular type. (You could also use the Type criteria discussed in step 5 to limit files by type.) The following are some examples of how to use wild cards to look for groups of related files:

Entry	What It Finds
*.xls	Files with XLS extension (Excel worksheet files)
d*.xls	Excel worksheet files with file names beginning with the letter d (for example, DRAFT1.XLS)
report??.txt	TXT files beginning with file names starting with *report*, followed by two more characters (for example, REPORT23.TXT)

To reuse the same search criteria as one used previously, click the arrow at the end of the Named text box and select the name search criteria you want to use from the list.

FIG. 44.16

Specify information about files you are searching for in the Find dialog box.

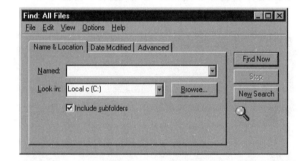

3. Specify where Find should look for the file in the Look In text box.

   You can type a pathname in the text box, select from the entries in the drop-down list, or click the Browse button to select the location to which you want to restrict the search.

   Select the Include Subfolders option if you want to include the subfolders of whatever folders you selected in the search.

 To search an entire drive, select the drive letter from the drop-down list and select Include Subfolders.

4. To limit the search to files created or modified within a specific time period, click the Date Modified tab (see Figure 44.17).

   You can restrict the search to files created or modified between two specified dates, or you can search for files created or modified during a specified number of months or days prior to the current date.

5. Click the Advanced tab to refine your search even more (see Figure 44.18).

6. Select a file type from the Of Type drop-down list to restrict the search to a specific type of file. The types listed here are the registered file types discussed in "Registering Documents So They Open Applications" later in this chapter. These include document types created by application programs, as well as various types of files needed by Windows such as icons, control panels, and fonts.

7. Enter a text string in the Containing Text text box to search for files containing a specific string of text. If you enter several words separated by spaces, Windows treats the entry as a phrase and finds only documents containing those words in that order.

FIG. 44.17

You can narrow your search to a specified time period using options on the Date Modified page.

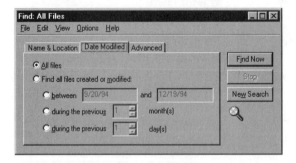

FIG. 44.18

Restrict your file search to files containing specific text or files of a specific size on the Advanced page of the Find dialog box.

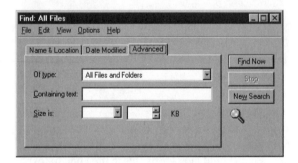

8. Specify the size of the file in the Size Is box. You can specify that the file be exactly a particular file size, or at least (or at most) a specified size. Select from the drop-down list to select which of these options to use, and then specify a size in the Size Is box.

9. When you have finished setting up your search parameters, click the Find Now button.

The Find dialog box expands at the bottom to show the results of the search (see Figure 44.19). If your search parameters were very specific, the search may take a few moments, especially if you told Find to look for files with a specific text string. All files matching the search specifications are listed, along with their location, size, and file type.

Use Find to do large-scale or disk-wide file deletions. You can use a search parameter that searches for a specific file type, such as *.XLS, or search for all old files, those files prior to a specific date. When the files display in the bottom of the Find window, use Quick View or view the file's properties to decide which files you want to delete.

At this point, you can perform all the same operations on any of the found files that you can on a file in Explorer. To work with a file in the Find dialog box, select the file and choose the File menu, or click the file with the right mouse button to open the shortcut menu. You can open, print, preview, move, copy, delete, rename, or view the properties of the file. You also can drag-and-drop the file to any folder in Explorer. This is handy if the file you located is in the wrong folder, and you want to quickly move it to the correct folder. The Edit menu contains commands for cutting and copying files, and for all the files, or all but the selected files.

FIG. 44.19

The results of a search are listed at the bottom of the Find dialog box.

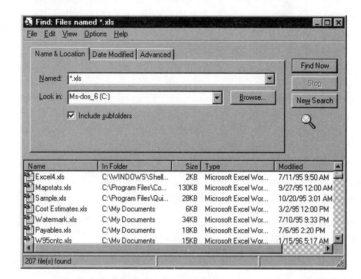

Searching Through Compressed ZIP Files

Find will search for file names within files compressed with PKZIP or a PKZIP-compatible compression program. This can be very useful if you archive files in ZIP format and later need to find a specific file that is within a ZIP file.

The reason Find can do this is that the file names within a ZIP file are not compressed. The file names are stored in the ZIP file as text. You can use Find to search through the contents of the ZIP files for specific names.

To search for a file name within a ZIP file, follow these steps:

1. Click Start, Find, Files or Folders.
2. Choose the Options menu and make sure that Case Sensitive is not selected.
3. Select the Name & Location tab. Specify the drive to search and select the Include Subfolders check box. Type ***.ZIP** in the Named edit box.
4. Select the Advanced tab. Type the file name in the Containing Text edit box. Wild cards will not work.
5. Click the Find Now button.

When Find displays a list of ZIP files containing the file name, you can use Quick View Plus to view all the files in the ZIP file. Utilities such as PKZIP for Windows from PKWare selectively unzip a single file from the ZIP file you found.

Saving the Search Criteria

You can save the search criteria as well as the results in an icon on your desktop. You also can save just the search criteria without saving the results. If you want to save the results with the search criteria, choose Options, Save Results so that Save Results is selected and shows a check mark. To save the criteria, and the results if you specified that, choose File, Save Search. The saved criteria, and the results if you specified them, will appear on your desktop as a document icon. You can label the icon by changing its name.

To open the Find dialog box using the saved criteria and result, double-click the icon. The Find dialog box will show the criteria and results as they were when saved. To redo the search, click Find Now.

The View menu has the same commands as Explorer for selecting how you want the files to be displayed in the results pane and for sorting the list of files.

The Options menu has two commands for fine-tuning your search. Choose the Case Sensitive command if you want Find to distinguish between upper- and lowercase characters in any text you specified in the Containing Text text box.

If you want to set up a new search, click New Search to clear the criteria for the current search. Now you can enter the criteria for the new search.

Customizing Explorer's Appearance

Windows offers many options for changing how the Explorer window looks. You can change how folders and files are listed; hide or display the toolbar and status bar; sort the folder and file icons by name, type, size, or date; hide the display of certain types of files; and make other changes to the Explorer window. Any changes you make remain in effect until you make new changes, even if you close and reopen Explorer.

N O T E   If you're used to opening multiple Windows in File Manager, take note of the fact that you can't do that in the Explorer. For most work, you don't need to open multiple windows in Explorer because you can drag from any file or folder in the right pane into any drive or folder in the left pane. You can display drives or folders in the left pane by clicking their + sign without disturbing the contents of the right pane. Should you ever need to have multiple windows in Explorer, just open additional copies of Explorer. You can then copy or move files between them. ▪

 T I P   Most of the settings and preferences you choose for viewing a folder remain with that folder. The next time you open that folder it will have the same settings.

Changing the Width of Panes

Use the mouse to change the size of the left and right panes of Explorer. To change the width of the two panes of the Explorer window, move the mouse pointer over the bar dividing the two panes (the mouse pointer changes to a double-headed arrow), hold down the left mouse button, and drag the bar left or right to adjust the size of the two panes to your liking. However, you can't hide one pane or the other completely as you could in Windows 3.1 File Manager.

Changing the Status Bar

The status bar at the bottom of the Explorer window provides information on the item you select. If you select a folder, for example, you see information on the number of items in the folder and the total amount of disk space used by the folder. You can hide the status bar if you don't use it to make more room for displaying files and folders. To hide the status bar, choose View, Status Bar. Choosing this command again displays the status bar.

Hiding the Toolbar

The tools on the toolbar are shortcuts for commands you otherwise access with menu commands. These tools are discussed in the appropriate sections in this chapter. If you don't use the toolbar, you can hide it by choosing View, Toolbar. To display the toolbar, choose the command again.

Changing How Folders and Files Display

When you first start using Explorer, notice that folders and files are represented by large icons in the right pane of the window, as shown earlier in Figures 44.4 and 44.5. You also can display files and folders as small icons, as a list, or with file details.

To change the way folders and files are displayed, follow these steps:

1. Open the View menu.
2. Choose one of the following commands:

Command	Result
Large Icons	Large icons
Small Icons	Small icons arranged in multiple columns
List	Small icons in a single list
Details	Size, type, and date modified

The currently selected option appears in the View menu with a dot beside it. Figure 44.20 shows files displayed using small icons.

If the toolbar is displayed, you also can click one of the four tools at the right end of the toolbar to change how items are displayed.

 TIP To automatically adjust column widths in the Detail view of Explorer to show the full content width, double-click the line between the column heads.

When you select the Details option, information on the size, type, and date the folder or file was last modified appears in columns next to the item in the list, as shown in Figure 44.21. You can change the width of these columns by moving the mouse pointer over the line that divides the buttons at the top of each column (the mouse pointer changes to a double-headed arrow), holding down the left mouse button, and dragging the line to change the width.

FIG. 44.20

You can view more files and folders in Explorer when you use small icons.

FIG. 44.21

To see information on the folders and files in the Explorer window, choose the Details view. Resize columns by dragging the line between header titles.

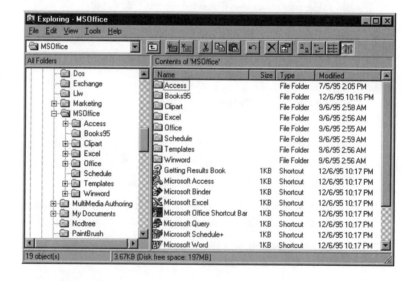

Arranging File and Folder Icons

If you select either the Large Icons or Small Icons option for displaying your files and folders, you can choose to let Windows automatically arrange the icons, or you can move the icons around to locate them wherever you want. To arrange the icons automatically, choose View,

Arrange Icons. If a check mark appears next to the Auto Arrange command in the submenu, the command is already selected. If not, select Auto Arrange. The icons are now automatically arranged in a grid. If you want to arrange icons at any location in the right pane, deselect Auto Arrange. Some people prefer to have their files and folders arranged in an order of priority, frequency of use, or some other creative arrangement. Figure 44.22 shows files grouped by usage. Some are forecasting files and others are budgetary files.

If the Auto Arrange command is not enabled, you can quickly arrange your icons in a grid by choosing View, Line Up Icons.

Part
X

Ch
44

FIG. 44.22
When Auto Arrange is off you can arrange icons in any way you want.

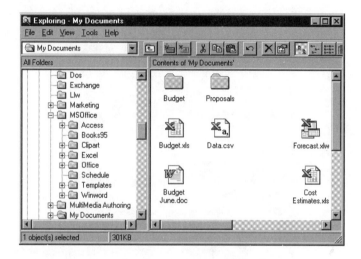

Sorting Files and Folders

You can sort the files and folders in the right pane of Explorer by name, type, size, and date. To sort the items in the Explorer display, follow these steps:

1. Choose View, Arrange Icons.

2. Select one of the four options from the submenu:

Command	Result
By Name	Sort folders and then files by their names
By Type	Sort folders and then files by the type column (this may not be the same as file extension)
By Size	Sort folders and then files by their sizes
By Date	Sort folders and then files by their dates

If you selected the Details option for displaying your folders and files, you can quickly sort the list of items by name, size, type, and date modified by clicking the button at the top of the column you want to sort by. Click Size, for example, to sort the list of items by size.

TIP When you see a list in Windows 95 and the list headings appear to be buttons, try clicking them to sort the information according to the column on which you click. Each click toggles between ascending or descending order.

Displaying or Hiding Different File Types

You can change several other options in the View Options dialog box. To change these options, follow these steps:

1. Choose View, Options to display the Options dialog box (see Figure 44.23).

FIG. 44.23
You can change several options on the View page of the Options dialog box.

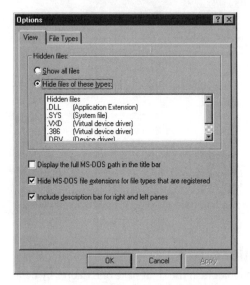

2. Select Show All Files to list all file types in the Explorer window. Or select Hide Files of These Types to hide the display of several types of system files.

   Hiding these files, which you normally don't have to deal with, shortens the list of items displayed for some folders, and also prevents you and other users from accidentally deleting or moving crucial system files.

3. Select the Display the Full MS-DOS Path in the Title Bar option if you want to see the full DOS path for the folder selected in the left pane.

4. Select the Hide MS-DOS File Extensions for File Types that Are Registered option if you don't want the extensions for files associated with a particular program to be displayed. (In Windows, a file's icon indicates what program it is associated with, if any; so you may have no reason to see file extensions.)

5. Select the Include Description Bar for Right and Left Panes option to display a descriptive bar at the top of the right and left panes of the Explorer window. The Description Bar shows you such information as the drive letter and pathname for the current view.

6. Click OK when you have finished making the selections you want.

Starting Explorer at Specific Directories or Files

One of Explorer's potentially annoying features is that, when it opens, it displays the directory or resource of the object from which it was opened. For example, if you right-click Start and choose Explore, then Explorer opens displaying the contents of the Start menu folder. If you right-click the My Computer icon on the desktop and choose Explore, then Explorer opens displaying the contents of My Computer. While this design is understandable, many of us expect or would like Explorer to open in a folder we designate or in the last folder in which it was used. Use the following tips and you'll be able to create shortcuts that open Explorer the way you want.

Opening Explorer at Specific Folders or Files

Opening Explorer from a command line enables you to use switches that control how Explorer opens. The command line can be entered in the Target box of a shortcut's Property sheet, entered from an MS-DOS prompt, or typed within an MS-DOS batch file. Understanding how these switches work enables you to open Explorer in the following ways:

- In a single pane, Open view, or with the double pane in the Explorer view.
- With full access to all folders or restricted to a *root* folder or UNC.
- With a folder open and no file selected or with a specific file selected.

N O T E Be sure that you type a comma between each switch. Long file names or UNC names entered in the Target line of a shortcut's property sheet do not need to be enclosed in quotes. ■

The syntax for using switches with the Explorer is:

```
Explorer /e,/root,<object>,/select,<sub object>
```

These switches do the following:

Switch	Description
/n	Opens a new window even when a window is already open in the same folder.
/e	Without /e Explorer opens in the single pane Open view seen from My Computer. With /e Explorer opens with two panes.

continues

continued

Switch	Description
/root,<object>	Specifies the highest level folder shown in Explorer, and then opens in this folder. Explorer is restricted to the root folder and its subfolders. Use a local path or UNC name. If no root is specified the Desktop is used.
/select,<sub object>	The object specified by <sub object> is selected when Explorer opens. The object can be a file, folder, or resource. Specify the path or UNC unless it is specified by /root.

Opening Explorer and Restricting It to a Folder A lot of file management time is spent scrolling up and down through the left pane of Explorer looking for the same two or three frequently used folders. With the following trick, you can create shortcuts that open Explorer to the specific folder you want. Two or three of these shortcuts on your desktop or Start menu will save a lot of time.

The *root* switch opens Explorer to the folder or UNC path that you specify, but it also restricts the user to that root and all the subfolders underneath it.

Follow these steps to create a shortcut that opens in the folder you want:

1. Create a desktop shortcut to EXPLORER.EXE in the Windows folder.
2. Right-click the shortcut icon and choose Properties.
3. Select the Shortcut tab.
4. Modify the Target line to read:

   `C:\WINDOWS\EXPLORER.EXE /e,/root,C:\my documents`

   This opens Explorer in the double-pane window like the one shown in Figure 44.24. Notice that the /root switch forces Explorer to display only the My Documents folder and its subfolders. Use the following command line to open a single pane folder window:

   `C:\WINDOWS\EXPLORER.EXE /root,C:\my documents`

FIG. 44.24

Open Explorer in a double-pane view with unlimited scope or restricted to a folder as shown here.

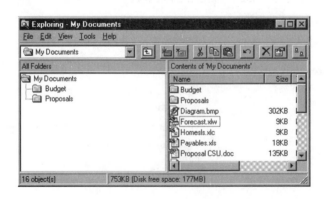

5. Change the icon by clicking the Change Icon button if you wish, then click OK.

6. Relabel the shortcut icon to indicate the view that it opens.

When you want to open Explorer to the folder designated by the root switch, just double-click the shortcut. To copy a file or folder into that folder, just drag-and-drop the file or folder onto the shortcut.

Opening the Explorer and Selecting a File   To open an Explorer window and display a specific file, create a shortcut icon as described in the previous section. Open the shortcut's Property sheet and select its Shortcut tab.

Part
X

Ch

44

In the Target line enter a line similar to:

```
C:\WINDOWS\EXPLORER.EXE /select,C:\my documents\schedule.xls
```

If you have restricted Explorer to a root folder with a dual pane view, then your command line might look something like this:

```
C:\WINDOWS\EXPLORER.EXE /e,/root,C:\my documents,/select,schedule.xls
```

The resulting windows look like Figure 44.25.

FIG. 44.25

Explorer windows can be restricted to a folder and have a specific file or folder selected when they open.

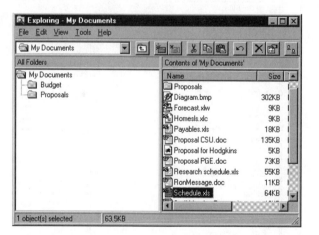

Customizing Explorer for Side-by-Side Views or Program Groups

While Explorer is very powerful, there are a few things about the old File Manager and Program Manager that some people still miss. One of the nice features of the Windows 3.x File Manager was its capability to display side-by-side windows. This enabled you to quickly drag-and-drop files between widely separated folders. Although you can drag-and-drop between folders in Explorer, it's sometimes more awkward to do so. The following section shows you how to use Explorer switches and a batch file to create a shortcut that opens side-by-side Explorer windows.

Some people prefer the Windows 3.x Program Manager as a way of viewing programs and documents they wish to start. If you prefer to see your programs and documents grouped on the desktop you will want to see how easy it is to create a programs group that duplicates everything in the Programs submenu of your Start menu.

Opening Side-by-Side Folder Windows from a Desktop Shortcut

The following procedure creates an MS-DOS batch file that opens two folder windows and positions them side-by-side, as shown in Figure 44.26. A shortcut to the batch file enables you to rerun it whenever you need it. To use this batch file you won't need to minimize the other programs that are running.

To create the side-by-side folder batch file, follow these steps:

1. Double-click My Computer to open a single pane window. Choose View, Options then select Browse Folders by Using a Single Window and choose OK.

FIG. 44.26

Run side-by-side folder windows from a batch file whenever you want.

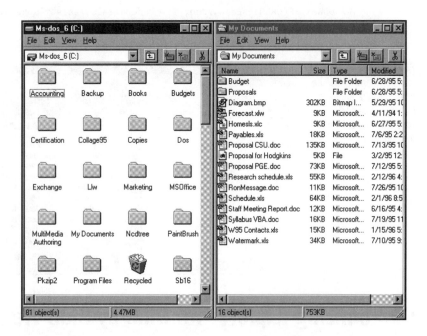

2. Create an MS-DOS batch file by clicking Start, Accessories, Notepad and entering two Explorer command lines that open folder windows into the drives or folders you want. If you want the windows to open side-by-side, the initial folder for each window must be different. If the folders are the same they will open on top of each other. Save this batch file with the extension BAT.

For example, to open two folder windows with one showing C:\ and the other showing C:\MSOffice, you would use:

```
Explorer C:\
Explorer /n,C:\MSOFFICE
```

In this example, the first line opens a folder window at the C: drive. The second line opens a new folder window at C:\MSOffice.

3. After you have saved the batch file, you can create a shortcut directly from the batch file by right-clicking the batch file and choosing Properties. Select the Program tab and change the name at the top of the sheet. This name is a descriptive name to help you if it does not appear as the file name. Select Minimize from the Run drop-down list. Select the Close on Exit check box. These actions prevent the batch file window from displaying. Choose OK.

Windows automatically creates a shortcut because you modified the batch file's properties. The shortcut is stored in the same folder as the original batch file.

4. Drag the shortcut onto the desktop, if you want it available from the desktop, or add it to the Start menu.

5. Close or minimize all programs and run the batch shortcut by double-clicking it.

6. When the two folder windows appear, click the window you want on the left, then right-click the taskbar in a clear area and choose Tile Vertically. Set any viewing options for the windows, such as column widths, then close each window. If these windows display different folders the next time they are opened, they will open in the same position and with the same viewing options.

To run your batch file, double-click the shortcut you created. If you opened both windows into the same folder the windows will open using the position and viewing options of the last window you closed in step 6.

Creating Windows 3.1-Like Program Groups

Some people who used Windows 3.1 really liked the way the Program Manager visually grouped their programs and documents. If you prefer this method of starting and visualizing your programs and documents, follow these steps to quickly create a folder window displaying groups of programs and document files that are in your Start menu. Figure 44.27 shows the window which duplicates the contents of the Programs menu.

FIG. 44.27
Put the contents of your Start, Programs menu in a window with a single click.

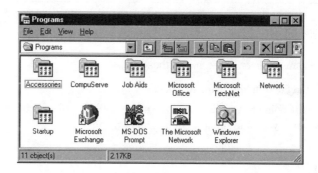

Part
X

Ch
44

To create a window duplicating the contents of the Programs submenu of the Start button, double-click the PROGRAM.GRP file in the Windows folder. A Group Conversion window displays while the group file converts into a folder window. When it's done you see a single pane window displaying the contents of the Start, Program menu. Adding or removing programs or documents to the Start, Program menu automatically updates the contents of the window.

Working with Long File Names

Windows 95 gives you the capability to type file and folder names up to 255 characters long and include spaces. This makes understanding file and folder names much easier than older versions of Windows or DOS.

> **CAUTION**
>
> Although a file name can be up to 255 characters long, you shouldn't make them longer than 50 to 75 characters because the full path name cannot be more than 260 characters. From a usability standpoint, file names that are too long are difficult to type and difficult to read in a list.

 You can display or hide the three-character file extension by choosing View, Options, and then clicking the View tab and deselecting the option Hide MS-DOS File Extensions for File Types that Are Registered. This will not hide file extensions for applications that are not registered.

Both of these improvements do not restrict your ability to use Windows files with older Windows or DOS systems that do not use long file names. An abbreviated version of the long file names enables files to be backward-compatible.

Renaming Files and Folders

As part of your efforts to keep the files and folders on your computer organized, you may want to rename a file or folder. This is easy to do in Explorer.

 If you're using a keyboard, you can rename a file or folder by selecting it and then either choosing File, Rename, or pressing F2.

To edit or rename a file or folder, follow these steps:

1. Click the file or folder name to select it.
2. Pause the pointer over the text in the name until the pointer changes to an I-beam and click where you want the insertion point in the text.

CAUTION

If you accidentally double-click the file name, the program for that file opens and loads the file. To return to naming the file, close the program and click once on the file name.

3. Edit using normal Windows editing methods. Press Enter to complete your edit.

If you should change your mind while typing in a new name, just press the Escape key to return to the original name. If you have already pressed Enter and the file has been renamed, click the Undo button in the toolbar, choose Edit, Undo, or press Ctrl+Z.

Part

X

Ch

44

CAUTION

If you change the three-letter DOS file extension for a name, you will see a Rename alert box with this message: If you change a file name extension, the file may become unusable. Are you sure you want to change it? This box warns you that by changing the extension you will not be able to double-click the file and open its program. You can still open the file from within the application by choosing File, Open.

Do not type file extensions when you rename files if file extensions are being hidden. If extensions are hidden and you rename the text file VACATION to be BIKING.TXT, the file will actually be renamed as BIKING.TXT.TXT.

Using Long File Names with Older Windows and DOS Systems

Folders and files with long names can be used on older Windows and DOS systems. The *FAT (File Allocation Table)*, an area on the disk that stores file information, has been especially modified to store both old-style 8.3 file names as well as long file names.

CAUTION

Beware of using MS-DOS-based or previous Windows versions of hard disk utilities, file management software, or file utilities with Windows 95. In most cases, long file names will be destroyed and you may lose data.

Some programs that will cause problems with Windows 95 are the Windows 3.x versions of:

- Norton Utilities™ by Symantec
- PC Tools™ by Central Point Software, Inc.
- Microsoft Defragmenter for MS-DOS versions 6.0, 6.2, 6.21, or 6.22
- Stacker 4.0 by STAC Electronics

These companies have released Windows 95-compatible upgrades for their utilities. Check with these companies for the correct version to use with Windows 95.

If you must run an old backup or disk management utility with Windows 95, use the LFNBK utility to remove long file names from the disk. After using the old utility you can restore long file names. LFNBK is described in the troubleshooting section at the end of Chapter 48, "Backing Up and Protecting Your Data."

CAUTION

Long file names cannot use the following characters:

/ \ : * ? " < > |

When you use a long file name, Windows automatically creates a file name fitting the 8.3 convention. This 8.3 file name is saved in its normal location in the FAT so that older Windows and DOS systems can still use the 8.3 file name.

You can see the MS-DOS file name that will be used for a file by right-clicking the file name, choosing Properties, and selecting the General tab. Figure 44.28 shows the File Properties sheet. The long file name is shown at the top of the box; the MS-DOS name appears near the middle.

FIG. 44.28

Find out about a file by right-clicking its name and then choosing Properties.

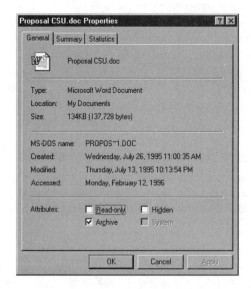

The rules used to convert long file names to 8.3 file names are

1. Remove spaces and any period except the right-most period.

2. Create the first portion of the name by taking the first six characters in the long file name and adding a *numeric tail* by adding a tilde (˜) followed by the number 1. If a file in the same directory already uses that number, increase the number to 2. Continue trying numbers through 9. If that does not yield a unique name, take the first five characters and create a unique numeric tail using numbers from 10 to 99.

3. Create the file extension by taking the first three characters after the last period. If the long file name does not have a period, there won't be a file extension.

Administering Long File Names in a Mixed-Name Environment

If you are working in an environment that uses Windows 95 as well as computers that still use the 8.3 naming convention, there are a number of things you can do to lessen the confusion caused by mixed names.

- Familiarize yourself with the LFNBK utility and use it with any pre-Windows 95 disk or file utilities that you use on Windows 95 files. Upgrade to Windows 95 utilities as soon as possible.

- Users should check the resultant 8.3 file name if they have any doubt about the resolution of a long file name down to an 8.3 file name. See the MS-DOS file name by opening a file's Property sheet and checking the MS-DOS name on the General page.

- Modify your Windows 95 computers so they truncate long file names at the first eight characters rather than truncating at six letters and adding the ~# numeric tail. Many users prefer this modification because it enables you to use the first eight characters of a long file name as part of the MS-DOS file name. To learn how to modify the Registry so the numeric tail is not used on MS-DOS file names, see "Modifying the Registry to Truncate Long File Names," later in this chapter.

- Create a naming convention for files and train your users on using it and understanding its importance.

If you decide to create naming conventions for your users, here are some possible conventions:

- Make the first six characters of long file names significant and unique. In this way each file's 8.3 file name will be readable and unique. In the following table you can see the difference between how long file names convert.

Non-Unique Leading Six Characters	
Long File Name	**8.3 Equivalent**
Sales Report Jan.Xls	SALESR~1.XLS
Sales Report Feb.Xls	SALESR~2.XLS
Sales Report Mar.Xls	SALESR~3.XLS

Unique Leading Six Characters	
Long File Name	**8.3 Equivalent**
Jan Sales Report.Xls	JANSAL~1.XLS
Feb Sales Report.Xls	FEBSAL~1.XLS
Mar Sales Report.Xls	MARSAL~1.XLS

- Create the long file name and the 8.3 name within the same name. Start long file names with the first six characters (eight if you modify the registry) of the MS-DOS file name, use underscore characters (_) to fill extra spaces up to the first eight characters, type a long file name, and then end with a period and the three letter extension. Use underscore characters to fill unused spaces in the first eight characters. Do not use blank spaces. This method makes it easy to read the 8.3 name, yet you can still do complex searches with Find on text in the long file. See the examples in the following table.

Long Files Names Compatible with 8.3 Names	
Long File Name	**8.3 Equivalent**
JanRpt__Sales Report.DOC	JANRPT~1.DOC
BdgtA___Budget Dept A.XLS	BDGTA_~1.XLS

Modifying the Registry to Remove Numeric Tails from File Names

Many people find it difficult to read and remember the MS-DOS file names that have *numeric tails*. The numeric tail is the tilde (~)and number at the end of an MS-DOS file name; for example, SALESR~1.XLS. Windows 95 adds a numeric tail when it creates an 8.3 file name from a long file name. These tails are designed to make sure that long file names can be converted to unique 8.3 names.

With a simple modification to the Registry you can get rid of the Windows habit of adding numeric tails. The lack of a numeric tail not only makes file names easier to read, it also gives your file name space for two more characters.

To modify the registry so Windows does not use numeric tails,

1. Click Start, Run and type **Regedit**, then choose OK to open the Registry Editor.
2. Expand the HKEY_LOCAL_MACHINE branch by clicking the + sign to its left.
3. Expand all branches in the following path:
   HKEY_LOCAL_MACHINE\System\CurrentControlSet\Control\FileSystem
4. Select FileSystem in the left pane.
5. Choose Edit, New, Binary Value, then type **NameNumericTail** and press Enter. Your entry, NameNumericTail, appears in the name column.
6. Double-click NameNumericTail. In the Edit Binary Value dialog box that appears type a **0** and choose OK. The value 00 should appear in the value column to the right of NameNumericTail.
7. Close the Registry Editor.

The next time you start Windows, MS-DOS file names will be created by truncating long file names to the first eight valid characters. Numeric tails will only be used if there is another file with the same name in the same folder.

Working with Long File Names in MS-DOS

If you use a DOS command from the command prompt, such as `dir` to list a directory containing files with long names, you see the normal file information as well as the long file names. The long file name is displayed in the far right column when using the DOS `dir` command.

When working from the MS-DOS command line you can use either the 8.3 or the long file name assigned to each file. Use long file names in MS-DOS command lines as you would 8.3 names. If the name includes spaces, put quotes around the entire path.

From the MS-DOS prompt, the default command line character limit is 127 characters. Command lines cannot be longer than 127 characters. To enable longer command lines add the following line to CONFIG.SYS:

```
shell=c:\windows\command.com /u:255
```

If your computer already has the SHELL command in the CONFIG.SYS file then change the /u switch to a value of 255.

If your computer does not have a CONFIG.SYS file in the root, create one by opening Notepad, typing the line as shown, then saving the text file to your boot disk root folder with the name CONFIG.SYS.

The command line will now be limited to 255 characters. This limit includes the MS-DOS command, switches, spaces, quotes, and long file name. You will be able to use 255 character command lines in all MS-DOS virtual machines running in Windows 95. Making this change will not enable MS-DOS on non-Windows 95 computers to use long file names.

Part

X

Ch

44

Synchronizing Files with the Briefcase

With the proliferation of home computers, laptop computers, and networks, you may often find yourself working on the same file on different computers. The inherent difficulty in working with the same file at more than one location is keeping the files synchronized—that is, making sure that the latest version of the file is at both locations. This used to be a daunting and dangerous task. It is not too difficult to accidentally copy the older version of a file on top of the newer version, rather than the other way around. *Briefcase*, makes the task of synchronizing files in different locations much easier.

N O T E If you frequently transfer files between computers, must maintain synchronized files, or want to control one computer from another, consider using LapLink for Windows 95. Its features are more robust, it updates files faster, and it operates over more communication media than Briefcase. ■

Briefcase is really a folder with some special features. When you want to work on files at a different location—for example, on your laptop while you are away from your office—you first copy the files from your desktop computer into Briefcase. You then transfer Briefcase to your laptop and work on the files in Briefcase. When you return to the office, you transfer Briefcase back to your desktop and issue a command that automatically updates any files on your desktop that were modified while they were in Briefcase. The files on your desktop are then synchronized with the files in Briefcase.

The Briefcase procedure works whether you transfer Briefcase using a floppy disk, keep Briefcase on one of two computers that are physically connected, or use Briefcase to synchronize files across a network.

Installing the Briefcase

Unless you chose the Portable option when you were setting up Windows, or specified the installation of Briefcase in a custom installation, you will not have the Briefcase feature. One way to check to see if you do have the Briefcase feature installed is to look for a Briefcase icon on your desktop. However, the Briefcase icon may have been moved or deleted, so a second way to check is to right-click in a folder or on the desktop. Choose New, and if the Briefcase appears as an item, choose Briefcase. If a new Briefcase appears, the Briefcase feature is installed.

> **CAUTION**
>
> If Briefcase is already installed in your Windows 95, Briefcase will not appear in the Accessories portion of the Components list in Add/Remove Programs as described in step 4 of the following instructions. Briefcase will only appear if it has not been previously installed. Once Briefcase is installed it cannot be uninstalled with Add/Remove Programs. This is to prevent the accidental loss of data from a Briefcase.

Creating a New Briefcase on the Desktop

If your PC does not already include a Briefcase on your desktop, you can easily create a new Briefcase. To create a Briefcase, follow these steps:

1. Decide where you want the Briefcase to be created (on the desktop, in a floppy disk folder, in a folder on the hard disk, and so on).

2. Right-click in the location in which you want the Briefcase created. If you want the Briefcase created on the desktop, for example, right-click the desktop.

3. From the pop-up menu, choose New, Briefcase. Windows 95 will create a Briefcase and add an icon for it in the location you have selected.

4. If you want to rename the Briefcase, click the Briefcase icon to select it, then click the Briefcase's description. Type a new description and press Enter.

As previously explained, you can create as many Briefcases as you like. By default, Windows 95 creates a Briefcase called My Briefcase on your desktop. You can rename the default Briefcase to suit your preferences.

Synchronizing Files with a Laptop or Another Computer on the Network

You can use Briefcase to keep files synchronized between a laptop and a desktop computer. This is useful because you may update files on the laptop while it is disconnected from the desktop. Upon reconnecting the two computers, you can ask Windows to synchronize the files between the two computers—comparing and updating files between the two computers. The most up-to-date file replaces the unchanged file. If files on both computers have been changed, you will be asked to choose which file should replace the other.

> **CAUTION**
>
> Be sure that the times and dates are correctly set on any computer on which you use synchronization. Incorrect dates or times could cause the wrong file to be overwritten.

Keeping synchronized files between your laptop and desktop computers is most convenient if they can be physically connected by a cable or network. Physically linking two computers is a much faster way to transfer files than by using a floppy disk. Using Briefcase helps you keep the files you are using on both computers synchronized. You can work on either the file on the original computer or the file in Briefcase, and use the Update command to keep the files synchronized.

Part

X

Ch

44

 The recommended approach is to put Briefcase on the computer you use less often.

You may have two computers on which you need to keep synchronized files, but you don't have the computers connected. You can still keep files synchronized by putting Briefcase on a floppy disk and using the disk to move the Briefcase between computers. You can use this method to synchronize files between your work computer and your home computer or between your desktop and laptop computers. Although it's not as fast as synchronizing files between two connected computers, it works well if you are not working with a large number of files and don't have the means to physically connect the computers.

To synchronize files on two computers that are connected by cable or network or that use a floppy disk to transfer the Briefcase, follow these steps:

1. Copy the files and folders you want to use on both computers into Briefcase.

   The simplest way to copy the files to Briefcase is to drag-and-drop them on the My Briefcase icon on the desktop.

 The fastest way to move the Briefcase is to right-click the My Briefcase icon, click Send To, and then click the floppy drive you want to move Briefcase to.

2. Move Briefcase to the computer on which you will be working with the Briefcase files. If your computer is not connected to the other computer, move the Briefcase to a floppy disk.

   Once you move the Briefcase it will not be located on the original desktop. It can only be at one place at a time.

   The idea is to move, not copy, Briefcase onto the other computer, so that it exists in only one location. An easy way to move Briefcase is to select the My Briefcase icon with the mouse, drag it to the new location with the right mouse button, and choose Move Here from the shortcut menu that appears.

3. If you are using a floppy disk, transfer the floppy disk to the other computer you want to work on.

4. Open and edit the files in Briefcase, as you normally would.

   If Briefcase is on a floppy disk and the other computer you are working on has Windows installed on it, you can transfer the files to the hard disk on that computer to speed up editing. Drag the files to the hard disk, and after you have edited them, drag the files back to Briefcase.

If you are working on computers that are physically connected, open and edit the files from Briefcase. You can work on the files on your portable or laptop even when it is not connected to the desktop.

> **CAUTION**
>
> If the other computer you are working on does not have Windows, you shouldn't transfer them to the hard disk. Open and edit them in the Briefcase on the floppy disk. Otherwise, you'll defeat the purpose of using Briefcase for keeping the files synchronized.

5. Once you are finished editing the files and you need to synchronize the files between the two computers, reconnect the computers if a cable or network connects them.

    If Briefcase was on a floppy disk, you can open Briefcase from the floppy disk or move Briefcase back to the desktop of the original computer. Then open Briefcase.

    Double-click the My Briefcase icon to open it (see Figure 44.29).

FIG. 44.29

Use My Briefcase to keep files in different locations synchronized.

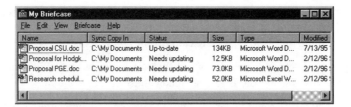

> **N O T E** By default, My Briefcase displays files in the Details view. This view is much like the Details view in Explorer with two additional columns. The Sync Copy In column lists the location of the original file. The Status column indicates whether the file is up-to-date, or whether it's older or newer than the original. Like the other columns in the Detail view of a folder, you can sort the list by clicking the column headings. ▪

6. Choose Briefcase, Update All. Or, select only those files you want to update and choose Briefcase, Update Selection. The Update My Briefcase dialog box appears, as shown in Figure 44.30.

7. Check the proposed update action for each file as it is synchronized with its corresponding file on the other computer.

    The default update action is to replace the older version of the file with the newer version. If you want to change the update action for a file, right-click the file name and change the action using the pop-up menu that appears (see Figure 44.31).

8. Click the Update button to update the files. (The computers must be connected for you to update the files.)

FIG. 44.30

All files that need to be updated are listed in the Update My Briefcase dialog box.

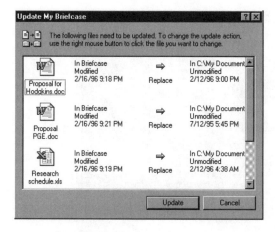

FIG. 44.31

Change the update action that will be applied to a file by right-clicking it and selecting the desired action.

Checking the Status of Briefcase Files

You can check the update status of the files in the Briefcase at any time. To check the status of a file or folder in Briefcase, open My Briefcase by double-clicking it. Examine the Status column in the window.

If you have the Briefcase files displayed in a view other than Details, you won't see this Status column. To check the status, you can choose View, Details to switch to Details view. Or you can select the file to check and choose File, Properties, and then click the Update Status tab (see Figure 44.32). The middle portion of the Update Status page shows the status of the file in the Briefcase on the left and that of the original file on the right. If the files are the same, Up to Date is indicated in the center. If the files are not the same, Replace is shown in the center along with an arrow. The arrow points to the file that is out-of-date and should be replaced.

From within this Properties sheet, you can update the file (as described in the preceding section) by choosing Update. You also can prevent a file from being updated (which is discussed in the next section) by choosing Split from Original.

You can choose Find Original to open the folder with the original file, without having to work your way through the hierarchy of folders in Explorer or My Computer.

FIG. 44.32

In this figure, the copy of Proposal PGE.doc in C:\My Documents is newer than the copy in the Briefcase, so Windows indicates that the copy in the Briefcase should be replaced.

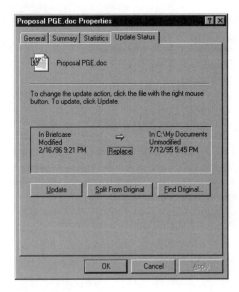

TROUBLESHOOTING

If you have Briefcase or the folder with the original open, the status may not be updated immediately. Choose View, Refresh both in My Briefcase and in the folder containing the original file. This ensures that the status indicates any recent changes.

Preventing a File from Synchronizing

You may want to break the connection between a file in Briefcase and its original file, so that when you issue the Update command, the two copies of the file are not synchronized. You may want to do this to preserve the original file or if the portable file is now a file that has changed into a document unrelated to the original.

To split a file from its original, follow these steps:

1. Open Briefcase and select the file you want to split.
2. Choose Briefcase, Split From Original.

   Notice that the file is now referred to as an orphan in the Status field of the Briefcase window.

You also can split a file by clicking the Split from Original button on the Update Status page of the Properties sheet.

Registering Documents So They Open Applications

When you register a file type with Windows, you tell Windows that the file type has a certain MS-DOS extension and that a particular program should be used to open the file. The most useful reason for registering a file type is that you can then double-click any file of that type, and the file will be opened using the program you have instructed Windows to use.

T I P If you want to open a file with a program other than the program it's associated with, hold down the Shift key and right-click the file. The context menu displays an Open With command. Choose this command to see a list of programs you can use to open the file.

N O T E If you learn how to create and edit your own file types, you can customize the context menu that appears when you right-click a file. For example, you might want to add an extra Open association to choose between opening an HTML document in a browser or editor. ■

If you double-click a file and the file opens in a program, the file is registered with that program. If Windows does not have a program associated with the file you double-clicked, the Open With dialog box shown in Figure 44.33 opens.

FIG. 44.33

Double-clicking an unassociated file type displays the Open With dialog box which prompts you for the program to run.

To register the file type with a program, follow these steps:

1. Type a description of the file type in the Description edit box. The description displays under the Type column in Explorer for all files with this extension.

2. Scroll through the Choose the Program list to the program you want to open the file in and click the program. If the program is not shown in the list, click the Other button and select the program's EXE file from an Open dialog box.

3. If you want to open other files of this type with the same program, check the Always Use This Program to Open This File check box.

4. Choose OK.

TROUBLESHOOTING

If after double-clicking a file, it opens in a program other than the program you expected it to open in, you need to change the program this file type is registered with. To do this, open the Options dialog box from Explorer, select the File Type sheet, and edit the association for that file type.

Using Explorer with Shared Resources on a Network

If you are using Windows on a network, you can share resources with other users in your workgroup and use resources that other users have designated as shared. You can open the files in any folder that has been designated as shared by another user, and you can share any of your folders so that the files in that folder can be used by other users. You can use Explorer to designate resources on your computer as shared and to browse the shared resources in your workgroup or on your entire network.

Browsing Shared Folders

You browse a shared folder using Explorer in the same way you browse a folder on your computer.

To browse a shared folder, follow these steps:

1. Under Network Neighborhood in the left pane of Explorer, find the computer on your network on which the folder you want to browse is located.

   If a plus sign appears next to the name of the computer, click the plus sign to display the shared resources on that computer (see Figure 44.34).

   Shared resources can include folders, entire drives, CD-ROM drives, and printers, as you can see in Figure 44.34.

2. Select the shared folder to display its contents in the right pane of Explorer, as shown in Figure 44.35.

3. To open a shared file from Explorer, double-click the file name in the right pane.

Sharing Resources on Your Computer

You can designate any folder on your computer as shared. When you share a folder, you can assign a *share name* and *password* to that folder. You also can specify what type of access users have to the shared folder. Once you have shared a folder, other users have access to the files in that folder. The computers that have the folders you want to share must be on and logged in to the network.

FIG. 44.34

View the shared resources on another user's computer in Explorer.

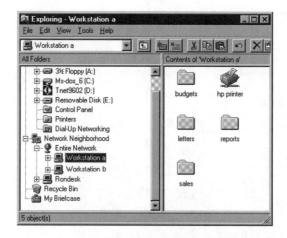

FIG. 44.35

View the contents of a shared folder by selecting it in Explorer.

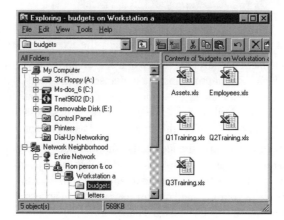

To share a folder, follow these steps:

1. In Explorer, select the folder you want to share.

2. Right-click the folder, and then click Sharing to display the Sharing page on the Properties sheet.

3. Select the Shared As option, as shown in Figure 44.36.

4. You can accept the default share name for the folder or type a new name in the Share Name text box.

5. Enter a comment in the Comment text box, if you want.

   The comment appears in the Details view of your computer when other users select it in Explorer or Network Neighborhood. Comments can help users locate shared information.

FIG. 44.36

Designate a folder as shared on the Sharing page of the Properties sheet.

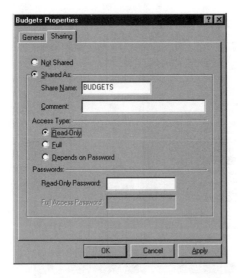

6. Select one of the Access Type options to specify the access for the shared resource.

   You can grant users two levels of access to a shared folder. If you want users to be able only to read files and run programs in a folder, select the Read-Only option. If you want users to be able to read, modify, rename, move, delete, or create files and run your programs, select the Full option. If you want the level of access to depend on which password the user enters, select the Depends on Password option.

   If you want to limit access to the files in the shared folder to certain users, assign a password to the folder and give the password to only those users. If you select the Depends on Password option, you need to enter two passwords—one for users who have read-only access to your files and one for users with full access. If you want all users to have access to your files, don't assign a password.

7. Click OK.

You can share an entire disk drive by selecting the drive and following the preceding steps.

You can quickly tell if you have designated a folder as shared by looking for a hand beneath its folder icon in Explorer or Network Neighborhood, as shown in Figure 44.37.

To change the properties of a shared folder, right-click the folder and change the share name, comment, access privileges, or password for the shared folder.

CAUTION

If the Sharing tab is not visible when you open the Properties sheet, you must enable file and printer sharing services.

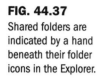

FIG. 44.37
Shared folders are indicated by a hand beneath their folder icons in the Explorer.

Shared folders—

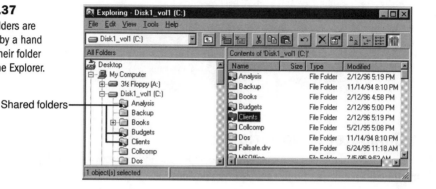

Stop Sharing a Folder

To stop sharing a folder, follow these steps:

1. Select the folder you want to stop sharing.
2. Right-click the folder, and then click Sharing.
3. Select the Not Shared option and click OK.

Mapping a Network Drive

Windows has greatly simplified working with networks by listing all shared resources in Explorer and Network Neighborhood. You no longer have to map a drive to the shared folder. However, if you prefer to map a drive to a shared resource on another computer, you can still do it. The mapped drive appears under My Computer, just like any other drive. This makes it easy for you to access files on another computer, while making it obvious that the files are in a drive on the network.

To map a drive to a shared folder, follow these steps:

1. Select the shared folder you want to map in Explorer or Network Neighborhood.
2. Right-click the folder, and then click Map Network Drive. The Map Network Drive dialog box appears, as shown in Figure 44.38.
3. By default, Windows assigns the next available drive letter on your computer to the folder you select to map. To assign a different letter, click the drop-down arrow and select a letter from the list.
4. If you want to automatically reconnect to this shared folder at log on, select the Reconnect at Startup option.
5. Click OK.

To remove the mapping for a shared folder, click the Disconnect Network Drive button in Explorer or Network Neighborhood, select the network drive you want to disconnect, and click OK. Or right-click on the drive in the left pane of Explorer and click Disconnect.

Part
X

Ch
44

FIG. 44.38

You can map a shared folder to a drive letter in the Map Network Drive dialog box.

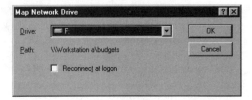

Finding a Computer on Your Network

If you know its name, you can quickly find a computer on your network by using the Find Computer command. To find a computer on your network, follow these steps:

1. Open the Start menu; then choose Find, Computer. Or, in Explorer, choose Tools, Find, Computer.

2. Enter the name of the computer you want to find in the Named text box of the Find: Computer dialog box, as shown in Figure 44.39.

FIG. 44.39

Find a computer on your network using Find: Computer.

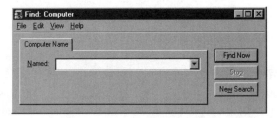

3. Click the Find Now button. The dialog box expands, listing the location of the specified computer if it is found on the network, as shown in Figure 44.40.

4. To open a browse window displaying the shared files and folders on the found computer, double-click the name of the computer at the bottom of the dialog box, or right-click the name and click Open.

FIG. 44.40

The location of the found computer is listed at the bottom of the Find: Computer dialog box.

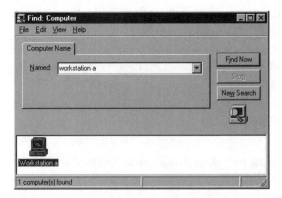

Using Network Neighborhood to View Network Resources

When you install Windows and you are connected to a network, you see an icon for Network Neighborhood on your desktop. When you first open Network Neighborhood by double-clicking its icon on the desktop, the Network Neighborhood appears, as shown in Figure 44.41.

FIG. 44.41
The Network Neighbor-hood window displays all the resources on your network.

To view the shared resources on a particular computer on your network, double-click the icon for the computer to open a new window. You can continue this process to open shared folders and view the contents. Many options discussed in the sections on using Explorer earlier in this chapter are also available in Network Neighborhood. You can, for example, change the way files are displayed; add or remove the toolbar; and move, copy, and delete files.

N O T E If you have file sharing enabled for your computer, it will appear in Network Neighborhood. However, you can't access your own computer from within Network Neighborhood. Use Explorer or My Computer to access your computer. ▓

By default, each time you open a folder, a new window appears. This can result in a desktop full of windows and lots of confusion. If you prefer to have a single window open for browsing files, with the contents of that window changing as you open new folders, choose View, Options; and then click the Folder tab, select the Browse Folders by Using a Single Window option, and click OK.

 When browsing folders using a separate window for each folder, you can hold the Ctrl key while double-clicking the subfolder and prevent a new window from opening. The original window becomes the subfolder. This can help to minimize desktop clutter.

Whether you use Explorer or Network Neighborhood to work with the files on your network depends on your style of working. Try them both and see which works best for you. ●

CHAPTER 45

Adding New Hardware to Windows 95

Installing Plug and Play hardware

Learn how to take full advantage of Windows 95's revolutionary Plug and Play technology.

Installing legacy (non-PnP) hardware

This guide to working with older hardware helps you avoid troublesome conflicts during installation.

Troubleshooting hardware installation

When things go wrong, this section helps you get out of trouble and back to work.

Windows 95 brings a host of important new capabilities to the desktop PC, including the new Plug and Play (PnP) technology. Anyone who has stayed up all night or stayed in all weekend trying to get a new sound card to work will tell you that. PCs are built specifically for flexibility and upgrades, yet installing an adapter card can be a grueling and sometimes futile exercise.

Microsoft recruited the participation of companies such as Intel, Compaq, Phoenix Technologies, and others to develop an industry standard for managing PC hardware and peripherals. Windows 95 Plug and Play enables PCs, peripherals, and the Windows 95 operating system to communicate with each other, allowing for automatic configuration of hardware.

Plug and Play can take the complexity out of hardware installations, but there is a catch—for Plug and Play to work to its full potential, the PC's motherboard, add-in cards, and operating system must all be Plug and Play-compliant. But even if your hardware is not PnP-compliant, Windows 95 is able to make educated guesses about your PC's configuration to ease installations. ■

TROUBLESHOOTING

If you have upgraded a sound card or other device that uses Windows 3.1 drivers, the new sound card may not be detected by the Add New Hardware Wizard. This occurs because Windows 95 is still seeing the reference to the older card's 16-bit drivers in the SYSTEM.INI file. To resolve the problem, you must go into SYSTEM.INI with a text editor such as NOTEPAD.EXE, and remove the lines referring to the 16-bit drivers. Run the Add New Hardware Wizard, and the new sound card or other device should be set up correctly.

This problem occurs because Windows 95 still looks into DOS/Windows 3.x configuration files to maintain compatibility with 16-bit applications. During setup, Windows 95 looks to CONFIG.SYS, AUTOEXEC.BAT, and SYSTEM.INI files to check for legacy drivers.

This chapter helps you understand how Plug and Play works—and more importantly, what to do when it doesn't. You learn how to use the Add New Hardware wizard and other tools to work with peripherals that are not Plug and Play-compliant. You also learn how to handle conflicts.

Installing Plug and Play Hardware

Plug and Play can make adding peripherals easy for users of all levels of expertise. With the proper hardware, installing peripherals can be as simple as plugging in an add-in card and starting up the PC. This section guides you through the steps involved in setting up a Plug and Play device. You also learn how Plug and Play technology works.

How Windows 95 Plug and Play Works

Because it addresses so many components in the PC, Plug and Play is a complex technology. Plug and Play enables all parts of the PC to communicate to each other, from the low level BIOS to the various add-in cards. When Windows 95 starts, the operating system and PC go through a series of steps to establish configurations, arbitrate conflicts, and record changes.

The Components of Plug and Play   To understand how Plug and Play works, you have to know what elements are involved. Four major technologies work together under Plug and Play:

- *System BIOS (basic input/output system).* The system BIOS is the low-level code that boots your system, detects the hard disk, and manages basic operations. Plug and Play systems employ a specially tuned BIOS that has the intelligence to detect hardware and manage configuration changes.

N O T E   Under the Plug and Play specification, PnP BIOSes are identified as Plug and Play BIOS version 1.0a or later. To find out what BIOS version you have, look for the BIOS information on your monitor at the beginning of the boot-up process. ■

- *Operating system.* The operating system interacts with the BIOS and hardware, playing a critical role in Plug and Play. Windows 95 is the first Plug and Play operating system, but Microsoft intends to bring the technology to Windows NT in the future.

- *Hardware peripherals.* To be Plug and Play-compliant, adapter cards and other hardware must include circuitry that stores configuration data and allows interaction with other PnP components. The PCI add-in cards, by definition, are PnP-compliant, while ISA and EISA cards must be specifically designed for PnP. External peripherals such as modems or printers can be PnP as well.

- *Device drivers.* Drivers let your peripherals talk to Windows 95. Under Windows 95's Plug and Play, hardware must employ 32-bit *virtual device drivers* (called VxDs), as opposed to the 16-bit, real-mode drivers used under DOS/Windows 3.x.

N O T E The 32-bit VxDs for most devices are supplied by the hardware vendors. If the appropriate driver is not available on the Windows 95 CD-ROM or disks, contact your peripheral manufacturer to get the latest PnP-compliant drivers. ■

Walking Through the PnP Process Each time you boot up the system a series of steps occurs that launches the Plug and Play process. All the hardware on the system is checked at boot time, so if new hardware has been installed, it will be detected and the appropriate steps taken by the PnP system.

This list details the steps that Windows 95 goes through during system startup, as follows:

1. The system BIOS identifies the devices on the motherboard (including the type of bus), as well as external devices such as disk drives, keyboard, video display, and other adapter cards that are required for the boot process.

2. The system BIOS determines the resource (IRQ, DMA, I/O, and memory address) requirements of each boot device. The BIOS also determines which devices are legacy devices with fixed resource requirements, and which are PnP devices with flexible resource requirements. Note that some devices don't require all four resource types.

N O T E Microsoft uses the term *legacy device* to refer to older hardware peripherals that do not comply with the Plug and Play specification. As a general rule, any ISA card bought before 1995 is probably a legacy device. ■

3. Windows 95 allocates the resources remaining after allowing for legacy resource assignments to each PnP device. If many legacy and PnP devices are in use, Windows 95 may require many iterations of the allocation process to eliminate all resource conflicts by changing the resource assignments of the PnP devices.

4. Windows 95 creates a final system configuration and stores the resource allocation data for this configuration in the registration database (The Registry).

5. Windows 95 searches the \WINDOWS\SYSTEM directory to find the required driver for the device. If the device driver is missing, a dialog box appears asking you to insert into drive A the manufacturer's floppy disk containing the driver software. Windows 95 loads the driver into memory and then completes its startup operations.

Note that Windows 95 makes educated guesses about the identity and resource requirements of legacy devices. Windows 95 includes a large database of resource settings for legacy devices, enabling it to detect and configure itself to a variety of existing hardware. However, this detection is not perfect, and it forces dynamic PnP peripherals to be configured around the static settings of legacy hardware.

Understanding Plug and Play Hardware

Of course, Windows 95 Plug and Play works best on systems properly equipped to support it. This section helps you to determine if your existing PC is Plug and Play-ready; and if not, what you can do to upgrade it. This section also can help you to determine whether a new system you plan to buy is PnP-compliant.

Determining Whether Your PC Supports Plug and Play   So is your PC Plug and Play? To make that claim, a system must have a BIOS that conforms to Plug and Play version 1.0a or later. Vendors generally began building Plug and Play into motherboards at the beginning of 1995, so older PCs probably won't support direct PnP features.

N O T E   Even if your BIOS is PnP-compliant, you won't have a true Plug and Play system until all the peripherals in your system are PnP too. Remember, legacy devices force Windows 95 to make educated guesses about their requirements, and their resources can't be dynamically allocated. ■

How can you find out if your Windows 95 system is PnP-ready? Go to Windows 95's System Properties sheet and do the following:

1. Click the Device Manager tab of the System Properties sheet to display Devices by Type. (Click the View Devices by Type option button if necessary.)

2. Double-click the System Devices icon in the device list to expand the System Devices list.

3. If your PC supports Plug and Play, you see a Plug and Play BIOS entry (see Figure 45.1). The I/O Read Data Port for ISA Plug and Play Enumerator item appears regardless of whether your PC is Plug and Play.

4. Double-click the Plug and Play BIOS icon to open the Properties sheet for the Plug and Play BIOS.

5. Click the Driver tab to display the device driver (BIOS.VXD) that Windows 95 uses to connect to the PnP feature of your system BIOS (see Figure 45.2).

6. To leave the sheet, click OK, and then click OK on the System Properties sheet.

What does a Plug and Play BIOS do exactly? As the cornerstone of PnP functionality, the BIOS adds three major enhancements to conventional PC BIOS:

■ *Resource management* handles the basic system resources: direct memory access (DMA), interrupt requests (IRQs), input/output (I/O), and shared memory address ranges. Resource management allows various devices to access limited system resources without causing conflicts. The Plug and Play BIOS resource manager configures boot devices on the motherboard and any PnP devices in the system.

FIG. 45.1
Check the System Devices list to determine whether your PC has Plug and Play BIOS.

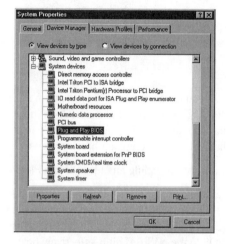

FIG. 45.2
Click the Driver tab to check the properties of Windows 95's Plug and Play BIOS device driver.

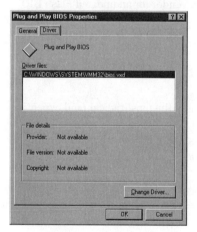

Part
X

Ch
45

■ *Runtime management* of configuration is new to PCs. PnP BIOS includes the capability to reconfigure devices after the operating system loads. This feature is particularly important for notebook PCs that have PCMCIA (also known as *PC Card*) devices that you can change at will. Previously, the operating system considered all devices detected by the BIOS to be static, which required restarting the system anytime a PC Card or other device was swapped out.

■ *Event management* detects when devices have been removed or added to the system while the computer is running. The PnP BIOS 1.0a provides event management, such as detecting when your notebook PC is connected to a docking adapter. (Note that installing or removing desktop add-in cards while the PC is running is not a safe practice.) Event management relies on runtime management to reconfigure the system.

CAUTION

Some brands of computers whose motherboards were produced in 1994 display messages during the boot process indicating that the motherboard supports Plug and Play. Many of these motherboards, however, have early versions of the PnP BIOS, which do not conform to the 1.0a specification. Even if your computer displays a PnP message during the boot process, check Device Manager for the Plug and Play BIOS entry to verify that you have PnP BIOS 1.0a.

Upgrading to Plug and Play   If you have an older 486 or Pentium PC, you may not be able to take advantage of Plug and Play. The problem is that the BIOS in these systems was written before there was a PnP standard to support. Still, you may be able to upgrade your PC to support PnP, so that future installations of PnP-compliant hardware go more smoothly.

Generally, there are three options for upgrading an older PC to a Plug and Play BIOS:

- *Flash the BIOS*. This is an option for those systems with a Flash BIOS, a nonvolatile memory chip (NVRAM) that retains BIOS instructions when the power is turned off. Updating a Flash BIOS is as easy as running an upgrade utility from a floppy disk. The utility writes a newer BIOS to the NVRAM chip, effectively turning your PC into a PnP system. Contact your system vendor for an updated Flash BIOS.

- *Replace the BIOS chip*. If your system is two years old or more, you probably don't have a Flash BIOS. But you may be able to replace the BIOS chip, which is often seated into a socket on the motherboard. You'll need to call your PC or motherboard vendor about a PnP BIOS upgrade kit, which lets you pull the existing BIOS chip(s) and plug in the replacement(s).

- *Replace the motherboard*. This is the most radical (and expensive) approach, but it's the only solution if the BIOS chip is soldered directly onto the motherboard and is not Flash-upgradable. You need to make sure the new motherboard fits into your system's chassis and accepts your existing add-in cards, memory, and processor.

N O T E   While a motherboard upgrade can update older BIOSes to Plug and Play, it may make more sense to wait to purchase a new system. A new PC comes with updated peripherals such as a larger hard drive and faster graphics board, which improve overall system performance. ■

Purchasing a Plug and Play System   Owners of older PCs may have to do a little investigating to determine if their systems support Plug and Play, but new systems should be PnP-compliant right out-of-the box. Now that Microsoft has committed to bringing PnP to its other Windows operating system—Windows NT—the presence of PnP on Intel-compatible PCs becomes even more important.

Making sure you have a PnP-ready PC is not difficult. Generally, any machine that displays the "Designed for Windows 95" logo is PnP-compliant. Lacking that logo, look for the following:

■ *Plug and Play BIOS 1.0a or later.* Also make sure that the system uses a Flash BIOS, because future updates to the PnP specification or other system architectures may require a BIOS upgrade.

■ *PCI bus expansion slots.* Unlike ISA peripherals, all PCI cards are PnP-compliant. Even in non-PnP systems, PCI cards arbitrate configuration among themselves, and offer the further convenience of being software configurable. Also, the VESA Local Bus (VLB) standard is on the wane as Pentium systems replace 486s, which makes VLB peripherals harder to find.

You should also check if the ISA peripherals installed in the PC, such as sound boards or modems, are PnP-compliant. Remember, the presence of non-PnP or legacy hardware in your system makes the task of hardware configuration more difficult and prone to failure. You should also check on the CD-ROM and fixed disks to ensure that they also are designed for the specification.

TROUBLESHOOTING

Your PCI graphics card may show an IRQ conflict in the System Properties sheet. Under Plug and Play, PCI cards can share IRQs; however, Windows 95 does not support PCI cards that try to share IRQs with non-PCI devices. While Windows 95 display drivers do not require IRQ resources, PCI graphics cards request an IRQ to maintain full compatibility. As a result, all PCI graphics cards attempt to assign an IRQ. You must use Device Manager to assign a new IRQ setting to the device that is conflicting with the PCI graphics card.

If Device Manager shows a resource conflict with a PCI-to-ISA bridge, know that there is no conflict here. If your Plug and Play BIOS reports both a PCI and an ISA bus, the Device Manager may report a conflict with that component. Users see an exclamation point in a yellow circle next to the PCI-to-ISA bridge entry in Device Manager. However, the PCI and ISA buses both work normally. There is no actual conflict. If you want, you can contact your hardware vendor to see if an updated Plug and Play BIOS is available that will only report a PCI bus.

Installing Plug and Play Hardware

If you've been through a few nightmarish upgrades, you'll find installing a PnP adapter card into a PnP-compliant PC to be a refreshing experience. To install both a new card and its 32-bit VxD driver, do the following:

1. Turn off power to the PC.

2. Open the case and install the adapter card, following the instructions provided with the card.

3. Close the case and turn on your PC.

4. Insert the driver software floppy disk in your A or B drive, if requested, and follow the steps for installing the driver software.

5. Restart Windows 95, if requested.

Part
X

Ch
45

It's that easy. If the driver for your card is included with Windows 95, you may not need the card's floppy disk; Windows 95 automatically sets up the driver for your device. (Note that in this case, you may need to put the Windows 95 CD-ROM or requested floppy disk into the appropriate drive so the bundled VxD can be loaded.)

TIP Windows 95 and your hardware may both provide a 32-bit VxD for your device. Compare the dates of the driver files using Explorer, and install the more recent file.

The same basic procedure applies for PnP-compatible external devices, such as printers, scanners, or external modems. If your PC has PnP-compliant serial and parallel ports, you will follow a procedure similar to the one in the preceding list. When you add or change a peripheral device, you don't need to open the PC, and in some cases (modems, for example), a new driver is not required.

Installing Legacy (Non-PnP) Hardware

As a Plug and Play operating system, Windows 95 may eventually make even complex upgrades a simple manner of plugging in a card and booting to a new configuration. But the existence of millions of add-in cards and external peripherals with no PnP support means that that day is still some time in the future. Understanding this, Microsoft has gone to great effort to ensure that non-PnP peripherals are adequately supported under the new regime.

The effort seems to have paid off. While installing legacy devices can still be tricky, the experience is simpler and less hazardous than under 16-bit Windows 3.x. This section shows you how to install legacy devices.

How Windows 95 Operates with Legacy Hardware

Windows 95 cannot fully automate the configuration of legacy devices; however, it does interact with non-PnP devices to ease the process. Detection routines, for example, allow Windows 95 to recognize popular add-in cards such as Creative Labs Sound Blaster boards, even though they lack PnP capability. The System Properties sheet, meanwhile, provides a one-stop shop for determining hardware conflicts, editing resource setting values, and optimizing performance. Finally, Windows 95's automated handling of PnP devices makes managing the remaining legacy hardware that much easier.

Almost all PC adapter cards require at least one interrupt request (IRQ) level and a set of I/O base memory addresses for communication with your PC's processor. Some cards require one or more DMA (Direct Memory Access) channels for high-speed communication with your PC's RAM. The IRQ's, I/O memory, and DMA channels collectively are called *device resources*.

Legacy adapter cards use the following two methods for setting device resource values:

- *Mechanical jumpers* that create a short circuit between two pins of a multipin header. Jumpers are commonly used to designate resource values for sound cards, and they must be set to match the resource settings of Windows 95. If jumper settings do not match those set in Windows 95, the device will not operate.

■ *Nonvolatile memory (NVM)* for storing resource assignments. Nonvolatile memory—such as electrically erasable, programmable read-only memory (EEPROM)—retains data when you turn off your PC's power. Network adapter cards and sound cards commonly use NVM. Usually, you must run a setup program for the card to match the board settings to those of the operating system.

N O T E   PCI adapter cards do not have jumpers or nonvolatile memory to designate resource values. Instead, the system BIOS and Windows 95 automatically allocate resources needed by PCI adapter cards during the boot process. ■

The following sections describe how Windows 95 deals with a variety of legacy adapter cards. Later chapters of this book describe in detail the installation process for specific device types, such as modems, CD-ROM drives, and sound cards.

Part

X

Ch

45

Legacy Device Detection During Windows 95 Setup

When you run Windows 95's setup program, Windows 95 attempts to detect all the hardware devices in your PC, including legacy devices such as ISA sound cards and network adapters. It then installs 32-bit protected mode drivers for peripherals for which updated drivers are available. However, Windows 95 often keeps references to real-mode (16-bit) device drivers in the CONFIG.SYS and AUTOEXEC.BAT files, which are used when the system runs DOS software in DOS-only mode.

If Windows can't identify the legacy device, you need to install the device manually. This procedure is described in the section "Installing Legacy Cards After Setting Up Drivers," later in this chapter.

Setting Resource Values for Legacy Adapter Cards

You must enter the IRQ, I/O base address, and DMA channel of a new adapter card to values that do not conflict with the resource values that are already assigned to system devices, PCI slots, or other legacy adapter cards. One of the problems with the basic design of IBM-compatible PCs is that only 16 interrupts are available, and the majority of these interrupts are likely to be in use. Therefore, your choice of IRQs is limited.

N O T E   The word "base" in I/O base address refers to the location at which the block of I/O addresses for the adapter card begins. The actual number of address bytes occupied by the I/O system of the adapter card varies with the type of card. The I/O addresses are separated by 16 bytes, and most adapter cards require fewer than 16 bytes of I/O address space. ■

Table 45.1 lists the PC's IRQs and most common use of each interrupt level.

Table 45.1 Interrupt Assignments and Options for ISA Cards Installed in 80×86-Based PCs

IRQ	Function	Most Common Use
0	Internal timer	Dedicated; not accessible
1	Keyboard	Dedicated; not accessible
2	Tied to IRQ9	Dedicated; see IRQ9
3	Second serial port	COM2 and COM4; usually assigned to a modem
4	First serial port	COM1 and COM3; usually for a serial mouse
5	Second parallel printer	Often used for bus mouse, network, and scanner cards
6	Floppy disk drives	Dedicated; do not use
7	First parallel printer	Used by some scanner cards; otherwise available
8	Time-of-day clock	Dedicated; not accessible
9	IRQ2 on 80×86 computers	IRQ2 is rerouted to IRQ9; often shown as IRQ2/9
10	Unassigned	Good choice for sound card, if offered
11	Unassigned	Not a common option; use if 12 is assigned
12	Usually unassigned	Sometimes dedicated to an IBM-style mouse port
13	80×87 coprocessor	Dedicated; do not use even if an 80×87 is not installed
14	Fixed-disk drive	Dedicated; do not use
15	Usually unassigned	Used for secondary disk controller, if installed

Assigning IRQs is a real shell game, with many legacy devices being limited to just two or three specific IRQ numbers. In addition, many ISA boards won't support high IRQ numbers (any setting above IRQ9), which further limits your options.

TIP When you install a new legacy device, you should assign it the highest IRQ number that it will support, leaving the lower IRQs for cards that don't support interrupts above IRQ9 or IRQ10. The Sound Blaster 16 audio adapter card, for example, supports only IRQ2/9, IRQ5 (default), IRQ7, and IRQ10.

Virtually all PCs come with two serial port devices (COM1 and COM2) and one parallel port (LPT1) device. The COM1 is usually occupied by the serial mouse, unless your PC has a separate IBM PS/2-compatible mouse port that requires an assignable interrupt. The default interrupt for the Sound Blaster and most MPC-compatible audio adapter cards is IRQ5, the same setting preferred by many network adapters. Although IRQ7 is assigned to the second parallel printer (LPT2), few users have two printers, and printers seldom require an interrupt—so IRQ7 is a good candidate when space gets tight.

TIP If you can't get sound on a networked PC, it may be that the network and sound cards are conflicting. The IRQ5 is the preferred setting for both network adapters and sound cards, which makes this problem very common.

N O T E Most legacy PC adapter cards use jumpers to set resource values. Cards that store resource settings in nonvolatile RAM require that you run their setup applications to set IRQ, I/O base address, and DMA channel (if applicable). If the setup program unavoidably installs real-mode drivers for the device, don't forget to disable the real-mode drivers by adding temporary REM prefixes before restarting Windows 95. See the section "Changing Resource Settings" later in this chapter. ▪

Part
X

Ch
45

Installing Adapter Cards with Automatic Detection

The easiest way to install a new legacy card in a Windows 95 system is to use the Add New Hardware Wizard's automatic detection feature to identify your added card. The wizard also is capable of determining if you have removed a card. Auto-detection is best suited for PCs that have few or no specialty adapter cards, such as sound and video capture cards.

The following steps describe the automatic-detection process in installing a Creative Labs Sound Blaster AWE 32 card:

1. Set nonconflicting resource values for your new adapter card, using jumpers or the card's setup program.

2. Shut down Windows 95, and turn off the power on your PC.

3. Install the new adapter card in an empty ISA slot, and make any required external connections, such as audio inputs and speaker outputs for sound cards.

4. Turn the PC power on, and restart Windows 95.

5. Launch Control Panel, and double-click the Add New Hardware icon to start the Add New Hardware Wizard (see Figure 45.3).

FIG. 45.3

The Add New Hardware Wizard provides a step-by-step guide to installing new devices into your PC.

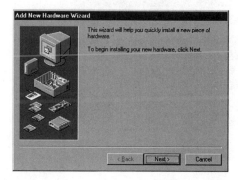

6. Click the Next button. The wizard dialog box appears. You can choose manual or automatic hardware detection and installation. Accept the default Yes (Recommended) option (see Figure 45.4).

FIG. 45.4

The Add New Hardware routine lets you choose between automatic or manual hardware detection. Be warned that automatic selection can take a while, particularly on slower machines.

7. Click the Next button to display the wizard's boilerplate (see Figure 45.5).

FIG. 45.5

The wizard warns you that detecting installed hardware is not without its perils.

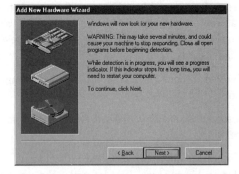

8. Click the Next button to start the detection process (see Figure 45.6).

After a few minutes of intense disk activity, often interspersed with periods of seeming inactivity, the wizard advises you that detection is complete (see Figure 45.7).

FIG. 45.6

The wizard detection-progress dialog box tells you when detection is complete.

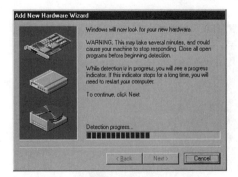

FIG. 45.7

The wizard has finally finished the detection process.

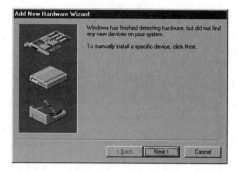

9. Click the Details button to display what the wizard detected. Figure 45.8 shows that the Sound Blaster AWE-32 was detected.

   If the wizard does not detect your newly installed card, you must install the card manually. Click Cancel to terminate the automatic detection process.

FIG. 45.8

The wizard detected the new Sound Blaster AWE-32 sound card.

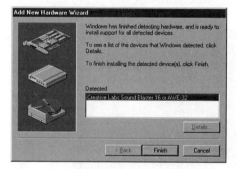

10. Click the Finish button to install the required drivers from the Windows 95 CD-ROM or floppy disks. The message box shown in Figure 45.9 indicates the expected medium, in this case, the Windows 95 CD-ROM.

FIG. 45.9

If the driver software isn't available on your hard drive, Windows 95 prompts you to install the media that contains the drivers.

11. Insert the Windows 95 CD-ROM into the drive, and click OK to install the drivers.

12. If Windows 95 can't find the required device driver file in the expected location, you will be prompted to browse for the necessary files.

13. When driver installation is complete, a message box advises you that system settings have changed and asks whether you want to restart Windows 95. Click Restart Now so that your driver change takes effect.

Installing Legacy Cards After Setting Up Drivers

The alternative to automatic device detection is to install the new adapter card after you install its driver software. The advantage to this method is that you can determine in advance resource settings that don't conflict with existing devices.

The following steps describe the process of reinstalling the drivers for the Sound Blaster 32-AWE card:

1. Launch the Add New Hardware Wizard from Control Panel, and click the Next button in the opening dialog box to display the wizard dialog box. Here you choose between manual and automatic hardware detection and installation (refer to Figure 45.4).

2. Choose the No option to select manual installation; then click the Next button to display the wizard's Hardware Types dialog box (see Figure 45.10).

FIG. 45.10

The Add New Hardware Wizard's Hardware Types dialog box lists a variety of adapter card categories.

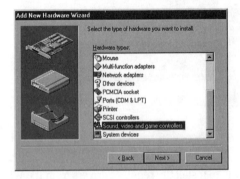

3. Select the card type in the Hardware Types list; then click the Next button to display the Manufacturers and Models dialog box (see Figure 45.11).

FIG. 45.11

The wizard dialog box lists manufacturers and models of devices whose drivers are included with Windows 95.

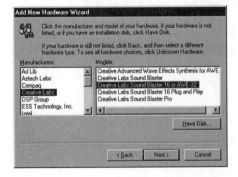

4. Make the appropriate selections in the Manufacturers and Models list boxes; then click the Next button to display the default settings for the new device.

N O T E If you don't see the manufacturer or model in the list boxes, you need a floppy disk or CD-ROM that contains Windows 95 drivers for your device (Windows 3.1 or later drivers won't work). If you have the required Windows 95 drivers, click the Have Disk button to install the drivers from floppy disk or CD-ROM. If you don't have Windows 95 drivers, click the Cancel button to terminate the installation. ■

5. Windows 95 can't determine what resource value settings you made for your new or replacement adapter card, so the default settings for the device appear in the wizard's Resource Settings dialog box (see Figure 45.12). You should write down or print these default settings.

FIG. 45.12

Default values for the Sound Blaster AWE-32 card appear when you open the Resource Setting dialog box.

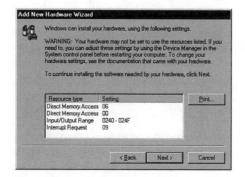

6. Click the Next button to display the System Settings Change message box (see Figure 45.13).

If the default settings in the preceding step correspond to the resource settings of your card, click the Yes button to shut down Windows 95. If you haven't installed the card (which is the normal situation for manual device detection), turn off the power to your PC, install the card, turn the power back on, and restart Windows 95 with the new card activated.

If any of the resource values in the preceding step are incorrect, or you receive a "resource conflict" message, click the No button in the System Settings Change message box so that you can alter the resource values as necessary.

FIG. 45.13

The System Settings Change message box gives you the option to restart Windows 95.

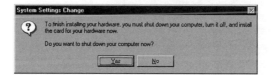

Part

X

Ch

45

7. Open Control Panel's System Properties sheet, click the Device Manager tab, and expand the entries for the type of device that you're installing. Exclamation points superimposed on the device's icon(s) indicate that the device is not yet fully installed or has been removed from your PC.

8. If you're replacing a card, entries for both cards appear in the Device Manager list. To remove the old entry, select the entry and click the Remove button. A message box requests that you confirm the removal process (see Figure 45.14).

FIG. 45.14

Windows 95 asks for confirmation before you remove a device from the Device Manager.

9. Double-click the entry for the new adapter card to display the Properties sheet for the device.

10. In the Resource Settings list box, select the resource whose value you want to change; then click the Change Settings button to display the Edit Interrupt Request dialog box for the resource.

11. Use the spin buttons of the Value text box to select the value that corresponds to the preset value for your adapter card. If a conflict with the existing card occurs, the card that has the conflicting value is identified in the Conflict Information text box (see Figure 45.15).

12. Change the Value setting to a value that displays No devices are conflicting in the Conflict Information box; then make the corresponding change in the card, using the jumpers or nonvolatile RAM. (Turn off power to your PC before making jumper changes.) Figure 45.16 shows an I/O base address setting changed to remove a conflict at Input/Output Range 0260-026F.

FIG. 45.15

Change the IRQ setting for the new adapter card to avoid a conflict.

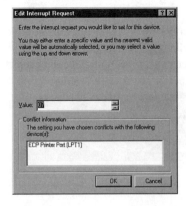

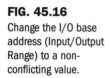

FIG. 45.16
Change the I/O base address (Input/Output Range) to a non-conflicting value.

13. After making all the changes necessary to remove resource conflicts, click OK to close the resource's Edit Input/Output Range dialog box, and then click OK to close the Properties page for the specific device.

14. Click OK to close the System Properties sheet.

15. Shut down and restart Windows 95 so that your new settings take effect.

The process of manually installing a legacy device described in the preceding steps appears to be complex, but it is a much more foolproof method than the one used by Windows 3.x. For example, the capability to detect potential resource conflicts before the new setting is locked in helps eliminate many problems associated with installing new devices under Windows 3.x.

N O T E   Windows 95 includes drivers for an extraordinary number of popular devices but not for low-volume products, such as digital video capture and MPEG-1 playback cards. Most manufacturers of specialty legacy devices should provide 32-bit protected-mode drivers for Windows 95. You can find updated Windows 95 drivers on manufacturer's forums on CompuServe, America Online, and The Microsoft Network, as well as on World Wide Web sites. ■

Removing Unneeded Drivers for Legacy Devices

If you remove a legacy device from your PC and don't intend to reinstall it, it's good Windows 95 housekeeping to remove the driver for the device from the Device Manager list. Follow these steps to remove the Device Manager entry for permanently removed adapter cards:

1. Double-click Control Panel's System icon to open the System Properties sheet.

2. Click the Device Manager tab and double-click the icon for the hardware type of the device removed to display the list of installed devices. An exclamation point superimposed on a device icon indicates a removed or inoperable device.

3. Click the list item to select the device you want to remove and then click the Remove button.

4. Confirm that you want to remove the device by clicking OK in the Confirm Device Removal message box.

If you have more than one hardware configuration, a modified version of the Confirm Device Removal message box appears. Make sure the Remove from All Configurations option button is selected; then click OK to remove the device and close the message box.

Troubleshooting Hardware Installation

Windows 95 is clearly superior to Windows 3.x when it comes to installing and managing hardware, but it is not perfect. The peaceful coexistence that Windows 95 tries to foster between PnP and legacy devices can break down into bitter conflict, particularly when new legacy hardware is being installed. But Windows 95 does provide a wealth of tools for managing these conflicts when they occur. This section helps you troubleshoot hardware installation problems under Windows 95 with tips for using the Device Manager and other tools.

Understanding the Device Manager

The Device Manager displays all the system components in hierarchical format, enabling you to dig down to individual devices and subsystems. In essence, the Device Manager is the user interface for the Windows 95 Registry. But unlike working in The Registry, the Device Manager is designed to avoid the kind of catastrophic crashes that making changes in The Registry can cause.

The Device Manager gives you quick access to hardware configurations for virtually all the devices in your PC. To open the Device Manager, double-click the System icon in Control Panel and click the Device Manager tab. You will see a list of items, some with a plus (+) sign to the left. This plus sign indicates that more detailed device information is available. Selecting the plus sign expands the display to show any listings below that item.

The Device Manager displays hardware information from two separate perspectives, by device type and by device connection. By default, Device Manager opens with the View Devices by Type option button selected (see Figure 45.17). In this mode, similar devices are grouped under a single item, such as the entry under Ports (COM & LPT). Clicking the View Devices by Connection option button shows the same information, but now most of the devices appear under the Plug and Play BIOS item (see Figure 45.18).

To access the configuration for a sound card, do the following:

1. Go to the Device Manager page of the System Properties sheet.
2. Click the plus (+) sign found next to the Sound, video, and game controllers item.
3. Click the specific sound hardware item that appears on the sheet.
4. Click the Properties button to display the tabbed properties sheet for the sound hardware device.

Changing Resource Settings

After you are at the General page of a device's properties sheet, you can access the IRQ, I/O address, and DMA resource settings by clicking the Resources tab. Here you see the resources that are currently assigned to that device. Any conflicts are indicated with an asterisk next to the resource having a problem.

FIG. 45.17

The Device Manager provides two views of the devices installed in the PC.

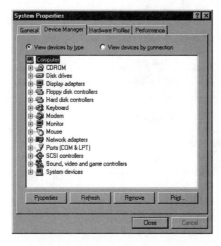

FIG. 45.18

The second option button lets you view components by their physical connections in the system.

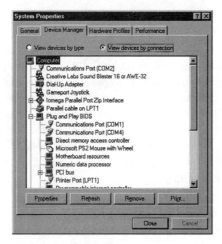

To change the resource settings for a device, do the following:

1. In the Resource settings box, click the resource item you want to view or edit.
2. Uncheck the Use automatic settings check box (see Figure 45.19).
3. Click the enabled Change Setting button.
4. In the Resource Edit dialog box, click the spinner buttons to switch among system resources.

Part

X

Ch

45

FIG. 45.19

Before you can make changes to device settings, you must disable the Use Automatic Settings item.

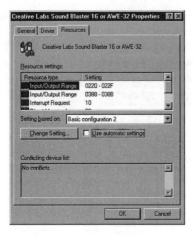

> **N O T E** Device Manager shows all the resources, indicating those that are already in use by another peripheral. Be sure you don't create a conflict by assigning a resource to a device that is already being used by another device. ■

TROUBLESHOOTING

You might get a `Resource conflict` message when you install a Plug and Play adapter card. Most PC adapter cards require at least one I/O base address and one or more interrupts. (The section "Setting Resource Values for Legacy Adapter Cards" describes I/O base addresses and interrupts.) Most adapter cards support only a few of the available I/O base addresses and interrupts. If you already have several legacy adapter cards in your PC, you may have a situation where the I/O base addresses or, more likely, the interrupts supported by the new card are occupied by existing legacy cards. In this case, you need to change the settings of one or more of your legacy cards to free the required resource(s) for use by your new card.

The worst-case condition occurs in PCI bus PCs where all of the available interrupts are assigned before you install the new card. (In many PCI-bus PCs, PCI slots consume one interrupt each, whether the slot is in use or not.) The only solution in this instance is to free an interrupt by reconfiguring your PC's system BIOS to reassign an interrupt from an unused PCI slot. Obviously, this action disables that slot, rendering it useless. If your system BIOS does not permit reconfiguration, you must remove an existing adapter card to free an interrupt.

You can get an effective roster of system settings by double-clicking the Computer icon at the top of the Device Manager tree. Doing so brings up the Computer Properties sheet, which features two tabs: View Resources and Reserve Resources (see Figure 14.20).

FIG. 45.20

The Computer Properties sheet provides a bird's-eye view of your systems resource status.

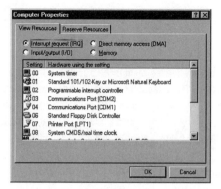

The View Resources tab displays these four option buttons that cause the page to display the status of key system resources:

- Interrupt Request (IRQs)
- Direct Memory Address (DMA)
- Input/Output (I/O)
- Memory

Clicking the option button brings up a scroll down list of occupied settings and the device which is using it.

N O T E The View Resources page of the Computer Properties sheet is an excellent place to get an overview of your system's resource status. ■

The Reserve Resources page lets you view any resources that have been excluded from use by hardware devices (see Figure 45.21). You also can use this page to reserve resources. For example, follow these steps to reserve IRQ12 (some older BIOSes won't recognize an IRQ12 devices unless it is a PS/2 mouse):

FIG. 45.21

The Reserve Resources page lets you set aside key resource settings to avoid conflicts.

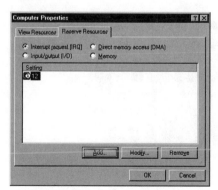

TROUBLESHOOTING

Your system could hang during shutdown when a system BIOS expects a PS/2-style mouse port to occupy IRQ12, but a software-configured PnP adapter occupies it instead. You need to change the software-configurable device in Device Manager to another IRQ number. You might also consider reserving IRQ12 in Device Manager, so Plug and Play does not later assign a device to that resource. Also consider getting a BIOS upgrade that enables you to make full use of IRQ12.

1. Click the Reserve Resources tab.
2. Click the Interrupt Request (IRQ) option button.
3. Click the Add button to bring up the Edit Resource Setting sheet (see Figure 45.22).

FIG. 45.22

Set the resource to reserve in the Edit Resource Sheet.

4. Use the spinner controls to select the IRQ you want to change.
5. Click OK to change the settings.
6. If a device is currently logged into the IRQ being reserved, the Resource Conflict Warning sheet will apprise you of the possible problem and ask for confirmation (see Figure 45.23).

FIG. 45.23

If Windows 95 detects a device already using the resource being reserved, it will warn you and ask for confirmation.

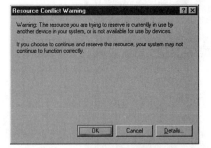

Checking for Resource Conflicts with the Device Manager

The Device Manager is an excellent tool for resolving hardware resource conflicts, enabling you to see if any devices are experiencing a conflict. Device Manager displays an exclamation point or a strikethrough symbol through the icon of any item with a conflict, allowing you to quickly zero in on problems. The symbols indicate different situations:

- *Exclamation point inside a yellow circle*. Indicates a device that is experiencing a direct conflict with another device.
- *Red X symbol*. Indicates a device that is disabled, either due to a conflict or by user selection.

Hardware Problems with the Registry Editor

If you have a problem that changing resources won't solve, the card supplier's product-support staff will need additional information about your system. The primary source of system information in Windows 95 is The Registry. All device information that appears in the Device Manager is obtained from entries in The Registry.

Part
X

Ch
45

> **CAUTION**
>
> Viruses can cause Windows 95 to report hardware conflicts. You should sweep your system for viruses regularly, particularly when you encounter unexpected problems.

N O T E You should be able to manage most hardware problems without resorting to editing The Registry. Windows 95's Device Manager provides tools for managing hardware conflicts. ■

To examine The Registry, you need to set up and use The Registry Editor (REGEDIT.EXE) application. REGEDIT is not a Start menu choice because Microsoft did not intend all users to access its settings directly. Entering incorrect settings into REGEDIT can cause the system to fail to boot up.

1. Open the Start menu, and choose Run.
2. Type **REGEDIT** to open the Registry Editor.
3. Choose Find, Edit to open the Find dialog box.
4. In the Find What text box, type the keyword for the card in question; then click the Find Next button to locate the first instance of the keyword.

   The support person usually gives you the keyword on which to search. The phrase **sound blaster**, for example, finds all references to Sound Blaster hardware in The Registry.
5. The first or second instance of the keyword is likely to display the Plug and Play device assignment data for the card. Press F3 to find the successive instances of the keyword. Figure 45.24 shows the PnP device data for the Sound Blaster 16 card.
6. Pressing F3 should turn up additional instances of Registry entries for the device in question. Figure 45.25 shows The Registry entry that defines the driver for the Line Input device of the Sound Blaster 16, SB16SND.DRV.

FIG. 45.24

The Windows 95 Registry Editor displays Plug and Play device assignment values for a Sound Blaster 16 card.

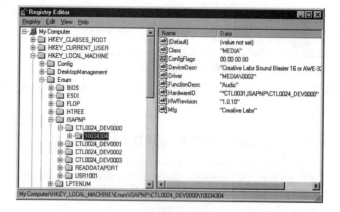

FIG. 45.25

Continued searching in RegEdit displays the settings of the driver for the Line Input device of the Sound Blaster 16 card.

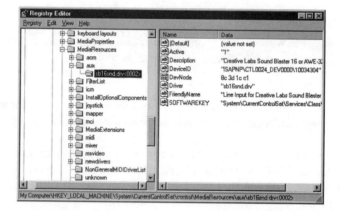

> **CAUTION**
>
> Using the Windows 95 Registry can be dangerous. If you enter an improper value, it can disable key system components and even prevent your system from rebooting altogether.

Unfortunately, it is not possible to cover all the various things that can go wrong during hardware installation under Windows 95. Many problems are the result of interactions between specific types of hardware. If you discover a problem with hardware you are installing, you should seek guidance from the vendor. They should know about potential driver updates and other fixes that can help resolve the problem.

TROUBLESHOOTING

Most PCs with recent system BIOS automatically detect an additional drive connected to the primary IDE controller as a primary slave drive. If you have an older BIOS, you need to use the PC's BIOS setup application to specify the type of drive installed (number of cylinders, number of heads, landing zone, and other drive parameters). If you connect a third drive to a PC with a recent BIOS, you need to enable the secondary IDE controller in the BIOS setup program so BIOS can recognize the drive. IDE CD-ROM drives connected to sound cards usually can be installed as secondary, tertiary, or quaternary IDE drives. Use the default (secondary) setting for an IDE CD-ROM if you don't have a secondary IDE controller in your PC; if your PC has a secondary IDE controller, use the tertiary I/O base address and interrupt for the CD-ROM.

CHAPTER 46

Controlling Printers

Microsoft has packed a great deal of experience into the features of the Windows 95 printing system. To appreciate this system, take a brief look at the new feature changes Microsoft has made to enable faster printing while producing a higher quality output. Although some changes, at first glance, appear to be ho-hum, don't be fooled. Windows 95's new print model is both faster than its predecessors and designed with the user in mind. ■

How to install and delete printers

You learn how to install a new printer using the Add Printer Wizard or Plug and Play, and how to delete a printer already installed on your system.

How to configure your printers

Use the properties sheet to customize the settings for your printer, including the printer port configuration, sharing capabilities, paper handling, and graphics settings.

How to print from Windows applications

Find out how to start a print job from a Windows application and to manage print jobs using the Print Manager.

How to use the special printing features for laptop and docking station users

Set up a hardware profile that allows you to manage print jobs when you are not connected to your printer.

How to solve common printing problems

Look here to learn about the tools that come with Windows 95 for diagnosing printing problems and for a list of common printing problems you can use to troubleshoot your printer.

This chapter discusses each of the new printing features and how they work in concert to produce a quality print job:

■ *Rapid return from printing* is enabled by the 32-bit printer drivers, preemptive spooler, and enhanced meta file spooling.

■ *Deferred printing* enables you to configure your computer to conveniently print to a file when you are on the road or away from your printer. After you reattach the printer, simply release the print files to the appropriate printer.

■ *Bi-directional printer communications* sends print files to your printer and listens for a response. Windows can quickly identify a printer that cannot accept a print file.

■ *Plug and Play* supports the addition of new printers by quickly identifying the brand and model of a printer and assisting you in configuring the appropriate drivers for that printer.

■ *Extended capability port support* enables Windows 95 to use the latest in high-speed parallel-port technology to connect your printer.

Installing and Deleting Printers

The printer installation process depends largely on the make and model of your printer. The following sections describe how to fully install a printer—with an emphasis on the specific areas in which you can expect to find printer differences. The following sections use the HP LaserJet IIIP printer configured with 5M of internal RAM and an HP PostScript cartridge as an example.

Installing a New Printer

Before you install a printer, you should follow these preliminary steps:

■ Determine your printer's make and model (for example, Hewlett-Packard IIIP).

■ Refer to the printer manual, or print a test page using the printer's test feature, to find the amount of RAM contained in your printer (for example, 2M).

■ Identify the type of communications interface required to connect your printer to the computer (for example, serial, parallel, or a special interface).

■ Identify any special features or functions supported by your printer, such as PostScript-compatibility. Some printers are multimode and may require installation as two separate printers (such as the HP LaserJet IV with PostScript option).

■ Find the location of a suitable port on your computer to connect your printer. The selected port must correspond to the same port type required by your printer (that is, serial to serial, parallel to parallel).

This information is required by the Windows Add Printer Wizard later in the installation process.

Installing a Printer with the Add Printer Wizard The Windows 95 print architecture incorporates a printer installation wizard to step you through the labor-intensive chore of installing a printer.

To use the Add Printer Wizard, follow these steps:

1. Open the Start menu and choose Settings, Printers. If the control panel is open, double-click the Printer folder. The Printers window appears, showing each installed printer as an icon (see Figure 46.1). Don't worry if you don't have any installed printers yet, the window also includes the Add New Printer icon. The program associated with the Add New Printer icon is the Add Printer Wizard.

FIG. 46.1
Start a printer installation by opening the Printer folder.

2. Double-click the Add New Printer icon to start the Add Printer Wizard. Windows displays the initial Wizard screen.
3. Choose Next. Windows displays the Add Printer Wizard screen shown in Figure 46.2.

FIG. 46.2
The Add Printer Wizard steps you through the printer installation procedure by first asking whether you are installing a local or network printer.

4. Choose the Local Printer option to install a printer attached directly to your computer. Choose Next. The screen shown in Figure 46.3 appears.

Part

X

Ch

46

FIG. 46.3
Select the make and
model of the printer you
are installing from the
lists provided.

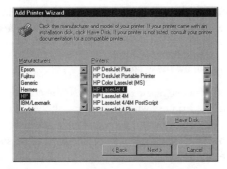

5. Locate the make and model of your printer by scrolling through the Wizard's screen lists (Windows 95 has drivers that support over 300 printers).

   If you're adding a printer after initial installation of Windows 95, you need the Windows 95 installation disks or CD. Windows will ask for these if it does not have an existing driver available. You also can use a manufacturer's disk to install custom printer drivers.

   If you are installing a new driver for an existing printer, click the Have Disk button and locate the new driver in the Install From Disk dialog box. Choose OK.

TIP Many laser printers are Hewlett-Packard compatible and many dot-matrix printers are Epson compatible. If you can't get a driver or the Generic selection driver doesn't work well, try one of the commonly emulated printers.

Scroll the screen on the far left to select your printer's manufacturer. Then select the appropriate printer model. If your printer isn't on the list, you can install it by choosing either the generic printer or the Have Disk button. If your printer came with its own software driver, insert the disk from your printer manufacturer and choose the Have Disk button to complete the requirements of this screen.

Once you have made your printer selection, click Next to display the screen shown in Figure 46.4.

FIG. 46.4
Select the printer port
to which you want to
attach the printer.

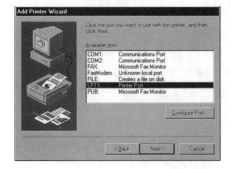

6. Provide the printer port information. The Wizard screen shown in Figure 46.4 displays ports based on the survey Windows did of your computer hardware. You may have several COM and LPT ports. Refer to the list of information you compiled before you started the installation and choose the port to which you want to attach the printer. The port selected in Figure 46.4 is LPT1, a very typical selection.

7. Choose the Configure Port button. The Wizard displays the Configure Port window (see Figure 46.5). The window contains a check box that enables Windows 95 to spool your MS-DOS print jobs. This is the only configuration in the Add Printer Wizard for the LPT1 port. This check box should always be selected to enable MS-DOS printing, unless your MS-DOS applications prove to be incompatible with Windows 95 printing. Select the Check Port State before Printing check box if you want Windows 95 to determine whether the printer port is available prior to starting the print job.

FIG. 46.5

Configure your parallel printer port to enable MS-DOS applications to use the same driver.

8. After you configure the port, choose OK and then Next to open the dialog box shown in Figure 46.6. Use this dialog box to name the new printer and define it as your default printer, if desired. In the Printer Name field, type the name of the printer. The name can be as many as 128 characters and can contain spaces and nonalphanumeric symbols. The printer's name should include location or ownership.

FIG. 46.6

The printer name and default status are specified using this Wizard screen.

N O T E If you have access to two printers of the same type, add unique identifiers to their names, such as "HP LaserJet Series II Room 5, Building 10" and "HP LaserJet Series II Room 25, Building 15." ■

9. Choose Yes to set this printer as the system default. By setting this printer as your default, you instruct all applications to use this printer, unless you tell the application to use a different printer. (You can set the default to any other installed printer at any time.) Click Next to continue. The final Wizard screen appears (see Figure 46.7).

Part
X

Ch
46

FIG. 46.7

Printing a test page is the final step in configuring and testing your printer installation.

10. Specify whether you want to print a test page. Printing a test page tests the overall operation of the printer based on the settings you just entered. Choose Yes and click Finish to print the test page.

N O T E The test page contains information specific to your printer, its configuration, and the drivers Windows uses to interface with it. After this page is printed, save it for future reference. If others use your computer, you might have to return to a known installation configuration someday.

You also can get information on your printer using the MSINFO32.EXE utility located in the \Program Files\Common Files\Microsoft Shared\MSInfo folder. Run this utility and click Printing in the left pane of the Microsoft System Information window to view information on all installed printers. ■

Installing a Plug and Play Printer Plug and Play printers interact with Windows to automatically configure printers by using a dialog box transparent to the user. Many printer manufacturers have cooperated with Microsoft to not only make configuration easier, but to automatically update the software when you make changes to the printer hardware configuration.

If your printer is Plug and Play compatible, see Chapter 45, "Adding New Hardware to Windows 95," for an explanation of how Plug and Play devices are installed.

Renaming an Existing Printer

You can quickly rename printers named during installation using the Printers folder. The Printers folder displays all installed printers; their individual names are located immediately below the printer's icon (refer to Figure 46.1).

To rename a printer after it is installed, follow these steps:

1. Open the Printers folder by opening the Start menu and choosing Settings, Printers. If the Control Panel is open, double-click the Printers folder.

2. Select the desired printer and choose File, Rename. Or, click the printer name, wait a second, and click a second time.

   Windows creates a text box around the printer name and highlights that name.

3. Change the name by typing a new name or editing portions of the existing name.

4. When finished, press Enter. The new printer name is used throughout the Windows operating system.

Deleting an Existing Printer

You can delete an installed printer from the Printers folder, which displays all installed printers as icons. To delete a printer from the Printers folder, follow these steps:

1. Select the printer you want to delete and press the Delete key.

   Windows opens a dialog box and asks whether you're sure that you want to delete the printer.

2. Choose OK; the printer is now deleted. Windows then asks whether it can remove the associated software from your hard disk.

> **CAUTION**
>
> If you have a similar printer that could use the same drivers, do not remove the software. Deleting the associated software might remove that driver from use by other printers.

3. Choose OK to remove the deleted printer's software driver.

The printer and its driver are now removed. Windows signifies this event by removing that printer icon from the Printers folder.

N O T E If you plan to reattach this printer in the future, do not remove the software drivers. This can save you time when reattaching the printer. ▪

N O T E If a new driver becomes available for your printer, you can update your existing driver using the Add Printer Wizard. A new driver can add new capabilities, correct bugs, or increase the performance of your printer. In step 5 of the steps in the section "Installing a Printer with the Add Printer Wizard," choose the Have Disk button to specify the location of the new driver, and then continue as if adding a new printer.

One source for new drivers is the printer manufacturer. Most manufacturers have a private BBS or a site on CompuServe or the Internet where you can download updated drivers. Check your printer manual for online addresses. You also can find updated drivers in the Windows 95 Driver Library (W95DL), which is available at several online locations:

- CompuServe: **GO MSL**
- Microsoft Download Service (MSDL): (206) 936-6735
- Internet (anonymous FTP): **ftp.microsoft.com** (SOFTLIB/MSLFILES directory)
- The Microsoft Network: Go To Other Location MSSL, then double-click Microsoft Windows Software Library and then Microsoft Windows 95 Software Library
- World Wide Web: **http://www.microsoft.com/windows/software** ▪

Part

X

Ch

46

Configuring Your Printer

By now, you have installed one or more printers for use by Windows 95 applications. Both Windows and MS-DOS applications can use these resources without further effort. The initial installation of the printer created a default configuration. You might want to make changes to that configuration. Because few default configurations satisfy all printing requirements, you might want to change the printer's configuration frequently.

TIP If you change printer settings frequently, you can install duplicate printers and configure each printer with its own set of properties. This eliminates repeated property changes.

> **NOTE** Windows 3.1 provided a setting to change the priority of background printing. This feature does not appear in Windows 95. However, the print spooler in Windows 95, which uses 32-bit device drivers and DLLs, handles background printing much more smoothly than Windows 3.1 did, obviating the need to optimize the background printing settings. ■

Options for Your Printer

Printer properties are preset during installation of the printer. The preset values for the many variables might not meet your current printing needs. You might also have to make changes to meet special printing needs or to solve any performance problems that arise.

Like many other printing issues discussed in this chapter, the exact options available depend on the capabilities of your printer. The following discussion focuses on the basic procedures; you must adapt these to fit your specific printer.

To change printer options, open the Printer Properties sheet (see Figure 46.8). Use one of these two methods:

■ If the Print Manager for the printer whose options you want to change is open, choose Printer, Properties.

FIG. 46.8

Use the General page of the Printer Properties sheet to get and specify basic information about the printer.

- Open the Printer control panel and select the printer whose options you want to change. Choose File, Properties or right-click the printer icon and choose Properties from the shortcut menu.

This sheet has several tabbed pages. The settings on each page depend on the manufacturer, printer model, and printer options.

The Printer Properties sheet typically contains the following information. (The details of these tabs will change with different printers.)

- *General page*. Enables you to identify your printer, print a test page, and choose a separator page to separate print jobs of different users. Each page includes a user name and job-specific information such as date, time, and file name.

- *Details page*. Contains controls to attach or change ports, add or delete ports, change time-out periods, and specify how Windows will process print files. Use the Details page to configure enhanced meta file printing and the spooler.

- *Sharing page*. Enables a printer to be shared with other workstations attached to your computer over a network.

- *Paper page*. Provides several controls that set the printer's default paper handling, orientation, and number of pages to be printed.

- *Graphics page*. Sets the resolution, halftone capabilities, scaling, and other options that define how the printer treats graphic files.

- *Fonts page*. Enables you to adjust how fonts are treated by Windows for this printer. Configurable fonts include printer, cartridge, and software fonts.

TIP Be certain to accurately configure the available printer memory. An incorrect value in this variable can change the speed of your printouts or cause your printer to time out or fail during printing sessions.

- *Device Options page*. Configures the options associated with the printer's hardware, such as the printer memory capacity settings, page protection, and other device-specific options. The number and type of controls are specific to the printer's make, model, and hardware.

TROUBLESHOOTING

In Windows 95, the settings in your programs for the number of copies to be printed override the setting on your printer. To print multiple copies, change the setting in the program from which you are printing.

WordPad and Paint do not support printing multiple copies, so if your printer does not support printing multiple copies, this option will not be available.

continues

Part

X

Ch

46

continued

When you try to print a page you may receive the message Not enough memory to render page. If your printer has bi-directional communication with your computer, there may be a problem with the amount of memory the printer driver detected. To have Windows 95 recheck the printer for memory, follow these steps:

1. With the printer online, open the Start menu and choose Settings, Printers.

2. Right-click the icon for the printer you want to check and choose Properties.

3. Select the Device Options tab and choose the Restore Defaults button.

4. Click OK.

Printing with Color

Microsoft uses licensed Image Color Matching (ICM) technology from Kodak to create an image environment that treats color consistently, from the screen to the printed page. The Windows ICM goal is to be able to repeatedly and consistently reproduce color-matched images from source to destination.

ICM provides more consistent, repeatable quality among various brands of printers and scanners and provides a higher quality color rendering (the term *color* includes grayscale rendering). To fully benefit from ICM technology, choose a color printer that is compliant with Kodak's ICM specifications.

Setting Color Printing Properties Figure 46.9 shows the Graphics page of the Printer Properties sheet for a color printer. The controls on this page allow you to configure your printer to produce the best color possible.

- ■ *Resolution*. This drop-down list box specifies the number of dots per inch (dpi) that the printer can produce. The higher the dpi, the clearer the graphics.

- ■ *Dithering*. This error-correcting tool used by Windows 95 more accurately represents an object's color and grayscale.

- ■ *Intensity*. This brightness control lightens or darkens a printout to more accurately reflect its screen appearance and to compensate for deficiencies in toner or paper quality.

To access the color settings for a color printer, click the Color button. Use the Graphics—Color dialog box to set ICM compliance alternatives (see Figure 46.10).

Use the color settings to adjust the level of compliance of your printer with the ICM standards. The dialog box is also useful for trial-and-error adjustment of color printer output quality. Following is a list of the settings:

- ■ *Color Control*. A macro command that enables you to direct the printer to print only black and white or to specify whether you want ICM technology.

FIG. 46.9
The Graphics page of the Printer Properties sheet for a color printer lets you adjust color and output quality.

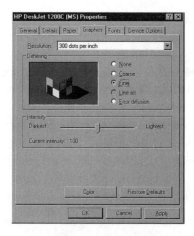

FIG. 46.10
Display this box by choosing the Color button on the Graphics page.

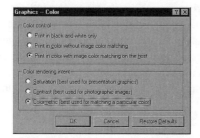

■ *Color Rendering Intent.* Provides the best ICM settings for three of the major uses of color printing: presentations, photographs, and true-color screen display printing. Select the choice that works best for your purpose.

Using the 32-Bit Subsystem

Naturally, a 32-bit application is faster than its 46-bit equivalent. However, in Windows 95, 32-bit performance means more than speed; it also means safety. 32-bit applications run in their own address space so a failure in one application doesn't propagate to others. Because printing is a resource-dependent function, 32-bit performance results in better use of your resources. It permits Windows 95 designers to provide a more robust, feature-rich user interface.

When using the 32-bit printing subsystem, you will find the following differences in Windows 95 versus Windows 3.1 performance:

■ *Return from Printing.* When an application prints, it shares memory and resources with the print system. In the Windows 32-bit architecture, 32-bit applications do not share the same memory—each has its own virtual memory resources. Virtual memory, combined with the faster performance of 32-bit drivers, results in the printing subsystem quickly releasing resources. 32-bit printer drivers share existing resources more equitably, resulting in smoother background printing.

- *System Stalls.* Because the printing subsystem runs in its own 32-bit virtual processor, a printing failure no longer locks out other applications. Another benefit from this design is that Windows can clean up resources after a print failure.

- *Printing Independence.* 32-bit virtual drivers enable Windows to support each printer with an individual, dedicated Print Manager. Multiple Print Managers result in the independent configuration of each printer and maximize the use of all printers without the need for frequent reconfiguration.

To verify that all Windows 95 printing components are 32-bit, perform the following checks:

- Using the Port Configuration dialog box, verify that all port drivers are VXD files. The VXD extension designates a virtual device driver.

- Using the Print Manager Properties sheet, print a test page from the General page. The test page displays the name and version of the current printer driver. Verify that the version of the driver is the latest available for Windows 95. As a general rule, this driver should also have a VXD (virtual device driver) extension. If your drivers are not VXD, check with your printer manufacturer to obtain the latest releases of these drivers. Then perform the Add a Printer installation procedure using the new drivers.

Using Enhanced Meta File Spooling (EMF)

The new enhanced meta file (EMF) feature appears to fall in the "so-what" category—or does it? Historically, PostScript printing has employed meta files to produce excellent hard copy results. A printer meta file contains specific printer instructions to produce a hard copy printout. Many printer manufacturers use proprietary meta file formats, such as PostScript, to produce their best results. Now meta files can be created in the operating system and be standardized for most printers.

The EMF Process   An application submits a print stream to Windows. If the printer is configured to support enhanced meta files, the print stream is converted into a series of high-level printer instructions.

The process of changing a print stream to a meta file converts each page into a series of printer-recognizable macro instructions. Printing EMF files transfers much of the processing overhead from the computer to the printer. Windows uses its 32-bit graphics device interface (GDI) and its device independent bitmap (DIB) engine to create the image to print.

Print Spooling   Print spooling creates a temporary disk file that stores print files—Windows only stores these files until it has finished printing. The spooler is an integral part of the Windows 32-bit print architecture. The spooler itself is a 32-bit virtual device driver.

An application sends a print stream to Windows for printing. The printer driver reviews the printer configuration and verifies that the spooler is required. The spooler creates a memory-mapped file on the system's hard disk to store the application's print stream. Although this process takes time, it uses fewer system resources for a shorter period of time than sending the print stream directly to the printer.

Using the spooler enables Windows to smooth out background printing and return resources to the application more quickly.

Configuration of the EMF Print Spooler   The enhanced meta file (EMF) print spooler is responsible for converting your documents into a printable format prior to sending them to the printer. The spooler is important because it affects both printing speed and how quickly Windows returns control to you after printing.

N O T E   You cannot configure PostScript printers using the EMF print spooler. PostScript is itself a substitute for EMF, and Windows will only configure RAW for PostScript printers. ■

To use the spooler, follow these steps:

1. From a desktop shortcut printer icon or the Start menu, choose Settings and start the Print Manager. Select a non-PostScript printer.

2. Choose Printer, Properties.

3. Select Spool Settings. Windows displays the Spool Settings dialog box (see Figure 46.11).

   The Spool Settings dialog box has four controls: spooler printing, bypassing the spooler, spooler formats, and printer communications.

FIG. 46.11

The Spool Settings dialog box provides controls to modify the operation of the Windows printer spooler.

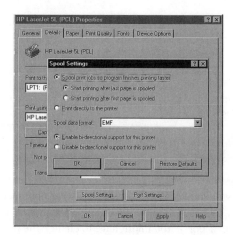

Part
X

Ch
46

4. Select the Spool Print Jobs So Program Finishes Printing Faster option. Selecting this option enables the spooler.

   Alternatively, select Print Directly to Printer; this option disables the spooler.

5. If you selected the Spool Print Jobs So Program Finishes Printing Faster option, you can then choose when you want Windows to start printing during the spooling process. Printing after the last page is spooled provides the smoothest background printing, even though you wait longer for the printout.

6. Specify EMF in the Spool Data Format drop-down list box (the RAW option saves the print stream to a spooler, but does not convert the print stream to EMF format). Select RAW when printing to a PostScript printer or to a printer with a proprietary meta file print driver. The EMF setting should produce superior results on most printers. However, if your printing slows down or produces poor-quality graphics, try the RAW setting for possible improvement.

7. Select the Enable Bi-Directional Support option or the Disable Bi-Directional Support option to specify whether Windows can communicate in both directions with the attached printer. If a printer cannot support any level of bi-directional communications or is not attached, the correct choice is Disable Bi-Directional Support. In all other cases, the appropriate choice is Enable Bi-Directional Support, which allows the Print Manager to monitor the printer status during the printing process.

N O T E   To take advantage of bi-directional printer communication, you must have a bi-directional printer using an IEEE 1284-compliant printer cable, your printer port must be configured to PS/2 mode (versus AT-compatible mode), and your Windows 95 printer driver must support bi-directional communication. ▨

TROUBLESHOOTING

If you are using the RAW spool data format and you shut down Windows 95 before the print job has finished spooling, the job may be canceled without warning. Use the EMF spooling format to receive a warning message when you close Windows 95 before a print job has finished spooling.

Configuring the Printer Port

In addition to configuring settings that affect the printer itself, you can make a few configuration changes to the port to which the printer is attached. These options vary depending on which port you use to print. The most common printing port is an LPT port, usually LPT1 (or LPT2, if you have a second LPT port). You might have to change the printer port if you attach a printer to a serial port or add a printer switch.

Follow these steps to change the configuration options for port LPT1:

1. Open the Start menu and choose Settings, Control Panel.

2. Double-click the System icon.

3. Windows displays the System Properties dialog box; choose the Device Manager tab to configure printer ports (see Figure 46.12).

FIG. 46.12

The Device Manager tab of the System Properties sheet identifies the port, its present state of operation, and the hardware configuration being used.

4. Double-click the Printer Ports icon to show the attached ports. Choose the printer port whose configuration you want to change, such as LPT1 or COM1. For this example, choose LPT1. If your printer is attached to another parallel port or a COM (serial) port, choose that port instead.

5. Click Properties. The Printer Port Properties sheet shown in Figure 46.13 appears. Note that Printer Port Properties are divided among three tabs: General, Driver, and Resources.

FIG. 46.13

The General page of the Printer Port Properties sheet provides current status and information about the port's hardware.

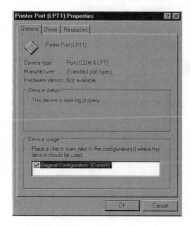

Part

X

Ch

46

6. Choose the Driver tab.

7. Verify that the driver file selected on the Driver page is the most current printer driver available (see Figure 46.14). Note that the VXD extension signifies a 32-bit virtual driver that can be expected to provide the best performance. If you have a driver with a DRV extension, you are not using a 32-bit driver. Check with your printer manufacturer for the latest version.

FIG. 46.14

The Driver page of the Printer Port Properties sheet provides the name and version of the currently installed port driver.

8. To install a different driver, click Change Driver. Windows displays the Select Device dialog box shown in Figure 46.15. Use this dialog box to load a new driver from either a vendor-supplied disk or to choose a previously installed driver. If you have a vendor-supplied disk that contains the new port driver, choose Have Disk.

FIG. 46.15

Select a new or existing printer port driver.

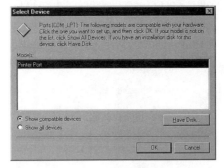

9. Windows displays an instruction window that directs you to insert the manufacturer's disk in drive A. The window also allows you to browse and select a driver from another location. Windows requests a vendor disk. Insert the appropriate disk and click OK. Otherwise, click Cancel to stop the installation process. Windows installs the vendor software and links it to the selected printer port.

The Resources page contains detailed information about the printer port's addresses and any configuration conflicts. Review this information to verify that Windows has properly installed the driver. In the background, Windows cross-checked the ports configuration with the system startup settings. Windows can and does spot configuration problems, but doesn't necessarily notify the user that there's a problem. The resources contain the Input/Output Range of addresses. The addresses of the LPT1 port are shown under the Setting column. If a device uses an interrupt, that interrupt is also shown. If Windows spots a problem, it will designate that a conflict exists and list the information in this window. You can then choose alternative configurations to test other configurations.

To configure the printer port, click the Resources tab. The critical information is the Conflicting Device List (see Figure 46.16). This list contains all items that conflict with your printer port. When installing new hardware, always verify that its address and interrupts do not conflict with existing hardware properties.

FIG. 46.16

The Resources page of the Printer Port Properties sheet displays detailed hardware information vital to port operation and the diagnosis of communications problems.

Part
X

Ch
46

You should normally choose Use Automatic Settings. If you have any conflict problems, the Settings Based On list box shown in Figure 46.16 provides several optional configurations that Windows can use to configure the printer port.

To use this control, first deselect the Use Automatic Settings check box. You then can use the Settings Based On option to select from a list of Windows configurations. Each configuration shows the port configured to different devices and interrupts. As each configuration is considered, problems associated with the new configuration are shown in the Conflicting Device List information box at the bottom of the page.

N O T E Carefully review the hardware properties for all devices to identify potential conflicts. Windows cannot discover and display all problems in normal operation. Use the Device Manager to check for conflicting devices; doing so can prevent problems later. ■

Most printer installations do not require changes to the printer port settings. However, unusual address conflicts from older equipment or Enhanced Capability Ports (ECP) technology provide more configuration options. The number of possible decisions and potential conflicts between pieces of hardware increase as the number of options increase. Select OK to complete the port configuration.

Printing from Applications

When you print from an application under Windows 95, you use the same commands and techniques available under previous versions of Windows; however, there have been changes. Application printing now takes less time, the operating system releases your resources quicker, and the color/grayscale found in the printer output is substantially more consistent and accurate. However, many details of the printing architecture are transparent to application users.

Basic Windows 95 Printing Procedures

Depending on the application from which you are printing, you may have some slightly different printing options. This section looks at the printing options available to all applications written for the Windows 95 operating system. The two most common Windows 95 applications are WordPad and Paint, included with Windows 95. The options you see in these applications are the same as the options in many Windows 95 applications.

To print from an application, follow these steps:

1. Load the file to be printed.

2. Initiate the print command. In most Windows applications, do this by choosing File, Print. Figure 46.17 shows a typical Print dialog box. The controls in this dialog box let you specify the portion of the file to be printed and the printer designated to complete the job.

FIG. 46.17

A typical application's Print dialog box lets you send a print job to a specific printer.

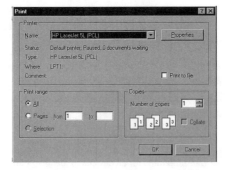

3. Select the desired printer from the Name list box.

4. Specify the number of copies you want to print in the Number of Copies text box.

5. Define the print range in the Print Range area. By default, most applications choose All as the print range.

TIP The sheets-of-paper icon next to the Collate option shows whether the print job will be collated.

6. If you are printing more than one copy of the document, you can have the copies collated (each copy of the multipage document is printed completely before the next copy of the document). To collate copies, select the Collate check box. If you don't select this option, all the copies of each page are printed together. The Collate option is not available in all applications.

7. To output the printer information to a print file, select the Print to File check box. Print files were used in earlier versions of Windows to store print jobs, but Windows 95 uses Deferred Printing to create its own spooled print file, eliminating the need to check this box. Print files also are used for transferring printouts between computers with dissimilar applications.

8. To initiate the links between your application and the Windows print drivers, click OK. Your application should now begin printing the specified document.

If you change your mind and don't want to print, click Cancel to return to the document without making any changes or starting the print job.

This basic printing procedure applies to most applications, even if their Print dialog boxes are slightly different than the one shown in Figure 46.17. Some applications have additional options, as discussed in the next two sections.

Part
X

Ch
46

N O T E If you plan to print to a file frequently, set up a bogus printer. For example, set up a second PostScript printer to create EPS files. Use the Options, Printer Setup command (or the Printers application in Control Panel) to install a new printer; accept the current driver if you already have a PostScript printer installed or add the PostScript driver if you don't have one installed. When you get to the step in the Add Printer Wizard in which you are asked to select a port (refer to Figure 46.4), select the FILE option. When you're ready to print from the application, choose File, Print Setup to select the bogus printer and then print the document. The Print to File dialog box will appear, in which you can specify the name and folder for the print file. ■

Applications with Special Print Options

Some applications take the basic printing features in Windows 95 and add a few features of their own. This section looks at some of the additional features you may find in other programs, with Word 97 as an example. Although these features vary from application to application, this section should give you an idea of what to look for.

Figure 46.18 shows the Word 97 Print dialog box.

FIG. 46.18

The Print dialog box in Word 97 includes several enhancements not found in the standard Windows 95 Print dialog box.

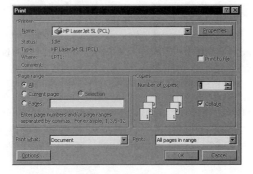

Here is a quick summary of some of the additional (and different) options provided by this application compared to the standard Windows 95 printing options:

- *The Current Page option in the Page Range section.* When this option is selected, Word prints the page in which the insertion point is currently located.

- *An enhanced Pages option.* This enhanced option allows you to specify a page range in the variable box located to the right of the *Pages* label. The range can be individual pages separated by a comma, a page range separated by a hyphen, or both.

- *The Print What drop-down list.* In Word, you can select to print the document itself or other information such as summary, annotations, and styles.

- *The Print option.* From this drop-down list, you select to print odd, even, or all pages in the range.

- *The Options button.* When you click this button, Word displays the Options dialog box, opened to the Print tab. Use this dialog box to set printing options specific to Word.

N O T E For a more complete discussion of Word's printing features, see Que's *Special Edition Using Microsoft Word 97.* ■

Keep in mind that the options described here are not the same in all applications.

Windows 3.1 Applications with Special Print Options

The other common type of Print dialog box you may encounter is from a Windows 3.1 application that has a customized dialog box, such as the one for Word 6 shown in Figure 46.19.

FIG. 46.19

The Word 6 Print dialog box is still styled like a Windows 3.1 Print dialog box.

Most options in this dialog box are the same as those shown in Figures 46.17 and 46.18. However, there are some differences:

- There is no status entry or comment field that describes the printer's current activity.
- You select a different printer by clicking the Printer button and selecting from a dialog box instead of choosing a printer from a drop-down list.
- There is no Properties button.

As with the other printing options discussed in this chapter, the options displayed in the Print dialog box vary from application to application.

Managing Print Jobs

Like Windows 3.1, Windows 95 offers the option of printing directly to the configured port or using its 32-bit Print Manager. For most applications, the Print Manager provides facilities to better manage the printing of documents.

The Print Manager

To start the Print Manager, open the Start menu and choose Settings; then choose Printers and double-click the icon for the printer you want to manage in the Printer control panel (see Figure 46.20).

FIG. 46.20

The Printers control panel has icons for each of your installed printers as well as the icon to add a new printer.

Part
X

Ch
46

 To create a desktop shortcut for your printer, see "Creating a Desktop Printer Icon" later in this chapter.

Unlike Windows 3.1, Windows 95 uses a separate Print Manager for each printer. Therefore, make certain that you choose the correct Print Manager to view the status of your print jobs.

The Print Manager shown in Figure 46.21 displays the current printer status for each print job.

FIG. 46.21

Each printer has its own Print Manager; make sure that you select from the Printer control panel the correct printer for the print jobs you want to check.

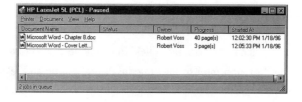

The printer status includes the following information:

■ The Document Name section shows the name of each application that has submitted a print job, as well as the name of each document job in the print queue.

■ The Status column describes the current condition of each print job, such as paused or spooling.

■ The Owner column gives the user's name associated with each document. A print job on your printer may belong to someone else when you share your printer.

■ The Progress column shows the relative progress of each job in the print queue. The progress of each job monitors the printing of each document and provides information concerning the number of pages printed and the number of pages left to print.

 By default, print jobs are listed in the order they entered the queue. You can sort them according to name, status, owner, progress, or start time by clicking the appropriate column heading.

■ The Started At column provides the time and date when each job entered the queue. This is important for users with deferred print jobs.

Controlling Printing

The Print Manager coordinates and schedules the printing of files received from your applications. These applications may be Windows-based or MS-DOS based.

The Print Manager pull-down menus provide you with the following capabilities, all of which are described in the next several sections:

■ Pause printing

■ Purge printing

■ Work offline

■ Set printer as default

■ Change a printer's properties

■ Pause a selected document's printing

■ Cancel a selected document's printing

■ View the status bar

■ Access windows Help

N O T E   If you are using a network printer, you can cancel only your own print jobs. You cannot pause the printing, even of your own documents. Canceling someone else's print jobs or pausing printing requires network supervisor rights. ▪

Pausing Printing   Pausing a printer temporarily stops print jobs from being sent to a printer. Once a paused printer is restarted, all pending print jobs are started and sequentially sent to the printer. This feature is useful when changing toner or performing printer maintenance.

To pause printing, choose Printer, Pause Printing. The Print jobs are paused and the Print Manager's title bar displays Paused.

To restart printing, choose Printer, Pause Printing again, which is now prefaced by a check mark. The Pause Printing check mark disappears and printing resumes.

 You can exit Print Manager without purging print jobs, unlike in Windows 3.1. All print jobs in progress will continue printing. Paused print jobs will remain in the print queue and can be resumed by reopening Print Manager and releasing them. In fact, you can shut down Windows 95 when a print job has been paused and it will not be lost from the print queue. When you restart Windows, a message box appears informing you that your printer has print jobs pending and a flashing "Printers Folder" button appears in the taskbar. To resume printing, choose Yes, to pause printing choose No, and to cancel the print job(s), choose Cancel.

Purging Print Jobs   The Purge Print Jobs command permanently removes all queued print jobs. Choose Printer, Purge Print Jobs. The documents listed by the Print Manager disappear.

TROUBLESHOOTING

Purging print jobs stops Windows 95 from sending print jobs to the printer. However, it does not purge the print jobs currently being processed by the printer. You may have to reset the printer to terminate unwanted printing.

Working Offline   Windows 95 enables you to initiate a print job without being physically attached to a printer. This feature is known as Deferred Printing, or Working Offline. Deferred Printing is available for network printers and laptop computers. Deferred Printing tracks deferred print jobs and releases them under configuration control when the computer is connected to the printer locally or networked, or attached through a docking station.

 The Work Offline command is only available for laptop computers and network printers. Use the Pause Printing command to delay printing on a computer that uses a local printer. See the section "Pausing Printing" earlier in this chapter for more information on that option.

Part

X

Ch

46

N O T E   The spooler must be turned on for you to use Deferred Printing. ■

To configure a printer to work offline, choose Printer, Work Offline. A check mark appears in front of the Work Offline command. The Printer is now configured to work offline and defer printouts. The Print Manager changes its title to read User Intervention Required. This information is then placed in the status line of each print job being sent to this printer. The Print Manager defers printouts until you change the status of the Work Offline flag.

To change the status of the Work Offline flag, choose Work Offline for a second time. The check mark disappears and the deferred printouts are sent to the printer.

The taskbar normally displays a printer when a document is being printed. If deferred documents are pending, the icon changes to include a question mark circled in red.

To print documents that have been deferred, follow these steps:

1. Physically connect the target printer to the system by putting the laptop in the docking station or connecting to the network printer.
2. From the Print Manager window, choose Printer, Work Offline to remove its check mark.

   If you have multiple printers configured, be sure to select the correct printer before releasing the print jobs.
3. Verify that printing begins immediately to the target printer and that the deferred print jobs are no longer displayed by the Print Manager.

Setting a Default Printer   If you have more than one printer available (either locally or on a network), you can choose a default printer. All applications use the default printer, unless you choose another from within the application.

To set a printer as the default, start that printer's Print Manager and then choose Printer, Set as Default. A check mark appears next to the Set as Default command on the pull-down menu, signifying that this printer is now the Windows default printer.

To remove the printer as the system default, select the Set as Default option again to reset the flag. Alternatively, from the Print Manager of another printer, select the Printer, Set as Default command. Windows allows only one default printer.

Pausing a Document   You may pause a document to stop the Print Manager from sending it to the printer. Pausing suspends processing of the print job, but it does not stop the document from being spooled. The Print Manager displays a list of documents being printed; any paused print jobs are labeled Paused.

To pause documents, choose them from the list of documents in the print queue, then choose Document, Pause. The selected documents now display a Paused status.

To release a paused document, repeat the preceding steps. The paused status toggles off, and the selected documents no longer display a Paused status.

Canceling a Document from Printing   You also can permanently remove selected documents from the list of documents being printed. To cancel documents, choose one or more documents from the documents in the print queue; then choose Document, Cancel.

> **CAUTION**
>
> When you cancel a document, Windows immediately removes that document from the print queue. You do not receive a confirmation prompt. You might try Pause first and make certain you want this document's printout terminated.

Turning the Status Bar Off and On   The status bar lists the status of the print queue and contains the number of print jobs remaining to be printed. To turn off the display of the status bar, choose View, Status Bar. Repeat this action to turn the status bar display back on. The Status Bar option is a standard Windows toggle control; if the option is not preceded by a check mark, the status bar is not visible.

Closing Print Manager   To close the Print Manager, choose Printer, Close; or click the Close button.

 Closing the Print Manager in Windows 95 does not purge the associated print jobs (unlike Windows 3.1). Printing continues based on the Print Manager's settings.

To rearrange the print queue, select a document, drag it to the correct queue position, and drop it. Dragging and dropping a document in the print queue works only with documents that are not currently being printed.

Drag-and-Drop Printing from the Desktop

A new feature of the Windows 95 operating system is the ability to print a document without first initiating the associated application or the File Manager. Using desktop icons, you can quickly launch print jobs from the desktop.

In earlier versions of Windows, printing used a four-step operation: open an application, load a file, initiate printing, and finally, shut down the application after printing. Windows 95 uses a two-step printing procedure that is quick and convenient. However, before you can print from the desktop, you must take certain steps to set up your system.

Creating a Desktop Printer Icon

Before you can drag and drop documents to desktop icons, you must first create the icons. Although some icons are automatically created during Windows setup, printer icons are not.

Part

X

Ch

46

To create a shortcut icon for a printer, follow these steps:

1. Open the Start menu, choose Settings, Printers. You also can open the Printers folder by double-clicking the Printers icon in the Control Panel window. The Printer's folder is now open.

2. Select the desired printer, drag it onto the desktop, and release it.

3. Windows displays a question window that asks permission to create a shortcut (see Figure 46.22). Answer Yes; the shortcut icon is created. If you answer No, the icon disappears from the desktop.

FIG. 46.22

A Windows question window asks your permission to create a shortcut.

After you have created the shortcut to the printer, you can modify it by creating a shortcut key or changing the icon. Modifying shortcuts is discussed in Chapter 44, "Managing Files."

Print from the Desktop

After you create a shortcut icon on the desktop for your printer, you can print any document from the desktop. To print from the desktop, simply open a folder that contains a printable document and select that document. Drag the document's icon to a printer desktop icon and drop the file there.

Make sure the document is associated with an application and the application is available to Windows, or your printing will be terminated.

Another way to quickly print a file is to add a shortcut for your printer to the SendTo folder (which is in the Windows folder). You can then right-click a file in the Explorer or a folder window, choose Send To, and choose the printer from the Send To list. If you have multiple printers or multiple configurations for the same printer, add shortcuts for each one to the SendTo folder.

Windows starts the associated application configured to handle that file type. Windows executes that application's print command. Once the printing has been committed to the background print spooler, Windows releases the associated application, closes it, and background prints the spooled files.

TROUBLESHOOTING

Drag-and-drop printing is not supported by File Manager when running in Windows 95. Use the Explorer or a folder window if you want to print using drag-and-drop.

Desktop Printing of Multiple Documents

Using Windows, you can print several files at once by dragging them to the shortcut icon on the desktop. Follow these steps to print several files at once:

 You can select and print multiple documents created using different applications.

1. Select several documents to print.
2. Drag the selected documents to the desktop printer icon.
3. Drop the documents on the icon.
4. The message window shown in Figure 46.23 appears. Click Yes to print. Click No only if you want to stop all documents from printing.

FIG. 46.23
This message window asks permission to print the multiple documents.

Windows starts each of the applications associated with the selected documents and begins printing.

N O T E Before trying to print multiple documents, check whether your system has the resources (memory and disk space) to support the number of applications Windows has to open to print the files. ■

Printing from MS-DOS Applications

Windows provides support for printing from MS-DOS applications in much the same way it does for printing from Windows applications. Although EMF support for MS-DOS applications is not supported, the print stream is spooled using the RAW setting for the print spooler. The result is a faster return to MS-DOS applications and the ability to mix Windows and MS-DOS print streams (avoiding contention problems that occurred under Windows 3.1).

Part
X

Ch
46

The major change Windows 95 brings to MS-DOS applications is direct access to the Windows print spooler. MS-DOS applications no longer compete for a share of the printer; you can actually use the Print Manager to queue your MS-DOS printouts with those of Windows applications.

When you print from an MS-DOS application in the Windows environment, the DOS application spools print jobs to the 32-bit print spooler, which takes the output destined for the printer port and spools it before printing. Windows automatically installs the print spooler for MS-DOS applications; the spooler is transparent to users. Although your MS-DOS printouts automatically use the 32-bit spooler, they cannot be processed into Enhanced Meta Files.

Printing from a Docking Station

Every time you start Windows, it performs an inventory check of all attached hardware. Windows also provides a choice of configurations during startup (that is, it lists the configurations it recognizes). You must choose one of the selections from this list.

You can configure Windows to work offline when the computer is undocked and online when the computer is docked. You can set the system configurations for the printer port to be configured only when the laptop is attached to the docking station. You also can configure the port to be automatically unavailable when the system is being used as a laptop.

Configuring a Hardware Profile

A hardware profile specifies whether Windows will use a specific peripheral. Hardware profiles provide a tool that you can use to specify the hardware configurations to operate your system. Hardware configurations are created and changed through the Control Panel's System icon.

Because the printer is not a system resource, it isn't part of the hardware configuration. However, the printer is attached to the system through the LPT1 port. This port *is* a system resource and can be configured to be available when the computer is in a docking station. The port also can be configured as unavailable when the system is used as a laptop.

Use the following steps to create the hardware profile:

1. Open the Start menu; choose Settings, Control Panel.
2. Double-click the System icon. The System Properties sheet appears.
3. Choose the Hardware Profiles tab. The tab contains a text window with a single item: Dock 1. When Windows is first installed at a docking station, it creates the Dock 1 setting in the text window.
4. Select the Dock 1 setting and click Copy.

N O T E   Windows automatically detects most docking stations and creates a Dock 1 profile. Even if you initially install Windows on a laptop, Windows checks the system components each time it starts and creates profiles automatically when it finds changes. ▪

5. Change the name of the newly created configuration from Dock 1 to **Lap Top** or some other name that indicates that the laptop isn't in its docking station. Click OK.

6. Choose the Device Manager tab from the System Properties sheet.

7. Select the port (COM or LPT) from the Device Manager page.

8. Choose the printer's port (LPT1) and choose Properties.

   The Printer Port (LPT1) Properties sheet that appears contains a Device Usage block with a hardware configuration window (see Figure 46.24). The Device Usage block now contains two hardware configurations: the initial Dock 1 and the new Lap Top. The two items are check box controls. A check in the Dock 1 box directs Windows to include port LPT1 in its hardware configuration whenever a docking station has been detected.

FIG. 46.24

The Printer Port Properties sheet shows which hardware profile is currently configured.

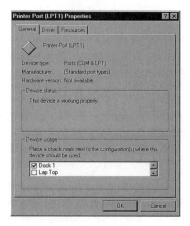

9. Check the Dock 1 box. Leave the Lap Top box unchecked.

10. Reboot your Windows system. During initial boot-up, Windows asks for a configuration. Choose Lap Top.

To verify that you have configured the hardware profile correctly, do not change the hardware and follow these steps:

1. Open the Start menu; then choose Settings, Control Panel.

2. Double-click Device Manager.

3. Select the port (COM or LPT) from the Device Manager page.

4. Note that the printer port is now offline, signified by a red X through the port's icon. Printing now results in a diagnostic message that the printer is not attached. The Print Manager deletes all print files. Therefore, you must set the printer to Work Offline so the system will save all print files.

Part
X

Ch
46

Repeat the process first by rebooting Windows, this time selecting the Dock 1 configuration setting. The printer port returns. The saved print files can then be released for printing.

Common Printer Problems

The most useful tool in identifying and correcting printer problems is a thorough knowledge of your printer's installation and properties. During installation, test your printer and the wide range of properties available to better identify a starting point for dissecting most problems.

Windows provides fundamental troubleshooting aid with Bi-Directional Printer Communication. If a printer can talk to its drivers, many potential causes for problems can be routinely identified.

Advance preparation is always an excellent safeguard against any computer problem. The following checklists can be useful when you are diagnosing a local printer problem.

Before the Problem: Initial Preparation

Following initial installation of the printer, perform these steps:

1. Make a test-page printout and save the resulting printout for future use. The test page can contain important configuration information including the current printer driver, memory size, and port information. On PostScript printers, it will contain version level and settings.

2. If your printer can perform a self test, make a printer self-test printout. For most printers, this test page contains the printer's internal configuration. This information may contain the number of pages printed, memory size, a list of configured options, and internal software revision level. Save the printout for future use. This information may be useful in describing your printer to its manufacturer at a later date, for upgrading or troubleshooting.

3. Note the proper configuration of your printer's indicators: the Ready or Online light and the display status.

4. Make a record of your printer's internal menu settings for paper size, orientation, interface, and so on.

5. Record the installation results and the information from the Printer Properties screens.

Diagnosing the Problem: A Checklist

For a local printer, perform the following steps to start diagnosing a problem:

1. Verify that all cabling is free of nicks, tears, or separations.

2. Verify that all cabling is fully inserted and locked at both the computer and the printer ends.

3. Verify that the printer is online and that all proper indicators are lit (for example, that the Online or Ready indicators are lit).

4. Verify that the printer is properly loaded with paper and that there are no existing paper jams.

5. Verify that the printer has toner (laser), ink (inkjet), or a good ribbon (dot-matrix).

6. Verify that cabinet doors and interlocks are closed and locked.

7. Verify that the printer's display, if available, shows a normal status.

8. Verify that the Windows printer driver can communicate with the printer using the Printer Properties screens. You should be able to print a test page to verify communication. If you cannot print a test page, Windows generates a diagnostic message providing you with a starting point to locate the problem.

9. Verify that the Windows Printer Properties screens display the same information that was contained in the Properties screens when you installed the printer.

10. Attempt to print to the errant printer using another application and a different type of print file (for example, print a text file or a graphics file).

Troubleshooting Tools

If the basic troubleshooting steps listed in the preceding section fail, Windows comes with three important tools you can use to further investigate printer problems. The first tool is Windows 95's new Help file. Initiate the Help file from the Print Manager's Help menu. Then select the Troubleshooting icon.

The Troubleshooter steps you through several of the most probable causes of printing problems (see Figure 46.25). Primarily, this tool verifies that the printer can communicate with the computer. If basic communication is lost, none of the software tools can provide any real assistance. You must resort to hardware exchange until you resolve which component or components are defective. However, with the exception of toner and paper problems, most printing problems are not hardware failures; the problems are primarily software settings or corrupted printer drivers.

Part
X

Ch
46

FIG. 46.25

The Windows Print Troubleshooter assists you in isolating problems using logical fault-isolation techniques.

The Windows 95 Print Manager provides a diagnostic tool that can aid you during the process of equipment interchange. The information on this screen varies (Windows provides as much detail as possible about the problem). The increased amount of information is a result of the Bi-Directional Communications between the computer and the printer. For those printers without bi-directional capability, you will receive a standard "Unable to print" diagnostic.

If you click the diagnostic's Retry button, Windows continues to monitor the printer's status at approximately five-second intervals. If you click the Cancel button, the diagnostic discontinues and the Print Manager pauses the print file.

The third troubleshooting tool is the Enhanced Print Troubleshooter, shown in Figure 46.26. This software application steps you through your problem by asking you questions concerning the problem. As you answer each question, you are provided with a range of possible alternatives to help you narrow in on the potential source of the problem. Clicking the hot buttons next to the most accurate answer brings up another screen with additional insight and questions. This tool is a Windows 95 executable file named EPTS.EXE, which is located in the \Other\Misc\Epts folder on the Windows 95 CD-ROM. Copy all the files in this folder to the \Windows\System folder on your hard disk and run the program by double-clicking EPTS.EXE in the Explorer or a folder window. You also can type **epts.exe** in the Start Run dialog box.

FIG. 46.26

The Enhanced Print Troubleshooter steps you through a printer problem using questions in plain English.

TROUBLESHOOTING

If your first print job of a Windows 95 session always seems to take longer than subsequent print jobs, remember that the print spooler must be started the first time you print a file. Depending on your system configuration, this can take several seconds—adding to the time it takes to print your first file. After the print spooler is started, subsequent print jobs take less time.

CHAPTER 47

Installing, Running, and Uninstalling Windows Applications

Install 16-bit applications in Windows 95

Install applications that were written for the Windows 3.x environment.

Install Windows 95 applications

Learn how to use Setup to install Windows 95 applications.

Add and remove Windows component applications

Use the Add/Remove Programs icon in Control Panel to install and uninstall individual components of Windows 95 without having to reinstall Windows 95 from scratch.

Uninstall applications

Learn how to uninstall a Windows application in Windows 95 automatically, using the Add/Remove Programs icon, or manually, if Windows 95 can't do it automatically.

Windows Applications are bigger, more powerful, and much more complex than DOS-based applications were in the old days. They've become so intertwined with the operating system that it's hard to tell where the dividing line is between Windows and an application. And nearly every Windows application has the potential to interact with any other Windows application on your system.

Not surprisingly, the process of installing and removing applications has grown more complex as well. Fortunately, as application installation grew more complicated, application developers turned to automated setup programs to handle most installation chores. Windows 95 adds new features to further automate adding and removing applications. ■

Understanding How Windows Runs Applications

Windows 95 runs applications designed specifically for Windows 95. It also can run most Windows 3.1 applications, DOS-based applications, and applications designed for Windows NT. Windows 95 no longer requires the traditional CONFIG.SYS, AUTOEXEC.BAT, and .INI files for configuration information. However, for backward-compatibility, Windows 95 uses settings from INI files and maintains its own versions of CONFIG.SYS and AUTOEXEC.BAT to support loading real-mode device drivers.

Although Windows 95 runs various kinds of applications successfully, it provides different kinds of support for each category of application. Windows applications fall into one of two general categories: 32-bit applications (designed for Windows NT and Windows 95) and 16-bit applications (designed for Windows 3.1 and lower versions). This section describes how Windows 95 runs these two types of programs.

Support for Win32 Applications

Windows 95 offers several significant advantages over Windows 3.1. Some advantages, such as preemptive multitasking and multithreading support, are available only to 32-bit applications.

Support for long file names is one feature of Windows 95's 32-bit operating system that is available to any application designed to make use of it. All Windows 95 applications let you create file names containing as many as 255 characters, allowing you to assign files names such as "First Quarter Sales Results" rather than "1QSALES." Theoretically, program developers can adapt 16-bit applications to use long file names as well. However, don't expect many older Windows applications to add long file name support; the programmers are likely to concentrate on converting the application to full-fledged 32-bit status instead of spending time on minor upgrades.

Most applications benefit from Windows 95's 32-bit architecture, which makes memory addressing more efficient. In addition, Windows 95 runs each 32-bit application in its own memory space. Ordinarily, such details are of interest only to programmers. However, these advantages have a side effect that all users will appreciate. If a 32-bit application hangs or crashes, the problem is isolated, confined to the application's own address space, and thus unlikely to affect other running applications. You can exit the problem application and, without even rebooting, have Windows 95 clean up the affected memory.

Advantages of Preemptive Multitasking and Multithreading   Despite appearances, single-processor computers can't really perform multiple tasks from several different applications all at the same instant. Generally, PC computers perform only one operation at a time, but do so very fast. But, if the applications are designed to break operations into small tasks, the operating system switches between tasks from several applications so quickly that it seems that all the applications and their processes are running simultaneously.

Programmers designed Windows 3.1 applications to surrender control of the CPU voluntarily at various points of execution, enabling Windows to switch to another task. This is called *cooperative multitasking*. However, some applications were more cooperative than others. If an application was reluctant to share CPU capacity with other applications, Windows 3.1 couldn't do much about it.

Preemptive multitasking enables the Windows 95 operating system to take control away from one running task and pass it to another task, depending on the system's needs. The system doesn't have to wait for an application or process to surrender control of the CPU before another application can take its turn.

With preemptive multitasking, Windows 95 doesn't depend on the foresight of application programmers to ensure that an application performs multitasking successfully. Windows 95 has more power to arbitrate the demands of various running applications.

Multithreading enables an application to create and run separate concurrent *threads* or processes and thus handle different internal operations. Each process gets its own share of Windows 95's multitasking resources. For example, a word processing application might use one thread to handle keyboard input and display it on-screen. At the same time, a separate thread can run in the background to check spelling while another thread prints a document.

Some Windows 3.1 applications implemented their own internal multithreading, with varying degrees of success. Windows 95 makes multithreading an integral feature of the operating system, available to all 32-bit applications.

Increased System Resources   In Windows 3.1, attempting to launch an application when there was insufficient system resources often resulted in Not Enough Memory errors even though there was ample RAM and disk memory available. In Windows 3.1, things like having lots of installed fonts, running in high resolution, and high color display modes taxed system resources. You don't have this problem in Windows 95 with 32-bit applications.

Windows 95 doesn't remove the limitation on system resources completely, but the improvement is dramatic. One way Windows 95 makes more system resources available is to store many data structures in 32-bit memory regions (heaps) instead of in the 16-bit graphical device interface (GDI) and USER heaps used in Windows 3.1 (which are limited to 64K). As a result, the system limits on certain types of programming information, such as timers, COM and LPT ports, and data in list boxes and edit controls, are now unlimited. Windows 95 still limits other kinds of programming information, such as for Windows menu handles, items per list box, and installed fonts, but those limits are significantly higher than in Windows 3.1. As a result, you can run more applications, create more windows, use more fonts, and so on—all without running out of system resources. For instance, as I write this I have two very large, resource-hungry applications running, plus a communications program, a personal organizer, Explorer, and CD Player. That's more than enough to exhaust system resources in Windows 3.1 and precipitate a flurry of error messages. But in Windows 95 I still have more than 80 percent of the available system resources free.

Support for Windows 3.1 Applications

Most Windows 3.1 applications run in Windows 95 without modification or special settings. Microsoft claims that 16-bit Windows applications run at least as well in Windows 95 as in Windows 3.1.

Windows 3.1 applications continue to use cooperative multitasking; they cannot use Windows 95's preemptive multitasking and multithreading. However, 16-bit applications benefit from the advantages Windows 95 derives from 32-bit device drivers and 32-bit subsystems, such as the printing subsystem, which uses multitasking at the operating system level.

Windows 3.1 applications running in Windows 95 all run in the same virtual machine and share the same address space—just as they do when running in Windows 3.1. As a result, they don't share the same crash protection as Windows 95 applications. If one 16-bit application hangs or crashes, it's likely to affect other 16-bit applications that are running at the same time. In other words, any application failure that requires rebooting or restarting Windows 3.1 requires you to shut down all the 16-bit applications you're running. However, a failure of a 16-bit application does not affect 32-bit applications, and Windows 95 probably can clean up after an errant 16-bit application without requiring a reboot to recover System Resources and clear memory.

Windows 3.1 and Long File Names

You may wonder what happens to the long file names you assign to files in Windows 95 programs if you open and save these files in 16-bit Windows or DOS programs that don't support long file names. Fortunately, Windows 95 uses a technique called *tunneling* to preserve long file names when you open these files in 16-bit programs. Although you won't be able to view the long file names or assign new long file names in these programs, at least you won't lose the existing long file names.

 If you work in an environment that uses both 8.3 and long file names, you will want to understand some of the administrative issues involved in using both. In addition, you may want to modify the Windows Registry to make it easier to work in a mixed name environment. Many users are bothered by truncated long file names that end with a ~1 tail. By modifying the Registry, you can make Windows truncate file names to eight characters. To learn more about long file names and modifying the Registry for truncated names, see the sections "Administering Long File Names" and "Modifying the Registry to Remove Numeric Tails from File Names" in Chapter 44, "Managing Files."

When you save a file with a long file name in a 16-bit program, it is saved with the truncated 8.3 version of the name that Windows 95 assigned when you created the long file name. However, Windows 95 is smart enough to recognize that this is happening and to reassign the original long file name to the newly saved file. The technique is called *tunneling* because the long file name "tunnels" from the old version of the file to the new without being affected by the assigning of an 8.3 file name by the 16-bit program.

There are utilities available that add the capability to use long file names in older programs. Norton Navigator has a feature that enables long file names in many 16-bit Windows programs. Be aware that some Windows programs, such as Excel 5 and Word 6, do not use common Windows 95 dialog boxes (such as File Save As and File Open), which are common to applications using the Windows 95 interface. Such applications may not fully benefit from these utilities. In these cases, you may be able to enter a long file name in the File Name text box but not be able to view long file names.

Installing Applications in Windows 95

To install a Windows application you usually use a setup program or install utility. Installing DOS-based applications is a different matter. These setup programs for Windows applications take care of all the details of installing the application. You don't have to concern yourself with creating directories, copying files, and integrating the application into Windows. A manual installation of a major software suite is beyond the capabilities of the average user, and a dreaded chore for even the most advanced user.

What Does Setup Do?

A typical setup or installation program begins by prompting you for some information and then installs the application automatically. The better setup programs provide feedback during installation to keep you informed of what they're doing to your system and the progress of the installation. Depending on the complexity of the application you are installing, the setup program might give you an opportunity to select various options and customize the installation. The program might limit your input to accepting or changing the path where you install the application, selecting whether to install various optional components, or specifying configuration settings for the new application.

After receiving your input, the setup program proceeds to perform some or all of the following steps automatically:

- Searches for an existing copy of the application it's about to install and switches to upgrade mode if appropriate.
- Scans your system to determine whether your hard disk has enough room for the necessary files and perhaps checks for the existence of special hardware or other system requirements.
- Creates folders and copies files. Often, the setup program must expand files that are stored in a compressed form on the distribution disks.
- Creates a shortcut that you can use to launch the application.
- Adds a folder and/or shortcuts to your Start menu.
- Updates Windows configuration files.
- Updates the Windows Registry.

Part

X

Ch

47

- Registers the application as an OLE server.
- Registers the application's file types so Windows can recognize the file name extensions for the application's document and data files.
- Installs fonts, support utilities, and so on.
- Configures or personalizes the application.

What If There's No Setup Program?

A few Windows programs don't include a setup utility to install the application—the developer just didn't supply one. An example could be a small utility program for which installation consists of copying a couple of files to your hard disk and perhaps adding a shortcut to your Start menu to launch the application. You'll find instructions for installing the application in an accompanying manual or README file.

The installation instructions may assume that you're installing the program in Windows 3.1, not Windows 95. Fortunately, this isn't a serious problem. Most of the procedures for installing an application in Windows 3.1 work equally well in Windows 95. For instance, although Windows 95 supplies new tools for managing files, the underlying process of creating directories (folders) and copying files is the same in both Windows 95 and Windows 3.1. Also, for backward compatibility, Windows 95 includes full support for WIN.INI and SYSTEM.INI files, so any additions that you're instructed to make to those files should work as expected.

There are two common manual installation procedures that you must adapt for Windows 95. First, if the Windows 3.1 installation instructions require that you create a file association in File Manager, you must substitute the Windows 95 equivalent of registering a file type. See "Registering File Types so Documents Open Applications" in Chapter 44 to learn how to register file types. Second, instead of creating a program item in Program Manager, you add a program to the Start menu.

Using Windows 3.1 Applications in Windows 95

According to Microsoft, Windows 95 features full backward-compatibility with 16-bit Windows 3.1 applications, and thus you can install and use Windows 3.1 applications in Windows 95 without modification. And in fact, with only rare exceptions, Windows 3.1 applications do indeed run successfully in Windows 95.

 For a current list of programs with known incompatibility problems with Windows 95 and suggested fixes or workarounds, read the file PROGRAMS.TXT in the Windows folder. You can also search for compatible software programs at the following site on the Internet:

http://www.microsoft.com/windows/thirdparty/compat.htm

If you encounter a compatibility problem with a legacy application—an older application designed for a previous version of DOS or Windows—running in Windows 95, check with the application's developer for a patch or work-around for the problem. In some cases, perhaps the only solution is an upgrade to a Windows 95 version of the application.

TIP There is an application called MKCOMPAT.EXE, located in the Windows\System folder that helps fix Windows 3.X programs that are not completely compatible with Windows 95. Use the Find command to find MKCOMPAT.EXE, double-click it to start it, and use the File, Open command to open the EXE file you are having trouble with. Systematically check and uncheck items in the window and try running the program again. You can access additional items by choosing File, Advanced Options.

Using this program is a matter of trial-and-error; there is no Help facility to guide you. Call the software development company that created the Windows 3.x program and ask if it knows the MKCOMPAT parameters to make the program run or if it has a Windows 95-compatible version.

Installing Windows 3.1 Applications

The installation instructions for most Windows 3.1 applications direct you to use the Run command to start the setup program and install the application. The instructions might mention that you can find the Run command on the File menu in either Program Manager or File Manager. However, in Windows 95, you find the Run command on the Start menu. The setup program is usually on disk 1 of the installation disks or in the root directory if the program is on a CD-ROM.

N O T E You might prefer a different technique for launching the Setup program. Open the My Computer window and double-click the drive icon for the drive that contains the installation disk. Then locate the Setup program's icon and launch the program by double-clicking it.

When you use this technique, you need not type the command in the Run dialog box to start the Setup program. This technique also lets you scan the disk for README files before installing the application.

Part

X

Ch

47

> **CAUTION**
>
> Save a copy of your AUTOEXEC.BAT and CONFIG.SYS files before installing any new DOS or Windows 3.x application. After you install a Windows 3.x or DOS application, it is a good idea to check your AUTOEXEC.BAT files to see if any unnecessary programs or configuration lines were added. For example, some applications add a line that loads SHARE.EXE or SMARTDRV.EXE, neither of which are needed in Windows 95. Not only do these programs waste memory, you may have problems with your system if they are loaded.

Of course, the setup program for a legacy application is tailored to Windows 3.1 rather than Windows 95. For example, the installation program offers to create Program Manager groups (see Figure 47.1) and update INI files. Fortunately, you can just accept those options when the program offers them. Windows 95 intercepts Program Manager updates and automatically converts them to Start menu shortcuts. Windows 95 also transfers WIN.INI and SYSTEM.INI entries into the Registry.

FIG. 47.1

If you run this Setup program in Windows 95, the program will be added to the Start menu, which is the equivalent to program groups in Windows 3.x.

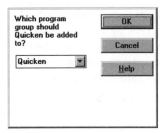

If you install Windows 95 as an upgrade to Windows 3.1, the Setup program should take care of such issues. The Windows 95 Setup program automatically transfers information about your existing applications to the Registry when you install Windows 95 into your existing Windows 3.1 directory. As a result, you shouldn't have to reinstall applications.

Setting Up Existing Applications in a Dual-Boot Configuration

If you choose to create a dual-boot system by installing Windows 95 in a folder separate from Windows 3.1, Windows 95 won't know about any Windows 3.1 applications already on your disk. Just adding those applications to your Start menu isn't enough to let you run them successfully in Windows 95.

> **CAUTION**
> Before reinstalling a Windows 3.1 application in Windows 95, be sure to note the directory in which the application is currently installed. You must specify *exactly* the same directory when you reinstall the application. Otherwise, you might waste valuable disk space by having two copies of the same application on your system.

In some cases, it may not be necessary to have a separate copy of an application on your hard disk to use it in Windows 95 as well as Windows 3.1. However, most applications expect to find certain initialization and support files in the Windows folder. If you attempt to run the application from Windows 95, it expects to find those files in the Windows 95 folder. But if you installed the program under Windows 3.1, those files are in the Windows 3.1 folder, not in the Windows 95 folder. In some cases, if you copy the Windows 3.1 applications' initialization and support files to the Windows 95 folder, you can run the applications. But usually, you have to reinstall your Windows 3.1 applications in Windows 95 before you can use them. You certainly need to reinstall an application if it uses features such as OLE. However, the application may not run in Windows 3.x when you do this.

The bottom line is that you need to find out for each Windows 3.x application whether or not it will run in both Windows 3.x and Windows 95 without installing the program twice. You should first try creating a shortcut to the application in Windows 95 and see if the application runs. If not, copy the initialization and support files to the Windows 95 folder and try again. If the application still won't run from Windows 95, reinstall it in Windows 95. Then, if the application doesn't run in Windows 3.x, you will have to reinstall from Windows 3.x, using a different directory than the one used when you installed it in Windows 95.

TROUBLESHOOTING

When you try to use the same application under both Windows 3.1 and Windows 95 on a dual-boot system, the application may "forget" changes you make in the application's user preference settings. If you change user settings in an application when running it under Windows 3.1, they may not be there when you run the application under Windows 95—and vice versa. Even though there's only one copy of the application on your hard disk, you may have two sets of the initialization files where user preference settings are stored; one each in the Windows 3.1 and Windows 95 folders. The application uses the settings from (and stores revised settings in) the initialization files it finds in the default Windows folder for the version of Windows you're running at the time. Unfortunately, there's no way to keep two sets of initialization files in sync automatically.

With some applications, however, you may be able to specify the location of the INI file, in which case you can point to one common INI file (in either the Windows 95 or Windows 3.1 folder). Another possible solution is to move the INI file to the application directory. And a third workaround is to specify the folder containing the INI file as the startup folder for that application.

Running Windows 3.1 Applications

After installing a Windows 3.1 application in Windows 95, you can launch and run the application just like any other Windows application. Windows 95 changes the application's appearance automatically, giving it the new Windows look (see Figure 47.2). The application window's title bar has the new format, complete with the new style of Minimize, Maximize, and Close buttons, and most buttons and other window elements take on the three-dimensional look.

Beneath the superficial appearance changes, the application works the same as it did under Windows 3.1. Windows 16-bit applications continue to use a shared memory space in Windows 95, so they can't preemptively multitask the way the newer 32-bit Windows 95 applications can. The application benefits from some Windows 95 performance improvements such as increased system resources, improved memory management using the Virtual Machine Manager, and some 32-bit Windows subsystems, including the print and communication subsystems. However, to take maximum advantage of the features and capabilities of Windows 95's 32-bit operating system, you must upgrade to a new version of the application. In the meantime, you can continue to use your 16-bit Windows 3.1 applications effectively and efficiently.

FIG. 47.2

Running a Windows 3.1 application in Windows 95 gives the program an automatic facelift. However, despite the change of appearance, the application performs the same as in Windows 3.1.

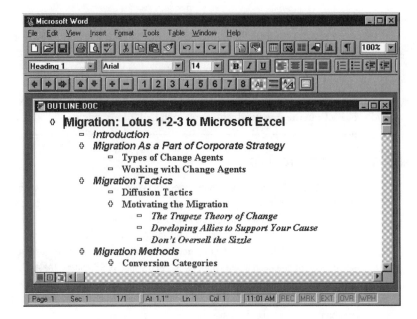

Installing Windows 95 Applications in Windows 95

To take full advantage of the improvements in performance that Windows 95 offers, you have to upgrade to the Win32-based versions of your applications. By doing this you will benefit in several ways.

One new feature of Windows 95 is an optional way to start an application's setup program: a new Install Programs Wizard accessible via the Add/Remove Programs icon in the Control Panel. The Add/Remove Programs dialog box provides a common starting point for adding and removing Windows applications and Windows system components and accessories.

To run the Install Programs Wizard and use it to install a Windows application, follow these steps:

1. Open the Start menu and choose Settings, Control Panel. This opens the Control Panel window shown in Figure 47.3.

2. In the Control Panel window, double-click Add/Remove Programs to open the Add/Remove Programs Properties sheet shown in Figure 47.4. By default, the Install/Uninstall tab is active.

3. To start the Install Program Wizard, choose Install.

4. When the Install Program from Floppy Disk or CD-ROM dialog box appears (see Figure 47.5), insert the application's distribution disk (the first floppy disk or CD) in the appropriate drive and click Next.

FIG. 26.3

The Windows 95 Control Panel contains a Wizard to make installing applications easier.

FIG. 26.4

The Add/Remove Programs Properties dialog box is the master control for adding and removing applications.

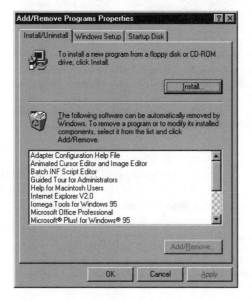

5. The Wizard searches the disk's root directory for an installation program (usually named SETUP.EXE or INSTALL.EXE) and displays the command line in the Run Installation Program dialog box (see Figure 47.6).

FIG. 26.5

The Install Program Wizard takes you through each installation step.

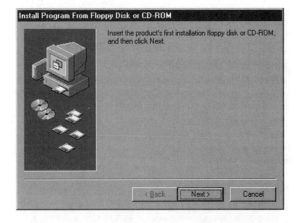

FIG. 26.6

Usually the Wizard finds the application's setup program on the disk.

6. If the Wizard fails to find the setup program (perhaps because it is in a subdirectory) or you want to run a different setup program (perhaps from a network drive), you can choose Browse and select a different file in the Browse dialog box (see Figure 47.7). Choose Open to insert the selected file name in the Wizard.

FIG. 26.7

If the Wizard needs help locating the setup program, you can browse for the correct file.

7. After the correct command line for the setup program appears in the Run Installation Program dialog box, click Finish to start the setup program and begin the application installation.

The application's setup program then installs the application. You'll need to respond to several prompts during the installation process. If the setup program includes a Windows 95-compatible uninstall feature, the Wizard notes this and adds the new application to a list of programs that you can remove automatically.

Adding Windows' Component Applications

The Add/Remove Programs icon in Control Panel lets you install and remove Windows components and accessories as well as applications. Therefore, you can reconfigure your copy of Windows 95 without reinstalling it.

Adding and Removing Windows Components

To use the Windows Setup feature to add or remove a Windows component, follow these steps:

1. Open the Start menu and choose Settings, Control Panel.

2. Open the Add/Remove Programs Properties sheet by double-clicking the Add/Remove Programs icon.

3. Click the Windows Setup tab to display a list of Windows components as shown in Figure 47.8.

FIG. 26.8

The Windows Setup page of the Add/ Remove Programs Properties sheet lets you add and remove parts of Windows.

Part
X

Ch
47

In the Components list box, a check mark next to an item indicates that the component is already installed on your system. If the check box is gray, the Windows component is composed of more than one subcomponent and some (but not all) subcomponents are currently installed. For instance, in Figure 47.8, only some of the subcomponents (accessories such as Calculator, Paint, and WordPad) of the accessories component are installed. To see what's included in a component, choose Details.

4. Select a component in the Components list box. The Description box in the lower portion of the dialog box displays a description of that component and tells you how many of the available subcomponents are selected.

5. If the component you selected consists of more than one subcomponent, choose Details to open a dialog box listing the subcomponents. (For example, Figure 47.9 shows the Accessories dialog box listing the subcomponents of the main Accessories component.) In some cases, a subcomponent will have additional subcomponents, which you can view by choosing Details again.

FIG. 26.9

The Accessories dialog box lists a component's parts. By choosing Details, you can narrow your selections.

6. Mark components for installation or removal by clicking the check box beside that item in the Components list. Adding a check mark to a blank check box marks that item for installation. Conversely, clearing a checked box instructs Windows to uninstall that component.

7. If you're selecting subcomponents in a dialog box you opened by choosing a Details button, click OK to close that dialog box and return to the Add/Remove Programs Properties sheet.

8. When the check marks in the Components lists specify the components that you want composing your Windows system, choose Apply in the Add/Remove Programs Properties sheet. You'll need to supply the Windows Setup disks or CD when prompted.

TROUBLESHOOTING

If you clear a check box for a component that was checked when you run Windows Setup, this tells Windows to remove the component, rather than to not install it. This can be confusing the first time you run Setup again to add new components. Leave those components that are already installed checked unless you want to uninstall them.

Installing Unlisted Components

Eventually, you might want to install a Windows component that doesn't appear on the Components list in the Windows Setup tab of the Add/Remove Program Properties sheet. For example, you might want to install one of the system-management utilities from the Windows 95 Resource Kit.

To install a Windows component not listed in the Components list box, open the Add/Remove Program Properties sheet, click the Windows Setup tab, and choose the Have Disk button at bottom of the dialog box. This opens the Install From Disk dialog box (see Figure 47.10).

FIG. 26.10

When adding Windows components from a supplemental disk, you must supply the full path to the correct INF file.

In the Copy Manufacturer's Files From field, specify the path to the setup information file (INF) for the Windows component that you want to install. (The setup information file tells Windows Setup what is available to install and how to do it.) You can either type the path and file name or choose Browse and select the file in the Browse dialog box. After specifying the correct path, click OK. Windows opens the Have Disk dialog box (see Figure 47.11), which lists the components available for installation. Check the ones that you want to install, then choose Install. You might have to supply disks and browse for needed files when prompted.

Windows not only installs the component, but also adds the component to the Components list in the Windows Setup tab. Later, you can remove the component just like any other in the list.

Installing components for DOS applications is different from the procedure used with Windows. In most cases, installing many of the major DOS applications requires suspending Windows 95 and switching to the "exclusive" DOS mode.

TIP   To get into DOS mode, click Start, Shut Down. When the Shut Down Windows dialog box appears, select Restart the Computer in MS-DOS Mode? Option and click Yes.

Part
X

Ch
47

FIG. 26.11

The Have Disk dialog box lists the Windows components available on the supplemental disk, or at least the components described in the INF file that you selected.

Running Applications

After you install the application's and Windows' accessories, Windows 95 gives you many options for launching them. The technique that you choose depends on your personal preferences, working style, and what you're doing at the time.

The various methods for launching applications are discussed in more detail in Chapter 43, "Windows Navigation Basics," and Chapter 44, "Managing Files." The following is a summary of the techniques:

- Choose the application's shortcut from the Start menu.

 To modify the properties of the shortcut for an application, right-click the shortcut and choose Properties. Select the Shortcut tab in the Properties dialog box. Here you can specify a folder for the application to start in and a shortcut key for starting or switching to the application from the keyboard. You can also specify whether you want the application to start in a window, maximized or minimized.

- Create and use a shortcut on the desktop.
- Right-click the application's icon in Windows Explorer or the My Computer window, then click Open in the context menu.
- Double-click the application's icon in the My Computer window or Windows Explorer.
- Choose the Run command from the Start menu and then type the path and file name of the application's executable file.
- Choose the Run command from the Start menu, then drag an EXE file from My Computer or Network Neighborhood and drop the file into the Run dialog box.
- Use the Windows 3.1 Program Manager and run the application by double-clicking its program item.

N O T E Windows 95 includes updated versions of both Program Manager and File Manager. The optional 3.1 interface adds applications to the Program Manager during installation. If you opt for the Windows 3.1 interface, you also can add program items to the Program Manager manually.

If you want to start Windows 95 in the Program Manager, you need to install Windows 95 using the Custom option. Choose User Interface in the Computer Settings dialog box and then choose Change. Select Windows 3.1 (Program Manager) and choose OK. If you have already installed Windows 95, add a shortcut to PROGMAN.EXE to the \WINDOWS\STARTUP folder. PROGMAN.EXE is located in the \WINDOWS\ folder. ■

- Open a document or data file associated with the application. When you open a file, Windows launches the application automatically and then opens the file in that application. There are as many ways to open files as there are ways to launch applications. For instance, you can open files in Explorer, by choosing a recently used file from the Documents submenu on the Start menu, or by double-clicking a shortcut on your desktop.

- For a bizarre twist, try this method of launching a Windows application. You can open an MS-DOS window and type the command at the DOS prompt to start the application. You would expect to get an error message saying the program requires Windows to run. But, instead, Windows 95 launches the Windows application for you. You must include the extension for the application's file name, otherwise Start will search for a folder matching the file name and open that folder in Explorer if it finds one. When you exit the Windows application, the DOS window will remain open.

- Finally, you can be in an MS-DOS window and open a document in a Windows application by typing the following:

  Start *pathname\documentname*.ext

  If the document has been registered with a Windows application, the application will open and the document will load.

T I P You can set up more than one association for any one file type. By doing this, you will have a choice in the context menu (the right-click menu) of which application you want to use when opening this type of file. You may, for example, want to be able to open an Excel XLS file with either Excel or 1-2-3. By default, when you right-click a file with the XLS extension in My Computer or Explorer and select Open, the file will be opened in Excel.

TROUBLESHOOTING

Windows 95 does not allow you to modify the properties of the actual EXE file for Windows applications. You can create a shortcut for the application and then use the Shortcut tab in the Properties dialog box for that shortcut to specify a working directory.

Part
X

Ch
47

Removing Windows Applications

Installing a Windows application can be a complicated venture. Windows applications are often tightly integrated with the operating system. Installing such applications not only requires copying the application's files into the application's own directory, but also adds numerous support files to your Windows directory and changes Windows' settings. Fortunately, nearly all applications provide setup programs to automate the installation process.

Removing an application can be similarly complicated. Finding all the support files and settings added or changed during the application's installation can be nearly impossible. Fortunately, many application setup programs now offer an uninstall option to automate the process when you need to remove the application from your system.

> **CAUTION**
>
> Even uninstall programs can lead to problems. If a program installed a DLL file that is also used by another program, when you uninstall the program, the DLL will be removed and then the remaining program won't run because of the missing file.

Windows 95 takes this welcome trend a step further by adding a facility to remove applications. That facility is in the same Control Panel dialog box that you use to install applications and Windows components.

Removing Applications Automatically

Windows 95's Add/Remove Programs Wizard adds to the capability of individual setup programs by tracking an application's components in the Registry. This lets Windows delete an application's files and settings but still identify and retain any files that another application might share and use.

> **N O T E** Only applications that provide uninstall programs specifically designed to work with Windows 95 appear in the Install/Uninstall tab of Add/Remove Programs. ■

 T I P Use the keywords *uninstall, deinstall,* and *remove* to search for uninstall instructions in the online Help for the application you want to remove. Search through the application directory for any README files that might describe how to remove a program.

To uninstall an application automatically, start by opening the Control Panel and double-clicking the Add/Remove Programs icon. This opens the Add/Remove Programs Properties sheet—the same sheet used to install the application (see Figure 47.12).

The lower portion of the dialog box lists applications that you can remove. To remove an application, select it from the list and choose Remove. After you confirm that you want to remove the program, Windows runs the selected application's uninstall program.

FIG. 26.12

In the Add/Remove Programs Properties sheet, you can remove applications as well as install them.

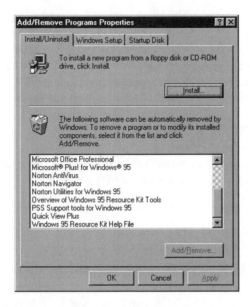

Removing Applications Manually

If you want to remove an application from your system, just hope that it's one that Windows can remove automatically. Removing an application manually can be difficult, and possibly dangerous. It is very difficult to know if a file you are deleting for one program is also used by another program. If you are not careful, you can end up disabling programs inadvertently and then have to reinstall them.

Removing Files from the Application Directory   Getting rid of the files in an application's own folder is fairly straightforward. In fact, that should probably be the first step in removing an application manually.

Many applications install support files in the Windows directories. It's nearly impossible to tell what application added which files, and to make matters worse, several applications can share the same files. If you ignore the files in the Windows folders when you remove an application, you can leave numerous orphaned files on your system needlessly consuming hard disk space. However, if you make a mistake and delete the wrong file or one that another application also uses, you might render the other application unusable.

If you find support files in your Windows folder that you think are unnecessary, copy them to a separate folder before you remove them. If you don't encounter any problems after a few months, you can delete that folder.

Removing Orphaned DLLs   *Dynamic link library files (DLLs)* are files associated with one or more applications that contain subroutines used by these applications. When you install a new application, chances are one or more DLLs are placed somewhere on your hard disk. Because there is no easy way to know to which application a particular DLL belongs, and where all the

Part

X

Ch

47

DLLs for an application are located, it is difficult to know what DLLs to get rid of when you manually uninstall an application. To make things more complicated, sometimes a DLL is used by more than one application, so if you delete that DLL when you remove one of those applications, you may adversely affect the other applications. This is a major benefit of having an automatic uninstall feature for a Windows application that knows what DLLs to remove when you remove the application.

 Never immediately delete a DLL after manually uninstalling a program. The DLL may be used by other programs that you aren't aware of. A safer practice is to copy the DLL to a disk and delete it from your hard disk. Make a small TXT file with the same name as the DLL telling from which directory the DLL was removed. If any program displays a message saying the DLL you removed is needed, you can copy it back to its original directory.

Here are a few tricks that can help you determine if it is safe to remove a DLL that you suspect is associated with an application you have removed and no longer needed:

- Right-click the DLL in Explorer or My Computer and choose Quick View. Look through the header information for clues indicating which applications use it. If it seems that the only application using the DLL is the one you removed, it is probably safe to delete the DLL.
- Search for references to the DLL in the headers of EXE files, using the Find command. Follow these steps to search through application headers:
    1. Click Start, Find, Files and Folders.
    2. Select the drive you want to search and type ***.DLL;*.EXE** in the Named text box. This tells Find to search for all files with either the DLL or EXE extension.
    3. Check the Include Subfolders option and make sure the Options, Case Sensitive option is not selected.
    4. Select the Advanced tab and type the name of the DLL you are checking for in the Containing text box. Do not include the file extension.
    5. Choose Find Now.

All EXE and DLL files containing the name of the DLL file you specified will be listed in the Find dialog box. If no files are found, you can feel reasonably secure about deleting the DLL.

Before you delete any DLL, even if one or both of the methods just described indicates that it is probably safe to do so, it is a good idea to rename the DLL or move it to a floppy disk. If you don't have any trouble running your applications for a period of time, you can get rid of the DLL. Otherwise, restore any DLLs that appear in error messages when you try to run an application.

There are several commercial utilities available for helping you uninstall applications, including MicroHelp's UnInstaller 32-bit, Quarterdeck's CleanSweep 95, and Vertisoft's Remove-It for Windows 95. Be sure to get the Windows 95 versions of these programs that are designed to modify the Registry when you uninstall a program. These utilities will also uninstall Windows 3.x programs.

Removing References to Applications in System Files   Often an application adds lines to the WIN.INI, SYSTEM.INI, CONFIG.SYS, and AUTOEXEC.BAT files when you install the application. This is mainly true for Windows 3.x applications, because the system information for Windows 95 applications is stored in the Registry. After you have removed an application, search through these files for references to the application. Delete these references to keep your system files from becoming cluttered with unused information.

> **CAUTION**
>
> You should always back up your system files before you edit them, in case you accidentally delete lines that affect how other programs run.

If you get an error message informing you that a particular file is missing after you have removed an application, it may be because there is still a reference to this file in one of the system files. Use Notepad to look through your system files for references to the deleted file.

 Click Start then Run and type **Sysedit** in the Open text box. The System Configuration Editor opens with windows displaying your WIN.INI, SYSTEM.INI, CONFIG.SYS, and AUTOEXEC.BAT files. You can view, edit, and save any of these files using the Sysedit.

Part
X

Ch
47

Removing Shortcuts and Folders from the Start Menu   After you remove an application's files from your hard disk, you want to get rid of any shortcuts that pointed to the application. To delete a shortcut icon from your desktop, simply drag and drop the shortcut onto the Recycle Bin icon on your desktop.

To remove the application from the Start menu, click the Start button and choose Settings, Taskbar. Then, in the Taskbar Properties sheet, click the Start Menu Programs page. Next, choose Remove to open the Remove Shortcuts/Folders dialog box (see Figure 47.13).

The Remove Shortcuts/Folders dialog box, like the Windows Explorer, displays a hierarchical list of folders and files. To expand the display and show a folder's contents, you can click the plus sign beside the folder. Select the folder or shortcut that you want to delete, then choose Remove. To remove other items, repeat the process as necessary. When you finish removing items, click Close.

Removing File Associations   After you remove an application, you can remove any associations that might have existed between file extensions and the defunct application. After all, you don't want Windows to try to launch the nonexistent application when you double-click a document file.

To remove the link between a file extension and an application, start by opening the My Computer window. Next, choose View, Options to open the Options dialog box, then click the File Types tab. You then see the screen shown in Figure 47.14. Scroll down the Registered File Types list and select the file type that you want to delete, then choose Remove. Windows asks you to confirm your choice. If you answer Yes, Windows abolishes the registration of that file type.

FIG. 26.13

After removing an application, open the Remove Shortcuts/ Folders dialog box to remove the application's folder and shortcuts from your Start menu.

FIG. 26.14

Using the Options dialog box to remove a file type registration is easier and safer than editing the Registry directly.

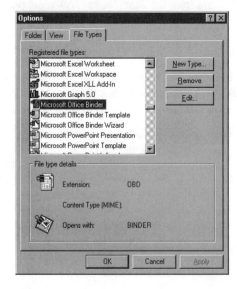

CHAPTER 48

Backing Up and Protecting Your Data

Part of any successful file management routine includes creating duplicate copies of data for backup. Virus protection is another critical component of good file management. *Viruses* are computer programs written for the purpose of interrupting or destroying your work.

The backup program that comes with Windows enables you to create backups onto a removable storage device such as floppy disks, a tape, or a removable hard disk. Windows does not include a virus protection program at this time, so you need to find a reliable third-party program that protects your system from this modern-day scourge. ∎

How to back up your files

Learn how to copy one or more files from your hard disk to another disk (usually a floppy disk, a tape drive, or another computer on your network).

How to verify that files are backed up correctly

This chapter explains how to compare files on your backup disks with the original files to ensure their validity.

How to use your backup files

Learn how to restore your backed-up files to any location you choose (including their original locations).

How to protect your system from viruses

This chapter discusses viruses and ways you can protect your system against them.

Backing Up Your Files

The Windows Backup program automatically creates a duplicate image of your hard disk's data on a magnetic tape or spreads an image across multiple floppy disks. During the backup operation, each disk in the set is filled to capacity before the next disk is requested. The collection of all these duplicates files and folders is referred to as the *backup set*.

As hard disks grow in capacity, it becomes more and more laborious to use floppy disks to back up your data. A much more convenient method is to use a tape backup system. You may be able to back up your entire hard drive with one tape. With tape backups, you also avoid the inconvenience of having to sit at your computer swapping floppy disks. In fact, you can initiate the backup when you leave for lunch; when you return, it will be done.

CAUTION

You put the entire concept of having secure data at risk if your backups are not kept in a safe location, physically separate from the original data. For a small company, the physical location for the backup set can be a safe deposit box or the president's house. For a large company, there are services that pick up tapes and store them in disaster-proof vaults. I personally know of two instances in which the backups were lost along with the original system. In one case, a thief stole the backup floppy disks that sat next to the computer. In the other case, the fire that destroyed the legal firm's computers also destroyed their backups, which were in a closet in an adjacent room.

N O T E   In the last few years, several new options for backing up large amounts of data have appeared on the market. The ubiquitous Iomega Zip drive is a very convenient way to back up moderate amounts of data (a Zip disk can hold 100M of data). Iomega's Jaz drive disks can hold up to 1G, ideal for today's large-capacity hard drives. Removable disk media such as these are much faster than tape drives and more convenient to use. Unlike the slow sequential file access on tape drives, the Iomega drives enable you to quickly access files randomly, like you do on a hard drive. Software for backing up your hard drives comes with both to these products. For more information, visit Iomega's Web site:

http://www.iomega.com/ ■

N O T E   Backup does not install as part of a typical or minimum installation. If Backup is not installed and you want it, refer to Chapter 47, "Installing, Running, and Uninstalling Windows Applications," on how to add programs. On the Windows Setup page of the Add/Remove Programs Properties sheet, look for Backup in the Disk Tools items in the Components list. ■

To start the backup program, open the Start menu and click Programs, Accessories, System Tools, and finally Backup. When you first start Backup, you may see a Welcome to Microsoft Backup dialog box that describes the process of making backups. You can select the Don't Show This Again check box if you don't want to see this dialog box again. You also may see a message box that reads `Backup has created a Full System Backup file set for you`. This means that until you specify otherwise, Backup marks all files and folders to be part of the backup. It's a very good idea to do a Full System Backup at least once a week or once a month, depending on the value of your data and how often program configurations change.

 T I P Create a Full System Backup occasionally. It has all the configuration and Registry files necessary to rebuild your system from a disaster.

Once you get past these initial dialog boxes, the Backup dialog box appears, as shown in Figure 48.1.

FIG. 48.1

Windows Backup creates duplicate copies of files and folders, compares backups to original files, and restores duplicate files and folders.

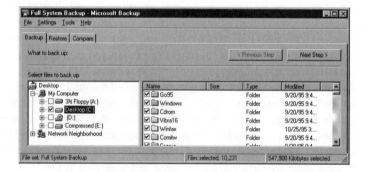

The three basic functions of Backup are divided into tabbed pages in the Backup dialog box:

- *Backup.* Copies one or more files and folders from your hard disk.

- *Compare.* Compares the files in a backup set to make sure that they match the source files on the hard disk.

- *Restore.* Copies one or more files from your backup set to the hard disk or to another floppy disk.

In addition to these major functions, several other operations can be accessed from the pull-down menus:

- The File menu enables you to load and save setup files that define settings to be used when backing up and restoring files. The File menu also enables you to print a list of files contained in a backup set.

- The Settings, File Filtering command enables you to filter the folders or file types you want to include in a backup set (this command is discussed in detail later in this chapter). Using the Settings, Options command, you can set various options for each of the major functions, as well as options that effect the program generally.

- The Tools menu contains commands for working with tapes.

Part

X

Ch

48

Understanding Backup

Before you implement a backup strategy, you need to understand the difference between *full* and *incremental* backups, the two types of backups that you can perform with Windows Backup. When you carry out a full backup, all files and folders on the selected drive are backed up. With a full backup set, you can completely restore your system to its original state in the event of a catastrophe. The disadvantages to a full backup are that it can take a lot of time and storage space if you have many files on your hard drive. The first step of your backup strategy, however, should include a full backup.

With an incremental backup, only those files that have changed since the last full or incremental backup (whichever was last), using the same backup set, are backed up. Typically, you start a backup cycle with a full backup and then periodically perform an incremental backup, using a different set of floppy disks or a new tape for each incremental backup. Each incremental backup set will contain only those files that have changed since the previous backup. If you need to completely restore your hard disk, you need the full backup set and all the incremental backup sets. The advantages of using incremental backups is that it takes much less time and less space than a full backup. The disadvantages are that you must use a new set of disks (or a new tape) each time you perform an incremental backup, and restoring your hard disk is more complicated, since you need to use each of the incremental backup sets, in addition to the full backup set, to be sure that you get the most recent version of a file.

> **CAUTION**
>
> To back up all the files you need to completely restore your system, including essential system files used by Windows 95, you need to use the *Full System Backup Set*. This is the only way to safely back up all the files you need to rebuild your system after a catastrophe. Selecting the drive you want to back up in the Select Files to Back Up pane *will not* back up important system files needed to fully restore your system.

N O T E   You may be used to using *differential backups* in your backup schedule. A differential backup backs up all files that have changed since the last *full* backup (not just the files that have changed since the last differential backup). Windows 95 does not support differential backups, so you will have to change your backup strategy to one using incremental backups. ■

 T I P   Creating a full backup is important to preserving your entire system. Full backups take care of merging Registry settings and the file replacements necessary when restoring a Windows system.

An Overview of How to Back Up Your Hard Disk

The Backup program makes it easy to name different sets of backup files so that you don't have to select the files and folders each time. When you aren't using your computer (at lunch time, when you return phone messages, or when you leave work), you can start a backup.

Here is the general procedure for creating a backup:

1. Have enough formatted floppy disks or tapes to store the backup.
2. Start Windows Backup.
3. Select the name of a backup set you previously created. Alternatively, manually select the drives, files, and folders you want to back up.
4. Select the Next Step button, then select the destination to which you want to back up—a tape, a floppy disk drive, or another hard disk.
5. Start the backup.

When Backup is finished, you should store the backup media in a safe location physically separate from the computers.

 TIP For an extensive list of tape drives compatible with Backup, choose Help, select the Contents tab, then select the Using Tapes for Backup item. You also find a list of drives that are not compatible with Backup.

Windows Backup supports the following tape drives and backup devices:

- Hard disks
- Network drives
- Floppy disks
- QIC 40, 80, and 3010 tape drives connected to a primary floppy disk controller
- QIC 40, 80, and 3010 tape drives, manufactured by Colorado Memory Systems and connected to a parallel port

 TIP If you own a tape drive manufactured by Colorado Memory Systems that is not supported by Windows 95 Backup, contact Colorado Memory Systems (970-669-8000) for information on a free upgrade to the backup software that came with your backup unit that is compatible with Windows Backup. Or, connect to Colorado's Web site at **http://www.hpcc920.external.hp.com/cms/index.htm**.

Backup supports compression using the industry-standard QIC-113 format. It can read tapes from other backup programs that use the same format with or without compression. Full backups can be restored to a hard disk of another type.

Part
X

Ch

48

Preparing a Backup Schedule

When you back up important or large amounts of data, it's important to have a backup schedule and a rotation plan for the backup tapes.

Basically, the backup schedule for most businesses should consist of a full system backup followed by incremental backups spread over time. Should your computer ever completely fail, you can rebuild your system using the full backup (restores Windows, the system Registry, all applications, and their data files as they existed on a specific date). You can then use the incremental backups (which store only changed files) to restore the latest versions of any files that changed after the full backup. Do a full system backup once a week and an incremental backup daily.

Never use one set of tapes for all your backups. If you have only one set of tapes, composed of a full backup and incrementals, creating another backup means that you overwrite one of the previous backups. Should the tape fail or the computer fail during backup, you might be left with no backups capable of restoring your system.

Some companies create a full system backup every day. At the end of the week, the tapes are taken to an offsite vault and a new set of tapes are started. Multiple sets of backup tapes are used and rotated between the onsite and offsite storage locations.

Backing Up Files

Running a backup operation consists of selecting the files you want to back up, specifying the destination for the backup files, and starting the backup. The files that you select for backup will be stored in a single backup file with the extension QIC. To perform a backup, follow these steps:

 TIP Whenever you frequently work with the same files and settings, save them as a file set.

1. Open the Start menu and click Programs, Accessories, System Tools, Backup.

2. Click the check box for the drive containing the files you want to back up in the left pane of the Backup window.

   In Figure 48.1, local drive C is selected. The files and folders on the drive are displayed in the right pane. You can expand and collapse the hierarchical display in the left pane by clicking the plus (+) and minus (−) signs next to the folders.

3. Select the files and folders you want to back up. If you want to back up using a file set you have previously named, choose File, Open File Set and select the file set you want to back up.

   You can select all the files in a folder by clicking the check box next to the folder's name in the left pane of the Backup dialog box.

   To view the files and folders inside a folder, in the left pane open the folder containing the folders or files you want to view, then in the left pane click the name of the folder whose contents you want to see; its contents are displayed in the right pane. You can then select individual files or folders inside that folder.

   To select the entire drive, click the box next to the drive in the left pane.

   If you select a folder with many files, a File Selection dialog box momentarily appears, notifying you that file selection is in progress; the box displays the number of files and their total size as the selection progresses.

The total number of files currently selected and their cumulative size appears in the status bar at the bottom of the window.

4. When you have finished selecting the files and folders you want to back up, click the Next Step button.

5. Select the destination for the backup files (see Figure 48.2).

   If you select a tape drive, the volume name for that tape appears in the Selected Device or Location box. If you select a disk drive, this box shows the drive letter or path, such as A:\.

FIG. 48.2

Select the destination for the files you want to back up.

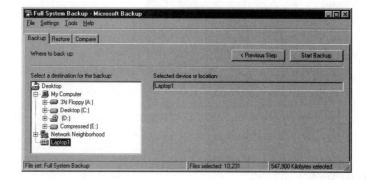

6. Save the file settings for this backup set if you will be doing this backup frequently.

7. Click the Start Backup button.

8. Type a name for the backup set in the Backup Set Label dialog box that appears (see Figure 48.3). This will be the name of the file containing all the files you have selected for backup.

   If you want to prevent unauthorized people from restoring the backup and stealing your data, click the Password Protect button in the Backup Set Label dialog box and enter a password.

   Give the backup set a meaningful name that will identify the data for you, in case you need to restore or compare it. Names can include spaces, symbols, and numbers. You may want to use a name such as **Accounting, full backup 5/10/97**.

CAUTION

If you forget the password you assign to your backup set, there is no way to use that backup set.

When you have specified a backup label and an optional password, choose OK. The Backup message box appears (see Figure 48.4), showing you the progress of the backup operation. You can cancel the operation by choosing the Cancel button.

If you are backing up to floppy disks, a message box prompts you when you need to insert the next disk, if necessary.

Part
X

Ch
48

FIG. 48.3

Name the backup set in the Backup Set Label dialog box.

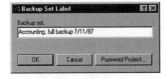

FIG. 48.4

You can monitor the progress of a backup operation in the Backup message box.

9. When the message box appears informing you that the backup operation is complete, click OK. Click OK again to return to the Backup dialog box.

TROUBLESHOOTING

Windows Backup does not support disk spanning with the Zip drive. In other words, if your backup set requires more than one Zip disk, Backup won't work. You can use the backup software that comes with your Zip drive to back up an entire disk onto Zip disks.

Using Backup to Create an Archive   The Backup program is a handy way to archive files. Suppose that you want to make room on your hard disk by deleting some files you aren't currently using but want to use at a later date. Use Backup to archive the files to floppy disks or a tape, then delete the files from the hard disk. If you need the files later, use the Restore function to put them back on your hard disk.

Using Backup to Copy Files to Another Computer   You also can use Backup to transfer folders and files to another computer. The benefit of using Backup for this task is that it takes care of spreading the files across multiple floppy disks when necessary, and it preserves the arrangement of folders so you can duplicate your folder organization on another computer. If you purchase a laptop, for example, you can use Backup to transfer the information on your desktop computer to the laptop, including the arrangement of your folders.

Scheduling Backups Using System Agent

You can schedule your backups to run automatically when you are not working with your computer using the System Agent that comes with Microsoft Plus! for Windows. The System Agent has a default schedule for running some of the disk utilities that come with Windows 95, so you can schedule additional programs to run at specified times. To schedule Backup to run automatically, follow these steps:

1. Create a backup set following the steps outlined in "Saving File Sets" later in this chapter.

   Before you save the backup set, choose Setting, Drag and Drop and clear the Confirm Operation Before Beginning and Quit Backup After Operation Is Finished options. Choose OK.

2. Exit Backup.

3. Click Start, Programs, Accessories, System Tools, and then System Agent.

4. Choose Program, Schedule a New Program.

5. Type the following in the Program text box:

   "C:\Program Files\Accessories\Backup.exe" C:\Program Files\ Accessories*setname.set*

   Setname.set is the name of the backup set you created.

6. Choose the When to Run button and schedule when you want Backup to run.

7. Exit System Agent.

Be sure to leave your computer running if you have scheduled Backup to run after you leave work. You can create two different schedules: one that does a full backup, perhaps once a week, and another that does daily incremental backups.

Changing Backup Settings and Options

You can change several settings and options that affect your backup operations. To change the settings and options for the backup operation, follow these steps:

1. Open the Settings menu and choose Options.

2. Click the Backup tab to open the dialog box shown in Figure 48.5.

3. Change or select from the following options and then choose OK:

FIG. 48.5

Use the Backup page in the Settings—Options dialog box to change the settings and options that affect the way backup operations work.

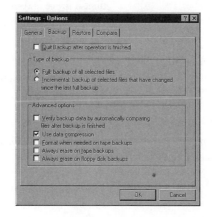

Part
X

Ch
48

Option	Function
Quit Backup After Operation Is Finished	Closes Backup when the backup operation is completed. Use this option when you use the System Agent to run automatic backups.
Full: Backup of All Selected Files	Backs up all selected files, regardless of whether the file has changed since the last backup. Use this option the first time you run a backup of your hard disk.
Incremental: Backup of Selected Files that Have Changed Since the Last Full Backup	Only backs up selected files that have changed since the last full backup. Use this option between full backups.
Verify Backup Data by Automatically Comparing Files After Backup Is Finished	Compares each file that is backed up with the original file to verify accurate backup.
Use Data Compression	Compresses files as they are backed up to allow more files to be backed up on a tape or floppy disk.
Format When Needed on Tape Backups	Automatically formats an unused tape before backup operation. This only works on tapes that have not already been formatted.
Always Erase on Tape Backups	Erases the tape on backup. When this option is not selected, backups are added to the tape if there is room.
Always Erase on Floppy Disk Backups	Automatically erases floppy disks before they are used in a floppy disk backup operation. When this option is not selected, backups are added to the floppy disk if there is room.

Saving File Sets

If you back up the same set of files regularly, you can save the settings for that file set. Saving backup settings saves you the trouble of reselecting the files and destination each time you want to back up the files.

To save a file set, follow these steps:

1. Open the Backup dialog box and in the Backup page select the files you want to back up, as described earlier in this chapter. Click the Next Step button.

2. Select the destination for the backup files from the Select a Destination list.

3. Choose File, Save As. The Save As dialog box appears (see Figure 48.6).

FIG. 48.6

Name your file set with a recognizable name for what it contains and when it was created.

4. Type a name for the backup set in the File Name text box.

5. Choose the Save button.

6. Choose the Start Backup button if you want to continue the backup operation and create a backup using the file set you just specified.

If you make changes to an existing file set, choose the File, Save command to save the file set with the same name without opening the Save As dialog box.

To open a file set for use in a backup operation, follow these steps:

1. Open the Backup dialog box, then click the Backup tab. Choose File, Open File Set to display the Open dialog box shown in Figure 48.7.

FIG. 48.7

Open a file set to use in a backup or restore operation from the Open dialog box.

Part
X

Ch
48

2. If you can't see the file set you want to open, open the folder that contains the file set.

3. Select the file set and choose Open.

The file set is opened, and the files named in this file set are selected in the Backup dialog box.

TROUBLESHOOTING

After setting up a backup set and performing the backup, you might be unable to save the settings for the backup set. You need to save the backup set after you have selected the files to backup and the destination for the backup but before you start the backup. Once you start the back up by clicking the Start button, you will not be able to save the file set.

Filtering Folders and File Types Included in Backup Operations

Backup's file filtering commands enable you to filter out specific folders and types of files so they are not included in the backup set. These commands can save you a lot of time when you are creating a file set to be backed up.

You may not want to include all the files on your hard disk in a backup operation. If you want to back up all but a few folders, you need only specify the folders you *don't* want to include in the backup set. In most cases, you don't need to include program files in your daily backups, because you can always reinstall your programs if your system crashes. You can dramatically reduce the number of disks you use in a backup if you limit the file set to data files only.

To exclude files of a specific type or date from a backup, follow these steps:

1. Choose Settings, File Filtering. The File Filtering—File Types dialog box appears, as shown in Figure 48.8.

FIG. 48.8

You can exclude files of a specific type or files with specific dates.

2. To exclude files modified between two dates, select the Last Modified Date check box. Enter From and To dates that *exclude* the files you do not want copied.

TIP

If you want to exclude all but a few of the file types in the File Types list, click Select All, hold the Ctrl key, and click the types of files you don't want to exclude.

3. To exclude specific file types from the backup operation, select the types of files you want to exclude from the File Types list and click Exclude. Continue to select file types and click the Exclude button until all the file types you want to exclude appear in the Exclude File Types list at the bottom of the dialog box.

   To select all of the file types in the list, click Select All.

4. To delete a file type from the list in the Exclude File Types box, select the file type and click Delete.

5. To clear the Exclude File Types box, click Restore Default.

6. When you finish making your selections, choose OK.

Changing the General Settings in Backup

You can change two options in Backup that affect the backup, restore, and compare functions. To change these options, choose Settings, Options. Select the General tab to open the dialog box shown in Figure 48.9.

- Select the Turn on Audible Prompts option if you want to hear beeps from your computer's speaker during backup, compare, and restore operations.

- Select the Overwrite Old Status Log Files option to replace the old status log with the new one generated by the current backup. The status log records errors and completions of file backups.

FIG. 48.9
Use the General page in the Settings—Options dialog box to change the settings and options that affect the way Backup's operations work.

Backing Up with a Simple Drag-and-Drop

Drag-and-drop is an easy way to back up your files if you have created file sets (as described earlier in this chapter in the section "Saving File Sets"). You can drag a file set and drop it onto the Backup icon, or you can double-click a file set name. Either of these actions immediately starts the backup. With the appropriate settings, the entire backup operation can go on in the background and you can continue to use the computer for other tasks.

T I P Backing up data is so important that if you are an experienced Windows user, you may want to set up other users' computers with drag-and-drop backup so that they can easily protect their data.

To prepare Backup for drag-and-drop operation, follow these steps:

1. Choose Settings, Drag and Drop to open the Settings—Drag and Drop dialog box shown in Figure 48.10.

FIG. 48.10

Change the Backup settings to make drag-and-drop backup operate in the background while you work.

2. Change or select from the following options and then choose OK.

Option	Function
Run Backup Minimized	After dragging a file set onto the Backup icon, the Backup window minimizes.
Confirm Operation Before Beginning	Displays a message showing which files will be backed up. Asks you to confirm that you want the files backed up.
Quit Backup After Operation Is Finished	Quits Backup after the file set is backed up. Use this option when you use the System Agent to run Backup automatically.

If Backup is operating in the background, you do not see it as a window on-screen. If you need to stop a backup that is in the background, display the taskbar and click the Backup button. A dialog box displays the current backup status and gives you the opportunity to cancel the backup.

N O T E If you have multiple file sets, but you don't want them all as shortcuts on your desktop, you can still start them quickly to do a backup. In the Windows Explorer or My Computer window, double-click the name of the file set you want to back up. You are prompted whether you want to make a backup; the backup runs with the settings specified for that file set. ■

Before you can create backups with a drag-and-drop procedure, you must display the Backup program icon. You can open the Program Files\ Accessories folder in a window in Windows Explorer or My Computer. A more convenient method is to create a shortcut to BACKUP.EXE and display it on your desktop.

If you also want a quick way to find and display the SET files that specify your file sets, create a shortcut to the directory containing the SET files. Use the Find command (available on the Start menu) to find all files that end with SET, then create a new folder and drag the SET files into the new folder. Now create a shortcut to this folder and put that shortcut on the desktop (see Figure 48.11).

FIG. 48.11
Once drag-and-drop is enabled, backing up is as easy as dropping a file-set icon onto the Backup shortcut.

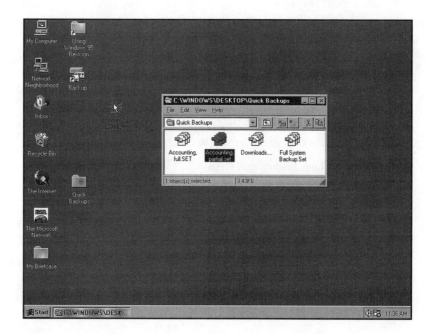

N O T E Normally, the file sets are stored in the Program Files\Accessories folder. ■

To back up a file set, you only need to double-click the shortcut to the folder containing the file sets. This opens the folder containing the file sets as a Window on your desktop. Figure 48.11 shows such an open folder. Now drag the file set you want to back up onto the shortcut to BACKUP.EXE and drop it. You are prompted whether you want to continue with the backup operation. Respond by clicking Yes or No.

Part
X

Ch
48

Formatting and Erasing Tapes

If you use tapes to do your backups, Backup includes two tools for working with tapes. When you purchase a new tape, you must format the tape before you can use it, just as you format a floppy disk. The Format Tape command formats a tape for you. If you want to erase the contents on a tape before you use it for a new backup operation, you can use the Erase Tape command.

To format a tape, follow these steps:

1. Insert the tape in the tape drive.

2. Open the Backup dialog box and choose Tools, Format Tape. If the Format Tape command is grayed out, choose the Redetect Tape command, which enables Backup to detect the tape.

3. When the Format Tape dialog box appears, type a name for the tape and choose OK. You use this name to identify the tape relative to other tapes you use.

    Formatting begins. The progress of the formatting operation is displayed in the Format Tape dialog box. Formatting a tape can take a long time; you may want to start the formatting operation when you are going to be away from your desk for an extended period.

4. When the message box appears telling you the operation is complete, choose OK. Choose OK again to return to the Backup dialog box.

To erase a tape, follow these steps:

1. Insert the tape in the tape drive.

2. Open the Backup dialog box and choose Tools, Erase Tape. If the Erase Tape command is grayed out, choose the Redetect Tape command, which enables Backup to detect the tape.

3. Choose Yes when the confirmation message box appears. The progress of the erase operation is displayed in the Erase dialog box.

4. When the message box appears telling you the operation is complete, choose OK. Choose OK again to return to the Backup dialog box.

Restoring Files

You can restore all the files from a backup set or select specific files or folders to restore. You also can choose where you want to restore the files.

To restore files, follow these steps:

1. Open the Backup dialog box and click the Restore tab (see Figure 48.12).

2. Select the drive containing the backup files from the left panel of the window.

3. Select the backup set containing the files you want to restore from the right pane. If you have more than one backup file on a floppy disk or tape, select the one containing the files you want to restore. A single backup file, with the extension QIC, contains the files you backed up.

4. Click the Next Step button.

5. Select the folders or files you want to restore as shown in Figure 48.13.

FIG. 48.12

In the Restore page of the Backup dialog box, select the files you want to restore.

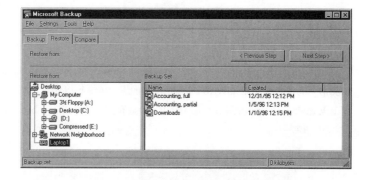

FIG. 48.13

You can select all or part of a backup set when you restore.

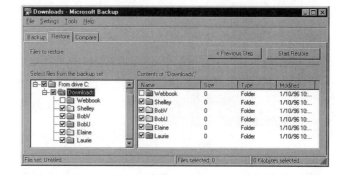

6. Click the Start Restore button. The Restore message box appears, showing you the progress of the restore operation (see Figure 48.14).

   By default, the files are restored to their original location. You can choose to restore the files to another location by changing one of the restore options, as described next.

FIG. 48.14

The Restore message box keeps you informed about how the restore operation is progressing.

7. When the Operation Complete message box appears, choose OK.

Restoring Files to Other Locations

You can restore files to locations other than their original location (the location from which they were initially backed up). To restore files to an alternate location, follow these steps:

1. Choose Settings, Options.

2. Click the Restore tab.

3. Select the Alternate Location option and choose OK.

4. Perform steps 1 through 6 of the restore procedure described in the preceding section (stop just before you have to click the Start Restore button).

5. Click the Start Restore button. The Browse for Folder dialog box appears (see Figure 48.15).

FIG. 48.15

Select the location to which you want to restore files from the File Redirection box.

6. Select the location to which you want to restore the files and choose OK.

7. When the Operation Complete message box appears, choose OK.

Changing Restore Settings and Options

You can change several settings and options that affect your restore operations. To change the settings and options for the restore function, follow these steps:

1. Choose Settings, Options.

2. Click the Restore tab to open the dialog box shown in Figure 48.16.

3. Change or select from the following options and then choose OK.

Option	Function
Quit Backup After Operation Is Complete	Closes Backup when the restore operation is completed. Use this option if you use the System Agent to run the restore operation automatically.
Original Locations	Restores files to their original locations.
Alternate Location	Restores files to an alternate location. (See "Restoring Files to Other Locations" earlier in this chapter.)

Alternate Location, Single Directory	Restores files to a single directory at an alternate location. Doesn't duplicate original folder structure.
Verify Restored Data by Automatically Comparing Files After the Restore Has Finished	Compares each file to the file on disk or tape after it is restored to check for accuracy of restore.
Never Overwrite Files	Files that are already on the destination location are not overwritten during a restore operation.
Overwrite Older Files Only	Only files that are older than the files in the backup set are overwritten during a restore operation.
Overwrite Files	All files are overwritten during a restore operation. Use the Prompt Before Overwriting Files check box to specify whether you want to be prompted before a file is overwritten.

FIG. 48.16

Use the Restore page in the Settings–Options dialog box to change the settings and options that affect the way restore operations work.

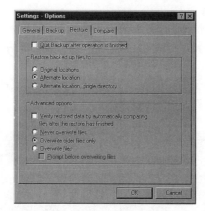

TROUBLESHOOTING

If you restored your system using Full System Backup.Set, some of your settings, such as the icon arrangement on my desktop and the custom colors you had selected, might not have been properly restored. Some custom settings, including settings for colors, sounds, desktop themes, icon arrangement, and pointers, are saved in the Registry each time you shut down and restart Windows 95. When you do a full system restore, the original custom settings are restored in the Registry, but they are

continues

continues

overwritten by the current settings (the default settings) when you restart your computer after the restoration. You must manually restore these custom settings. A few other settings, namely the desktop pattern, wallpaper, and screen saver, will be properly restored only if you restart your computer immediately after you finish the restoration. Otherwise, these settings will automatically be overwritten by the default settings.

Verifying Backup Files

The first time you use a series of disks or a tape for a backup, or any time you want to be absolutely sure of your backup, you should do a comparison. When you compare backups to the original files, you verify that the backup copies are both readable and accurate. To perform a compare, follow these steps:

1. Open the Backup dialog box and click the Compare tab.
2. From the left pane of the dialog box, select the device containing the backup files you want to compare (see Figure 48.17).
3. From the right pane, select the backup set containing the files you want to compare.
4. Click the Next Step button.
5. Select the files or folders you want to compare to the original files.
6. Click the Start Compare button. The Compare message box informs you of the progress of the compare operation.
7. Choose OK when the Operation Complete message box appears; choose OK again to return to the Backup dialog box.

FIG. 48.17
Use the Compare function to verify the accuracy of your backup operations.

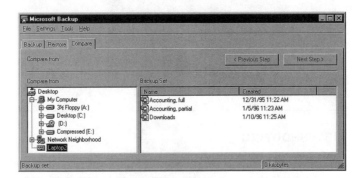

Changing Compare Settings and Options

You can change several settings and options that affect your compare operations. To change the settings and options for the compare function, follow these steps:

1. Choose Settings, Options.
2. Click the Compare tab to open the dialog box shown in Figure 48.18.

FIG. 48.18

Use the Compare page in the Settings—Options dialog box to change the settings and options that affect the way compare operations work.

3. Change or select from the following options and then choose OK.

Option	Function
Quit Backup After Operation Is Finished	Closes Backup when the compare operation is completed. Use this option if you use the System Agent to run the compare operation automatically.
Original Locations	Compare files to files at their original locations.
Alternate Location	Compares files to files at an alternate location.
Alternate Location, Single Directory	Compare files to files in a single directory at an alternate location. Doesn't look for duplicates of the original folder structure.

Protecting Your Files from Viruses

You need to take measures to protect your computer from viruses, a scourge of the modern-day computer world. In addition to backing up your system regularly, you should obtain an anti-virus program and make a habit of using it on a regular basis to protect your files against infection, especially if you frequently introduce files onto your hard disk from outside sources.

Understanding How Viruses Damage Your Computer

A *computer virus* is a program designed to do damage to either your computer or your computer's data. Viruses make copies of themselves and spread from one computer to another.

There are three ways in which viruses can be transmitted between computers:

■ Loading and running infected software

■ Booting up with an infected floppy disk

■ Opening a document or template file that has a macro virus attached to it

Part
X

Ch
48

It used to be the case that viruses were only transmitted by one of the first two routes. With the arrival of macro viruses, it has become much more difficult to insulate your system from viruses. Now you can get a virus by simply opening an infected Word for Windows or Excel document or template file. If there is a macro virus attached to the document, all the documents you open from that point on will become infected with the virus. If you commonly exchange documents with other users, you must take precautions against this new type of virus.

The best approach for protecting yourself against viruses is to install one of the anti-virus programs that are available. Used correctly, a good anti-virus program can protect you against the vast majority of known viruses before they damage your computer. Symantec's Norton Anti-Virus for Windows and McAfee Associates' VirusScan are well-respected virus protection programs. Both of these companies provide virus-definition updates that you can download from their Web sites to protect your system against the many new viruses that are constantly arriving on the computing scene.

ON THE WEB

Visit the following Web sites for more information on the preceding products:

http://www.symantec.com

http://www.mcafee.com

TROUBLESHOOTING

If you use the Full System Backup.Set backup set to restore files, the system Registry files are restored automatically, regardless of which files you select for restoration. This backup set is designed to fully restore your system in the event of a disaster. You need to create another backup set that does not include the system files. You can create a backup set for all the files on your hard disk, excluding the system files, by selecting the drive in the Select Files to Back Up pane. You can then do partial restores from this set without restoring the system files.

ON THE WEB

For an excellent selection of links to anti-virus software sites, connect to the Web at

http://www.primenet.com/~mwest/software.htm

PART XI

Appendixes

A Tips and Tricks for System Administrators   1039

B The CD-ROM   1051

C Business Sites on the Web   1055

Tips and Tricks for
System Administrators

If you are an administrator responsible for the deployment and support of Microsoft Office 97, there's some information about the product and also about the product's relationship to the operating system that you might find useful.

Office 97 runs on Windows 95, Windows NT 3.51 (with SP 5 installed), and Windows NT 4 (SP 2 recommended). Client computers must have a 486 or higher processor and meet the following minimum requirements for RAM to run a single Office application with no other applications running: 8M RAM for Windows 95, 16M RAM for Windows NT. Because it would be highly unusual to establish workstation configurations that expected users to single-task, you should plan on a configuration of 16M RAM for Windows 95 and 32M RAM for Windows NT for efficiency. Actually, my own recommendation is to double these numbers for real productivity.

For clients running Windows 95 and Windows NT 4, Microsoft Office 97 supports profiles, and you can use the Policy Editor to establish options such as default file-saving types throughout the organization.

The Office 97 Resource Kit comes with a number of template files with system policies that can be useful for customizing Office installations. The templates include policies for default file types when saving, messages about policies that appear in the Office Assistant cue cards, pointers to network paths for shared files such as templates, and other handy policy changes. ■

Installation

If you want to roll out Office from a network installation point, it's a good idea to invest in the Office 97 Resource Kit in order to get your hands on the Network Installation Wizard. This is a safe way to change the information in the .INF and .STF files for a customized setup.

> **CAUTION**
>
> Don't try to modify the .INF and .STF files yourself, even though they look like ASCII files. They are formatted very precisely with tabs, position of text, and so on.

The .INF file holds configuration details about the following installation procedures (this is not a complete list):

```
[Source Media Descriptions]
<disk number>, <disk label>, <file>, <path>
[Default File Settings]
INF FILES AND INSTALLATION
[Languages]
[Setup Files - Core]
[Setup Files - Network]
[Setup Files - Admin]
[RMapiNT Setup]
[RMapi95 Setup]
[Setup Files - NonAdmin]
[DA ODBC 32 bit]
[Help PSS]
[VBA 94 Files]
[PPT Typical Design Templates Typical]
[User Files]
[Admin Workdir Files]
[AccIA95 Templates]
[Lotus Notes Converter]
[Spell]
[Hyphenation]
[Acc Language Ref]
[VBA ACC Help]
[VBA ACC Remove]
[Acc Sample Apps]
[Nwind HTML]
[Acc User Assistance]
[Acc Wizards]
[Acc Wiz Data]
[dbwiz bmps]
[styles bmps]
[Acc Help Core]
[Grammar]
```

```
[Thesaurus]
[Equation Editor]
[Fonts]
[Templates]
[Text Converters]
[Wizards]
[VBA 97 Help]
[EXCEL Main Files]
[Excel Template Document]
[EXCEL Briefcase Files]
[Retain Previous Gallary Default]
[Delrina Fax]
[Clean XL Start]
[MAPI]
[EXCEL Main Help]
[EXCEL Main Help TBR]
[EXCEL VBA Help]
[EXCEL VBA Help TBR]
[EXCEL Examples]
[Data Map Main]
[Data Map Data]
[Data Map Font]
[Data Map Help]
[Unicode Wrapper]
[DA ODBC Thunking]
[EXCEL ODBC Add-in]
[EXCEL Query]
[EXCEL Query Add-in]
EXCEL Query Help and Cue Cards]
[DA ISAM Excel]
[DA ISAM Text]
[DA ISAM xBase]
[DA Brazos ISAM dBase Installer]
[DA Brazos ISAM Excel Installer]
[DA Brazos ISAM FoxPro Installer]
[DA Brazos ISAM Text Installer]
[DA SQL Server]
[Code Page Translator]
[EXCEL dBase Examples]
[DA Brazos Help]
[EXCEL Templates
[EXCEL Access Link]
[EXCEL Analysis ToolPak]
[EXCEL Autosave]
[EXCEL Lookup]
[EXCEL File Converter Macro]
[EXCEL Sum If]
[EXCEL Report Manager]
[EXCEL Solver]
[EXCEL Template Wizard]
[EXCEL Update Links]
[EXCEL Quattro Pro Converter]
[PPT8 Help]
[PPT8 vba]
[PPT8 vba TBR]
[Macro Template Support]
```

continues

continued

```
[Macro Templates]
[Translators]
[Geniographics
[WP Help]
[Winword Help]
[Word Sched Converter]
[Word Address Conv]
[Org Chart]
[Acc Calendar OCX]
[Acc Cal OCX help]
[Brief Replication Files]
[PPT8 Typical Content Templates Reg]
[PPT8 Typical Content Templates]
[PPT8 Content Web Pages Templates]
[PPT8 Additional Content Templates Reg]
[PPT8 Additional Content Templates]
[Acc Wiz Dev]
[Acc Min Wizards]
[DbWiz Templates]
[Word Forms]
[Acc Exe Last]
[Clipart Setup]
[PPT8 Popular ClipArt Files1]
[Truetype Fonts]
[Exchange Server1]
[Holidays and Forms]
[rhelp_help]
[Lotus Organizer]
[Lotus Organizer Converters]
[RMapi95 MSMAIL4]
[RMapiCommon ConfigFiles]
[RMapi95 MAPI]
[RMapi95 SystemFiles]
[RMapi95 HELP]
[RMapi95 Win95Help]
[RMapiCommon MSMAIL4]
[RMapiNT MSMAIL4]
[RMapiNT MAPI]
[RMapiCommon MAPI]
[RMapiCommon SystemFiles]
[RMapiNT HELP]
[RMapiCommon Win95Help]
[RMapiCommon Win95Help Admin]
[Sched Plus Core]
[Old Msmail Files]
[Old Msmail WinDir Files]
[Old Msmail SysDir Files]
[Help Core]
[DA Convdsn]
[DSN Remove]
[Clipart Cags]
[ArtGallery]
[EXCEL WEB FORM]
[EXCEL HTML]
```

```
[EXCEL HTML DLL]
[Graphics Filters]
[Graph Core Files]
[Graph Gallery File]
[Graph VBA Help Files]
[Graph VBA Help Files TBR]
[Graph Help Files]
[Graph Help Files TBR]
[Office AutoCorrect List]
[VBA Office Help]
[MS Info]
[EMail Template]
[Word Borders]
[Word Main Files]
[Word Mail Templates]
[Word Mail OFTs]
[Word VBA Help]
[Word Web Core]
[Word Web Template]
[Word Web Help]
[Word Web Help Cleanup]
[Word Web Styles]
[Word Web Forms]
[Word Web Dialogs]
[Word Backgrounds]
[Word Bullets]
[Word Lines]
[Word Web OCX]
[Word Web TWD]
[Run Query Files]
[Binder Files]
[Binder Help Files]
[Binder VBA Help Files]
[Binder Help Companion Files]
[Binder Help Remove]
[Binder Sys]
[Binder Templates]
[DA MSVCRT]
[Outlook Templates]
[Office DLLs]
[Internet-Lycos]
[Office System]
[MOM Files]
[Office Help]
[Online Docs]
[PPT Sounds]
[PPT8 xlators]
[PPT8 reg files]
[PPT8 system files]
[PPT8 blank presentation]
[PPT8 core files]
[PPT8 content templates]
[PPT8 design templates]
[ppview32.exe]
[PPT Web Files]
[Bookshelf Truetype Fonts]
```

continues

continued

```
[Bookshelf 96 SRG]
[Bookshelf Shared Files]
[Bookshelf 96 Integration Files]
[Bookshelf Book Files]
[Bookshelf Bookmm1 Files]
[VBA Files]
[VBE Files]
[Imager Files]
[Imager Effects]
[Imager SelfReg File]
[Imager Help Files]
[Imager Sys]
[Custom Dictionary]
[rcore_sound]
[rcore_group]
[rcore_recall]
[rcore_convert]
[rcore_headers]
[rcore_addins]
[rcore_singles]
[rcore_readme]
[Old Outlook Files]
[rcore_schdplus_shortcuts]
[rcore_mailrec_shortcuts]
[File Open Indexer]
[DA DAO]
[DA DAO Help]
[MFC First]
[Word Mail]
[Office Assistant ACT Files]
[Office Assistant ACP Files]
[Office Assistant ACT Files Admin]
[Ie30]
[Msroute]
```

The .STF file controls the installation configuration, displays installation messages, and imports information to the Registry.

The Network Installation Wizard walks you through the decision-making process (changing the data in the .INF file) and when you approve the final decisions, the .STF file is modified.

> **CAUTION**
>
> If you choose to customize your installation with the Network Installation Wizard, be sure to back up the .INF and .STF files before beginning.

You can give your modified .STF file a new name, but you cannot change the name of the .INF file (the .STF file refers to it). Then tell your client installation setup procedure the name of the .STF file to use. You have three choices for performing a network-based installation to your client machines:

- *Interactive*, in which client users connect to your network installation point and run Setup. The information and defaults that are displayed reflect any changes you've made with the Network Installation Wizard.
- *Batch*, in which you run a batch file for Setup that uses your customized .STF file. The client user begins the set process by running the batch file, and all the .STF file information is used for default settings. The client user does not participate in the decisions.
- *Push*, in which you initiate Setup from the network to the client workstation. The easiest way to establish a Push installation is to put the Setup command into logon scripts.

You can run Setup from the command line (choose Run on the Start menu or Program Manager) with parameters that specify options. Some of the parameters you might have a need for are:

/a	Create administrative installation point (run from CD only).
/b *number*	Skip the Setup dialog box and use the number to indicate the installation type: 1=Typical; 2=Custom; 3=Run from CD or Run from Network Server.
/c *"number"*	Skip the Product ID for OEM Certificate dialog box and use the number you specify in the parameter.
/f	Create all files with 8.3 format instead of long file names.
/g(+) *"file"*	Generate a log file to record details of the Setup process. If (+) is specified, append new information to any existing log file instead of overwriting.
/gc(+) *"file"*	Same as /g but adds all calls and returns from any custom actions to the log (the log file can be extremely large with this parameter enabled).
/k *"number"*	Skip the 11-digit CD key dialog box and enter the number specified in the parameter.
/n *""*	Forces a prompt for a user name when no default user name exists in the Registry.
/n *"name"*	Specifies the user name to use when no default user name exists in the Registry.
/o *""*	Prompts for an organization name when none exists in the Registry.
/o *"name"*	Specifies the organization name to use when no default organization names exist in the Registry.
/q *{option}*	Specifies the level of user interaction for batch mode installations: 0=no dialog boxes except for final one; 1=no dialog boxes; t=no Setup user interface elements appear.
/r	Reinstall an application (maintenance mode only).
/s *"folder"*	Overrides default source with the specified folder.

continues

continued

/u	Removes Office and prompts for removal of shared components.
/u {a}	Removes Office; shared components are removed without prompting.
/x "*file*"	Creates network installation log file which tracks the number of installations made from the administrative installation point (overriding any values in the .STF file).
/y	Proceeds as if installing, setting Registry entries, but copies no files to the user's disk (use to restore Registry values).

Workgroup Administration of Applications

Sharing applications and application documents across the network is a basic need, and administrators should have some understanding about the way Office 97 implements these features.

Access Workgroup Administration

Access has a great deal of built-in security that can be used to protect databases. Depending upon your needs, you can use security measures that range from casual to extremely strict.

Secure Startup Options   *Startup options* are one good way to restrict access to various menu and toolbar functions. To impose startup options, you must first create a startup form and a custom menu bar. Then you can use the Startup dialog box—accessed from the Tools menu—to restrict access:

- In the Display Form box, enter the name of your startup form.
- In the Menu Bar box, specify the name of your menu bar.
- In the Advanced section (click Advanced to get there), deselect all but the following: Display Status Bar, Allow Viewing Code After Error.
- Use Visual Basic to set AllowBypassKey to False so that users cannot use the Shift key to bypass the Startup settings.

Password Protect Databases   *Database passwords* are an easy and common way to enforce document protection, but there are some perils:

- Forgetting the password is fatal. Keep a list of database names and associated passwords. (Don't tape the list to your monitor; that sort of kills the whole point.)
- You cannot synchronize a replicated database that has a password.

Protect Source Code   To protect source code, save the copy of the database that is used by clients as an .MDE file. This eliminates the VB source code. The code is compiled and works just fine. Make sure you have a copy of the full database, complete with code, in some secure place.

> **CAUTION**
>
> The real problem with an .MDE file is when it is used for a database with tables and you need to modify the design. It's best to use .MDE files for front-end structures (tables go into the back-end).

Encrypt Databases   You can encrypt a database with the User-Level Security Wizard. If you encrypt the database using the same file name, the original file is deleted once the encryption process has completed successfully (it is not deleted if there are any errors).

There are two problems with encrypted databases:

- Working with the database is quite a bit slower.
- You cannot compress it with programs such as WinZip. (Well, you can run the compression without error, but the size of the file is the same after you've finished compressing it).

Workgroup Permissions   Microsoft Access employs user-level security procedures rather than share-level, similar to the way your Windows NT network is secured. Permissions are assigned to the objects in a database (including the database itself). When a user accesses any object (form, table, or so on), the user permission for the object is checked. (Wait, there is one share-level security measure—password protection for a database.)

The information about users, groups, and their associated permissions is held in the *workgroup information file*. This file contains the names of users, groups (including the users that make up each group), the logon password for each user, and the SID of each user and group. (*SID* is a machine-generated binary string that identifies a user or group as a unique entity.) The location of the workgroup information file is stored in the Windows Registry.

The workgroup information file is created with the Workgroup Administrator (WRKGADM. EXE) which is found in \%Windows95root%\System or \%WindowsNTRoom%\System32.

Locking Options   By default, when you turn on locking, Access does not really lock records (even though the specifications call it a record-locking application). It really locks a 2K page of records (2,048 bytes to be exact) which may actually overlap multiple records. In a network environment, you might want to open recordsets differently, using one of these options:

- *No Locks*, which means locking is only in effect at the moment a record is saved. If two users are editing a record simultaneously, when they attempt to save the changes the first one there wins. The second user is notified and can either discard the changes or wait and look at the newly saved data and begin editing again. This locking method is called *optimistic locking*.
- *Edited Record Lock*, which means a record is locked when a user begins to edit it. However, it is not the record that is locked; it is the page containing that record, so there is every chance additional records may be locked. This locking method is called *pessimistic locking*.
- *All Records Lock*, which locks everything. This is most useful if you are performing frequent batch updates (and also when you are doing maintenance on tables).

You can also set locking defaults for the individual objects in a database (use the Tools, Options dialog box).

Excel Workgroup Administration

Excel 97 has some security features you can implement over and above any security you want to impose from the operating system level. However, all security for Excel documents is shared-level; there is no user-level security available (unlike Access). For a large multi-user environment, this does not offer the most robust level of security.

The RC4 encryption routine is available with Excel 97, which is more robust than the previous encryption scheme (XOR). Incidentally, RC4 is illegal in France so if the operating system Regional Settings applet is set to France, XOR encryption will be implemented.

Lost or forgotten passwords for Excel workbooks are fatal, so administrators should insist on a list of file names and passwords.

PowerPoint Workgroup Administration

PowerPoint does not provide any security features for documents, and administrative efforts aimed at securing documents must be performed within the operating system.

One administrative task that may come up from time to time is the implementation of video conferences that are set up to view a PowerPoint presentation. The presentation conference can take place over the LAN, the Internet, or a combination of both. In order to establish a presentation conference, PowerPoint 97 or PowerPoint 95 must be running on Windows 95 or Windows NT on each node.

For nodes connected to the same LAN, the computer configuration must include TCP/IP networking protocol. Presentation conferencing requires the Pptconference network port (port 1711). If you have PowerPoint 95 nodes, they must use the Conference network port (531), or else compatibility will be a problem.

For nodes connected via the Internet, the connection must be through an ISP or direct. You cannot have a presentation conference through a proxy server.

The Presentation Conference Wizard in PowerPoint allows users to start the conference from their own computers. However, the order in which things occur and how they occur must be planned in advance (and overseen) by an administrator.

There are some special considerations you have to be aware of if you want to include PowerPoint 95 users in a presentation conference. First, the presenter must save the presentation in PowerPoint 95 format or in dual format (95/97). Not only must the conference be running on the Conference network port, but the operating system and the application must be expecting that port. That means changing the registry for PowerPoint 97 users. Edit the registry as follows: in

HKEY_LOCAL_MACHINE\Software\Microsoft\Office\8.0\PowerPoint\DLL Addins\Conference the current value of the ServiceName entry is "pptconference." Change that value to "conference."

Word Workgroup Administration

Word 97 provides RC4 encryption, replacing its previous encryption routine, Office 4.x.

Word 97 provides a number of easy-to-use features that are helpful in a workgroup environment:

- Templates and styles provide consistency.
- Master/Sub document features are handy when a number of people have to work together on a large document.
- The new features in Track Changes make it easier to figure out who's been working in a document and what they did.
- Document comments make sharing less confusing (especially when connected to the Track Changes feature).
- Saving multiple versions of a document in the same file makes it convenient to track the history of a document.

You can establish a configuration that places some files on the network server. For example, if you store templates on the server, it's very easy to add or modify a template and ensure consistency. ●

The CD-ROM

The CD-ROM that accompanies this book is filled with
several useful files, including HTML versions of several
additional best-selling Que titles, custom Excel templates,
Internet Explorer 3.092, and much more. (You can view
and navigate the CD-ROM with any browser, but if you
don't have one installed on your system, the first thing you
should do is install the copy of Internet Explorer 3.02
that's on the CD-ROM.)

There are four categories of files on the CD, and within
those categories you'll find plenty of great information,
both to increase your productivity with Office 97 or just to
satisfy your curiosity. ■

Books

You'll find several books on the CD, all in HTML format so you can browse through them using hyperlinks and all the other bells and whistles that help you find the information you need quickly and easily:

■ *Platinum Edition Using Windows 95* gives you all kinds of nifty information, tricks, tips, and explanations for getting the most out of that operating system.

■ Selected chapters from *Special Edition Using Windows NT 4.0 Workstation* provide wonderful information on running, managing and administering Windows NT 4 computers.

■ *Office 97, Excel 97, Word 97*, and *Access 97 Quick References* are a great place to find quick answers on basic Office 97 features and functions.

■ *Special Edition Using FrontPage 97* gives you a complete education on using Microsoft FrontPage 97 for Web page development.

■ *Special Edition Using Internet Explorer 3.0* will get you completely up-to-speed on all facets of installing, configuring, and running Microsoft's popular Web browser.

Templates and Wizards

You'll be amazed and delighted by the templates and wizards we've provided, and all of them add power, efficiency, and productivity to your Office 97 applications. This collection from Village Software® will make you the envy of all your Office-using friends. The real-world solutions to business and personal needs make this collection a valuable asset.

Software

We've included a robust assortment of software that will make your life in front of the computer easier, more productive, and more fun:

■ Xerox's Pagis Pro 97—Trial Version (used for scanning and organizing documents)
■ PointCast Client
■ An array of Microsoft Office 97 Viewers
■ PaintShop Pro
■ Fore Front's WebPrinter
■ ActiveX Control Pad, along with ActiveX Controls
■ Adobe Acrobat Viewer 3.0
■ Crt (Telnet Utility)
■ Symantec's WinFax Pro 8.0

Internet Utilities

With all the time you spend on the Internet (and you'll be spending more and more time there), we thought you'd appreciate some useful utilities:

- *Cute FTP* is one of the most powerful, easy-to-use FTP applications we've come across.

- *IE 3.02* is included so you have access to a powerful, stable browser.

- *The Office Web Directory* is a collection of Web sites that provide information, help, tricks, tips, and advice about getting the most out of Office 97.

- We've included a software package that gives you the opportunity to join Earthlink, one of the best-known Internet Service Providers.

Installation instructions for all of these files can be found on the CD. Check the README files for specific details. ●

App

B

Business Sites on the Web

This appendix is a listing of business resources you can find on the Internet. Whether you're just in the planning and startup phase of your business, involved in international trade, need legal or accounting assistance, or are interested in the latest trade shows and conferences, you'll find a Web site that can help you find answers. ■

Business Startup and Planning

America's Brightest

http://www.americasbrightest.com/

This Santa Monica-based organization describes itself as the "one-stop shop" for small businesses and working professionals. A subscription-based service with a one-month free trial, America's Brightest offers a giveaway and a wide range of discussion groups.

Big Dreams

http://vanbc.wimsey.com/~duncans/

Big Dreams is an online newsletter dedicated to individuals starting their own business. Visit the site and play the Business Game to ask yourself key questions about your new business, or take a look through current and archived issues for topical articles.

BizTalk

http://www.biztalk.com/

BizTalk is an electronic magazine devoted to small business. Departments include news, finance, law, politics, technology, and more. *BizTalk* runs contests to provide seed money for startups.

Business Plan Resource File

http://www.aifr.com/startup.html

Sponsored by the American Institute for Financial Research, this site is designed to help emerging business with their first business plan. A full compendium of general advice is offered in addition to having information on interactive business plan software.

Business Research Lab

http://spider.netropolis.net/brl/brl1.htm

This site is dedicated to the development of market research, an essential element for startups. Filled with tips and articles on conducting surveys and focus groups, the site also has a large number of sample surveys on file.

BuyersZone

http://www.buyerszone.com/index.html

BuyersZone is an online buyer's guide for businesses. It includes articles on what to look for in everything from 401(k) plans to voice mail systems. Also featured is The Inside Scoop which offers the latest tips and stories of "buying disasters."

CCH Business Owner's Toolkit

http://www.toolkit.cch.com/

CCH (Commerce Clearing House) features articles on Small Office, Home Office (SOHO) guides to everyday business, coupled with a comprehensive listing of business tools, including model business forms, financial templates, and checklists.

Education, Training, and Development Resource Center for Business and Industry

http://www.tasl.com/tasl/home.html

This page, sponsored by Training and Seminar Locators Inc., offers help in finding business education resources. An index of qualified training providers and information about products and services is included.

Internal Revenue Service

http://www.irs.ustreas.gov/

An important step in planning your business is to establish your tax status and potential responsibilities. The new IRS site has a special "Tax Info for Business" section with many helpful tax guides, including the Tax Calendar to keep track of special deadlines; a Business Tax Kit, a downloadable package of forms and publications; and the interactive Tax Trails for Business.

LinkExchange

http://www.linkexchange.com/

LinkExchange is an online advertising network that claims more than 100,000 members. If you have a Web site to promote, you can join for free; you then display ads for other members, and they display ads for you. There are also low-cost paid services.

Marketing Resource Center

http://www.marketingsource.com/

A free service of Concept Marketing Group, Inc., the Marketing Resource Center has an extensive articles library on planning your business, marketing tools and contacts, a database of industry associations, and links to online business magazines.

Marketshares

http://www.marketshares.com/

Marketshares tracks the best commercial and corporate Web sites. You can use their built-in search engine or browse their categories including Arts & Entertainment, Business & Technology, Finance & Money, and Travel & Transportation. Most links include a paragraph describing the site.

App
C

PRONET

http://www.pronett.com/

PRONET is a Multilingual Interactive Business Centre: The corporate philosophy is to help small- to medium-sized businesses grow by helping them use the Internet as a natural extension of their communications and marketing programs.

Occupational Safety and Health Administration

http://www.osha.gov/

Aside from a wealth of information on health and safety regulations and statistics, the OSHA site features software advisors that you can download on confined space standards, and asbestos regulations to help you figure out your requirements.

Small Business Advisor

http://www.isquare.com/

A terrific collection of articles for the new businessperson forms the core of this site. Example titles include "Don't Make These Business Mistakes," "Getting Paid," and "Government Small Business Resources." You'll also find tax advice and a glossary of business terms.

Small Business Workshop

http://www.sb.gov.bc.ca:80/smallbus/workshop/workshop.html

Sponsored by the Canadian government, this site has a host of articles for any business around the world. Areas include Starting Your Business, Marketing Basics, Planning Fundamentals, Financing Your Business, and Basic Regulations.

Tax Planning

http://www.hooked.net/cpa/plan/index.html

"An ounce of prevention…" is certainly worth more than a pound when it comes to taxes. This site specializes in information on tax planning—for individuals, businesses, and even an IRS audit. Take the tax challenge to find out how much you don't know about taxes.

Tax Prophet

http://www.taxprophet.com/

Hosted by Robert Sommers, the tax columnist for the *San Francisco Examiner*, the Tax Prophet has a number of FAQ files on tax issues and tax information for foreigners living in the U.S. The Interactive Tax Applications is very informative; try the Independent Contractor versus Employee Flowchart to check your job status.

U.S. Small Business Administration

http://www.sbaonline.sba.gov/

SBA Online is your online resource to government assistance for the small businessman. The site is organized into special areas on Starting, Financing, and Expanding Your Business as well as other information on SCORE, PRONET, and local SBA links.

Business Financing

Angel Capital Electronic Network

http://www.sbaonline.sba.gov/ADVO/acenet.html

Angel Capital Electronic Network (ACE-Net), the Internet-based network, is sponsored by the SBA's Office of Advocacy. The site gives new options for small companies seeking investments in the range of $250,000 to $5 million.

America Business Funding Directory

http://www.businessfinance.com/

America Business Funding Directory is the first search engine dedicated to finding business capital. You can search categories ranging from venture capital to equipment lending to real estate, as well as a private capital network of accredited investors.

Bankruptcy FAQs

http://site206125.primehost.com/faqs.html

Sponsored by Gold & Stanley, P.C., commercial bankruptcy lawyers, this site answers many basic questions about the ins-and-outs of bankruptcy from all perspectives. Topics include "How to Recover Money" and "10 Things to Do When a Bankruptcy Is Filed."

Closing Bell

http://www.merc.com/cb/cgi/cb_merc.cgi

Closing Bell provides a daily e-mail message containing closing prices and news for a personalized portfolio of market indices, mutual funds, and securities from the three major U.S. exchanges. Visitors can also sign up for news alerts during the day for followed companies.

Computer Loan Network

http://www.clnet.com/

Borrowers can use this Web site to add a loan Request for Proposal (RFP) directly to the CLN MortgageNet mortgage multiple listing service. Mortgage brokers, lenders, banks, and secondary marketers will search the system, locate your RFP, and then find ways to offer you a lower note rate than your currently quoted rate, if possible.

App
C

Currency Converter

http://www.oanda.com/cgi-bin/ncc

This interactive Web page is designed to allow you to see current conversions for 164 currencies. Convert your U.S. dollars to everything from the Albanian lek ($1 = 155 leks) to the Zambian kwacha ($1 = 1,310 kwacha). You can also check the previous day's rates or download a customizable currency converter.

EDGAR Database

http://www.sec.gov/edgarhp.htm

EDGAR, the Electronic Data Gathering, Analysis, and Retrieval system, performs automated collection, validation, indexing, acceptance, and forwarding of submissions by companies and others who are required by law to file forms with the U.S. Securities and Exchange Commission (SEC). Its primary purpose is to increase the efficiency and fairness of the securities market for the benefit of investors, corporations, and the economy. EDGAR is also a great resource of filing examples.

Export-Import Bank of the U.S.

http://www.exim.gov/

The Export-Import Bank offers programs on loans and guarantees, working capital, and export credit insurance. All the necessary application forms can be found online here with additional literature on importing from and exporting to various countries around the world.

FinanceNet

http://www.financenet.gov/

FinanceNet was established by Vice President Al Gore's National Performance Review in Washington, D.C. in 1994 and is operated by the National Science Foundation. This site features a listing of government asset sales including a subscription to daily sales.

Financial Women International

http://www.fwi.org/

Founded in 1921, Financial Women International serves women in the financial services industry who seek to expand their personal and professional capabilities through self-directed growth in a supportive environment. FWI's vision is to empower women in the financial services industry to attain their professional, economic, and personal goals, and to influence the future shape of the industry.

National Credit Counseling Service

http://www.nccs.org/

The National Credit Counseling Service's Web site features news about its Debt Management Program for businesses and individuals, as well a full range of information on credit, budgeting, and financial planning.

Prospect Street

http://www.prospectstreet.com/

Prospect Street is a venture capital firm specializing in resources for high-tech entrepreneurs: information technology, software, the Internet, and wireless communications. Its site has links to investment, stock, and technical research sources.

Securities and Exchange Commission

http://www.sec.gov/smbus1.htm

This page of the SEC site opens its small business area where you can find information on taking your small business public. In addition to a complete Q&A, you'll also find current and pending initiatives of interest.

App
C

U.S. Tax Code On-Line

http://www.fourmilab.ch/ustax/ustax.html

This Web page allows access to the complete text of the U.S. Internal Revenue Title 26 of the Code (26 U.S.C.). To make cross-referencing easy, hyperlinks are embedded throughout the text.

International Business and Trade

Asia-Pacific Economic Cooperation

http://www.apecsec.org.sg/

Based in Singapore, this organization's Web site carries information on the 18-member countries' economies, information on intellectual property rights overseas, and a financial procedures guidebook with government procurement outlines.

Bureau of Export Administration

http://www.bxa.doc.gov/

A key element of this site is the EAR Marketplace, a one-stop source for timely Export Administration Regulations data, including a current, searchable copy of the Export Administration Regulations online. You can also find current information on U.S. encryption policy here.

Central and Eastern Europe Business Information Center

http://www.itaiep.doc.gov/eebic/ceebic.html

CEEBIC is a primary information source for doing business in the emerging markets of central and eastern Europe. Each country has a full profile that includes market research and business and trade opportunities. A recently added page features tax and VAT rates for the area.

Contact! The Canadian Management Network

http://strategis.ic.gc.ca/sc_mangb/contact/engdoc/homepage.html

This bilingual (English and French) site features links to more than 1,500 Canadian small business support organizations. Here you'll also find a small business handbook on doing business in Canada and information on cross-cultural business strategies.

The Electronic Embassy

http://www.embassy.org/

The Electronic Embassy provides information on embassies for every country with special attention to those on the Internet. There is also an International Business Center that spotlights commercial and nonprofit organizations providing goods, services, or opportunities to international markets.

ExporTutor

http://web.miep.org/tutor/index.html

Is your business export ready? Follow this site's 10-Step Road Map to Success in Foreign Markets, developed by Michigan State University's International Business Center, to find out. There's also a Quick Consultant with valuable information on everything from Accounting to Value Chain Analysis.

India Market Place

http://www.indiaintl.com/

Here you'll find in-depth information on doing business in India, Indian business news updated every business day, extensive information about trade shows being held in India, and links to India-based business management resources, directories and databases, and associations.

TrADE-Net Italy

http://www.tradenet.it/

Italy is filled with small- to medium-sized companies known for their quality and desire to export. TrADE-Net Italy has a searchable industry directory organized by category—perfect for finding your company just the right import item.

Venture Web—Japan

http://www.venture-web.or.jp/

Searching for a Japanese connection? Whether you're looking for a partner in Japan or marketing your availability to the Japanese market, you can submit your request for posting on the site. Other areas of the site have information on export/import regulations and human resource links.

Web of Culture

http://www.worldculture.com/index.html

The Web of Culture is a wonderful site to visit before working with or going to a new country. The site includes information on business, religion, resources, and holidays. There's even a very visual page about gestures and their meanings in different countries.

App
C

Job Opportunities and Labor Resources

AFL-CIO

http://www.aflcio.org/

The AFL-CIO Web site focuses on information on unionization and other labor-related issues. New sections include an Executive Pay Watch, Ergonomics, Working Women, and Summer Jobs for Seniors.

America's Job Bank

http://www.ajb.dni.us/

A multi-state project of the public Employment Service, America's Job Bank is for both employers and employees. A section on Occupational Employment trends offers in interactive outlook handbook and answers to many surveys such as, "What's the fastest growing occupation?"

Computer Register

http://www.computerregister.com/

If you're in the market for computer consultants or related services, check out these extensive advertisements, including employment. Classifieds are provided for both job seekers and employers.

CareerPath.com

http://www.careerpath.com/

CareerPath.com posts more than 400,000 new jobs on the Internet every month, and is updated daily by newspapers across the U.S. You can search their help wanted database by category, newspaper, and keyword.

Department of Labor

http://www.dol.gov/

The government site has information on minimum wage regulations, labor protections and welfare reform, and small business retirement solutions. Visitors can access "America's Job Bank" as well as such for regulatory and statutory information.

Ernest & Young's Virtual HR Office

http://www.idirect.com/hroffice/

This site is a resource center for the human resource professional which includes a chat room, bulletin board, newsletter, and links to other HR sites in both the U.S. and Canada.

E-Span

http://www.espan.com/

Connecting the right person with the right job is what E-Span is all about. Visitors can access a resume database, a reference and resource library, and information on career fairs.

JobWeb

http://www.jobweb.org/

Run by the National Associations of Colleges and Employers, JobWeb lists jobs, employer profiles, and career planning resources. One resource, the Catapult, offers a variety of career assessment tools.

National Center for Employee Ownership

http://www.nceo.org/

The National Center for Employee Ownership (NCEO) is a private nonprofit organization. The NCEO site is a leading source of information on employee stock ownership plans (ESOPs), stock options, and other forms of employee ownership.

Telecommuting, Teleworking, and Alternative Officing

http://www.gilgordon.com/

This site features telecommuting information from around the world, and from many different perspectives, on the subjects of telecommuting, teleworking, the virtual office, and related topics. Includes a FAQ section and listing of upcoming events.

Legal and Regulatory

American Law Source Online (ALSO)

http://www.lawsource.com/also/

This site is notable because it has links to all American online legal systems, including the federal judiciary and all 50 states and territories. ALSO has equally far-reaching coverage of Canadian and Mexican law.

Business Law Site

http://members.aol.com/bmethven/index.html

Sponsored by Methven & Associates, the Business Law Site covers federal and state statutes, and legal research sites for both business and high-tech law. You can also find a full compendium of tax forms, information on international law, and a listing of legal research sites.

App
C

Corporate Counselor

http://www.ljx.com/corpcounselor/index.html

The Corporate Counselor has resources including daily news, columns, and articles on employment law, securities, antitrust, and other business issues.

Department of Labor Poster Page

http://www.dol.gov/dol/osbp/public/sbrefa/poster.htm

A fixture in every American workplace finds its online equivalent: the Department of Labor mandatory notices. So far, you can download posters for the minimum wage requirements, OSHA, the Family Leave Act, and the Equal Opportunity Act. All posters are in PDF format; you'll need a PDF reader like Adobe Acrobat (**http://www.adobe.com**).

International Trade Law

http://itl.irv.uit.no/trade_law/

Sponsored by the Law Department at Norway's University of Tromsø, you can search this site for virtually any subject related to international trade law. Typical topics include Dispute Resolution, Customs, Protection of Intellectual Property, GATT, and other free trade treaties.

The Legal Information Institute

http://www.law.cornell.edu/

Sponsored by Cornell University, the Legal Information Institute Web site houses its collection of recent and historic Supreme Court decisions, hypertext versions of the full U.S. Code, U.S. Constitution, Federal Rules of Evidence and Civil Procedure, and recent opinions of the New York Court of Appeals complete with commentary. Fully indexed and searchable.

QuickForms Online

http://www.quickforms.com/

QuickForms is an easy-to-use interactive system that drafts sophisticated agreements automatically weighted in your favor. Answer and view questions online, and you have your draft agreement in 10 minutes. A wide range of contracts are available.

Magazines Online

Advertising Age

http://www.adage.com/

All the information you could ever need about the movers and shakers of advertising. The site features a section on getting the most out of your Web site called NetMarketing as well as the DataPlace, featuring industry reports and statistics.

Barron's Online

http://www.barrons.com/

In addition to complete contents of their weekly publication, *Barron's Online* features the ability to examine most companies mentioned in their articles through the Barron Dossiers. *Barron's Online* requires a free registration.

BusinessWeek

http://www.businessweek.com/

BusinessWeek's online only content includes Maven, the interactive computer shopper, and BW Plus with listings of the best business schools, business book reviews, and articles on the computer industry and the Information Age. You can also access BW Radio, which provides hourly market reports in RealAudio format.

Disgruntled

http://www.disgruntled.com/

Describing itself as "The Business Magazine for People Who Work for a Living," *Disgruntled* provides an irreverent look at being employed. There's even a Boss Button on every page which takes you to a proper-looking spreadsheet when the boss is looking over your shoulder.

Entrepreneurial Edge Online

http://www.edgeonline.com/

Articles aimed at the innovative entrepreneur fill this site. You also find a Pointers from the Pros section, a SmallBizNet (with a full digital library), and the Interactive Toolbox, a series of self-calculating worksheets and benchmarking and assessment tools.

Fast Company

http://www.fastcompany.com/

A new edge business magazine with a host of "how-to" articles: how to make a group decision like a tribe, how to deal with the issues of dating and sexual harassment on the job, how to choose a career counselor, how to disagree (without being disagreeable), and more.

Financial Times

http://www.usa.ft.com/

The online edition of the *Financial Times* is divided into three sections: News & Comment, with "tastes" of articles from the newspaper as well as stock market info updated every 30 minutes; Themes & Topics, for categorized articles; and Connect & Respond, where online visitors can find services, such as recruitment advertising and library of annual reports.

Forbes Digital Tool

http://www.forbes.com/

In addition to current and archived articles from *Forbes*, this Web site features the Toolbox, a collection of reports and indices; ASAP, *Forbes'* supplement on the Information Age; Angles, a section on media and politics; and access to a free Investment Monitor.

Fortune

http://www.pathfinder.com/fortune/

Can't wait to see if you made the 500 this year? Check out the digital version of the famous survey as well as online areas dedicated to the stock market, mobile computing, managing your money, and information technology. You'll also find a special Fortune Forum for exchanging views on investing and related matters.

Hispanic Business Magazine

http://www.hispanstar.com/

This site covers information for business owners and professionals with a Hispanic interest. There is also a national resume referral service, a market research area focusing on the U.S. Hispanic economic market, and a special events department that provides a calendar of events.

Inc. Online

http://www.inc.com/

Self-described as the "Web site for Growing Companies," *Inc. Online* is actually several minisites, including Inc. itself, with articles and archives; Business & Technology, with statistics to benchmark your business; and Local Business News, where you can choose from more than 25 U.S. cities for local business news and resources.

MoneyWorld Online

http://www.money-world.net/

MoneyWorld Online features investing information and tips on the most promising investment opportunities. *MoneyWorld* offers "hot-pick" IPOs, a series of long and short picks and growth industry surveys.

Red Herring

http://www.herring.com/mag/home.html

Red Herring provides business information for the technology and entertainment industries with a special focus on emerging markets. Their online site features an Entrepreneurs Resource Center with workshops on the unique challenges facing business startups.

Success Magazine

http://www.SuccessMagazine.com/

The *Success* site includes a searchable archive of past articles, a survey of the best 100 franchises (with links), and the Source, a compendium of business-related links, organized by subject.

The Wall Street Journal—Small Business Suite

http://update.wsj.com/public/current/summaries/small.htm

Although the interactive *Wall Street Journal* is a subscription service ($49 per year), this service is free. Articles of interest to small business are the primary feature here along with a series of discussion groups, Web resources, and a business locator.

Marketing and Market Research

American Demographics/Marketing Tools

http://www.marketingtools.com/

At the American Demographics/Marketing Tools Web site, you can check out consumer trends, tactics and techniques for information marketers, or access *Forecast*, a newsletter of demographic trends and market forecasts.

American Marketing Association

http://www.ama.org/

AMA is a national organization of marketing professionals. Their Web site features a special section on Internet marketing ethics as well as a calendar of events, publications, and information on regional chapters.

Business Intelligence Center

http://future.sri.com/

What type of person is your customer? The Values and Lifestyles (VALS) program at SRI Consulting, hosts of this site, studies consumers by asking questions about their attitudes and values. You can answer an online questionnaire to determine your VALS type—and see how you fit with other consumers.

Business Wire

http://www.businesswire.com/

Business Wire is a leading source of news on major U.S. corporations, including Fortune 1000 and NASDAQ companies. You can look up a company, category, keyword, or region and find all the pertinent business news. You can sign up for their service online.

Commando Guide to Unconventional Marketing and Advertising Tactics

http://199.44.114.223/mktg/

This online reference covers such topics as how to market survey your competition, doing your own professional marketing and business plan, referral systems, barter exchanges, print advetorials, and telemarketing.

First Steps: Marketing and Design Daily

http://www.interbiznet.com/nomad.html

Developed by the Internet Business Network, First Steps contains a rich source of articles on market research and industry analysis regarding business-to-business transactions. Much of the marketing and design work is Internet-oriented.

International Public Relations

http://www.iprex.com/

IPREX specializes in international public relations. Its areas of expertise include business-to-business, crisis management, energy and environment, and technology. Its news section has valuable information on public relation trends.

Market Facts and Statistics

http://www.mightymall.com/sevenseas/facts.html

This 1996 survey covers the countries of the world's population, gross national product, and growth rate. Each country has a small paragraph on its economy and markets. The information is organized by major regions: Asia, Western Europe, Central Europe, Middle East, Atlantic, and West Indies.

Marketing Resource Center

http://www.marketingsource.com/

Sponsored by the Concept Marketing Group, the Marketing Resource Center maintains an articles archive with more than 250 business-related articles. Their Tools of the Trade section links to an association database and software for general business and project management.

Retail Futures

http://e1.com/RF/

Sponsored by the Institute for Retail and Merchandising Innovation, this site carries information on tracking customer preferences, category and brand management, regional marketing, and store and product design issues.

Sales Leads USA

http://www.abii.com/

This site is run by American Business Information, Inc. which specializes in generating company profiles. Free services include searching for businesses or people by name with American Directory Assistance or searching by type of business with American Yellow Pages.

Selling.com

http://www.selling.com/

This site is dedicated to salespeople and their needs. Here, you'll find a collection of selling concepts and exercises written by salespeople, for salespeople.

Sharrow Advertising & Marketing Resource Center

http://www.dnai.com/~sharrow/register.html

You have to register at first to visit this site, but it's well worth it; the Advertising Parody section is worth the time by itself. The BizInfo Resource Center has an overview of database marketing, a direct mail profit spreadsheet, and information on approaches to integrated marketing.

Top Marketing Tips, Tricks, and Techniques

http://www.disclosure.com/marketing/toptricks.html

What's the inside scoop? Check out this site, sponsored by Disclosure, Inc., for all the skinny on advertising, direct marketing, marketing law, marketing management, promotions, public relations, trade shows, and telemarketing.

U.S. Census Bureau

http://www.census.gov/

The Census Bureau is a great site to gather social, demographic, and economic information. The site has more than 1,000 Census Bureau publications featuring statistical information on such topics as the nation's population, housing, business and manufacturing activity, international trade, farming, and state and local governments.

World Business Solution

http://thesolution.com/

The World Business Solution is a free marketing manual available from TheSolution.com. There's also a section devoted to downloadable or lined handy forms and reference.

Nonprofit Information

Charity Village

http://www.charityvillage.com/cvhome.html

Hundreds of pages of news, jobs, resources, and links for the Canadian nonprofit community. Sponsored by Hilborn Interactive, Inc. this site is updated daily in both French ("Rue Principale") and English ("Main Street").

Council on Foundations

http://www.cof.org/index.html

The Council of Foundations is an association of foundations and corporations gathered to promote responsible and effective philanthropy. You'll find information on the various types of foundations as well as a Community Foundation Locator service.

The George Lucas Educational Foundation

http://glef.org/welcome.html

The George Lucas Educational Foundation, a tax-exempt, charitable organization based in Nicasio, California, was established to facilitate the innovative uses of multimedia technologies to enhance teaching and learning. The site has frequently updated information about innovative efforts to change education.

The Gen-X Group

http://www.globalserve.net/~genxgrp/

Gen-X Group is a not-for-profit Christian organization promoting charities and nonprofit organizations on the Internet. The site features a short course on how and why nonprofit organizations can get on the Web.

The Grantsmanship Center

http://www.tgci.com/

The Grantsmanship Center specializes in training for grant writing and fundraising. Much of the site is designed to support their courses around the country. The site also contains a cross-referenced database of state and federal funding.

IdeaList

http://www.contact.org/

This site features a global directory of nonprofits with links to more than 10,000 sites in 110 countries. There is also an online library of tools for nonprofits, with information about fundraising and volunteering, accounting and management, legal issues, and nonprofit support organizations.

Nonprofit Resources Catalog

http://www.clark.net/pub/pwalker/

A personal project by the head of United Way Online, this site features meta-links (links to pages of links) dedicated to Interlink sites that benefit nonprofits. Categories include Fundraising and Giving, General Nonprofit Resources, and United Ways on the Internet.

Patents, Trademarks, and Copyrights

Basic Patent Information

http://www.fplc.edu/tfield/ipbasics.htm

Sponsored by the Franklin Law Center, this compendium of resources offers beginning information for artists, independent inventors, Internet authors and artists, programmers, and small business owners, including information on how to avoid being burned by fraudulent invention promotion schemes.

Copyright Clearance Center

http://www.copyright.com/

Copyright Clearance Center (CCC) is a not-for-profit organization created at the suggestion of Congress to help organizations comply with U.S. copyright law. CCC offers a number of catalogs that you can search to see if a work is registered.

Copyright Website

http://www.benedict.com/index.html

This lively site provides real-world, practical, and relevant copyright information including a look at famous copyright infringement cases, copyright fundamentals, and distribution of copyright information over the Web.

Intellectual Property Center

http://www.ipcenter.com/

News and information on intellectual property issues dominate this site. Government statutes and decisions are highlighted, along with memos from law firms on intellectual property issues.

Nerd World: Copyrights & Patents

http://www.nerdworld.com/users/dstein/nw427.html

This site provides a resource of links to many patent attorneys and intellectual property law firms from around the world. A recent survey showed many contacts in the U.S., Canada, and Japan.

App

C

Patent Application Drafting

http://w3.gwis.com/~sarbar/patapp01.htm

This Web site gives an overview of the steps necessary for writing a patent application, section by section. Aside from covering the statutory legal requirements, Intellectual Property Attorney R. Lawrence Sahr gives insightful comments on the target audience for your patent: the patent office itself.

Patent Pending Resource

http://silkpresence.com/patents/

Sponsored by the patent law firm of Ogram & Teplitz, this site covers new patents law, a FAQ on provisional patent application that allows the "Patent Pending" label to be used. There are also online forms that ask a patent attorney's questions before you schedule a visit.

U.S. Patent Office

http://www.uspto.gov/

The home page for the U.S. Patent Office gives you access to downloadable patent application forms and searchable databases. These include both the U.S. Patent Bibliographic Database (U.S. patents issued from January 1, 1976 to July 8, 1997), and the AIDS Patent Database (full text and images of AIDS-related patents issued by the U.S., Japanese, and European patent offices).

Procurement and Contracting

Acquisition Reform Network

http://www-far.npr.gov/

The Acquisition Reform Network (ARNet) provides services to members of the government acquisition community, both public and private sector. Its resource center, the Federal Acquisition Virtual Library, provides links to numerous other federal acquisition resources on the World Wide Web. Numerous opportunities are also listed.

BidCast

http://www.bidcast.com/

BidCast is a subscription service that allows you to browse and search thousands of U.S. federal government bids. You can sign up with the e-mail service for personal notification. There is a free trial section that allows you to look at Commerce Business Daily listings.

Business Information and Development Services (BIDS)

http://www.bidservices.com/newindex.html

BIDS is an electronic publishing and consulting firm which informs small businesses about upcoming government contract opportunities and provides assistance in the procurement process. Their site offers information from both the Commerce Business Daily (U.S.) and Supply and Services Open Bidding Service (Canada).

Commerce Business Daily

http://www.govcon.com/public/CBD/

A sophisticated search engine for finding government procurement opportunities. You can search for a procurement or award under a specific category, by contract value or by a search phrase. You can even specify the level of "fuzziness" the engine uses to find items bearing a close similarity to your search criteria.

Electronic Commerce Program Office (ECPO)

http://www.arnet.gov/ecapmo/

The Electronic Commerce Program Office (ECPO) is a multi-agency group assembled under the co-leadership of the General Services Administration and the Department of Defense to implement Electronic Commerce/Electronic Data Interchange (EC/EDI) for the federal acquisition programs. An online tutorial can help you get started.

Electronic Commerce Resource Center

http://www.ecrc.ctc.com/

The ECRC Program promotes awareness and implementation of Electronic Commerce and related technologies into the U.S.-integrated civil-military industrial base. Downloadable products can be found in the Electronic Commerce Testbed.

Environmental Protection Agency Procurement

http://www.epa.gov/epahome/Contracts.html

Visit this site for a full listing of business opportunities and EPA acquisition resources. In addition to covering policy and procedure, you can also find an acquisition forecast and a special section devoted to small business opportunities.

FAA Acquisition Center

http://www.faa.gov/asu/asu100/acq-reform/acq_home.htm

After you've checked out the FAQ page on supplying to the Federal Aviation Administration, visit FAST, the FAA Acquisition System Toolset. FAST is a interactive databank designed to guide users through the FAA's new Acquisition Management System (AMS); it contains examples, templates, instructions, tips, policy documents, and other automated tools.

Federal Acquisition Institute

http://www.gsa.gov/fai/

Trying to find your way through the maze of federal acquisition? Pay a visit to the Federal Acquisition Institute, a one-stop acquisition training shop. Here you can sign up for the FAI Online University or download a Contract Pricing Reference Guide.

General Services Agency

http://www.gsa.gov/

The GSA's mission is to provide expertly managed space, supplies, services, and solutions at the best value to Federal employees. In addition to full information on buying practices, you can also visit its online shopping service, GAO Advantage.

Government Accounting Office

http://www.gao.gov/

The U.S. General Accounting Office (GAO) is a nonpartisan agency that conducts audits, surveys, investigations, and evaluations of federal programs. You can sign up for daily reports through the GAO Daybook service or visit the GAO FraudNET for allegations of fraud, waste, abuse, or mismanagement of federal funds.

App
C

Government Contractors Glossary

http://www.kcilink.com/govcon/contractor/gcterms.html

An excellent resource for finding your way through the verbiage of government contracts. A special Acronym Table appears at the end of this guide to enable you to identify the full meaning of the most common government acronyms.

National Technology Transfer Center

http://www.nttc.edu/

The National Technology Transfer Center's task is to take technologies off laboratory shelves and put them to work in U.S. businesses and industries where taxpayers get even more benefits from their investments. Full database services, a training center, and links to other business assistance sites are hallmarks of this Web site.

State and Local Procurement Jumpstation

http://www.fedmarket.com/statejump.html

This invaluable Web page gives you links to procurement sources for all 50 states, not to mention Washington, D.C. and Guam. Most states also have some local listings for specific cities as well as economic development links supplying market data.

U.S. Business Center

http://www.business.gov/

This one-stop shop is designed to streamline interactions between businesses and the government. Common questions and answers are organized by subject, and an expert tool area gives you forms and guidance in everything from Disaster Assistance to Finding a Zip Code.

U.S. Post Office

http://www.usps.gov/business/

The Post Office wants to give you the business! This Web site provides an overview of doing business with the USPS and even tells you how to submit an unsolicited bid. You can download the Procurement Manual, as well as check out business opportunities.

U.S. Veteran Affairs

http://www.va.gov/osdbu/

The online Department of Veteran Affairs site promotes increased use of small and disadvantaged businesses, including acquisition opportunities. A focus of this site is the VA's 1997 Forecast which supplies marketing information useful to the small businessperson in selling his goods and services, both to the VA and to the VA's large prime contractors.

Small Office/Home Office (SOHO)

America's Small Business Finance Center

http://www.netearnings.com/

Sponsored by Net Earnings, Inc., this one-stop shop offers business advice on insurance policies and prices, and on applying for loans and credit cards. You can also sign up for online payroll service here.

American Express Small Business Exchange

http://www.americanexpress.com/smallbusiness/

The American Express Small Business Exchange offers online classifieds (buying and selling); expert advice where you can ask a specific question, browse the categories, or check out the tip of the month; and business planning and resources with information on starting, managing, or expanding your business.

App
C

Bathrobe 'til 10

http://www.slip.net/~sfwave/

This guide for the home professional offers articles and information for the solo self-employed. Concerned about word use? Pay a visit to the Grammar Queen to clear up those business correspondence blues.

Biz$hop

http://www.bizshop.com/

Biz$hop is a virtual company specializing in helping entrepreneurs achieve success in their own businesses. There are numerous reports and free business resources available—be sure to download the free "First 25 Business Decisions" report.

BizResource.com

http://www.bizresource.com/

Dedicated to encouraging small businesses and entrepreneurs, BizResource offers an ongoing series of business tips (both via e-mail and archived online), a business chat area, and a series of audio, video, and computer resources.

Business@Home

http://www.gohome.com/

An electronic magazine dedicated to the working-from-home community, Business@Home includes articles on opportunity, marketing, and technology. Its Cool Tools department reviews recent hardware and software important to the general home office worker, while the Consultant's Corner focuses on the consultants' work experience.

Business Resource Center

http://www.morebusiness.com/

This site hosts an excellent four-part primer with advice and activities to get you thinking about your business, its customers, development, and marketing. In addition, you can find templates and worksheets here for press releases and business plans.

Business Start Page

http://www.wp.com/fredfish/

Here's a great place to start your business day. This site offers a virtual desktop where you can find everything at your fingertips: Yellow, Blue, and International page telephone directories, links to shipping companies, a reference library, and a series of tips and tricks.

Center for Family Business

http://199.103.128.199/fambiznc/cntprovs/orgs/necfb/

Run by Northeastern University, this site features an ongoing series of articles on running a family business (both home and office- or store-based). You'll find lots of information here on family business issues including generational change, sibling rivalries, and how to balance family and business priorities.

EGOPHER—The Entrepreneur Gopher

http://www.slu.edu/eweb/egopher.html

Sponsored by St. Louis University, EGOPHER is designed for people and organizations interested in new, small, or entrepreneurial businesses. A variety of Top 10 lists for entrepreneurs is available along with topical business resources and access to core research journals in entrepreneurship.

Electronic Money Tree

http://www.soos.com/$tree/

Aimed at the Internet savvy (or those who want to be) entrepreneurs, the Electronic Money Tree consists primarily of a digest of articles. Sample articles include "Can SOHO Really Compete?," "Biz Tips," "Better Press Releases," and "Time Management."

Entrepreneur's Bookstore

http://kwicsys.com/books/

There are more than 600 information reports offered at this site, most from $1 to $2 each. The reports are categorized. Sample topic areas include Mail Order, Multilevel Marketing, Legal, and Direct Response TV.

Entrepreneur Magazine's BizSquare

http://www.entrepreneurmag.com/

This site is chock-full of information for the SOHO businessperson. Visit the Resource Center to check out the online Franchise 500 and Business Opportunity 500 lists. Then go to the SOHO Mall for all your business-related software, books, magazines, and audio or videocassettes.

EntreWorld

http://www.entreworld.org/

The EntreWorld site is organized by business level. Visit the Starting Your Business area for information on business planning, finding the right people, or creating products that win loyalty. Running Your Business is devoted to later-stage companies with information on expanding your customer base and exit strategies.

FranInfo

http://www.frannet.com/

Thinking about franchising? Visit FranInfo's site to find information on buying a franchise or franchising your own business. The site has several self-tests to determine if you're ready for franchising, as well as a listing of franchises for sale.

Guide to the Small Business Administration

http://www.geocities.com/WallStreet/2172/

Before you dive into the SBA bureaucracy, you might want to visit this site first. There are lots of details covering the various SBA programs available, with information to help you find just the right one for your business.

Heath's Computer and Telecommunication Acronym Reference

http://www.sbri.com/acro2.htm

Visit this site before your next cocktail party where you want to impress others with statements like, "My GOSIP is about to go LUNI on Harv's LANE." Or maybe when you just want to find out what all those jargonese initials mean.

Home Office Association of America

http://www.hoaa.com/

There's power in numbers—even if you're working alone. The Home Office Association of America offers group health insurance, a long-distance calling plan, a debt collection service, home business and equipment insurance, and more. Be sure to visit their 50 Great Home Office Startup Ideas page.

App

C

Home Office Links

http://www.ro.com/small_business/homebased.html

A full compendium of Web links for small and home-based offices including franchises, business opportunities, reference material, newsgroups, searching tools, and services for small business. Links to just about anything related to small- and home-based business can be found here.

Home Office Mall

http://www.the-office.com/

A centralized location for products and services catering to the home office professional. Find everything from computers for rent to computer furniture, to networks for female executives.

Home Realtors Information Network

http://www.realtors.com/

About the only thing all home business have in common is the home. This Web site, sponsored by the National Association of Realtors, has almost 900,000 listings of homes around the country—and, of course, a search engine to help you find your dream office.

NetMarquee Family Business NetCenter

http://nmq.com/

This site supplies news and information for owners and executives in family-owned businesses. There is a calendar of events, weekly articles, and a listserve for ongoing discussion related to family businesses.

Offshore Entrepreneur

http://www.au.com/offshore/

With the motto, "Neither profit, nor opportunity, have any borders," the Offshore Entrepreneur takes you through the promise, pitfalls, and profit of basing your business in another country. The site offers abundant information on tax-planning and forming an off-shore corporation.

Opportunities for Women in Small Business

http://www.mindspring.com/~higley/project.htm

One path around the glass ceiling is to open your own business. This site is dedicated to helping women choose and run a business. There are profiles of successful women, as well as financial and legal advice and tips on how to avoid failure.

Resource Center for Home-Based Businesses

http://www.masseypub.com/

Learn from someone who made the home-based business dream come true. Featuring information on self-published brochures, this site offers a FAQ section, details on seminars, and an area devoted to mail order scams.

Retail Business Resource Center

http://www.retailadvz.com/

Looking for a site where you can learn from the experts? The Retail Business Resource Center offers theme-oriented live business chats, live workshops, and even a business therapist offering real-world solutions to real-world problems.

Small Business Innovative Research

http://www.sbir.dsu.edu/

Small Business Innovative Research is a federally supported program aimed at funding small businesses with money from Federal agency and department's R&D divisions. This site assists small companies in applying for that funding by answering questions and providing online tests.

App
C

SOHO America

http://www.soho.org/

SOHO America is a small business benefits association. In addition to news of interest to the small office/home office market, this site offers a comprehensive list of health benefits, business tools, and personal discounts available to members.

Your Small Office

http://www.smalloffice.com/

This site is the online presence of *Small Office Computing* and *Home Office Computing* magazines and features articles from their magazines. The Web site visitor will find a great number of reviews of network, computer, and office equipment as well as a full "How To" department covering everything from Startup to Sales and Marketing.

U.S. Chamber of Commerce Small Business Institute

http://www.uschamber.org/programs/sbi/index.html

The U.S. Chamber of Commerce runs a Small Business Institute with a variety of resources both for free and for sale. There are self-study programs on Mastering Your Business on the Internet and the Small Business Institute Series, as well as information on the SOHO Conference.

Travel and Transportation

Airlines of the Web

http://w2.itn.net/airlines/

Where can you find a listing of *all* the airlines, both passenger and cargo? At the Airlines of the Web site, of course. Passenger airlines are categorized by region, and you can also find airline-related information like 800 numbers and a link to a real-time reservation service.

American Airlines

http://www.americanair.com/aa_home.htm

The American Access Web site takes a full-service approach. Here, you can plan your travel, check out Advantage frequent flier miles, take advantage of the NetSaver fares, and download Personal Access, American's Windows-based software program that brings you dedicated AAdvantage information, travel planning, and up-to-the-minute information and specials.

American Movers Conference

http://www.amconf.org/

The American Movers Conference is an association of 3,000 professional moving companies in the U.S. Their site has information on how to prepare your move, how much a "self-haul" might cost, and listings of movers across the country.

Continental Airlines

http://www.flycontinental.com:80/index.html

Continental On-Line's main claim to fame is its C.O.O.L. Travel Assistant which can be used to schedule and book airline travel on Continental, Continental Express,, and Continental Micronesia as well as more than 40 rental car companies and 26,000 hotels around the world.

FedEX

http://www.fedex.com/

Not only can you now track your overnight package online, but you can also use their interactive rate finder, and even ship packages via the Internet to more than 160 countries from the U.S. and Canada. There's also a searchable database of drop-off locations and downloadable software for managing your shipping, including the airbill printing.

HomeBuyer's Fair

http://www.homefair.com/home/

While most of this site is dedicated to helping you buy or sell your home, the HomeBuyer's Fair has some amazing interactive tools in its Popular Exhibits area. There's a Salary Calculator for comparing the cost of living in hundreds of U.S. and international cities, a Moving Calculator for figuring the cost of a move, and a Relocation Crime Lab for comparing crime statistics.

InterKnowledge Travel Network

http://www.interknowledge.com/

When your business takes you to an exotic locale—meaning you've never been there before—stop by the InterKnowledge Travel Network site first. The site is characterized by beautiful images and full details on geography, culture, and climate.

Northwest Airlines

http://www.nwa.com/

This Northwest Airlines site has information on CyberSavers, their online low-cost tickets, as well as regular travel and frequent flier information. A full slate of vacation packages rounds out the site.

U.S. Air

http://www.usair.com/

Tune into the U.S. Air Web site to schedule and book a flight or check your frequent flyer miles. An extensive area of the site is devoted to its U.S. Airways Cargo service where you can use the software to track shipments with real-time information from airport drop-off to pickup.

United Parcel Service

http://www.ups.com/

Interactive functions featured at the UPS site include package tracking, cost-estimating, a drop-off locator, and pick-up scheduling. UPS also makes available free software for all of these functions as well as up-to-the-minute zone and rate charts.

Trade Shows and Conferences

EXPOguide

http://www.expoguide.com/

If you're thinking about selling your product through a trade show, stop by this site first. It has a full listing of trade shows, conferences, and exhibitions as well as comprehensive coverage of show services and associations. Although primarily intended for trade show managers, there's still plenty of information here for exhibiting companies.

App
C

CD Information

http://www.cd-info.com/CDIC/Industry/TradeShows.html

Today, much of computing and information storage and retrieval revolves around the CD-ROM. This site is CD-centric and lists many upcoming exhibitions, conferences, seminars, and workshops in a month-by-month format.

Guide to Unique Meeting Facilities

http://www.theguide.com/

A terrific resource for meeting planners, The Guide to Unique Meeting Facilities covers colleges and universities, retreat centers, camps and lodges, and cultural and historical venues, as well as traditional conference centers. There is also a Hot Date/Cool Rate area to highlight facilities with open, economical dates.

Major Trade Shows in Asia

http://www.tdb.gov.sg/trshow/tr_menu.html

You can start your search for Asian trade shows here, either by country, industry, or by date. Fourteen countries, including Brunei, China, Japan, South Korea, and Vietnam, and more than 25 different industries are covered.

Trade Show Central

http://www.tscentral.com/

Sponsored by the International Association for Exhibition Management, Trade Show Central gives you easy access to information on more than 30,000 trade shows. Its searchable database links to an e-mail notification service where you can request more information. Its AudioNet connection broadcasts and archives keynote speeches from major events.

Wall Street Directory

http://www.wsdinc.com/index.html

Wall Street Directory offers a wide range of information for traders and investors. To see its up-to-the-minute conference information, select the Seminars-Shows-Conventions category and click the Search by Category button.

Small Business Administration Upcoming Events

http://www.sbaonline.sba.gov/gc/events.html

Organized on a monthly basis, the SBA keeps a listing of many business-related seminars and conferences. Although not hot-linked, all conferences have telephone contact information. Free seminars are prominently noted.

EventWeb

http://www.eventweb.com/

A free mailing list service for meeting, conference, and trade show promoters. Sample articles include "How to Exhibit at a Virtual Trade Show," "Expanding Educational Horizons in the Online World," and "Promote Your Speakers—Inexpensively!"

Tradeshow News Network

http://www.tsnn.com/

The Tradeshow News Network allows you to search for a trade show in the U.S. by location, date, or industry. Its Trade Show Education department offers tips on both exhibiting and attending, as well as an Ask the Expert section.

Virtual Online Trade Show

http://www.volts.com/

This site promotes the Virtual Trade Show concept, and is aimed at both exhibition managers and exhibitors. Exhibitors can see how they can save money, broaden their exposure, and communicate with their customers. ●

Index

Symbols

^ (caret) operator, VBA, 671

: (colon) range operator, Excel, 168

: (colon) command, VBA Immediate window, 660

, (comma) union operator, Excel ranges, 168

= (equal sign), assigning HTML attributes, 775

_ (underscore) in variable names, 659

16-bit applications, 996-997

3-D cell ranges (Excel), 180
  Currency format, 180
  formulas, 181-183

32-bit applications, 994-995
  multithreading, 994-995
  preemptive multitasking, 994-995
  printing subsystem, 971-972
  system resources, 995

A

\<A> tag (HTML), 778

ABS(x) function (Word forms), 82

absolute comparison (Validation Rule property), 355

absolute references
  Excel formulas, 186
  URLs, 791

accepting task assignments (Outlook), 529-530

Access
  add-ins, Linked Table Manager, 372
  Briefcase Replication, 16

Compact utility, 15
connecting with Excel, 274-275
  FROM clause, 292-293
  GROUP BY clause, 293
  modifying databases from Excel, 290-291
  ORDER BY clause, 293
  pivot tables, 276-280
  SELECT statement, 291-292
DAO (Data Access Objects), 275
  installation, 275-276
  sample application, 296-301
data sharing, 37
databases
  converting, 24
  encrypting, 1047
  security during conversion, 25
Datasheet view, 372
  customization, 374-375
  navigating, 375-376
  switching to Form view, 374
Expression Builder, 442
  control references in macros, 457-458
filters, 15, 381-382
  Advanced Filter/Sort window, 386-388
  Filter by Input, 383-386
Form view, 372
  forms, creating, 372-374
  navigating, 375-376
  switching to Datasheet view, 374
forms
  macros, 458-460
  multiple table forms, 441-442
HTML files, 15
hyperlinks, 15
importing
  compared to linking, 368
  data sources, 368-369
  manipulating data, 371-372
  mechanics of, 369-371

linking
  compared to importing, 368
  data sources, 368-369
  manipulating data, 371-372
  mechanics of, 369-371
lookup fields, 15
macros
  assigning command buttons, 458
  conditions, 451-452
  controls, 455-458
  creating, 449-451
  Expression Builder, 457-458
  macro sheets, 446-449
  naming, 453-455
  rows of actions, manipulating, 455
  use, 458-460
mailing labels, 424-426
modules, 15
Object Browser, 16
objects
  Application object (VBA), 629
  recordsets, 282
  unbound objects, converting, 25
protecting source code, 1046
queries, 390
  action queries, 407-408
  action queries, appending records with, 410
  action queries, creating tables with, 411-412
  action queries, deleting records with, 408-409
  action queries, updating records with, 409-410
  calculations, 401-403
  column width, 397
  creating, 290
  criteria, expressions, 400-401
  criteria, identifiers, 398-400

criteria, operators, 398-400
criteria, setting, 397-398
Design view, 390-391
fields, adding, 393-394
fields, deleting, 394-395
fields, hiding, 396-397
fields, moving, 395
fields, naming, 395-396
fields, viewing, 396-397
joining, 392
properties, 403-405
QBE, 391
relationships, 392-393
Simple Query Wizard, 405-406
sort order of results, 401
tables, adding to queries, 391
records
data entry, 376-377
deleting data, 378
editing data, 378
locking, 1047
relational databases, 274
Relationship Editor, 434
Repair utility, 15
replicas, 15
reports
AutoReport, 414-417
columnar reports, 415
customization, 427-428
Design view, 428
e-mail, 430
HTML, 429-430
macros, 458-460
multiple table reports, 442-444
printing, 423
Reports Wizard, 417-423
tabular reports, 416-417
sorts, 379-380
multiple sorts, 380-381
unsorting records, 381
SQL, 290
sending SQL to Access,
293-295
temporary queries, 295-296
subroutines
DialogHandler, 284-286
Driver, 280-282
GetQueryNames, 282-284
ImportData, 286-290
tables, 75
creating, 347-348
data types, 348-351
data types, changing, 363
Datasheet view, 346-348
Design view, 346, 348-349
editing, 362-363
field-level properties, 351-358
fields, arranging, 363
fields, deleting, 363
fields, naming, 363
importing, 360-361

indexes, 356-357
linking, 361-362
Mail Merge (Word), 115
many-to-many relationships,
435
one-to-many relationships, 434
one-to-one relationships,
435-436
primary key, 347, 349
properties, changing, 363
queries, 440-441
relationships, 364-365, 436-439
table-level properties, 357
troubleshooting
converting databases, 25
data types, 363
linking tables, 372
mailing labels, 424
queries, 405
user-level security, 1047
wizards
Command Button, 458
Input Mask, 354
Lookup, 351
Mailing Label, 424-426
Publish to the Web, 429-430
Report, 37
Reports, 417-423
Table, 346, 358-360
workgroup administration,
1046-1048

AccessLinks add-in (Excel), 37

Accessories Shortcut Bar, 32

accounting software, 763-765

**ACCPAC Plus for DOS A/R
(accounting software), 764**

ACE-Net (Web site), 1059

**Acquisition Reform Network (Web
site), 1074**

**Action Buttons command
(PowerPoint Slide Show
menu), 575**

action queries (Access), 407-408
records
appending with action queries,
410
deleting, 408-409
updating, 409-410
tables, creating, 411-412

**Action Settings dialog box
(PowerPoint), 575**

Activate method
Excel objects, 625, 628
Word objects, 622

**Active Elements command
(FrontPage 97 Insert menu),
837**

**Active Server Pages (ASP),
703-706**

ActiveX Controls, 649-652, 802
ActiveX Control Pad, 806
objects, inserting in HTML
files, 807-808
Script Wizard, 805
scripts, editing with ActiveX
Control Pad, 808-809
VB Script, 699
connecting to scripts, 804-805
Layout control, 809-810
editing, 810-812
inserting in HTML files, 810
<OBJECT> tag, 802-803
<PARAM> tag, 803-804
PowerPoint slide shows, 578
troubleshooting, 812

**Add Constraint dialog box
(Excel), 320, 329**

**Add Custom Chart Type dialog
box (Excel), 139**

Add method (Excel objects), 625

Add New Hardware Wizard
installing legacy cards, 948-951
troubleshooting, device detection,
936

Add Printer Wizard, 963-966

**Add Scenario dialog box (Excel),
305**

**Add Table command (Excel Table
menu), 261**

**Add Template dialog box (Word),
66**

Add Toolbar dialog box, 36

**Add Watch command (VBA
Debug menu), 668**

add-ins
Access, Linked Table Manager,
372
AutoMap Streets Plus, 767-769
Excel
AccessLinks, 37
ATP (Analysis ToolPak), 314
SBFM, 762
Solver, 324
Virus Search, 11

**Add-Ins command (Excel Tools
menu), 37**

**Add/Remove Programs Wizard,
1010**

**Adding an Object dialog box
(Publisher), 733**

**AddMenu macro action (Access),
446**

<ADDRESS> tag (HTML), 777

Address Book (Outlook)
  adding contacts to, 505
  data source for Mail Merge
    (Word), 116
  sending e-mail with, 505-507

Address property (Excel objects),
  627

Administrative Setup (network
  installation), 10

ads, creating with PageWizard
  (Publisher), 736-739

Advanced dialog box (Outlook),
  516

Advanced Filter (Excel lists),
  239-242

Advanced Options command (File
  menu), 999

Advertising Age (Web site), 1066

AFL-CIO (Web site), 1063

Airlines of the Web (Web site),
  1082

aligning
  controls on forms, 654
  icons, 865
  objects (Publisher), 723-724

Allow Zero Length property
  (Access), 356

ALSO (Web site), 1065

America Business Funding
  Directory (Web site), 1059

American Airlines (Web site),
  1082

American Demographics/
  Marketing Tools (Web site),
  1068

American Express Small Business
  Exchange (Web site), 1077

American Law Source Online
  (Web site), 1065

American Marketing Association
  (Web site), 1068

American Movers Conference
  (Web site), 1082

America's Brightest (Web site),
  1056

America's Job Bank (Web site),
  1063

America's Small Business
  Finance Center (Web site),
  1077

Analysis ToolPak, *see* ATP

AND (x,y) function (Word forms),
  82

Angel Capital Electronic Network
  (Web site), 1059

animating PowerPoint objects,
  552, 570
  Animation Effects toolbar, 552-553
  configuring for multimedia, 594
  custom animation, 553-554
  Preset Animations, 553

Animation Player (PowerPoint),
  581

Animation Effects toolbar
  (PowerPoint), 17,
  552-553

Answer report (Excel Solver), 334

antivirus software, 1036

appending records (Access), 410

<APPLET> tag (HTML), 778

Application collection (Access),
  629

Application directory, removing
  applications from, 1011

applications, 994-997
  Access, *see* Access
  Backup, *see* Backup
  backward-compatibility, 994
  buttons, creating for Shortcut
    Bar, 30
  creating shortcuts for, 863
  dual-boot configurations,
    1000-1001
  Excel, *see* Excel
  failed responses, 877
  incompatibility problems, 998
  installing, 997-998
    Install Programs Wizard,
      1002-1004
    setup programs, 997-998
  interfaces, 30-31
  minimizing, 877
  MKCOMPAT.EXE, 999
  Office 97-compatible applications,
    39
  opening files, 927
  Outlook, *see* Outlook
  PowerPoint, *see* PowerPoint
  reducing to buttons on taskbar,
    862
  removing, 1010-1014
    automatically, 1010
    DLLs (Dynamic Link
      Libraries), 1011-1013
    file associations, 1014
    folders, 1013
    from Application Directory,
      1011
    from Startup folder, 849
    manually, 1011-1014

references to applications,
  1013
  shortcuts, 1013
running, 1008-1009
  at startup, 847-849
starting
  Explorer, 868
  from Start menu, 859-860
  My Computer, 869
  shortcuts, 864
  taskbar buttons, 861
startup appearance, 849
switching between via taskbar,
  861-862
Win32
  multithreading, 994-995
  preemptive multitasking,
    994-995
  support for, 994-995
  system resources, 995
Windows 3.1, 996
  backward-compatibility,
    998-1001
  dual-boot configurations,
    1000-1001
  installing, 999-1000
  long file names, 996-997
  reinstalling, 1000
  running, 1001
Windows component
  adding, 1005-1006
  installing unlisted
    components, 1007
  removing, 1005-1006
Word, *see* Word

Applications Shortcut Bar, 32

ApplyFilter macro action
  (Access), 446

applying styles (Word), 70-71

Appointment object (Outlook),
  699

Archive attribute, 900

Archive command (Outlook File
  menu), 481

archives, creating with Backup,
  1022

archiving folders (Outlook),
  480-482

arithmetic operators, Access
  queries, 398-405

Arrange Icons command (View
  menu), 870, 909

Arrange Icons menu commands
  Auto Arrange, 873
  By Date, 909
  By Name, 909
  By Size, 909
  By Type, 909

Arrange menu commands (Publisher)
Layout Guides, 721
Line Up Objects, 724

arranging
icons, 872-873
files, 908-909
folders, 908-909
windows, taskbar, 877
see also sorting

array formulas (Excel)
constants, 191-194
functions, 188-190
using as arguments for functions, 190-191

arrays
VBScript, 689
VBA
Dim statement, 670
ReDim statement, 671

Asia-Pacific Economic Cooperation (Web site), 1061

Ask (Word field), 119, 122-123

Ask the Active Platform Pro (Web site), 707

ASP (Active Server Pages), 703-706

assigning
categories (Outlook), 509
tasks (Outlook), 528-529

ATP (Analysis ToolPak), 314
Exponential Smoothing, 315-316

Attach Template dialog box (Word), 64

attaching templates to documents (Word), 64-65

attributes
Archive, 900
Hidden, 900-901
HTML, 775
Read Only, 899-900
System, 900-901
see also properties

audio
PowerPoint, 587-589
Clip Art Gallery, 595
configuring playback, 596-598
outside sources, 596
Publisher
sound clips, editing, 742-745
sound clips, inserting, 740-742

Auditing command (Excel Tools menu), 204

auditing formulas (Excel)
invalid data, tracing, 207-208
tracers, 204-206
tracing dependents, 206

Auto Arrange command
Arrange Icons menu, 873
View menu, 909

AutoArchive (Outlook), 480-481

AutoComplete (Word), 12

AutoContent Wizard (PowerPoint), 579

autocorrelation (Excel forecast), 321-322

AUTOEXEC.BAT files, installing Windows 3.1 applications, 999

AutoFilter, Excel lists, 236-239

AutoFormat command (Access Format menu), 428

AutoMap Streets Plus, 18, 767-769

AutoNumber data type, Access tables, 350
Field Size property, 352
New Values property, 353

AutoReply (Outlook Out of Office Assistant), 514-515

AutoReport (Access), 414
columnar reports, 415
tabular reports, 416-417

AutoShape command (PowerPoint Format menu), 556

AutoShapes (PowerPoint), 548
placing text on, 555-557

AutoSummarize (Word), 12

AutoText (Word), 68

AVERAGE ( ) function (Word forms), 82

.AVI files (PowerPoint), 590

axes, Excel charts
category axis, 150-151
value axis, 150-151
vertical axis, defining, 162-164

B

<B> tag (HTML), 774, 776

Background and Text Colors command (Publisher Format menu), 754

backgrounds (FrontPage 97), 827-828

Backup, 1016-1027
archives, creating, 1022
backups, creating, 1019
drag-and-drop method, 1027-1029

file backups, 1020-1022
filtering files, 1026-1027
full backups, 1018
hard disks, 1018-1019
incremental backups, 1018
restoring files, 1030-1035
changing restore settings, 1032-1034
compare settings, 1034-1035
to other locations, 1031-1032
troubleshooting, 1033
verifying backup files, 1034
saving file sets, 1024-1026
settings, changing, 1023-1024, 1027
starting, 1016
tapes, 1029-1030

Backup dialog box, 1017, 1024

Backup Set Label dialog box, 1021

backups
creating, 1019
differential, 1018
drag-and-drop method, 1027-1029
File menu, 1017
files, 1020-1022
full, 1018
hard disks, 1018-1019
incremental, 1018
Iomega Zip drive, 1016
passwords for file sets, 1021
restoring files, 1030-1035
changing restore settings, 1032-1034
compare settings, 1034-1035
to other locations, 1031-1032
troubleshooting, 1033
verifying backup files, 1034
saving settings, 1024-1026
schedule preparation, 1019-1020
scheduling with System Agent, 1022-1023
settings, changing, 1023-1024, 1027
tape, 1016
tapes
Backup program, 1029-1030
formatting, 1029
troubleshooting, 1026
viruses
protecting computer from, 1035-1036
transmittal, 1035

backward-compatibility, 994, 998

Balance Sheet reports (SBFM), 766

Bankruptcy FAQs (Web site), 1059

bar charts (Excel), 150

Barron's Online (Web site), 1066

baselines (Excel forecasts), 315
  autocorrelation, 321-322

Basic Patent Information (Web site), 1072

batch files, creating side-by-side folder, 914-915

Bathrobe 'til 10 (Web site), 1077

Beep macro action (Access), 447

BidCast (Web site), 1074

<BIG> tag (HTML), 776

Big Dreams (Web site), 1056

bin operator (Solver), 330

Binary Value command (New menu), 920

Binder
  creating binders, 46-47
  customization, 57-58
  documents, printing, 11
  file sharing
    e-mail, 55-56
    Internet, 56
    networks, 55
  menu bar, 48
  opening binders, 47
  previewing binders, 51
  printing binders, 51
    headers/footers, 52-53
    landscape documents, 54-55
  sections
    deleting, 50
    editing, 48-49
    organizing, 49
    printing, 52
    selecting, 49-50
    unbinding, 50
    viewing contents, 47
  status bar, 58
  templates, 57

Binder Options command (Binder File menu), 57

Binder Page Setup command (Binder File menu), 52

Binder Page Setup dialog box (Binder), 52

BIOS, Plug and Play, 936-940

Biz$hop (Web site), 1077

BizResource.com (Web site), 1077

BizTalk (Web site), 1056

<BLOCKQUOTE> tag (HTML), 777

<BODY> tag (HTML), 775

boilerplate text (Word), 68

Bookmark command (Word Insert menu), 101

bookmarks, Word indexes, 101

booting into MS-DOS, 857

BOOTLOG.TXT, troubleshooting Windows 95 startup, 855

**
 tag (HTML), 774, 778**

breakpoints (VBA), 669

Briefcase, 884
  Briefcase Replication (Access), 16
  creating on desktop, 922
  files
    splitting, 926
    status checks, 925-926
    updating, 925
  installing, 922
  synchronizing files, 921-923

Briefcase command (New menu), 922

Briefcase menu commands
  Split from Original, 926
  Update All, 924

Browse for Folder dialog box, 1032

Browsed at a Kiosk slide show option (PowerPoint), 575

browsing
  folder contents, 884-885
  shared folders, 928

bubble charts (Excel), 153

Bureau of Export Administration (Web site), 1061

Business Information and Development Services (Web site), 1074

Business Intelligence Center (Web site), 1069

Business Law Site (Web site), 1065

Business Plan Resource File (Web sites), 1056

Business Research Lab (Web site), 1056

Business Resource Center (Web site), 1078

Business Start Page (Web site), 1078

Business Wire (Web site), 1069

Business Works (accounting software), 765

Business@Home (Web site), 1077

BusinessWeek (Web site), 1066

buttons
  activating programs, 861
  reducing applications, 862
  see also Shortcut Bars; toolbars

BuyersZone (Web site), 1056

By Date command (Arrange Icons menu), 909

By Name command (Arrange Icons menu), 909

By Size command (Arrange Icons meun), 909

By Type command (Arrange Icons menu), 909

bypassing
  Startup group at startup, 849
  Startup menu, 853
  Windows 95 Login dialog box, 846
  Windows 95 logo during startup, 846

Byte setting (Fields Size property), 352

C

Calculated Field command (Excel Formulas menu), 269

calculated fields, creating for Excel pivot tables, 268-270

Calculated Item command (Excel Formulas menu), 267

calculated items, Excel pivot tables, 266-268

Calculation fields, Word forms, 81-83

calculations, Access queries, 401-403

Calendar view (Outlook), creating fields, 487

calendars, creating with PageWizard (Publisher), 735-736

Call command (VBA), 662

CancelEvent macro action (Access), 447

canceling
  file selections, 890
  print jobs, 985
  see also undoing

Caption property (Access), 355

Caption property (forms), 652

Card view (Outlook)
  combination fields, 490
  designing folder views, 483

sorting
  by column, 466-467
  by field, 467-468
  creating new views, 468-470
PCI, Plug and Play compliance, 941
sound boards, installing, 945-951
caret (^) operator, VBA, 671
Case command (Word Format menu), 785
Case Sensitive command (Options menu), 906
Cash Flow reports (SBFM), 766
categories (Outlook)
  adding, 508-509
  assigning, 509
  e-mail, assigning categories to messages, 510
  folders
    searching by category, 511-512
    viewing by category, 510
Categories command (Outlook Edit menu), 508
category axis (Excel charts), 150-151
CCH Business Owner's Toolkit (Web site), 1057
CD Information (Web site), 1084
cells (Excel)
  cell drag-and-drop, 176
  character capacity, 13
  formulas
    absolute references, 186
    arguments, using arrays as, 190-191
    constants for array formulas, 191-194
    functions, using with array formulas, 188-190
    mixed references, 187-188
    naming, 194-198
    refreshing links, 201-202
    relative references, 186-187
    relative references, naming with, 198-199
    sheet-level names, 195
    troubleshooting links, 202-203
    workbook-level names, 196
    workbooks, linking, 200-201
  indenting text, 14
lists, 234-235
  Advanced Filter, 239-242
  AutoFilter, 236-239
  Data Forms, 248-250
  database functions, 246-247

formulas, 242-243
natural language formulas, 243-245
ranges
  3-D ranges, 180
  copying, 177
  Currency format for 3-D ranges, 180
  formulas for 3-D ranges, 181-183
  hyperlinks, 177, 183
  moving, 176
  multiple selections, 169-172
  naming, 172-173
  reference formulas, 177
  reference operators, 168
  selecting, 174-175
rotating text, 14
scenarios, 304
  creating, 305-307
  hiding, 306
  protecting, 306
  summarizing, 307-310
Cells property (Excel objects), 628
Center for Family Business (Web site), 1078
Central and Eastern Europe Business Information Center (Web site), 1062
Central Differencing (Excel Solver), 340
Change AutoShape command (PowerPoint Draw menu), 548
Change or Apply Style dialog box (Publisher), 716
Changing Cells (Excel Solver), 326-328
character formatting tags (HTML), 776-777
Charity Village (Web site), 1071
Chart menu commands (Excel)
  Chart Options, 158
  Source Data, 156
Chart Options command (Excel Chart menu), 158
Chart Wizard (Excel), 14
charts (Excel)
  bubble, 153
  category axis, 150-151
  data labels, 158
  data markers, 164-165
  designing templates, 139-141
  Error Bars, 165-166
  macros for labelling, 158-161
  plotting data series, 155-157
  value axis, 150-151

vertical axis, defining, 162-164
XY (Scatter), 152
check box control (VBA), 641
Check Box Form Field Options dialog box (Word), 84
check boxes
  FrontPage 97, 840
  Word forms, 84
CheckGrammar method (Word objects), 622
CheckSpelling method (Word objects), 622
CHIDIST function (Excel), 218
Choose Columns dialog box (Excel), 258
<CITE> tag (HTML), 777
classes (VBA objects), 664
ClassID (VBScript), 691
CLEAN function (Excel), 263
Clear Grid command (Access Edit menu), 405
Client/Server Central (Web site), 682
Clip Art Gallery
  network installation, 10
  PowerPoint
    audio, 595
    video, 589-590
Clipboard
  Clipboard Viewer, 38
  copying between applications, 38-39
  VBScript, 688
ClipMate, 38, 54
Close event (Word objects), 623
Close macro action (Access), 447
Close method
  Excel objects, 625
  Word objects, 623
Close Program dialog box, displaying, 879
Closing Bell (Web site), 1059
<CODE> tag (HTML), 776
Code view (Script Wizard), 808
collapsing folders, 885
collating print jobs, 979
colon (:), range operator in Excel, 168
colon (:) command, VBA Immediate window, 660

color
  printing
    configuring color printing
      properties, 970-971
    Image Color Matching (ICM)
      technology, 970
  text on Web pages (Publisher),
    754

Colorado Memory Systems
  telephone number, 1019
  Web site, 1019

Column charts (Excel), 150

**COLUMN function (Excel),
212-214**

**columnar reports, Access
AutoReport, 415**

columns, Access tables, 397

**combination fields (Outlook),
490-491**

**combo box control (VBA),
641-642**

**comma (,), union operator in
Excel ranges, 168**

**Command Button Wizard
(Access), 458**

**Commando Guide to
Unconventional Marketing and
Advertising Tactics (Web site),
1069**

commands
  Arrange Icons menu
    Auto Arrange, 873
    By Date, 909
    By Name, 909
    By Size, 909
    By Type, 909
  Arrange menu (Publisher)
    Layout Guides, 721
    Line Up Objects, 724
  Briefcase menu
    Split from Original, 926
    Update All, 924
  Chart menu (Excel)
    Chart Options, 158
    Source Data, 156
  Data menu (Excel)
    Filter, 236
    Form, 248
    Get External Data, 246
    PivotTable Report, 253
    Refresh Data, 134
    Template Wizard, 143
  Debug menu (VBA)
    Add Watch, 668
    Step Into, 669
  Draw menu (PowerPoint)
    Change AutoShape, 548
    Group, 548
    Rotate or Flip, 550

Edit menu
  Categories (Outlook), 508
  Clear Grid (Access), 405
  Delete Rows (Access), 401
  Find, 857
  Go To (Access), 376
  Invert Selection, 889
  Links (PowerPoint), 561
  Links (Word), 42
  Paste Special (Word), 40
  Select All, 889
  Undo, 917
  Undo Delete, 893
File menu
  Advanced Options, 999
  Archive (Outlook), 481
  Binder Options (Binder), 57
  Binder Page Setup (Binder),
    52
  Create New Publication
    (Publisher), 748
  Delete, 894
  Empty Recycle Bin, 896
  Exit, 899
  Get External Data (Access),
    369
  Import and Export (Outlook),
    482
  New (Word), 67
  Open, 999
  Open Binder (Binder), 47
  Open File for Editing, 898
  Open File Set, 1020
  Open Search (Outlook), 478
  Preview (FrontPage 97), 831
  Preview Web Site (Publisher),
    757
  Print, 902, 978
  Print Binder (Binder), 51
  Properties, 899, 925
  Publish Form As (Outlook),
    539
  Publish FrontPage Web
    (FrontPage 97), 822
  Publish to Web (Publisher),
    758
  Publish Web Site to Folder
    (Publisher), 758
  Quick View, 898
  Rename, 916
  Restore, 895
  Return Data to Microsoft
    Excel (Excel), 262
  Save As, 1025
  Save As (Word), 68
  Save as HTML (Excel), 779
  Save as HTML (PowerPoint),
    580, 781
  Save as HTML (Word), 779
  Save Binder As (Binder), 57
  Save Search, 906
  Save Search (Outlook), 478

Send (Access), 423
Send To (Binder), 56
Send To (PowerPoint), 38
Find menu
  Computer, 932
  Files, 902
Form menu (Outlook)
  Control Toolbox, 536
  Display This Page, 693
  Rename Page, 693
Format menu
  AutoFormat (Access), 428
  AutoShape (PowerPoint), 556
  Background and Text Colors
    (Publisher), 754
  Case (Word), 785
  Font (Word), 785
  Freeze Columns (Access), 376
  Selected Data Series (Excel),
    164
  Selected Plot Area (Excel),
    220
  Style (Word), 71
  Style Gallery (Word), 65
  Unfreeze All Columns
    (Access), 376
Formulas menu (Excel)
  Calculated Field, 269
  Calculated Item, 267
Go menu (Binder), Show Web
  Toolbar, 56
Help menu (Excel), Financial
  Manager Help Topics, 762
Insert menu
  Active Elements (FrontPage
    97), 837
  Bookmark (Word), 101
  Copied Cells (Excel), 179
  Cross-reference (Word), 98
  Cut Cells (Excel), 179
  Field (Word), 95
  Form Field (FrontPage 97),
    839
  Index and Tables (Word), 93
  Module (VBA), 660
  Movies and Sounds
    (PowerPoint), 590
  Name (Excel), 173
  Object (PowerPoint), 559
  Page (Publisher), 712
  Page Numbers (Publisher),
    716
  Picture (Word), 786
  Procedure (VBA), 660
  Reports (Access), 415
  Rows (Access), 401
  Table of Contents (FrontPage
    97), 836
  Timestamp (FrontPage 97),
    835
  UserForm (VBE), 636

New menu
  Binary Value, 920
  Briefcase, 922
  Folder, 870, 891
  Shortcut, 863
Options menu
  Case Sensitive, 906
  Results, 906
Printer menu
  Close, 985
  Pause Printing, 983
  Properties, 973
  Purge Print Jobs, 983
  Set as Default, 984
  Work Offline, 984
Program menu, Schedule a New
  Program, 1023
Query menu (Access)
  Delete Query, 408
  Run, 410
  Show Table, 391
  Update Query, 409
Record menu (Access)
  Filter, 382
  Remove Filter/Sort, 381
  Sort, 380
Records menu (Excel)
  Edit Column, 262
  Sort, 261
Section menu (Binder)
  Delete, 50
  Next Section, 49
  Previous Section, 49
  Print Preview, 51
  Select All, 50
  Unselect All, 50
Send To, 875-877
Settings menu
  Control Panel, 846, 851
  Drag and Drop, 1023, 1028
  File Filtering, 1017, 1026
  Options, 1017, 1027
  taskbar, 861, 1013
Slide Show menu (PowerPoint)
  Action Buttons, 575
  Custom Animation, 570
  Rehearse Timings, 567
  Slide Transition, 565
  View on Two Screens, 572
  View Show, 569
Start menu
  Programs, 46
  Run, 857, 862, 999, 1008
Table menu (Excel), Add Table,
  261
Tools menu
  Add-Ins (Excel), 37
  Auditing (Excel), 204
  Data Analysis (Excel), 315
  Design Checker (Publisher),
    755

Design Outlook Form
  (Outlook), 487, 693
Erase Tape, 1030
Find, 902, 932
Find (Outlook), 477
Format Tape, 1030
Go To, 885
Goal Seek (Excel), 311
Macro (Access), 16
Macro (Word), 83
Mail Merge (Word), 110
Protect Document (Word), 76
Redetect Tape, 1030
Relationships (Access), 364,
  436
Scenarios (Excel), 305
Services (Outlook), 507
Snap To (Publisher), 723
Solver (Excel), 320, 325
Templates (Word), 64
Unprotect Document (Word),
  77
Verify Hyperlinks (FrontPage
  97), 831
VBA, Call, 662
View menu
  Arrange Icons, 870, 909
  Auto Arrange, 909
  Conditions (Access), 451
  Details, 907, 925
  Field Chooser (Outlook), 484
  Font, 899
  Forms Toolbar (FrontPage
    97), 839
  Group By (Outlook), 471
  Immediate Window (VBA),
    648
  Landscape, 899
  Large Icons, 907
  Line Up Icons, 909
  List, 907
  Object Browser (VBA), 649
  Options, 916, 933
  Options (Explorer), 30
  Page Break Preview (Excel),
    13
  Page View, 899
  Properties Window (VBE),
    637
  Refresh, 887, 926
  Replace Window, 899
  Show Fields (Outlook), 483
  Small Icons, 907
  Sort (Outlook), 467
  Sorting and Grouping
    (Access), 428
  SQL View (Access), 405
  Status Bar, 907
  Toolbar, 870, 884, 907
  Toolbars (Word), 76, 88
  Watch Window (VBA), 668

Commerce Business Daily (Web
  site), 1074
Common Dialog control (VBA),
  649-652
Compact utility (Access), 15
Compare (Word field), 119
Compare tab (Backup dialog box),
  1017
comparison operators (Solver),
  329
compatibility
  backward-compatibility, 994, 998
  incompatibility problems, 998
compound criteria (Access
  queries), 400-401
compound documents
  comparison of linking and
    embedding, 42
  creating, 40-42
  tracking links, 42
compression, troubleshooting
  Windows 95 startup, 857
Computer command (Find
  menu), 932
Computer Loan Network (Web
  site), 1059
Computer Properties sheet,
  troubleshooting hardware
  conflicts, 954-956
Computer Register (Web site),
  1063
computers
  finding on networks, 932
  sharing resources, 928-931
  viruses
    protection, 1035-1036
    transmittal, 1035
concordance method of indexing,
  100
conditional fields, Word Mail
  Merge main document,
  120-121
conditional formatting (Excel), 14
conditions, Access macros,
  451-452
Conditions command (Access
  View menu), 451
conference presentations
  (PowerPoint), 573-574
CONFIG.SYS file, 856
  installing Windows 3.1
    applications, 999

configuring
accounting software for SBFM, 763-764
backup settings, 1023-1024
Office Assistant, 19
PowerPoint
audio playback, 596-598
self-running slide shows, 575

Confirm File Delete dialog box, turning off, 897

Confirm Folder Delete dialog box, 894

Confirm Operation Before Beginning option, 1028

Conjugate method (Excel Solver), 340

connecting frames (Publisher), 713-714

constants, Excel array formulas, 191-194

constraints (Excel Solver), 328-331

Contact object (Outlook), 699

Contact! (Web site), 1062

contacts (Outlook)
adding names to Contacts folder, 504-505
Address Book
adding to, 505
sending e-mail with, 505-507
creating e-mail for contacts, 498-499
creating from e-mail messages, 496-497

Continental Airlines (Web site), 1082

contiguous ranges (Excel), 169

Continued references (Publisher), 714-716

Control Panel, 884

Control Panel command (Settings menu), 846, 851

Control Toolbox (VBA), 647

Control Toolbox command (Outlook Form menu), 536

Control Toolbox toolbar (PowerPoint), 578

controls
aligning, 654
macros (Access), 455-458
sizing, 654
tab order, 653

Convergence (Excel Solver), 338

converting
Access databases, 24
Excel files, 23-24
to HTML
Excel spreadsheets, 779-780
PowerPoint presentations, 781-782
Publisher documents, 782-784
Word, 779
macros (Word), 22
PowerPoint
objects, 560-561
files, 25-26
Publisher documents for Web, 759
unbound objects (Access), 25
Word documents, 22-23

Copied Cells command (Excel Insert menu), 179

Copy Disk dialog box, 893

Copy method
Excel objects, 627-628
Word objects, 624

copying
between applications (Clipboard), 38-39
disks, 893
Excel
cell ranges, 177
from Excel to Access, 38
files, 891-892
folders, 891-892

CopyObject macro action (Access), 447

Copyright Clearance Center (Web site), 1072

Copyright Website, 1073

CorelDRAW!, rotating PowerPoint slide images, 54

Corporate Counselor (Web site), 1065

Council on Foundations (Web site), 1071

Count property (Excel objects), 624

COUNT( ) function (Word forms), 82

COUNTA function (Excel), 210

coupons, creating with PageWizard (Publisher), 739

Create Data Source dialog box (Word), 111

Create New Data Source dialog box (Excel), 256

Create New Publication command (Publisher File menu), 748

CreateObject function (VBScript), 691

criteria (Access)
expressions, 400-401
identifiers, 398-400
operators, 398-400
setting, 397-398

Cross-reference command (Word Insert menu), 98

Cross-reference dialog box (Word), 98

cross-references, Word documents, 98

Currency Converter (Web site), 1060

Currency data type, Access tables, 350

Custom Animation command (PowerPoint Slide Show menu), 570

Custom Animation dialog box (PowerPoint), 553

Custom Header dialog box (Binder), 53

Customize dialog box, 33

customizing
Access
Datasheet view, 374-375
reports, 427-428
animations (PowerPoint), 553-554
Binder, 57-58
Explorer, 906-911
arranging icons, 908-909
changing file display, 907-908
changing folder display, 907-908
displaying file types, 910-911
hiding file types, 910-911
hiding toolbar, 907
pane widths, 906-907
sorting folders, 909-910
status bar, 907
to open side-by-side windows, 914-915
to start programs like Program Manager (Windows 3.x, 915-916
forms (Outlook), 535-538
Help, 20-22
Publisher
Design Gallery, 732-734
Web page text color, 754
Shortcut Bars
adding, 35
appearance of bars, 33
buttons, adding, 34
buttons, arranging, 34
buttons, creating, 34

buttons, customizing, 34-35
creating custom bars, 36
buttons, deleting, 34
deleting, 35
hiding, 32-33
positioning bar, 31-32
saving configurations, 37
Solver (Excel), 337-338
toolbars
macro buttons, 604-605
Word, 89-91
Web pages (Publisher), 749

Cut Cells command (Excel Insert menu), 179

Cut method (Word objects), 624

cutting between applications, 38-39

D

DacEasy (accounting software), 764

damping factor (Excel forecasts), 318-320

DAO (Data Access Objects), 275
DialogHandler subroutine, 284-286
Driver subroutine, 280-282
GetQueryNames subroutine, 282-284
ImportData subroutine, 286-290
installation, 275-276
sample application, 296-301
setting up Access structures, 276-280
VBA, 673-674

Data Analysis command (Excel Tools menu), 315

Data Form dialog box (Word), 111

Data Forms, Excel lists, 248-250

data labels, Excel charts, 158
macros for creating labels, 158-161

data markers, Excel charts, 164-165

Data menu commands (Excel)
Filter, 236
Form, 248
Get External Data, 246
PivotTable Report, 253
Refresh Data, 134
Template Wizard, 143

data sharing
Access, 37
Excel, 37
PowerPoint, 38

data source (Word Mail Merge), 109
Access tables, 115
Excel worksheets, 115
Outlook Address Book, 116
records
filtering, 117
selecting, 117-118
sorting, 118
types of, 115-116
Word tables, 114-115

data types (Access)
changing, 363
tables, 348-351
AutoNumber, 350
Currency, 350
Date/Time, 350
Hyperlink, 351
Memo, 350
Number, 350
OLE Object, 350
properties, 351-358
Text, 349
Yes/No, 350

Database (Word field), 119

database driver, Excel Template Wizard, 142-143

database functions (Excel), 246-247

databases (Access), 274
converting, 24
encrypting, 1047
FROM clause, 292-293
GROUP BY clause, 293
modifying databases from Excel, 290-291
ORDER BY clause, 293
protecting source code, 1046
queries, 390
action queries, 407-408
action queries, appending records with, 410
action queries, creating tables with, 411-412
action queries, deleting records with, 408-409
action queries, updating records with, 409-410
calculations, 401-403
column width, 397
criteria, expressions, 400-401
criteria, identifiers, 398-400
criteria, operators, 398-400
criteria, setting, 397-398
Design view, 390-391
fields, adding, 393-394
fields, deleting, 394-395
fields, hiding, 396-397
fields, moving, 395
fields, naming, 395-396
fields, viewing, 396-397

joining, 392
properties, 403-405
QBE, 391
relationships, 392-393
Simple Query Wizard, 405-406
sort order of results, 401
tables, adding to queries, 391
records, locking, 1047
security during conversion, 25
SELECT statement, 291-292
sending SQL to, 293-295
temporary queries, 295-296
see also Access; tables

Datasheet view (Access), 346-348, 372
customization, 374-375
data entry, 376-377
navigating, 375-376
switching to Form view, 374

Date/Time data type, Access tables, 350
Format property, 353

DAVERAGE function (Excel), 246-247

DCOUNT function (Excel), 247

Debug menu commands (VBA)
Add Watch, 668
Step Into, 669

debugger (VBA), 666-668
breakpoints, 669
stepping through code, 668-669

Decimal Places property (Access), 353-355

Default Paragraph Font style (Word), 70

Default Value property (Access), 355

Deferred Printing, 983-984

Define Views dialog box (Outlook), 484

DEFINED(x) function (Word forms), 82

defining
axes (Excel), 162-164
data sources, Excel pivot tables, 256-258
scenarios (Excel), 305-307

delaying e-mail message delivery (Outlook), 525

Delete command
Binder Section menu, 50
File menu, 894

Delete Query command (Access Query menu), 408

Delete Rows command (Access Edit menu), 401

DeleteObject macro action (Access), 447

deleting
buttons
from Shortcut Bars, 34
from toolbars (Word), 91
data from Access tables, 378
fields (Access), 363
queries, 394-395
files, 893-895
from MS-DOS prompt, 894
purging, 897
restoring, 895-897
system, 895
folders, 893-895
joins (Access), 393
printers, 967
records (Access), 408-409
sections (Binder), 50
Shortcut Bars, 35
shortcuts, 864-865

Department of Labor (Web site), 1064

Department of Labor Poster Page (Web site), 1065

Description property (Access), 404

deselecting, *see* **selecting**

Design Checker (Publisher), 755-757

Design Checker command (Publisher Tools menu), 755

Design Gallery (Publisher), 730
creating custom galleries, 732-734
editing objects, 731
inserting objects on pages, 730-731
Web pages, 752

Design Outlook Form command (Outlook Tools menu), 487, 693

Design view (Access), 346
queries, 390-391
reports, 428
tables, 348-349
data types, 349-351

designing templates (Excel)
charts, 139-141
worksheets, 137-138

desktop, 846, 869-874
accessing, 870-871
Briefcase, 922
folders, creating, 870
icons, 862-867
aligning, 865
arranging, 872-873
removing, 871

selecting, 871
see also icons
keyboard, 873-874
multiple profiles, 847
printing (drag-and-drop), 985-987
creating printer shortcut icons, 985-986
multiple documents, 987
shortcuts, 863, 870-871
opening side-by-side windows from, 914-915

Desktop Shortcut Bar, 32

Details command (View menu), 907, 925

Device Manager, 954-956
determining Plug and Play compatibility, 938
printer ports, configuring, 975
removing device drivers, 951-952
troubleshooting hardware installation, 952
checking for resource conflicts, 956-957

DGET function (Excel), 247

dialog boxes
Action Settings (PowerPoint), 575
Add Constraint (Excel), 320, 329
Add Custom Chart Type (Excel), 139
Add Scenario (Excel), 305
Add Template (Word), 66
Add Toolbar, 36
Adding an Object (Publisher), 733
Advanced (Outlook), 516
Attach Template (Word), 64
Backup, 1017, 1024
Backup Set Label, 1021
Binder Page Setup (Binder), 52
Browse for Folder, 1032
Change or Apply Style (Publisher), 716
Check Box Form Field Options (Word), 84
Choose Columns (Excel), 258
Close Program, displaying, 879
Confirm File Delete, turning off, 897
Confirm Folder Delete, 894
Copy Disk, 893
Create Data Source (Word), 111
Create New Data Source (Excel), 256
Cross-reference (Word), 98
Custom Animation (PowerPoint), 553
Custom Header (Binder), 53
Customize, 33
Data Form (Word), 111
Define Views (Outlook), 484
Drop-Down Form Field Options (Word), 84

Edit Binary Value, 920
Edit Rule (Outlook), 515
Field (Word), 95
Field Chooser (Outlook), 484
File Filtering—File Types, 1026
File Selection, 1020
Filter (Outlook), 474
Find, 904
opening, 906
Format Tape, 1030
Hyperlink (Publisher), 750
Import File to FrontPage 97 Web, 821
Index and Tables (Word), 93
Insert ActiveX Control (ActiveX Control Pad), 807
Insert Calculated Item (Excel), 267
Insert Page (Publisher), 712
Install from Disk, 1007
Join Properties (Access), 392
Layout Guides (Publisher), 721
Line Up Objects (Publisher), 724
Link (Access), 370
Links
PowerPoint, 561
Word, 42
Login, 846
Make Table (Access), 411
Mark Index Entry (Word), 100
Mark Table of Contents Entry (Word), 92
Modify Location (Binder), 58
Move Items (Outlook), 479
New Office Document, 28
New Query (Access), 390
New Report (Access), 415
New Style (Word), 74
New Table (Access), 346
New Toolbar (Word), 90
Not Responding, 877
Open Data Source (Word), 115
Open With, 901
Options, 910, 928
Other Designs (Publisher), 734
Print, 978
Word 6 features, 980-981
Word 97 features, 979-980
Print Binder (Binder), 51
Publish Form As (Outlook), 539
Pushpin Properties (AutoMap Streets Plus), 769
Query Options (Word), 117
Query Properties (Access), 403
Record Macro (Word), 103
Relationships (Access), 364
Remove Shortcuts/Folders, 1013
Save As, 1025
Excel, 23
Word, 23
Scenario Summary (Excel), 308
Scenario Values (Excel), 306

Select a Folder (Publisher), 758
Select Folder(s) (Outlook), 477
Set Up Show (PowerPoint), 571
Settings—Drag and Drop, 1028
Show Table (Access), 436
Slide Transition (PowerPoint), 568
Solver (Excel), 325
Spool Settings, 973
Style (Word), 71
Table Properties (Access), 357
Tables of Contents Options (Word), 94
Templates and Add-ins (Word), 64
Text Form Field Options (Word), 79, 85
Update My Briefcase, 924
Use Address Book (Word), 116
VBA, use in, 649-652
View Summary (Outlook), 483
Welcome, 847
Welcome to Microsoft Backup, 1016

DialogHandler subroutine (Access), 281, 284-286

differential backups, 1018

Dim statement (VBA), 670

directories, removing applications from, 1011
see also folders

disabling Welcome to Windows 95 screen, 847

Disgruntled (Web site), 1066

disks
errors, 850-854
floppy disks
copying, 893
moving files to, 892
hard disks
backups, 1018-1019
troubleshooting Windows 95 startup, 857
startup disks, 850-854
creating, 851
restarting Windows 95 from, 857-858

Display This Page command (Outlook Form menu), 693

displaying
Close Program dialog box, 879
drives, 884
file extensions, 916
file properties, 899
file types, 910-911
files, changing display, 907-908
folder properties, 899

folders, 885
changing display, 907-908
taskbar, 847
toolbar, 884

DLLs (Dynamic Link Libraries), removing, 1011-1013

DMAX function (Excel), 247

DMIN function (Excel), 247

Do...While loops (VBA), 666

Doctor HTML, 796

Document Maps (Word), 12

documents, 28
Binder documents, printing, 11
compound documents, 40-42
comparison of linking and embedding, 42
tracking links, 42
creating, 28-30
opening, 30
Explorer, 868
from Start menu, 860-861
My Computer, 869
with shortcuts, 864
running at startup, 847-849
Word
converting, 22-23
cross-references, 98
document mapping, 96-98
global templates, creating, 66
headings for tables of contents, 92-93
indexes, 99-103
styles, applying, 70-71
styles, creating, 73-74
styles, modifying, 71-73
tables of contents, creating, 93-94
tables of contents for multiple documents, 95
tables of contents, updating, 95-96
template conflicts, resolving, 66-67
templates, attaching, 64-65
templates, creating, 67-68
templates, previewing, 65
templates, saving, 67
user templates, 67
workgroup templates, 67
see also files; Word

Documents collection (Word objects), 620
events
Close, 623-624
Open, 623
methods
Activate, 622
CheckGrammar, 622

CheckSpelling, 622
Close, 623
Open, 623
Save, 623
SaveAs, 623
SendMail, 623
properties
Font Selection, 624
PageSetup, 621
Path, 621
ReadOnly, 621
Saved, 621
SaveFormat, 621-622

Double setting (Field Size property), 352

DPRODUCT function (Excel), 247

Drag and Drop command (Settings menu), 1023, 1028

drag-and-drop
backups, 1027-1029
copying files, 892
moving files, 892
printing from desktop, 985-987
creating printer shortcut icons, 985-986
multiple documents, 987
printing, 986

dragging objects in Outlook, 494
appointments, creating from messages, 496
contacts
creating e-mail for, 498-499
creating from messages, 496-497
dragging objects outside Outlook, 501-502
journal entries
creating, 507
creating from messages, 497-498
notes
creating, 499
sending as e-mail messages, 500
to public folders, 531
to Tasks folder, 495-496
text, 500

DRAM (Dynamic RAM), 586

Draw menu commands (PowerPoint)
Change AutoShape, 548
Group, 548
Rotate or Flip, 550

Draw Table tool (Word), 12

Driver subroutine (Access), 280-282

drivers
 printers
  deleting, 967
  extensions (DRV/VXD), 976
  installing, 976
  installing printers, 964
  sources, 967
  VXD (virtual device drivers),
   972
 removing, Device Manager,
  951-952
 Windows 95 Driver Library
  (W95DL), 967

drives
 displaying, 884
 searching for files, 903-904

**Drop-Down Form Field Options
 dialog box (Word), 84**

**drop-down list boxes, Word
 forms, 84-85**

**drop-down menus (FrontPage
 97), 840**

DSTDEV function (Excel), 247

DSTDEVP function (Excel), 247

DSUM function (Excel), 246-247

**dual-boot configurations,
 1000-1001**

DVAR function (Excel), 247

DVARP function (Excel), 247

Dynamic RAM (DRAM), 586

**Dynamic Link Libraries (DLLs),
 1011-1013**

dynasets (Access), 390, 440

E

/e switch, 911

e-mail
 Binder, 55-56
 distributing Mail Merge
  documents (Word), 126-128
 Exchange Server, managing
  mailbox, 514
 Outlook
  adding to Contacts folder,
   504-505
  appointments, creating from
   messages, 496
  assigning categories to
   messages, 510
  AutoReply, 514-515
  contacts, adding to Address
   Book, 505
  contacts, creating e-mail for,
   498-499

 contacts, creating from
  messages, 496-497
 creating tasks, 495-496
 delaying message delivery,
  525
 forms, 539
 Inbox Assistant, 514, 519-520
 journal entries, creating from
  messages, 497-498
 notes, sending as e-mail
  messages, 500
 Out of Office Assistant,
  514-518
 redirecting replies, 525
 Rules, 515-518
 sending e-mail with Address
  Book, 505-507
 tracking messages, 523-525
 voting messages, 520-522
 reports
  Access, 423, 430

E-Span (Web site), 1064

Echo macro action (Access), 447

EDGAR (Web site), 1060

Edit Binary Value dialog box, 920

**Edit Column command (Excel
 Records menu), 262**

Edit menu commands
 Access
  Clear Grid, 405
  Delete Rows, 401
  Go To, 376
 Find, 857
 Invert Selection, 889
 Outlook, Categories, 508
 PowerPoint, Links, 561
 Select All, 889
 Undo, 917
 Undo Delete, 893
 Word
  Links, 42
  Paste Special, 40

**Edit Rule dialog box (Outlook),
 515**

editing
 Design Gallery objects
  (Publisher), 731
 file names, 916-917
 FrontPage 97
  files, 823-825
  graphics, 826-827
 Layout control (ActiveX), 810-812
 macros, 607-609
  Word, 104-105
 PowerPoint
  grouped objects, 549
  video, 591-593
 records (Access), 378

 Registry, removing numeric tails
  from file names, 920
 scripts with ActiveX Control Pad,
  808-809
 sections (Binder), 48-49
 shortcut names, 864-865
 sound clips (Publisher), 742-745
 styles (Word), 71-73
 tables (Access), 362-363

**Editor (FrontPage 97), 817,
 822-823**

**EDO (Extended Data Out) RAM,
 586**

**Education, Training, and
 Development Resource Center
 for Business and Industry (Web
 site), 1057**

EGOPHER (Web site), 1078

**The Electronic Embassy (Web
 site), 1062**

**Electronic Commerce Program
 Office (Web site), 1074**

**Electronic Commerce Resource
 Center (Web site), 1075**

**Electronic Money Tree (Web site),
 1078**

<EM> tag (HTML), 776

<EMBED> tag (HTML), 778

embedding, 39-40
 compound documents, creating,
  40-42
 documents in Binder, 48
 files sizes, 41
 PowerPoint, 560
  manipulating embedded
   objects, 561
 versus linking, 42

**EMF (enhanced meta file)
 spooling (printing), 972-974**

**Empty Recycle Bin command
 (File menu), 896**

**encrypting databases (Access),
 1047**

**Enforce Referential Integrity
 property (Access), 364**

**enhanced meta file (EMF)
 spooling (printing), 972-974**

***Entrepreneur* Magazine's
 BizSquare (Web site), 1079**

***Entrepreneurial Edge Online*
 (Web site), 1066**

***Entrepreneur's* Bookstore (Web
 site), 1078**

EntreWorld (Web site), 1079

envelopes, printing with Mail Merge (Word), 126

Environmental Protection Agency Procurement (Web site), 1075

EOF( ) function (VBA), 672

equal sign (=), assigning HTML attributes, 775

Erase Tape command (Tools menu), 1030

Ernest & Young's Virtual HR Office (Web site), 1064

Error Bars (Excel charts), 165-166

error trapping (VB Script), 691

errors
disk, ScanDisk, 850-854
Windows 95 startup, 856
see also troubleshooting

events
Document object (Word)
Close, 623-624
Open, 623
VBScript, activating, 690-691
VBA, 673

Events Wizard (Outlook), 695

EventWeb (Web site), 1085

Excel
add-ins
AccessLinks, 37
ATP (Analysis ToolPak), 314
cells
cell drag-and-drop, 176
character capacity, 13
conditional formatting, 14
indentation, 14
rotating text, 14
charts
bubble, 153
category axis, 150-151
data labels, 158
data markers, 164-165
Error Bars, 165-166
macros for labelling, 158-161
plotting data series, 155-157
value axis, 150-151
vertical axis, defining, 162-164
XY (Scatter), 152
connecting with Access, 274-275
FROM clause, 292-293
GROUP BY clause, 293
modifying Access databases, 290-291
ORDER BY clause, 293
SELECT statement, 291-292
DAO (Data Access Objects), 275
installation, 275-276
data sharing, 37

files, converting, 23-24
forecasting
autocorrelation, 321-322
baselines, 315
creating forecasts, 315-316
damping factor, 318-320
error in prior forecast, 316
regression-based forecasts, 318
formulas, 14
absolute references, 186
arguments, using arrays as, 190-191
constants for array formulas, 191-194
dependents, tracing, 206
functions, using with array formulas, 188-190
Goal Seek, 310-314
invalid data, tracing, 207-208
mixed references, 187-188
naming, 194-198
refreshing links, 201-202
relative references, 186-187
relative references, naming with, 198-199
sheet-level names, 195
tracers, 204-206
troubleshooting links, 202-203
workbook-level names, 196
workbooks, linking, 200-201
functions
CHIDIST, 218
CLEAN, 263
COLUMN, 212-214
COUNTA, 210
database functions, 246-247
Excel 4.0 functions, 230-231
FDIST, 220-224
FIND, 213
FREQUENCY, 218-220
GROWTH, 314
INDEX, 211-212
INDIRECT, 214-215
IRR, 227-229
LINEST, 220-224
MATCH, 213, 215-217
MAX, 212
NORMDIST, 218-220
NPV, 225-227
OFFSET, 210-211
profitability indexes, 229
R^2, 221-224
ROW, 212-214
TREND, 314
VLOOKUP, 215-217
lists, 234-235
Advanced Filter, 239-242
AutoFilter, 236-239
Data Forms, 248-250
database functions, 246-247

formulas, 242-243
natural language formulas, 243-245
macros
command buttons, 638-639, 644-645
forms, 636-637
InputBox function, 646
MsgBox function, 642-644
recording, 634-636
text box controls, 639-641
objects
Activate method, 625, 628
Add method, 625
Address property, 627
Cells property, 628
Close method, 625
Copy method, 627-628
Count property, 624
Formula property, 628
Name property, 626
Open method, 625
ReadOnly property, 625
Save method, 625
SaveAs method, 625
Saved property, 625
Sort method, 628
VBA, 674-677
Visible property, 626
Worksheets collection, 626
page breaks, 13
pivot tables
calculated fields, creating, 268-270
calculated items, 266-268
creating, 253
data sources, defining, 256-258
DialogHandler subroutine, 284-286
Driver subroutine, 280-282
external data sources, 255-256
fields, 253
GetQueryNames subroutine, 282-284
ImportData subroutine, 286-290
limitation of calculated fields, 270
Microsoft Query, 256
page fields, 263-264
Query window, 260-263
Query Wizard, 258-260
refreshing, 255
retrieving data from Access databases, 276-280
ranges
3-D ranges, 180
copying, 177
Currency format for 3-D ranges, 180
formulas for 3-D ranges, 181-183

hyperlinks, 177, 183
moving, 176
multiple selections, 169-172
naming, 172-173
reference formulas, 177
reference operators, 168
selecting, 174-175
rows, capacity, 13
SBFM, 762-763
accounting software,
configuring, 763-764
importing data, 765-766
reports, 766
software considerations,
764-765
scenarios, 304
creating, 305-307
hiding, 306
protecting, 306
SBFM, 767
Solver, 331
summarizing, 307-310
Solver
Automatic Scaling, 339
Central Differencing, 340
Changing Cells, specifying,
326-328
Conjugate method, 340
constraints, 328-331
forecasts, damping factor, 319
linear searches, 339
Newton method, 340
nonlinear searches, 339
Precision edit box, 337-338
quadratic estimates, 340
reports, 333-337
Show Iteration Results, 339
solutions, 331-333
tangential estimates, 340
Target Cell, specifying,
325-326
spreadsheets, converting to
HTML, 779-780
tables, 75
templates, 132, 135-136
building with Template
Wizard, 143-146
charts, designing for, 139-141
database driver for Template
Wizard, 142-143
entering data in, 146
template elements, 133-135
Template Wizard, installing,
141
workbooks, opening, 132-133
worksheets, designing for,
137-138
troubleshooting
cell ranges, 183
charts, 157
Goal Seek, 314

links, 202-203
Solver, 340
Template Wizard, 148
wizards
Chart, 14
Internet Assistant, 779
PivotTable, 255
Query, 14, 258-260
Template, 141
workgroup administration, 1048
worksheets, Word Mail Merge,
115

Exchange Server
e-mail
delaying message delivery,
525
Inbox Assistant, 519-520
managing mailbox, 514
Out of Office Assistant,
514-518
redirecting replies, 525
tracking messages, 523-525
voting messages, 520-522
forms, 541
public folders, 531
adding items to, 531-532
manipulating items in, 532-533
tasks, 526
accepting assignments,
529-530
assigning, 528-529
ownership, 526-527
tracking owners, 527-528
updates, 527

Exit command (File menu), 899

Expand Slide (PowerPoint), 16

expanding folders, 885

Explorer (Windows), 882-887
applications, starting, 868
creating documents, 29
customizing, 906-911
arranging icons, 908-909
displaying file types, 910-911
file display, 907-908
file types, hiding, 910-911
folder display, 907-908
pane widths, 906-907
side-by-side windows, 914-915
sorting folders, 909-910
starting programs like
Program Manager
(Windows 3.x), 915-916
status bar, 907
toolbar, hiding, 907
documents, opening, 868
filename extensions, viewing, 30
files
opening, 901-902
viewing, 882-887

sharing resources, 928-933
browsing shared folders, 928
finding computers, 932
mapping network drives, 931
viewing network resources,
933
starting, 882, 911-913
toolbar, hiding, 907

**Explorer (FrontPage 97),
818-819**
files, importing, 821-822
importing Web site elements,
819-820
publishing Web pages to servers,
822
views, 820

EXPOguide (Web site), 1083

**Exponential Smoothing (Excel),
314, 315-316**

**Export-Import Bank (Web site),
1060**

ExporTutor (Web site), 1062

Expression Builder (Access), 442
control references in macros,
457-458

**expressions, Access queries,
400-401**

**Extended Data Out (EDO) RAM,
586**

F

**FAA Acquisition Center (Web
site), 1075**

Fast Company (Web site), 1067

**FAT (file allocation table), long
file names, 917**

Favorites Shortcut Bar, 32

**fax, distributing Mail Merge
documents (Word), 126-128**

FDIST function (Excel), 220-224

**Federal Acquisition Institute
(Web site), 1075**

FedEX (Web site), 1082

Field Chooser (Outlook), 537

**Field Chooser command (Outlook
View menu), 484**

**Field Chooser dialog box
(Outlook), 484**

**field codes (Word Mail Merge),
113**

Field command (Word Insert menu), 95

Field dialog box (Word), 95

Field Size property (Access), 352-353

fields
Access
arranging, 363
deleting, 363
lookup fields, refreshing, 15
naming, 363
queries (Access), 393-397
relationships, 364-365
calculated fields, creating for
Excel pivot tables, 268-270
Calculation, Word forms, 81-83
Mail Merge (Word)
Ask, 122-123
conditional fields, 120-121
Fill-In, 125
If, 123-124
inserting fields in main
document, 118-120
Outlook
combination fields, 490-491
creating, 486-488
formula fields, 488-490
pivot tables (Excel), 253
see also data types

figure tables (Word), 96

file allocation table (FAT), 917

file extensions
displaying, 916
hiding, 916
removing, 1014
typing, 917

File Filtering command (Settings menu), 1017, 1026

File Filtering—File Types dialog box, 1026

File Manager (Windows 3.x), 882

File menu
backups, 1017

File menu commands
Access
Get External Data, 369
Send, 423
Advanced Options, 999
Binder
Binder Options, 57
Binder Page Setup, 52
Open Binder, 47
Print Binder, 51
Save Binder As, 57
Send To, 56
Delete, 894
Empty Recycle Bin, 896

Excel
Return Data to Microsoft
Excel, 262
Save as HTML, 779
Exit, 899
FrontPage 97
Preview, 831
Publish FrontPage Web, 822
Open, 999
Open File for Editing, 898
Open File Set, 1020
Outlook
Archive, 481
Import and Export, 482
Open Search, 478
Publish Form As, 539
Save Search, 478
PowerPoint
Save as HTML, 580, 781
Send To, 38
Print, 902, 978
Properties, 899, 925
Publisher
Create New Publication, 748
Preview Web Site, 757
Publish to Web, 758
Publish Web Site to Folder,
758
Quick View, 898
Rename, 916
Restore, 895
Save As, 1025
Save Search, 906
Word
New, 67
Save As, 68
Save as HTML, 779

File Selection dialog box, 1020

file sharing
Binder
e-mail, 55-56
Internet, 56
networks, 55
Excel
protecting workbooks, 15
workbooks, 14

files, 882
AUTOEXEC.BAT, 999
backups, 1020-1022
Backup program, 1016-1027
changing restore settings,
1032-1034
compare settings, 1034-1035
creating, 1019
differential, 1018
File menu, 1017
filtering files in Backup,
1026-1027
full, 1018
hard disks, 1018-1019

incremental, 1018
Iomega Zip drive, 1016
passwords for file sets, 1021
restoring, 1030-1035
restoring to other locations,
1031-1032
saving settings, 1024-1026
schedule preparation,
1019-1020
scheduling with System
Agent, 1022-1023
settings, changing, 1023-1024
tape, 1016
troubleshooting, 1026
verifying, 1034
batch, creating side-by-side folder
batch files, 914-915
BOOTLOG.TXT, 855
Briefcase
splitting, 926
status checks, 925-926
updating, 925
CONFIG.SYS, 856
installing Windows 3.1
applications, 999
copying, 891-892
deleting, 893-895
from MS-DOS prompt, 894
purging, 897
restoring, 895-897
system, 895
displaying
changing display, 907-908
types, 910-911
file-name extensions
viewing in Explorer, 30
finding, 902-906
saving search criteria, 906
searching compressed ZIP
files, 905
hiding, 910-911
icons, 885-887
arranging, 908-909
managing with My Computer,
887-888
names, 890
administering long file names,
919-920
long, 916-921
MS-DOS, 917-918, 920-921
multiple files, 890-891
removing numeric tails from,
920
renaming, 916-917
typing file extensions, 917
undoing, 917
Windows, 917-918
Windows 3.1 long file names,
996-997
opening
from Explorer, 901-902
unrecognizable, 901-902
with applications, 927

previewing
  landscape, 899
  QuickView, 897-899
printing, 902
properties
  changing, 899-901
  displaying, 899
read-only, 900
registering types, 927-928
saving as set, 1020-1021
selecting, 889-890
sorting, 909-910
starting Explorer from, 911-914
synchronizing with Briefcase,
  921-923
SYS, 856
SYSTEM.DAT, 856
troubleshooting
  opening with applications, 928
  restoring, 1033
viewing (Explorer), 882-887
viruses
  protecting computer from,
    1035-1036
  transmittal, 1035
ZIP, searching for files in, 905
see also documents

Files command (Find menu), 902

Fill-In (Word field), 119, 125

Filter command
Access Record menu, 382
Excel Data menu, 236

Filter dialog box (Outlook), 474

**Filter property (Access), 358,
404**

filtering
files in Backup operations,
  1026-1027
lists (Excel)
  Advanced Filter, 239-242
  AutoFilter, 236-239
records, Word Mail Merge data
  source, 117

filters
Access, 15, 381-382
  Advanced Filter/Sort window,
    386-388
  Filter by Input, 383-386
views (Outlook), 474-476

FinanceNet (Web site), 1060

financial functions (Excel)
IRR, 227-229
NPV, 225-227
profitability indexes, 229

**Financial Manager Help Topics
command (Excel Help menu),
762**

Financial Times (Web site), 1067

**Financial Women International
(Web sites), 1060**

Find command
Edit menu, 857
Tools menu, 902, 932
Outlook, 477

Find dialog box, 904
opening, 906

FIND function (Excel), 213

Find menu commands
Computer, 932
Files, 902

finding
computers on networks, 932
files, 902-906
  saving search criteria, 906
  searching compressed ZIP
    files, 905
folders, 902-906
  saving search criteria, 906
  searching compressed ZIP
    files, 905
see also searches

**FindNext macro action (Access),
447**

**FindRecord macro action
(Access), 447**

First Steps (Web site), 1069

**Flash BIOS, upgrading to Plug
and Play, 940**

floppy disks
copying, 893
moving files to, 892

**flowing text into frames
(Publisher), 713-714**

**Folder command (New menu),
870, 891**

folders, 882
Briefcase, 884
  creating on desktop, 922
  installing, 922
  synchronizing files, 921-923
browsing contents of, 884-885
collapsing, 885
Control Panel, 884
copying, 891-892
creating, 891
creating shortcuts for, 864
deleting, 893-895
displaying, 885
  changing display, 907-908
expanding, 885
finding, 902-906
  saving search criteria, 906
  searching compressed ZIP
    files, 905
hiding, 885

icons, 885-887
  arranging, 908-909
mapping network drives to, 931
moving, 891-892
My Computer, 884
  managing files with, 887-888
names, renaming, 916-917
Network Neighborhood, 883-884
opening, 885
  shortcuts, 912-913
  at startup, 848
Outlook, 478
  archiving, 480-482
  creating, 479
  designing views, 483-485
  moving items into, 479-480
  public folders, 531-533
  searching by category,
    511-512
  shortcut icons, 479
  tasks, 526-528
  viewing by category, 510
Printers, 884
  deleting printers, 967
  renaming printers, 966-967
properties
  changing, 899-901
  displaying, 899
Recycle Bin, 883-884
  deleting files, 893-895
  emptying, 896
  restoring deleted files, 895-897
  sizing, 896-897
removin
  from Start menu, 1013
  from Startup folder, 849
selecting, 884, 889-890
shared folders, browsing, 928
sharing on computers, 928-931
sorting, 909-910
starting Explorer from, 911-914
Startup
  removing programs/folders
    from, 849
  troubleshooting, 849
startup appearance, 849
viewing in Explorer, 882-887

Folders view (FrontPage 97), 820

<FONT> tag (HTML), 776

Font command
View menu, 899
Word Format menu, 785

**Font Selection property (Word
objects), 624**

fonts, sizing, 899

footers
Binder documents, 11
binders, printing, 52-53

**Forbes Digital Tool (Web site),
1067**

forecasting (Excel)
  autocorrelation, 321-322
  baselines, 315
  creating forecasts, 315-316
  damping factor, 318-320
  error in prior forecast, 316
  regression-based forecasts, 318

<FORM> tag (HTML), 778

Form command (Excel Data menu), 248

Form Field commands (FrontPage 97 Insert menu), 839

Form menu commands (Outlook)
  Control Toolbox, 536
  Display This Page, 693
  Rename Page, 693

Form view (Access), 372
  data entry, 376-377
  forms, creating, 372-374
  navigating, 375-376
  switching to Datasheet view, 374

Format menu commands
  Access
    AutoFormat, 428
    Freeze Columns, 376
    Unfreeze All Columns, 376
  Excel
    Selected Data Series, 164
    Selected Plot Area, 220
  PowerPoint, AutoShape, 556
  Publisher, Background and Text Colors, 754
  Word
    Case, 785
    Font, 785
    Style, 71
    Style Gallery, 65

Format property (Access), 353

Format Tape command (Tools menu), 1030

Format Tape dialog box, 1030

Format When Needed on Tape Backups option, 1024

formatting
  backup tapes, 1029
  HTML
    character formatting, 776-777
    paragraph formatting, 777
  text
    for Web pages (Word), 785-786
    Publisher, 714

forms
  Access
    creating, 372-374
    Filter by Form, 383-388
    macros, 458-460
    multiple table forms, 441-442

  controls
    aligning, 654
    sizing, 654
    tab order, 653
  Excel
    cells, conditional formatting, 14
    command buttons, 638-639, 644-645
    InputBox function, 646
    macros, 636-637
    MsgBox function, 642-644
    text box controls, 639-641
  Exchange Server, 541
  input forms (FrontPage 97), 838-841
  Organization Forms Library, 540
  Outlook
    customization, 535-538
    fields, creating, 486-488
    moving, 538
    properties, 536
    sample forms, installing, 533
    saving, 538-540
    use, 533-534
    VB Script, 693-697
  PowerPoint, 654-655
  properties, 652-653
  VBA, events, 673
  Word, 74-75
    Calculation fields, 81-82
    check boxes, 84
    creating forms, 75-76
    drop-down list boxes, 84-85
    help, 85
    implementation, 86
    Invoice template, 78-79
    macros for fields, 82-83
    protecting, 76-77
    saving, 77
    templates, 77-78

Forms Toolbar command (FrontPage 97 View menu), 839

formula fields (Outlook), 488-490

Formula property (Excel objects), 628

formulas (Excel), 14
  3-D cell ranges, 181-183
  absolute references, 186
  arguments, using arrays as, 190-191
  constants for array formulas, 191-194
  functions, using with array formulas, 188-190
  Goal Seek, 310-314
  lists, 242-243
  mixed references, 187-188
  naming, 194-198

  natural language formulas in lists, 243-245
  refreshing links, 201-202
  relative references, 186-187
    naming formulas with, 198-199
  sheet-level names, 195
  tracers, 204-206
    invalid data, tracing, 207-208
    tracing dependents, 206
  troubleshooting links, 202-203
  workbook-level names, 196
  workbooks, linking, 200-201
  see also calculations

Formulas menu commands (Excel)
  Calculated Field, 269
  Calculated Item, 267

Fortune (Web site), 1067

<FRAME> tag (HTML), 778

frame control (VBA), 642

frames (Publisher)
  disconnecting frames, 714
  flowing text into, 713-714
  formatting text, 714
  frame capacity, 712
  text wrap, 725-726

FranInfo (Web site), 1079

Freeze Columns command (Access Format menu), 376

FREQUENCY function (Excel), 218-220

FROM clause (Access queries), 292-293

FrontPage 97, 814-818
  Editor, 817, 822-823
  Explorer, 818-819
    files, importing, 821-822
    importing Web site elements, 819-820
    publishing Web pages to servers, 822
    views, 820
  files, editing, 823-825
  graphics
    backgrounds, 827-828
    editing, 826-827
    image maps, 829-830
  hyperlinks, 828-829
  Image Composer, 819
  Image toolbar, 825
  interactive Web pages, 834
    input forms, creating, 838-841
    search engines, 837-838
    tables of contents, 836
    timestamps, 835-836
  Personal Web Server, 817
  templates, 841-842
  troubleshooting, 831
  Web pages, saving, 830-831

full backups, 1018

functions
Calculated fields, Word forms, 82
Excel
array formulas as arguments for functions, 190-191
CHIDIST, 218
CLEAN, 263
COLUMN, 212-214
COUNTA, 210
database functions, 246-247
Excel 4.0 functions, 230-231
FDIST, 220-224
FIND, 213
FREQUENCY, 218-220
GROWTH, 314
INDEX, 211-212
INDIRECT, 214-215
IRR, 227-229
LINEST, 220-224
MATCH, 213, 215-217
MAX, 212
NORMDIST, 218-220
NPV, 225-227
OFFSET, 210-211
profitability indexes, 229
R^2, 221-224
ROW, 212-214
TREND, 314
using with array formulas, 188-190
VLOOKUP, 215-217
queries (Access), 403
VB Script, 689
CreateObject, 691
creating, 697-698
Is testing functions, 688
Unicode standard, 690
VBA, 663
EOF( ), 672

G

Gen-X Group (Web site), 1071

General Services Agency (Web site), 1075

The George Lucas Educational Foundation (Web site), 1071

Get External Data command
Access File menu, 369
Excel Data menu, 246

GetQueryNames subroutine (Access), 281-284

global names (Excel formulas), 196

global templates (Word), 62
creating, 66

Go menu commands (Binder), Show Web Toolbar, 56

Go To command
Access Edit menu, 376
Tools menu, 885

Goal Seek (Excel), 310-314

Goal Seek command (Excel Tools menu), 311

GoToControl macro action (Access), 447

GoToPage macro action (Access), 447

GoToRecord macro action (Access), 447

Government Accounting Office (Web site), 1075

Government Contractors Glossary (Web site), 1076

grammar checking (Word), 12

Grantsmanship Center (Web site), 1072

graphics
FrontPage 97
backgrounds, 827-828
editing, 826-827
image maps, 829-830
PowerPoint presentations on Internet, 581
Publisher
Design Gallery, 730
text wrap, 726
Web pages, 751-752
Web pages, 793
Doctor HTML, 798
Word, Web pages, 786
see also objects, PowerPoint

graphics accelerators, PowerPoint multimedia, 586

Great Plains (accounting software), 765

GROUP BY clause, Access queries, 293

Group By command (Outlook View menu), 471

Group command (PowerPoint Draw menu), 548

grouping
objects
PowerPoint, 548-549
Publisher, 719
views
Outlook, 471-474

groups (Publisher), creating, 719-721

GROWTH function (Excel), 314

Guide to the Small Business Administration (Web site), 1079

Guide to Unique Meeting Facilities (Web site), 1084

H

<H1>...<H6> tags (HTML), 777

hard disks
backups, 1018-1019
troubleshooting Windows 95 startup, 857

hardware
legacy adapter cards, installing
automatic detection, 945-948
installing after setting up drivers, 948-951
removing uneeded drivers, 951-952
setting resource values for adapter cards, 942-943
legacy devices, 942-952
detection during Setup, 943
setting resource values for adapter cards, 943-945
Windows 95 operation, 942-943
Plug and Play, 938-942
determining Plug and Play support, 938-941
installing, 941-942
purchasing new systems, 940-941
troubleshooting resource conflicts, 954
upgading to Plug and Play, 940
see also Plug and Play
profiles, laptop printing (docking stations), 988-990
troubleshooting installation, 952-959
changing resource settings, 952-956
checking for resource coflicts, 956-957
Device Manager, 952
Registry Editor (REGEDIT.EXE), 957-959
Windows 95 startup, troubleshooting installation, 856

<HEAD> tag (HTML), 775

headers (Binder), 11
printing, 52-53

headings, Word tables of contents, 92-93

Heath's Computer and Telecommunication Acronym Reference (Web site), 1079

Help
customizing, 20-22
Microsoft on the Web, 20-22
Office Assistant, 18-20
VBA, 681
Word forms, 85

Help menu commands (Excel), Financial Manager Help Topics, 762

Hidden attribute, 900, 901

hiding
Explorer toolbar, 907
fields, Access queries, 396-397
file extensions, 916
file types, 910-911
folders, 885
scenarios (Excel), 306
Shortcut Bars, 32-33
status bar (Explorer), 907

Hispanic Business Magazine (Web site), 1067

Home Office Associate of America (Web site), 1079

Home Office Links (Web site), 1080

Home Office Mail (Web site), 1080

Home Realtors Information Network (Web site), 1080

HomeBuyer's Fair (Web site), 1082

Hourglass macro action (Access), 447

<HR> tag (HTML), 778

<HTML> tag, 775

HTML (HyperText Markup Language), 11, 774-775
Access reports, 15, 429-430
ActiveX Controls
Layout control, 809-812
objects, inserting in HTML files, 807-808
scripts, editing with ActiveX Control Pad, 808-809
attributes, 775
converting documents
Excel, 779-780
PowerPoint, 781-782
Publisher, 782-784
Word, 779
file management
relative references, 791
staging, 791

FrontPage 97, 814
PowerPoint slide shows, 17, 580-582
tags, 774
character formatting, 776-777
<OBJECT>, 802-803
paragraph formatting, 777
<PARAM>, 803-804
<SCRIPT>, 804
special function, 778
troubleshooting, 779
VBScript, 699-703
W3C (World Wide Web Consortium), 810
Web page structure, 775-776
Word
creating pages with, 784
graphics, 786
hyperlinks, 786-787
tables, 787
text, 784-786

Hyperlink data type, Access tables, 351
Allow Zero Length property, 356

Hyperlink dialog box (Publisher), 750

hyperlinks, 11
Access, 15
Excel cell ranges, 177, 183
FrontPage 97, 828-829
Publisher, 749, 752-754
testing, 793
verifying, 797
Word, 786-787

Hyperlinks view (FrontPage 97), 820

I

<I> tag (HTML), 776

ICM (Image Color Matching) technology, 970

Icon view (Outlook), sorting
by column, 466-467
by fields, 467-468
creating new views, 468-470

icons
activating, 874
aligning, 865
arranging, 872-873
desktop, 862-867
files, 885-887
arranging, 908-909
folders, 885-887
arranging, 908-909
removing, 871

selecting, 871
multiple icons, 871
shortcuts, 885
see also shortcuts

IdeaList (Web site), 1072

If (Word field), 120, 123-124

IF() function (Excel), 197

IF(x,y,z) function (Word forms), 82

If...Then...Else loops (VBA), 665-666

IIS (Internet Information Server), 703, 817

Image Color Matching (ICM) technology, 970

Image Composer (FrontPage 97), 819

image maps (FrontPage 97), 829-830

Image toolbar (FrontPage 97), 825

<IMG> tag (HTML), 778

Immediate window (VBA), 648-649, 658
: (colon) command, 660

Immediate Window command (VBA View menu), 648

Import and Export command (Outlook File menu), 482

Import File to FrontPage 97 Web dialog box, 821

ImportData subroutine (Access), 286-290

importing
Access
compared to linking, 368
data sources, 368-369
manipulating data, 371-372
mechanics of, 369-371
Excel, SBFM, 765-766
files to FrontPage 97 Explorer, 821-822
tables to Access, 360-361
Web site elements into FrontPage 97, 819-820

Inbox Assistant (Outlook), 514, 519-520

Inc. Online (Web site), 1067

Income Statement reports (SBFM), 766

incremental backups, 1018

indenting text (Excel), 14

Index and Tables command (Word Insert menu), 93

Index and Tables dialog box (Word), 93

INDEX function (Excel), 211-212

Indexed property (Access), 356-357

indexes (Word), 99
creating, 101-102
marking items for indexing, 99-101
multiple indexes, creating, 103
page ranges, 101
switches for field codes, 102
viewing index marks, 101

India Market Place (Web site), 1062

INDIRECT function (Excel), 214-215

Information Viewer, 466
fields
combination fields, 490-491
creating, 486-488
formula fields, 488-490
folders, designing views, 483-485
sorting
by column, 466-467
by field, 467-468
creating new views, 468-470

Information Viewing, folders, 478
archiving, 480-482
creating, 479
moving items into, 479-480
shortcut icons, 479

inner joins (Access), 364

input forms (FrontPage 97), 838-841

Input Mask property (Access), 353-355

Input Mask Wizard (Access), 354

InputBox function (VBA), 646

Insert ActiveX Control dialog box (ActiveX Control Pad), 807

Insert Calculated Item dialog box (Excel), 267

Insert menu commands
Access
Reports, 415
Rows, 401
Excel
Copied Cells, 179
Cut Cells, 179
Name, 173
FrontPage 97
Active Elements, 837
Form Field, 839

Table of Contents, 836
Timestamp, 835
PowerPoint
Movies and Sounds, 590
Object, 559
Publisher
Page, 712
Page Numbers, 716
VBA
Module, 660
Procedure, 660
VBE, UserForm, 636
Word
Bookmark, 101
Cross-reference, 98
Field, 95
Index and Tables, 93
Picture, 786

Insert Page dialog box (Publisher), 712

inserting
ActiveX Controls on Web pages, 802-803
ActiveX Control Pad, 807-808
Layout control, 810
buttons on toolbars, 91
fields
main document (Word Mail Merge), 118-120
queries (Access), 393-394
Publisher
Design Gallery objects on pages, 730-731
hyperlinks on Web pages, 752-754
pages, 712-713
sound clips, 740-742

Install from Disk dialog box, 1007

Install Programs Wizard
installing Windows applications, 1002-1004
starting, 1002

installing, 10
applications, 997-998
Install Programs Wizard, 1002-1004
setup programs, 997-998
Briefcase, 922
DAO, 275-276
Excel AccessLinks add-in, 37
legacy adapter cards
automatic detection, 945-948
installing after setting up drivers, 948-951
removing unneeded drivers, 951-952
setting resource values for adapter cards, 942-945
legacy hardware, 942-952

networks, 10-11
Office 97, 1040-1046
Plug and Play hardware, 941-942
printers, 962-966
Add Printer Wizard, 963-966
configuring ports, 965
drivers, 964, 976
Plug and Play printers, 966
test pages, 966
sample forms (Outlook), 533
troubleshooting hardware installation, 952-959
changing resource settings, 952-956
Device Manager, 952
Registry Editor (REGEDIT.EXE), 957-959
unlisted Windows components, 1007
Windows 3.1 applications, 999-1000
Windows 95, 857-858
wizards, Template (Excel), 141

instances (VBA objects), 664

int operator (Solver), 330

INT(x) function (Word forms), 82

Integer setting (Field Size property), 352

Intellectual Property Center (Web site), 1073

IntelliMouse, 11

interactive Web pages (FrontPage 97), 834
input forms, creating, 838-841
search engines, 837-838
tables of contents, 836
timestamps, 835-836

interfaces, 30-31

InterKnowledge Travel Network (Web site), 1083

Internal Revenue Service (Web site), 1057

International Public Relations (Web site), 1069

International Trade Law (Web site), 1065

Internet
file sharing (Binder), 56
HTML, 774-775
attributes, 775
character formatting tags, 776-777
Excel spreadsheets, converting, 779-780
page structure, 775-776
paragraph formatting tags, 777
PowerPoint presentations, converting, 781-782

Publisher documents,
converting, 782-784
relative references, 791
special function tags, 778
staging, 791
tags, 774
Word, creating Web pages
with, 784-787
Word documents, converting,
779
ISPs, 792
PowerPoint slide shows, 579-580
Publisher
blank Web pages, 751
converting documents for
Web pages, 759
Design Checker, 755-757
graphics, 751-752, 752
hyperlinks, 752-754
placing pages on Web servers,
757-759
previewing Web pages, 757
text, 751
text color, 754
Web Site PageWizard, 748-751
Web Publishing Wizard, 794-796

Internet Assistant (PowerPoint),
580-582

Internet Assistant Wizard (Excel),
779

Internet Explorer, 20

Internet Information Server (IIS),
703, 817

Internet Service Providers (ISPs),
792

intersection operator (Excel), 168

Invert Selection command (Edit
menu), 889

Invoice template (Word), 78-79

Iomega Zip drive, 1016

IRQs
conflicts
PCI graphics cards, 941
troubleshooting, 952-956
legacy adapter cards, 944-945

IRR function (Excel), 227-229

ISPs (Internet Service Providers),
792

J-K

JobWeb (Web site), 1064

Join Properties dialog box
(Access), 392

joining queries (Access), 392

journal entries (Outlook)
automatic journal entries, 504-507
creating, 508
creating from e-mail messages,
497-498
dragging objects to create, 507
options, 503-504

Journal entry object (Outlook),
699

jumpers, 942-945

keyboard, 873-874
activating icons, 874
selecting files, 889

keyboard execution of macros,
613-614

L

labels
Excel charts, 158
mailing labels (Access), 424-426
printing with Mail Merge (Word),
126

Landscape command (View
menu), 899

landscape documents, printing
binders, 54-55

laptops
printing from
creating hardware profiles,
988-990
from docking stations, 988-990
Work Offline (Deferred
Printing) command, 983-984
synchronizing files between
desktop computer and, 922-923

Large Icons command (View
menu), 907

layering objects (Publisher),
716-718

Layout control (ActiveX),
809-810
editing, 810-812
inserting in HTML files, 810

layout guides (Publisher),
721-722

Layout Guides command
(Publisher Arrange menu), 721

Layout Guides dialog box
(Publisher), 721

legacy devices, 937, 942-952
adapter cards, installing
automatic detection, 945-948
installing after setting up
drivers, 948-951

setting resource values,
942-943
setting resource values for
adapter cards, 943-945
detection during Setup, 943
drivers, removing, 951-952
NVM (nonvolatile memory), 943
Windows 95 operation, 942-943

Legal Information Institute (Web
site), 1065

Letter Wizard (Word), 12

LFNBK utility, 919

<LI> tag (HTML), 774, 777

libraries, Windows 95 Driver
Library (W95DL), 967

Limits report (Excel Solver), 335

line charts (Excel), 152

Line Up Icons command (View
menu), 909

Line Up Objects command
(Publisher Arrange menu), 724

Line Up Objects dialog box
(Publisher), 724

linear searches (Excel Solver),
339

LINEST function (Excel),
220-224

LINEST( ) function (Excel), 188

Link dialog box (Access), 370

Linked Table Manager (Access),
372

LinkExchange (Web site), 1057

linking, 39-40
Access
compared to importing, 368
data sources, 368-369
manipulating data, 371-372
mechanics of, 369-371
tables, 361-362
compound documents, creating,
40-42
files sizes, 41
PowerPoint, 560
manipulating linked objects,
561
tracking links, 42
versus embedding, 42
Web pages, see hyperlinks
workbooks (Excel)
formulas, 200-201
refreshing links, 201-202
troubleshooting links, 202-203

Links command (Edit menu)
PowerPower, 561
Word, 42

Links dialog box
PowerPoint, 561
Word, 42

list box control (VBA), 641

List command (View menu), 907

List view (Script Wizard), 808

lists (Excel), 234-235
Advanced Filter, 239-242
AutoFilter, 236-239
Data Forms, 248-250
database functions, 246-247
formulas, 242-243
natural language formulas,
243-245

local templates (Word), 62

locking records (Access), 1047

Login dialog box, 846

**logos, creating with PageWizard
(Publisher), 739-740**

long file names, 916-921
administering, 919-920
FAT (file allocation table), 917
MS-DOS, 917-918, 920-921
renaming files, 916-917
Windows, 917-918
Windows 3.1, 996-997

**Long Integer setting (Field Size
property), 352**

**lookup fields (Access), refreshing,
15**

Lookup Wizard (Access), 351

loops (VBA), 659-660
Do...While, 666
If...Then...Else, 665-666

M

Macro command (Tools menu)
Access, 16
Word, 83

macros
Access
assigning command buttons,
458
conditions, 451-452
controls, 455-458
creating, 449-451
Expression Builder, 457-458
macro sheets, 446-449
naming, 453-455
rows of actions, manipulating,
455
use, 458-460
automatic execution, 614

buttons
customizing, 605-607
inserting on toolbars, 604-605
creating, 602-604
editing, 607-609
Excel
command buttons, 638-639,
644-645
data labels, 158-161
InputBox function, 646
MsgBox function, 642-644
recording, 634-636
text box controls, 639-641
forms
controls, aligning, 654
controls, sizing, 654
Excel, 636-637
PowerPoint, 654-655
properties, 652-653
tab order of controls, 653
keyboard execution, 613-614
manipulating VBA code, 611-612
methods, 610
objects, 610-611
subroutines, 609-610
variables, 609
Word
converting, 22
editing, 104-105
fields in forms, 82-83
recording, 103-104
running, 104

Mail Merge (Word), 108
data source, 109
Access tables, 115
Excel worksheets, 115
Outlook Address Book, 116
records, filtering, 117
records, selecting for data
source, 117-118
records, sorting for data
source, 118
types of, 115-116
Word tables, 114-115
e-mail distribution, 126-128
envelopes, 126
fax distribution, 126-128
Mail Merge Helper Wizard,
110-113
main document, 109, 113
Ask field, 122-123
conditional fields, 120-121
field codes, 113
Fill-In field, 125
If field, 123-124
inserting fields in, 118-120
merging to a new document, 126
printing documents, 126
testing merges, 124-125

**Mail Merge command (Word
Tools menu), 110**

**Mail message object (Outlook),
699**

mailbox, *see* e-mail

**Mailing Label Wizard (Access),
424-426**

**main document (Word Mail
Merge), 109, 113**
Ask field, 122-123
conditional fields, 120-121
field codes, 113
Fill-In field, 125
If field, 123-124
inserting fields in, 118-120

**Major Trade Shows in Asia (Web
site), 1084**

**Make Table dialog box (Access),
411**

**managing files with My Computer,
887-888**

**manual timing of slide shows
(PowerPoint), 565-566**

**many-to-many relationships
(Access tables), 435**

mapping network drives, 931

**Mark Index Entry dialog box
(Word), 100**

**Mark Table of Contents Entry
dialog box (Word), 92**

**Market Facts and Statistics (Web
site), 1069**

**Marketing Resource Center (Web
site), 1070**

Marketshares (Web site), 1057

**marking items for indexing
(Word), 99-101**

**MAS90 (accounting software),
765**

**MATCH function (Excel), 213,
215-217**

**mathematical operators, Access
queries, 398-400**

**mathematical operators (VBA),
671**

MAX function (Excel), 212

MAX( ) function (Word forms), 82

**Max Records property (Access),
405**

**Maximize macro action (Access),
447**

MDRAM (Multibank DRAM), 586

Media Player, 591-593

Memo data type, Access tables, 350
Allow Zero Length property, 356

memory, 49
NVM (nonvolatile memory), 943
printers, 970

menu bars (Binder), 48

MergeField (Word field), 120

MergeRec (Word field), 120

MergeSeq (Word field), 120

merging documents, *see* **Mail Merge (Word)**

messages, *see* **e-mail**

meta files, 972-974

metering manual presentations (PowerPoint), 570-571

methods
Document object (Word)
Activate, 622
CheckGrammar, 622
CheckSpelling, 622
Close, 623
Open, 623
Save, 623
SaveAs, 623
SendMail, 623
Range object (Excel)
Activate, 628
Copy, 628
Sort, 628
Selection object (Word), 624
VBA, 664
Workbooks object (Excel)
Activate, 625
Add, 625
Close, 625
Open, 625
Save, 625
SaveAs, 625
Worksheets object (Excel), 627

methods (VBA), 610

Microsoft Exchange Server, *see* **Exchange Server**

Microsoft IntelliMouse, 11

Microsoft Media Player, 591-593

Microsoft Office Developer forum (Web site), 656

Microsoft Office Small Business Edition, *see* **SBE**

Microsoft on the Web, 20-22

Microsoft Query, 256

MIN( ) function (Word forms), 82

Minimize macro action (Access), 447

minimizing
applications, 877
windows, 871

mixed references (Excel formulas), 187-188

MKCOMPAT.EXE, 999

MOD (x,y) function (Word forms), 82

Modify Location dialog box (Binder), 58

Module command (VBA Insert menu), 660

modules (Access), 15

Modulus operator (VBA), 671

MoneyWorld Online **(Web site),** 1068

motherboards, upgrading to Plug and Play, 940

mouse operations, 875

.MOV files (PowerPoint), 590

Move Items dialog box (Outlook), 479

MoveSize macro action (Access), 447

Movies and Sounds command (PowerPoint Insert menu), 590

moving
cell ranges (Excel), 176
fields, Access queries, 395
folders, 891-892
Outlook
forms, 538
items into folders, 479-480

MS-DOS
failure to boot in, 857
long file names, 917-918, 920-921
printing, 987-988
prompt, deleting files from, 894

MsgBox function (VBA), 642-644

MsgBox macro action (Access), 447

MSINFO32.EXE utility, 966

Multibank DRAM (MDRAM), 586

multimedia (PowerPoint)
action settings, 593
animation, configuring, 594
audio, Clip Art Gallery, 595
audio, configuring playback, 596-598
audio, outside sources, 596
Clip Art Gallery, 589-590
guidelines for, 587-589
hardware requirements, 586-587
video, .AVI files, 590

video, .MOV files, 590
video, Clip Art Gallery, 589-590
video, editing, 591-593

multiple users, desktop, 847

multitasking, Win32 applications, 994-995

multithreading, Win32 applications, 994-995

My Computer, 884
managing files with, 887-888
opening documents, 869
starting applications, 869

N

/n switch, 911

Name command (Excel Insert menu), 173

Name property (Excel objects), 626

Name property (forms), 652

names
files, 890
administering long file names, 919-920
long, 916-921
MS-DOS, 917-921
multiple files, 890-891
removing numeric tails from, 920
renaming, 916-917
typing file extensions, 917
undoing, 917
Windows, 917-918
Windows 3.1 long file names, 996-997
folders, renaming, 916-917
printers, 966-967
shortcuts, editing, 864-865

naming
fields (Access), 363
queries, 395-396
formulas (Excel), 194-198
relative references, 198-199
sheet-level names, 195
workbook-level names, 196
macros (Access), 453-455
ranges (Excel), 172-173
sections (Binder), 47

National Center for Employee Ownership (Web site), 1064

National Credit Counseling Service (Web site), 1061

National Technology Transfer Center (Web site), 1076

natural language formulas (Excel lists), 243-245

navigating Datasheet view (Access), 375-376

Nerd World (Web site), 1073

NetMarquee Family Business NetCenter (Web site), 1080

Netscape Navigator, testing Web pages, 793

Network Installation Wizard, 10, 1040

Network Neighborhood, 883, 884
viewing network resources, 933

networks
Excel, sharing workbooks, 14
file sharing (Binder), 55
installing software, 10-11
mapping drives, 931
Office 97, installation, 1040
sharing resources, 928-933
browsing shared folders, 928
finding computers, 932
mapping network drives, 931
viewing network resources, 933
workgroup administration
Access, 1046-1048
Excel, 1048
PowerPoint, 1048-1049
Word, 1049

Never Overwrite Files option, 1033

New command (Word File menu), 67

New menu commands
Binary Value, 920
Briefcase, 922
Folder, 870, 891
Shortcut, 863

New Office Document dialog box, 28

New Query dialog box (Access), 390

New Report dialog box (Access), 415

New Style dialog box (Word), 74

New Table dialog box (Access), 346

New Toolbar dialog box (Word), 90

New Values property (Access), 353

NewMacros (Code) dialog box (Word), 104

newsletters (PageWizard), 736

Newton method (Excel Solver), 340

Next (Word field), 120

Next Section command (Binder Section menu), 49

NextIf (Word field), 120

non-contiguous ranges (Excel), 169

Nonprofit Resources Catalog (Web site), 1072

nonvolatile memory (NVM), legacy devices, 943

Normal style (Word), 70

Normal template (Word), 62

NORMDIST function (Excel), 218-220

Northwest Airlines (Web sites), 1083

Not Responding dialog box, 877

NOT(x) function (Word forms), 82

Note object (Outlook), 699

notes (Outlook)
creating, 499
sending as e-mail messages, 500

NPV function (Excel), 225-227

nudging objects (Publisher), 724-725

null value (VBA), 663

Number data type, Access tables, 350
Field Size property, 352

NVM (nonvolatile memory), legacy devies, 943

O

<OBJECT> tag (HTML), 778
ActiveX Controls, inserting, 802-803

Object Browser
Access, 16
VBA, 649

Object Browser command (VBA View menu), 649

Object Linking and Embedding, see OLE

Object menu (PowerPoint Insert menu), 559

objects
Access
recordsets, 282
unbound objects, converting, 25
ActiveX Controls
inserting in HTML files, 807-808
Layout control, 809-812
PowerPoint
animation, 552-554, 570
AutoShapes, 548
converting, 560-561
grouped objects, editing, 549
grouping, 548-549
inserting from other applications, 560
rotating, 550-552
stacking, 546-547
properties, 875
Publisher
aligning, 723-724
grouping, 719
layering, 716-717
layout guides, 721-722
nudging, 724-725
ruler guides, 722-723
snapping objects to guides, 723
VBScript, 691-692
Err, 691
Outlook object model, 699
VBA, 610-611, 618-619, 664-665
Activate method, 622, 625, 628
Add method, 625
Address property, 627
Application (Access), 629
Cells property, 628
CheckGrammar method, 622
CheckSpelling method, 622
classes, 664
Close event, 623-624
Close method, 623-625
Copy method, 624, 627-628
Count property, 624
creating, 674
Cut method, 624
Documents collection, 620
Excel, 674-677
Font Selection property, 624
Formula property, 628
instances, 664
Name property, 626
Office Assistant, 630-632, 678-680
Open event, 623
Open method, 623, 625
PageSetup property, 621
Paste method, 624
Path property, 621
Presentation (PowerPoint), 629

properties, 619
ReadOnly property, 621, 625
Save method, 623, 625
SaveAs method, 623, 625
Saved property, 621, 625
SaveFormat property, 621-622
SendMail method, 623
Slides (PowerPoint), 629-630
Sort method, 628
Visible property, 626
Word, 677-678
Worksheets collection (Excel), 626

Occupational Safety and Health Administration (Web site), 1058

ODBC Timeout property (Access), 404

Office 97, installation, 1040-1046

Office 97-compatible applications, 39

Office Art, 12

Office Assistant, 18-20
configuring, 19
objects, 630-632
VBA, 678-680

Office Resource Kit, installing software, 10

Office Shortcut Bars, see Shortcut Bars

Office VBA Central (Web site), 656

OFFSET function (Excel), 210-211

Offshore Entrepreneur (Web site), 1080

<OL> tag (HTML), 777

OLE (Object Linking and Embedding), 39, 40
comparison of linking and embedding, 42
compound documents, creating, 40-42

OLE Object data type, Access tables, 350

one-to-many relationships (Access tables), 434

one-to-one relationships (Access tables), 435-436

Open Binder command (Binder File menu), 47

Open command (File menu), 999

Open Data Source dialog box (Word), 115

Open event (Word objects), 623

Open File for Editing command (File menu), 898

Open File Set command (File menu), 1020

Open method
Excel objects, 625
Word objects, 623

Open Search command (Outlook File menu), 478

Open With dialog box, 901

OpenForm macro action (Access), 447

opening
binders, 47
documents, 30
Explorer, 868
from Start menu, 860-861
My Computer, 869
with shortcuts, 864
files
from Explorer, 901-902
unrecognizable, 901-902
with applications, 927
Find dialog box, 906
folders, 885
at startup, 848
shortcuts, 912-913
workbooks (Excel), 132-133
see also starting

OpenModule macro action (Access), 447

OpenQuery macro action (Access), 447

OpenReport macro action (Access), 447

OpenTable macro action (Access), 447

operators, Access queries, 398-405

Opportunities for Women in Small Business (Web site), 1080

Options command
Explorer View menu, 30
Settings menu, 1017, 1027
View menu, 916, 933

Options dialog box, 910, 928

Options menu commands
Case Sensitive, 906
Results, 906

OR (x,y) function (Word forms), 82

ORDER BY clause, Access queries, 293

Order By property (Access), 358, 405

Organization Forms Library, 540

Original Locations option, 1032, 1035

OSHA (Web site), 1058

Other Designs dialog box (Publisher), 734

Out of Office Assistant (Outlook), 514
AutoReply, 514-515
Rules, 515-518

outer joins (Access), 364

Outline view (PowerPoint), 16

Outlook, 17
Address Book, data source for Mail Merge (Word), 116
categories
adding, 508-509
assigning, 509
e-mail, assigning categories to messages, 510
folders, viewing by category, 510
searching folders by category, 511-512
contacts
adding to Address Book, 505
sending e-mail with Address Book, 505-507
dragging objects, 494
appointments, creating from messages, 496
contacts, creating e-mail for, 498-499
contacts, creating from messages, 496-497
dragging objects outside Outlook, 501-502
journal entries, creating from messages, 497-498
notes, creating, 499
notes, sending as e-mail messages, 500
text, 500
to Tasks folder, 495-496
e-mail
adding to Contacts folder, 504-505
delaying message delivery, 525
Inbox Assistant, 514, 519-520
Out of Office Assistant, 514-518
redirecting replies, 525
tracking messages, 523-525
voting messages, 520-522
Excel, 75

Exchange Server, managing mailbox, 514
fields
  combination fields, 490-491
  creating, 486-488
  formula fields, 488-490
folders, 478
  archiving, 480-482
  creating, 479
  designing views, 483-485
  moving items into, 479-480
  shortcut icons, 479
forms
  customization, 535-538
  moving, 538
  properties, 536
  sample forms, installing, 533
  saving, 538-540
  use, 533-534
Information Viewer, 466
  filtering, 474-476
  grouping, 471-474
  searches, 477-478
  sorting, 466-470
journal entries
  automatic journal entries, 504-507
  creating, 508
  dragging objects to create, 507
  options, 503-504
public folders, 531
  adding items to, 531-532
  manipulating items in, 532-533
tables, 75
tasks, 526
  accepting assignments, 529-530
  assigning, 528-529
  ownership, 526-527
  tracking owners, 527-528
  updates, 527
troubleshooting
  Address Book, 506
  dragging objects, 499
  filters, 476
  forms, 540
  saving changes, 501
  views, 469
VBScript, 692
  forms, creating, 693-697
  functions, creating, 697-698
  object model, 699
wizards
  Events, 695
  Import and Export, 482
Output All Fields property (Access), 404
OutputTo macro action (Access), 447

Overwrite Files option, 1033
Overwrite Old Status Log Files option, 1027
Overwrite Older Files Only option, 1033

P

<P> tag (HMTL), 777
Page Break Preview command (Excel View menu), 13
page breaks (Excel), 13
Page command (Publisher Insert menu), 712
page fields (Excel pivot tables), 263-264
Page Numbers command (Publisher Insert menu), 716
page ranges for Word indexes, 101
Page View command (View menu), 899
pages (Publisher), adding, 712-713
PageSetup property (Word objects), 621
PageWizard (Publisher)
  ads, creating, 736-739
  calendars, creating, 735-736
  coupons, creating, 739
  logos, creating, 739-740
paragraph formatting tags (HTML), 777
<PARAM> tag (HTML), 778
  ActiveX Controls, inserting, 803-804
partitioning, 857
passwords, 1021
Paste method (Word objects), 624
Paste Special command (Word Edit menu), 40
pasting between applications, 38-39
Patent Application Drafting (Web site), 1073
Patent Pending Resource (Web site), 1073
Path property (Word objects), 621

pausing print jobs
  Pause command (Document menu), 984-985
  Pause Printing command (Printer menu), 983
PCI cards, 941
Peachtree for DOS (accounting software), 765
Personal Web Server (FrontPage 97), 817
Personal Web Server (PWS), 703
Picture command (Word Insert menu), 786
Picture property (forms), 652
PictureAlignment property (forms), 653
PictureSizeMode property (forms), 653
Pie charts (Excel), 151
pivot tables (Excel)
  calculated fields, creating, 268-270
  calculated items, 266-268
  creating, 253
  data sources, defining, 256-258
  DialogHandler subroutine, 284-286
  Driver subroutine, 280-282
  external data sources, 255-256
  fields, 253
  GetQueryNames subroutine, 282-284
  ImportData subroutine, 286-290
  limitation of calculated fields, 270
  Microsoft Query, 256
  page fields, 263-264
  Query window, 260-263
  Query Wizard, 258-260
  refreshing, 255
  retrieving data from Access databases, 276-280
  scenarios, 308
PivotTable Report command (Excel Data menu), 253
PivotTable Wizard (Excel), 255
placeholders (PowerPoint), 555
<PLAINTEXT> tag (HTML), 776
Platinum for Windows 4.02 (accounting software), 765
Plug and Play, 935-938
  BIOS, 936-940
  determining Plug and Play support, 938-941
  hardware, 938-942
    installing, 941-942
    troubleshooting resource conflicts, 954

printers, installing, 966
purchasing new systems, 940-941
upgrading to Plug and Play, 940
VxDs (virtual device drivers), 937

Plus!, System Agent, 1022-1023

PnP, *see* **Plug and Play**

polynomial trendline, 222

Pop-up Menu control (ActiveX), 803

ports, printers, 965, 974-978

positioning Shortcut Bars, 31-32

PowerPoint
Animation Effects toolbar, 17
Animation Player, 581
data sharing, 38
embedding, 560
  manipulating embedded
    objects, 561
files, converting, 25-26
forms, 654-655
HTML files, 17
Internet Assistant, 580-582
linking, 560
  manipulating linked objects,
    561
multimedia
  action settings, 593
  animation, configuring, 594
  audio, Clip Art Gallery, 595
  audio, configuring playback,
    596-598
  audio, outside sources, 596
  guidelines for, 587-589
  hardware requirements,
    586-587
  video, .AVI files, 590
  video, .MOV files, 590
  video, Clip Art Gallery,
    589-590
  video, editing, 591-593
objects
  animation, 552-554, 570
  AutoShapes, 548
  converting, 560-561
  grouped objects, editing, 549
  grouping, 548-549
  Presentation (VBA), 629
  rotating, 550-552
  Slides (VBA), 629-630
  stacking, 546-547
presentations, converting to
  HTML, 781-782
printing from Binder, 54
self-running slide shows, 574-575
  action buttons, 575-578
  configuration, 575
  Internet presentation, 579-580
  starting, 578-579

slide shows, 564
  ActiveX Controls, 578
  adjusting transitions, 569
  animation, 570
  conference presentations,
    573-574
  metering manual
    presentations, 570-571
  multiple computers, 572-573
  running, 571-574
  Slide Navigator, 573
  testing timing, 569
  timing, 564-567
  transitions, 567-569
slides, 16
text
  AutoShapes, placing on,
    555-557
  placeholders, 555
  text boxes, 555
toolbars
  Animation Effects, 552-553
  Control Toolbox, 578
troubleshooting
  AutoShapes, 557
  linking and embedding, 562
  multimedia, 591
views
  Outline, 16
  Slide Sorter, 565
wizards
  AutoContent, 579
  Presentation Conference, 574
WordArt, 557-560
workgroup administration,
  1048-1049

<PRE> tag (HTML), 777

**preemptive multitasking, Win32
applications, 994-995**

**Presentation Conference Wizard
(PowerPoint), 574**

**Presentation object (PowerPoint),
629**

**Preset Animations (PowerPoint),
553**

**Preview command (FrontPage 97
File menu), 831**

**Preview Web Site command
(Publisher File menu), 757**

previewing
binders, 51
files
  landscape, 899
  QuickView, 897-899
templates
  Excel, 146
  Word, 65

Web pages
  FrontPage 97, 831
  Publisher, 757
  Word, 786
see also viewing

**Previous Section command
(Binder Section menu), 49**

**primary key, Access tables, 347,
349**

**Print Binder command (Binder
File menu), 51**

**Print Binder dialog box (Binder),
51**

Print command (File menu), 902

Print dialog box, 978
Word 6 features, 980-981
Word 97 features, 979-980

**Print Preview command (Binder
Section menu), 51**

Printer menu commands
Close, 985
Pause Printing, 983
Properties, 973
Purge Print Jobs, 983
Set as Default, 984
Work Offline, 984

**Printer Port Properties sheet,
975-977**

**Printer Properties sheet,
968-969**
General page, 968
Graphics page, 971

**printers, adding to Send To
menu, 902**

printing, 978-981
binders, 51
  headers/footers, 52-53
  landscape documents, 54-55
  previewing, 51
canceling print jobs, 985
collating, 979
color
  configuring color printing
    properties, 970-971
  Image Color Matching (ICM)
    technology, 970
configuring printers, 968-978
  32-bit printing subsystem,
    971-972
  bogus printers, 979
  color printing properties,
    970-971
  EMF (enhanced meta file)
    spooling, 972-974
  Image Color Matching (ICM)
    technology, 970

ports, 974-978
Printer Properties sheet, 968-969
default printers, setting/ removing, 984
Deferred Printing, 983-984
deleting printers, 967
drag-and-drop printing from desktop, 985-987
creating printer shortcut icons, 985-986
multiple documents, 987
printing, 986
drivers
deleting, 967
extensions (DRV/VxD), 976
installing, 964, 976
sources, 967
VxD (virtual device drivers), 972
files, 902
installing printers, 962-966
Add Printer Wizard, 963-966
configuring ports, 965
drivers, 964
Plug and Play printers, 966
test pages, 966, 990
laptops
creating hardware profiles, 988-990
docking stations, 988-990
Work Offline (Deferred Printing) command, 983-984
Mail Merge documents (Word), 126
MS-DOS applications, 987-988
new Windows 95 printing features, 962
outputting to files, 979-992
pausing print jobs
Pause command (Document menu), 984-985
Pause Printing command (Printer menu), 983
ports, configuring, 965, 974-978
Print Manager, 981-985
canceling print jobs, 985
closing, 985
default printers, setting/ removing, 984
diagnostic tool, 992
pausing print jobs, 983-985
purging print jobs, 983
status bar, turning on/off, 985
working offline, 983-984
print queue, rearranging, 985
renaming printers, 966-967
reports (Access), 423
sections (Binder), 52
spooling, 972-973
test pages, 966, 990

troubleshooting, 990-992
Enhanced Print Troubleshooter, 992
memory, 970
Print Manager diagnostic tool, 992
Print Troubleshooter, 991
purging print jobs, 983
viewing printer information with MSINFO32.EXE utility, 966
Word 6, 980-981
Word 97, 979-980
PrintOut macro action (Access), 447
Procedure command (VBA Insert menu), 660
procedures (VBA), 660
PRODUCT (x,y) function (Word forms), 82
profitability indexes, 229
Program Manager (Windows 3.1), 915-916
programming, *see* **VBScript; VBA**
Programs command (Windows Start menu), 46
programs, *see* **applications**
Programs Shortcut Bar, 32
Project Explorer (VBA), 646-647, 658
PRONET (Web site), 1058
properties
Access tables, 351-352
Allow Zero Length, 356
Caption, 355
changing, 363
Decimal Places, 353-355
Default Value, 355
Enforce Referential Integrity, 364
Field Size, 352-353
Filter, 358
Format, 353
Indexed, 356-357
Input Mask, 353-355
New Values property, 353
Order By, 358
Required, 356
Validation Rule, 355-356
Document object (Word)
Font Selection, 624
PageSetup, 621
Path, 621
ReadOnly, 621
Saved, 621
SaveFormat, 621-622

files
changing, 899-901
displaying, 899
folders
changing, 899-901
displaying, 899
forms, 652-653
Outlook, 536
objects, 875
VBA, 619
viewing, 875
queries (Access), 403-405
Range object (Excel)
Address, 627
Cells, 628
Formula, 628
shortcuts, setting, 865-867
VBA objects, 664
Workbooks object (Excel)
Count, 624
ReadOnly, 625
Saved, 625
Worksheets object (Excel)
Name, 626
Visible, 626
see also attributes
Properties command (File menu), 899, 925
Properties window (VBA), 647
Properties Window command (VBE View menu), 637
Prospect Street (Web site), 1061
Protect Document command (Word Tools menu), 76
protecting
forms (Word), 76-77
scenarios (Excel), 306
source code (Access), 1046
public folders (Outlook), 531
adding items to, 531-532
manipulating items in, 532-533
Publish Form As command (Outlook File menu), 539
Publish Form As dialog box (Outlook), 539
Publish FrontPage Web command (FrontPage 97 File menu), 822
Publish to the Web Wizard (Access), 429-430
Publish to Web commands (Publisher File menu), 758
Publish Web Site to Folder (Publisher File menu), 758
Publisher, 17
Design Gallery, 730
creating custom galleries, 732-734

editing objects, 731
inserting objects on pages, 730-731
groups, creating, 719-721
objects
aligning, 723-724
grouping, 719
layering, 716-717
layout guides, 721-722
nudging, 724-725
ruler guides, 722-723
snapping objects to guides, 723
pages, adding, 712-713
PageWizard
ads, creating, 736-739
calendars, creating, 735-736
coupons, creating, 739
logos, creating, 739-740
sound clips
editing, 742-745
inserting, 740-742
text
Continued references, 714-716
disconnecting frames, 714
flowing into frames, 713-714
formatting, 714
frame capacity, 712
layering text boxes, 717-718
text wrap, 725-727
wrapping, 725-727
troubleshooting
Continued references, 716
grouped objects, 738
Web pages, 758
video clips, 745
Web pages
blank Web pages, 751
converting documents for, 759
converting existing
documents to, 782-784
Design Checker, 755-757
graphics, 751-752
hyperlinks, 752-754
placing on Web servers, 757-759
previewing, 757
text, 751
text color, 754
Web Site PageWizard, 748-751
wizards, Web Publishing, 758

publishing Web pages to servers (FrontPage 97), 822

Purge Print Jobs commands (Print menu), 983

purging deleted files, 897

PWS (Personal Web Server), 703

Q

QBE (Query By Example), 391

quadratic estimates (Excel Solver), 340

queries (Access), 390, 440-441
action queries, 407-408
records, appending, 410
records, deleting, 408-409
records, updating, 409-410
tables, creating, 411-412
calculations, 401-403
creating, 290
criteria
expressions, 400-401
identifiers, 398-400
operators, 398-400
setting, 397-398
Design view, 390-391
Excel pivot tables, 276-280
fields
adding, 393-394
column width, 397
deleting, 394-395
hiding, 396-397
moving, 395
naming, 395-396
viewing, 396-397
FROM clause, 292-293
GROUP BY clause, 293
joining, 392
modifying databases from Excel, 290-291
ORDER BY clause, 293
properties, 403-405
QBE (Query By Example), 391
relationships, 392-393
SELECT statement, 291-292
sending SQL to, 293-295
Simple Query Wizard, 405-406
sort order of results, 401
tables, adding to queries, 391
temporary queries, 295-296
see also pivot tables

Query menu commands (Access)
Delete Query, 408
Run, 410
Show Table, 391
Update Query, 409

Query Options dialog box (Word), 117

Query Properties dialog box (Access), 403

Query Wizard (Excel), 14, 258-260

Quick View, exiting, 899

Quick View command (File menu), 898

Quick View Plus, 897

Quick View, previewing files, 897-899

QuickBooks (accounting software), 765

QuickForms Online (Web site), 1066

QuickShelf Shortcut Bar, 32

Quit macro action (Access), 447

R

R² value (Excel functions), 221-224

radio button control (VBA), 641

radio buttons (FrontPage 97), 839

RAM, PowerPoint multimedia, 586

Range object (Excel)
methods
Activate, 628
Copy, 628
Sort, 628
properties
Address, 627
Cells, 628
Formula, 628

range operator (:), Excel, 168

ranges (Excel)
3-D ranges, 180
Currency format, 180
formulas, 181-183
copying, 177
hyperlinks, 177, 183
moving, 176
multiple selections, 169-172
naming, 172-173
reference formulas, 177
reference operators, 168
selecting, 174-175

Ratio reports (SBFM), 766

Read Only attribute, 899, 900

read-only files, 900

ReadOnly property
Excel objects, 625
Word objects, 621

Record Locks property (Access), 404

Record Macro dialog box (Word), 103

Record menu commands (Access)
Filter, 382
Remove Filter/Sort, 381
Sort, 380

recording macros, 602-604
Excel, 634-636
Word, 103-104

records
Access
appending with action queries, 410
data entry, 376-377
deleting data, 378
deleting with action queries, 408-409
filters, 381-388
multiple sorts, 380-381
simple sorts, 379-380
unsorting, 381
updating with action queries, 409-410
Mail Merge (Word)
filtering for data source, 117
selecting records for data source, 117-118
sorting records for data source, 118

Records menu commands (Excel)
Edit Column, 262
Sort, 261

Recordset Type property (Access), 404

recordsets (Access), 282

Recycle Bin, 883-884
deleting files, 893-895
restoring deleted files, 895-897
emptying, 896
sizing, 896-897

Red Herring (Web site), 1068

Redetect Tape command (Tools menu), 1030

ReDim statement (VBA), 671

redirecting e-mail replies (Outlook), 525

reducing applications to buttons on taskbar, 862

reference formulas (Excel), 177

reference operators (Excel), 168

references to applications, removing, 1013

referential integrity (Access), 364

Refresh command (View menu), 887, 926

Refresh Data command (Excel Data menu), 134

refreshing
lookup fields (Access), 15
Excel
refreshing links in workbooks, 201-202
pivot tables, 255
windows, 886

REGEDIT (Registry Editor)
accessing, 957
troubleshooting hardware installation, 957-959

registering file types, 927-928

Registry
editing, 920
lost/failed files, 856
troubleshooting hardware installation, 957-959

regression-based forecasts, 318

Rehearse Timings command (PowerPoint Slide Show menu), 567

reinstalling, *see* **installing**

relational databases, 274

Relationship Editor (Access), 434

relationships (Access), 364-365, 436-439
many-to-many, 435
one-to-many relationships, 434
one-to-one, 435-436
queries, 392-393

Relationships command (Access Tools menu), 364, 436

Relationships dialog box (Access), 364

relative comparison (Validation Rule property), 356

relative references (Excel formulas), 186-187
naming formulas, 198-199

relative references (HTML), 791

Remove Filter/Sort command (Access Record menu), 381

Remove Shortcuts/Folders dialog box, 1013

removing
applications, 1010-1014
automatically, 1010
DLLs (Dynamic Link Libraries), 1011-1013
file associations, 1014
folders, 1013
from Application Directory, 1011

manually, 1011-1014
references to applications, 1013
shortcuts, 1013
icons, 871
numeric tails from file names, 920
programs/folders from Startup folder, 849
Windows components, 1005-1006
see also deleting

Rename command (File menu), 916

Rename macro action (Access), 447

Rename Page command (Outlook Form menu), 693

renaming, *see* **names; naming**

RepaintObject macro action (Access), 447

Repair utility (Access), 15

Replace Window command (View menu), 899

replicas (Access), 15

Replication ID setting (Field Size property), 352

Report Wizard (Access), 37

reports
Access
AutoReport, 414-417
columnar reports, 415
customization, 427-428
Design view, 428
e-mail, 430
HTML, 429-430
macros, 458-460
multiple table reports, 442-444
printing, 423
Reports Wizard, 417-423
tabular reports, 416-417
Excel, SBFM, 766
Solver (Excel), 333-337

Reports command (Access Insert menu), 415

Reports Wizard (Access), 417-423

Requery macro action (Access), 448

Required property (Access), 356

Resource Center for Home-Based Businesses (Web site), 1081

restarting, *see* **starting**

Restore command (File menu), 895

Restore macro action (Access), 448

Restore tab (Backup dialog box),
1017

restoring
archives (Outlook), 482
deleted files, 895-897
files
backups, 1030-1035
changing restore settings,
1032-1034
compare settings, 1034-1035
to other locations, 1031-1032
troubleshooting, 1033
verifying backup files, 1034
minimized applications, 877
minimized programs, 871

Results command (Options
menu), 906

Retail Business Resource Center
(Web sites), 1081

Retail Futures (Web site), 1070

RetrieveNow ( ) subroutine
(Access), 296

Return Data to Microsoft Excel
command (Excel File menu),
262

right-clicking (mouse operation),
875

/root, <object> switch, 912

Rotate or Flip command
(PowerPoint Draw menu), 550

rotating
objects (PowerPoint), 550-552
text (Excel), 14

ROUND (x,y) function (Word
forms), 82

ROW function (Excel), 212-214

rows (Excel), 13

Rows command (Access Insert
menu), 401

ruler guides (Publisher),
722-723

Rules (Outlook Out of Office
Assistant), 515-518

Run Backup Minimized option,
1028

Run command
Access Query menu, 410
Start menu, 857, 862, 999, 1008

Run Permissions property
(Access), 404

RunApp macro action (Access),
448

RunCode macro action (Access),
448

RunCommand macro action
(Access), 448

RunMacro macro action (Access),
448

running
applications, 994-997, 1008-1009
backward-compatibility, 994
Win32, 994-995
applications at startup, 847-849
documents at startup, 847-849
macros
Access, 458-460
automatic execution, 614
keyboard execution, 613-614
slide shows (PowerPoint), 571-574
timing, 569
Windows 3.1 applications, 1001

running macros (Word), 104

RunSQL macro action (Access),
448

S

<S> tag (HTML), 776

Safe mode, starting Windows 95,
853-854

Sales Analysis reports (SBFM),
766

Sales Leads USA (Web site),
1070

<SAMP> tag (HTML), 776

Save As command (File menu),
1025
Word, 68

Save As dialog box, 1025
Excel, 23
Word, 23

Save as HTML command
(File menu)
Excel, 779
PowerPoint, 580, 781
Word, 779

Save Binder As command (Binder
File menu), 57

Save macro action (Access), 448

Save method
Excel objects, 625
Word objects, 623

Save Search command
(File menu), 906
Outlook, 478

SaveAs method
Excel objects, 625
Word objects, 623

Saved property
Excel objects, 625
Word objects, 621

SaveFormat property
(Word objects), 621

saving
backup settings, 1024-1026
files as set, 1020-1021
forms
Outlook, 538-540
Word, 77
search criteria, 906
Shortcut Bar configurations, 37
templates (Word), 67
Web pages (FrontPage 97),
830-831

SBE (Small Business Edition),
17-18

SBFM (Small Business Financial
Manager), 762
accounting software, configuring,
763-764
Excel, 762-763
importing data, 765-766
reports, 766
scenarios, 767
software considerations, 764-765
supported accounting software,
763

ScanDisk, troubleshooting
Windows 95 startup, 850-854

Scatter charts (Excel), 152

Scenario Summary dialog box
(Excel), 308

Scenario Values dialog box
(Excel), 306

scenarios (Excel), 304
creating, 305-307
hiding, 306
protecting, 306
SBFM, 767
Solver, 331
summarizing, 307-310

Scenarios command (Excel Tools
menu), 305

Schedule a New Program
command (Program menu),
1023

scheduling backups, 1019-1020
System Agent, 1022-1023

scoping variables (VB Script),
690

<SCRIPT> tag (HTML), 778, 804

Script Editor (VB Script), 694

Script Wizard (ActiveX Control
Pad), 805

Scrollbar properties (forms), 652

search engines for Web pages (FrontPage 97), 837-838

searches
files, 902-906
compressed ZIP files, 905
saving search criteria, 906
folders (Outlook), searching by category, 511-512
views (Outlook), 477
see also finding

Section menu commands (Binder)
Delete, 50
Next Section, 49
Previous Section, 49
Print Preview, 51
Select All, 50
Unselect All, 50

sections (Binder)
deleting, 50
editing, 48-49
organizing, 49
printing, 52
selecting, 49-50
unbinding, 50
viewing contents, 47

Securities and Exchange Commission (Web site), 1061

security
Access
records, locking, 1047
user-level, 1047
converting Access databases, 25
file sharing, Excel workbooks, 15
forms, protecting in Word, 76-77
virus protection, 11

Select a Folder dialog box (Publisher), 758

Select All command
Binder Section menu, 50
Edit menu, 889

Select Folder(s) dialog box (Outlook), 477

select queries (Access), 409-410

SELECT statement (Access queries), 291-292

/select, <sub object> switch, 912

Selected Data Series command (Excel Format menu), 164

Selected Plot Area command (Excel Format menu), 220

selecting
cell ranges (Excel), 174-175
files, 889-890
folders, 884, 889-890
icons, 871

records for Mail Merge (Word)
data source, 117-118
sections (Binder), 49-50

Selection object (Word), 624

SelectObject macro action (Access), 448

self-running slide shows (PowerPoint), 574-575
action buttons, 575-578
configuration, 575
Internet presentation, 579-580
starting, 578-579

Selling.com (Web site), 1070

Send command (Access File menu), 423

Send To command, 875-877
File menu
Binder, 56
PowerPoint, 38

Send To menu, adding printers to, 902

SendKeys macro action (Access), 448

SendMail method (Word objects), 623

SendObject macro action (Access), 448

Sensitivity report (Excel Solver), 335

Services command (Outlook Tools menu), 507

Set (Word field), 120

Set Up Show dialog box (PowerPoint), 571

SetMenuItem macro action (Access), 448

Settings menu commands
Control Panel, 846, 851
Drag and Drop, 1023, 1028
File Filtering, 1017, 1026
Options, 1017, 1027
Taskbar, 861, 1013

Setup, 1045
device detection, 943
network installation, 10

setup programs, installing Windows applications, 997-998

SetValue macro action (Access), 448

SetWarnings macro action (Access), 448

SGRAM (Synchronous Graphics RAM), 586

sharing
resources on computers, 928-931
resources on networks, 928-933
browsing shared folders, 928
finding computers, 932
mapping network drives, 931
viewing network resources, 933

Sharrow Advertising & Marketing Resource Center (Web site), 1070

sheet-level names (Excel formulas), 195

Shortcut Bars
application buttons, 30
customization
adding bars, 35
adding buttons, 34
appearance of bars, 33
creating buttons, 34
creating custom bars, 36
creating more bars, 32
customizing buttons, 34-35
deleting bars, 35
deleting buttons, 34
hiding bars, 32-33
positioning bar, 31-32
rearranging buttons, 34
saving configurations, 37
opening documents, 30
see also toolbars

Shortcut command (New menu), 863

shortcuts, 862-867
creating folders on desktop for storage, 870
creating for
applications, 863
desktop, 870-871
folders, 864
creating to open folders at startup, 848
deleting, 864-865
desktop, 914-915
double-clicking, 863
icons, 885
names, editing, 864-865
opening documents, 864
opening folders, 912-913
printers, 985-986
removing from Start menu, 1013
setting properties, 865-867
starting applications, 864
troubleshooting, 864
see also icons

Show Fields command (Outlook View menu), 483

Show Table dialog box (Access), 436

Show Table command (Access Query menu), 391

Show Web Toolbar command (Binder Go menu), 56

ShowAllRecords macro action (Access), 448

showing, *see* **displaying; viewing**

ShowToolBar macro action (Access), 448

shutting down computer, 956

side-by-side folder batch files, creating, 914-915

SIGN(x) function (Word forms), 82

Simple Query Wizard (Access), 405-406

Simply Accounting for Windows (accounting software), 765

Single setting (Field Size property), 352

Site Builder Workshop (Web site), 806

sizing
controls on forms, 654
fonts, 899
graphics (FrontPage 97), 827
Recycle Bin, 896-897

SkipIf (Word field), 120

Slide Show menu commands (PowerPoint)
Action Buttons, 575
Custom Animation, 570
Rehearse Timings, 567
Slide Transition, 565
View on Two Screens, 572
View Show, 569

Slide Sorter view (PowerPoint), 565

Slide Transition command (PowerPoint Slide Show menu), 565

Slide Transition dialog box (PowerPoint), 568

slides (PowerPoint)
Expand Slide, 16
objects
animation, 552-554
AutoShapes, 548
converting, 560-561
embedding, 560-561
grouped objects, editing, 549
grouping, 548-549
linking, 560-561
rotating, 550-552
stacking, 546-547

self-running slide shows, 574-575
action buttons, 575-578
configuration, 575
Internet presentation, 579-580
starting, 578-579
slide shows, 564
ActiveX Controls, 578
adjusting transitions, 569
animation, 570
conference presentations, 573-574
metering manual presentations, 570-571
multiple computers, 572-573
running, 571-574
Slide Navigator, 573
testing timing, 569
timing, 564-567
transitions, 567-569
Summary Slide, 16
text
AutoShapes, placing on, 555-557
placeholders, 555
text boxes, 555
WordArt, 557-560

Slides object (PowerPoint), 629-630

<SMALL> tag (HTML), 776

Small Business Administration Upcoming Events (Web site), 1084

Small Business Advisor (Web site), 1058

Small Business Edition, 17-18

Small Business Financial Manager, *see* **SBFM**

Small Business Innovative Research (Web site), 1081

Small Business Workshop (Web site), 1058

Small Icons command (View menu), 907

smoothing (Excel forecasts), 315-316

Snap To command (Publisher Tools menu), 723

snapping objects to guides (Publisher), 723

SOHO America (Web site), 1081

Solver (Excel)
Automatic Scaling, 339
Central Differencing, 340
Changing Cells, specifying, 326-328
Conjugate method, 340
constraints, 328-331

forecasts, damping factor, 319
linear searches, 339
Newton method, 340
nonlinear searches, 339
Precision edit box, 337-338
quadratic estimates, 340
reports, 333-337
scenarios, 331
Show Iteration Results, 339
solutions, 331-333
tangential estimates, 340
Target Cell, specifying, 325-326

Solver command (Excel Tools menu), 320, 325

Solver dialog box (Excel), 325

Sort command
Access Record menu, 380
Excel Records menu, 261
Outlook View menu, 467

Sort method (Excel objects), 628

sorting
Access
query results, 401
records, 379-381
files, 909-910
folders, 909-910
records for Mail Merge (Word)
data source, 118
views (Outlook)
by columns, 466-467
by field, 467-468
creating views, 468-470
see also arranging

Sorting and Grouping command (Access View menu), 428

Sound Blaster, installing AWE 32 card, 945-951

sound boards (cards), installing, 945-951

sound clips (Publisher)
editing, 742-745
inserting, 740-742

Source Data command (Excel Chart menu), 156

speaker presentations (PowerPoint), 572

Split from Original command (Briefcase menu), 926

splitting Briefcase files, 926

Spool Settings dialog box, 973

spooling print jobs, 972-974

SQL (Structured Query Language), 290
Access
importing tables to, 360-361
linking tables, 361-362

queries, 391
sending to Access, 293-295
queries, temporary queries, 295-296

SQL View command (Access View menu), 405

stacking objects
PowerPoint, 546-547
Publisher, 716-717

staging (HTML files), 791

Start menu, 858-861
opening documents, 860-861
opening programs from, 859-860
removing folders, 1013
removing shortcuts to applications, 1013

Start menu commands
Programs, 46
Run, 857, 862, 999, 1008

starting
applications
Explorer, 868
My Computer, 869
shortcuts, 864
Start menu, 859-860
taskbar buttons, 861
Backup, 1016
documents from Start menu, 860-861
Explorer, 882, 911-914
Install Program Wizard, 1002
self-running slide shows (PowerPoint), 578-579
Windows 95
alternate mode, 852-853
BOOTLOG.TXT, 855
bypassing Login dialog box, 846
bypassing logo, 846
bypassing Startup group, 849
bypassing Startup menu, 853
compression, 857
controlling program/folder appearance, 849
failed boots, 857
hard disk, 857
hardware, 856
incorrect application starts, 857
lost/failed system Registry, 856
missing files, 856
opening folders at startup, 848
partitioning, 857
restarting from startup disk, 857-858
running applications at startup, 847-849

running documents at startup, 847-849
Safe mode, 853-855
ScanDisk, 850
startup disk, 850
Startup menu, 852-853
testing with Step-by-Step mode, 855-856
troubleshooting, 849-854, 856-857
see also opening

startup disks
creating, 851
restarting Windows 95 from, 857-858
troubleshooting Windows 95 startup, 850-854

Startup folder
bypassing at startup, 849
removing programs/folders from, 849
troubleshooting, 849

Startup menu, 852-853

Startup Position property (forms), 653

State and Local Procurement Jumpstation (Web site), 1076

statements (VBA)
Dim, 670
Do...While, 666
If...Then...Else, 665-666
ReDim, 671

statistical functions (Excel)
FDIST, 220-224
FREQUENCY, 218-220
LINEST, 220-224
NORMDIST, 218-220
R^2, 221-222

status bar (Explorer), 907

Status Bar command (View menu), 907

status bars (Binder), 58

status checks, Briefcase files, 925-926

Step Into command (VBA Debugger menu), 669

Step-by-Step mode, testing Windows 95 startup, 855-856

stepping through code (VBA), 668-669

Stock Ticker control (ActiveX), 803

Stockholders' Equity reports (SBFM), 766

StopAllMacros macro action (Access), 448

StopMacro macro action (Access), 448

<STRIKE> tag (HTML), 777

<STRONG> tag (HTML), 777

Structured Query Language, *see* SQL

<STYLE> tag (HTML), 778

Style command (Word Format menu), 71

Style dialog box (Word), 71

Style Gallery command (Word Format menu), 65

styles (Word), 68-70
applying, 70-71
creating, 73-74
Default Paragraph Font, 70
modifying, 71-73
Normal, 70
shortcut keys, 72

<SUB> tag (HTML), 777

subroutines, 609-610
VBA, creating, 660-663

Success Magazine (Web site), 1068

SUM( ) function (Word forms), 82

summarizing scenarios (Excel), 307-310

Summary Slide (PowerPoint), 16

<SUP> tag (HTML), 777

support
Win32 applications, 994-995
Windows 3.1 applications, 996

switches
index field codes (Word), 102
opening Explorer, 911-912

switching between
Access views, 374
programs, taskbar, 861-862

synchronizing files with Briefcase, 921-923

Synchronous Graphics RAM (SGRAM), 586

SYS file, 856

System Agent, scheduling backups, 1022-1023

System attribute, 900-901

system files, deleting, 895

system resources, 995

SYSTEM.DAT file, 856

T

tab control (VBA), 642

tab order of controls, 653

TabIndex property (forms), 653

Table menu commands (Excel),
Add Table, 261

**Table of Contents command
(FrontPage 97 Insert menu),
836**

**Table Properties dialog box
(Access), 357**

Table view (Outlook)
combination fields, 490
designing folder views, 483
sorting
by column, 466-467
by field, 467-468
creating new views, 468-470

**Table Wizard (Access), 346,
358-360**

tables
Access, 75
action queries, creating with,
411-412
adding to queries, 391
creating, 347-348
data entry, 376-377
data types, 348, 349-351
data types, changing, 363
Datasheet view, 346, 347-348
deleting data, 378
Design view, 346, 348-349
editing, 362-363
editing data, 378
field-level properties, 351-358
fields, arranging, 363
fields, deleting, 363
fields, naming, 363
filters, 381-388
importing, 360-361
indexes, 356-357
linking, 361-362
Mail Merge (Word), 115
many-to-many relationships,
435
multiple sorts, 380-381
navigating, 375-376
one-to-many relationships, 434
one-to-one relationships,
435-436
primary key, 347, 349
properties, changing, 363
queries, 440-441
relationships, 364-365, 436-439
relationships, defining,
392-393
reports, 414

simple sorts, 379-380
table-level properties, 357
unsorting records, 381
Excel, 75
Word, 12
Mail Merge, 114-115
Web pages, 787
see also databases

tables of contents
FrontPage 97, 836
Word
creating, 93-94
headings, identifying, 92-93
multiple documents, creating
for, 95
tables of figures, 96
updating, 95-96

**Tables of Contents Options dialog
box (Word), 94**

TabStop property (forms), 653

**tabular reports (Access),
AutoReport, 416-417**

tags (HTML), 774
character formatting, 776-777
<OBJECT>, inserting ActiveX
Controls, 802-803
paragraph formatting, 777
<PARAM>, inserting ActiveX
Controls, 803-804
<SCRIPT>, 804
special function, 778

**tangential estimates (Excel
Solver), 340**

tape backups, 1016

tapes
Backup program, 1029-1030
formatting, 1029

**Target Cell (Excel Solver),
325-326**

Task object (Outlook), 699

Taskbar
arranging windows, 877
buttons
activating programs, 861
reducing applications, 862
command (Settings menu), 861
displaying, 847
switching between programs,
861-862

**Taskbar command (Settings
menu), 1013**

tasks (Outlook), 526
accepting assignments, 529-530
assigning, 528-529
ownership, 526-527
tracking owners, 527-528
updates, 527

**Tasks folder (Outlook), dragging
objects to, 495-496**

**Tasks view (Outlook), creating
fields, 487**

Tax Planning (Web site), 1058

Tax Prophet (Web site), 1058

**Telecommuting, Teleworking, and
Alternative Officing (Web site),
1064**

Template Wizard (Excel)
building templates, 143-146
database driver, 142-143
entering data in templates, 146
installing, 141

templates
Binder, 57
Excel, 132, 135-136
building templates with
Template Wizard, 143-146
charts, designing for, 139-141
database driver for Template
Wizard, 142-143
entering data in templates, 146
template elements, 133-135
Template Wizard, installing,
141
workbooks, opening, 132-133
worksheets, designing for,
137-138
FrontPage 97, 841-842
Word, 62
attaching templates to
documents, 64-65
creating documents based on
templates, 63
creating templates, 67-68
forms, 77-78
global templates, creating, 66
Invoice template, 78-79
previewing templates, 65
resolving template conflicts,
66-67
saving templates, 67
user templates, 67
workgroup templates, 67

**Templates and Add-ins dialog box
(Word), 64**

**Templates command (Word Tools
menu), 64**

testing
merges (Word Mail Merge),
124-125
printers (printing test pages), 966,
990
slide show timing (PowerPoint),
569

Web pages
  graphics, 793
  hyperlinks, 793
  Netscape Navigator, 793
Windows 95 startup, Step-by-Step
  mode, 855-856

text
  dragging in Outlook, 500
  editing (FrontPage 97), 823-825
  Excel
    indenting, 14
    rotating, 14
  PowerPoint
    placeholders, 555
    placing text on AutoShapes,
      555-557
    text boxes, 555
  Publisher
    color on Web pages, 754
    Continued references, 714-716
    disconnecting frames, 714
    flowing into frames, 713-714
    formatting, 714
    frame capacity, 712
    layering text boxes, 717-718
    pages, adding, 712-713
    text wrap, 725-727
    Web pages, 751
  Word, Web pages, 784-786

text box control (VBA), 639-641

**Text data type (Access tables),
349**
  Allow Zero Length property, 356
  Field Size property, 352

**Text Form Field Options dialog
box (Word), 79, 85**

**Timestamp command (FrontPage
97 Insert menu), 835**

**timestamps (FrontPage 97),
835-836**

**timing slide shows (PowerPoint),
564-565**
  automatic timing, 566-567
  manual timing, 565-566

<TITLE> tag (HTML), 775

tolerance (Excel Solver), 338

**Toolbar command (View menu),
870, 884, 907**

toolbars, 11
  Animation Effects (PowerPoint),
    17
  displaying, 884
  Explorer, hiding, 907
  FrontPage 97, Image, 825
  macro buttons
    customizing, 605-607
    inserting, 604-605

PowerPoint
  Animation Effects, 552-553
  Control Toolbox, 578
Word
  creating, 89-91
  Forms, 76
  viewing, 88-89
  see also Shortcut Bars

**Toolbars command (Word View
menu), 76, 88**

Tools menu commands
  Access
    Macro, 16
    Relationships, 364, 436
  Erase Tape, 1030
  Excel
    Add-Ins, 37
    Auditing, 204
    Data Analysis, 315
    Goal Seek, 311
    Scenarios, 305
    Solver, 320, 325
  Find, 902, 932
  Format Tape, 1030
  FrontPage 97, Verify Hyperlinks,
    831
  Go To, 885
  Outlook
    Design Outlook Form, 487,
      693
    Find, 477
    Services, 507
  Publisher
    Design Checker, 755
    Snap To, 723
  Redetect Tape, 1030
  Word
    Macro, 83
    Mail Merge, 110
    Protect Document, 76
    Templates, 64
    Unprotect Document, 77

**Top Marketing Tips, Tricks, and
Techniques (Web site), 1070**

**Top Values property (Access),
404**

**tracers (Excel formulas),
204-206**
  invalid data, tracing, 207-208
  tracing dependents, 206

tracking
  links, 42
  Outlook
    e-mail messages, 523-525
    task owners, 527-528
    voting message responses
      (Outlook), 522

**Trade Show Central (Web site),
1084**

TrADE-Net Italy (Web site), 1062

**Tradeshow News Network (Web
site), 1085**

**TransferDatabase macro action
(Access), 448**

**TransferSpreadsheet macro action
(Access), 448**

**TransferText macro action
(Access), 448**

**transitions (PowerPoint slide
shows), 567-569**

**TRANSPOSE( ) function (Excel),
189**

TREND function (Excel), 314

TREND( ) function (Excel), 193

troubleshooting
  Access
    converting databases, 25
    data types, 363
    linking tables, 372
    mailing labels, 424
    queries, 405
  ActiveX Controls, 812
  Add New Hardware Wizard,
    device detection, 936
  backups, 1026
  double-clicking shortcuts, 863
  Excel
    cell ranges, 183
    charts, 157
    Goal Seek, 314
    links, 202-203
    Solver, 340
    Template Wizard, 148
  files
    opening with applications, 928
    restoring, 1033
  FrontPage 97, 831
  hardware installation, 952-959
    changing resource settings,
      952-956
    checking for resource coflicts,
      956-957
    Device Manager, 952
    Registry Editor
      (REGEDIT.EXE), 957-959
  HTML, 779
  IRQ conflicts, 941
  memory, 49
  Outlook
    Address Book, 506
    dragging objects, 499
    filters, 476
    forms, 540
    saving changes, 501
    views, 469
  PowerPoint
    AutoShapes, 557
    linking and embedding, 562
    multimedia, 591

printing, 990-992
  Enhanced Print
    Troubleshooter, 992
  memory, 970
  Print Manager diagnostic tool,
    992
  Print Troubleshooter, 991
  purging print jobs, 983
Publisher
  Continued references, 716
  grouped objects, 738
  Web pages, 758
shortcuts, creating for folders, 864
shutdown, 956
Startup folder, 849
VBScript, 703
VBA, 621, 643, 677
Windows 95 startup, 849-857
  alternate mode, 852-853
  BOOTLOG.TXT, 855
  compression, 857
  failed boots, 857
  hard disk, 857
  hardware, 856
  in Safe mode, 854-855
  incorrect application starts,
    857
  lost/failed system Registry,
    856
  missing files, 856
  partitioning, 857
  ScanDisk, 850
  startup disk, 850
  Startup menu, 852-853
Word
  Mail Merge, 112
  toolbars, 91
see also errors
\<TT\> tag (HTML), 777
Turn on Audible Prompts option,
  1027
turning off Confirm File Delete
  dialog box, 897

U

\<U\> tag (HTML), 777
U.S. Air (Web site), 1083
U.S. Business Center (Web site),
  1076
U.S. Census Bureau (Web site),
  1071
U.S. Chamber of Commerce
  Small Business Institute (Web
  site), 1081
U.S. Patent Office (Web site),
  1073

U.S. Post Office (Web site), 1076
U.S. Small Business
  Administration (Web site),
  1059
U.S. Tax Code On-Line (Web
  site), 1061
U.S. Veteran Affairs (Web site),
  1076
\<UL\> tag (HTML), 777
Unauthorized FrontPage Support
  Site (Web site), 842
unbinding sections (Binder), 50
unbound objects (Access),
  converting, 25
underscore (_) in variable names,
  659
Undo command (Edit menu), 917
Undo Delete command (Edit
  menu), 893
Unfreeze All Columns command
  (Access Format menu), 376
Unicode standard (VB Script),
  690
union operator (,), Excel, 168
Unique Records property
  (Access), 404
Unique Values property (Access),
  404
United Parcel Service (Web site),
  1083
UNIX, 792
Unprotect Document command
  (Word Tools menu), 77
Unselect All command (Binder
  Section menu), 50
Update All command (Briefcase
  menu), 924
Update My Briefcase dialog box,
  924
Update Query command (Access
  Query menu), 409
updating
  records (Access), 409-410
  tables of contents (Word), 95-96
upgrading Plug and Play, 940
URLs (Uniform Resource
  Locators)
  relative references, 791
  testing for broken links, 793
Use Address Book dialog box
  (Word), 116
Use Data Compression option,
  1024

user comments, 11
user templates (Word), 67
UserForm command (VBE Insert
  menu), 636

V

validating Web pages, 796-799
Validation Rule property (Access),
  355-356
value axis (Excel charts),
  150-151
\<VAR\> tag (HTML), 777
variables
  VBScript, 688
    scoping variables, 690
  VBA, 609, 659
    creating, 669-671
VB Pro (Web site), 656
VBScript
  Active Server Pages, 703-706
  ActiveX Control Pad, 699
  arrays, 689
  Clipboard, 688
  comparing to VBA, 684-687
  error trapping, 691
  events, activating, 690-691
  functions, 689
    CreateObject, 691
    Is testing functions, 688
    Unicode standard, 690
  objects, 691-692
  Outlook, 692
    forms, creating, 693-697
    functions, creating, 697-698
    object model, 699
  resources, 707
  Script Editor, 694
  troubleshooting, 703
  variables, 688
    scoping variables, 690
  Web browsers, 699-703
  Windows Scripting Host, 706
VBA (Visual Basic for
  Applications)
  commands, Call, 662
  comparing to
    VB Script, 684-686
    Visual Basic, 681-682
  Control Toolbox, 647
  controls, 641-642
    aligning, 654
    sizing, 654
    tab order, 653
  DAO, 673-674

debugger, 666-668
    breakpoints, 669
    stepping through code,
        668-669
dialog boxes, 649-652
events, 673
data labels (Excel), 158-161
Excel macros
    command buttons, 638-639,
        644-645
    InputBox function, 646
    MsgBox function, 642-644
    recording, 634-636
    text box controls, 639-641
form properties, 652-653
forms
    Excel, 636-637
    PowerPoint, 654-655
functions, 663
    EOF(), 672
help, 681
Immediate window, 648-649, 658
    : (colon) command, 660
loops, 659-660
macros
    automatic execution, 614
    buttons, customizing, 605-607
    buttons, inserting on toolbars,
        604-605
    creating, 602-604
    editing, 607-609
    keyboard execution, 613-614
manipulating code, 611-612
mathematical operators, 671
methods, 610, 664
null value, 663
Object Browser, 649
objects, 610-611, 618-619, 664-665
    Activate method, 622, 625, 628
    Add method, 625
    Address property, 627
    Appliation (Access), 629
    Cells property, 628
    CheckGrammar method, 622
    CheckSpelling method, 622
    classes, 664
    Close event, 623-624
    Close method, 623, 625
    Copy method, 624, 627-628
    Count property, 624
    creating, 674
    Cut method, 624
    Documents collection, 620
    Excel, 674-677
    Font Selection property, 624
    Formula property, 628
    instances, 664
    Name property, 626
    Office Assistant, 630-632,
        678-680
    Open event, 623
    Open method, 623, 625

PageSetup property, 621
Paste method, 624
Path property, 621
Presentation (PowerPoint),
    629
properties, 619
ReadOnly property, 621, 625
Save method, 623, 625
SaveAs method, 623, 625
Saved property, 621, 625
SaveFormat property, 621-622
SendMail method, 623
Slides (PowerPoint), 629-630
Sort method, 628
Visible property, 626
Word, 677-678
Worksheets collection
    (Excel), 626
procedures, 660
Project Explorer, 646-647, 658
Properties window, 647
resources, 655-656, 682
statements
    Dim, 670
    Do...While, 666
    If...Then...Else, 665-666
    ReDim, 671
subroutines, 609-610
    creating, 660-663
troubleshooting, 621, 643, 677
variables, 609, 659
    creating, 669-671
VBE, 634
Word macros, 103-105
writing files to disk, 671-672

VBE (Visual Basic Editor), 634

**Ventur Web-Japan (Web site),
1063**

**Verify Hyperlinks command
(FrontPage 97 Tools menu),
831**

verifying backup files, 1034

video
    PowerPoint, 587-589
        .AVI files, 590
        editing, 591-593
        .MOV files, 590
    Publisher, 745

Video RAM (VRAM), 586

View menu commands
    Access
        Conditions, 451
        Sorting and Grouping, 428
        SQL View, 405
    Arrange Icons, 870, 909
    Auto Arrange, 909
    Details, 907, 925
    Excel, Page Break Preview, 13
    Explorer, Options, 30
    Font, 899

FrontPage 97, Forms Toolbar, 839
Landscape, 899
Large Icons, 907
Line Up Icons, 909
List, 907
Options, 916, 933
Outlook
    Field Chooser, 484
    Group By, 471
    Show Fields, 483
    Sort, 467
Page View, 899
Refresh, 887, 926
Replace Window, 899
Small Icons, 907
Status Bar, 907
Toolbar, 870, 884, 907
VBA
    Immediate Window, 648
    Object Browser, 649
    Watch Window, 668
VBE, Properties Window, 637
Word, Toolbars, 76, 88

**View on Two Screens command
(PowerPoint Slide Show), 572**

**View Show command
(PowerPoint Slide Show menu),
569**

**View Summary dialog box
(Outlook), 483**

viewing
    in Explorer, 882-887
    fields, Access queries, 396-397
    folders (Outlook), viewing by
        category, 510
    index marks (Word), 101
    network resources, 933
    object properties, 875
    scenarios (Excel), 306
    section contents (Binder), 47
    toolbars (Word), 88-89
    see also previewing

views
    Access tables
        Datasheet, 346-348
        Design, 346
    Explorer (FrontPage 97), 820
    Information Viewer, 466
        archiving folders, 480-482
        combination fields, 490-491
        creating folders, 479
        designing folder views,
            483-485
        fields, creating, 486-488
        filtering, 474-476
        folders, 478-482
        formula fields, 488-490
        grouping, 471-474
        searches, 477-478
        sorting, 466-470

PowerPoint
Outline, 16
Slide Sorter, 565

virtual device drivers (VxD), 972

Virtual Online Trade Show (Web site), 1085

virus protection, 11

Virus Search add-in, 11

viruses
antivirus software, 1036
protecting computer from, 1035-1036
transmittal, 1035

Visible property (Excel objects), 626

Visio (Web site), 656

Visual Basic
comparing to VBA, 681-682
PowerPoint slide shows, 578

Visual Basic Editor (VBE), 634

Visual Basic for Applications, *see* VBA

VLOOKUP function (Excel), 215-217

voting messages (Outlook), 520-522

VRAM (Video RAM), 586

VxD (virtual device drivers), 972
Plug and Play, 937

W

W3C (World Wide Web Consortium), 810

Wall Street Directory (Web site), 1084

***Wall Street Journal* (Web site), 1068**

Watch Window command (VBA View menu), 668

Web browsers (VB Script), 699-703

Web documents, 11
PointPoint, 17

Web of Culture (Web site), 1063

Web Page Wizard (Word), 784

Web pages
ActiveX Controls, 802
ActiveX Control Pad, 806-809
connecting to scripts, 804-805
Layout control, 809-812
<OBJECT> tag, 802-803
<PARAM> tag, 803-804

FrontPage 97, 814-818
Editor, 817-818, 822-823
Explorer, 818-819
files, editing, 823-825
Image Composer, 819
image manipulation, 825-830
input forms, 838-841
interactive Web pages, 834-838
Personal Web Server, 817
saving, 830-831
templates, 841-842
graphics, verifying existence, 793
HTML, 774-775
attributes, 775
character formatting tags, 776-777
Excel spreadsheets, converting, 779-780
page structure, 775-776
paragraph formatting tags, 777
PowerPoint presentations, converting, 781-782
Publisher documents, converting, 782-784
relative references, 791
special function tags, 778
staging, 791
tags, 774
Word, creating with, 784-787
Word documents, converting, 779
hyperlinks, testing, 793
ISPs, 792
Netscape Navigator, 793
Publisher
blank Web pages, 751
converting documents for, 759
Design Checker, 755-757
graphics, 751-752
hyperlinks, 752-754
placing on Web servers, 757-759
previewing, 757
text, 751
text color, 754
Web Site PageWizard, 748-751
validating, 796-799
Web Publishing Wizard, 794-796

Web Publishing Wizard, 794-796

Web Publishing Wizard (Publisher), 758

Web sites
Acquisition Reform Network, 1074
ActiveX Gallery, 802
Advertising Age, 1066
AFL-CIO, 1063
Airlines of the Web, 1082
America Business Funding Directory, 1059

American Airlines, 1082
American Demographics/ Marketing Tools, 1068
American Express Small Business Exchange, 1077
American Law Source Online, 1065
American Marketing Association, 1068
American Movers Conference, 1082
America's Brightest, 1056
America's Job Bank, 1063
America's Small Business Finance Center, 1077
Angel Capital Electronic Network, 1059
antivirus software, 1036
Asia-Pacific Economic Cooperation, 1061
Ask the Active Platform Pro, 707
Bankruptcy FAQs, 1059
Barron's Online, 1066
Basic Patent Information, 1072
Bathrobe 'til 10, 1077
BidCast, 1074
Big Dreams, 1056
Biz$hop, 1077
BizResource.com, 1077
BizTalk, 1056
Bureau of Export Administration, 1061
Business Information and Development Services, 1074
Business Intelligence Center, 1069
Business Law Site, 1065
Business Plan Resource File, 1056
Business Research Lab, 1056
Business Resource Center, 1078
Business Start Page, 1078
Business Wire, 1069
Business@Home, 1077
BusinessWeek, 1066
BuyersZone, 1056
CCH Business Owner's Toolkit, 1057
CD Information, 1084
Center for Family Business, 1078
Central and Eastern Europe Business Information Center, 1062
Charity Village, 1071
Client/Server Central, 682
Closing Bell, 1059
Colorado Memory Systems, 1019
Commando Guide to Unconventional Marketing and Advertising Tactics, 1069
Commerce Business Daily, 1074
Computer Loan Network, 1059
Computer Register, 1063

Contact!, 1062
Continental Airlines, 1082
Copyright Clearance Center, 1072
Copyright Website, 1073
Corporate Counselor, 1065
Council on Foundations, 1071
Currency Converter, 1060
Department of Labor, 1064
Department of Labor Poster Page, 1065
Disgruntled, 1066
Doctor HTML, 796
E-Span, 1064
EDGAR, 1060
Education, Training, and Development Resource Center for Business and Industry, 1057
EGOPHER, 1078
Electronic Commerce Program Office, 1074
Electronic Commerce Resource Center, 1075
The Electronic Embassy, 1062
Electronic Money Tree, 1078
Entrepreneur Magazine's BizSquare, 1079
Entrepreneurial Edge Online, 1066
Entrepreneur's Bookstore, 1078
EntreWorld, 1079
Environmental Protection Agency Procurement, 1075
Ernest & Young's Virtual HR Office, 1064
EventWeb, 1085
EXPOguide, 1083
Export-Import Bank, 1060
ExporTutor, 1062
FAA Acquisition Center, 1075
Fast Company, 1067
Federal Acquisition Institute, 1075
FedEX, 1082
FinanceNet, 1060
Financial Times, 1067
Financial Women International, 1060
First Steps, 1069
Forbes Digital Tool, 1067
Fortune, 1067
FranInfo, 1079
Gen-X Group, 1071
General Services Agency, 1075
The George Lucas Educational Foundation, 1071
Government Accounting Office, 1075
Government Contractors Glossary, 1076
Grantsmanship Center, 1072
Guide to the Small Business Administration, 1079
Guide to Unique Meeting Facilities, 1084

Heath's Computer and Telecommunication Acronym Reference, 1079
Hispanic Business Magazine, 1067
Home Office Associate of America, 1079
Home Office Links, 1080
Home Office Mail, 1080
Home Realtors Information Network, 1080
HomeBuyer's Fair, 1082
IdeaList, 1072
Inc. Online, 1067
India Market Place, 1062
Intellectual Property Center, 1073
InterKnowledge Travel Network, 1083
Internal Revenue Service, 1057
International Public Relations, 1069
International Trade Law, 1065
JobWeb, 1064
Legal Information Institute, 1065
LinkExchange, 1057
Major Trade Shows in Asia, 1084
Market Facts and Statistics, 1069
Marketing Resource Center, 1057, 1070
Marketshares, 1057
Microsoft Office Developer forum, 656
MoneyWorld Online, 1068
National Center for Employee Ownership, 1064
National Credit Counseling Service, 1061
National Technology Transfer Center, 1076
Nerd World, 1073
NetMarquee Family Business NetCenter, 1080
Netscape Navigator, 793
Nonprofit Resources Catalog, 1072
Northwest Airlines, 1083
Occupational Safety and Health Administration, 1058
Office VBA Central, 656
Offshore Entrepreneur, 1080
Opportunities for Women in Small Business, 1080
Patent Application Drafting, 1073
Patent Pending Resource, 1073
PRONET, 1058
Prospect Street, 1061
QuickForms Online, 1066
Red Herring, 1068
Resource Center for Home-Based Businesses, 1081
Retail Business Resource Center, 1081
Retail Futures, 1070

Sales Leads USA, 1070
Securities and Exchange Commission, 1061
Selling.com, 1070
Sharrow Advertising & Marketing Resource Center, 1070
Site Builder Workshop, 806
Small Business Administration Upcoming Events, 1084
Small Business Advisor, 1058
Small Business Innovative Research, 1081
Small Business Workshop, 1058
SOHO America, 1081
State and Local Procurement Jumpstation, 1076
Success Magazine, 1068
Tax Planning, 1058
Tax Prophet, 1058
Telecommuting, Teleworking, and Alternative Officing, 1064
Top Marketing Tips, Tricks, and Techniques, 1070
Trade Show Central, 1084
TrADE-Net Italy, 1062
Tradeshow News Network, 1085
U.S. Air, 1083
U.S. Business Center, 1076
U.S. Census Bureau, 1071
U.S. Chamber of Commerce Small Business Institute, 1081
U.S. Patent Office, 1073
U.S. Post Office, 1076
U.S. Small Business Administration, 1059
U.S. Tax Code On-Line, 1061
U.S. Veteran Affairs, 1076
Unauthorized FrontPage Support Site, 842
United Parcel Service, 1083
VB Pro, 656
VBScript, 707
Ventur Web-Japan, 1063
Virtual Online Trade Show, 1085
Visio, 656
Wall Street Directory, 1084
Wall Street Journal, 1068
Web of Culture, 1063
Your Small Office, 1081

WEEKDAY( ) function (Excel), 191

Welcome dialog box, 847

Welcome to Microsoft Backup dialog box, 1016

Welcome to Windows 95 screen, 847

wildcard operators
Access queries, 399
finding files, 903

Win32 applications, 994-995

windows
   arranging (Taskbar), 877
   minimizing, 871
   refreshing, 886

Windows 3.1
   applications, 996
      backward-compatibility,
         998-1001
      dual-boot configurations,
         1000-1001
      installing, 999-1000
      long file names, 996-997
      reinstalling, 1000
      running, 1001
   Program Manager, customizing
      Explorer to open programs like,
      915-916

Windows 3.x, File Manager, 882

Windows 95
   failed applications, 877
   installing, 857-858
   starting
      alternate mode, 852-853
      BOOTLOG.TXT, 855
      bypassing Login dialog box,
         846
      bypassing logo, 846
      bypassing Startup group, 849
      bypassing Startup menu, 853
      compression, 857
      failed boots, 857
      hard disk, 857
      hardware, 856
      incorrect application starts,
         857
      lost/failed system Registry,
         856
      missing files, 856
      opening folders at startup, 848
      partitioning, 857
      program/folder appearance at
         startup, 849
      restarting from startup disks,
         857-858
      running applications at
         startup, 847-849
      running documents at startup,
         847-849
      Safe mode, 853-855
      ScanDisk, 850
      startup disk, 850
      Startup menu, 852-853
      testing with Step-by-Step
         mode, 855-856
      troubleshooting, 849-857

**Windows 95 Driver Library
(W95DL), 967**

Windows Backup program, *see*
Backup

Windows component applications
   adding, 1005-1006
   installing unisted components,
      1007
   removing, 1005-1006

Windows Explorer, *see* **Explorer**

**Windows Explorer, see Explorer
(Windows), 882-887**

**Windows Scripting Host
(VBScript), 706**

wizards
   Access
      Command Button, 458
      Input Mask, 354
      Lookup, 351
      Mailing Label, 424-426
      Publish to the Web, 429-430
      Report, 37
      Reports, 417-423
      Simple Query, 405-406
      Table, 346, 358-360
   Add Printer Wizard, 963-966
   Add/Remove Programs, 1010
   Excel
      Chart, 14
      Internet Assistant, 779
      PivotTable, 255
      Query, 14, 258-260
      Template, 141
   Install Program, 1002
   Network Installation, 10, 1040
   Outlook
      Events, 695
      Import and Export, 482
   PowerPoint
      AutoContent, 579
      Presentation Conference, 574
   Publisher
      PageWizard, 735-740
      Web Publishing, 758
      Web Site PageWizard, 748-751
   Script Wizard (ActiveX Control
      Pad), 805
   Web Publishing, 794-796
   Word, 63
      Letter, 12
      Mail Merge Helper, 110-113
      Web Page, 784

Word, 62-63
   AutoComplete, 12
   AutoSummarize, 12
   AutoText, 68
   boilerplate text, 68
   converting documents to HTML,
      779
   cross-references, 98
   data sharing, 38
   document mapping, 96-98
   Document Maps, 12

documents
   converting, 22-23
   tables of figures, 96
Excel, 75
forms, 74-75
   Calculation fields, 81-82
   check boxes, 84
   creating, 75-76
   drop-down list boxes, 84-85
   help, 85
   implementation, 86
   Invoice template, 78-79
   macros for fields, 82-83
   protecting, 76-77
   saving, 77
   templates, 77-78
grammar checking, 12
indexes, 99
   creating, 101-102
   marking items for indexing,
      99-101
   multiple indexes, creating, 103
   page ranges, 101
   switches for field codes, 102
   viewing index marks, 101
macros
   converting, 22
   editing, 104-105
   recording, 103-104
   running, 104
Mail Merge, 108
   Access tables as data sources,
      115
   Ask field in main document,
      122-123
   conditional fields in main
      document, 120-121
   data source, 109
   e-mail distribution, 126-128
   envelopes, 126
   Excel worksheets as data
      sources, 115
   fax distribution, 126-128
   Fill-In field in main document,
      125
   filtering records for data
      source, 117
   If field in main document,
      123-124
   inserting fields in main
      document, 118-120
   Mail Merge Helper Wizard,
      110-113
   main document, 109, 113
   merging to a new document,
      126
   Outlook Address Book as data
      source, 116
   printing documents, 126
   selecting records for data
      source, 117-118

sorting records for data
source, 118
testing merges, 124-125
types of data sources, 115-116
Word tables as data sources,
114-115
objects
Activate method, 622
CheckGrammar method, 622
CheckSpelling method, 622
Close event, 623-624
Close method, 623
Copy method, 624
Cut method, 624
Documents collection, 620
Font Selection property, 624
Open event, 623
Open method, 623
PageSetup property, 621
Paste method, 624
Path property, 621
ReadOnly property, 621
Save method, 623
SaveAs method, 623
Saved property, 621
SaveFormat property, 621-622
SendMail method, 623
VBA, 677-678
Print dialog box features, 979-980
styles, 68, 69-70
applying, 70-71
creating, 73-74
Default Paragraph Font, 70
modifying, 71-73
Normal, 70
shortcut keys, 72
tables, 12, 75
tables of contents
creating, 93-94
headings, identifying, 92-93
multiple documents, creating
for, 95
tables of figures, 96
updating, 95-96
templates, 62
attaching to documents, 64-65
creating, 67-68
creating documents based on,
63
global templates, creating, 66
previewing, 65
resolving conflicts, 66-67
saving, 67
user templates, 67
workgroup templates, 67
toolbars
creating, 89-91
viewing, 88-89
troubleshooting
Mail Merge, 112
toolbars, 91

Web pages
creating, 784
graphics, 786
hyperlinks, 786-787
tables, 787
text, 784-786
wizards
Letter, 12
Mail Merge Helper, 110-113
Web Page, 784
workgroup administration, 1049
**Word 6, Print dialog box features,
980-981**
WordArt (PowerPoint), 557-560
**Work Offline command (Printer
menu), 984**
**workbook-level names (Excel
formulas), 196**
workbooks (Excel)
linking with formulas, 200-201
refreshing links, 201-202
sharing on networks, 14
templates, 132, 135-136
opening workbooks, 132-133
template elements, 133-135
Workbooks object (Excel)
methods
Activate, 625
Add, 625
Close, 625
Open, 625
Save, 625
SaveAs, 625
properties
Count, 624
ReadOnly, 625
Saved, 625
workgroup administration
Access, 1046-1048
Excel, 1048
PowerPoint, 1048-1049
Word, 1049
workgroup templates (Word), 67
worksheets (Excel)
lists, 234-235
Advanced Filter, 239-242
AutoFilter, 236-239
Data Forms, 248-250
database functions, 246-247
formulas, 242-243
natural language formulas,
243-245
Mail Merge (Word), 115
templates, designing, 137-138
**Worksheets object (Excel),
624-626**
**World Wide Web Consortium
(W3C), 810**

**wrapping text (Publisher),
725-727**
**writing files to disk (VBA),
671-672**

X-Y-Z

**XE field codes (Word indexes),
99-101**
<XMP> tag (HTML), 777
XY (Scatter) charts (Excel), 152

**Yes/No data type, Access tables,
350**
**Your Small Office (Web site),
1081**

Zip drives, 1016
**ZIP files, searching for files in,
905**

SOLVE YOUR BUSINESS PROBLEMS

If you need the right tool for your business task, go to the experts Microsoft chose to create their sample Excel applications. And it's not just Excel expertise--Village Software has authored Que book sections covering VBA (and VBScript) development across the rest of Office, too. Village Software's pre-built Business Solutions unlock the value of Microsoft Office for your company. For some free Village Software FastStart products, see the CD-ROM accompanying this book. For other great Village Software products, visit our website.

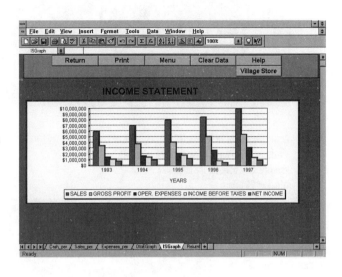

Our products are Microsoft Office Compatible, so you know they'll behave reliably. Our network of business experts also provides the in-depth knowledge necessary to create tools that will work for *your* business.

CUSTOM PROGRAMMING FROM INDUSTRY EXPERTS

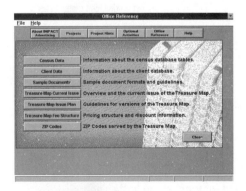

Village Software also provides custom development services. Our clients range from Fortune 500 clients to small businesses, and include projects such as automated intranet-based sales reporting for world-wide enterprises, financial systems in Excel and Access, and automated contact management in Outlook. To request a quote for a custom job, visit Village Software's customization website at www.villagesoft.com/custom.

Special prices for Que book readers!

Check out Que® Books on the World Wide Web
http://www.quecorp.com

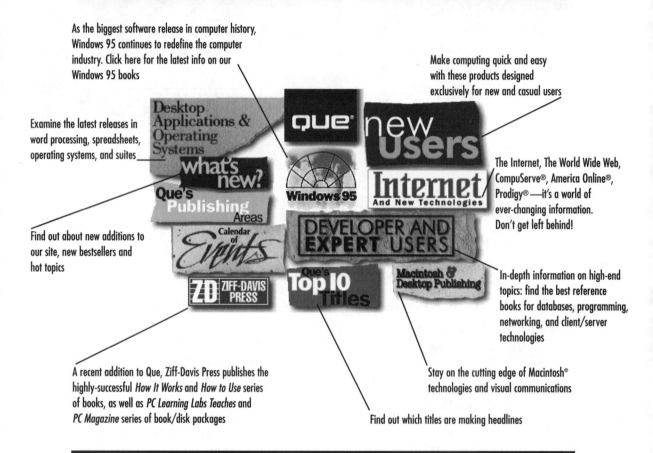

As the biggest software release in computer history, Windows 95 continues to redefine the computer industry. Click here for the latest info on our Windows 95 books

Make computing quick and easy with these products designed exclusively for new and casual users

Examine the latest releases in word processing, spreadsheets, operating systems, and suites

The Internet, The World Wide Web, CompuServe®, America Online®, Prodigy® —it's a world of ever-changing information. Don't get left behind!

Find out about new additions to our site, new bestsellers and hot topics

In-depth information on high-end topics: find the best reference books for databases, programming, networking, and client/server technologies

A recent addition to Que, Ziff-Davis Press publishes the highly-successful *How It Works* and *How to Use* series of books, as well as *PC Learning Labs Teaches* and *PC Magazine* series of book/disk packages

Stay on the cutting edge of Macintosh® technologies and visual communications

Find out which titles are making headlines

With 6 separate publishing groups, Que develops products for many specific market segments and areas of computer technology. Explore our Web Site and you'll find information on best-selling titles, newly published titles, upcoming products, authors, and much more.

- Stay informed on the latest industry trends and products available
- Visit our online bookstore for the latest information and editions
- Download software from Que's library of the best shareware and freeware

Complete and Return this Card
for a *FREE* Computer Book Catalog

Thank you for purchasing this book! You have purchased a superior computer book written expressly for your needs. To continue to provide the kind of up-to-date, pertinent coverage you've come to expect from us, we need to hear from you. Please take a minute to complete and return this self-addressed, postage-paid form. In return, we'll send you a free catalog of all our computer books on topics ranging from word processing to programming and the internet.

Mr. ☐   Mrs. ☐   Ms. ☐   Dr. ☐

Name (first) ☐☐☐☐☐☐☐☐☐☐☐   (M.I.) ☐   (last) ☐☐☐☐☐☐☐☐☐☐☐☐☐☐☐☐

Address ☐☐☐☐☐☐☐☐☐☐☐☐☐☐☐☐☐☐☐☐☐☐☐☐☐☐☐☐☐☐☐

☐☐☐☐☐☐☐☐☐☐☐☐☐☐☐☐☐☐☐☐☐☐☐☐☐☐☐☐☐☐☐

City ☐☐☐☐☐☐☐☐☐☐☐☐☐☐   State ☐☐   Zip ☐☐☐☐☐ ☐☐☐☐

Phone ☐☐☐ ☐☐☐ ☐☐☐☐   Fax ☐☐☐ ☐☐☐ ☐☐☐☐

Company Name ☐☐☐☐☐☐☐☐☐☐☐☐☐☐☐☐☐☐☐☐☐☐☐☐☐☐☐☐☐

E-mail address ☐☐☐☐☐☐☐☐☐☐☐☐☐☐☐☐☐☐☐☐☐☐☐☐☐☐☐☐☐

1. Please check at least (3) influencing factors for purchasing this book.

Front or back cover information on book .... ☐
Special approach to the content .... ☐
Completeness of content... ☐
Author's reputation .... ☐
Publisher's reputation .... ☐
Book cover design or layout .... ☐
Index or table of contents of book .... ☐
Price of book.. ☐
Special effects, graphics, illustrations .... ☐
Other (Please specify): _____ ☐

2. How did you first learn about this book?

Saw in Macmillan Computer Publishing catalog .... ☐
Recommended by store personnel .... ☐
Saw the book on bookshelf at store .... ☐
Recommended by a friend .... ☐
Received advertisement in the mail .... ☐
Saw an advertisement in: _____ ☐
Read book review in: _____ ☐
Other (Please specify): _____ ☐

3. How many computer books have you purchased in the last six months?

This book only .... ☐   3 to 5 books .... ☐
2 books .... ☐   More than 5 .... ☐

4. Where did you purchase this book?

Bookstore .... ☐
Computer Store .... ☐
Consumer Electronics Store .... ☐
Department Store .... ☐
Office Club .... ☐
Warehouse Club .... ☐
Mail Order .... ☐
Direct from Publisher .... ☐
Internet site .... ☐
Other (Please specify): _____ ☐

5. How long have you been using a computer?

☐ Less than 6 months   ☐ 6 months to a year
☐ 1 to 3 years   ☐ More than 3 years

6. What is your level of experience with personal computers and with the subject of this book?

	With PCs	With subject of book
New	☐	☐
Casual	☐	☐
Accomplished	☐	☐
Expert	☐	☐

Source Code ISBN: 0-7897-1301-2

7. Which of the following best describes your job title?

Administrative Assistant .... ☐
Coordinator .... ☐
Manager/Supervisor .... ☐
Director .... ☐
Vice President .... ☐
President/CEO/COO .... ☐
Lawyer/Doctor/Medical Professional .... ☐
Teacher/Educator/Trainer .... ☐
Engineer/Technician .... ☐
Consultant .... ☐
Not employed/Student/Retired .... ☐
Other (Please specify): _____ ☐

8. Which of the following best describes the area of the company your job title falls under?

Accounting .... ☐
Engineering .... ☐
Manufacturing .... ☐
Operations .... ☐
Marketing .... ☐
Sales .... ☐
Other (Please specify): _____ ☐

9. What is your age?

Under 20 .... ☐
21-29 .... ☐
30-39 .... ☐
40-49 .... ☐
50-59 .... ☐
60-over .... ☐

10. Are you:

Male .... ☐
Female .... ☐

11. Which computer publications do you read regularly? (Please list)

_____
_____
_____
_____
_____
_____
_____
_____
_____
_____

Comments: _____
_____
_____

Fold here and scotch-tape to mail.

Licensing Agreement

By opening this package, you are agreeing to be bound by the following:

The software product contained on this CD is copyrighted and all rights are reserved by the publisher and author. You are licensed to use this software on a single computer. You may copy and/or modify the software as needed to facilitate your use of it on a single computer. Making copies of the software for any other purpose is a violation of the United States copyright laws. THIS SOFTWARE IS PROVIDED FREE OF CHARGE, AS IS, AND WITHOUT WARRANTY OF ANY KIND, EITHER EXPRESSED OR IMPLIED, INCLUDING BUT NOT LIMITED TO THE IMPLIED WARRANTIES OF MERCHANTABILITY AND FITNESS FOR A PARTICULAR PURPOSE. Neither the publisher nor its dealers or distributors assumes any liability for any alleged or actual damages arising from the use of this program. (Some states do not allow for the exclusion of implied warranties, so the exclusion may not apply to you.)